MW01012684
FALSE
CREEK

The Chuck Davis History of Metropolitan Vancouver

The Chuck Davis History of Metropolitan Vancouver

Chuck Davis

Harbour Publishing

1 2 3 4 5 — 15 14 13 12 11

Harbour Publishing Co. Ltd.
P.O. Box 219, Madeira Park, BC, V0N 2H0
www.harbourpublishing.com

Printed and bound in Canada

With support from the City of Vancouver's 125th Anniversary Grants Program and the participation of the Government of Canada.

Canada Council for the Arts · Conseil des Arts du Canada

Harbour Publishing acknowledges financial support from the Government of Canada through the Canada Book Fund and the Canada Council for the Arts, and from the Province of British Columbia through the BC Arts Council and the Book Publishing Tax Credit.

Library and Archives Canada Cataloguing in Publication

Davis, Chuck, 1935

The Chuck Davis History of Metropolitan Vancouver.

Includes bibliographical references and index.
ISBN 978-1-55017-533-2

1. Vancouver Metropolitan Area (B.C.)—History. 2. Vancouver Metropolitan Area (B.C.)—Biography. I. Title. II. Title: History of Metropolitan Vancouver.

FC3847.3.D38 2011 971.1'33
C2011-904626-1

Contributors & Staff

Published by Harbour Publishing Co. Ltd.

Publisher—Howard White

Managing editor—Anna Comfort O'Keeffe

Photo editor—Peter Robson

External coordinator—Allen Garr

Designer—Roger Handling, Astrid Handling / Terra Firma Digital Arts

Production manager—Teresa Karbashewski

Lead editor—Audrey McClellan

Substantive editors—Audrey McClellan, Margaret Tessman

Contributing authors—

1757–1993: Chuck Davis

1994–2003: Elaine Park

2004–2007: Allen Garr

2008–2011: Eric Villa-Gomez and Stephen Ullstrom

Sidebar contributors—Martin and Jennifer Butler, Chuck Davis, Chris Gainor, Tom Hawthorn, Bob Mackin, Jim Taylor, Annie Mayse, Susan Mayse, Stephen Ullstrom

Subject consultants—

Chinese-Canadian history: Larry Wong, Jim Wong-Chu

First Nations history: Bruce Granville Miller

Japanese-Canadian history: Masako Fukawa, Stan Fukawa

Additional research and writing—Daniel Francis, John Gibbs, Nicola Goshulak, Andy Hill, Robert Ingves, Megan Lau, Arianna McGregor, Marysia McGilvray, Jim McGraw, Malcolm Page, Stephen Ullstrom

Production assistants and photo research—Natalia Cornwall, Stephen Ullstrom, Joyce Wan

Copy editors and proofreaders—Cheryl Cohen, Maureen Nicholson, Sarah Weber, Patricia Wolfe

Indexers—Ellen Hawman, Megan Lau, Arianna McGregor, Stephen Ullstrom, Joyce Wan

Marketing—Marisa Alps, Berglind Kristinsdottir

Photo page 1: Granville Street, Aug. 24,1946.
City of Vancouver Archives, CVA 586-461
Photo page 2-3: Coal Harbour showing the Vancouver Rowing Club, 1913.
City of Vancouver Archives, Pan NXVIII. W.J. Moore photo
Endsheets: Detail of "Bird's Eye View of the City of Vancouver, 1898."
City of Vancouver Archives, Map 547.

Support

Harbour Publishing wishes to acknowledge the following organizations for their support of *The Chuck Davis History of Metropolitan Vancouver*:

Vancouver 125

Pacific News Group

City of Vancouver Archives

Vancouver Public Library Special Collections

Tourism Vancouver

BC Bookworld

Financial Contributors

Harbour Publishing also wishes to recognize the following businesses and individuals whose financial contributions helped to complete this project:

Shell Busey's House Smart Referral Network

Al Westnedge

Yosef Wosk

Frank Anfield

C.J. Banfield

Glenda Bartosh

Richard Bowen, Lynne Bowen

Eleanor Boyle

John James Carney

Gwendolyn M. Dick

Judy Fladell

Allen Garr

Jean Gosse

Elizabeth Hawkins

Barbara Hughes

Doreen M. Imredy

Judith Knox

Jeanine Lucas

Olive McEwan

Jim McGraw

Wayne Norton

Joseph Planta

Marion S. Poliakoff

Toshiko Quan

Oluf P. Skow

Kathleen Stewart

Mary-Lou Storey

Greg Trammel

Shurli Tylor

Larry Wong

Sponsors

As his final gift to Metropolitan Vancouver the late Chuck Davis spent almost a decade researching and writing this book. His only funding during this period came from generous and community-spirited individuals and firms who sponsored specific years in the chronology. To these early supporters we owe a deep debt of gratitude.

Lead Sponsor
The Vancouver Board of Trade

1827-1885
The Oppenheimer Group

1886
Canadian Imperial Bank of Commerce (CIBC)

1887
The Salvation Army

1888
Fasken Martineau LLP

1889
Capilano Suspension Bridge

1897
KPMG LLP

1899
In honour of Sam Promislow 1899-1976

1902
Tourism Vancouver

1903
H.Y. Louie Co. Ltd.

1905
Institute of Chartered Accountants of British Columbia

1907
British Columbia Automobile Association (BCAA)

1908
Kearney Funeral Services

1909
Gwen Newton in tribute to Robert Clark

1910
The McElhanney Group

1911
Borden Ladner Gervais LLP (BLG)

1912
PricewaterhouseCoopers LLP (PWC)

1913
The Historic Ramada Limited Hotel on West Pender

1917
Deeley Harley-Davidson Canada

1918
Canadian National Railway Company (CN)

1919
Real Estate Board of Greater Vancouver

1920
Architectural Institute of British Columbia (AIBC)

1922
The University of British Columbia (UBC)

1923
Odlum Brown Ltd.

1924
A-Ace Limousine / www.gerrymcguire.com

1927
Allied Holdings Ltd.

1928
Vancouver Regional Construction Association (VRCA)

1929
Robert Allan Ltd., Naval Architects and Marine Engineers

1930
Acme Protective Systems Ltd.

1933
City of Vancouver Archives

1936
Vancouver Historical Society

1937
All Nations Stamp & Coin

1943
Vancouver Foundation

1945
London Drugs

1946
TCG International Inc. (TCGI)

1947
Vancouver City Savings Credit Union (Vancity)

1948
Vancouver Fire & Security Ltd.

1949
Beedie Construction Company Ltd.

1950
Univar Canada

1951
Industrial Alliance Pacific Insurance and Financial Services Inc.

1952
In Memory of Catherine MacKinnon 1952-1972

1953
Kal Tire

1954
Gore Mutual Insurance Company

1956
Ebco Industries Ltd.

1957
Pacific Western Brewing Company

1958
Ritchie Brothers Auctioneers

Sponsors *(continued)*

1960
McCarthy Tétrault LLP

1961
The Jim Pattison Group

1962
BC Hydro

1963
Boston Pizza

1964
Tree Island Industries Ltd.

1965
Simon Fraser University (SFU)

1966
Sierra Systems Group Inc.

1967
Commonwealth Insurance Company

1968
Algo Communication Products Ltd.

1969
Tom Lee Music Company Ltd.

1970
DDB Canada

1972
DuMoulin Boskovich LLP

1973
Alexander, Holburn, Beaudin and Lang LLP

1974
Bruce Allen Talent

1975
Urbanics Consultants Ltd.

1976
Canada Wide Media Ltd.

1977
Western Mechanical Services (1977) Ltd.

1978
Abbey Window Coverings / Springs Window Fashions

1979
AXA Pacific Insurance Company

1980
Polygon Homes Ltd.

1981
HSBC Bank Canada

1982
The History Group Inc.

1983
Canada Place Corporation

1984
Morrison Productions

1986
Concord Pacific

1987
Placer Dome / Barrick Gold

1988
Rogers Plus

1989
Blake Cassels & Graydon LLP

1990
Bosa Development Corp.

1991
Mint Records Inc.

1993
Quasar Design & Data Management Inc.

1994
Langara College

1995
Vancouver Public Library

1997
Galiano Island Books

1999
Vancouver Film Studios Ltd.

2001
Spirit of Vancouver (Vancouver Board of Trade)

2002
Coast Capital Savings Credit Union

2003
channel m Multivision Television

2004
The McLean Group

2005
The Landing

2006
Vancouver Airport Authority

2007
Rennie Marketing Systems

2008
FCV Technologies Ltd.

2010
Tourism Vancouver

2011
TELUS Communications Company

CONTENTS

Foreword

Chuck Davis had a story he liked to tell about his mania for trying to make the people of the Vancouver region more aware of their history. He was delivering a slide show to a class of grade four, five and six students and put up an image showing the statue of Captain George Vancouver, which stands in front of City Hall.

"Who can tell me who that man is?" he asked.

One hundred voices shouted out with complete confidence, "George Washington!"

He wondered if this was some kind of an anomaly and made sure to ask the same question at every school he went to. Out of forty-nine schools he visited all over metropolitan Vancouver, only once did he encounter a student who could identify the man after whom Vancouver was named.

He recounted this experience every chance he got because it said everything he wanted to say about the kind of work he was doing and why he felt it was needed. Not only is the general awareness of Vancouver history much lower than it should be, among children and adults both, we end up filling the vacuum with the history of our neighbours. Chuck became so famous for promoting the story of Vancouver and its environs at every chance that the media took to calling him "Mr. Vancouver," but he never referred to himself as a historian. He had great admiration for historians and hugely valued the work done by scholars more formally trained than himself (he left school in grade six) but he was appalled by the communication gap between them and the general public. This was doubly disastrous because in his mind the story that our historians and educators were sitting on was such a good one.

Chuck Davis, "Mr. Vancouver," with Captain George Vancouver—not George Washington! *Alan Twigg*

As one of British Columbia's most versatile media figures, Chuck was well positioned to do something about this, and once he set his mind to it, stirring up popular interest in the past became his mission in life. He promoted it on his CBC Radio programs and devoted his newspaper columns to it. He began doing school tours and writing books—eighteen counting this one—including histories of North Vancouver District and Port Coquitlam and two voluminous urban encyclopedias, *The Vancouver Book* (1976) and *The Greater Vancouver Book* (1997). Sometime in the 1990s he began work on the present book, which he described as "the capstone of my writing career." In it he intended to tell the world everything he had learned in his long love affair with Vancouver history, but in a lively, readable way that would reach out to all those Vancouverites who had grown up knowing more about George Washington than George Vancouver. When asked to describe the new book by his colleague Tom Hawthorn, he said the book would be "fun, fat, and full of facts."

"Just like you," said Hawthorn.

Putting everything he wanted the world to know about Vancouver in one place proved a daunting task, and Chuck was forced to extend the publication date year after year but he was having fun doing the thing he loved so he didn't worry. Then time ran out. At age seventy-four Chuck was diagnosed with inoperable cancer and given only weeks to live. It was completely characteristic of Chuck that the greatest concern he felt upon receiving this news was about finishing his book. He spent a couple of anxious weeks making public appeals for help before a number of his admirers, including myself, were able to convince him he should just take the work as far as he could and rest assured we would finish it if necessary. Sadly that did prove necessary, but I like to think that when he shuffled off to that great archive in the sky on November 20, 2010, he took comfort in the knowledge his great scheme would live on.

Taking over somebody else's labour of love is not to be done lightly and the fact it has turned out as well as it has is a credit to many people, most notably Chuck himself. Not simply because he laid down a foundation that made it hard for us to go astray, but because he left behind an ocean of good will that made our work immeasurably easier. The City of Vancouver bestowed a $20,000 grant on the project, enabled by the good offices of Chuck's second family, the Vancouver Historical Society. The Vancouver Public Library, the Vancouver Archives and the Pacific Newspaper Group donated what must be the largest assemblage of Vancouver-area photographs ever published in one book. Busy movers and shakers like Allen Garr, Rick Antonson, Penny Ballem, Sam Sullivan, Scott Anderson, Paul Whitney, Alan Twigg and Yosef Wosk went out of their way to clear our path forward and many of Chuck's former colleagues from the scribbling trades stepped up to finalize the text, including Elaine Park, Allen Garr, Susan Mayse, Annie Mayse, Jim Taylor and Tom Hawthorn. The dedicated crew at Harbour Publishing performed with their customary excellence but one who deserves special mention is Managing Editor Anna Comfort O'Keeffe, into whose lap fell responsibility for delivering on the rash promises made by her boss, and who is chiefly responsible for pulling together the myriad threads left loose by Chuck's passing. She was ably abetted by editor Audrey McClellan and photo editor Peter Robson. Many more made important contributions, and we have attempted a more complete list on the staff and contributors page.

Finally, this book would not exist without the sponsors who made financial contributions, especially those who supported Chuck by underwriting individual years, foremost among them the Vancouver Board of Trade. We have accorded these supporters a special place of honour in the foregoing pages.

So here it is. It might not be exactly as Chuck would have done it, but over 80 percent is his own work and we feel we can say with confidence the finished product fits the description, "fun, fat and full of facts." We hope you enjoy it. And Chuck, old buddy, wherever you are, rest in peace. Your work is done.

Howard White, Publisher

Acknowledgements

Harbour Publishing is most grateful to Chuck Davis himself, for his unwavering enthusiasm for Vancouver's history and his determination to complete this project. He was the inspiration to the team who stepped forward to finish *The Chuck Davis History of Metropolitan Vancouver*. First among these was Elaine Park, who enthusiastically volunteered to research and pen the largest portion of incomplete entries.

In addition, we are thankful to Allen Garr and Eric Villa-Gomez who also stepped in to complete missing years, as well as to writers Chris Gainor, John Gibbs, Tom Hawthorn, Andy Hill, Stephen Hume, Robert Ingves, Bob Mackin, Annie Mayse, Susan Mayse, Marysia McGilvray, Malcolm Page, Jim Taylor and Stephen Ullstrom for their help with sidebars and filling in the missing pieces.

We are also extremely grateful to Jean Barman for her early guidance and to Masako Fukawa, Stan Fukawa, Bruce Granville Miller, Larry Wong and Jim Wong-Chu, who were all extremely generous with their time and knowledge.

Special thanks to editors Audrey McClellan and Margaret Tessman, who skilfully pulled all the elements together, as well as to proofreaders Cheryl Cohen, Maureen Nicholson, Sarah Weber and Patricia Wolfe.

Administrative duties were handled admirably by Regina Kasa and Sue Longhi.

Photo editor Peter Robson deserves special thanks for so ably taking on the enormous task of illustrating this book. Thanks too, to Allen Garr, a long-time friend of Chuck Davis, who, in addition to pitching in with writing and research, performed essential ambassadorial services. Our sincere thanks to Leslie Mobbs, City Archivist and Director of Records and Archives for the City of Vancouver; Heather Gordon at the City of Vancouver Archives; Debbie Millward, Manager of the News Research Library at the Pacific News Group and Shelagh Flaherty, Director of the Central Branch of the Vancouver Public Library. Without the support of their organizations, this book would not have been possible.

When it came down to digging for photos, Kate Bird of the Pacific News Group once again demonstrated the expertise and dedication for which she is renowned (sorry we kept crashing your computer). Special thanks also to Kim McArthey and Kate Russell of the Vancouver Public Library and the many helpful archivists at the City of Vancouver Archives, including Megan Schlasse, Jeannie Hounslow and Chak Yung. Their extensive knowledge of their archival holdings and generous advice added greatly to the book.

Others who helped with photos include Jim Wong-Chu; Hugh Ellenwood, archives manager at White Rock Museum & Archives; Daniel Francis, writer/editor; Carrie Schmidt, librarian and archivist at Vancouver Maritime Museum; Vickie Jensen of Westcoast Words; Ryan Gallagher, reference specialist at Surrey Archives; Rollie Webb, maritime expert; Pippa Van Velzen of Port Coquitlam Heritage; Cristopher Wright; Jennifer Yuhasz, archivist for the Jewish Museum and Archives of British Columbia; Candice Bjur of UBC Archives; Henri Robideau; and Arianna McGregor, who helped to collect and file images.

It should also be noted that this book would not be the same without the contributions of hundreds of talented photographers who have captured the people, events and neighbourhoods of metropolitan Vancouver over decades. They are too numerous to name here, but credits appear in the photo captions when known. Our sincere apologies to anyone who may have been overlooked.

Thanks too to all those who helped to research and write nearly five hundred photo captions—including Daniel Francis, Nicola Goshulak, Megan Lau, Arianna McGregor, Jim McGraw, Stephen Ullstrom and copy editor Cheryl Cohen. We are also grateful to all those who worked tirelessly to compile a detailed and useful index—Megan Lau, Arianna McGregor, Stephen Ullstrom, Joyce Wan, Ellen Hawman, Teresa Karbashewski.

Roger Handling and Astrid Handling of Terra Firma Digital Arts also deserve special thanks for an elegant page design.

We are grateful to Ariba Dalal of Quasar Design and Data Management for technical expertise in hosting Chuck Davis's website, www.vancouverhistory.ca.

Special thanks to the Vancouver Historical Society, including Scott Anderson, Bruce Watson and Paul Flucke. Rick Antonson, Penny Ballen, Gregor Robertson, Sam Sullivan, Alan Twigg, Paul Whitney and Yosef Wosk provided crucial leadership at key junctures. Many thanks to Vancouver 125 and all the generous sponsors.

To anyone whom we may have overlooked in these acknowledgements, we sincerely apologize for any omissions and thank you too.

And finally, to Edna and Stephanie Davis, who did everything possible to assist despite difficult circumstances—thank you.

Preface

The Chuck Davis History of Metropolitan Vancouver belongs to all of us. Those of us who live here come to understand our home in new and interesting ways. Those of us from away are rewarded with a portrait of a major North American urban region encouraging us to rethink the taken-for-grantedness of where we live. Those of us stimulated by others' adventures and foibles are entertained and satisfied by the many stories and anecdotes. And those of us who have followed Chuck Davis's long career as Vancouver's historian take pride in a job well done.

Much of the appeal of *The Chuck Davis History of Metropolitan Vancouver* lies in its open and inviting approach. The book does not pretend to interpret the past for us, although inevitably any account reflects to some extent its creator's interests and assumptions. *The Chuck Davis History* is a chronological compendium of both familiar and little known facts and information about the southwest tip of British Columbia, a densely populated area of 21 incorporated municipalities and almost 3,000 square kilometres housing half the Canadian province's 4.5 million people. While Vancouver is the best known of the components, it is numerically and spatially a small part of this larger whole.

The Chuck Davis History of Metropolitan Vancouver is the emanation of a single individual's long-lived love affair with the place about which he writes. In the tradition of Vancouver's first archivist, Major J.S. Matthews, as chronicled by Daphne Sleigh in the aptly titled *The Man Who Saved Vancouver*, Chuck Davis was determined to salvage as much detail as possible about the history of Metro Vancouver at a time when few others were so engaged. Chuck arrived on the West Coast as an impressionable nine-year-old child in 1944 and, while he subsequently bounced around from place to place, he never really left. His career in radio in Victoria, Prince Rupert and Vancouver and as a columnist for Vancouver's *Province* newspaper gave him entryways to fact-finding into which he, like Major Matthews before him, rushed enthusiastically and wholeheartedly. Chuck wanted to know, and to share, everything about everything. While he somewhat moderated his goal over time having only, it is said, 64 book projects in his "to do" drawer at the time of his death in late 2010, he never surrendered his dream in respect to Metro Vancouver.

Chuck Davis introduced Vancouverites to their city in the best-selling *Chuck Davis's Guide to Vancouver* and companion *Kids! Kids! Kids! And Vancouver* co-written with Daniel Wood. Published in 1973 and 1975, well before the guidebook genre took off in respect to Vancouver, these were personalized introductions to the streets, sites, restaurants, shopping and entertainment possibilities that engaged Chuck and therefore should do so for us as well. Today the pair are important historical documents testifying to the enormous changes that have subsequently overtaken the city.

By the time of the two books' publication, Chuck Davis had envisaged and was editing the first of two very popular urban almanacs whose impressive lists of contributors on every possible topic speak to the wide-ranging respect he had acquired. *The Vancouver Book* appeared in 1976, *The Greater Vancouver Book* in 1997, their ragtag appearance on our book shelves today testifying to their enduring utility as references. Chuck also authored several other volumes on aspects of Vancouver and Metro Vancouver even as he was turning his mind to the large magnum opus we now hold in our hands.

Those of us who have followed the course of *The Chuck Davis History of Metropolitan Vancouver* over the past decade, including occasional queries by an ever-enthusiastic Chuck over some detail or the other, have had a glorious ride. Chuck embraced computer technology as a means to organize his seemingly endless mounds of data, described by a friend as the world's largest gerbil nest. Chuck's "History of Metropolitan Vancouver" website chronicling the project's progress became a staple of many of our lives. Every time we consulted it for some bit of information, we were once again caught up in his enthusiasm and persistence. Chuck's respect for accuracy assured us that whatever we found there would be as reliable as any "'fact" could ever be. The project was in its final stages of completion at the time of Chuck's death and has been brought to publication through the support of friends and fellow historians who have filled in some of the remaining sections in the spirit in which he would have written them. Just as Chuck was always willing to share some anecdote or incident catching his fancy—"Say, did I ever tell you the story of ...?"—those who knew him now did so in his honour.

Chuck Davis's wish that *The Chuck Davis History of Metropolitan Vancouver* be "fun, fat, and full of facts" has been done proud by Harbour Publishing. The book testifies to what we as single individuals can accomplish should we set our mind to it and also to the coming of age of a significant component of British Columbia, Canada and North America. While other more interpretive histories of Metro Vancouver will come along, as well they should, as Chuck Davis's mantle passes on, their authors will be hard pressed to match the exuberance, good will and pure enjoyment he brings to the city and region of his dreams.

Jean Barman
Vancouver, 2011

Lions Bay
BOWEN ISLAND
Horseshoe Bay
WEST VANCOUVER
NORTH VANC
99
1
Upper Levels Hwy.
Marine
Capilano
City of North Vancouver
Dee
Lonsdale
Dollarton Hw
Burrard Inlet
Stanley Park
Georgia
Howe
Hastings
7A
Grandview
7
Kingsway
99A 1A
Granville
VANCOUVER
Marine
Strait of Georgia
Vancouver International Airport
Richmond Freeway
91
RICHMOND
Lulu Island
No. 3
Fraser River
DEL
Scale: 1:285,000
km
0 1 2 4 6 8 10
TSAWWASSEN

METROPOLITAN VANCOUVER
VER
Belcarra
Anmore
COQUITLAM
7A
Port Moody
RNABY
Lougheed Hwy.
7
7
Port Coquitlam
Pitt Meadows
Lougheed Hwy.
1
Maple Ridge
New Westminster
7
Fraser
1A
1
Abbotsford
91
SURREY
99A
10
10
City of Langley
1A
LANGLEY
White Rock

1757-1885

1757

Before Vancouver. Difficult as it is to imagine now, this is the landscape that young Spanish explorer José Maria Narváez would have seen when he arrived in the Vancouver area in 1791, beating British Captain George Vancouver by just a year. *Jim McKenzie illustration*

An entry followed by [camera icon] references a related photo or illustration.

1757

June 22 George Vancouver was born in King's Lynn, Norfolk.

1782

Smallpox spread via trade routes from Mexico north to Puget Sound, the Strait of Georgia and the Fraser Canyon, decimating Native populations.

1791

April 1 HMS *Discovery*, under the command of Capt. George Vancouver, sailed from Falmouth to explore the Pacific coast of North America.

July 5 Spanish explorer Lieutenant José Maria Narváez, the first European to see this area (he beat George Vancouver by a year), anchored west of Point Grey and explored the mouth of the Fraser River. [camera icon]

1792

April 30 Capt. George Vancouver in HMS *Discovery* entered the Strait of Juan de Fuca.

June 13 Vancouver entered and explored Burrard Inlet, which he named Burrard's Channel. He had a friendly encounter here with local Coast Salish people.

June 22 Captain Vancouver and Spanish captain Dionisio Galiano, who was also leading an exploring expedition, were startled to meet each other at what is now English Bay. The two men hit it off, and Vancouver named Spanish Banks as a tribute. [camera icon]

1808

July Simon Fraser and his men, who had just descended the river that would later be named for

Right: Hard-boiled explorers. A surprise encounter at sea on the morning of June 21, 1792, resulted in George Vancouver sharing breakfast with Dionisio Galiano, commander of the Spanish vessel *Sutil*. The *Sutil* and another Spanish vessel, the *Mexicana*, had been at anchor off Point Grey, site of modern-day Vancouver, when a longboat approached, flying British colours. It was Captain Vancouver, back from explorations up the coast. He and Galiano agreed to continue their exploration of the coast together. *Gordon Miller illustration*

Vancouver's First Neighbourhoods

Anthropologists believe the first humans settled what is now Vancouver about 10,000 years ago as the ice age that earth scientists call the Wisconsin Glacial Episode ended. But there's no scientific consensus as to whether the first inhabitants came by sea or by land. Persuasive evidence argues that the first peoples moved down a deglaciating coast and then followed rivers from the retreating Cordilleran ice sheet deep into the province's Interior valleys in pursuit of abundant fish and game. However, others make a strong case that Interior valleys were first inhabited by peoples travelling an ice-free inland route who then descended rivers to the coast. The Stó:lō people, who take their name from the Fraser River itself, believe their occupation of Vancouver's landscape began in time immemorial with the arrival of sky creatures who transformed ancestral animals. Although divided into distinct tribal groups, the Stó:lō are unified by a common language; all speak variations of Halkomelem with the people who occupied the region of what's now Metro Vancouver speaking the Hun'qmyi'num' dialect. The Squamish of North Vancouver speak a distinct language although they are part of the Coast Salish group that includes Halkomelem speakers. The Squamish originally occupied the region around the head of Howe Sound but expanded into the Vancouver area in the mid-19th century.

At the time of recorded contact with Europeans in the late 18th century, the Stó:lō tribes occupying what is now the Vancouver area were the Xwméthkwiyem, rendered in English as the Musqueam, who lived at the mouth of the Fraser River; the Kwikwetl'em who lived on the Coquitlam River and Coquitlam Lake; the Q'éytsi'i, anglicized as Katzie, who lived in the Pitt River watersheds; the Qw'ó:ntl'an or Kwantlen who lived around what is now New Westminster; the Sxa'yeqs, or Skayuks, of the Stave Lake watersheds; the Mathekwi of Matsqui; the Q'ó:leq' of Whonnock and the Sne'kwōmes, or Snokomish, who lived in the area around what is now White Rock. However, many of these populations moved during the tumultuous years following European contact. When a Hudson's Bay Company trading post was established at Fort Langley in 1827, the Qw'ó:ntl'an, Q'éytsi'i, Sne'kwōmes, Sxa'yeqs and Q'ó:leq' all moved closer to the source of trade goods and as a consequence of depopulation from introduced epidemics.

By the time of European settlement in the mid-1850s, the Vancouver area was largely occupied by the Musqueam people, whose villages extended from the Fraser River delta around Point Grey, False Creek, the West End, Stanley Park and along Burrard Inlet. They heavily utilized shellfish, salmon and trout that spawned by the hundreds of thousands in small creeks long since paved over and diverted through culverts, hunted elk, bear, deer and sea mammals. Today, although village sites are remembered only as names that seem strange to the present inhabitants—Kullukhun, "the stockade;" Tha'thulum, "shivering woman rock;" Khapkhepayum, "cedar place"—the Stó:lō, Squamish and other bands of the Vancouver region are a vigorous and flourishing group of First Nations that include some of the most prosperous, politically active and culturally resurgent aboriginal communities in British Columbia.

An early view of downtown, this 1868 image shows a First Nations dwelling in what is now trendy Coal Harbour, close to Robson and Georgia Streets.
City of Vancouver Archives, St Pk N4

(Sources: *A Stó:lō Coast Salish Historical Atlas; Early Human Occupation in British Columbia; Handbook of North American Indians: Northwest Coast*)

Contemporary First Nations bands and their populations in the Vancouver area include:

Squamish	3,794
Musqueam	1,234
Katzie	505
Tsleil-Waututh	477
Tsawwassen	291
Matsqui	249
Kwantlen	207
Semiahoo	85
Kwickwetl'em	74

(Source: Indian and Northern Affairs Canada, interactive map, http://fnpim-cippn.inac-ainc.gc.ca/index-eng.asp)

Fraser, explored the native village at Musqueam. Men of the village chased them off, and the Europeans retreated back up the river.

1816

H and C King in Woolwich manufactured what became Stanley Park's Nine O'Clock Gun.

1824

James McMillan of the Hudson's Bay Company, with a party of men, struck out into the Interior from the mouth of the Nicomekl River in Surrey. They went up the Nicomekl until their boats could go no farther, then portaged to the Salmon River, which flows into the Fraser about 50 kilometres (31 miles) east of its mouth. McMillan marked a tree at that location—he called it the Hudson's Bay Tree—and when he returned two-and-a-half years later, he found that tree and built the first Fort Langley beside it.

1825

March 19 The Hudson's Bay Company opened Fort Vancouver on a bluff above the north bank of

1825

Vancouver's First Tourist

The first European who indisputably set eyes on what is now Vancouver was a modest Spanish marine pilot not long out of his teens. The year was 1791, and José Maria Narváez (born in Cadiz in 1768) was in command of the tiny naval schooner *Santa Saturnina*, about the size of a modern 12-metre yacht, although considerably broader in beam. Small enough that it could be propelled by eight oarsmen when becalmed, the little vessel nevertheless carried a crew of 22, including soldiers from Don Pedro Alberni's garrison of Catalonian volunteers stationed at Nootka.

On secret orders from the Spanish viceroy in Mexico, *Santa Saturnina* was part of an expedition, led by Lt. Francisco de Eliza, sent to gather intelligence and map the unknown waters beyond the Strait of Juan de Fuca, which had been explored as far as Haro Strait by Manuel Quimper in 1790. Although Spain had laid claim to the territory, it was worried about the English (who believed their claim dated from expeditions by Sir Francis Drake in 1579 and James Cooke in 1778), the Russians (who had established forts in Alaska) and even the French (who had sent an exploratory mission to the Northwest Coast in 1786).

The *Santa Saturnina* left Nootka in the company of Eliza's 16-gun ship *San Carlos* on May 5, 1791. In July, Narváez became the first known European to sail into the Strait of Georgia, where he took note of fresh water about 3 kilometres (2 miles) out to sea and deduced the presence of a large river. Narváez never did see the Fraser River, whose freshet he had correctly identified, but he did see the site of present-day Vancouver, anchoring off Point Grey. He incorrectly thought the point was an island and charted it as Ysla de Langara on what is the oldest known map of the region to survive.

Narváez and the Spanish crews are estimated to have rowed and sailed more than 10,000 kilometres (6,200 miles) as they explored the Strait of Georgia, which they named Canal de Floridablanca, Howe Sound (Bocas del Carmelo), Burrard Inlet (Boca de Floridablanca), Point Atkinson (Punta de la Bodega) and Point Roberts (Ysla de Zepeda). Narváez traded with the Musqueam and made contact with the Squamish at the head of Howe Sound, where an old tale recounted by historian B.A. McKelvie tells of an encounter between Squamish warriors and dead men aboard two floating islands festooned with cobwebs. Spanish coins were found among the Squamish "until quite recent times," McKelvie reported in the mid-20th century.

Narváez charted Nanaimo harbour on the east coast of Vancouver Island and continued north to Comox and Cape Lazo, then explored Desolation Sound on the mainland, named Texada and Lasqueti Islands, mapped the Canadian Gulf Islands and the San Juan Islands and returned to the base at Nootka.

In 1792, English naval captain George Vancouver renamed most of the landmarks recorded by the crew of *Santa Saturnina*. The Spanish withdrew as their empire declined, and the British presence grew as their empire ascended. Since victors write the history, Narváez was consigned to the historical footnotes, and Vancouver left his name on the city that arose on the shores of Boca de Floridablanca.

Looking askance at her bovine companion, this cow peers out of a former storehouse at Fort Langley, in a 1924 photo. The Hudson's Bay Company established Fort Langley in 1827. A successful agricultural and salmon exporting business began there in 1833.
Leonard Frank photo, Vancouver Public Library VPL 4244

the Columbia River, where the city of Vancouver, Washington, is now located, directly across the river from Oregon state. The fort became the HBC's western headquarters. It was situated on the north bank of the Columbia because the traders thought that river would eventually become the border between Canada and the United States.

1827

July 30 A group of two dozen HBC men began constructing the first Fort Langley. Among them were two Hawaiians or Kanakas (the term *Kanaka* is the Polynesian word for "human being"), Como and Peeohpeeoh. After 13 or 14 years, Como returned to Fort Vancouver, where he worked until his death in 1850. Peeohpeeoh, who raised a large family, stayed in the vicinity of Fort Langley for the rest of his life.

1833

February 20 James Murray Yale took command of Fort Langley, and a Hudson's Bay Company farm was established at Langley Prairie. The farm was very successful, shipping salted salmon to Hawaii.

1834

Toronto was incorporated (as York).

1835

October The Hudson's Bay Company steamship *Beaver* left England. Six months later, in April 1836, it became the first steamship to reach the eastern Pacific Ocean.

1838

June 28 Victoria was crowned Queen of Great Britain, succeeding King William IV.

1843

July The Hudson's Bay Company established Fort Camosun at the southern end of Vancouver Island. By December it had been renamed Fort Victoria.

Don't be too quick to judge this ship by its appearance. The intrepid SS *Beaver*, which reached the West Coast in the spring of 1836 after a six-month journey from England, gained the honour of becoming the first steamship to reach the eastern Pacific Ocean.
City of Vancouver Archives, Bo P354. Photo S.J. Thompson

1848

Measles and dysentery swept through Stó:lō settlements on the Fraser River.

1853

Alexander McLean operated the first dairy farm in metropolitan Vancouver at Ladner. After being flooded out in 1853, McLean moved his family and their 50 cows to the west bank of the Pitt River in what is now Port Coquitlam.

1856

Three cannons were shipped to British Columbia from England as part of a larger shipment to "the provinces of Canada." One of them was today's Nine O'Clock Gun.

1857

John "Gassy Jack" Deighton, born in Hull, Yorkshire, started working on the West Coast as a steamship operator in the late 1850s.

December 28 James Douglas, governor of the colony of Vancouver Island, established in 1849, proclaimed the British Crown's control of mineral rights on the mainland.

1858

August 10 A crew of men under the direction of A.C. Anderson, director of road operations, began constructing the first road on the British Columbia mainland. It ran from Tsawwassen Beach, south of Ladner, overland to Fort Langley.

The government reserve that later became Stanley Park was set aside. Much of it was logged over the next decade.

1859

February 14 Queensborough was proclaimed the site of the new capital of British Columbia. In July, the town was renamed New Westminster. (Historical coincidence: Oregon became a state on the same day.)

May 1 St. John the Divine Anglican Church was consecrated at Derby, near Fort Langley. Because there were not yet any local sawmills, the church was built of imported California redwood.

The Birthplace of British Columbia

November 19, 1858 James Douglas proclaimed mainland British Columbia a Crown colony of Great Britain. The announcement was made in Fort Langley, the provisional capital, a remote, muddy outpost at the farthest fringes of the Hudson's Bay Company's continent-spanning fur trade empire.

Faced with a stampede of prospectors up the Fraser River after the discovery of gold in the gravel bars was bruited about San Francisco, Douglas, governor of the colony of Vancouver Island, had unilaterally annexed the territory that would become BC—without the permission of the government in London. Now, in a drenching, bone-chilling rain, Douglas had gathered the admiral commanding the Royal Navy's Pacific squadron, stationed at Esquimalt; David Cameron, the chief justice of Vancouver Island; and Matthew Baillie Begbie, the new judge of BC, to preside over the reading of the Royal Proclamation affirming and formalizing his earlier decision to extend British administrative authority over the mainland north of the 49th parallel. First Douglas read Queen Victoria's commission of Begbie as the new judge, then Begbie read the commission appointing Douglas governor of the mainland colony, then Douglas revoked the HBC's powers over its old fur trading territory, proclaimed the British Columbia Act dissolving New Caledonia and creating a new colony, indemnified officers of the government from any irregularities during the procedure and proclaimed British law to be in force.

Only 31 years earlier, already anticipating the loss of the Oregon Territory to the Americans, a party of 25 HBC fur traders—three clerks, twelve French Canadians, one Metis, two Hawaiians, two Iroquois, two "other Indians," an Orkneyman and an Irishman, led by Chief Factor James McMillan—had made its way up the Fraser River and chosen a site where the current was deep enough for a ship to anchor. McMillan had reconnoitred for the first HBC trading post on the lower Fraser in 1824. Now he picked a place near the meandering stream the Kwantlen called T'salkwakyan and which later settlers would call the Salmon River, about 16 kilometres (10 miles) up the Fraser from the mouth of the Pitt River. The site was strategically positioned to take advantage of an ancient portage between the Salmon and the Nicomekl River, which provided another access route to the sea at Boundary Bay.

The party arrived on July 24, 1827, on the HBC schooner *Cadboro*, a ship smaller than many Native war canoes, and began clearing the site the next morning. There was haste to get the defensive palisades up because the party had been given an apocalyptic warning by a Kwantlen chief, who told them that should they try to settle, they'd be annihilated. Once Fort Langley was in place—two log bastions towered above palisades that enclosed a rectangle about 40 metres (130 feet) by 30 metres (100 feet)—trading, not warfare, was the order of the day for both sides. By September 15 a storehouse had been built and filled with trade goods; then winter quarters were constructed for the garrison. Still, despite the wealth and power of the HBC, the company's hold on the lower Fraser was fragile and tenuous. On October 11 the fort's journal records a war party of 86 Cowichans from Vancouver Island passing upriver on the way to raid the Chilliwacks. On October 18 the journal reports the Cowichans' return: the head of a slain warrior dangling from the bow of the lead canoe; the others laden with booty and enslaved women and children. Gradually, however, the practice of raids and counter-raids, slave-taking and inter-tribal warfare, which occasionally involved the HBC, diminished.

In 1839 the fort was relocated 5 kilometres (3 miles) upstream to take advantage of more suitable farmland. It burned down the following year and was relocated again, close to the present site. In 1858, Douglas had plans drawn up for a town named Derby, adjacent to Fort Langley. It was to be the capital of the new colony of BC, but the next year Richard Moody, commander of the Royal Engineers, deemed it militarily indefensible. He chose a site at what became New Westminster instead. Fort Langley continued to play a key role as a provisioning post during the early years of the gold rush but was increasingly overshadowed by New Westminster and Vancouver. It ceased operation in 1886 and largely fell into ruin. In 1955 it was declared a national historic site and some buildings were reconstructed, and today the surrounding village offers tourists a collection of historic structures, antique shops and sidewalk cafes.

June 13 Coal was discovered in an area of Burrard Inlet that was promptly named Coal Harbour.

Governor Douglas adopted a policy of "benevolent assimilation" of Native people. Over the next decade, members of BC First Nations began entering the wage economy.

The Royal Engineers arrived in British Columbia. They had a great impact on the development of the Lower Mainland, overseeing the construction of roads and bridges. One of the roads they built, North Road, led from the capital of New Westminster to Burrard Inlet. Today it's the oldest road in metropolitan Vancouver and is the boundary between Burnaby and Coquitlam.

By Christmas 1859, eight months after arriving in New Westminster, the Royal Engineers had built a theatre there. The fare at the Theatre Royal was mostly light farces, comedies, minstrel shows, songs, dances and skits.

1860

April 11 Samuel Maclure, son of a Royal Engineer surveyor, was reputedly the first white child born in New Westminster. He went on to become one of BC's most renowned early architects, designing many buildings in Vancouver including Aberthau (now the Point Grey Community Centre), Brock House at UBC and Gabriola in the West End.

July 17 New Westminster was incorporated. It's the oldest incorporated municipality west of Ontario.

The colonial government banned the sale of alcohol to Native people.

Streets Paved by Gold

Spring news of gold discoveries on the Fraser River attracted more than 30,000 American and other prospectors to the British Columbia mainland.

The seeds of the rush were sown a year earlier and related 35 years later by John Sebastian Helmcken in his memoir. Helmcken, a physician with the Hudson's Bay Company, was at dinner with James Douglas, HBC chief factor and governor of Vancouver Island, who produced a small bottle containing tiny flakes of gold that had been traded at an HBC fort on the North Thompson River. Everything to which they were accustomed was about to change, Douglas told his dinner companions.

"This was the first gold I saw and probably the first that arrived here," Helmcken wrote. "A few weeks after this Mr. Douglas showed us a soda-water bottle half full of scaly gold, which had been collected I think by the Indians of the North Thompson. The Legislature existed at this period but took no heed of these discoveries."

More gold was found on the lower Fraser River in February 1858, and then word leaked out of the San Francisco mint where the earlier dust and flakes were sent for refining. Two months later, 30,000 California miners were stampeding to the Fraser River, soldiers were deserting from the US Army, sailors were abandoning their ships in Puget Sound, sawmills and logging camps in Oregon and Washington were idled for want of men, wives were left on their farms. Some fought their way through a bloody Indian war in the interior of Washington but most took overloaded steamships to Fort Victoria—on one day 1,800 passengers embarked in San Francisco—where they were compelled to wait for the Fraser's spring freshet to subside. There were no boats to the mainland, so miners built their own in a frenzy of sawing and hammering. Helmcken remembered, "These boats were built exactly of the shape of coffins and in these frail craft very many started for the Fraser."

The motley flotilla rowed, paddled and sailed to Mayne Island, camping in Miner's Bay until the Strait of Georgia was calm enough to chance a crossing to the Fraser mouth. Then the men battled a river in full flood to Fort Langley. "Some got there—some were lost and doubtless some caught by the Indians, the inmates murdered. No one can have any just or correct idea of the number who perished—they were never heard of more and of course in the main were unknown to other miners—these in turn scattering throughout the country only had their attention, time and industry occupied by the excitement and madness of looking for gold."

Douglas, too, took note of the dangers, writing that "a great many canoes have been dashed to pieces and their cargoes swept away by the impetuous stream, while of the ill-fated adventurers who accompanied them, many have been swept into eternity."

But with rich gold finds on almost every gravel bar—from June to September the Fraser produced more gold than the entire first year of the California gold rush in 1848—the flood of prospectors, instead of abating, continued upstream, into the Cariboo and then the Kootenays. Among them was John Fox Damon, a reporter with the *Victoria Gazette*, who wrote with authority about the perils of the journey up the Fraser. To maintain control, the British Parliament created the mainland colony of British Columbia, and in February 1859 Colonel Richard Moody and the Royal Engineers arrived to establish the new colony's capital at what would become New Westminster. Later that year Moody had a road built from New Westminster to Burrard Inlet (today's North Road), and in 1860 or possibly 1861 a reserve was established that later became the Hastings Townsite. By 1862, in the wake of the gold rush, the first settlers had a homestead in what is now Vancouver, and a timber pre-emption on the north shore of Burrard Inlet began a thriving lumber industry.

Between 1858 and 1863, $10 million in gold poured out of the Fraser River watershed. During the 1860s, $30 million in gold flowed from the Cariboo. The tiny outposts on Burrard Inlet boomed and merged to become a new town, then a city. With the coming of a transcontinental railway, it surpassed New Westminster and Victoria as the commercial centre of British Columbia. By 1887, a year after its incorporation, the great newspapers of London had dubbed Vancouver "the Constantinople of the West."

The fortunes of the mining industry established by the "annus mirabilis"—the year of wonders—that was 1858 have waxed and waned with commodity prices; other rushes have come and gone; coal, copper, lead, zinc and other metals have had their day, but it can safely be said that the way to Vancouver's place as Canada's third-largest city was paved by gold.

Golden era. In 1862 prospector Billy Barker discovered gold in Williams Creek, leading to the foundation of Barkerville, a gold-rush town that grew to be the largest in western Canada for a short time. This 1862 photograph shows a gold escort preparing to leave the bustling settlement. *BC Mining Museum*

Hand fallers. Standing tall in 1885 to fell a Douglas fir in Kitsilano, these two men were engaged in one of the first major industries of Vancouver—logging.
Harbour Publishing Archives

1861

February 13 BC's longest-lasting newspaper published its first issue. New Westminster's *British Columbian* folded in November 1983 after more than 122 years. Just over a week later, on February 21, it noted the arrival of 12 Chinese on the vessel *Otter* and 40 more on the vessel *Caledonia*.

March 17 Won Alexander Cumyow was born in Port Douglas, at the head of Harrison Lake. He was the first Chinese baby born in what became Canada. His father, Won Ling Sing, was one of the first Chinese migrants to arrive in BC from California, attracted by the discovery of gold on the Fraser River.

The first Chinese laundry, the Hi Sing House, was established in New Westminster.

Hugh McRoberts established Richmond (or Richmond View) Farm on Sea Island. He was the first white settler on the island, and his farm was one of BC's earliest and largest farms.

The Kwantlen hosted a great potlatch on McMillan Island near Fort Langley. Nearly 4,000 people attended.

Father Leon Fouquet of the Oblates established St. Mary's Catholic mission near what is now the city of Mission. The Oblates built a school that opened in 1863 with 42 Stó:lō boys in attendance. In 1868 the Sisters of St. Ann opened a convent school for girls at the mission.

1862

October A Yorkshire potter named John Morton saw a chunk of Burrard Inlet coal on display in a New Westminster shop window and wondered if there might be fine clay near that coal, suitable for pottery. There was clay, but of a quality suitable only for bricks. Morton and two associates—William Hailstone and Morton's cousin Sam Brighouse—preempted about 225 hectares (550 acres) on November 3, at a price equivalent to $2.50 per hectare ($1.00 per acre), with a view to becoming brickmakers. Some thought they spent far too much money for the remote "Brickmaker's Claim," and one newspaper report derisively described them as "three greenhorn Englishmen." The "three greenhorns" built a cabin near the north foot of today's Burrard Street and began to raise cows.

Right: Three Greenhorns. Now prosperous about thirty years after becoming pioneers, (left to right) William Hailstone, Sam Brighouse and John Morton decided to try their hand, in 1862, at brick-making, in what is now the West End. Their contemporaries laughed them off as greenhorns, but the investment in land, at least, paid off when the CPR bought them out.
City of Vancouver, Port P775. J.D. Hall photo

A stone obelisk was erected

this year to mark the spot on the 49th parallel at Point Roberts from which all survey work would proceed eastward. The road running directly north from this point was named Coast Meridian Road. Today Coast Meridian runs through the city of Port Coquitlam.

Colonel Richard Moody of the Royal Engineers named Lulu Island in Richmond in honour of 16-year-old Lulu Sweet, a visiting member of a touring English musical revue.

Elsewhere in BC

Billy Barker found gold at Williams Creek in central British Columbia. By 1870 more than 100,000 people had travelled the Cariboo Wagon Road to reach the bustling town of Barkerville. For a brief time it was said to be the largest town west of Chicago and north of San Francisco.

Smallpox broke out in Victoria

and spread through the region. Coast Salish people, many of whom lived on the Lower Mainland, had a lower mortality rate than other aboriginal people due to vaccination programs, but the epidemic decimated the Native population.

Also in Canada

August 18 Simon Fraser died in St. Andrews West, Canada West, near what is now Cornwall, ON.

Lumber ships. After Sew Moody and Captain Stamp started sawmills in the 1860s, Burrard Inlet filled with windjammers loading lumber.
City of Vancouver Archives, Mi P47

1863

The BC contingent of the Royal Engineers was disbanded. Many of the officers returned to England, but almost all of the rank and file opted to stay behind in order to claim the land grants promised them.

1864

November 9 The first shipment of lumber left Burrard Inlet for a foreign port as more than 250,000 board feet set sail for Australia.

Lumberman Sewell Prescott Moody, originally from Maine, purchased Burrard Inlet Mills on the north shore of Burrard Inlet, renamed it Burrard Inlet Lumber Mills (though it was commonly known as Moody's Mill) and turned it into a going concern. The settlement that sprang up around the mill became known as Moodyville. It was just east of today's Lonsdale Road.

Frederick Seymour became governor of British Columbia.

1865

January 14 Seattle was incorporated.

April 11 The first telegraph message was transmitted from Moody's Mill on the North Shore to New Westminster.

April 14 The first telegraph message from the outside world arrived at Burrard Inlet, telling of the assassination of US president Abraham Lincoln.

July 30 The first religious service was held on Burrard Inlet, conducted for the men of Moodyville by the Rev. Ebenezer Robson, a Methodist.

August 15 The New Westminster library was established with books donated by the Royal Engineers.

1866

August 6 The Crown colonies of Vancouver Island and British Columbia were united under the name British Columbia. The new colony's capital was New Westminster. Frederick Seymour became governor of the united colony.

1867

June On the south shore of Burrard Inlet (at the north foot of today's Dunlevy Street), and with the help of British financing, Edward Stamp established Stamp's Mill, Vancouver's first major industrial development. Stamp built a flume from Trout Lake to the sawmill to sustain its steam-driven machinery.

July 1 Canadian Confederation.

Politicians away to the east created a new country called Canada, naturally inspiring thoughts it might eventually stretch from sea to sea.

1868

May 25 The capital of the colony of British Columbia was moved from New Westminster to Victoria.

July 18 Ada Young married Peter Plant at Moody's Mill, with the Rev. Edward White presiding over this first marriage among the non-Native population of Burrard Inlet.

August 8 William and Thomas Ladner purchased 65 hectares (160 acres) each on the banks of the Chilukthan Slough. The purchase was recorded at New Westminster.

1869

July Maximilian "Maxie" Michaud arrived at Burrard Inlet. He had walked to Vancouver from Montreal. When he got here, aged about 30, he bought the New Brighton Hotel from

Gassy Jack

September 30 John "Gassy Jack" Deighton arrived in a rowboat. The Yorkshire-born Deighton, with a complexion, said a chum, of "muddy purple," and a gift of the gab that gave him his nickname, rowed into Burrard Inlet from New Westminster with his Native wife, her mother, her cousin, a yellow dog, two chairs and a barrel of whiskey.

The canny Deighton jovially greeted the men who worked at Stamp's Mill. He knew the nearest drink for these thirsty fellows was a 5-kilometre (3-mile) row east up the inlet to North Road, then a 15-kilometre (9-mile) walk along that rude trail through the forest to New Westminster. (Encounters with bears on the road were not at all uncommon in those days.) Deighton announced to the millworkers that they could have all they could drink if they helped him build a bar. The Globe Saloon was up within 24 hours.

The locals had a nickname for Deighton, who was endlessly and garrulously confident of the area's future. They called him "Gassy Jack." That led, the story goes, to the area around his saloon—a gathering spot for millworkers and visiting sailors—being nicknamed, in turn, Gastown. (There are other theories for the origin of the name, one associated with a nearby pocket of natural gas.)

Joseph Trutch, BC's chief commissioner of lands and works, refused to recognize existing aboriginal reserves and ordered them re-surveyed and reduced. He reversed Governor Douglas' policy of allowing aboriginal people to pre-empt land, and three years later wrote a memorandum denying the existence of aboriginal title. Native chiefs protested and petitioned the government and the monarch in England, to little avail.

Gastown. Vancouver began with a saloon. It was near this tree at the corner of Carrall and Water Streets that the garrulous barkeep John "Gassy Jack" Deighton opened his first watering hole, servicing the workers from the nearby Hastings Mill. In 1870, the year this photograph of Water Street was taken, the informal little hamlet of Gastown was surveyed and officially anointed the Township of Granville.

Dominion Photo Co. photo, Vancouver Public Library VPL 24322

Left: Vancouver's first postmaster was Maximilian "Maxie" Michaud, who made the astounding trip from Montreal to Vancouver by foot, arriving in July 1869. After buying the New Brighton Hotel (the two-storey building), Maxie established the city's first unofficial post office in its kitchen. *Vancouver Public Library, Special Collections, VPL 151. H.T. Devine photo*

its owner, Oliver Hocking. The first unofficial post office in what is now Vancouver was located in the kitchen of the hotel. It opened July 2, with Maxie as postmaster.

James A. Raymur took over Captain Edward Stamp's sawmill and renamed it Hastings Mill (in honour of Rear Adm. George Fowler Hastings, commander of the Royal Navy's North Pacific station at Esquimalt from 1866 to 1869). When he first cast eyes upon the squalor and haphazardness of the mill and its surroundings, he gazed about him in horror and delivered one of the great Vancouver quotes: "What is the meaning of this aggregation of filth?" He cleaned it up fast.

Gastown's first jail was two cells built of logs. It stood in what is now Gaoler's Mews in Gastown.

A Kanaka family settled on a large pebble beach in Coal Harbour (where the Westin Bayshore Hotel now stands at the foot of Denman Street). Their homestead came to be known as Kanaka Ranch. When John Morton, one of the three greenhorns, tried to dispossess the family in 1895, they took the case to court, which in 1899 sustained their right to the land.

Sir Anthony Musgrave became governor of British Columbia.

1870

March 1 Granville, known colloquially as Gastown (after Gassy Jack Deighton), came into being. The townsite, which had been surveyed in February, was named for Granville George Leveson-Gower, 2nd Earl Granville, colonial secretary at the time. Sixteen years later it was renamed Vancouver.

Portuguese Joe Silvey, an illiterate whaler from the Azores, opened Hole-in-the-Wall, a saloon catering to thirsty millworkers, at the corner of Water and Abbot Streets.

1871

February 10 John Linn, one of the Royal Engineer sappers who built our first roads, received 60 hectares (150 acres) of land in return for his military service. Linn, who was described as "a strapping Scottish stonemason," settled with his wife and six children at the mouth of a creek on the north shore of Burrard Inlet. The creek and many other North Shore features came to be named for him—though the name was misspelled.

July 20 British Columbia joined the Canadian Confederation.

Gassy Jack Deighton raised a Canadian flag over his saloon, the first to be seen in this area. Joseph William Trutch was appointed the first Lieutenant-Governor.

November 13 John Foster McCreight was elected first premier of the province of BC.

With a gun salute and trumpets and horns, British Columbia entered the Canadian Confederation in 1871. Canada got its western coastline, and BC its debt removed and a trans-Canada railway. *Robert J. Banks illustration. British Columbia Archives, PDP 00501*

December 26 The Masons' Grand Lodge of British Columbia was inaugurated.

The first salmon cannery was set up along the Fraser River.

British common law held fish to be an open-access resource, but restrictive regulations diminished aboriginal peoples' access to and control of salmon.

1872

June 12 Superintendent John Jessop visited the school at Fort Langley. The teacher, James Kennedy, was in the process of being fired, the school was about to close because of mosquitoes, and there were no maps or blackboards.

October The first bridge was built across False Creek.

December 23 Amor De Cosmos became premier of British Columbia.

British Columbia placed an agent-general in London to further the aims of the province in the United Kingdom.

The province amended the Qualification and Registration of Voters Act to bar Chinese and First Nations people from voting in provincial elections. To become a lawyer, members of the BC bar had to appear on the provincial voters' list, so Chinese and First Nations were effectively banned from practising law, although many did without provincial sanction, hiring white lawyers to act as their "front." It wasn't until the late 1940s, when the franchise was returned, that many minority Canadians, including the Chinese and First Nations, were called to the bar.

1873

April 26 The District of Langley was incorporated,

with James Mackie as the first warden. (Before 1881, the head of a municipal council in BC—equivalent to today's mayor—was appointed to the office and was called a warden.)

December 13 Henry Osborne Alexander was born at Hastings Mill, the first white male born on Burrard Inlet.

December 22 Moody's Mill on the North Shore burned to the ground, but was quickly rebuilt with lumber and bricks purchased from the Hastings Mill, its competitor across the inlet.

Some say the McCleery farmhouse, built this year and demolished in 1956, was the first house constructed within the boundaries of what would become the city of Vancouver. But the three greenhorns—John Morton, Sam Brighouse and William Hailstone—had built their cabin near the north foot of what is now Burrard Street in 1862. (The McCleery land is a golf course today.)

The *Eleanora*, built from a scow and powered by an engine from a threshing machine, began service as a ferry across Burrard Inlet. The engine was later fastened with chains attached to a buoy so it could be located if it fell through the hull mid-trip. Locals nicknamed it the *Sudden Jerk*.

"Navvy Jack" Thomas built the first house on the waterfront in what would become West Vancouver and married the daughter of a Squamish chief. (The house was moved and still stands, much altered, at 1768 Argyle St.)

John Sullivan Deas, a free black man from Carolina, opened a cannery on what would later be called Deas Island. Deas sold out in 1878 and left BC.

1874

February 11 George Anthony Walkem of the Cariboo became BC premier when Amor de Cosmos resigned to sit as an MP in Ottawa.

A genteel oasis on a wild coast, the McCleery farmhouse was built in 1873, one of the first buildings within the current boundaries of Vancouver. The farm is now the McCleery Golf Course, in Kerrisdale along the Fraser River. *City of Vancouver Archives, CVA 677-347*

Left: Vancouver's first ferry started across Burrard Inlet in 1873. Named the *Eleanora*, it was more commonly known as the *Sudden Jerk*.
Harbour Publishing Archives

April 1 Henry Harvey became the official postmaster for Granville townsite, replacing the unofficial postmaster, Maximilian Michaud.

A stagecoach line came into service between Burrard Inlet and New Westminster.

Hundreds of Coast Salish people rallied in New Westminster seeking a settlement of the "land question"— the demand by BC's Native people to have their title and rights to their lands and resources recognized and respected. Also this year the chiefs of the Lower Fraser produced a petition in which they expressed their discontent over land settlement in BC, and the federal minister of the Interior, David Laird, presented their concerns to the Privy Council in England.

A loophole discovered in the act disenfranchising Chinese voters gave previously registered Chinese the right to vote, and in the 1874 Lillooet by-election, money was spent freely to court their vote. Two years later, the BC legislature closed the loophole and amended the Municipal Act to prohibit Chinese from voting in any election for mayor, reeve, councilor, or alderman. Since the Dominion government used the provincial voters list for federal elections, this effectively barred the Chinese from voting in any elections.

1875

May 29 John "Gassy Jack" Deighton died.

1876

February 1 Andrew Charles Elliott became BC premier.

Albert Norton Richards was appointed Lieutenant-Governor of the province.

A census of Stanley Park found about 80 "Skwamish" people living there. Their chief was Supple Jack.

The Joint Indian Reserve Commission, with representatives of the Dominion and provincial governments, was established to create Indian reserves in British Columbia. The commission made its decisions after discussions with, but without the consent of, First Nations, disregarding aboriginal title and rights.

1877

Manzo Nagano, born in Kuchinotsu, Nagasaki, a seaman on a British vessel, jumped ship in New Westminster and took up permanent residence in Canada, the first recognized Issei (first-generation Japanese person) in the country. He teamed up with an Italian fisherman and fished for salmon in the Fraser River. He also worked as a lumberman before moving his family to Victoria in the 1890s, where he ran a gift shop, a Japanese food store and a small hotel. He became one of the first BC producers of salted humpback (pink) salmon which he exported to Japan. In 1923, when fire destroyed his life's work, he returned to his village in Japan and died there a year later.

1878

June 25 George Anthony Walkem became BC premier again.

June 29
Burrard Inlet's first newspaper appeared, the *Moodyville Tickler*. It had a very brief, tongue-in-cheek existence. For example, the more you paid for your obituary, the more glowing it became.

The BC legislature passed a resolution prohibiting the employment of Chinese on public works. This employment policy remained effective until 1947. Later in the month the government tried to impose an annual head tax of $60 on

Chinese residents in the province, but the canneries, in need of cheap Chinese labour, successfully lobbied to delay its implementation and it was subsequently disallowed by the Dominion government on the grounds that it would interfere with trade and commerce between China and Canada.

1879

George Apnaut, a Kanaka or native Hawaiian, was elected to one of the first Maple Ridge town councils. Apnaut was one of several Kanakas who in the late 1850s squatted at the mouth of a creek (which came to be known as Kanaka Creek) that emptied into the Fraser River near Fort Langley. When the CPR laid its tracks along the Fraser River, the little Kanaka community was obliterated. The last house was gone by 1912.

1880

January 5 Joseph Shannon was appointed the first warden of Surrey.

May Work on the rail line from Yale to New Westminster began.

December 31 A New Year's Eve ball was held at Deighton House (the hotel built by Gassy Jack Deighton) in Granville.

The first general store in Ladner's Landing

began as a supply tent on a wharf. During the 1880s, Thomas McNeely built it into a prosperous business.

In the 1880s, Kyuzo Kawamura became the first Japanese shipwright to offer his carpentry skills on the Fraser. He and other boat builders who followed him would fish during the summer and build skiffs on cannery premises during the winter when there was little opportunity for other employment.

1881

February Surrey council began to offer a bounty of $2.50 for bears.

April 15 The *Senator*, a steam tug built at Moodyville, made its maiden voyage. The tug ferried passengers, mail and occasionally cattle across Burrard Inlet.

May 15 St. James Anglican Church at Granville was consecrated. It was destroyed in the Great Fire of 1886.

September The influential *London Truth* newspaper editorialized: "British Columbia is not worth keeping.

It should never have been inhabited at all. It will never pay a red cent of interest on the money that may be sunk in it."

The CPR brought over 17,000 Chinese workers to Canada to spend the next four years working on the western section of the transcontinental railway. They were paid a dollar a day, when non-Chinese were paid from $2 to $2.50 a day. The Chinese were also forced to buy their supplies from the CPR store and to build their own camps.The western section was considered the most dangerous and difficult to build, and at least 600 Chinese died in the process of laying track through the Rocky Mountains—more than four for every mile of track.

The first municipal hall was built at Surrey Centre. It was used until 1912.

"Captain Jack, the Poet Scout" brought a Wild West show to New Westminster.

Clement Francis Cornwall, a rancher from the Cariboo, was the new Lieutenant-Governor.

1882

February 4 Electricity came to BC, lighting up the Moodyville sawmill

on the north shore of Burrard Inlet. These were the first electric lights on the Pacific coast north of San Francisco, and the mayor and council of Victoria made a special trip to see them.

June 13 Robert Beaven became BC premier.

The first confirmed case of leprosy in the Chinese community was discovered in New Westminster. A

Coal Peddler to Company Tycoon

Chinese entrepreneur Yip Sang (born September 6, 1845) arrived in Vancouver and found work as a peddler—selling sacks of coal door to door—then as a bookkeeper, timekeeper and paymaster for the Canadian Pacific Railway Supply Company. He quickly worked his way up the ranks and became a superintendent of Chinese labourers. By 1888, Yip had started his own business, the Wing Sang Company, which provided labour contracting as well as import/export to and from the Far East. The company's 1889 building at 51–67 East Pender is the oldest in Chinatown.

Yip became a naturalized British subject in 1891. One of Vancouver's most successful merchants in the early Chinatown, he helped establish the Chinese Benevolent Association of Vancouver and the Chinese Board of Trade of Vancouver, and he later became Life Governor of the Vancouver General Hospital. His wealth allowed him to support four wives and to raise 23 children. Generations of Yips have grown up in Vancouver, and hundreds of Yip Sang's descendents live throughout North America.

Chinese labourer infected with the disease was found hiding beneath the crawl space of the city hall. He had been shunned by his community, and when he was found he was hanged and burned in the hope of preventing the spread of the infection. (In 1891, a leper colony was established on D'Arcy Island, near Victoria. It was in operation until 1924.)

St. John the Divine Anglican Church was floated across the river to Maple Ridge from its original location at Derby (near Fort Langley). Built in 1859, it still has an active congregation and is the oldest functioning church in BC.

The English Cannery began operating in Steveston. This salmon cannery was sold to Henry Bell-Irving in 1891. Four years later it burned down and, upon rebuilding, was named the Phoenix Cannery. The site is now part of the Britannia Heritage Shipyard.

Spratt's Oilery, a floating fish oil plant and cannery, was established in Coal Harbour. Employees used dynamite to catch herring.

The Red Cross Brewing Company, built on the Granville waterfront, was likely the area's first brewery. By 1892 Red Cross was shipping all over the province and was outselling the imported brands...imported, that is, from eastern Canada and featuring familiar names like Molson, Carling and Labatt.

1883

January 29 William Smithe became premier of BC.

February 2 The first sale of Port Moody lots was held at New Westminster. By March there were 11 houses there.

March 12 *Duke of Abercorn* unloaded a shipment of rails from Cardiff, Wales, at Port Moody; they were destined for the CPR.

December 12
The first local telephone call was made—between Port Moody and New Westminster.

The Elgin Hotel was built in Port Moody. Along with a floating boarding house and the Caledonian Hotel, the Elgin provided accommodation for the men building the CPR.

John Irving of New Westminster bought out the Hudson's Bay Company's ships and formed the Canadian Pacific Navigation Company.

Teacher Agnes Cameron hung a sign on the Hastings Mill school door: "Irate Parents Will Be Received After 3 p.m."

1884

March 17 The K de K steam ferry began the first ferry service between New Westminster and Brownsville (now part of Surrey). The ferry licence was sub-let to Angus Grant of New Westminster, who built the ferry and named it after a close friend with the unusual name of Knyvett de Knyvett.

April 19
The Dominion government passed an anti-potlatch law to ban this custom, central to Northwest Coast First Nations' culture, which Europeans believed prevented the Natives from becoming "civilized." Although it failed to stop the practice, the law stayed in place until 1951.

June 20 Sacred Heart Roman Catholic Church was consecrated at Ustlawn, the Indian mission village in North Vancouver. It replaced a tiny chapel built in 1868 by those

Originally named Sacred Heart, Greater Vancouver's oldest surviving Catholic church was built in North Vancouver in 1884 for the Squamish Nation members who had converted. Seen here in an 1890s photo, the church was rededicated as St. Paul's in honour of the second Catholic bishop of Vancouver when the church was renovated in 1910. *City of Vancouver Archives, SGN 50. Photo Charles S. Bailey*

members of the Squamish Nation who had converted to Catholicism. A second spire was added in 1910 when renovations were made, and the church was rededicated as St. Paul's. You can still see it on the North Shore skyline.

August 6 William Van Horne, the CPR's head man, visited Granville.

September 16 CPR president Van Horne asked the railway's directors to choose the township of Granville (Gastown), not Port Moody, as the terminus of the new railway. Port Moody went ballistic. Van Horne also recommended that Granville be renamed Vancouver.

The story, likely true, is that an excited Van Horne was rowed around what became Stanley Park by Lauchlan Hamilton, the CPR's local land commissioner (another version has realtor Alexander Wellington Ross at the oars), and, gazing about him in wild surmise, exclaimed aloud that the city was destined to be a great one and must have a name commensurate with its greatness. Nobody would know where "Granville" was, Van Horne told whoever was rowing, but everyone knew of Captain Vancouver's Pacific explorations and would instantly know where this important new link in world shipping was located.

The CPR received a land grant of 25,000 acres (more than 10,000 hectares) in exchange for extending the transcontinental rail line to Granville/Vancouver. Some 6,000 of those acres (2,500 hectares) were in the city itself.

The choice of Vancouver as the Pacific terminus for the CPR ensured the town's dominant role in BC.

August What may be the first use in print of the name "Vancouver" for our city appeared in a Portland, OR, newspaper story.

December 18 The name "Vancouver" for our city was mentioned in a Montreal newspaper.

December 23 Pioneer Lumber Co. of Port Moody was incorporated, the first of several lumber companies to operate in that area.

A massive cantilever bridge, destined to carry the CPR across the Fraser at Lytton, arrived in sections at Port Moody. It had been transported by ship from Britain.

A forest fire swept through the future West Vancouver from Hollyburn to Eagle Harbour.

Canoe Pass school opened in Delta with Frederick Howay (later to become known as a judge, orator and historian) as the first teacher.

Huge, knot-free beams, 34 metres (112 feet) long by 70 centimetres (28 inches) square

The employees of Yick Lung Jin, Merchant Tailors, seen in this 1900 photo, would have been affected by the Chinese immigration head tax first imposed in 1885. Starting at $50, the tax doubled in 1901, and then jumped to $500 in 1903.
Vancouver Public Library, Special Collections, VPL 9498

were shipped to Beijing's Imperial Palace from Burrard Inlet sawmills.

The Oppenheimer brothers set up their food wholesaling company in Vancouver. It is now the Oppenheimer Group, Vancouver's oldest locally owned company.

1885

July 20 The federal government's Act to Restrict and Regulate Chinese Immigration into Canada received royal assent. Among other restrictions, it required every Chinese person entering Canada to pay a head tax of $50 (this was raised to $100 in 1901 and to $500 in 1903, a prohibitive amount), and was the first of many enactments to discriminate against Vancouver's large Chinese population. The result (intended): many men who pioneered in the goldfields of BC or worked to build the CPR could not now bring their families over from China to join them.

Fall The CPR's Lauchlan Hamilton began his survey of, and street building in, Vancouver. A plaque on the building at the southwest corner of Hastings and Hamilton Streets marks the occasion and location.

October 6 A resolution of Richmond council provided that white labour only would be employed on municipal works contracts. Similar resolutions were passed in many Greater Vancouver municipalities in the late 19th century.

November 7
The CPR's last spike was driven at Craigellachie.

December 25 Dominic Charlie was born (or baptized) near Jericho Beach. He became locally famous for his ability to forecast the weather. He and his half-brother collected Squamish legends for publication.

Seraphim "Joe" Fortes arrived in Vancouver, aged about 20, as a crewman aboard the *Robert Kerr*. Originally from Barbados, he jumped ship to settle here and began to teach local people, especially kids, how to swim.

Charles Henry Cates settled in Moodyville and began hauling stone in a 240-foot steam scow called *Spratt's Ark*. He later acquired two tugs and began shipbuilding and towboating.

Shigekichi Hayakawa became the first Japanese to obtain an independent fishing licence—one not attached to a cannery.

The first public wharf was built near Steveston at London's Landing.
The *Telephone* offered the first regular steamboat service, calling daily at points on both banks of the South Arm en route to New Westminster.

The first church in Surrey, Christ Church Anglican, near Cloverdale, was built in seven weeks.

Surrey council retained a lawyer for an annual fee of $50.

1886-1899

1886

Vancouver went from creation to cremation in two months, burning to the ground 16 days after the establishment of a fire department. But the city endured. And its most enduring feature—Stanley Park—resulted from the city council's first decision.

April 6 The City of Vancouver was incorporated. The ceremony, held in Jonathan Miller's house, was delayed when it was discovered no one had thought to bring paper on which to write down the details. Someone had to run down the street to the stationery store.

April 27
Margaret Florence McNeil was the first white child born in Vancouver.

May 3 Vancouver's first municipal election. It was an at-large vote that elected 10 aldermen and a mayor, Malcolm MacLean. There was no voters list, and 499 votes were cast. (The population of the city was about 1,000, but only people who owned property or rented property worth at least $300 were eligible to vote.) In one of the first bylaws passed by council, five wards were created, each electing two aldermen for one-year terms of office.

May 12
The first meeting of Vancouver's first city council.

The first piece of business: a petition to lease from the federal government a 400-hectare (1,000-acre) military reserve that the city would use as a park. Today it's Stanley Park. Council also offered the job of chief of police to John Stewart, a night watchman.

May 15 Lauchlan Hamilton began to survey what would become Granville Street. (Hamilton named the street for the colonial secretary of the time.)

Vancouver's First Newspaper

January 15 The first issue of the city's first newspaper, the *Vancouver Herald*, appeared. Note that it bears the name "Vancouver" more than two months before incorporation.

One interesting item was an advertisement placed by George Black, proprietor of the Brighton Hotel at Hastings, BC, located at what is now the north foot of Windermere Street. "This fine and commodious new Hotel," the ad read, "has been recently completed, and is furnished with every convenience for the comfort of guests. The situation and accommodations are unsurpassed on Burrard Inlet, which has become the most fashionable WATERING-PLACE in British Columbia. The prospect is charming, the sea breezes are invigorating, and the facilities for Boating and Bathing are excellent. Private sitting and dining rooms. Suites of apartments for families or parties.

"The Bar is entirely detached from the main building...Buses to and from New Westminster twice a day." We think the "buses" referred to are what we would call stagecoaches.

George Black was already familiar for his butcher shop on the tiny city's waterfront. No beef or pork here, though. Black went into the forest surrounding the city to bag deer and an occasional elk, sold their meat from his shop or from a rowboat he took out to meet visiting ships. He was famous for his gambling prowess, too, and for the horse races he sponsored down muddy Granville Street.

(The *Herald*'s last issue appeared October 12, 1887.)

May 28 Vancouver's first fire department, Volunteer Hose Company Number One, was formed.

June 1 J.W. Ross' *News* began to publish.

The first CPR passenger train arrived in Port Moody from Montreal across the newly completed transcontinental line on July 4, 1886. Port Moody was supposed to be the Pacific terminus for the railway, but history had already passed the tiny community by. Just a few months earlier, CPR general manager W.C. Van Horne had completed a secret deal with the provincial government to move the terminus down the inlet to Vancouver in return for a sizable grant of free land at the site. *City of Vancouver Archives, Can P3*

The Great Fire. A lone tent on a ghostly, burned-out wasteland illustrates the hope that lived on after Vancouver was devastated by fire in 1886, two months after incorporation. Within a few days the newspaper was printing again and Vancouver was on its way to recovery. *City of Vancouver Archives, LGN 455. Photo J.A. Brock and Harry T. Devine*

The Great Fire

June 13 A furious, swift fire destroyed Vancouver in a time variously reported between 20 and 45 minutes, when flames from a brush-clearing fire blew into tinder-dry brush to the west of the city. At least eight people died; some accounts claim 28. About 1,000 wooden buildings—virtually the entire city—were totally consumed. Said an eyewitness, "The city did not burn, it was consumed by flame. The buildings simply melted before the fiery blast...The fire went down the sidewalk on old Hastings Road, past our office, so rapidly that people flying before it had to leave the burning sidewalk and take to the road; the fire travelled down that wooden sidewalk faster than a man could run."

The city's volunteer firefighters had only axes, shovels and buckets. It wasn't enough. The heat was ferocious: the bell of St. James Anglican Church, which had warned so many, was turned to a molten lump of slag when the church itself burst into flame. (The melted bell can be seen today at the Vancouver Museum.) The ship *Robert Kerr*, now a coal hulk, was blown from its mooring and came to a stop near the foot of Dunlevy Street, where it served as a refuge for people jumping into the inlet to escape the fury of the fire.

There are a hundred stories of the fire, but this one has always stayed with me: Lauchlan Hamilton, the CPR land commissioner and city alderman, dashed to his office, collected "the most valuable papers," shoved them in a sheaf under his arm and ran into a cauldron of fire, "breathing air as hot as cinders." When Hamilton reached safety, he saw that the papers, still under his arm, were charred black.

June 17 Four days after the fire, the *News* was back on the streets.

July 4 CPR Locomotive No. 371, having been placed on the train at North Bend, BC, hauled the first Pacific Express into Port Moody. The first scheduled passenger train to cross Canada from sea to sea had travelled for five days, 19 hours. It was one minute late.

July 13 Vancouver city council passed bylaw No. 258 to regulate the use of bicycles, which must henceforth not exceed 8 miles per hour.

July 26 The first inward cargo to the port of Vancouver arrived: tea from China.

July 30 Vancouver's first fire engine, the *M.A. MacLean*, a 2-tonne (5,000-pound) Ronald steam pumper—ordered a week after the Great Fire—arrived at Port Moody. A four-horse team hauled it over miles of dusty roads via New Westminster to Vancouver, where it arrived August 1. With its accompanying four hose reels and 760 metres of 6-centimetre hose (2,500 feet of 2½-inch hose), it cost $6,905. The engine was placed in service "under canvas" until the new firehall was built.

August 11 The first major fire fought by the Vancouver Fire Brigade (VFB) was at Spratt's Oilery, a fish oil plant and cannery at the north foot of today's Burrard Street (described as "a considerable distance from town"), near midnight. There were no horses available to pull the engine to the fire site, so the firefighters had to pull it themselves.They were not able to save the oilery, but they did prevent the fire from spreading.

September 1 Vancouver's first bank, the Bank of British Columbia (no connection with the later bank of the same name), opened.

September 13 The St. Andrew's and Caledonian Society of Vancouver was formed. It's still active today, the oldest Scottish organization in the city. Here's a startling statistic: On St. Andrew's Day, November 30, 1887, the society held a grand St. Andrew's Ball in McDonough Hall at the southeast corner of Hastings and Columbia. Of the 1,000 or so people who lived in Vancouver at the time, 400 attended. In a rainstorm.

Also in 1886

The first badges for the Vancouver City Police were made of American silver dollars, with one side smoothed down and engraved *Vancouver City Police*. A pin was soldered onto the other side.

The city's first graveyard, at Brockton Point, was closed as Stanley Park began to be developed.

William Macdougall's *Advertiser* began publishing in Vancouver.

For a brief time Vancouver, with a population of about 1,000, had three daily newspapers.

The Oppenheimer brothers' food wholesaling company built a warehouse that today is home to Bryan Adams' recording studio. It is also the oldest brick building in the city.

Chinese labourers were stranded in British Columbia following the completion of the CPR rail line. Many migrated south, settling in Vancouver, New Westminster and Victoria. A number moved east to cities such as Calgary, Toronto and Montreal in search of job opportunities and less discrimination.

The oldest brick building in modern-day Vancouver was constructed in the same year as the devastating Great Fire—1886. Originally a warehouse for the Oppenheimer brothers' food wholesaling company, the building is now home to Bryan Adams' recording studio.
City of Vancouver Archives, Bu P683

1887

The city's conflicted relationship with Asia was on display in a year that combined the emergence of Pacific trade with mob attacks on Chinese workers. And a new Board of Trade set to work lobbying governments on taxation.

January 17 The first Hudson's Bay store opened in the city on Cordova Street, on property leased from the CPR. Shelves held what were advertised as the "necessities of life": saws, axes, lanterns and provisions.

February 24 The Vancouver Anti-Chinese League held a meeting in reaction to the rumour that hundreds of Chinese had landed in Vancouver. When twenty-four Chinese arrived from Victoria, a crowd of 300 to 400 whites marched through the snow to the Chinese camp at the western end of Coal Harbour. To escape the onslaught, some of the Chinese jumped into the icy water and the rest were chased onto the CPR right-of-way without shelter. Not satisfied, part of the mob returned to Vancouver and set fire to some of the Chinese buildings on Carrall Street. These and other disturbances led to the suspension of the city charter and the dispatch of special constables from Victoria.

March 16 The First Baptist Church of Vancouver opened on Cordova Street.

March 31 The first issue of the *News-Advertiser* appeared. It was created when the *Advertiser*, owned by F.L. Carter-Cotton, merged with the *News*. Both papers were about a year old. The big front-page story: "A Demented Chinaman."

April Vancouver's first band concert was held at the Methodist Church on Water Street, opening with "The Maple Leaf Forever."

May The CPR main line was extended 20 kilometres (12.2 miles) along Burrard Inlet to Vancouver.

May 23 The first CPR passenger train arrived in Vancouver from Montreal. Locomotive 374, attached to the train at Port Moody, brought it in with Peter Righter at the throttle. (It is often thought No. 374 pulled the train right across the country.

Decked out for Queen Victoria's Golden Jubilee and celebrating its ocean-to-ocean journey, the first CPR cross-country passenger train arrived in Vancouver in 1887.
City of Vancouver Archives, Can P6

Nope, just from Port Moody.) The first passenger to step down onto the platform was a 21-year-old Welshman named Jonathan Rogers. He became a major developer in the city. The Rogers Building, the attractive white terracotta building at the northeast corner of Pender and Granville, was one of his.

June 13 SS *Abyssinia*, chartered by the CPR, arrived from Asia with a cargo of tea, silk and mail bound for London, England. This marked the beginning of the trans-Pacific, trans-Atlantic trade using the new railway. With Vancouver as the trans-shipment point, the *Abyssinia*'s cargo got from Yokohama to London in 29 days. Back then that was FAST: water-only transport of the same cargo normally took about 45 days. The *Abyssinia* showed that Vancouver was going to be an important Pacific Rim port.

July 1 Vancouver was made a customs port of entry.

Summer CPR surveyor Lauchlan Hamilton rowed his wooden canoe south across False Creek to pitch a tent on the forested south slope. While plotting road survey lines through the bush he looked back across the water at the brand-new city of Vancouver rising against the backdrop of the imposing North Shore mountain range and determined the new subdivision should be called "Fairview."

August 8
The first electric lights were turned on in Vancouver.

September 22 A group of Vancouver businessmen—merchants, lumbermen, bankers and manufacturers—held a meeting and decided to form a Board of Trade. Within a month they had drawn up a list of goals and objectives. Besides calling for a land registry office, courthouse, more schools, playgrounds and mail delivery, the board wanted direct taxation abolished by both civic and provincial governments.

December 14 The Vancouver Reading Room opened its doors on the upper floor at 136 Cordova St. W. In April 1889 it became a free library.

Elsewhere in BC

April 1 A.E.B. Davie became premier after the death of William Smithe.

Hugh Nelson, a lumberman, was appointed Lieutenant-Governor.

Also in 1887

The Salvation Army began in Vancouver with four ladies known as the Hallelujah Lassies.

Hugh Boyd, a Richmond farmer and the settlement's first warden (like a mayor), was awarded a medal for the best wheat grown in the British Empire.

Surrey appointed E.T. Wade as its first police constable. A year later they bought him handcuffs and a gun.

There was a typhoid outbreak in Delta, due partly to river pollution caused by salmon canneries.

There were about 16 canneries operating in the Lower Fraser.

Jones Tent and Awning was founded by Charles H. Jones. The company lasted for nearly a century.

Shishido Yo became the first Japanese woman to settle in Canada. She and her husband Washiji Oya, a seaman, opened a store on Powell Street.

Two years later their son Katsuji was the first *nisei* (second-generation Japanese) born in Canada.

Shinkichi Tamura opened a toy shop at the corner of Cordova and Carrall. In 1904 he established a silk goods store on Granville Street. He built the New World Hotel in 1913. He expanded his business from Vancouver to Osaka and Kobe, Japan. A banker, financier and merchant, Tamura was one of the most successful Japanese businessmen of the pre-World War II period. The New World Hotel was still in use a century later. Renamed Tamura House in 2002, it housed a 110-bed facility for the homeless run by the St. James Community Seniors Society.

The first Sikhs to see British Columbia likely arrived this year when Punjabi soldiers from Hong Kong regiments travelled through Canada after celebrating Queen Victoria's Diamond Jubilee in London. The visitors were impressed with the beautiful landscape, the lush vegetation and the favourable climate of the province. When they returned home, the soldiers spread the word about opportunities in this new land, and by the turn of the century South Asians were immigrating to BC.

Comings and Goings

Gihei Kuno arrived in Vancouver on board the SS *Abyssinia*. A trained carpenter, he settled in Steveston and built boats after the fishing season was over. He also operated a grocery store and a rooming house. Seeing the opportunities in the new country, he wrote to the young men in his home village (Mio, Wakayama prefecture) and enticed them to join him in Steveston. Many countrymen from other parts of Japan followed, and he became known as the father of Japanese settlement in Canada. Kuno died on August 12, 1916, and was buried in his home village. (We've also seen 1888 as Kuno's year of arrival.)

Colonel Richard Moody, who commanded the force of Royal Engineers who either built or contracted our first roads and bridges, died at about age 74 in Bournemouth, England.

The CPR opened the original Hotel Vancouver at the corner of Granville and Georgia Streets in 1887. This may appear in the photograph to be the middle of nowhere, but the company planned to shift development of the new city toward its own lands west and south of the original townsite. *City of Vancouver Archives, SGN 4. Charles S. Bailey photo*

1888

The year's high points were the official openings of Stanley Park and the first Hotel Vancouver, both signs that the city's social and business culture was maturing.

January 30 Work began on a dam on the Capilano River to create a water supply for Vancouver. When the dam was completed, the water was sent through a pipeline lying on the bottom of Burrard Inlet.

February 7 Vancouver's oldest union, Local 226 (Vancouver) of the International Typographical Union, received its charter.

Likely May
The first Hotel Vancouver opened.

July 5 Mayor David Oppenheimer opened St. Luke's Hospital in Vancouver. The facility was consecrated by Ven. Archdeacon Woods. Sister Frances Redmond ran BC's first nursing school here, as well as Vancouver's first social services centre.

July 10 John B. Rivet, blacksmith and wheelwright, opened a shop in Trounce Alley.

Left: The desire for a fresh and steady supply of water for Vancouver led to the building of the Capilano Dam in North Vancouver in 1888. The water was then piped under Burrard Inlet. The dam was replaced in 1954, by the Cleveland Dam. *City of Vancouver Archives, Ci Dept P37. Photo Harry T. Devine*

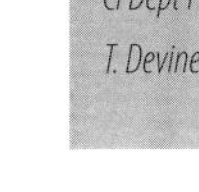

The SS *Beaver*, Ship for All Seasons

July 26 A strong tide was running into the First Narrows and the wind freshened, as Capt. George Marchant brought the venerable SS *Beaver* out of Vancouver Harbour that evening, bound for Thurlow Island. The ship's ungainly paddlewheels, mounted to the front of the hull and driven by a pair of 35-horsepower steam engines, churned as the ship struggled with buffeting wind and current. Trying to swing inside a huge tidal eddy, Captain Marchant hugged the southern shore. It was a fatal mistake on a lee shore.

The most historic ship on the West Coast struck hard on the rocks of Prospect Point. A passing steamer, the SS *Muriel*, went to the *Beaver*'s assistance but was unable to pull the paddlewheeler off. With the hold already half full of water, the crew scrambled over the bow and waded ashore.

The wreck lay in the shallows, accessible to souvenir hunters who stripped the hulk bare. One enterprising fellow named Charles McCain took 500 kilograms (1,100 pounds) of bronze and copper fittings that he later made into commemorative coins, key chains and jewellery. A consortium of Victoria businessmen had plans to retrieve the ship, dismantle it and ship it to Chicago for reassembly as an exhibit in the 1893 World's Fair. But in June 1892, almost 100 years to the day since Captain George Vancouver had sailed past the same point, the wake from the passing steamer *Yosemite* dislodged the wreck and it slipped into deep water and sank.

After 53 years as a steamer on the West Coast, the SS *Beaver* ran aground in 1888 at Prospect Point and was abandoned. The ship had been vital in its day for coastal fur trading and transportation. Its wreck is now a training site for underwater archeologists. *City of Vancouver Archives, Bo P155. Baily Bros. photo*

Commissioned for the Hudson's Bay Company at the beginning of the steam age, the *Beaver* was the first steamship on the West Coast of North America. During 53 years of service it had been present at almost every major event in the early history of BC. Gunboat for punitive expeditions against Indian tribes, diplomatic flagship, supply ship, Royal Navy hydrographic survey ship, general freighter, grimy towboat—the *Beaver* had done just about everything and been just about everywhere.

The ship was launched from the Blackwall shipyards on the Thames, near London, in 1835 and was one of the marvels of its day. The *British Daily Colonist*, reminiscing about the old ship in 1892, not long before it sank for good, recalled that King William had been among the 160,000 Londoners who turned out to see the *Beaver* slip down the ways. The engines and boilers, the newspaper reported, had been built by the son of James Watt, who invented the steam engine. But the ship was rigged as a sailing vessel for the journey around stormy Cape Horn to Astoria at the mouth of the Columbia River. The journey took 163 days with the paddlewheels in the hold, to be mounted on arrival.

When an influx of American settlers made it clear that the British would have to withdraw from the Oregon Territory, the *Beaver* was on the exploratory mission that in 1843 founded Fort Victoria, future capital of a future province. On January 5, 1853, the *Beaver* carried Governor James Douglas and 20 Royal Marines to Nanaimo to demand for trial two men who had murdered a shepherd in Saanich. Faced with a large, hostile band of Cowichans and Nanaimos, Douglas offered an ultimatum: give up the murderers and live in peace or "I will burn your lodges and trample out your tribes." The murderers took to the woods. Metis woodsmen from the Victoria Voltigeurs tracked them through the snowy woods. They were captured, brought aboard the *Beaver*, tried and found guilty, and a gallows was erected on Protection Island where they were hanged. A year later, on November 27, 1854, the *Beaver* delivered the first 75 settlers to Nanaimo, then just a defensive bastion and seven log buildings.

On November 18, 1858, the *Beaver* carried the official party to Fort Langley for the founding of a new colony on the mainland. The next day it fired the 18-gun salute that marked the birth of British Columbia. A year later it played a role in launching the Pig War, a 12-year standoff between the British and the Americans over who owned the San Juan Islands. On June 15, 1859, the *Beaver* carried a party from Fort Victoria to San Juan Island for a picnic. Among them was senior HBC official A.G. Dallas, who on landing learned that American settler Lyman Cuttler had shot a company pig rooting in his garden. The starchy Dallas demanded compensation. The Americans refused and landed a company of troops from Oregon; the British responded with two warships and 800 men; both sides dug in and the armies faced each other—and frequently dined together—until 1872, when the German emperor was asked to arbitrate and awarded San Juan to the United States.

Not all the *Beaver*'s adventures were stately. Historian Alan Morley tells of George Black, Gastown's first butcher, who once kept a pet bear. When the bear grew large and obstreperous, Black chained it and shipped it to Victoria aboard the *Beaver*. In mid-voyage the bear got loose, the crew took to the rigging and, Morley says, the old ship experienced a lively hour or two before Bruin was penned up again.

Today a plaque marks the spot where the *Beaver* foundered; the Vancouver Maritime Museum has an exhibit that features the ship's anchor, paddlewheel shaft and boiler; and the wreck site has been used in recent years to train divers in underwater archeology.

July 15 The *News-Advertiser* had this note: "Mr. W.A. Cumyow, formerly a merchant in Yale and Victoria, and who has lived recently in Westminster, has now opened an office in the new block at the corner of Cordova and Homer streets, and, as will be seen by his advertisements, will act as Chinese and English translator and accountant, also as real estate and custom house broker, conveyancer, etc." In 1861, Won Alexander Cumyow was the first Chinese baby born in Canada. (A note on newspaper style of the time: New Westminster is often referred to simply as Westminster.)

July 26
The first steamer on the West Coast, the Hudson's Bay Company's *Beaver*, ran aground on Prospect Point. After 53 years, her days of service ended.

September The first Surrey Fall Fair was held on the grounds of the municipal hall. The fair ended in a deficit, so winners accepted reduced prizes and promised to attend the next year.

September 27
Stanley Park was officially opened, Mayor David Oppenheimer presiding.

September 29 J.C. McLagan established the *World*, a daily newspaper.

The result of the first decision that Vancouver's first city council made back in 1886, Stanley Park was officially opened by Mayor David Oppenheimer on September 27, 1888. The establishment of the park was a sign of the city's growing maturity. It remains an iconic Vancouver landmark. *City of Vancouver Archives, LGN 1048. Photo Harry T. Devine*

Also in 1888

David Oppenheimer, who was mayor of Vancouver from 1888 to 1891, was elected by acclamation for two of his four one-year terms.

Surrey council paid for residents to be vaccinated against smallpox—the outbreak was contained, with only four deaths in Surrey.

The Delta Agricultural Society was founded for the purpose of holding an annual agricultural fair. A harness-racing track was built on the fairgrounds.

Moodyville's steamer *Eliza* was making five round-trips a day from Moodyville to Vancouver, and one to Hastings. The fare was 25 cents each way. With increased access, the North Shore's population began to grow.

The West School was built at Burrard and Barclay.

The first part of the CPR roundhouse in Yaletown was built.

Today it's a community centre and home to Locomotive No. 374.

McDonough Hall was built at the southeast corner of Hastings and Columbia. "The upper floor," said city archivist Major J.S. Matthews, "was a social centre for grand events in those early days." It later became the Cosy Corner Grocery.

Hastings Park was granted in trust to the city by the province, with the site to be used as a public park.

Henry Avison, the first employee of the Vancouver Park Board, lived with his family in Stanley Park in the 1880s. He cut the first trails and roadways in the park, and the Avison Trail in Stanley Park is named for him.

January 1889 marked the opening of the first Granville Street Bridge. This image will be unfamiliar to today's commuters, however, since the bridge used now is the third in its place.
City of Vancouver Archives, SGN 20

1889

In a year when Shakespeare and Lord Stanley came to Vancouver, the city got its first running water from the North Shore. And labour leaders organized to fight for the nine-hour workday.

January 4 The first Granville Street Bridge opened. (The current bridge is the third.)

March 5 The Vancouver Board of Trade held its first banquet in the Hotel Vancouver, at a cost of $12.50 per plate. That amount also got you a quart bottle of Mumm's Extra Dry Champagne.

March 14 The Vancouver Real Estate Board was formed. Today it's known as the Greater Vancouver Real Estate Board.

March 26 A small crowd gathered at Georgia and Granville Streets and watched as a valve was turned and fresh Capilano River water began to gush out. The *News-Advertiser* wrote: "Water from the water works dam of the Capilano River, ten miles from the place of writing in this city, crossed the Narrows Monday night at 11:10 o'clock, at 1 o'clock had filled the mains on Georgia street and at 2 o'clock had reached Westminster avenue [Main Street]." Vancouver had its water.

September The Vancouver Fire Department finally got horses to pull its fire engine. Since the summer of 1886 the firefighters had had to pull the engine themselves.

Elsewhere in BC

August 2 Pioneer New Westminster newspaper publisher John Robson became premier on the death of A.E.B. Davie.

Fire Wagon. In September 1889 the Vancouver Fire Department got horses for its fire engine so the firefighters could finally stop pulling it themselves.
Bailey Bros. photo. Vancouver Public Library VPL 19788

September 28 The windjammer *Titania* departed Steveston with canned salmon for direct shipment to Britain. Until this voyage, local canneries had imported and exported via Victoria.

Also September 28 Vancouver's first city hospital opened, a 35-bed wooden building at Beatty and Cambie Streets.

October 29 Governor General Lord Stanley (the same man who gave us the Stanley Cup) dedicated Stanley Park during the first visit of a GG to British Columbia. An observer at the dedication wrote: "Lord Stanley threw his arms to the heavens, as though embracing within them the whole of one thousand acres of primeval forest, and dedicated it 'to the use and enjoyment of peoples of all colours, creeds, and customs, for all time.'" His statue, in Stanley Park, immortalizes that gesture.

November 16 The Union Steamship Company was formed from the consolidation of the Moodyville ferry company and Burrard Inlet Towing Company.

December 5 *Richard III* opened at the Imperial Theatre, the first Shakespearean production in the city.

Also in 1889

John Howe Carlisle became chief of the Vancouver Fire Department. He served as chief for an astonishing 42 years. Carlisle was the first recipient of Vancouver's Good Citizen Award (1922).

New Brunswick-born Jay Russell and Victoria-born Len DuMoulin formed Russell and DuMoulin law firm. Today it's known as Fasken Martineau DuMoulin (part of the international firm Fasken Martineau) and is the biggest law firm in Vancouver.

The Trades and Labour Council was formed for the purpose of establishing a nine-hour workday.

The Marpole Midden was discovered by a road crew building an extension of Granville Street. Over the next several years, archeologist Charles Hill-Tout excavated the refuse heap, which contained mostly mollusk shells, but also tools, weapons and skeletal remains that date back to 400 BC. It turned out to be one of the largest village sites ever discovered in North America.

Comings and Goings

Benjamin Tingley Rogers (born in Philadelphia on October 21, 1865) came to Vancouver. He established the BC Sugar Refinery, wresting all sorts of concessions from city councillors anxious to have new industry.

June Writer Rudyard Kipling first visited Vancouver.

Katsuji Oya became the first *nisei* (second-generation Japanese) to be born in Canada.

1890

Signs of Vancouver's progress this year included the construction of a sugar refinery, the beginning of modern transit and the opening of the first high school.

January Vancouver's first high school opened.

May 12 The New Westminster Salmonbellies organized as a field lacrosse club.

June 13 Won Alexander Cumyow voted in the provincial election in spite of legislation disenfranchising Chinese voters. Although Cumyow's name appeared again on the 1898 BC voters list, he was not allowed to exercise his franchise. He next voted in 1949, after the legislation had been repealed.

June 28 Vancouver's electric streetcar system began running from the Granville Street Bridge to Union

Electric streetcars became the symbol of a modern city. Vancouver inaugurated its street railway system in June 1890. By 1907, the year this photograph was taken, tracks ran through downtown to Stanley Park, out to Kitsilano and south down Main Street, or Westminster Avenue as it was then called. The photo shows three of the green-painted cars trundling north up Westminster toward Keefer Street, still sharing the roadway with horse-drawn wagons. *Vancouver Public Library, Special Collections, VPL 7231. Philip Timms photo*

Right: The original BC Sugar refinery (pictured) produced its first sugar in 1891. The brainchild of American Benjamin Tingley Rogers, the plan was to import raw sugar from Australia, Asia or Central America, and refine it for the growing western Canadian market. The plan worked: Rogers Sugar remains a popular brand, and the refinery a local industry. *City of Vancouver Archives, Bu P216*

Street and Westminster Avenue (now Main Street).

July 8 The first foundation stone of the BC Sugar refinery, established by B.T. Rogers, was laid. (That building no longer exists.)

Also in 1890

Future BC premier John Oliver rented out the first steam thresher in Delta

and transported it from farm to farm on the new main roads of the municipality.

Japanese fishermen started experimenting with new techniques: seining for chum salmon, jigging for ling cod in Burrard Inlet and holding live fish in a tank to ensure a steady supply of fresh fish for market.

G. Oya opened a Japanese provisions store in Vancouver to cater to the increasing number of immigrants.

Comings and Goings

April Shiga Aikawa and Yasukichi Yoshizawa left Vancouver in a skiff to look for fishing grounds in northern waters. It took them 42 days to reach the mouth of the Skeena, where they became the first and second Japanese to fish in the north. Their exploits fired the imaginations of those on the Fraser, and within five years hundreds of Japanese fishermen joined them on the Skeena and Nass Rivers.

November 12 The first shipment of raw sugar for the BC Sugar refinery, 226 tonnes (250 tons), arrived on board the SS *Abyssinia* from the Philippines.

Right: Four years after opening the Hotel Vancouver, the CPR opened a world-class opera house in 1891 on Granville Street just south of the hotel. The 1,200-seat theatre attracted an impressive roster of performers over the years, including Sarah Bernhardt, Dame Nellie Melba and Nijinsky and the Ballet Russe. In 1935 it became a cinema called the Lyric, which remained in operation until 1960 when the building was demolished to make way for Pacific Centre. *City of Vancouver Archives, Bu P8. Photo courtesy of Bailey Bros.*

1891

The growing city got an opera house this year, and the world's most famous actress came to entertain. And a squatter named Sam shot the sheriff.

January 2 Electric streetlights were switched on in New Westminster, drawing power from a plant fuelled by sawdust.

January 14 Lieutenant-Governor Hugh Nelson proclaimed the former military reserve in Burnaby to be Central Park and set it aside for recreation. (The park was named after Central Park in New York, where Julia Oppenheimer, wife of Vancouver's mayor, was born.)

January 29 Mayor David Oppenheimer was invited to tour the brand-new BC Sugar refinery. Oppenheimer had donated the land on which the refinery sat.

February 9

The 2,000-seat Vancouver Opera House, built for $100,000 by the CPR, opened on Granville Street. The city's population was 13,000! It was an astonishingly grand edifice for such a tiny town, but

an indication of the CPR's optimistic view of the future.

March 10 H.O. Bell-Irving formed the Anglo-British Columbia Packing Company.

June 12 Ross McLaren Sawmills at Millside (later known as Fraser Mills), built in 1889, finally began operation.

July 1 The Douglas border crossing, named after Sir James Douglas, was established.

August 22 Coquitlam was incorporated.

August 29 The first councillors for North Vancouver District were sworn in. Moodyville decided not to be part of the new municipality, which stretched from Horseshoe Bay to Deep Cove.

September 26
Squatter Sam Greer, after whom Greer's Beach (Kitsilano Beach today) was named, shot the sheriff who came to evict him. While that official healed, Sam and his family were ousted, his buildings levelled and he spent some time in jail.

September 26 The first British Columbia amateur athletic meet was held at Brockton Point.

October 1 The Westminster and Vancouver Tramway Co. began Canada's first interurban line, running from (where else?) Vancouver to New Westminster.

November 27 The Great Northern Railroad from Seattle reached the south shore of the Fraser at New Westminster.

At a time when logging and canneries were the only significant industries, the Great Northern Cannery opened in West Vancouver in 1891. It operated until 1969, and is now a fisheries research station.
City of Vancouver Archives, SGN 1547. Photo C. Bradbury

Also in 1891

The Great Northern Cannery was built near Sandy Cove in West Vancouver, where the fisheries research station now stands. It operated until 1969.

There were 13,000 residents in Vancouver. In six years it had grown from a population of 400.

For the first time the non-aboriginal population of BC outnumbered the aboriginal population.

Richmond's Methodist Minoru Chapel was built, the first church on Lulu Island.

The first telephone line in Richmond was installed at a Steveston store. Messengers were sent from the store to fetch the person for whom the call was intended while the caller waited.

New connection. The lower mainland gets a little bit smaller with the first interurban line from Vancouver to New Westminster.
City of Vancouver Archives, LGN 1161. Photo BC Electric Railway Company photographer

A map was drawn showing the proposed boundaries of Burnaby. It took in all of Point Grey and what is now South Vancouver. Today, Burnaby's mayor has a copy hanging on the wall of his or her office.

When the federal Department of Fisheries and Oceans refused to issue fishing licences to Natives living along the Fraser River in the Cowichan Indian Agency, many of the younger generation of Lamalchi (now know as the Hwlitsum) relocated to reserves in the Fraser Agency. Their primary residence was a house at Hwlitsum, near Ladner and Canoe Pass, still occupied by band members today.

Comings and Goings

April 28 The CPR's *Empress of India* arrived in the city for the first time.

September 21 Sarah Bernhardt starred in *Fedora* at the Vancouver Opera House.

September 21 E.H. Wall of New York demonstrated the Edison gramophone for the first time in Vancouver at Manor House.

Empress of the Ocean

April 28 The CPR's *Empress of India* arrived in the city for the first time after sailing around the world with ports of call at Hong Kong, Shanghai, Nagasaki and Kobe.

The arrival of the first of the Canadian Pacific Railway's new state-of-the-art steamships—intended to set the benchmark for reliability, speed and opulent passenger service between Asia and Canada's West Coast—was a momentous event. The last of the great clipper ships, with their raked hulls and acres of canvas, were still in service sailing from New Westminster to Australia and China, but for all their grace and power they were hostage to the winds, while steamers like the *Empress of India* were not.

As the 19th century drew to a close, the British Empire was at its zenith, bound together by the commerce that pulsed along vast sea lanes protected by the Royal Navy, the most powerful military force of its day. If Britannia ruled the waves with cruisers and battleships, the fast steamships that delivered the Royal Mail had come to symbolize the prosperity, security and technological prowess of the world's reigning mercantile superpower.

In 1887, completion of CPR's trans-continental railway provided a strategic transportation link between Asia and Britain that proved as important in its day as the Panama Canal would later be. Suddenly, instead of beating around Cape Horn under reefed sails or taking the long voyage around Africa, cargo could cross the Pacific, speed across Canada by train and continue across the Atlantic, cutting months from the voyage. And so even before the railway was finished, the CPR had in place a maritime service linking Asia to Vancouver.

After winning a trans-Pacific mail contract from the British government, the company commissioned the gleaming white *Empress of India*, the first of a fleet of eight fast steamers that carried passengers and high-value cargo. On its first arrival in Vancouver, the *Empress of India* discharged 486 passengers and 1,640 tonnes of tea, silk, rice and opium from a berth at the foot of Granville Street. By the end of 1891, two other ships, the *Empress of China* and the *Empress of Japan*, had joined the *Empress of India* in what became a lucrative trade for the CPR.

Perishable, easily damaged raw silk was shipped from Asia to Vancouver aboard the *Empresses*, then loaded onto specially designed CPR express freight trains that featured airtight cars finished with specially treated woods and lined with paper to protect the precious cargo. Once loaded, the cars were sealed and the silk trains sped across Canada to the garment industries of Montreal and New York. The only passengers were armed guards who rode the trains to defend against possible hijackings, and these express freights had priority over all other rail traffic—even a VIP train carrying a future King of England had to wait on a siding for a silk train to roar past.

Eight *Empresses* saw service on the trans-Pacific run, with the *Empress of Russia*, *Empress of Asia*, *Empress of Canada*, *Empress of Australia* and a second *Empress of Japan*, later renamed the *Empress of Scotland*, joining the original three. However, there were never more than four of the ships in service at any one time. All the *Empresses* were requisitioned for military service in the world wars. Displaced by airlines, the trans-Pacific passenger service by luxury steamer was never resumed.

1892

A retail name that became a Vancouver institution for the better part of a century got its start this year. And a premier who fought to get BC out of British hands and into Confederation met an ignominious end.

February 15 J.C. Keith, a North Shore realtor, received financing to build a road on the north shore of Burrard Inlet from Howe Sound to Indian Arm. Work began, but a depression halted it, and the road, especially in its less-travelled stretches, began to deteriorate. That's why Keith Road runs in bits and pieces.

March 3
Charles Woodward opened his first store, selling dry goods, near Westminster (Main) and Hastings in Vancouver.

Elsewhere in BC

July 2 Theodore Davie, brother of former premier A.E.B. Davie, became premier upon the death of John Robson.

Edgar Dewdney, who developed the plans for New Westminster and established the Dewdney Trail from the Fraser River to the Similkameen and later the Kootenays, became Lieutenant-Governor of BC. After his term as L-G he surveyed the route for a railway between Hope and Princeton. It was built nearly 20 years later, operating as the Kettle Valley Railway.

The Country Boy Who Made Good

March 3 Charles Woodward opened his first store, selling dry goods, near Westminster (Main) and Hastings in Vancouver. He ultimately parlayed that corner store into one of western Canada's most successful department store chains.

One of five children, Woodward was born on a farm about 100 kilometres (60 miles) northwest of Toronto on July 19, 1852. He was carefully tutored in modern agricultural techniques by his English-born father and educated at Mono College in Ontario's Wentworth County. He married Elizabeth Anderson in 1873 and left home at 22 to homestead with his wife and two young children before travelling to the Prairies in 1882 to try his hand at cattle trading. When that didn't work out he returned to Ontario and farmed on Manitoulin Island, where he opened the first Woodward's Store.

Following heavy losses in a fire that destroyed his lumber business, Woodward closed the store—yet paid off all his creditors to the penny. Then he moved to Vancouver and opened his new store just in time for the Panic of 1893, a financial crisis on Wall Street precipitated by overbuilding and the collapse of a railroad bubble. The panic triggered a series of bank failures. The depression that followed was the worst US economic crisis until the Great Depression, with unemployment topping 18 percent (and in some cities exceeding 25 percent among industrial workers), accompanied by sometimes violent civil and labour unrest. "For the first time Vancouver saw misery on its doorstep and starvation in its streets," wrote historian Alan Morley. "By the spring of '94 the churches all through town were feeding hundreds at soup kitchens, and hundreds sought warmth in the public library."

To make things worse, there was a disastrous flood in the Fraser Valley during the spring of 1894. Yet Woodward's Store survived, selling groceries, boots and shoes while renting out unused space in the building. Despite the general economic stagnation, the retail operation proved so successful that it expanded into the entire building and was perfectly positioned to exploit the boom that accompanied the Klondike gold rush in 1897. At that time it moved to 624 Westminster. The original building was torn down in 1985.

By 1902 Woodward was doing so well that he expanded the business again, incorporating as Woodward Department Stores Ltd. The new enterprise relocated to a new building at the corner of Hastings and Abbot, where it opened as an emporium featuring 20 departments, "each one...so complete in itself that it may be said to represent an independent store." Originally a four-storey wood frame building with a brick facade, it added two storeys in 1908 and expanded seven more times until it reached more than 60,000 square metres (645,000 square feet) of floor space. A second department store opened in Edmonton in 1926.

Woodward was a civic-minded man, active in fraternal organizations and service clubs, and deeply interested in matters of community development. He was also an innovative marketer. He held the first one-price sale day—25 cents—in 1910 after buying a competitor's inventory at auction. This was the inspiration for Woodward's famous $1.49-day sales in the 1950s. In the 1920s a miniature Eiffel Tower was constructed on the Vancouver department store's roof with a light so bright it could be seen on Vancouver Island. In the 1930s, Christmas displays, which became legendary in western Canada, were placed in storefront windows.

When Charles Woodward died in 1937, his son William Culham "Willy" Woodward, who was born in 1885, succeeded him as president. Willy had joined the family business as a bookkeeper in 1907 and worked his way up to senior management. Under his leadership the chain opened a store that anchored Park Royal in West Vancouver. Willy also served as a director of the Bank of Canada and the Royal Bank and was appointed Lieutenant-Governor of BC in 1941. When he retired in 1956, his son Charles N. "Chunky" Woodward became president of Woodward's.

The chain expanded to Victoria in 1951, New Westminster in 1954, Oakridge Mall in 1959, Calgary in 1960 and Surrey in 1966. It also had stores in smaller BC centres. In 1974 the company's net sales topped $500 million. But the rapidly changing retail market caused problems, and in 1987 Woodward's posted its first financial loss since going public in 1950. Chunky resigned in 1989 and died in 1990, not living to see the historic family company declare bankruptcy in 1993 and vanish from Vancouver's business landscape.

The old Woodward's site was the subject of several development plans over the succeeding years, eventually opening in 2010 as a blend of commercial businesses and upscale condominiums that the city and province hoped would revitalize the neighbourhood.

March 25 Lawyer Edward Pease Davis founded Davis and Company.

April 30 The first election was held in the new municipality of South Vancouver. W.J. Brewer was elected first reeve. (Brewers Park is named for him.) South Vancouver's life was brief. It vanished on New Year's Day 1929 when it amalgamated with Vancouver.

September 22 A provincial order-in-council created the municipality of Burnaby.

October 10 A Women's Christian Temperance Union children's home opened at Dunsmuir and Homer in Vancouver.

November 1 Vancouver Firehall No. 3 opened on Broadway, west of Westminster Avenue, with a hand-drawn hose reel. The firefighters had no horses to pull their wagons, but they did have a telephone!

November 4 The first New Westminster Farmers' Market opened, attended by reeves and pioneer settlers from throughout the Fraser Valley.

November 5
Golf arrived in Vancouver with the formation of the Vancouver Golf Club (no relation to the present VGC). The six-hole course was built on links-type lands at Jericho.

November 15 The first assizes were held in Vancouver, with Judge John Foster McCreight presiding.

November 20 The *News-Advertiser* had this wonderful item: "The man Bennett, who was taken in charge Friday night as a lunatic, was much quieter toward midnight, but on Saturday forenoon he got worse again and was taken to New Westminster. He is a wood-turner by trade and worked in the Sehl-Hastie Erskine factory in Victoria. He seems to have become deranged through trying to invent a plan by which round, square or triangular pieces could be shaped on the one lathe."

December 5 The Terminal City Club was formed in Vancouver. It was known then as the Metropolitan Club and met in a building at the southwest corner of Hastings and Richards.

Also in 1892

James Machin became the second librarian of the Vancouver city library, succeeding George Pollay.

New West School was built at Burrard and Helmcken.

A new main post office opened at Pender and Granville.

Musqueam people hosted a potlatch and gave away thousands of dollars' worth of goods.

Sadanosuke Hayashi was credited with initiating the salt salmon chum industry.

I. Yamamoto operated the first boat works in Steveston.

Yoichi Tanabe apprenticed with a Chinese tailor in Vancouver, then opened the first Japanese tailor shop in Canada.

Fred Cope was elected mayor, the youngest in Vancouver's history (he was 32).

Comings and Goings

June 29
BC premier John Robson died in London, England, as a result of getting his finger caught in a cab door. Infection set in and... Robson was succeeded by Theodore Davie.

December 8 Future movie actor John Qualen was born in Vancouver. He appeared in more than 140 films, most famously as Muley in *The Grapes of Wrath* (1940). He has likely been seen most often, however, as Berger, the little fellow who wants to sell freedom fighter Victor Lazlo a ring in *Casablanca*.

This new main post office was built in 1892 at the corner of Pender and Granville. It immediately lent a permanent air to the young city. *City of Vancouver Archives, Bu P429.3*

Left: Elite retreat. The original Vancouver Club was an exclusive social retreat for the city's elite, located in this building on West Hastings close to the homes of many of its members. The extension on the left is the club pavilion, added in 1903. The original was replaced in 1913 by the building that still stands.
Philip Timms photo, Vancouver Public Library VPL 5145

1893

A national retailer claimed a downtown location that it still holds. And Vancouver's civic leaders created a club that still helps define the city's establishment.

March 25 The Vancouver Club was organized. The members adopted a constitution on this date and agreed on rules and regulations for club members. An 1889 attempt to form the club had not been successful, but many of the same men were involved in this second and successful venture.

June 9 Canadian-Australasian service was inaugurated with the steamer *Miowera.*

June The Vancouver library (called the Free Reading Room and Library) moved to 169 West Hastings St.

August 26 Edward Holmes completed a walk from Montreal to Vancouver.

October 6
The Hudson's Bay Company opened a new store

at Georgia and Granville. They've been at that corner ever since—but not in that building!

October 31 Vancouver Firehall No. 3 got its first horse-drawn hosewagon but still had no horses. When a fire broke out, the firefighters had to borrow horses from the city waterworks to pull the wagon.

Left: When the Hudson's Bay Company opened its store at the corner of Georgia and Granville in 1893, as shown here, it was a smaller version of the store so familiar to Vancouver residents today. Actually, this red-brick building was not even the first HBC outlet in the city. The company had been running its original store in Gastown for six years before it moved to this uptown site.
City of Vancouver Archives, Bu N417

Also in 1893

The Fraser River Fishermen's Protective Association was established. In the late 19th century the Fraser was fished by sail- and oar-powered gillnet boats, owned mostly by canneries.

Roedde House was built at 1415 Barclay in the West End of Vancouver. Today the charmingly preserved heritage structure is a museum, open for visits by the public.

Pictured here in 1957 and now the centrepiece of Barclay Heritage Square in the West End, Roedde House was originally built for Vancouver's first bookbinder, Gustav Roedde, in 1893. Since the City of Vancouver bought it in 1966, the heritage building has been expertly restored, and it is now open to the public as a museum.
City of Vancouver Archives, Bu P508.93. Photo A.L. Yates

The first telephone line was installed to Ladner's Landing in Delta. The switchboard was in Thomas McNeely's store.

A wharf built at the southern end of No. 5 Road in Richmond became known as Woodward's Landing. Two times a week, a boat left from here for New Westminster.

Land held by Mr. Austin (now the Vancouver Golf Club on Austin Road) was assessed for tax purposes at $20 per acre.

The first Japanese settlement in New Westminster was formed near the mill at Sapperton.

Alfred Horie Construction was established in Vancouver. The company is still in operation as the AHC Group.

Right: Christ Church, shown here in 1894 shortly before its completion, served the city's second Anglican congregation. It was built at the corner of Burrard and Georgia, on land purchased from the CPR, to serve a growing population in the West End. It became a cathedral in 1929.
City of Vancouver Archives, Ch P73

1894

An Anglican cathedral and a Roman Catholic hospital got their start in Vancouver. But the big news was disaster in the Fraser Valley.

January 22 The first school in Burnaby opened in the Edmonds neighbourhood.

April 17 The Art, Historical and Scientific Association, forerunner of the Vancouver Museum, was founded. The first donation was a stuffed swan.

May The Fraser River flooded, and many families in the Fraser delta were moved. There was some loss of life and much damage to dykes, bridges and railway lines. Some canneries were swept away. The valley was paralyzed for a week. This was the greatest flood in BC's recorded history. The gauge at Mission read 25.8 feet (nearly 8 metres), compared to the 24.6 feet (7.5 metres) of the famous 1948 flood. But property damage was much less in 1894: there was less property to damage!

August The cornerstone of Christ Church was laid in Vancouver. (It became a cathedral later.)

October 12
A party of hikers climbed a North Vancouver mountain. When they shot a blue grouse there, they decided to call it Grouse Mountain.

Great flood. This man is helpless to save the rail line as he floats in the wake of the greatest flood to ever strike BC, in May 1894. Charged by snow melt, the Fraser River flooded, paralyzing the valley for a week.
City of Vancouver Archives, Out P288. Photo George W. Edwards

Patient haven. St. Paul's Hospital was built by the Sisters of Providence, a Catholic religious order, at the invitation of Bishop Paul Durieu. Its location on Burrard Street at Comox was originally so remote from the centre of the city that patients arrived along a rutted wagon trail. By 1905, when this photograph was taken, an additional 50 beds had been added to the original 25.
Vancouver Public Library, Special Collections, VPL 5147. Philip Timms photo

December 21 Construction started on St. Paul's Hospital in Vancouver.

Also in 1894

Robert Alexander Anderson was elected mayor.

A Mrs. Thomson began the first kindergarten in Vancouver, on Georgia Street.

Alfred Wallace, who had established a boatbuilding operation in his backyard, opened a small shipyard on False Creek, just east of the north end of the Granville Street Bridge.

Thomas Kidd of Richmond was elected the first MLA for the municipality.

The Japanese Christian Endeavour Society of Seattle sent Rev. Masutaro Okamoto to work in Vancouver and Steveston during the fishing season. Previously he had worked among the fishermen of Skeena and established a mission in Victoria and a Sunday school in Vancouver.

The city of Vancouver adopted a bylaw to limit the sale of fresh produce to "permanent" places of business. The intent was to restrict the Chinese market gardeners and peddlers who went door to door to sell their produce.

1895

America's greatest wit came to town on a pay-off-the-creditors tour. And money changed hands following the discovery of gold in what is now suburban Richmond.

January 1 William H. Malkin arrived in Vancouver in the midst of a recession. "When I came here," he said in a 1937 speech, "half the stores were vacant, there was only a population of 17,000, and the future of the city was far from being assured." In 1929–30, W.H. was mayor of a much larger city, whose future he did much to assure.

January 6 General William Booth, founder of the Salvation Army, visited Vancouver.

August 2 Delta Creamery's first shipment of butter reached Vancouver Island.

August 15 American writer Mark Twain, 60, came to the Opera House on a speaking tour and made audiences laugh so long and loud that parts of his commentary couldn't be heard. Twain had a bad cold at the time, and a famous photograph shows him laid up at the Hotel Vancouver, chatting with writers

Elsewhere in BC

March 4 John Herbert Turner became premier.

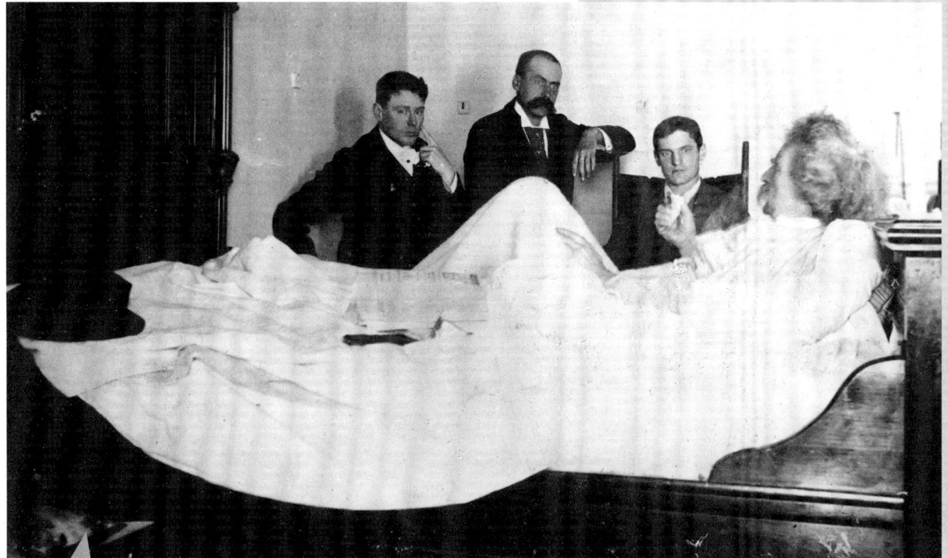

Mark Twain visited Vancouver's Opera House in 1895 as part of a speaking tour arranged to pay off his sizable debts. This famous photograph shows Twain laid up with a bad cold at the Hotel Vancouver, chatting with local reporters. *City of Vancouver Archives, Port P329. Photo George T. Wadds*

from the local newspapers. (Twain had declared bankruptcy in 1894 and was touring to raise money to pay off debts, incurred by his investments in new technology and a publishing house.)

Fall Richmond bored to find artesian water. When none was found by 310 metres (1,008 feet), the project was abandoned.

November 6 A newspaper report said, "Miles of claims have been staked on Lulu Island as a result of the discovery of gold. The first assay is reported to have yielded $10,000 a ton."

Also in 1895

Henry Collins became mayor. He had lost the election in 1894, and in 1895 was unable to campaign due to an accident shortly before the race began, but he still managed to beat his opponent by nearly 400 votes.

The Provincial Elections Act deprived Japanese and South Asians, then known as East Indians, of the right to vote in provincial elections. Because municipal and federal voters lists were based on the provincial list, the act denied them the right to vote in any elections and denied them entry into civil service jobs or professions like law, pharmacy and teaching, which required that members be on the voters list.

The Vancouver Lawn Tennis Club was formed.

The first letter boxes were installed on Vancouver streets.

Jacob Grauer, who had been a butcher in Vancouver since 1886, moved to a 120-hectare (295-acre) farm on Sea Island. Five years later he purchased another 260 hectares (640 acres) on Boundary Bay, where he grazed beef cattle and sheep, and grew feed for his Sea Island dairy herds. Grauer's meat products were later marketed under the Frasea Farms label. His sons worked with him in the business, and several became prominent Vancouver-area citizens: George was said to be the first white boy born in Mount Pleasant; Rudolph was reeve of Richmond (1930–49); and Albert ("Dal") became president of BC Electric and chancellor of UBC.

Chinese Canadian merchants established the Chinese Consolidated Benevolent Association, which became the political centre for the Chinese community in Vancouver. The Chinese Board of Trade was also formed.

The Canadian Japanese Association was established. It encouraged immigrants to become naturalized Canadians.

In the summer of 1907 women tennis players were still wearing full-length skirts and high-necked blouses to bat the ball around at the Vancouver Lawn Tennis Club, which had been formed in the West End in 1895. In 1914 the club purchased land from the CPR and moved to its present location at the corner of Fir and 16th. Club membership at the time read like a who's who of the city elite. *City of Vancouver Archives, CVA 677-242*

The Japanese Christian Endeavour Society opened a mission at the corner of Pender and Abbot Streets in Vancouver to minister to Japanese immigrants in BC. It relocated to Jackson and Powell Streets and became the Japanese Methodist Church and then the Powell Street United Church.

Y. Aoki opened a logging camp at Indian River, employing some 45 Japanese. He was joined by two other immigrants who opened camps in Port Moody and North Vancouver. Most of the products were exported to Japan.

The Oldest Chinese Grocery

Ling Chung Lam opened the Hong Wo General Store in the heart of Steveston's cannery row. The store, which had one of the first telephones in Steveston, sold all the daily necessities for the cannery workers and fishermen in the area, including meat, vegetables, fruits, dry goods, candy, clothing and hardware. Lam later branched into labour contracting, supplying cannery workers from the local Chinese community; he also bought 40 hectares (100 acres) of farmland nearby and owned several greenhouses, which supplied his store with locally grown potatoes, beans, tomatoes, cucumbers and cauliflower. The Lam family operated the store from 1895 to 1971, making it the longest-running general store in BC. A small settlement of Chinese and Japanese cannery workers and fisherman developed in the area between the Hong Wo Store and the Pacific Coast Cannery.

Also in Steveston, Isaburo Tasaka and his partner Shiozaki started a salted salmon operation in Steveston; the Gyosha Dantai (later the Japanese Fishermen's Benevolent Society) was organized to represent the nearly 2,000 Japanese fishermen on the Lower Fraser, about a third of the total fishing population; and Steveston's first Methodist church was built on land and with funds provided by Umejiro Yamamura. Labour was provided by Japanese Canadian fishermen. When a severe typhoid fever epidemic broke out, the mission was turned into a hospital and treated 26 Japanese and 12 Natives. The mission also operated a Japanese language school and conducted religious services.

1896

A man who would be elected mayor nine times arrived in Vancouver, apparently fleeing a fraud investigation in the United States. And city council passed a bovine bylaw.

March The Stanley Park Brewery began operations in Vancouver.

August 8 Jinsaburo Oikawa arrived in Canada from Miyagi in northern Japan. Two years later he started a chum salmon salting operation in Sunbury, 27 kilometres (17 miles) upriver from Steveston. He sold his products to Japanese and Chinese railway workers and loggers. In 1899 he returned to his home village to recruit villagers to come to Canada and expand his business. In 1902 he moved to Don Island, in the Fraser River, to continue the salmon salting operation. He also experimented with sujiko (fish roe) for export to Japan. On his next recruitment trip in 1906, he brought 82 recruits on the *Suian Maru*. They landed on Vancouver Island and were apprehended because they did not have the proper immigration papers, but a clerk at the Japanese consulate negotiated their entry. Oikawa returned to Japan in 1917; many of the people he brought to Canada remained here.

September 17 Louis D. Taylor, 39, arrived in Vancouver. In 1910 he was elected mayor...and then again in 1911, 1915, 1925–28 and 1931–34. For much of that time, mayors served one-year terms, so he won nine elections. Historian Daniel Francis has recently discovered that Taylor came to Vancouver to escape an investigation into his actions as an employee at a Chicago bank. This remained a secret throughout Taylor's time in the city.

October 26 Vancouver council set at 25 the maximum number of cows allowed per owner within city limits.

November 7 Burnaby hired its first law enforcer, at $2 a day, to police rowdyism, notify owners of swine running at large, and enforce the wide tire bylaw for wagons. He was dismissed for lack of funds in April 1897.

Also in 1896

The Hudson's Bay Company closed Fort Langley, one of the early Lower Mainland settlements,

and James Douglas' first choice as the capital of the new colony of British Columbia in 1858 (it lost out to New Westminster).

W.H. Malkin Co. was founded, with premises at 115 Water St. It was said that in those days, the water came right to the warehouse door of the wholesale grocery company. Malkin later moved to number 57.

Tokutaro Chikamura and Tsukichi Kato purchased 230 Powell St., becoming the first Japanese immigrants to own property on Powell.

The Vancouver Board of Trade lobbied for steamship service to northern points to promote trade and open the country.

1897

The first movies came to town as men were heading north to the Klondike Gold Rush. And two former mayors—Vancouver's second and third—died.

January 3
Prisoners in Vancouver's chain gang went on strike to protest having to work clearing the city's lanes.

April 15 The BC Electric Railway Company was formed and took control of the interurban tram system, which it operated until 1953.

July 22 Union Steamship SS *Capilano* sailed for the Klondike, the first Vancouver ship to go in response to the news that gold had been discovered in Rabbit Creek (later Bonanza Creek) near Dawson City, Yukon, in August 1896.

August 2 The movies came to Vancouver, with an Ethiopticon Kinetoscope moving-picture exhibition at Market Hall, together with Edison's "speaking phonograph."

October 2 News reached the city of the death September 19 on the Skagway Trail of former Vancouver mayor Fred Cope.

October 21 Pauline Johnson read her poetry at Homer Street Methodist Church. Sir Charles Tupper was in the audience. Until three months earlier he had been Canada's prime minister.

December The Royal Bank came to Vancouver as the Merchants Bank of Halifax, headquartered at the southwest corner of Hastings and Richards.

December 31 David Oppenheimer, Vancouver's second mayor—and one of the best—died.

Also in 1897

The McKinnon family settled in a Vancouver neighbourhood that Mrs. McKinnon would later suggest be named after Kerry's Dale, their former home in Scotland. We spell it Kerrisdale.

Alexander McDonald Paterson came to Delta to run the Paterson farm called Inverholme. He later served as Delta's reeve for 28 years. The Inverholme schoolhouse (now preserved on Deas Island) was built in 1909 on the Paterson farm.

Rev. Goro Kaburagi, ordained in the United States, became the first Japanese Christian minister in Canada. To spread his beliefs, Kaburagi began publishing the *Bankuba Shuho* (*Vancouver Weekly*) in July. It was renamed the *Kanada Shinpo* (*Canada News*) in November 1903, and on March 1, 1904, it became the first Japanese-language daily in Canada, with Kaburagi its full-time editor.

Canine power. With its prime location on the West Coast, the population of Vancouver doubled during the Klondike gold rush as would-be miners streamed through. In this photograph, boys and men gather to admire a dogsled and snowshoes from the Vancouver Hardware Co.—and the mismatched team of dogs.
Vancouver Public Library, Special Collections, VPL 19781. Bailey Bros photo

Left: A local fleet takes advantage of the fishing boom at the mouth of the Fraser River. *City of Vancouver Archives, Out P550. Photo S.J. Thompson*

The Chinese revolutionary leader Sun Yat-sen visited Vancouver.

This was a bonanza year for the fishing industry: as many as 14 ships lined up at Steveston's wharves to load canned sockeye for European markets. The catch exceeded the canning industry's capacity, and surplus fish (for which the fishermen were not paid) were tossed into the Fraser to rot.

A new and larger Japanese Fishermen's Hospital was built with $1,800 collected by the Gyosha Dantai. The hospital had a dispensary, clinic, minor operating room, general ward for more than 30 people and two small rooms for special patients. Japanese families were assessed $8 per year to cover operating costs. This entitled participants to full medical coverage, including consultations, medicine and hospital beds, although they had to pay for operations separately. This may have been the first "medical insurance" in North America.

William Templeton was elected mayor in his second try for the office. He had lost to David Oppenheimer in 1890.

Thomas Robert McInnes was named Lieutenant-Governor.

1898

Another Lower Mainland community was devastated by another fire, the Nine O'Clock Gun was fired for the first time—nine hours early—and Vancouver's longest-surviving newspaper began publication.

March 1 The Gordon sisters, Jessie and Mary, established Crofton House School for girls.

March 26 The first issue of the *Vancouver Daily Province* appeared. It quickly became the biggest paper in town.

March 28 Vancouver's first long-distance telephone (local and long-distance telephones were separate instruments then) was installed in the offices of the *Province*.

June 24 Vancouver papers reported that lady cyclists following the new "bloomer" fashion were finding it hard to gain admission to respectable places while wearing them.

July 1 The single-scull championship of the world was held in Vancouver Harbour. Jake Gaudaur beat Vancouverite R.V. Johnston.

July 8 This joke appeared in the *Province*:

"I say, waiter, this salmon cutlet isn't half so good as the one I had here last week."

"Can't see why, sir, it's off the same fish."

August 6 The first pay telephones in Vancouver were installed at English Bay. Cost: five cents.

September 10–11 The entire downtown section of New Westminster, including almost all the commercial section, was burned in a great fire. Hundreds were left homeless.

Fire struck New Westminster on the night of September 10, 1898. Flames spread from a steamboat moored on the waterfront to the docks and then through the centre of the city. By morning, most of the downtown was in ashes, including Holy Trinity Church, which had been dedicated in 1860. In this photograph of the church's charred remains, the historic bells can be seen in the lower right, damaged by the fire then hacked apart by souvenir hunters. Within a year most of downtown New Westminster had been rebuilt and the church was subsequently restored. *Vancouver Public Library, Special Collections, VPL 8750. Stuart Thomson photo*

1898

When Hastings Was the Main Drag

August 11 The *Province* reported that "Hastings Street, from Granville to Westminster Avenue [today's Main Street] is destined to be 'the' street in Vancouver there is no doubt. As has already been pointed out, between Cambie and Granville streets, 234 feet is being built upon, leaving only 702 feet vacant in the four lots. With the continuation of the tram line down Hastings Street, east from Cambie Street to Westminster Avenue, an immense impetus will be given to that portion of the business centre of the city. Vancouver is the biggest city on the Pacific coast and besides being the metropolis of British Columbia, is surely destined to be the third of the three largest cities in the Dominion of Canada—the Liverpool of the west.

"By far the most important building now in the course of erection in Vancouver is the Canadian Pacific Railway's magnificent new depot which is being built to fill the pressing need of several years...The building will be roofed in before the autumn rains commence and will be finally completed in the spring." (Note: The depot referred to is not the present building.)

October 7 John Schulberg presented BC's first moving pictures in a rented store on Cordova Street.

Also October 7 This appeared in a local paper: "The residents of Fairview, south end of Cambie street bridge, are to be congratulated in having a letter box placed at the corner of Seventh Avenue and Ash street. Mr. Foote has instructions to collect once per day, 10:45 a.m. and Sundays at 7 a.m."

Nine o'clock gun. A cannon was installed in Stanley Park in this shed near Brockton Point in 1894. Every evening at nine o'clock the gun was fired by a telegraph operator typing a key to close the circuit. The shed was demolished in 1936 and the mechanism was modernized, but the Nine O'Clock Gun still booms out across Burrard Inlet every evening.

City of Vancouver Archives, St Pk P121. Leonard Frank photo

October 15 The Nine O'Clock Gun was fired for the first time in Stanley Park. But not at 9 p.m. It was at noon.

November 14 The *Province* reported: "Despite the fact that a campaign was inaugurated in Vancouver against nickel-in-the-slot machines [i.e., jukeboxes] they are back again in large numbers."

Elsewhere in BC

February 10 The legislative buildings in Victoria opened. The *Victoria Times* called it "a theatre for the great deeds of legislators and administrators yet unborn." Yeah, right.

April 18 Henry Dallas Helmcken (MLA for Victoria) introduced a bill to extend provincial voting rights to women in BC. However, the bill ran into stern opposition from James Mutter (MLA for Cowichan-Alberni), who asserted that the female brain was two ounces lighter than a man's. The bill was defeated.

August 15 Charles Augustus Semlin became premier.

Also in 1898

James Ford Garden was elected mayor and remained in office until the new century began.

Vancouver city now had 25,000 residents.

James Skitt Matthews arrived in Vancouver. His methods were chaotic, his research was occasionally shaky and his temper was terrible, but he amassed a collection of general memorabilia from the city's past that is quite simply titanic. We owe him an unpayable debt.

The 500-seat Sing Kew Theatre opened. Situated between Shanghai Alley and Canton Alley, it became the centre of vibrant nightlife and entertainment for early residents of Chinatown.

1899

The first automobile arrived in Vancouver. And for the first time the city sent young men off to war.

January 22 Bishop Durieu consecrated St. Paul's Boarding School on the Mission Reserve in North Vancouver. Natives there helped fund and build the school, which was demolished in 1959.

June 24 Chief Dan George was born in North Vancouver.

July 6 Vancouver aldermen in horse-drawn carriages toured city sewer works under construction.

July 16 Archbishop Adélard Langevin laid the cornerstone of the Church of Our Lady of the Holy Rosary. In 1916 the church was elevated to a cathedral, Holy Rosary Cathedral, which is one of the city's most prominent and striking landmarks.

July 29 The first council meeting was held in Burnaby's first municipal hall, a small wooden structure built at a cost of $906. It was at the corner of Vancouver Road (Kingsway) and Edmonds.

September 26 BC's and Vancouver's first automobile,

a steam-powered vehicle that cost $650, appeared on a Vancouver street. The first motorist was contractor William Henry Armstrong, who took Mayor James Ford Garden for a ride. "The beautiful horseless carriage," wrote one reporter, "answered the steering gear to a hair's breadth as with rubber tires it noiselessly rolled along the asphalt with a motor power entirely hidden from view like some graceful animal curving its way in and out of the traffic."

Left: Steamy trip. Vancouver's first car would have turned heads when it arrived in 1899. The Stanley Steamer—an early model steam-driven car—was bought by W.H. Armstrong for George M. Taylor, pictured here with his wife. *City of Vancouver Archives, Trans P28*

September 29 Harry L. Salmon billed himself as the "Leading Tobacconist" in a big newspaper ad. In order to attract a large clientele to his new shop at the corner of Cordova and Cambie Streets, he announced that "every lady visiting the store will be presented with her choice of the following gifts: A Fine Havana Cigar, Puritano Fino; A Fine Cigar Shield to fit vest pocket; a fine Tin of Navy Cut Tobacco, or a Souvenir Fan."

September The Vancouver Fire Department became a fully paid department, with its 22 firefighters receiving $15 a month.

October 24 Seventeen Vancouver volunteers were among 60 men from BC who left on a CPR train to join the Canadian contingent going to the Boer War, which began on October 11.

Also in 1899

Vancouver High School affiliated with McGill University and took the name Vancouver College.

St. John the Divine, the first church in Burnaby, was built in what is now Central Park. It burned down in 1904, and another church was built on the same site a year later.

Fraser River canneries packed more than 300,000 cases of salmon this year, reflecting the Fraser's position as one of the world's most important salmon rivers.

A logging operation began on Black Mountain in West Vancouver. A flume carried logs from Whyte Lake to the sea. Oxen were also used on the few skid roads in the area, one of which became Keith Road.

Francis Caulfeild, recently arrived from England, settled at Skunk Cove (later renamed Caulfeild), where he planned a village in keeping with the beautiful surroundings—and with the whole waterfront reserved as a public park. Caulfeild built a water system served by Cypress Falls, and by 1909 was offering lots for summer homes.

J.M. Fromme was the first homesteader in Lynn Valley.

The BC Fishermen's Union was established.

The Beatty Street Drill Hall was built.

Members of the Cadet Corps and a bugle band perform drills on the Cambie Street Grounds opposite the Beatty Street Drill Hall. The hall, which opened at the turn of the century, resembles a medieval castle, complete with turrets, battlements and brick-and-granite walls which are 3 feet thick. The grounds became known as Larwill Park and for a time served as the city's main bus depot, but the drill hall still looks much as it did a hundred years ago. *Vancouver Public Library, Special Collections, VPL 6797. Philip Timms photo*

The first CPR station, a tiny building, was moved from the north foot of Howe Street to 10 Heatley St. CPR worker William Alberts, who had been badly injured on the job, was allowed to move into the old, unused station and use it as a rent-free residence for the rest of his life. He lived there for 50 years.

The St. Mungo Cannery was built on River Road in Delta, atop what later proved to be an important archeological site.

1900-1909

DRY GOODS
CROCKERY
GROCERIES
MANTELS
Limited
WOODWARD DEPARTMENT

1900

The Vancouver tradition of commuting to the North Shore began when a ferry service was inaugurated. And there was conflict between Caucasian and Japanese fishermen.

May 10 First meeting of the recently incorporated Japanese Fishermen's Benevolent Society (formerly Gyosha Dantai) at the Phoenix Cannery in Steveston.

May 12
The ferry to North Vancouver began operation,

providing the first regular service between North Vancouver and the south shore of Burrard Inlet. Later renamed *North Vancouver No. 1*, the boat ended up as a private residence, beached on a small island near Tofino.

June 9 John Oliver, a future premier, began his political career as the MLA for Delta.

July 1 Fishermen on the Lower Fraser went on strike. Overfishing by Americans was partly to blame for depleted salmon stocks, as fish traps remained legal in Washington state until 1934. During the strike there was hostility between the white fishermen's union and the Japanese fishermen who lived in cannery houses and depended on the canneries for food. On July 22 the militia was called in to keep the peace, and 160 soldiers from the Duke of Connaught's Own arrived in Steveston. By July 30 the strike had been broken and everyone was back fishing.

August 5 A letter to the editor of the *Province*: "There are few residents in the city and particularly in the West End who are not disturbed in their slumbers from 5 a.m. by the fearful and nerve-killing noises made by the crows. A vote should be taken as to whether the people want crows or not."

Glamourless streetcar. Public transit came early to Vancouver, but it wasn't always pretty. No. 25, in this picture from Denman Street in 1895, had shallow, lengthwise seats to prevent people from sticking their feet out. The seats were reported to be so shallow that "women, when once seated, could not rise again." *City of Vancouver Archives, M-3-18.2.*

September 5
Riverfront lots in Surrey between 10 and 13 acres were advertised at "$105 per lot, irrespective of acreage."

An 80-acre (approximately 32 hectares) farm, partly cleared, with farmhouse and small orchard was advertised at $40 per acre. A schoolteacher's salary in Surrey at the time was $60 to $100 a month.

October 19 Tomekichi Homma, the first president of the Gyosha Dantai, applied to Thomas Cunningham, Collector of Votes in Vancouver, to be put on the voters list. Cunningham refused, citing Section 8 of the Provincial Elections Act: "No Chinaman, Japanese, or Indian shall have his name placed on the Register of Voters for any Electoral District, or be entitled to vote at any election." Homma, a naturalized British subject and a boarding-house keeper in Vancouver, sued the BC government. The Supreme Courts of BC and Canada ruled in his favour and ordered that Homma's name be entered on the voters list, but in 1903 the Judicial Committee of the Privy Council in London, Canada's highest court of appeal at the time, reversed these decisions. The Homma case was the beginning of a long struggle for voting rights for Japanese citizens.

October 21 The bells at Holy Rosary Church (it was not yet a cathedral) were blessed by a papal delegate visiting Vancouver. The church was built (in 490 days) of sandstone from Gabriola Island.

Elsewhere in BC

February 28 Joseph Martin became premier. He lasted 106 days—the shortest term of any BC premier.

June 15 Lieutenant-Governor Thomas McInnes called on James Dunsmuir to serve as premier.

Thomas McInnes, who had been meddling in provincial politics—dismissing two premiers and being censured by the legislature—was himself dismissed, the only L-G in BC's history to lose his job. Sir Henri-Gustave Joly De Lotbinière was appointed to succeed him.

Elsewhere in Canada

September 6 W.A.C. Bennett was born in New Brunswick.

Chez Bay. Another Vancouver landmark was born in 1900 with the construction of the new Hudson's Bay Company building at Georgia and Granville, replacing the Bay's old red-brick structure from 1893. More than a century later, the store is still a familiar part of the downtown core, although it has since been expanded.
City of Vancouver Archives, Duke of C and Y P7

November 1 Mrs. Shimizu organized a ball at the Hotel Vancouver in honour of Her Imperial Majesty, the Empress of Japan.

December 30
A big civic parade in Vancouver welcomed troops home from the Boer War.

Also in 1900

At the turn of the 20th century, fish canneries were largely responsible for the ethnic diversity in the Fraser delta area. Chinese men, often brought to Canada as indentured labourers by a "China boss," butchered and canned the fish; Native and Japanese women cleaned the fish and filled the cans; and Native, Japanese and European men fished. More than 200 cannery and fishery workers were needed to process 1,200 cases a day (57,600 pounds, about 26,000 kilos).

Cannery owners formed the Fraser River Canners Association to protect their interests against dissatisfied fishermen.

The Dewdney Trunk Road was built on the north bank of the Fraser.

The name of the West School was changed to Dawson School.

The Canadian Pacific Railway financed a film to promote Canadian immigration to the west. It took two years to complete because the filmmakers weren't allowed to show snow.

Canada's first "Japan Town" began emerging in the area around Hastings Mill, between Powell Street and Westminster Avenue (now Main Street). It was home to about 500 Japanese millworkers and mushroomed with small businesses including boarding houses for Japanese men, hotels, stores, barber shops, blacksmiths, cleaners, fish markets, greengrocers and restaurants. Institutions such as the Japanese consulate (1889) and the first Japanese newspaper, *Bankuba Shuho* (1897), were already established.

1901

The social calendar contained a couple of major entries: the first royal visit and an inaugural party at the city's premier mansion.

January Canadian Pacific Railway bought out the Canadian Pacific Navigation Co. and its fleet of 14 vessels. The resulting CP coastal service became known as BC Coast Steamships.

March 25

Vancouver requested and was granted $50,000 from US steel magnate and philanthropist Andrew Carnegie to build a library.

Carnegie agreed to give the funds only if the city furnished a site and agreed to support the library at a rate of $5,000 a year. The city council accepted the Carnegie gift and its conditions. A site was chosen at the corner of Hastings Street and Westminster Avenue (now Main Street) for the new Carnegie Library, which opened in October 1903.

April 10 J.C. McLagan, founder and editor of the *Vancouver Daily World*, died. His widow, Sara Ann McLagan, became the first woman publisher of a daily newspaper in Canada. She was also managing editor, editorial writer, proofreader and occasional reporter. Sara McLagan was an interesting woman in her own right. She came here from Ireland in 1858, age three. Her father taught her telegraphy. When she was 12, a major forest fire threatened their Matsqui home, but Sara tapped a message through to New Westminster and that brought help. At age 14 she took over the New Westminster telegraph station.

Left: Sara McLagan, owner of the *Vancouver World*, was the first woman to run a daily newspaper in Canada. She and her husband, John, had got it going in 1888 and when he died she carried on with the help of her brother Fred, the business manager. The *World* was one of three dailies in the city, and the only evening paper. Under her direction it was a voice for the women's suffrage movement and for the city's underprivileged. McLagan sold the business to Louis Taylor in 1905, established the successful Clayburn brickworks with her brothers and—in her 60s—went to France to work for the Red Cross during World War I. She died in 1924. *City of Vancouver Archives, Port P636. Photo George T. Wadds*

June 23 Snow in South Vancouver!

July 23 Mr. and Mrs. B.T. Rogers had a housewarming party at their new mansion, Gabriola, on Davie Street. Designed by Samuel Maclure, it was the grandest home in the city. Benjamin Tingley Rogers was one of the city's leading industrialists, founder of the sugar refinery. After he died in 1918, Gabriola was converted into apartments and gradually deteriorated. Saved from demolition in the 1970s, it has since housed a series of restaurants.

July 24 The *Province* reported that from June 1, 1900, to May 31, 1901, St. Paul's Hospital had admitted 561 patients, discharged 506 of them, and still had 35 in beds. Some 25 patients had died, 11 of them within three days of entry. Catholics numbered 153, Protestants 383, and other religions 25. Males? 393. Females? 165. Fifty patients had been admitted with typhoid fever, and seven of them had died. The statistics go on for two long and detailed columns.

Elsewhere in the World

January 22 Queen Victoria died and Edward VII became king.

September 30 Vancouver's first royal visit began with the arrival of the Duke and Duchess of Cornwall and York (later King George V and Queen Mary). A report from the time said: "The city was gaily bedecked with flags and bunting, the display being the most spectacular the young city had ever seen." Events included a visit to Hastings Sawmill, "at which latter place they saw a forest giant being cut up."

November 19 Headline in the *Province*: "Klondike Revolution?" The newspaper reported that the *San Francisco Call* had "devoted its entire front page to the story of the unearthing of a huge conspiracy. It declares that a plot exists to overthrow the Yukon government and establish a republic with Dawson as the capital. It is said that the conspirators are at Dawson, Skagway, Vancouver, Victoria and Seattle, and that 5,000 miners are awaiting a signal to overcome the mounted police."

We checked the date of this story and yes, it was November 19, not April 1. The *Province* went on to report that other San Francisco newspapers later denounced the story as "a gigantic fake."

Also in 1901

Vancouver's population was 29,000, up from 13,000 ten years earlier.

The census recorded 365 people living in North Vancouver, and the *British*

Columbia Directory described the area as a "suburban townsite." In Steveston there were 396 Japanese men, most of whom were single or had families in Japan. There were 46 Japanese women, only one of whom was single, and 23 children under the age of 16. Twelve of the children had been born in Canada, the rest in Japan. Two enterprises listed in the census were Japanese owned: the Fishermen's Hospital and George Isomura's boat works.

Thomas O. Townley was elected mayor. He was swept out the next year because people saw him as the mayor of "saloons and gambling and kindred matters."

This was a peak year for salmon. Forty-nine canneries operated on the Lower Fraser and nearly a million cases were packed.

The Moodyville mill closed after being the largest single source of export income for BC for 20 years. It was cheaper to move the mill to the source of logs than the other way round.

As a result of pressure from the Vancouver Board of Trade, when a five-day steamer service from Seattle to Skagway was inaugurated, it included a stop at Vancouver.

The City Hospital was incorporated under the name Vancouver General Hospital.

1902

Vancouver was linked to Australia by undersea cable, and the city's first attempt to promote tourism began. The first union local for women workers was established at a time when the extent of pay disparity was decried even by male labour leaders.

January 20 The Royal Brewing Company took over a small brewery near the Cedar Cottage interurban railway station and started brewing heavy English ale.

March 29 With Mayor Thomas Neelands presiding, Grand Master F.M. Young of the BC Grand Lodge of Masons laid the cornerstone of the Vancouver Free Library, now Carnegie Centre, at Westminster (now Main) and Hastings.

May 27 Vancouver's baseball team beat the University of California team 4–2 at Powell Street Grounds (now Oppenheimer Park, and still used for baseball).

May The British Columbia Packers Association was established with the purchase of 42 canneries, and Alexander Ewan became the first president. Today BC Packers is western Canada's largest seafood company. Among its most famous products is Clover Leaf salmon, first sold under that name in 1889.

June 27
The Vancouver Information and Tourist Association—precursor to today's Tourism Vancouver—began operations at 439 Granville St.
A shingle hanging outside read: "Headquarters for visitors and tourists—Free information bureau."

Elsewhere in BC

November 21 Edward G. Prior became premier of BC. He was in office until June 1903, about seven months. Prior Street in Vancouver is named for him.

Elsewhere in the World

May Canadian-born Edmund Augustine Smith filed his first patent application for the Smith Butchering Machine, a mechanized fish-butchering machine he had invented that cut off the heads and fins, and gutted the bellies, of 60 to 75 salmon per minute. Nicknamed the "Iron Chink," the machine required three men to operate it and replaced 30 Chinese labourers working with knives. It was first used at Steveston's Gulf of Georgia Cannery in 1906.

June 25 The *Province* reported that "grave fears" had been expressed over the rapidly deteriorating condition of King Edward VII, with death expected at any time. The story took up the entire front page. The king pulled through and lived another eight years.

July 1 The first train of the Vancouver and Lulu Island Railway arrived in Steveston. Operated by the CPR principally to serve the canneries, the line became known as the "Sockeye Limited," although it was not used to transport the canned salmon: the canneries still preferred shipping by boat. The line ran along today's Arbutus Corridor between False Creek and the Fraser River to the foot of Oak Street, where a trestle bridge crossed to Richmond; the rails then proceeded through the countryside to Steveston's salmon canneries. The railway served Steveston for 50 years.

July 28 Al Larwill was given notice to move from the Cambie Street Grounds. "He has lived in the small cottage on Cambie Street Grounds since the year of the fire [1886]," reported the *Province*. "Every game known to Britons has been played on the grounds, and Al was the father of them all. Baseball gloves, lacrosse sticks, footballs, cricket bats and all kinds of athletic paraphernalia found a ready storehouse in his shack. Al's dining room was the dressing room for every team that played on the grounds. Now that Vancouver is to buy the land from the CPR and enlarge, grade and level the park, it will be necessary for 'Old Forty' to move." We haven't yet learned the reason for his nickname, but you'll be pleased to learn that the grounds were renamed Larwill Park. The "park" was the site of Vancouver's bus depot until the 1990s, when it was converted to a parking lot.

August 9 The first BC chapter of the Imperial Order of the Daughters of the Empire (IODE) was established in Vancouver on the occasion of Edward VII's coronation.

September 12 Charles Woodward, who had opened a small store on Westminster Avenue (now Main Street) in 1892, incorporated Woodward's Department Stores. Three days later, excavations began at the northwest corner of Hastings and Abbott Streets for the construction of a four-storey emporium. The lot itself (big enough to hold a building 20 metres/66 feet wide on Hastings and 40 metres/132 feet long on Abbott) hadn't cost Woodward much: it was a swamp 2.5 metres (8 feet) below the sidewalk elevation. The city drained it for him. The new store threw open its doors on November 4, 1903.

This log dam was part of the Buntzen Lake power project that brought the first hydroelectricity to Vancouver in 1903. Water from Coquitlam Lake flowed into Buntzen Lake, renamed after the general manager of the BC Electric Railway Company, Johannes Buntzen, then down penstocks to a generating plant on Indian Arm.
City of Vancouver Archives, S-4-13

October 31
The Pacific Cable from Vancouver to Brisbane, Australia, the last piece of Britain's global telegraph network, was completed.

Sir Sandford Fleming sent the first message over the line, and Vancouver's mayor, Thomas Neelands, wired greetings to King Edward VII. The Vancouver Board of Trade had lobbied hard for this connection to the "All Red Line," so called because it linked the British Empire, indicated by red or pink on maps, around the world.

November 21 Entertainment seekers were informed they could see *The Eruption Of Mount Pelee—By Electricity* at the Edison Electric Theatre on Cordova Street. This was a reconstruction, in a studio, of an actual natural disaster. John A. Schulberg opened the theatre, believed to have been Canada's first permanent cinema, this year. According to movie historian Michael Walsh, "It offered the latest in novelty entertainment—short, silent pictures that moved and occasionally told stories."

December 17 "The Privy Council of Great Britain has reversed the decision of the Full Court in British Columbia," the *Province* reported on its front page, "and has decided that it is within the power of the Legislature of the province to prevent Japanese from voting." The case had been launched two years earlier by a Vancouver man named Tommy Homma, a naturalized British subject. "He applied to the Collector of Voters in Vancouver to have his name placed on the list, but the Collector refused...The Electoral Act provides that no Chinese, Japanese or Indian shall have his name placed on the list."

Also in 1902

L.I. Dundas logged Capitol Hill in Burnaby using oxen.

Burnaby pioneer Charles F. Chaffey built his family home, Fir Grove, at Vancouver (now Kingsway) and Chaffey. Chaffey-Burke Elementary School in Burnaby is named for him and for another pioneer, William Burke.

Tsunejiro Okamura became the first Japanese photographer in Canada when he opened a photography shop in New Westminster. He landed in Vancouver in 1891, learned English and worked in a photographic shop to learn his craft.

John A. Cates launched the Terminal Steamship Company, providing ferry service to points on Howe Sound.

Cates had his brother George E. Cates build a luxury steamer at his False Creek shipyard. The *Britannia,* with its plush-covered seats and full dining service, could carry several hundred passengers.

Posh cruising. The Terminal Steamship Company's *Britannia*, shown here passing the much smaller West Vancouver passenger ferry, was the classiest excursion vessel of its day. In the dining room waiters dressed in formal attire served three-course meals on linen tablecloths. The *Britannia* cruised to Bowen Island and many other spots around Howe Sound.
Vancouver Public Library, Special Collections, VPL 7199. Philip Timms photo

Work restarted on Keith Road on the North Shore, but two bridges were swept away by creek flooding just after completion.

Peter Larson built the Hotel North Vancouver on West Esplanade. It became the community centre, where public gatherings were held. Larson Avenue in North Vancouver is named for Peter Larson.

The District of North Vancouver opened its first school at 4th and Chesterfield.

The influx of new residents meant two teachers were needed. Renamed Central School, it grew rapidly. The school building, at 333 Chesterfield Ave., later became city hall, including a court room and jail cells. Today it is Presentation House.

With assistance from the Japanese consul, Goro Kaburagi, a Christian minister, started an elementary school for children of Japanese ancestry. In 1906 it became the Vancouver Japanese School on Alexander Street.

James Skitt Matthews, 24, who eventually became Vancouver's first official archivist, fell ill with typhoid and spent three months in Vancouver General Hospital. There he met the woman who years later became his second wife.

The first European resident in Kitsilano, realtor Theodore Calland, built the mansion Edgewood (now demolished) just west of the CPR property at Boundary Street, now Trafalgar Street.

The Marpole Bridge, a low-level rail bridge, was built over the North Arm of the Fraser River

to carry the Vancouver and Lulu Island Railway (a CPR line). Today the bridge and track are leased by the Southern Railway of BC. (There was also a bridge here for vehicle traffic, built in 1901. By the 1950s it had become a real bottleneck. More and more people were using it to get to the airfreight terminal on Sea Island, but it had to be raised for marine traffic—records show that in 1954 it was opened 7,015 times! The vehicle bridge was dismantled in 1957 after the Oak Street Bridge was opened. Today's Arthur Laing Bridge, opened in the mid-1970s, was built higher and longer on the same alignment.)

Stó:lō people, under the supervision of the Oblate Fathers from St. Mary's Mission in Mission, completed construction of the Church of the Holy Redeemer on McMillan Island at Fort Langley.

The Shirt, Waist and Laundry Workers International Union established a local in Vancouver, the first union organization for women workers in Vancouver. Also this year, the Trades and Labour Council heard a complaint that a local hatmaker had employed a woman apprentice without pay for a year, then offered her $1 a week at a time male workers were making $10

Left: The Rat Portage Lumber Company shingle and sawmill went into operation at the foot of Fir Street on the south side of False Creek in 1902. It was owned by entrepreneur William Lamont Tait. False Creek, with its sawmills, railyards and shipbuilding operations, was becoming the industrial heart of the city.
City of Vancouver Archives, Mi P39

to $15 and other female workers made $2. "No young woman could live a virtuous life on $2 a week," the Labour Council declared.

The first BC table tennis championship was played in Vancouver. Men, women and boys competed.

Governor General Lord Aberdeen commissioned artist James Blomfield to work on a modified version of Vancouver's coat of arms. In 1902 Aberdeen presented this work to the visiting Duke and Duchess of Cornwall. Today's arms are a modified version of Blomfield's design.

William Lamont Tait, lumberman and financier, opened Rat Portage Lumber, a shingle and sawmill on False Creek. Tait's Shaughnessy mansion, Glen Brae, is now Canuck Place.

Comings and Goings

New Westminster pioneer **James Kennedy,** born in Ireland in 1817, died. Both an architect and a builder, Kennedy designed and constructed many of the city's first buildings. His wife was the first white woman in New Westminster. Kennedy Elementary is named for him.

1903

The headlines featured gunfire with the killing of a union activist, the shooting of a wolf in a West End henhouse and a murder of crows in Stanley Park. And two city landmarks were opened: the Carnegie Library and the Woodward's department store.

January 6 Vancouver Business College opened with four students.

January 29 Headline from the *Province*: "Good Work of the Tourist Association Already Showing Results". "It is confidently expected that during the month of June there will be 5,000 visitors to the city. The chief attraction during that month will be the meeting of the General Assembly of the Presbyterian Church in Canada, which will convene here on the 10th."

March 6 The *Province* reports on a "Handsome Book on Vancouver." It's a 1903 publication by the Tourist Association, titled *Vancouver, The Sunset Doorway*. "The...booklet is a credit to the city. From the handsomely lithographed covers to the smallest detail of illustrating the art-mechanical work has been well done. In its hundred pages there is every possible detail of information, from the physical features of the city and its environments, to sketches of its growth and history since the days when Vancouver was a hamlet... special articles, like those on Coast Indians and Vancouver's Chinatown, present descriptions of native and Oriental life in original and striking character. There are dozens of photographs...By the end of the week 5,000 copies of the booklet will have been mailed by the secretary to all parts of the world."

March 10 Fraser River Sawmills was formed

and operated out of the old Ross McLaren mill in Port Coquitlam. The company grew to become the largest lumber shipper in the British Empire.

April 15 Union activist Frank Rogers was shot and killed on a Vancouver street. His killer was

Elsewhere in BC

June 1 Richard McBride became premier when E.G. Prior resigned. He won the provincial election in October and remained premier through three more elections, until December 1915—the longest term to that point.

Elsewhere in the World

The Pacific Coast League (baseball) was established. Vancouver finally got a PCL team in 1956.

At the urging of Shinkichi Tamura, one of the most successful Japanese businessmen of the pre-World War II period, Canada participated in Japan's National Industrial Exposition. As a result, the first consignment of Canadian wheat was shipped to Japan.

Standing pretty in mid-air, these early tourists enjoy North Vancouver's first tourist attraction, the steel-cable suspension bridge built over the Capilano River in 1903. It replaced the original bridge of hemp rope and cedar planks. *City of Vancouver Archives, CVA 371-211*

never identified. Rogers had worked on the city docks, helped build the longshoremen, railway, and fishermen unions and had been active in the 1900 fishermen's strike on the Fraser River. The shooting happened in the midst of unrest among rail workers, with longshoremen striking in sympathy.

Summer A steel-cable suspension bridge, the first commercial tourist attraction in North Vancouver, was built over the Capilano Canyon, replacing an earlier, rougher version.

August 26 The Art, Historical and Scientific Association, headed by president Sara McLagan, agreed to hand over its collection to the City of Vancouver, a prelude to the creation of a city museum.

Fall The first North Vancouver District Municipal Hall was built at the corner of 1st Street and Lonsdale Avenue. Since incorporation in 1891 the council had been meeting in various buildings over in Vancouver, except for one obligatory meeting a year in the district.

October 1 The Vancouver Public Library, now with more than 8,000 books, moved into the Carnegie Library building at Westminster (now Main) and Hastings. This was the city's main library until 1954. Today it's a community centre for the Downtown Eastside, a very busy place that contains, among other things, a library!

Also on October 1 The *Province* described an event that occurred at the corner of Burnaby and Cardero Streets in the West End. Mr. W.S. Holland, who lived at that corner, heard a disturbance at 3 a.m. in the chicken shed behind his residence. His "entire poultry colony," he said, began to squawk. Mr. Holland got out his shotgun and blasted away at what looked like a large dog chasing his chickens. Then he went back to bed. When he got up later that morning he found a dozen dead hens...and one big dead timber wolf. Repeat: at the corner of Burnaby and Cardero!

October 8 The first Mission to Seamen, a social centre for sailors, was established in St. James Hall in Vancouver.

November 3 Crows made the news with a plan to allow sportsmen into Stanley Park "to exterminate the pest."

A bounty of "five cents per head up to 5,000 head" was offered, and the park was closed to the public as the huntsmen did their work. Although a bylaw banned the discharge of firearms within the park, officials said they would look the other way. (And today? Every day as dusk falls, about 5,000 to 8,000 crows gather near the Willingdon exit on Highway 1 in Burnaby.)

November 4 Charles Woodward opened a four-storey department store

Gift of words. The American steel tycoon and philanthropist Andrew Carnegie funded more than 2,500 public libraries around the world. One of them—this ornate sandstone pile at the corner of Hastings and Main—was in Vancouver. Built with a $50,000 grant from Carnegie, the three-storey library opened in 1903 with a collection of 8,000 books, and continues to serve the community today. The building to the left of the library is the Old Market Building in which the offices of Vancouver City Hall were located on the second floor until 1929. *Vancouver Public Library, VPL 3433. Philip Timms photo*

1903

Woodward's branches out. On November 1903, Charles Woodward opened a four-storey emporium on the corner of Hastings and Abbott, expanding his business from the original, modest department store on Westminster Avenue (now Main Street). *Vancouver Public Library, Special Collections, VPL 6701. Philip Timms photo*

at the northwest corner of Hastings and Abbott Streets.

November 12 The *Province* reported on the Royal Bank's new building at Hastings and Homer. The building was erected by Jonathan Rogers, after whom the Rogers Building at Pender and Granville was named, and one of the architects was Sydney Morgan Eveleigh, after whom a tiny downtown street is named. The new bank had the first safety deposit box in the city and two, count 'em, two teller's cages.

November 13 The secretary at Vancouver General Hospital reported that the hospital's expenditure during October was $2,492.16. The house surgeon reported that there were 38 patients (26 males and 12 females) in the hospital at the beginning of the month.

November 18 The first military cadet corps in Vancouver, the Vancouver High School Cadet Corps, was gazetted to the militia as a unit.

Vancouver's Grandfather of Electricity

December 17 The first hydroelectric powerhouse on the mainland went into operation.

When Vancouver's first streetcars went into service in 1890 the electricity required to run the system was generated by a little steam powerhouse on what is now Union Street (a block south of Georgia, east of Main.) As the city and the service grew, more power was needed. So the BC Electric Railway Co. started looking for a spot near the city where hydroelectric power could be generated. It found the perfect spot at what was then called Trout Lake (or Beautiful Lake), just east of Port Moody, and built a tunnel to carry water there from Coquitlam Lake. The difference in water levels between the two lakes—Coquitlam was nearly 10 metres (33 feet) higher—provided the motive force to generate the power. An annual rainfall of about 3.7 metres (145 inches) didn't hinder the effort.

The BCER's general manager, Johannes Buntzen, a Dane, supervised construction of the system. Buntzen's work didn't end when the powerhouse began operating: he went before Vancouver city council and urged members to attract industries that could use this new source of power. Buntzen has been called the grandfather of electricity here, and everyone was so pleased with the results they renamed the lake after him.

Also in 1903

The Royal Vancouver Yacht Club was formed. It catered to both power and sail.

The three Latta brothers scaled both peaks of the Lions.

Hearing that climbers often used ropes for mountaineering ascents, they packed some along but had no idea of how to use them and finally threw them away. Their technique was to grasp the small shrubs and bushes growing out of the cracks in the rock, a style that would be considered rather poor form today!

Stained-glass depictions of Spenser, Milton and Shakespeare were installed in the Carnegie Library. They're there to this day, beautiful things.

The first taxi, described as a "wheezy, two-cylinder Ford," was driven in Vancouver by H. Hooper.

A recession ended, and North Vancouver District Council was at last able to raise enough money to rebuild the Capilano and Seymour bridges, destroyed 10 years earlier.

Ladner's Landing changed its name to Ladner.

Ladner was never incorporated as a town or village but has always been a part of Delta. It has never had a government of its own and has no official boundaries.

A new railway line connected Cloverdale and Port Guichon, near Ladner, making it possible to travel from Brownsville in North Surrey to Victoria by railway (and, presumably, rail ferry). The trains were infrequent and often very late.

The population of Delta reached 2,000, including 350 Chinese men, mostly cannery workers, who lived in a Chinatown along the dyke.

Thomas Sullivan and his brother Henry acquired the timber rights to the land at Johnston and Bose in Surrey. The area is known to this day as the Sullivan District.

The head tax on Chinese immigrants was increased to $500 per head. The result (intended): immigration virtually stopped.

H.Y. Louie Co. began life as a tiny grocery and restaurant supply company founded by Hok Yat Louie.

It grew to become one of the primary food wholesalers in the Chinese community and one of the most successful Chinatown businesses. It grew even more under the stewardship of Hok Yat's son, Tong Louie, who took over in 1959.

The Saba brothers, Mike and Alex, from Beirut, opened a shop on Hastings Street near Woodward's. They specialized in silks.

Mankichi Iyemoto settled in the Fraser Valley and started farming. He was followed by other Japanese Canadians who established themselves successfully as berry farmers. The earliest farms were around Port Haney, near Maple Ridge.

Harvey Hadden, philanthropist, bought 65 hectares (160 acres) in Capilano Canyon, sight unseen, from architect Sydney Morgan Eveleigh. He built Hadden Hall there, described as "a sort of Garden of Eden in the forest." Today the clubhouse of Capilano Golf and Country Club is on the site where Hadden's home once stood.

Comings and Goings

Nicolai Schou, the first elected reeve of Burnaby, died in office.

Alfred Graham Ferguson, the first chairman of the Vancouver Park Board, died in San Francisco.

Henry John Cambie, Canadian Pacific Railway engineer, moved to Vancouver. He was in charge of CPR surveys from 1876 to 1880. His survey from the Yellowhead Pass to Port Moody set the route to the lower Fraser. Cambie Street is named for him.

John Wallace deBeque Farris came to Vancouver at age 24 as the city's first Crown prosecutor.

John Lawson, the "Father of West Vancouver," came west from Ontario as a conductor with the CPR.

Future poet Robert Service ended up in Vancouver, flat broke, after a temporary job on a Duncan dairy farm. He got a job with the Canadian Bank of Commerce here.

Road builder Francis V. Guinan moved to Vancouver.

The *Princess Victoria* arrived in Vancouver from England. As a fast and luxurious liner, she set the pattern for the BC Coast Steamship service.

1904

The aging, white-haired bandit known as the Grey Fox pulled off Canada's first train robbery in the Fraser Valley.

January 20 The Canadian government disallowed a BC act restricting Chinese immigration.

May 20 A small schoolhouse opened in Lynn Valley with 18 pupils attending.

June Konstantin "Alvo" von Alvensleben, Prussian count and financier, arrived in the city. He made a living here first by painting barns, repairing fish nets and shooting ducks and geese, which he sold to the Vancouver Club at 35 cents each. Later he made a fortune as a stock promoter and became a prominent social figure.

July 23 The first bridge to span the Fraser opened.

It joined New Westminster to Brownsville (now part of Surrey). Hailed as the engineering feat of the century and built for $1 million by the provincial government, it carried trains on the lower span and vehicles and pedestrians on the upper, and was just wide enough for two hay wagons to pass.

An engineering marvel and a revolution in Lower Mainland transportation, the first bridge to span the Fraser River opened in 1904, connecting New Westminster to Brownsville (Surrey). Trains, vehicles and pedestrians could all cross, though when the Patullo Bridge opened in 1937, the upper deck was removed and the New Westminster Bridge modified to carry only trains.
City of Vancouver Archives, M-2-71

July 25 The Bank of Nova Scotia opened its first branch in Vancouver at 418 West Hastings St.

September 10 Bill Miner held up a train at Silverdale, near Mission, and escaped across the line into Washington's Whatcom County. Miner, known as the Grey Fox because of his white hair and sly ways, was one of those outlaw figures who became a favourite of the public. He was immortalized in a BC movie in 1982.

The Grey Fox, Bill Miner, was an outlaw who gained great popular support in his lifetime. He successfully pulled off one of Canada's first train robberies at Silverdale in 1904, escaping across the border into Washington. He was later captured near Kamloops following his second BC heist in 1906, but escaped prison only a year into his 25-year sentence.
Mary Spencer photo, Vancouver Public Library VPL 748

November St. Andrew's Presbyterian Church was built on Lower Keith Road in North Vancouver, and Rev. J.D. Gillam became the first minister of any denomination to settle on the North Shore.

Elsewhere

Jack London's novel *The Sea Wolf* was published. Wolf Larsen, the title character, was allegedly based on a BC sealing captain, Alexander McLean, who sometimes lived in Vancouver.

April 19 It's not local, but the item is irresistible. A great fire in Toronto caused $10 million in damage (likely equivalent, at the very least, to 10 times that today) and destroyed great sections of the city.

Also in 1904

Frank Kerr opened the first movie house in New Westminster. He frequently had to glue the film together when it broke.

The Steveston Land and Oil Company was formed to drill for oil on Lulu Island.

Charles Cates built a wharf in North Vancouver and handled cargo from California destined for the Klondike.

Pioneer settler Miss Harriet Woodward opened her private school on the northeast shore of Deer Lake. She also started a post office in her home, which she ran for the next 45 years.

In municipal politics, William J. McGuigan was elected mayor. And the number of wards in Vancouver was increased from five to six.

After buying up a number of the smaller telephone companies throughout the province, the Vernon and Nelson Telephone Company changed its name to the British Columbia Telephone Company.

Five thousand Indian men (almost all Sikhs) began to arrive in BC. Most found work in lumber mills.

Shanghai Alley and Canton Alley, two narrow parallel blocks in the area south of Dupont (now Pender) at Carrall Street, became the social and cultural hub of Chinatown, modelled after the vibrant narrow streetscapes common in the home country. Restaurants, tailor and barber shops, social halls and meeting places, a 500-seat theatre and several tenements crowded the self-contained alleyways. In the 1920s Chinatown's hub shifted eastward. During the dirty thirties the area fell on hard times, and many property owners (including Yip Sang, who held several properties in the alley) who could not afford to pay their taxes had their properties foreclosed by the city. By the late 1940s both Canton Alley and much of the once-vibrant Shanghai Alley were demolished.

Comings and Goings

May 11 Future provincial archivist W. Kaye Lamb was born in New Westminster. He had an extraordinarily distinguished career: provincial archivist and librarian of British Columbia from 1934 to 1940, university librarian of the University of British Columbia from 1940 to 1948, Dominion archivist of Canada from 1948 to 1968 and the first national librarian of Canada from 1953 to 1967. He died August 24, 1999, at age 95.

Fill 'er Up

John Hendry, manager of Hastings Sawmill, telephoned Imperial Oil, managed by Charles Merle Rolston, to purchase gas for his new automobile. In 1955, city archivist Major J.S. Matthews (who in 1907 was working for Imperial Oil) recalled what happened next: "There had arrived in Vancouver a queer-looking vehicle called an *automobile*. We had read about them in magazines. One day the telephone rang. The call came from the Hastings Sawmill and the speaker asked if we had any gasoline which could be used in automobiles.

"The office boy replied that we had three kinds: one was '74'-brand Baume gasoline and was supplied to drug stores, who sold it to ladies for cleaning their gloves; the second kind was deodorized stove gasoline, used in plumber's firepots for heating soldering irons; and the third kind was benzine, used for dissolving lacquer in the salmon canneries along the Fraser to prevent the salmon cans from rusting.

"The office boy went to the warehouse and told the foreman, Bud Mulligan, to send a four-gallon can of '74' down to John Hendry, manager of the mill. That can was the first gasoline ever sold in British Columbia for motorcar use."

1905

The city got its first pro baseball team and its first bathhouse at English Bay, and there was an automobile race around Stanley Park. But there was also a problem with bears at Broadway and Westminster (today's Main Street).

January Vancouver High School (later King Edward) opened.

June Louis D. Taylor and "others" bought the *Vancouver World* from Sara McLagan.

July 4 The first interurban tram arrived in Kerrisdale.

July 10 Construction started on the first buildings at Colony Farm, the agricultural arm of the Coquitlam Mental Hospital, informally called Essondale (now Riverview Hospital). The farm won contests across Canada for the quality of its produce and livestock.

September 4 The family of Chris Peters was thrown into a panic by the visit of a large brown bear. The Peters resided, and Mr. Peters had his shoe store, at the corner of Westminster and 9th Avenues in Vancouver—now the corner of Broadway and Main. Not too many bears are seen at that intersection these days!

Labour Day
The first auto club race around Stanley Park.

Eleven cars started, five finished; all the finishers were Oldsmobiles.

September 14 In a report on activities at Stanley Park, the *Province* noted that the "superintendent reported the following animals had been donated to the park's zoo: A monkey, Roy G. Stephens, 1700 Ninth avenue; a large seal, W. Swallow, 664 Granville; four grass parakeets, Mrs. Bulwer, 1728 Georgia street; a fawn, W.T. Massey, 833 Pender street; a raccoon, W. Selp, 621 Sixth avenue east; a canary, Mrs. Clark, 1555 Robson; a seal, Mayor Buscombe; a black bear, G.W. Wagg, 108 Water street."

September 16 A newspaper report: "The Fraser River is full of sockeyes, and ten canneries are packing today to the full capacity of their respective plants, according to reports received from Steveston and other cannery centres this morning. The average catch of sockeyes last night was probably two hundred fish to the boat...fishermen reported that the water is teeming with salmon."

Also in 1905

Glassware merchant Frederick Buscombe became mayor of Vancouver.

The first professional baseball team, the Beavers, was formed in Vancouver.

The first bathhouse was built by the park board at English Bay at a cost of $6,000.

Construction began on a new main post office. Today it's part of Sinclair Centre.

Alfred Wallace incorporated Wallace Shipyards and submitted a proposal to build a new yard on property he had bought on the North Shore. By the end of World War II, under his son Clarence, it had become Canada's biggest shipbuilding firm.

Steveston, meanwhile, became the centre for Japanese boat builders, as

The Park Board built Vancouver's first bathhouse on the beach at English Bay in 1905, at a cost of $6,000. In 1931 the original wooden structure (shown here) was replaced by the concrete English Bay Bathhouse that today's beachgoers still use. *City of Vancouver Archives, SGN 302*

T. Atagi established Atagi Boat Works. In 1907 the Tanaka, Yamanaka, Sakamoto and Nakade boat works started, and in 1914 the Kishi Brothers' boat works. In 1942 they were all taken over by non-Japanese.

McDowell's Drug Store opened next to McMillan's Grocery at 1st Street and Lonsdale in North Vancouver. It was run by the same family until 1973.

One branch of Delta's Taylor family opened a post office in Ladner. The family would continue to operate it for 56 years, to 1961, passing it on from father to son to daughter-in-law.

A tract of land between White Rock and Crescent Beach, formerly known as Blackie's Spit, was named Ocean Park by Surrey pioneer H.T. Thrift. He bought the land on behalf of a wealthy Winnipeg philanthropist who wished to develop it for the Methodist Episcopal church.

The first Buddhist temple in Canada opened at the Ishikawa Hotel on Powell Street.

The Institute of Chartered Accountants was established in Vancouver.

Comings and Goings

March 5 UBC administrator Walter Gage was born in South Vancouver.

Charles Kingsford-Smith, aged 8, arrived in Vancouver with his family. (They weren't here long.) Later he became the first man to pilot a plane across the Pacific Ocean. A school in Vancouver is named for this Australian aviator.

1906

By summer, Vancouver residents could watch moving pictures of the San Francisco earthquake, which had occurred two months earlier. There was a deadly ship collision off Stanley Park. And machines started replacing workers in the salmon canneries.

May 1 The telephone came to North Vancouver, and that made a difference to the ferry system. Until the ferry terminal hooked up to the telephone line, the wharfinger used a system of calls with a bugle to let consignees know when their goods had arrived: two toots for McMillan's Grocery, three for Larson's Hotel, a long and two shorts for the *Express* (newspaper) and two long toots for the butcher.

June 1 The Vancouver Athletic Club opened.

June 2 On page 3, the *Province* had an advertisement for the Opera House, which was showing "moving pictures" of the San Francisco earthquake and fire of April 18.

June 6 The Vancouver Board of Trade complained about "execrable" telephone service.

July 3 Chief Capilano of the Squamish Nation went to London to

Right: Aboriginal stand. Chief Joe Capilano (front row, fifth from left) poses in North Vancouver with fellow chiefs and companions before setting off to England to meet King Edward VII. The delegation presented concerns about aboriginal land rights to the king, but received no firm response. *City of Vancouver Archives, In P41.1*

Elsewhere in BC

May 11 The Grey Fox, Bill Miner, and his accomplices were captured near Kamloops by a Royal Northwest Mounted Police posse, three days after their second train robbery in BC. Miner was sentenced to 25 years in the New Westminster Penitentiary, but he escaped the next year.

James Dunsmuir, coal baron and former premier, became Lieutenant-Governor.

Elsewhere in Canada

A young man named Ernest Poole built a farmhouse in his hometown of Stoughton, SK—his first construction job. He went on to build his company into one of Canada's largest, PCL Construction, which has been active for decades in BC.

meet King Edward VII and Queen Alexandra. The chief, accompanied by Cowichan and Cariboo chiefs, presented a petition to the king concerning aboriginal land rights. Chief Capilano later reported the delegation was warned such matters might take as long as five years to settle.

July 21 The wooden steamer *Chehalis* sank when it was rammed by the CPR's Seattle–Vancouver steamship *Princess Victoria* near Brockton Point. Eight men died.

August 13 The owners of all houses on Dupont Street were given 30 days to put a stop to their activities. (They were running brothels.) But by the end of October the brothels were back in operation.

August 15 Electricity became commonly available in North Vancouver after a cable was laid across the Second Narrows.

August 22 Vancouver's Canadian Club was formed. An inaugural luncheon was held on September 25 at the Hotel Vancouver with Governor General Earl Grey as guest of honour.

September 3 Streetcars began operation in North Vancouver and served the area for 40 years. From the ferry wharf, one line went along Queensbury Avenue to 19th Street, one went up Lonsdale to 21st Street, and another went west to Keith Road and Bewicke Avenue.

September The Japanese Methodist Church (later Powell Street United Church), at the corner of Jackson and Powell, was dedicated. On the upper floors were classrooms for night classes as well as dormitories for single men.

Also in 1906

A new provincial courthouse was built at 800 West Georgia, replacing the original courthouse in Victory Square. The new building was designed by Francis Rattenbury. The last case to be tried here was in 1979, and in 1983 the building became the new home of the Vancouver Art Gallery.

David Spencer opened his first Vancouver store.

Alfred Wallace opened his shipyard in North Vancouver. Under various names (Wallace Shipyards, Burrard Dry Dock, Versatile Pacific, etc.) it eventually become the North Shore's largest industry, building scores of ships during both World Wars.

Richmond's school districts merged, and the Richmond School Board was formed. The board then ruled that only children whose parents owned property were eligible to attend public school. As most Japanese lived in houses owned by the canneries, their children did not qualify. The Japanese community responded by building and operating its own four-room school in Steveston. When it opened

Left: Until 1907 East Pender was known as Dupont Street and was home to the city's red light district. By day it was a busy commercial thoroughfare at the entrance to Chinatown. At night the red lights winked on and mobs of men thronged the wooden sidewalks in search of female company in the brothels that occupied the two-storey clapboard buildings. In 1906 police closed the Dupont Street brothels, though they simply moved to adjacent neighbourhoods.
Vancouver Public Library, VPL 6729. Philip Timms photo

As compelling signs of Vancouver's and British Columbia's maturity and dominance, impressive public buildings were commissioned throughout the 1890s and early 1900s. In this 1906 photo, the provincial courthouse, now the art gallery, is under construction, designed by then-popular architect Francis Rattenbury.
City of Vancouver Archives, M-11-34

Posing in front of Canada's first gurdwara, or temple, in this 1936 picture, these Sikhs first organized in 1906 into the Khalsa Diwan Society. The society became the focal point for religious, social and political activity within the Indian community, and was able to build the temple in 1908. *The Voyage of Komagata Maru* by Hugh Johnston

in 1909, Nobutaro Takashima was the principal, and Japanese teachers were hired to teach the Japanese curriculum. Around 1914, a Mrs. Chilton was hired to teach English.

At Lord Strathcona School in Vancouver, meanwhile, Japanese Canadian students were enrolled in a public school alongside white students for the first time.

The Japanese Consulate opened Vancouver's first Japanese language school, the Vancouver Kyoritsu Nippon Kokumin Gakko, at 439 Alexander St. in Japantown. The sole teacher taught 30 pupils. By 1935 there were 967 pupils registered, and they met daily for two hours.

There was another huge salmon run this year, and the Smith butchering machine was introduced at Steveston's Gulf of Georgia Cannery. It took the place of a 30-man gang of Chinese cannery workers and came to be known as the "Iron Chink."

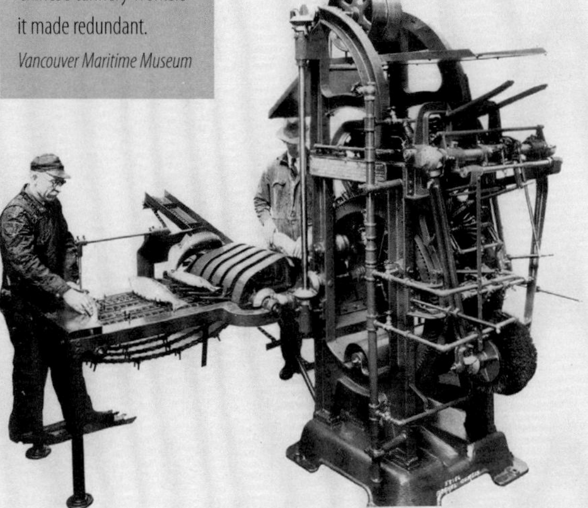

The introduction of the Smith butchering machine in 1906 revolutionized the salmon-canning industry on the coast. Developed in Seattle by E.A. Smith, the machine greatly accelerated the rate at which fish could be cut up in preparation for canning. The machine was known as the Iron Chink because of the number of Chinese cannery workers it made redundant. *Vancouver Maritime Museum*

The Khalsa Diwan Society was established in Vancouver. This organization became the voice for the city's Indian community and a focus for religious, social and political activity. In 1908, the society built Canada's first gurdwara (temple) at 1866 West 2nd Ave. in Vancouver to serve as a gathering place for Indians of all faiths.

Comings and Goings

Al Jolson, 20, performed at the Grand Theatre.

1907

The city got its first police car and the country's first gas station, and the fire chief, always aware of the danger of conflagrations, ordered three motorized firefighting units. In a conflagration of a different sort, the short-lived Asiatic Exclusion League attacked Chinese and Japanese residents. And a Seattle moviemaker shot the earliest surviving film of Vancouver.

February Henry Birks and Sons of Montreal, the famed jewellers, bought out George Trorey's jewellery store at the northeast corner of Granville and Hastings, keeping Trorey on as manager. Trorey's clock on the sidewalk outside became a Vancouver landmark, better known as the Birks' clock. It's still ticking away at Granville and Hastings a century later...on the southeast corner!

April 12 The Vancouver Stock Exchange was incorporated by an act of the provincial legislature.

May 7 William Harbeck, a Seattle moviemaker, mounted a camera on the front of a BC Electric Railway tram and filmed the journey along Granville and Hastings, along Westminster Avenue (now Main Street) to Carrall, Powell, Cordova and Cambie, Robson and Davie. This is the earliest surviving film of Vancouver, and it is fun and exciting to see streets full of horse-drawn wagons; men, every one of them wearing a hat, strolling into long-gone shops; women hurrying along in their dark, ground-length skirts; and the occasional recognizable sign: Knowlton Drugs, P. Burns (meat packer), the Edison Grand Theatre, Woodward's and "Cascade: A Beer Without Peer." Gone is the second CPR station at the foot of Granville,

Although there were smiles in 1923 while the good times rolled, the Vancouver Stock Exchange was not always favourable toward the Vancouver business community. Started in 1907, the exchange hit several rough patches with the Depression, a mining scandal, World War II and then more scandals in the 1970s and 1980s. The exchange ceased as an independent entity in 1999 when it was merged with the Alberta Stock Exchange to form what is now the TSX Venture Exchange. *Courtesy PNG*

Trorey's Jewellers and the original *Province* newspaper building. The film was discovered in the basement of an abandoned building in Australia! It had apparently been dumped there by movie house managers along with other movies no longer wanted. And Andrew Martin, of the Vancouver Public Library's Special Collections division pinpointed the date the film was made. He found a *Province* story, dated May 8, 1907, that described the filming. It jauntily reported that Vancouverites had been "Stricken with Kinetoscopitis." (Copies of this film are available for loan at the Vancouver Public Library.)

May 11
The University Women's Club of Vancouver was founded by eight graduates.

May 13 The small, central core of North Vancouver business and industry broke away and formed its own municipality, the City of North Vancouver. The residents felt their area would be more prosperous on its own. As a result of the break, North Vancouver District was deprived of its water system, municipal hall, ferry terminal and ferry, firefighting and

Elsewhere in BC

February 2 Surrey's John Oliver became leader of the opposition in the BC legislature after the first provincial election to be run on party lines.

Elsewhere in Canada

December 6 The first recorded flight in Canada of a heavier-than-air machine took place at Baddeck, NS, when Thomas Selfridge was lifted into the air in a tetrahedral kite, the *Cygnet*, designed by Alexander Graham Bell.

A White Man's Country

September 7 A protest rally at the city hall (Main and Hastings), staged by Vancouver's Asiatic Exclusion League, turned into a riot as a white mob rampaged through Chinatown and Japantown. The riot was immediately followed by a general strike of Vancouver's Asian workers. The city's timber industry, hotels and private homes suffered from the withdrawal of so many of the workers they depended on. William Lyon Mackenzie King, then deputy minister of Labour, led a Royal Commission to investigate the losses sustained by Chinese and Japanese merchants. The Chinese were awarded $3,000 for property damage and over $20,000 for business losses; $9,000 was awarded to the Japanese. During 1907, the BC legislature passed an act preventing Asians from entering professions, and buying property in parts of Vancouver.

On Monday, the *News-Advertiser* and *Province* reported on the "Saturday night excitement." The *Province* noted that "the Chinese of Vancouver armed themselves this morning as soon as the gun stores opened. Hundreds of revolvers and thousands of rounds of ammunition were passed over the counter to the Celestials before the police stepped in and requested that no further sale be made to Orientals...Few Japanese were seen buying arms, but a bird's-eye view today of the roofs of Japanese boarding-houses and stores in the Japanese district disclosed the fact that the Orientals are prepared for a siege. Hundreds of bottles are stored on the roofs, and these with stones, clubs, and bricks will be hurled at the whites in the streets below should any further trouble occur." The *Province* opined that "this province must be a white man's country...We do not wish to look forward to a day when our descendants will be dominated by Japanese, or Chinese, or any color but their own."

In a move that quickly made them unpopular, the Asiatic Exclusion League rioted against the Chinese and Japanese communities in 1907 while marching on city hall. Asian workers immediately went on strike, and a Royal Commission was quickly called, which provided some compensation to these Chinese businesses with boarded-up windows. Meanwhile, the league disbanded only five days after the riot. *University of British Columbia Library courtesy PNG*

road-making equipment, even the cemetery. In return, the city paid some of the district's outstanding liabilities.

May 31 A dozen Vancouver businessmen formed the Vancouver Exhibition Association, with a goal of developing a fair to showcase Vancouver to the world.

Spring John Lawson settled his family in Navvy Jack Thomas' house, which became known as Hollyburn.

Five years later, Lawson was instrumental in getting West Vancouver to secede from North Vancouver.

June 10 The newly constituted District of North Vancouver held its first council meeting in Lynn Valley Schoolhouse. A new municipal hall, on Lynn Valley Road, was completed in 1911.

Canada's First Gas Station

The first gas station in Canada opened at Cambie and Smithe Streets. Sometime this year it occurred to employees at the Vancouver office of the Imperial Oil Co. that the usual method of fuelling automobiles to this time—namely, carrying a sloshing bucket full of gasoline up to the vehicle and pouring it through a funnel into the tank—was somewhat dangerous. So Charles Rolston, manager of Imperial's local office, built a small open-sided shed of corrugated iron next to the storage yard. Atop a tapering concrete pillar he placed a 13-gallon (59-litre) kitchen water tank fitted with a glass steam-gauge, with 1-gallon (4.5-litre) increments marked off by white dots. The tank was gravity fed, being connected to Imperial's main storage tank. The filling hose was a 10-foot (3-metre) length of garden hose, which the attendant drained with thumb and finger after filling a car.

The first attendant was Imperial's former night watchman, J.C. Rollston, who had been in poor health. His co-workers believed he would improve in the sun and open air. They bought a barroom chair for him and set him down by the "pump." Canada's first gas station was now in business. The late city archivist J.S. Matthews (who worked for Imperial Oil at the time) said that, in the beginning, a busy morning would see three or four cars show up.

June 13 The Presbyterian theological college, Westminster Hall, was founded.

June 24 Formation of Jericho Country Club.

August 1 The Vancouver Stock Exchange opened at 849 West Pender with 12 charter members. Three months to the day later its president, C.D. Rand, said, "Many applications to list stocks of doubtful merit have already been made to the Exchange, but have been promptly turned down by your executive, and this policy will be adhered to while we remain in office."

Douglas Lodge was built in 1912 as the Bank of Commerce Building at Granville and 12th. It continues today as a heritage apartment block. Emily Carr used to teach a friend painting here, and John Candy and Arthur Erickson, among other celebrities, have been residents. *Vancouver Public Library, Special Collections, VPL 5006. Leonard Frank photo*

August 14 The first newspaper reference to the Vancouver Police Department's first automobile.

The car got its first use exactly one week later, on August 21, when one Richard Goddlander, "a well-known police character," was charged with public intoxication and given his first automobile ride. Destination: the city jail.

September 12 The Asiatic Exclusion League was disbanded.

September 30 Vancouver city council was discussing street names and decided to commemorate battles. So what had been Campbell Street became Alma Road (Crimean War); Richards Street became Balaclava (also a Crimean War battlesite); Cornwall, the second street with that name, became Blenheim to recall the Battle of Blenheim; Lansdowne became Waterloo; and the old Boundary Street that divided District Lot 192 and the CPR grant became Trafalgar.

December 1 W.J. Timmins, proprietor of the new Pantages vaudeville theatre on Hastings Street, was up from Tacoma to "look over the work." The 1,200-seat theatre opened in early 1908.

Also in 1907

Alexander Bethune, a shoe merchant, was mayor. He had been an alderman for five years. During Bethune's term, Vancouver council asked the Dominion government for use of the Kitsilano Indian Reserve.

Firehall No. 6 was built at 1001 Nicola and Firehall No. 2 was built at 270 East Cordova.

John Howe Carlisle, chief of the Vancouver Fire Department, arranged to purchase three motorized firefighting units, in the face of some amused, and some not-so-amused, opposition. His was a daring move. The company making these units—Seagrave of Columbus, OH—had just begun their manufacture, and very few fire departments in North America were making the switch. Vancouver's was the first in Canada.

The Jewish congregation B'nai Yehudah (Sons of Israel) held its first services in a small rented home, at 14 West Cordova St. It was legally incorporated as Schara Tzedeck in 1917.

Japanese residents of Vancouver built an arch to honour the visit of His Imperial Highness Prince Fushimi.

Jiro Inouye, a graduate of Waseda University in Tokyo, left the Oriental Trading Company in Vancouver, bought 8 hectares (20 acres) of land and became the first Japanese landowner in Haney. He pioneered the strawberry industry and encouraged immigrants to take up farming.
In 1919 he established the Haney Nokai (farmers' association), which became the model for other farming co-operatives in the Fraser Valley.
His wife, Kane Inouye, meanwhile, formed a women's club where Japanese women could gather to discuss mutual problems and learn English and Canadian customs.

Tynehead Hall, the first community hall in Surrey, was built.

Dominic Burns, brother of Pat Burns of the meat-packing empire, built a slaughterhouse this year in Vancouver. It was torn down in 1969 and the man in charge of the demolition said it was the toughest building to destroy he had ever seen. One item: the brick walls were 36 centimetres (14 inches) thick.

B.T. Rogers, the sugar refiner, donated a pair of marble statues to the Terminal City Club. They're still there.

Richard Carmon Purdy opened his first chocolate shop on Vancouver's famed Robson Street. Today Purdy's Chocolates has over 50 locations in BC, Alberta and Ontario.

The *Daily Province* had a circulation of just over 15,000, the highest in town, and cost five cents.

Comings and Goings

August 8 Train robber Bill Miner escaped from the penitentiary in New Westminster.

October 5 Rudyard Kipling made his third and final visit to Vancouver.

October 14 The famous American bandleader and composer John Philip Sousa performed here with his band—all 55 of them. The performance would have set you back $1.75 for the best seats.

William H. Ladner, the well-known Delta pioneer (and reeve from 1880 to 1906) died at 81. Ladner was named for him.

1908

A boxing kangaroo was an added attraction at the Pantages Theatre, and the New Westminster Salmonbellies won their first national trophy. The Bellies are still playing lacrosse and still winning.

March 19 The first Vancouver Horse Show was held at the Drill Hall.

May 16 This advertisement appeared on page 12 of the *News-Advertiser*: "Manager George Calvert, of the Pantages Theatre, takes great pleasure in announcing that there will be an extra act on the bill this afternoon and this evening, namely 'Jeff,' the Boxing Kangaroo. This animal is claimed to be an adept in the boxing line, in fact almost as good if not better than an ordinary boxer and he has proved a great attraction wherever he has appeared. This is an act that will greatly please the ladies and children and there should be a large turnout of them at all the performances to-day."

June The first hospital to serve the North Shore was opened, a tiny six-bed facility at St. Andrews and 15th Street.

September 9 The British Columbia Refining Company in Port Moody was incorporated. It refined oil shipped from California.

September 20 The Rev. W.A. Davis conducted Sunday service in John Lawson's home for a group of Presbyterians, Methodists, Baptists and Congregationalists.

October 5 In Steveston, fire consumed "China town," leaving 300 people homeless,

The King of English Bay

July 21 Members of the Vancouver Athletic Club interrupted Seraphim "Joe" Fortes at supper in his cottage near the Alexandra Park bandshell and escorted him to the pavilion at English Bay where, at a surprise meeting, he was presented with a handsome gold medal in recognition of his "splendid" service as swimming instructor and lifeguard. As news of the event spread down the promenade, a large crowd gathered and cheered "lustily."

Earlier in June, Fortes had plunged into the sea in his best Sunday suit to rescue a young swimmer—the latest in more than 100 lives he was credited with saving during his 30-odd years on the beaches of Vancouver.

Born in Barbados in 1865 (or perhaps it was 1863 in Port of Spain in the Republic of Trinidad and Tobago—both dates and places are cited in reputable sources, although the 1901 census gives Trinidad), Fortes came to Vancouver from Liverpool in 1885 aboard the barque *Robert Kerr*. The voyage took 11 months, the captain died en route and the sailing vessel was wrecked on San Juan Island and had to be towed to Vancouver. The ship was condemned and anchored off Gastown as a hulk, where it later served as a refuge for people fleeing the Great Fire of 1886. Fortes ran Vancouver's first shoeshine stand and later worked as a bartender and porter at the Bodega Saloon and the Alhambra Hotel, where he earned a reputation for his excellent cocktails and for his ability to subdue rowdies and dissuade excessive drinking.

He had become an accomplished competitive swimmer during his five years in England and soon volunteered his talents as a qualified swimming instructor for children at English Bay, eventually quitting his job to spend all his time at the beach. "English Bay Joe" swam every morning and drank a cup of sea water—his "medicine." "Joe belonged to the beach—and the beach to Joe," wrote historian Alan Morley in 1961. "From dawn to dark and long after dark, he was host to picnickers, chaperone to courting couples and a terror to the bum and the hoodlum." In 1901 he was appointed Vancouver's first official lifeguard and was much loved by the thousands of children he taught to swim ("scarce a tyke who was raised in Vancouver in the '90s or 1900s but learned to swim with Joe's hamlike fist gripping the back of his or her cotton bathing suit," observed Morley) and whose lives he frequently saved. In 1910, for example, he fearlessly swam into the bay to rescue two little boys, James Ellehalt, 8, and Albert Dempsey, 7, who were being swept out to sea in a small boat.

When Fortes died in 1922, he was honoured with the largest public funeral in Vancouver's history. In 1926 the citizens of Vancouver subscribed to a memorial drinking fountain in Alexandra Park. Designed by sculptor Charles Marega in bronze and granite, it was low enough for the smallest children to drink and was inscribed, simply, "Little children loved him." Fortes was named Vancouver's Citizen of the Century by the Vancouver Historical Society during the city's centennial year in 1986, and a branch of Vancouver Public Library on Denman Street bears his name.

Elsewhere in Canada

Restrictions were placed on Japanese immigration for the first time. The Hayashi-Lemieux "Gentlemen's Agreement" between Britain and Japan restricted Japanese immigration to 400 male immigrants and domestic servants per year, plus returning immigrants and their immediate family. Since wives and children were exempt from the restrictions, married men were able to send for their wives and unmarried men found mates through the "picture bride" system. Thus, 1908 marked the beginning of the "family building" phase for the Japanese community.

half of them Japanese. Fire is the most feared hazard of early settlements with wooden structures, and there were several other major fires in Steveston. Chinatown had also been razed a year earlier, on April 5, 1907, leaving approximately 100 people homeless, mostly Chinese, some Japanese and three Caucasians. On October 8, 1901, shops were destroyed, and on May 14, 1918, the most disastrous fire occurred, leaving 600 homeless.

November 1 The federal Ministry of Militia and Defence renewed the lease of Stanley Park to Vancouver for

Portrait of the artist. As a young artist, Emily Carr taught art classes in Vancouver from 1906 to 1910. After spending time in France, she returned in 1912 to paint and to continue teaching. But reception of her work was mixed and, for mainly financial reasons, she moved back to Victoria in 1913. *Vancouver Sun*

Gold and Blue and a Hullabaloo

"My girl's a hullabaloo, she wears the Gold and Blue," went one of the early songs from the University of British Columbia, a forward-thinking institution which even before it was incorporated in 1908 had taken steps to ensure that female students would be protected from the gender-based intolerance and prejudice that continued to afflict more venerable institutions. The famous colours, representing the golden sunset and blue sea from the provincial coat of arms, were officially adopted by the students in 1921 after a campaign by the student newspaper, the *Ubyssey*, but they'd been worn by sports teams since 1915.

The first notion that British Columbia might benefit from a university of its own was put forward in 1877 by John Jessop, the provincial superintendent of education, but the province's population was small, money was tight and the proposal was ignored by legislators. The idea was revived in 1890 when Premier John Robson's government passed An Act Respecting the University of British Columbia, founding a provincial university. Lieutenant-Governor Hugh Nelson even appointed a chancellor—Dr. Israel Powell—and a convocation was called. It met and recommended a far-sighted amendment to the act: that "no woman shall, by reason of her sex, be deprived of any advantages or privileges accorded to other students of the University."

However, a wrangle between Vancouver and Victoria MLAs over the distribution of seats in the legislature meant no decision could be reached about where a university should be located. When Robson died of blood-poisoning after crushing a finger in a carriage door in 1892, the idea of a BC university once again fell into dormancy.

In the interval, high schools in Vancouver and Victoria affiliated with McGill University in Montreal. While this arrangement enabled several hundred students to acquire the higher education they might otherwise have been denied, it was not ideal—and that led to the 1908 act of incorporation.

The province appointed a panel of distinguished educators from outside BC to propose an appropriate site for the new university, and by fall 1910 it had agreed on Point Grey; land was set aside there for the campus. The province also set aside 11.74 square kilometres (4.5 square miles) to be subdivided and used to underwrite the costs of the university. (In 1907 the provincial legislature had passed an act endowing a future provincial university with 800,000 hectares/2,000,000 acres of land in the BC Interior as well.) During the Great Depression, the university returned control of the Point Grey lands to the province. Part of the area was developed for housing, part accommodated the university and the rest remained undeveloped forest. (In 1988, 763 hectares/1,885 acres were transferred by the province to the Greater Vancouver Regional District for Pacific Spirit Regional Park.)

Competitive plans for university buildings at Point Grey were called in 1912, and the first convocation of the university-to-be elected a chancellor. A president was appointed in 1913, and by 1914 work had begun on a science building for the new university in Point Grey. In the meantime, higher education needs were met by McGill University College, which had been operating in two buildings next door to Vancouver General Hospital since 1912. On September 30, 1915, UBC replaced McGill at the Vancouver General site and, due to wartime austerity, continued with a skeleton staff and a student body almost entirely depleted of men.

Relocation from the so-called Fairview Shacks was delayed, and on October 28, 1922, students and supporters held a huge rally in downtown Vancouver and marched to Point Grey. This "Great Trek" persuaded the province to move ahead with construction, and classes began at the present site of UBC in 1925. Expansion has been constant ever since, with the addition of faculties of law (1945), graduate studies (1948), medicine (1950), forestry (1951), education (1956) and commerce (1957). Altogether there are 12 faculties and a score of schools and research institutes.

Today UBC occupies two main campuses in Vancouver and Kelowna, has a downtown presence at UBC Robson Square and shares the Great Northern Way campus—an innovative collaboration with Simon Fraser University, Emily Carr University of Art and Design and the BC Institute of Technology—southeast of downtown. The university enrolls almost 55,000 students—more than 7,500 of them international students—grants more than 10,000 degrees each year and boasts 250,000 alumni in 120 countries.

99 years, renewable. This was also the year the first tourist bus service began operating in the park.

Also in 1908

Point Grey municipality was formed.

Shaughnessy Heights was subdivided by the CPR.

The sale of opium was prohibited.

The North Vancouver Land and Improvement Company cleared Grand Boulevard in North Vancouver and planted shrubs. The boulevard was conveyed to the City of North Vancouver for parkland, around which a high-class residential area was planned.

Members of the BC Mountaineering Club made the first known ascent of Mount Seymour on the North Shore.

Richmond built its first high school at Bridgeport. With four rooms, the school was considered huge. The first class graduated in 1911.

Surrey formed its first police force, responsible for welfare issues, collecting poll and business taxes and investigating local crime.

The New Westminster Salmonbellies won their first national prize, the Minto Cup, which from 1901 to 1909 was awarded to the champion senior men's lacrosse team in Canada. (The Salmonbellies won the cup in 1909 too.)

The largest agriculture fair ever held in the province was opened in New Westminster. By this time, Fraser Valley fruit was being canned and shipped all over the world.

1909

Vancouver was in the throes of real estate speculation, which led to a name change for 9th Avenue, which became Broadway. The second Granville Street Bridge opened and the city's first mechanized ambulance killed a pedestrian on its first test drive.

January 7 The first export shipment of grain was made out of Vancouver. Some 50,000 bushels of wheat from the prairies went to Australia.

March 10 The new world heavyweight boxing champion, Jack Johnson, visited Vancouver for an exhibition bout at the Vancouver Athletic Club against an opponent named Victor McLaglen. It was Johnson's first fight after winning the title. Trivia: McLaglen, 26, later became a well-known movie actor.

March 15 The first freight train travelled the new Great Northern Railway track (Blaine, WA, at one end, New Westminster at the other) along the White Rock foreshore, precipitating real estate speculation and a building boom. A customs post was opened at White Rock.

March 29 Longshoremen struck for higher pay. They wanted 35 cents per hour for daywork and 40 cents per hour for nightwork.

May The name of 9th Avenue was changed to Broadway. There were a number of Americans involved in the

A Lawsuit for the Record Book

March 9 Hugh Magee, pioneer Point Grey farmer, died in Point Grey, aged 83. He was born June 4, 1826, in what is now Northern Ireland and moved to Upper Canada (Ontario) in 1843. Here he married Isabella Crawford in 1850. In 1857 he sold the farm and took his family, which now included three young children, to California. They travelled by sea via New York, across the Isthmus of Panama (no canal yet) and then by ship again to San Francisco. Hearing news of the Fraser River gold strike in 1858, the family headed to New Westminster.

By 1861 they were living at Rosehill on the Burnaby/New Westminster border, where 10th Avenue intersected with the North Arm Trail (Marine Drive). Magee found the land in that area too marshy for farming, although a later tenant of that land, Rose Hill Farm, established a dairy farm and sold milk there.

By October 1864 Magee had settled west of Marpole, the first to farm on the North Arm of the Fraser. He bought a home in New Westminster and floated it down the Fraser on a barge to a spot near what is now the foot of Blenheim Street. In 1902 the Magees cleared a road (known as Magee Road until the name was changed to 49th Avenue) through the forest from Blenheim Street to newly constructed Granville Street. The CPR also applied the name "Magee" to a station on the interurban line from Vancouver to Steveston.

Hugh Magee left an estate valued at more than $100,000 and a will with instructions that kept lawyers and the courts busy for the next 53 years. It took until the last of his 15 children had died before the estate was finally settled in 1962. The Magee name lives on in Magee High School, which had its beginnings in 1913 when Point Grey established its first high school.

Drawing a full crowd on race day in 1912, the Minoru racetrack in Richmond proved a popular hit when it opened in 1909. *City of Vancouver Archives, CVA 371-328. Photo W.J. Cairns*

Elsewhere in BC

August 25 The Canadian Pacific Railway opened its new line over Kicking Horse Pass near Field, BC. The route featured two spiral tunnels, bypassing the former switchback with its 4.4 percent grades.

The Indian Rights Association was formed and worked on behalf of Native rights until 1916.

Railway contractor Thomas Wilson Paterson was appointed Lieutenant-Governor.

city's real estate boom, and they felt that Broadway (after Broadway in New York City) would, in archivist Major J.S. Matthews' words, "help promote some mysterious advantage."

May 5 Robert Clark, merchant, died in Vancouver, aged 65. Born in Lanarkshire, Scotland, in 1845, his first job was in a grocery store, but then he learned the shipbuilder's trade. On May 1, 1871, he left Scotland for Canada. He built the first steamer that sailed on Lake Manitoba ("Going into the forest," the 1906 BC *Illustrated News* related, "he picked out the trees, hewed the lumber and with help whip-sawed the lumber. He then built and launched the boat and delivered her to the owners, a craft one hundred feet in length."), then moved to the US and worked in various cities until he came up to Victoria in 1875. In 1880 he opened a menswear store in Nanaimo, moving it to Yale a year later. His store there burned down. In 1886, when the CPR was on its way to Vancouver, he moved there too and opened a new store on Hastings Street. The *Illustrated News* noted: "He built his present store [also on Hastings], ninety by one hundred and thirty-two feet, and in it he carries a full and complete line of men's furnishing goods, carefully selected. He is the pioneer clothing merchant of this place." Clark was instrumental in the creation of the Vancouver Board of Trade in 1887, after the devastating fire of 1886 that destroyed much of the city.

May 24 Vancouver's first marathon was run.

The location was Recreation Park, 11 runners took part, and the race was won by Vancouver's Will Chandler in a time of 3 hours, 22 minutes. There were 2,500 spectators, and Mayor Charles Douglas fired the starting pistol. One of the timekeepers was prominent local jeweller George Trorey, manager of Vancouver's Birks store.

June The first moving picture theatre in North Vancouver opened at Larson's Pavilion.

August 21 Minoru racetrack, named after King Edward's Epsom Derby winner, opened in Richmond, with 7,000 people on hand.

September 6 Governor General Earl Grey officially opened the new

The West Vancouver Transportation Company launched its first ferry in 1909. It putted across the inlet in the hands of Captain Alfred Alexander Findlay and engineer Harry Lawson Thompson and could carry 35 passengers. *Vancouver Public Library, Special Collections, VPL 6744. Philip Timms photo*

Right: The impressive residence in this 1912 image is Hycroft, which was built in 1909 by General Alexander McRae and his wife, Blanche. Considered the grandest home in the fashionable Shaughnessy neighbourhood in the McRaes' time, the building is still one of the most beautiful in the city today, and is currently owned by the University Women's Club.

R. Broadbridge photo. Vancouver Public Library VPL 13689

Granville Street Bridge. Lady Grey cut the ribbon. The new bridge, which lasted until 1954, extended from Pacific to 4th, east of the original bridge.

September 28 The first contingent of 110 French Canadians from Quebec's lumber industry arrived by train to work at Fraser Mills. Their residential settlement, built with company help, became known as Maillardville, in honour of community leader Father Edmond Maillard.

October 6
Vancouver took its first mechanized ambulance out for a test drive and ran over an American tourist, killing him.

October 20 "The Vancouver branch of the Canadian Women's Press Club," the *Province* reported, "held its first regular meeting yesterday afternoon. The club has been formed with the object of bringing together all women writers of the City." One of the founders of the local branch was Lily Laverock, one of the most interesting of all Vancouver pioneers. The Edinburgh-born Miss Laverock (she was Miss Laverock to everyone) had arrived as a child with her parents and went on to become the first female general reporter in the city. She worked first at the *World* and later became women's editor of the *News-Advertiser*. Later still she became an impresario, and an impressive one.

October The first bank in Surrey, a branch of the Bank of Montreal, opened in Cloverdale.

November 8 The West Vancouver Transportation Company began a ferry service across the inlet with the 35-passenger *West Vancouver*. The pier was at the foot of 17th Street, on land, owned by John Lawson (one of the company's founders), that is now John Lawson Park.

December Professor Teja Singh established the Guru Nanak Mining and Trust Company, providing an economic foundation for the Sikh community in Canada. The organization had 251 members, and the leading Sikhs of the time sat on its board of directors. The goals of the trust were to look after the economic welfare of Sikhs by investing in businesses, real estate and farms, banking and homes construction. All members shared in risk and profits. Rather than accept unemployment during slow periods, many men were willing to assume the risks of management. In agriculture, this might mean leasing a field crop, such as potatoes, from a farmer and harvesting it, with every member of the harvest gang taking a share of the profits—if there were any. The principal investment, in such a case, was labour. Most Sikhs took it upon themselves to look after their fellow Sikhs; this helped strengthen the community and provided members and new immigrants with a social safety net.

Also in 1909

Charles Stanford Douglas won the mayoralty, beating four other candidates, a record number to that time. Among the vanquished was Louis D. Taylor, who won a year later.

General Alexander McRae and his wife, Blanche, built Hycroft at 1489 McRae.

It was the grandest home in Shaughnessy, costing $100,000 at a time when $3,000 would buy you a new house. The McRaes turned it into a glittering social centre. Owned today by the University Women's Club, it is still one of the most beautiful buildings in the city, inside and out.

When the streetcar line was extended from downtown Vancouver to Boundary Road, developers began promoting Vancouver Heights (which, despite its name, was on the Burnaby side of the line) as an exclusive subdivision that would rival Shaughnessy Heights. For example, Overlynn, the Charles J. Peter mansion at 3755 McGill St., was built at a cost of $75,000.

Realizing the growing importance of Vancouver as a port, and anticipating that its fame would spread to many faraway places, the Vancouver Board of Trade advocated the city build a new city hall.

This was a fiscally feverish year in the city. An alley corner on Hastings Street was sold for $100,000, while one property owner refused an offer of $250,000 for a corner on Robson and Granville Streets. Bank of Toronto officials at the time deplored "the wild speculation which has taken place in real estate."

The Cecil Hotel opened on Granville Street.

The Grandview Methodist Church was built at 1895 Venables. Later, it become a United Church and was eventually converted into the Vancouver East Cultural Centre, the "Cultch."

Wigwam Inn, at the north end of Indian Arm, was built by German-born financier Alvo von Alvensleben. By 1913 it was popular enough to have daily boat service provided by the sternwheeler *Skeena*.

The Vancouver Police Department began its first mounted patrol in Stanley Park.

Perhaps the patrolmen saw the first eight pairs of grey squirrels, a gift from New York City. The squirrels' descendants now inhabit most of the park's 400 hectares (1,000 acres).

The Chinese Benevolent Association was founded and moved into its own new building at 108 East Pender.

A directory of Japanese immigrant business showed 568 businesses in the Powell Street area. One of those may have been Koji Nakasuka's dry-cleaning and dyeing plant, the first in Vancouver operated by a Japanese. Nakasuka did the pressing, his wife did the mending, adjusting and fitting, and their children managed the counter and made deliveries.

The Vancouver School Board began to offer night school courses. Some 966 people signed up.

The work of the Surrey Women's Institutes began. The institutes welcomed new settlers and assisted with such projects as libraries, parks, youth training and dental clinics.

The No. 18 Field Ambulance unit, Army Medical Corps, was founded.

After many years of unsuccessfully drilling to find its own water, Richmond entered into an agreement to have its water supply piped from New Westminster's reservoir.

The interurban railway was extended from Eburne in Richmond to New Westminster.

Wigwam Inn was a luxury resort that opened at the north end of Indian Arm in 1909. It was owned by B.F. "Benny" Dickens, a Vancouver advertising executive, and Alvo von Alvensleben, a flamboyant German entrepreneur who made, and lost, a fortune in the pre-war real estate boom in the city. Although it attracted many famous visitors, the resort was not a success and it changed hands often over the years. Since 1986 it has been used as an outstation by the Royal Vancouver Yacht Club. *City of Vancouver Archives, LGN 1028*

English Bay pier was built.

The North Pacific Lumber mill at Barnet was destroyed by fire. A modern plant was constructed to handle 150,000 board feet a day. Separate accommodation was built for Caucasian, Chinese and Sikh workers, and Barnet, although a part of Burnaby, became a company townsite.

Charles S. Davies arrived in Port Coquitlam from England and became a contractor and builder, involved in such projects as the city hall and the Commercial Hotel. He later became an alderman and then mayor.

Pitt Meadows got its first school and first telephone.

The BC Electric Railway purchased plans for two open-air sightseeing cars from the Montreal Tramways Company for 25 cents and constructed them in the BCER's New Westminster shops.

The Vancouver Labour Council joined the Canadian Trades and Labour Council.

The Clayburn brick works were producing 30,000 bricks a day.

Fred Hinckleton built the first shack on Grouse Mountain. It quickly became a rendezvous point for hikers wanting food and refreshments.

Comings and Goings

October 14 Famed American politician William Jennings Bryan lectured at the Vancouver Opera House.

Sculptor Charles Marega arrived in Vancouver, accompanied by his wife Berta. Many of his sculptures are still prominent around the city, including the Lions Gate Bridge lions, the Edward VII fountain by the Vancouver Art Gallery and the statue of George Vancouver at city hall.

Frederick Begg arrived in Vancouver from Lindsay, ON, and with his brother Frank as partner established the Begg Motor Company, the city's first car dealership.

1910-1919

1910

The first Pacific National Exhibition opened with attractions that would be illegal today. Louis D. Taylor won his first of eight mayoral elections. And the first airplane flight west of Winnipeg took place. That airplane would later lose a race to a horse.

Right: A crowd of 3,500 witnessed western Canada's first airplane flight in Richmond's Minoru Park on March 26, 1910. Perhaps overcome by the grandeur of this moment, pilot Charles K. Hamilton (far right) later made the gesture of pitting his biplane against a racehorse—unfortunately for his reputation, the horse won.
Vancouver Public Library, Special Collections, VPL 23378. Dominion Photo Co.

February 9 Ewing Buchan, a Vancouver banker, had his version of "O Canada" sung at a meeting of the Canadian Club. Buchan's lyrics became popular in BC but were eventually supplanted by those of Robert Stanley Weir.

February 28 Vancouver's main post office moved to a new building at the northwest corner of Granville and Hastings. This building displayed "Edwardian Baroque dignity, with columns, a clock tower and a granite facade." Today it is part of Sinclair Centre.

March 12 An explosion at a dynamite plant on Bowen Island killed five workers and was felt in Nanaimo.

March 25 The first airplane flight west of Winnipeg took place at Minoru Park in Richmond, with 3,500 spectators. Pilot Charles K. Hamilton flew a Curtiss pusher biplane. On March 26, Hamilton flew from Minoru to New Westminster and back. He later challenged a racehorse to a one-mile race which, much to Hamilton's embarrassment, the horse won by 10 seconds.

Elsewhere in BC

March 4 At Rogers Pass a CPR rotary snowplough and hundreds of workers were clearing snow and debris from an avalanche when a second avalanche swept down from above, killing 62 people, 32 of them Japanese.

April 20 A man in Surrey was fined $10 for speeding in his 1907 Marion car. He was travelling at 12 miles per hour.

May 6 The Vancouver chapter of the IODE commissioned sculptor Charles Marega to create a fountain in tribute to King Edward VII, who died on this day, succeeded by George V. Today the fountain stands next to the Vancouver Art Gallery, on the east side of Hornby Street.

May A "site commission" established by the provincial government began to tour British Columbia in search of a suitable location for the province's first university. It eventually chose Point Grey.

June North Vancouver Yacht Club held its first long-distance race for the Cates Cup, won by W.S. Buttar's *Ysidro*.

July 1 The first baseball game between teams from two Japanese communities featured the Victoria Nippons vs. the Vancouver Nippons. Although sumo wrestling is Japan's national sport and the martial arts are practised in many Japanese Canadian communities, baseball is the most popular sport among Japanese Canadians.

July 4 W.G. McElhanney founded the engineering firm that still bears his name. The McElhanney Group of companies has offices in western Canada, Newfoundland and Indonesia.

July Vancouver's Westminster Avenue—so called because it led to New Westminster at the time—was renamed Main Street. (Its original name was False Creek Road.)

August 15 At Exhibition Park, the Vancouver Exhibition opened to the public for the first time. We know it today as the Pacific National

Left: The renowned Pacific National Exhibition opened for the first time on August 15, 1910. It was originally called the Vancouver Exhibition, and as a sign of its prestige, the first festival was opened by Prime Minister Wilfrid Laurier. *Vancouver Public Library, Special Collections, VPL 20974*

Exhibition. Prime Minister Wilfrid Laurier presided over the official opening ceremony on August 16. The *News-Advertiser* wrote, "Petrified women, sacrificial crocodiles from the sacred river Ganges, and dusky negroes who dodge swiftly thrown baseballs, to say nothing of the numerous Salome dancers, Spanish Carmens, Dutch comedians and chorus girls are some of the attractions being offered the visitors at the fair this week."

October North Vancouver's Board of Trade held its first annual banquet. Streetcars and a special ferry ran overtime for this occasion.

Also in October
All-night street lighting first illuminated North Vancouver.

November 9 We now call it Central City Mission, but when they laid the cornerstone on this date—in a driving rain—it was just the Central Mission. Clerics from a number of local churches were there. The mission has since housed thousands and fed millions. On July 24, 1993, it moved from 233 Abbott St. to a new location at 415 West Pender.

November 23 The Royal Canadian Navy's HMCS *Rainbow* steamed into Vancouver's harbour this afternoon. It was the first RCN warship to visit the port, and the city gave the *Rainbow* and the 189 crew members a big welcome.

November 24 The BC Electric Railway Company issued a call for tenders for its new passenger station and office block at the southwest corner of Carrall and Hastings Streets. Old-timers will recall that the interurban cars actually ran through the ground floor of that office block, which still stands.

December 10 Father Edmond Maillard, after whom Maillardville was named, opened Our Lady of Lourdes Church there.

December 21 Hastings Townsite ratepayers voted to join Vancouver.

Also in 1910

An interurban railway was put through on the south side of the Fraser River expressly to carry valley farm produce between New Westminster and Chilliwack. It ran through the centre of what is now the City of Langley and sparked growth at Innes Corners/Langley Prairie. The BC Electric substation here is still admired by architects.

Louis D. Taylor was elected mayor of Vancouver for the first time. He made a habit of it, winning eight mayoral elections in all.

Vancouver city police agitated for a six-day week. The request was shelved.

Left: In 1910 sawmill owner W.L. Tait built a palatial home in the Shaughnessy Heights district. This neighbourhood, developed as a subdivision for the super-rich by the CPR, was the most fashionable pre-war address in the city. Tait called the house Glen Brae, a reflection of his Scottish background, though local wags knew it as Mae West House, a reference to the prominent domes. *Leonard Frank, Vancouver Public Library VPL 8956*

Fraser Mills was renamed Canadian Western Lumber Company and went on to become the biggest lumber company in the British Empire.

Sacred Heart Catholic Church, consecrated in 1884 at Ustlawn, the Indian mission village in North Vancouver, had a second spire added during renovations this year and was rededicated as St. Paul's. It's a familiar North Shore landmark to this day.

Vancouver's first skyscraper, the Dominion Trust Building at Hastings and Cambie, was completed.

It was the tallest building in the British Empire for a time, and its construction motivated the Vancouver Fire Department to purchase its first motorized aerial ladder, a 1909 Seagrave 23-metre (75-foot) tractor-aerial ladder, first of its type built by the Seagrave Company.

Right: Early skyscraper. Vancouver's first skyscraper, at 13 storeys, was the Dominion Trust Building. When it opened in 1910, it was the tallest building in the British Empire and a symbol of the city's pre-war energy and prosperity. It was owned by the Dominion Trust Co., a major player in the booming real estate market. By the time this photograph was taken, however, in 1915, the economy had taken a nosedive, taking with it the Dominion Trust, whose general manager had killed himself shortly before the company went bankrupt. The building survived, and still dominates the corner of Hastings and Cambie with its striking mansard roof and colourful terracotta exterior.

R. Broadbridge photo, Vancouver Public Library VPL 8393

Knox Presbyterian Church (later Knox United Church) began holding services in the Southlands district.

An Anglican Church conference held in London provided a large grant to establish a theological school in Vancouver.

The Oblate Fathers opened their third Vancouver church on 12th Avenue just west of Main Street in Mount Pleasant. Built in the neoclassical revival style, St. Patrick's had twin cupolas and a grand entry portico with Ionic columns. That church has now been replaced by a newer building facing onto Main Street.

The three-year-old City of North Vancouver had 5,000 residents.

North Vancouver High School opened. For many years it was the only high school on the North Shore.

West Vancouver's John Lawson donated land at 18th and Marine Drive for a building to house a church (Presbyterian) and Hollyburn School.

The North Shore hospital moved to a bigger 15-bed building at 151 East 12th St.

The Associated Charities of Vancouver started a West End creche (as child-care facilities were then called).

The city of South Vancouver was incorporated. Its northern boundary was 16th Avenue.

Henry Thomas Thrift, Surrey's municipal clerk, donated land for a new school building.

Kerrisdale Avenue was named at the request of Mrs. McKinnon, whose family had settled in that area in 1897. Kerrisdale commemorated their home in Scotland, Kerry's Dale.

The Cedar Cottage neighbourhood took its name from an interurban train stop, which took its name from a nearby home built in the 1890s. Cedar Cottage residents have always been proud to live in the only Vancouver neighbourhood that has its own lake (Trout Lake).

Southlands, a lavish Marine Drive mansion, was built for the wholesale grocer W.H. Malkin. It was the first built in that area.

Fairacres was built in Burnaby as a home for realtor Henry Ceperley and his wife, Grace, a Michigan heiress. Since 1967 it has been home to the Burnaby Art Gallery.

The Vancouver Block went up at 736 Granville. Its lofty clock is a downtown landmark.

The Hospital for the Mind (known as Essondale until 1966, when it was renamed Riverview Psychiatric Hospital) opened in Coquitlam. Colony Farm, operating out of a hay barn on 400 hectares (1,000 acres), was part of the hospital. Sixty patients were admitted the first year. They worked on the farm to provide food for themselves and staff.

Columbia Bitulithic was founded and headquartered in Coquitlam. The company built roads throughout the province and was responsible for much of the Vancouver road network.

The 6th Field Company Canadian Engineers was established in North Vancouver.

A visitor to Vancouver's east side reported that a "Piccola Italia," or Little Italy, had been established in the area around present-day Main Street. There were about 1,000 Italians in Vancouver at the time.

B'nai Brith was established in Vancouver.

The Canadian Immigration Act specifically barred immigrants from India.

The wood-hulled, steam-powered tug *Haro* was built in Vancouver for the harbour service of BC Mills (Hastings Mill).

The Bank of Vancouver was established. It was liquidated just five years later because it could not attract a significant deposit base.

The first BC Federation of Labour was formed. Twenty-six delegates, mainly from the Lower Mainland, pledged to seek the eight-hour day, favoured industrial unionism and endorsed socialism. This federation was disbanded in 1920.

Car dealer H. Hooper made a record automobile trip from Chilliwack to New Westminster in two hours and ten minutes. There were no roads as such.

Bob Brown, who became known as Vancouver's "Mr. Baseball," bought the Vancouver Beavers for $500. He was the club's owner, president, manager and shortstop.

Two sculpted lions were placed in front of the provincial courthouse in Vancouver. They were created by John Bruce, a Scot. Each weighed 15 tonnes (about 16 tons) and cost $4,000.

Phyllis Munday, 15, began Vancouver's first Girl Guide company with her mother.

Woodward's held its first one-price sale day, 25 Cents Day, a forerunner of $1.49 Day.

Comings and Goings

August Major-General Baden-Powell visited North Vancouver and inspected a gathering of local Boy Scouts.

With a solemn and majestic background for this formal portrait, a bandmaster of the Seaforth Highlanders poses with one of the two lions at the courthouse (now the art gallery). The lions were placed in 1910. *City of Vancouver Archives, LGN 525.*

November 17 Anna Pavlova, one of the most famous ballerinas who ever lived, danced in Vancouver.

Notable deaths: **Chief Joe Capilano** died on March 11; **James Edwin Machin**, Vancouver's first librarian, died March 31.

Architect Woodruff Marbury Somervell arrived in Vancouver from Seattle. Over the next few years he designed sugar king B.T. Rogers' mansion, Shannon; the now-vanished Birks Building (southeast corner of Georgia and Granville); the BC Electric building at Hastings and Carrall; and the Toronto-Dominion Bank at Hastings and Seymour.

An itinerant young English actor named William Pratt arrived in Vancouver. Among his earliest non-acting jobs here: carpenter at the Vancouver Exhibition. Later he moved to Hollywood and changed his name to Boris Karloff.

1911

Vancouver got the provincial courthouse on Georgia Street (now the Vancouver Art Gallery) and a new Cambie Street Bridge, while a commercial building boom saw the start of construction on the Sylvia Hotel at English Bay. Commercial Drive and Marine Drive received their modern names, and a visiting troupe of entertainers included a young man named Charlie Chaplin.

January 1 Hastings Townsite, the residents of which had voted to be annexed by Vancouver, became part of the city. (Today's Glen Drive was the western edge of the townsite.) As well, a small chunk of Canadian Pacific Railway property called "No Man's Land" was annexed by the city. South Vancouver ratepayers also voted in favour of annexation by Vancouver (1,914 to 200), but the provincial government refused to permit it, saying Vancouver was already overburdened with administration problems.

February 24 The first Vancouver Automobile, Motor Boat and Accessory Exhibition opened.

February 27 *North Vancouver Ferry No. 3* was launched from Wallace Shipyards, the first self-propelled boat of any size to be built in North Vancouver.

February **George Cunningham, aged 21, opened his first drugstore at Denman and Nelson. He eventually commanded a 52-store empire.**

March Construction began on the 83-metre (270-foot) World Building on the southeast corner of Pender and Beatty Streets, the present-day Sun Tower. John Coughland and Sons of Vancouver fabricated 1,135 tonnes (1,250 tons) of steel for what was then the tallest building in the British Empire. It held that title until 1914, when the Royal Bank of Canada eclipsed it with a 20-storey office building in Toronto. (The caryatids on the World Building, the *Nine Maidens*, were created by sculptor Charles Marega.)

April 28 William Templeton, who later became the first manager of the Vancouver Airport, built and flew a homemade biplane at Minoru Park racetrack. This was the first plane built and flown in Greater Vancouver.

Will Templeton flew his homemade biplane at the Minoru Park racetrack in Richmond in 1911. His was the first plane to be built in Greater Vancouver. *City of Vancouver Archives, Trans P39*

June 12 Real estate developers expected to get a boost in sales when the BC Electric Railway activated the Burnaby Lake interurban line.

June 24 The first nine holes of the Vancouver Golf Club in Coquitlam were opened for play. The clubhouse was the old Austin farmhouse, with a dormitory for golfers who missed the last tram back to Vancouver or New Westminster.

June The *Sea Foam* was added to the West Vancouver Transportation Company ferry fleet, with a capacity of 60 passengers. The vessel was sometimes used to tow freight barges hauling West Vancouver residents' furniture and effects.

July 1 The bells of Holy Rosary Cathedral rang their first full peal to commemorate the coronation of King George V. The only English-hung (that

Elsewhere in the World

February 24 Bill Miner, the Grey Fox, who had pulled off one of Canada's first train robberies near Silverdale in the Fraser Valley in 1904, was captured in Georgia and sent to the state penitentiary. He died there two years later.

is, free-swinging) church bells in the city, the eight bells were called into use for ceremonial occasions including weddings, funerals and ordinations. A full peal, in which the bells ring through more than 5,000 changes without a break, takes three hours.

July 11 Wallace Shipyards, the major employer in North Vancouver, was destroyed by fire. It was rebuilt almost immediately.

July 27 The *Province* reported that one-third of Vancouver's population had passed through the gates of Stanley Park during the week of July 10–16, making it "one of the most popular pleasure resorts the Terminal City possesses." During the week mentioned, "a census of every person entering the park was taken. A count was also taken of every auto, saddle horse, bicycle, dog, hack, and in fact every rig or conveyance...Sunday, the final day of the count, was of course the heaviest day of the week. On that day 21,738 pedestrians, 191 autos, 52 hacks, 367 rigs, 58 saddle horses, 148 bicycles and 173 dogs passed through the gates."

July North Vancouver Tennis Club held its opening tournament on its courts at 23rd and Lonsdale (today the site of the Harry Jerome Community Recreation Centre).

September 15 North America's biggest bank-vault robbery to date happened right in little old New Westminster.

Five men—or was it three? accounts differ—bound and gagged a janitor at the city's sole Bank of Montreal branch and got away with more than a quarter of a million dollars. Multiply that by about a hundred to gauge the impact today. The *Province* cartoonist had a field day with the heist. One of his drawings showed two cops interviewing an elderly neighbour. "Have you seen any suspicious persons?" they ask. "Yes," she says, "there was two reporters here this morning."

September 25 Park Drive in East End Vancouver—so called because it ended at Clark Park—was renamed Commercial Drive. The name was changed thanks to real estate promoters who wanted to bring into prominence what they predicted would be a great commercial thoroughfare.

October 18 The first elementary school in West Vancouver opened for classes. One source says it was in a large tent erected for use by the Presbyterian church. There were 14 pupils.

December Charles Marega's bust of David Oppenheimer, Vancouver's second mayor, was placed near the entrance to Stanley Park. (Oppenheimer had presided at the opening of the park.)

December 20 Lester and Frank Patrick opened the world's largest artificial-ice rink in Vancouver.

Known as the Denman Arena, it burned down in 1936.

Also in 1911

Construction began on a number of buildings, including St. George's School at 3851 West 29th Ave.; the Vancouver Rowing Club in Stanley Park; Point Atkinson Lighthouse; the Stanley Park Dining Pavilion; the First Baptist Church at 969 Burrard; B'nai Yehudah (Sons of Israel), Vancouver's first synagogue, at Pender and Heatley; the Sylvia Hotel, 1154 Gilford; the Rogers Building at the northeast corner of Granville and Pender; and a tea house at the Capilano Suspension Bridge.

In 1911 construction began on the permanent home—seen in this 1913 photo—for the Vancouver Rowing Club. An 1899 amalgamation of the Vancouver Boating Club and the Burrard Inlet Rowing Club, the VRC is the oldest amateur sports organization in Vancouver. *City of Vancouver Archives, Sp P102.1. W.J. Cairns photo*

Right: Pauline Johnson was already the most famous poet in Canada when she moved to Vancouver in 1909. She had been born on the Six Nations Reserve in Ontario, and she began her public readings in 1892—and for many years toured Canada, the US and England—as the Indian Princess, enthralling her audiences with poems about aboriginal life. Her collection of aboriginal tales, *Legends of Vancouver*, was published in 1911 to raise money for her treatment for cancer. When she died in 1913, thousands of people lined Georgia Street for her funeral procession. Her ashes were buried in Stanley Park.
Cochran of Ontario photo, Vancouver Public Library VPL 9430

Teddy Lyons began his spieling for the BC Electric Railway. A conductor on the regular streetcars, Lyons was called in on short notice one day to work one of the specially constructed open-air sightseeing cars and was discovered to be a born showman. Thousands of people over the decades listened with fascination to Teddy's tales of the city's history, and groaned and laughed at his jokes as he pointed out the sights of the city. "There's the richest bird in Vancouver," he would tell his sightseeing passengers, pointing to a seagull flying overhead. "He just made a deposit on a brand-new Cadillac." It was corny and the passengers loved it as much as they loved the little groups of children who sang at corners where the car stopped, or the long narrow souvenir photos of the passengers taken by photographer Harry Bullen and sold on every trip. Teddy, who knew every historical corner of our town, kept it up for a jaw-dropping 39 years. He retired in 1950 and died February 27, 1955.

Vancouver's population reached 120,847, double what it had been five years earlier. A study found that 34 percent of Vancouver's population was British.

BOMA, the Building Owners and Managers Association of British Columbia, was formed. Today the association has more than 300 member firms that own or manage over $8 billion in commercial real estate in Vancouver alone, making it the largest commercial real estate industry association in BC.

A company called Harbour Navigation began operating small ferryboats on the Fraser River. The company is still around under the name Harbour Cruises Ltd.

Pauline Johnson published *Legends of Vancouver*.

The Canada Post Publishing Co. Ltd. was established. Not long after, it became Broadway Printers.

The *Journal of Commerce*, Vancouver's oldest magazine, began publishing. Billed as Western Canada's Construction Newspaper, it now publishes both digital and print editions.

Vancouver's first Italian newspaper, *L'Italia nel Canada*, appeared.

Dominion Construction was incorporated under the leadership of Charles Bentall.

The Holden Building was built on Hastings Street. It served as Vancouver's city hall from 1929 to 1936.

The Canadian Pacific Railway built Piers A and B on the Vancouver waterfront and added 12 more stalls to its roundhouse in Yaletown. As well, prompted by the imminent opening of the Panama Canal, the CPR announced plans to create a major shipyard at Westminster Junction (Port Coquitlam), complete with railway marshalling yards and an industrial complex.

London-born Helena Gutteridge arrived in Vancouver. She went on to organize the BC Women's Suffrage League and fought for (and won) passage of BC's first minimum wage act. (It varied by industry, but $13 to $15 a week was the range.) Gutteridge became Vancouver's first woman alderman.

The first suffrage convention was held in Vancouver at O'Brien Hall, with Mayor Louis D. Taylor as chairman.

A 71-hectare (175-acre) tract called the University Endowment Lands was carved out of the District Municipality of Point Grey's western tip.

The road that had been the old North Arm Trail, then River Road, became Marine Drive after Point Grey municipal council straightened and blacktopped it. The road was planned as a scenic loop around the Point Grey peninsula. It still is.

The western stretch of Dundas Street in Vancouver was renamed Powell Street to honour Dr. Israel Wood Powell who, among other good works, donated the site of Vancouver's first city hall.

A company called the Grouse Mountain Scenic Incline Railway was created to build a 2.5-kilometre (1.5-mile) rail line that would carry passengers up the mountain to a lavish resort hotel. The scheme collapsed as World War I loomed and it became impossible to obtain steel.

The Pacific Coast Hockey Association was founded. It folded in 1924.

The Lonsdale Theatre opened in North Vancouver.

Sculptor Charles Marega began teaching art to night school students.

Essondale mental hospital's Colony Farm was considered the best in the west, yielding over 630 tonnes (700 tons) of crops and nearly 91,000 litres (20,000 gallons) of milk. The farm provided therapy as well as food for its patients.

Japanese settlers began growing strawberries in Surrey. The nearby community hall came to be called Strawberry Hill. The berries were sent to canneries in New Westminster and Vancouver.

Surrey council passed a resolution to close the Serpentine and Nicomekl Rivers to navigation in order to construct dams for land reclamation, bringing the era of steamboats and log booms on these rivers to an end.

A real estate boom in what would become West Vancouver saw waterfront lots advertised for as much as $4,500.

The Cloverdale telephone exchange opened with 209 subscribers.

Donald Mann of the Canadian Northern Railway was knighted. Port Mann, named for him, was originally intended to be the railway's Pacific terminus. The Canadian Northern became part of the Canadian National Railway in 1923.

Burnaby hired two mounted policemen and set aside $250 for the purchase of two horses.

The Vancouver Fire Department was deemed by an international committee to be "one of the world's finest...as regards equipment and efficiency," behind only London, England, and Leipzig, Germany. The city had 11 firehalls and 191 firefighters.

The first power was produced from the concrete dam and 52.5-megawatt powerhouse located at the outlet of Stave Lake.

The Bank of Toronto and the Dominion Bank—which eventually merged—each opened second branches in Vancouver.

H.H. "Harry" Stevens became a Conservative MP for Vancouver. He served for nearly 30 years, including a stint as federal minister of trade and commerce.

The Vancouver Park Board, realizing the importance of playgrounds, established MacLean Park as the city's first supervised playground. The park was named for Vancouver's first mayor.

Wisconsin-born Julius Harold Bloedel began logging in BC.

Comings and Goings

February 6 Dr. Sun Yat-sen visited Vancouver on a fundraising campaign, staying at the Woods Hotel on East Hastings Street for a month. He also visited the Chinese Freemasons in Victoria, Nanaimo and Cumberland to solicit funds for the revolution against China's imperial rulers. Dr. Sun convinced the Vancouver Chinese Freemasons to re-mortgage their building and promised to make them his national political party if he became president of the new republic.

A political exile in this 1897 picture, Dr. Sun Yat-sen visited Vancouver in 1911 to raise money for his hoped-for revolution in China. The following year he briefly became the first provisional president of the Republic of China, though China remained fragmented and his political life rocky.
Courtesy Jim Wong-Chu

May 8 Fred Karno's entertainment troupe from England began a week-long engagement at the original Orpheum Theatre at Pender and Howe Streets. Among the performers: a 22-year-old not-yet-famous Charlie Chaplin.

Notable births: Actor and pianist **John Emerson** was born in Vancouver on March 13; **Mandrake the Magician** (Leon Mandrake), entertainer, was born in New Westminster on April 11; actress **Katherine DeMille** (born Katherine Lester) was born in Vancouver on June 29; Squamish chief **Simon Baker** was born on the Capilano reserve.

Nine-year-old Nat Bailey arrived in Vancouver with his family from Seattle. He launched the White Spot restaurant chain in 1928.

Samuel Brighouse, one of the three greenhorns, left Vancouver for England, where he died in 1913.

1912

The pace of urban life accelerated, with what may have been the city's first report of automobile congestion. Some people took to the sky: the city recorded its first passenger flight and its first parachute jump, though not with the same plane. The Vancouver police department got fingerprinting technology, its first police boat and its first female employees, but also had its first constable killed in the line of duty.

February 27 The Pacific Great Eastern Railway was incorporated to build and operate a railway from North Vancouver to Prince George. North Vancouver hoped to become the major railway terminus on the West Coast. The PGE was named after, and partly funded by, Britain's Great Eastern Railway, hence the odd name. The railway did not connect Vancouver with Prince George for 44 years—hence its nickname, "Prince George Eventually."

March 15 The municipality of West Vancouver was incorporated. Land for the city hall was donated by John Lawson, called by some the Father of West Vancouver. The municipality's population was 700, though it rose to 1,200 during the summers.

March 25 Constable Lewis Byers responded to a "drunk annoying" call on Powell Street. The drunk had a gun, and Byers was shot and killed—the first Vancouver police officer killed in the line of duty. Police closed in around a waterfront shack where the drunken Oscar Larsen had holed up and shot him dead.

Sporting times. The year 1912 started with a bang for sport fans. At the massive Denman Arena (pictured here), the Vancouver Millionaires beat the New Westminster Royals 8–3 in what was the first professional hockey game in Vancouver.
City of Vancouver Archives, Pan NXVIII. W.J. Moore photo

January 5 The first professional hockey game ever played in Vancouver was enjoyed by the crowd at the Patrick brothers' Denman Arena. The Vancouver Millionaires beat the New Westminster Royals 8–3.

January 28 Vancouver alderman R.P. Pettipiece addressed a crowd at the Powell Street Grounds. His topic was unemployment. The meeting was broken up by mounted police.

February 12 The first edition of the *Vancouver Morning Sun* appeared. In the 1920s it became an afternoon newspaper, the *Vancouver Sun*.

Elsewhere in BC

July 1 The Esquimalt and Nanaimo Railway on Vancouver Island was leased by the Canadian Pacific.

A joint Dominion/provincial Royal Commission on Indian Affairs (the McKenna/McBride commission) was appointed and charged with settling the "land question." Between 1913 and 1915 it toured the province to talk with aboriginal leaders. Some new reserves were created and others further reduced.

Elsewhere in Canada

August 28 A Canadian businessman named E.G. Rykert, who was well enough known in 1912 to be quoted on the country's future, spoke in Montreal after his return from a business trip to Europe. "Mr. Rykert," the *Province* reported, "declared that Canada was taking an increasingly important place before the eyes of the British public. 'When I was in London,' he said, 'I noticed one day that the newspaper bulletins announced in huge type that Borden would arrive at such and such an hour; not "Premier Borden of Canada," but just "Borden." This shows that the Canadian premier is now a British public character.' "

Elsewhere in the World

April 14–15 The *Titanic* sank.

July 14 Duncan Gillis, a 250-pound Vancouver policeman, became the first Olympic medal winner from BC, winning silver at Stockholm in the hammer throw with a toss of 48.39 metres (53 yards).

The lovely old Parker carousel, now at Burnaby's Village Museum, was built this year in Kansas.

March 30 The Vancouver local of the International Longshoremen's Association was formed, with 60 charter members.

March Emily Carr, back from a sojourn in France, exhibited paintings she created there in her gallery at 1465 West Broadway.

April 6 In the first municipal election in West Vancouver, Charles Nelson was elected reeve (mayor).

April 8 The West Vancouver Transportation Company, which had fallen on hard times, was taken over by the municipality. It continued to lose money for another 12 years.

April 21 A public memorial service was held at the Vancouver Opera House in aid of widows and orphans of the seamen of the *Titanic*.

April 23 A group of concerned, forward-looking men gathered in the council chambers of Vancouver City Hall, formed the Vancouver Mining Club and elected its first president, Robert R. Hedley. The group was later renamed the British Columbia and Yukon Chamber of Mines. On December 8, 2005, the name of the association was changed again, to the Association for Mineral Exploration British Columbia (AME BC).

April 24 Billy Stark was the pilot for the first passenger flight in BC. He flew his passenger, James Hewitt, a *Province* sports reporter, for 9 kilometres (6 miles) and eight minutes, soaring up to 200 metres (600 feet). The plane travelled at 65 km/h (40 mph), and Hewitt rode on a board strapped to the lower wing.

The Sylvia. Still a distinctive feature of Beach Avenue, the Sylvia Hotel was built in 1912 on English Bay as an apartment building. It was only later during the Depression and World War II that the building shifted to being a hotel.
R. Broadbridge photo, Vancouver Public Library VPL 9426

May 6 The memorial drinking fountain dedicated to King Edward VII was unveiled at the courthouse. In the beginning, little bronze cups were left for drinkers...but they kept getting stolen. The first drink was taken by Mayor James Findlay. Today the fountain is on the east side of Hornby next to the Art Gallery.

May 7 West Vancouver appointed its first police constable. Early police officers, when called to points west of town, had to take the bus.

May 24 Prof. Charles Saunders made the first parachute jump in Canada during a two-day aviation meet (tickets 50 cents, children 25 cents) at Hastings Park. Saunders had jumped from balloons before, but this was his first leap from a plane. The *Province* of May 25 explained that Prof. Morton (no first name given), who was supposed to have made the jump, had fallen ill and Saunders was called in at short notice. He leaped from 1,000 metres (3,500 feet) and didn't open the parachute until he had fallen 300 metres (1,000 feet). Needless to say, the crowd was thrilled. Both days of the meet featured aerobatics and races.

May 30 Cedar Cottage property owners voted for annexation by Vancouver.

May Enrollment commenced in the 6th Field Engineers of North Vancouver, under the command of Major J.P. Fell. The unit was a training and recruitment depot in the two World Wars and saw action on D-Day.

June 24 The *Vancouver Sun* reported that "the roads are getting crowded: the total number of automobiles...in Vancouver is 1,769."

July 1 Peter Greyell, a White Rock builder, opened a 50-room, four-storey hotel in that community with a luncheon for 300 guests.

July 9 Vancouver's progressive police department now had a chief's car, a detective car, a paddy wagon

A historic neoclassical landmark at 12th and Hemlock, Chalmers' Presbyterian Church was dedicated in 1912. It now houses Holy Trinity Anglican Church and Pacific Theatre.
City of Vancouver Archives, CVA 99-3495. Photo Stuart Thomson

and an ambulance. Later in the year the VPD got its first police boat. Even more important, it hired its first women employees: Nancy (or Lurancy) Harris and Minnie Miller (or Millar). Their salary was $80 a month. (Today Vancouver has well over 100 women police officers, in almost all ranks.) Police worked eight hours a day, seven days a week. They were expected to attend court on their own time, as well as "any celebrations or parades where their attendance was expected."

July 16 "Splash Day" in Burnaby celebrated the completion of the municipal waterworks system.

July 24 The BC Electric Railway Company held its first annual picnic at Hastings Park. The BCER had increased its trackage in Vancouver from 21 kilometres (13 miles) in 1900 to 170 kilometres (105 miles) this year, opening up vast areas of undeveloped land for single-family housing.

August 10 A story in the *Province* reported that the clock on the Vancouver Block, the brand-new white terracotta office building on Granville Street, was the largest in Canada. "The four faces of this clock are each twenty-two feet in diameter. The glass contained in the dial weighs four tons and is seven-eighths of an inch in thickness. The minute hands are eleven feet long and the hour hands about eight feet...The clock was erected by the Standard Electric Time Company of San Francisco at a cost of more than $10,000."

August 11 Chalmers' Presbyterian Church, at the southwest corner of 12th Avenue and Hemlock Street in Vancouver, was dedicated. "The new church," the *Province* reported, "has been specially planned to take a helpful part in the social life of the community. It has been planned and equipped as a seven-day-a-week church for the people. A gymnasium, swimming and shower baths, reading rooms and social parlors are included." Today this is Holy Trinity Anglican Church.

August 21 The University of British Columbia's convocation, the governing body of the university, held its first meeting. Dr. Francis Carter-Cotton was chosen first chancellor.

August 13
Vancouver's Great Auto Show opened as part of the Vancouver Exhibition

(what we now know as the PNE). "The man who is completely ignorant of the working of a car," the *Province* wrote, "and who would be unable to steer it even if his hand were placed on the wheel, will have an opportunity of learning in a few minutes the exact method by which auto locomotion may be effected."

August 23 or 25 Streetcar service started on Nanaimo Street between Hastings and Broadway. Also this year, streetcars began running out to Kerrisdale and down Oak Street to Marpole.

The Shannon, located at Granville and 57th, was the country estate for sugar magnate Benjamin Tingley Rogers. The design was ready by 1913, but the mansion wasn't finished until 1925. Modern plans include some development on the grounds for more residents, while preserving the heritage mansion and other buildings and gardens.
Arlen Redekop / The Province

Left. Arch supreme. When the Duke of Connaught, Governor General of Canada, and his wife, the Duchess, visited Vancouver in September 1912, residents pulled out all the stops. It was customary to erect arches to welcome dignitaries, but even by the standards of the time this one, seen here at the corner of Hamilton and Pender with an honour guard, was a whopper. *City of Vancouver Archives, CVA 677-502*

August 24 Woodward's Department Stores bought a 26-metre (86-foot) lot fronting on Hastings Street with plans to double the size of the existing store at the northwest corner of Abbott and Hastings. The lot cost $400,000, or $4,500 per front foot, which the newspapers said was "a record price for inside property in that section of the business district of Vancouver."

September 2 Burnaby's Oakalla Prison Farm was officially opened. Its first inmate was William Daley, sentenced to serve a year of hard labour for stealing some fountain pens.

September 14 Lynn Valley Park was officially opened in the District of North Vancouver,

with band concerts given by the North Vancouver City Band. One piece of more than usual interest was entitled *The Echoes of the Lynn,* composed by Miss G. Strickland, age 15. The 6th Field Engineers of North Vancouver made their first appearance as an honour guard. A small suspension bridge, 50 metres (165 feet) above Lynn Creek, was a highlight of the park and is still a favourite feature of what is now Lynn Canyon Park, one of the most popular parks in the Lower Mainland.

September 15 From the front page of the *Province*: "The provincial police has received from Ottawa the apparatus required for registering the marks of human finger tips, and hereafter this method of identification of criminals will be part of the regular procedure at the provincial capital... All records will be photographed and a copy sent to Ottawa so that the Dominion police will by and by have a complete collection of impressions of the finger tips of the criminal section of the travelling public."

September 18 The original Lumbermen's Arch (note the plural, not "Lumberman's") loomed over the intersection of Hamilton and Pender Streets to honour the visit to Vancouver by the Duke and Duchess of Connaught. The Arch was built and donated by the BC Lumber and Shingle Association for the royal visit. A huge Douglas fir, bark left on, was sawn into eight logs—each a metre (3 feet) in diameter and 6 metres (20 feet) long—which were stood on end and topped with a flag-bedecked pediment. The newspapers claimed "there was not a nail in the whole of it." After the royals left, the Arch was disassembled, taken to Stanley Park and put back together again. By late 1947 it had deteriorated and was demolished. The present much simpler version—a single leaning log—was put in its place in 1952. (Incidentally, the Arch's designer was Captain G.P. Bowie, who was killed at Ypres on July 7, 1915.)

Fall The architectural firm Sharp and Thompson won the competition for the contract to design the new Point Grey site for the University of British Columbia.

It built the first four original campus buildings and became the university's official architectural firm. Over the years partners came and went as the firm evolved into Thompson, Berwick, Pratt and Partners.

November 25 Point Atkinson Lighthouse "flashed into being," replacing an older version installed by the Dominion government in 1875. The lighthouse horn, which sounded every 53 seconds in foggy weather, came to be known as Old

Shining light. The Point Atkinson Lighthouse began service in 1912, replacing an earlier light, at the point where Burrard Inlet meets Howe Sound. The lighthouse is today preserved in what is now Lighthouse Park in West Vancouver, along with the last stand of old-growth forest in the area. *Vancouver Public Library, Special Collections, VPL 71342.*

Wahoo by the locals. Lighthouse Park was originally set aside as a timber preserve to provide fuel for the lighthouse and its steam fog alarm. As a result, the park has never been logged and retains many of its original native trees and plants.

December 12 Richmond's town hall burned to the ground. A new town hall was built in Brighouse in 1919.

December 20 The Rex Theatre, described in the papers as "the most modern movie house in the world," opened on Hastings Street.

Not only an eatery. The iconic Downtown Eastside restaurant The Only opened on Hastings in 1912 and survived until 2009, when it closed amid allegations of drug dealing on its premises. In 2011 the non-profit Portland Hotel Society was planning to reopen the restaurant in its original location, with its original menu, by early 2012, after building renovations. *Steve Bosch/Vancouver Sun*

Also in 1912

James Findlay beat Louis D. Taylor to become mayor for a year.

Construction began on the Birks Building

at the southeast corner of Georgia and Granville. The handsome structure was designed by architect Woodruff Marbury Somervell. Its demolition in 1974 caused an uproar.

BC Breweries Ltd. built a new brewery at West 12th Avenue and Yew "on the wooded outskirts of the city beside a creek flowing through a duck-filled marsh." (This is now Connaught Park.)

Douglas Lodge was built at 2799 Granville as the Bank of Commerce Building. It has been used for business and as an apartment, and some of its famous residents include John Candy, Arthur Erickson and Sarah McLachlan.

Surrey, Burnaby and Delta built new municipal halls this year. Surrey's spacious hall was designed by C.H. Clow and built in Cloverdale. Today it's a cultural and seniors' centre. Burnaby shared its hall with the RCMP from 1935 to 1956, and then with the library. Delta's Tudor-style structure, designed by A. Campbell Hope, now houses the Delta Museum and Archives at 4858 Delta St.

The Great Northern Railway—now the Burlington Northern Santa Fe—built a station in White Rock. When passenger service was withdrawn from White Rock in 1975, the BNR gave the station to the city. It now houses the White Rock Museum and Archives, at 14970 Marine Dr.

The Stanley Park causeway was built.

The Only Restaurant, famed for its humble surroundings and generous helpings of seafood, opened on Hastings Street.

Seven Indo-Canadian millworkers were killed in Port Moody when a freight train was routed, in error, onto a siding where the workers were loading freight cars.

The Clachan (Gaelic for "meeting place") tea room was built at Dundarave in West Vancouver and run by Jessie and Helen Stevenson. A second floor added in 1914 allowed for overnight guests. The Clachan went through several incarnations as a restaurant, and today is the Beach House.

Lawyer E.P. Davis built a mansion, designed by architect Samuel Maclure, on extensive grounds near the tip of Point Grey. Davis named it Kanakla, a West Coast native word meaning "house on the cliff." It was renamed in honour of Dr. and Mrs. Cecil Green, who bought the house in 1967 and generously donated it to UBC. The complex is now known as Cecil Green Park.

The Vancouver Fire Department, always in the forefront, took delivery of its first motorized pump, a 5,700-litre-(1,250-gallon)-per-minute engine that remained in service for almost 40 years. Meanwhile, Coquitlam formed a volunteer fire brigade.

The Wallace Shipyards opened in North Vancouver, replacing the yard that had burned down in July 1911.

Construction began on pedestrian tunnels under Vancouver General Hospital. The first tunnel was built to connect laundry services to the hospital. There are now about 1.6 kilometres (1 mile) of tunnels under VGH. There was also construction at St. Paul's Hospital as work commenced to add a 120-bed expansion.

The Burnaby branch of the Victorian Order of Nurses (VON) was formed to provide community nursing care at a time when there were few doctors and a rapidly expanding population. Also this year, the Registered Nurses Association of British Columbia was founded.

H.R. MacMillan was named BC's first chief forester.

A.J.T. Taylor founded Taylor Engineering, which was involved in many large-scale projects throughout BC. Taylor went on to promote development of West Vancouver's British Properties and construction of the Lions Gate Bridge in the 1930s. West Vancouver's Taylor Way is named for him.

In sports, the Shaughnessy Heights Golf Club opened at West 37th Avenue and Oak Street, and the Vancouver Curling Club was established.

Con Jones, an ex-bookie from Australia, built a home for his Vancouver field lacrosse team, a wooden structure completely surrounding the field of play, which was bounded by Renfrew, Oxford, Kaslo and Cambridge Streets. Soccer was also played for more than 50 years at what became known in 1942 as Callister Park. It was demolished in 1971.

An area by Brockton Oval in Stanley Park was set aside for an "Indian village." Two totem poles and the Thunderbird house-posts were donated at the time.

Nine metres (30 feet) below VanDusen Botanical Gardens is an enormous abandoned reservoir that was built in 1912. Its rust-stained concrete vaults once held nearly 14 million litres (3 million gallons) of city drinking water. The reservoir was abandoned and sealed in the early 1970s.

Comings and Goings

August 28 Hardial Singh Atwal was born in Vancouver, the first Canadian-born Sikh.

September 18 Canada's Governor General, the Duke of Connaught (a famous soldier and a son of Queen Victoria), visited Vancouver with the Duchess to officiate at the ceremony naming the brand-new Connaught Bridge—a name that never caught on. Everyone called it the Cambie Street Bridge. The royals were accompanied by their daughter, Princess Patricia, the woman for whom the Princess Patricia's Canadian Light Infantry (PPCLI) is named; she was the regiment's colonel-in-chief.

September 20
French actress Sarah Bernhardt performed in Vancouver—in French.

October 14
Thomas Wilby and his driver, Jack Haney, arrived in Vancouver, the first people to drive across Canada in an automobile.
They had left Halifax on August 27 in a brand-new Reo. After leaving Vancouver, they carried on to the Pacific Ocean at Alberni on Vancouver Island. With the roads the way they were then, this really was an epic journey: the trip took 49 days. Wilby wrote a book about this trip called *A Motor Tour Through Canada.*

Two of the three greenhorns, died in 1912: John Morton, 78, in Vancouver on April 18; William Hailstone, 82, in Newcastle-on-Tyne, England, on July 12.

1913

Right: Elegance. The CPR began construction of the second Hotel Vancouver on the site of the first at Granville and Georgia. When it opened in 1916 it set a new standard of elegance for the city with a cavernous lobby, glass-enclosed rooftop tea garden and oak-lined ballrooms. At 500 rooms it was the largest hotel in the city.
Vancouver Public Library, Special Collections, VPL 12022. Leonard Frank photo

In spite of a financial depression, construction continued—and when a Native band sold reserve property in Kitsilano, the land jumped 10-fold in value when subdivided. Poet Pauline Johnson became the first—and last—person to be buried in Stanley Park.

January 31 Prisoner Joseph Smith, who had killed guard J.H. Joynson in 1912, was executed at the BC Penitentiary, the first and only hanging there. (Most executions occurred at Oakalla.)

January The *North Shore Press* newspaper began publishing.

February Vancouver city police, who had agitated for a six-day week in 1910, tried again. Their request was shelved and they continued to be on duty seven days a week.

March 7 Poet Pauline Johnson died of breast cancer at age 52 in the Old Bute Street Hospital, Vancouver. Before she died, she had asked to be buried in Stanley Park, which was her favourite place in Vancouver and which she immortalized in her poems. The city granted this request, and the Women's Canadian Club began raising funds for a cairn to mark the resting place of her ashes.

Also March 7 Port Moody was incorporated as a city. Civic elections were held April 3. P.D. Roe, the owner of a local sawmill, was elected the first mayor by acclamation.

March 17 The Vancouver Opera House, which opened in 1891, reopened as the Orpheum (not the present one) with vaudeville acts. (In July 1935 it became the Lyric, showing talking pictures.) The building stood where Sears is today on Granville Street.

April 17 Baseball's Athletic Park was dedicated.

Bob "Mr. Baseball" Brown had built this fine wooden ballpark at the southeast corner of 5th and Hemlock (he cleared the land himself), and 6,000 fans filled every seat to watch the Vancouver Beavers beat the Tacoma Tigers 8–4. The first admission prices were 25 and 50 cents.

A Hotel for the Century

Construction on one of Vancouver's most beautiful (and now vanished) buildings, the second Hotel Vancouver, began early in 1913.

An article in the April 25, 1914, issue of *Engineering Record* gave some of the details: "The original wood-frame building [referring to the first Hotel Vancouver, which had opened for business in 1888] had been from time to time extended by additions until it covered an area of about 60,000 square feet (5,570 square metres), on most of which the structure stood five storeys high. In designing the new hotel, limitations were put on the work by two conditions: First, a city ordinance had just been passed placing the maximum height of buildings at 120 feet with the allowance of a tower eight storeys higher covering one-third the ground area; and second, the railway company [the hotel was owned by the CPR] required that the business of the hotel should not be interfered with during the construction period."

The building's stepped construction resulted in just 44 of the hotel's 500 rooms being without an exterior view. Building this big beauty took well over two years. It opened to the public in 1916.

Elsewhere in BC

August Massive amounts of rock were accidentally blasted into the Fraser River during construction of the Canadian Northern Railway, and a slide at Hell's Gate prevented a record sockeye run from reaching its spawning grounds. One result was famine among the Native people who relied on Fraser River salmon for food.

Elsewhere in the World

September 8 Bill Miner, the Grey Fox, died in a Georgia prison.

April 18 The City of Port Coquitlam celebrated Inauguration Day, marking its incorporation as a city, breaking away from the District of Coquitlam. Its population of 1,500 took as its motto "By Commerce and Industry We Prosper." The first mayor was James Mars. Coquitlam lost a bit more of its territory as tiny Fraser Mills also broke away.

April 22 Vancouver's Rotary Club was organized, with 94 members. It was the first Rotary Club in the area, and only the third in Canada.

April Artist Emily Carr rented Vancouver's Drummond Hall and showed 200 paintings before returning to Victoria to live on family property.

May 16 An act of Parliament created the Vancouver Harbour Commission. The first commissioner was Frank Carter-Cotton.

May The North Vancouver Rowing Club was launched.

May 27 The Capilano light was installed on the north side of the entrance to Vancouver Harbour. It was destaffed in 1946 and replaced with a beacon.

June 18 The Fraser Valley Milk Producers Association was formed. Today it's Dairyland.

June 28 The *Vancouver World* reported: "Throwing open its doors this week to the travelling public, the Hotel Connaught, one of Vancouver's very finest hostelries, was at once favored with the support which so fine a place really deserves." Today the Connaught is known as the Historic Ramada West Pender.

This imposing edifice at the corner of Pender and Beatty was first called the World Building for its inaugural tenant, the *Vancouver World*. After that newspaper folded, the *Vancouver Sun* occupied the building for many years and it became known as the Sun Tower. From 1968 to 1996 it was occupied by the Geological Survey of Canada, but "Geological Survey of Canada Tower" never caught on. *R. Broadbridge photo, Vancouver Public Library VPL 8388*

July 12 The Pacific Highway opened. It ran from the Fraser River bridge to the US border. A new customs office opened at the border in a tent, which was later replaced by a permanent wooden building. The highway was paved in 1923.

July North Vancouver's city hall at 1st and Lonsdale was remodelled as a post office. Council moved to temporary quarters in the Keith Block.

September The recently paved Vancouver Road was renamed Kingsway and opened with great fanfare and a parade of automobiles. A local newspaper wrote: "The new highway between Vancouver and New Westminster passing through South Vancouver and Burnaby is now complete...It is a broad, magnificent road, and by none will it be more appreciated than motorists, who, to the number of six hundred, made the trip between the two cities on the day the road was opened. There is a famous London highway of this name, and it is thought our Kingsway is named for that one."

November 3 The Alcazar Theatre opened at 639 Commercial Dr. with the comedy *Too Much Johnson*. Later, it was renamed the York Theatre.

November 8 The doors of the "elegant and vast" new Birks store opened at Georgia and Granville. An advertisement cited the name of the managing director, George Trorey, reminding us that when Birks came to Vancouver in 1907 they purchased his jewellery shop at the northeast corner of Hastings and Granville...and with it the famous clock.

December 4 An Ayrshire cow named Flossie was given an award by the Canadian Ayrshire Breeders Association for producing 11,655 pounds (more than 5 tonnes) of milk and 446 pounds (200 kilograms) of butterfat over 314 consecutive days. Flossie was owned by the Shannon Brothers of Cloverdale.

Mansions, Yachts and the Hudson's Bay

A general financial depression began, and the previous years' frenetic pace of building slowed dramatically. There was still some construction going on, though.

The Hudson's Bay erected a new building at Georgia and Granville to replace the 1893 structure. This one is the familiar white building, but not as big as the current Bay at that corner. More was added in later years.

Conservative Hall, later called Dundarave Hall, was built on Marine Drive in West Vancouver and used for community social activities. It has also served as a cabaret, a church, a furniture store and restaurant.

Three schools opened this year: Hollyburn, the first purpose-built school in West Vancouver; Lord Tennyson, at West 10th and Cypress; and David Livingstone Elementary, named for the Scottish explorer and missionary. The latter had eight classrooms.

Businessman Philip Gilman built a grand mansion on Jericho Beach. Known today as Brock House, it operates as a seniors' centre next to the Royal Vancouver Yacht Club.

The Campbell River Lumber Company, with about 250 workers, built a mill in White Rock a mile east of the railway station.

West Vancouver built a ferry terminal at the foot of 14th Street. In 1989 it was designated a heritage building with exhibition space for art shows.

Edgar George Baynes built the Grosvenor Hotel, then became the manager.

St. Mary's Church was established at 2498 West 37th Ave. in Kerrisdale.

Also in 1913

Truman Smith Baxter was elected mayor. He won the post again in 1914, beating Louis D. Taylor, but lost to Taylor in 1915.

To widen Pender Street, the city expropriated land on either side of the road, demolishing Chang Toy's grocery warehouse and leaving him with a narrow strip of land. No compensation was offered. Toy was furious. Instead of selling his prime location cheaply to his neighbour, he hired architects Brown and Hillam to design a building for the site. The result was the Sam Kee Building, six feet, two inches wide (less than 2 metres wide), which is the world's narrowest commercial building. A series of bay windows increased the useable width of the upper floor, while the basement, lit with glass blocks set in the pavement to augment lighting, extended under the sidewalk and ran the length of the building, doubling the square footage. This building, situated at the corner of Pender and Carrall Street, was restored in 1986 by the current owner, Jack Chow, and architect Soren Rasmussen.

Sandheads #16 Built on the US east coast in 1880 as the *Thomas F. Bayard* (named in honour of a Delaware senator), this two-masted schooner had been a pilot ship in Delaware Bay, then a gold rush freighter, running between Puget Sound and Alaska from 1898 to 1906, and finally a seal hunter out of Victoria from 1907 to 1911 before becoming a lightship.

C.H. Cates Ltd. was incorporated. Cates Tugs was controlled by the Cates family until 1992, when it was bought by US entrepreneur Dennis Washington, owner of the Montana-based Washington Corporation.

Native residents of Kitsilano Indian Reserve sold its 29 hectares (70 acres) to the government for $218,750. The land was valued at $2 million when divided into residential lots.

An island with the Granville Street Bridge running over it, but still looking a bit waterlogged in this 1916 photograph, Granville Island was created in 1913 from a mud flat through the dredging of False Creek.
City of Vancouver Archives, Pan N95. W.J. Moore photo

Granville Island, once a mud flat, reached island status this year thanks to the miracle of dredging.

Barnard Street, named after Frank Stillman Barnard, president of the BC Express Co., was often confused with Burrard Street, and so was renamed Union Street.

Streetcar service connected Vancouver to North Burnaby.

The 11th Regiment, Irish Fusiliers of Canada was formed.

The Zionist and Social Society was formed.

Eric Hamber became president of Hastings Sawmills Company.

Gordon Wismer, a future attorney general, began his law practice in partnership with Gerald G. "Gerry" McGeer.

Huge crowds turned out at Shaughnessy Golf Club to watch Harry Vardon play.

Vardon was the only six-time winner of the British Open.

Frederick "Cyclone" Taylor joined the Pacific Coast Hockey Association, giving the new league the credibility it needed. He played for Vancouver until his retirement in 1921. One of the great hockey players, he scored 194 goals in 186 games.

Queen's Park in Burnaby was renamed Confederation Park to commemorate Canadian Confederation. The park is at Willingdon and Penzance.

Launched in 1913 in response to the popularity of the Wigwam Inn on the northern shore of Indian Arm, the sternwheeler *Skeena* prepares for its return trip to Vancouver. *City of Vancouver Archives, LGN 546. Photo Richard Broadbridge*

Comings and Goings

April 11 Vancouver's Mr. Showbiz, Hugh Pickett, was born in Vancouver.

July 31 Alys Bryant, a visiting American aviatrix, flew a plane at Minoru Park in Richmond, the first woman in Canada to make a solo flight.

July 31 Samuel Brighouse, Vancouver and Lulu Island pioneer and one of the three greenhorns, died.

October 13 Journalist and newspaper executive Stuart Keate was born in Vancouver. In the opening pages of his autobiography *Paper Boy* (1980), Keate described his early life, providing a really interesting look at the Vancouver of this era.

December 6 Jonathan Miller III, a Vancouver pioneer—our first constable and first postmaster—died at age 79.

Frank Wesbrook became the first president of the University of British Columbia.

1914

As Vancouver sent soldiers off to the Great War, a UBC employee in Germany to buy books for the university was arrested on suspicion of spying. There was fighting in Vancouver Harbour as Sikh immigrants on the *Komagata Maru* were turned away from Canada. And the mayor banned a British music hall entertainer whose act included display of her ankle.

January 1 The first train of the North Shore Division of the Pacific Great Eastern Railway ran from North Vancouver to Dundarave in West Vancouver. By July 1 the PGE line had been extended to Whytecliff station. The interior section started at Squamish and went north, but it was not connected to the North Shore line, which was used mostly by residents or holiday-makers rather than for freight.

January 2 The first PGE train derailment occurred, on the second day of operation, at 24th Street in West Vancouver.

January 5 Lots "close to beach" were advertised in the *Semiahmoo Gazette*, priced from $125 to $1,500.

March 2 A St. David's Day banquet was given by the Welsh community at Pender Hall.

April 1 Sixteen-year-old Jack Kong, a houseboy, was scolded by his employer, Mrs. Charles Millard, for burning the breakfast porridge. She ordered him to cook some more, but Kong refused because the task would make him late for school. According

Elsewhere in BC

April 7 The last spike of the Grand Trunk Pacific Railway (between Winnipeg, MB, and Prince Rupert, BC) was driven one mile east of Fort Fraser. By 1919 the GTPR had been nationalized by the federal government and folded into Canadian National Railways with the Canadian Northern Railway.

December 17 Frank Stillman Barnard became Lieutenant-Governor of British Columbia.

Elsewhere in Canada

May 29 The *Empress of Ireland* sank in the St. Lawrence River after colliding with the Norwegian collier *Storstad*. She went down within 15 minutes, with the loss of 840 passengers and 172 crew members. Among the 462 survivors was Arthur Delamont, 22, who became famous locally as the originator and leader of the Kitsilano Boys Band. Arthur's brother Leonard was one of the victims.

August 5 Canada declared war on Germany and Austria–Hungary.

A wave of Italian immigration, which had started in 1900, ended with the advent of World War I. Ukrainian immigration dried up too, as most Ukrainians in Canada came from the western Ukraine, which was controlled by the Austro-Hungarian Empire. Many Ukrainians in Canada were classed as enemy aliens and either interned or required to report regularly to the RCMP.

Vancouver resident Julia Willmothe Henshaw and her husband Charles became the first couple to drive through the Rocky Mountains. She was famous as the author of the 1898 novel *Hypnotized*. (I read it; don't bother.)

Elsewhere in the World

June 28 In Sarajevo, Bosnia, a young radical assassinated Archduke Franz Ferdinand of Austria and his wife. This incident precipitated World War I.

August 4 While in Germany to buy books for the University of British Columbia's first serious library (rather than acquiring them haphazardly as gifts), J.T. Gerould was arrested as a spy. After much delay, Gerould was finally deported to Switzerland.

August 15 The Panama Canal opened, considerably shortening ocean journeys between British Columbia and Europe and spurring the Port of Vancouver's growth in grain exports. Today we ship more grain than any other Canadian port.

to Kong, Mrs. Millard seized a bread knife and threatened to cut off his ear. He grabbed a chair to defend himself. As she lunged for him, he hit her with the chair and knocked her dead. Fearing her death would be viewed as murder, Kong cut up the body in the cellar and burned it in the furnace. However, when the police confronted Kong with the evidence, he quickly confessed. Fearful families started to discharge their houseboys, and a sensational trial ensued. The prosecution alleged premeditated murder, with the chair story as a cover-up; the defence countered that Kong had only acted in self-defense and had better opportunities to commit murder without leaving such a messy trail of evidence behind. In the end, the jury found him guilty of manslaughter and sentenced him to life in prison. After serving seven years of his life sentence, Kong was deported to China in 1921.

April 24 Pitt Meadows was incorporated.

May 9 From the *Coquitlam Star*: "The new $50,000 two-storey Terminal Hotel on Busteed Avenue [in Port Coquitlam] will be completed early next week."

May 19 Myrtle and Alex Philip, originally from Maine, began to build a fishing lodge on 4 hectares (10 acres) they'd bought (for $700) on the northwest shore of Summit Lake (later named Alta Lake). When they first visited the area a few years earlier, it took a while to get there: a steamship trip from Vancouver to Squamish, an overnight stay in Brackendale and then a two-day trek along the Pemberton Trail on rented packhorses. But 1914 was also the year the Pacific Great Eastern railway reached the area. Soon the Philips' Rainbow Lodge, the first fishing/vacation lodge of any size in the Whistler area, became the most popular summer resort west of the Rockies. It was famed for its hospitality, and as many as 100 people could stay there at a time. The Philips ran the resort until they sold it in 1948.

June 11 The Pageant of Vancouver, a huge two-day musical-historical extravaganza, began at the Horse Show Building.

June 26 The *Province* had a story on a "Made in BC" exhibition at Spencer's Department Store.

War duty. At attention, though perhaps on the wrong side of the world, these men man a gun emplacement at Ferguson Point, Stanley Park that was erected once World War I began.
City of Vancouver Archives, ST Pk P228.1

A lasting blot on Canada's immigration record, the *Komagata Maru* arrived from India in Vancouver in 1914 specifically to challenge the exclusionary immigration policy. Except for those already with resident status, the ship and its passengers were finally forced back to India after a two-month standoff.
Vancouver Public Library, Special Collections, VPL 6232. Leonard Frank photo

Gunboat Diplomacy in Burrard Inlet

May 23 The ship *Komagata Maru* arrived and anchored in Burrard Inlet with 376 Indians (12 Hindus, 24 Muslims and 340 Sikhs) aboard. Canadian regulations at the time limited immigration from South Asia, and the ship had been chartered by a Sikh businessman specifically to challenge those rules. All but 20 passengers (those who already had resident status) were refused permission to leave the ship. They were also refused food and water, but local supporters managed to supply them.

Attempts by local mobs to push the ship out to sea with a tugboat were foiled when passengers seized control of the vessel and threw a hail of Japanese-made bricks at the mob. (One of those bricks is preserved at the Vancouver Museum.) Vancouver's mayor at the time, Truman Baxter, organized an anti-Asian rally, and in June a board of inquiry found all the passengers inadmissible. However, the ship would not leave without supplies for the return voyage. In July an armed boarding party stormed the ship but was unable to capture it.

Finally the new Royal Canadian Navy was called in—for its first official task—and on July 23 the *Komagata Maru* was forced to steam away with its passengers, back to India.

July 30 Columbia Bitulithic, founded in 1910 and headquartered in Coquitlam, was awarded a $71,815.52 contract to pave Victoria Road (now Victoria Drive) from Kingsway to 43rd Avenue.

August 4 World War I began; as a result, the Vancouver Stock Exchange suspended trading for two months.

Seen here camped on a field in Blackwell, Kent, England, the 29th Vancouver Battalion, nicknamed the Tigers, were organized in 1914 by Col. Henry Seymour Tobin. Members went on to distinguish themselves in battle in World War I, and in civilian life after the war.
City of Vancouver Archives, LGN 546. Photo Richard Broadbridge

August 10 Dr. Leonard S. Klinck, dean of agriculture, 37, was the first faculty member appointed by UBC. He had visited Vancouver to consult with UBC President Wesbrook and ended up being hired. After Wesbrook's unexpected death in 1918, Klinck became the second president and held the post for 25 years. Klinck supervised the war-delayed move to the Point Grey campus from the "Fraserview Shacks." He died in West Vancouver on March 27, 1969.

August 21 The first troop train left Vancouver for the war in Europe.

August Food merchants in North Vancouver sold out as hoarding began because of the war.

September 5 Capt. Alexander McLean drowned in False Creek after he fell overboard from his tug. Alexander allegedly inspired the character Wolf Larsen in Jack London's novel *Sea Wolf*.

September 11 The Royal Purple Of Canada (Vancouver Lodge No. 1), the women's auxiliary of the Elks, was established.

October 20 The Vancouver School of Pharmacy was established.

October 27 Port Coquitlam City Hall opened. With expansion in the 1980s that modernized and more than doubled the space, the building is now one of the handsomest government structures in the Lower Mainland.

October The Vancouver Police Pipe Band was formed. It is the senior police band in Canada, and third-oldest in the world, after the Edinburgh and Glasgow police bands. It's the official civic band for Vancouver. Members travel to many national and international competitions and parades at their own personal expense on their vacation time.

Fall New Westminster raised the 47th, 121st and the 131st battalions.

November 1 or 2 Col. Henry Seymour Tobin organized and commanded the 29th (Vancouver) Battalion. It earned the nickname "Tigers" for the members' gallant conduct. One of Tobin's Tigers, Bob Hanna, won a Victoria Cross for exceptional bravery. Tobin himself was decorated for distinguished service. Among the battalion's survivors were Sherwood Lett, later chief justice of BC (1955–64), and Oscar Orr, who became a well-known judge. Tobin returned too and, among other things, was president from 1939 of Vancouver Breweries. He died in 1956.

November 13 Col. Albert Whyte, agent for the developers of White Cliff City in West Vancouver, requested the area be renamed Whytecliff.

November 20 A "French Cabaret" was held at the Avenue Theatre in aid of the Women's Employment League.

December 1 Owners and officers of SS *Novgorod*, a ship of the Russian Volunteer Fleet, hosted a luncheon for "commercial interests" of the city. The menu included Consommé Czar Nicholas avec petites pâtés.

Also in 1914

The Pacific Construction Company took over shipbuilding yards in Port Coquitlam. It built several wooden ships during World War I and was briefly one of the Lower Mainland's four largest shipyards.

Baron von Mackensen, who had built a "castle" at Port Kells in Surrey, was arrested on suspicion of being a German spy. Before the war he had hosted community Christmas parties, but in 1914 he raised the German flag over his castle. After the war he was deported.

Membership in the Vancouver Board of Trade rose to 1,000. A special act of Parliament had created the Vancouver Harbour Commission, and the Board of Trade persuaded the federal government to dredge First Narrows for shipping.

The first Girl Guide company in Burnaby was formed at South Burnaby High School. The girls rolled bandages, knitted socks, sponsored a bed in Royal Columbian Hospital and printed a newspaper, *News from Home*, which they sent to local men at the front.

The Vancouver Elementary School Teachers' Association was established.

Bayview School opened at Collingwood and 7th.

Attracted by its deep anchorage, fresh water and good price, Imperial Oil began constructing BC's first oil refinery at Ioco. (Ioco is an acronym of Imperial Oil Company.)

A concrete bridge was built across the Capilano River.

Dundarave Pier was built in West Vancouver.

The Vancouver Park Board and the federal government authorized construction of the first section of the Stanley Park seawall.

Anticipating the economic opportunities to be created by the 1914 opening of the Panama Canal, H.H. Stevens built Vancouver's first grain elevator on the waterfront. It was initially dubbed Stevens' Folly, but Stevens was vindicated as Vancouver became Canada's largest grain exporter.
City of Vancouver Archives, CVA 99-3495. Photo Stuart Thomson

The Canadian Northern Railway built a line across Lulu Island from Queensborough to Steveston. A few years later, peat fires destroyed much of this railway.

The third CPR station opened at 601 West Cordova. Contractor was Westinghouse, Church, Kerr and Co. Today the beautiful old building is the western terminus for the SkyTrain and the West Coast Express, and the southern port for the SeaBus.

Province publisher Hewitt Bostock was appointed to the Senate.

The Architectural Institute of British Columbia (AIBC) was founded.

The main Oakalla Prison was opened. (A smaller version had opened in 1912.)

By 1914 there were 243 households in Shaughnessy Heights, 80 percent of which were listed in the Vancouver social register.

Paine Hardware moved to 90 Lonsdale in North Vancouver. This funky store, with its jaw-dropping variety of tools and such, much of the stock old-fashioned and hard to get, became a North Vancouver landmark. Tragically, its interior was destroyed by fire in 1998.

The Vancouver and District Joint Sewerage and Drainage Board was incorporated.

About 14 kilometres (9 miles) upstream from the Fraser, a dam built on the Coquitlam River this year diverted most of the river's water flow for electricity and blocked sockeye salmon from reaching their spawning habitat in Coquitlam Lake.

Vancouver Harbour's first grain elevator was built at the foot of Woodland Drive. The brainchild

The third CPR station, which is now the transit hub Waterfront Station, was built in the neoclassical style in 1914.
Vancouver Public Library, Special Collections, VPL 257

of local MP H.H. Stevens, who saw the opportunity provided the local economy by the Panama Canal, the elevator was dubbed "Stevens' Folly" by the less far-sighted.

Malcolm McLennan became Vancouver's chief constable.

Justice Samuel Davies Schultz was appointed to the Vancouver County Court, the first Jew named to the bench in Canada.

Goodman Hamre began a bus service between New Westminster and Aldergrove. A year later he expanded the service with a line from New Westminster to White Rock.

The Laundry Workers Union was organized locally.

The Asahi Baseball Club, composed of Japanese Canadians, began playing at what is now Oppenheimer Park and became the most popular team in the Lower Mainland, with a legion of Japanese and non-Japanese fans. The club won the Pacific Northwest Championship for five consecutive years, beating bigger Caucasian teams.

The Asahi baseball team drew its members from the Japanese Canadian community and was known as the best baseball team in the city. Between 1919 and 1940 the Asahi won 10 city championships. They were known for playing "brain ball"; smaller than many of their opponents, they relied on speed and tactics rather than powerful hitting. *Japanese Canadian National Museum*

A new generation of Canadian-born residents of Vancouver's Chinatown formed the Chinese Canadian Club. The members of the society were mainly English-speaking and locally born, in their mid-to-late teens, and interested in socializing and meeting new friends rather than discussing the political or social issues of the day. The club premises included a reading library, and members were instrumental in the formation of a soccer team.

William Charles Hopkinson, an immigration officer working out of the provincial courthouse (today's Vancouver Art Gallery), was murdered by a local Sikh who was infuriated by Hopkinson's actions during the *Komagata Maru* incident. Some say Hopkinson's ghost still wanders the building.

Fred Deeley Sr., who had arrived in Vancouver in 1913, opened Fred Deeley Ltd. in a 3.5-metre-wide (12-foot) store at 1075 Granville. He sold BSA motorcycles. In 1916 he acquired the city's Harley-Davidson franchise (now the oldest dealership in Canada), and by 1925 he owned a motorcycle shop, a bicycle shop and one of Canada's larger car dealerships.

John Hendry, who had bought Hastings Mill about 25 years earlier, renaming it BC Mills, Timber and Trading, had the satisfaction of knowing that by 1914 it had become the largest company of its kind in the northwest, with 2,000 employees. Among other things, the company shipped doors, sashes and blinds.

The book *British Columbia from Earliest Times to the Present* appeared. Written by Frederick William Howay, it was the standard history of BC until Margaret Ormsby's 1964 work, *British Columbia: A History*.

Alex Mitchell, who in 1899 bought Stanley Park Stables (at Seymour and Dunsmuir), the taxi business of his day, with 86 horses, 40 rigs, 7 hacks and 2 tallyhos, went bankrupt. The major causes: World War I and the popularity of the automobile.

Comings and Goings

Early February English music hall great Marie Lloyd visited Vancouver. Trouble! The mayor banned her performance. Too risque! (At one point she lifted her floor-length gown up two inches to reveal a watch on her ankle.)

December 8 Former Vancouver mayor (1898–1900) James Garden died at age 67.

Some significant births: movie actor **John Ireland** on January 30; **William Rathie**, the first Vancouver mayor (1963–66) actually born in the city, April 1; conductor **John Avison**, who founded the CBC Chamber Orchestra, April 25.

A 22-year-old actor named Basil Rathbone performed in Vancouver with the Frank Benson Shakespeare Co. He later became famous in the movies as Sherlock Holmes.

Ruth St. Denis and Ted Shawn, two of the pioneers of modern dance, made the first of many visits to Vancouver.

Ivor Frederick Ackery arrived in Vancouver with his mom. As Ivan Ackery, he managed the Orpheum Theatre from 1935 until 1969.

1915

The University of BC opened with its first lectures in temporary "shacks." In a fit of intramural rivalry, the mayor hijacked a former US president from the Board of Trade. And Vancouver won the Stanley Cup.

January 11 Mewa Singh was hanged in New Westminster. In the wake of the 1914 *Komagata Maru* incident, members of Vancouver's Sikh community had felt a particular enmity for William Hopkinson, a local customs official who had formerly served with the Calcutta Police Force. Mewa, who supported India's independence movement and the passengers of the *Komagata Maru,* shot Hopkinson to death at the provincial courthouse in Vancouver in 1914. A hall in the Ross Street Sikh Temple is named for Mewa.

Cyclone Taylor of the Vancouver Millionaires. *Stuart Thomson/City of Vancouver Archives, CVA 99-778*

Mighty Millionaires. The only year Stanley Cup glory has come to Vancouver was 1915, the year the Vancouver Millionaires defeated the Ottawa Senators in the championship. The Millionaires fought again for the cup in 1918, 1921 and 1922, but lost each time. *City of Vancouver Archives, CVA 99 – 126*

February 15 The Imperial Theatre opened a brand-new musical comedy, *Fifty Years Forward.* Among its predictions for 1965: a female mayor in Vancouver.

March 12 In support of striking Vancouver longshoremen, dock workers in Seattle and other West Coast ports boycotted all ships going to or coming from Vancouver.

March 26

The Vancouver Millionaires, led by high-scoring Cyclone Taylor, won the Stanley Cup in the Denman Arena, sweeping the Ottawa Senators in three games (it was a best-of-five series).

March The first class in BC for deaf students met in a room in the old Mount Pleasant School on East 8th Avenue. There were nine boys and girls, ranging in age from 9 to 16 years. Mabel Bigney, who had come from the Halifax School for the Deaf, was the teacher. (Seven years later deaf students—62 of them by then—got their own building.)

Elsewhere in BC

January 23 The last spike of the Canadian Northern Railway (running from Quebec to Vancouver) was driven at Basque, BC, near Ashcroft. This line was eventually absorbed into what became the Canadian National Railway.

December 15 Vancouver lawyer William John Bowser (1867–1933), Conservative, became premier, succeeding Sir Richard McBride. Bowser served less than a year, to November 23, 1916.

Elsewhere in Canada

September 11 William Cornelius Van Horne, former CPR president, who supervised construction of the railway across Canada and who named Vancouver (it had been Granville), died at age 72 in Montreal.

Elsewhere in the World

French inventor George Claude was granted patents for neon light this year. This would later have an important effect on Vancouver.

Done in by a fire, the original Cambie Street Bridge stands broken in this 1915 photo.
City of Vancouver Archives, SGN 996.4. Photo W.J. Moore

April The creosoted wood deck of the Cambie Street Bridge caught fire, and a 24-metre (80-foot) steel side-span collapsed. (This was obviously not the current bridge!)

May With World War I continuing to rage in Europe, North Vancouver city council made enquiries of all not-yet-naturalized city residents of German or Austrian birth to determine if they should be interned or deported.

June A sports ground was opened at Mahon Park in North Vancouver.

Spring To avoid violating American neutrality, a Seattle company, British Pacific Engineering, built submarines for Russia at top-secret plants in Burnaby and Vancouver.

Once completed the hulls were dismantled and shipped to Petrograd (Saint Petersburg) for reassembly.

July 1 The first Georgia Viaduct opened to extend Georgia Street over the CPR's Beatty Street yard. It was named the Hart McHarg Bridge, commemmorating a World War I hero, but the name didn't catch on. The viaduct was badly made, and in later years chunks began to fall off, startling pedestrians below.

July 30 The White Rock pier was officially opened.

The first portion—191 metres (628 feet) long—had been opened in 1914, and another 300 metres (985 feet) was added this year. Legend has it that locals wanted a solid pier instead of the earlier floating version, so they invited the appropriate federal official to inspect the dock, carefully choosing a time when the tide was at its highest. The dock heaved mightily, and the alarmed official speedily approved a permanent pier anchored to the ocean floor. The pier was rescued from demolition in 1976 and is kept in good repair.

August 11 The North Shore's Marine Drive was opened by Premier Richard McBride, providing access to previously secluded areas such as Caulfeild.

August 26 North Vancouver City Hall relocated in the old Central School, whose staff and pupils had moved to the new Queen Mary's School. Council intended this to be a temporary home but ended up meeting there for decades. The old school/city hall is now Presentation House, home of the North Vancouver Museum and Archives, a theatre and a photographic gallery.

August 28 The first Canadian Northern

Working in broad daylight, but otherwise top secret, these men in either Vancouver or Burnaby in 1915 work on submarines destined for Russia. The scheme was devised by an American firm, which wanted to make a buck while respecting American neutrality in World War I.
Mariner's Museum, Newport News, VA

Peerless pier. Begun in 1914, and then added to the following year, the White Rock pier was officially opened on July 30, 1915. As seen in this 1920s picture, the pier and beach were popular places to play.
White Rock Museum and Archives 1993-106-46

Pacific Railway through-train from the east arrived in Vancouver.

The railway later became part of the Canadian National Railway, but its terminal is still here, now named Pacific Central Station.

August The Canadian Japanese Association sent a wire to Prime Minister Borden "to volunteer for service to fight for king and country." Anticipating a positive response, a Japanese Volunteer Corps of 202 men began training in Vancouver under Captain Robert Colquhoun and four officers of the Canadian Army Service Corps. The Japanese community covered the cost of the three-month training session and maintenance of the volunteers. However, when Yasushi Yamazaki (or Yamasaki), president of the CJA, went to Ottawa, the volunteers' offer was refused and the group dissolved. After being rejected in BC, the following year, 196 Japanese travelled to Alberta to join Canadian battalions of the British army. When they were shipped to Europe, 54 were killed and 92 wounded. The Japanese community in BC also purchased $230,000 worth of war bonds.

September 30 Frank Wesbrook, first president of the University of British Columbia, moved into his office at the Fairview Shacks, a ramshackle collection of wooden buildings at West 10th and Laurel in the Fairview neighbourhood. Wesbrook commented: "We take occasion this morning to congratulate ourselves that, though the Empire is at war, such a good beginning of the university has been possible." There were 379 students in three faculties: Arts and Science, Applied Science, and Agriculture. An Officers Training Corps was established at UBC this year, and the university's Alma Mater Society was formed on October 12.

Winter The Hoffar-Beeching Shipyard at 1927 West Georgia (at the foot of Cardero Street on Coal Harbour) began assembling aircraft when the Hoffar brothers, Henry and Jimmie, fitted floats to the Curtiss Jenny belonging to Billy Stark, Vancouver's first licensed pilot. Two years later, Boeing bought the brothers out.

Adapting to new technology and local geographical realities, Vancouver got its first home-built seaplane in 1915 when the Hoffar Brothers, of the Hoffar-Beeching Shipyard, attached floats to the Curtiss Jenny owned by Vancouver's first licensed pilot, Billy Stark. This started a new industry, and continued when the brothers built their first seaplane from scratch a year later.
City of Vancouver Archives, Air P73.1

1915

Mayor Louis Taylor (at right, holding hat low) escorts former US president Teddy Roosevelt through a throng of well-wishers to a waiting limousine. Roosevelt, who had arrived aboard the CPR, was stopping off briefly in the city on his way to San Francisco. At the time he was a controversial figure in the US for his outspoken advocacy of an American entry into the war against Germany. Speaking from the back of the car, he told the crowd that Canadians should be proud that they had responded to "the great rallying call of Empire." *City of Vancouver Archives, CVA 99-1276. Photo Stuart Thomson*

Also in 1915

The year began with Louis D. Taylor as mayor. He was succeeded at the end of the year by Malcolm Peter McBeath, who had been a Vancouver alderman from 1912 to 1914. Several of the city's great stories concern Taylor. When former US president Theodore Roosevelt and his wife visited Vancouver on a holiday in 1915, the Vancouver Board of Trade did not include Mayor Taylor in the official reception at the CPR station. (Board members didn't like him.) Undaunted, Taylor boarded the train at an earlier stop, greeted the Roosevelts, introduced himself and chatted amiably with them as they came into Vancouver. The train stopped at the station, the Board of Trade party surged forward...and Mayor Taylor stepped down onto the platform. He introduced the Roosevelts to the open-mouthed board members, then whisked the former US president and his wife off for a drive around Stanley Park. (Daniel Francis recounted this story in his lively book *LD: Mayor Louis Taylor and the Rise of Vancouver*.)

In his essay "Report on the Planning of Greater Vancouver," eminent planner Thomas Adams noted that the city was "unique both in regards to natural beauty and business prospects," but was "suffering in a special degree from haphazard growth and speculation in real estate, notwithstanding the progress that has taken place in the last few years in regard to the control of sanitary matters and local improvements." In 1919 Adams established the Town Planning Institute of Canada.

The newly-created Harbour Commission gave Ottawa one dollar for False Creek sandbars and received clearance to reclaim the land. What was beginning to be created was Granville Island.

Ivor W. Neil began a sightseeing bus and taxi service in Vancouver.

The Vancouver Exhibition (today's PNE) had become a permanent fixture in Hastings Park, housing nearly a dozen buildings and an athletic field. The 1915 exhibition also had a new feature: $50,000 in prizes.

James Inglis Reid, who had come to Vancouver from Scotland in 1906, opened his own butcher shop at 559 Granville. The store became famous for its haggis; its meats, including Ayrshire bacon, Belfast ham, black pudding and oatmeal-coated sausage; and its sign: "We hae meat that ye can eat."

Alexandra Park bandstand opened on Beach Avenue at Burnaby Street in the West End.

The name "Seaton Street" disappeared from the Vancouver landscape as the road became a simple extension of Hastings Street west of Burrard. Lauchlan Hamilton had bestowed the name in 1886 after picking it at random from a BC map. Because a lot of wealthy folk lived along Seaton at the time, it was also known as Blueblood Alley.

The 255 hectares (630 acres) of Moodyville, the first independent settlement on the North Shore, joined the City of North Vancouver, giving the city its present shape. The following year the abandoned Moodyville sawmill was destroyed by fire.

Wallace Shipyards and North Shore Iron Works won contracts to produce high-explosive shells.

Brazil established a consulate in Vancouver.

Professor Frederick Wood, the first BC-born educator at UBC, founded the Player's Club there this year. The troupe produced its own very popular shows in downtown Vancouver.

Helena Gutteridge convinced the Vancouver Trades and Labour Council to support equal pay for equal work in its constitution.

There was a woman's hardball team in Vancouver in 1915. They were called the Minnehahas.

Comings and Goings

January 29 Richard Henry Alexander, former manager of the Hastings Mill, died at 70 in Seattle.

February 2 Golfer Stan Leonard, said to be British Columbia's greatest golfer, was born in Vancouver. In the late 1920s, Leonard caddied at Shaughnessy Heights for 50 cents.

February 25 Israel Wood Powell died. A surgeon and politician, he was also the first chancellor of UBC, first president of the BC Medical Council and first grand master of the freemasons' Grand Lodge of BC. From 1872 to 1889 he was superintendent of Indian affairs in BC, and fought for aboriginal land and water rights. He donated the site for Vancouver's first city hall. Powell Street and the community of Powell River were named for him.

May 15 Walter Moberly, a surveyor and explorer who helped set out the CPR's route through the west, died. (An oddity: he also designed New Westminster's first sewer system.)

July 7 Captain G.P. Bowie, who designed the original Lumbermen's Arch (note the plural), erected at Pender and Hamilton for the 1912 visit of the Duke of Connaught, was killed at Ypres.

With their store decked in spruce boughs for the holiday season, the staff of James Inglis Reid Meat Market are ready in 1922 for the Christmas shoppers. Opened in 1915, the store became famous for its Scottish specialties. *Vancouver Public Library, Special Collections, VPL 10644. Leonard Frank photo*

1916

The University of BC conferred its first degrees, and women made headway at city hall. The park board embarked on a century of planting trees on Vancouver streets. And Lost Lagoon was marooned.

Right: Vancouver's first seaplane, built from scratch in Coal Harbour in 1916 by the Hoffar Brothers, was copied from a British magazine. Jimmie Hoffar taught himself how to fly it.
City of Vancouver Archives, Air P73.2

February 14 The first trans-Canada telephone call was placed—between Vancouver and Montreal.

The circuit ran 6,763 kilometres (4,200 miles) through Buffalo, Chicago, Omaha, Salt Lake City and Portland, OR. A telephone line for an all-Canada connection was not completed until 1932.

March 8 Sock Day in Vancouver. The IODE collected socks for men at the front.

April 21 The first congress of the new British Columbia Chess Association began in Vancouver. The winner of the tournament was entitled to be called the Chess Champion of British Columbia. J.M. Ewing, a Scot by birth, was the first champion.

May 4 UBC held its first convocation for conferring degrees. Among the graduates was Uchida Chitose, the first Japanese Canadian to graduate from a Canadian university. She earned her teacher qualification from the Vancouver Normal School but had to move to Alberta to get a teaching position.

May 16 The *Vancouver World* had an item about the new post office—Postal Station C—which opened on this date at 15th Avenue and Main Street. Today it's known as Heritage Hall, home of several community organizations and a meeting hall for local events.

June 2 *The Buzzer*, that publication you get on the buses and SkyTrain in the Lower Mainland, began publishing.

July The second Hotel Vancouver, a spectacular building, opened at the southeast corner of Granville and

Elsewhere in BC

November 23 Harlan Carey Brewster was elected BC premier. Two other decisions by BC's voters this day were notable: we approved Prohibition in the province, to come into effect October 1, 1917, and we also approved giving women the vote. Brewster died in office on March 1, 1918.

December 13 Canadian Pacific Railway opened its 8-kilometre-long (5-mile) Connaught Tunnel beneath Mount MacDonald at Rogers Pass. The avalanche-plagued route over the summit of Rogers Pass was abandoned. (An avalanche here on March 4, 1910, had killed 62 workmen.)

The Allied Indian Tribes of British Columbia was formed to pursue the Indian land question, replacing the Indian Rights Association.

Elsewhere in the World

A little-known episode in the life of Vancouver's Major James Skitt Matthews: While Matthews was in hospital in London, England, recovering from severe war wounds, he devised a method of compressing paraffin wax and sawdust into walnut-sized pellets that, when ignited, gave off enough heat to boil a quart of water. Matthews called them Fire Cubes. The Anglo-American Oil Co. made and sold millions, but without making a profit. The army's commander-in-chief, General Sir Douglas Haig, ordered Matthews to supply enough for the army to test in the trenches, but then the war ended and demand for the Fire Cube flickered out. Some 17 years later, Matthews became Vancouver's first city archivist.

Georgia. It had a brief life as a hotel, closing in May 1939 when the present Hotel Vancouver opened. It was demolished in 1949.

Labour Day Two PGE trains collided in West Vancouver. One of them, the No. 2, built in 1910 in Philadelphia, was restored and is now at the West Coast Railway Heritage Park near Squamish.

September An application by Miss Rose Peers for membership in the North Vancouver Board of Trade created controversy. However, she was finally accepted as the first female member.

Fall The Hoffar Brothers, Henry and Jimmie, built a "hydroplane," as seaplanes were then called, copying the design from a photo of an Avro biplane they had seen in the British periodical *Flight*. Jimmie taught himself how to fly it.

Also in 1916

Vancouver aldermen voted to open civic offices to women.

Surrey council hired its first female employee. Miss C.E. Bauer worked in the Collectors and Assessors Office.

Facing a labour shortage due to the war, Fraser Valley fruit growers and the Mission Board of Trade considered asking the federal government to temporarily suspend the head tax on Chinese immigrants. David Whiteside, Liberal MLA for New Westminster, condemned the action as "short sighted," and the New Westminster Trades and Labour Council also protested and accused Asian fruit and vegetable growers and vendors of taking advantage of the war situation to gain "control of the food supply of the province." The BC Consumer league eventually recruited 3,000 women as berry pickers to alleviate the problem. During 1915–16 only 20 Chinese arrivals paid the head tax.

Holy Rosary Church, built in 1910, became a cathedral.

Malcolm McBeath, 35, was elected mayor, one of the city's youngest.

The city passed a bylaw reducing the number of aldermen per ward from two to one. Until this year, aldermen hoping to be elected by a particular ward had been required to live in that ward, but another new bylaw eliminated this requirement.

The people of the Squamish Nation, who had lived for generations in scattered villages on Howe Sound, the Squamish River and Burrard Inlet, migrated to the inlet for jobs and consolidated into one band. The Halkomelem people of the Burrard Reserve, who speak a different Coast Salish language, did not join them, although the two groups have many links.

The *Mabel Brown*, a wood-hulled, five-masted auxiliary schooner, was built in North Vancouver for the Canada West Coast Navigation Co. The name "Mabel Brown" was given to a class of lumber-carrying sailing ships built on the Pacific coast. Eighteen were built.

West Vancouver began its municipal bus service, which became known as the Blue Buses.

The first annual regatta was held at Dundarave pier in West Vancouver.

The Dewdney Trunk Road reached Deroche.

Lumber and shipping magnate Robert Dollar purchased 40 hectares (100 acres) of land at Roche Point on the North Shore. He built a large lumber and shingle mill there, which began operations in 1917, as well as houses for his workers, a school, post

The bowels of the *Mabel Brown* are shown under construction in North Vancouver in 1916. The name was eventually given to a class of lumber-carrying sailing ships, among the last of an era before steel hulls and mechanical engines took over. *City of Vancouver Archives, Air P73.2*

Dollarton mill. The Canadian Robert Dollar Company bought the land for its sawmill operation in North Vancouver, out toward Deep Cove, in 1916. Employees lived in an adjacent village site known as Dollarton, which in 1918 was linked by road to central North Vancouver. Dollar was a Scottish-born lumberman who developed a significant trans-Pacific trade in lumber from the Dollarton mill. This is a view of the interior of the mill not long before it closed in 1942.

Vancouver Public Library, Special Collections, VPL 4119. Leonard Frank photo

office, community hall and store. The settlement became known as Dollarton.

Eric Hamber became president of BC Mills, Timber and Trading, which was owned by his father-in-law, John Hendry. (Hamber had married Hendry's daughter Aldyen in 1912.)

Someone proposed building a dam and two sets of locks for the Second Narrows, suggesting that this would simplify the bridging problem and eventually turn the upper harbour into a freshwater lake, with a canal east to Pitt River. You may have noticed this plan was not carried out.

The mainland portion of Eburne was renamed Marpole, after CPR official Richard Marpole, who lived in Marpole at the time on Marpole Avenue.

The responsibility for street planting of trees, shrubs, etc., in Vancouver passed to the Board of Parks and Recreation.

Stanley Park's Lost Lagoon became landlocked, an artificial lake created by construction of a causeway. It got its curious name (now inaccurate) from poet Pauline Johnson, who remarked how the lagoon disappeared at low tide.

Granville Island, once a mud flat, reached island status this year thanks to the miracle of dredging. It was 14.5 hectares (36 acres) in size and 3 metres (10 feet) above high-water mark, with 80 industrial lots. Rents were from $500 to $1,500 per acre each year.

The Vancouver Institute was founded to offer lectures during the winter term. It is still going strong, offering lectures at the UBC campus during the fall and spring academic terms.

John Ridington (born in West Ham, England), hired by UBC as a cataloguer in its library in 1914, was appointed the university's first librarian. Over the next seven years he expanded the holdings from 700 books to 55,000. By the end of his term of office there were 125,000 volumes.

Thomas Carlyle Hebb was appointed professor of physics at UBC. He served until 1938, and the university's Hebb Building was named for him.

The UBC Botanical Garden was established. Today it is the oldest university botanical garden in Canada, set in a coastal forest and featuring 30 hectares (70 acres) of plants from around the world, including 400 species of rhododendron.

Stanley Park's Lost Lagoon was separated in 1916 from the sea by a causeway, turning it into an artificial lake. The lake received its name from writer Pauline Johnson, who remarked how the lagoon disappeared at low tide.

City of Vancouver Archives Pan N54. W.J. Moore photo

Open for industry after being created in 1913 by dredging False Creek, Granville Island features the Vulcan Iron Works in this 1917 picture. It would be a few more years before all the land was utilized.
Dominion Photo Co. photo, Vancouver Public Library VPL 20405

It was a busy year in theatre. The Vancouver Shakespeare Society was formed, as well as Mussoc, the University of British Columbia Musical Theatre Society. Mussoc alumni include Ruth Nichol, Jane Mortifee, Brent Carver, Richard Ouzounian, Jeff Hyslop, Patrick Rose, Ann Mortifee, Victor Young, David Y.H. Lui and Margot Kidder. The UBC Player's Club was also born and was one of the only theatre troupes for much of the city's early history.

The Canada Chinese Labour Association was formed with the aim of improving workers' knowledge and increasing their authority in the workplace. In order to educate its members, the association offered English proficiency classes, a speech-making club and a newsletter. By 1918, it had 600 members. The same movement also spawned the Chinese Vegetable Peddlers Association and the Chinese Shingle Workers' Union.

Comings and Goings

November 8 June Hovick was born in Vancouver. As June Havoc she became a well-known actress. Her sister, Gypsy Rose Lee, was born in Seattle. In the musical *Gypsy*, the character Baby June is based on June Havoc.

December 17 Frank Griffiths, radio and TV station owner and sports executive, was born in Burnaby.

Actor John Drainie was born in Vancouver. Orson Welles later called him the greatest radio actor in the world.

Ma Murray, the famous newspaper publisher, moved with her family to the Ioco area (briefly). In 1921 they moved back to Vancouver.

Notable deaths: Lumberman **John Hendry** died on July 17; **Charles R. Shaw**, the first reeve of Burnaby, died at age 82 in Ann Arbor, MI; **Thomas Haney**, after whom Haney was named, also died (he had arrived in 1876 and established a brickyard that remained in operation until 1977).

1917

As Caucasian women gained the right to vote in provincial elections, all residents lost the legal right to drink alcohol. Vancouver firefighters went on strike and won a wage increase. The police chief was shot dead. And endless construction of the Stanley Park seawall began.

March 20 Malcolm MacLennan, Vancouver's chief constable, was shot and killed at 522 East Georgia St. while attempting to arrest Bob Tait, a heavily armed drug addict. PEI-born MacLennan, 43, had been chief only since 1914. Ironically, he was an early proponent of medical assistance, rather than criminal prosecution, for drug addicts. He was also the first chief to hire a non-Caucasian constable (Constable Raiichi Shirokawa). Tait also killed an innocent passerby, George Robb, eight years old.

Perhaps unaware that a year later they would receive the right to vote (except for Asian or First Nations women), these young women do jobs that had traditionally been done by men. The reason? Labour shortages during the war. The venue? The Imperial Oil gas station at Broadway and Granville in 1916. *Vancouver Public Library, Special Collections, VPL 13212*

April 9 The BC and Yukon Hotels Association was incorporated.

May 17 Wallace Shipyards launched the *War Dog*, the first steel ocean-going freighter to be built on Burrard Inlet.

The first steel ocean-going freighter to be built on Burrard Inlet was the *War Dog*, seen here riding at ease in the water in 1917, the year it was launched. *City of Vancouver Archives, CVA 99-620. Stuart Thomson photo*

Elsewhere in BC

January 1 The Workmen's Compensation Act of British Columbia took effect.

April 4 Women could now vote in BC...unless they were aboriginal or Asian. The next day the *Province* carried the news deep within a report from the legislature, preceded by some news on agricultural matters.

October 1 Prohibition came into effect in BC. It was overturned in a plebiscite on October 20, 1920.

A massive snowslide blocked the PGE railway line and cut off the Whistler Valley for six weeks.

Elsewhere in Canada

August 29 The Migratory Birds Convention Act received royal assent. Before the act came into effect, a good hunter could take up to 2,000 birds a year in the Fraser delta and earn a comfortable income selling waterfowl to the local market.

November 16 The federal government took over the Canadian Northern Pacific Railway. It became part of Canadian National in 1918.

December 17 Called by some the bitterest election in Canadian history, the 1917 federal election was fought mainly over the issue of conscription. Sir Robert Borden's Unionist government, a coalition, was elected with a strong majority. (Borden's Conservatives had won the 1911 election.) Major J.S. Matthews, future Vancouver archivist, served as the deputy returning officer in Belgium during the election.

Left: Detailing the tragic consequences of the devil drink that could lead a man to senselessly kill his wife, this early Prohibitionist material did its work, with Prohibition being in effect for three years, from 1917 to 1920. *Vancouver Public Library VPL 18999*

June BC Electric Railway workers went on strike.

June 14 The Schara Tzedeck congregation at Heatley and Pender was legally incorporated and renamed (it was originally B'nai Yehudah). David Marks served as first president until 1921. (His daughter Sadie later gained fame as radio comedian Mary Livingstone.)

June 17 The Pantages Theatre opened at 20 West Hastings and was proclaimed one of the continent's best vaudeville houses.

July 2 Tsutae Sato, educator, arrived in Canada to teach at the Nippon Kokumin Gakko, the Japanese School on Alexander. For a lifetime of work in education, Sato was named to the Order of Canada in 1978.

July 7 Vancouver Fire Department firefighters went on strike for better pay and conditions. City council grumbled but finally agreed to their demands.

July 16 Float-plane builder Jimmie Hoffar took the sports editor of the *Province* up to 600 metres (2,000 feet) in the H-1.

July 19 Helen MacGill became the first woman to be appointed a judge of the juvenile court.

July North Vancouver civic employees formed a union. A month later, ferry employees, firemen and police received wage increases.

August 8 During a business trip to Portland, Vancouver's Alvo von Alvensleben was arrested. It seems British intelligence officials had sent a list of "dangerous German spies" to the US Justice Department and Alvensleben's name topped the list. US officials interned him near Salt Lake City on suspicion of being a German spy. He was not released until March 1920, 15 months after the war ended.

August 31 Last issue of the *News-Advertiser*, a newspaper that had first appeared in 1887.

September 1 Robert Cromie, who had bought the *News-Advertiser*, amalgamated it with his *Morning Sun*.

Also in 1917

Stonemason Jimmy Cunningham began building what became the Stanley Park seawall. Born in 1878 on the Isle of Bute, Scotland, Jimmy came to BC in 1910 and had served in World War I with the Canadian Expeditionary Force. In 1932 he became the Vancouver Park Board's master stonemason with a special task: to secure Stanley Park's shores.

The Pantages Theatre opened in 1917, at a time when vaudeville drew crowds. This 1926 photo shows the theatre front wired to dance with bright lights advertising The Still Alarm show. *Dominion Photo Co. photo, Vancouver Public Library VPL 22311*

H. Nelson Menzies joined James Inglis Reid in his Granville Street butcher shop. Menzies introduced the Scottish sausages that made Reid's shop famous.

The Food Floor in the Woodward's store at Hastings and Abbott became the largest in the world under one roof.

Fletcher's Fine Foods began operating in Vancouver.

The number of salmon in the Fraser was down significantly because of a 1913 slide that blocked the river. The Fraser's cannery industry was badly affected, and many canneries closed.

Helen Emma MacGill, Canada's first woman judge, was appointed to the bench of the juvenile court in Vancouver.

Evlyn Farris became the first woman on the UBC board of governors. She served with distinction for more than 20 years.

Sanford Crowe was elected the second MP for Vancouver, joining H.H. Stevens.

The Capilano Timber Company was formed and ran a logging railway up the Capilano Valley to bring out the red cedar for which the valley was famous. One of its bridges, the Houlgate Creek Trestle (named for R. Kerr Houlgate, one of the company owners), was 120 metres (400 feet) long and nearly 30 metres (90 feet) high. The company's mills were destroyed by fire in June 1932, closing down the business.

In the lumber camps of Surrey, members of the Industrial Workers of the World (IWW) union went on strike for better camp conditions, a nine-hour day and higher wages. They went back to work after winning all but the bid for higher wages.

By 1917, George Cowan, a Vancouver lawyer, had purchased 400 hectares (1,000 acres) on Bowen Island. He built cottages for family and friends on this land.

The West Vancouver Horticultural and Agricultural Association was formed.

At a cost of $5,250, "the Barn" was built at Main Mall and Agronomy Road on the UBC campus. Initially a classroom for returning World War I soldiers, it later became the horticulture facility for generations of undergraduate students in agriculture. After a long battle to save this heritage building, in 1967 it was converted (at a cost of $62,000) into a faculty, staff and student cafeteria.

First published under the unpromising title *Anonymous*, the monthly UBC newspaper soon became the *Ubi Cee*. It changed the spelling of that name in 1918 to *Ubyssey*.

Another publication that appeared this year was *British Columbia Mountaineer*, a biennial journal of the British Columbia Mountaineering Club.

The *Malahat*, a wooden, five-masted auxiliary schooner was built in Victoria as a lumber carrier. According to Rob Morris, editor of *Western Mariner* magazine, during the US prohibition era the *Malahat* "became known as the 'Queen of Rum Row,' sailing...out of Vancouver, often with 60,000 cases of liquor on board." She was wrecked in 1944.

The Grand Central Hotel in Marpole found a new use this year as the Provincial Home for Incurables, mainly tuberculosis patients. It was in use until 1965.

A study at Essondale mental hospital showed that syphilis was the cause of the mental illness of 10 percent of patients.

Kitsilano High School was built at 10th and Trafalgar.

The Vancouver Fire Department became fully motorized, the first fire department in a major city in Canada, and possibly on the continent, to achieve this distinction.

Workers finished filling in False Creek east of Main Street.

Sólskin (Sunshine), an Icelandic Canadian women's group, was formed to give aid to Icelandic Canadians serving in World War I.

Comings and Goings

May 21 Actor Raymond Burr was born in New Westminster. He became famous on TV's *Perry Mason* and later *Ironside*.

We think Stan Laurel performed in Vancouver in the spring of 1917. He had appeared in Seattle on March 18.

Famed dancer Vaslav Nijinsky appeared with Diaghilev's Ballets Russes at the Opera House in Vancouver.

Toronto-born financier Austin Cotterell Taylor, 28, arrived in BC, where he eventually became one of the province's wealthiest men.

1918

The city's celebration of the end of the war to end wars was muted by the Spanish flu epidemic, which killed hundreds of residents, and by the loss of more than 340 people when the *Princess Sophia* sank. Vancouver Centre voters elected the province's first female MLA. And the pilot survived Vancouver's first plane crash in civilized fashion.

January 5 Dallas Murray "Dal" Richards was born. Named for Dr. Dallas Perry, the man who delivered him on this date at Vancouver General Hospital, Dal Richards went on to play music for us for 70 astonishing years.

January 24 Mary Ellen Smith was the first woman to run and win election as an MLA in BC. She won a by-election in the Vancouver Centre riding. This was also the first time women could vote in a provincial election...although Native and Asian women were still disenfranchised.

Left: Down time. Enjoying quiet domesticity at home, Mary Ellen Smith was a formidable activist in public, being the first woman to be elected an MLA in British Columbia. She won the by-election for Vancouver Centre in 1918.
City of Vancouver Archives, Port N31. Photo Walter H. Calder

January A cannery in Steveston, built in 1889–90, was converted into a shipyard. Today it is known as Britannia Heritage Shipyard, the oldest surviving collection of cannery/shipyard buildings on the Fraser.

February 28 Vancouver's firefighters became the first Canadian members of the International Association of Firefighters, headquartered in Washington, DC.

February The vessel *War Puget* was launched, the first for Lyall Shipyards of North Vancouver.

March 6 John Oliver, a Delta farmer who had been minister of agriculture and railways, became premier of BC when Premier Harlan Brewster died. "Honest John" presided over the establishment of government-run liquor stores. People called them "John Oliver's Drugstores." Oliver in the Okanagan is named for him. He held

Elsewhere in BC

April 14 Daylight Saving Time was introduced to British Columbia. (The first season ended October 26, 1918.)

October 25 *Princess Sophia* sank, the worst disaster in BC's coastal history. The ship, part of CP's BC Coast Steamships service, struck a reef in Lynn Canal during a severe snowstorm off the Alaskan coast. The crowded luxury steamer was thought to be safe, anchored firmly on the reef, and several other vessels on the scene accepted Captain L.P. Locke's decision not to attempt an evacuation of the *Sophia*. The passengers, most from the Yukon, played cards and wrote letters. After 40 hours, however, as the wind and waves increased, the *Sophia* slipped off the reef during the night and sank. All those aboard, more than 340 people, including at least 63 crew, died. The only survivor was an oil-soaked dog found later wandering on the shore.

Bruce Hutchison, 17, began his lifelong career in journalism as a high school sports reporter for the *Victoria Times*. He joined the *Vancouver Sun* in 1938.

Frank Barnard, streetcar system founder and incumbent Lieutenant-Governor, was knighted by King George V. He was described as "a living link" between industrialized BC and colonial days before the arrival of the railroad.

Elsewhere in Canada

May 24 The Canadian Parliament gave women the right to vote in federal elections.

Ontario, Manitoba, Saskatchewan and British Columbia passed laws that made it illegal to hire white women in Chinese-owned restaurants and laundries. Chinese communities challenged these laws in the courts. In 1919 the Cooks and Waiters Union complained that Chinese restaurateurs often disguised their proprietorship by giving their business "white" names and hiring white waitresses. On the other hand, many hotels and restaurants owned by white businessmen, hired Chinese help because they were willing to work longer hours at lower pay.

Glove salesmen checking the new stock before they head off to work, these men were part of a long local tradition at Watson Gloves. Founded in 1918, the company still makes more than 1,000 gloves daily.
Photos courtesy of Watson Gloves

the office of premier until his death in 1927.

April Watson Gloves was founded by John Watson and Wayne Stanley. Every weekday Watson cut the strong Canadian leather and Stanley sewed it into gloves. On Saturdays the two men went to the wharves and sold the gloves they had crafted that week to workers gathered at Vancouver's docks. The company is still going strong and makes more than 1,000 pairs of gloves daily.

May 10 The blackest day in Vancouver Fire Department history: No. 11 hosewagon, en route to an alarm, struck a streetcar at East 12th Avenue and Commercial Drive. Four of the hosewagon's five-man crew died.

May 14 The worst fire in Steveston's history destroyed three canneries, three hotels, numerous residences and much of the retail district. The Chinese and Japanese sections south of Moncton Street were razed, leaving 600 homeless. At least 600 Chinese and Japanese residents were left homeless, and Japanese fishermen lost 20 boats and 100 nets stored in the Star and Lighthouse Canneries. Damages from the fire were assessed at $500,000.

May 18 Five ships left Vancouver to take 800,000 bushels of wheat to Europe. This was the first grain shipment out of Vancouver via the Panama Canal.

May 27 The Geological Survey of Canada opened its Vancouver office under Charles Camsell, who kept an eye on prospecting and mining development throughout BC and Yukon and worked closely with the provincial Department of Mines. The office was an immediate success as prospectors, exploration geologists and mining engineers availed themselves of its maps and reports, as well as its highly relevant library and the staff's geological expertise.

May The provincial government took over the PGE Railway on the North Shore when it ran into financial trouble. The service had become unreliable, and the railway had shown no sign of attempting to complete the Howe Sound portion of its track.

June 17 Benjamin Tingley Rogers, sugar manufacturer, died in Vancouver, aged 52. His handsome mansion, Gabriola, on Davie Street, was sold, and Mrs. Rogers moved into Shannon, a new mansion in Shaughnessy.

June and July A summer of labour unrest: an eight-day strike at North Shore Shipyards in June was followed by a streetcar strike and a Dominion postal workers strike in July.

August 2 The Vancouver Trades and Labour Council conducted a widely observed 24-hour general strike, the first in Canadian history, in memory of martyred labour leader Albert "Ginger" Goodwin. The strike ended after a riot by returned soldiers, who broke into the Labour Temple and badly beat up two men, who were forced to kiss the flag.

September 4 Vancouver's first plane crash. An H-2 flying-boat—an aircraft with a hull-shaped fuselage that allowed it to land on or take off from water—crashed in the West End after its engine failed at 450 metres (1,500 feet). Piloting the little plane was Lt. Victor Bishop of the RAF, a seasoned pilot who had seen (and would see more) action in World War I. Bishop's plane dropped like a stone and fell on the roof of a house owned by Dr. J.C. Farish at the corner of Bute and Alberni Streets. Bishop was not seriously injured. In fact, he stepped out of the plane into the upstairs hallway of the house and, with the assistance of one of the residents, walked down the stairs to the front door and outside through a gathered crowd to a waiting ambulance.

September 8 Hotelier Tommy Roberts was shot dead by a masked intruder during a card game in Vancouver.

What goes up... Surveying the damage, these two men consider Vancouver's first plane crash. The pilot landed on top of a house in the West End, and walked downstairs to a waiting ambulance. *City of Vancouver Archives, Air P31. Photo Frank Gowen*

September 9 The Surrey Board of Trade was established.

September 24 Port Coquitlam held a sale of property for arrears of taxes. There were not many buyers so the city retained ownership of much of the land, gradually selling it off in the 1920s.

October 5 The Spanish flu epidemic, which killed more people during World War I than the war itself, hit Vancouver. The first reaction was overconfidence and even a bit of levity as the "grippe" seemed to be under control. The *Province* editorial cartoonist had early fun with weird ways to beat the bug. The levity soon stopped. Churches and theatres closed; shopping was banned. By November 14 there were 400 dead in Vancouver alone. The worst was not over until the end of November.

October 17 The *Ubyssey*, the University of BC's student paper, first appeared under that name. The paper began as a staid and sober weekly, but that soon changed. (Trivia: Actress Rita Hayworth was born the same day.)

October 19 Dr. Frank Wesbrook, first president of the University of BC, died at 50. He was an immensely popular man, and his death at such an early age was particularly saddening. He was succeeded by Leonard Sylvanus Klinck, who served until 1944.

November 11
Greater Vancouver celebrated the Armistice and the end of the Great War.

The streets were jammed with thousands of celebrants.

November 12 Adam Urias dePencier, Anglican priest, bishop of New Westminster, president of the Anglican Theological College, received the Order of the British Empire from King George V.

December 7
A moderate earthquake tremor stopped the clock on the Vancouver Block on Granville Street.

December 13 The Terminal City Club, a prominent private club for businessmen, burned its mortgages and notes in a lively and crowded ceremony. "Mayor [Robert] Gale," the *Province* reported, "called on two of the original endorsers of the notes, Messrs. John Ross and George E. Trorey...[They] were given the original documents, whereupon matches were promptly applied and the notes burned merrily while the orchestra struck up Keep the Home Fires Burning." The club, formed December 5, 1892, built the Metropolitan Building as its home in 1909, renting out upper floors for offices.

December 15 Vancouver established its first traffic department. Constables directing traffic wore white gloves.

Peace parade. Parading downtown for victory and empire, these revellers celebrate the armistice on November 11, 1918, at the end of World War I. *City of Vancouver Archives, CVA 99-781. Photo Stuart Thomson*

Also in 1918

The *Province* newspaper donated funds to develop a park on land that had been left vacant at Cambie and Hastings Streets when the old provincial law courts were demolished. At that time, the *Province* offices were right across the street from the new park, which was named Victory Square to commemorate victory in World War I.

The Workmen's Compensation Board's head office was moved from Victoria to 402 Pender St. in Vancouver to facilitate faster handling of claims for the majority of claimants. In 1929 the offices moved again, to 411 Dunsmuir.

Easthope Brothers of Vancouver developed a four-cycle heavy-duty marine engine for the Fraser River fishing industry. Costing about $150 each, the Easthope engines soon became famous.

Right: A 2-cylinder model (8–14 hp), 118 cubic-inch Easthope engine designed for cruisers and light boats, including the small gillnet fishing vessels. A local Vancouver company started in 1906, Easthope engines were soon famous and widely used.
Vancouver Sun

Robert H. Gale was elected mayor of Vancouver and served until 1921.

Following formation of the Vancouver City Hall Employees Association, and fearful that communist unions would take over workplaces and society in general, the city set up a conciliation committee during Gale's tenure to settle disputes between itself and its employees.

Shipbuilding on False Creek was now Vancouver's largest industry.

The first issue of *Harbour and Shipping* appeared. It is now the oldest magazine published in British Columbia.

Vancouver city council imposed a $100 licence fee on Chinese market gardeners and produce peddlers. The peddlers formed a Vegetable Sellers' Association and appealed all the way to the Supreme Court, claiming the fee would cause them undue hardship. As well, white customers submitted a petition to council, arguing that the fee would force up consumer prices. Eventually negotiations brought the licence fee down to $50.

The Opsal Steel building, originally occupied by Columbia Block and Tool Co., was built.

The first Parent Teachers Association in Vancouver was organized, between Dawson and Aberdeen schools.

Dr. Robert Edward McKechnie, a distinguished surgeon, became UBC's second chancellor. He retained that office until his death in 1944.

Garnet Gladwin Sedgewick, a Shakespearean scholar, joined UBC's English department. In 1920 he became head of the department. The university's Sedgewick Library is named for him.

Realtor Henry Ceperley bequeathed Vancouver's second supervised playground.

Harry Gardiner, the "Human Fly," climbed up the outside of the World Building (known today as the Sun Tower).

Provincial botanist John Davidson founded the Vancouver Natural History Society.

Comings and Goings

Famed actress Sarah Bernhardt appeared at the Orpheum. Huge crowds the first day tapered off when people realized she acted in French. (Note: The most expensive ticket was 85 cents.)

Shipshape. As evidence that shipbuilding was now Vancouver's largest trade, four ships lie side by side in the False Creek shipyards in this 1918 panorama.
City of Vancouver Archives, Pan N49A.2. Photo W.J. Moore

1919

While labour strife shut down much of the city, the Vancouver Symphony Orchestra got its start. Lumbermen's Arch was installed in Stanley Park.

January 30 The Native Daughters of BC was formed in Vancouver. The group's objective was to pay tribute to the pioneers and history of the province. Today it operates the Hastings Mill Store Museum at the north foot of Alma Street.

March 3 Pioneer aviator William Boeing flew a sack of mail from Vancouver to Seattle in the first international air mail delivery between Canada and the United States. The publicity stunt was hatched by pioneer druggist E.S. Knowlton to promote the Vancouver Exhibition and was carried out with the co-operation of postal officials and the Royal Vancouver Yacht Club, where Boeing docked his plane and picked up the mail. W.A. Turquand, manager of the Hotel Vancouver, J.T. Little, director of the Vancouver Exhibition, and Chief Constable William McRae oversaw the handover of the mail sack, which contained, among other missives, a letter from the mayor of Vancouver to his Seattle counterpart.

June 3 A general strike began in Vancouver. At its height more than 10,000 workers were on strike, including some civic employees. In North Vancouver, shipyards closed and streetcars halted.

July 19 A great Peace Celebration and Parade were held in Vancouver, including a Thanksgiving service in Stanley Park, led by Premier John Oliver and Vancouver mayor Robert H. Gale.

Post-haste. Neither snow, nor rain, nor heat, nor gloom of night... nor borders! The first international airmail delivery from Seattle lands at the Royal Vancouver Yacht Club. *City of Vancouver Archives, Trans P44. Photo Stuart Thomson*

August 29 The original Lumbermen's Arch, at its new location in Stanley Park, was dedicated in memory of its designer, Captain G.P. Bowie, who was killed at Ypres on July 7, 1915. First erected at Pender and Hamilton for the 1912 visit of the Duke and Duchess of Connaught, the arch had been moved to Stanley Park shortly afterward. Eventually it began to deteriorate and was demolished on December 3, 1947, to be replaced by the present, much simpler version.

Also August 29 Twenty-five-year-old prisoner Alex Ignace was the first person hanged at Oakalla.

Summer The shady Henry Green, who never answered personal questions and refused to have his photograph taken, convinced social leader Mary Isabella Rogers to help underwrite his subscription orchestra. That was the origin of the Vancouver Symphony Orchestra.

September The new Rotary Clinic for Chest Diseases was officially opened to provide free medical care

Elsewhere in BC

Edward Gawler Prior, a mining engineer, soldier, politician and former BC premier, became Lieutenant-Governor of BC.

The federal government's By-Election Act of 1919 theoretically gave the franchise to all Asians. This "oversight" caused the provincial government to pass an amendment that disqualified those who lacked the provincial franchise (i.e., Asian and Native people) unless they were veterans of the Canadian Armed Forces. As a result, 20 Chinese Canadian veterans of World War I gained the right to vote.

The BC legislature also amended the Factories Act to prevent laundries from operating between 7 p.m. and 7 a.m. When white laundry owners complained about lax enforcement and accused Chinese launderers of defying the act by working on statutory holidays, the government replaced token fines with penalties that rose to $200 for second violations and included jail sentences for those who did not pay.

Calm before the storm. An early incarnation of the Vancouver Symphony Orchestra poses on April 25, 1920 at the old Orpheum Theatre. Alas, the organizer, Henry Green, skipped town a year later with all of the money. It wouldn't be until 1930 that the VSO would resurrect. *City of Vancouver Archives, CVA 99-5311. Photo Stuart Thomson*

for children. This was an outpatient clinic for the treatment and prevention of tuberculosis, the dreaded "white death" so prevalent early in the century.

November 1 The first train arrived at the brand-new Canadian National Railway station facing Main Street in Vancouver this evening. First to leave (also today) was the Transcontinental Express, headed for Toronto.

November 19 The city's newspapers published a five-page section listing the lots seized for non-payment of taxes that were to be auctioned off. There were more than 2,000 pieces of property on the list, and some of them were seized for overdue taxes totalling less than $10.

November 20 Francis L. Carter-Cotton, 75, walked into English Bay and drowned himself. The former newspaper publisher, MLA, cabinet minister and first chancellor of UBC had suffered two serious strokes in 1919, one just weeks before his death.

Also in 1919

A group of Chinese soccer players formed a team in 1919, went on to play in the "mainstream" league and ended up winning some major tournaments. This was the Chinese boys' first chance to compete on a level playing field; before they established the team they were treated as outsiders, second-class citizens in Vancouver. (Kathryn Gretzinger recounted their story in her award-winning radio documentary *A Level Playing Field* in 1999.)

Japanese Canadians held 3,267 commercial fishing licences for the Lower Fraser, about half the licences issued. The Federal Department of Marine and Fisheries announced that it would "gradually eliminate Orientals from the fishery" and issue licences to only "whites" and "Indians." By 1925, close to 1,000 licenses had been stripped from Japanese Canadians. (Note of interest: At this time a commercial fishing licence for the Fraser River cost $5.)

Proud winners of the 1933 Mainland Cup, the Chinese Student Soccer Team—formed in 1919 and playing until 1942—proved to be a vehicle for gaining some equality with the white community. In this tournament, they beat favourites UBC Varsity 4–3 in a wet and exhilarating match. *Courtesy Robert Yip*

(B.C.) MAINLAND CUP CHAMPIONS - 1933

Standing L to R William Lore, Gibb Yip, Jackson Louie, Jack Soon, Shupon Wong, Horne Yip, Charlie Louie, Gim Jang, George Lam
Sitting, L to R Lim On, Dock Yip, Art Yip, Quene Yip, Frank Wong, Buck Sing

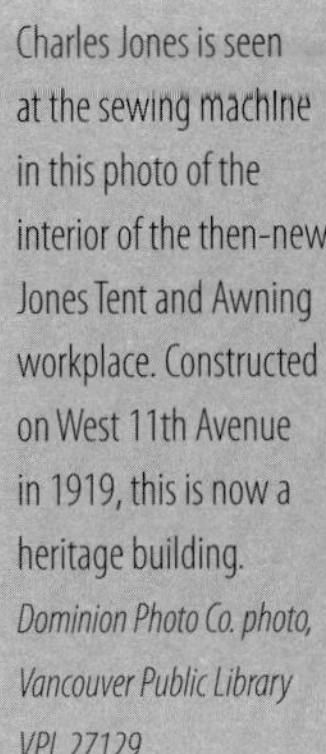

Charles Jones is seen at the sewing machine in this photo of the interior of the then-new Jones Tent and Awning workplace. Constructed on West 11th Avenue in 1919, this is now a heritage building. *Dominion Photo Co. photo, Vancouver Public Library VPL 27129*

Eggs at the farmers' market in New Westminster cost $1 a dozen.

Times were good for Surrey farmers, as prices forced up by the war had not yet fallen.

The Vancouver Real Estate Board, which had suspended operations during World War I, resumed its activities. It has been going ever since.

Arthur Mars became mayor of Port Coquitlam. His brother James had held the office earlier.

David William Poppy, who had been reeve of Langley Municipality from 1908 to 1913, became reeve again.

A new town hall was built in the Brighouse area of Richmond, replacing one that had burned to the ground in 1912.

Blythe Rogers, eldest son of BC Sugar Company founder B.T. Rogers, built the stylish Tudor home originally called Knole at the northwest corner of 57th and Marine. He died soon after at the age of 26.

The discount store arrived. Selling items from bankruptcy closeouts, ends of lines and overstocked inventory, Samuel Joseph Cohen opened the first Army and Navy Store at 44 West Hastings. It moved to its 300 West Hastings location in 1939.

The Jones Tent and Awning building went up at 2034 West 11th Ave. It is now a heritage building.

Henry Angus became a member of the UBC faculty. The Henry Angus Building (Faculty of Commerce and Business Administration) was named for him.

The Kiwanis Club of Vancouver was established. In the Lower Mainland today there are 17 branches with more than 10,000 members.

The annual publication *Scarlet and Gold* first appeared, produced by and for veterans of the RCMP, Vancouver Division.

Ivor W. Neil, who had been operating a sightseeing bus and taxi service in Vancouver since 1915, took over Goodman Hamre's White Rock bus service.

Cooper and Smith Towing began operations on the Fraser River. In 1932 the company became Westminster Tug Boats Inc.

The Vancouver Japanese Language School decided to discontinue its instruction of general subjects and focus on Japanese language instruction only. As a result, children attended regular Canadian public schools in English and learned Japanese language after school.

Comings and Goings

Early August Captain Ernest C. Hoy, DFC, of Vancouver took off from Minoru Park on Lulu Island and flew to Calgary. Said in one sentence, it sounds unimpressive. These days a trip like that takes about an hour and a quarter. For Captain Hoy it took 16 hours and 42 minutes. His flight was the first ever made across the Canadian Rockies. This was also the first airmail delivery across the Rockies—from Richmond to Golden, Calgary and Lethbridge.

September 22 Edward, Prince of Wales, 25, visited Vancouver. There was a civic reception and a military ball at the arena in the evening—tickets were $5. The prince visited other areas of Greater Vancouver and opened the New Westminster Exhibition. Before the ball he attended a dinner as a guest of the Vancouver Club. Members went to great lengths to impress the prince and make him feel at home, painting the ladies' lavatory; providing an electrical display of Edward's motto *Ich Dien*; arranging for HRH's favourite flowers (sweet peas); and engaging the services of Mr. Copley's orchestra, which was tucked away in the dining room's bay window. (The prince went on to become King Edward VIII, but abdicated in 1936.)

1920-1929

1920

A float plane base opened at Jericho Beach, and the city's Yellow Taxi company began business with a single cab. Prohibition was voted down in BC. And a New Year's Day tradition got its start at English Bay.

This group of brave swimmers are shivering at the water's edge at English Bay on the first day of 1939, preparing to participate in the annual Polar Bear Swim. The origins of the swim go back to 1920 when Peter Pantages, owner of the Peter Pan Cafe on Granville Street, rounded up a few hardy souls to follow him into the water. It has been a New Year's Day tradition ever since. *City of Vancouver Archives, CVA 371-836*

January 1 The Polar Bear Club swim was started by Peter Pantages. Every New Year's Day for more than 90 years now, several hundred cold-defying people have leapt screaming into the chilly waters of Vancouver's English Bay, dressed only in their bathing suits or other more unorthodox attire.

January A traffic count on the Fraser River bridge revealed that more than 13,000 trains—passenger, freight and mixed—had crossed during the previous year (an average of more than 35 a day). By comparison, 65 automobiles per hour was the highest count for the upper span.

February 3 The Vancouver harbour police were formed.

War sentinel. Now surrounded by cherry trees, the striking Japanese Canadian War Memorial was installed in 1920 in Stanley Park to commemorate the Japanese Canadian volunteers who fought in World War I. *City of Vancouver Archives, CVA 99-3280. Photo Stuart Thomson*

February 4 North Vancouver mountaineers Don and Phyllis Munday married. By 11 a.m. they were climbing one of the local mountains.

April 2 A striking Japanese Canadian War Memorial, designed by Vancouver architect James Benzie, was dedicated in Stanley Park. The monument commemorated the 190 Japanese Canadians who volunteered to fight for Canada in World War I. Of those, 146 were killed or wounded. During the battle of Vimy Ridge, fought over four days in April 1917, Sergeant Masumi Mitsui of Port Coquitlam led his troop into battle with such distinction that he was awarded the Military Medal for Bravery. A Japanese Canadian entrepreneur, Koichiro Sanmiya, sold war bonds to raise money for the memorial, which still stands, surrounded by flowering cherry trees.

April 18 Henry Osborne Alexander died in Vancouver. Alexander was the first white male born on Burrard

Elsewhere in BC

October 20 British Columbians voted to end prohibition in the province, three years and 19 days after it began.

December 24 Walter Cameron Nichol, editor and proprietor of the *Daily Province*, became Lieutenant-Governor of British Columbia, the only journalist so honoured to date.

During the 1920s, the BC Native population reached its lowest number.

Elsewhere in Canada

May The Group of Seven, an informal association of landscape painters, formed in eastern Canada.

The Canadian Air Board was created to govern aviation in Canada.

Elsewhere in the World

January 16 Prohibition started in the United States. It ended in 1933.

Inlet—on December 13, 1873, at Hastings Mill. He was called to the bar in 1896 and practised in Vancouver, later becoming a judge. On January 10, 1908, when two South Vancouver neighbours came to court over ownership of a rooster, Magistrate Alexander ordered the bird turned loose on the street to decide for itself where it belonged.

April 22 A chapter of the IODE started in West Vancouver.

May 22 Irish-born George McSpadden, Vancouver's first building inspector and assessor, died here at age 54. In 1900 he took a census of Vancouver's population, which was just over 23,000 people. He built his residence at Commercial Drive and Charles Street in East Vancouver, and a street and park near there are named for him.

June 8 Welsh-born CPR executive Richard Marpole died in Vancouver at age 69. He was the CPR's manager when the first passenger trains crossed Canada and was the first in North America to prepare timetables based on a 24-hour system. An exciting episode in his life: he was a member of the posse that caught the Grey Fox, Bill Miner, on May 11, 1906, after Miner's second BC train robbery.

July Construction of the Peace Arch began, directed by W.E. Simmons of Vancouver. Work was halted in November to give the concrete time to set, then resumed in June 1921.

August 5 Fire destroyed much of downtown Port Coquitlam. It started above the firehall, ironically—in the residence of the fire/police chief. Half the city's buildings along the Dewdney Trunk Road were destroyed. No one was injured.

August 13 Garibaldi Park was officially opened. Why was a BC park named for an Italian patriot? According to place-name experts G.P.V. and Helen B. Akrigg, "Mount Garibaldi was named by an Italian serving as a sailor on a survey ship, the mountain being on view on Garibaldi's birthday [July 4]. All we can say with certainty is that the name, whatever its origins, was officially conferred by Captain Richards of HM survey ship *Plumper* sometime around 1860." The park was later named for the mountain.

Also in 1920

In the Colebrook area of Surrey, loggers cut down a big tree (84 metres/276 feet high). In it they found an eagle's nest that was too large for a farm wagon to haul away.

UBC surrendered over 800,000 hectares (2 million acres) of land in the Cariboo region of BC, which had been given as an endowment by the provincial government, and took instead 1,200 hectares (3,000 acres) adjacent to the university's site—the University Endowment Lands.

Richmond's Minoru Park, closed during World War I, reopened as Brighouse Park, named for pioneer Samuel Brighouse, a Lulu Island farmer and one of the three greenhorns. (Minoru was the name of the horse, raced by King Edward VII, that won the Epsom Derby in 1909.)

Short Street in Kitsilano (it was one block long) was renamed Greer Street in honour of pioneer Sam Greer. In 1952 it was renamed again and is now Fleming Street.

Five-pin bowling (invented by Tom Ryan of Toronto) came to the Lower Mainland of BC. By 1945 it had overtaken ten-pin in the number of its followers.

In Vancouver, a referendum brought in an experiment with proportional representation, which was then being tried out in a number of North American cities. Three years later, in 1923, another referendum brought back the eight-ward, single-member system.

The fifth annual South Vancouver Horticultural Association and Farmers' Institute featured a honey competition and goat show.

Casa Mia, a spectacular mansion on Southwest Marine Drive, was built for George C. Reifel, the namesake of

Right: One of Vancouver's most famous heritage houses, Casa Mia, on Southwest Marine Drive, was built in 1920 by George Reifel. He was a Vancouver brewing magnate, and bought the land that is now the Reifel bird sanctuary on the Fraser River. *Photo by Kim Stallknecht/* Vancouver Sun

the waterfowl sanctuary on Westham Island, near Ladner.

Capt. John Cates sold his resort complex on Bowen Island—including the Hotel Monaco, Terminal Hotel and the Terminal Steamship ferry fleet—to the Union Steamship Company of BC and moved to the province's Interior. On summer weekends as many as 5,000 passengers boarded the boats to Bowen.

By 1920 Horseshoe Bay had become a summer destination for many campers, picnickers and weekend fishermen, who travelled there by train for a 50-cent fare on a regular 30-minute service. Cabins—often wood frames covered with canvas—were built during the summer and rented out.

Called Chai-hai by the Squamish people, Horseshoe Bay was developed as a summer resort in 1909, but it was the arrival of the PGE railway in 1914 that made it a popular recreational destination in the ensuing years. By the early 1930s Dan Sewell Sr. was operating a marina and a hotel and the bay was getting a reputation as a sport fishing mecca. *Leonard Frank photo, Vancouver Public Library VPL 16437*

In the 1920s the Blue Funnel Jitney Service charged 50 cents for a trip from Port Coquitlam to New Westminster.

In North Vancouver City, Fire Chief Sparks (yes, that really was his name) and his entire force went on strike—and were dismissed.

The Union Bank (architect: Woodruff Marbury Somervell—that's one man) opened at Hastings and Seymour. Today it's a Toronto-Dominion branch.

Of the 31 businesses in Steveston in 1920, 17 were owned by Japanese Canadians.

Kamejiro Edamura, who trained as a watchmaker in Japan, opened a jewellery store on Vancouver's Main Street with his son Tomegoro.

The CNR built a low-level bridge over the North Arm of the Fraser. Friend (and train buff) Jim McGraw confirms the bridge is still in daily use. "Most of the time the bridge is left open (for marine traffic) and only closed for trains. The trains are locals that access the Lafarge cement plant and other newer industry on the south side of Lulu Island via a spur line. The main portion of the line turns west on Lulu Island servicing various industries in North Richmond. The only place to see the bridge is when you drive on River Road (the one in Richmond, not Delta). The road follows the southern shore of the North Arm of the Fraser and you actually drive under the bridge's approach."

Arrests for prostitution in Vancouver, which numbered 20 in 1900, had increased to 500 by this year.

Belgium became the third country to appoint a consul to Vancouver. (The first two were Chile in 1892 and Brazil in 1915.)

The Children's Protective Association initiated the removal of Chinese students from the classroom.

A little two-room schoolhouse called Strathcona Heights was built on a rocky slope at 5300 Maple St. There's still a school on that property today: Quilchena Elementary.

The Anglican Theological College was formed, amalgamating Latimer Hall and St. Mark's Hall.

A group of artists, educators and art patrons formed the British Columbia Art League to lobby the provincial and city governments for a school. The Vancouver School of Decorative and Applied Arts opened its doors in 1925. Today it's called the Emily Carr University of Art + Design.

Jericho Beach became a military air station for flying boats following the war. This photograph shows a Curtiss seaplane belonging to the Royal Canadian Air Force at the base in 1925. Aircraft from the station carried out forest and fishery patrols, fought forest fires, conducted aerial photography and generally kept an eye on the coast from the air. *Library and Archives Canada, PA-133584*

The Architectural Institute of British Columbia (AIBC), founded in 1914 under the Friendly Societies Act, was incorporated in 1920 under the Architects Act.

The local Field Brigade, Royal Canadian Artillery, was established.

Two service organizations established chapters in Vancouver: Hadassah, the Women's Zionist Organization of America; and the Gyro Club, a "fraternity of friendship."

The first BC Federation of Labour was disbanded when workers across western Canada joined the One Big Union, which organized everyone. The OBU had a short life.

Etsu Suzuki established the first Japanese labour union, the Nihonjin Rodo Kumiai, a general union of all Japanese workers regardless of their occupation. Suzuki was a journalist for *Tairiku Nippon* (*Continental Times*), published in Vancouver. He became the publisher of *Rodo Shuho* (*Labour Weekly*).

Yellow Taxi began doing business with a single car owned by Roy Long, a lawyer.

Jericho Beach Air Station was established. Seaplanes from Jericho surveyed the coast and provided flight training.

David Lambie "Davey" Black became club pro at Shaughnessy Golf Club, a job he held for 25 years.

An oil well was drilled in Surrey to a depth of 370 metres (1,220 feet) before it was abandoned. Several attempts to strike oil in subsequent years also met with failure.

J.B. Leyland became reeve of West Vancouver. He served for 10 years.

Comings and Goings

October 17 The first plane to fly right across Canada arrived in Richmond from Halifax. It had taken 10 days to make the trip. At the controls: two Canadian Air Force pilots.

Yvonne Millicent Firkins, a theatre producer and director born in Worcester, England, arrived in Vancouver. She became a powerful figure in local theatre and in 1964 opened the Arts Club Theatre.

Liverpool-born Gerald Rushton, 22, arrived in Vancouver and began working for the Union Steamship Company. He stayed with the company for 38 years and became an expert on the coast's maritime history, writing two histories, *Whistle up the Inlet* and *Echoes of the Whistle*.

Significant births: **James Doohan**, born in Vancouver on March 3, was best known as Scotty in the original *Star Trek* series; **Robert Bonner**, future attorney general, was born on September 10.

Notable deaths: **Chang Toy**, Vancouver businessman, died in China on a business trip at age 64 (Chang built the famous Sam Kee Building in Chinatown, the narrowest commercial building in the world); **John Wesley Sexsmith**, successful farmer and pioneer in Richmond, died, aged 90; Haida artist **Charles Edenshaw** died—he trained the maternal grandfather of equally famed native artist Bill Reid, who was born this year; **David Spencer**, founder of the Spencer's Department Store chain, died in Victoria in March, age 82.

1921

The city extended its hands across the US border with the dedication of the Peace Arch. Music patrons became victims of a symphonic scam artist. And Vancouver lost the Stanley Cup.

March 12 The Capitol Theatre opened at 820 Granville St. Unlike the Pantages and Orpheum Theatres, which were built to house vaudeville and live theatre, the Capitol was a pure movie palace, a lush theatre that originally seated 2,500. It was equipped with a huge Wurlitzer organ to accompany the movies. Calvin Winter and his Capitolians played at the opening.

Left: The originals. Glee clubs, when they were cool the first time around, trod the boards at the beautiful Capital Theatre, which first opened as a cinema. Such clubs traditionally sang short songs in trios or quartets. *City of Vancouver Archives, CVA 99-3439. Photo Stuart Thomson*

March 21 The first game of the 1921 Stanley Cup series,

a best-of-five contest between the Ottawa Senators and the Vancouver Millionaires, took place at the Denman Arena. The attendance for game one was 11,000, setting a new world record for the largest crowd to see a hockey game. The Senators won the cup three games to two.

April 18 Fitzgerald McCleery died at age 82 in Vancouver. With his brother Samuel, he built the trail from New Westminster to Point Grey for a salary of $30 a month. In September 1862 the brothers were the first to farm the Fraser delta lands. Their first 15 head of cattle were shipped from Oregon. Dairy products were canoed to New Westminster and carried by steamer to Fraser logging camps. In the 1950s the McCleery farm became a golf course. Fitzgerald kept a diary of his life in BC, now part of the collection of the Vancouver City Archives.

Spring Henry Green, who had convinced social leader Mary Isabella Rogers to help underwrite his subscription orchestra (the genesis of the Vancouver Symphony Orchestra), skipped town with the orchestra's money, never to be heard from again.

June 14 Jenny Dill and her husband, Frank, arrived in Vancouver. They had left Halifax on February

Elsewhere in BC

June 15 A brief and ineffective period of prohibition that had started in BC in 1917 came to an end; from this date on the provincial government controlled the sale of spirituous and malt liquors.

The postwar census, taken just two years after World War I ended, showed the number of BC residents who declared their German origin had declined by nearly 40 percent. In public, people of German ancestry now spoke English only. Beginning this year, all Germans entering Canada had to register as enemy aliens, although this regulation was short-lived.

Elsewhere in Canada

April 15 The Canadian Bar Association, a professional, voluntary organization formed in 1896, was incorporated by a special act of Parliament.

December 6 The first federal election in which women had the vote. William Lyon Mackenzie King defeated Arthur Meighen's Conservatives to win his first term as prime minister. His was also the first minority government in Canadian history. King's Liberals held 116 seats; the opposition's seats totalled 119.

The Western Canada Hockey League was founded. Its name was changed to the Western Hockey League in 1926; later that same year it became the Prairie Hockey League. It folded in 1928. The Vancouver Maroons were in the league from 1924 to 1925.

Julian Hedworth George Byng, Viscount Byng of Vimy, became Governor General of Canada. He served until 1926. Lord Byng School was named for him.

Elsewhere in the World

June 10 Prince Philip was born on the island of Corfu, a Greek island in the Mediterranean.

Regal cruiser. The *Princess Louise*, at 3,630 tonnes, was the largest passenger ship ever built in BC. It joined the Princess fleet of elegant coastal steamers owned by Canadian Pacific and used to make the night run between Vancouver and Victoria. During the summer it was a cruise ship, carrying tourists north to Skagway, Alaska.
City of Vancouver Archives, CVA 99-2229. Photo Stuart Thomson

1 and walked across Canada, one of three teams in a race across the country. The Dills were the second team to arrive, but they had started walking seven days after the team that arrived first, and had taken four fewer days for the journey. The walkers faced terrible storms, wolves, wildcats, defective footwear...It was a real adventure and the whole country followed their every step.

July Seven hundred tourists camped in Central Park in Burnaby. These "autoists," as the newspapers called them, came from as far away as eastern Canada and the United States, and the municipality considered putting in shower baths and laundry "wash houses." The camp closed in about 1927.

August 29 The Canadian Pacific Railway's *Princess Louise,* the largest passenger ship ever built in BC, was launched at Wallace Shipyards. It was built for the CPR's northern service and was the only "Princess" designed and built in Vancouver. The *Louise* had a record run of 40 years without an incident before being sold in 1955 to become a restaurant in Long Beach, CA, where it sank in 1990.

September 6 The Peace Arch was dedicated before a vast crowd at the Douglas Crossing on the BC–Washington border. BC's Premier Oliver attended, along with nearly 400 other people from Victoria, who arrived in a boat that anchored at Blaine. In a pleasant hands-across-the-border gesture of friendship, Victoria's 72nd Seaforth Highlanders band played the US national anthem, and the Bellingham Elks band played "God Save the King."

October 28 A sudden flood wave crashed down on the village at Britannia Beach and swept away 50 of its 100 houses, killing 35 people. "It was at 9:30 o'clock on Friday night that the disaster happened," the *Province* reported. "The creek had been growing more turbulent and, with the melting of the snow in the higher levels, the waters became uncontrollable. A dam was washed out and then a railroad fill went, and the debris carried away houses...Shrieks of the victims were heard above the roar of the flood."

Also on October 28 Port Coquitlam was going through rough times. A fire in 1920 razed half the town's commercial buildings along Dewdney Trunk Road. On this date more buildings and a bridge were lost when the Coquitlam River flooded. Several businesses and St. Catherine's Church were swept downstream. The church and the barbershop came to rest on a sandbar. By the end of the year PoCo was virtually bankrupt, and council had to sell the city's fire engine. This was a bad move as a year later fire wiped out another section of downtown.

Upholding peace. The Peace Arch at the US border south of Vancouver commemorates peaceful relations between Canada and the United States. Schoolchildren from British Columbia and Washington State raised money to pay for the arch, and the names of the young donors are embedded in the structure.
City of Vancouver Archives, Arch P11

Left: A brutal wake-up call, the Anderson and Peterson houses lie strewn about in Howe Sound in 1920, the morning after an unexpected wave from a swollen creek swept through Britannia Beach. *PNG*

Also in 1921

The University of British Columbia appointed its first dean of women, Mary Louise Bollert. Bollert was one of the founders of the BC Teachers Federation—inspired, in part, by the desire to push for pay equity for women teachers. UBC named Mary Bollert Hall, now used by the university's Development Office, in her honour. Bollert retired in 1941 and ran unsuccessfully for the provincial Liberals that year in Vancouver–Point Grey. Born in Guelph, ON, in 1884, she died August 1, 1945, in Vancouver.

A fellow named John Putnam visited Vancouver, saying he was going to put the city on the moviemaking map. He somehow got hold of a stack of city stationery and sent invitations to kings and prime ministers all over the world, telling them to come here (at the city's expense) for a vast celebration to begin the project. A few people replied with thanks before a couple of white-coated gentlemen showed up to escort Mr. Putnam back to the Seattle hospital from which he had escaped.

Menchions Shipyards launched the *Norsal*, which it had built for the Powell River Co., a major forest products firm. A contemporary story reported that the boat was "the largest power yacht of its type built on this coast, being 132 feet over all...with a draft of about eight-and-a-half feet... The boat is twin-screw with two 200-h.p. Fairbanks-Morse engines of the semi-diesel type, which are expected to give her a speed of 15 miles an hour." The *Norsal* made its maiden voyage in May 1922. In 1945 the boat was sold to lumberman J. Gordon Gibson, who renamed it *Maui Lu* and sailed it to Hawaii.

The bronze memorial *Winged Victory* was erected outside the Canadian Pacific Railway station on Cordova Street in Vancouver. The work commemorated the 1,100 CPR employees who had lost their lives in World War I. Copies of the memorial went up in Winnipeg in 1922 and at Montreal's Windsor Station in 1923. After World War II a plaque was added to the statues as a tribute to soldiers in that war. The sculptor, commissioned by the railway after a nationwide search, was the grandly named Coeur de Lion MacCarthy.

The east half of False Creek was filled to create the yards of the Great Northern (now Burlington Northern) and the Canadian Northern Pacific (now part of Canadian National Railways) railways. A bridge, built in the 1870s, that crossed the creek was removed.

The Sannie Transportation Company began a ferry service between Horseshoe Bay and Snug Cove on Bowen Island. It started with three round trips a day, more on weekends. The fare remained at 25 cents for the next 30 years.

Laura Emma Jamieson organized a branch of the Women's International League for Peace and Freedom.

Scottish-born Lily Laverock began her work as an impresario in Vancouver. Over the next couple of decades this former newspaper writer (Vancouver's first woman reporter) brought to the city, through her International Celebrity Concerts, such figures as Geraldine Farrar, Jascha Heifetz, Fritz Kreisler, Nellie Melba, John McCormack, Maurice Ravel and Sergei Rachmaninoff, and such ensembles as the Don Cossack Singers and the Ballet Russe de Monte Carlo, an effort that made a profound contribution to the musical life of Vancouver. She suspended her concert sponsorship at the beginning of World War II and retired in the early 1950s.

The Vancouver Little Theatre Association, possibly Canada's oldest continuously operating community theatre company, was formed. Its first play, *Lonesome Luke*, was directed by Frederic Wood and presented in a 200-seat auditorium at Templeton Hall at Pender and Templeton.

Richmond won top prizes for its agricultural produce at the Vancouver and Victoria Exhibition. Both the quality and the diversity of produce—grain, forage crops, vegetables, berries, tree fruits and dairy—was evident.

The *Province* had this Daily Chuckle: Jenkins was sitting down to breakfast one morning when he was astounded to see in the paper an announcement of his own death. He rang up friend Smith at once. "Halloa,

Smith!" he said. "Have you seen the announcement of my death in the paper?"

"Yes," replied Smith. "Where are you speaking from?"

The Schara Tzedeck (Gates of Righteousness) synagogue was opened next to Vancouver's first synagogue, B'nai Yehudah (Sons of Israel), which was stuccoed over so it would match the new building. The site is irreverently known as Beth Condo, since the old building eventually became, as a part of the gentrification of Strathcona neighbourhood, a compact of privately owned apartments.

The staff at St. Paul's Hospital devised a machine that controlled ether administration in the operating room.

Vancouver General Hospital dropped its policy of shunting Chinese patients to the basement.

Four Sisters of the Immaculate Conception arrived from Montreal to set up a school for Chinese children in Vancouver. In 1924 they added a medical dispensary, and four years later they constructed a hospital at 236 Campbell Ave., which became Mount Saint Joseph Hospital when it moved to its Prince Edward Avenue location.

The Fire Wardens Branch, responsible for inspections, enforcing fire bylaws and investigating fires, was formed in Vancouver. It replaced a police sergeant who had enforced fire bylaws part-time for many years.

The Association of Professional Engineers of British Columbia was formed to establish the qualifications necessary to practice.

The Vancouver Central Lions Club was founded.

It is the oldest Lions Club in British Columbia and the second-oldest in Canada. Today there are 26 Lions Clubs in Vancouver, 55 in the Lower Mainland. As well, there are about 25 Lions Ladies Clubs, the first of which was established in 1937.

Leon Johnson Ladner, lawyer, a founder of UBC convocation and of Ladner, Downs, one of Vancouver's largest law firms, became the Liberal Conservative MP (yes, you read that right) for Vancouver South. He served to 1930.

Angus MacInnis, politician, began his long public service with election to the Vancouver School Board. He went on to become an MP for Vancouver East. (MacInnis Park in East Vancouver was named for Angus and his wife Grace.)

Ronald Bick Lee, businessman and community leader, founded Foo Hung Co., a leading importer of Asian goods.

Hilda G. Howard, under the pseudonym Hilda Glynn-Ward, wrote one of the most offensive racist novels published in BC. *The Writing on the Wall*, published by the Sun Publishing Company, depicts Vancouver's white population dying after consuming vegetables and sugar to which the local Chinese merchants had purposely added typhoid germs. The Chinese and Japanese population remained healthy because members had been "inured to [typhoid] by countless generations of living without sanitation."

William Lamont Tait, lumberman, died. He had arrived in Vancouver on February 13, 1891, and later opened Rat Portage Lumber, a shingle and sawmill on False Creek (1902–10). Tait was one of the first businessmen to hire workers from India and the False Creek Indian reserve. His Shaughnessy mansion, Glen Brae, built in 1910, had one of the city's first elevators. Today Glen Brae is Canuck Place, a children's hospice.

Fritz Ziegler established Ziegler Chocolate Shops.

Comings and Goings

April 29 Famed contralto Ernestine Schumann-Heink left Vancouver for a tour of the Far East.

Henry John Cambie, railway engineer, retired. (He wasn't a locomotive engineer, but, rather, worked out the railway's routes.) Cambie Street was named for him.

William Ferriman Salsbury, railway executive, stepped down as the CPR Pacific Division's treasurer after 35 years. An east-side street was named for him.

Ioco was developed as a community near the head of Burrard Inlet for employees of the Imperial Oil Company, which had operated a refinery at the site since 1915. The name Ioco comes from the company's initials.
City of Vancouver Archives, Pan N140B. Photo W.J. Moore

1922

Revellers woke up on New Year's Day to find the main rule of the road had been reversed. Student activism arrived this year as angry university students took to the streets. Radio arrived too, with six stations signing on by the end of the year.

Executive yacht. Sleek against the Coastal Mountains, the *Norsal*, launched in 1922 and the largest yacht of its type and time on the coast, was built to transport executives of the forestry firm Powell River Co. *City of Vancouver Archives, CVA 447-2508. Photo Walter E. Frost*

January 1

At 2 a.m., motor vehicles in British Columbia began driving on the right-hand side of the street. The change went surprisingly smoothly; there were no accidents.

February 4 Joe Fortes, celebrated English Bay lifeguard, died aged about 57. His funeral at Holy Rosary Cathedral was the most heavily attended in Vancouver history to that time, with thousands outside the packed church. A small fact about Joe that stays with you: he had, for all his life, one small well-thumbed book by his bed, apparently the only book he ever read: *The Imitation of Christ* by Thomas à Kempis. Joe arrived in Vancouver in 1885, jumped ship to settle here and, being an excellent swimmer, began to teach local people, especially kids, how to swim. He taught hundreds and hundreds of them, and they loved him for it. In 1901 he was appointed Vancouver's first official lifeguard and was credited with more than 100 rescues. In 1986 the Vancouver Historical Society named Fortes the Citizen of the Century.

Guarding English Bay. The city named Joe Fortes the first official lifeguard and special constable at English Bay beach in 1901. Originally he lived in a squatter's shack near the Sylvia Hotel, but in 1905 he moved to a small cottage near the bandstand in Alexandra Park. Still, his real home was the waterfront, where he taught children to swim and kept on eye on things generally.
City of Vancouver Archives, CVA 677-440

February 15 The investment firm Odlum Brown was incorporated.

February 18

Brothers M.J. Lannon and P.J. Ryan founded Vancouver College.

February 21 James Welton Horne died in Vancouver, aged 68. Born in Toronto, he achieved business success in Manitoba, then moved to Coal Harbour in March 1885 and invested in real estate, profiting as the CPR approached. As founder of the BC Electric Railway, Horne developed the street railway and interurban between New Westminster and Vancouver. Over his career, he was a Vancouver city councillor, provincial MLA and park board commissioner.

March 22 The *Weekly Optimist* (now the *Delta Optimist*) began publishing in Delta, operated by the Dunning family.

March 31 William Henry Armstrong died in Vancouver, aged 64. He was born September 18, 1857, in Stratford, ON. After 1902 his firm, Armstrong, Morrison and Balfour, built the Fraser River bridge at New Westminster, the Great

Elsewhere in BC

Government-owned liquor stores flourished in the province after they were introduced in 1921. There were 51 stores by March 1922, including seven in Vancouver.

In a move to curtail Japanese fishermen, fishing licences to "other than white, British subjects and Indians" were cut by up to 40 percent. Japanese Canadian fishermen formed the Amalgamated Association of Fishermen, chaired by Shinya Yoshida of the Steveston Fishermen's Association, to launch a court case against the restrictions They won their case in the Supreme Court in 1926, but the government enacted legislation to allow the discrimination to continue. The case went on to the Privy Council in England in 1929, where the fishermen won again, but by then many had left BC.

Broadcasting on All Frequencies

March 15 One consequence of Vancouver's always competitive newspaper market was the sudden proliferation of radio stations in the spring of 1922. Evolving technology and a creative interpretation of government regulations led to a no-holds-barred race to be the first Vancouver station to broadcast.

That honour went to the *Province*'s Station FE (later CKCD), which signed on March 13 at 8:30 p.m., broadcasting news and recorded music from the Merchant's Exchange Building to points as far away as High River, AB. The *Vancouver Sun*'s CJCE (later CKMO) went on the air two days later, and the *Vancouver Daily World*'s CFYC began reporting news and stocks on March 23.

Historian Charles Bruce described Vancouver's first radio broadcast as "an average news-day at the *Province*. A gang in Cork threatened to shoot Michael Collins. In Johannesburg radicals from the Rand mine war fired at General Jan Smuts. India faced political disaster, Salmon Arm fruit-men were sore at low prices, and fire swept the main street of Summerland. Fatty Arbuckle went on trial for the third time at San Francisco, MPs welcomed Agnes Macphail as the first woman to reach the House of Commons, and in Nova Scotia a Boston professor produced a new theory on the fire-setting Antigonish ghost. The weather was cloudy with rain."

According to the *Province*, a radio set to pick up the broadcasts could be had for $25 or, in a pinch, made at home. Radio in the early 1920s was more a sideline for newspapers than a commercial advertising prospect, so product endorsement was limited, at least in Vancouver. If listeners grew bored with local news, they could flip their dials to more distant stations and stories, picking up broadcasts from as far away as Oakland and San Francisco. Edmonton's CJCA and Calgary's CFAC, both also launched in 1922, were early commercial successes.

Vancouver's first live music broadcast was courtesy of the *Sun*'s CJCE when Miss Emma Heit, a stage performer from the Pantages Theatre, sang "Maytime" with accompaniment. The station was co-operated by Sprott-Shaw Community College's School of Wireless Telegraphy and remained student-run for much of its existence.

"I was introduced to broadcasting through CKMO. I was hired as an announcer," former student broadcaster Earle Connor told Dennis Duffy, a BC radio historian. "Within three weeks, I was chief engineer, because the chap who had been the engineer decided he could make more money if he went back as a wireless operator on the rumrunners. I stayed with them for about a year. The pay was $45 a month—when I got it. Occasionally the Sprotts would go off on their yacht in the summertime, and we'd work three months before they'd come back and sign the cheques."

It was August 1, 1925, before the Canadian National Railway radio station (CNRV) began broadcasting in Vancouver, and another 11 years before it became the CBC.

In the first rush to put stations on the air, broadcasters changed their call signs several times, broadcast with impromptu equipment, ran multiple call signs from the same station, broadcast on the same frequencies and launched "phantom stations" that were not truly independent entities, all symptoms of the frenzy to be first on the air.

Northern Railway bridge across False Creek, and early Granville and Main Street bridges, and paved many of Vancouver's streets. Armstrong caused a sensation in Vancouver in 1899 when he brought in the first steam-powered automobile.

April 24 Thomas Ladner, farmer and salmon canner, died at age 84 in Vancouver. Born at Trenant Park in Cornwall, England, he came to BC in 1858. Ten years later, with his brother William, he was the first to pre-empt land on the site of Ladner.

May 1 The Department of Education, spurred by a request from the Vancouver School Board, took over the education of deaf and blind children in the province. On May 1 the deaf students, 62 of them, moved into the new school at Jericho Beach. The blind students followed in September. The British Columbia School for the Deaf and the Blind had begun.

Also May 1
Richmond's first May Queen, Violet Thompson, was crowned at Brighouse Park.

June 22 Ontario-born grocer Robert Kelly died in Vancouver, aged about 60. He came to Vancouver in 1890 and worked for Oppenheimer Brothers before co-founding Kelly, Douglas and Co. Ltd., a wholesale grocery firm on Water Street in Gastown, in 1896. Five years later his partner, Frank Douglas, drowned en route from Skagway to Vancouver when his ship hit an iceberg and sank. Frank's brother Edward took over his role in the company. The firm introduced its own coffee in 1896, and its trade name, Nabob, became a household word. Kraft bought the brand in 1994, and it's now the second-biggest-selling roast and ground coffee brand in Canada.

September 12 William Farrell, the first president of BC Telephone, died in Vancouver, aged about 68. Born in Huddersfield, England, he came to Vancouver in 1891 and with associates formed the nucleus of the BC Telephone Company. In 1948 the William Farrell Building was built at Seymour and Robson as the company's head office.

Which university? University of British Columbia students, illustrating that spelling is important, form big letters with their bodies after taking part in a "Great Trek" to Point Grey to protest the delay in moving to their new campus.
University of British Columbia Archives [UBC 1.1/862]

September Johan (Johannes) Buntzen, the first general manager of the BC Electric Railway, died in Copenhagen at age 63. He came to Vancouver in the early 1890s, managed early development of the BCER from 1897, supervised engineering and electrical work at what became known as Buntzen Lake, and was in charge of the Lake Coquitlam powerhouse that provided Vancouver's electricity. He resigned from BCER in 1909 and retired to Copenhagen, his birthplace.

October 9 Robert McBeath, who had won the Victoria Cross in action in France in 1917

and was now a Vancouver police constable, was shot to death after jumping on the running board of a car and attempting to arrest the driver, Frank Deal, for drunk driving.

October 28 Students at the University of BC, frustrated by the provincial government's endless delays in moving them out to their new (and uncompleted) campus at Point Grey, took part in the "Great Trek." Nearly 1,200 of them, angry at having to study in the big and drafty Fairview Shacks on Willow Street, paraded through downtown Vancouver streets, led by the band of the Irish Fusiliers. The students then boarded streetcars that took them to Alma Road (now Alma Street) and the gates of the campus. The male students boarded Broadway West streetcars, while the women went on 10th Avenue cars. They continued their procession along the dirt trail that led through the forest to the unfinished site, joined forces at Point Grey and assembled to form a huge "UBC" with their bodies for the benefit of photographers. The government responded by authorizing a $1.5-million loan to resume construction. Even so, it wasn't until 1925 that the students could finally move in.

Fall Sumas Lake was pumped dry and the fertile land beneath claimed for farming, becoming the richest, most efficient, dairying and berry- and hop-growing region of the province. This ended centuries of Native use of the lake for hunting and fishing.

December 15
It became the law: women could now serve on juries in BC.

December 21 Isaac Oppenheimer, Vancouver businessman, died in Spokane, WA. He was one of the four Oppenheimer brothers who thrived here. In 1886 he opened a wholesale grocery warehouse in the Oppenheimer Bros. Building at Powell and Columbia, Gastown's oldest brick building (now owned by singer Bryan Adams). Oppenheimer Bros. became BC's largest business of its type and exists today as the Oppenheimer Group, Vancouver's oldest locally owned company. Isaac was an alderman from 1887 to 1889, with some of his term overlapping with his brother David's mayoralty.

Poet's memorial. Two First Nations men, Mathias Joe (left) and Dominic Charlie, gather at Pauline Johnson's memorial cairn in 1961. The writer was much loved, evidenced by the 1922 erection of the cairn despite her request that no such memorial be raised.
Gordon F. Sedawie photo, Vancouver Public Library VPL 13271

Also in 1922

After his wife, Grace, died, realtor Henry Ceperley sold their home, Fairacres, at Deer Lake in Burnaby and used the money to build Ceperley Playground in Stanley Park.

Electric power came at last to West Vancouver after seven years of appeals to the BC Electric Company.

Pacific Stages Transport began a bus route from Vancouver to Port Moody and Port Coquitlam. The service was later extended to Haney and eventually became Pacific Stage Lines. BC Electric formed its own intercity bus operation, BC Rapid Transit.

Charles Edward Tisdall, a walnut farmer, was Vancouver's first and only mayor selected under the system of proportional representation, in which the candidate for city council who got the most votes became mayor. He succeeded Robert Gale.

A memorial to poet Pauline Johnson, carved from natural rock by James McLeod Hurry, was unveiled near Ferguson Point in Stanley Park. The Women's Canadian Club had begun raising funds in 1913 for this cairn, which marks the resting place of the Mohawk poet's ashes. Incidentally, Johnson specifically decreed in her will that no memorial be raised.

The Shaughnessy Heights Building Restriction Act, which prohibited the division of single-family dwellings into apartments or housekeeping rooms, was passed in the provincial legislature.

Jacob Grauer established the Frasea Dairy Farm on Sea Island. It became Richmond's largest dairy farm, with 500 cows at one point. The farm was shut down in 1954 to make way for the expansion of Vancouver International Airport.

There was one automobile for every 12 people in Vancouver.

Baseball's Vancouver Beavers of the four-city Northwestern League disbanded. The team had won pennants in 1911, 1914 and 1922, then went into decline. It played at Athletic Park, at West 5th and Hemlock.

Tom Fyles, a postman, became the first person to complete a winter ascent of the Lions.

Canadian Pacific's *Empress of Japan* ended its service. This *Empress,* which first arrived in Vancouver on June 22, 1891, crossed the Pacific 315 times, steaming more than 4 million kilometres (2.5 million miles) and setting trans-Pacific speed records that were unchallenged during the ship's 22 years of active service. The *Empress* sat in Vancouver's harbour four more years before being sold.

Historian Frederick Hubert Soward, 23, began teaching in UBC's history department. In his early years he was known as "the boy wonder." Soward continued working until 1966 and headed the department from 1953 to 1963.

Anne Margaret Angus wrote the first UBC student play (*The High Priest*) performed by the University Players' Club.

Vancouver's first Good Citizen Award was given to fire chief John Howe Carlisle.

The Vancouver Business and Professional Women's Club was founded.

Ontario-born Gordon Wismer, who had arrived in Vancouver in 1907, established his own law firm in Vancouver. He became one of BC's best-known criminal lawyers and was the province's attorney general in the 1930s and 1940s.

With her husband, Ephraim, Anne Sugarman founded the Reform Jewish Sunday School. She had a full life, detailed in *Pioneers, Pedlars, and Prayer Shawls* by Cyril E. Leonoff.

Minnesota-born George Frederic Strong, 25, began to intern at Vancouver General Hospital. He became internationally known as a heart specialist. The G.F. Strong Centre is named for him.

Future senator Thomas Reid was elected a councillor in Surrey.

The vaguely castle-like building on the east side of Main at East 15th, which began life in 1916 as Postal Station C, became the Dominion Agriculture Building, a function it filled until 1962. It was vacant for three years and then was occupied by a special investigation branch of the RCMP until 1976. The building was vacant again until 1982 and fell into disrepair, but then a non-profit group was formed to restore it as a community centre, Heritage Hall, which opened in 1983. A funky fact: plant and animal fossils can be seen in the marble walls.

The wooden-hulled tug *Master* was built in Arthur Moscrop's False Creek Shipyard.

Presently maintained by an enthusiastic non-profit society, *Master* is the only Moscrop tug that has not been redesigned and that still uses its original steam engine. It attends maritime festivals and is docked in the Maritime Museum's Heritage Harbour, representing the steam towboats of the early 20th century.

H.R. Budd became president of the Vancouver Real Estate Board.

The Vancouver Information and Tourist Association changed its name to the Greater Vancouver Publicity Association.

Comings and Goings

According to historian Cyril Leonoff, "Benny Kubelsky was playing the Orpheum circuit in 1922, along with the Marx brothers, and accompanied Zeppo Marx to a family Passover seder in the home of David Marks, a Vancouver tailor. There he met the Marks' daughter Sadie. The couple married in 1927 and in the heyday of radio, under the stage names of Jack Benny and Mary Livingstone, became a world-renowned comedy team."

Arthur William Delamont, 30, came to Vancouver. Born in Hereford, England, as a young man he was active in the Salvation Army Band in Moose Jaw, SK. After his arrival here, he played trumpet at the Pantages vaudeville theatre and went on to lead the Kitsilano Boys' Band.

Notable births: radio personality **Jack Cullen** on February 16; restaurateur **Frank Baker** of the Attic restaurant on June 24; **George Henry Reifel,** who later donated a portion of Reifel Island to the Crown to maintain the George C. Reifel Migratory Bird Sanctuary, named for his father, on July 22.

The *Master* is the last surviving steam tug on the coast. It was built for Captain Herman Thorsen by Arthur Moscrop, considered the premier tugboat builder of his time, and launched at the Beach Avenue Shipyard in False Creek in 1922. The *Master* towed logs and barges from up the coast to mills in the Lower Mainland. The black diamonds on the tug's funnel in this photograph are the insignia of the Marpole Towing Co., which bought the *Master* in 1940. Retired in 1959, the vessel has been restored and is on regular display at the Vancouver Maritime Museum.
Vancouver Public Library, Special Collections, VPL 57549

1923

The park board addressed the issue of squatters in Stanley Park, a decades-long ban on most Chinese immigration took effect, and when the first sitting US president to visit Vancouver spoke, a huge crowd turned out to hear what would be one of his last speeches.

February 27 The *Surrey Gazette*, a weekly, began publication in White Rock.

March 2 Joseph "Fighting Joe" Martin, former BC premier (for three and a half months in 1900), died in Vancouver, aged 70. Born in Ontario in 1852, Martin, a former Manitoba MLA and cabinet minister, began practising law in Vancouver in 1897 and was elected MLA for Vancouver City in 1898. After Lieutenant-Governor McInnes forced Premier Semlin to resign in February 1900, Martin became premier. Four months later he was defeated by James Dunsmuir. He moved to England in 1908 and was elected to the British House of Commons in 1910. Back in Vancouver he tried (and failed) to get elected as an Asiatic Exclusion League candidate and lost out in a bid to become mayor. He became one of the city's largest landowners.

March 19 The BC Electric Railway inaugurated a motorbus line on Grandview Highway.

March 26 The *Province* published a special edition to mark its 25th year as a Vancouver daily.

March The CNR station had just been completed and the park board started work on an undeveloped parcel of land in front of the station, at the corner of Main and Terminal. Sir Henry Thornton, the first president of the CNR, provided a special track to bring sand and black soil from Chilliwack. Upon completion, the park—outfitted with benches and rare trees—was named after Thornton.

April When city engineer F.L. Fellows drew up plans for the proposed Canadian National and Great Northern Railways' passenger stations, he found himself with a nameless thoroughfare on his plan. Since it led to the stations, he thought Station Street would be a

A registration certificate, required under the Chinese Immigration Act of 1923 for Chinese living in Canada, shows Canadian Immigration stamps from 1925, 1931 and 1937. Until the act was repealed in 1947, Chinese immigration was practically banned. *Vancouver Public Library, Special Collections, VPL 30626*

Elsewhere in BC

John Turner, premier of BC from 1895 to 1898, died (no relation to the former prime minister).

Elsewhere in Canada

July 1 A new Chinese Immigration Act came into effect, virtually banning Chinese immigration to Canada. Only diplomats, people born in Canada, students and merchants were allowed to enter. During the 24 years that the act was enforced, only 44 Chinese arrived in Canada. Chinese Canadians long referred to July 1 as "Humiliation Day," and many refused to join in Dominion Day celebrations. The act was not repealed until 1947, and then only wives and children under 18 of Canadian citizens were admitted. Chinese were not able to come to Canada on the same basis as other immigrants until 1967.

Restrictions on Japanese immigrants continued. The quota (established in 1908) was reduced from 400 to 150 annually, but members of the immediate family were exempt from that quota...until 1928. After that year, family members were included in the quota of 150, virtually halting immigration from Japan.

The Canadian Northern Railway became part of the Canadian National Railway.

Elsewhere in the World

March 3 The first issue of *TIME* Magazine appeared.

Left: Vancouver's first motorbus, painted the familiar dark green colour of the BC Electric Company, hauls a load of local dignitaries on its inaugural run in March 1923. The vehicle had a 30-horsepower engine, hand-cranked of course, hard rubber tires and candles in lieu of a defroster. In the thick fogs so common in the city in those days, off-duty drivers came in to act as fog pilots, standing in the doorway to warn their partner back onto the road or trotting ahead trailing a white handkerchief. *City of Vancouver Archives, Trans P101.1*

good name. Fellows also named Terminal Avenue.

July 23 Sixteen Squamish-speaking bands were amalgamated into the Squamish Indian Band.

July 27 The official opening of the Prospect Point Signal Station, which was installed in Stanley Park to regulate all shipping in and out of Vancouver's harbour. The Signal Station, a two-storey structure, was made redundant by the construction of the Lions Gate Bridge, which opened in November 1938.

August Southam assumed control of the very successful Vancouver *Province.*

September 4 West Vancouver High School opened in the Hollyburn elementary school building.

September 8 A knee-slapper in today's *Province*:

Foreman: Yes, I'll give ye a job sweepin' and keepin' the place clean.

Applicant: But I'm a college graduate.

Foreman: Well, then maybe ye better start on somethin' simpler.

September 14 Nine-year-old Stuart Keate (future publisher of the *Vancouver Sun*) was listening to a radio broadcast of the heavyweight boxing championship between Jack Dempsey and Luis Firpo, "the Wild Bull of the Pampas." In his

Honest John Hosts Wobbly Warren

July 26 US President Warren Harding visited Vancouver, the first sitting president to do so. Premier John Oliver and Mayor Charles Tisdall hosted a luncheon in his honour at the Hotel Vancouver. More than 50,000 people crowded into Stanley Park to hear him speak, thrilled that such an important figure was visiting.

Exactly one week later, on August 2, Harding died of heart failure in San Francisco. The city was shocked and saddened, and the Kiwanis Club initiated a fundraising drive to pay for a grand memorial to Harding, who was a Kiwanian. The monument, designed by Vancouver sculptor Charles Marega (also a Kiwanian), was erected in Stanley Park at the site where the president spoke. It's still there today. (Harding was succeeded by Vice-President Calvin Coolidge.)

Shipping guide. Perched on the highest point of Stanley Park, the Prospect Point Signal Station was opened in 1923 to guide ships into the harbour. Long since decommissioned, the site is now a popular lookout, famed for its magnificent views. *City of Vancouver Archives, St Pk N93.1. Photo W.J. Moore*

Lotusland to Lalaland

September 3 The Great Pacific Highway opened in Cloverdale, linking Vancouver with California. "A smooth unbroken highway, dustless and rutless," the *Province* reported, "now undulates evenly from Vancouver to Los Angeles, linking two nations and joining three states to the Province of British Columbia." The new link, the *Province* said, was now the world's longest paved road. (Drive down 176th Street in Surrey and you link to I-5 in Washington. That route is this road.)

The road benefited from a planting effort by the Kiwanis Club of Vancouver, which put in 1,150 ornamental trees to hide some ugly clearcuts left by decamped lumber companies. At the end of the formal ceremonies, "one side of the highway through the village was then overspread with flax seed and borax for dancing. The Vancouver pipers piped, the New Westminster band played, and the many hundreds present danced gaily."

Flax seed and borax???

autobiography *Paper Boy*, Keate recalled that "when Firpo knocked Dempsey out of the ring, I dashed into nearby Granville Street and stopped the first car I could find. 'What's up, son?' asked the driver. 'Firpo has just knocked out Dempsey and won the heavyweight championship of the world,' I cried. Which, in retrospect, was an authentic harbinger of the career to come: I was not only first with the news, but had it totally wrong!" (After being knocked through the ropes, Dempsey returned to the ring and knocked Firpo down twice in the second round, finally knocking him out.)

October 1 The first ship of the Canadian government's mercantile marine left Vancouver with grain bound for Britain.

December 5 Radio was used for the first time in a Vancouver mayoralty election campaign. Candidate W.R. Owen, a former blacksmith, gave a 10-minute speech over Station CJCE. He won the election.

December 12 The Rotary Club held its first Christmas Carnival.

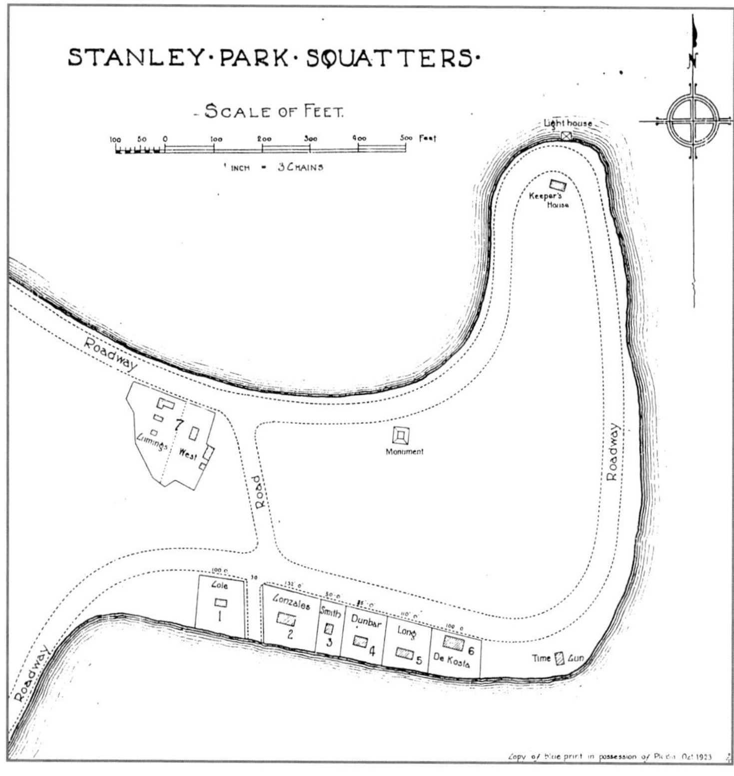

Acknowledging "squatters" in Stanley Park, the Vancouver Park Board in 1923 issued a map showing their whereabouts along the water. *City of Vancouver Archives, Map 649*

Also in 1923

Vancouver's population topped 130,000, a growth of 13,000 in two years.

The Vancouver Park Board issued a map showing the location of "squatters" in Stanley Park. The city had launched a court case in 1921 to expel these eight families, of aboriginal and European ancestry, from the park; the families appealed their eviction but lost the case in 1925. They were allowed to remain in their homes for a fee of a $1 a month until they were finally evicted in 1931. However, siblings Agnes and Tim Cummings at Brockton Point somehow managed to avoid eviction and remained in their home in the park until they died in the 1950s.

Diesel engines began to be used locally in tugboats this year, according to Agnes Rothary, writing in 1943 in *Ports of British Columbia.*

The oldest local functioning amateur sports organization in Vancouver, the Meralomas, was established as the Mermaid Swim Club. As other sports were added to the club, the name

"Meraloma" was coined from "mer" for mermaid, "al" for alpha and "om" for omega. The last "a" was added for the sound.

The Alcazar Theatre, built on Commercial Drive in 1913, was taken over by Vancouver Little Theatre. (The Alcazar has also been known as the York, the New York and the Raja.)

Burnaby got its first fire truck, a Model T Ford converted in his garage by mechanic (and fire truck driver) Bill Banks. He later converted a 12-cylinder Packard limousine.

Pacific Stage Lines and the BC Rapid Transit Company, subsidiaries of BC Electric Railway, began regular passenger service in the Fraser Valley.

The Burnaby Civic Employees Union Memorial Fountain was erected, designed by William Williamson of Westminster Monumental Works. Made of BC granite, the fountain was erected to honour union members killed in World War I. Originally located on Kingsway near Edmonds at the old Municipal Hall, in 1974 it was moved to Burnaby Village Museum.

The Women's Institute, a province-wide group of community-minded women, sparked the idea of creating a Crippled Children's Hospital in Vancouver. The name changed to Children's Hospital in 1947.

The Canadian Daughters League was established

with approximately 30 members. It is a fraternal and benevolent organization whose members believe in Canada and its people. Today it has about 300 members in British Columbia. There are three branches in the Lower Mainland with about 90 members.

The *Westender* first appeared (as the *West Ender*). Today it has a circulation of about 58,000.

The big wooded area adjacent to the University Endowment Lands, known today as Pacific Spirit Regional Park, was once a source of timber for the Hastings Sawmill. The logging, which started in 1860, ended this year. Then the land was endowed to the university. You can see second-growth Douglas fir, western red cedar, western hemlock and more here.

Ocean Park got its first post office.

It was featured in Ripley's "Believe it or Not" as the smallest in the world. People wrote from distant places just to get the postmark.

Writer Steve Gatensbury was born in New Westminster. He started work in the sawmill industry at 16. His "fly on the wall" history of the BC logging history is called *Once, To Learn It: A Lighthearted Account of a Fifty Year Adventure in the BC Lumber Industry*. He also wrote *Queensborough: Images of an Old Neighbourhood* about New Westminster.

Executive and judge J.V. Clyne, 21, graduated from UBC. He had worked summers as a cowboy, sawmill labourer, deckhand and placer gold miner, and went on to study marine law at the London School of Economics. He was called to the BC bar on January 8, 1927, and was

Pint-sized P.O. Good things come in small packages, luckily, for the Ocean Park Post Office, deemed to be the smallest in the world at the time.
City of Surrey Archives

appointed to the BC Supreme Court in 1950.

Scottish-born William Marr Crawford, shipping executive, was named president and managing director of Empire Stevedoring, BC's largest waterfront employer.

Vancouver boxing promoter Charles "Pop" Foster began training a future world welterweight champion, 17-year-old Jimmy McLarnin, who had been selling newspapers on the street in Vancouver.

British-born Charles Cleaver Maddams, a Mount Pleasant settler, who in 1888 had bought 2 hectares (5 acres) on the south shore of False Creek, transferred his Maddams Ranch to the Vancouver Park Board to cover his taxes.

Ballantyne Pier was completed, two years after work began in 1921. Although only a cargo storage and loading facility for Vancouver's busy port, the original pier was designed to look more like a triumphal gateway to the city than a warehouse.

Construction began on the Main Library, the science building, a power plant and several "semi-permanent" buildings at UBC; the Centre Lawn building at Essondale; and a bridge across the Second Narrows (not the present bridge).

Milk output at Colony Farm at Essondale, the mental hospital, reached almost a million pounds (453 tonnes). Among the more notable of the 62 Holsteins there was Colony Grebegga Valdessa, two years old, who produced 28,371 pounds (nearly 13 tonnes) of milk, a world record for her age group. (That's nearly 78 pounds/35 kilograms a day!)

Star milker. Colony Grebegga Valdessa—a lean, mean, milk-making machine—produced 78 pounds of milk a day for the Colony Farm at Essondale, a mental health facility.
Riverview Hospital Historical Society

Mrs. Tom Routley, president of Port Coquitlam's Women's Institute, thought it would be a good idea to have a joint May Day involving both PoCo schools, James Park and Central. Held alongside the Coquitlam River and ruled over by May Queen Evelyn Mars, it was the first Community May Day. It has been held every year since without a break and is likely the city's biggest annual event.

Port Coquitlam paid tribute to the men it lost in World War I with the construction of a cenotaph. It stands today in the park in front of city hall.

Coquitlam joined the Greater Vancouver Water Board. Annual rates were introduced: 75 cents for houses without bath, $1.15 for houses with.

Comings and Goings

Notable births: architect **Ron Thom** in Penticton on May 15; writer and teacher **Robert Harlow** in Prince Rupert on November 19.

December 9 Thomas George Shaughnessy, after whom the old-money Vancouver neighbourhood was named, died in Montreal, aged 70. Born in Milwaukee, WI, in 1853, Shaughnessy became a railroader and in 1882 was recruited over a glass of beer as general purchasing agent for the CPR. He became the railway's president in 1898 and held the job for 20 years. He was knighted in 1901 and became Lord Shaughnessy in 1916.

Fritz Ziegler, who had established Ziegler Chocolate Shops in 1921, died. His widow Wanda became president and grew the chain from three to eleven Lower Mainland stores.

1924

The news was dominated by a murder mystery involving high society, corruption and racism, and there was an ever-changing cast of newspapers and radio stations to keep Vancouver updated on developments. Meanwhile, the man who later created an iconic Vancouver restaurant chain started selling hot dogs.

March 11 Robert Cromie, owner of the *Vancouver Sun*, bought the *Vancouver World*, which had been in financial difficulty for some time, from Charles Campbell. Two months later, Campbell started publishing the *Evening Star*, with Victor Odlum, 44, as publisher and editor-in-chief. Now Vancouver had four dailies. A month and a half later, Campbell sold the *Star* to Odlum.

April 27 Mayor William Reid Owen presided over a ceremony unveiling the cenotaph at Vancouver's Victory Square. A memorial to Vancouver's soldiers who died in France, its inscription reads "Their name liveth for ever more / Is it nothing to you—All ye that pass by." At an annual ceremony on November 11,

Left: Courthouse Square. Prior to World War I, Victory Square was known as Courthouse Square, being the site of an impressive domed provincial courthouse. This building was demolished just prior to the war and the law courts moved uptown to Georgia Street. The site was redeveloped as a park after the war, using money donated by the Southam family, owners of the *Province* newspaper, located in a building across Cambie Street. When the cenotaph was added, the name was changed to Victory Square. *City of Vancouver Archives, CVA 99-1477. Photo Stuart Thomson*

Elsewhere in BC

July 29 North Vancouver's Phyllis Munday became the first woman to ascend Mount Robson.

October 29 From the *Province*: "A westbound Canadian Pacific Railway train heading for Vancouver was hit by an explosion...and among the five dead were Doukhobor leader Peter Verigin, 65, and John McKie, the newly elected MLA for Grand Forks." The cause of the explosion was never officially determined, but some speculate it was intentional and that Verigin was the target. The paper commented: "With the death of Peter Verigin...the breakup of one of the greatest communistic organizations in the world is forecast here."

Elsewhere in Canada

January 26 The Red Ensign became Canada's official flag.

Parliament passed the United Church of Canada Act, uniting the Methodists, Congregationalists and Presbyterians into the largest Protestant church in Canada. The act came into force on June 10, 1925.

Elsewhere in the World

August 9 A painting of President Warren Harding speaking to a huge crowd in Stanley Park on July 26, 1923, was presented to the US National Museum. The *Vancouver Sun* had commissioned the work by John Innes, a well-known Vancouver artist.

September 28 Two US planes landed in Seattle, having completed the first flight around the world.

Elsewhere in the Universe

August 21 The planet Mars was closer to Earth than it had been for many years, which lent exciting credence to the *Province*'s front-page story: "Mysterious signals picked up at Point Grey wireless station during the past few weeks culminated this morning in a recognized group of sounds which lead the operators to believe that Mars has succeeded in establishing communication with the earth. Four distinct groups of four dashes came in over the ether at 7:12 a.m., when Mr. W.T. Burford was on duty. These dashes were not in any known code but started on a low note, gradually ascending and concluding with a 'zipp.' The signals were not sent by spark nor continuous wave and the theory that Mars has at last managed to 'get through' is gaining support."

Right: Wong Foon Sing, the Chinese "houseboy," was front-page news in the *Vancouver Sun* when he was arrested for the murder of Janet Smith. Before his formal arrest he was abducted by a group of vigilantes who tried to beat a confession out of him. Given the anti-Asian racism of the time, it was no surprise that Wong was the prime suspect, but there was never any evidence that he did it. The case reached all the way to the floor of the provincial legislature, where alarmed politicians tried to pass a law to protect white women from having to work alongside Asian men. Eventually the hysteria died down, though the murderer was never identified.
Barrett/PNG

Remembrance Day, former service members gather here to honour their fallen comrades.

May 21 Manzo "Jack" Nagano, the first Japanese immigrant in BC (and possibly in Canada), died at age 69 in Kuchinotsu, where he had been born in 1855. At 22 he worked as a cabin boy on a British ship travelling from Nagasaki to New Westminster, arriving in 1877. He fished for salmon on the Fraser and later worked on the Gastown docks. He ran businesses in Yokohama, Seattle and Victoria, and pursued several ventures, including a hotel for Japanese immigrants. He prospered as an exporter of salted salmon. A mountain near Rivers Inlet was named for him in 1977.

June 20 Storekeeper Harry Eburne died in South Vancouver. In February 1875 he came to BC with his foster parents, and six years later, aged about 25, he opened the first general store and post office at the Sea Island end of the Fraser River. Originally named North Arm, the settlement was renamed Eburne and, later, Marpole.

June 21

Lady Alexandra, the flagship of Union Steamship Company's new excursion fleet, arrived from Scotland,

where it had been built and launched in February. With accommodation for 1,400 picnickers, *Lady Alexandra* was on the Howe Sound to Bowen Island run until 1953. Renamed *Princess Louise II*, the vessel served as a floating restaurant in Coal Harbour from 1959 to 1972, when new American owners towed it to Redonda Beach, CA, to become a gambling hall. Damaged in a storm there in 1980, the boat was scrapped.

July 1 On the first anniversary of enforcement of the Chinese Immigration Act, all Chinese-owned shops were closed for a day of mourning. All public amusements and activities were forbidden to Chinese residents, who were told not to watch the Dominion Day parade. Chinese leaders lectured on the Immigration Act and its humiliation of the Chinese Canadians.

WRIT OUT IN 'PEG SCANDAL

Thousands of Tons Paid for Never Delivered, Charge

WINNIPEG, May 1.—A writ was issued late yesterday in the court of King's bench by Solicitor General of Can- ...ainst the Canadian Coal ...ompany Ltd., claiming ...t of $106,628, alleged ...e been overpaid by the ...ment on contracts by ...endant company for the ...of coal to the Tuxedo barracks since 1920.

CHARGED WITH MURDER

WONG FOON SING

Wong Foon Sing, Chinese house-boy, who disappeared from the Baker home where Janet Smith was murdered, was found wandering on Marine Drive early this morning. He was apprehended and charged with murder.

MA... EXCE... FORECA...

Wild Exciteme... vails When Re... Announced

OTTAWA, May 1... twenty-four days of de... House of Commons thi... ing adopted the budg... majority of thirty-sev... vote was: For, 123; aga...

...OVA SCOTIA

THOUSANDS ARE

Murder in Shaughnessy Heights

July 26 Janet Smith was found murdered in the Shaughnessy Heights home of her employer F.L. Baker, a socially prominent exporter of pharmaceutical drugs. The Point Grey municipal police were summoned to investigate what at first appeared to be the suicide of the 22-year-old Scottish nursemaid. The police botched the case, and only the suspicions of the city's Scottish community reopened it. Sensational revelations involving the city's elite and political corruption revealed the widespread racism in Vancouver society.

A Chinese houseboy, Wong Foon Sing, had found the body, and on March 20, 1925, he was kidnapped by a group of vigilantes dressed in the hooded apparel of the Ku Klux Klan. For six weeks, he was shackled to the floor of an attic room in Point Grey and subjected to frequent beatings, death threats and other forms of intimidation to force a confession. (The kidnappers later turned out to be a group of police officials, a detective and members of the Scottish cultural organizations.) After Wong was released by the kidnappers, he was taken into custody by the police and charged with the murder of Janet Smith. Attorney General A.M. Manson later confided to a reporter that he knew the houseboy was innocent, but the Crown wanted to use his trial to flush out the real murderer, an admission which persuaded a Vancouver grand jury to order Wong released for lack of evidence. This crime and its astonishing aftermath were on the front page of local papers every day for months.

The murderer was never found, but Wong Foon Sing paid the ultimate price. His reputation in tatters and job prospects bleak, on January 1926 he chose to return to China.

July 28 Canada's Governor General Julian Hedworth George Byng, better known as Viscount Byng of Vimy, visited the municipality of Point Grey to lay the foundation stone for Lord Byng High School. A young student, Frances Dowman, presented a bouquet to the GG, who'd received a lot of bouquets for his service in World War I, which included commanding the Canadian Corps in the famous attack on Vimy Ridge in April 1917. There were five teachers and about 100 students at Lord Byng High School (compared to more than 1,000 today), but they weren't in the building when school began in September. For five months Lord Byng students attended classes at nearby Lord Kitchener School, finally moving into their newly completed building in March 1925. (Incidentally, the NHL's Lady Byng Trophy—awarded for sportsmanship combined with excellence—was donated by Byng's wife.)

October 21 CFYC carried a speech given by Prime Minister Mackenzie King at the Denman Arena in downtown Vancouver. This is considered to be Canada's first federal political broadcast.

The golfer who appears to be playing in the wilds of Vancouver in this 1927 picture is actually on the Hastings Golf Course, which opened in 1924. It survived until 1954, when the Empire Stadium was built on its grounds. *City of Vancouver Archives, CVA 99-1616. Photo Stuart Thomson*

Also in 1924

Twenty-two-year-old Nat Bailey hawked peanuts at local baseball games. When local car owners discovered the scenic loop through Vancouver along newly paved Marine Drive and Granville Street, Bailey was inspired to transform his 1918 Model T truck into a travelling lunch counter, which he parked every Sunday at Lookout Point on Southwest Marine Drive. Hungry sightseers crowded around, paying a dime for a hot dog or a nickel for an ice cream. On a hot summer day in 1924, one customer leaned out of his car and shouted, "Why don't you bring it to us?" That was the inspiration. Four years later, Nat Bailey proudly welcomed guests to the first White Spot drive-in.

The Hammond Cedar Products Company baseball team of the Dewdney League won the BC baseball championship. Harry Butler was the star pitcher. Harry's son Tom (long famous in Vancouver public relations circles) told us that his father, "like all his teammates, had a job in the sawmill at 40 cents an hour...but he got a $5 bonus for every game he pitched and won."

Hastings Golf Course opened. It lasted to 1954, when the British Empire Games took over the space.

The Pacific Coast Hockey Association folded, merging with the Western Canada Hockey League. The PCHA had been founded in 1911 by Frank and Lester Patrick with three teams: the New Westminster Royals, the Victoria Aristocrats and the Vancouver Millionaires.

Ranjit Mattu, star athlete, born in 1916 in the Punjab, came to Vancouver. He graduated with a BA from UBC as a star athlete in rugby and football. He coached Canadian high school football and later junior football to 1949. His Vancouver Blue Bombers were the Dominion champions of 1947, the first such championship won by Vancouver.

In community politics: William Reid Owen, the first blacksmith in the Mount Pleasant neighbourhood, became mayor of Vancouver, the first mayoralty candidate to use radio in his campaign in 1923. (He beat Louis D. Taylor, who beat him the next year for his fourth mayoral term.) J.M. Fromme, known as the "Father of Lynn Valley" because he built the first house there in 1899, became reeve of North Vancouver District. Thomas Reid became reeve of Surrey, a post he held for the next 10 years.

Lunch to go. The first incarnation of White Spot, this was a Model-T truck that a young Nat Bailey in 1924 transformed into a mobile lunch counter where tourists could buy hot dogs and ice cream at Lookout Point in Point Grey. *Photo by George Mittlestead, Courtesy White Spot and Triple-O: The White Spot Story, by Constance Brissenden*

Archimandrite Antonin Pokrovsky founded the Holy Resurrection Russian Orthodox Church in Vancouver. (An archimandrite in the Eastern church is either "the superior of a large monastery or group of monasteries" or an honorary title given to a celibate priest.)

Anne Sugarman was the founding president of the Vancouver Council of Jewish Women. The Vancouver Jewish Community Chest was also organized this year.

The Kinsmen Club of Vancouver was founded.

Charles Edward Findlater, 31, who came to Vancouver from England in 1918 to teach voice and piano, founded the Wesley Sunday School Choir. Ten years later it was renamed the Elgar Choir. Findlater conducted it until 1974.

Michigan-born Edgar Stewart Robinson, 27, was named head of the Vancouver Public Library. He ran the system for the next 33 years.

M.Y. Williams, a Canadian geologist, began the collection that today is the UBC Geological Museum.

Forest Lawn Cemetery opened.

Lansdowne Park, a horse racing track that opened on Lulu Island in Richmond, was named for a former Governor General. The peat bog on which the track was built acted like a sponge, and horses were known to run slower at high tide. Sam Randall, Thoroughbred racing promoter, ran the track from 1924 to 1945.

Hazing was banned at UBC.

Esther Fong Dickman became the first Canadian Chinese woman to graduate from UBC.

The Vancouver Judo Club was established with Steven Shigetaka Sasaki as sensei (instructor). Named the Tai Iku Dojo, it was the first recorded judo dojo in BC. Members practised in the living room of Mr. Kanzo Ui until the dojo moved to Dunlevy Street the following year. In 1926, Tomoaki "Tom" Doi and Takeshi Yamamoto, students of Sasaki, opened the first judo dojo in Steveston. Judo flourished throughout BC, and in 1932 the RCMP opened its own judo dojo at the Heather Street barracks. Sasaki became the force's official judo instructor, and 11 officers under his tutelage earned their first-degree black belts.

North Vancouver High School, which had opened in 1910 and was for many years the only high school on the North Shore, moved to its own building at 23rd and St. Georges.

Alexander Russell Lord began teaching at Vancouver's Normal School. In 1950 he retired as principal. Awarded the Fergusson Memorial Award in 1950 for his "outstanding contribution to education in BC," an elementary school in Vancouver is named for him.

Lansdowne race. The horses galloping toward the finish line were photographed in July 1928 in Lansdowne Park, which had been built in Richmond in 1924. The site is currently home to the shopping mall Lansdowne Centre. *City of Vancouver Archives, CVA 99-1742. Photo Stuart Thomson*

Charles Brakenridge became the Vancouver city engineer and ended up being the longest serving, holding the post for 22 years.

The Burrard Inlet Tunnel and Bridge Company ran into legal and financial difficulties. By the end of this year the municipalities of West Vancouver, Vancouver and the two North Vancouvers owned all the stock in the company.

Capt. John Cates returned from the BC Interior to Bowen Island to construct a house and run a hotel at Crescent Beach.

Harbour Navigation built the *Harbour Princess*, the first diesel-powered passenger boat on the coast, which carried passengers and freight to Wigwam Inn (up Indian Arm).

The Hotel Vancouver dismissed its Chinese workers, replacing them with whites. A year later, with the introduction of the minimum wage for sawmills, many Chinese workers were dismissed. In 1928, restaurant workers came under the minimum wage legislation, which further discouraged the hiring of Chinese, who would have been paid the same as whites.

Aero Garment Ltd. (originally the Vancouver Shirt and Overall Manufacturing Company) was founded. Vancouver's largest privately owned clothing manufacturer became one of the most successful Chinese businesses of its day. Owned by Charles Chan Kent, it was the first to manufacture permanent-press clothing in Canada.

The Japanese labour union newspaper *Minshu* (The Daily People) began publication under the leadership of Etsu Suzuki. It was closed down in 1941 after Japan bombed Pearl Harbor.

Curling became an Olympic sport for the first time in Chamonix, France. France, Great Britain and Sweden were the only countries to participate.

Comings and Goings

March 20 Sara Ann McLagan, newspaper publisher, died in Vancouver, aged about 69. She took over the *Vancouver Daily World* when her husband, John McLagan, founder and editor of the *World*, died in 1901. Sara Ann was the first woman publisher of a daily newspaper in Canada.

June 25 HMS *Hood* visited Vancouver. A Tyee potlatch was held during the 10-day visit. Three months later, in Topsail Bay, NL, the ship hosted a "Miss World" competition with 25 competitors. The winner was Miss Honolulu, followed by Miss Vancouver in second place and Miss Melbourne in third.

Notable births: department store executive **Charles "Chunky" Woodward** on March 23; **Arthur Erickson**, BC's most renowned architect, on June 14; **Lucille Johnstone**, executive at Rivtow and a legend in BC business, on November 11.

Henry Avison, the first employee of the Vancouver Park Board, died in Prince George at age 69. He cut Stanley Park's first trails (one is named for him), was its first zookeeper (the zoo was a bear tied to a tree), designed the park's first gardens and lived in a lodge by its entrance.

1925

The University of BC finally moved to its Point Grey campus, and Vancouver staked its first claim to being Hollywood North. Motorists could now drive to the North Shore across a bridge at the Second Narrows. And the local chapter of the Ku Klux Klan made news.

January 5 Newspaper report (included only because of the accused's age): "Bail in a dope case will be set at $5,000. L. O'Neil, 87, is to be arraigned before Magistrate Findlay in Police Court and charged with trafficking in narcotics under the Drug Act. Police will state that O'Neil did a brisk trade with a number of women, the tip to his activities coming from three women arrested recently."

January 8 A man was attacked by a shark in the First Narrows.

Newspaper readers woke up January 8, 1925, to the exciting news that a Vancouver city worker, repairing the underwater Seymour mains, had been attacked by a 7-foot shark. After a 15-minute fight, the city worker won, using an iron bar. The shark was hoisted ashore and destroyed.
The Province

City Diver Battles For His Life Against Shark

HAS NARROW ESCAPE ON BED OF INLET

JOHN G. BRUCE.

MAY HOLD UP WATER BILL

John Bruce Kills Sea Monster 90 Feet Under Water.

Fought Off Ferocious Attacks With Iron Bar For 15 Minutes.

NINETY feet below the turbulent surface of the Second Narrows, John G. Bruce, diver for the city, engaged in repairing the Se, mour mains, Wednesday afternoon, had the battle of his marine career with a seven-foot shark—and won. The black-grey monster was landed on the Seymour wharf just east of the site of the Second Narrows bridge, where it attracted considerable attention. The carcass was destroyed today. The diver has had several fights with devil fish, killing two recently.

MADE THREE ATTACKS.

"It was early in the afternoon while I was surveying the pipes for possible leaks that the shark appeared," said Bruce, in relating the story of the fight, with the reluctance characteristic of the seaman, "and I saw the dark shadow of his form coming for me.

January 17 The first organized game of football was played in Vancouver.

Two teams, one junior and the other senior, were put together at the University of British Columbia. The juniors were the first into the field of play, beating a team named the Tillicums 17–5. The seniors followed a week later, losing 7–6 to St. Mark's, the campus theological college.

February 7 Eleven crew members returning to the Japanese ship *Idzumo* drowned in fog-choked Burrard Inlet after their small ship's boat collided with a barge. A memorial service was held February 11 at Wesley Church.

March 20 The Ku Klux Klan popped up in the news when vigilantes dressed in their hooded apparel kidnapped a Chinese houseboy who worked in the house where Janet Smith was murdered a year earlier. They finally let him go when they realized he was innocent. The racist and anti-Catholic, anti-Jewish, anti-trade-union Ku Klux Klan, which started in the southern United States, had and has its followers

Elsewhere in BC

North Vancouver mountaineers Don and Phyllis Munday climbed Mount Arrowsmith on Vancouver Island. From the summit they spied a huge peak in the distant northeast, towering above all its neighbours. Their resolution to reach "Mystery Mountain" resulted in years of expeditions to what is now called Mount Waddington—at 4,019 metres (13,186 feet) the highest point wholly within BC. Don Munday described their attempts in an exciting 1948 book, *The Unknown Mountain*.

Elsewhere in Canada

June 10 The United Church of Canada was born, a union of Congregationalists, Methodists and two-thirds of the Presbyterians of Canada. It became the largest Protestant Christian church in Canada. An inaugural service, the first United Church service in Vancouver, was held on this date at St. Andrew's Presbyterian to celebrate the union.

October 17 Edward Flickenger, and Dr. Perry Doolittle arrived in Vancouver. On September 8, 1925, Flickenger, the Ford Motor Car Company's chief photographer, and Doolittle, founder of the Canadian Automobile Association (and now known as "the father of the Trans-Canada Highway"), had left Halifax in a brand-new 1926 Ford Model T. They drove 7,700 kilometres (more than 4,780 miles) across Canada to Vancouver. It was the first time an automobile had travelled completely across the country. For 800 kilometres (nearly 500 miles) they had to fit the Model T with railroad wheels because there was no road.

November 4 Canadian National diesel electric car No. 15280 completed a run from Montreal to Vancouver in a total elapsed time of 72 hours and an actual running time of 67 hours 7 minutes. (Compare that to the 39 days taken by the automobile.)

Headquarters of the Ku Klux Klan in Vancouver was, briefly, the Shaughnessy mansion built by lumber baron William Lamont Tait and known as Glen Brae. (Tait and his wife had died by then.) The hooded racists called the house their Imperial Palace and, according to neighbours, used to march around the garden carrying crosses of red electric lights. But the group soon faded away, in part because the national secretary absconded with the treasury.

City of Vancouver Archives,CVA 99-1496. Photo: Stuart Thomson

in Canada. The Klan was strongest in Saskatchewan in the late 1920s, but there was a chapter in Vancouver in 1925. KKK membership in Vancouver was said to be 8,000 at its peak—this is likely an exaggeration. At any rate, a local bylaw was passed prohibiting mask wearing and the number of Klan members dwindled to about 200.

March For five months Lord Byng students had been attending classes in the nearby Lord Kitchener School building. They moved into their now completed building this month. This is also the year that Lady Byng donated the cup, named for her, that is given each year to the NHL player who combines sportsmanship with excellence.

April 6 Sam Greer died, aged about 82. In 1882 this pugnacious 39-year-old Irishman (his nickname was "Gritty") established a farm on 65 hectares (160 acres) of land at Kits Beach. It came to be called Greer's Beach. But the land wasn't his. It belonged to the province, which in 1884 gave it to the CPR. Now Sam, his wife and their six kids were squatters. He refused to move. In 1887 the sheriff came, and Sam shot the sheriff. While that official healed, Sam and his family were ousted and his buildings levelled, and he spent some time in jail.

May 7 The *Beaver* memorial at Prospect Point was unveiled.

It commemorated the Hudson's Bay Co. steamship and HBC development of the West Coast.

June 12 The *Sun* had an item on page 2 about Vancouver Day. The *Province* followed with a story the next day. This first tribute to the city's pioneers was marked by the unveiling of a drinking fountain at the corner of Carrall and Water Streets. June 13 was chosen for the celebration because it was the day in 1792 on which Captain Vancouver explored Burrard Inlet and the date in 1886 on which the Great Fire occurred. Mayor Louis D. Taylor said that the event would be marked annually. But there's no other reference to Vancouver Day until June 13, 1929, four years later. And the 1929 report seems to be the last time the day was heard of.

August 11 Radio CNRV began broadcasting from a studio in the CNR train station.

The railway ran a national network heard on its trains all across the country. It eventually became the

Law courts. Its new location a sign that the downtown was shifting west, the provincial courthouse opened on Georgia Street in 1911, replacing the original law courts on Hastings Street. The original architect was Francis Rattenbury, who had also designed the Parliament Buildings in Victoria. "Ratz" was at the centre of a social scandal in the 1920s, when he divorced his first wife and married a woman nearly 30 years his junior. This photo of the north face of the law courts shows the King Edward VII fountain, sculpted by Charles Marega. It was later moved around to the west side of the courthouse, which since 1983 has housed the Vancouver Art Gallery.

City of Vancouver Archives, M-11-74.

The Bridge of Sighs

November 7 Before the Ironworkers Memorial, another bridge crossed Burrard Inlet at the Second Narrows. The North Shore municipalities joined to finance the project, and the *Vancouver Morning Sun* of November 6, 1925, devoted great swaths of print to the bridge, which opened to traffic the next day. (3,000 cars crossed it on opening day.) The *Sun* story made special mention of chief engineer William Smaill, who also designed the bridge. "To his skill and experience," the *Sun* wrote, "was due, to a very great extent, the outstanding success that attended the work from the start to the finish."

Not quite. Marine traffic was directed to pass beneath the bridge in the shallows near the shore, rather than out in deeper water. A barge going under on September 13, 1930, at low tide, became stuck beneath the span. Witnesses looked on in helpless horror as the tide began to rise, the barge began to crush against the bridge and the bridge began to buckle. No one was hurt, but the span was out of commission for four years.

The crossing was hit often by ships—three collided with it before the barge incident—and came to be known as "The Bridge of Sighs." It was gone by 1970.

The original Second Narrows Bridge featured two lanes for motor-vehicle traffic divided by a central railway track. When it opened in 1925 it provided the first road link to the North Shore; the Lions Gate Bridge would not be built for another decade. Unhappily, its structural drawbacks left it prey to regular accidents and closures, the longest lasting four years. *City of Vancouver Archives, CVA 371-2831*

CBC! Also this year, Arthur "Sparks" Holstead, who had been granted a licence to operate a 10-watt radio station, CFDC, in Nanaimo in 1923, brought the station's transmitter to Vancouver in a suitcase and went on the air. The federal government's broadcasting regulator objected and ordered him to stop transmitting, but public petitions demanded his return, and the station signed back on.

October 1 The Vancouver School of Decorative and Applied Arts opened its doors. Today it's known as the Emily Carr University of Art + Design. (The seed for the institute was planted in 1921 when a group of artists, educators and art patrons formed the British Columbia Art League to lobby the provincial and city governments for an art gallery and art school.)

November 2 A story in the *Province* told of plans to construct the Dominion Marine Observatory on Grouse Mountain. It would be built "when the highway to the top of the mountain is completed," according to the *Province*, which added that Mr. Edward Mahon, "well-known English businessman," would pay for the installation of the Mahon reflecting telescope. Thanks to "the clear and steady atmosphere" on the mountain, this telescope would "place the observatory at a single bound in the very forefront of the famous observatories of the world." The highway was finished in the spring of 1927, but nothing more was heard of the project.

Also in 1925

The University of British Columbia campus finally opened at Point Grey and granted its first honorary degrees this year. One of the graduates this year was 20-year-old Walter Gage, who earned his BA. His 50-year association with the university culminated in his retiring as president in 1975.

Gordon Shrum (born in Smithville, ON, on June 14, 1896) drove from Toronto in a Model T to teach at the physics department at UBC. He was 29. He taught at the university for nearly 40 years, heading the department for 23 of them.

Another graduate this year was Albert Edward "Dal" Grauer, 19, who earned his BA. He was president of the BC Electric Railway in the 1940s.

Burnaby's first fire department, made up of volunteers, was formed in South Burnaby. The chief of police also acted as fire chief.

Arthur Whalley opened a service station, general store and soft drink stand in Surrey. When Pacific Stage Lines opened a bus stop there, they called it Whalley's Corner. The name Whalley was officially adopted in 1948 for the community that sprang up around the establishment.

The Devonshire Hotel opened at the northeast corner of Georgia and Hornby Streets. (On July 5, 1981, it was brought down in a spectacular controlled explosion.)

The American Can Company Building at 611 Alexander St., admired by architects, was built. It was rehabilitated by architect Bruno Freschi in 1988.

The Koo family established what is now J.B. Hoy Produce, a family-operated store in the Kerrisdale neighbourhood of Vancouver, where operators wear white smocks to set out the veggies.

One-year-old Pacific Airways, under founder Don MacLaren, operated its upcoast fishery patrols from a flying-boat base at Jericho Beach.

Richard Cormon Purdy, who had started his chocolate business in 1907, sold the firm to Hugh Forrester.

Albert O. Koch, called the father of Congregation Beth Israel, came to Vancouver from New York via Montreal and at age 31 launched National Dress Co., Vancouver's first garment manufacturing plant.

Adam Urias dePencier, Anglican priest, became the archbishop of New Westminster.

The first neon lights flickered on in Vancouver, installed by enterprising Granville Street merchants.

In a 1925 Progress edition, the *Point Grey Gazette* said there was nothing in Point Grey between 16th Avenue and the Fraser River "other than the few scattered houses in that corner of the municipality bounded by Oak, Cambie, 16th and King Edward." (King Edward is equivalent to 25th Avenue.) In other words, there was nothing between King Edward and the Fraser River but forest. The article also refers to the "Muskee-Ehm Indian Reserve." Point Grey municipality was created in 1908 and merged with Vancouver in 1929. The editor of the newspaper, by the way, was Earle Birney.

The Giant Dipper roller coaster began operating at Vancouver's Hastings Park. It cost $65,000, was almost a kilometre long and its cars reached speeds of over 60 kilometres an hour (almost 40 mph). The longest sheer drop was 18 metres (60 feet). It was torn down on March 6, 1948, to make room for an extension of the racetrack.

By special arrangement with the Hudson's Bay Company, four-point blankets were sold to tourists for $18 a pair at the gas station at Fry's Corner, the junction of Fraser and Pacific Highways in Surrey.

Twenty-six-year-old Ivor Ackery got a job as an usher at the Capitol Theatre. Ten years later, as Ivan Ackery, he became general manager of the Orpheum Theatre, a job he held for more than 30 years.

Vancouver's John Edward "Jack" Underhill, 23, became Canada's top male badminton star, winning numerous BC and national championships over the next two decades.

Charles and Martha Lovell moved from Agassiz to Port Coquitlam. They are mentioned here because they raised five daughters, named for the flowers their mother loved: Daisy, Rose, Lily, Violet and Pansy.

R.C. "Harry" Galer, who had been a hard-working alderman on Port Coquitlam council for several years, was elected mayor. (The R.C. stood for Roger Charles.) Immensely popular, he served as PoCo's mayor for 20 years. He died in 1968 at age 94.

Vancouver's Locarno Crescent was named this year in honour of the Locarno Pact (1925), the outcome of a multinational conference on the establishment of guaranteed borders in Europe. Locarno is a town in Switzerland.

Film historian Michael Walsh writes that *The Winds Of Change*, a 1925 drama directed by Frank Lloyd, began the tradition of Hollywood producers filming on location in Vancouver. The movie was a gold-rush melodrama in which Capilano Canyon stood in for the Klondike.

Harold Merilees, called Vancouver's first great ad man, began at the advertising department in Spencer's Department Store.

Comings and Goings

March 23 Wilson Duff, anthropologist, was born in Vancouver. His entire career centred on the study of Northwest Coast Indians.

Rudolph Valentino came to judge a tango contest in the dance pavilion near Stanley Park.

1926

In the midst of a building boom, the city started planning for a population of a million. Stanley Park lost its tallest Douglas fir, a chalet on Grouse Mountain attracted Vancouver's wealthy, and Babe Ruth came to town and appeared on stage with the mayor and the police chief.

The Plan Was an Unplanned Triumph

February 1 Vancouver City Council established the Vancouver Town Planning Commission, following passage of the province's Town Planning Act. The act gave councils the authority to prepare official town plans and coordinated transportation plans; establish and enforce zoning regulations; consider any matters dealing with the physical development of the municipality. The first commission was made up of nine citizens, Mayor Louis D. Taylor, and representatives from the school, harbour, park and sewer boards. It hired Harland Bartholomew and Associates, town planning consultants from St. Louis, MO, to prepare a comprehensive town plan for Vancouver.

Bartholomew's report, submitted in December 1929, began, "Few cities possess such a combination of nearby natural resources, a splendid harbor, a terrain ideally suited for urban use, an equable climate, and a setting of great natural beauty." He planned for a city of 1 million people focused on the "great seaport" of Burrard Inlet. The Fraser River banks and False Creek would be industrial. Businesses would spread evenly over the central business district to "prevent undue traffic congestion," and the nearby West End would provide apartments close to jobs.

According to Dr. Ann McAfee, a Vancouver city planner from 1974 to 2006, "The Bartholomew Plan was never formally adopted by City Council. Nevertheless, over the years, much of Bartholomew's vision was realized." The most recognizable evidence of the Bartholomew Plan today is the central boulevard down Cambie Street, south of King Edward.

January 19 Charles Gardner Johnson, called "the father of Vancouver's shipping industry," died in Vancouver, aged 68. Born February 8, 1857, near Dunblane, Scotland, he went to sea in 1870. In the 1880s he left seafaring to farm in Manitoba. This did not work out well, and on September 5, 1885, he arrived in Vancouver, broke, and went to work for the CPR as a labourer. In 1886 he opened a shipping and insurance agency, the first in the city. C. Gardner Johnson and Co., at Hastings and Granville, became one of the city's major shipping agents.

January 27 The newly created West Vancouver Town Planning Commission banned the construction of temporary waterfront shacks and unsightly summer camps. It also banned industry, and West Vancouver became a residential suburb of Vancouver.

January 31 Final day of business at the assay office at 501 Granville (in the old post office).

April 25 Newspaper headline: Vancouver's Building Activity Shatters All Records.

May Howard and Alma Fletcher opened West Vancouver's first theatre, the Hollyburn, on Marine Drive near 18th Street.

July Anatole Portnoff was one of a group of Russian immigrants who arrived this month in Vancouver aboard the *Empress of Canada*, only to discover that the passports issued to them by the British consulate in Harbin were not sufficient to get them into the country. They were ordered to remain aboard the *Empress* and return with it to Russia. But Archimandrite Antonin Pokrovsky, who had founded Holy Resurrection Church in Vancouver in 1924, took an interest in their plight. As Portnoff described it: "I will never forget the moment: we were standing on the upper deck, admiring the beautiful morning and the city we were not destined to live in, when we spotted a majestic figure—a gray-haired elder, a Russian monk, advancing toward the ship along the pier. We could not believe our eyes that in this faraway country, thousands of miles from our native land, we were actually seeing a Russian Batyushka, with a big cross on his chest, wearing a kamilavka. He walked straight to us, and we all rushed to him to get his blessing." With the help of Fr. Antonin and a local businessman from Russia, the immigrants were allowed to stay in Canada.

September 19 The first seaplane flight from Montreal to Vancouver ended in the city. It had taken eight days.

Elsewhere in BC

Randolph Bruce, who had made a fortune in mining and devoted much of his life to good works and public service, was appointed Lieutenant-Governor.

Elsewhere in the World

Seattle-born Sadie Marks, who lived for a time in Vancouver and first met Benny Kubelsky here in 1922, met him again in Seattle. They hit it off, got married and went on to entertainment fame, he as Jack Benny, she as Mary Livingstone.

September 30 The Vancouver Women's Building at Thurlow and Alberni was dedicated.

September Hide Hyodo Shimizu was the only teacher of Japanese ancestry hired to teach in a public school in BC. Born in Vancouver in 1908, Hyodo completed first year at UBC, transferred to the Vancouver Normal School, received her teaching certificate and began teaching Grade One at Lord Byng School. She was limited to teaching Japanese Canadian students only. In 1942 she was appointed supervisor of the school system in the internment camps in BC.

September Here's an interesting excerpt from a September 1926 report by Constable W.J. Hatcher of the BC Provincial Police, Westminster District, regarding the policing of Port Coquitlam: "At times the auto traffic is very heavy on the Dewdney Trunk Road, a count at different times shows that from 250 to 300 an hour pass along this highway, especially on Sunday afternoons and evenings." Constable Hatcher appended a statement of expenditures for the month: salary was $106.50, office supplies totalled $12.75, travelling expenses amounted to $6.30, equipment was 60 cents, and "prisoners meals" cost $2.64. There is no indication of how many prisoners were fed that month.

October 14 Thomas John Janes, stagecoach owner and driver, died in Vancouver, aged 71. He arrived in Granville (later Vancouver) on October 31, 1883, and opened a butcher shop, then began operating Janes Stage, the first stagecoach line to carry passengers between New Westminster and Vancouver. The route was along Westminster Avenue (now Main Street and Kingsway).

The original Tomahawk Barbecue, opened in 1926 in North Vancouver, was an early drive-in restaurant in the Vancouver area—"the first," according to its website—though business still mainly consisted of sit-down customers at the lunch counter. *Courtesy Tomahawk Restaurant*

November 2 The Society of Notaries Public of BC was incorporated. Membership in the society was optional until 1956, when statutory amendments made it compulsory.

November After the 1925 construction of the bridge across the Second Narrows, industrialist W.C. Shelly had a vision that a popular resort could be placed atop Grouse Mountain if a road could be built to make it easier to get up there. Shelly, who had made his fortune in the bakery business (with 4X Mills and Canadian Bakeries Ltd.), established Grouse Mountain Highway and Scenic Resort Ltd. to build the road and a chalet at the end of it. Grouse Mountain Chalet opened in November, a magnificent wooden structure, built—without a nail—by Scandinavian craftsmen. There was a huge stone fireplace, bearskin rugs, fine furniture and dining ware. The popularity of the place "was particularly evident on Saturday nights," a fan wrote, "when a trail of limousines streamed up the highway to deliver guests for the evening." Shelly's group also commissioned Tom MacInnes to write a book, *Chinook Days*, to mark the opening of the highway. It's an old-fashioned combination of local Native legends and early Vancouver history.

December Vancouver shoppers had a brand-new department store. David Spencer opened his nine-storey

Swish chalet. Once the North Shore became accessible through the construction of the Second Narrows Bridge, W.C. Shelly built a luxurious chalet resort at the top of Grouse Mountain, as seen in this 1926 photo. *City of Vancouver Archives, Out P230*

Right: A lighthouse without a keeper? The Brockton Point (shown here) and Prospect Point lighthouses were converted to automatic. *City of Vancouver Archives, S-5-6*

building at the corner of Hastings and Richards Streets. The store went five storeys below street level as well, providing customers with 29,700 square metres (320,000 square feet) of shopping space...and Spencer's toyland offered a paradise for children.

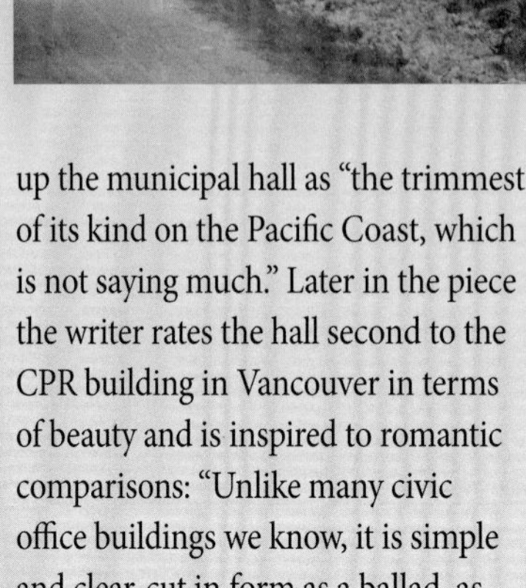

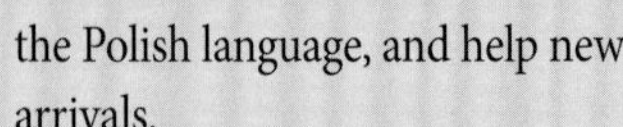

Also in 1926

The local newspaper world got complicated: Victor Odlum's *Evening Star* became the *Morning Star* and took over the *Morning Sun*'s circulation. The *Evening Sun* (which had been the *World*), took over the *Evening Star*'s circulation. The city was now back to three papers: the *Morning Star*, the *Evening Sun*, and the *Province*—the latter the biggest of the three.

Meanwhile, Henderson's Directory listed six radio stations in Vancouver: CNRV, run by the Canadian National Railway for its train passengers, operated from studios in the CNR station on Main Street; CFYC was operated by Commercial Radio Ltd; CFCQ (later CKMO) operated out of 500 Beatty, home of the Sprott-Shaw Radio Co., which had been teaching the technical aspects of radio for years; CKFC was a "United Churches" station; CKCD was owned by the *Province* newspaper; and CFDC was owned by the Sparks Co. CFDC had gone on the air in Nanaimo in 1923 but moved to Vancouver in 1925 and changed its name to CKWX, the oldest existing call letters in local radio.

Prospect Point and Brockton Point lighthouses were destaffed, converted to automatic control.

The *Richmond Record* ran an article titled "Our Town Hall Luck," summing up the municipal hall as "the trimmest of its kind on the Pacific Coast, which is not saying much." Later in the piece the writer rates the hall second to the CPR building in Vancouver in terms of beauty and is inspired to romantic comparisons: "Unlike many civic office buildings we know, it is simple and clear-cut in form as a ballad, as firm and strong in line and colour."

Butcher shop owner James Inglis Reid set up a $25,000 fund for Vancouver General Hospital as a memorial to his teenaged son Knox, who drowned off Bowen Island. The fund was used for therapeutic services for boys.

The Greater Vancouver Water District was incorporated. The first chief commissioner was Ernest Albert Cleveland, after whom Cleveland Dam was named. (In 1991 the GVWD was folded into the Greater Vancouver Regional District.)

By the 1920s the Dutch immigrant community in metropolitan Vancouver had become large enough to organize major social events. In 1926, Holland Society members aided in the establishment of the first of BC's 36 Christian Reformed Churches.

The Council of Jewish Women opened a neighbourhood house in Strathcona.

Seven friends started the Polish Friendship Society in Vancouver to maintain the Polish identity, preserve the Polish language, and help new arrivals.

The Vancouver Board of Trade made a grant to the University of British Columbia for the purpose of establishing a faculty of commerce. It also assisted in the formation of the Canadian Chamber of Commerce.

The tallest Douglas fir ever recorded in Stanley Park, 99 metres (325 feet) tall, toppled.

The North Burnaby Board of Trade was established.

The first Japanese union, the Nihonjin Rodo Kumiai, was admitted to the Vancouver Trades and Labour Council as the Japanese Camp and Millworkers Union.

The first of several Ladies Auxiliaries to the Fraternal Order of Eagles was founded in 1926. (They are attached to but entirely independent of the men's Aeries.)

The Soroptimist International club, founded in 1921 in Oakland, CA, saw its first Vancouver chapter established this year. The Soroptimists now have 16 chapters in metropolitan Vancouver. The club's name was coined from the Latin *soror* meaning "sister" and *optima* meaning "best," loosely interpreted as "the best for women." The club is a nonpolitical service organization for business and professional women who wish to give something back to their communities.

North Vancouver mountaineers Don and Phyllis Munday came within 18 metres (60 feet) of the top of Mount Waddington, BC's highest peak.

The mining company Placer Development Limited was incorporated this year in Vancouver. In 1987 it merged with Dome Mines Limited to form Placer Dome.

Charles H. Scott became principal of the Vancouver School of Decorative and Applied Arts, a post he held until his retirement in 1952. Jock MacDonald, one of the first abstract painters in Canada, came to Vancouver, aged about 29, to teach at the school.

The Native Sons of British Columbia published *Romance of Vancouver*.

Yasutaro Yamaga organized the Maple Ridge Berry Growers Co-operative Exchange in Haney, the first agricultural producers' co-operative whose membership consisted of both Japanese and non-Japanese farmers.

A wooden truss bridge was constructed over the Coquitlam River to link the Dewdney Trunk Road with Pitt River Road. (That stretch of the Dewdney is now part of the Lougheed Highway.) The truss bridge replaced an old plank bridge that had been closed for two years for reasons of safety. The new bridge was painted red, and the "Red Bridge" became a prominent PoCo landmark, keeping the name even when it was painted in other colours. (Its modern replacement has been deliberately coloured red.)

Charles Davies became an alderman in Port Coquitlam. He held that office for 21 years. Then he was elected mayor and served in that capacity for another 9 years, an unbroken 30 years of service to the city.

Built by the CPR in what was then wide-open space, the Langara Golf Course and clubhouse opened in 1926. The Vancouver Park Board bought the property in 1973, and it is now an urban haven for golf enthusiasts.
City of Vancouver Archives, Bu N322. Photo W.J. Moore

Whistler's first sawmill was built by the Barr brothers on Green Lake. At its peak it employed up to 50 men and gave the PGE more business than any other stop on the line.

Langara Golf Course was established southeast of 49th and Cambie.

Three Scandinavians, Oscar Pearson, Ole Anderson and Andrew Israels, built Hollyburn Lodge to promote the recreational potential of Hollyburn mountain. They hauled lumber salvaged from the old Naismith Mill buildings, a mile down the mountainside.

Hudson's Bay Company extended its store at Granville and Georgia. The original 1893 store at that corner was demolished and an addition created that echoed the style of (and was seamlessly attached to) the adjacent 1913 store.

John Hendry Park on the east side (the park that surrounds Trout Lake) was donated to the city by Aldyen Hamber, daughter of Hastings Sawmill owner John Hendry (for whom the park was named), and her husband Eric Hamber, a future Lieutenant-

In a major building project at the Hudson's Bay store at Granville and Georgia, an addition was seamlessly added in 1926, creating the imposing block seen today.
City of Vancouver Archives, Bu P77. Photo Gowen Sutton Co. Ltd.

Mayor Louis Taylor as catcher was in campaigning mode for this appearance with Babe Ruth, the Yankee slugger. Nine days later he would face re-election for the first two-year term in the city's history. (Until then mayors were elected annually.) Whether or not Ruth's visit had anything to do with it, Taylor successfully held onto office for his sixth term.
City of Vancouver Archives, CVA 1477-107. Photo Dominion Photo

Governor of BC. Meanwhile, Douglas Park was established in the Riley Park/South Cambie neighbourhood. It had been a Chinese vegetable farm—and before that a small milk ranch, and before that a pasture to feed the oxen of logger Jerry Rogers, and before that, forest.

The Joe Fortes Memorial Drinking Fountain was placed in Alexandra Park. Much of the cost had been raised from pennies donated by local schoolchildren—hundreds of whom had been taught to swim by Joe. The bronze-granite fountain was designed by Charles Marega.

The road to Whytecliff and Horseshoe Bay was opened, as was a park at Whytecliff Point, called Rockcliffe at first. A tea room with a dance floor was built about where the present lookout is.

Pacific Stage Lines opened a new depot at Dunsmuir and Seymour with ticket offices, inside bus bay for loading, restaurant, travel agency and more.

King George School became Magee School to avoid confusion with another school named King George in Vancouver. The new name commemorated Hugh Crawford Magee, a successful pioneer farmer who took up land in Point Grey in the 1860s, the first farmer to settle on the North Arm of the Fraser. Magee died in 1909.

Dr. Herbert Nowell founded the Dominion Herbal College. Now located in Burnaby, it's the oldest college of its kind in North America.

On the death of her husband J. Stewart Jamieson, Laura Jamieson succeeded him as Burnaby Juvenile Court judge, the first BC woman in this position.

The Vanderpant Gallery opened on Robson Street. Run by photographer John Vanderpant, it became a centre of intellectual life in the city for more than a decade.

The Asahi baseball team won the Terminal League Championship—the first of several league championships it amassed over the next 15 years.

Comings and Goings

January Wong Foon Sing, a houseboy in the Shaughnessy home in which nanny Janet Smith was murdered in 1924, and who was an early suspect in the killing, returned to China.

November 5 Queen Marie of Romania (a granddaughter of Queen Victoria) paid a visit. En route to Vancouver from Seattle, the queen stopped at Samuel Hill's home in Blaine, went into the kitchen and prepared pancakes and honey for the family. Her train left at 10 a.m. for Vancouver, where she was greeted by the mayor and Lieutenant-Governor. She briefly toured the city before attending a luncheon given by the Women's Canadian Club, an event the *Province* covered, listing the names of every member of every committee involved in the do. Afterwards she visited UBC, and that evening she went to a banquet, where she was escorted into the hall by Scottish bagpipers. The next morning the train again stopped at Blaine and Queen Marie visited the Peace Arch, erected to commemorate the 100th anniversary of peace between the United States and Canada. (Sam Hill was one of the driving forces behind the Arch.)

November 29
Baseball's Babe Ruth hammed it up on stage in Vancouver during a personal appearance tour of North America. He posed as a batter, with Vancouver mayor Louis D. Taylor crouching behind him as catcher, and the city's chief of police umpiring.

Future businessman Jack Diamond, 17, arrived in Vancouver from Poland with a straw suitcase and the clothes on his back.

Francis William Caulfeild, an English land developer, made his last visit here, aged about 86. He never lived in BC but in 1899, attracted by the beauty of the coast, purchased waterfront property east of Point Atkinson, in an area called Skunk Cove. He renamed it Caulfeild (thanks!) and developed it as a "charming Old World community," with winding lanes (later roads) following the natural contours of the wooded slopes. Caulfeild died in London in 1934 at age 94.

Notable deaths: **Susanna Gertrude Clarke Mellon**, a long-time supporter of arts and worthy causes and a founder (in April 1894) of the Art, Historical and Scientific Society, died in Vancouver on June 17, aged about 82; **Zebulon Franks**, storekeeper and the first Jewish religious leader in Vancouver, died here, aged about 62.

1927

Two Vancouver institutions had their start, with the openings of the lavish Orpheum Theatre and the fabled Hotel Georgia. One of Vancouver's deadliest fires destroyed a West End apartment building. And a future king who took an afternoon ride on the PNE roller coaster liked it so much he went back in the evening.

January 22 The cornerstone of Grace Hospital was laid.

February The first permanent branch of the Vancouver Public Library opened in Kitsilano at 2375 West 4th Ave. VPL now maintains an extensive system of 22 branch libraries throughout the city.

March 7 Golden Ears Provincial Park was created.

April 15 Rudolph Verne formed the first ski club in western North America, the Hollyburn Pacific Ski Club. Members claimed Hollyburn was "the finest territory for Cross-Country Skiing in the Dominion." The first organized ski competition was held from April 15 to 17.

April 15 Charles Trott Dunbar died in Vancouver, aged about 66. Dunbar arrived in Vancouver in 1888 and in 1906 was promoting development of Dunbar Heights, with lots "selling like hotcakes." On February 3, 1910, he won approval from the BC legislature to incorporate the Port Moody, Indian Arm and Northern Railway. A year later, 100 men were employed grading the CPR line from Port Moody to the north side of Burrard Inlet opposite Barnet, along his proposed route.

Currently rebranded as the Rosewood Hotel Georgia, the historic Georgian Revival-style building opened in 1927, towering over the corner of Georgia and Howe.
City of Vancouver Archives, Hot N36

May 7 Official opening of the Hotel Georgia. Historian and writer Sean Rossiter has unearthed an astonishing wealth of facts about the hotel and its staff and guests, who included Edward, Prince of Wales (later the abdicating King Edward VIII); George, Duke of Kent (later King George VI); John Barrymore; John Wayne; Bob Hope; Bing Crosby; Frank Sinatra; Nat King Cole, who integrated the hotel; Marlene Dietrich; Katherine Hepburn; and Beatrice Lillie. My favourite story describes the sharp-witted Lillie sailing into her room, followed by a flock of reporters. She spots a pigeon on the windowsill, opens the window and asks the pigeon, "Any messages?"

May A 9 p.m. curfew was introduced in North Vancouver City as vandalism got out of hand.

July 4 CPR Piers "B" and "C" were officially opened as part of Canada's Diamond Jubilee festivities.

July 8 One of the worst fires in Vancouver's history for loss of life occurred at the Royal Alexandra Apartment at Bute and Comox Streets.

Elsewhere in BC

August 20 John Duncan MacLean became premier on the death of John Oliver.

Elsewhere in Canada

The federal government amended the Indian Act to make it illegal to obtain funds or legal counsel to argue for Native land claims. The Allied Indian Tribes, formed in 1916 to lobby for Native rights, dissolved and indigenous resistance went underground.

Elsewhere in the World

May 20 Charles Lindbergh took off from New York and aimed his *Spirit of St. Louis* for Paris. On May 21 Lindbergh landed in Paris and the world went nuts.

The biggest theatre of its time in Canada, the 3,000-seat Orpheum opened in 1927, dazzling visitors with its gigantic chandelier and costly decorations. On show at the time of this photo were "Gene Austin Victor Record Star" and other big Orpheum acts, and Richard Dix in *Shanghai Bound*.
Vancouver Public Library, Special Collections, VPL 11036. Stuart Thomson photo

A painter's varnish and thinners caught fire and turned the building into an inferno in which eight people died.

July 21 Yip Sang (also known as Yip Chun Tien), a Chinatown pioneer, died in Vancouver. An orphan, he sailed by junk from Hong Kong to San Francisco at age 19; worked 17 years as a dishwasher, cook and cigar maker; then came to Canada in 1881 and settled in Vancouver's Chinatown. At first he sold sacks of coal door to door. He established the Wing Sang Co. in 1888, and the next year he built the Wing Sang Building (51–67 East Pender), the oldest standing structure in Chinatown. In the early 1900s as a CPR contractor, Yip supplied labourers in BC and Alberta and sold rail and steam tickets. He was married four times and had 19 sons and four daughters. His family donated his papers to the Vancouver City Archives. Yip Sang is prominently featured in *Saltwater City*, Paul Yee's excellent history of Chinatown.

August 17 John Oliver, premier of BC, died in office at age 71. He was born July 31, 1856, the son of a lead miner, in Church View Cottage in Hartington, England. When the mine closed in 1870 the family immigrated to Canada, where John worked as a labourer on the CPR before becoming a farmer and then a politician. He was an early reeve of Delta and became premier in 1918, a post he held until his death. James Morton wrote his biography in 1933: *Honest John Oliver: The Life Story of the Honourable John Oliver, Premier of British Columbia, 1918–1927.*

September 2 The Rogers Building at Pender and Granville, erected in 1912 and there to this day, was sold for $1 million, the city's largest real estate transaction to that time. The purchaser was General Frank "One-Arm" Sutton. The 10-storey white terracotta building was named for Jonathon Rogers, a Welsh-born

A Palace on Granville

November 7 The Orpheum Theatre opened its doors only eight months after breaking ground, and Vancouverites lined up around the block to see Marie White and the Blue Slickers, followed by a comic revue, dance and a short film (Phyllis Haver in *The Wise Wife*).

When local businessman J.F. Langer agreed to build the Orpheum for the San Francisco theatre chain of the same name, he had grand plans: a master architect, crystal chandeliers, silk wall hangings, gold leaf, air conditioning, a $45,000 organ—the theatre was to be the greatest of Vancouver's great vaudeville houses, lit in neon, with all the latest technology, equipped to show "photoplays."

His plans were, for the most part, realized. The architect—his name was Marcus Priteca, and he was born in Scotland—designed dozens of entertainment palaces in his long career, imbuing them with a richness that still dazzles visitors, and he outdid himself with this glorious "Spanish renaissance" (the description is loose) picture house. A gigantic chandelier, imported from Czechoslovakia, threw its light upon the thousands of seats below, the ceiling of the upper lobby was inspired by an Indian temple, and costly paintings and hangings surrounded early theatregoers on every side.

The theatre was, as intended, the belle of the 1920s ball, suggesting palatial opulence beyond even her competitors' wildest dreams. The final bill for construction and furnishing was somewhere near $1.25 million, most of it visible; the gold-leafed ceiling alone was worth $100,000. Stars of stage and screen often attended premieres, or just dropped by to say hello, and the overall atmosphere of effortless glamour was a roaring success.

In the audience on opening day was a 14-year-old kid named Hugh Pickett who went on to have a long association with the Orpheum and Vancouver's entertainment industry generally.

Twenty-eight-year-old Ivan Ackery happened to be manager at a rival theatre, the Victoria on Victoria Drive near East 43rd. "I remember going down Granville Street that year, and I thumbed my nose at the Orpheum," he reminisced in later years. "Oh, I was so jealous." He had no idea that about eight years later they'd put him in charge of running the place.

Another theatre that opened this year was the Columbia in New Westminster. Like the Orpheum the Columbia offered a combination of vaudeville, movies and live music. And like the Orpheum it eventually became a movie house. Today, after extensive refurbishing, it is the Burr Theatre, named in recognition of New Westminster-born actor Raymond Burr.

contractor who—in a nice illustration of the importance the arrival of the Canadian Pacific Railway would be to the city—was the first person to step down onto the platform when the first passenger train pulled in in May 1887. "I feel that I am parting with an old friend," Rogers said about the sale.

September 21 One of the CPR silk trains derailed near Yale.

When these trains, carrying silk from Asia, sped east across the country, all other trains were shunted to sidings to let them pass. Even a special train carrying Prince Albert (the future King George VI) west on a royal visit was moved aside to let the silk through. So a derailment of one of these trains got a lot of attention. Ten cars of silk came thundering off the rails 3 kilometres (2 miles) east of Yale, and five of them ended up in the Fraser River. The value of the silk in the submerged cars was estimated at $1.5 million. This was the first accident in 20 years of the service. "During the past few months," the *Province* said, "an enormous amount of silk has been despatched from Vancouver. It averaged a monthly value of $25,000,000 to $30,000,000."

November 5 Woodward's had a big advertisement in the *Vancouver Sun*. Headlined "36 Years of Continuous Progress," the ad showed the company's expansion over the years, with a drawing of the first store on Main Street in 1891. The first store at the "present location" (Hastings and Abbott) had opened in 1903 with just over 4,000 square metres (43,560 square feet). The 1927 store had more than 33,000 square metres (357,108 square feet), more than eight times larger. Much of the ad was devoted to explaining Woodward's fight against the "price combines." "The old timers," the copy says, "will remember our fight against the Drug combine in the early days when we stood alone...At present there is a Tobacco combination trying to cut off our supplies unless we raise our prices. This we refuse to do."

November 8 The *Province* reported that "the last two totems preserved at the Musquiam [sic] Reserve, Point Grey, were presented to UBC on Thanksgiving Day by Chief Tsem Lano at the final event on Varsity's annual 'homecoming' celebration programme."

November The dragon figurehead of the *Empress of Japan* was installed on a concrete pedestal overlooking the First Narrows entrance to the harbour. The ship itself, which criss-crossed the Pacific from 1891 to 1922, had been scrapped in 1926 and the figurehead dumped. Frank Burd, publisher of the *Province* at the time, learned of its disposal and with a handful of like-minded people decided to rescue it. A plaque was attached, stating the figurehead was a gift to the citizens of Vancouver. The weather treated the dramatic old dragon badly, and in 1960 it was replaced with a fibreglass copy. The original has been carefully restored and is on display in the Maritime Museum.

Too striking a symbol to be tossed, the dragon figurehead of the *Empress of Japan* was rescued from the scrap heap and installed in 1927 overlooking the First Narrows entrance to the harbour.
City of Vancouver Archives, CVA 447-284. Photo Walter E. Frost

Also in 1927

Vancouver's population was rising by about 1,000 people a month.

Kew Ghim Yip began to practise medicine in Chinatown. He had been born in Vancouver in 1902 but had taken his medical training at Queen's and interned as a doctor in Ann Arbor, MI, because of BC restrictions on Asian hospital interns. Yip treated patients for more than 40 years, from 1927 to 1968.

J.M. McCallan's home at the northeast corner of West 67th Avenue and Hudson Street, built in 1912, became Vancouver's first Children's Hospital.

The Salvation Army opened what is now called "old Grace Hospital" at 26th Avenue and Heather Street. The cornerstone for that building was to be laid by Premier John Oliver, but he was ill that day, so Vancouver banker Mayne Hamilton and architect Enoch Adams performed the ceremony.

Voters in North Vancouver City and North Vancouver District approved a new hospital bylaw. The North Vancouver General Hospital opened in 1929.

Ethlyn Trapp, radiologist, born July 18, 1891, in New Westminster, earned her MD this year at McGill. She went on to have a distinguished career, becoming the first woman president of the BC Medical Association (1946–47).

Yacht club. Ready except for the landscaping, the permanent clubhouse for the Royal Vancouver Yacht Club was built in 1927 at Jericho Beach.
City of Vancouver Archives, BU N321. Photo W.J. Moore

The Royal Vancouver Yacht Club, formed in 1903, opened a permanent clubhouse at Jericho Beach on English Bay. Since 1905 it had been in a two-storey floating clubhouse in the shelter of Deadman's Island.

Leon Mandrake, born in 1911 in New Westminster, began touring with his magic show. By the 1940s he had become a top box-office attraction.

The Greater Vancouver Publicity Association answered 24,000 phone calls for information this year. In comparison, the association's successor, Tourism Vancouver, handled 2.5 million inquiries in 2004, a combination of phone calls; email, mail, and web inquiries; and in-person inquiries at the visitor centre.

Kiyoko Tanaka-Goto opened a brothel on the upper floor of 35 West Hastings. She ran the place, with 12 girls, from 1927 to 1941. Her story, recounted in *Opening Doors*, an excellent collection of oral histories, is a fascinating look at the Vancouver of the time.

The North Burnaby Public Library opened with 125 books.

Major J.S. Matthews, soon to become the city's archivist, ran unsuccessfully for the Vancouver Park Board (he ran again, again unsuccessfully, in 1928). At the time he was director of the Art, Historical and Scientific Society, the predecessor of the Vancouver Museum.

Louis D. Taylor got elected mayor. Again.

A young Grouse summer employee, 17-year-old Lindsay Loutit, formed the Grouse Mountain Ski Club to provide new skiers with lessons and equipment rentals.

The C.D. Howe Company built the Alberta Wheat Pool grain elevators at the foot of Cassiar Street.

Greeks in Vancouver (there were about 2,000 at the time) joined to found the St. George Orthodox Hellenic Community.

B'nai Brith Women was founded.

Kosaburo Shimizu was ordained by the United Church and went to work at the Powell Street United Church, which soon became one of the focal points of activity for the Japanese community in Vancouver. Shimizu was born September 13, 1893, in Tsuchida, Japan, and came to BC about 1906.

Furnished apartments at Burrard and Thurlow rented for $45 to $80 per week.

UBC began collecting ethnographic material, much of which is now preserved at the Museum of Anthropology on the university campus.

Comings and Goings

April 9 A banquet was held at the Hotel Vancouver in honour of visiting Governor General Viscount Willingdon of Ratton, who had assumed the office on October 2, 1926. Willingdon Avenue in Burnaby is named for him.

April 26 Arctic explorer Roald Amundsen visited Vancouver. He told of his dirigible flight over the North Pole.

August 16 The Prince of Wales (later King Edward VIII) and his brother Prince George (later the Duke of Kent and, still later, King George VI) visited Vancouver. It was Edward's third time here. The first was in 1919, the second 1924. While he was here, Edward tried out the Giant Dipper roller coaster at the Pacific National Exhibition one afternoon and liked it so well he returned in the evening.

Notable births: scientist and politician **Pat McGeer** on June 27; future mayor **Thomas "Tom Terrific" Campbell** on October 5; politician **Grace McCarthy** on October 14; sculptor **Jack Harman**.

Notable deaths: **Carl Gottfried "Charles" Doering**, who established the Doering and Marstrand Brewery and ran the Stag and Pheasant saloon on Water Street, died in Vancouver on April 15 at age 71; **Phil Jackman**, one of the Royal Engineers who came to BC from England in 1859, died aged 92. After the corps disbanded in 1863. Jackman stayed behind, building roads and acting as New Westminster's one-man police force, toting drunken miscreants to jail in a wheelbarrow.

1928

Vancouver runner Percy Williams returned from the Olympics with two gold medals and was greeted with a waste-paper parade (the Vancouver equivalent of a ticker-tape parade) on Granville Street. The city got its first automated traffic light and its first White Spot restaurant. And the mayor nearly lost his head.

January 1 St. Francis-in-the-Wood Anglican Church in Caulfeild, West Vancouver, was consecrated. It was designed by Henry A. Stone, a local resident, businessman and early benefactor of the Vancouver Art Gallery.

Also January 1

Sixteen-year-old Ivy Granstrom made her first entry into the chilly waters of English Bay in the Polar Bear Swim. Miss Granstrom, blind from birth, went on to appear at 77 consecutive Polar Bear events.

January The General Gordon School Band was formed in Kitsilano under the direction of 36-year-old Arthur W. Delamont, once a Salvation Army trumpet player (as a younger man he played in an English band led by the composer Edward Elgar). It later became the famous Kitsilano Boys Band. Delamont led the band for five decades.

January The Women's Institute Hospital for Crippled Children at 8264 Hudson St. admitted its first patient.

March 1 Capt. W.D. "Davey" Jones, the first man appointed to fire the Nine O'Clock Gun, died at age 85...at, appropriately, 9 p.m.

March 19 The Japanese Hall and Japanese School at 475 Alexander St. was dedicated and played a vital role as a community gathering place. It's still there, a heritage building.

March Fenwick Fatkin staged a display of daffodils in the community hall at Bradner, in conjunction with local growers. Bradner became known as a floral centre and in 1932 held its

Elsewhere in BC

April 23 Agnes Deans Cameron died. There's a movie in her life. She was born in Victoria on December 20, 1863, and died there at age 64, but spent a good deal of time in Vancouver and was the city's first woman high school teacher and first woman principal. She was once fired for allowing students to use a ruler during a drawing exam. But that's not the whole story. In her mid-40s she travelled 16,000 kilometres (almost 10,000 miles) up the Mackenzie River to the Arctic Circle and wrote a book about the trip, *The New North: An Account of a Woman's 1908 Journey through Canada to the Arctic.* It was a smash.

July 18 "After twelve years of Liberal rule," the *Province* reported, "the people decided it was time for a change." Did they ever! The Tories, under Simon Fraser Tolmie, 61, took 32 of the province's 48 seats, including every seat in Vancouver and Victoria. Tolmie was a veterinarian who had once been chief inspector of livestock for the Dominion. He was premier from August 21, 1928, until November 15, 1933. Duff Pattullo became leader of the opposition.

July 20 On the *Province*'s front page: **Trio Conquers Mystery Mountain, Straddling Knife-edged Peak Higher Than Man Has Ever Climbed In B.C.** The "mystery" mountain was Mount Waddington, the highest peak wholly within British Columbia, and the climbers were Don and Phyllis Munday of Vancouver and A.R. Munday of Winnipeg. The paper's headline was not quite accurate; the Mundays themselves never claimed to have conquered the mountain. What they had reached was the second highest of Waddington's peaks. The next year the Mundays began using skis to explore the immense snowfields of the mountain. This marked the beginning of widespread ski exploration in the Coast Range. (Climbers Fritz Wiessner and Bill House were the first to climb Waddington's main peak, in 1936.)

Seen here on Mount Victoria in the Rockies in 1925, Vancouver mountaineers Don and Phyllis Munday shot to fame when the Vancouver *Province* claimed in 1928 that they had peaked Mount Waddington, the tallest mountain in BC. In actual fact, they had only reached Mount Waddington's second-highest peak.
The Province

Elsewhere in the World

May 31 Australian aviators Charles Kingsford-Smith and Charles Ulm, along with Americans Harry Lyon and James Warner, took off from Oakland, CA, to make the first flight across the Pacific Ocean. Kingsford-Smith briefly lived in Vancouver with his family when he was a young boy. A year later he flew from Ireland to Harbour Grace, NL, becoming the first man (non-solo) to cross both oceans by air. A school in the city has been named in his honour. It's at 6901 Elliott St.

1928

In the 18th major bridge accident in three years, the *Norwich City* struck the Second Narrows Bridge in 1928. Fed up, shipping interests took the bridge owners to court—and won—but the bridge remained. *City of Vancouver Archives, CVA 99-1826. Photo Stuart Thomson*

first flower show, attended by huge crowds, with a grand concert and dance in the evening.

April 23 The *Norwich City* struck the Second Narrows bridge in the 18th major bridge mishap in three years. Shipping interests took the Burrard Inlet Tunnel and Bridge Company to court, maintaining the bridge was a hazard to navigation. The Privy Council found against the bridge company, but the bridge remained.

May 7 The 95-foot *St. Roch* was launched by Burrard Dry Dock. Built for the RCMP of Douglas fir and Australian "iron bark," and reinforced to withstand ice pressure, the ship was designed as an Arctic supply and patrol vessel.

May 25 A 6-cylinder, 125-horsepower La France pumper was placed in service at Firehall No. 11. Built by La France Fire Engine and Foamite Ltd. in Toronto, it weighed 5 tonnes (5.5 tons), cost $14,945 and was in service until December 8, 1966. For many years after that, people walked by it or let their children play on it at Ceperley Park. "Then," according to VFD's Rob Jones-Cook, "during the summer of 2004 the Vancouver Park Board hired a group of students to refurbish it. They have done a wonderful job and it is now 'assigned' to Stanley Park Fire Department where...many more children for many more years will have the fun of 'driving' old Shop No. 77 to fires."

June 16 Nat Bailey, who had been selling snack food to motorists off the back of his truck at Lookout Point on Southwest Marine Drive, established a permanent restaurant in a small log hut at 67th and Granville, calling it the White Spot Barbecue. Over the years it grew into a large dining room, but many of his patrons preferred to eat their "Triple-O" burgers in their cars: the first White Spot drive-in.

July 1 Vancouver's longest-serving postmaster, G.H. Clarke, began his term. He served to March 30, 1947, or 18 years, 8 months.

July Gordon Farrell, 38, became president of the BC Telephone Company. His father, William, had been the company's first president.

August 1 Surrey held its third annual municipal picnic on Bowen Island. Over the years, some 500 to 600 people would attend the event each year, taking a day trip to Pitt Lake, Bowen Island, Sechelt or even Victoria. Union Steamship Company boats were hired and special trains

Mounties' ship. The *St. Roch*, pictured quiet in its berth, was launched in 1928 and built to withstand the Arctic ice as an RCMP Arctic supply and patrol vessel. *City of Vancouver Archives, Bo N243. Photo Charles H. Smith*

Upgrading from a drive-in hot dog stand, Nat Bailey opened the first White Spot Restaurant in 1933 on Granville and 67th, launching a franchise that continues today.
City of Vancouver Archives, CVA 99–4930. Photo Stuart Thomson

laid on by GNR or BCER. The picnics continued until 1946, when the influx of new residents made them impractical.

August 14 The fireboat *J. H. Carlisle*, named for the long-serving fire department chief, was launched with retiring Chief Carlisle proudly looking on. The boat was put into service September 1 at No. 16 Station at the south foot of Drake Street.

August 25 A BC Airways Ford Trimotor, the biggest airliner in Canada at the time, crashed into Puget Sound while trying to fly under the fog after a passenger challenged the pilot for being reluctant to take off. All seven aboard were killed. BC Airways had begun flying the Trimotor from Lulu Island on a route between Seattle and Vancouver in early August.

Also August 25 A statue of the famed Scottish poet Robert Burns (1759–96) was unveiled in Stanley Park by the Rt. Hon. Ramsay Macdonald, the former British prime minister. The bronze and granite statue is an exact replica of one standing in Burns' birthplace in Ayrshire, Scotland. (Local Scots annually mark Robbie Burns Day on January 25, but it was in the 1930s that fervour was particularly marked. Even the Chinatown Lions' Club organized an annual Burns dinner, complete with haggis served with a sweet and sour sauce.)

August A private company, the Vancouver Armoury Association, was formed to raise funds and acquire land to build an armory. The association built the shell of the structure, then turned it over to the Crown. This complicated procedure—made necessary because Parliament was reluctant to spend money on new facilities in the aftermath of World War I—gave us Bessborough Armouries at 2025 West 11th. The official opening was not until March 27, 1934, when the Governor General, the Earl of Bessborough, dedicated this structure that was named for him.

August The Rev. J.W. Ogden, an amateur artist of some skill, wrote a letter to the *Province*, an angry, impassioned attack against "the notorious Group of Seven," a collection of whose paintings had recently arrived from Ottawa.

September 8 According to the *Vancouver Star*, the first airmail from eastern Canada (Ottawa) arrived in Vancouver.

September 14 Olympic dual gold-medal winner

Percy Williams came home to what Premier Simon Tolmie described as "perhaps the most remarkable home-coming in the history of British Columbia." Thousands of people jammed Granville Street from the Canadian Pacific Railway station to Georgia Street to cheer Percy on. "The demonstration affected spectators in the Fairfield Building," one newspaper report said, "to such an extent that they tore up the contents of waste paper baskets, and sent the fluttering scraps out over the crowds as confetti." Williams, a King Edward High grad, won gold medals at the Amsterdam Olympics for the 100- and 200-metre races. He is still the only Canadian to win two gold medals in track and field.

Raised high by cheering teammates, gold medal-list Percy Williams of Vancouver had won both the 200- and 100-metre dash at the 1928 Amsterdam Olympics.
Vancouver Public Library, Special Collections, VPL 13295

October 17 Voters in Vancouver, Point Grey and South Vancouver okayed amalgamation of the three communities, to take effect January 1, 1929. Vancouver's southern boundary, which had previously been 16th Avenue, was now the Fraser River.

October 18
Vancouver got its first automated (i.e., not manually operated by a police officer) traffic light.

October 20
The first talking motion picture to be shown in Vancouver, *Mother Knows Best*, opened at the Capitol Theatre on Granville Street.

November 11 Regular services commenced at Canadian Memorial Church in Vancouver, 10 years to the day after the Armistice. Rev. G.O. Fallis, who was a chaplain in France during World War I, built the church as a peace memorial to the soldiers who died in that war. Funds for the church and its 10 stained glass windows (one for each province and the Yukon) were collected from Canadians across the country with the aim of making this a truly national church. The organ in the church was donated by Americans in memory of their countrymen who died serving in the Canadian armed forces.

November 29 The North Vancouver section of the Pacific Great Eastern Railway was closed. The line, which ran between North Vancouver and Horseshoe Bay, had opened in 1914, but it began losing money soon after the road to Horseshoe Bay was completed in 1926.

December 2 Campbell Sweeny died in Vancouver on his 82nd birthday. Born in Philipsburg, QC, he arrived in the city in 1887 to manage the first Bank of Montreal, became superintendent of the bank's BC branches in 1901 and retired in 1914. He was involved in the city in a great many other ways, as one of the original governors of UBC, a president of the Vancouver Board of Trade, honorary life president of the Vancouver Club, sportsman and, later, sports executive. His interests were many: cricket, lacrosse, rowing, rugby, tennis and more.

December 4
Vancouver mayor Louis D. Taylor blew a silver whistle to signal the start of construction on the present Hotel Vancouver.

December An interim receiver was appointed to oversee William Shelly's Grouse Mountain Highway and Scenic Resort Ltd. (By the summer of 1935 the property and everything on it—road, chalet, light and power lines, water and sewage systems, unfinished buildings—reverted to the District of North Vancouver for non-payment of $20,000 in taxes.) This was a better year for Shelly on the political front: he was elected to the BC legislature, and Premier Simon F. Tolmie appointed him finance minister and minister of industry. He was later named president of the executive council—the cabinet.

Also in 1928

The old Hastings Mill, site of Vancouver's first real industry, was demolished.

The last of the Fraser River riverboats stopped running, superseded by vehicular traffic.

Planning for a new airport began this year. Sea Island was selected as the site to replace Vancouver's original airport, a 16-hectare (40-acre) piece of land south of what is now Alexandra Road.

Union Steamship Company built a hundred cabins on Bowen Island to promote visits to the island. A handful still exist.

The National Harbours Board built a railway tunnel below Esplanade west of Lonsdale in North Vancouver. Now owned by BC Rail, the tunnel is 499.8 metres long (1,640 feet) and runs from St. Andrews Avenue to Chesterfield.

The CPR began ferry service from Steveston to Sidney on Vancouver Island. Fog, ice and floods hampered the service.

A blizzard of anecdotes swirl around Louis D. Taylor, Vancouver's most frequently elected mayor, but it would be hard to beat this 1928 gem: Taylor was aboard the first airplane flight from Victoria to Vancouver, or, more precisely, from Victoria to a landing field at Minoru Park in Richmond. The arrival of the Ford Trimotor attracted the park's racetrack crowd as the plane taxied toward them. Mayor Taylor leaped out of the plane and began to stride forward toward the crowd. He was struck by the plane's propeller, still whirling, and suffered a skull fracture. A few weeks later he was up and about, apparently as good as ever. Aviation pioneer Don MacLaren, his tongue firmly in cheek, later commented: "It sliced off the top of his head, you know, and knocked him unconscious. They said if he'd had an ounce more brains he'd have been a dead man."

The BC Electric Co., which started in 1903 and controlled local electric lighting, streetcar firms and gas companies, was purchased by Montreal-based Power Corporation.

Pitt Meadows got electric light.

Jane Kilmer was the first woman elected to Port Coquitlam city council (beating Vancouver to that distinction by nine years). She continued winning for most of the next 40 years except for a two-year spell in 1946–48 when she lost by three votes. She was the longest-serving woman alderman in BC history. Her actual terms on council add up to 34 years, and in all that time she missed only about 10 meetings.

The Building and Construction Industries Exchange of BC was founded, largely to clean up unscrupulous bidding practices in the city. It's now known as the Vancouver Regional Construction Association.

The United States established a consulate in Vancouver.

In sports and recreation, the UBC Thunderbirds won the provincial football championship under their coach, Dr. Gordon Burke. Soccer's New Westminster Royals captured the Lower Mainland's first national title. Golfer David Lambie "Davey" Black, 44, won the first BC Open. He was the pro at Shaughnessy Golf Club from 1920 to 1945. Vancouver's Crystal Pool was opened. "Coloured" people (including Chinese and Japanese swimmers) could not use it, although that would eventually change.

After shipping knocked out the aerial telephone cable, a submarine cable was laid to link Vancouver with West Vancouver. It was now possible to phone from Horseshoe Bay to Vancouver.

An acrobat died at the Orpheum Theatre after a fall

in a vaudeville act. Some say his ghost haunts the theatre still.

The Royal Vancouver Yacht Club's Eight Bells Club was formed this year for club members seeking a burial at sea—actually just off the RVYC's Point Grey location. Family and friends of the deceased sail out and pour the ashes into the bay, then return to the club and have an informal social.

Already in motion, a girl raises her arms to dive into the Crystal Pool. Opened in 1928, the Crystal was originally racially segregated, but that would change in 1945. It was replaced in 1974 by the Vancouver Aquatic Centre. *City of Vancouver Archives, CVA 99-2215. Photo Stuart Thomson*

Tudor Manor. Another elegant building to grace the beach, the heritage Tudor Manor was completed in 1928 in the West End. *City of Vancouver Archives, Bu N411. Photo W.J. Moore*

Names of the deceased are engraved on a bell that hangs in the yacht club bar. A bell is traditionally rung eight times at the end of a watch, thus the name.

The Ukrainian Labour-Farm Temple Association, known for its mandolin orchestra and choir, built a community hall at 805 East Pender at Hawks.

The Wilderness Patrol, directed by J.P. McGowan, was released this year. According to film historian Michael Walsh: "Made to sidestep British film quota legislation, this quickie silent Western featured Winnipeg-born screen cowboy Bill Cody riding the North Vancouver range."

Vancouver Terminals Ltd. recommended a long line of cement docks on the Vancouver shore from Wreck Beach to Jericho. "It is a malodorous mistake," they said, "on the part of pretty town planners that for all time the entire waterfront must be gummed up and reserved for hot dog and fried onion joints, and allocated as a pleasaunce of yellow sands for tourists and ladies in scant attire and the like. WE WANT BUSINESS!" (That word "pleasaunce" means "a pleasant spot.")

Charles Cleaver Maddams died in Vancouver aged about 73. In 1888 he bought 2 hectares (5 acres) on the south shore of False Creek in Mount Pleasant, and in 1890 he established Maddams Ranch, which, in its day, was the pride of the community. Because of nearby Chinese farms, he named the area China Creek. In 1923 he transferred the ranch to the park board to cover his taxes. Maddams Street, originally a Mount Pleasant trail, was named for him.

Japanese residents of Steveston built a Buddhist temple.

It had been in the works for several years, but construction was delayed due to fear it would antagonize the local Christian population or lead to Japanese fishermen losing their licences. Seijiro Kiba built the temple, with assistance from Tsunematsu Atagi, to serve the local membership of about 200 families. The land cost $3,000 and the building $5,000. There was still animosity between white and non-white, particularly Asian, residents of the city. In 1928, 142 Vancouver businesses, including three of Vancouver's biggest department stores, petitioned the provincial government to let municipal councils limit the number of shops owned by non-white, and a year later numerous Chinese businesses decided to close on Sundays to avoid further anti-Chinese agitation.

Famous Players Canadian Corporation bought the suburban theatres owned by the Langer Circuit—the Kitsilano, the Windsor, the Alma, the Victoria Road and the Kerrisdale—as well as the "New Orpheum," which had opened on November 7, 1927. Ivan Ackery, doorman at the Capitol Theatre, was promoted to manager of the Victoria Road Theatre at Victoria and 43rd. He noted in his autobiography, *Fifty Years on Theatre Row*, that his new salary was "something in the neighbourhood of $25 a week."

Comings and Goings

January 26 The famous Romanian violinist Georges Enesco appeared at the Vancouver Theatre. This was an early engagement sponsored by impresario Lily Laverock.

Notable births: country singer **Evan Kemp** on January 22; future mayor **Jack Volrich** on February 27; broadcaster **Jim Cox** on August 7.

Notable deaths: **John Francis Bursill**, former Fleet Street journalist, *Vancouver Sun* columnist (under the pen name Felix Penne), poet and founder of the Collingwood Free Library, died in Burnaby on February 8 aged about 80. Bursill had come to Vancouver in 1905, aged about 60, to join his eldest son in East Collingwood; **Henry John Cambie**, railway engineer, whose CPR survey from Yellowhead Pass to Port Moody set the route to the lower Fraser, died in Vancouver on April 23, aged 91 (Cambie Street was named for him); **Walter Cameron Nichol**, founder of *Saturday Night* magazine (1887), newspaperman and BC's 12th Lieutenant-Governor, died in Victoria on December 19.

1929

Vancouver became the third-largest city in Canada. The Vancouver stock exchange planned a new building—just in time for the stock market collapse. Winston Churchill visited the city. And aviator Charles Lindbergh didn't.

January 1

The municipalities of Point Grey and South Vancouver amalgamated with the city. When newly elected mayor W.H. Malkin walked into his office on January 2, 1929, he was the chief executive of a city that had, overnight, grown in population by more than 50 percent to become the third largest in Canada, with 240,000 residents. The expanded city now also had 12 aldermen, one for each of 12 oddly shaped new wards. Their boundaries ran in arrow-straight lines north and south, ignoring neighbourhoods.

Also January 1 Alfred Wallace died in North Vancouver, aged 63. He came to Canada in 1889 and two years later was building fishing boats in False Creek. He started Wallace Shipyards in 1905 and ran it for more than 20 years. In 1921 Wallace built the *Princess Louise* for the CPR fleet, the first contract awarded to a local firm. During World War I the company built merchant and naval vessels. By the end of World War II, under Alfred's son Clarence, it was Canada's biggest shipbuilding firm.

January 2 The first meeting of the new Vancouver city council following amalgamation. Mayor W.H. Malkin, a wholesale grocer, paid a warm tribute to his predecessor, Louis D. Taylor, giving him credit for the

Elsewhere in BC

In 1922 the number of fishing licences sold to "other than white, British subjects and Indians" had been cut by up to 40 percent. Local Japanese fishermen took their case to court and won, but the provincial government enacted legislation to allow the discrimination to continue. The case went to the Privy Council in England in 1929. The fishermen won, but only half of them were still around when the decision was handed down this year.

Elsewhere in Canada

October 18 The Judicial Committee of the Privy Council in England, Canada's highest court at the time, ruled that women were, after all, persons. A word of explanation: in April 1928 the Supreme Court of Canada had ruled that women were not persons. The judges expanded on the judgment, ruling that, "by the common law of England, women were under a legal incapacity to hold public office." That paternalistic ruling was overturned today, thanks in part to crusaders like Nellie McClung and Emily Murphy.

Elsewhere in the World

February 14 St. Valentine's Day massacre in Chicago, where Al Capone's gang killed seven members of a rival organization.

May 6 The first Oscars were awarded in Hollywood.

October 25 The New York Stock Exchange collapsed and launched a severe economic crisis in the US and, soon after, Canada and much of the rest of the western world. The Great Depression had begun. In 1929, volume on the Vancouver Stock Exchange was 143 million shares. That number dropped to 10 million in 1930.

December 17 The *Empress of Japan II* was launched in Glasgow. Considered Canadian Pacific's finest trans-Pacific liner, it was 4 metres (13 feet) longer and 2 metres (6 feet) wider than the *Empress of Canada*, more luxurious, faster and much less expensive to operate. It arrived in Vancouver in August 1930 to commence regular crossings to Asia via Honolulu but, unfortunately, the worldwide depression had a severe impact on both passenger and cargo numbers for Canadian Pacific's Empress line, and the service ended within a few years. The *Empress of Japan II* was requisitioned as a troop ship in 1939 and its name was changed to *Empress of Scotland*.

Popeye, the Sailor Man, made his first appearance.

Kodak made its first 16 mm film.

The first grocery store in North America to allow their customers to help themselves to the merchandise, the Piggly Wiggly franchise exploded across the continent in the early 1920s. However, after hitting financial trouble, the company was broken up, with the Canadian portion being sold to Safeway in 1936. *Dominion Photo Co. photo, Vancouver Public Library VPL 25055*

amalgamation. Malkin's two years in office would be efficient, if unexciting.

February 6 John Hess Elliott, pioneer, died in Vancouver, aged 65. He arrived in the city in 1898. In addition to building numerous homes in the Fairview neighbourhood at the turn of the century, Elliott is known for helping establish Savary Island as a vacation destination. When World War I began he enlisted with the 242nd Battalion Canadian Expeditionary Force. At the age of 53 he chose to fight in the trenches of Europe alongside men less than half his age. He was severely wounded in battle and, shell-shocked, was unable to remember his own name. Evacuated to a hospital in England, Elliott remained unidentified until a fellow soldier recognized him and sent word home to his wife and family that he was alive. He was brought back to Vancouver on a stretcher, a decorated veteran.

February 7 Coloured motion pictures (without artificial tinting) were shown for the first time in Vancouver at Kodak's store on Granville Street.

February 14 Daniel Loftus Beckingsale died in London, England, aged 82. He came to Vancouver in June 1886 and became the first port doctor and an early health officer. Beckingsale formed the Vancouver Reading Room, predecessor of the public library.

May 31 An ad for Piggly Wiggly stores in the *Province* showed 28 locations in Vancouver, one in West Vancouver, one in Victoria and one in New Westminster. Safeway purchased the chain in 1936.

June 1 An artist's conception of the new (second) Stock Exchange Building appeared in the *Sun*. The building would be at the northwest corner of Pender and Howe Streets.

June 3 The Peter Pan Restaurant opened at 1180 Granville. According to the *Sun* headline, "Thousands Inspect New Cafe." A photo showed the staff lined up out front. This restaurant, soon to become a city landmark, was started by Peter Pantages of Polar Bear Swim fame.

Granville landmark. Located downtown on Granville, the Peter Pan Cafe was soon a local favourite and city landmark. It was started by Peter Pantages (far right), of the Polar Bear Swim fame. *Vancouver Sun*

Also June 3 The Orpheum Theatre (the present one) ran an ad for a new Mary Pickford film, *Coquette*, "her first 100% Talking Picture, and the usual big bill of Radio-Keith-Orpheum Vaudeville." Incidentally, the theatre was now called the RKO Orpheum.

July 13 A race was held in Vancouver with some of the world's top runners, including Olympic gold medallist Percy Williams. Two days later this story appeared in the *Vancouver Sun*: "Eddie Tolan of the University of Michigan, 100 and 200 yard sprint champion of the United States, today charged he was the victim of a 'hometown decision' when he was adjudged beaten by Percy Williams in Vancouver last week. Tolan made the statement while passing through Windsor. He said he had pictures which show him leading Williams by close to a foot at the finish." The official top three finishers on that "muddy horse race track" were (1) Percy Williams, (2) Eddie Tolan and (3) Frank Wykoff.

July 27 On a stop in Seattle during a tour of North America following his famous solo flight across the Atlantic, Charles Lindbergh refused an invitation from Vancouver mayor Louis D. Taylor to fly into Vancouver because, said Lindbergh, "your airport isn't fit to land on." That embarrassed Vancouver and prompted the push to build one that was fit. It opened in 1931.

July The provincial exhibition buildings in New Westminster burned down. The fair was due to open in September, so they put up big tents instead.

Establishing a local presence, Boeing opened up shop in 1929 in the former Hoffar-Beeching Shipyard. On order were B1Es—"flying boats"—and a luxury yacht, the *Taconite*, built for William Boeing. *City of Vancouver Archives, CVA 99-2344. Photo Start Thomson*

July A serious fire occurred in Ladner's Chinatown, which stretched along the riverfront and consisted of more than a dozen buildings. Half were destroyed in the blaze, which was reported in the *Ladner Optimist* newspaper: "Fanned by a tremendous wind, the fire burned like lightning through the dry wood and the damage was all done before firefighting equipment from Vancouver could reach the scene. Calls for help came soon after the blaze was discovered. Its origin is unknown."

August 8 Samuel Maclure died in Victoria, aged 69. The son of a Royal Engineer and brother of Sara Ann McLagan, he is considered the most gifted of early BC architects. Maclure designed some 150 buildings either alone, with his firm or in partnership with others, and he designed many Shaughnessy Heights homes before World War I.

August 24 Boeing of Canada opened a plant on Coal Harbour and bought the Hoffar-Beeching Shipyard at 1927 West Georgia. In 1930 they began to build planes there, but this year the shipyard built the *Taconite*, a luxury yacht, for William Boeing. The boat was all teak and 125 feet in length. It is still in Vancouver, still looks beautiful and is available for charters.

August 27 Well, it sounded good. Some local histories indicate that the *Graf Zeppelin*, the most famous airship of the 1920s, visited Vancouver—specifically, Coal Harbour—on August 27, 1929. Alas, a closer examination of papers of the day revealed the truth: the zeppelin didn't get here. "Plans of Dr. Hugo Eckener to bring the Graf Zeppelin over Vancouver and Seattle," the *Province* reported, "were upset by two occurrences. Dense fog in the North Pacific forced the airship south in order to get her bearings, and a slight attack of ptomaine poisoning caused the commander to hasten to Los Angeles." The huge airship had just completed "one of the most spectacular flights of all time, a non-stop 5,800 miles across the Pacific Ocean from Japan." It had taken just over 78 hours.

September 1 Vaudeville was drawing smaller audiences all across North America. As a result, from this date the operation of the Orpheum Theatre in Vancouver (the present one) was shared by former competitors Orpheum Circuit and

Famous Players. Orpheum Circuit would finally accept the decline and fall of vaudeville and sell the theatre outright to Famous Players in 1931 as a movie house. Vaudeville could still be enjoyed for a few more years in Vancouver, mainly at the Beacon Theatre, but its glory days were over.

Smiling for the camera, a full house of dancers and diners pack out the Commodore Cabaret (now the Commodore Ballroom). The Commodore, which first opened in 1929, is one of Vancouver's premier live-music venues today, although it has opened and closed and changed hands many times over its eight-decade history. *King Studio photo, Vancouver Public Library VPL 70488*

British Lion Dines on Grouse

September 2 Did you know Winston Churchill was once here? Back on September 2, 1929, Winnie—described as "the former chancellor of the exchequer and holder of a dozen other cabinet positions in Great Britain"—arrived in New Westminster to open its exhibition. Some 40,000 people turned up to see him. The following day he travelled to Haney "for an inspection of British Columbia's lumber industry." His host was the Honourable Nels Lougheed, provincial MLA and an executive of the Abernethy Lougheed Logging company, who gave him a demonstration of BC logging methods.

Next on Winnie's agenda? A trip up Grouse Mountain, where he dined at the chalet. On September 3 he gave a talk at the Vancouver Theatre on Granville Street. The next day he went to Victoria to see the Esquimalt dry dock, add a brick to the Anglican cathedral and plant a hawthorn tree in Beacon Hill Park.

December 3 The Commodore Cabaret (known today as the Commodore Ballroom) opened on Granville Street. Owners Nick Kogas and John Dillias began a tradition of showcasing local bands and international touring artists.

December 14 Henry Tracy Ceperley died at age 79. He was born January 10, 1850, in Oreonto, NY, and arrived in Vancouver around 1885. Ceperley Rounsefell and Co., established the next year, became one of BC s largest real estate/insurance firms. Ceperley encouraged the CPR's William Van Horne to promote in Ottawa the idea of a municipal park on what was a federally owned military reserve. That park, which we know as Stanley Park, opened on September 27, 1889. Ceperley's Deer Lake home is now the Burnaby Art Gallery.

December 17
Unemployed men raided the city relief office in Vancouver.

The effects of the Great Depression, which began with the New York Stock Exchange crash less than two months earlier, were beginning to be felt locally.

December 18 Burnaby's first street lighting was turned on, illuminating Hastings Street from Boundary to Gilmore.

Oh, You Pratt!

October 4 In the Vancouver Archives is a handwritten letter, dated October 4, 1929, carefully inscribed by Lauchlan Hamilton (77 at the time) during a brief visit to the city. Hamilton was a CPR surveyor who laid out much of downtown Vancouver. His letter is addressed to J. Alex Walker of the town planning commission. It was written more than 40 years after his survey:

"I cannot say that I am proud of the original planning of Vancouver," Hamilton wrote, after explaining that the shortness of his visit precluded a personal meeting with Walker. "The work, however, was beset with many difficulties. The dense forest, the inlets on the north and False Creek on the south, the pinching in of the land at Carrall Street" and so on, and so on.

If you look at a map of Vancouver, you'll note that east-west streets such as Hastings and Pender turn at an angle as they pass Cambie and enter the downtown peninsula. Presumably Hamilton didn't want to have the streets make that bend. In his letter to Walker he complains that his "original plan" for the direction of the streets in the city's downtown peninsula had to be altered because a property owner named Pratt refused to go along with Hamilton's design. What that design was we haven't discovered after several hours of research.

The archives holds a collection of field survey books used by Hamilton and those working for him. It's fascinating to leaf through those brittle, yellowing pages and see the pencilled notes and drawings made over 120 years ago as the surveyors decide to cut a "Granville Street" through here and a "Nelson Street" through there. The pages are covered with scribbled computations and little memos, each street plan carefully dated. The survey of Granville south of Nelson, for example, began March 15, 1885. The corner of Cambie and Hastings was laid out on April 30, 1886. If you're a surveyor and you haven't seen these little books, by all means visit the archives and ask to have a look.

The Empress of Hastings and Gore

The British Guild Players, Vancouver's leading professional theatre company before World War II, produced its first show. On opening night, the leaders of the company, the husband-and-wife team of David Clyde and Dorothy Hammerton (who became better known as Fay Holden) received telegrams of congratulations from key figures of the era, such as Laurel and Hardy and J.M. Barrie.

David and Fay had enjoyed successful stage careers in Scotland and England as well as Boston and New York in the United States throughout the 1920s. In 1929, in partnership with playwright and actor Norman Cannon, they moved to Vancouver, where they bought and refurbished the Empress Theatre at the corner of Hastings and Gore Streets, the largest stage west of Chicago at the time. Their productions, usually frothy comedies, were big hits, attracting Vancouverites who sought an escape from daily life during the Depression. A 1933 *Vancouver Sun* article noted that, between the stage hands, electricians, designers and actors, the Empress Theatre had a payroll of $1,500 a week, which qualified it as a significant employer in Vancouver.

David and Fay lived at the corner of Ontario Street and East 51st Avenue and insulated their home with expired theatre posters and advertising signs. In addition to their theatrical success with the British Guild Players, the couple helped establish Vancouver's early reputation as Hollywood North by working regularly in the local film industry and in Hollywood itself from the mid-1930s onward, appearing in over 120 movies. David Clyde had small parts in the musical *Rose-Marie*, *The Philadelphia Story* and *Now Voyager*, among many others. Fay Holden found fame playing Mickey Rooney's mother in the Andy Hardy films.

They ran the theatre company from 1929 to 1938 before moving to Hollywood as their film careers became more demanding. The Empress Theatre itself was dismantled in 1940. The British Guild Players featured many high-profile actors, including Dorothy Somerset (who initiated the UBC Theatre program), Sydney Risk (who created the Everyman Theatre in the 1940s) and such stars of the period as Basil Radford.

The company's theatrical legacy continues in Fay and David's old Vancouver neighbourhood, as one of Canada's leading theatre and film acting and production programs, Studio 58, is based at Langara College, located directly across Ontario Street from their home.

Vancouver's first art deco building, the Georgia Medical-Dental Building (left) was erected in 1929 at the corner of Georgia and Hornby. Featuring whimsical ornaments along natural, medical and mythological themes, the building was demolished in 1989 despite an intense bid to save it. *Vancouver Public Library, Special Collections, VPL 12170. Leonard Frank photo*

Also in 1929

Earle "Mr. Good Evening" Kelly started his broadcasts for the *Province*'s radio station CKCD. He earned that nickname for his lugubrious introduction to his program. Kelly became known as Canada's first personality broadcaster.

The Vancouver Unemployed Worker's Association was formed.

The Georgia Medical-Dental Building, the first art deco-style building in Vancouver, was built at the northwest corner of Georgia and Hornby Streets. It was richly embellished with whimsical ornaments like plump little terracotta owls and other birds, lions and horses. The building was adorned with medical, religious and mythological symbols around the main door. Following an intense but unsuccessful public campaign to save it, the handsome structure was demolished on May 28, 1989, by a controlled explosion, viewed by a huge throng in the surrounding streets.

The Alpine Club of Canada conducted a ski tour of Mount Seymour. Vigorous development followed.

The provincial Public Library Commission applied for, and received, a grant of $100,000 from the Carnegie Corporation to test an idea for five years: providing library services to a rural population. The result, still active, was the Fraser Valley Public Library.

The Pacific National Exhibition opened its first permanent amusement park. Happy Land was near the racetrack and offered rides and games. It lasted to the end of the 1957 season and was replaced in 1958 by the bigger Playland.

The Holden Building on East Hastings, built in 1911, became Vancouver's

Glory days (round 1). The R-class sloop *Lady Van* won the Lipton Cup Regatta, finally beating Seattle's long-time champion *Sir Tom*. The *Lady Van* went on to win the cup again in 1934 (when this photo was taken), 1937, 1938, 1939 and 1940. War ended this long-standing race between Seattle and Vancouver, and the *Lady Van* ended up derelict in Seattle. But, restored by the Boatbuilding Heritage Society of BC, the *Lady Van* raced again and won against Seattle's restored *Pirate* in the resurrected 2010 Alexandra Cup.

city hall, a title it would hold until the current city hall opened in 1936. The Holden Building was also temporarily home to the city's archives. The city hall from 1897 to 1929 was a now-vanished building immediately south of the Carnegie Library on the west side of Main Street.

UBC's social work program began,

the third university social work program established in Canada after Toronto's (1914).

Mary Louise Bollert, the University of British Columbia's dean of women, became president of the Confederation of University Women.

Annie Jamieson was first elected to the Vancouver School Board. She served to 1946. An elementary school in Vancouver is named for her.

Christ Church, the oldest surviving church in the City of Vancouver, which was built between 1889 and 1895, became an Anglican cathedral.

Vancouver Drydock built *Lady Van*, a racing yacht, for Royal Vancouver Yacht Club members who wished to compete for the 1929 Lipton Cup. Built to a C.E. Nicholson design, the *Lady Van* won the cup. The yacht continued to compete under subsequent owners, including Lt.-Gov. Eric Hamber, and was sold to Seattle interests in the 1940s.

United Church minister Andrew Roddan was appointed to Vancouver's First United Church, "the church of the open door." Roddan was an early advocate of low rent and housing projects on the city's east side, welfare services for the poor and a fresh-air camp on Gambier Island.

Charles Montgomery Tate celebrated the 50th anniversary of his service as a Methodist priest. Tate, who was affiliated with St. Andrew's-Wesley United Church, had been a missionary to the first church in Vancouver built by Native residents (1876).

Comings and Goings

March 31 Actor Lee Patterson was born in Vancouver. His film career spanned the last half of the 20th century, from 1953 to 1994.

Notable deaths: **G.F. Baldwin**, city pioneer, former city comptroller and the first city clerk, died on June 12; **Thomas Plimley**, pioneer Vancouver auto dealer, died in Victoria aged about 58; **Peter Righter**, who was at the throttle when locomotive No. 374 brought the first Canadian Pacific Railway passenger train into Vancouver on May 23, 1887, died at age 77.

Mary Riter Hamilton, a World War I battlefield artist, arrived in Vancouver to teach art.

Ben Wosk, future furniture merchant, arrived from Russia with his family.

1930-1939

1930

Two separate ship collisions put the accident-prone Second Narrows bridge out of commission. Meanwhile, two building that opened this year—the Marine Building and the Stanley Theatre—are still standing and still among the city's most admired buildings.

Right: Green Timbers. The original gravel-paved Old Yale Road and Old Yale Wagon Road carves its way through Green Timbers, the last turn-of-the-century virgin forest. Now known as the Pacific Highway, the forest was clear-cut before it could be declared a park. Commercial reforestation began in 1930.
City of Surrey Archives

March 1 The Fraser Valley Public Library Demonstration began, with Dr. Helen Gordon Stewart as director. The Carnegie Corporation of New York donated $100,000 to establish a rural library and a bookmobile for five years. After the funds were exhausted in 1934, Valley residents, despite the Depression, voted to pay a new tax to continue the service—and the first regional library in North America was born.

March 15 A group of people gathered in Green Timbers Urban Forest to plant more than 120 baby trees, the beginning of commercial reforestation here. Victor Harbord-Harbord, a *Province* reporter covering the story, planted a Douglas fir for the paper. Sixty years later, at an anniversary ceremony at Green Timbers, two of Harbord-Harbord's great-grandchildren romped and chased each other beneath the very tree planted by their late great-grandfather. Columnist Chuck Davis planted another tree for the *Province* on that day in 1990.

April 4 The *Vancouver Sun* reported that "no time is to be lost on the construction of the new $225,000 theatre on south Granville street for Mr. Frederick Guest, of Hamilton, Ontario...The detail plans and specifications for the theatre are approaching completion in the offices of architects Hodgson and Simmonds...The new playhouse will have a seating capacity of 1,250 and will be ultra-modern in every respect...equipped with the latest for talking pictures and also a pipe organ." They're talking about our old friend the Stanley Theatre, which opened this year at 2750 Granville St.

April 28 Hewitt Bostock died at Monte Creek. We can thank him for the *Province*, although he wouldn't recognize the paper today. Born May 31, 1864, in Surrey, England, he graduated in law from Cambridge but, oddly, took up ranching when he came to Kamloops in 1888. In 1894 he started a newspaper in Victoria, the *Weekly Province*, and later sent an associate to Vancouver to test the climate for a competitor to the *World* and the *News-Advertiser*. On March 26, 1898, the *Daily Province* appeared and quickly became the biggest paper in town. Bostock became an MP and was later Speaker of the Senate.

April 29 An editorial in the *Province*: "Our handling of the Oriental problem has not only had more than a trace of injustice in it; it has been ineffective as well. We have hunted the Orientals out of the fishing industry and they have gone to the woods and they have gone to the farms. We have made it uncomfortable for them on the farms, and they have gone into business in the cities. We haven't diminished their numbers; we have simply pushed them about."

April A ship called the *Losmar* tore away the south span of the Second

A 10.5-hectare (25-acre) garden, an initiative of Washington state, was installed on the American side of the Peace Arch.

Percy Williams of Vancouver, who had won two gold medals at the 1928 Olympics, ran the 100 metres in 10.3 seconds, setting a world record that would last until 1941. He also won the 100-yard race in the first British Empire Games, held at Hamilton, ON. That race effectively ended his career when he tore a muscle in his thigh. He did compete in the 1932 Olympics but didn't make it out of the heats.

In other sports, the UBC women's basketball team, representing Canada, won the women's world championship in Prague, beating France 18–14 in the final. A crystal vase signifying the world title is on display at UBC. And Jean Gordon, a Vancouver laboratory technician, won the Women's World Cup of ten-pin bowling at Jakarta, Indonesia.

Top left: Big bash. Coming through a little off course, the *Losmar* tore away the south span of the original Second Narrows Bridge in April 1930.
City of Vancouver Archives, Br P9.5

Below left: KO'd. Finishing the job started by the *Losmar* a few months beforehand, the *Pacific Gatherer*—towed by the tug *Lorne*—knocked out the centre span of the Second Narrows Bridge on September 13, 1930. Repairs were not attempted.
Vancouver Public Library, Special Collections, VPL 10141. Leonard Frank photo

Narrows bridge, putting it out of commission. On September 13 the *Pacific Gatherer* finished the job, taking out the fixed centre span. No attempt was made to reconstruct the bridge.

May 3 Premier Simon Fraser Tolmie opened Capilano Bridge, which replaced the concrete bridge built across the Capilano River in 1914. Marine Drive was now classified as a primary highway.

Also May 3 A letter appeared in the *Province* suggesting that bells be put on automobiles as a safety feature, to sound continuously when the vehicle was going downhill.

May There were bright spots during the Depression years: in May 1930 Dominion Bridge opened a plant in Burnaby to produce steel for construction. Clients included Vancouver's Marine Building, the Alberta Wheat Pool and Second Narrows bridge repairs.

July 12 A "city market" opened at the corner of Main and Pender Streets.

July 29 The old Hastings Mill store, one of the few buildings to escape the fire of 1886, was placed on a scow and towed south by the tug *Alert*, under the direction of Capt. Charles Cates. The snug little structure was safely beached at high tide on the shores of Point Grey, near Alma Road, where it became a museum, run by the Native Daughters of British Columbia, Post No. 1. It makes for a truly interesting visit to the past. Don't miss the stories, pictures and drawings of the Great Fire.

August 21 Newspaper reports said the annual per capita income for BC residents was $4,339.

August 26 The Vancouver Women's Aeronautic Association was organized, the first in Canada.

September 7 The oldest surviving bowling centre in Canada, Commodore Lanes and Billiards, in the basement at 838 Granville St., opened under the direction of Frank Panvin. And here's a remarkable story, told by reporter Gordon McIntyre: "From opening day until Frank Panvin's death in 1962, the only time staffer Mitz Nozaki spent away from the alley was when the Canadian government interned him at Shuswap Lake with other Japanese Canadians during World War II."

Still shining with bright lights, Canada's oldest bowling centre, Commodore Lanes and Billiards, opened downtown in 1930 in the basement of 838 Granville Street.
City of Vancouver Archives, CVA 99-4117. Stuart Thomson photo

September 30 The first iron lung was donated to Vancouver General Hospital.

The iron lung was a device that helped patients with severe respiratory problems breathe.

October 23 Contact! The Vancouver branch of the Aviation League of Canada, an organization promoting the growth of the air industry, began formal proceedings. Maj. D.R. MacLaren, DSO, was unanimously elected president at a meeting at the Hotel Georgia. Ten committees bristled with high-powered local names, including William Templeton (first manager of the Vancouver Airport); Gen. Victor Odlum; Gen. A.D. MacRae (his Hycroft is a famous Shaughnessy mansion); financier Austin Taylor; newspaperman R.J. Cromie; Duncan Bell-Irving and more.

An art deco masterpiece, the Marine Building opened to much awe in 1930. It was once the tallest building in the British Empire, but has long been overshadowed. *City of Vancouver Archives, Bu P346. Otto Fernand Landauer photo*

October The Marine Building opened. It is the most famous and, in the opinion of many, still the most beautiful building in Vancouver, an art deco masterpiece. A Toronto bond-trading house, G.A. Stimson, believed Vancouver would become a major West Coast port and decided to erect an office building near the waterfront to accommodate the city's marine-related businesses. A site was found at the foot of Burrard Street, and a local architectural firm, McCarter and Nairne, was commissioned to realize the vision. The architects conceived of it as a great crag of a building, rising from the sea, although it is now almost totally hidden by a forest of modern skyscrapers. For more than a decade it was the tallest building in the British Empire. A.J.T. Taylor, managing director of British Pacific Properties in West Vancouver, moved into the lavish penthouse with his wife in 1930, but Mrs. Taylor eventually decided she didn't like heights, so they moved out. The space is occupied by offices today.

Risking All for the VSO

October 5 The Vancouver Symphony Orchestra performed for the first time at the Orpheum Theatre, although it wasn't until 1976 that the group would make the Orpheum its permanent home. The conductor was Allard de Ridder, who put up his $3,000 life savings—a tremendous amount in 1930—to guarantee the musicians' wages for this first concert and led the orchestra until 1940.

De Ridder was born in 1887 in Dordrecht, Holland. He received his music education in Holland and at the Cologne Conservatory; was a guest conductor in Arnhem, The Hague and Amsterdam; and was later conductor of Amsterdam's National Opera and assistant conductor of the Los Angeles Philharmonic. He was also a violist with the Boston Symphony Orchestra and the LA Phil. In 1941 he moved to Toronto where he joined the Hart House String Quartet and taught at the Royal Conservatory of Music before founding the Ottawa Philharmonic Orchestra in 1944. He retired to Vancouver in 1951.

This was also the year the Vancouver Junior Symphony (currently known as the Vancouver Youth Symphony Orchestra) was conceived and formed by flautist Cyril Haworth.

November 3 Vancouverites scoffed at the claim of a Veronia, OR, sawmill that it was sawing up the world's tallest tree,

a 70-metre (230-foot) specimen from an unnamed species. "That is only a toothpick," the *Province* huffed, "compared with the giant Douglas fir that was cut near Vancouver in 1895, measured at 415 feet. The size of this tree established a record for all time." Alas, not so. Guinness gives that title to an Australian eucalyptus at Watts River, Victoria, Australia, that was reported in 1872. It was 132.6 metres (435 feet) tall when it was discovered, already on the ground, and may have been over 150 metres (500 feet) originally.

November 20 The Canadian National Institute for the Blind opened its Vancouver headquarters on Broadway.

November 21 Vancouver got its first shipment of "Lillybet" dolls, modelled after five-year-old Princess Elizabeth—who is Queen Elizabeth II today.

November 22 Spencer's Department Store held a giant toy parade with Santa Claus and a retinue of storybook people.

Also on November 22 A letter appeared in the *Daily Province* suggesting it would be a good idea to have traffic lights at Main and Kingsway.

November 24 Gustav Roedde, printer and book binder, died in Vancouver, aged 70. He was born January 7, 1860, in Groß-Bodungen, west of Nordhausen, Germany. Roedde came to Vancouver via Cleveland, San Francisco and Victoria and opened the city's first book bindery in 1886. He had Roedde House built in 1893, the second house on the block, after Barclay Manor next door. Custodians of the house believe its architect was Francis Mawson Rattenbury, designer of the Vancouver Art Gallery (formerly the courthouse) and Victoria's Parliament Buildings and Empress Hotel. Roedde's wife, Matilda, is said to have complained, "I wish that Rattenbury had given us a basement." The house was sold to H.W. Jeffreys in 1927 and later became a boarding house. The City of Vancouver bought it in 1966. Called Roedde House and charmingly restored, it is now used for community activities.

December 6 The first airmail to Asia left Vancouver.

December 8 Work began on the Burrard Bridge, it opened July 1, 1932.

Also in 1930

Construction began in Richmond on what is today Vancouver International Airport. William Templeton, the first manager of the airport, had been on the committee that chose Sea Island as the location. When construction began he published a brochure that read, in part: "The day is not far distant when giant airliners and dirigibles will leave this harbor for far-away China, Japan, and even Australia, while large multi-motored planes will carry the passengers and mails which arrive here from these distant countries...faster than the winds themselves and higher than the birds which fly." (The "harbor" reference reflected the fact that much of the early airport's traffic was "flying boats.")

The BC Electric Co., which was already operating Terminal City Cabs, took over Yellow Cabs, which began

A grand sovereign surging through the water, the *Empress of Japan* was considered to be the finest trans-Pacific liner produced by the Canadian Pacific Steamships Ocean Services company. It arrived in Vancouver in 1930, and began regular trips to Asia via Honolulu. *Dominion Photo Co. photo, Vancouver Public Library VPL 23254*

A Port Coquitlam landmark until its demolition in 2008, the Wild Duck Inn underwent "Tudor Revival" touches and was moved near the Lougheed Highway in 1930. But it wasn't until owner Will Routley added a 100-seat pub in 1931 that business soared.

Port Coquitlam Heritage and Cultural Society

doing business here in 1920 with a single car owned by Roy Long.

Will Routley added Tudor Revival touches to his Wild Duck Inn in Port Coquitlam. He also moved the inn upstream slightly, to its present location near the Lougheed Highway. In 1931 he added a 100-seat pub and saw business soar.

The new Ford automobiles were on display at the Hotel Vancouver. They sold for $540.

The Fraser Highway became part of the Trans-Canada Highway.

The New Westminster Exhibition closed for good this year, which caused a rise in attendance at the Pacific National Exhibition.

The PNE Forum was constructed at a cost of $300,000. It was the largest artificial ice surface in North America at the time.

The Vernon Block at 225–255 East Broadway was built. It's now a heritage structure, as is the Memorial Park South Fieldhouse at 5950 Prince Albert, also built in 1930.

Jaywalking was banned in Vancouver.

Mae Garnett, about 55, joined the *Vancouver Sun*. She was one of the first female general news reporters in western Canada (she wrote for the *Albertan*, *Edmonton Bulletin* and *Vancouver News-Herald*).

Henry Forbes Angus, 39, who had joined UBC in 1919 as an assistant professor of economics, was named the university's head of economics, political science and sociology.

Enrolment at UBC topped 3,000, and the university cleared 120 hectares (nearly 300 acres) between Chancellor Boulevard and Spanish Banks for development. However, the Depression was in full flower and the plans died because the university couldn't afford to build the necessary infrastructure.

The University Golf Club opened for play.

The first school of psychiatric nursing opened in BC.

A world record for egg laying was set by "No Drone, No. 5H," a hen from the Whiting farm in Surrey. She laid 357 eggs in 365 days. "No Drone" was preserved for posterity and her stuffed form put on display at the World Poultry Congress in Rome, Italy, in 1934. In 1954 the Whiting family presented the stuffed hen to the Langley Museum.

Deadman's Island, so named because it was once the site of Native burial grounds (and was later used by white settlers for the same purpose), was the subject of much dispute until 1930, when the federal government leased the island to the city. It is now the site of HMCS *Discovery*, home of Vancouver's naval reserve.

St. Andrew's-Wesley United Church opened at Burrard and Nelson. Its name shows it was a merger of two churches, one Presbyterian, the other Methodist, the result of the formation of the United Church of Canada five years earlier.

Arthur Laing, born in Eburne on September 9, 1904, was elected to the Richmond School Board. He served to 1943, including eight years as chairman, then entered federal politics in 1949.

Solomon Mussallem was elected reeve of Maple Ridge. He served until 1934, then again from 1936 to 1943, and for a third time from 1946 to 1953.

Rudolph M. Grauer became reeve of Richmond. He held that post to 1949.

One of our favourite entries: Labour activist William Arthur "Bill" Pritchard was arrested in 1920 and found guilty of seditious conspiracy following an inflammatory speech during the Winnipeg General Strike in June 1919. He spent a year in jail. Ten years later he was elected reeve of Burnaby and served until 1932.

As a form of unemployment relief, Surrey council gave one day's work a week to single men, and two days a week to married men, as long as

Left: Granville Island was flourishing as the 1930s got going, churning out anvils, band saws, bolts, steel rivets, cement, paint, boilers, barrels, chains and rope for the forest and mining industries.
City of Vancouver Archives, Dist N116.2

weather conditions permitted and until the allotted sum of $10,000 had been used up.

Burnaby's Town Planning Commission was established. Burnaby also held its first annual Better Baby Contest to promote child welfare. Judges were the medical health officer and the school board doctor.

Richmond became a member of the Greater Vancouver Water Board. The municipality had been plagued over the years by broken, corroded or frozen pipes as it tried to transport fresh water across bridges or over the bed of the Fraser to Sea and Lulu Islands.

Seton Academy, a Catholic girls' school, opened in Overlynn, a grand Tudor Revival manor designed by Samuel Maclure. The house, at 3755 McGill St. in Burnaby, was built in 1909 for Charles J. Peter, a prosperous dry goods merchant. The Sisters of Charity of Halifax bought the house in 1927 to use as their convent and school. In 1970, when the school closed, Action Line Housing Society bought Overlynn and developed seniors' housing on the property. Burnaby Council designated the mansion a heritage structure in 1995.

Granville Island was flourishing. Over 1,000 people were working six days a week in the island's factories, producing materials for the province's forestry and mining industries.

Of 55 businesses in Steveston, 31 were owned by Japanese residents, who this year paid half the cost ($20,000) to build a new 14-room school in the community.

Archeologists found 200 skeletons in the ancient Marpole Midden.

The Britannia copper mine began a five-year reign as the largest copper producer in the British Empire.

With the help of money raised by the Women's Auxiliary, founded in 1929, Vancouver's Greek community built St. George's Greek Orthodox Church at 7th and Vine in Kitsilano. A Sunday School and a Greek language class were established at the same time.

The UBC Thunderbirds made history in Athletic Park, at 5th and Hemlock, the first sports ground in Canada to be equipped with floodlights. An exhibition game against the Hamilton Tigers was the first football game in the country to be played under lights.

Don Bradman, the legendary Australian cricketer, described the cricket pitch adjacent to Brockton Oval in Stanley Park as the most scenic in the world.

The Vancouver Bach Choir was formed by Herbert Mason with 130 members. It immediately became the largest choir in the city; it is now also the oldest.

Comings and Goings

April 4 American band leader Paul Whiteman arrived in Vancouver and was amazed to learn that Canadian immigration authorities refused to allow his orchestra to perform at two dance dates, although they could perform at a concert. Whiteman said "all or nothing" and left for Seattle on the 6th.

December 15 Mrs. Victor Bruce visited British Columbia during the last leg of her around-the-world flight, taking off from Vancouver's temporary airport on Lulu Island at noon. The "daring British aviatrix" arrived in Victoria shortly after 1 p.m. and went for lunch with Lt.-Gov. R. Randolph Bruce. (We don't think they were related, although one of the guests at the luncheon was the Rev. Montague Bruce, a cousin of the flyer.) Later that afternoon she flew to Seattle, and then on to San Francisco. "She had an exciting experience," ran one newspaper report, "when she made a forced landing in Iraq. The Baluchi tribesmen were friendly, and after dancing with them she was escorted over the desert to Jask."

Notable births: **Allan King**, film director, who caused a sensation in 1969 with his documentary *A Married Couple*, which followed the real-life couple Bill and Antoinette Edwards, February 6; **Anne Macdonald**, arts advocate, March 18; **Dave Barrett**, future BC premier, October 2; **Betty Keller**, writer and arts coordinator.

1931

As the Depression took hold, there were reports of hobo jungles, "communist" rallies, wage rollbacks and the creation of charitable organizations. But there was also the official opening of Vancouver's first proper airport, designed by an enthusiastic amateur.

Right: The Native Daughters of BC rescued the Hastings Mill store when they heard it was about to be demolished, along with the mill. They had it barged to its present site at the foot of Alma Street, where it functions as a pioneer museum. During the Great Fire of 1886, this building, which dates to 1865, functioned as a hospital and morgue. *Leonard Frank photo, Vancouver Public Library VPL 7972*

January 10 A story in the *Province*, headlined "New Record for Number of Autos," reported that "motor tourist travel into British Columbia from United States showed a big increase in 1930 over 1929, according to reports from the Greater Vancouver Publicity Bureau. Entering British Columbia through the ports of Pacific Highway, Douglas and Huntington," the story continued, "came 128,856 cars, carrying a total of 417,581 passengers. This was an increase of more than 7,000 cars and more than 26,000 passengers over the previous year." By the way, a brand-new Chrysler Straight Eight sedan was going for $1,950 FOB Detroit, in 1930.

January Work began on a tunnel under downtown Vancouver that was meant to keep Canadian Pacific Railway trains off the city's streets. The tunnel opened in 1932.

February 19 Henry Ogle Bell-Irving died at age 75. H.O. was born January 26, 1856, in Dumfriesshire, Scotland, and came to Canada at age 27 as a surveying engineer for the CPR. He was briefly an architect in pre-fire Vancouver, then opened a general store in Gastown. By 1891 he was into the canning business that made his fortune: he became Canada's largest exporter of canned salmon.

We owe some of our knowledge of the early look of this area to his accomplished amateur watercolours. He left half of his own paintings to the provincial archives.

February Harvey Hadden died in London, England, aged 79. A wealthy Englishman born in Nottingham in 1851, he first visited Vancouver in 1891 and became a major property

Elsewhere in BC

The Native Brotherhood of British Columbia was formed. Its official mandate was to improve the socio-economic conditions of Indian people in BC, and it organized protests on fishing, lands, taxation and social issues. The organization's founding declaration avoided any mention of aboriginal title, but unofficially it sought recognition of aboriginal title to ancestral lands.

John W. Fordham Johnson, banker and president of BC Sugar, became Lieutenant-Governor.

Elsewhere in Canada

Citizenship was granted to Japanese people in Canada. They could not yet vote, although an exception was made for those Japanese Canadian soldiers who had fought for Canada in World War I.

Elsewhere in the World

January 23 World-famous ballerina Anna Pavlova, who had so thrilled Vancouver audiences in 1910 and in two subsequent visits, died of pneumonia at the Hôtel des Indes in The Hague in the early hours of January 23. She was nine days short of her 50th birthday.

December 11 Statute of Westminster, granting legal and political independence to Commonwealth countries.

Alfred Butts devised a word game he first called Lexico, but that we know today as Scrabble.

owner here before 1913. In 1928 he donated land at Kits Beach that became Hadden Park, and in his will he bequeathed $500,000 for Vancouver parks. In 1957 parks at Georgia, Adanac, Woodland and McLean were purchased with this money.

March 11 Koichiro Sanmiya died in Vancouver aged about 51. He was born *c.* 1880 in Sendai, Japan, and arrived in Vancouver in 1907. He owned the Strand Hotel restaurant and established the K. Sanmiya Co. (an importer/exporter of Japanese goods) and *Canada Daily Newspaper*, a Japanese-language paper. In the 1920s he started the Vancouver Malt and Sake Co. and was issued the only distiller's licence in BC. Sanmiya was a founder and president of the Canadian Japanese Association (Nipponjin Kai, now the Japanese Canadian Association). He sponsored the Asahi baseball team and raised funds for the war memorial to Japanese Canadian soldiers in Stanley Park.

March 19 The Franciscan Sisters of the Atonement began a Catholic Japanese Mission School for Japanese residents of Steveston, where the nuns ran a nursery, Sunday school and English classes. When the Steveston Japanese were interned at Greenwood during World War II, the mission closed down.

April Rachel Goldbloom, philanthropist, died in Vancouver aged about 66. She was born in New York *c.* 1865 and married William Goldbloom in 1882. Nell, their daughter, was the first Jewish girl born in Winnipeg. In the first decade of the 1900s they moved to Vancouver, and their home at 540 Burrard became the centre of Jewish community life—almost every Jewish organization of that time was said to have been started there. Goldbloom was described as a "one-woman philanthropic organization." See the book *Pioneers, Pedlars, and Prayer Shawls* by Cyril E. Leonoff.

May 16 Alexander Mitchell, the first farmer in Greater Vancouver, died on Mitchell Island, aged 84. Born May 8, 1847, in Masham County, QC, Mitchell arrived in BC in April 1877. He settled in Moodyville and later took out squatter's rights on Richmond's small Mitchell Island, which was named for him. He was active in municipal politics and represented South Vancouver's Ward 3 as councillor. He was secretary of the school board and later a councillor for Richmond's Ward 5.

June 24 William John Brewer died in Vancouver, aged about 90. Brewer arrived in the Vancouver area from Australia in 1870, and in 1884 he purchased 10.5 hectares (25 acres) in what is now the Cedar Cottage district. He moved to the South Vancouver area after the Great Fire of 1886 destroyed his Granville Street business. He was elected a Ward 4 alderman in 1889 and elected the first reeve of the new municipality of South Vancouver on April 30, 1892.

June 25 Dugald Campbell Patterson died in Vancouver, aged 71. He was born January 2, 1860, in the village of Partick, Scotland, and came to Canada in 1884. By 1894 he had settled in the newly formed municipality of Burnaby, where he built a pioneer homestead and farm on what is now the northeast section of Central Park. He co-founded

The Do-It-Yourself Airport

July 22 Vancouver Airport and Seaplane Harbour opened, with Premier Simon Fraser Tolmie officiating. A crowd of 55,000 people turned up for the four-day ceremonies. The complex covered 192 hectares (474 acres). Most of the 3,000-odd passengers during the first year were there for sightseeing flights, but aviation historian Sean Rossiter calculates that about 536 arrived from other points on the 309 incoming flights—309 incoming flights? That's nearly one a day!

A great Vancouver story tells of how William Templeton, the airport's first manager, saved thousands of dollars by laughingly declining the services of an American design firm and doing the job himself for about $14. One reminder of his 1931 work: Cowley Crescent, which circles the first terminal: Templeton laid a light bulb down on the plans and traced around it with a pencil. That's why Cowley looks the way it does. (Templeton had shown initiative before: with his brother and a cousin to help, he built and flew a home-made biplane at Minoru Park racetrack on April 28, 1911, our first local plane.) His tireless promotion got the airport off to a strong start.

Takeoff. Its runways ready to receive planes, the newly opened Vancouver Airport is surveyed in this 1931 panorama. Altogether 55,000 people showed up for the four days of opening festivities. *City of Vancouver Archives, Pan N05A. Photo W.J. Moore*

These Vancouverites, photographed in 1980, are enjoying the outcome of a decision made decades earlier to build a saltwater swimming pool at Kitsilano Beach. A crowd of 5,000 turned up for the 1931 opening.
Ken Oakes / Vancouver Sun

the park, was the first postmaster of Edmonds in 1909, was elected a school trustee in 1912 and developed a plan to preserve ravines for parks. Patterson Avenue and Patterson SkyTrain station in Burnaby are named for him, and Patterson House, once the family home, is designated a heritage building in Burnaby.

July 3 **Canada's first baseball game played under lights took place at Athletic Park in Vancouver.**

July 12 The Crescent Beach Hotel in White Rock was selling fresh crab salad for 50 cents.

August 2 There was what the *Province* called a "Communist demonstration" near the Cambie Street Grounds. From the same paper, one of the more compelling leads we've ever seen: "One person in every 300 in British Columbia is insane."

August 15 The Kitsilano saltwater swimming pool opened. The largest of its kind in North America, the pool measured 200 by 60 metres (650 by 200 feet), cost $50,000 to build and was opened in perfect weather by a crowd of 5,000 people, who waited impatiently for the inevitable speeches to end before diving in.

August 23 Sanford Johnston Crowe, contractor, died in Vancouver aged 63. He was born on February 14, 1868, in Truro, NS, and moved to Vancouver in 1888. Crowe retired in 1909 and was elected alderman (1909–15). He was vice-president of the Vancouver Exhibition Association, served as Vancouver's second Member of Parliament and was appointed to the Senate in 1921. Crowe Street is named for him.

Summer About 1,000 unemployed and homeless men were living in hobo "jungles" around the Canadian National and Great Northern Railway yards east of False Creek. They arrived or left by hopping a train, and those who stayed in Vancouver built shacks with discarded tin signs, lumber, cardboard or other materials, insulated with paper.

October 5 The Vancouver Art Gallery opened on West Georgia, a few blocks west of its current location, in a 1911 art deco building. Sculptor

Vancouver had a new art gallery to celebrate in 1931, on West Georgia. The gallery sparkled for its grand opening, in a 1911 art deco building a few blocks away from its current location.
Leonard Frank photo, Vancouver Public Library, Special Collections, VPL 10926

Charles Marega was commissioned to create large busts of Michelangelo and Leonardo da Vinci to flank the entrance, as well as a frieze of medallions showing famous artists. Today the VAG is the fifth-largest gallery in the country and holds the world's largest collection of works by Emily Carr.

October 10 West Vancouver agreed to sell 4,000 acres (more than 1,600 hectares) to the British Pacific Properties syndicate (financed with money from the Guinness family of brewery fame) for $75,000, about $18.75 an acre. It's worth a tad more today.

October

Strikers at Fraser Mills, protesting repeated wage rollbacks, were dispersed by mounted police charges.

November 8 The *Province* published a commentary on Adolf Hitler and his appeal to Germany's disenchanted youth. World War II was still eight years in the future.

November 22 Hugh Boyd, Richmond's first reeve, died in Bangor, Ireland, aged about 89. He was born in 1842 in County Down and came to BC in 1862, lured by the Cariboo gold rush. He was elected reeve of Richmond in 1880 and served to 1886, then left for Ireland in 1887 to live near Belfast. Boyd criss-crossed the Pacific Ocean 12 times after his retirement. Richmond was named in honour of the Yorkshire birthplace of his wife Mary, née McColl.

December 16 Elizabeth "Betsy" Flaherty, a buyer for Spencer's Department Store, got her flying licence. Flaherty was born in about 1878, which would have made her about 53, the oldest female pilot in Canada. She was a passenger on Trans-Canada Airlines' first cross-Canada flight in 1937, and was a charter member of the "Flying Seven," an all-woman flying club that began in 1936.

December

Greater Vancouver residents formed the Common Good Cooperative Society to engage in a "war against poverty." The self-help society operated a store, grew food on vacant land and helped many through the worst of the Depression. The credit union movement in BC is an offshoot of the society.

Also in 1931

Coloured comics in the *Province* included Rock-Age Roy, Harold Teen, Smitty, Gasoline Alley, Little Orphan Annie and The Gumps.

The entrance fees at Vancouver Golf Club had been $100, with dues of $6 a month, but during the Depression the dues were reduced to a dollar a month and 20 cents each time you played. Caddies earned about 75 cents for four hours' work.

Louis D. Taylor, mayor of Vancouver from 1910 to 1911, in 1915 and again from 1925 to 1928, was elected yet again. This stretch, which lasted to 1934, would be his last.

The UBC golf clubhouse opened at 2545 Blanca. Today it has Canada's only provincial golf museum, housing classic clubs, old trophies and prints

Mayoral touch. A city presence who just kept coming back, Mayor Louis D. Taylor pins a tassel on an interested party while canvassing for disabled children.
City of Vancouver Archives, CVA 1477-168. Dominion Photo

The new, art deco English Bay Bathhouse was built in 1931, replacing the old one built in 1905. Recently restored in 2002, the house is still used by thousands of visitors each year.
City of Vancouver Archives, Be P10. Joseph Frederick Spalding photo

from the early days of golf. There is a library and archives, with more than 1,200 books, 100 volumes of clippings and photos, and video footage of great BC golf moments, including Ben Hogan in the 1967 Masters tournament.

George Burrows began to supervise Vancouver's beaches and pools, a job he held until 1971. A cairn donated by lifeguards and dedicated to Burrows can be found near the bathhouse at Kitsilano Beach.

Bandleader Mart Kenney, who began his career in the late 1920s with the CJOR Radio Orchestra and with Len Chamberlain at the Hotel Vancouver, formed a group called Mart Kenney and the Western Gentlemen for a one-off engagement at the Alexandra Ballroom in Vancouver. The rest is, as they say, history. ("I was the Bryan Adams of 1944," Kenney once said.) In March 2000, to mark his 90th birthday and nearly 70 years in showbiz, Kenney released a new CD of original music.

Actor John Qualen, born December 8, 1899, in Vancouver, appeared in *Street Scene*, his first movie. He went on to perform in more than 140 films. His father, the pastor of First Scandinavian Church (Lutheran) on Prior Street from 1898 to 1900, was against his son's acting career.

Margaret Ormsby, born in Quesnel in 1909, earned an MA in history at the University of British Columbia. She went on to become the doyenne of British Columbia history.

The *Ubyssey*, the student newspaper at UBC, was shut down over a censorship issue and printed a fake funeral notice. The memorial read: "Sacred to the memory of Free Speech."

Mount Seymour's first ski mountaineering hut was built.

James Skitt Matthews, 53, became the city's unofficial archivist (and in 1933 the first official one). His methods were chaotic, his research was occasionally shaky and his temper was terrible, but Matthews amassed a body of work on the city's past that is quite simply titanic. We owe him an unpayable debt. His second wife, Emily, helped him in his tireless efforts to collect city memorabilia and reminiscences.

Harold Merilees, "Vancouver's first great ad man," moved from Spencer's Department Store—where he had worked since 1925—to the BC Electric Railway Company, and eventually became the firm's manager of public information.

The newly created Vancouver Town Planning Commission published a short pamphlet for high school students that described its goal and methods. "The idea of planning is to prevent waste; it is a scientific attempt to direct the growth of the various components, residential, industrial and business, that go to make up a city along sane, and as far as can be foreseen, permanent lines."

Comings and Goings

February 22
Pianist/ composer Sergei Rachmaninoff performed in Vancouver.

May 23 Lorne Parton, journalist, was born in New Westminster. He became a *Province* reporter and columnist in 1952.

November 9 Future judge Stu Leggatt was born.

December 31 Politician and broadcaster Rafe Mair was born.

1932

The Great Depression settled like a sodden shroud on the city. Thousands were on relief (34,000 at the peak), and hundreds more were riding the rods into town on every freight train (the author's father was one of them). Reporter Alan Morley counted 1,250 men in the breadline at First United Church. The city's relief cost for 1931–32 was over $1.3 million. A symbol of the economic downturn: the unfinished state of the Hotel Vancouver.

February Victor Odlum killed the *Star,* a morning paper, when the printers refused to take a pay cut. Now the city was back to two newspapers, the *Sun* and the *Province,* both evening broadsheets. Some former *Star* staffers, including Gus Sivertz and J. Edward Norcross, started up a new paper, the *News,* on November 1, 1932. It lasted five months, but Sivertz, Norcross and others then launched the *Vancouver News-Herald.*

March 31 The advent of sound didn't entirely kill off silent movies. On this date the Beacon Theatre (the old Pantages) on Hastings Street was showing the 1915 classic *Birth of a Nation.*

April 13 Sister Frances (Mrs. Fanny Dalrymple Redmond), the city's first public health nurse, died in Vancouver aged about 80. She was born in England and arrived in Vancouver not long after the Great Fire of June 13, 1886. Sister Frances was a nurse at St. James Church and was called the "Florence Nightingale of the City" for her nursing care during the smallpox epidemic of the 1890s.

Hard times. As a sign of the times, throngs of men are seen gathering at Victory Square in downtown Vancouver in this July 1932 photo. They were seeking jobs that did not exist during the Depression.
City of Vancouver Archives, Re N2.2.

April 25 The *Sun* reported that the Vancouver General Hospital maternity department had broken all previous records for the number of babies born there in one day: 11. The previous record was 8. "It was," said the *Sun,* "the busiest day doctors and nurses have had in the history of the department. One wee Japanese and 10 white babies, including a set of twins, form the record-breaking crew, six of whom are boys and five girls."

May 4 A large demonstration by the unemployed occurred at Vancouver City Hall.

Elsewhere in Canada

August 1 The Co-operative Commonwealth Federation (CCF), forerunner of the NDP, was founded in Calgary. Its first leader was James Woodsworth.

It became possible for the first time this year—thanks to the "Copper Highway"—to place a call to the other side of Canada without having it route through American cities. When the first trans-Canada telephone call (from Vancouver to Montreal) was placed in 1916, the circuit ran 6,763 kilometres (about 4,200 miles) through Buffalo, Chicago, Omaha, Salt Lake City and Portland, OR.

Elsewhere in the World

December 25 Greater Vancouverites listened to the first Christmas radio message from the sovereign as George V spoke from Sandringham.

At the Los Angeles Olympics, Duce McNaughton, a Magee High School grad who led his school to the first-ever provincial boys' basketball championship, won the high jump, while the Vancouver Rowing Club, coached by Bob Johnston, won a bronze medal in the double sculls event. One of the crew was Ned Pratt, soon to be a well-known architect. His partner was Noel de Mille.

May 16 Robert Dollar, lumber baron and steamship lines president, died in San Rafael, CA, aged about 88. "The Pacific's Grand Old Man" was born in 1844 in Falkirk, Scotland, and came to eastern Canada at 14. By age 19, Dollar was an experienced lumberjack. He moved to California in 1888 and bought *Newsboy,* the first in a shipping empire of more than 100 vessels. In 1912 he established the Canadian Robert Dollar Co. in Vancouver to run the fleet of the Dollar Steamship Line. Timber stands bought from the BC government supplied his sawmill on Burrard Inlet. The Dollar flag, a white dollar sign on a red background, was known worldwide.

May 27 The Vancouver Junior Symphony (now the Vancouver Youth Symphony Orchestra) gave its first performance.

July 17 The first CPR trains began to run through a tunnel under downtown Vancouver, built to get the trains off city streets. That same tunnel is used today by SkyTrain. It was built by Northern Construction Co. and J.W. Stewart for $1.6 million. The tunnel is 6 to 24 metres (20 to 80 feet) below the surface and 1,395.72

A year after this tunnel was being dug under the downtown core in 1931, the first CPR trains rolled through during an attempt to get the trains off city streets. Decades later, SkyTrain is using such tunnels.
Leonard Frank photo, Vancouver Public Library VPL 12419

Bridge to future. Another sign of the city's progress and maturity, the Burrard Bridge was opened on Dominion Day, July 1, 1932, to great fanfare and excitement.
City of Vancouver Archives, CVA 99-2656. Stuart Thomson photo

A Sugar Bridge and a Potlatch House

July 1 With "a snip of a pair of golden scissors in the hands of Mayor Louis D. Taylor," one of the local papers reported, "Vancouver's $3 million Burrard Bridge was opened to the public...Hardly was the ribbon cut in front of the devouring eyes of movie cameras, than thousands of pedestrians and hundreds of cars surged across the magnificent white structure in a procession of triumph, celebrating another step in Vancouver's progress." The Kitsilano Boy's Band played; so did the Fireman's Band, and an RCAF seaplane zoomed under the bridge "to the great amazement of the congregated thousands." At a civic reception later, in the Hotel Vancouver, a replica of the bridge was unveiled. It was made of sugar.

The architect of the concrete version was G.L. Thornton Sharp, of Sharp and Thompson. It was Sharp who was responsible for the most noticeable physical feature of the bridge, those tall galleries in the middle. "Both central piers," Sharp told a reporter, "were designed and connected with an overhead gallery across the road. This helped to mask the network of steel in the truss from the two approaches, and has been treated as an entrance gateway to the city." (So if you've ever wondered what those two big concrete structures were for, the answer is they're to hide all that messy steel. The story that people once lived in apartments inside one or both of them is an urban myth.) The bridge piers have provision for a rapid transit vertical lift span beneath the highway deck, but it was never installed.

Busts of Captain Vancouver and Harry Burrard jut out from the bridge's superstructure (there's a *V* under Vancouver's bust, a *B* under Burrard's), a gleaming and colourful coat of arms welcomes the visitor and—bridge engineer John Grant's inspiration—there are huge lamps at both ends of the span, a tribute to Canada's World War I prisoners of war, who huddled around open fires in their prison camps.

One small change that resulted from the construction of the Burrard Bridge: Cedar Street disappeared. When the bridge went in, it connected to Cedar Street south of the bridge. The name Burrard was simply extended and Cedar disappeared. On the northern approach to the bridge, road crews paved over the ruins of Chip-kaay-am, Chief George's potlatch house.

metres (4,500 feet) in length, following an elongated S-curve from the west portal on Burrard Inlet (now the Waterfront terminal for SkyTrain), left up to Thurlow, and back south under Dunsmuir to Cambie, where it curves almost due south, ending at the east portal near the Georgia Viaduct. A new eastern portal was built to the north of the original when the tunnel was rebuilt for SkyTrain use. Most of the original tunnel floor was slightly lowered to accommodate stacking the east- and west-bound tracks of the SkyTrain just inside the new portals.

August 20
New regulations allowed Vancouver beer parlors to remain open from 9:30 a.m. to 11:30 p.m.

September 17 Vancouver's new coroner's court and city morgue opened at 238–240 East Cordova. Today that little building is the Vancouver Police Museum.

October Construction began on homes in the British Properties in West Vancouver. At the height of the Depression, this project gave 150 local men steady employment.

October
The province established relief camps for single unemployed men, of which there were many: more than 6,000 by 1934.

November 13 The Vancouver Garrison dedicated a plaque marking the site of the city's first drill hall. It's in the lobby of the Shelly Building, across Pender from the Old Sun Building. A small contingent of BC men left from this location to fight in the Boer War in 1899.

November 21 The *Province* cited a local young "artiste" and "promising composer" named Jean Coulthard.

December 8 Businessman (and ex-politician) H.H. Stevens walked around Stanley Park on his 54th birthday. He continued his birthday walk for 40 years. His last was on December 8, 1972, when he was 94. He died June 14, 1973.

December 20 Burnaby, battered by the Depression, defaulted on its bond payments and went into receivership on December 31—where it would stay until 1942. North Vancouver District suffered the same fate. Like a lot of struggling places in North America, the district—its tax base hammered by the loss of major industries and the lucrative ferry service to North Vancouver City—collapsed into bankruptcy. One old-timer recalled jigging for salmon in local streams to have something for dinner. Some 75 percent of landowners saw their property revert to the municipality for unpaid taxes. The district was placed under the control of a commissioner, Charles Tisdall, and did not have representative government again until 1951. According to Bettina Bradbury, who studied conditions in Burnaby during the Depression, "22 per cent of the district's population ended up on welfare and almost half of its taxpayers could not afford to pay taxes."

Also in 1932

The *Richmond Review* newspaper began publication.

Mrs. J.R. Paton won first prize for her griddle scones at the Surrey Agricultural Fair.

In the 1932–33 season, Vancouver shipped out 96,869,841 bushels of wheat, making it the world's largest grain port.

Oreste and Agnes Notte, originally from Italy, moved to Vancouver from Victoria and opened a bakeshop at 14th and Granville. Three years later they moved the shop, called Notte's Bon Ton, downtown.

The MV *Scenic* began service as the only floating post office in the British Empire, delivering mail to people living up Indian Arm. Known as the Burrard Inlet TPO (travelling post office), it served until 1968.

Scenic P.O. Serving an isolated population along Burrard Inlet and Indian Arm, the MV *Scenic* was launched in 1932 to become the only floating post office in the British Empire. It served until 1968, a year before this photograph was taken. *City of Vancouver Archives, CVA 447-8015. Walter Edwin Frost photo*

Construction on the new Hotel Vancouver—which the Canadian National Railway had started in 1928—ground to a halt in 1932, a victim of the Depression. The work site would remain dormant for five years.
City of Vancouver Archives, CVA 99-3708. Photo Stuart Thomson

Future judge Angelo Branca, 29, became Canadian amateur middleweight boxing champion. "I was a tough little bastard," he said, "tough as hell and all solid muscle."

An outside worker for Surrey Municipality this year was paid between 37.5 cents and 56.25 cents an hour.

The Burrard Inlet Tunnel and Bridge Company went bankrupt, and ownership of the Second Narrows bridge (the first one) eventually passed to the Crown.

Cooper and Smith Towing, which had started operations on the Fraser River in 1919, became Westminster Tug Boats and began to specialize in boat handling in Burrard Inlet.

The Vancouver Concert Orchestra, a predecessor to the CBC Vancouver Chamber Orchestra (now the National Broadcast Orchestra), was formed by John Avison. "In those days," Avison once told a *Province* interviewer, "we played a lot of light music, and we used to do radio shows from the CN station and the Hotel Vancouver." Avison took over his new duties with enormous enthusiasm. He did everything: chose the repertoire, conducted, selected the players and handled the contracting. (He was also a superb accompanist on piano and performed with many of the internationally recognized performers who visited Vancouver.)

York House School, a private school for girls, was founded by Lena Cotsworth Clarke, who named the school after her hometown, the ancient cathedral city of York in England. York, in turn, was named for the House of York, whose symbol is the white York rose, which the school adopted as part of its crest.

Thanks to local aviation pioneer Don MacLaren and Canadian Airways, Vancouver residents could now fly to Victoria for $20 on a luxurious eight-seat Sikorsky S-38 amphibian. There were two or three return flights each day from an office at the foot of Cardero Street on Coal Harbour. Unfortunately, the Sikorsky was not designed to withstand the effects of salt water. Within two years it was "just one gob of corrosion," according to maintenance engineer Rex Chandler.

Winona Grace Woodsworth, 26, married Angus MacInnis, a Labour MP from Vancouver. Grace MacInnis, daughter of J.S. Woodsworth (founder of the CCF, precursor to the NDP), went on to become one of Canada's most famous—and effective—politicians, first elected in 1941.

The Great Depression forced a reduction in UBC operating grants from the provincial government. Students mounted a successful publicity campaign against a suggestion that the university be closed; still, the budget was reduced from $626,000 to $250,000, and salaries were also reduced.

The Depression just kept on coming. In 1928 the Canadian National Railway began building a huge chateau-style hotel at Georgia and Hornby Streets, but a depressed economy halted construction this year. The building stood uncompleted for five years. We know it today as the Hotel Vancouver.

The Jewish Administrative Council was established, and Ephraim and Anne Sugarman founded Congregation Beth Israel. Cyril Leonoff, chronicler of local Jewish history, notes that, "with the growth of the second generation, Canadian-born and schooled, a demand arose for the formation of a modern congregation without segregation of the sexes and with greater English-speaking content. This led in 1932 to the inauguration of a Conservative congregation, Beth Israel (House of Israel), which reconciles the traditional values of Judaism with modern forms."

In sports, 17-year-old Stan Leonard won the BC Amateur golf championship for the first time. The Vancouver Curling Club affiliated with the Forum. A seaside pool was built at Stanley Park's Second Beach. Reginald "Pop" Phillips brought the box version of lacrosse ("boxla") to BC.

The children of pioneer William Henry Ladner erected a plaque on the clock tower in Delta beside the museum. William and his brother Thomas Ellis Ladner were the first settlers in the area named for them.

Dr. Harry Warren began teaching at the BC and Yukon Chamber of Mines; his students were prospective prospectors. Warren was vice-president of the chamber from 1939 to 1951 and president from 1952 to

1954. He was equally well known as an amateur sports executive.

At one time, if you had turned off every electrical installation Lennox Mackenzie designed in Vancouver, half the city would have been plunged into darkness. His work, which began this year, included lighting the Stanley Park causeway, a lot of street lighting, and the exterior lighting on city hall, all the city's major hospitals, and many hotels, stores, factories, apartment blocks, houses and office buildings.

North Shore citizens donated shrubbery and plants from their own gardens to complete the landscaping of the North Vancouver General Hospital, which had opened in 1929.

Farmers from the drought-stricken Prairies loaded their families into old vehicles and began to come west. Many squatted in Surrey, and some of them eventually bought land and became established.

The Women's Auxiliary to the Rotary Clinic for Chest Diseases, founded in 1921, changed its name to the Rotary Women's Auxiliary. It remained a separate entity and financially independent of the Rotary Club.

William Woodward became honorary colonel of the 15th Field Regiment (RCA).

BC Motor Transportation and BC Rapid Transit, both subsidiaries of the BC Electric Railway, were merged under the umbrella of Pacific Stage Lines, a wholly owned BCER subsidiary and one of the largest intercity bus companies in Canada.

Alberta-born Gerald "Cap" Hobbis, 14, traded a bunch of old magazines for his first bicycle. He repaired it in his basement and sold it to his first customer, Fred Bramley, for $10. Cap became a hugely successful bicycle retailer.

Ben Wosk, originally from Vradiavka, Russia, began dealing in old stoves from a small shop on Granville. He later became a major furniture dealer.

Ivan Ackery, manager since 1930 of the Dominion Theatre on Granville Street, began to show his promotional drive. In his autobiography, *Fifty Years on Theatre Row,* Ackery wrote, "I began to do some good promotion work while at the Dominion. There was a 1932 Gracie Fields movie called *Looking on the Bright Side* that hadn't been doing too well in early showings on the circuit, so we really went to work on it. We worked with the newspaper, giving free passes to the film to cooperative advertisers; we got free window space in shops, where we hid free passes among the merchandise and lucky customers would find them on making purchases. I worked with eight music stores in the city, having them feature Gracie Fields records and sheet music, and went on CKMO with a great radio man and Fields fan, Billy Brown. A cousin of Gracie's played piano in Vancouver, and we got him to come on the radio broadcast at CKMO and two other radio stations. In short, we blitzed it!" Empire Films, which had made the picture, broadcast Ivan's results in a notice to other film folk: "Ackery did it—so can you! I.F. Ackery...[sold] the Greatest Number of Paid Admissions ever recorded for that theatre...Ackery is no magician, just a wide-awake manager, but he did transform a Double-Feature Policy theatre into an Extended Run House." As reward for his efforts, Ackery was transferred to Victoria to manage the Capitol Theatre there.

Comings and Goings

April 13 Famed pianist Ignace Paderewski performed at the Vancouver Arena. Eight years later he was at the head of the Polish government-in-exile during World War II.

A Major legacy. Recognized as the official city archivist, Major J.S. Matthews (second from right) ensured the survival of life as it was in Vancouver. Also pictured on this drive through Stanley Park is Verne Wellburn, the driver of the 910 Russell, August Jack Khahtsahlano (far right) and his wife, Mary Ann.
Deni Eagland / Vancouver Sun

The Australian XI touring cricket team played BC at Brockton Point. Don Bradman, the greatest batsman of all, played there and described the ground as the loveliest in the world.

One of BC's most famous artists, Jack Shadbolt arrived in Vancouver and went on to teach at the Vancouver School of Art for nearly 30 years.

Notable births: **William Richards "Bill" Bennett**, who went on to become BC's 27th premier, was born in Kelowna to W.A.C. and May Bennett on April 14; entrepreneur **Peter Toigo** was born in Powell River on September 9; **Iona Campagnolo**, the province's first female Lieutenant-Governor, was born on Galiano Island on October 18; broadcaster, politician and ombudsman **Barrie Clark** was born in the Okanagan on November 17.

Michael W. Brighouse, one of Lulu Island's largest landowners, died. His father was pioneer Samuel Brighouse.

1933

Established in 1933—during the Depression—in the expectation that a relatively undeveloped province like British Columbia would need some heavy equipment, Finning Tractor and Equipment Company (pictured here *circa* 1950s) went on to become the world's largest dealer of Caterpillar products (now Finning International).
Courtesy Finning

Vancouver boasted of having the lowest cost of living among Canadian cities. A new daily newspaper began publication with a young Pierre Berton as city editor, while the first serious attempt to integrate immigrants began with an annual festival. Men, meanwhile, were allowed to go topless on the beaches.

January 4 Finning Tractor and Equipment Company Ltd. was incorporated.

January 17
The *Vancouver Sun* turned its newsroom over to students from the University of British Columbia. Staff of the *Ubyssey*, the student newspaper, took over the layout, placement of stories, editorial and sports pages, and more. The front-page story with the most space devoted to it asked several distinguished citizens whether a university education gave a person an advantage in the workplace. The answer, not surprising given that all the people interviewed were UBC teachers, was that it did. Familiar names pop out of the *Ubyssey* roster of 30 who worked on the paper that day: Norman Hacking, Dick Elson and 19-year-old Stu Keate, who became the *Sun*'s publisher 31 years later.

May 29 The Chinese Students soccer team won the BC Mainland Cup, beating the UBC Varsity squad 4–3. The win sparked exuberant celebrations in Chinatown, with bands playing and firecrackers exploding. The day after victory, Vancouver's Chinese community held a parade and declared a holiday. Free tea and dim sum were served to all. Originally formed in 1920 by local high schoolers from prominent pioneer Chinese families, the club had previously won the Iroquois Cup (1926) and the Wednesday League Cup (1931). They

Elsewhere in BC

November 15 Thomas Dufferin Pattullo (1873–1956), Liberal, became premier. "Duff" served to December 9, 1941.

Elsewhere in the World

January 30 Adolf Hitler was named chancellor of Germany.

November 26 Singer Robert Goulet was born in Lawrence, Massachusetts. He was a star in Vancouver's Theatre Under the Stars.

December 5 Prohibition in the US, which began in 1920, was repealed.

Orange Crates and Pocket Combs Make a Newspaper

April 24 The first issue of the *Vancouver News-Herald* appeared, operated largely by editorial staff fired by the short-lived *Star*. The new paper faced formidable competition: the *Province*'s circulation at the time was 90,265 and the *Sun*'s somewhere in the 60,000 to 70,000 range. The *News-Herald*'s started at 10,000 and peaked at 40,000, but the paper lasted until 1957.

A lot of well-known local newspaper people worked for the *News-Herald* in its 24 years of life: Pierre Berton was its first city editor at age 21, and others involved were Barry Broadfoot, Himie Koshevoy and Clancy Loranger, to name a few.

From its first four-page issue the paper struggled. Reporters sat on orange crates, and two or three would share one typewriter. The second-hand press quit, and the first issue had to be cranked out manually. The staff used their pocket combs to fold the sheets. They rented a tiny building at 426 Homer St. and knocked a hole in its wall to get to the typographical shop next door.

On September 20, 1954, the paper shortened its name to the *Herald* and moved into a new, larger building on Georgia Street. Then newspaper magnate Roy Thomson bought the paper and, less than three years later, citing expenses, shut it down. The last issue was June 15, 1957.

went on to win the Spalding Cup in 1937. The team disbanded in 1942.

Also May 29 Vancouver boxer Jimmy McLarnin won the world welterweight championship, kayoing Young Corbett.

Left: Vancouver-raised Jimmy McLarnin, known by such nicknames as "Baby Face" and the "Baby-faced Assassin," became the world welterweight champion in 1933 after knocking out reigning champion Young Corbett III in the first round. *Courtesy PNG*

May 30 A publication called *Unemployment and Relief, City of Vancouver* (available in the city archives) had this note on 1933 shopping: "Vancouver offers the greatest inducement to the family working-man...the cost of living there being the lowest among eight of the chief cities of Canada for which complete data is available. For slightly less than $15 a week the working-man with a family of five can pay rent for a six-roomed house with modern conveniences, fuel and food bills."

June 9 Vancouver City Council voted to allow men to go topless on city beaches.

June 13 June 13 is unofficially called Vancouver Day because a number of events important to the city occurred on this date. In 1792, for example, Captain George Vancouver explored and christened Burrard Inlet. (He named it for a navy friend, Harry Burrard, back in England. Burrard was never here.) On June 13, 1859, a seam of coal was discovered at Coal Harbour, which is why it has that name. On June 13, 1886—just two months after incorporation—Vancouver burned to the ground in the Great Fire, and most recently, on June 13, 1933, Major James Skitt Matthews declared the Vancouver City Archives officially open.

July 3 In mid-Depression Burnaby, police were called out when more than 100 unemployed people "interfered" with a sheriff's order to evict a family from its house in the 4200 block Eton Street.

August 10 Mrs. Victor Spencer introduced her eldest daughter, Louise, at a "fete" at Aberthau, their Point Grey residence. Guests mingled under a specially erected marquee. (Today Aberthau is the Point Grey Community Centre.)

August 25 A non-stop flight from Vancouver to Kingston took off today. The flight ended on the 26th.

September 21 The first Vancouver Folksong and Dance Festival began. The brainchild of Mrs. John T. McCay, the festival brought together the people and culture of all ethnic groups in Vancouver, Croats and Czechs, Slavs and Hungarians, Greeks, Scandinavians, Mexicans, Armenians, Austrians, Estonians, Chinese, Poles, Japanese, Germans... Mrs. McCay asked members of each community to bring a treasured item of their culture for the first year. The result was a display of astonishing beauty. After the first year, Vancouver's Native people were the hosts, and singing and dancing were added to the program, which encouraged the British Vancouverites to join in with morris dances and madrigals.

October 21 The first successful suicide leap off Vancouver's Burrard Bridge. Many more followed. (We were living through the Great Depression, which explains a lot.) Reading back through the files, at times it seems there were lineups of people waiting their turn to jump. Because the bridge isn't quite high enough to guarantee a speedy end, the more usual result was severe injury.

December 14 The Canadian movie *Crimson Paradise* had its world premiere at the Capitol Theatre in Victoria. The moviemaker had trouble getting bookings for the film in local cinemas, which were dominated by US product. We cite this Victoria event because Ivan Ackery was the manager at the Capitol at the time, and insisted on showing it. Vancouver film historian Michael Walsh writes that Ackery was given three nights, chosen because they were traditionally the worst in box-office terms. Ackery turned the local showing into a smash, and the movie had to be held over. (*Crimson Paradise*, incidentally, was the first Canadian feature film with sound. It has disappeared without trace.) It was promotional savvy such as this that eventually led to Ackery's elevation to manager of the Orpheum in 1935.

December 16 Voters approved a plan to build a bridge across the First Narrows.

The full tutti. Nat Bailey turns his White Spot on Gransville and 67th into a full indoor dining restaurant. He had opened it in 1928 as a drive-in restaurant.
Constance Brissenden, Triple O: The White Spot Story

Also in 1933

Dan Sewell of Horseshoe Bay converted a Briggs and Stratton household appliance motor to his boats and began one of the first powerboat and sport-fishing operations on the coast.

The Canada Rice Mill in Richmond was built, a new source of tax revenue and employment in the midst of the Depression.

Radio CJOR moved to the Grosvenor Hotel, 840 Howe Street, and operated for years out of the hotel's basement. The station became a real force in local radio in the 1930s, with broadcasters like Ross and Hilda Mortimer, Dorwin Baird, Billy Browne Sr. and Jr. and Vic Waters. Waters eventually became program director and hired future broadcasting stars like Red Robinson, Jack Webster and Brian "Frosty" Forst.

Carnegie Library closed for a couple of months in 1933. There was no money. (In 1935 the library's appropriation was nine cents more than it had been in 1934.)

The Vancouver School of Decorative and Applied Arts became simply the Vancouver School of Art.

Nat Bailey's White Spot No. 1 restaurant opened on Granville at 67th Avenue. He had opened a drive-in hotdog barbecue stand at that location in June 1928.

Comings and Goings

March 12 Philip Owen was born in Vancouver. He got into politics in 1978 as a park board commissioner and was elected to council by 1986. In November 1993 he became the city's 42nd mayor, serving to 2001.

August 14 J.S. Woodsworth, leader of the brand-new Co-Operative Commonwealth Federation (CCF), precursor of the NDP, spoke to crowds in the arena about the new party.

November 5
American entertainer Texas Guinan, a big star in her day,

died of amoebic dysentery at Vancouver General Hospital, failing to rally after an operation. She was just 43, and was in town with her show. (She had appeared here years before.) She was a singer and nightclub owner, famous in the 1920s for greeting her club patrons with "Hello, sucker!" Her clubs were continually being shut down and she was continually being arrested. "I'm nature's gift to the padlock makers," she once said. Somehow in Prohibition days you could always get a drink at Texas' clubs.

1934

As residents continued to struggle financially, Prime Minister R.B. Bennett came to town to declare Canada a success in weathering the Depression. A street photographer who became a Vancouver institution began taking pictures of passersby on Granville Street, and the Pacific National Exhibition gave away its first prize home.

January 1 There was a riot in Chinatown as "more than 1,000 Orientals and white men" battled savagely. Police reserves fought for more than an hour to disperse the mobs before the fire department was called to assist with high-pressure hoses. Cause of the riot was apparently an altercation between a Chinese taxi driver and his Occidental passenger. The driver allegedly struck the white man on the head with a hammer.

January 5 The Vancouver Library Board accepted city council help to reopen the library's reading room, closed for most of 1933 from lack of funds.

January 16 As it had done the year before, the *Sun* invited staff of the *Ubyssey*, the student newspaper at UBC, to edit the paper. Some of the *Ubyssey* staffers involved were Archie Thompson, John Cornish, Pat Kerr, Boyd Agnew, Nancy Miles, Norman Hacking (editor-in-chief of the *Ubyssey*), Alan Morley, Jack Paul, Darrel Gomery, Zoe Browne-Clayton and Dick Elson. Alan Morley's name leaps out: in 1961 he wrote the first (and still, in some ways, the best) Vancouver history: *Vancouver: From Milltown to Metropolis*.

January 19 Prime Minister R.B. Bennett spoke to the Vancouver Board of Trade's 47th anniversary dinner at the Hotel Vancouver. Among his words: "Canada is a world example of successful weathering of this depression." Yeah, right.

January Almost 4,000 passengers were ferried from the city to the Ambleside ferry dock on a single day in January 1934. Their destination: the trailhead on Hollyburn Mountain, popular with skiers and hikers.

March 24 "Jack" Drainie (more well known later as John) appeared in Maxwell Anderson's *Elizabeth the Queen*, a play produced by the Vancouver Little Theatre Association. Future judge J.V. Clyne played Sir Walter Raleigh.

May 13 Acting Premier A. Wells Gray cut the ribbon on a 25-bed children's hospital at 250 West 59th Ave. The official opening ceremony had been delayed for months by a scarlet fever outbreak.

May 21 William H. Malkin, former mayor and wholesale food merchant, turned the sod to mark the start of construction on Marion Malkin Bowl in Stanley Park. The bowl was his gift to the city as a memorial to his wife Marion, who had died in 1933. "It replaced an old circular bandstand which stood on the very same spot," Malkin recalled in a 1952 interview. "So many people were wondering why we had a village-style bandstand in a beautiful, big-city park that I decided something must be done about it." The "something" was a donation of $8,000, plenty of money in those Depression days. The shell of the structure was patterned after the famous Hollywood Bowl, and the original stage was 16.5 metres (54 feet) wide.

May Vancouver boxer Jimmy McLarnin, who had won the world welterweight championship in 1933, lost it to Barney Ross. He regained it from Ross in September but lost it, to Ross again, in May 1935.

June The Fraser Valley Union Library District, the first regional library in North America, was established with headquarters in Chilliwack. The per capita tax rate to finance the system was set at 35 cents annually. The financial hardship for the young system was offset by an agreement among the participating communities to provide rent-free space. (In 1950 the rate was raised to 40 cents.)

July 1 The first United Airlines flight arrived at the Vancouver Airport.

Elsewhere in Canada

May 28 The Dionne quintuplets were born in Callender, ON.

Victoria-born Lynn Patrick, 22, whose name is mostly associated with hockey, signed with football's Winnipeg Blue Bombers. In the first game he set a season record for the team with a 68-yard touchdown reception.

Elsewhere in the World

May 29 Future BC premier Bill Vander Zalm (1986–91) was born in Noordwykerhout, the Netherlands. His family came to Canada in 1947. His full birth name was Wilhelmus Nicholaas Theodore Marie Vander Zalm.

Arriving on Dominion Day (now Canada Day), the first United Airlines flight, and the first modern, all-metal airliner in the city, landed at the Vancouver Airport, making Vancouver even more accessible to the rest of the world.
City of Vancouver Archives, CVA 1376-81

The move brought Vancouver air links with most of the continent and introduced the first modern airliner, the all-metal Boeing 247, capable of speeds up to 290 kilometres an hour (180 mph).

July 8 The Vancouver Symphony Orchestra gave its first performance at Malkin Bowl

to celebrate the performing space's official opening. In later years Theatre Under the Stars (TUTS) made the Bowl its home, and a group called the Home Gas Orchestra played there often.

Out on a beautiful summer day in Stanley Park, these concertgoers are enjoying the 1934 generosity of businessman and former mayor William H. Malkin, who built the Malkin Bowl in memory of his wife, Marion.
City of Vancouver Archives, CVA 1184-1963. Photo Jack Lindsay

July 13 Coquitlam councillor Thomas Douglas was shot dead at his North Road gas station. Because he was a socialist—he had run provincially for the United Front, a socialist party—some thought the murder had political overtones.

September First radio broadcasts of local lacrosse games.

November 17 R.H. Pooley, a Conservative MLA, made the *Province*'s front page with a charge that "professors at the University of British Columbia are teaching communism to our boys and girls... Those same professors are flourishing under the capitalist system. They are paid high salaries, but ask them to take a 10 per cent cut and they are the first to kick." UBC president Leonard Klinck said he didn't take Pooley very seriously. "Communism is dealt with, but it is never taught in the sense that Mr. Pooley means. After all, we can recognize the existence of a thing without preaching it."

November The reconstructed Second Narrows bridge opened, with an 85.3-metre (280-foot) lift span replacing the fixed spans damaged by the *Losmar* and *Pacific Gatherer* in 1930. Though ships still hit the bridge, it was never closed for more than 10 days. After the Ironworkers Memorial Second Narrows Crossing opened in 1960, the original bridge was closed to car traffic and sold to the CNR for a dollar in 1963. It was dismantled in 1970.

December 13 Gerald Grattan "Gerry" McGeer, 46, was swept into the mayoralty with the largest lead in Vancouver history: 25,000 votes out of 44,000 cast. He defeated Louis D. Taylor, the most elected mayor in the city's history. The McGeer victory put an end to Taylor's political career.

Also in 1934

Howard Rodgers operated a water taxi and rescue boat from Horseshoe Bay, running mercy missions for the Britannia Mines.

Amsterdam-born Dorothy Gretchen Steeves, 39, one of the founders of the CCF, was elected MLA for North Vancouver, one of seven original CCF members in BC. She held the seat for 11 years.

Convicts in the BC Penitentiary refused to work unless given wages, then went on a rampage, destroying prison property. It was the first disturbance of any note at the prison, but it would not be the last.

A long row of horse chestnut trees was planted on 17th Street in West Vancouver by Boy Scouts to commemorate the visit from England of Scout leader Lord Baden-Powell.

Berta Marega, sculptor Charles Marega's wife, died. "From that time," according to art historian Peggy Imredy, "regardless of his commissions and work, life appeared drained from him."

The Pacific National Exhibition gave away a home as part of the inaugural Prize Home Lottery, the first time such a significant prize had been awarded. The prize was valued at more than $5,000 including home, East Vancouver lot and furnishings (from Eaton's).

The Jewish Congress was founded in Vancouver.

The Kiwassa Club of Vancouver was formed by 100 wives of members of the Kiwanis Club of Vancouver.

St. Peter's Cathedral on Blackwood Street in New Westminster, built in 1886, was battered beyond repair by a powerful storm. A new church was planned.

Radio station CRCV appeared, headquartered on Station Street off Main. It had been CNRV, the CNR station, but was now run by a new entity, the Canadian Radio Broadcasting Commission, which in 1936 would become the Canadian Broadcasting Corporation or CBC.

Lily Alice Lefevre, poet and philanthropist, presented a $5,000 scholarship and gold medal to UBC in memory of her husband, Dr. John Matthew Lefevre (1853–1906). They had come to Vancouver in 1886, when Dr. Lefevre became surgeon general for the CPR's Pacific Division.

Deaf and blind Charlie Crane enrolled as a special student at UBC. He proved

Happy snapper. Standing behind his signature camera waiting for his next customer to walk down Granville Street, Foncie Pulice was a Vancouver institution for 45 years.. *George Diack/Vancouver Sun*

For a Lasting Souvenir

Granville Street today is not the place it once was. Storefronts have been pulled down, put up, redone and the blue-collar bustle has given way to nightclubs and world-class restaurants. But one missing piece of old Granville is not architectural; it's extremely human.

Walking up from Robson in 1934 or 1952 or 1969, you couldn't avoid Foncie. The enterprising photographer would snap your picture on the street and hand you a card that read, "Call and see a natural living photo of you and your friends for a lasting souvenir." If you felt inclined, you could pick up the pictures the next day, three for a dollar.

Foncie Pulice (the family pronounces it "police") worked all day, every day, charming passersby and making 40 cents on every hundred snaps, his enormous Electric camera flashing away at couples, families, anyone out and about. The faces he captured are those of an older, less polished Vancouver: businessmen, teenagers, tourists and dockyard labourers, relaxed and comfortable, often smiling, in the Granville sun or rain.

Journalist Stephen Hume tells the story of a Foncie snap—a young sailor and his girl out on the town in, perhaps, 1940—that found its way into a naval mural. The painting wound up in a seniors' home in Victoria, where the original sailor, now an old man, recognized himself and his late wife, 60 years later.

At the height of his success, Foncie was taking perhaps 4,000 snaps a day and running three businesses. He took pictures on Granville Street, at the Pacific National Exhibition, in Stanley Park, elsewhere. And during the war, as he told a *Province* interviewer in 1979, "the public couldn't get film, you see, so the street photographers were all they had. Servicemen would come home on leave, they'd have pictures taken. Families would get together, we'd take their picture." For some families he was essentially a portrait studio, taking appointments—always on the street—and offering multiple sizes of print.

Pulice wasn't the only one doing this at the time. Sidewalk photographers were taking candid shots of individuals, couples, families and other groups as they walked down main streets in many Canadian cities. What made Pulice unique in the trade was the length of time he kept at it: 45 years. A fixture of the Vancouver streets, he spent over four decades recording the changing face of Vancouver before hanging up his camera in 1979. Many of his photos are now in the Vancouver Museum.

Built in Coquitlam in 1934 by future BC Lieutenant-Governor Eric W. Hamber as a country retreat and hunting lodge, the opulent Minnekhada Lodge is now part of a regional park and is open to the public. *Leonard Frank photo, Vancouver Public Library VPL 12447*

outstanding in athletics, particularly in wrestling.

Bobby Jones, considered along with Jack Nicklaus one of the century's best golfers, visited Vancouver and played at Shaughnessy Heights Golf Club.

Jack Short, 25, began his astonishing run of broadcasting race results over CJOR. (He had started in 1933 on another station.) Too tall and lanky to succeed as a jockey, he called nearly 50,000 races at Exhibition Park, broadcast live for CJOR radio. He invariably signed off his broadcasts with the famous catchphrase "Adiós amigos!" Jack wrapped it up in 1976.

Eric W. Hamber built Minnekhada Lodge in Coquitlam as a country retreat and hunting lodge. Home to two Lieutenant-Governors—Hamber (1936–41) and Clarence Wallace (1950–55)—the estate has also hosted royalty and is now part of a GVRD park. The estate was named by an early owner, lumberman Harry Jenkins, who combined Sioux words meaning "rattling water."

Rintaro Hayashi and Yuiche Akune established the Steveston Kendo Club, the first in Canada. The club achieved a reputation of excellence but was disbanded in 1942 when members were relocated to internment camps away from the coast.

Jessie Columbia Hall, daughter of pugnacious pioneer Sam Greer, received Vancouver's Good Citizen Award.

Her long career of volunteerism included working with the Children's Aid Society, Vancouver Welfare Federation, Women's Auxiliary of Christ Church and others. During World War I she provided supplies for a French field hospital. She was the first woman to serve as a member of a Vancouver jury and also served as president of the Burrard Women's Conservative Club and Victorian Order of Nurses.

Dorothy Somerset, who had arrived in Vancouver from Australia in 1921, began as a director with the University Players' Club. She was a prominent theatre figure here for more than 50 years.

Two other women arrived in Vancouver this year and became major forces on the art scene. Mildred Valley Thornton was an artist and art critic; June Roper had been a dancer in Europe and became an influential dance teacher.

Local poet and social activist A.M. Stephen wrote the poem "Vancouver," which was published in the Province and later widely anthologized. Here is an excerpt:

Vancouver

Who can snare the soul of a city
  in a butterfly net of words?
Who can melt steel and concrete
  into the flowing matrix of song?
Yet there is a word-symbol,
  if it can be found,
There is a sign and a password
  in the plastic stuff of mind,
  an image behind the veil,
  that can reveal the meaning of a city.
Nineveh, Babylon, Rome—
  the sound of them is an echo in an
  empty room,
  stirring the dust of dead men's
  bones.
Vancouver—
  the sound of it is a wave,
  breaking on the shores of the future.

Comings and Goings

February 1 The Vienna Choir Boys performed in Vancouver. They appeared again in 1935, presented by New York impresario Sol Hurok.

June 15 Singer Arnie Nelson was born. He was a child star on CKNW.

Notable deaths: **Alphonse E. Savard**, commercial portrait photographer, died on May 1, aged about 70; **Frank E. Harrison**, former postmaster, died on July 5; **Joseph Moore Steves**, who developed BC's largest Holstein herd and supplied milk for Vancouver until the cattle were sold during the Depression, died on January 9. (Steves was the second son of William Herbert Steves, who founded Steveston.)

1935

The year was marked by marches and rallies of the unemployed—prompting use of the Riot Act—and the "On to Ottawa" trek to lobby for better conditions. Construction began on the current city hall with a controversial design and location, while a plebiscite changed the face of city politics by eliminating the ward system. This was also the year I (Chuck Davis) was born.

January 2 Gerry McGeer took office as mayor of Vancouver. He was voted into office on a promise to fight crime, and to do away with slot machines, gambling, bookmaking, white slavery and corruption in the police force.

January 21 Vancouver got 43 centimetres (17 inches) of snow, one of the snowiest 24 hours in the city's history. One result: the roof of the Hastings Park Forum collapsed. There were no injuries.

January A severe snow and ice storm, together with flooding, hit the Fraser Valley, cutting communication and transportation links and causing much other damage.

February 4 *West Vancouver No. 5* ferry sank after colliding with the CPR's *Princess Alice* off Prospect Point. A woman passenger lost her life.

March 1 In Burnaby, the BC Provincial Police took over from the municipal police. They enforced the law there until August 1950, when the RCMP took over.

March 11 The Bank of Canada was founded. Its first home in Vancouver was in Page House at 330 West Pender St., famous for its stained glass ceiling. There was a machine gun in the bank to defend its assets against bank robbers.

March 19 Thomas Owen Townley, former Vancouver mayor (1901), died in Florida at age 72. After losing in a bid for a second term he became registrar of land titles in Vancouver, a position he had held previously in New Westminster. He is also remembered as the commander of Vancouver's first militia.

Elsewhere in Canada

September 5 Charlotte Acres became the first Canadian woman to win a world professional swimming championship. She won the 5-mile (about 8-kilometre) swimming contest at the Canadian National Exhibition.

October 14 In the federal election, William Lyon Mackenzie King became prime minister. H.H. Stevens of Vancouver won the sole seat for his Reconstruction Party, out of 174 candidates. And Mayor Gerry McGeer was elected the Liberal MP for Vancouver–Burrard.

December Ottawa was reported to be considering raising unemployment insurance to $10 per week. This would give clients the same income as old age pensioners.

Elsewhere in the World

January 11 Aviator Amelia Earhart began a trip from Honolulu to Oakland, CA, becoming the first woman to fly solo across the Pacific Ocean.

March 28 F.M. Rattenbury, 67, the architect who gave Vancouver the courthouse now occupied by the Vancouver Art Gallery, was murdered. Rattenbury came to BC at age 25 and was quickly commissioned to design the provincial legislature, then the Empress Hotel and the Vancouver courthouse. But then commissions began drying up and "Ratz" got into real trouble when he began an affair with a younger married woman named Alma Pakenham. They both divorced and fled to England, where the family's 19-year-old chauffeur, who had also begun an affair with Alma, bashed in Rattenbury's head with a mallet.

November 6 Aviator Sir Charles Kingsford-Smith went down somewhere in or near "the shark-infested Bay of Bengal." He had been on a mail flight from Allahabad, India, to Singapore, an over-water distance of 2,188 kilometres (1,360 miles). Stories of his disappearance dominated newspapers in late 1935. He was never found. At the suggestion of city archivist Major J.S. Matthews, an elementary school at 6901 Elliott in Vancouver was named for Kingsford-Smith.

March 21 John Grove died, aged about 71. Grove served as lighthouse keeper at Prospect Point and later at Brockton Point (1895–1930). From 1888 he lived in a cottage on the rocks until the station was electrified in January 1926. To make extra money, Grove ran a lemonade stand for tourists, but the park board complained and the stand was closed down.

March Standard Oil purchased 22 hectares (55 acres) of land at the north foot of Willingdon in Burnaby for a refinery. The company moved quickly to purchase local oil distribution companies, acquire service stations, establish dealerships, start a new refinery (which processed California crude oil) and acquire a tanker, the *BC Standard*. The present-day company that inherited the Standard Oil mantle in this part of the world is Chevron.

April Unemployed men converged on Vancouver from labour camps around the province, marched to Victory Square and demanded financial assistance from the city. The mayor had the spokesmen arrested, then read the Riot Act to the assembled workers, who marched away. Police raided worker headquarters that evening, and a riot ensued. Police on horseback were called out to control it. McGeer was firmly on the side of the moneyed interests fearful of communist takeover, which alienated many of his former supporters, who sympathized with the strikers.

April 15 A Grand Rally of Boy Scouts and Girl Guides at Hastings Park welcomed Lord and Lady Baden-Powell.

May 4 Edward Faraday Odlum, author and scientist, died in Vancouver, aged 84. He came to the city on April 15, 1889. Odlum built the first electric arc light used here (for football games) and the first public telephone. In 1892 he was elected alderman. He was author of *A History of British Columbia* (1906), president of the Art, Historical and Scientific Association of Vancouver and father of Victor Odlum, soldier and newspaper publisher.

June 3 A thousand unemployed men boarded freight cars in Vancouver to begin the "On to Ottawa" trek protesting conditions for the unemployed. They were turned back at Regina. A story on the first page of the *Province* the next day included the following statistics: "A total of 6,255 single men were in relief camps in British Columbia last December 31, and 3,536 last April 30, according to a return tabled in the House of Commons. Since the date of inception of relief camps in the province in October, 1932, until last September, the average government expenditure for each man per day was $1.30, the return showed."

June 18 Wearing his Victoria Cross and Military Medal and carrying the Union Jack, James "Mickey" O'Rourke led a parade of 1,000 striking waterfront workers in what has come to be known as the Battle of Ballantyne Pier. City police responded with tear gas and billy clubs.

July 10 An ad in the *Province* proclaimed that "a vote for the CCF candidate is a vote to give the Chinaman and Japanese the same voting right that you have! A vote for a Liberal candidate is a vote against enfranchisement."

July 26 The Lyric Theatre on Granville Street opened as a movie house. It originally opened in 1891

Swarming the boxcars in 1935 to start the "On to Ottawa" protest, 1,000 jobless men sought justice and fair jobs six years after the stock markets had crashed in 1929. The men had been labouring in make-work camps under harsh conditions in remote areas of western Canada and were finally on strike. Perceived as a communist revolt, the protest was crushed by the RCMP in Regina. *National Archives Canada*

as the Vancouver Opera House and became the Orpheum (not the present one) in 1913, offering vaudeville acts. The Lyric closed in December 1960 and was demolished to make way for Pacific Centre.

July 31 Tragedy at Alta Lake when a Boeing flying boat piloted by W.R. McCluskey, manager of Pioneer Airways, crashed while attempting a takeoff from the lake. Aboard were three passengers, UBC dean Reginald W. Brock, his wife Mildred, and a man named David Sloan. McCluskey and Brock were killed on impact. Mrs. Brock died en route to hospital, and Sloan died 10 days later in hospital. Making the crash particularly sad was the fact that two of the Brocks' sons, David and Tommy, witnessed it. Reginald Brock was one of Canada's leading geologists. He had been director of the Geological Survey of Canada from 1907 to 1914 and was one of the first four teachers hired by UBC president Frank Wesbrook.

August Fourteen Chinese potato trucks crashed barricades at Marpole Bridge that were erected to prevent their delivering their produce to wholesalers. The BC Coast Vegetable Marketing Board had been established a year earlier to restrict the Chinese gardeners' share of the market, and the barricades were one of the tactics it used. The farmers driving the trucks were ultimately released without charges because the Crown failed to prove the produce they were transporting was for local sale.

Summer The Kitsilano Showboat began operation as a forum for amateur talent that continues to this day.

September 20 George Henry Cowan, lawyer, author and public speaker, died in Vancouver, aged about 77. He practised law, was appointed Queen's Counsel for the Dominion government in 1896 and King's Counsel for the BC government in 1905. An anti-Asiatic, he drafted the Chinese Head Tax law. He was the author of *Better Terms for British Columbians* (1904), a founder of Vancouver's Conservative Association and MP for Vancouver from 1908 to 1911. In 1896, while campaigning by boat to represent Burrard in the federal election, Cowan was impressed by the southeast tip of Bowen Island. He bought 46 hectares (114 acres) there in 1899, and by 1917 had 400 hectares (1,000 acres), on which he

Showtime. Superimposing a splash of fun on an awe-inspiring view, the Kitsilano Showboat opened in 1935 to provide a venue for amateur talent. Nearly 80 years later, the show goes on. Vancouver Sun

City Hall—"That Modernistic Monstrosity"

October 5 Ground was broken to mark the start of construction of the new city hall, Vancouver's sixth. The silver spade used in the ceremony to start the digging was presented by Alderman Halford Wilson to a beaming Mayor Gerry McGeer.

Just a few months into his first term in 1935 McGeer led the fight to place a new city hall in the block bounded by Cambie Street, West 12th Avenue, Yukon and West 11th, then occupied by Strathcona Park. A squabble over the building's location had been going on for a decade. McGeer favoured the Strathcona Park site for several reasons: it was high, so the building would be seen from many parts of the city and would itself provide good views; the city already owned the land, and there would be lots of room for the building and landscaped grounds around it; it would spark an extension of the Cambie streetcar line and that, in turn, would spur development of the area; and it would cement links with the recently annexed municipalities of South Vancouver (the northern boundary of which had been just four blocks south, on 16th Avenue) and Point Grey.

McGeer also led the decision to accept the design submitted by the architectural firm of Townley & Matheson, a design that was not greeted with unanimous cries of admiration. One letter to McGeer (now in the City Archives) read: "Have you no eye for beauty? Why put up an eyesore and...a pile of concrete like that modernistic monstrosity pictured in the local papers? It looks just like Nelson's Laundry. It is a crime to put up a filthy looking structure like that...On such a beautiful site it is doubly bad." A special bond issue was announced to raise money for the $1-million building, but it ran into severe opposition from the business community. Most of the opposition to the Strathcona site had come from local businessmen, who wanted city hall downtown so they wouldn't have to go so far to get to it.

Another letter writer harrumphed, "We do not relish the idea of going some two-and-a-half miles from the centre of the business section of this city to do business in this proposed new city 'pile.' Change your location to the Central School site, and we do not think you will have too much trouble selling your bonds."

If those businessmen had prevailed, today's city hall would be in that "Central School site," the block bounded by Pender and Dunsmuir, Cambie and Hamilton, and immediately north of the Queen Elizabeth Theatre.

built cottages for family and friends. Cowan Road on Bowen Island is named for him.

October Work began on the Pattullo Bridge

(it opened November 15, 1937).

November 8 The *Province* had an interesting front-page story: a local 15-year-old had left home in 1932 to go swimming in the Fraser River. He never returned. His parents had reconciled themselves to the fact he drowned. He showed up three years later; said he'd been working on a farm in Toronto.

Also November 8 The City of Vancouver Archives received a gift from the CPR: an inch of the rail from Craigellachie, site of the last spike.

November 11 The cornerstone for St. James Anglican Church at Gore and Cordova Streets was laid on Remembrance Day, with the ceremony conducted by the Most Rev. A.U. dePencier, archbishop of New Westminster. The church's architect was Adrian Gilbert Scott, who was apparently influenced by a building he had seen in Cairo, Egypt.

November 15 A young schoolboy named Jack Cullen bought (for 35 cents) his first record, a song called "Don't Give Up the Ship," warbled by Dick Powell. In future years "Boy Disc Jockey" Jack Cullen's collection of records, transcriptions and discs became one of the world's largest, and his late-night CKNW show, *The Owl Prowl*, was hugely successful.

November 22 James Ramsay, biscuit maker, died in Vancouver, aged 68. In 1891 (or 1892) he moved to Vancouver and established Ramsay Bros. and Co., manufacturer of biscuits, candies and syrup. A Vancouver alderman and MLA, Ramsay was chair of the Vancouver School Board for ten years, a president of the YMCA and a Vancouver General Hospital board member. His many activities included a term as president of the Canadian and the BC manufacturer's associations.

December Vancouver voters decided to end the ward system.

Turnout was only 19 percent of eligible voters, but 69 percent of them supported the at-large electoral system. In March 1936 the provincial government amended the city's charter accordingly. The *Vancouver Sun* interviewed city clerk Fred Howlett about the low voter turnout and reported on December 11 that "interest in the election seemed slacker than he had ever seen in his experience dating back to 1910, including 24 previous contests." Explanations offered: "no popular public issue" and "light rain."

Also in 1935

The BC Archives began to collect its substantial holdings of radio broadcast recordings from privately owned radio stations in Vancouver, Victoria and the BC Interior, as well as the CBC. These include acetate disc recordings from the period 1935 to 1960.

Bandleader Mart Kenney and his Western Gentlemen gained national renown with a series of CBC radio programs, notably the Sunday night favorite *Sweet and Low*. That show began this year, broadcast live and heard right across the country from the original Hotel Vancouver's ritzy Spanish Grill. (In later years Kenney would again perform in the Spanish Grill, this time in the present Hotel Vancouver. That dining room is now called Griffins.)

The Fairleigh family built the Hollywood Theatre, and began to run it.

The *Vancouver Sun* began to campaign for a convention bureau. Said alderman J.J. McRae: "Our merchants need the business that conventions bring, and our city can stand a little of the cheer that throngs of visitors bring to the city."

The first provincial curling championship was held. Joe Dundas of Vancouver won.

A special committee of the BC Medical Association was formed to investigate what could be done about an increasing incidence of cancer and lack of treatment facilities. Dr. C.W. Proud, a pioneer in treatment and research in cancer, set the objective of forming a cancer institute. The BC Cancer Foundation was incorporated under the Canadian Societies Act, and funds were borrowed to purchase 3.5 grams of radium, a precious commodity.

The Depression was taking a toll on the Chinese community as 80 percent of Chinese workers were unemployed. The Anglican Church Mission set up a soup kitchen in Chinatown, and the Chinese Benevolent Association appealed to city council for assistance. The Provincial Workers Council and Chinese Workers Protective Association petitioned jointly for the relief of unemployed Chinese. In response, the provincial labour department sent 217 destitute Chinese back to China because the cost of passage was deemed cheaper than ongoing relief payments.

Fraserview Golf Course, the first public golf course in Vancouver,

Little Orpheum Ackery

Ivan Ackery became manager of the Orpheum Theatre, a position he held until 1969.

The young British-born entrepreneur shaped the childhood of a generation. He may have been best known for his advertising stunts—walking down Granville Street with a cow and a sign reading "There's a great show at the Orpheum and that's no bull" was particularly popular—but to the city's children, Ackery's greatest achievement was not the sell but the product.

Against the grim backdrop of Depression-era Vancouver, Ackery's Orpheum was a child's passport into paradise: not just the wonderful escape offered by the films themselves, but the still-glamorous theatre where they were treated as princes and princesses, and, indeed, crowned kings and queens by lottery at the end of every month.

Henry Lee, seven years old in 1937, later recalled his first trip: "This was the Great Depression, and we were a very, very poor family. All I had heard about was the palaces that my dad described to me in China. This was the first time I'd seen something in actual form, and it staggered me, it absolutely staggered me." He wasn't alone. Though many families had to save for a week to attend a movie—admittance was 10 cents—the experience was deeply memorable, perhaps more memorable than the onscreen antics.

Denny Boyd wrote in the *Vancouver Sun*, "The rose-red carpeting led to the dramatic split stairway to the upper foyer, light cascading down from the chandeliers and the wall sconces. There were balustrades and ornate arches, pillars and colonnades, coffered and domed ceilings...I didn't know Ivan Ackery then, only what he gave us. I sensed that someone was being terrifically kind to us on those Saturday mornings in the Depression, giving us two features, 30 minutes of cartoons, a Pete Smith Specialty and the newsreel, all for a dime. We were made welcome. Nobody shushed us when we screamed as the giant tarantulas crept up on Tarzan."

Having survived the greatest economic crisis of the century, "Little Orpheum Ackery" continued to run the Orpheum as a successful venture for many years, bringing in stars and premieres by the dozen, not to mention employing usherettes in costume—matched, of course, to his features—among other marketing feats. Yet he still had one great last act up his sleeve.

In the 1970s, when a construction boom was sweeping Vancouver and the great old theatres of Granville's vaudeville heyday were settling into ruin and decay, the Orpheum was slated to be torn down to make way for a boxy multiplex. Ackery and impresario Hugh Pickett launched a campaign to save the last of the movie palaces. Their campaign, backed by thousands of Vancouverites, was successful.

The Orpheum became a civic theatre, home to the Vancouver Symphony, and was renovated for live, amplified performance—not without some difficulty. A new false ceiling in the original style was suspended from the roof. On April 2, 1977, the Orpheum once again opened its doors to a crowd waiting to be delighted, and once again they were.

Ivan Ackery died in 1989, a day short of his ninetieth birthday. He was a war hero at 15, having lied about his age to enlist during World War I and having fought at Vimy Ridge. He was a star in Vancouver; he'd met Cary Grant and Marilyn Monroe and shared drinks with the boisterous Gary Cooper and the demure Princess Margaret. Yet these events are only a footnote to the obituary of the man who can be described, without irony, as a hero of the silver screen.

opened. In the early 1950s a residential development was built west of the course and named Fraserview. The development's curved streets were named after famous golf courses of the world.

Comings and Goings

August 10 Visiting author Will Durant spoke at the Auditorium.

England's Joyce Wethered, 34, considered by many the best female golfer ever, broke the course record at Jericho with a 73. (An indication of her skill: the great golfer Bobby Jones said: "I have never played against anyone and felt so outclassed.")

Notable births: **Joy Kogawa**, daughter of an Anglican minister, was born Joy Nozonie Nokayama in Vancouver on June 6 (her superb award-winning 1981 novel *Obasan* is a story of the Japanese Canadian internment); poet **Patricia Louise "Pat" Lowther** was born in Vancouver, July 29; writer/broadcaster **Chuck Davis** was born in Winnipeg on November 17 (he came to Vancouver in 1944); novelist and poet **George Bowering** was born in the Okanagan, December 1.

May 4 Frank William Hart died in Prince Rupert, aged 78. Hart's Swedish family had come here from the US, and in 1887 he built the city's first theatre, Hart's Opera House, on Carrall Street. It presented amateur shows, touring companies, variety and vaudeville and was also a roller-skating facility.

Architect Thomas Hooper died in Vancouver. Some of his work includes the Winch Building (now part of Sinclair Centre), the Spencer Building on Cordova, and the rear addition (Robson Street side) to the Vancouver courthouse. A number of well-known architects apprenticed in his office, including J.Y. McCarter, architect of Vancouver's Marine Building.

December J.S. Ross, the first editor of the *Vancouver Daily News* (1886), died.

Golfers' treat. Fraserview Golf Course, the first public golf facility in Vancouver, opened its front nine holes to the public, making it accessible to all who wished to be frustrated by the clever sport. *City of Vancouver Archives, CVA 392-439*

1936

The city celebrated its Golden Jubilee with the opening of a new city hall and a new church that was later described as the best building in Vancouver. The main sports arena burned down just hours after thousands watched a controversial boxing match.

January 20
Vancouver's radio stations went off the air to mark the death of King George V. A memorial service was held on January 28 at Malkin Bowl.

January 31 Mount Seymour Provincial Park, then only 274 hectares (about 680 acres), was opened.

March 17 Charles Edward Tisdall, alderman, died in office, aged 69. Tisdall was born April 9, 1866, in Birmingham, England, and arrived in the city in April 1888. He was mayor of Vancouver from 1922 to 1923, selected under a system of proportional representation in which the candidate for city council getting the most votes became mayor. His long record of public service (he had earlier been a Conservative MLA, a park board member and an alderman) no doubt helped in his mayoral run.

March 27 George Emery Cates, shipbuilder, died in Vancouver. Born December 6, 1861, in Machias, MA, Cates began working at age nine. After learning shipbuilding in New York City, he was employed on a schooner as a cook. Cates arrived in Vancouver in 1896 and started Cates Shipyards, where he built the 500-ton steamship *Britannia*, Klondike scows and a 500-horsepower electric plant.

April 25 Charles Woodward, retailer, predicted that "within 40, at the outside 50, years Vancouver will be the largest city in Canada."

May 24
Civic Golden Jubilee celebrations, marking the city's 50th birthday, began in Vancouver.

June 4 Jubilee celebrations sparked articles in local newspapers on the city's early days. On this date the *Vancouver Sun* had an interesting

Elsewhere in BC

May 1 Eric Hamber, athlete and business executive, became Lieutenant-Governor.

Elsewhere in Canada

May 22 The Japanese Canadian Citizens League sent four *nisei* to Ottawa to appear before the House of Commons Franchise Revision Committee in an attempt to secure political and economic rights for the Japanese community. The motion to allow Hide Hyodo (a schoolteacher at Lord Byng School in Steveston), Minoru Kobayashi (an insurance agent in Steveston), Dr. Edward Banno (a Vancouver dentist), and Dr. Samuel Ichiye Hayakawa (professor of English at the University of Wisconsin, who later became president of San Francisco State College) to speak to the committee was voted down.

Elsewhere in the World

January 20 King George V died. He was succeeded by Edward VIII, who, 324 days later abdicated because he "found it impossible to carry the heavy burden of responsibility and to discharge [his] duties as King... without the help and support of the woman" he loved. The woman was, of course, Wallis Simpson, an American divorcee, and neither the royal family, the British political establishment or the Church of England would accept her as Edward's wife. Edward's brother Albert Frederick Arthur George, Duke of York, became King George VI, and his 10-year-old daughter, Elizabeth, became next in line of succession.

August 1 The Olympic Games began in Berlin. Vancouver diver George Athans, Sr. competed in these games, and Percy Norman coached the Canadian swimming team. Covering the event for the *Vancouver Sun*: 28-year-old Erwin Swangard. And sitting in the stands observing the activities: German Chancellor Adolf Hitler.

Major Austin Cotterell Taylor, who bred racehorses at his A.C.T. Stock Farm in Milner (now part of Langley), did a lot to establish Thoroughbred horseracing in BC. In 1936, his Indian Broom was second favourite in the Kentucky Derby, finishing a hard-driving third.

article about the early rivalry between Vancouver and Port Moody. It quoted Edward Mallandaine, editor of the 1887 *British Columbia Directory*, who wrote: "The new town called Vancouver will, no doubt, be of some detriment to Port Moody." The *Sun* noted that "the words were written before the first CPR train arrived at Vancouver, but already Vancouver had a population nearly three times as great as Port Moody's, the city which, up to a year or two before, had every reason to expect that it would be the terminus of the Canadian Pacific Railway and, therefore, the metropolis of the Canadian Pacific Coast...Several men who later become well-known citizens of Vancouver lived then at Port Moody," and "more than 100—that is, approximately half of the males listed in the Port Moody section of the directory were employees of the CPR, about twice as many men as the company was employing at that date in Vancouver."

June The BC Coast Vegetable Marketing Board began seizing shipments of potatoes, grown by Chinese farmers, that were stored in Vancouver warehouses. Ladner farmers Chung Chuck and Mah Lai went to the BC Supreme Court for an injunction against the board, and when the board continued to stop trucks, the farmers asked that board officials be jailed for contempt of court. At the time, Chinese peddlers were petitioning city council for protection from inspectors who were deliberately dumping their produce on the street for "inspection purposes." In January 1937 the Privy Council ruled that provincial laws regulating the marketing of tree fruits and vegetables (which had the intended effect of stifling Chinese farmers) were invalid, prompting Chinese Canadian farmers and wholesalers to sue the marketing board for levies it had unlawfully collected.

Lined up in anticipation of the festivities to begin, Vancouverites in 1936 were eager to celebrate their city's first 50 years. *Philip Timms photo, Vancouver Public Library VPL 67000*

July 2 Mayor Gerry McGeer laid the cornerstone for the new city hall.

July 18 The Chinese community erected a Chinese Carnival Village at Pender and Carrall to celebrate the Vancouver Jubilee. A replica seven-storey pagoda and a traditional Chinese gate were imported from China for the occasion, and Grace Kwan was elected Jubilee Queen. The Chinese village became one of the Jubilee's most popular attractions. For most non-Chinese, it was the first introduction to the Chinese community in their city.

August 10 John Irving, steamship captain, died in Vancouver, aged 81. The son of Captain William Irving, John was born November 24, 1854, in Portland, OR, and came to New Westminster with his family in 1858. At 16 he joined his father's steamboat business, taking over a year later when his father died. By 1883 John was head of Canadian Pacific Navigation, a consolidation of the Irving and Hudson's Bay Company lines, and in 1890 he launched Columbia and Kootenai Steam Navigation, buying and building boats. CPR bought both lines, which became the BC Coast Service and the BC Lake and River Service, respectively. Irving then founded John Irving Navigation, which he sold in 1906 to White Pass Railway. John Irving was MLA for Cassiar from 1894 to 1901.

August 19 Max Baer fought in Vancouver's 10,000-seat Denman Arena, and the *Province*'s Bill Forst wrote a funny column about Baer's terrified opponent, James J. Walsh, who billed himself as the Alberta Assassin: "Obviously scared to death, Mr. Wobbly Walsh didn't even wait for a good excuse to 'dive.' He dashed out of his corner in a terrified frenzy of energy, wrapped both arms around Baer's middle and hung on. Baer jostled and jolted, wrestled and wriggled. Finally Walsh let loose, and apparently quite dizzy as a result of his minute and a half of waltzing, rolled to the floor. He was so dizzy he couldn't get up again, try as he might (or maybe he didn't). At the count of ten he made a quick recovery."

Right: Flying aces. Demonstrating air defence, the Flying Seven—an all-female flying group—took to the air one day in November 1936 and then kept at least one airplane over Vancouver throughout each 24-hour day. During World War II the group was instrumental in training women in parachute and aircraft maintenance.
City of Vancouver, CVA 371-478.

Baer's manager, Ancil Hoffman, had suspected Walsh wouldn't last long and had Buddy Baer dressed for action. Buddy boxed 10 rounds with his older brother. It was the first time the two Baers appeared together in the ring.

August 20 A few hours after the Baer fight, the Denman Arena burned down,

taking with it 25 years of memories. The Vancouver Millionaires won the 1915 Stanley Cup in the arena. Dempsey and Braddock had fought there, Rudolph Valentino had judged a beauty contest and Sir Arthur Conan Doyle (creator of Sherlock Holmes) had given a speech in the building. Also destroyed in the blaze were three adjacent shipbuilding plants. No lives were lost. City Fire Marshal J.A. Thomas fumed to the newspapers that the building had been the worst fire trap in Vancouver "ever since it was built." "If it had started to burn with the crowd still in it," he said, "the death toll could easily have reached 1,000."

In celebration of Vancouver's Golden Jubilee, an 8-foot-high statue of Captain George Vancouver was unveiled in 1936 in front of the new city hall building, which was still under construction at the time. Doing the honours was Sir Percy Vincent, the visiting Lord Mayor of London.
City of Vancouver Archives, Mon P78

Also on August 20 A 2.5-metre (8-foot) statue of Captain George Vancouver was unveiled at Vancouver City Hall by the visiting Lord Mayor of London, Sir Percy Vincent. Sir Percy also presented a civic mace to the city. The bronze and granite statue (carved by Charles Marega) and the mace are still at city hall. Among the other gifts the Lord Mayor brought: "a sprig from a tree in the orchard where a falling apple gave Isaac Newton the idea that led to his theory of gravity." Hmm. I wonder where that sprig is today? (Incidentally, a few days before Mayor Gerry McGeer welcomed Sir Percy, he [McGeer] had been made an honorary Squamish chief.)

August 22 The Army of the Common Good, a self-help group formed

during the Great Depression, created the "Common Good Credit Unit" with six charter members and $10.25 in deposits. This is considered the beginning of the credit union movement in BC. Within two months, deposits at the Common Good Credit Unit more than doubled, to $25.10. The first loan, for $27, was made May 22, 1937.

August 29 Visiting Governor General Lord Tweedsmuir officiated at the opening of the Seaforth Armoury (Tweedsmuir, whose name was John Buchan, was the author of a bestselling mystery, *The Thirty-Nine Steps.*) A day later he was seated among the congregation for the first service held in St. James Anglican Church, at Gore and Cordova. The *Province* wrote that Tweedsmuir "joined in the response and bowed humbly in prayer, hardly to be distinguished from the commoners around him." A lot of people, architect Arthur Erickson among them, say this is the best single building in Vancouver. It is the third church of the same name in Vancouver. The first one burned in the Great Fire of 1886 (its melted bell is a treasured artifact at the Vancouver Museum), and the second lasted until this building opened.

October 2 UBC Stadium opened.

November We're not sure if the Flying Seven, an all-women flying group, was formed in November, but we do know that it conducted its first "fly-over" this month. The Flying Seven Canadian Women Pilots flew out of Sea Island. During World War II, club members trained women in parachute packing, fabric work and other aspects of airplane care. Some of the trainees joined Boeing's Vancouver plant or the RAF's women's division. One of the original members, Betsy Flaherty, who had received her flying licence on December 16, 1931, aged about 53, was the oldest female pilot in Canada. During the

The new Vancouver City Hall at Cambie and 12th was completed on December 1, 1936. Nine days later, a municipal election decided the first mayoral occupant, George Clark Miller, who won as an independent promising to stop political "bickering."
Province *Newspaper photo, Vancouver Public Library VPL 40212*

1936 fly-over, the seven women took turns flying, keeping at least one plane aloft over the city for 24 hours as a demonstration of air defence.

December 1
Vancouver's new city hall opened for business.

Each lock plate on the outer doors displayed the Vancouver coat of arms, and each doorknob bore the monogram of the building. The ceiling on the second floor of the rotunda was gilded with gold leaf from several BC mines. In March 1976, city hall was designated a heritage building. The building's architects were Townley and Matheson.

December 4 The *News-Herald* was lavish in its praise of Vancouver's new city hall, describing it as "a temple of justice." (In the same edition of the newspaper was an advertisement for a local restaurant advising that it featured "All White Help.")

December 9 A civic election decided that the first mayor to occupy Vancouver's brand-new city hall—he would move in January 2, 1937—would be George Clark Miller, who had been an alderman. The *Province* described the mayoral fight as a "stiff one" and said that it "divided the east and west sections of the city into opposing camps." Miller defeated L.D. McDonald, C.E. Thompson and former mayor Louis D. Taylor, 79, in the first election under the at-large system, which replaced the previous ward system. (Gerry McGeer had been elected to the federal Parliament in 1935 so did not run in the civic election.)

Also in 1936

Vancouver's main post office, at the northwest corner of Hastings and Granville, underwent a major expansion: a tunnel was built to the CPR station and the lobby was richly refurbished in bronze, cedar, terracotta and marble.

The *Hollyburn* was built for the West Vancouver Municipal Ferry system, the last vessel to join the fleet. It was sold to Harbour Navigation in 1945 and became an excursion vessel, and celebrated its 50th birthday during Expo 86.

The Vancouver Historical Society was incorporated.

There was a triple hanging (three prisoners in one day) at Oakalla, and several double hangings during the year.

The National Harbours Board took over the Port of Vancouver. The same

The Sheet Metal Workers Local 280 had this 12-foot rocket designed in 1936 for a parade celebrating Vancouver's 50th anniversary. The intent was to symbolize "the role played by craftsmanship and transportation in the growth of Vancouver." It now stands at the southwest end of the Cambie Street Bridge.
Vancouver Public Library, Special Collections, VPL 16850. Stuart Thomson photo

Carved by Chief Joe Capilano of North Vancouver, the Thunderbird Dynasty Pole was dedicated in 1936 at Prospect Point in Stanley Park. It was erected to commemorate the fateful meeting of the Squamish people and Captain George Vancouver on June 12, 1792. The pole was a popular tourist destination until it succumbed to carpenter ants. *Philip Timms photo, Vancouver Public Library VPL 4931*

year, Major B.D.C. Treatt, a British expert in coastal defence, assessed the port and recommended measures for defence in case of attack by Japan. Treatt carried out a similar review for Cape Breton in 1936.

Plimley Motors, a British car dealership, opened in Vancouver. Car ownership was gradually increasing, but many people felt operating costs were still too high. Gas was selling for 25 cents a gallon in the city—that's 6.6 cents per litre.

Hilker Attractions, Vancouver's first concert agency, began operations. Run by Ontario-born Harry Hilker and his Vancouver-born son Gordon, 23, the agency brought in more than 1,000 performers, including Yehudi Menuhin, Paul Robeson and Isaac Stern.

Several recreational facilities opened, including New Brighton Outdoor Pool and the Capilano Golf and Country Club opened in West Vancouver.

Canadian Airways decided to compete with United on the Seattle–Vancouver run, starting out with aging biplanes, but then graduating to Lockheed 10 Electras, among the fastest airliners of the time.

As part of the city's Golden Jubilee celebrations, six new totem poles joined two that had been erected at Brockton Point in 1912. Two have since been moved to the Royal BC Museum and replaced with replicas or new poles. Also this year, the Thunderbird Dynasty Pole was dedicated at Prospect Point. Carved by Chief Joe Capilano of North Vancouver, the pole commemorates the meeting of the Squamish people and Capt. George Vancouver near the mouth of the Capilano River on June 12, 1792.

The Industrial Building at the Pacific National Exhibition, built in 1910 at a cost of $50,000, was demolished. It was described as "flashy, but badly constructed." Despite—or, perhaps, because of—the Depression, attendance at the fair continued to climb: it hit 377,000 this year. (Average attendance during the 1920s was about 200,000.)

Chaldecott Road was renamed King Edward Avenue. It was originally named for F.M. Chaldecott, a solicitor, early settler in Point Grey and one of the organizers of the Municipality of South Vancouver.

The Vancouver Park Board declared that Oppenheimer Park was the only park where political, religious or other views could be publicly voiced. It was a favourite rallying point for Depression-era rallies and demonstrations.

The Greater Vancouver Publicity Association changed its name to the Greater Vancouver Tourist Association. (Today it's Tourism Vancouver.)

Notte's Bon Ton pastry shop, famous for its cakes and confections, moved from West 14th and Granville to the downtown Granville Street location it would occupy for the next 65 years.

Right: Game of stars. In the spirit of camaraderie, Vancouver and Hollywood cricket teams pose together in this 1936 photo, when the Hollywood team came up for a game. Reflecting the British force behind the Hollywood cricket scene, stars such as Errol Flynn (front row, far left with pipe), Nigel Bruce (next to Flynn) and C. Aubrey Smith (front and centre, also with pipe) are pictured. *City of Vancouver Archives, Port P1494.2. Photo Stuart Thomson*

The undoubted star of Vancouver's Golden Jubilee Open was famous golfer Byron Nelson. But a local boy, Vancouver amateur Ken Black, won the title with an astonishing eight-under-par 29 on Shaughnessy's final nine.

Shinkichi Tamura, banker and builder, died in Japan, aged about 73. He came to BC in 1888 and worked at a sawmill, later establishing the Sien Ban export company and the New World Hotel, and becoming Japantown's foremost banker. He was Canada's first trade commissioner to Japan and was the only Japanese listed in the 1911 *Who's Who in Western Canada*. In July 2001 the St. James Community Service Society bought the New World Hotel for low-income housing and renamed it Tamura House.

The Lost Lagoon Fountain went into action. It had been purchased from Chicago, a leftover from that city's world fair. When it was installed, some city residents complained about the expenditure of $35,000 in the depths of the Great Depression.

George Moir, provincial minister of education and provincial secretary, a Liberal MLA since 1933, campaigned for health insurance coverage for those living on $1,800 a year or less. Although opposition from doctors killed the proposal, it was the basis of the BC Hospital Insurance Act.

Comings and Goings

July 4 In cricket news: a Hollywood XI visited the city to play a Vancouver XI at Brockton Point, after the Vancouver team visited Hollywood the previous year. Playing for Hollywood were, among others, Errol Flynn (attracting a lot of attention), Boris Karloff and C. Aubrey Smith.

When it was installed in 1936, the Lost Lagoon Fountain added a touch of elegance to Stanley Park. The fountain had been purchased as a leftover from the Chicago World Fair.

City of Vancouver Archives, St Pk N142.08. Photo W.J. Moore

August 12 A giant of Canadian music, Sir Ernest MacMillan, came to the city as a guest conductor of the Vancouver Symphony Orchestra. Sir Ernest was principal of the Toronto Conservatory of Music, dean of the faculty of music at the University of Toronto and conductor of the Toronto Symphony Orchestra. He'd become Sir Ernest the year before, the first person knighted outside the UK for contributions to music.

The Hoboken Four, a singing quartet, appeared at the Orpheum as part of a tour by the Major Bowes Amateur Hour. One of the four was a skinny 20-year-old named Frank Sinatra. He wrote his mom while here, telling her how much he missed Hoboken.

Notable births: **David Suzuki**, Canada's best-known scientist; **Rolf Knight**, historian of working-class history; **Norbert Vesak**, Vancouver's first modern dance professional.

Notable deaths: **Sir Francis Stillman "Frank" Barnard**, founder of Vancouver's streetcar system, managing director of BC Electric Railway and Lieutenant-Governor (1914–19), died in Esquimalt on April 11, aged about 80; **Robert James Cromie**, founder of the *Vancouver Sun*, died in Victoria on May 11, aged 48; **Frank Cornwall McTavish**, orthopedic surgeon and provincial secretary of St. John's Ambulance, died November 8, aged about 64; **Hugh Crawford Magee**, first farmer to settle on the North Arm of the Fraser and a pioneer Point Grey farmer, died December 2, aged about 78 (he was also the namesake of Magee Secondary School); **Jacob Grauer**, pioneer and father of BC Electric president Dal Grauer, aged about 75.

1937

When Vancouver elected its first female councillor as a socialist party candidate, the business community responded by forming the Non-Partisan Association, which would dominate civic politics for most of the century. As construction began on the Lions Gate Bridge, a factory on Coal Harbour started making warplanes. And sliced bread became the city's newest best thing.

February 2 Eudora Jane Lochead died in North Vancouver. She had opened Hastings Grove Store, the first general store in the area, in 1911. Above the store she ran a rooming house with 20 bedrooms (tents outside housed the overflow). In 1913 she opened a second store at Sperling and Hastings, with a post office added March 1, 1914.

March 5 First mention of "marihuana" in a Vancouver newspaper.

The story in the *Province* reported that traces of hemp were found in a dead man's stomach.

March 22 Fire destroyed the business and editorial offices of the *Vancouver Sun* at 125 West Pender, with damage set at more than $200,000. There was just one casualty: the janitor suffered minor burns and smoke inhalation. *The newspaper came out on time that day*. The *Sun* moved into the Bekins Building across the street and bought the building May 18. We still know it today as the old Sun Tower.

Right: Trailblazer. A long-time political and labour activist, Helena Gutteridge addresses a crowd during labour unrest in this 1938 photo. In 1937 Gutteridge had become the first woman ever elected to Vancouver city council. *Vancouver Public Library, Special Collections, VPL 13333*

March 24 Helena Gutteridge of the Commonwealth Co-operative Federation (CCF) became the first woman ever elected to Vancouver city council, but she had been politically active long before that. Gutteridge came to Vancouver from England in 1911 and organized the BC Women's Suffrage League, fighting for votes for women. In 1915 she convinced the Vancouver Trades and Labour Council to support equal pay for equal work in their constitution, and in 1919 she united labour with women's groups and won passage of BC's first minimum wage act. (It varied by industry, but $13 to $15 a week was the range.)

March 31 Construction began on the Lions Gate Bridge, then the longest suspension bridge in the British Empire, to give better access to the British Properties. More than 300 men were employed in the construction.

May 12 A Coronation Day service was held at Brockton Point in Stanley Park to celebrate the accession to the throne of George VI and Queen Elizabeth. Alderman Jonathan Rogers planted the King George VI oak in the park.

Elsewhere in BC

Richard Arlen, Lilli Palmer and Antoinette Cellier starred in a movie filmed in and around Revelstoke. *Silent Barriers* is about building the CPR through the Rockies, and there are a lot of familiar names portrayed: William Van Horne, Sir John A. Macdonald, Major Rogers, James Hill... The movie plays fast and loose with the facts, but it's fun to watch.

Elsewhere in the World

May 6 Something went terribly wrong as the mighty German passenger zeppelin *Hindenburg* attempted a mooring at Lakehurst, NJ. The airship burst into flames and crashed. The famous film of that disaster has been seen countless times since.

May 27 The Golden Gate Bridge opened in San Francisco.

June 22 Alabama-born Joe Louis, 23, faced world heavyweight champion James J. Braddock in a title bout at Chicago's Comiskey Park. Although he was dropped early in the fight, Louis rose from the canvas to score an eighth-round knockout.

June 3 The Duke and Duchess of Windsor were married in France.

July 2 Aviator Amelia Earhart, three weeks short of her 40th birthday, went missing on a flight over the South Pacific. She was never found.

Under construction in 1937—and a long drop to the drink—the Lions Gate Bridge was a private venture built to give better access to the British Properties in West Vancouver.
City of Vancouver Archives, Br P81.2

May 22 The Palomar Supper Club opened at Burrard and Georgia in Vancouver at precisely 9 p.m. Music was provided by the DeSantis Swing Orchestra. A *Vancouver Sun* story May 25 reported that "several hundred couples were on hand early to dance to the music and enjoy their first sight of this ultra-modern and exceptionally beautiful indoor entertainment place."

June 2 Charles A. Woodward, department store founder, died in Vancouver, aged 84. He was born July 19, 1852, on a farm near Hamilton, ON. In 1891 he visited Vancouver and bought two lots for a store, then moved here in 1892 and opened his first store where Georgia meets Main. The big Hastings Street store opened in 1903, known later especially for its Woodward's Food Floor, the first self-serve food floor on the continent. In a day when grocery stores were small, this gigantic emporium was—the right word—exciting. In 1910 the store held its first one-price sale day, 25 Cents Day, a forerunner of $1.49 Day. Woodward was a one-term Liberal MLA at age 71. When he died, his son William took over. Charles A. Woodward was named to the Canadian Business Hall of Fame in 1966.

June 16 The federal government announced a contract for 11 Blackburn "Shark" warplanes to be built by Boeing at Coal Harbour for the Royal Canadian Air Force.

July Robert Shun Wong, a teenage model plane builder, flew the full-scale, single-seat Pietenpol airplane that he had built himself in his family's apartment on 124 Market Alley in Vancouver's Chinatown. With the help of his younger brother Tommy and a magazine article that showed him how to build the plane, he gathered all the parts in sections (it was not unusual to see the wings, rudder and other pieces in the hallway outside their apartment) and found a used engine at the auto wreckers. The brothers assembled the aircraft at the Boeing plant on West Georgia Street, where an air force officer examined their work and gave it an official aircraft designation: CF BAA. In later years the brothers joined the RCAF and became flight instructors. After the war, they purchased some used aircrafts and opened their flying school, Central Airways, on Toronto Island. It became the largest flying school in Canada. The brothers sold the business in 1982 but their legacy was that most of the Trans-Canada Airline pilots were former students. (Wong was the second Chinese person to successfully build and fly an airplane, following in the footsteps of Fung Joe Guey, who designed and constructed a biplane in Oakland's Chinatown in 1909.)

July 19 Sliced bread came to Vancouver, eight cents a loaf. It was the greatest thing to hit the city since...since...

August 4 The Oak movie theatre opened with great fanfare at Kingsway and Marlborough—tickets were 25 cents for adults and 10 cents for children. Hailed as a masterpiece of "art moderne," it operated until 1968.

September 1 Pilots Billy Wells and Maurice McGregor completed a round-trip from Vancouver to Seattle and back for a brand-new airline, Trans-Canada Air Lines. Trans-Canada was founded by the federal government. Don MacLaren was its first employee and Lockheed 10s were its first aircraft. It offered regular intercity and transcontinental air mail services from Vancouver.

September 29 A shipment of food left BC for the Prairies, which was suffering through the worst of the Great Depression.

September A.E. Crickmay shot a 235-pound (over 100-kilogram) bear at 234 East 15th St. in North Vancouver.

November 12 "The Vancouver Non-Partisan Association was formed at a luncheon meeting at Hotel Vancouver today," the papers reported, "when a large group of representative citizens met to discuss the action of the CCF (Co-operative Commonwealth Federation) in nominating a party slate for the municipal elections in December." In the late 1990s the NPA was the dominant force in Vancouver civic politics: the mayor and all 10 councillors were members.

November 15 The Pattullo Bridge opened to traffic.

Premier Duff Pattullo, wielding a welder's torch, ceremonially cut a metal chain across the roadway. Length of the $4-million bridge, including approaches: 2,400 metres (7,880 feet). Its clearance above the Fraser: 48 metres (160 feet). The 25-cent toll on the bridge was not removed until February 12, 1952. Said Premier Pattullo at the opening: "It is a thing of beauty." Yeah, right. On the first day the Pattullo opened, 5,000 cars crossed it. Today average weekday traffic is more than 60,000 vehicles. The Pattullo Bridge caused a boost in population of areas to the south for many thousands who found houses in Vancouver too costly.

November 18 Julia Willmothe Henshaw died at Caulfeild in West Vancouver, aged about 68. She settled in Vancouver with her husband in about 1887 and became an editor of the *Province* and a columnist for the *Vancouver Sun*. Mrs. Henshaw wrote several important plant studies, including *Mountain Wild Flowers of Canada* (1906) and *The Wild Flowers of B.C.* (1908). She won the Croix de Guerre for her work as an ambulance driver in France during World War I.

November 24 A benefit tea was held in Vancouver for Chinese war refugees from the Sino-Japanese War.

Also in 1937

The Lougheed Highway was completed.

The Federal Building, which housed federal government offices, was built. Today it's part of Sinclair Centre and is one of the few remaining art deco buildings in the city.

With more than 3,000 patients in care, insulin shock and Metrazol therapy (no longer used) were introduced at Essondale mental hospital, the first full-time dentist was appointed, a new nurses' home was built and the first psychologist was appointed.

Welcome link. Opened in 1937 by its namesake, Premier Thomas Pattullo, the Pattullo Bridge made Surrey accessible to the masses in the Vancouver area, allowing them to buy houses they could not otherwise afford. *Vancouver Public Library, Special Collections, VPL 11091. Leonard Frank photo*

Industries listed for this year in Surrey include sawmills, CNR shops, a gypsum plant, tannery, grain elevators, fishing, brick plant, farming, summer resorts and golf courses.

In 1937 a total of 538 people were squatting on the Vancouver waterfront in houseboats, shacks and tents. Their numbers continued to grow over the next two years, despite the city's attempts to destroy their homes.

Nat Bailey, who had opened the White Spot Barbecue at 67th and Granville in 1928, replaced it with the White Spot Restaurant and Drive-in. The legend began.

Maurice A. Gaudry opened his Morray's Fountain Lunch at the corner of Smithe and Seymour Streets. "When I started," he told the *Province*'s Aileen Campbell, "I sold a cake donut and a coffee for a nickel and did it for two or three years—others raised, but I stuck by it." He bought the site in 1969 and sold it to the city in 1977 for $350,000.

Vancouver's Foon Sien Wong, a legal translator and interpreter, was named publicity agent of the Chinese Benevolent Association's aid-to-China program during the Sino-Japanese War.

Suichi Kusaka graduated from the University of BC with the Governor General's medal for the highest marks. He went on to work under physicist Robert Oppenheimer at Berkeley and under Albert Einstein at Princeton.

Centre Park, a 1,200-seat softball diamond, opened at Broadway and Fir. It was demolished in 1950.

Seventeen-year-old Bob Smith from Winnipeg, the city's first jazz disc jockey, began playing big-band 78s on the CJOR program *Hilites*. This was also the year Edmonton-born radio pioneer Bill Rea, 28, came to Vancouver and began at CJOR. He launched CKNW in 1944.

Pictured sawing through a log, this squatter was one of hundreds who lived on the Vancouver waterfront during the Depression. Over the years, the squatters not only remained but grew in number, despite city attempts to destroy their homes.
City of Vancouver Archives, Wat P128

The Vagabond Players were formed in New Westminster. They still perform; since 1950 their home has been the Vagabond Theatre (now Bernie Legge Theatre) in Queens Park, New Westminster. The troupe has produced more than 250 plays and won over 30 awards at the Regional and Dominion Drama Festivals.

South African-born Ethel Wilson, who came to Vancouver in 1898, an orphan at the age of 10, began writing. She submitted (at age 49) a magazine piece for the left-leaning *New Statesman and Nation* titled "I Just Love Dogs."

City archivist J.S. Matthews and native elder August Jack Khahtsahlano compiled a map showing "Indian Villages & Landmarks: Burrard Inlet & Howe Sound Before the White Man Came." It's at the Vancouver City Archives.

Jung Jin Sow, superintendent of a local Chinese school, presented a Chinese perpetual calendar he had created, the first of its kind, to the Vancouver City Archives.

Comings and Goings

May A squadron of three airplanes and 150 decorated Japanese Canadian fishing boats gathered at the mouth of the Fraser to greet Prince and Princess Chichibu of Japan, en route to the coronation of King George VI of England.

August 2 Dr. Norman Bethune spoke in Vancouver for the Canadian Blood Transfusion Service.

Notable births: **Jack P. Blaney**, president emeritus of Simon Fraser University, was born in Vancouver on February 24; broadcaster **Robert "Red" Robinson** was born in Comox on March 30—he started broadcasting on Vancouver's CJOR when he was 17; **Harold Steves** was born May 29, the fourth generation of the Steves family on the original Steveston site in Richmond.

1938

Tensions lingered in the final years of the Depression. Vancouver police used tear gas and clubs on "Bloody Sunday" to evict hundreds of unemployed men who had occupied a federal building demanding relief and jobs, and politicans in BC tried to limit Asian business licences as well as immigration from China and Japan. On a lighter note, the Cave Cabaret opened in December.

January 7 Fogs were more frequent and thicker in Vancouver in the 1930s and '40s. The *Province* printed a cartoon depicting a lady lost in dense Vancouver fog.
The lady (peering at a dim figure): "Is this Yew?"
A gentleman: "Your guess is as good as mine, lady, but I think it's me—how about yourself?"

January 12 Annie Charlotte Dalton, poet, died in Vancouver, aged 72. She was born December 9, 1865, in Birkby, Huddersfield, England, and arrived in BC in 1904 with her husband, Willie Dalton. The Dalton home became a meeting place for writers and readers. Left partially deaf by a childhood illness, Annie Dalton was known as "the Poet Laureate of the Deaf" for her work on their behalf. She was made a member of the Order of the British Empire in 1935, the only woman poet so honoured at the time.

February 19
A mysterious big bang was heard in Vancouver. It woke thousands of people, yet no cause was ever found.

March 10 Carlisle Street (near Renfrew and Hastings) was named for retired fire chief J.H. Carlisle. Fire department historian Alex Matches notes that "it is one of very few streets in the city which has no addresses, only the backs of buildings on adjacent streets."

April 17 The English Bay pier was demolished.

May 12 Juvenile court judge Helen Gregory MacGill, the first female judge in BC, became the first woman to receive an honorary LLD from UBC.

June 12 Robert Errol "Bob" Bouchette, *Sun* columnist, died. He wrote the column "Lend me your

Elsewhere in BC

June Harold Winch, MLA for Vancouver East, became the leader of the CCF in BC.

December 9 The BC legislature voted to encourage the federal government to pass the Oriental Exclusion Act. Also this fall, the provincial government passed the Credit Union Act, allowing for the official designation of chartered credit unions throughout BC.

Elsewhere in Canada

November 13 A BBC broadcasting official visiting Toronto heard the Vancouver-based Mart Kenney orchestra there and liked it so much he arranged a worldwide broadcast for the ensemble. Kenney played music by Noel Coward, Ray Noble and other British and Canadian composers. NBC's Blue Network also featured the program the next day.

December 30 The *Province*'s music critic R.J. (Rhynd Jamieson), an acknowledged hater of "swing" music, agreed to take part in a mock trial of the genre on CBC Radio's *National Forum*. The radio audience was to be the jury. R.J. was the prosecutor; Graham MacInnes, art critic of *Toronto Saturday Night*, and CBC conductor Percy Faith appeared for the defence. Swing, said R.J., was "a menace to real musical development in its true sense." Take that, Tommy Dorsey!

Elsewhere in the World

August 19 The Ballet Russe sailed from London, bound for Australia. The *Province* reported that with the troupe went Alexandra Denisova, "one of the youngest, yet one of the most talented of the famous dancers." The local angle was that the 15-year-old Denisova was, in truth, a Vancouver girl named Pat Meyers. Because world opinion at the time was that the best dancers came from Russia, it was a tradition to give the ballerinas Russian names. Young Pat, who lived in Dunbar, "practiced dancing for eight hours each day." Like many local dancers, Meyers (and her 16-year-old sailing mate Rosemary Deveson—a.k.a. Natasha Sobinova) was a student of Vancouver teacher June Roper, and was among the first of more than 60 dancers that Roper sent from Vancouver to international ballet companies and to Hollywood.

Left: The English Bay pier was a fixture of the West End beach from its construction in 1909 to its demolition in 1938. It featured a glassed-in pavilion at its end where live dance bands played during the summer evenings.
City of Vancouver Archives, Be P73.2. Gowen Sutton Co. Ltd. photo

ears," in which he harangued the 1930s establishment to do more about poverty, joblessness and relief camps. Bouchette was described as "a shining knight out of time in the harsh world of the Depression." A victim of his own depression, he drowned himself off Second Beach.

June 19 In an event that came to be called "Bloody Sunday," Vancouver police evicted 700 unemployed men from the Post Office (now Sinclair Centre), injuring 39 and arresting 22. The workers, led by Steve Brodie, had occupied the building for six weeks, demanding federal relief. After the occupiers were ousted by police using clubs and tear gas, more than 5,000 demonstrators marched through the downtown to the east side, smashing store windows and causing considerable damage. Two other groups of unemployed men had occupied the Art Gallery and Hotel Georgia. All three buildings were occupied on May 20; the men in the hotel left shortly after, but those in the Art Gallery remained until June 19, when provincial NDP leader Harold Winch negotiated their departure.

July 1 The 1st Avenue Viaduct opened to traffic.

July 27 The Pier "D" fire, largest and most famous of Vancouver's many large waterfront fires, raised four alarms, destroyed the CPR pier (about where the SeaBus terminal is today) and buried one of the firefighters' hosewagons under tons of debris.

July 29 QUEEN ANNE SETS OUT TO SEA. That was the headline on a *Province* story about Annabelle Mundigel, "a frequent participant in the Polar Bear swim," who made the paper's front page with a bold venture: to swim from Vancouver to Snug Cove, Bowen Island. The 19-year-old

The CPR pier—or Pier "D"—morphed into smoke and flames on July 27, 1938, setting a new standard for Vancouver waterfront fires.
City of Vancouver Archives, CVA 1376-40. Photo Joseph Bertalino

was "clad in black trunks and a light woollen, apple-green singlet, well greased, with ears plugged," when she slipped into the waters of English Bay at 9 a.m. She was not alone on the 27-kilometre (17-mile) swim: her brother Jack, armed with a chart especially prepared for him by the Union Steamship Company, guided her to the best currents, and her parents were in another boat. The time of the swim: 7 hours, 15 minutes. Her nourishment: one chocolate bar. What that 1938 story didn't reveal, and what Ann Mundigel (who became Mrs. Ann Meraw of Maple Ridge) told us a few years ago, was that a few metres off shore she tugged off her swimsuit, handed it to her mother in the escorting rowboat and did the rest of the swim clad only in lard. Just outside Snug Cove she struggled back into the swimsuit and was met by a small, but cheering, crowd.

A decades-long fixture of the Vancouver nightclub scene, the Cave Supper Club was famous for its papier-mâché stalactites and live music. From 1938 to its closure in 1981, it played host to such diverse performers as Duke Ellington, Johnny Cash and Bachman-Turner Overdrive.
Vancouver Sun

August 17 A restaurant called C.K. Chop Suey at 123B East Pender was in the news for defying a civic licence cancellation order issued two days earlier. The reason for the cancellation: the restaurant employed two white waitresses. The owner, Charlie Ting, told officials the waitresses were employed in the cafe when he took it over in May and he wasn't aware of an agreement between the city's mayor, George Miller, and Chinatown restaurants not to employ white help. The city ordinance that prohibited white women from working in Chinese-owned restaurants had passed in 1937, to the outrage of Chinese establishments. A delegation of 16 waitresses from three restaurants marched to city hall on September 24, 1937, to protest the bylaw, but the mayor refused them a hearing. Restaurant proprietors had their licences revoked if they failed to observe the law. In 1939, city council decided that white women were allowed to work in Chinese-owned restaurants that served "English meals to English customers."

August 21 The *Province* published a letter to the editor from one signed "Waterfront": "Sir: Why is there all this fuss and trouble about the garbage dump on False Creek Flats? I fail to see how anyone can approve discharge of refuse in the heart of the city, even if it is in an industrial area. There are thousands of people living close to the flats and this ill-smelling property is at their very back doors. Why does Vancouver fail to follow the example of many large eastern cities which tow their garbage out to sea and dump it?...Let's see if our garbage can't be dumped far out in the Gulf of Georgia. That's where it belongs."

September 3 New Brunswick-born Roy W. Brown, about 58, was appointed the editorial director and vice-president of the *Vancouver Sun*. He had been editor of the *Province*. (When he was 11, Brown had been the youngest pupil ever to enroll in Vancouver High School.)

September 24 Railway builder and World War I general John William Stewart died in Vancouver. Born in 1862 in Sutherlandshire, Scotland, Stewart arrived in Canada in 1882. He was a partner in Foley, Welch and Stewart, the largest North American railway contracting firm, which built much of the Grand Trunk Pacific line and began the Pacific Great Eastern and parts of the CNR. In World War I, General Stewart commanded 13 battalions, organized railway troops and built railways in France, but he was described by those who knew him as "shy and retiring."

October 1 Air Travel Week began, proclaimed to mark the establishment of Trans-Canada Airlines' Vancouver-to-Winnipeg airmail service. This was also the year runway lights were installed at Vancouver Airport, seven years after it opened.

October 14 Capt. Charles Henry Cates died, aged 78. He was born December 15, 1859, in Machias, ME, two years before his brother George Emery Cates. Charles hauled stone from Gibsons and Squamish quarries to help rebuild Vancouver after the Great Fire of June 13, 1886. He built the first wharf on the North Shore and in 1913 formed C.H. Cates Towing, later Charles H. Cates and Son (1921), one of the oldest and largest towage and "lightering" firms on Burrard Inlet.

October 22
Mart Kenney and his Western Gentlemen instructed dancers at the Hotel Vancouver in a new dance craze, the Lambeth Walk.

November 14 Members of the Vancouver Board of Trade were taken on an inspection tour of the soon-to-open brand-new Hotel Vancouver (the present one).

November 23 Vancouver city council lost its bid to change the city charter in order to limit licences for businesses run by Asians.

November *The New Canadian* was established as "the Voice of the

The longest suspension bridge of its time in the British Empire, Lions Gate Bridge opened for pedestrians on November 12, 1938. The toll was five cents per person. Two days later, the bridge opened to vehicles, for 25 cents. The tolls continued until 1963, when the Guinness family, of beer fame, sold the bridge to Vancouver. *City of Vancouver Archives, Br P21. Leonard Frank photo*

Lions Gate Bridge

November 12 At 8:50 a.m. the Lions Gate Bridge was opened to pedestrian traffic. The first "civilian" to cross the bridge appears to have been one R.F. Hearns of Caulfeild in West Vancouver. Hearns, described by the *Province* as a "bespectacled but sprightly" retiree, wasn't supposed to get onto the bridge until the official opening time of 9 a.m., but a soft-hearted gateman heeded his plea that there was snow on the ground and it was awfully cold, and let him pass. Hearns held ticket No. 2, cost five cents.

Ticket No. 1 was possessed by 75-year-old Mary Sutton, who had risen at 6 a.m. and walked to the bridge through the snow from her home at 1665 West 7th. "When I was halfway across Granville bridge," she told *Province* reporter Stuart Keate, "a young fellow came along and gave me a lift. I arrived at the Lions Gate at a quarter to eight." She didn't set out to walk across the bridge until exactly 9:00, so after solemn deliberation we have to give the palm to Mr. Hearns. (He told Keate he had also bought the first BC Electric ticket on the interurban railway out to Burnaby Lake.) The two pioneers likely nodded to each other as they passed, Miss Sutton walking north, Mr. Hearns walking south. Some 6,950 pedestrians crossed the bridge on the weekend before cars were allowed over.

The first "civilian" to *drive* over the bridge, on November 14, was another North Shore resident, C.H. Chamberlain of Lower Capilano, who got to the toll gate on the north side at 4 a.m. "Bound to be the first to cross, you know," he said.

Negotiations to build this beautiful span had gone on for 10 years. A lot of people hated the idea of a busy road through the heart of Stanley Park, but it was the Depression, and the bridge was just too powerful an economic idea to quash. Vancouver engineer W.G. Swan played a significant role in the design and construction of the bridge, as he had done with the Pattullo Bridge in 1937. The bridge cost the Guinness brewing interests about $6 million to build, an investment they thought worth the price because it would spur development of their British Properties lands on the North Shore.

They were right. The bridge brought an immediate boost to the fortunes of the North Shore, even before it was officially opened on May 26, 1939, by King George VI and Queen Elizabeth.

The bridge opened with just two lanes. It wasn't long before that was changed to three, with the middle lane reserved for passing. In 1963 the provincial government bought the bridge for $6 million and soon removed the tolls that had been imposed from the beginning. Overhead lane-control signals enabled traffic in the centre lane to be reversed at will. Today more than 52,000 vehicles cross the bridge on a typical weekday.

Second Generation," the first English-language newspaper for the Japanese community. Various *nisei*, including Ken Adachi, Irene Uchida, Muriel Kitagawa, and Toyo Takata, wrote for the paper at one time or another, and it was the only Japanese newspaper allowed to publish during World War II. When the government realized that official orders had to be published in both Japanese and English, Takaichi Umezuki was added as the Japanese editor. (An English-language paper for the Chinese community, *The Chinese News Weekly*, had begun publishing in 1936.) *The New Canadian* published its final issue in Toronto in 2001, 63 years after it first appeared.

December 15 "Vancouver's smart set," the *Province* reported, "will 'go underground' this evening, when to the strains of Earl Hill's orchestra, the Cave Cabaret opens in Vancouver at 9 o'clock. Opening night visitors will step into a realistic replica of a cavern, complete with stalactites, subdued lighting and pirate treasure. They will dance on a gleaming floor constructed to the most scientific methods." The Cave was *the* spot for Vancouver nightlife for many years and the constant haunt of the *Sun*'s self-described "saloon columnist," Jack Wasserman.

Also in 1938

The Teahouse at Ferguson Point in Stanley Park was built as an officers' mess for a military defence garrison manned by the 15th Coast Artillery Regiment. After the war the city operated it as a summer tea house. In 1971 entrepreneur Brent Davies leased the building and turned it into a place of fine dining with a spectacular view.

The Ford Motor Company built an assembly plant in Burnaby. During World War II it produced military vehicles. It was demolished in 1988 to make way for Station Square.

Shaughnessy's Angus Street gained the reputation of being a lovers' lane, but city electrician Thomas Martin complained that "Cupid is breaking more street lights than hearts." Remedies and suggestions ranged from "No Necking" signs to "a street reserved for spooning."

Months after arriving in Vancouver from Austria, brothers-in-law John G. Prentice and L.L.G. "Poldi" Bentley established Pacific Veneer, a furniture and panelling veneer company. They built a small mill, which employed 28 people, on the Fraser River in New Westminster. By 1939 they employed 1,000 workers. Today the firm is known as Canfor, which in 2010 had nearly 5,000 employees and revenues of $2.4 billion.

Another city street made the news this year: Macdonald Street was shown

As a car is fitted together on the assembly line, this 1938 photo depicts the early days of the Ford Motor Company's assembly plant in Burnaby. The plant lasted until 1988, when it was demolished to create Station Square. *Leonard Frank photo, Vancouver Public Library VPL 14463*

on an 1886 map of the city, but now a mini-controversy developed over the spelling of the name, with many claiming it should be "McDonald." The question was soon settled: the street was originally named for Prime Minister Sir John A. Macdonald.

Thomas Carlyle Hebb, a professor of physics at UBC since 1916, retired. The Hebb Building, opened October 24, 1963, as a teaching addition to the Physics Department, was named for him.

UBC's Alma Mater Society established a low-power radio station, CITR.

An anonymous $50,000 donation allowed the BC Cancer Foundation to establish a treatment centre, the British Columbia Cancer Institute, where 288 patients were treated in the first year. The first chairman of the board of governors was former mayor W.H. Malkin, who served until 1945. Dr. A. Maxwell Evans was named head of the institute and stayed for 33 years. (One wonders if the anonymous donor was W.H. Malkin himself, who was a very prosperous grocery wholesaler and jam maker.)

Vancouver's first neighbourhood house grew out of the Alexandra Orphanage in Kitsilano, incorporated in 1894, which was only the 36th non-profit society in BC. By the 1930s the orphanage was in decline as the trend was clearly toward placing children in foster homes rather than orphanages. In 1938 the orphanage was closed, to reopen a couple of months later as the Alexandra Neighbourhood House.

Sam Tyson and Alex McKenzie built *Tymac No. 2*, which was used for the next two decades to carry passengers from the foot of Columbia Street to Britannia Mines, church camps and summer resorts around Howe Sound. The boat's doors, window frames and trim were made with 200-year-old teak from the Canadian Pacific liner *Empress of Japan*. *Tymac No. 2* later operated as a False Creek ferry (1984–86), a Vancouver Harbour tour boat (1986–89), and a tour boat out of Steveston (1990s).

In the wake of a scandal involving fraudulent assay results from a listed mining company, trading at the Vancouver Stock Exchange collapsed to 30 million shares from 120 million the year before.

The Vancouver Art Gallery board was reluctant to buy an Emily Carr picture, priced at $400, because, according to arts writer Tony Robertson, "it wasn't art as they understood art. They were eventually persuaded it was and paid up."

Some familiar performing arts groups got their start this year: Dorothy Somerset founded the UBC Summer School of Theatre, and Ira Dilworth founded the CBC Vancouver Chamber Orchestra. Meanwhile, social leader and Vancouver Symphony Orchestra supporter Mary Rogers wondered aloud why only 100 people in a city of 250,000 contributed to the VSO's financial well-being.

The BC government began a two-year project to develop a park on the Canadian side of the Peace Arch.

Tong Louie, the son of Hok Yat (H.Y.) Louie graduated from UBC with a Bachelor of Science degree in agriculture. This faculty had been recommended to him because it would lead to a profession with no racial bias (unlike law, medicine, teaching in public schools, working for the government, etc., which at that time were not open to Chinese). He chose soil science as his major and studied food technology, which helped him immensely when he took over the family's food wholesale business after his father's death. Louie became the first Chinese director of the Royal Bank of Canada as well as head of the Vancouver Board of Trade and the Business Council of BC. In 1976 he bought London Drugs.

Two women enter Vancouver's first cancer clinic at the corner of Heather Street and 11th Avenue, *circa* 1945. The clinic was established in 1938 by the BC Cancer Foundation thanks to an anonymous $50,000 donation. *Courtesy BC Cancer Foundation*

Comings and Goings

Notable deaths: railway executive and former alderman **William Ferriman Salsbury** died in Victoria on January 5 (a street in Vancouver is named for him); **Frederick Buscombe**, former mayor, died on July 21, aged 75; **Lily Alice Lefevre**, poet, hostess, philanthropist and one of the founders of the Vancouver Art Gallery, died in Vancouver on October 17, aged 85; **Henry Torkington "Harry" Devine**, photographer, died in Vancouver on December 17, aged 73.

1939

As World War II started, Vancouver's harbour was armed and coastal ships were converted to military use. This was the year the current Hotel Vancouver opened and rotary dial telephones came to town. The Vancouver Police Department, meanwhile, declared a losing war on the world's oldest profession.

January 11 BC Premier Duff Pattullo, in Ottawa, told the federal government that BC wouldn't object to the "infiltration" of a small number of European refugees into Canada "if they can be readily absorbed." The *Sun* noted the he was definitely opposed to any large movement.

January 13 Front page headline in the *Sun*: "Two Guns to be Placed at First Narrows."

January 14 Deputy-Chief Grundy of the Vancouver Police Department was demoted in a shakeup of the force, and the *Sun* reported "War Declared on Vice." The spread of venereal disease prompted Police Chief W.W. Foster to launch another crackdown by his "morality squad" with the goal of the "absolute suppression of prostitution."

January 23 Sculptor Charles Marega's lions were installed at the south approach to Lions Gate Bridge. Marega was unhappy with the work: he had wanted the lions to be of bronze, but budget restrictions forced him to use concrete. Two months later, on March 24, Marega died suddenly. He had just finished teaching a class at the Vancouver School of Art and collapsed while putting on his coat to go home. He was 68. Among his other work: the Joe Fortes fountain, the Edward VII fountain by what is now the Vancouver Art Gallery, the busts of Burrard and Vancouver on the Burrard Bridge, the statue of Vancouver at city hall and the bust of David Oppenheimer near the park board offices.

January 31 E.H. Grubbe retired from the Bank of Montreal at Main and Hastings after 45 years in banking, 40 of them in BC.

Elsewhere in Canada

March 1 The official inauguration of airmail service between Montreal, Toronto and Vancouver.

September 10 Canada declared war on Germany.

Mid-December The first contingent of the Canadian Active Service Force left for Europe. The second contingent left January 2, 1940. Wartime security measures forbade any indication of where they left from.

The 2850 Hudson locomotive that drew King George VI and Queen Elizabeth across Canada this year so impressed the king with its power that he gave his approval for these locomotives to carry the "Royal" designation. Hence, the "Royal Hudsons." Incidentally, 2850 carried the royal couple on CPR lines from east to west, then CNR lines on the return voyage.

Chinese Canadians volunteered for military service in World War II, but the Canadian government classified them as "allied aliens," subject to investigation, and refused to consider them for active combat service. Meanwhile, Chinese Canadian organizations raised hundreds of thousands of dollars for both the Chinese and Canadian war efforts.

Elsewhere in the World

July 4 Lou Gehrig's "luckiest man on the face of the earth" speech at Yankee Stadium.

September 1 Hitler invaded Poland, igniting World War II.

September 3 Britain and France declared war on Germany.

December 18 Winston Churchill, First Lord of the Admiralty, spoke to the world in a broadcast from London. "The First Contingent of the Canadian Expeditionary Force, safely escorted across the Atlantic by the main battle fleet, was disembarked at a British port." Churchill revealed the progress of the Canadian soldiers in the course of his report on the sinking of the German battleship *Graf Spee*.

February 24 The first Fireman's Ball was held in Burnaby. Admission was $1 a couple.

March 6 A vehicle testing station opened. Vancouver Mayor Lyle Telford drove the first car through.

May 24 The CPR bade a musical farewell to the second Hotel Vancouver and entered into a joint management contract with the CNR to run the new Hotel Vancouver, two blocks west, which opened today. Construction of this third version had been delayed by the Depression, but workers rushed to complete it in time for the royal visit of King George VI and Queen Elizabeth. The king and queen stayed overnight at the new hotel.

May 26 King George VI and Queen Elizabeth officially opened the Lions Gate Bridge.

A Chinatown street dance celebrated their visit.

July 3 The province granted the second charter to a BC credit union, the Amalgamated Civil Servants Credit Union of Vancouver. The first BC charter, by the way, was awarded on June 9, 1939, to Powell River Credit Union. The already-existing Common Good Credit Unit, formed in 1936, was third.

June 5 From the *Vancouver Sun*: "Joe Gonsalves, Pioneer, Dead. Joe Gonsalves, 82, who came to Vancouver when it was known as Gastown 65 years ago, died Saturday night in St. Paul's Hospital, to which he was admitted several weeks ago.

A contemporary Vancouver landmark at West Georgia and Burrard, the third Hotel Vancouver—now the Fairmont Hotel Vancouver—was opened in 1939 to great fanfare by the CNR.
City of Vancouver Archives, CVA 99-5030. Photo Stuart Thomson

"Mr. Gonsalves' home was at Pender Harbor, where he had lived for the last 35 years. He came to Vancouver in 1874, when he was about 17. At 12 he had left his home on the Island of Madeira after he had prevailed on a sea captain to let him travel on his ship.

"For several years he was a squatter in Stanley Park and his five daughters and one son were all born at Brockton Point. As he lay in the hospital, his mind still alert, despite his age, he recalled early days of Vancouver and the British Columbia coast."

August 3 Radiotelephones were installed in Vancouver police cars.

August 26 Local militia in North Vancouver stood by the guns at First Narrows as world war threatened.

September Vancouver's harbour was placed under the control of the Royal Canadian Navy. All ships passing into the harbour had to stop and report to naval launches.

September Factories and workers on Granville Island, the industrial heart of the city, began operating

Seen training at the armoury in this September 1939 photo, the Seaforth Highlanders were one of the first Canadian regiments to deploy once war was declared. After serving in England during the Battle of Britain, they saw combat in 1943 in Italy and then in the Netherlands, where they were the first Allied unit to enter Amsterdam after Germany's surrender.
City of Vancouver Archives, CVA 99-2957. Photo Stuart Thomson

around the clock, producing defence equipment such as anti-torpedo nets, minesweeping equipment and rigging ropes for the merchant fleet. And for the first time women were hired at the factories.

September 10 German-speaking citizens pledged their loyalty to Canada at a mass meeting in Moose Hall.

October 11 Dr. Leonard Klinck, UBC president, opened the city's first public aquarium at the old English Bay Bathhouse. The star was Oscar the Octopus. Manager of the aquarium was an American named Ivar Haglund, who later moved to Seattle and opened a restaurant called Ivar's Acres of Clams. (A restaurant, eh? Anyone here seen Oscar?) The aquarium closed in 1956.

October 18 A committee of prominent men from the Lower Mainland approached Surrey council, and successfully petitioned to rename the Peace Arch Highway. The new name: the King George VI Highway.

November 21 A 50th anniversary banquet was held to celebrate craft unionism in the Lower Mainland.

December 2 Vancouver welcomed its first dial telephones.

Also in 1939

James Lyle Telford, 50, became mayor of Vancouver, succeeding George Miller. Telford was no stranger to politics, having represented the CCF in the provincial legislature, but he resigned from the CCF once elected, stating that he felt civic office should be free of party politics.

The *Prince Robert*, built in 1930 for the Canadian National Railway's Vancouver-to-Alaska cruise service, carried the king and queen from Victoria to Vancouver this year and then was converted by the Royal Canadian Navy to an armed merchant cruiser. In 1940 the *Prince Robert* seized the German freighter *Weser* off Manzanillo and brought it to Esquimalt as a prize of war, then continued wartime service around the world until 1945.

Boeing built a plant on Sea Island for the production of Canso and Catalina and later B-29 superfortress aircraft. At the peak of production it employed more than 6,000 people.

Soon after the start of World War II, Richmond's Japanese residents, among others, began raising money for the National Defence fund.

St. Peter's Catholic Church, at the corner of Royal Avenue and Fourth Street in New Westminster, was built this year in the California Mission style. Some statues in the church are survivors from the old St. Peter's

Having opened soon after war was declared in September 1939, the Boeing plant on Sea Island was in full swing by the time this 1942 photo was taken. Employing 6,000 people at its peak, most of them women, the plant built Canso, Catalina and B-29 superfortress aircraft. It shut down quickly after V-J Day, leaving many workers stunned and highlighting the abnormal economic and labour situation that existed during the war.
Dominion Photo Co. photo, Vancouver Public Library VPL 25925

Cathedral, built in 1886 on Blackwood Street and damaged beyond repair in 1934: among them, the Blessed Mother and Child, St. Joseph and St. Peter. The crucifix over the altar is also from the old cathedral.

UBC students provided nearly $80,000 to build the university's first student union building, a memorial to the late dean of applied science, Reginald W. Brock, and his wife, killed in a 1935 airplane accident.

Karl Jacobs, a Canadian movie stunt man, built Steelhead Lodge in Coquitlam as a secluded getaway for Hollywood stars. Some of the present streets in the River Springs neighbourhood were named for famous visitors: Gable, Novak and Flynn.

George Adams was a contractor who built the Carnegie Library at Main and Hastings, early parts of the Vancouver General Hospital, and the W.H. Malkin warehouse (now the Old Spaghetti Factory). He bought lot 492 at Tunstall Bay on Bowen Island, built a house and moved there with his family this year. The island's Adams Road is named for him.

Appraised at $75,000 in 1920, Glen Brae, the William Lamont Tait mansion at 1690 Matthews, sold this year for $7,500.

Monks of the Benedictine order moved into Fairacres, a handsome twin-gabled Tudor Revival house in Burnaby, that had been built for Grace and Henry Ceperley in 1910.

One of the odder railway stories in BC history happened this year. First, you need to know that one local result of the Great Depression was that Grouse Mountain had become home to a small colony of squatters. They built a small village of log cabins up there—nearly 100 of them—and as the economy improved, that little settlement began turning into what the locals called "Ski Village." Enter a fellow named Kent Ford, who proposed a sprocket railway from Mosquito Creek up to the village. However, Ford's proposal ran into a vexing problem: with exquisitely inconvenient timing, World War II started after construction had begun, and Ford was unable to get enough steel. He must have been a formidable optimist: without even pausing for breath he continued to build his railway—with one track of steel, the other of wood. It didn't work. Curiously enough, an attempt to build a railway up Grouse nearly 30 years earlier had foundered for exactly the same reason: a lack of steel because of a world war!

Steveston voted to stay "dry."

A herring reduction plant was installed in the Gulf of Georgia Cannery to produce fishmeal and fish oil, used for many industrial and agricultural purposes.

North Shore Neighbourhood House opened.

Seeking soldiers. A sign that two years into the war Canada still needed troops, this 1941 recruitment centre in Victory Square (downtown Vancouver between W. Hastings and W. Pender) seeks to pull on patriotic heartstrings by its proximity to the cenotaph and the watchful gaze of Winston Churchill. *City of Vancouver Archives, Mil P265*

Queen Elizabeth Park was named for Queen Elizabeth the queen consort. Sitting atop an extinct volcano, this former rock quarry is a beauty spot, a riot of colour with flowers, shrubs, rare trees and more on every side. The Bloedel Conservatory, Seasons Restaurant and so on, were added in later years.

The Van Tan nudist club was established, the first such club in the Lower Mainland.

Comings and Goings

January 31 The Harlem Globetrotters visited Vancouver.

The Nazi invasion of Czechoslovakia caused a great exodus—political leaders, businesspeople, professionals and intellectuals fled. Theodor, Otto, Leon and Walter Koerner were among those who came to British Columbia. With their background in forestry, the four brothers formed the Alaska Pine and Cellulose Company. It was Walter Koerner's idea to rename western hemlock, which had not been a popular wood for construction, "Alaska pine."

1940-1949

1940

A Vancouver newspaper picture of departing troops became the most famous Canadian photograph of the war. As troops departed, young children evacuated from Britain began arriving in the city. So did one of their older countrymen: novelist Malcolm Lowry moved into a waterfront shack on Burrard Inlet to write—and drink. To lighten the clouds of war, Theatre Under the Stars started in Stanley Park, and bandleader Dal Richards began a 25-year (!) booking at the Hotel Vancouver.

January 3 The T. Eaton Company announced that demolition of the old Hotel Vancouver at Georgia and Granville would start immediately. The company wanted to locate its new department store on the site. But the hotel was used for vets after the war, so this 1940 plan must have been postponed.

February 16 Orpheum Theatre manager Ivan Ackery proudly hosted the Canadian premiere of *Gone with the Wind*. Vivien Leigh's daughter happened to be attending a private school here, and she was in the audience (unannounced, at her mother's insistence).

February Canada's first all-Chinese-language school was dedicated at 571 East Georgia St.

April 11 Greater Vancouver shipyards began to build corvettes and minesweepers for action in the Atlantic. Some passenger ships were converted for military use.

May 1 Dal Richards, his 11-piece band and an unknown 13-year-old singer named Juliette were booked to replace Mart Kenney at the new Hotel Vancouver's Panorama Roof Ballroom. An initial six-week contract stretched into 25 years of regular performances and broadcasts at The Roof.

Also May 1 Coquitlam held its first May Day festival.

May 9 In UBC's 25th annual convocation, the largest graduating class in the school's history was "capped" at the university theatre. Chancellor R.E. McKechnie congratulated 389 young men and women.

July 22 Elementary Training School Number 8 at the Vancouver Airport, part of the Commonwealth Air Training Plan, began training its first batch of pilots.

August 6 The first season of Theatre Under the Stars began in Stanley Park's Malkin Bowl. The program featured *The Geisha*, *As You Like It* and *Midsummer Night's Dream*. Reserved seats were 50 cents, unreserved 25 cents. We needed TUTS, because the other news was generally bad (the *Province*'s front-page headline today was "Nazis Groom Air Blitzkrieg Forces"). A big crowd showed up for the performance: 4,000 if you read the *Province*, 12,000 if you read the *Sun*.

Elsewhere in BC

June 29 The "Big Bend" Highway, linking Revelstoke and Golden and completing the last piece of the western section of the transcontinental highway, was officially opened. It was now possible to drive across Canada *within* Canada.

July 3 The *Province* reported that five Canadian Pacific locomotives of the "Royal" class would soon be hauling passenger trains between Revelstoke and Vancouver. "First of the five, No. 2860, reached Field Monday for delivery to the British Columbia district, and No.'s 2861, 2862, 2863 and 2864 will follow in short order. It was one of this type, No. 2850, which was assigned last summer to the royal train, and it hauled the gleaming blue and silver unit all the way from Quebec to Vancouver in what proved to be the longest single run ever achieved by any locomotive."

Elsewhere in the World

May 10 In Great Britain, Winston Churchill became prime minister.

May 24 – June 4 The Battle of Dunkirk and the evacuation of Allied troops from France took place.

July The Channel Islands became the only British territory occupied by Nazi Germany. Vancouver's Channel Islanders' Society began fundraising activities to help refugees from Guernsey and Jersey.

September 7 The London blitz began as German bombers pounded the city.

September 4 Georgia Sweeney (or Sweney), first teacher at Hastings Mills school, died in Santa Paulao, CA, in her 80s. Sweeney was a graduate of a girl's seminary in Victoria and was an accomplished musician and artist, although her admirers noted she "could also milk a cow." Her pencil sketches are in the Vancouver City Archives. She taught classes at Hastings Mills in 1872, then left for San Francisco. She married in the early 1880s.

Right: *Wait for Me, Daddy.* One of the most iconic photographs from World War II just happened to have been taken in New Westminster by *Vancouver Province* photographer Claud Detloff. *Life* magazine later named it among the top 10 pictures of the 1940s. It shows a boy running after his marching father on October 1, 1940.

City of Vancouver Archives, LP 109. Photo Claude Detloff

October 1 The *Province*'s Claud Detloff took the famous *Wait for Me, Daddy* photograph, which became the most reproduced Canadian picture of World War II.

Life magazine named the photo, which showed a boy running after his marching dad in the New Westminster brigade, one of the 10 best pictures of the 1940s. Wisconsin-born Detloff began his career with the *Minneapolis Journal*. He came to Canada and joined the *Province* in 1936, when he was about 37. He later become chief photographer at the paper.

October 16 The King George VI Highway was officially opened

under that name (previously it had been known as the Peace Arch Highway). Among the crowds of people on hand were Premier Duff Pattullo; Elmer Johnston, president of both the BC Automobile Association and the Vancouver Tourist Association; Surrey reeve J.V. Leyland; and a bunch of the usual suspects. "Scores of cars," the *Province* reported, "lined the highway on both sides of the Peace Arch to witness the colourful opening ceremony." (The population of Surrey this year, by the way, was about 15,000.)

November 10 "Cap" Hobbis opened his first bicycle store in New Westminster. He eventually owned 12 Cap's Bicycle Shops throughout the Lower Mainland and later established a bicycle museum at the first store.

December Iwakichi Sugiyama, co-owner with Senkichi Fukuyama of the Burrard Fishing Company and Howe Sound Fisheries, became the first Asian person to vote in a civic election in Vancouver. The *News-Herald* reported that Sugiyama voted as the authorized agent of his company. Sugiyamja also operated a saltery on Galiano, which processed herring, salmon and salmon roe. It was a self-contained operation that included a machine shop, supply store, bunkhouses, mess hall with a full-time cook, and an *ofuro* (Japanese bath).

December 15 Mary Agnes Joe Capilano (her Native name was Lay-kho-lote or Lahullette or La-yulette), Squamish matriarch, died on the Capilano Indian Reserve, North Vancouver, at age 104. She was born in 1836 at Potlatch Creek on Howe Sound. Her grandfather, George Mathias, had welcomed George Vancouver off Point Grey on June 13, 1792; her father was Chief Skakhult. Known as "the Indian Princess of Peace," she was an authority on the genealogy of coastal tribes and was considered a great orator in her language. She was married to Joe Capilano. Throughout her long life she travelled everywhere by dugout canoe.

Also in 1940

Vancouver's Major-General Victor Odlum, about 60, was given command of the 2nd Canadian Infantry Division. Odlum, who had fought in the Boer War and World War I, was slow to adapt to modern warfare, and a year later Prime Minister Mackenzie King offered him the position of high commissioner (in effect, ambassador) to Australia. The PM told the House of Commons that "in view of the situation in the Orient the government had decided the best possible appointment to the Australian post should be made," adding that "nobody was so well qualified for the post as Gen. Odlum if he could be persuaded to accept."

Albert O. Koch, whose National Dress Company was Vancouver's first garment manufacturing plant, started a chain of dress stores called Lauries.

During the war years, many single women from the Prairies came to work in Fraser River canneries, living in company bunkhouses, each of which had a matron in change. Many of the women married local fishermen and stayed on.

Also during the war, the US government extracted peat moss from Delta's Burns Bog to use in magnesium fire bombs.

By 1940, Saba's had become the largest retail house in western Canada specializing in silks. The Saba family arrived in Nanaimo in 1888, then moved to Vancouver. Mike Saba (born about 1861 in Beirut) opened Saba Brothers on West Hastings with his younger brother Alexander (born April 7, 1881, in Beirut) in November 1903. Two years later the store moved to the 500 block of Granville. Mike retired in 1921, selling his shares to Alex.

The Empress Theatre, which stood at the northwest corner of Hastings and Gore, was demolished, and thereby hangs a tale...about Anna Pavlova. She was called the greatest dancer who ever lived, and her 1910 appearance in Vancouver was met with rapturous praise. One tiny memento of her visit to Vancouver came to light in a curious way many years after she died in 1931. She had performed at the Empress, and when they tore that theatre down, one of the workmen noticed a flash of soft colour in the debris. He reached down and picked up a tiny powderpuff. Stitched on it, in faded golden letters, was a single word: Pavlova.

Australia-born educator Violet Dryvynsyde, who had come to Vancouver with her family in 1930, founded the private Athlone School

Celebrity venue. The glorious Empress Theatre, at the corner of Hastings and Gore, made its place in history by hosting Anna Pavlova, deemed the greatest dancer who ever lived. *Vancouver Public Library, Special Collections, VPL 21112. Dominion Photo*

Right: Stuck in ice, as it was for most of the voyage, the RCMP ship *St. Roch* waits for clear sailing on its two-year journey from Vancouver to Sydney, NS, through the Northwest Passage. Its return journey in 1944 via a different route and in the right season took only 86 days, and made the *St. Roch* the first ship to travel the passage in both directions. The ship is now on permanent display at the Vancouver Maritime Museum. *City of Vancouver Archives, Bo P304*

Bottom right: British novelist Malcolm Lowry and his wife Margerie found a measure of peace in Dollarton, on the coast near North Vancouver, where they lived in a squatter's shack. It was here that Malcolm completed his masterpiece, *Under the Volcano*, which drew on his turbulent time in Mexico. *Vancouver Public Library, Special Collections, VPL 30484*

for Boys with six students. By the time of her death in 1969, the school at 49th and Arbutus had 230 students.

Ernest Cleveland, chief commissioner of the Greater Vancouver Water District since 1926, had turned 65 on May 12, 1939, and so had reached retirement age. But his work was considered so important that special legislation was passed allowing him to continue on the job. He served for 12 more years. The Cleveland Dam on the Capilano River is named for him.

The Cambie Street boulevard was installed, a legacy of the Bartholomew plan (see the entry about this plan in 1926).

Kingsway was widened to four lanes.

Vancouver architect Ned Pratt was instrumental in launching the modern era in house design locally when he produced the drawings for artist B.C. Binnings' largely self-designed West Vancouver house.

Journalist Alan Morley published *The Romance of Vancouver*, a collection of stories on earliest Vancouver. The stories had earlier appeared as a series in the *Sun*.

Comings and Goings

June 23 The *St. Roch*, built in North Vancouver in 1928 as an RCMP patrol ship for Western Arctic operations, sailed from Vancouver, en route to Sydney, NS, by way of the Canadian Arctic. The trip took two years, and the return voyage made this the first vessel to travel the Northwest Passage in both directions. Because of wartime security, the *St. Roch*'s departure went unreported.

July 8 Our notes show this or July 9 as the date of the arrival of the first young British war evacuees in Vancouver, but there was also a story about them in the May 7 *Sun*. Thousands of children were evacuated from Britain for the duration of World War II.

Malcolm Lowry, novelist, born July 28, 1909, in New Brighton, near Liverpool, England, moved into a squatter's shack at Dollarton, on the north shore of Burrard Inlet, and began to complete his masterwork, *Under the Volcano*—counted by many as one of the great books of modern literature.

Lawren Harris, one of the Group of Seven, moved to Vancouver from Ontario at about age 54 and lived here until his death on January 29, 1970. He is considered one of the great Canadian painters of the 20th century.

Notable deaths: **Edward Beaton Cook**, pioneer contractor (he built the Bank of BC building at Hastings and Richards—the city's first bank, which had no connection to the present bank of that name—the Imperial Building at Seymour and Hastings, Douglas Lodge at Granville and one of the city's first large apartment buildings at West 12th Avenue), died in Vancouver on May 2, aged about 87; **Angelo Calori**, the proprietor of Gastown's Europe Hotel (the famous "flatiron" building at the convergence of Alexander and Powell), died on May 7 in Vancouver at age 81.

1941

This was the year the war really arrived. The city was already busy with war bond and blood donation drives when Japan bombed Pearl Harbor, triggering a crackdown on Japanese Canadians. With the coast a potential war zone, blackout curtains and gas masks became part of life in Vancouver. Early victims included motorists who collided with others because headlights had been painted blue.

January 14 At an emergency meeting of the Japanese Canadian Citizen's League, Yoshiaki "Sunshine" Sato, a fisherman from New Westminster and a reserve soldier for five years with the 47th Westminster Regiment, vented his frustrations: "After rapping us right and left about disloyalty, this so-called Canadian democracy owes us the chance to prove our loyalty." However, only 35 Nisei who lived outside BC were allowed to enlist in the Canadian forces. (These 35 were quietly allowed to remain in the service after Pearl Harbor.)

January 31 West Coast shipyards received the first orders for 10,000-ton cargo ships

that would convey war material and food to war-ravaged Europe. Most shipyards worked 24 hours a day, seven days a week. The West Coast climate allowed work to continue year-round. As a result, Lower Mainland shipyards built more than half the ships Canada supplied to the war effort.

February 11 One of the key figures in local history, Canadian Pacific Railway land commissioner, surveyor and alderman Lauchlan Alexander

Elsewhere in BC

September 5 William Culham Woodward, 56, was sworn in as BC's Lieutenant-Governor. Woodward was the son of retailer Charles Woodward and the father of Charles "Chunky" Woodward. He ran the Woodward's chain with his brother Percival Archibald Woodward until 1956, when Chunky became president of the company.

November 26 W.A.C. Bennett was first elected to the BC legislature as Conservative member for the Okanagan.

December 9 John Hart was elected Liberal premier of the BC coalition government, a position he held until he retired in 1947.

Elsewhere in Canada

February 28 Wartime Housing Limited (WHL) was incorporated. Between 1941 and 1947 WHL built and managed rental units across Canada for war industry workers and veterans. On the North Shore 750 single-family homes were built, as well as barracks-type apartments for single workers, Westview School, a recreation centre and a firehall.

This was an optimistic posting: Vancouver's Leonard Marsh became a research advisor to the federal committee on postwar reconstruction. It took four more years to be "postwar," but they were ready!

Elsewhere in the World

April 12 Bob Ito, a Japanese Canadian boy, less than 10 years old, won in one category and came second in another at the annual Eisteddfod festival.

May 24 The German battleship *Bismarck* sank HMS *Hood* (which had visited Vancouver in June 1924). There were only three survivors from the British ship.

May 27 The Royal Navy sank the *Bismarck*.

November 14 Dateline Washington: "A space magazine editor predicts that 20 years from now the nations of the world will be supporting 2,000 men on missions 'all over the solar system.' The cost of these missions will be so great... that the nations will have no room left in their budgets for the costs of war." Dr. Franco Fiorio, editor of the Italian-language magazine *Missili & Razzi*, was speaking to the American Rocket Society. Maybe he meant to say 200 years.

December 7 Japan bombed the US naval base at Pearl Harbor, Hawaii. Canada declared war on Japan the same day.

December 8 Britain and the US declared war on Japan.

December 11 The US declared war on Germany and Italy.

The Lower Mainland turned into the largest Canadian producer of ships after an order came on January 31, 1941, to build 10,000-ton cargo vessels.
City of Vancouver Archives, M-7-36. Photo W.J. Moore

Hamilton, died in Toronto, aged 88. Hamilton worked with crews that surveyed the western reaches of the Canada–US border and established many Prairie townsites. He arrived in Vancouver in 1883, and as a city councillor (1886–87) he proposed Stanley Park and laid out its perimeter. Hamilton Street was named for (and by) him.

February 28 Vancouver's new YMCA building opened on Burrard Street.

February A delegation of 23 residents of the Dunbar–Southlands neighbourhood, an exclusively white, middle-class area, visited city hall with an 83-signature petition and urged city council to "take instant steps... against the intrusion of the Oriental into desirable residential districts." Tong Louie had touched off the furor by purchasing a house at 5810 Highbury Street, intending it to be the matrimonial home for his soon-to-be wife, Geraldine. Alderman Halford Wilson urged council to draft a bylaw to prevent Asians from owning, or even renting, property in places other than "their own recognized localities" (with an exception to accommodate white people who employed Asian houseboys). Fortunately, times were changing, and many of Louie's university schoolmates, like the well-connected Arthur Laing, rallied around him, working publicly and behind the scenes. But the single most influential endorsement came from Tong's Highbury Street neighbours, such as Amy Leigh and her father, who resisted peer pressure and welcomed the couple into their neighbourhood. The protest gradually subsided and a significant colour barrier was broken.

April 23 Burrard Dry Dock laid the keel of the SS *Fort St. James*, the first of its North Sands 10,000-ton cargo vessels. It took nine months to complete. The last North Sands ship, begun in March 1943, took just three and a half months. Even though thousands of workers were new to the shipbuilding industry, mass-production techniques quickly enabled the formation of an efficient workforce.

May 18 A thousand Air Raid Precaution volunteers put on a public demonstration at Mahon Park in North Vancouver. Chief Warden G. Robert Bates made the mock air raid as realistic as possible—complete with low-flying bomber and incendiary devices.

May 22 Vancouver had its first trial blackout.

The keel of the SS *Fort St. James* was laid on March 23, launching the North Sands ships. Mass-production techniques quickly allowed efficiency to improve so that the last North Sands ship built, in 1943, took only three and a half months, compared with the nine months needed for the first ship.
Vancouver Public Library, Special Collections, VPL 15600

Crowding in for the unveiling of the grand prize—a new boat—these eager participants, circa 1955, are part of a long history of fishing derbies at Sewell's marina in Horseshoe Bay. At the first salmon derby in 1937, the grand prize was a "clinker row boat" built by Dan Sewell himself, with funds going toward constructing a new community hall in Horseshoe Bay.
Courtesy Sewell's Marina

July 19 The first twilight horse races were run at Hastings Park.

August 16 A Narvaez Pageant was held in West Vancouver to commemorate the 150th anniversary of the sighting of this shore by the Spanish explorer José Maria Narváez. (Narváez's visit preceded George Vancouver's by a year.) Earlier in the year, Vancouver City Council had adopted the name Narvaez Drive for a west-side street, on the recommendation of the Town Planning Commission. The street looks down on the waters first navigated by the Spaniard in the summer of 1791.

August 26 The *Vancouver Sun* took over management of the annual Salmon Derby, with its headquarters at Dan Sewell's marina in Horseshoe Bay.

September 15 In the pouring rain at the old Athletic Park at 5th and Hemlock, the Vancouver Grizzlies football team in their all-red uniforms registered their first and only regular season win of their only season. It was a 7–6 victory over the Saskatchewan Roughriders on a touchdown by Jack Horne. Their season stats were one win, seven losses. But to put it in context, they played eight games in 33 days, and at one point played four road games in nine days.

September 18 The Asahi baseball team played its last game.

Team members were exiled to internment camps for the duration of the war, along with others of the Japanese Canadian community of the Lower Mainland. The Asahi, formed in 1914, never played again.

September 23 *Province* columnist Jimmy Butterfield died in Penticton. He was born about 1879 in London, England, and began his daily column, *The Common Round*, in 1923. Butterfield's work stood out because at a time when newspaper style could be stiff and long-winded, he wrote about local doings in a voice that sounded personal. In the 18 years he produced his column, he only once explained the origin of its name. It seems the minister at his church in England consistently misquoted an old verse that ran: "It's the daily round, the common task, that makes life all you need to ask." The minister recalled it as "the common round, the daily task." An odd coincidence: on the very day Jimmy told his readers the story behind his column's name, September 23, 1941, he died.

October 21 Four women from Vancouver were among five women elected to the 48-seat BC Legislative Assembly, a record.

Tilly Rolston (Vancouver–Point Grey) was elected as a Conservative (though in 1951 she crossed the floor to join W.A.C. Bennett in the new Social Credit party), Liberal Nancy Hodges was elected in Victoria City, Grace MacInnis (Vancouver–Burrard) was elected for the Co-operative Commonwealth Federation, and fellow CCFers Dorothy Steeves (North Vancouver) and Laura Jamieson (Vancouver Centre) were re-elected.

October 25 *North Vancouver No. 5*, the last car ferry built for the North Vancouver Ferry system, was launched in False Creek.

October 27 The troop transport *Awatea* (Maori for "Eye of the Dawn") left Vancouver for Hong Kong with troops of the Winnipeg Grenadiers and the Royal Rifles of Canada.

October 28 Mrs. W.W. Southam pressed the control button to set in motion the first of two new presses at the *Province*. Her husband, W.W., was the newspaper's production manager.

November 12 The first person to donate blood to the Red Cross in Vancouver was a "bantamweight" New Westminster grocer named Jimmy Muir. "Last week," the *Province* reported, "the mayor (Jack Cornett) drew Muir's name from a hat and gave him the honor of being the first person in Vancouver to contribute blood in the Red Cross 'blood bank.'"

Just in time for Christmas, gas masks went on sale in Vancouver on December 14, 1941. In this 1943 photo, young children at school practise putting them on, part of the city's efforts to be prepared for an attack.
City of Vancouver Archives, CVA 586-1228. Photo Coltman, Don Steffens Colmer

Another early donor was David Smith, of West 12th Avenue, "a carpenter in the Boeing factory on Coal Harbour, where 500 workmen have each offered a pint of blood." The blood was to be sent to the war zones.

December 8 The electric flame at the Stanley Park war memorial commemorating the Japanese Canadian contribution during World War I was switched off after Canada declared war on Japan. It was not switched on again until 1985.

December 14
Gas masks went on sale to the general public.

Schoolchildren did their part by taking part in drills and learning to study with the masks on.

Also in 1941

J.W. Cornett became mayor of Vancouver, succeeding Lyle Telford and serving until 1946. A Vancouver street was named for him, and Wenonah Street was named for his daughter.

Highway 7 (the Lougheed) first appeared on a map.

Semiahmoo Park was established in White Rock with land leased from the Semiahmoo Indian band. The band later protested unfair terms in its agreement with the municipality.

Surrey municipality had acquired so much land in lieu of unpaid taxes during the Depression that it gave away lots to generate tax income from them.

Einar Neilson founded Lieban, a retreat for artists and intellectuals, on Bowen Island.

The 1,178-seat Vogue Theatre opened at 918 Granville Street as the Odeon theatre chain's "prestige" movie house—a response to the Capitol and the Orpheum, which were operated by Famous Players.

Horse racing in Richmond suffered a blow when Brighouse Park was closed after attendance fell because of the war and the opening of Hastings Park on the Pacific National Exhibition grounds in Vancouver.

In Greater Vancouver this year, four out of five homes did *not* have all of the following: a car, a telephone, a radio and a vacuum cleaner.

Most German Canadians in the Lower Mainland, who had been interned when the war began in 1939, had been released by 1941.

The federal government took over operation of the airport. Ottawa underwrote the Sea Island Boeing plant this year, and two new 1.5-kilometre (1-mile) runways were built.

William Crawford, the president and managing director of Empire Stevedoring, BC's largest waterfront employer, donated his yacht *Fyfer* to the Canadian Navy for war use. Crawford served without pay as a civilian consultant to the ministry of shipping during the war.

Vancouver's Alexander Duncan McRae—who had distinguished himself in World War I—was named national chair of the Canadian War Services Fund.

Comings and Goings

September 23 Famed actor Basil Rathbone (still the best Sherlock Holmes in the movies) visited Vancouver as part of a war bond drive.

November 9 The Westminster Regiment sailed for overseas service.

December 18–20
Gracie Fields performed at Exhibition Gardens.

Notable writers born in 1941: **Allen Garr** on November 6; **Marion Crook**, who became a specialist in the

Despite swearing their "unswerving allegiance to Canada," Japanese Canadians were swiftly interned and their property seized after the declaration of war with Japan in December 1941. Under the claim of protecting Canadian shores from Japanese attacks, more than 1,000 Japanese fishing boats were confiscated, as seen in this photo of an idle fishing fleet. *Dominion Photo Company photo, Vancouver Public Library VPL 26951*

The War against Japan

December 8 "British Columbia went to war against Japan Sunday," the *Province's* Paul Malone wrote, " a few minutes after the first bombs fell on Honolulu and the Philippines." All military bases were on the alert, and leaves were cancelled. As defence against aerial attack, blackout curtains were strung across windows and car headlights were painted blue, causing night-time collisions.

"RCMP and Provincial Police swiftly rounded up dangerous enemy aliens while spokesmen for British Columbia's 24,000 Japanese declared their unswerving allegiance to Canada." The government arrested 38 Japanese who were allegedly dangerous to national security, impounded 1,137 fishing boats owned or operated by Japanese Canadians, and closed 59 Japanese language schools in the province and the three Japanese language newspapers published in Vancouver.

A *Province* editorial the next day suggested the quarrel "is with Japan, not with the Japanese nationals here or people of Japanese blood. To these, in a very difficult situation they are compelled to face, is due every consideration."

In spite of this call for reason, merchants in Vancouver's "Japan Town" district immediately suffered a drop in business, broken windows, and attempted arson. Insurance companies cancelled policies carried by Japanese. The CPR dismissed employees of Japanese ancestry, as did mills and factories throughout the West Coast.

By December 16, all people of Japanese origin, regardless of citizenship, were required to register with the Registrar of Enemy Aliens. Penalties for non-compliance included fines up to $200 or imprisonment of two months. (This was in addition to the registration that had taken place from March to August of 1941, in which people of Japanese ancestry over 16 years of age had been required to register with the RCMP. They were issued colour-coded registration cards—white for Canadian born; pink for naturalized Canadians; yellow for Japanese nationals—that contained vital statistics, a photo, fingerprints and a registration number.)

lives (and travails) of teens, in New Westminster; and **Tamio Wakayama**, who was born in New Westminster but spent his early childhood in an internment camp at Tashme, BC.

Notable deaths: **Walter Henry Grassie**, a jeweller who arrived by CPR train in Port Moody in July 1886 and came to Vancouver by boat (his first shop was a little wooden building on Cordova Street), died in Vancouver on April 3, aged 80; **Frederick S. Maclure**, brother of newspaper publisher Sara Ann McLagan and architect Samuel Maclure, died at Iona Island on November 25, aged about 77 (he was born *circa* 1864 in New Westminster); **John Howe Carlisle**, Vancouver's first fire chief, died in Burnaby on November 28, aged 84; **J.M. Fromme**, Father of Lynn Valley, who in 1899 built the first house in the valley and who from 1924 to 1929 was the reeve of North Vancouver District, died at age 83.

1942

The Pacific National Exhibition grounds became the transit centre for thousands of Japanese Canadians who, as "enemy aliens," were stripped of their property and shipped to internment camps inland. As part of the war effort, Shaughnessy mansions were used as multi-family dwellings and the Nine O'Clock Gun was silenced to save gunpowder. With rationing in effect, meanwhile, there was a stampede when 500 women competed for 300 pairs of nylon stockings.

January 7 Won Joe Quoy, the first Chinese jockey to race professionally in BC, died at the ripe old age of 76. Joe was born about 1865 in New Westminster to parents who had come from California following the gold rush, and his was the second name in the "as native-born under Section 18" of the Chinese Immigration List of 1923, following the entry for his older brother, Won Alexander Cumyow, who was the first baby of Chinese origin born in Canada. Their father ran a store in New Westminster and owned several horses. The first races in New Westminster were held on Columbia Street, then unpaved. Joe was 12 years old and 90 pounds when he first raced. He rode at tracks in BC, including Langley and Nanaimo, and in Seattle, Portland and Walla Walla. After putting on weight, he turned to sulky riding. Later in life, Won Joe Quoy became a merchant, running a small New Westminster tobacco store on Columbia Street with his brother Frank. After the fire of 1898 destroyed the store, he announced "Business as Usual" within two days.

January 10 The Vancouver Fire Department's "inhalator" crew, the Rescue and Safety Branch, was put in service. Over the years, these men saved many lives.

January 22 The federal government announced plans for an RCAF storage depot on the Kitsilano Indian Reserve west of Burrard Bridge.

March 3 The City of Vancouver began acquiring land from Stanley Park to Burrard Street.

Elsewhere in BC

January 13 W.A.C. Bennett, Conservative MLA for South Okanagan, gave his first speech in the legislature.

Elsewhere in Canada

August 24 The Wartime Prices and Trade Board began issuing ration books covering the purchase of sugar, coffee and tea.

October 11 After two hard, slogging years fighting the Arctic ice, the *St. Roch*, which had left Vancouver on June 23, 1940, arrived in Sydney, NS.

December 21 Butter was rationed.

Elsewhere in the World

August 19 Vancouver's Colonel Cecil Merritt became the first Canadian in World War II to win the Victoria Cross. His citation reads, in part, "For matchless gallantry and inspiring leadership whilst commanding his battalion during the Dieppe raid on the 19th August, 1942. From the point of landing, his unit's advance had to be made across a bridge in Pourville which was swept by very heavy machine-gun, mortar and artillery fire: the first parties were mostly destroyed and the bridge thickly covered by their bodies. A daring lead was required; waving his helmet, Lieutenant Colonel Merritt rushed forward shouting, 'Come on over! There's nothing to worry about here.'"

November 20 The Alaska Highway (then called the Alcan Highway) was officially opened.

December 2 Physicist Enrico Fermi split the atom.

The 1942 bombing of England's Canterbury Cathedral had one unusual result. Shattered fragments of the 11th-century stained glass from the cathedral were given to wartime parishioner Archdeacon Greig, who later settled in Vancouver. The sanctuary and chancel memorial windows at St. John's Shaughnessy Anglican Church at Nanton and Granville Streets in Vancouver are made of those fragments. "They were taped together by matching colors," writes Faith Bloomfield, "and the windows, measuring two feet by seven feet, are now installed in the sanctuary above the choir stalls." (Faith Bloomfield is a member of the Bloomfield family, which contributed so much to stained glass work in this city.)

Waving goodbye to friends and family with brave smiles on their faces, Japanese men leave Vancouver in 1942 for destinations in the BC Interior and the Prairies. Stripped of their rights and property, they would not be allowed back until 1949.
Province newspaper photo, Vancouver Public Library VPL 1384

The Japanese Canadian Internment

January to November On January 14, fearful that Canada might be the next target of Japanese attacks after Pearl Harbor, and suspicious that collaborators might be harboured aboard Japanese boats in Steveston, the federal government announced that all Japanese Canadians were to be removed from the West Coast to government camps.

One of every three Canadian residents of Japanese ancestry lived in Greater Vancouver. The Powell Street district had the greatest concentration, with approximately 5,000, but there were also significant numbers of Japanese Canadians living in Fairview on the south bank of False Creek, along the south shore of English Bay, in Kitsilano and Marpole, near the banks of the North Arm of the Fraser River, around Heaps Sawmill, and around the Celtic and Great Northern fish canneries.

On March 26, Hastings Park was closed to the public and turned into an internment camp and "processing centre" for more than 8,000 Japanese Canadian citizens. Less than a week later, on April 1, the government began to move them from the West Coast to internment camps in the Interior and points east. The government had already taken 1,337 of their fish boats "into custody" and now confiscated their houses, businesses and other property (including cars, radios and cameras). The owners received little or no compensation. Newspapers were suppressed, language schools were closed, and a light in a Stanley Park monument built to honour Japanese Canadian soldiers who had fought bravely and with high casualties for Canada in World War I was turned off.

Of the 76 students of Japanese ancestry registered at the University of British Columbia in 1941–42, 69 were Canadian-born. The seven who were born in Japan had to withdraw, and Nisei (second-generation) students were allowed to remain only long enough to write their final examinations. Some transferred to universities east of the Rockies, but not all institutions would accept them.

Hide Hyodo, the only teacher of Japanese ancestry in the BC public school system, organized classes for the children at Hastings Park, under the auspices of the BC Security Commission. "I was still continuing to teach daily at Steveston, so every other day after school I'd rush from Steveston, and in the long interurban tram ride to Hastings Park look over the schedule and make assignments for the next two days...then I'd have to rush home by curfew time, and get ready for my evacuation, too." On October 23 she was one of the last to board the train that took her from Vancouver. Her first stop was Tashme, where she helped organize schools in the internment camps. Her next stop was New Denver in the Kootenays where she remained as supervisor of the school system in the detention camps. The rest of her family was dispersed to eastern Canada.

Dr. Masajiro Miyazaki was interned in the Bridge River–Lillooet area, where he served as the doctor for 1,000 internees. Miyazaki had arrived in Vancouver on June 29, 1913, aged about 13, and had taken part in UBC's Great Trek in 1922. He practised medicine in Vancouver until 1942. In 1945 the town of Lillooet petitioned for his release to replace its deceased doctor. Miyazaki received the Order of Canada in 1977.

Masumi Mitsui, who had received the Military Medal for Bravery while fighting for Canada in 1917, was forcibly moved, with his family, from their 7-hectare (17-acre) Port Coquitlam chicken farm to an internment camp in Greenwood, BC.

Vancouver writer Roy Miki, a third-generation Japanese Canadian, was born this year, six months after his parents had been shipped from Haney to a sugar beet farm in Manitoba.

The *New Canadian*, an English-language newspaper for the Japanese community, moved to Kaslo, a "ghost town" on Kootenay Lake. It became the primary source of information between various camps and across the country for Japanese Canadians trying to connect with friends and relatives. It was also the means by which government directives were announced in both English and Japanese.

By the end of October the removal of all Japanese from the 100-mile "security zone" was complete.

1942

Grim evidence of wartime internment policies, these cars lined up near Hastings Park in Vancouver were seized in 1942 by the government while their owners were sent inland. Also seized were 1,137 fishing boats, along with cameras, radios, houses and other property. Little, if any, compensation was ever paid until 1988, when the federal government offered an apology and money to living survivors. *Province newspaper photo, Vancouver Public Library VPL 1358*

May 1 Canadian Pacific Airlines was born when Canadian Pacific Railway amalgamated 10 northern bush plane companies. The company's first planes were Canadair C4 Argonauts and then DC6s. The new airline focussed at first on servicing routes within the province from the airport on Sea Island in Richmond. It soon expanded into the far northern reaches of the other provinces and territories.

Right: Put together by the Canadian Pacific Railway from 10 smaller bush plane companies, Canadian Pacific Airlines was launched in 1942. It quickly became a company to be reckoned with, expanding to the west with record-setting flights to Australia and Tokyo and then turning its sights to eastern Canada. It was not to last, however; after being rebranded as CP Air in 1968, the airline was sold to Canadian Airlines in 1987. *City of Vancouver Archives, CVA 586-2283. Photo Coltman, Don Steffens Colmer*

May 20 William Marr Crawford, master mariner, died in Vancouver, aged about 59. He was born in 1883 in Limekilns, Fife, Scotland, and came to Canada in 1911. He joined Empire Stevedoring, BC's largest waterfront employer, as manager and in 1923 was named president and managing director. In 1930 he launched the *Fyfer*, "the finest private yacht on the Pacific," and in 1941 donated it to the Canadian Navy for war use. During World War I, Captain Crawford served, without pay, as marine master to the ministry of shipping; he served as a civilian in the same role during World War II.

July 1 Alexander Maitland Stephen, writer and poet, died in Vancouver, aged about 60. He was born in 1882 in Hanover, ON. In his early years,

Stephen tried ranching and mining as well as rural teaching. He was wounded in World War I. Back in Vancouver he opened an engineering company. He was a progressive social activist, a nationally known critic and the author of two novels, plays, romances and poetry. His 1934 poem "Vancouver" was widely anthologized.

July 28 The Nine O'Clock Gun was silenced to save gunpowder.

August 9 A.D. McRae sold his Hycroft mansion in Shaughnessy, built at a cost of $109,000 in 1909, to a grateful federal government for $1. (The McRaes faced rising costs for upkeep, and the war made it difficult to hire staff.) Shaughnessy Military Hospital was full to bursting with convalescent soldiers, and Hycroft was put to immediate use to handle the overflow. It served as an auxiliary to the hospital for 18 years. Then a new wing was added to Shaughnessy, and Hycroft sat empty for two years, until the University Women's Club bought it. The club has occupied it ever since. Incidentally, women were not allowed to hold mortgages in their own right at the time, so the club was required to pay for the house in full. It took members a year to raise the money. In its original configuration, Hycroft was a 30-room home (11 of the rooms were bedrooms) with a coach house, stables, a swimming pool, an Italian garden and more, all on 2 hectares (5.2 acres).

September 13 According to military historian Peter Moogk, "it was a hazy Sunday when a fish-packer sailed in across the 'examination line' from Point Atkinson to Point Grey, oblivious to the wartime crisis. As the boat chugged on towards the First Narrows, the gunners at the fort received a message to fire a 'stopping round' ahead of the boat to compel the master to come to a stop and to identify himself. It was customary on such occasions to fire a non-explosive, solid shell that would kick up a large splash in front of the offending vessel... When one of the 12-pounder guns of the fort fired the 'stopping round,' the shell hit a wave and started to ricochet across the water at an oblique angle. Beyond the fish-packer in English Bay was the *Fort Rae,* a 9,600-ton freighter that had been launched the month before and was still on its sea trials. The skipping round hit the freighter above the waterline. As the shell passed through the number 3 hold it turned sideways and punched out a hole below the waterline on the other side. At first this was not noticed. The ship was evidently on its way back to the Burrard Dry Dock when the captain received word of flooding in the hold. He beached the freighter on the north shore, just inside the First Narrows. It remained there, on the tidal flats, until it could be patched up and floated off."

Stand-in. Pausing for a photo from deep within a ship, this was one of the hundreds of women who were hired—beginning in September 30, 1942—to fill labour shortages at the Burrard Dry Dock in North Vancouver. The end of the war, while a joyous time, was also a time of sadness for these workers as they were let go to make room for the returning men.
City of Vancouver Archives, CVA 586-1153. Photo Coltman, Don Steffens Colmer

September 30 The first group of women workers was hired by Burrard Dry Dock in North Vancouver.

At the peak of wartime activity, 1,000 of the yard's 13,000 workforce were women.

November 6 One of the lions in front of the provincial courthouse (carved in 1908 by John Bruce), the one on the west side, was damaged by a bomb. The culprit was never caught.

November From the minutes of the Building Owners and Managers

Association of BC: "Mr. Marshall, Regional Coal Controller, addressed the Association, conveying to members the seriousness of the present coal shortage. He stated that supply was 33 per cent short of requirements and suggested that office building temperatures should range from 64 to 68 degrees maximum. In fact, the coal shortage became so acute that the Yorkshire Building sent a letter to its tenants urging heat conservation."

Aiming for the sky, this Lower Mainland anti-aircraft crew in 1943 are ready for whatever the Japanese and Germans throw their way. At the peak of their popularity in 1942, batteries were located in Steveston, Point Grey and Ambleside, among other locations. *City of Vancouver Archives, CVA 1184-629. Photo Jack Lindsay*

Also in 1942

Baseball's Capilanos—named after the Capilano Brewery and owned by beer magnate Emil Sick of Seattle—stopped playing because of wartime travel restrictions.

Austin Cotterell Taylor was named chair of the BC Security Commission, which, among other activities, administered the internment of local Japanese. In 1947 Taylor received the CBE for his wartime service.

The fishing industry was declared an essential service during the war, and workers were exempt from conscription. Convicts were released to work on the fish boats.

Granville Island was declared crucial to the war effort and closed to the public to protect island industries from saboteurs.

Military historian Peter Moogk has noted that the Lower Mainland's coastal batteries were "at their peak in 1942...from Steveston to Point Atkinson, [they] were manned by 720 gunners, supported infantry regiments, and auxiliary units. Anti-aircraft batteries of 40 mm. and 3.7-inch calibre guns appeared at Point Grey, Little Mountain, Ambleside and elsewhere."

Darshan A. Sangha, born in 1917 in Langeri, Punjab, India, became the first person in Vancouver's Sikh community to be drafted.

A small number of Chinese Canadian volunteers with special skills were allowed into active service.

Most of these men served as pilots and in Special Operations, where their language skills allowed them to work behind enemy lines in Asia. It wasn't until the summer of 1944 that Chinese Canadians in BC were included in the army drafts.

Much of Surrey's strawberry crop was lost when Japanese farmers were

interned. To fill the gap left by the departure of the Japanese Canadian workforce, many people came from the Prairies, which had been slower to recover from the Depression.

Commercial blueberry farming began in Pitt Meadows.

The Workmen's Compensation Board opened the Rehabilitation Centre in Vancouver to treat injured workers. During the last three months of the year an average of 262 workers were treated daily at the centre.

The Ovaltine Cafe opened at 251 East Hastings. The cafe has survived intact with coffee counter, booths, mirrors and varnished woodwork and was a frequent location for scenes in CBC-TV's hit series *Da Vinci's Inquest.*

The Shriners' Gizeh Temple was moved from Victoria to Vancouver.

Burnaby finally came out of its Depression-mandated receivership.

Since December 31, 1932, Burnaby had been administered by a provincially appointed commissioner. Now residents could once again elect a reeve and council.

Wartime housing shortages prompted the federal government to issue an order-in-council allowing Shaughnessy homes to be split up into smaller units. That order-in-council remained in force until 1955.

The Dollar Mill at Roche Point on Indian Arm closed down. The mill, established in 1916 by shipping magnate Robert Dollar, had been a major employer for many years.

Vancouver writer Earle Birney won the first of his two Governor General's Awards for poetry, for his book *David and Other Poems.*

At Essondale mental hospital, 34 patients died from tuberculosis. This was also the year electro-convulsive shock therapy (ECT) was introduced at Essondale.

Gordon House, one of the city's oldest neighbourhood houses, opened in the West End. (Alexandra House preceded it by four years.)

Vancouver's first Kinette Club, a women's counterpart to the Kinsmen Club, was established.

Harold Elworthy and Stan McKeen formed Straits Towing with the one-tug Preston-Mann fleet and McKeen's Standard Towing.

Emily Carr donated 145 paintings and sketches to the Vancouver Art Gallery.

Andrew Roddan had an exhibition of his paintings. The well-known United Church minister was also a gifted amateur painter, charter member of the Vancouver Art Gallery and supporter of local artists.

Saba's, the largest retail house in western Canada specializing in silks, experienced a riot when 500 women stampeded the store to buy 300 pairs of nylon stockings. No one was hurt.

Comings and Goings

May 20 The *Crosline*, launched in Seattle on June 22, 1925, for the Crosby Direct Line Ferries Company, arrived from Washington state to join the Burrard Inlet ferry fleet. The vessel, which could carry 300 passengers and 65 cars, was purchased to help transport shipyard workers to their jobs on the North Shore. In 1947, after the war, the *Crosline* was sold to the ferry system of the Washington State Department of Highways, which rebuilt the boat and used it until 1967. Then the *Crosline* did time as a warehouse on Lake Union until it was sold in 1975 and moved to Coos Bay, OR, to be used as a restaurant. That venture fell through, and the boat's superstructure was removed to become a shore-based warehouse. Eventually the remaining timbers and planks became part of a fishing boat and a dock.

Some people born in 1942 who had an impact on the city: newspaper publisher **Don Babick** (January 18); broadcaster and Mount Pleasant organizer **Dave Adair** (June 21); DJ, VJ, actor and interviewer **Terry David Mulligan** (June 30); industrialist **Edgar Kaiser** (July 5); journalist and newspaper executive **Don MacLachlan** (November 5); actor, broadcaster, author and X-Kalay administrator **David Berner** (November 18).

Notable deaths: **John Murray Jr.**, 82 or 83, who was known as "Mr. Port Moody" and who named the streets of the municipality (his father, John Sr., was Port Moody's first settler); **Con Jones**, an ex-bookie from Australia, tobacco retailer (known for the slogan "Don't argue: Con Jones sells fresh tobacco") and sports entrepreneur.

1943

With round-the-clock shipyard production at its height, Vancouver's war efforts included commando practices on Kitsilano Beach and police seizure of cameras and film from people caught taking pictures of the waterfront. And Emily Carr paintings were selling at the Vancouver Art Gallery for $50.

March 18 Construction began on the *Fort Columbia*, first of the Victory ships to be built by Burrard Dry Dock. With oil-fired boilers, they were cheaper to run than coal-fired North Sands ships, although some Victory ships were built to run on either fuel. The company built 34 Victory ships in a little over two years. 

Below right: Stone frigate. HMCS *Discovery*, the landlocked naval base on Deadman's Island in Stanley Park. *Colin Price / The Province*

Elsewhere in BC

January 1 The sale of whipping cream was forbidden in British Columbia, a result of World War II rationing restrictions.

Elsewhere in Canada

January 4 Effective this date, boys who had reached the age of 17 were allowed to enlist for training in active units or formations of the Canadian Army. They were paid 70 cents per day.

Elsewhere in the World

March 31 *Oklahoma!* premiered on Broadway.

July Canadian mining tycoon Sir Harry Oakes was murdered in the Bahamas.

September 3 Italy surrendered.

Hockey's Lynn Patrick joined the New York Rangers, coached by his father Lester Patrick, and scored 13 goals in his first season.

Also March The canoe called *Houmiltichesen*, built by Jericho Charlie (Chin-nal-set), was presented as a gift to the City of Vancouver by the BC Loggers' Association and the Consolidated Red Cedar Shingle Association of BC. They had purchased it from August Jack Khatsahlano, Jericho Charlie's stepson.

May 3 From the *Province*, page 6: "City police Sunday seized two cameras and a quantity of film from persons taking photographs in prohibited waterfront areas.
"A Lt.-Cdr. of the U.S. Navy lost his camera and film when he was stopped by police at Prospect Point in Stanley Park.

"Two girls, photographing each other at the North Vancouver ferry wharf, were required to turn over their picture-taking equipment.

"A man reported to be taking pictures of English Bay from Queen Mary School grounds, Fourth and Trimble, could not be found when police searched the district Sunday."

May 15 Six paintings by Emily Carr went on sale at an exhibition of works by Carr and others at the 33rd Annual Exhibition of the BC Society of Fine Arts at the Vancouver Art Gallery. The Carrs were priced at $50 each.

June 13 Sir Gerald Burrard, a descendant of Harry Burrard, the friend of George Vancouver after whom Burrard Inlet was named, presented a telescope to the city. (Gerald Burrard was famous for his knowledge of weaponry. He has

Busy waters. Vancouver's importance as a wartime shipbuilding centre—with more than half of the ships built in Canada at this time—is revealed in this 1944 panorama of its bustling shipyards. *City of Vancouver Archives, Pan P77*

written on shotguns, sporting guns and rifles.)

June 26 The cornerstone was laid for HMCS *Discovery* on Deadman's Island, Stanley Park.

June Burnaby endorsed a "closed shop" for civic employees—the third municipality in Canada to do so, and the first in BC. (A closed shop is one in which the employer hires only union members in good standing.)

July 14 Langley Memorial Hospital was incorporated.

August 19 First annual exhibition of the Vancouver Gladiolus Society.

August 25 Stanley Park was rededicated. Frank Plant drove the official party to the ceremonies. He had driven Lord and Lady Stanley and Mayor and Mrs. Oppenheimer to the original dedication 55 years earlier. The 1889 ceremony was re-created at the same spot. Playing the role of Mayor David Oppenheimer was his great-nephew David Oppenheimer.

September 13 The West Vancouver Parks Board was established.

September 23 A great news item appeared in the *Province*: "When Mr. and Mrs. E.R. Valleau purchased a property on Burke Street in Burnaby they proceeded to build a home. That was last February. Just the other day when Mr. J.H. Treaves purchased a lot, he discovered he owned the Valleau home. Arrangements for the transfer are being completed, and Mr. and Mrs. Valleau will soon have title to their home. They had mistakenly built their home on the adjoining piece of property."

October 4 Frederick William Howay (born Howie) died in New Westminster, aged 75. He was born in London, ON, and moved to BC with his family in 1870. Frederick practised law, becoming a county court judge (1907–37). He wrote books and articles establishing him as the leading BC historian of his generation. He was president of the Art, Historical and Scientific Association of Vancouver (1910–15), a precursor of the Vancouver Museum. His *British Columbia from Earliest Times to the Present* (1914) was the standard history of BC into the 1950s.

October 6 Vancouver's water supply was chlorinated.

October 21 Percy W. Evans died in Los Angeles, CA. Evans came to BC from England in 1888 and with his brother and cousin opened a fuel and cement firm, Evans, Coleman and Evans, on Columbia Street. They sold the firm in 1910. With his brother, Evans also owned Vancouver's Stanley and Manitoba Hotels, with an interest in the Plaza Theatre building.

November 11 After being silent for some time because of wartime shortages, Vancouver's famous Nine O'Clock Gun resumed firing.

There were a few more days of silence, then it was back to regular operation.

November 13 Newspapers reported that the Dominion Bank Building, the 15-storey office structure at the northwest corner of Cambie and Hastings, had been purchased by Samuel J. Cohen, president of the Army and Navy Department Stores, and would be remodelled as a modern department store after the war. Wonder whatever happened to that idea? (Samuel Cohen's granddaughter, Jacqui Cohen, says that it was never intended to be a department store. "He bought it because the price was right.")

November Edelweiss Credit Union was established in Vancouver to serve the area's German community. In May 2001 it joined with the Fraser Valley Credit Union to become BC's fifth-largest credit union, with assets of more than $1 billion and a new name: Prospera Credit Union.

December 25 Edmund Shorey Knowlton, pioneer druggist, died in Vancouver, aged about 75. Born in Newboro, ON, Knowlton came to BC in 1896 and opened Knowlton's Drug Store in 1897. The store moved to a succession of sites on Westminster (now Main Street) and Hastings until settling in at 1911 at 15 East Hastings. Knowlton served as a president of the Pharmaceutical Association of BC. Knowlton's opened a second drugstore in West Vancouver by 1948. In 1965 the name was changed to Knowlans Drugs, but its original name was restored in 1970.

Also in 1943

Kitsilano Beach was used for rehearsing commando beach assaults. Still, the receding danger of attack brought a gradual reduction in local defences so trained personnel could be sent to bolster the Canadian army in Europe, which was now in continuous action.

The Ukrainian Labour-Farm Temple Association was once again allowed to carry out its activities. In 1940 the ULFTA's community hall at 805 East Pender in Strathcona was one of 108 such buildings seized because of the association's opposition to Canadian involvement in the war. The ULFTA supported the Soviet Union, which had yet to join the Allied effort against Nazi Germany. Now that the Russians were deeply involved in the war, the ban was lifted. (In 1946 the ULFTA changed its name to the Association of United Ukrainian Canadians.)

The precursor of the Vancouver Volunteer Centre was formed in 1943. It was initially charged with mobilizing women for the war effort and providing accommodation for children evacuated from Britain and for those whose mothers worked on the assembly line. The Women's Voluntary Service, as it was known at the time, began by helping 37 agencies and registering 267 volunteers. By the end of the war approximately 10,000 volunteers were involved.

Burnaby Hospital had a humble beginning. A group of Burnaby citizens interested in building a local hospital met and formed a fundraising committee; $6,000 was raised by door-to-door canvass. That prompted the city to provide more funds and the hospital was on its way. (Burnaby's population at the time was 35,000, and the average weekly wage was $33.81).

John Henderson (1880–1968) began 21 years' service as a Vancouver school trustee. He was named Vancouver's Good Citizen in 1961 because of his long service in a score of organizations and for many personal deeds. An elementary school is named for him.

The Vancouver Foundation was established. The key figure in its creation was W.J. VanDusen, lumber magnate and philanthropist. Whitford Julian VanDusen came from Tara, ON, where he was born July 18, 1889. His long, solid work in the lumber industry from 1912 to 1969 (much of it beside H.R. MacMillan) was deservedly overshadowed by his remarkable philanthropy. The Vancouver Foundation now distributes about $60 million annually and supports a wide range of issues from arts and culture to the environment, education, health, and children, youth and family. Today it is Canada's largest community foundation with an endowment fund worth roughly $800 million. (VanDusen also paid for and donated

Canadian commandos race onto Kitsilano Beach in 1943, rehearsing for the day that enemies might attack. However, as the threat seemed to recede, local defences were reduced so that trained personnel could join the real fight happening in Europe.
City of Vancouver Archives, CVA 586-1214. Photo Coltman, Don Steffens Colmer

Wartime neighborhood. Burkeville, a residential enclave on Sea Island next to the airport, is a time-capsule of World War II architecture. The small, "no-frills" cottages, most of which have since been modified by their owners, were sponsored by the federal government. *Courtesy Smith Bros. and Wilson (BC) Ltd.*

the land now occupied by Vancouver's VanDusen Botanical Garden. He died here December 15, 1978.)

The Southlands Riding Club was incorporated. Today it sits on just over 7 hectares (17 acres) beside the McCleery Golf Course in South Vancouver. The original clubhouse, once an abandoned fisherman's net-storage hut on Deering Island, was dismantled and carried piece by piece, by members on horseback, to its present site.

H.R. Butler was club champion at the old Shaughnessy Golf Club this year.

Construction began on Burkeville, west of Airport Road in Richmond.

The federal government built 328 houses for employees at the Boeing plant on Sea Island. Indeed, the community was named for the Boeing president, Stanley Burke, and streets were named for airplane manufacturers. After the war, Boeing sold the houses to returning veterans.

Toronto-born Elmore Philpott, 47, joined the *Vancouver Sun* and began a political affairs column that lasted to 1961.

Squamish political leader Andy Paull established the North American Indian Brotherhood (NAIB) to organize Native people across Canada to fight for civil rights without loss of Indian rights. Paull had figured prominently in the Allied Tribes of BC and the Native Brotherhood of BC. Like those earlier associations, NAIB was suppressed by federal and provincial governments that discouraged Native organizing and fundraising.

Vancouver-based E.J. Ryan Contracting, one of Canada's largest contractors, filed for bankruptcy.

On the death of her husband, R.J. Sprott, Anna Ethel Sprott became president of the Sprott-Shaw Schools of Commerce, Radio and Telegraphy. She was the founder of the West Coast Radio School.

Only three students graduated from the Vancouver School of Art.

Comings and Goings

March 2 RAF/RCAF war ace "Buzz" Beurling, "King of the Air over Malta," visited Vancouver.

June 6 Theatre director Bill Millerd was born in West Vancouver.

1944

As Canadian troops pushed across Europe after D-Day, one Vancouver soldier achieved fame through poetry while another went to Buckingham Palace to collect a Victoria Cross. A new radio station—destined to become the biggest—initiated hourly newscasts to deliver war news.

Right: Responsible for preserving a great deal of Vancouver's history through his photography, Leonard Frank seemed to be in all places at once with his "action reflex camera" and his keen, loving eye.
Bernard Frank. L.11025, Jewish Museum & Archives of BC

January A strike at BC Electric lasted three weeks. Streetcars stopped running.

February 23
Leonard Frank, photographer, died, aged about 74.

He came here from Germany in 1892, aged 22, looking for gold, but that didn't work out. Then he won a lottery in which first prize was a camera. Frank's father, a professional photographer, taught the craft to young Leonard, and he began to take pictures. For 50 years he took pictures. His nearly 50,000 images captured a now-vanished British Columbia with astonishing clarity and beauty. I swear you can see the stubble on the lumberjacks' cheeks. Enjoy this extraordinary body of work in Cyril Leonoff's multi-award-winning 1990 book *Leonard Frank: An Enterprising Life.*

March 26 Mayor Jonathan Webster "Jack" Cornett attended a Vancouver ceremony marking the 123rd anniversary of Greek independence.

June 30 Charles Hill-Tout, ethnologist, died in Vancouver, aged 85. He was born September 28, 1858, in Buckland, England, and came to Canada's West Coast in the 1890s. It was Hill-Tout who realized Vancouver's Marpole Midden was the largest of its kind in North America. He founded his own school, Buckland College, on Burrard Street. After approximately a decade at Buckland, Hill-Tout gave up education and moved to a farm in the Abbotsford area, where he subsequently opened and operated a mill that produced railway ties for the CPR. Throughout this time he worked as an amateur anthropologist with a particular interest in the Salish people. He was a member of the Royal Society of Canada and served as president of its anthropological section, and he was also president of the Art, Historical and Scientific Association of Vancouver (forerunner of the Vancouver Museum). Hill-Tout is said to have suggested the name Kitsilano for a Vancouver neighbourhood, modifying the name of the Squamish chiefs.

August 14
Vancouver City Council adopted Odessa, Ukraine, as a sister city.

To mark the occasion the Vancouver Symphony Orchestra gave a concert of Russian music. (That likely made a lot of Ukrainians angry, but they were a Soviet socialist republic at the time.)

August 15
Radio station CKNW signed on (unofficially) at 1230 on the dial,

with 250 watts of power, after on-air testing that had started April 1. NW, now at the 980 frequency, has been one of the top-rated radio stations in

Elsewhere in the World

June 6 D-Day. More than a thousand planes and gliders began dropping paratroopers into Normandy in the dark hours before dawn. The push to recapture the Nazi-occupied continent was under way.

October 21 Vancouver's Private Ernest Alvia "Smokey" Smith, a Seaforth Highlander, won the Victoria Cross for bravery in action in northern Italy. On December 21 the *Province* reported: "'Smokey' Smith wants to get home to New Westminster. He has his Victoria Cross. The excitement of a private investiture at Buckingham Palace is over. Now he's getting impatient. 'Five years is a long time to be overseas,' Canada's first buck private to win the VC in this war, said in a London interview today." When Smith died at his home in Vancouver on August 3, 2005, he was the last living Canadian recipient of the Victoria Cross. He lay in state at the House of Commons and was given a full military funeral on August 13.

Strange Harvest

September 28 Some weeks after D-Day, sitting alone at midnight in a military vehicle in St. Omer, France, Chaplain Stanley Higgs of Vancouver, then attached to the 6th Canadian Light Anti-Aircraft Regiment, was writing a poem. It was a tribute to 3rd Canadian Infantry Division, which was hurrying toward Antwerp and Brussels. The division had stopped to rest at St. Omer, about 30 kilometres (19 miles) southeast of Calais, and Stan Higgs was thinking about its men. He had been with them during their advance to the Falaise Gap, when Canadian and Polish troops had met with fierce resistance. Now the men were enjoying some well-earned R and R.

Taken sometime after D-Day—the historic day in June 1944 on which the Allies began their long push to break the German hold over Europe—this photo shows soldiers disembarking from their transport into the surf on the French coast. *Dominion Institute*

"There was a film being shown to the men in a barn in one of the fields there," Stan recalled. "It was a very fine film called *Blossoms in the Dust*. There is a wonderful scene where Greer Garson, in the character of the woman whose real-life story the film told, rises up in the public gallery of the Texas state legislature to argue for the rights of children born out of wedlock. Her extraordinary enunciation and spirit inspired me. After the movie I went back and sat in my vehicle and stared out through the window and began to think of a poem. It occurred to me that unless someone recorded what 3rd Division had done as they fought their way east, no one would know. So by the light of a coal-oil lamp I started to write it out."

He finished the poem, which he titled "Strange Harvest," at three in the morning on September 28, 1944. It first appeared two days later in *Flak*, the regiment's weekly bulletin. The reaction was immediate, and it was good. The regiment's commanding officer likened Stan's poem to "In Flanders Fields," the classic elegy of World War I. The Red Cross asked to use it. Less than a month later the BBC was broadcasting it around the world, read by Canadian war correspondents Matthew Halton and Gerry Wilmot against a musical background. "The next thing I knew," Stan said, "I got a letter from a friend in Barkerville, in BC, and he'd heard it there on the Armed Forces Network." A recording of the poem was made by Vancouver broadcaster Bill Herbert.

Stan's poem, written by flickering lamplight in a truck on the shell-pocked fields of northern France, had gone around the world. It's a long poem, too long for full inclusion here, but its flavour is established immediately in the first section:

Strange Harvest

A Tribute to 3rd Canadian Infantry Division

Dip gently your scythe, good reaper
O'er the fields of Calvados,
Tread softly Normandy's furrowed earth
From Epron to the coast,
For the harvest is not all the yield of the soil,
Nor the furrows the mark of the plough,
But the earth's rich red is the blood of the dead
The dead who are sleeping now.
They came from the sea, like you and me,
But they beached on a steel-rimmed coast
They carved their way through the Hun at bay,
And blasted the tyrant's boast
That no might could breach the wave-locked shore,
No Allied foot gain hold;
The sea would be red with the blood of the dead,
The dead who had been too bold

the Greater Vancouver area for the past 40 years. No one would have predicted it given the unpromising beginnings. CKNW was a tiny station playing "cowboy" music on the second floor of a nondescript hotel in New Westminster, far from the big boys in Vancouver. However, owner Bill Rea launched many innovations with his new station: he initiated hourly newscasts—a local first—because he knew we wanted news of our troops overseas; he kept NW on 24 hours a day, another first; he started a people-on-the-street show called *Roving Mike* that lasted for decades; and he established the Orphans' Fund, which has raised millions for local kids. What an impact Bill Rea made on local radio!

September 11
The first child-care centre was set up for children of soldiers.

September 15 A new product called "contact lenses" arrived in Vancouver.

September 18 Film producer Walter Wanger described Vancouver-born Yvonne De Carlo (real name Peggy Middleton) as the "most beautiful girl in the world."

September 30 A second BC Federation of Labour was founded, succeeding the original one which had disbanded in 1920.

October 16 The RCMP ship *St. Roch* arrived in Vancouver from Halifax via the Northwest Passage, the first ship to have sailed the passage in both directions. The outward journey took 28 months but the return only 86 days. The *St. Roch* also became the first ship to traverse the passage in a single season. Sgt. Henry Larsen captained the 95-foot (29-metre) RCMP schooner, and his extensive knowledge of Arctic waters allowed him to chart the optimum route—although severe ice conditions stretched the west-to-east voyage to more than two years. Today the *St. Roch* is open to public view at the Maritime Museum.

October 21 (Trafalgar Day) HMCS *Discovery*, a naval training base, was officially opened on Deadman's Island, which is now connected to Stanley Park by a short causeway.

North Vancouver City finally emerged from receivership, which had started December 31, 1932, during the Great Depression.

The Children's Health Centre was built at Vancouver General Hospital.

Dr. R.E. McKechnie, long-time chancellor of UBC, died. He was succeeded by Eric Hamber, who held the post for seven years.

Leonard Klinck stepped down after 25 years as president of UBC. He was succeeded by Dr. Norman A.M. MacKenzie. Klinck had come to UBC in 1914 as dean of the Faculty of Agriculture. He became president in 1918 after the sudden death of President Frank Wesbrook and saw the university through a difficult period, successfully managing the development of Point Grey campus and a strong faculty.

Harry Letson donated 150,000 engineering books and periodicals to UBC.

The BC Research Council, founded by the provincial government, was established on the UBC campus to operate laboratory facilities, conduct industrial research and help develop technologies that would be useful to BC. The council was a catalyst for innovation in the province.

Volume at the wartime Vancouver Stock Exchange bottomed out at 11 million shares this year, with brokers devoting themselves to selling Canadian government Victory bonds.

The Restaurant and Foodservices Association of BC was formed in Vancouver to deal with problems created by rationing during World War II.

Beer magnate Emil Sick of Seattle bought Athletic Park, where his Capilano baseball team played, and renamed it Capilano Stadium.

International Artists' Film Corporation signed a 20-year lease with Burnaby for a 16-hectare (40-acre) production location on Canada Way near Willingdon.

The White Rock Players acting troupe was formed.

Erwin Swangard became foreign editor of the *Province*.

Also in 1944

Local Doukhobors held a prayer vigil on the courthouse steps for 13 of their brethren imprisoned in Oakalla.

A forest fire swept down Black Mountain in West Vancouver, covering about 1,800 hectares (7 square miles). It was finally stopped just 275 metres (300 yards) above Eagle Harbour.

Howard Simons established the engineering firm H.A. Simons to serve the forest products industry. At last count it had completed more than 10,000 projects in more than 70 countries.

Surrey schoolteachers asked for a pay raise. Students with summer jobs in war industries were making more than their teachers.

Les Gilmore of Richmond harvested 900 bushels of potatoes per acre, the highest yield per acre in Canada.

Comings and Goings

April 23 Jack Benny brought his regular cast—Mary Livingstone, Phil Harris, Rochester, Dennis Day and announcer Don Wilson—up from New

Right: Comedian Jack Benny (second from left) and his wife, Mary Livingstone (left), enjoy a break with some colleagues while in Vancouver to tape Benny's radio show. *City of Vancouver Archives, CVA 1184-517. Jack Lindsay photo*

York to broadcast his famous radio show from Vancouver. What made the show particularly notable was that Mary Livingstone (real name Sadie Marks) had grown up in Vancouver. Mary got a lot of comic mileage out of Jack's age. He was forever 39. That led to exchanges like this:

Jack: You know, Mary, being in Vancouver brings back memories to me, too. When I was in vaudeville, I played the Orpheum Theatre many a time. Did you know that?

Mary: Did I *know* that? Jack, every time you played here, didn't you notice a little girl in the third row in the aisle seat, with long blonde pigtails and a pink ribbon in her hair?

Jack: Well, I'll be darned! Was that you?

Mary: No, that was my mother.

Jack: *Now cut that out!*

Vancouver mayor Jack Cornett popped in as a special guest, and Jack, who played up his reputation as a cheapskate, began to pester him about the toll charge (25 cents) on the Lions Gate Bridge. Jack wondered if it might be possible to drop the toll so he could see Grouse Mountain up close, instead of always through his telescope. The mood got serious for a moment as Jack echoed Mayor Cornett's plug for Canada's Sixth Victory Loan, a fundraising campaign to help the war effort. Jack visited Vancouver often and helped raise funds to save the Orpheum Theatre.

Also this year, golfing great Ben Hogan participated in a wartime fundraiser at Shaughnessy Golf Course.

December Winnipeg shopkeeper George Davis and his nine-year-old son Charlie arrived in Vancouver. When he grew up, Charlie became a broadcaster and writer.

1945

As the city celebrated the end of the war, women were dismissed from wartime industrial jobs. Also this year, a ship exploded in the harbour, breaking windows across downtown, and fire destroyed Vancouver's baseball stadium. City council ended its racial segregation of a city swimming pool.

March 6 The freighter *Greenhill Park* exploded in Vancouver Harbour, killing eight men and breaking hundreds of downtown windows. Debris from ths ship fell as far away as Lumbermen's Arch in Stanley Park. The vessel was towed to Siwash Rock, where the fire was finally extinguished. A later inquiry pointed to improper stowage of flammable cargo and explosives, and improper use of matches. The ship was rebuilt at Burrard Dry Dock and as the *Phaeax II* continued working until 1967.

April 18 A pre-school for deaf children began at Lord Tennyson School.

April 30 Fire destroyed Capilano Stadium in Vancouver, continuing past midnight into May 1. The stadium was rebuilt quickly.

May 7 At 7:04 a.m. air raid sirens began to blare out all over Greater Vancouver to mark VE Day: Victory in Europe. Now attention would turn to defeating Japan.

June 11 Gerry McGeer was named to the Senate.

July 12 That's the date on a photograph of 23-year-old 2nd Lieutenant Molly Bobak at work painting in London, England. Born in Vancouver, Molly Lamb studied at the Vancouver School of Art from 1938 to 1941. In November 1942 she enlisted as a draughtsman in the Canadian Women Army Corps (CWAC), the only woman to be hired as an official war artist. She was posted to Holland after V-E Day and painted the work and experiences of female soldiers overseas.

July 14 A remarkable story by the *Province*'s Jean Howarth told of a young man named Ivan Knopski—he ran a concession stand at St. Paul's Hospital—who was building his own

A large explosion rocked Vancouver on March 6, 1945, when a freighter in the harbour, the *Greenhill Park*, blew out its third hold. It had been packed in part with the chemical sodium chlorate (used in bleaching, explosives and fertilizer), whiskey and signal flares. Whiskey fumes were ignited by sailors trying to see in the dark while siphoning the deadly drink. Dramatic fireworks ensued from the flares, downtown windows shattered, and pickles—another cargo item—rained down. Eight men were killed, and many more wounded. *City of Vancouver Archives, CVA 586-3567. Photo Coltman, Don Steffens Colmer*

house at the corner of Main Street and East 29th Avenue. Knopski was blind. "His neighbors, as they watched him building, didn't believe that. They were sure he was boasting, that he had some sight left. But when they heard his hammer going on into the night till 11 and 12 and no lanterns around, then they knew he must be telling the truth."

July 20 Businessman A.J.T. Taylor died in New York, aged 57. Alfred James Towle Taylor was born in Victoria on August 4, 1887. In 1912 he founded Taylor Engineering, which built large projects around the province. He promoted the development of British Pacific Properties and the construction of Lions Gate Bridge in the 1930s. Taylor

Elsewhere in BC

March 2 Emily Carr died in Victoria, aged 73. She was born there on December 13, 1871, and lived there much of her life. She studied art in San Francisco, England, and France, and between 1900 and 1913 she lived off and on in Vancouver, where she taught art, painted and tried, unsuccessfully, to interest locals in her work. In 1899 she travelled to Ucluelet on Vancouver Island, the first of many trips to paint Native sites. In 1913 she returned to Victoria and ran a boarding house until the late 1920s, when she was invited to participate in *Canadian and West Coast Art, Native and Modern*, a show at Ottawa's National Gallery. This show brought her popular attention and also put her in contact with other Canadian artists. Later in life, encouraged by her friend Ira Dilworth, she began writing about her life and experiences. Carr won the Governor General's Award for non-fiction in 1941 for *Klee Wyck* and was awarded an honorary degree by UBC in 1945.

The provincial government created the BC Power Commission, which began extending electricity into rural areas.

The provincial government passed a law giving the vote to Asians who were Canadian citizens and had fought in World War II.

Elsewhere in Canada

February 20 The first family allowance cheques were mailed by the federal government.

May 16 Prime Minister Mackenzie King opened the federal election campaign with a speech from Vancouver broadcast over Radio CBR (now CBU).

September 5 Cipher clerk Igor Gouzenko walked out of the Soviet embassy in Ottawa. He revealed the existence of a Soviet spy ring in Canada. This has sometimes been called the event that marked the onset of the Cold War.

Elsewhere in the World

March Anne Frank, 15, died in Bergen-Belsen concentration camp in Germany. Her *Diary of a Young Girl* was published in 1952.

April 6 Coevorden, the Dutch city from which Captain George Vancouver's family derived its name, was liberated from Nazi occupation by Canadian forces. In a happy coincidence, April 6 is the City of Vancouver's birthday!

April 12 US president Franklin D. Roosevelt died.

April 25 The United Nations began operations in New York City.

July 16 The first atomic bomb was exploded in a test at Alamogordo, NM.

August 6 The atomic bomb was dropped on Hiroshima.

August 9 The atomic bomb was dropped on Nagasaki.

August 14 Japan surrendered and World War II ended. The victory was wildly celebrated in Greater Vancouver...and, oh yes, elsewhere, too.

September 10 A news report datelined Portland, OR: "Following consultations with Dr. Gerald Wendt, noted scientist, the Pacific Northwest Trade Association...approved appointment of a committee to collaborate with its fisheries committee in consulting with University of Washington scientists and others on the advisability of utilization of the atomic bomb to blast out Ripple Rock, navigation hazard on Canada's route to Alaska." Yikes! The rock was later taken out with conventional explosives.

Left: Piled on for a good time, these revellers celebrate the Allies' victory in Europe on May 7, 1945. From here, the focus shifted to defeating Japan and ending the war on the Pacific front. *Province newspaper photo, Vancouver Public Library VPL 42798*

worked for the British ministry of aircraft production in London during World War II. Taylor Way in West Vancouver was named for him.

August 1 Mary Louise Bollert died in Vancouver, aged about 61. Born in 1884 in Guelph, ON, she was a graduate of the University of Toronto (BA, 1906) and of Columbia University (MA, 1908). Bollert was director of women's education and social welfare programs in Toronto, then dean of women at Regina College from 1914 to 1921. She was appointed the first dean of women at UBC in 1921 with a salary far below that of male deans. She was a founder of the BC Teachers Federation, a delegate to many international women's conferences (one of 12 deans of women invited to tour Japan in 1934) and president of the Confederation of University Women (1929–30).

August 4 Foam on beer glasses in BC beer parlours was now limited by law to half an inch.

August 7 A headline in the *Province*: "City Man Says He Discovered Atomic Power!" News of the atom bomb's destruction of Hiroshima brought forth an intriguing tale: "Convinced," the paper reported, "that an invention of his that 'draws power out of the air' is basically the same as the atomic bomb, Louis P. Isaacs, 1184 Nelson street, said today he had written a letter to His Majesty the King appealing for protection of his inventor's rights. Mr. Isaacs has driven himself on a bicycle chassis powered by a device which, he says, harnesses electricity from the air; he claims to have developed heat with it and to have lit lamps."

August 22 Locomotive 374, which pulled the first CPR passenger train into Vancouver in 1887, arrived in the city for a last run before being put on outdoor display in Kitsilano.

September 2 All internment camps except New Denver were ordered closed, and settlements of shacks were bulldozed. However, the Japanese Canadians who had been interned there since 1942 were not allowed to return home. Japanese Americans had left US internment camps and returned to the coast early in 1945, but Japanese Canadians were ordered to move "east of the Rockies" or agree to be "repatriated" to Japan. When Yoshiji Takahashi left New Denver internment camp to reclaim his farm in Mission after the war ended, he was sentenced to a year in Oakalla Prison in Burnaby. Akihide Otsuji was also sentenced to one year of hard labour in 1948 after he returned to the coastal area. It wasn't until March 31, 1949, that the Canadian exile was actually over, and the New Denver office of the BC Security Commission, which administered the internment, remained open until 1957.

September 8 Henry Reifel died in Vancouver, aged 76. He was born April 2, 1869 in Spiyer, Bavaria. Reifel immigrated to the US in 1886 and began his brewing career in Portland and San Francisco. He came to Vancouver in 1888 and began a brewery at Main and 16th on Brewery

"They were really just skeletons"

August 30 Sub-Lieutenant William K.L. Lore, originally from Victoria, was the first Allied officer ashore in Hong Kong. Lore was the first Chinese Canadian in the Royal Canadian Navy and the first officer of Chinese descent in all the navies of the British Commonwealth.

It had not been easy. He volunteered for the navy in 1940, '41 and '42 but was not accepted until 1943. Because he had learned to build and maintain radios during the Depression, he was assigned to intelligence operations and then assigned to the staff of Rear Admiral Sir Cecil Harcourt, who was the first to arrive in Hong Kong harbour after Japan's surrender. Because of his ability to speak Cantonese, Lore was choseen to be the first British officer to land in Hong Kong.

He was not only present when the Japanese officially handed over the colony, but was also sent with two other officers to liberate the prisoners of war held by the Japanese at the Sham Shui Po prison camp.

"I went into the first building I came to and it was very dark," he recounted in a 1994 interview shortly before he died. "There were about 40 men in there, Canadians, sitting at tables and so forth. Because I was coming in from the light I don't think they could see much; just an Asian in uniform. I said, 'Hi, you guys, don't you want to see a Canadian?' Then they ran forward and saw my cap badge.

"They were really just skeletons. You could see their bones through their skin. Then they were crying and weren't ashamed of crying. And finally I cried too because they were telling me what they had suffered."

Lore remained in the Canadian navy as an intelligence officer until 1957. He then settled in Hong Kong and worked as an insurance salesman before becoming a lawyer in 1962. He died in 1994.

Dancing down the street, and not at all minding the traffic jam, Vancouverites celebrate VJ Day—Victory over Japan—on August 15, 1945.
Vancouver Public Library, Special Collections, VPL 30420. Dominion Photo Company

Creek. By 1908 he had built Canadian Brewing and Malting (at 11th and Yew) and later amalgamated several companies into Vancouver Breweries, which he sold to Carling O'Keefe. Reifel developed a technique to produce malt from rice and opened Anglo-Japanese Brewing in Japan. He sold his brewing interests on retirement in 1933. He donated the property for the original Vancouver Art Gallery on Georgia Street, a few blocks west of the present gallery.

September 14 Three members of the Vancouver Fire Department were killed fighting a fire in the McMaster Building on Homer Street.

October 28 Tomekichi Homma died in an internment camp in Slocan, BC, aged 80. He was born June 6, 1865, in Onigoshi-mura, Chiba-ken, Japan, and came to Canada at age 18. He settled in Steveston and from 1897 to 1899 was chairman of the Japanese Fishermen's Benevolent Society, which built the first hospital in Steveston. He also fought for Japanese Canadian voting rights, winning in the Canadian Supreme Court but losing at the British Privy Council. Homma started the first Japanese newspaper in Vancouver. An elementary school in Richmond is named for him.

November 5 The Boeing Aircraft factory on Coal Harbour—pretty much inactive as the war ended—was to be sold to BC Packers, likely for use as a maintenance plant for the fishing fleet.

November 6 Vancouver City Council cancelled an order that had established separate swimming days at Crystal Pool for non-white people. The pool, the *Province* reported, "is now open to everyone, all the time, regardless of race, creed, or colour. Vancouver Park Board commissioners at a special meeting voted to withdraw previous rules about special days for whites, negroes, and Orientals."

December 8 Jonathan Rogers, pioneer, contractor and philanthropist, died in Vancouver, aged 80. He was born July 30, 1865, on Plas Onn farm in Denbighshire, Wales. He learned to speak English at age 16. Rogers was the first person to step down onto the platform from the first CPR passenger train to arrive at Vancouver on May 23, 1887. He eventually built up more than 300 metres (1,000 feet) of frontage along Granville and Hastings, including the Rogers Building (1911), the handsome white terracotta building at the northeast corner of Granville and Pender. He was a Vancouver alderman in 1906 and again in 1911. As a Vancouver parks commissioner and chair (1908–43), he maintained Stanley Park in its natural state. Rogers Park, named in his honour, is on East 7th Avenue.

December Burrard Dry Dock let go the last of its female workers.

A thousand women (out of a workforce of 13,000) had worked at the plant, where, at the war's height, 34 Victory ships were built in 26 months. (When victory was announced, some women workers found themselves in tears, knowing their jobs had ended and that, despite a fight by their union to keep them on, the returning men would necessarily put them out of work.)

Also in 1945

Thirty-year-old Sam Bass borrowed money to buy Schoff's Drug Store at Main and Union in Vancouver, renaming it London Drugs. Bass, the son of Jewish immigrant farmers from Kiev, Ukraine, had been born on a farm near Winnipeg on April 25, 1915. He had been an RCAF pharmacist during World War II and was actually heading for California when he stopped over in Vancouver and bought the store. A pioneer in his field, he created the first modern drugstore in BC and was the first pharmacy discounter. Bass sold the chain to a US firm in 1968. He was a strong supporter of Jewish charities and community affairs before he died in Vancouver on November 8, 1990, at age 75. (Today London Drugs is owned by Vancouver-based H.Y. Louie and has 75 stores in western Canada.)

George Frederick Curtis became the first dean of the fledgling law faculty at the University of British Columbia. After a number of years spent in private practice in Halifax and teaching at Dalhousie University, Curtis was hired by UBC to head a faculty that had little money, no classrooms and no library. He brought in judges and practitioners as voluntary lecturers and remained as dean for 26 years, stepping down in 1971. The George F. Curtis Building at UBC is named for him.

After his return from a German prisoner-of-war camp, Saskatchewan-born Art Seller took advantage of the postwar flying boom: in partnership with Harold Foster, whom he later bought out, he formed the Royal City Flying Club at Vancouver Airport. It had one war-surplus Tiger Moth. Later, a second Moth was added.

W.H. Malkin stepped down as chair of the board of governors of the BC Cancer Institute and was succeeded by Dr. A. Maxwell Evans, who served for 33 years.

The first Cloverdale Rodeo took place.

The magazine *BC Outdoors* began publishing.

The United Fishermen and Allied Workers Union was organized.

Weldwood's manufacturing operations in British Columbia began this year when a predecessor company, Western Plywood, began producing fir and poplar plywood in a Vancouver plant.

Aragon Recording opened at 615 West Hastings. One of its founding partners, broadcaster and musician Al Reusch, acquired sole ownership of the three-room space in 1954.

In 1945 the city agreed to provide $1 million for a new main library to replace the 1901 Carnegie building. The new building didn't open, however, for another nine years.

Poet Earle Birney won the second of his Governor General's Literary Awards for poetry, for his book *Now Is Time.*

Vancouver-born movie actor John Ireland, 30, appeared in his first film, *A Walk in the Sun.*

Mary Pack, a home-schooling teacher who was dismayed by the lack of services for physically handicapped children in Vancouver, started the BC Spastic Society. In 1948 it became the BC Division of the Canadian Arthritis and Rheumatism Society.

Italy-born Joe Philliponi (born Filippone), about 32, opened the Penthouse dinner club at 1019 Seymour. It's still there, nearly 70 years later. Philliponi was shot to death in his office on September 18, 1983.

Foon Sien Wong, a spokesman for Chinese rights, began a campaign to get the vote for Chinese Canadians.

Comings and Goings

September 1 Visiting movie actress Yvonne De Carlo (born Peggy Yvonne Middleton on September 1, 1922, in Vancouver) celebrated her birthday at the Hotel Vancouver's Panorama Roof. She was appearing here as part of Yvonne De Carlo Week in the city. De Carlo had appeared in, among other films, *Salome, Where She Danced* (the 1945 role that made her a star) and as a handmaiden in the 1942 Hope/Crosby comedy *Road to Morocco*. Howard Hughes made his first visit to Vancouver about this time, at the controls of his own plane. We can date the visit because he met (and, some say, romanced) the lovely Miss De Carlo while here. De Carlo died in California in 2007.

Cariboo Digest, precursor to *BC Outdoors* magazine began circulation in 1945. *Courtesy BC Outdoors magazine*

Notable births: publisher and writer **Howard White** was born in Abbotsford on April 18; novelist and poet **George Payerle** was born in Vancouver on August 21; broadcaster **Bill Good Jr.**; impresario and manager **Bruce Allen**; and teacher, writer and editor **Catherine Kerr** were also born in Vancouver this year.

1946

In the aftermath of war, the city's Dominion Day celebration was world class, but some people had less to celebrate. Vancouver struggled to provide housing for veterans, and thousands of people of Japanese descent were deported. This was also the year the first parking meter was installed.

January 26 There was an extreme housing shortage, and homeless World War II veterans took matters into their own hands, occupying the old (and vacant) Hotel Vancouver, two blocks east of the present hotel. They used the building until 1948.

February 14 ELEVEN 'HUSH-HUSH' TROOPS DOCK HERE was the headline on a story in the *Vancouver Sun* about the arrival from Australia of 11 Canadian soldiers who had served in the Pacific war. The war was over, but these men were still "under orders not to talk about their military activities." We know today what four of them had been doing: Sgt. Norman Lowe and Sgt. Louis King of Vancouver, Tpr. Douglas Mar of Port Alberni and Sgt. Douglas Jung of Victoria, all Chinese Canadians, all volunteers, had served with distinction in a "secret Chinese Guerrilla unit" in the East Indies. Their story is even more amazing when we consider the fight Chinese Canadians had to wage to be accepted into the Canadian armed forces. Douglas Jung, who won the Burma Star in the war, went on to become the first Chinese Canadian veteran to receive a university education under the auspices of Veteran's Affairs, and the first Chinese Canadian lawyer to appear before the BC Court of Appeal. In 1957 he became Canada's first Chinese Canadian MP.

March 21 Central Auto and Window Glass Shop opened its doors for business. The shop was at 26 McInnis St. (rear of Fogg Motors) in New Westminster. It went on to become TCG, one of the biggest companies in BC.

April 22 It snowed in Haney, perhaps the latest date on record for that town. And here's a coincidence linked to that snowfall that we really like, related by Nicole Parton, widow of the late *Province* columnist Lorne Parton. "This story is almost unbelievable," she says, "but is completely true." On their first date, Nicole writes, "Lorne (who was 15 years my senior) asked me when I was born. I replied that my birthday was April 22, 1946. His jaw dropped, and for a few moments he stared at me in amazement, unable to speak. 'Then I've got something to show you,' he said, pulling out his wallet. With trembling hands, he extracted a small black-and-white photograph he'd taken as a boy of 15. He was living in Haney at the time, and on the Easter Monday he took the photograph, there was a late snowfall. Thinking how beautiful the spring trilliums were as their noses poked through the snow, Lorne pressed the date into the snow with gravel: *April 22, 1946*. When the photos were developed, he tucked that particular picture into his wallet without really knowing why. He carried the photo in his wallet for 27 years, until our first date in 1973. When he pulled the photo from his wallet, we both had a sense that we were destined to be together."

April 30 As part of the city's Diamond Jubilee (60th anniversary) celebrations, the Vancouver Park Board hosted a dinner at the Stanley Park dining pavilion for nine "Jubilarians," all born in Vancouver in 1886 after incorporation.

June 4 Louis D. Taylor, former mayor, died in Vancouver, aged 88. Louis Denison Taylor, born July 22, 1857, in Ann Arbor, MI, was a very interesting fellow. In 1896 he hurriedly left Chicago, where he was in banking, with criminal charges pending against him for accepting deposits when he knew his bank was insolvent. And for a brief period he was married to two women at the same time. He only *looked* like Caspar Q. Milquetoast. Taylor arrived in Vancouver on September 17, 1896. He was one of the city's most popular mayors, serving seven times between 1910 and 1934. He worked to amalgamate Point Grey, South Vancouver and Vancouver, though he was not in office when amalgamation happened, in 1929; he opened the airport at Sea Island; and he supported the establishment of an archives for the city.

June 23 An earthquake felt mostly on Vancouver Island stopped the clock on the Vancouver Block, just as a 1918 quake had done.

Elsewhere in BC

October 1 Mining engineer Charles Arthur Banks was sworn in as BC's Lieutenant-Governor.

Elsewhere in the World

January 10 The first meeting of the United Nations was held in New York City.

A US-based chain of convenience stores adopted the name 7-Eleven this year to reflect the fact the stores were open from 7 a.m. to 11 p.m. Today virtually all 7-Elevens are open 24 hours a day.

July 1 This Dominion Day was the first national holiday since the end of the war, and Vancouver celebrated with a spectacular parade in the world's largest outdoor theatre, built at Brockton Point. Two hundred and fifty thousand people attended.

Also July 1 Steveston held its first Salmon Festival, and Sophie Kuchma, the first Salmon Queen, was crowned. Sophie won the title by selling the most tickets to the festival at 10 cents each.

July 7 Vancouver's first Jewish home for the aged, Louis Brier Home, was opened by comedian and humanitarian Eddie Cantor, who gave a benefit performance in its support. Today the home is at 1055 West 41st Ave.

July 28 Beth Israel Cemetery was consecrated.

August 30 The Cascades Drive-In Theatre opened in Burnaby. Cars arrived two hours before the showing of *Home in Indiana* (a 1944 movie) was to begin. The theatre closed in 1980, and the site is now occupied by the Cascade Village condominium.

August Walter Mulligan, a Vancouver police officer with the force since 1927, was named head of the department's Criminal Investigation Bureau. Mulligan became chief of the department in 1947.

September 19 C.D. Howe, the "Minister of Everything" (in this case, transport), officiated at a ceremony in honour of the arrival of the first scheduled overseas plane from Australian National Airways (which later became Qantas), and the establishment of an air route around the world through the Commonwealth.

The first of its kind in Canada, the Cascades Drive-In Theatre opened in 1946 and quickly became a Burnaby landmark. When this photo was taken in 1949, the featured attraction was the 1948 film *The Noose Hangs High*, starring the comedy team of Bud Abbott and Lou Costello. The novelty eventually wore off, though, and the Cascades closed in 1980. Vancouver Sun

October 11 Quoted in the *Province*, Cecil Alton, chairman of a special advertising committee of the Vancouver Tourist Association, said: "At least 1,000,000 American tourists will have visited Vancouver this year." And the number of visitors to Bowen Island reached an all-time high of 101,000.

October 28
Effective today, milk sold in Vancouver had to be pasteurized.

November 23 Boys band leader Arthur Delamont was named Mr. Good Citizen of 1946, a popular decision. Delamont is always associated with the Kitsilano Boys Band (founded in 1927), but that group was just one of seven he was leading when this award was made. The others were the bands of West Vancouver, North Vancouver, Point Grey, Grandview, Fairview and the University of BC.

December 10 West Vancouver voted to discontinue the ferry service to Vancouver.

Also in 1946

With the war over, Vancouver Airport was returned to civic control.

The first sail-past of the West Vancouver Yacht Club took place at Sandy Cove.

Troll's fish and chips opened in Horseshoe Bay. (A restaurant was opened on the same site in the early 1950s, and it was enlarged in 1962.)

The *Pamir*, the last working sailing ship in BC waters, was towed out of Vancouver Harbour with a load of coal for Australia.

The Registered Nurses Association of BC (RNABC) obtained its first certification at St. Paul's Hospital in 1946.

Earle Birney began teaching literature at UBC. He continued until 1965,

Vancouver got its first parking meters in 1946. The fee was a nickel an hour. Police checked the meters in the beginning, but responsibility was transferred to a civilian force in 1976 for more effective enforcement. Vancouver parking has not been the same since. *City of Vancouver Archives, CVA 586-4816. Photo Coltman, Don Steffens Colmer*

starting Canada's first creative writing department along the way (in 1963). Harry Adaskin came to UBC this year too, to establish the faculty of music. Adaskin headed the department for 12 years and spent 15 more as a professor.

The first female physician was appointed at Essondale mental hospital.

The parking meter came to Vancouver, charging one nickel for one hour's parking.

Following five years as a pilot in the RCAF, Jack Bell became the first commercial grower of cranberries in BC. He planted 1.2 hectares (3 acres).

The famous 2400 Motel on Kingsway opened.

This was a year of shortages everywhere. In Cloverdale and White Rock (still a part of Surrey), 264 people were waiting for telephones.

Comings and Goings

Four thousand people of Japanese descent were exiled to Japan.

February 7 The great American bass Paul Robeson performed at the Orpheum, and 3,000 fans in the sold-out theatre kept him coming back for more and more. The *Sun*'s Stanley Bligh, in a warm review, commented: "In addition to his great success in the artistic field, the eminent Negro has won an outstanding place in the world by his firm stand on the question of racial equality, his knowledge of languages, international economics and his wide sympathy for the oppressed peoples of the whole globe." That sympathy would later get him into trouble.

June 8 CKNW's John Ashbridge was born. It's Ashbridge's rich baritone you hear on the PA during Canucks' games.

July 13 Canada's new Governor General, Field Marshal Viscount Alexander of Tunis, visited British Columbia. He was our last British GG, and one of the most popular, a genuine war hero. Alexander had become a major-general in the British Army in 1937 at age 45, the youngest of that rank, and had a distinguished record in World War II—including commanding the rearguard during the Dunkirk evacuation, where he was the last man to leave France. He led the invasions of Sicily and Italy, and was commander-in-chief in the Mediterranean from 1942. All of which perhaps explains why he became the only white man in the history of the Pacific coast to become, with full tribal rites, a Native chief. While he was here, Alexander received a Kwakiutl thunderbird headdress and ceremonial blanket, and became Chief Nakupunkim.

Notable deaths: **Charles Cotterell**, who was with the CPR for 47 years, died in Vancouver on February 14, two months after he retired, aged 68; **Earle Kelly**, a *Province* reporter and night editor who did nightly newscasts seven nights a week on the *Province*'s own station, CKCD, from 1929 to 1946 (thousands of BC radio listeners knew him as "Mr. Good Evening") died on April 15; **George Alexander Walkem**, shipbuilder, died in Burnaby on December 13, aged 64. Walkem was president of West Coast Shipbuilders, Vancouver Iron Works, West Coast Salvage and Construction and Gulf of Georgia Towing; was elected reeve (mayor) of Point Grey in 1923; and was MLA for Richmond–Point Grey (1924–28) and Vancouver (1928–33). His ashes were scattered over English Bay from the tug *George A. Walkem*.

Right: Wet work. Heirs to Jack Bell's pioneering work in 1946 as the first BC commercial grower of cranberries, these workers round up part of BC's multimillion-dollar cranberry crop in Delta. Because berries are small, and the vines low to the ground, the "wet harvest" method is preferred. For this, the fields are flooded so that the berries float to the top. *Peter Battistoni / Vancouver Sun*

1947

Public opinion led to a Canadian military retreat from Stanley Park, and a children's petition against a war tax on candy led to a price reduction on chocolate bars. Chinese Canadians got the right to vote again. There was talk of a downtown parking shortage. And while two iconic radio programs got their start this year, a Vancouver nurse wrote Canada's first million-selling hit song.

January 31 The centennial of Congregation Schara Tzedeck took place in 2007,

but the building associated with the congregation—the synagogue at Oak and West 19th—got its start on this day, when Vancouver mayor Gerry McGeer officiated at the sod-turning ceremonies. Vancouver's Jewish community had been worshipping in a 600-seat synagogue at the corner of Heatley and Pender since 1921, but now many of the city's Jews were living near and around Cambie and Oak Streets, so this new synagogue was built to be closer to them. The synagogue, dedicated as a memorial to Jewish war veterans, is still the largest Orthodox synagogue in Vancouver.

February 1 Winnipeg-born Bob Smith made his debut as host of the CBC radio show *Hot Air*. Robert Norman Smith was born January 15, 1920, in Winnipeg and heard his first jazz recording at 13, a clarinet piece from a Noel Coward play on a CKMO program, *British Empire*. He came to Vancouver in 1927 but left (temporarily) during the war, joining the RCAF and later serving with US forces in the South Pacific. Virtually all the jazz recordings Bob played on *Hot Air* were from his own collection. He hosted the show out of the CBC Vancouver studios for 35 years, until 1982, when he left because of the onset of Parkinson's disease. He died in 1989. *Hot Air* is still going and is Canada's longest-running radio program.

February 10 An era ended as the last ferry travelled across Burrard Inlet to West Vancouver,

then returned to the downtown terminal. The last ferry to North Vancouver ran in 1958.

February 26 Vancouver Police constables Charles Boyes and Oliver Ledingham were shot dead by three bank robbers near the Great Northern Railway roundhouse on the False Creek flats. Detective Percy Hoare was injured. Hoare managed to shot and kill one of the robbers. The other two were soon arrested, and one was hanged later in 1947.

March 31 The Eburne Post Office closed. It had been active since 1892.

April 19 Writer Daniel Francis was born in Vancouver. He wrote about 80 percent of the entries in the splendid *Encyclopedia of British Columbia*—10 years of research and writing. Said Terry Glavin in the *Georgia Straight*: "The EBC is lively, serious, profusely illustrated, authoritative, funny, and a thing we should all be proud of...No household in British Columbia should be without one." In the 1980s Francis was a contributor to *The Canadian Encyclopedia*. He also wrote the 2004 biography *L.D.: Mayor Louis Taylor and the Rise of Vancouver* and *Seeing Reds: The Red Scare of 1918–1919*, published in 2010.

Reflecting the population shift of the Jewish community from the downtown to the area around Oak and Cambie, Mayor Gerry McGeer officiates in 1947 at the ground-breaking ceremonies for a new synagogue for Congregation Schara Tzedeck. The synagogue was dedicated as a memorial to Jewish war veterans, and remains the largest Orthodox synagogue in Vancouver. *Vancouver Public Library, Special Collections, VPL 44401*

May 10 Vancouver schoolchildren circulated a petition calling for an end to wartime taxes on candy. In response, the price of chocolate bars was lowered from 8 cents to 7 cents.

June 15 Environmental commentator Patrick Moore was born in Port Alice. Moore was one of the founders of Greenpeace and served as its president for many years. Later, as a director for the Forest Alliance of BC, he became a spokesperson for the logging industry, a fact that enraged some environmentalists. One group created a website titled *Patrick Moore is a Big Fat Liar*, listing ten "lies." It wasn't long before Moore created a responding site titled, of course, *Patrick Moore is NOT a Big Fat Liar*, to rebut their charges.

Elsewhere in BC

January 1 The Japanese population of BC was reduced to 6,776 people—two-thirds the pre-war figure.

April 28 A Trans-Canada Airlines Lockheed Lodestar disappeared in southwestern BC with 15 people on board. None survived. Not until September 1994, more than 47 years later, was the crash site discovered on Mount Cheam near Chilliwack.

August Not really local, but irresistible: A Mayne Island woman cut open a fish today and found a photograph of "a beautiful woman" in the fish's belly.

December 29 Liberal Byron "Boss" Johnson became premier of BC. Boss was a nickname that reflected Johnson's Danish heritage, not his political domination. He headed a coalition government that had high hopes. "Great things are in store for the people of British Columbia," he said. There isn't room here to explain how those great things didn't happen, but the coalition's problems led directly to the rise of the Social Credit party and a fellow named William Andrew Cecil Bennett. Johnson served until August 1, 1952, when he was defeated by Bennett in an election.

Elsewhere in Canada

January 1 The Canadian Citizenship Act came into force. Before this date, Canadians were British subjects, but this statute introduced the idea of Canadian citizenship as an entity independent of British subject status. The act also repealed many of the anti-Asian measures enacted over the previous half century, including the Chinese Immigration (Exclusion) Act of 1923, the Chinese Head Tax, and the Continuous Journey Act.

The Citizenship Act gave Chinese Canadian citizens the right to vote, which they had lost in about 1875. It also extended the franchise to Canadians of South Asian origin. Japanese Canadians and aboriginal people were still excluded.

July 18 The federal government appointed Justice Henry Bird of the BC Supreme Court to inquire into Japanese Canadians' losses resulting from the Custodian of Enemy Property selling their possessions and businesses at less than market value and from theft of their property. The onus was on the Japanese Canadians to provide evidence that the custodian had been negligent and had failed to take proper precautions to prevent property being lost, stolen or destroyed after the owners were interned. The terms of reference excluded losses caused by deterioration of property, losses prior to the assumption of control by the custodian, losses from the forced sale of fishing boats and other losses such as "goodwill." Those who had been "repatriated" to Japan were not eligible to file a claim. By 1950, the Bird Commission had awarded $1.3 million in claims to 1,434 Japanese Canadians, less than a quarter of the $5 million in losses claimed. Bird rejected the National Japanese Canadian Citizens Association's appeal that further claims be considered and that there be indemnity for general losses. Fishermen who had their boats sold off at a fraction of their worth, and countless others who saw their life's work destroyed, remained uncompensated.

Elsewhere in the World

June 24 US pilot Kenneth Arnold was flying above the Cascade Range in Washington state when he spotted nine silver disc-shaped objects in the sky ahead. These objects performed incredible aerial manoeuvres unlike anything Arnold had ever seen. He reported his sighting to the media, likening the discs to saucers, and the "flying saucer" era began.

November 20 Princess Elizabeth and Prince Philip were married.

Candy kerfuffle. Determined to get back their five-cent candy bars, and willing to ridicule those who had caved in to the big candy corporations, these children were part of the 1947 nationwide protests against an inflationary three-cent rise in candy-bar prices. Cold War paranoia prevailed, with allegations that some children were associated with the National Federation of Labour Youth, a Communist organization. But in the end the price of chocolate bars was lowered—by one cent. Vancouver Sun

August 11 Vancouver mayor Gerry McGeer died, aged 59. His death came as a shock: he'd been back in office just a little over seven months. The vigorous and ebullient McGeer passed quietly, lying on a sofa in the den of his home at 4812 Belmont. Alderman Charles Jones took over the mayor's chair.

August 26 With the war over, the former officers' mess at Ferguson Point was converted into a house for the commander of the military district. However, the public attitude was that we wanted all of Stanley Park back, including unrestricted access to Ferguson Point. The park was federal government property leased to the city, but in the interests of good public relations the commander, Brigadier E.C. Plow, left. The house became the Teahouse at Ferguson Point and has since been incorporated into the restaurant on the site.

September 13 The *Sun* reported today that the City of Vancouver had conducted a survey and discovered more than 18,500 automobiles were driven in downtown Vancouver every day—"and there would be more than that if there was sufficient parking space." The survey determined that 6,000 drivers used their cars for transportation to work in the downtown. "Another 12,500 persons drive down for shopping, business calls and sales calls." (In the early 2000s, Vancouver's Traffic Engineering Department reported that an average of 273,410 vehicles entered downtown every day, nearly 15 times the 1947 total.) But that 1947 survey covered more than traffic. It also revealed that the average shopper would be willing to pay 10 cents an hour for parking, 15 cents for two hours "and 35 cents for all-day accommodation." We had parking meters back then, and the rate was 5 cents for an hour. (And the average wage was about $175 a month.)

October 10 *Province* headline: BIGGER HASTINGS TRACK—GIANT DIPPER DOOMED. "The Happyland Giant Dipper will be torn down to make way for a new 5½ furlong racetrack costing $200,000, to be built at Hastings Park in time for the races next summer. The announcement was made today by Mackenzie Bowell, president of the Pacific National Exhibition. The present track is a half-mile affair (four furlongs). The new track will be pear-shaped. Estimated at $200,000 at present costs, the price of the new track may rise before it is completed... Head of the stretch of the new track will be approximately where the popular Giant Dipper is now. The present concrete and steel grandstand will remain, but a new roof will be built...Mr. Bowell is doubtful if a new Giant Dipper will be built."

October 15 A late-night radio show called *Owl Prowl* began on CKMO, with a brash young DJ named Jack Cullen. "The show started October 15, 1947," Jack recalled in 1994. "It ran from ten p.m to one a.m. It was much more hit-parade oriented than today...I was a movie buff, and I subscribed to all the music and entertainment papers: *Billboard, Variety, Metronome, Downbeat*... and I used all this stuff. I sold my own spots ($1.50 or $2): I'd hustle by day, broadcast by night. The show

Dipping no more. Nearly a mile long, and so thrilling that the future King Edward VIII thundered down its tracks twice during a visit in 1927, the Happyland Giant Dipper was nevertheless demolished in 1948 to make room for an extension of the Hastings Racetrack. Children were saddened by the news, the *Vancouver Province* noted. But the odds were that some adults rejoiced at the thought of the following season's betting. *John Mackie collection PNG*

clicked so quick. In six months I was laughing...I was making about $1,000 a month. In 1948 that was good." In 1949, lured away by Bill Rea, Cullen took *Owl Prowl* to CKNW.

November 6 Woodward's Department Store expanded.

November 14 Vancouver's William Munavish, safecracker, became the first Canadian to be declared a habitual criminal.

November 21 After a test period, Vancouver's first FM station, CBU-FM 105.7, officially went on the air.

December 3 The old Lumbermen's Arch was demolished.

There were fears it might collapse and injure park visitors. Originally erected at Pender and Hamilton for the 1912 visit of the Duke of Connaught, it was moved to Stanley Park and dedicated on August 29, 1919, to its designer, Captain G.P. Bowie, who was killed during World War I.

Also in 1947

Vancouver native William "Bill" Gun Chong, known as "Agent 50," was awarded the British Empire Medal, the highest military honour given by the British government to non-British citizens. He was the only Chinese Canadian to receive this honour for his work behind enemy lines in Hong Kong during World War II. By chance, he found himself in Hong Kong when Japan took over the city in December 1941. Chong volunteered with the British Army Aid Group, an intelligence unit. As Agent 50 he served under extremely dangerous and hostile conditions in China, leading escapees from occupied territory and transporting medical supplies. He was captured by the Japanese three times and escaped each time.

Returning Chinese Canadian veterans, who were allowed to cast their vote during the war, formed the Chinese Veterans Organization and began to press the federal government for full citizenship.

Vancouver-born composer Jean Coulthard was invited to teach theory and composition at the University of British Columbia, a position she held until she retired in 1973. She had begun composing music at age nine and wrote for orchestra, opera, voice and chamber music, among others. Her citation, upon receiving a 1994 Order of British Columbia, reads in part: "Jean Coulthard's belief that a composer has a special responsibility to the community resulted in works designed to be accessible to the wider public, including works for students." Among her students were Chan Ka Nin, Michael Conway Baker, Sylvia Rickard, Jean Ethridge and David Gordon Duke.

Elizabeth Clarke, a nurse at the Vancouver Hospital for Crippled Children, loved to read stories and poems to her little charges. One young boy was excited at seeing a sparrow on the windowsill by his bed, and that inspired Miss Clarke to write the poem "Bluebird on Your Windowsill." She later set it to music. The Rhythm Pals introduced the song on CKNW, and people loved it. Vancouver recording pioneer Al Reusch cut a version with Don Murphy, and eventually it was recorded by Doris Day, Wilf Carter and others. It became the first Canadian song to sell a million copies. Miss Clarke gave every dime of her royalties to children's hospitals across Canada.

The junior football Vancouver Blue Bombers became Dominion champions, a first for the city. Coach was Punjab-born Ranjit Mattu, a star athlete here in the 1930s and later.

Calgary-born Clyde Gilmour, 35, began contributing film reviews to CBC Radio in Vancouver. He had worked on various newspapers in western Canada, and during the war had served in the navy as news correspondent. Gilmour married Barbara Donald this year, moved to Toronto in 1954 and went on to host the popular program *Gilmour's Albums* for CBC Radio from 1956 to 1997.

The George Derby Veteran's Rehabilitation Centre opened in Burnaby. It began as part of the Shaughnessy Hospital complex to help "veterans reintegrate following the acute care phase of their recovery by offering physical and occupational therapy programs as well as job retraining and rehabilitation." The complex was transferred to the province in 1974, and in 1988 a new George Derby Centre opened as an intermediate-care facility with 300 priority access beds for veterans.

Comings and Goings

Jack Webster, 29, a pugnacious reporter from Glasgow, left the newspaper world of Scotland (where he'd started at age 14) and England and came to Vancouver to work at the *Sun*.

1948

The news was dominated by widespread and deadly flooding in the Fraser Valley. Modern trolley buses and two-way escalators went into service as the city moved into the future, and another tie with the past was lost as Gassy Jack Deighton's widow died, more than seven decades after the saloon owner who gave Gastown its name.

January 3 Art Jones and Ray Munro, photographers at the *Vancouver Sun*, both of them mad at *Sun* managing editor Hal Straight for some unremembered reason, went into business as freelancers in a company they called Artray. Their base of operations was 9 East Hastings St. An early assignment: photographing the flooding in the Fraser Valley (May). A vast collection of their photos was donated to the Vancouver Public Library.

March 6 Under a large photograph of an unhappy young man sitting among the rubble of the partially demolished Giant Dipper roller coaster, the *Province* ran this story: "They're tearing down the Giant Dipper at Vancouver's Hastings Park today to make room for the extension of the racetrack. This may be good news to adult followers of the galloping bangtails, but it's something close to a major tragedy for thousands of youngsters. Shown viewing the crumbling skeleton with nostalgia and sorrow is 14-year-old Bob. Said Bob, 'If they want to rip things apart in this town, why don't they start in on a few schools?' The Giant Dipper has been a top attraction at the midway since 1925. It cost $65,000...The longest sheer drop was 60 feet—a thrill credited with having hastened the ripening of many a beautiful friendship. In 1927 the Duke of Windsor, then the Prince of Wales, tried out the Dipper one afternoon and liked it so well he returned in the evening."

April 14 Two-way escalators in Vancouver's Hudson's Bay store made the newspapers.

April 18 The Ink Spots, starring Vancouver's Bill Kenny, started a two-week engagement at the Palomar, their first. The group had been booked for a June 1947 appearance, but some kind of problem with the booking agent meant they didn't appear. The

A novelty item, the new escalators at the Hudson's Bay store attracted crowds and the press when they started turning in 1948. *PNG*

Elsewhere in BC

July 31 "Canadians," said Mrs. Florence Aymond, speaking in Victoria, "speak the most consistent English in the world—even if it is consistently wrong." Mrs. Aymond, described as a well-known examiner in speech arts and drama, added "We tend to flatten our vowels and take the music out of our speech. But on the Coast, in Vancouver and Victoria particularly, vowels in general are very good. We have musical vowel sounds with affectation." Mrs. Aymond said Canadians tended toward harshness of speech and blamed it on the tremendous pace of living. Rushing, she said, tends to tighten the muscles, so that we scamp our words and don't take time to articulate.

Elsewhere in Canada

The federal government repealed the law that said Canadians could only vote in a federal election if they were allowed to vote in the provincial election of their home province. This meant that all Japanese-Canadians could finally vote federally.

Elsewhere in the World

January 30 Mahatma Mohandas Gandhi was assassinated.

July 31 Out of the London Olympics came a cheering story of the Canadian basketball team's victory over first Italy, then England: "The big, fast Italian team went into an early lead as the Canadians opened their bid for the zone title, but were soon overtaken through the efforts of 21-year-old Pat McGeer of University of British Columbia who led the team with 12 points."

November 14 Prince Charles was born at 9:14 p.m. London time, in Buckingham Palace.

Vancouver hosts its first boat show, proving you don't need water to appreciate a good boat. *Vancouver Public Library, Special Collections, VPL 83154. Artray photo*

last known performance of the Ink Spots with Bill Kenny was in Ottawa at the Gatineau Club on either October 31 or November 1, 1953. In 1989 the incarnation of the group with Bill Kenny was inducted into the Rock and Roll Hall of Fame.

April 26 Vancouver's first boat show.

May 9 The Women's Auxiliary to the Air Services dedicated a Remembrance Garden in Stanley Park "as a living memorial in honoured tribute to the service, sacrifice and achievement of our gallant airmen." A poem on a plaque in the garden reads:

Not here they fell who died a world to save
Not here they lie but in a thousand fields afar
Here is their living spirit that knows no grave
Not here they were — but are

July 14 The first "cottage" hospital opened at Langley Memorial Hospital with 35 beds.

August 10 Gassy Jack Deighton's widow, his second wife, died at age 90 on the North Vancouver Indian Reserve. Her Native name was Qua-Hail-Ya, but she was known to Jack and others as Madeline. The niece of Jack's first wife, Madeline was 12 years old at the time of her 1870 marriage to Deighton and was the mother of his only child, Richard Mason Deighton, born in 1871. Richard died in November 1875, six months after his father. To the end of her days, Madeline spoke fondly of Jack.

August 13 A ribbon-cutting ceremony opened the new Oakridge Transit Centre on West 41st Avenue just east of Oak Street. Civic and other dignitaries were taken on inaugural runs in the city's new Brill T-44 trolley

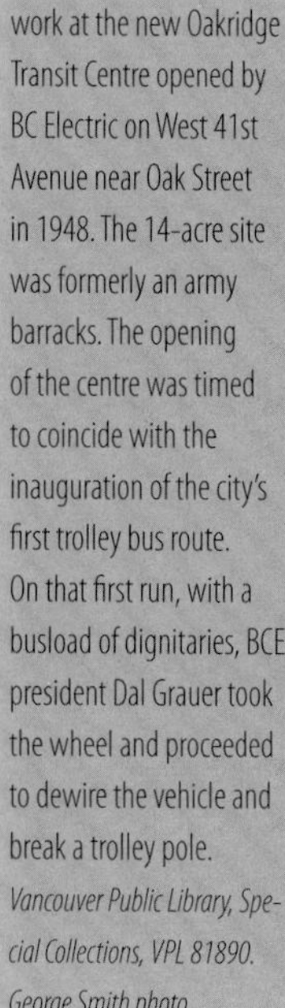

Right: Transit central. These dispatchers are at work at the new Oakridge Transit Centre opened by BC Electric on West 41st Avenue near Oak Street in 1948. The 14-acre site was formerly an army barracks. The opening of the centre was timed to coincide with the inauguration of the city's first trolley bus route. On that first run, with a busload of dignitaries, BCE president Dal Grauer took the wheel and proceeded to dewire the vehicle and break a trolley pole. *Vancouver Public Library, Special Collections, VPL 81890. George Smith photo*

Fraser River Floods—Again

May 24 The Fraser River overflowed its banks. Before the flood ended in early June it had wreaked enormous havoc: 10 people died, there was $20 million in damage (in 1948 dollars), more than 16,000 people lost their homes, rail service was disrupted for two weeks, and more than 80 bridges were washed away. Greater Vancouver was isolated from the rest of the country for days, as access via both railways and the Trans-Canada Highway was cut. Barnston Island was inundated and cattle had to be removed. Dead cattle floated downstream from Fraser Valley farms.

On May 31 Premier Byron Johnson declared a state of emergency in response to the flooding. Up and down the river, thousands of citizens and more than 3,000 troops laboured together, filling sandbags and dumping gravel, whatever it took to hold back the raging waters. The author was in Grade 8 at Maple Ridge High School in Haney at the time and remembers being sent out with schoolmates to help lay sandbags.

There had been a similar dramatic flood in the same areas more than 50 years earlier, with the water rising even higher, but the 1894 flooding occurred when there was far less to destroy.

Flood havoc. Working to get their vehicle unstuck and to higher ground, these farmers were caught in the midst of the great Fraser River flood of 1948. Cutting Vancouver off from the rest of the country by wiping out the railways and highway, the flood also killed 10 people, caused $20 million in damages (in 1948 dollars), and led to more than 16,000 people losing their homes. *Province newspaper photo, Vancouver Public Library VPL 44496*

buses. On August 15, BC Electric offered the public free rides on the new buses, and on August 16 the first of 30 new T-44s entered revenue service in the city. First passengers received a route map and an explanation of how the trolleys worked.

September 1 Vancouver's mayor, Charles Jones, died in office, just over a year after succeeding Gerry McGeer, who had also died in office. Alderman George Miller, who had been mayor in 1937–38, took over official duties until the end of the year. Charles Thompson became mayor in 1949.

October 3 Hallelujah Point in Stanley Park was officially named to commemorate the work over 60 years (1887–1947) of the Salvation Army in BC.

October 18
A small bust of former mayor Gerry McGeer was unveiled to stand on the north side of City Hall.

November 28 A ghostly image of a Seattle high school football game materialized on a four-by-five-inch screen at a home in West Vancouver's British Properties. As reported in the *Province* the following day, radio-shop proprietor E.A. Mullins had built the primitive set from a kit that cost $238. Nine viewers—Mullins' family and friends—gathered to watch the telecast from Seattle TV station KRSC, which later became KING-TV.

December 1 The T. Eaton Company took over the nine BC stores of the David Spencer chain. The president of the company, John David Eaton, visiting from Toronto, said the purchase wouldn't affect Eaton's plans to demolish the old Hotel Vancouver and build a modern store at Georgia and Granville. The newspapers held back the story of the sale because Chris Spencer, head of the Spencer chain, said he wanted to be the first to tell his employees. Spencer's, which began modestly in 1873 in Victoria, included stores in Vancouver, Victoria, New Westminster, Nanaimo, Courtenay, Duncan, Chilliwack and Mission. The Vancouver store had opened in 1906 on Hastings between Seymour and Richards and eventually expanded to take up the entire block.

Also in 1948

Sixty thousand daffodil bulbs were planted along the Stanley Park Causeway, a gift from the Netherlands to thank Canadian soldiers for helping to liberate their country from the Nazis.

Fort Point Grey, the last of Vancouver's World War II gun batteries, was dismantled and closed. A historic maker at the restored No. 1 Gun position tells the battery's history.

In response to the housing crisis after World War II, about 50 hectares (120 acres) of empty land near Grandview Highway and Boundary Road in Vancouver were quickly developed. Alderman Halford Wilson, chair of the civic street-naming committee, announced that the new streets would be named after wartime personalities, locations, battles and events. That gave us Worthington and Falaise Avenues; Dieppe, Anzio, Mons, Normandy, Seaforth and Maida Drives; and Vimy and Matapan Crescents. Malta Place completed the set. (Donald and Jack Worthington were soldiers, sons of a former alderman.)

Edmund Desjardins, a founding director of the G.F. Strong Centre, became its first manager, a post he held until 1979. He guided its development into an outstanding rehabilitation institution. Desjardins was confined to a wheelchair as a quadriplegic in 1944 as a result of a training accident at Sandhurst Military College in England. As chairman of the Architectural Committee for the Social Planning and Review Council of BC, Desjardins prepared and presented a comprehensive set of design standards for people with disabilities that was adopted by the City of Vancouver in its building bylaw. His design standards for accessibility were also incorporated into the province's building code. Desjardins was appointed to the Order of Canada in 1975.

Ron Thom, architect, graduated from the Vancouver School of Art.

This was a big year for Vancouver's Jennie Wong.

She entered a contest sponsored by the *Vancouver Sun*: first prize was a radio show on one of the participating stations. Audition tapes were judged by a panel consisting of Freddie Robbins, a New York City disk jockey; Frank Sinatra; and orchestra leader Claude Thornhill. Jennie won the contest and was given a half-hour Saturday afternoon program on CKMO, which she called *Jennie's Juke Joint*. Besides being the first Chinese Canadian disc jockey, she was also the first female DJ. Later she was the "weather girl" for CBC Edmonton's morning radio show before starting her own business doing theatrical and television makeup in Edmonton, a gig that lasted for 25 years!

A group of second-generation Chinese Canadian Vancouverites began publishing a bilingual (Chinese and English) community newspaper, *New Citizen*. In 1952 it moved to Toronto, but editor Roy Mah stayed behind to start up *Chinatown News*, which reflected the interests and aspirations of his generation.

Foon Sien Wong became president of the Chinese Benevolent Association and continued his campaign for the rights of Chinese Canadians. Although the 1923 Chinese Exclusion Act had been repealed in 1947, and Chinese Canadians had gained the vote and many rights of citizenship, Canada's immigration policy was still highly restrictive. For the next 11 years Wong made an annual pilgrimage to Ottawa and lobbied the federal government, regardless of political stripe, to relax these restrictions on Chinese immigration. His goal of fair treatment eventually coincided with the 1967 introduction of policy based on a universal point system for assessing prospective immigrants. In 2008 he was designated a National Historic Person by the National Historic Sites of Parks Canada.

The Welsh community raised enough money to send a hand-carved bardic chair to the Royal National Eisteddfod in Bridgend, Wales. Presented annually to the winning bard at the festival, the chair was made from black walnut and white cowhide and combined traditional leeks of Welsh Eisteddfod design with a West Coast Native design by Bill Calder.

According to singer Karl Norman, when the power failed during a production of the operetta *Naughty Marietta* at TUTS (Theatre Under the Stars) in Stanley Park, "the orchestra kept playing, and I kept singing, and people from the audience lined up their cars at the back of Malkin Bowl and lit the performance with their headlights."

Westlake Lodge on Hollyburn Mountain installed rope tows. Lift tickets were $1.50.

The Cloverdale Rodeo was enlarged but had to be postponed to Labour Day because of the Fraser floods.

North Vancouver District came out of receivership, its citizens now able to run the city themselves.

Bus service began in Burnaby, which now had many paved roads.

The airport was officially named the Vancouver International Airport.

Masters of Tapestry

The P.A. Woodward Foundation presented two large Gobelin tapestries, *Masters of the Spirit* and *Masters of Science*, to the university to hang in Woodward Biomedical Library. The tapestries were created in France.

Dr. William Gibson had purchased *Masters of Science* from Antoine Behna, a patron of the tapissers, who owned them. According to Gibson, "The only tapestries which [Behna] had allowed out of France were gifts to the Pope and President Truman. Nonetheless he showed me several others stored in his extensive barns.

"One of those caught my eye. It was entitled *Masters of the Spirit*—parallel to the one we had, but in this case the characters portrayed were great philosophers and writers of the past. He would not part with it however, for one of his oldest tapissiers, while working on this massive 16 x 11 feet beauty, suffered a cerebral haemorrhage at 68 years of age when he was only half finished the project. The disastrous stroke affected the man's perception so that the right half is a shambles compared with the left half which preceded it. M. Behna would not allow it to be sold lest people viewing it would make fun of his unfortunate weaver. I explained that I was a neurologist with scientific interest in this amazing result, and that my colleagues in far-off Vancouver had the same interest. Finally he agreed that in those circumstances we could buy it...Many physicians and psychologists have come to see it since."

The old Fraser Street Bridge was mechanized. Since 1905 the bridge, which connected Fraser Street in Vancouver with No. 5 Road on Lulu Island in Richmond, had been opened by hand whenever a ship needed to pass. There had been a low-level crossing to Mitchell and Lulu Islands since 1893, and when the new bridge was built in 1905, it included a connection to Mitchell Island en route. The deck on the bridge's small swing span was replaced with open steel grating in 1962, but by 1974 the Fraser Street Bridge was obsolete, replaced by the Knight Street Bridge.

Some of the year's changes at UBC: the Biological Sciences Building was built, and Premier John Hart opened the Physics Building (renamed the Hennings Building in 1963 in honour of Dr. A.E. Hennings, a UBC professor of physics for 29 years). An outstanding feature of the Hennings Building is the exterior granite columns. Garnet Gladwin Sedgewick, a Shakespearean scholar and member of UBC's English department since 1918, retired. UBC's Sedgewick Library, the former undergraduate library, was named for him.

Fourteen charter members signed a constitution, gathered $48 in assets and started Fraser Valley Credit Union (now Prospera Credit Union). The credit union ended 1948 with 53 members and assets of $2,441.35.

Jimmy Lovick, described as "the true giant" of Vancouver ad men, who had been active in local advertising since 1934, struck out on his own this year. He opened James Lovick and Company offices in Vancouver, Calgary, Toronto and Montreal. By 1958 Lovick and Company was the largest agency in Canada, with additional offices in Edmonton, London (ON), Halifax, New York and San Francisco. Lovick established his headquarters in his own building, a handsome structure at 1178 West Pender St.

Comings and Goings

July 30 In the *Province*: "Joy Coghill, one of Vancouver's best known actresses, is going to Chicago in search of her master's degree in directing and producing. Miss Coghill started acting as a child in Scotland where she went to school. When she came to Vancouver in 1940 she entered into dramatics and attended UBC where she graduated with a B.A. degree. Recently, she directed the UBC Players in *School for Scandal*."

September 22 Bing Crosby brought his hugely popular Philco radio show to Vancouver and recorded a benefit program for the Sunset Memorial Centre on East 51st Avenue. It aired October 13. Appearing with Bing on the show were jazz violinist Joe Venuti and actors Marilyn Maxwell, William Gargan and Ray Milland. This performance was unique in being the only program in the Philco series transcribed outside the United States. A song hit of the time was "Hair of Gold, Eyes of Blue." It began with the words "I came down from Butte, Montana," but Bing changed the lyrics on air to "I came down from West Vancouver." Before the show, incidentally, Crosby was made a full-blooded Indian "chief." The Squamish tribe made him an honorary member with the title "Chief Thunder Voice."

Notable births: **Gordon Campbell**, future BC premier, in Vancouver on January 12; **Brian Antonson**, future broadcast instructor (BCIT), in Burnaby on June 28; **Margaret Sinclair**, future wife of Prime Minister Pierre Trudeau, in Vancouver on September 10; **Marion Lay**, who became an Olympic athlete and promoted women's involvement in sports, in Vancouver on November 26.

1949

Japanese Canadians were allowed to return to Vancouver, four years after the end of World War II and seven years after they had been interned away from the coast. They were also given the right to vote, along with the province's First Nations people. And the first Native woman enrolled at UBC.

January 16 BC Electric discontinued streetcar service on the Kitsilano Beach run.

January 29 Harry Duker, chairman of the Vancouver Tourist Association fundraising campaign, told the *Sun* he was aiming for $75,000 in operating funds for 1949. "During the year 70,000 persons came to the association's headquarters at Georgia and Seymour for information."

January The second Hotel Vancouver, one of the city's most outstanding landmarks since it was built in 1914, was torn down. It was the largest wrecking job undertaken to that time in the British Commonwealth. "There is no alternative," read newspaper reports, "as no hotel operator is willing to buy, rehabilitate and operate it at his own risk."

The Dry Squad Raids Again

January 3 Police raided three local nightclubs.

The *Sun*'s front-page headline the next day was great: "Police Open War on Night Club Drinking." Imagine! People drinking liquor in a nightclub! Next thing you know, they'll be dancing!

Chief Constable Walter Mulligan warned that his dry squad men were "definitely going to tighten up on liquor drinking in cabarets." Detectives swooped down on three cabarets and confiscated 13 bottles of liquor from underneath tables. Five were seized from the Cave Cabaret, two from the Palomar (one of the men summonsed at the Palomar was well-known entertainer Fran Dowie) and four more at the Mandarin.

The BC Cabaret Owners' Association (COA) blamed "rabid prohibitionists." "These attempted curbs on drinking," they added, "will only drive drink into vice dens, autos and hotel rooms."

Much has changed in 62 years, and we can thank the officials of the COA, among others, for that. "Figuratively rubbing their hands," the *Sun* reported, "the COA said 'Good! At last we can fight a test case out in the open over B.C.'s ridiculous liquor laws."

March 5 Burrard Bridge engineer Major J.R. Grant reacted to a local art teacher's remarks that the bridge (opened in 1932) was a "monstrosity." Fred Amess of the Vancouver School of Art had told a Lions Club gathering that the bridge pillars were "ashcans with a gasoline station on top." Grant explained that the pillars "were built as large as they are on request from the harbormaster, who wanted them prominent to avoid a navigation hazard at the False Creek entrance." He went on to explain that the large base of the piers was required because at the time the BC Electric Railway

With no one willing to buy and rehabilitate it, the second Hotel Vancouver, opened in 1916, was destroyed in 1949. In its last years it served as army barracks during World War II, and then housed veterans, who squatted during a housing crunch.
Province newspaper photo, Vancouver Public Library VPL 42396

had planned running a railway on a lower deck beneath the roadway. (Grant admited, "That railway will never go in now. The BCER is no longer interested.")

June 15 Won Alexander Cumyow, age 88, cast his ballot in the provincial general election. He had voted provincially in 1890 as a young man, after the franchise had been taken away from the Chinese, but this was the first time he had voted since then. He also voted in the federal election held on June 27, 1949.

Left: Opened in 1932, the Burrard Bridge still managed to create controversy in 1949 when A.F. Ames of the Vancouver Art School called its pillars "ashcans with a gasoline station on top." Bridge designer Major John R. Grant retorted, explaining the rationale behind the design, and saying that he'd rather trust the "esthetic ideas of the engineer." *Leonard Frank photo, Vancouver Public Library VPL 6583D*

Elsewhere in BC

March 24 BC passed a bill giving the franchise to Japanese Canadians. This eliminated the legal basis for discrimination against them, so Japanese Canadians were now eligible to work in the civil service, practise law and pharmacy, serve on a jury and enter professions that were previously closed to them. Sixty years after the first immigrant arrived from Japan in 1877, Japanese Canadians could enter the mainstream of Canadian society.

March 31 The provincial government removed all restrictions on the movement of Japanese Canadian people. They could now return to the coast, though many did not.

April 1 Native people got the vote in BC, although on-reserve residents were not enfranchised federally until 1960.

June 15 Nisga'a Chief Frank Calder was elected to the BC legislature in the first provincial election in which Asian Canadians and First Nations people could vote.

August 21 The biggest quake in BC's recorded history, 8.1 on the Richter scale, occurred off the Queen Charlotte Islands. Its major force extended to the uninhabited area west of the islands, so damage was minimal. Centres 2,400 kilometres (1,500 miles) away felt the quake, and it was even detected in Jasper, AB. Seattle measured it at 7.2. The *Province* reported on the front page that a clock had stopped in the home of Mrs. Laurie Sanders, Imperial Street in Burnaby.

November 2 The Hope–Princeton Highway officially opened to traffic. Highway No. 3 closely followed the old Dewdney Trail, the interior route along which provisions were moved north, and gold and furs moved south.

Elsewhere in Canada

March 29 The sale of margarine was approved, but thanks to lobbying by the dairy industry (which feared, rightly, the new product would hurt sales of butter), it had to be coloured white, not yellow.

April 1 Newfoundland entered Confederation.

July 1 Canadian Pacific Airlines launched its inaugural flight to Sydney, Australia. On July 13 it carried the first all-Canadian airmail to Australia.

Elsewhere in the World

January 10 RCA Records introduced a new format for music recordings: seven-inch singles that ran at 45 rpm. The new records came with a large centre hole, which made it easier to mount on the spindle. New "drop-changer" players could play these records for 50 minutes without interruption.

April 7 The Rodgers and Hammerstein musical *South Pacific* premiered on Broadway.

August 16 Margaret Mitchell, the author of *Gone with the Wind*, was fatally injured when she was hit by a speeding taxicab near her home in Atlanta, GA.

Isaac Jacob casts his ballot in the provincial election on June 15, 1949. First Nations peoples in BC had received the franchise two and a half months earlier, making BC the first province to make this move. Status First Nations peoples did not receive the right to vote in federal elections until more than a decade later. *Vancouver Public Library, Special Collections, VPL 80953. Tom Christopherson pboto*

The first person of Chinese descent born in Canada (in 1861), Won Alexander Cumyow was also the only Asian Canadian to vote both before and after the Chinese regained the right to vote in 1947. Despite being disenfranchised in 1872, he still managed to vote in 1890 in a BC provincial election, and then again in 1949. Vancouver Sun

Also on June 15 Fire on the False Creek waterfront caused $1 million in damage.

June 25 Sod was turned for Woodward's Department Store at Park Royal.

July 23 In a story on local tourist activity, the *Province* ran a photo of "travel advisors" Doris Young, Alyse Francis and Anita Zanon. "They reply to all queries, even stupid ones, with courteous, sensible information," explained Hedley Hipwell, president of the Vancouver Tourist Association, who noted that they dealt with from 600 to 700 visitors a day. "In 1948 they answered 120,000 phone calls. In 1927 there were 24,000...Last year, the girls gave out 160,000 travel folders and maps, answered 11,400 direct and 50,000 letters from other tourist bureaus, 8,000 coupon advertisement enquiries. They wrote invitations to 9,000 convention prospects...One of VTA's biggest jobs is finding rooms for folk who arrive in Vancouver without reservations. It takes the full time of one advisor to find accommodation for them." Hedwell said tourism in Vancouver was a $30-million industry.

August 15 Kingsway was reopened as a six-lane highway between Vancouver and New Westminster. It was described as "strikingly handsome" in the newspapers.

September 10 Gloria Cranmer became the first First Nations woman to attend the University of British Columbia. She graduated in anthropology in 1956 and went on to become a filmmaker, writer and linguist, recording the culture and language of the Kwakwaka'wakw people. She worked to repatriate potlatch items confiscated from Northwest Coast nations and was a major force in establishing the U'mista Cultural Centre at Alert Bay, where she was the initial curator from 1980 to 1991. Her contributions to British Columbia Native life are remarkable.

October 22 The first "official" tree was planted at Queen Elizabeth Park. It was called Little Mountain Park back then, carved out of a rock quarry and chosen as the site of Canada's first civic arboretum. "The tree looked lonely and a trifle battered," the *Province* wrote. "Fittingly enough, it was a Pacific dogwood, the only tree emblematic of B.C. It stood in a grassy spot overlooking the smoke and skyscrapers of downtown Vancouver."

November 9 The body of Woodward's employee Blanche Fisher, 45 and unmarried, was discovered in False Creek near the Kitsilano Trestle. Suicide was first considered but was ruled out when police discovered that she was not wearing shoes, stockings or underwear, and that there were many bruises on her body. The killer was eventually identified as Frederick Ducharme, 34, a very odd and twisted piece of work, with a record for indecent exposure and bizarre behaviour that can't be described here and which was only hinted at in the more straitlaced newspaper reporting of the day. Miss Fisher's umbrella was found in his car, and articles of her clothing turned up in his squalid False Creek shack. Ducharme was found guilty of the murder and hanged on July 14, 1950.

November 11 Kerrisdale Arena was officially opened. One of the people on hand was Fred "Cyclone" Taylor, a Vancouver hockey legend, who was president of the Point Grey Community Centre Association at the time. Vancouver Park Board chairman Bert Emery, acting mayor R.K. Gervin and Harry Duker, who managed fundraising for the building, were also present.

November 27
The Capilano River, swollen by a violent rainstorm, swept away a large section of Marine Drive, at the time the only road link to West Vancouver. Part of the bridge over the Capilano was washed away as well, so army engineers from Sardis rushed in to build an emergency Bailey bridge. That was also washed away, and West Vancouver was cut off for 10 days.

December 1
Grouse Mountain chairlift opened, the first double chairlift in Greater Vancouver and the third in Canada. It replaced a two- to three-hour hike from the skiers' bus stop at the base of the mountain.

December 4 Dick Diespecker's radio column in the *Province*—which followed local and international radio personalities in precisely the way we cover TV and movie stars today—told us that "dynamic young sportscaster" Ray Perrault had left CJOR to join the radio department of the O'Brien Advertising Agency. Perrault later spent 43 years in BC and federal politics. He died in 2008 at age 82.

December 11 Boxer Jimmy McLarnin laid the cornerstone for Sunset Memorial Centre on East 51st Avenue. McLarnin had played a large part in the establishment of the centre (now the Sunset Community Centre.) When Stan Thomas, one of the people involved in the creation of the complex, went to Hollywood in 1947, McLarnin introduced him to Bing Crosby, a friend of McLarnin's. Bing agreed to come up to Vancouver in September 1948 to record his radio show here and kick off the centre's fundraising campaign. The show at the Forum was attended by 9,000 people.

December 23 Vancouver's Seaforth Highlanders held a farewell parade for Lieutenant-Colonel D.M. Clark, their commanding officer, who was retiring. The ceremony included an inspection by Brigadier J.M. Rockingham of the Seaforth's ski company.

December 29 We confess: we don't understand this story. A box called "The Thing" was put out to float in English Bay by the leaders of the Polar Bear Club. When it was brought in to shore on January 1, 1951, during the swim, it was opened to reveal an effigy of Stalin, which was ceremoniously burned.

Double the fun. Saving skiers a two- to three-hour hike, a double chairlift opened on December 1, 1949, on Grouse Mountain. Photographed in the fall of 1960, William and Emily Berry enjoy a ride up with their daughter Lynn. The raincoats were provided for protection from the elements, and at the top riders were encouraged to purchase the pictures of themselves.
Vancouver Public Library, Special Collections, VPL 80953. Tom Christopherson photo

Also in 1949

An American movie, part of which was filmed in Vancouver more than 50 years ago, was actually set in Vancouver! How often does that happen? The 1949 thriller *Johnny Stool Pigeon*, starring Howard Duff, Shelley Winters, Dan Duryea and Tony Curtis, told of international drug dealers tracked to their downtown Vancouver lair by a heroic US Treasury agent. (Drugs in Vancouver? Ha! Never happen.)

Charles Edwin Thompson became mayor of Vancouver. Born September 17, 1890, in Grey County, ON, Thompson was a hard character to pin down. He felt that civic improvements should be provided to citizens, but civil liberties were impaired during his term by a policy that required city employees to be screened for communist sympathies.

Comings and Goings

November 2 A civic banquet was held at the Hotel Vancouver for visiting Prime Minister Nehru of India.

George Woodcock moved to BC after spending the war working on a farm as a conscientious objector. Over the next 45 years he taught at UBC, was the first editor of *Canadian Literature* (the first periodical to be entirely devoted to Canadian writing) and published more than 100 books, including a biography of George Orwell, *The Crystal Spirit*, which won the Governor General's Award for non-fiction in 1966.

1950-1959

1950

A new war started on the Korean Peninsula. The city had its first submachine gun robbery. And it was a bad day in White Rock when residents woke up to find their namesake rock had been painted black.

January 3 The comic strip *Pogo*, a huge hit in the United States, where it first appeared on October 4, 1948, debuted in the *Vancouver Sun*.

January 13 Hedley Hipwell was returned for a fourth term as president of the Greater Vancouver Tourist Association. Hipwell also headed the BC Automobile Association. Both groups shared directors.

February The Crescent Beach Hotel burned down.

March 15 A new passenger terminal opened at Vancouver International Airport.

April 13 The Ridge Theatre opened at 3131 Arbutus.

Left: The Ridge Theatre, still screening everything from high-art films to low-brow animation festivals, livens up Arbutus Street.
Artray photo, Vancouver Public Library VPL 81242

Spring Vandals painted White Rock's white rock black, enraging citizens who had to pay for the cleanup.

Elsewhere in BC

February 14 Nancy Hodges, the first female Speaker of the House in the British Commonwealth, presided over the opening of the BC legislature. Hodges, a well-known Victoria journalist and women's rights advocate, served as MLA from 1941 to 1953. She was appointed to the Senate in 1953, the first MLA from BC to achieve that honour.

August 15 The BC Provincial Police force was dissolved after 92 years of service. Its duties were assumed by the Royal Canadian Mounted Police.

October 2 Clarence Wallace, president of Burrard Dry Dock, was sworn in as BC's Lieutenant-Governor. Two years later he found himself in the uncomfortable position of having to decide which party leader to call on—W.A.C. Bennett or Harold Winch—to form the provincial government.

Elsewhere in Canada

August 22 The first Canada-wide rail strike began. It ended by government order on August 30.

November Sargit Singh and Bob Bose of Surrey won the Canadian championship in potato judging at the Royal Winter Fair in Toronto.

The federal government revoked Order-in-Council P.C. 4364, which prohibited "enemy aliens" from immigrating to Canada. This meant the Japanese Canadians who had been deported to Japan were allowed to return. Eventually about one quarter of them did.

Elsewhere in the World

June 26 North Korea invaded South Korea, and the Korean War began.

August 15 Princess Anne was born.

October 2 The comic strip *Peanuts* first appeared.

At the British Empire Games in Auckland, New Zealand, North Vancouver's Bill Parnell won the mile event, setting a new games record with a time of 4:11.0. Parnell also won bronze in the 880-yard race. Vancouver's Jack Varaleau, a member of the Canadian Olympic weightlifting team from 1948 to 1952, won a gold medal in weightlifting at the games.

These officers are wearing the uniform of the BC Provincial Police, the force that patrolled the province until 1950, when it was replaced by the RCMP. The BCPP traced its origins back to the gold-rush days of the 1850s, when it was known as the BC Constabulary. The uniform, adopted in 1924, featured a khaki jacket and pants, with green trim and a Sam Browne belt.
Vancouver Sun

May Patricia Kronebusch became Cloverdale's first Rodeo Queen.

June 21 Mayor Charles Thompson received the deed to Hadden Park, in Kitsilano, on behalf of the children to whom Harvey Hadden had dedicated it.

August 7 The *Province* reported that a submachine gun was used in a Vancouver robbery: "Masked bandits held four B.C. Electric employees at bay with a sub-machine gun early today in a ticket office raid which netted only $59. It was the first time such a weapon had been used in a city holdup...Police said the raid on the B.C. Electric carbarns 'bullpen' at Thirteenth and Main was staged by two men at 3:30 a.m., when most streetcars were in for the night and about 15 minutes before the morning shift was due to arrive."

August 12 Van Waters and Rogers Ltd. was incorporated in Vancouver, the Canadian affiliate of a company founded in 1924 in Seattle by George Van Waters and Nat S. Rogers. Today the company, which deals in industrial chemicals, is known as Univar Canada.

August 29 Eccles-Rand Limited personnel checked out Vancouver's first atomic bomb shelter, which their firm had built in an unidentified Shaughnessy backyard.

September 1 A national CPR strike hit Port Coquitlam hard, as many residents worked in the marshalling yards there.

Also September 1 Park Royal Shopping Centre opened in West Vancouver, the first regional shopping centre in Canada. Originally on the north side of Marine Drive, it later expanded to the south. (Northgate Mall opened this same year in Seattle.)

September 21 Vancouver's city engineer John Oliver said he feared that unless the provincial and Dominion governments contributed to the cost of the Granville Street Bridge, the project would cost $3 million more than the original $8 million estimate. (In 1939 the cost had been estimated at $4 million.) In the end, neither government came through, and the final cost to the city by the time the bridge opened in February 1954 was $16 million.

September 29 Vancouver's Sunset Memorial Centre, at 404 East 51st Ave., was officially opened by singer Bing Crosby—via a telephone call from Hollywood. Bing was awfully fond of BC and used to come up here often to relax and fish, but he was filming at the time and couldn't get away. A year later he managed to visit the centre and drew a huge crowd. (The name today is the Sunset Community Centre.)

September 30 In spite of protests from local people, BC Electric ended tram service between New Westminster and Chilliwack. BC Electric contributed to the cost of establishing bus transportation, but businesses complained mail was slower.

September The fall assizes opened with the first Chinese juror, Jack Chan, on jury duty.

November 11 The West Vancouver Memorial Library opened. An earlier library had been opened in 1921 but closed during the Depression.

Fortunately yet to be used for its original purpose, the first backyard atomic bomb shelter for four was built by Eccles-Rand Limited in Shaughnessy Heights. It sported a lead-lined door and steel-reinforced six-inch-thick walls.
The Province

Also in 1950

Naranjan Grewall won a seat on Mission City Council, becoming Canada's first Sikh city councillor. In 1954 he made history again when he was elected mayor of Mission. Grewall, who owned and operated six sawmills, was a vocal critic of BC's cutting practices and forest management systems. He referred to holders of forest management licences as "Timber Maharajahs" and warned that within 10 years, three or four

Teddy Lyons' Last Run

September 17 The last run of Vancouver's open-air streetcars brought an end to the career of tour guide Teddy Lyons. These famous observation cars were built by BC Electric in 1909 in their New Westminster shops, and Teddy was a "spieler" aboard No. 124 from 1911 to 1950, an astonishing 39 years. He pointed out interesting sights, told corny jokes, passed along local history... he was famous, he was perfect. I recall going for one of those trips around 1947 with my dad. I've never forgotten one joke Teddy told, which involved a fisherman coming to a secluded pond and reading a sign there. "Well, I don't know if they do," he said and began to fish. A warden came along and pointed angrily to the sign. "Can't you read?" he demanded. It turned out the sign read "Don't Fish Here."

You had to be there.

His quick wit and non-stop humour became so well known the company even published a book of Teddy Lyons jokes. Someone calculated Teddy had travelled 930,000 kilometres (nearly 580,000 miles) through the city during his tour-guide career. Hamming it up to the end, Teddy yanked out a hankie to dry his tears for photographer Art Jones.

Last look. When observation car No. 124 made its final run, hundreds of people lined the route to wave farewell to a Vancouver institution. Known as the "rubberneck wagons," the two open-air cars were in service for 41 years. They used to stop at street corners, where gangs of children would sing and dance for the sightseers in return for a shower of coins. But the real attraction was Teddy Lyons and his fellow conductor Dick Gardiner, who kept his riders amused with a string of magic tricks.
City of Vancouver Archives, Trans P122

1950

Park Royal, the first shopping centre in Canada, was developed by the same land company that owned the British Properties and the Lions Gate Bridge. When it opened in 1950 on the north side of Marine Drive, there was parking for 700 cars and, as this photograph shows, Woodward's Department Store was the anchor tenant. Vancouver Sun

giant corporations would effectively control the industry in BC.

Japanese Canadian boatbuilders began returning to the coast, including Nakade, Atagi, Kishi, Yamanaka, Sakamoto and Mukai. Kishi had built the boat *Shelaine* for Dale and Eiji Maeda while he was interned at Christina Lake, and they had transported it by railway to the coast.

Chuck Hourston started Hourston Glascraft, one of the world's first fibreglass boatbuilders, this year in his North Vancouver garage. Hourston learned the trade at Hamish Davidson's boatbuilding shop at Georgia and Denman, which started building fibreglass boats in 1948 or 1949. Today, under the leadership of Chuck's son Bill, Hourston is the world's oldest continuously operating fibreglass boatbuilding company.

Hugh Pickett, with partner Holly Maxwell, took over the management of Famous Artists, representing and booking performing artists. Pickett eventually bought Maxwell's share of the business and ran it until 1982, when he sold the company to Jerry Lonn of Seattle.

Irving House, once home to Capt. William Irving and his family, was purchased by the city of New Westminster for use as a historic centre. It's still that today, a fascinating place at 302 Royal Ave.

Four-room Gleneagles School, the first in the area, opened near Horseshoe Bay.

The *Vancouver Sun* established Camp Gates on Bowen Island for its paper carriers, named for Herb Gates, the circulation manager.

A 13-kilometre (8-mile) double-lane road was completed to the top of Mount Seymour. Conscientious objectors had been put to work building the road up to the developing ski area during World War II. By 1954, skiing on the mountain was booming and more than 150 cabins had been built up there.

Zoning problems in Surrey grew more acute as farmers, businesses, industry and residents found their interests conflicting. It became necessary to set up a town planning committee at the municipal hall.

A modern sewage plant was installed at White Rock; 1,200 homes and businesses were connected with the disposal plant.

The first diesel train came to White Rock. In the 1950s there were three trains a day, at 9 a.m., 1 p.m. and 9 p.m. Residents could set their watches by them.

The Ukrainian Orthodox Church was built at 154 East 10th. It's a heritage building today.

J.V. Clyne, a prominent Vancouver lawyer, was appointed to the BC Supreme Court.

Comings and Goings

Vickers Haywood, the last survivor of the original Vancouver City Police, died. Haywood had been hired by Chief Constable Stewart in 1886.

1951

Louis Armstrong played Vancouver, and Princess Elizabeth and Prince Phillip paid a visit just months before she became queen. The law against Native potlatches was repealed after nearly seven decades. The battle against impaired driving benefited from the introduction of the "Drunkometer," and a former yo-yo champion began hosting a unique radio show on CJOR.

May 1 The RCMP took over the policing of Surrey from the BC Provincial Police with a cost-sharing agreement between the federal and municipal governments.

May 11 There was a demonstration at the Hotel Vancouver of the latest weapon in the war against impaired drivers: the "Drunkometer." ("Latest" is a relative term; the device was invented by US scientist Rolla Harger in 1931 and was the precursor of the Breathalyzer.) The Drunkometer determined the amount of alcohol in someone's breath. A person would blow into a balloon, and the air in the balloon was then released into a chemical solution. If there was alcohol in the breath, the chemical solution changed colour—and the greater the colour change, the more alcohol in the breath.

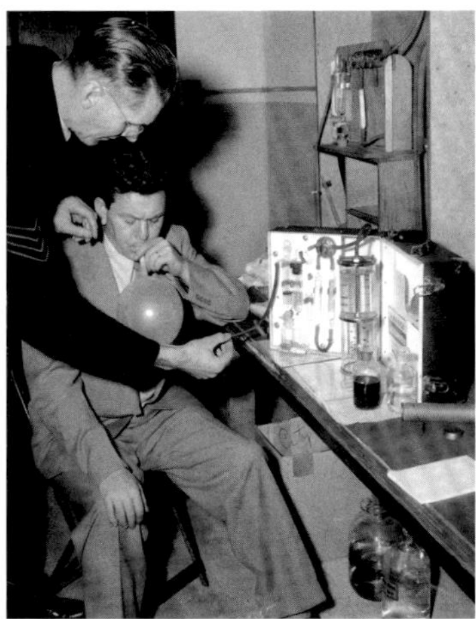

Left: Drunkometer. Demonstrating the latest Vancouver police weapon against drunk drivers—the Drunkometer—Ed Moyer, in this 1953 photo, blows into a balloon that Sergeant Rossiter then released into a chemical solution to measure the alcohol content. *Province newspaper photo, Vancouver Public Library VPL 42992*

Elsewhere in BC

September 1 Writer and activist Nellie McClung died at her home in Victoria, age 77.

The 1951 census for British Columbia showed, for the first time, more than a million people in the province: 1,165,200.

Major natural gas and oil fields were discovered near Fort St. John in the Peace River District.

Black Ball Ferries began a service between Gibsons and Horseshoe Bay with the MV *Machigonne* (passengers only) and the MV *Quillayute*.

Elsewhere in Canada

March 21 Trans Mountain (later called Trans Mountain Pipeline) was incorporated to build a pipeline that would carry crude oil from Edmonton to a Burnaby terminal. The first shipment of oil reached the terminal on October 17, 1953. The line was designed to transport up to 120,000 barrels a day," the *Province* reported, "with more than 50,000 barrels required to meet the daily needs of B.C." The $93-million pipeline stretched "through 718 miles (1,155 kilometres) of rugged country from the oil fields of Edmonton to a big tank farm in Burnaby."

The federal government revised the Indian Act, repealing the ban on Native people pursuing land claims and hiring lawyers to argue their claims in court. The act allowed aboriginal people to retain their status but also hold rights as Canadian citizens. The law forbidding potlatching was also repealed. The potlatch, a ceremony central to Northwest Coast Native culture, had been outlawed since 1884. (A potlatch held on McMillan Island in early September 1947, although illegal, had been heavily attended by Native people from all over the Lower Mainland.)

Elsewhere in the World

October 26 Rocky Marciano defeated Joe Louis at Madison Square Garden, New York.

December 24 The *Province* reported that Hollywood star Yvonne De Carlo "hasn't forgotten her home town." Miss De Carlo had started her own movie company, calling it Vancouver Productions. She'd made her first modest foray into showbiz as Peggy Middleton, an usherette in Ivan Ackery's Orpheum Theatre, then attended the Vancouver School of Drama and made her movie debut as a bathing beauty in 1942's *Harvard, Here I Come.*

1951

Oil link. Connecting the Alberta oilfields near Edmonton through the Rockies to Burnaby, BC, the Trans Mountain (later called Trans Mountain Pipeline) was said to be able to carry up to 120,000 barrels of oil a day.
The Province

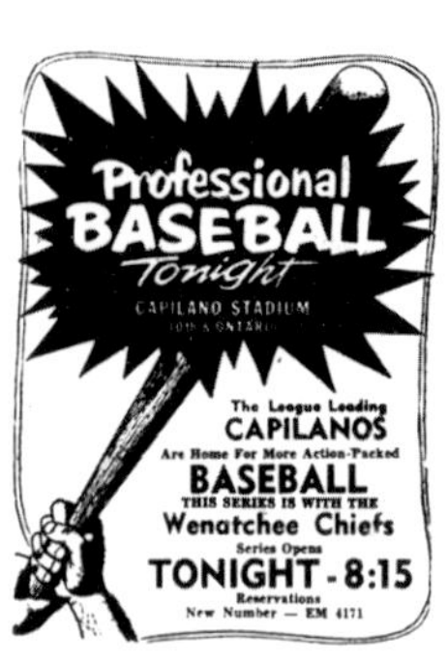

June 15 The new Capilano Stadium opened. The Vancouver Capilanos, managed by Bob Brown (Vancouver's "Mr. Baseball") defeated the Salem Senators 10–3. Capilano Stadium is known today as Nat Bailey Stadium.

June Harry Lee, the first Chinese Canadian architect, was registered.

August 21 Work started on China Creek Park.

August 24 The first Canadian Chess Championship began

a weeklong run at the Hotel Vancouver. A large number of chess-playing immigrants had come to Canada after World War II, and many of them ended up in Vancouver.

August Postal zones were introduced into Vancouver.

September 1 The comic strip *Mutt and Jeff* first appeared in the *Province*.

September 27 The Academy of Medicine opened in Vancouver.

October 31 The forest products firms MacMillan and Bloedel merged to form...aw, you guessed!

November 1 Lawrence Hall, site of primary education for the deaf, opened at the BC School for the Deaf and the Blind (later Jericho Hill School).

December High tides and gale-force winds combined to flood 490 hectares (1,200 acres) of farmland to a depth of 1.5 metres (5 feet) between the Serpentine and Nicomekl Rivers in Surrey. Repairs cost about $20,000, and the land suffered lower productivity for the next few years because of salt residue.

When it opened in 1951, Capilano Stadium was home to the Vancouver Capilanos baseball club, a member of the Western International League. By 1956, when this photo was taken, the home team had become the Mounties and played in the Triple-A Pacific Coast League. The '56 season ended on an unusual note when 59-year-old club manager Lefty O'Doul went to bat in the final game and hit a triple. Cap Stadium was renamed Nat Bailey Stadium in 1978, after the founder of the White Spot chain of restaurants.
PNG (above) and Vancouver Sun *(right)*

Posing in their potlatch finery, these First Nations people take part in an illegal potlatch in Quatsino, northern Vancouver Island, sometime between 1895 and 1898. An important part of coastal First Nations culture, potlatches were banned by the Canadian government in 1884 and not allowed again until 1951, though the ban did not stop them from being held.
City of Vancouver Archives A-15-20. Benjamin W. Leeson photo

Also in 1951

Fred Hume became mayor of Vancouver, even though he was living in West Vancouver. He had been mayor of New Westminster, his birthplace, from 1933 to 1942. Hume helped bring the British Empire Games to Vancouver in 1954 and helped the city land a minor pro baseball team in 1955. He owned the WHL's Vancouver Canucks from 1962 until his death in 1967 and lobbied for Vancouver to get its own NHL team.

The Lougheed Highway was completed, accelerating development on the north shore of the Fraser.

The Workmen's Compensation Board moved into a new head office at 707 West 37th Ave. One of its claims this year: a Vancouver man filed a claim for a head injury he said occurred when he bumped his head on a counter at work. Investigation proved that the man had struck his head on a pool table while retrieving a ball he had knocked off the table.

Eric Nicol began to write for the *Province*.

Legend has it that *Sun* writer Jack Wasserman was covering the royal visit somewhere in the Interior (before Princess Elizabeth and Prince Philip arrived in Vancouver) and, rushed for time, simply phoned in his notes. The notes were so good the *Sun* ran 'em as is. Then they gave him a man-about-town column, and he hit his stride.

A quote from Judge Angelo Branca's memoirs: "In 1951, after 565 convictions in six years against betting shops in Vancouver, the trade was flourishing as never before."

Albert O. Koch stepped down from his second term as president of Beth Israel Synagogue at 4350 Oak. He had held the post since 1938. (His first term was 1933–34.)

Japanese Canadians formed two cooperatives—Gulf of Georgia and Canadian Pacific—to process shrimp between December and March.

Japanese Canadian fishermen Yoshiaki Murao, Kumataro Sakiyama, Kasuichi Sakai and Ichiro Shiho introduced the concept of combined trolling and gillnetting. They rigged their gillnetters with trolling poles and gurdies and trolled for spring and

Pioneer ferry. Chugging along the coast is the MV *Quillayute*. It was the first ferry to run between Gibsons and Horseshoe Bay and was part of Seattle-based Black Ball Ferries, which launched its Canadian service in 1951. Black Ball provided the first real competition to Union Steamships, which had been plying the coast since 1889, but it was taken over in 1961 by what would become BC Ferries after a labour dispute led the provincial government to desire more control.
Vancouver Public Library, Special Collections, VPL 57946

coho salmon in Barkley Sound, on the west coast of Vancouver Island, until August. Then they returned to Steveston, replaced the trolling gear with net drums and rollers, and fished for late sockeyes, pinks, cohos and chums.

Comings and Goings

January 26 Louis Armstrong and the All Stars appeared at Exhibition Garden.

August 14 Baker W.C. Shelly died. He had made his fortune with 4x Bread and Canadian Bakeries Ltd., and in 1926 he attempted to develop a resort on Grouse Mountain, although that plan faltered two years later.

October 20 Vancouver enjoyed a visit by Princess Elizabeth and Prince Philip. The princess became queen less than four months later, in February 1952, following the death of her father, King George VI.

The Man Behind the Smilin' Buddha

Harvey Lowe started hosting *Call of China*, the first Chinese Canadian radio program, on CJOR. Lowe prepared and read stories of China, playing Chinese music between segments and building a bridge between Chinese and Caucasian residents of Vancouver.

Lowe had other claims to fame. In 1932, when he was 13, he began his career by winning the first World Yo-Yo Championship in London, England. After performing for the Prince of Wales (later Edward VIII) and Amelia Earhart, he toured England and France before returning home to Victoria. Five years later, when his mother suggested that he learn to speak Chinese, Lowe enrolled in a Shanghai university and was still there when the Japanese occupied the city. He started his broadcasting career there, reading the news on a radio station—which led to his own radio music show, *Hawaii Calls*.

Lowe returned to Canada when the communists took power China in 1949. He toured with his yo-yo, worked as a doorman at a Chinatown gambling club and bought a typewriter so he could write up stories about China. He showed those stories to local broadcasting legend Jack Short, and that led to *Call of China*, which ran until 1965.

In 1953 Lowe opened the Smilin' Buddha Cabaret on Hastings, and in the 1960s he was the stage manager at the Marco Polo, one of Vancouver's top nightclubs (he helped bring the Platters and the 5th Dimension vocal groups to Vancouver). Lowe performed his famous yo-yo routines at the Marco Polo and other nightclubs, even appearing on the *Smothers Brothers Comedy Hour*. When Robert Altman was filming *McCabe and Mrs. Miller* in Vancouver in 1971, one of the stars, Julie Christie, asked Harvey to show her the proper method for smoking opium.

In his final years, Lowe continued to act as an unofficial ambassador for the Chinese community, working in public relations and as a greeter at the airport. He died in Vancouver in 2009.

1952

A 21-gun salute at Brockton Point marked Queen Elizabeth's ascension to the throne, and W.A.C. Bennett was sworn in as premier, starting a historic 20-year run. Vancouver City Council voted to name a number of streets after golf courses.

January 25 At 8:30 p.m. CBR 1130 moved to 690 on the dial and changed its call letters to CBU. It's still there, as CBC Radio One.

February 7 A 21-gun salute was fired at Brockton Point to mark the succession to the throne of Elizabeth II.

February 12 Tolls were removed from the Pattullo Bridge.

April 4 Vancouver got its first taste of 3-D filmmaking with a really bad movie set in Africa, *Bwana Devil*, starring Robert Stack. Look out for that lion!

April 23 In her column in the *Vancouver Sun*, Penny Wise told of a visiting American who complained he couldn't find any restaurant in Vancouver that served something called a Caesar salad. Penny wrote that she'd never heard of such a thing. But she found a recipe for the salad and shared it with her readers. So we can date fairly specifically the Caesar's arrival on the local scene. The salad had been known in the United States for many years, but there is a dispute

Elsewhere in BC

The Kenney Dam was built on the Nechako River to provide hydroelectric power for Alcan's aluminum smelter in Kitimat. The dam flooded the lands of the Cheslatta people, and they were given only two weeks' notice to leave their homes. As well, the flow of the Nechako, a tributary of the Fraser River, was reduced by 75 percent, which severely affected salmon runs in the Fraser and its tributaries.

Elsewhere in Canada

January 24 Vincent Massey was sworn in as the first Canadian-born Governor General.

March 13 Susan Mendelson was born in Toronto. Few kitchens in BC lack at least one of her many cookbooks. The first, *Mama Never Cooked Like This,* sold 7,000 copies on its first day.

Elsewhere in the World

January The great American bass Paul Robeson gave a free concert at the Peace Arch. Robeson had performed at the Orpheum on February 7, 1946, and 3,000 fans in the sold-out theatre kept him coming back for more and more. But a hint of troubles ahead could be seen in an interview he gave the *Sun*, in which he commented, "I deeply believe Russia is now the world's most positive force for good, if we will help her." By 1952 the Cold War had the United States in a deep freeze, and Robeson's opinions, particularly his favourable view of the Communist Party (although he was never a member), resulted in a US refusal to allow him to return to Vancouver for another concert. He was stopped at Blaine, where local labour unions organized the free outdoor concert that attracted 25,000 people on the Canadian side, 5,000 on the US side.

February 6 King George VI, aged just 56, died, and his daughter Elizabeth, 25, became queen. She learned of his death while on a holiday in Kenya with her husband, Prince Philip. Vancouver and the rest of the British Commonwealth mourned the passing of the king. Her coronation took place on June 2, 1953.

May 12 Actor/director/producer Christopher Gaze was born in Leatherhead, England. He originated and still heads Bard on the Beach Shakespeare Festival, now an annual and much-loved tradition in Vancouver. Thanks to the efforts of Gaze and his staff, Bard receives less than 1 percent of its income from government grants.

November 1 The first H-bomb was detonated on Enewetak Atoll in the Pacific Ocean.

The Mau Mau rebellion began in Kenya. One observer was 14-year-old Gordon Wilson, a future BC politician.

Firoz Rasul, chairman emeritus of Ballard Power Systems, was born in Kenya.

A Hollywood movie titled *Hurricane Smith* starred two Vancouver-born actors, Yvonne De Carlo and John Ireland.

Arch attraction. The ever-popular Lumbermen's Arch was erected in Stanley Park in 1952, replacing the previous one, which was demolished in 1947 over fears that it might collapse.
City of Vancouver Archives Arch P50 Otto Landauer photo. Jewish Museum & Archives of BC

over when and where it originated and who created it.

July 15
The present Lumbermen's Arch was installed at Stanley Park,

replacing the original, which had been demolished in 1947.

July 18 The *Vancouver Sun* noted that the Vancouver Tourist Association (later called the Greater Vancouver Tourist Association) had no women on its board. A month later the *Sun* noted: "The postman rings four times daily, and statistically one-and-a-half persons per minute come into the over-crowded offices at the corner of Georgia and Seymour which house Vancouver's Tourist Bureau."

July Kerrisdale switched from trams to trolley buses.

September 4 Prime Minister Louis St-Laurent opened the Law Building at UBC.

October 19 The first sod was turned for St Anselm Anglican Church at Cleveland Way and University Boulevard.

Ocober 30 Burnaby General Hospital opened.

November 16 James Inglis Reid died today. He was 78. His famous high-ceilinged butcher's shop at 559 Granville, which opened in 1915, was almost as famous for its signs as for the special meats and haggis it sold. The most celebrated sign read "We hae meat that ye can eat." The meats included Ayrshire bacon, Belfast ham, black pudding and oatmeal-coated sausage. Reid was born in Scotland (Kirkintilloch) and came to Vancouver in 1906, at 32. Another Scot, H. Nelson Menzies, joined him in 1917.

Dorothy Somerset is welcomed to the stage during the opening night of the new Frederic Wood Theatre, featuring Earle Birney's *Trial of a City*. Wood was a founding member of the English department at the University of British Columbia and was instrumental in establishing Vancouver's early theatre scene. Somerset was the driving force behind creating the theatre, and behind establishing the theatre department at UBC. From left: Wood, Somerset, Birney, Art Sager, Allan Ainsworth, Don Erickson, Eric Vale, James Johnston, Blair Baillie, Nancy Woodworth, Philip Keatley, Elizabeth Keatley, Don Withrow and Bill Buckingham.
University of British Columbia Archives [UBC 20.1/24]

Early West End. The West End before the high rises moved in is revealed in this March 1952 aerial photograph.
Vancouver Public Library, Special Collections, VPL 81817. Art Jones photo

Long service was a constant at Reid's. When the shop closed in December 1986—forced out by Pacific Centre expansion—its manager, Gordon Wyness, had been there 41 years.

December 6 Frederic Wood Theatre at UBC officially opened. Joy Coghill, a member of Sydney Risk's Everyman Theatre company and a former student of Dorothy Somerset, directed Earle Birney's play *Trial of a City* (original title: *Damnation of Vancouver*) for the opening. The theatre's namesake, Freddy Wood, founded the University Players' Club and was its director from 1915 to 1931, annually touring a student show across BC (often the only live theatre seen in many towns). The club was disbanded in 1966 after the launch of UBC's theatre department. Wood also co-founded Vancouver Little Theatre with E.V. Young.

Also in 1952

Fred Amess became principal of the Vancouver School of Art.

The West Vancouver Chamber of Commerce was incorporated.

Lots in West Vancouver's British Properties were selling for between $2,000 and $5,000.

Vancouver City Council approved plans to name several city streets after famous golf courses. That gave us Seigniory, Leaside, Uplands, Bonnacord, Scarboro, Bonnyvale, Brigadoon and Bobolink.

The Mosquito Fleet was established.

It consisted of young men from Japanese Canadian fishing families who used flat-bottomed skiffs powered by outboard motors to fish out of Steveston, primarily in the Albion and South Arms flats. The fleet lasted until the 1960s, when the fishermen either graduated to larger boats or entered more permanent jobs on shore.

Comings and Goings

February 1 and 2 Louis Armstrong and the All-Stars appeared in the auditorium of Kitsilano High School.

February 11 Alan Twigg, founder of *BC Bookworld*, was born in Vancouver.

April 11–19 Duke Ellington played a gig at the Palomar Supper Club in Vancouver.

October 18–21 Sweet, dithery, US movie actress ZaSu Pitts, 58, appeared in Vancouver in *The Late Christopher Bean* with the Everyman Theatre. During her visit here, ZaSu was startled to learn Canada was not a British colony. The Internet Movie Database lists her in 204 movies.

October 20 Vancouver had two notable visitors today: Governor General Vincent Massey (our first Canadian-born GG) was in town, and so was singer Jeanette MacDonald, performing at the Georgia Auditorium.

Neon City

Vancouver may have been dormant during the Depression and World War II, but in the early 1950s it sprang back to life with new development that would make it an international city.

Postwar prosperity and exuberance created a building boom to house a growing population, supply shops to meet new consumer demands and provide hospitals, schools, churches, recreation centres and other amenities. Between 1951 and 1961 the City of Vancouver's population increased by 12 percent to 385,000. The population of the surrounding area increased by 87 percent.

Swaths of stucco-exterior houses were built on formerly vacant land in the Hastings Townsite area of eastern Vancouver and in Fraserview in the southeast. A hatching of schools followed to serve the baby boom children who came along between 1946 and 1964. And some residents, inspired by the Cold War, built private atomic bomb shelters—the first one appeared in a Shaughnessy backyard in 1950. Natural-gas and forced-air furnaces became popular, and where homeowners had once stored heating coal, wood or sawdust, they now built recreation rooms clad in fashionable knotty pine. Five movie theatres closed in the mid-1950s as families stayed home to watch the new television.

Modest three-storey apartments replaced the grand homes of wealthy West Enders, and in 1956 the four-year-old city planning department recommended a zoning change to permit apartment buildings over six storeys. Low-rise apartments also made an appearance in Kitsilano, Kerrisdale and Marpole.

Downtown Vancouver burgeoned with new commercial buildings and a forest of brilliant multicoloured neon signs that made the city the world's second-biggest collection of neon, after Shanghai, China. By the end of the decade neon, however, was falling out of fashion, and many business owners removed their neon signs. Streets became more traffic-congested, and one-way streets came into effect in the city core in 1957. Robson Street became known as Robsonstrasse as new residents arrived from Europe to patronize its chic shops and restaurants.

South of the city centre, on the north shore of the Fraser River, some of Vancouver's earliest farmland became the Shaughnessy Golf Course and the McCleery Public Golf Course. Despite a campaign to save the McCleery house, the first non-aboriginal home built in Vancouver was demolished in 1956. Hectares of market farms slightly farther east, many of them operated by Chinese farmers, gave way to residential neighbourhoods. Wai Chan, the city's last Chinese pushcart peddler, retired in 1953.

New industrial areas replaced old housing in East Hastings and around False Creek—the future site of Expo 86, which in its turn would displace other residents and businesses—and industrial developments took over farmland in the Still Creek and Grandview areas. An industrial park opened on Annacis Island, the Ioco refinery doubled in size and in 1968 Gulf Oil opened a refinery at Port Moody.

The British Empire and Commonwealth Games in 1954—scene of the under-four-minute Miracle Mile run by Roger Bannister and John Landy—left a legacy of athletic facilities including the 36,000-seat Empire Stadium, the Olympic-sized Empire Pool and the 250-metre Empire Oval, with its fast cycling track built of yellow cedar.

Other notable public buildings and works of the 1950s included the Queen Elizabeth Theatre and the Deas Island Tunnel (now the George Massey Tunnel), both visited by Queen Elizabeth on her 1959 tour. The Oak Street Bridge and a new Granville Street Bridge opened to handle increased traffic flow.

Wacky Races

August 1 William Andrew Cecil Bennett , who was born in New Brunswick, became premier of BC.

It sounds simple, but the swearing-in didn't happen until a month and a half after the election, which took place on June 12. The 1952 provincial election was held using a new multiple-choice voting system designed to keep the Co-operative Commonwealth Federation, led by Harold Winch, out of power. On June 13, only one MLA had been declared elected, and the ballot counting went on for weeks. It wasn't until July 14 that the results were official: the Social Credit Party had elected 19 members, the CCF 18, the Liberals 6 and the Conservatives 4. The Socreds did not have a leader at this point, so they held a caucus meeting on July 15 to elect one. Bennett won 10 of 19 votes cast and was named "premier-elect" by the *Sun*. But Lieutenant-Governor Clarence Wallace was not ready to make his choice. The CCF had a larger share of the popular vote and a longer history as a party. Wallace received conflicting advice from his counsellors and ultimately decided to call on Bennett to lead the province.

The new premier engineered the government's defeat less than a year later. Social Credit decisively won the 1953 election, and W.A.C. Bennett won five more election before his defeat on September 15, 1972. His 20-year term made him our longest-serving premier.

1953

Vancouver got local television in the form of the CBC and the cross-border station KVOS. The discovery of two murdered children in Stanley Park set off an enduring mystery, while a city weightlifter became the "world's strongest man."

January 6

Vancouver's longest wet spell began. It ended 29 days later. There was recorded rain on every one of those 29 days.

(On the same subject: believe it or not, no fewer than five cities in Canada have an average annual precipitation higher than Vancouver's paltry 111.3 centimetres (44 inches). Every major city from Quebec City east to St. Johns, NL, gets more annual precipitation than Vancouver.)

February 2 Mabel Ellen Boultbee (née Springer), *Sun* columnist, died at the Ritz Hotel in Vancouver, aged 77. The first white child born on Burrard Inlet (on April 29, 1875), she was the daughter of Mary Frances Miller (sister of Jonathan Miller, the first postmaster) and Benjamin Springer, manager of Moody's sawmill. A divorcee, she briefly ran a school with her sister, Eva, in the 1890s. A journalist for 30 years, she wrote the *Vancouver Sun*'s women's pages until just before her death. A prominent citizen and member of the Georgian Club, her apartment (shared with Eva) was a gathering place for the city's social elite of the 1930s and 1940s.

May 22 BC Electric opened the Dal Grauer substation, named for the company's president, on Burrard Street. The building attracted much admiration from architects for its modernism. (Today it's a condominium development.)

May 31 Christopher Spencer died in Vancouver, aged 84. He was born May 17, 1869, in Victoria, the son of David Spencer, founder of Spencer's Department Stores. "Mr. Chris" moved to Vancouver in 1907 to set up the branch here. After his father died in 1920, Chris was president of the company until T. Eaton Company purchased the Spencer stores in December 1948. Known for his public

Lewd and Filthy in a Court of Law

January 16 Police raided the Avon Theatre on Hastings Street, which was showing Erskine Caldwell's play *Tobacco Road*, and arrested five members of the cast, the director (Dorothy Davies), the manager of the Everyman Theatre troupe (Sydney Risk) and the owner of the Avon Theatre (Charley Nelson) for an allegedly indecent performance. The play included semi-nudity and simulated intercourse, and one of the cast, Doug Haskins, with his back to the audience, appeared to pee into a field. (The original play had premiered on Broadway in 1933 and is still one of the longest-running plays ever seen there, with 3,182 consecutive performances.)

The resulting trial featured a parade of witnesses—"ordinary people," university professors, clergy and even author Erskine Caldwell—who debated whether *Tobacco Road* was "lewd and filthy." Tom Dohm, later QC and president of the Vancouver Stock Exchange, acted for the defendants pro bono. Director Dorothy Davies took the stand for an emotional two hours of testimony in which she argued that the play did not pander to baser instincts but portrayed an aspect of life—a particularly ugly aspect, but life, nonetheless.

At the end of it, though, Magistrate W.W.B. McInnes found the cast, director and theatre owner Charley Nelson guilty. Sydney Risk, manager of the Everyman Theatre, was let off on a technicality. Vancouver County Court overturned the verdict on appeal, but the BC Court of Appeal reinstated the verdict when City Prosecutor Gordon Scott successfully argued that, among other things, County Court Judge James McGeer (brother of former mayor Gerry McGeer) had been "unduly influenced" by witnesses. There was no further appeal.

Elsewhere in BC

This year, according to the Workmen's Compensation Board (still called that in 1953), the total payroll in BC exceeded $1 billion for the first time.

Kal Tire was founded in Vernon. It is, among other things, Canada's largest retreader of truck tires.

Elsewhere in Canada

October 12 Frank Ogden—better known these days as Dr. Tomorrow—established the Canadian light-plane altitude record by flying a Mooney M-18 Scotsman to an altitude of 5,910 metres (19,400 feet). He set this "impossible" record with a conventional internal combustion engine by flying up until he ran out of gas, then gliding back. "It took place," Ogden once elaborated, "out of the Toronto Island Airport. The record has never been broken. Mainly, I suspect because most pilots are sensible enough to want 20 to 30 gallons of gas left in the tanks to get back. I...glided back to the same airport. With that plane that was not a problem." Ogden lives and works in Vancouver today.

Elsewhere in the World

May 29 Edmund Hillary and Tensing Norgay became the first to reach the top of Mount Everest, the world's tallest mountain.

June 2 Coronation in London of Queen Elizabeth II.

July 29 The Korean War ended.

Above left and right: BC Electric opened the Dan Grauer substation on Burrard Street in 1953 to rave reviews. Architectural historian Harold Kalman described it as "uncompromisingly modernist, with the brilliantly-colored workings exposed behind a transparent glass wall—which was replaced with opaque glass, following a minor explosion." *Art Jones, Artray photo, Vancouver Public Library VPL 82175(A)*

spirit and generosity, Christopher Spencer supported the University of BC, serving on the board of governors (1921–36) and in 1950 establishing the Chris Spencer Foundation to assist worthy students.

Spring A Women's Institute convention in Cloverdale passed a resolution calling for a National Health Scheme to give complete coverage for all Canadians.

Spring Television station KVOS ("Your Peace Arch Station") signed on in Bellingham, but found its real audience in Greater Vancouver. Rogan Jones' little "shoestring" station launched its programming with kinescope coverage of the coronation of Queen Elizabeth II. By the end of the year, sales of TV sets in Vancouver (at about $500 a pop) were in the tens of thousands, and residents with a $50 aerial or a pair of rabbit-ear antennae could watch three US-based stations: KING (channel 5), KVOS (channel 12) and KOMO (channel 4).

June 9 The Community Information Service, managed by Elaine Keene, opened its door and its phones. The background: the Community Chest and Council (now United Way), recognizing that it had become increasingly difficult to know where to turn for help with a problem, had determined that Vancouver needed an Information and Referral Service, a place where trained professionals would help people assess their situation and identify appropriate services to meet their needs. The Community Chest established a first-year budget of $7,300. The Rotary Club promised $2,500 and there was a personal donation of $200. The Junior League provided the remainder. Today the organization is known as Information Services Vancouver.

July 9 The Davis Cup tournament, the "world championship" of tennis, opened at the Vancouver Lawn Tennis and Badminton Club. The club was chosen because the Japanese team insisted on playing on grass courts, and none was available in the US.

September Vancouver alderman Anna Sprott became the first woman to serve as Vancouver's acting mayor.

October 12 Tilly Rolston died, aged 66. Tilly Jean Rolston was born in Vancouver on February 23, 1887. She entered politics as a Progressive Conservative MLA in 1941, but in 1951 she crossed the floor to sit as an Independent with W.A.C. Bennett for the remainder of the session. In the 1952 provincial election she was elected as the Social Credit candidate for Vancouver–Point Grey, and Bennett named her his education minister, the first Canadian woman to hold a cabinet post with portfolio.

October 23 The Burnaby Lake interurban tram line—the route of which roughly correlates with the Trans-Canada Highway today—closed after 42 years, replaced by a bus service. Charlie Martin, the first conductor on the original 1911 run, came out of retirement to act as conductor for the last run. The Vancouver–New Westminster interurban tram line—the route of which correlates with the Expo SkyTrain line—also closed after 63

Still the "world championship" of tennis despite the apparent low turnout, the American Zone stage of the Davis Cup was held at the Vancouver Lawn Tennis and Badminton Club in 1953 because the Japanese team insisted on grass courts, and none were available in the United States. The courts did not help, however; the Americans dominated, and went on to win the final against Belgium, which was held in Australia. *Vancouver Public Library, Special Collections, VPL 84752. Artray photo*

years, replaced by a bus service.

Most of the regular passengers were unhappy with the switch. Garageman William Setter of Cassie Street in South Burnaby said he'd been going home on the line for 30 years and considered the switchover to buses "organized chaos." Mr. and Mrs. C.C. Honour of New Westminster came along just for the last ride. Mr. Honour said he wanted to be "the last person off the last tram into the Royal City." But Mrs. Honour, the *Province* reported, was less enthusiastic. "I'd sooner ride our DeSoto," she said.

October 29
Cinemascope made its Vancouver debut at the Capitol with a showing of *The Robe*.

November 19 The present New Westminster City Hall opened.

December 2 On page 1 of the *Province*: "Bill Stone, 525 East Keith Road, North Vancouver, got his perfect cribbage hand the hard way Tuesday night. Playing with neighbor Bob MacKay, Stone had a king, pair of aces and a four in his hand as well as two fives. So he tossed the fives into his crib. MacKay had 6-7-8-8 and a 5 and a jack of spades. He threw the 5 and jack into the crib, the 5 of spades was cut and thus Stone had his perfect 29 hand."

December 9
The first Chinese Lions Club in North America was organized in Vancouver's Chinatown.

December 16
Vancouver's first television station, CBUT (channel 2), owned and operated by the CBC, was launched

when CBC chairman Davidson Dunton pushed a button at the station, a converted garage at the southwest corner of West Georgia and Bute Streets. CBUT began with network programming initially tape-delayed from Toronto.

Also in 1953

Winnipeg voted no, but Edmonton, Calgary and Regina—which had earlier balked—agreed to admit BC into the Western Interprovincial Football Union. What made the difference? A new 25,000-seat stadium was about to be built in Vancouver to house the 1954 British Empire Games.

The Babes in the Woods

The skeletons of two children were found in Stanley Park, covered with the remains of a woman's coat. Police determined they had been there since about 1947. The bodies were first believed to be those of a girl and a boy between 7 and 10 years of age, but study of their dental DNA in 1998 showed they were both boys, brothers in fact, but not twins. The misidentification hampered the investigation as contemporary reports of missing brothers were not followed up. Near the little bodies was a hatchet, later established as the murder weapon.

The skeletons were on display in the police museum for years, but retired VPD Sergeant Brian Honeybourn—who had made this crime a special study and instigated the DNA analysis—took the remains to a crematorium in the late 1990s. He then took a police boat out to the water off Kits Beach and scattered the children's ashes in the ocean. The Babes in the Woods murder, as the case is known, was one of the most shocking and disturbing in the city's history and is still unsolved. (The murder figures prominently in Timothy Taylor's highly praised novel *Stanley Park*.)

The football team formed the next year to play there was called the BC Lions.

Reporter Jack Webster, who'd worked for the *Sun* from 1947, was lured away by CJOR to do a show called *City Mike*. Webster was 35. His pugnacious style won him listeners quickly, and his hard-hitting daily reports on the Mulligan police scandal in 1955 made news themselves.

Gillnet fishermen on the Fraser objected to a government proposal to close the river to commercial fishing above Pattullo Bridge by mid-September each year. There were 650 gillnetters licensed to fish above the bridge, many of them Surrey residents. Their livelihood affected Surrey's economy.

The *Chinatown News*, a semi-monthly with text in English, began publishing.

The Benedictine monks' priory at Deer Lake became an abbey. Father Eugene Medved was the first abbott.

A breakwater installed at the head of the White Rock Pier helped to shelter small pleasure craft.

Nylon nets were introduced to the Fraser River fishing industry. They were stronger, lighter and more durable than the linen nets previously used.

Black Ball Ferries began service between Nanaimo and Horseshoe Bay.

Russell Baker, 43, a pioneer bush pilot, created Pacific Western Airlines from various other airlines he had established in BC and Alberta. Headquartered at the airport in Richmond, it grew to be the largest western regional air carrier, and in 1987 bought CP Air to form Canadian Airlines International. Russ Baker died November 15, 1958, in West Vancouver.

The Vancouver Incorporation Act was revised and renamed the Vancouver Charter. This act of the BC legislature incorporated the city and differentiated Vancouver from other municipalities in the province, which were created and governed by the provincial Municipalities Act. Vancouver's Town Planning Commission was formed.

Construction began on the Little Mountain Public Housing project—Vancouver's first attempt at financing rental projects for low-income families—which reached from East 33rd Avenue to East 37th, between Ontario and Main Streets. The architects were Sharp and Thompson, Berwick, Pratt.

Three founding trustees of the Richmond Hospital Fund met. Their

Seen here in about 1933, the *Lady Alexandra* was popular for ferrying picnickers between Howe Sound and Bowen Island until its retirement in 1953. It went on to be renamed the *Princess Louise II*, became a restaurant in Coal Harbour, and was then towed to California to become a gambling hall. *City of Vancouver Archives, CVA 374-92. Stuart Thomson photo*

Doug Hepburn: World's Strongest Man

August 30 Vancouver's Doug Hepburn won the world heavyweight weightlifting championship in Stockholm.

Hepburn was relatively small in the world of heavyweight weightlifters—1.75 metres (5 feet 9 inches) tall and weighing just 127 kilograms (280 pounds). Iran's Hossein Rezazadeh, by contrast, who won gold at the 2000 Olympics, weighed more than 147 kilograms (324 pounds) But the 26-year-old, Canada's only entry in Stockholm, did us proud at the competition, breaking the world record for the press. (A press is a lift in which the bar is brought to the shoulders and then, after a pause, is lifted overhead using only the arms.)

Hepburn's three lifts (the press, the snatch and the jerk) totalled 467 kilograms (1,030 pounds), and brought him the title of World's Strongest Man, a triumph for a guy who had to wear corrective footwear for a deformed foot, and who was teased cruelly as a kid because of his limping gait and his crossed eyes. Surgery fixed the eye problem; his prodigious discipline in training (he was totally self-taught) and his immense strength stopped the taunting. A year later he won another gold at the British Empire and Commonwealth Games in Vancouver. Hepburn died November 22, 2000.

total funds: $1,011. Two months after the meeting, 70 people at a public meeting approved formation of the Richmond Hospital Society.

Skiing was thriving: by 1953 five rope tows were active on Mount Seymour.

The Steveston Judo Club, a non-profit organization operated entirely by volunteers, was founded. It is now recognized as one of Canada's premier judo clubs, home to coaches and instructors of international calibre.

A program from the 1953 Canadian Ballet Festival carried a photo of a 14-year-old girl from Vancouver, described by New York critics as "one of the joys of the festival." Her name was Lynn Springbett. She's better known today as Lynn Seymour.

Eburne-born Arthur Laing, Liberal Member of Parliament for Vancouver South since June 1949, resigned to become BC Liberal leader. He was elected MLA in the June election, defeating Tilly Rolston in Vancouver–Point Grey. Laing retired as leader in 1959 and successfully re-entered federal politics in 1962. The Arthur Laing Bridge was named for him (on September 9, 1974, his 70th birthday).

Harold Winch, who had been a CCF MLA for Vancouver East since 1933—as well as leader of the BC CCF from 1938 and leader of the opposition from 1941—became Member of Parliament for Vancouver East for the CCF/NDP. He served to 1972. (A bitter rival of W.A.C. Bennett, he coined the nickname "Wacky.")

Portuguese immigration picked up when the Canadian government encouraged thousands of Portuguese to work in Canada's farming and fishing industries. Most of those who came were from the Madeira and Azores islands. Outside the Okanagan, the largest number of Portuguese live in metropolitan Vancouver (about 16,000 at last count), with a concentration on the east side. They have traditionally found work as labourers, carpenters, electricians, factory and service workers, and longshoremen; some eventually became small business owners.

The Vancouver Japanese Language School at 475 Alexander St. was returned to the Japanese community. From July 1942 to August 1947, the VJLS facilities had been occupied by the Canadian Armed Forces. In 1947 the government sold half the property and facilities to pay for maintenance expenses accumulated during the war. The remaining property was rented to the Army and Navy Department Store until 1952. The VJLS was the only property returned to Japanese Canadians of all the cars, homes, businesses, etc., confiscated after war was declared against Japan in 1941.

Brothers Ben and Morris Wosk, the president of Schara Tzedeck synagogue, chaired the synagogue's Burn the Mortgage campaign.

Comings and Goings

December 4 A heavily loaded Canadian Pacific Airlines DC-6B touched down at Vancouver International Airport at 12:42 a.m., becoming the first plane to fly non-stop from Tokyo to Vancouver. The airliner possibly set a second world aviation record in completing what CPA officials believed was the longest commercial airlines passenger flight in history. The 7,723-kilometre (4,800-mile) flight, with Captain James Black of West Vancouver at the controls, was completed in 13 hours and 51 minutes flying time. Today that same flight takes 8 hours and 25 minutes.

Right: Grand project. The present Granville Street Bridge opened on a miserable February day, but that didn't stop the crowds from turning out, or Mayor Fred Hume from bragging about "the largest single project ever attempted by the city." Vancouver Sun

1954

It was a banner year for sport as Vancouver hosted the Empire Games (the Miracle Mile run there is commemorated with a statue at Hastings Park) and, thanks to the new Empire Stadium, constructed for the games, entered the Canadian Football League with the BC Lions. It was also a good year for music as a new young DJ, Red Robinson, started playing rock 'n' roll music on CJOR.

January The Nine O'Clock Gun, which had been out in the open in Stanley Park for six decades, was housed in a granite and wire-mesh cupola.

February 4 The present Granville Street Bridge opened, replacing one that had served since 1909. A million cars crossed over the bridge in its first month. Mayor Fred Hume told a special luncheon at the Hotel Vancouver on opening day, "We're celebrating the official opening of the largest single project ever attempted by the city. As citizens of Vancouver we are entitled to crow a bit because we have accomplished this feat single-handed." He told the luncheon there had been "no formal assistance given by any other government body." At the end of the luncheon Alderman Birt Showler presented bridge worker Charles Geisser with the silver shears Geisser had used to cut the ribbon at the formal opening of the bridge a few hours earlier. The first "civilian" to drive over the 1954 bridge was the same woman who was first to drive over the second bridge in 1909. She had been widowed in between the two openings, so had a different name...but both times she was at the wheel of a brand-new Cadillac!

February 20 The Japanese Canadian Citizens Association was created to help facilitate the rebuilding of the Japanese Canadian community in BC.

March 2 The *Chinese Free Press* began to publish in Vancouver.

March 8 John Lawson, West Vancouver's first permanent white settler, died in Vancouver, aged 93. He was born April 15, 1860, in Cheltenham, ON, and arrived in BC in 1887. After 18 years as a railroad worker he bought property in the West Vancouver area in 1905. He planted holly trees by a "burn" (stream) on the property, coining the name Hollyburn. Lawson developed a ferry service to Vancouver in 1909, with the 35-foot launch *West Vancouver*, later replacing it with the *Sea Foam*, a 60-footer. He also established the first school at Capilano, was first postmaster and telephone agent, and was the second reeve of West Vancouver (1913). It has been said that the history of West Vancouver is the history of John Lawson.

April 16 "Professor Francis" died. He was an eccentric, erudite and cultured, who crashed parties of all kinds and became a fixture on the city's social scene. Less than elegantly dressed, he spoke at length (and with real knowledge) about any number of subjects.

May 12 A 24-year-old *Sun* reporter named Jack Wasserman began a new column on "the second front page" of the afternoon paper. Wasserman's column, often detailing the city's underbelly, became a hugely popular feature.

June 23 Vancouver voters okayed six-day shopping.

Elsewhere in BC

May 28 Margaret Jean Gee was the first Chinese Canadian woman to be called to the British Columbia bar. She was also the first Chinese Canadian woman Pilot Officer (Reserves) in the Royal Canadian Air Force.

July 15 A switch was thrown sending power from Kemano to the huge Alcan aluminum works at Kitimat. The project cost $275 million.

Elsewhere in the World

May 17 The US Supreme Court ruled that segregation was illegal in US public schools.

Built for the exciting 1954 Empire and Commonwealth Games, the Empire Stadium went on to play host to Elvis Presley and the Beatles, and became the home of the BC Lions and the Whitecaps.
Province newspaper photo, Vancouver Public Library VPL 43502

July 2 Vancouver's first cocktail bar opened on the first floor of the Sylvia Hotel.

July 21 With landscaping on the largest quarry at the future Queen Elizabeth Park completed, Mayor Fred Hume buried a time capsule beneath Centuries Rock in the park. It is to be opened in 2054. Mark your calendar.

July 30 The fifth British Empire Games opened at brand-new Empire Stadium, Canada's largest sporting facility.

We can thank Jack Diamond for the stadium. There wasn't enough money to finish the project, so Diamond assumed the role of organizer, enlisted the help of many of his business and social friends, and raised $360,000 privately to pay for the stadium's roof One casualty of the construction: Hastings Golf Course.

August 1 Journalist Tom Hawthorn wrote that "cabbie Dave King, driving for BC Radio Cabs, was taking a young woman to West Vancouver. When the cab slowed in traffic on the Lions Gate Bridge, she jumped out and, to King's horror, began climbing the railing. He raced over, dragged her to safety, shoved her in the car, and raced back to her West End address. The would-be suicide paid her fare, he told police later that day, and even tipped him 50 cents."

August 7 The "Miracle Mile" was run at the British Empire Games at Empire Stadium.

Roger Bannister of England, a medical doctor who had set a world record earlier with a sub-four-minute mile, beat John Landy of Australia in the first race in which the two racers ran the mile in under four minutes. This was also the first televised sports event broadcast live to all of North America. The race lived up to its billing: it was a thriller. Visit the British Columbia Sports Hall of Fame in BC Place Stadium to see a film of the event. Even after more than 50 years, the sight of those two men racing to the finish line is a pulse-pounder. And here's a historical curiosity: the *Province*'s publishing schedule was such that, even though the paper had a great full-page Bill Cunningham shot of the racers, it didn't publish the name of the winner. The results hadn't been officially confirmed by the time the paper went to press. (As everyone knows, it was Bannister.)

Also August 7 It was at that same 1954 Empire Games in Vancouver that one of the more dramatic races in Canadian sport history occurred. British marathoner Jim Peters,

The "mile of the century" thrilled spectators at the 1954 Empire Games as Roger Bannister and John Landy—up to then the only two runners who had broken the four-minute barrier—competed against each other for the first time. Amazingly, both again broke the barrier, with Bannister surging ahead to win after Landy made the mistake of looking back.
Photo Charles Warner

who was 15 to 20 minutes—about three miles—ahead of his closest competition, entered the stadium and collapsed just inside the gate. He struggled on, taking 15 minutes to go another 200 yards, falling several more times. When he crossed the finish line, one of the team assistants helped him off the track—but he had not actually finished the marathon. The line he crossed was for other track events. Peters was disqualified and immediately retired from the sport. The race was run on a hot and humid day, and Peters had had no water during his run; his collapse was the result of dehydration and heatstroke.

Winning touch. Hurtling for the team's first touchdown, Byron "By" Bailey proves that the BC Lions have what it takes to score as they play their inaugural game against the Winnipeg Blue Bombers.
Brian Kent / Vancouver Sun

August 25 The 45-bed Peace Arch Hospital opened in White Rock after six years of planning and fundraising by local residents.

August 28 The BC Lions played their first game.

The construction of Empire Stadium persuaded the Canadian Football League to grant Vancouver a franchise. The Lions didn't win their first game (they lost to the Western Interprovincial Football Union champion Winnipeg Blue Bombers 8–6), but *Province* columnist Jim Kearney wrote that to 20,606 paying customers at Empire Stadium, the Lions had proved they could score. The new team had actually led the Bombers briefly, thanks to a touchdown by fullback Byron "By" Bailey. "Johnny Mazur played the entire game at quarterback and showed his best form to date," Kearney wrote, and coach Annis Stukus praised his line of Arnie Weinmeister, Laurie Niemi, Chuck Quilter and George Brown. The Lions' early record was rocky: one win in their first 16 games. (Two months earlier, on June 7, future BC Lions great Lui Passaglia was born in Vancouver.)

September 4 Journalist Roy Brown died, aged about 74. He was born *circa* 1880 in New Brunswick and came to Vancouver as a small boy. At 11 he was the youngest pupil to enroll in Vancouver High School. In 1898 he worked as an office boy for the *News-Advertiser* and later as a cub reporter for the *World*. In 1899, at the *World*, Brown scooped the *Province* on property losses from the New Westminster fire. His biggest scoop was the 1918 sinking of CPR's *Princess Sophia* off Alaska, a tragedy that led to the loss more than 340 lives. He retired in 1938 as editor of the *Province*, and on September 3 was appointed editorial director and vice president of the *Vancouver Sun*.

September Robert "Red" Robinson, 17, started broadcasting on Vancouver's CJOR, playing music never before heard on local radio: rock 'n' roll and rhythm & blues. "In the Fall of 1954," Red later wrote, "Al Jordan left the show [*Theme for Teens*] and program manager Vic Waters, a great Deejay in his own right, asked me if I would like to try to maintain it. I jumped at the chance. Without question the first day on the air by myself was the most hectic and nervous time of my life. I knew this was it, this was going to mean a quick start toward my goal as a career Deejay or I was going to blow it entirely. I hit the air and kept on moving records through a full hour, on nervous energy alone. At the end of the hour the control room door flew open and Waters said the show was mine. He said the telephone reaction was great and he could live with what he had heard. What he had heard was a very immature voice, but a young man whose enthusiasm overcame a lack of announcing ability. I was totally hooked. I skipped school to learn everything there was to learn about broadcasting." The kids went nuts for Red's music, and in a year he had 54 percent of the audience. He emceed countless rock 'n' roll shows (Bill Haley and the Comets, Elvis, and the Beatles were the three biggest), co-ran an ad agency and emceed Timmy's Telethon for 22 years. His *Red's Classic Theatre* on KVOS-TV ran for 600+ episodes. He was elected to the Rock and Roll Hall of Fame in Cleveland in 1995, one of just three Canadian DJs honoured; inducted into the Canadian Association of Broadcasters Hall of Fame in 1997, and into the Rockabilly Hall of Fame in 2000.

October 12 The RCMP ship *St. Roch* returned to Vancouver, the first ship to circumnavigate North America.

October 14 Frank Everett Woodside, "Mining's Grand Old Man," died in Vancouver, aged 79. Born December 8, 1874, in Hamilton, PEI, Woodside left home at 16 to mine in Colorado and Rossland, BC. As secretary of the Western Federation of Miners he helped pass BC's eight-hour-day bill (1898). Woodside came to Vancouver in 1903. In 1910 he lobbied to end Hastings Townsite's ties with Burnaby and join Vancouver. The vote (which resulted in a "yes") was held at 2598 Eton, adjacent to the Woodside home (2594 Eton, now a heritage site). He was the first alderman for the Hastings Townsite area (1911–28). A charter member of the BC Chamber of Mines (1912), he was elected president in 1920. In 1922 "Big Frank" began a winter night school for prospectors. On retirement, he had been in mining for 60 years. A mountain in the Fraser Valley is named for him.

October 25 A fire heavily damaged UBC's Brock Hall.

It took three hours for the university's fire brigade and five trucks from Vancouver to quell the blaze. Before the fire forced them out and the roof collapsed, students swarmed into the building to haul out whatever they could. Dick Underhill (now running a law office on Bowen Island) was president of the Alma Mater Society, which had its offices in the building. "We were actually having a meeting at the time," he recalled, "and everyone pitched in to save things. There were some valuable paintings by B.C. Binning that we rescued, and I recall dashing into the AMS office to save some of the Society's records. Then all we could do was stand outside and watch the fire burning merrily." Students immediately started a drive to raise funds to fix the building. It was successful. The fire also sparked a drive for a metropolitan fire department that would coordinate firefighting services for the whole Lower Mainland.

October 26 In his *Province* column, Bill Dunford wrote: "A couple called Odlum look after a lighthouse in the Straits of Juan de Fuca. Recently they were expecting a child and figured that one way out of the name difficulty—and in keeping with their background and the tradition—was to call the babe after the first ship to pass their light after the blessed event.

"The babe arrived. Father, replete with binoculars, kept a vigil; a ship appeared. It was the *John F. Schwellenback*.

"They will try again."

November 8 The *Province* reported on page 1 that there was deep discontent with Police Chief Walter Mulligan. Many cops were quoted. Unrest simmered for another seven months.

Also in 1954

Richmond converted to a dial exchange from a manual telephone system. Cable television came to Horseshoe Bay.

Land expropriations began on Sea Island as Vancouver International Airport expanded.

One of the results: the end of the Frasea Dairy Farm, Richmond's largest. It had been established in 1922 by Jake Grauer, and at one time was home to 500 cows. One reason for the expansion: Trans-Canada Airlines (now Air Canada) introduced a fleet of Lockheed Super-Constellations for its Vancouver to Montreal flights. They carried 63 passengers, as well as

Looming up between the walls of Capilano Canyon, the Cleveland Dam—seen under construction in this photograph—opened in late 1954. The dam currently provides a third of Metro Vancouver's water, and is accessible to visitors as part of the Capilano River Regional Park. Province *newspaper photo, Vancouver Public Library VPL 632*

An Invisible Event

November 19 The Cleveland Dam was officially inaugurated. City archivist Major J.S. Matthews wrote that "the unveiling took place in a fog so dense that the large group of officials and spectators in attendance were completely obscured from sight; those forming the procession onto the causeway of the dam did so by following the person in front of them; the speakers addressed an audience they could not see, and the audience listened to speakers who were invisible."

The dam, a $10-million project on the Capilano River, was "the tallest of its type in Canada." The *Province* reported: "The giant concrete structure, and the natural valley facing toward the Lions, will control enough clean mountain water to supply the future needs of a 1,500,000 population. It towers 325 feet from the bottom of the gorge to the two-lane roadway which traverses its crest...Cleveland Dam will hold back an artificial lake 3 ½ miles long. In it will be 16-½ billion gallons of water." The Capilano River twists and turns through canyons and deep pools for eight kilometres (5 miles) below the dam before emptying into Burrard Inlet.

The dam was named for Ernest Albert Cleveland, Vancouver's first water commissioner, who was so highly regarded that when it came time for him to retire in 1940 (he had turned 65), special legislation was passed allowing him to continue on the job, which he did until his death in 1952, two years before the opening of the dam named for him.

Under the map is the world's largest map of its kind. The Challenger Map took George Challenger and his family seven years to build out of hand-cut pieces of plywood. The 80- by 76-foot topographical map amazed millions in the BC Pavilion at the Pacific National Exhibition, and is now looking for a new home. *Stanley Triggs photo, Vancouver Public Library VPL 85782D*

mail and freight, and travelled at 550 kilometres per hour (340 mph).

Vancouver council decided to rezone the slope above Kits Beach for apartments. Few home owners in the neighbourhood maintained their old houses, which led to the deterioration of the neighbourhood. This would have an unforeseen result: city historian Michael Kluckner has noted that "this affordable housing, the nearby beach, and vacant shops on 4th Avenue" made Kitsilano "the perfect home for Vancouver's hippie community of the Sixties and Seventies."

Baseball's Western International League folded, but at least the WIL's Capilanos went out as league champions.

Valley Curling Rink was opened in Cloverdale, but well water wouldn't freeze so Vancouver water had to be trucked in.

The *Province* newspaper commissioned the first composite photomap of the entire Lower Mainland. The scale was 1:63,360.

Japanese Canadian Buddhists purchased the Methodist church at 220 Jackson Ave. and began holding services there. In 1979 the Vancouver Bukkyo-kai was built on the same site.

The Challenger Map was completed.

It took George Challenger seven years and a million hand-cut pieces of plywood to construct a relief map of British Columbia, which was on display for years in the PNE's BC Pavilion. When Mr. Challenger died, his ashes were placed in a small urn and concealed under a plaque on the map's "Pacific Ocean." The map, disassembled after the BC Pavilion was demolished, is currently in limbo, although many people are working to find a new home where it can be reassembled and put back on public display.

The traffic department of the Vancouver Police formed a very popular motorcycle drill team, which soon became known as one of the top drill teams in the Pacific Northwest, performing in numerous cities and municipalities in BC and the US. The team still exists, travelling on its own time and responsible for all the expenses involved.

Comings and Goings

October 21 Hollywood columnist Hedda Hopper spoke at the *Vancouver Sun*'s Fashion and Beauty Clinic.

Notable deaths: **William Watts**, boatbuilder and founder (with partner Edward Trott) of Vancouver Shipyards, died in West Vancouver on May 8, aged about 92—their firm built the city's first steamboat, and in 1890 Watts won the BC rowing championship in a shell he built himself; **George Harvey Worthington**, physcian, alderman, and drugstore chain founder, on May 13, aged about 78.

Writer Malcolm Lowry, who had spent several years in a squatter's cottage near Dollarton on the North Shore, returned to England, where he died in 1957. While in that cottage Lowry wrote *Under the Volcano*, considered by many one of the great novels of the 20th century.

1955

This was the Vancouver Police Department's blackest year as the city learned of the police chief's systemic collection of payoffs from bootleggers. The chief resigned and two of his detectives shot themselves, one fatally. In happier news, the city hosted its first Grey Cup game.

March 15 The City of Langley was incorporated out of what had been the Langley Prairie area of Langley Township. A year earlier, nearly 800 of the 900 Langley Prairie residents had voted overwhelmingly to secede from the Township. Langley Prairie had become the commercial and business centre of Langley, but its political clout did not match its economic importance. The new city, with a population of 2,025, covered over 1,000 hectares (4 square miles).

March Reporter Ray Munro, frustrated by the *Province*'s refusal to print his allegations about Walter Mulligan, Vancouver's police chief, quit that paper and became the "Vancouver editor" of Toronto-based scandal sheet *Flash Weekly*.

April 24 "Amidst flashbulbs and the tears of fans" the last streetcar ran in Vancouver (it was on the Hastings route), ending 65 years of street railway service. Now the trolley bus was king. One of the passengers on that final run was Henry Ewert, an English teacher, who also rode the interurbans on their final day in 1958. Ewert has published several excellent books on public transit in this area. Especially appealing is *Vancouver's Glory Years: Public Transit 1890–1915*, written with Heather Conn and profusely illustrated.

July 17 A 69-year-old American leaped to his death from the Granville Street Bridge, the first suicide leap off the bridge that had opened a year and a half earlier.

July 22 Annacis Island, the first industrial park in Canada, was officially opened. The 490-hectare (1,200-acre) island had been owned since 1951 by Grosvenor

The end of a transit era came to Vancouver when the last streetcar, on the Hastings route, finished its run in 1955. About eight months beforehand, these passengers were photographed waiting to board at Hastings and Abbott. *Province newspaper photo, Vancouver Public Library VPL 43363*

When rail was still a popular way to travel, the CPR seized the advantage from its rival, the CNR, with the 1955 launch of The Canadian, a stainless-steel, domed ride from Vancouver to Montreal, which allowed passengers 360-degree views of the passing landscape. *Harbour Publishing Archives*

Elsewhere in BC

Harban Singh "Herb" Doman established Doman Industries Ltd. in Duncan on Vancouver Island. It became one of Canada's largest lumber companies.

Frank Mackenzie Ross, soldier, industrialist and rancher, became Lieutenant-Governor.

Elsewhere in Canada

January 7 The first television broadcast of the opening of Parliament.

March 17 A riot erupted in Montreal when Canadiens star Maurice "Rocket" Richard was suspended from play for the final days of the NHL season and the playoffs.

April 24 A new era in rail travel in Canada began when Canadian Pacific Railway introduced The Canadian, an "ultra-modern, lightweight, highly attractive stainless-steel streamlined train." The train offered the world's longest dome ride: 4,637 kilometres (2,880 miles) from Vancouver to Montreal.

June 3 Canadian Pacific Airlines inaugurated the first service between Vancouver and Amsterdam, over the North Pole. The 7,765-kilometre (4,825-mile) journey took 18 hours.

Elsewhere in the World

July 17 Disneyland opened in Anaheim, CA. A 10-kilometre (6-mile) traffic jam ensued.

Corruption, Trials and Tragedy

June 15 *Flash Weekly* hit the streets in Vancouver with sensational charges by Vancouver editor Ray Munro about illegal doings by the city's police chief, Walter Mulligan. Anticipating heavy demand, *Flash* printed 10,000 extra copies. They were gone within hours.

Munro accused Mulligan, and many of his men, of corruption. There was lots of opportunity for graft at the time. Vancouver in the late 1940s was a happening place: there was after-hours gambling; bookies collected bets in beer parlours, private clubs and hotels; and bootleggers were thriving. Wine and spirituous liquors were banned in restaurants and, believe it or not, in nightclubs, but revellers brought bottles into the clubs in brown paper bags and paid high prices for ice and mixers from proprietors who looked the other way. Proprietors, bootleggers and bookies, in turn, paid the cops to ignore the goings-on. The police officers who were not on the take were well aware of the kickbacks and had complained about them to reporters, politicians and the police commission as early as 1947, but nothing was done until Munro reported the allegations in *Flash*.

Mulligan sued Munro and *Flash*, but the police commission suspended Mulligan and asked the provincial attorney general to set up an inquiry into the allegations.

On June 24, Detective Sergeant Len Cuthbert, who was implicated in the scandal, pressed his service revolver against the left side of his chest, aimed for his heart and fired. He was rushed to hospital where emergency surgery kept him alive. The bullet, which went completely through him, had missed his heart by an eighth of an inch.

The Tupper Inquiry opened less than two weeks later, on July 5. It was headed by R.H. Tupper, QC, a Vancouver lawyer and the former head of the faculty of law at UBC, who told the public that his job was "to ferret out information, not to establish guilt and lay blame." Among the many witnesses called were several seasoned police officers. Jack Webster, who covered the inquiry for CJOR, cracked, "I had never seen so many big, burly men, whose memories were as sharp as tacks during any criminal trial, testify one after the other, 'I don't remember, I can't recall.'"

When Len Cuthbert took the stand in late July, still recovering from his suicide attempt, he suffered no memory loss and shocked the inquiry with his nervous recitation of bootleggers' payoffs made to cops and split with Mulligan. Equally devastating was the testimony of Detective Sergeant Bob Leatherdale, an honest cop who not only refused to go along with the payoff scheme but reported it to the city prosecutor, a judge and Mayor Charles Thompson—all of whom, according to *Flash* editor Ray Munro, sat on the report.

On August 5, Superintendent Harry Whelan shot himself just hours before he was to be cross-examined by Mulligan's lawyer. Whelan, who didn't survive, appeared not to be involved in the kickbacks but had told his wife he feared "they" would blame him for everything.

In October, Mulligan, who hadn't yet testified, asked to be relieved of his duties. He had discreetly applied for landed immigrant status in the United States, and in December he fled the country. He soon got a job as a limousine-bus dispatcher at the Los Angeles airport.

When the inquiry concluded on January 27, 1956. Tupper found that, with the exception of Cuthbert and Mulligan, he couldn't be sure of anyone else's guilt. What followed led Webster to label the commission a "whitewash." The attorney general's office ruled that it didn't have enough evidence to support Tupper's finding of corruption and could not take the case to court. That meant Mulligan would not be charged and was in fact free to return to Canada at any time. He did just that in May 1963, retiring to Oak Bay. Nobody ever went to jail. Mulligan died in Oak Bay in May 1987. His obit appeared in the *Sun* on page 19. The story was, after all, more than 30 years old by then.

Seen in an aerial photograph from 1955 while under construction, Annacis Island (on the right), opened officially that year as Canada's first industrial park. Annacis Island lies in the Fraser River between North Delta and Queensborough, a New Westminster neighbourhood located on the eastern tip of Lulu Island. *PNG*

International, which in turn was owned by the Duke of Westminster, one of Britain's wealthiest peers. More than 1,300 governmental, civic and business leaders were on hand. The July 21 *Vancouver Sun* reported that one factory was under construction, "with the possibility of a number of other firms also moving in." Today the island is home to a variety of industrial concerns and a major sewage treatment facility. Prior to industrial development, the island had been used for farming and fishing. It's hard to tell it's an island these days: the land is covered by buildings, warehouses, roads and bridges.

July A recording by Bill Haley and the Comets, titled "Rock Around the Clock," landed on CJOR DJ Red Robinson's desk. You know the rest.

August 26 The Vancouver Tourist Association became the Greater Vancouver Tourist Association. Also this year, former park board commissioner R. Rowe Holland told the association, and the *Vancouver Sun*, that he was "astounded" to find that information centre attendants at Stanley Park knew "nothing whatever" about the background of historic sites in the Greater Vancouver area. The same *Sun* story noted that the "question most frequently asked by visitors on tours of the city is: 'Where are the Mounties?'" And the paper also quoted GVTA member Jim Hughes' claim that Vancouver needed a full-time convention bureau.

September 21 Retired lumberman Leon J. Koerner and his wife set up the Leon and Thea Koerner Foundation, with funding of nearly $1 million, to finance educational, cultural and charitable projects.

October 6 Won Alexander Cumyow, court interpreter, died in Vancouver, aged 94. Born March 27, 1861, in Fort Douglas on Harrison Lake, he was the first Chinese Canadian born in Canada. He moved to New Westminster as a boy and later studied law. He was appointed a court interpreter in 1888 and served as the official Vancouver City Police court interpreter from 1904 to 1936. Cumyow spoke several Chinese dialects as well as Chinook. He was a community leader with the Chinese Empire Reform Association and other community groups, and a president of the Chinese Benevolent Society. He cast his first vote in 1890 and saw the vote taken away from the Chinese but lived to see it returned in 1947.

November 26 Vancouver hosted its first Grey Cup game.

Doug Walker's Montreal Alouettes faced Frank "Pop" Ivy's Edmonton Eskimos. Edmonton won 34–19.

After moving from Burnaby, monks of the Benedictine order settled in 1955 in their current home in Mission, BC. The Westminster Abbey community of monks in Mission is also home to the Seminary of Christ the King.
The Province

Also in 1955

The laying of gas pipes began in Surrey as BC Electric promised natural gas distribution for the Fraser Valley at Vancouver prices. BC Electric built the "largest gas turbine in the world" at Port Mann to generate electricity from natural gas.

Fort Langley was established as a National Historic Park and reconstruction began. The storehouse was the only surviving building and was restored as the trading store. It is possibly the oldest intact structure in BC (1840).

Andy Paull, Squamish Native leader, was honoured by Pope Pius XII for his contribution to the Catholic Church and to the Native people of Canada.

Stonemason Jimmy Cunningham, aged about 77, "retired." He had been working on the construction of the Stanley Park seawall since 1917 and eventually became supervisor of the work for the park board. After his retirement he continued to come down to the wall to keep an eye on things. He died September 29, 1963, and his ashes were secreted in an unmarked location within the wall.

The brothers of the Benedictine order, who had resided since 1939 in Fairacres at Deer Lake, moved to their present home at Westminster Abbey and Seminary in Mission.

George Adams died. He built the Carnegie Library at Main and Hastings, early parts of the Vancouver General Hospital and the W.H. Malkin warehouse, now the Old Spaghetti Factory. He bought lot 492 at Tunstall Bay on Bowen Island, built a house and moved there with his family in 1939. In 1950 he established a summer camp for *Vancouver Sun* carriers on the property. It was named Camp Gates in honour of the *Sun*'s circulation manager Herb Gates.

CBUT (the CBC's two-year-old television station) presented its first televised drama, *The Vise*, a one-act tragedy (1910) by Pirandello. It starred Derek Ralston, Peter Mannering, Valerie Cooter and Rae Brown, who would later be one of the cast members of the long-running CBC series *The Beachcombers*.

The *Clifford J. Rogers*, the world's first purpose-built container ship, left Vancouver for Skagway with its first shipment of 168 containers. The White Pass & Yukon Route, whose narrow-gauge railway connected Skagway, AK, with Whitehorse, YT, had developed the idea of container shipping in its Vancouver office and became the first company in the world to build a specialized cellular container ship and custom-designed rail cars to handle the metal containers. The *Clifford J. Rogers* served on the Vancouver–

Little Miss Sunbeam

Mel Cooper, broadcaster and salesman par excellance, was pursuing a reluctant client in 1955. He told me the story when I was researching the book *Top Dog! The History of Radio CKNW*: Through his contacts in the food industry, Mel learned Weston Bakeries was soon to introduce a new product onto grocery shelves in western Canada: Sunbeam Bread. It was an American innovation, and had been franchised to many bakeries south of the border. It was still unknown in Canada.

"We were on the outside looking in with the Weston people," Mel said. "I couldn't even get my calls to Jim Johnston answered. He was the key man. I went down to Seattle, where the Hanson Bread people had a Sunbeam franchise. I saw the drawing of the Miss Sunbeam girl on the package, and that gave me the idea. I came back to Vancouver, had an outfit made identical to the one on the package, the frilly little blue dress, then I hired a little girl and drove her to Weston Bakeries at Kingsway and Broadway.

"Now, remember, only Jim Johnston and his sales manager knew anything about the upcoming launch of Sunbeam Bread into this market. I sent the little girl up to his office, and I waited in my car outside. The girl is carrying a little package. The receptionist says, 'Well, who do we have here?' The girl says, 'My name is Little Miss Sunbeam, and I'm here to see Mr. Johnston.' The receptionist bounces up and into Johnston's office. 'There's someone out here you just have to see.' Johnston comes out, sees the little girl, and he's instantly charmed. He takes her into his office and she hands him the pretty little package.

"Inside it is a letter from me: 'Dear Mr. Johnston, my name is Mel Cooper, and I represent CKNW. We think we can sell a lot of bread for you in this market, etc., etc. I'm parked out on Broadway hoping to see you.'

"Well, he came down, invited me in, and we got that account."

Skagway route until it was sold to Greek owners in 1966. A year later, as the *Drosia*, it sank suddenly near Bermuda with the loss of eight crew members.

Vancouver-based West Fraser Timber began operations with the purchase by three brothers—Henry, William and Samuel Ketcham—of a small planer mill in Quesnel, BC. Today the company owns sawmills, plywood plants, veneer plants, pulp mills and MDF plants in BC, Alberta and the southern US and employs 6,700 workers.

Stan Leonard, BC's greatest golfer, belatedly joined the PGA tour full-time at age 40. Born February 2, 1915, by the late 1920s Leonard was caddying at Shaughnessy Heights for 50 cents. (This was before the 14-club limit when at least 20 clubs was not uncommon.) By 1932 at age 17, Leonard was BC amateur champion. He won 44 tournaments during his career.

Vienna-born forest products executive John Prentice, who had a deep passion for chess, became president of the Chess Federation of Canada, a post he held until 1971 (though his involvement with the game continued into the 1980s). Prentice's financial support and organizational ability led him to be called Canada's Mr. Chess. He died in 1987.

Vancouver doctor G.F. Strong was named president of the American College of Physicians and Surgeons.

With the inclusion of Richmond, the Fraser Valley Regional Library district covered an area of more than a million hectares (4,000 square miles), extending from Richmond to Hope, from Port Coquitlam to Agassiz and from the international border to the mountains north of the Fraser River.

Comings and Goings

May 10 Tommy Burns, the only Canadian to have been world heavyweight boxing champion, died while visiting Vancouver, aged 74. After retiring from the ring, Burns operated a pub in London and a speakeasy in New York. Then he renounced the sinful life and embarked upon the sawdust trail as an evangelist. On one of his evangelical tours he took a sidetrip to Vancouver to visit a friend, John Westway, and died here of a heart attack. They found on his body a calling card that read "Tom Burns, demonstrator of Universal Love." He was buried in Plot 3, Grave 451, of the Balsam Section of Ocean View Cemetery in Burnaby. Only four people attended the service—a boxing fan and his wife, plus two gravediggers. The grave had no marker for six years, until a sportswriter's campaign financed a plaque.

July 19
Judy Garland, 33, performed in Vancouver. A 12-year-old Vancouver girl, Connie Brent, was among the more than 5,000 fans in Exhibition Forum for the show, sponsored by B'nai Brith. Connie met with the star after the show and told her she wanted to learn how to sing "just half as good as you."

Notable deaths: **Thadeous Sylvester "Teddy" Lyons**, BC Electric Railway conductor, tour guide and "spieler," in Vancouver on February 27, aged about 66; **George Albert McGuire**, pioneer dentist and MLA, in Vancouver on July 2, aged 84; **Michael Saba**, silk merchant, in Los Angeles on July 10, aged about 94.

1956

Tourism was becoming a vital piece of the civic and provincial economy, bringing more revenue to the province than fishing or construction, and a new aquarium in Stanley Park, the first public aquarium in the country, was destined to attract even more visitors to the city. Construction started on a new central library, and construction of the PGE Railway to Prince George finally ended. Not all was rosy though. The crash of an airliner that went down in the Fraser Valley after leaving the Vancouver airport became the country's worst air disaster.

January 16 The Hastings East Community Centre was opened, and a new community centre opened in Cloverdale this year, four years after the old "Opera House" burned down.

March 20

The *Province* reported that three UBC students—Jane Gordon, Sharon Engelbeen and Debbie Wilkins—had mastered 1,000 facts about Vancouver.

"Their teacher is Mrs. Margaret Jones, staff supervisor of the Greater Vancouver Tourist Association." Among the facts: Vancouver's population included 3,929 residents of Russian extraction and 154 people who spoke only French; West Vancouver covered 32 square miles; local banks cleared $5 billion in 1954; there were 32 dance academies, 9 detective agencies, 2,225 apartment houses, 7 pawn brokers and 14 miles of waterfront in the city; and most important for tourism, Vancouver enjoyed an average of 1,663 hours of sunshine annually.

April 3 A bank robbery shootout at Cariboo Trail Shopping Centre in Coquitlam left one robber dead and a policeman injured. It was thought to be the first time a machine gun had been used in a local bank robbery.

April 19 Construction started on the main branch of the Vancouver Public Library at Robson and Burrard. This was also the year Burnaby Library was formally established.

Industry, Redefined

January 30 The *Province* reported that 90 million tourist dollars came into the province in 1955, $50 million of that into Vancouver, and calculated: "That adds up to 10 times as much as the wealth produced by gold mines in B.C.; almost three times as much as the salmon industry, and double Vancouver's record construction program."

On February 4, the *Vancouver Sun*'s Bill Fletcher, commenting on the *Province*'s figures, determined that Vancouverites spent 19 cents per capita to bring in its $50 million; Victoria spent 98 cents; San Diego, about the same size as Vancouver, 46 cents; Miami, $1.52; Tucson, $2.22; Palm Springs, $8.60; Honolulu ,$1.30. Fletcher also noted that, included in many plans to boost tourism was "a convention bureau set-up that could bring many millions to the Vancouver area in the normally slack winter months."

In April, an article by J.V. Hughes in *Western Business and Industry* magazine reported that "during the past 12 months, the [Vancouver Tourist] association office replied to more than 13,000 direct mail inquiries, and answered personal inquiries over the counter of more than 67,000. (Long ago we stopped counting our incoming phone calls.)"

On May 26 the *Sun* had more tourism statistics: "Average stay of the pleasure tourist here is 4.77 days. He spends $63.43." The business tourist spent more ($114.91) and stayed longer (5.44 days). In 1955, the *Sun* said, 65.2 percent of tourists travelling through Vancouver were from the United States and 12.5 percent of them had complaints: inadequate street and directional signs, poor weather, poor roads. Two out of three parties were in Vancouver for the first time.

A few days earlier, Clarke Todd, newly appointed manager of the convention department of the Vancouver Tourist Association, had told the papers he aimed to double Vancouver's convention trade.

Elsewhere in BC

August 23 After a failed attempt on August 10 (after 9 hours and 50 minutes the water was too cold for her to continue), Marilyn Bell became the first woman to swim the Strait of Juan de Fuca from Ediz Hook, near Port Angeles, WA, to Clover Point, near Victoria, on Vancouver Island. The 29.4-kilometre (18.3-mile) crossing took her 11 hours and 35 minutes. Bell, 18, was already famous as the first person to swim across Lake Ontario (1954) and the youngest person to swim across the English Channel (July 31, 1955).

September 25 Power was turned on in a new 150,000-volt hydro cable laid in the summer between the mainland and Vancouver Island.

Elsewhere in Canada

Ira Dilworth, 62, a scholar and broadcaster, who had been with the CBC in Vancouver since 1938, was promoted to director of all CBC English networks.

Elsewhere in the World

July 26 Egypt's president Gamal Nasser seized the Suez Canal.

It was perhaps a leap of faith when the Vancouver Aquarium opened in 1956 as Canada's first public aquarium, but with acts like this of a dolphin jumping for food, its popularity has proved enduring. Lesser known, but also important, is the aquarium's marine conservation, rehabilitation and research work.
City of Vancouver Archives, CVA 392-927

April 27 More than 8,000 fans watched Vancouver's newest sports team—baseball's Mounties of the brand-new Pacific Coast League—lose 2–1 to the San Francisco Seals in the club's home debut. The Mounties (formerly the Oakland Oaks) finished dead last in the eight-city circuit; pitcher Ernie Funk was 1 for 19. At the end of the season the Mounties were sold for $150,000 to a syndicate of businessmen, including Nat Bailey of White Spot fame. Shares in the club cost $25. Among the shareholders was Premier W.A.C. Bennett.

June 15 The Stanley Park Aquarium opened,

with the ribbon cut by Fisheries Minister James Sinclair. Sinclair's seven-year-old daughter Margaret was on hand (15 years later she married Canada's prime minister). The idea for the aquarium took root in 1951, when a private non-profit society, the Vancouver Public Aquarium Association, was formed (businessman Carl L.A. Lietze was the first president). It gained financial support from all three levels of government and the federal government has since recognized it as Canada's Pacific National Aquarium. When the Stanley Park aquarium opened, Vancouver's first aquarium, on English Bay since 1939, closed.

June 22 Burnaby's stylish new municipal hall opened near Deer Lake, in the geographical centre of the municipality. The first hall was built in South Burnaby in 1899, but 50 years later North Burnaby was the town's economic centre. Building at Deer Lake was a compromise between the two neighbourhoods. When the hall opened, the Burnaby detachment of the RCMP, which had occupied space in city hall since 1935, moved to its own building.

June 30 A tourist information booth opened at Marine and Capilano in North Vancouver. The first attendant was Frank Wilson. There's a booth there to this day.

July 5 Rochfort Henry "Tim" Sperling, electrical engineer, died in Vancouver, aged 80. Born in Yorkshire, he came to BC in 1896 and joined the BC Electric Railway. By 1905 he was general manager of BCER and was also GM of Vancouver Gas, Victoria Gas, Vancouver Power and Vancouver Island Power, replacing coal-burning plants with hydroelectric systems on the mainland and on Vancouver Island. He returned to England when World War I began and worked in aircraft production but eventually returned to live in Vancouver. Sperling Street in Burnaby is named for him.

August 1 A baby penguin was born at the Stanley Park Zoo, the first in Canada.

August 13 Letter carrier service began in White Rock.

October Charles Nanby Wynn "Chunky" Woodward, 32, grandson of Woodward's Department Store founder Charles A. Woodward and son of William Culham Woodward, was named president of the chain on his father's retirement. Chunky Woodward had joined the staff of his father's stores in 1946.

November 5 Edgar George Baynes, contractor and hotelier, died in Vancouver, aged about 86. He was born on a farm in Dunmow, Essex, England, in 1870 and ran away from home at age 13. Baynes came to Vancouver as a contractor in 1888. In 1893, with partner William McLeod Horie, he established Baynes and Horie. That firm built many Vancouver and BC public schools. In 1906 he established the Port Haney Brick Co. Baynes built the Grosvenor Hotel (once on Howe Street, now vanished) in 1913, and when the client couldn't pay for the work took the hotel over and worked as manager. The Vancouver Historical Society remembers Baynes with real warmth, because he provided a meeting place for them at no charge for more than 20 years. He was a parks commissioner for 15 years. He was also one of the first homesteaders in the Squamish River Valley.

November 28 Fred Hume was elected Vancouver's mayor for a fourth consecutive term, the first man to accomplish that.

December 9 All 62 people (59 passengers, three crew) aboard a Trans-Canada Airlines DC-4 Northstar heading to Calgary died when the plane slammed into Mount Slesse, in the Cascade Mountains near Chilliwack. Fifty minutes out of Vancouver the pilot had reported a fire in the No. 2 engine and was turning back. Flying on three engines, and 19 kilometres (12 miles) south of the assigned airway, the aircraft encountered a difficulty of some kind that led to the crew losing control. "The plane," wrote *Province* journalist Don Hunter, "remained hidden under deep snow, its disappearance a mystery for six months before the spring thaw revealed its presence." The wreckage was found on May 12, 1957, by a party of climbers who, on their return to Vancouver, notified the *Province*. The paper ran an Extra edition May 13 to announce the discovery of the wreckage. The *Province*'s Paddy Sherman, an experienced mountaineer, made subsequent visits to the crash site and testified at length before the resulting coroner's inquiry as an expert witness It was the worst air crash in Canada's history to that time. The wreckage still remains at the site, which is now a memorial.

December 22 A French adventurer completed a swim of the Fraser River from Prince George to New Westminster's Pattullo Bridge. (NOTE: In December!) A fellow named Fin Donnelly made the same excursion in 1995 to rase awareness of pollution in the Fraser. Fin did his swim in September. (We've also seen 1958 as the date for the Frenchman's swim.)

December 28 One of the odder human dramas that played out locally was the arrival of Christian George Hanna, a "man without a country," who arrived in Vancouver as a working stowaway aboard the Norwegian freighter *Gudveig*. Hanna, 23, was "not sure where he was born, nor who were his father and mother." He had been wandering around the world for months, unable to disembark because he had no papers to tell who he was. Something about his story captured the imagination and sympathy of Canadians, and there was a nationwide campaign to persuade Canada to take him in. And we did... until we discovered Hanna was actually Ahmed Aouad, an Egyptian. Then he got into trouble with convictions for indecent assault and public intoxication. He was deported.

December 29 The Japanese Fisherman's Hospital at 11900 No. 1 Rd. in Steveston, which the Army, Navy and Air Force Veterans in Canada, Unit 284, had bought in 1947, burned to the ground. ANAFV had converted the old hospital to a licensed club, which, in spite of large crowds and good sales, was always on the verge of bankruptcy due to a lack of integrity on the part of some managers.

December The McCleery farmhouse, built in 1873, was demolished by the Vancouver Park Board. The McCleery family farmed right up to this year, although Vancouver had acquired their farm in 1954. In 1959 it became a golf course, and in 1985 the Kerrisdale Historical Society erected a memorial cairn at the site of the house.

Also in 1956

Vancouver City Council rezoned the West End to allow significantly higher population density. This was in response to downtown businesses' concerns that they were losing customers to suburban shopping

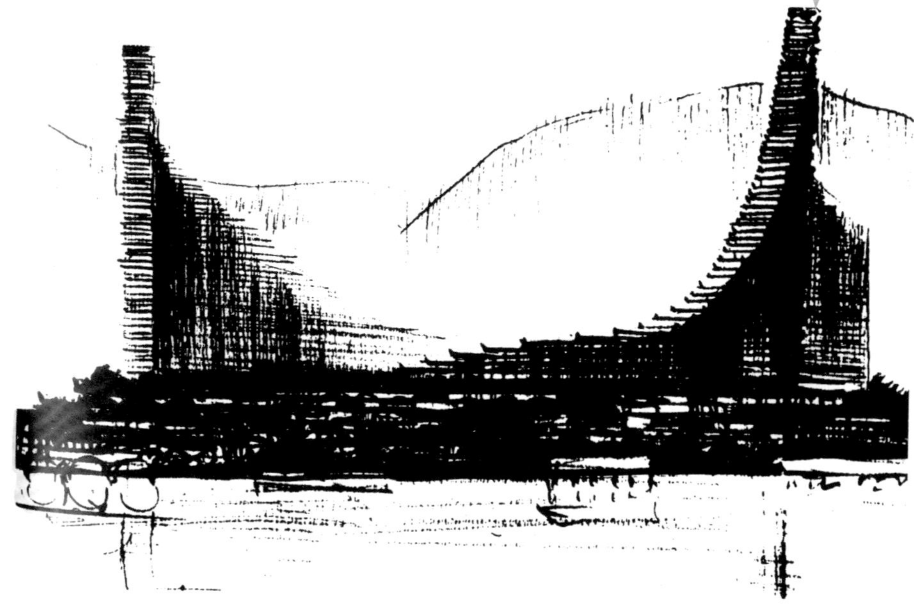

This is one Arthur Erickson plan that thankfully was not built: a plan to turn the West End into one giant apartment building, with twin towers on each end, as seen in this sketch. *Harbour Publishing Archives*

malls. Architect Arthur Erickson, 32, conceived a plan to turn the West End into one gigantic apartment building. Taras Grescoe has described his vision as "a stack of monster suites that culminated in hundred-storey twin peaks at either end of the downtown."

The Workmen's Compensation Board reported that, for the first time, the construction industry passed the lumber industry in number of injuries.

Bill Rea, who had started CKNW in 1944 and moved to California for health reasons in 1954, sold the station to accountant Frank Griffiths, who began to turn it into an empire. He left the running of 'NW to its capable staff but worked behind the scenes to establish a very much larger company that eventually became Western International Communications, with radio, TV, cable and more.

The first class of certified general accountants started studies at UBC. Although 107 students began, only 28 graduated and just two of those were women. One of them was Lucille Johnstone, who became a legend in BC business. She began working in 1944 as a tugboat operator for Rivtow and went on to become president and chief operating officer. By the time she left Rivtow in 1989, after 45 years, the company had reached sales of $250 million and had 1,500 employees. She died December 31, 2004, age 80.

The Squamish-to-Horseshoe Bay section of the PGE Railway was completed along Howe Sound, and the Horseshoe Bay-to-North Vancouver section was rebuilt. The railway had finally fulfilled its mandate to connect the Port of Vancouver to Prince George.

Dr. Gordon Shrum, already the head of UBC's physics department, became the university's dean of graduate studies. He held both posts until 1961 and then became the first chancellor of Simon Fraser University in 1962. Also at UBC: Ellen and Warren Tallman arrived from California to teach in the UBC English department. Their home became a centre of study and enjoyment of modern poetry in the city. Henry F. Angus ended 37 years as a member of the UBC faculty. He had been head of the economics, political science and sociology department since 1930 and the first dean of graduate studies since 1949. He became dean emeritus.

D.W. Poppy was elected reeve of Langley Township. His father, David William Poppy, had been reeve from 1908 to 1913 and again from 1919 to 1923.

The Vancouver Fire Department was described as having "the best fire department on the continent"

by the past president of the International Association of Fire Chiefs. The VFD won the National Fire Protection Association's Grand Award this year for having the most outstanding fire prevention program.

The Vancouver-based BC Cancer Institute launched a cervical screening program (the Pap smear program) across the province, under the direction of Dr. H.K. Fidler and Dr. David Boyes. The program sought to include all women in BC over the age of 20 and became a model for other countries.

Membership in the Society of Notaries Public of BC, incorporated November 2, 1926, became compulsory this year through statutory amendments that also gave the society full professional status with power to discipline members. Today British Columbia and Quebec are the only Canadian provinces where notaries are organized in a statutory self-governing society.

Bill Haley (centre) and the Comets, seen in this 1956 publicity handout and most famous for their 1954 song "Rock Around the Clock," played the first rock 'n' roll concert in Vancouver. Fans adored them, but the *Vancouver Sun* took a different stance, calling the concert "the ultimate in musical depravity." Vancouver Sun

Mary Pack, famous for her work in the fight against arthritis and rheumatism, was given the Post No. 2 Native Sons of BC Good Citizen Award. In 1953 she had received the Queen's Coronation Medal, and in 1974 she was named to the Order of Canada for her efforts.

Sikh priest Giani Harnam Singh died. He had run a pioneer lumber business and helped found the Akali Singh Sikh Temple. After his death his widow, Jagdish Kaur Singh, started a gravel truck business in Chilliwack. She became a director of Dhillon Holdings and owner of several dairy farms and landholdings in Chilliwack and Langley. A staunch supporter of Sikhism, she donated to charities worldwide.

Wanda Biana Selma Ziegler, about 82, president of Ziegler Chocolate Shops, retired. She had run the chain since 1923, when her husband, Fritz, died. Beginning with the three stores he had established, she gradually expanded to 11. On her retirement, the shops closed. Mrs. Ziegler died in Fort Langley on March 3, 1967, aged about 93.

Comings and Goings

June 27 DJ Red Robinson hosted Vancouver's first rock 'n' roll concert as Bill Haley and the Comets blew 'em away at Kerrisdale Arena. An estimated 6,000 fans screamed for more. The review the next day in the *Vancouver Sun* described the concert as "the ultimate in musical depravity."

June Sports journalist Jack Keating wrote that "Vancouver had what was termed its first 'Dream Game,' a game between two professional soccer teams rather than a professional against an amateur all-star team. Aberdeen played Everton to a 3–3 draw at Empire attracting 18,000 in the pouring rain." Moscow Lokomotive also came here in 1956 to play the Vancouver All-Stars—it was the first sports group to come to North America from the Soviet Union.

September 24 Entertainer Little Richard was mobbed by fans, and a riot nearly erupted during his show at Kerrisdale Arena.

December 5 The first Hungarian refugees, fleeing the Soviet occupation of their country, arrived in Vancouver. Among them was Professor Elod Macskasy (1919–90), who taught mathematics at UBC for more than 30 years and was BC's top chess player for most of that time. He won the Canadian Open Championship in 1958 and played on a number of Canadian Olympic chess teams. Another of the newcomers was sculptor Elek Imredy (1912–94), whose most well-known local work is *Girl in a Wetsuit*, seen by thousands as they pass by on the Stanley Park seawall.

Notable deaths: **Harry Hooper**, Vancouver's first taxi driver, died in Vancouver on January 11, aged 81; **Duff Pattullo**, Liberal MLA (1916–41) and premier (1933–41), who has been called the most significant of BC premiers, died March 29, aged 83; **Charles "Pop" Foster**, boxing promoter, who discovered and trained Vancouver's Jimmy McLarnin to become the world welterweight champion, died in Glendale, CA, on May 5, aged about 82; **Truman Smith Baxter**, former Vancouver mayor (1913–14) died in October, aged 88.

1957

The city opened the Oak Street Bridge to Richmond and a new central library that would serve for almost 40 years; UBC absorbed an entire forestry faculty from Hungary; and Vancouver lost a daily newspaper and elected the country's first Chinese Canadian MP. Elvis came to town, meanwhile, along with one-way streets.

January 24 One of the great stories in BC history began today when 200 students and 14 faculty members from the Forestry School in Sopron, Hungary, arrived at the Matsqui train station. Two months earlier, Sopron and other Hungarian cities had been invaded by Soviet troops. "Attempts to resist the approaching Soviet tanks," Professor Antal Kozak wrote, "were futile. About 450 students and 50 professors and their families left Sopron, fleeing across the open borders to Austria. Of these, about 250 were from the forestry school...The Faculty of Forestry at UBC offered to 'adopt' the Sopron University of Forestry and guaranteed its maintenance for five years until the current students graduated." By May 1961 the last Sopron class graduated. (They had started their classes in Hungarian, gradually upped the English content as they progressed.) Most of the 140 graduates decided to stay and work in Canada. The Sopron faculty and students were not, of course, the only Hungarian refugees here. At one point in 1957 there were 1,500 Hungarians housed at a camp at the Abbotsford airport.

February 16 Samuel Patrick Cromie died by drowning in a boating accident at Halfmoon Bay, north of Vancouver, aged 39. He was born

January 25, 1918, in Vancouver, the third son of Robert Cromie, who founded the *Vancouver Sun*. Samuel Cromie had worked his way up from the circulation department to become vice president/assistant publisher of Sun Publishing in 1955. He served in the RCAF during the war and was a Vancouver alderman on his return in 1946, at age 28, the youngest in Vancouver's history to that time. Cromie was described as "one of Canada's best-known newspaper men."

February 23 Premier W.A.C. Bennett opened a new school for the blind at Jericho (an extension of the existing school for the deaf and blind, which had been renamed Jericho Hill School in 1955).

February 24 William Culham Woodward died in Hawaii, aged 71. He was born April 24, 1885, in Gore Bay on Manitoulin Island, ON. At age 16 William was working for $15 a month as a Royal Bank clerk, but in 1908 he joined his father's department store, Woodward's, as bookkeeper. He served with the First Canadian Heavy Artillery in World War I before returning to the store. After his father died in 1937, William and his brother Percival Archibald Woodward ran the chain, with William as president. He was also BC's Lieutenant-Governor from 1941 to 1946. William's son Charles "Chunky" Woodward became president of Woodward's in 1956.

February 26 G.F. Strong, heart specialist, died in Montreal while en route to a meeting of the National Heart Foundation. It was four days after his 60th birthday. George Frederic Strong was born February 22, 1897, in St. Paul, MN. He interned at Vancouver General Hospital (1922–23), then served on its staff for the next 34 years. He was chair of the VGH medical board and a founder of the BC Cancer Foundation, the Western Society for Rehabilitation, BC Medical Research Institute, Vancouver Community Chest and the Family Welfare Bureau. G.F. Strong Centre in Vancouver is named for him.

April 15

A 14-square-kilometre (5.5-square-mile) chunk of South Surrey seceded as White Rock was incorporated.

It was named for a large white granite rock on the beach, a relic of the Ice Age.

May 1 BC Breweries became Carling Breweries (BC) Ltd. Two years later it became part of the Carling organization, with its head office in Toronto.

Elsewhere in BC

April 7 John Hart, financier and BC premier (1941–47), died in Victoria. He was Liberal MLA for Victoria City from 1916 to 1949 (except for a period from 1924 to 1933 when he did not run, for business reasons), was finance minister (1917–24 and 1933–47) and after World War II initiated a program of rural electrification and highway building, establishing the BC Power Commission (BC Hydro's forerunner). The Hart Highway from Prince George to Dawson Creek, was named for him.

Elsewhere in Canada

June 10 John Diefenbaker's Progressive Conservatives unexpectedly defeated Louis St-Laurent's Liberals in the federal election, forming a minority government. Less than a year later, Diefenbaker called a snap election and on March 31, 1958, the Tories won the largest landslide in Canadian history.

Elsewhere in the World

March 6 Ghana became independent, the first country in sub-Saharan Africa to do so.

June 27 Writer Malcolm Lowry (who had written much of his acclaimed novel *Under the Volcano* in Dollarton, on the north shore of Burrard Inlet) died, aged 47, in Ripe, Sussex, England, of an overdose of sleeping tablets. He was buried in the graveyard of the village church.

September 21 The TV series *Perry Mason*, starring New Westminster-born Raymond Burr, began on CBS-TV with "The Case of the Moth-eaten Mink." The series was immensely popular and ran for nine years.

October 4 The Soviet Union launched *Sputnik* and the space race.

Not local, but enlightening: in 1957 in the King County area of Washington state, nearly half of all workers in the county were employed in aerospace manufacturing related to the Boeing company!

The first Chinese Canadian MP in this country's history, Douglas Jung was elected by Vancouver Centre in 1957 and through re-election served until 1962. A Conservative in protest against the Liberals for their past racist legislation, Jung was also a Second World War veteran, a lawyer and a campaigner for enfranchisement. Vancouver Sun

May 3 The first person to be flown to the heliport atop the new main post office (still being built) was James Sinclair, the fisheries minister. He was met by Prime Minister Louis St-Laurent. The heliport was later closed: the aircraft were deemed too heavy for the roof.

May 26 Percy Norman, swimmer and swimming coach, died in Vancouver, aged 53. Born March 14, 1904, in New Westminster, Norman started his career as a promising marathon swimmer but chose to coach instead. He was considered Canada's top swimming and diving coach for many years, coaching the Canadian swim teams for the 1936 Olympic and 1954 British Empire and Commonwealth Games, winning six medals. He was the head coach of the Vancouver Amateur Swim Club at Crystal Pool from 1931 to 1955. Norman was inducted into the BC Sports Hall of Fame in 1967, and many of the swimmers he coached are also members of the hall. In 1960 the Vancouver Park Board named a pool for him at Riley Park.

May Pacific Press Ltd. was established in response to the rising costs of producing newspapers.

Management at the *Vancouver Sun* and the *Province* reached a deal to merge their mechanical and financial departments, a move that had been happening in two-newspaper cities all over North America. The papers were now produced in a single shared plant in the Sun Tower. Administrative offices were in the *Province*'s building at Victory Square. Federal regulators investigated the arrangement under the Combines Investigation Act and found it illegal but decided to allow it for economic reasons. The papers remained autonomous, and the *Province*, owned by Southam, became a morning daily. The *Sun* continued to appear as an evening paper for, successively, Sun Publishing, FP Publications and, briefly, Thomson Newspapers before it was also purchased by Southam in 1980.

June 10 Douglas Jung, born February 24, 1924, was elected to Parliament from Vancouver Centre, the first Chinese Canadian MP. Shortly after, Prime Minister John Diefenbaker appointed him to represent Canada at the United Nations as chair of the Canadian Legal Delegation. On September 7, 2007, a federal government building at the corner of West Pender and Burrard Street was named for him.

June 15 The final issue of the *Vancouver News-Herald* appeared. It had begun publishing in 1933.

July 1 The four-lane Oak Street Bridge on Route 99 opened to traffic. It became a vital link between Vancouver and Richmond and, along with the Middle Arm Bridge, replaced the old Marpole swing bridge over the North Arm of the Fraser. After the bridge opened, traffic began to move several blocks to the east and the business districts along Hudson Street and Marine Drive went into a swift decline. Tolls came off the bridge in 1959.

July 16 The *Sun* reported the death of Major John R. Grant, designer of the Granville and Burrard Street Bridges. He was 78. Grant was born in Elora, ON, and came to Vancouver after service in World War I. "In 1910," said the *Sun*, "he submitted his first design for a Burrard Street bridge, but the project was rejected on a civic plebiscite...He was designing engineer of the Seymour dam, Vancouver Heights reservoir, Vancouver Block and the Dominion Trust building." The Burrard Street Bridge was okayed in 1930 and Grant got the commission. The bridge opened

Behind the Glass Curtain

November 1 The Vancouver Public Library opened its new main branch at Burrard and Robson. The sleek, modernist structure was Vancouver's first glass curtain building, designed by architects H.N. Semmens and D.C. Simpson. It was awarded the Massey Medal, Canada's highest architectural honour.

The location was criticized by some at the time because of the lack of foot traffic, but almost from the beginning the building was too small. Designed to accommodate 750,000 volumes, with seating for 300 patrons, the branch soon had more than 5,000 patrons a day scrambling for the scarce chairs. And despite using the auditorium, several meeting rooms and much of the seating space for shelving, nearly a third of the collection was stored in the basement. However, the building served until May 1995, when the current main branch opened.

Tragically, the city's chief librarian since 1924, Edgar Stewart Robinson, who had campaigned for a new library for many years, died a week before it opened.

Showcase. Vancouver's award-winning new main library building, opened in 1957, was also Vancouver's first glass-curtain building. It remained open until 1995, when it was replaced by the current Central branch. *PNG*

July 1, 1932. "Highlight of the career of the slightly-built, gray-haired designer," the *Sun* concluded, "was the acceptance in 1949 of his plan for the new Granville Bridge, which cost $16.5 million."

August 17 The *Vancouver Sun* reported that American tourists were griping about the money exchange rate: they lost 5 and a half cents every time they cashed in a dollar!

August 26 The one-way street came to downtown Vancouver today. "Police and city traffic department officials worked feverishly to instal signs, paint traffic lines and tear down the temporary sign covers," and the *Province* predicted a great test of the system "when one of the greatest crowds in city history—100,000—packs Exhibition Park tonight and then heads home on unfamiliar one-way streets. B.C. Lions expect 25,000 for the game with Calgary Stampeders at Empire Stadium. An estimated 50,000 will attend the PNE and another 10,000 will watch racing." No special problems ensued, and no accidents were reported.

September 20 Julius Harold Bloedel died in Seattle, aged 93. He was born in March 1864 in Fond du Lac, WI. At age 17 he entered civil engineering but left due to money problems. He worked on a Wisconsin railway, then developed real estate in Sheboygan. With a $10,000 profit, he moved west in 1886. In 1890 he started Samish Logging in Bellingham Bay, WA. In 1911 Bloedel began logging in BC. He retired in May 1942 as president of Bloedel, Stewart & Welch in favour of his son Prentice Bloedel, but continued as board chair. In 1951 his company merged with that of H.R. MacMillan. His archives were donated to the University of British Columbia.

October 11 Earlier this year Anglican priest Stanley Higgs told the newspapers that general manager Cedric Tallis of the Vancouver Mounties baseball club would be in contempt of law if he pursued Sunday ball games. Sure enough, the Mounties were found guilty today and fined for playing baseball on Sunday.

November 2 The Steveston Community Centre was officially opened by Reeve E.R. Parsons and Leslie Peterson, provincial minister of education. The Steveston Community Society had worked tirelessly for 10 years to raise over $40,000 for the building. The Steveston Japanese Benevolent Society contributed $15,000 from monies received for the forced sale of the Japanese Hospital, the Gyosha Dantai offices and the Japanese Language School. The Japanese community requested that there be a dedicated room for judo and kendo.

December 8 George Henry Keefer died at Cobble Hill on Vancouver Island, aged about 92. He was born in 1865 in Bowling Green, ON. Keefer was prominent in BC railway construction for 50 years. In 1886 he cleared the CPR right-of-way from Port Moody to English Bay, mostly with the help of Stikine Indians. On June 12, 1886, looking for a campsite near today's Granville Bridge, he saw some dry brush and set it on fire to clean it up. On June 13, the "Great Fire" levelled Vancouver. He admitted his mistake many years later. (Some say this story is apocryphal.) Keefer Street in Chinatown is named for him.

December 9 William Grafton died in West Vancouver, aged 89. He was born February 6, 1868, in London, England, and came to Vancouver with two brothers in 1885. One of Bowen Island's first settlers, he launched the first Howe Sound ferry service around 1887 with a four-ton sloop. Grafton Lake and Grafton Bay are named for him.

Also in 1957

The Vancouver Police Department dog squad began with four dogs. Today all training for the squad is carried out in the city and by their own experts. The team's expertise has been recognized by other police forces in BC and the western US, which send their dogs and handlers to Vancouver for training.

A Mosquito Control Board was formed in Surrey. "The mosquitoes are still fighting back," an official reported.

An industrial area was zoned near Newton. North Surrey, where berry and chicken farms had formerly flourished, became almost all residential.

Numbered streets came to Surrey, consecutively upward from the 49th parallel. There is a "0" (Zero) Avenue in Surrey, right on the US border. Step off into the bush on the south side of 0 Avenue and you're in Washington. Lost in the conversion were many street names of historical interest, but it became a lot easier for people to find their way around this big city. Covering 317.40 square kilometres (122.5 square miles), it's the largest city in the BC Lower Mainland, with the second largest population (470,000 in 2010).

The Upper Levels Highway was completed on the North Shore.

The Vancouver Museum moved into the old Carnegie Library building when the new library moved into its new building.

Burnaby's Historical Society was formed and became the driving

Still a feature on the corner of Main and Hastings, the Carnegie building became the new home for the Vancouver Museum after the Vancouver Public Library moved to its new building in 1957. The museum moved to Vanier Park in 1967, and the Carnegie building went on to become a much-needed community centre. Vancouver Sun

Right: Moored at the mouth of the Fraser River for more than four decades, the *Sandheads No. 16* served as a sort of floating lighthouse, alerting boats to the location of the shifting sands of the delta. It was retired in 1957 after repairs were deemed too expensive, and sunk in 2002 after the Maritime Museum was unable to raise the necessary funds for restoration.
Vancouver Sun

force behind the creation of the city archives, museum and Heritage Advisory Committee.

The Nakade Boat Works was the most prolific in Steveston during the 1950s and 1960s, launching up to 10 boats a year.

The *Sandheads No. 16* lightship, at the mouth of the Fraser since 1913, ended its service. It was said to be the last 19th-century sailing ship on Canada's West Coast, and in 1978 it was purchased by the Vancouver Maritime Museum. However, the ship was riddled with dry-rot, and after several valiant but unsuccessful attempts to raise funds for restoration, it sank in False Creek in 2002 and was broken up by city workers.

Orville Fisher's mural, featuring the figure of Mercury, god of messages and glad tidings, was completed in the interior of the main post office, by the Homer Street entrance.

Wilfred John "Bill" Duthie, bookseller, opened Duthie Books at the northwest corner of Robson and Hornby. It speedily became the best-known bookstore in western Canada. Duthie had come to Vancouver in 1952 as the first regional book representative on the West Coast. An innovator, he dedicated an entire floor in his new store to paperback books, a marketing move unprecedented at the time. He was especially encouraging to emerging Canadian writers. The Bill Duthie Memorial Lecture is delivered annually at the Vancouver International Writers Festival. Born April 8, 1920, in Weston, ON, he died the day before his 64th birthday, sorely missed by the reading and writing fraternity. Duthie Books closed its last store in February 2010.

Bill Duthie, Vancouver bookseller extraordinaire, surrounded by his stock in this 1984 portrait, taken shortly before his death. Duthie opened his first store and revolutionized bookselling in Vancouver in 1957.
Steve Bosch / Vancouver Sun

The Quilchena Golf Course was opened to provide a place for Jewish golfers to play. They had been denied entry to other clubs.

Four parks in Vancouver were purchased through a bequest in the will of Harvey Hadden, who had died in England in 1931. The parks were on Georgia, Adanac, Woodland and McLean.

Comings and Goings

June 15 Malcolm Peter McBeath, mayor of Vancouver from 1915 to 1917, died, aged 76.

August 31 Elvis Presley performed one song at a packed Empire Stadium but left the stage when fans begin to battle with police. He returned to sing four more songs, none of which could be heard over the screaming. The next day, Presley's manager, Colonel Tom Parker, happily read aloud to the media a local newspaper account of the riot.

1958

British Columbia celebrated 100 years since the founding of the mainland colony of British Columbia. The festivities were tempered with tragedy as 19 people died when the under-construction Second Narrows Bridge collapsed. Both the historic ferry service to North Vancouver and the rail service to southern suburbs ended, but locals could now attend professional sports events on Sundays. And Vancouver became home to Canada's biggest roller coaster, a literal symbol of the year's ups and downs.

January 1 David Jones Greenlees was born in Richmond at 1:01 a.m. To mark the event the city named Greenlees Street in 1959.

January 9 J.V. Clyne was named chairman of MacMillan Bloedel, the giant forestry company, replacing H.R. MacMillan. Clyne had earlier resigned as a judge on the BC Supreme Court.

January 16 The *Sun* reported that Boyd Haskell, a 43-year-old Simpsons-Sears executive (he was the general manager of the Burnaby store), had been named president of the Greater Vancouver Tourist Association, succeeding George Bradley, president of Home Oil Distributors Ltd. The *Sun* also reported that "the association will spend $3,500 this year on a survey and analysis of its entire activities and workings." A few months later, on March 21, the *Province* reported that President Haskell had asked the City of Vancouver to increase its grant to the association from $40,000 to $75,000.

January The Esco Company of Oregon established its first Canadian alloy steel foundry in Port Coquitlam—the plant's accessibility to the CPR mainline facilitated the export of the finished product.

Also January Lots in the first subdivision at Lions Bay went on sale, and Charles and Mary Coltart started building the first home this spring. Development of this community 11 kilometres (7 miles) north of Horseshoe Bay was the dream of R.A. "Bob" Nelson, who bought land here in 1956. The dream became possible thanks to the completion of the Pacific Great Eastern (today BC Rail) line from West Vancouver to Squamish in 1956 and the construction of the Seaview (today Sea-to-Sky) Highway in 1958.

Also January Louie Gim "Gum" Sing (also known as Loy Sum Sing), a pioneer Chinese builder, died in Vancouver at 107. He was born June 6, 1850, in China and left a job in Hong Kong to work as the foreman of a CPR Chinese crew, arriving in Victoria on June 25, 1884. He helped lay the last track into Vancouver, survived the Great Fire and helped rebuild the city. He was noted for his great strength and education, and for fighting to preserve the rights of Chinese workers before the courts. In later years he took up truck farming on Lulu Island before settling in Chinatown.

February 28

The famed "interurban" tram lines had their final run today on the region's last remaining route, from Marpole to Steveston. According to Henry Ewert, BC Electric Railway historian, the last regularly scheduled train (whether single or multiple cars, they were always known as trains), consisting of car No. 1225, left Marpole at 12:30 a.m. The car was full, most of the passengers (Ewert included) being railway buffs. The same car made the last northbound return trip, leaving Steveston at 1:00 a.m., with a 1:30 a.m. arrival at Marpole. The passengers got off and the car went to the Kitsilano carbarn (under the south approach of the Burrard Bridge) for the last time, running along what we know today as the Arbutus corridor. Later the same day the interurban came to life again for a *ceremonial* last run. Two trains of two cars each made one last round trip, leaving Marpole at 11:00 a.m. Passengers were invited guests and municipal and BCE officials. The return trip paused at Brighouse for a luncheon hosted by the utility. After passengers were let off in Marpole, the

Elsewhere in BC

April 5 Ripple Rock was blown up. The twin peaks of Ripple Rock, lurking just below the surface of the waters in Seymour Narrows, north of Campbell River, had caused the sinking of more than 100 ships and the loss of more than 100 lives. The blast that blew the rock's top off was the largest non-nuclear explosion to that time.

July 1 Premier W.A.C. Bennett announced that BC would establish its own ferry service between Vancouver Island and the mainland. The move was prompted by labour strife in both the Black Ball and Canadian Pacific ferry systems.

Ritchie Bros., now the world's leading industrial auctioneer, held its first auction sale in a Kelowna, BC, Boy Scouts hall.

Elsewhere in Canada

Canadian Pacific Airlines became a jet airline when it bought turboprop Bristol Britannias.

Elsewhere in the World

January 31 Stung by the success of *Sputnik* (launched by the Soviet Union on October 4, 1957) the US launched its first satellite.

two trains made their way back to the Kitsilano carbarn, arriving at 3:00 p.m. The overhead trolley wires were removed in 1959 and more diesels were purchased. Those shiny new (in 1958!) diesel locomotives took over the BCER freight duties, and diesel buses of the company's intercity bus division, Pacific Stage Lines, began to handle passenger traffic.

February After seven years of negotiations, 110 owner-drivers of the Yellow, Star and Checker cab companies bought the 85-car Yellow Cabs Company Ltd.

March 12 Gordon Farrell, president of BC Telephone Company for 30 years, stepped down and was succeeded by Cyrus H. McLean.

March 14 The present main post office (architect Bill Leithead) opened at 349 West Georgia. Public Works Minister Howard Green and Postmaster-General William Hamilton jointly officiated. Hamilton arrived in a helicopter that landed on the rooftop heliport. The $13-million building, more formally known as the Vancouver Mail Processing Plant, was, at the time, the largest welded steel structure in the world.

April 19 Professional baseball tickets were sold on Sunday for the first time in Vancouver, at Capilano Stadium. On April 28 the Supreme Court of Canada upheld BC's approval of a Vancouver City Charter bylaw amendment permitting Sunday sports. Newspapers called it the end of the biggest public issue of the decade.

April Ladner was connected to Lulu Island via the Deas Island Tunnel (later renamed the George Massey Tunnel). Six sections comprising 663 metres (over 2,170 feet) of concrete and steel were sunk to construct the tunnel, which was opened to traffic later in the spring. The official opening was July 15, 1959. Until this time, river crossings were made via the Ladner–Woodward's Landing Ferry. Within 20 years after the opening of the tunnel, Delta's population had increased by 400 percent, and Ladner's Landing was turned from a rural enclave into a busy townlet.

May 28 The P&O liner *Chusan* arrived in Vancouver. One observer noted it was a historic event, re-establishing passenger vessel links with Asia that had lapsed for almost 20 years since the last voyages of the great CPR Empress liners. It was a big year for the late Dean Miller, who was retained as public relations representative for P&O. Dean first made his mark in the industry in 1954 when he represented a P&O subsidiary, the Orient Line, whose famous "O Boats"—*Oronsay*, *Orcades* and *Orsova*—included Vancouver in their Pacific itineraries. (P&O acquired 100 percent of the shares of the Orient Line in 1965 and retired the name). After P&O established Vancouver as a regular port in 1958, Dean made the maiden visit of each ship an extraordinary local event, and he eventually became synonymous with the industry itself. By the time of his death in 1997, Vancouver had become not merely a "port of call" but also one of the international cruise industry's principal ports of embarkation.

Disaster struck in 1958 when an accident caused several spans to fall during the building of the Second Narrows Bridge. In total, 19 people died and 20 were injured, leading the bridge to be renamed in 1994 the Ironworkers Memorial Second Narrows Crossing.
Ralph Bower / Vancouver Sun

June 17 The new Second Narrows Bridge collapsed during construction. Eighteen workmen and one rescue worker died and 20 more were injured. On June 17, 1994, the bridge was renamed in honour of these men and others who had worked on it. This bridge is now officially the Ironworkers Memorial Second Narrows Crossing.

July 13 The 100th anniversary of the creation of the (mainland) colony of British Columbia.

Among the centennial projects were the Maritime Museum and the Queen Elizabeth Theatre, which both opened in 1959. Mungo Martin, Henry Hunt and David Martin carved a 30.5-metre-high (100-foot) Kwakiutl totem pole. The original was presented to Queen Elizabeth II and stands in England's Windsor Great Park, while a duplicate pole was raised in Vancouver's Hadden Park, in front of the Maritime Museum. Some of the centennial events: 8,000 people celebrated at a barbecue atop Burnaby Mountain (a pavilion was built there as a centennial project); the Vancouver International Festival, a world-class performing arts showcase mixing local and international acts, became an annual event for the next decade.

August 13 The park board closed Vancouver beaches because of pollution.

August 30 Ferry service between Vancouver and North Vancouver ended, until the start-up of the SeaBus 19 years later. *North Vancouver Ferry No. 5*, built in False Creek in 1941 as the last car ferry for the North Vancouver ferry system, became the Seven Seas Restaurant. By the time the fondly recalled ferry service ended, it had carried more than 112 million passengers.

September 9 An exaltation of archbishops and bishops pitched in to put the finishing touches on the brand-new St. Mark's College on the UBC campus. Operated by the Basilian Fathers, St. Mark's was the first Roman Catholic college of university level in Vancouver.

September 10 The *Province* reported that "proposals for developing Tsawwassen Beach as the mainland terminus of the projected new Vancouver Island–Lower Mainland ferry service have been forwarded to the provincial government." The proposals included "a boat harbor and public beach. Site is on the Gulf of Georgia, about four miles (6.4 km) north of Point Roberts." The paper also said that Swartz Bay was one favoured Vancouver Island base.

October 5 The Surrey Centennial Museum opened. W.E. Ireland, provincial archivist, was there with his wife, a descendant of Eric Anderson, a Surrey pioneer whose log cabin is now part of the museum.

October The Hula Hoop craze hit Vancouver.

December 30 From Wilf Bennett's column in the *Province*:

> A Canadian on holiday in Paris was trying out his French in a restaurant.
>
> "Hi, garsong," he said after a lengthy study of the menu, "je desir Consomme Royal et un piece de pang et burr . . . no, dang it, half a minute! A piece of bang."
>
> The waiter said helpfully, "I'm sorry, sir, I don't speak French."
>
> "Very well," said the diner irritably, "for heaven's sake send me someone who can."

High roller. Playland's most popular roller coaster made its debut in 1958, designed by Carl Phare and built with Douglas fir. While it is certainly not the fastest or biggest coaster around, it more than makes up for that with ambience and thrills. *Vancouver Public Library, Special Collections, VPL 68820. Province newspaper photo*

December 31 A tunnel under Burrard Inlet? What a clever idea! Budgeted at $150 million, the idea was proposed to Vancouver City Council by Ald. Halford Wilson. The tunnel, conceived by the engineering firm H.H. Minshall and Associates, would run for 4.3 kilometres (2.7 miles) from a point on the North Shore about 800 metres (half a mile) east of Lions Gate Bridge to come out on False Creek flats just south of the Georgia Street Viaduct. Highways Minister Phil Gaglardi called the proposal a "pipe dream."

Also in 1958

The Buchanan Building—officially opened by Premier W.A.C. Bennett—became the new home of the liberal arts at UBC. The name honoured the late dean of arts and sciences, Daniel Buchanan, who died in 1950.

The largest roller coaster in Canada was built at the PNE grounds.

Shaughnessy Golf Course negotiated with the Department of Indian Affairs for a long-term lease of part of the Musqueam Indian Reserve. The Musqueam protested the terms when they learned of them, and in 1985 a Supreme Court of Canada decision upheld a $10-million award to the band because the department had not acted in the best interests of the Natives.

The Tunnel Town Curling Club opened four sheets of ice in a Boundary Bay air hangar.

The West Vancouver Recreation Centre opened at 780 22nd St.

In a poll taken on the North Shore, people in all three municipalities overwhelmingly supported building a new hospital. Lions Gate Hospital opened April 22, 1961.

Provincial birthplace. Designated a site of provincial and national importance as the "birthplace of British Columbia," Fort Langley—including the Big House pictured here—was restored in time for the BC Centennial celebrations in 1958. *Fort Langley National Historic Site*

A treehouse built by gently eccentric deaf twins Peter (1872–1949) and David Brown (1872–1958) on their heavily treed property in Surrey was demolished. They had lived in the treehouse for many years. A replacement of a quite different (more formal) design was installed. The twins planted many different kinds of trees on their property...more different kinds of trees, in fact, than existed anywhere else in BC. They left 24 hectares (59 acres) to Surrey, which turned the property into the charming Redwood Park.

Fred Steiner sold his Toronto radio store and moved to Vancouver. He opened a shop here and called it A&B Sound. Why A&B? A&A was taken. True story. He soon added music to the radios, televisions and stereos on sale, and by the 1980s A&B was known for having the best selection and lowest prices on records, cassettes and CDs in western Canada. In 2008 the company, which at its height owned more than 20 stores, went out of business.

Labatt's acquired Lucky Lager Breweries; Molson's bought out the American-owned Sick's brewery and became a major player in BC, with a plant at the south end of Burrard Bridge.

Thomas Reid, who in 1937 as the Liberal MP for New Westminster (1930–49) helped form the Fisheries Commission, and who was devoted to rehabilitation of the Fraser salmon run, was credited with the river's best run this year since 1905. BC packed more than a million cases.

Bill and Alice McConnell founded Klanak Press to produce quality limited editions of works by Canadian writers.The press emphasized design and typography as much as the writing and published a dozen books over the next 14 years by such authors as Marya Fiamengo, Ralph Gustafson, Anne Hébert, F.R. Scott and Jane Rule.

Radio CKWX started a locally shaped hit parade ("The Sensational Sixty"), the first in the city. Vancouver's hits were often different from those that appeared in *Billboard* and other trade publications, driven by the tastes of our own DJs like Dave "Big Daddy" McCormick and Red Robinson.

Comings and Goings

January 28 Queen Elizabeth, the Queen Mother, visited Vancouver briefly en route to New Zealand and Australia.

March 13 Prime Minister John Diefenbaker spoke to 8,500 people during an election rally at the Forum.

July 23 Princess Margaret visited. While here she opened the reconstructed Fort Langley.

July 28 Jazz giant Jack Teagarden recorded an album at the Orpheum Theatre. Its title: *Muskrat Ramble.*

August 4 The Oscar Peterson trio (Oscar Peterson, piano; Ray Brown, bass; and Herb Ellis, guitar) played a gig at the Orpheum Theatre. The concert was recorded, but the album wasn't released until 2003!

Notable deaths: **Henry "Harry" Frederick Reifel**, farmer and builder/owner (with his brother George) of the Commodore Block on Granville and the Vogue and Studio Theatres, in Vancouver on July 20, aged 62; **George James Bury**, CPR pioneer who rose from junior clerk to vice-president over a 40-year career, in Vancouver on July 20, aged 92 (he was knighted in 1917 for his service to the British war cabinet); **Frank Ross Begg**, Vancouver's first auto dealer, in Vancouver on September 16; **Russell Francis Baker**, pioneer bush pilot and founder of Pacific Western Airlines, in West Vancouver on November 15, aged 48.

Tim Cummings, the last aboriginal resident of Stanley Park, also died this year.

1959

Vancouver got its first shopping centre and the Queen Elizabeth Theatre, while the Queen herself came to town to open the Deas Island Tunnel. The city also became a tabloid dateline when 50-year-old actor Errol Flynn, a teenage girl in tow, died here. Sprinter Harry Jerome, meanwhile, broke his first world record, and golfer Stan Leonard was named "World Golfer of the Year."

January A four-day Chinese New Year celebration was held in Vancouver's Chinatown, sponsored by Chinese Canadian businessmen.

Also in January The *British Columbia Medical Journal* began publication.

March 16 The first ship to dock at Vancouver's brand-new Centennial Pier, operated by the National Harbours Board, was the *Lake Atlin*.

March Erwin Swangard was appointed managing editor of the *Vancouver Sun*. Swangard, who was born in Munich in 1908 and came to Canada in 1930, had worked for both the *Province* and the *Sun*.

May 6 Oakridge opened at Cambie Street and West 41st Avenue, the first shopping centre in the city. West Van's Park Royal had opened in 1950.

May 15
Vancouver's Harry Jerome broke the world record for the 220-yard dash, which had been set 31 years earlier by Percy Williams, also of Vancouver.

June 11 The Vancouver Maritime Museum opened.

June The University of British Columbia opened a new faculty club and social centre built with a gift from Mrs. Thea and Dr. Leon J. Koerner. The architect was Fred Lasserre, a UBC professor of architecture. As the campus residence for visiting royalty, the club has been honoured by the presence of both Queen Elizabeth and Prince Charles. Built at a cost of $750,000, the faculty club had both public and private dining rooms, a reading room, lounges, a music room, a snack bar, a games room and four salons. It was the centre of social activity for UBC faculty. Faced with financial insolvency, however, the club closed its doors in 1994. Five years later it sprang back to life as the Leon and Thea Koerner University Centre.

July 5 The Queen Elizabeth Theatre opened.

July 15 The *Delta Princess* made her last 10-minute run from Woodward's Landing in Richmond to Ladner. The construction of the Deas Island Tunnel made the service redundant.

Shopping first. Sitting pretty in its vast expanse of blacktop, the Oakridge Shopping Centre opened in 1959, the first such shopping centre in Vancouver. Vancouver Province

Elsewhere in BC

The Union Steamship Company, active in BC from the days of the Fraser River gold rush, was absorbed by Northland Navigation Company.

Elsewhere in Canada

May 4 Canadian Pacific Airlines started a trans-Canada service, Montreal to Vancouver.

June 26 Queen Elizabeth II and US president Dwight Eisenhower opened the St. Lawrence Seaway.

The death penalty was abolished in Canada.

Elsewhere in the World

January 3 Alaska became a state.

May 5 Lynn Seymour danced the lead in the Royal Ballet's *Swan Lake*. She also became a principal dancer in that British company. Born Lynn Springbett on March 8, 1939, in Wainwright, AB, Seymour had begun her training in Vancouver.

September 14 A Russian rocket hit the moon, the first time a human-made object had touched an extraterrestrial body.

November 16 *The Sound of Music* premiered on Broadway.

The Barbie doll was introduced.

July Westwood Motorsport Park opened in Coquitlam, at the time the only European-style racetrack in Canada. For 31 years the track hosted local, national and international motor racers. It closed in 1990 when the provincial government sold the land for residential development.

September 24 New Westminster mayor Beth Wood was presented with a gold key to the city of Long Beach, CA, to commemorate a softball contest between the two cities. "A great many people didn't seem to know where New Westminster is," Mayor Wood later told a laughing New Westminster council, "but they placed it soon enough after I told them that Vancouver was one of our suburbs."

October 11 William Harold Malkin, mayor of Vancouver in 1929 and 1930, died, aged 91. He was born July 30, 1868, in Burslem, Staffordshire, England. As mayor, Malkin established a committee to look into corruption and embezzlement in the city's Relief Department and worked to bring about changes in civic policy to benefit the working class. He later donated a 2.4-hectare (6-acre) park behind his Kerrisdale home to the city, as well as the money for construction of Malkin Bowl in Stanley Park, the latter dedicated to his late wife Marion.

Seen here under construction, the Deas Island Tunnel between Richmond and Ladner was officially opened in 1959 by Queen Elizabeth II. (It was later renamed the George Massey Tunnel after its main proponent.) Long considered impossible to build, the tunnel ended up being built on time and with one of the best safety records in BC. *PNG*

The Queen Buys Some Scissors

July 15 The Deas Island Tunnel (later renamed the George Massey Tunnel) was officially opened by Queen Elizabeth and Premier W.A.C. Bennett. Her Majesty participated in an ancient and curious ceremony with Premier Bennett: the premier handed the queen a costly pair of silver scissors, and she gave him a dime for them. The coin-for-scissors trade is an old British custom, which holds that if the giver of a cutting implement does not receive a coin in return, the friendship between the giver and the receiver will be cut.

The Queen and Prince Philip were busy during their brief visit here. Her Majesty also "graciously assented" to having the Queen Elizabeth Theatre named for her, then popped over to Victoria for a civic luncheon. There the royal couple met Archbishop William Mark Duke. Prince Philip was photographed shaking hands with him, inspiring the caption "Duke Meets Duke."

One unforeseen result of the tunnel opening: there was a sudden upsurge in visits by Canadians to Point Roberts, the tiny chunk of Washington state that, thanks to the 49th parallel, is accessible by land only through Canada. And why were they travelling there in the thousands? Sunday drinking. "Boozing Canadians leave Point Roberts a Hangover," one headline read. A popular bumper sticker read "Sunday Services at the Breakers." (The Breakers was a Point Roberts drinking hole.)

Another note of interest: when you drive through this tunnel under the Fraser River, you're traversing the lowest point on a public road in Canada. The roadbed is 20 metres (65 feet) below sea level.

Left: With flags waving gaily from the *St. Roch*, soon to become a permanent exhibit, children and dignitaries gather for the opening of the Maritime Museum. *Vancouver Maritime Museum*

November 18 Dr. Norman MacKenzie, the president of the University of British Columbia, announced that Leon Koerner, the retired chairman of Alaska Pine and Cellulose Ltd., had given the university $400,000 to pay for the construction of a graduate students' centre. The building, to be called Thea Koerner House in memory of Mr. Koerner's wife, who had died in July, was located on the West Mall, just west of the faculty club. The design, by architects C.E. Pratt and P. Kattfa of Thompson, Berwick & Pratt, won the Massey Gold Medal for Architecture in 1961. Dr. Koerner lived in the penthouse of the building during the summer months from the time the building was completed in 1961 until his death in 1972.

November 26 With CBC Television soon to go on the air in Vancouver, the *Province* ran a multi-page feature on the relatively new medium. One article told how to read a test pattern. "When the larger circle fills the screen and still remains perfectly circular, the largest possible picture is obtained and you still retain the proper aspect ratio (correct height as related to width). If by chance the circles are ovalled, picture distortion is occurring..." and so on and so on for three columns.

Also in 1959

A. Thomas Alsbury became mayor, the first to be born in the 20th century. He beat Fred Hume, who had held the position since 1951, by 11,000 votes.

Major league baseball player Brooks Robinson, born in Little Rock, AR, in 1937, was sent down to the Triple-A Vancouver Mounties by the Baltimore Orioles. "They sent me to Vancouver in the Pacific Coast League," Robinson later recalled. "I was shocked. That was the only time I was ever frustrated in baseball. My ego was really hurt...Yet it turned out to be the best thing that could have happened to me. I did very well at Vancouver and was brought back at the All Star break. And it was like night and day. I could hit! I had more confidence and I had gotten stronger physically, so I was no longer overmatched." Called the "ultimate third baseman" and the "human vacuum cleaner," Robinson was elected to the Baseball Hall of Fame in 1983, the only member of the hall to play for a Vancouver team.

Stan Leonard, once the pro at the Marine Drive Golf Club, was named World Golfer of the Year by the Golf Writers' Association in the US, the only Canadian to be so honoured.

More than 1,000 people attended the funeral of Andy Paull, Squamish leader, at St. Paul's Indian Catholic Church on the Mission Reserve in North Vancouver. Paull was active for many years in the fight for Native land claims and was the founder of the North American Indian Brotherhood.

St. Paul's Boarding School on the Mission Reserve in North Vancouver, consecrated January 22, 1899, by Bishop Durieu, was demolished. A residence for Native girls, Durieu Convent, was built next to St. Paul's Indian Catholic Church. It was demolished in October 1982.

The largest Catholic church in Vancouver, Our Lady of Sorrows, was built at 555 South Slocan St. The crest of the Servite Fathers was set in the floor of the sanctuary to honour the parish's founding fathers.

Dr. Harold Rice at St. Paul's Hospital built Canada's first heart-lung machine.

The BC Women's Hospital and Health Centre, at 4490 Oak St., had a new 99-bed wing officially opened by Lieutenant-Governor Frank Ross. Surrey Memorial Hospital opened, as did the Centennial Pavilion of

Vancouver General Hospital and the Centennial Wing at Burnaby Hospital.

VanCity Credit Union offered Canada's first open mortgage (a mortgage that can be prepaid or renegotiated at any time without financial penalty).

Chief Dan George (birth name: Teswahno) began his acting career at age 60. He appeared in the first production of *The Ecstasy of Rita Joe* by George Ryga (1967). His funny and dignified performance in the 1970 film *Little Big Man* earned him an Oscar nomination.

William Dale, director of the Vancouver Art Gallery, announced that there were only two or three works of art worthy of the name in the gallery's permanent collection. William Jarvis, a former National Gallery director, called the VAG's permanent collection, excepting Emily Carr, "pitiful."

Cycle of Flowering, a mural by Jack Shadbolt, was installed in the Queen Elizabeth Theatre restaurant.

Mildred Valley Thornton, artist and writer, stepped down after 16 years as art critic for the *Vancouver Sun*.

Phil Thomas, BC's leading folk music historian, and his wife Hilda started the Vancouver Folk Song Circle. Phil Thomas' books include *Songs of the Pacific Northwest* and *Twenty-five Songs for Vancouver, 1886–1986*.

Comings and Goings

February 5 Jennifer Granholm was born in Vancouver. She served as the governor of Michigan from 2002 until 2010.

Charming to the end. A man who was almost always surrounded by admirers, heartthrob Errol Flynn died suddenly in Vancouver at age 50 while visiting a friend. It turned out he had a host of hidden health problems. Vancouver Sun

The Death of Errol Flynn

October 9 Movie actor Errol Flynn arrived in Vancouver as a result of an earlier visit from an old friend, stock promoter George Caldough. Caldough had recently read about an American company that intended, through public subscription of $1.9 million, to finance a deep-sea treasure-hunting expedition off the coast of Spain. Caldough, his brain churning, began thinking about the *Zaca*, with Errol Flynn at the helm, searching for sunken Spanish gold. That would raise one hell of a public subscription.

In a fever of excitement and speculation Caldough flew to Hollywood and met Flynn.

He was shocked by the actor's appearance. As he later wrote in *Weekend Magazine*, "We hadn't met in two years, but he had aged 20...He followed me to Vancouver—accompanied by his 17-year-old friend, Beverly Aadland—after about 10 days. If anything, his appearance had deteriorated and he seemed to need help in just getting around. But his personal charm was unabated."

Flynn was supposed to go to New York for a TV show, but his famed disregard for time was in full flower. The Caldoughs half-heartedly tried for three days to get him on the flight to New York but they kept missing it. Finally—it was October 14, 1959—Flynn said he really did have to go and suggested they leave for the airport three hours early.

En route Flynn began to experience severe pain in his back and legs. Caldough, who was driving, veered off and headed for the West End apartment of a friend, Dr. Grant Gould. Astonishingly, not long after their arrival a few people materialized and another party began!

Flynn, who was standing against a wall to relieve the pain in his back, regaled the group with stories of the Hollywood figures he had known. Then he stopped and announced he was going to lie down for an hour and then would take everyone out for dinner. He moved into the doctor's bedroom and lay down on the floor.

When Beverly Aadland looked in on him a little later to see how he was, she found him trembling, his face blue. She could hardly hear his heart. Her screams brought the doctor...but it was already too late.

The death certificate, dated October 23, indicated myocardial infarction, coronary thrombosis, coronary atherosclerosis, liver degeneration, liver sclerosis and diverticulosis of the colon as the causes of death.

Flynn's autobiography came out that same year. It was titled *My Wicked, Wicked Ways*. They caught up with him in Vancouver. He was 50.

1960-1969

1960

The Vancouver Fire Department faced its largest modern fire when a False Creek sawmill burned. The Second Narrows bridge was opened, and Lord Stanley got a statue in his namesake park, 60 years after it was promised. The Vancouver tradition of open-line radio got its start, as did BCTV.

January 10 Richard Parmater "Parm" Pettipiece, labour union organizer and printer, died in Vancouver, aged about 84. Born in Ontario in 1875, Pettipiece began his printing career in 1890. He started papers in Revelstoke and Ferguson, BC, then came to Vancouver in 1901 and joined the *Province* in 1903, staying until 1954. He was editor of the *BC Federationist*, a labour publication, from 1912 to 1920. He served several terms on city council, and was a director of Vancouver General Hospital for 27 years. Pettipiece was also a four-term president of the International Typographical Union.

January 29 Donna Yee was named Miss Chinatown in the first beauty contest ever held in a Chinese Canadian community.

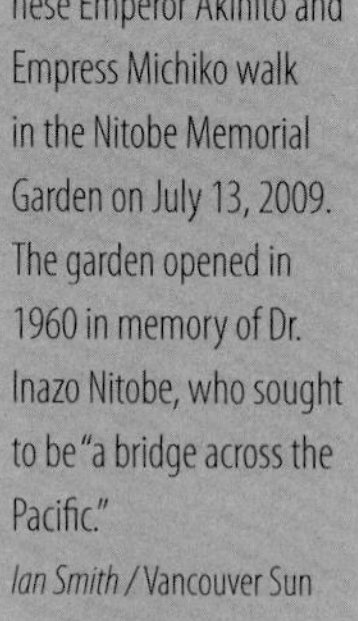

Bridging cultures. Japanese Emperor Akihito and Empress Michiko walk in the Nitobe Memorial Garden on July 13, 2009. The garden opened in 1960 in memory of Dr. Inazo Nitobe, who sought to be "a bridge across the Pacific."
Ian Smith / Vancouver Sun

February The Marco Polo (originally the Forbidden City Nightclub), run by brothers Alex and Hank Louie, opened the first Chinese food smorgasbord. A 10-course dinner cost $1.50. In 1964 the Marco Polo became a popular nightclub, bringing in acts from Las Vegas including Bill Haley, the 5th Dimension, Richard Prior and Pat Paulson.

April 1 Black Top Cabs, with 62 cars in its fleet, merged with 48-car Blue Cab to become the largest taxi operation in western Canada.

April 2 The Vancouver Opera Association, founded in 1959, began its presentations with a production of *Carmen*.

Also April 2 A "Tear It Down" party was held at the Point Grey Golf and Country Club as the old clubhouse was slated to go.

May 3 The Nitobe Memorial Garden was opened at UBC. Named for Dr. Inazo Nitobe, a Japanese international educator and Japanese representative to the League of Nations in the 1920s, it is considered the most authentic Japanese garden outside Japan. It was designed by landscape architect Kanosuke Mori. UBC notes that "the yatsu-hashi bridge in the iris garden has symbolic meaning. According to Japanese legend, devils can walk only in straight lines, so to be rid of the devils following you, you need only cross the zig-zaggy bridge and the devil will fall into the water. Since devils cannot stand the touch of water, you can carry on happily for the rest of your life."

May 19 A statue of Lord Stanley, after whom Stanley Park was named, was unveiled today by Governor General Georges Vanier in the park... and thereby hangs a tale. On October 19, 1889, someone (we're not sure who) wrote a letter promising a suitable monument to commemorate Governor General Lord Stanley's naming and dedication of the park. City archivist J.S. Matthews discovered that letter in 1950, more than 60 years after it was written, and realized the promise had not been fulfilled. So he began a fundraising campaign. It took another 10 years, but finally he raised enough money to commission the work. An observer at the 1889 dedication wrote: "Lord Stanley threw his arms to the heavens, as though embracing...one thousand acres of primeval forest, and dedicated it to the use and enjoyment of peoples of all colours, creeds, and customs, for all time." It was this expansive gesture that English sculptor Sydney Marsh captured.

June 1 Maximilian "Maxie" Michaud, hotelier, died in Langley, aged about 86. He was born about 1874 in Point Levis, QC. Michaud walked here from Montreal. He bought the Brighton Hotel (at the foot of today's Windermere Street in Vancouver) from Oliver Hocking and changed its name to the Hastings Hotel, promising "Travellers can be accommodated at all hours with good beds and meals. A good stock of liquors and cigars." Michaud's hotel—which also served as an early post office—became a popular spot with holidayers from New Westminster. He was "not exactly married" to his companion, Frisadie, who "charm[ed] all sojourners at the 'End of the Road.'"

Elsewhere in BC

June 15 BC Ferries began life officially as "BC Highways and Bridges Toll Authority Ferries." The authority began with two vessels—the MV *Tsawwassen* and the MV *Sidney*—which shuttled on the one route between Tsawwassen and Swartz Bay on Vancouver Island. There were 225 employees. Within a year it took over the Black Ball Ferries operation in Horseshoe Bay.

October 13 George Randolph Pearkes, a soldier who served in both World Wars, was sworn in as BC's Lieutenant-Governor. Pearkes won the Military Cross, the Victoria Cross, the Distinguished Service Order and the French Croix de Guerre in World War I. After World War II he was the MP for Nanaimo (1945–53) and Esquimalt–Saanich (1953–60).

Peter Toigo, Powell River–born entrepreneur, bought downtown Powell River from MacMillan Bloedel and built the town's first shopping centre.

Elsewhere in Canada

June 18 First Nations people won the right to vote in federal elections.

July 15 Running at a meet in Saskatoon for the University of Oregon, Harry Jerome set the world record of 10.0 seconds flat in the 100 metres.

August 10 The federal government proclaimed the Canadian Bill of Rights.

December 5 Canada admitted its two-millionth immigrant since World War II: 16-year-old Anette Toft came from Denmark with her mother and brother to rejoin her father, a dental technician, in Calgary.

Elsewhere in the World

February 1 In Greensboro, NC, four black students began a sit-in at a segregated Woolworth's lunch counter. This was the first of many non-violent protests throughout the US South.

May 1 The Soviet Union shot down a US U-2 spy plane. The pilot, Francis Gary Powers of the CIA, was captured.

August 16 Joseph Kittinger stepped out of a high-altitude balloon over New Mexico and parachuted 31,333 metres (102,800 feet), setting records for the highest-altitude jump, the longest freefall (25.7 kilometres/16 miles before opening his parachute) and the fastest speed attained by a human without motorized assistance (982 km/h or 610 mph). Those records still stand.

July 3 The Vancouver Fire Department battled its first five-alarm fire.

The conflagration destroyed the BC Forest Products plant and lumber storage facility on the south shore of False Creek. All firefighters and every piece of equipment, including both fire boats, tackled the fire. It still took them hours to put it out. Twelve firefighters were injured. One consequence of the fire: it spelled the end for that corner of Vancouver's industrial landscape. The city chose to rezone the land for housing and parks.

August 9 Vancouver experienced the hottest day in its 74-year history. The high was 33.3 degrees.

August 25 Premier W.A.C. Bennett opened the Second Narrows bridge. The cantilevered span of the main arch, at 335 metres (1,100 feet), was at the time the second longest in Canada.

September 22 From sportswriter Clancy Loranger's column in the *Province*: "Monday's meeting of Mounties' shareholders to vote on the sale of the baseball club to Milwaukee was hardly a sweetness and light

Just a couple of weeks shy of Premier W.A.C. Bennett's grand opening of the Second Narrows Bridge, Carl Stanwick (driver), Ben Handreth (resident engineer) and Dan Illingworth are photographed in (and on) the car they took on a trial drive on August 9, 1960. It was the first car to make the crossing. *Province newspaper photo, Vancouver Public Library VPL 39992*

session...There was one impressive bit, though. General manager Bob Freitas pointed it out: Not one shareholder, the so-called 'little guy' who invested his 25 or 50 bucks, asked what would happen to his money. 'Nobody even asked me privately,' said Bob in wonder. 'All they are interested in was keeping baseball here.'"

October 3 Helena Rose Gutteridge, suffragette, feminist, trade unionist, tailor, socialist and politician died in Vancouver, aged about 80. She was born about 1880 in London, England, and came to BC in 1911. She organized the BC Women's Suffrage League. Her interest in the working-class woman led to trade union activities, and she soon took a major role in the Vancouver Trades and Labour Council. Gutteridge joined the Co-operative Commonwealth Federation (CCF), became a champion of affordable housing and in 1937 was elected Vancouver's first woman alderman.

October 28 The Walter Koerner Library opened at UBC.

October 31 At 4:45 p.m. CHAN-TV signed on as Vancouver's first independent TV station, operating out of a temporary location at Richards and Davie Streets until the main studios in Burnaby were completed. The transmitter was on Burnaby Mountain. Initially the signal was poor: although it reached all of downtown Vancouver, it was inferior to that of incumbent stations CBUT (CBC) and KVOS-TV of Bellingham, WA, across the border. Art Jones, a former newspaper photographer, launched the station, which was known as BCTV (1971–2001) and then became Global BC.

December 7 William Carey Ditmars, contractor, died in Vancouver, aged 95. He built the Granville, Cambie and Fraser Street bridges and laid the substructure for Lions Gate Bridge. He received Vancouver's Good Citizen Award in 1928.

December The Lyric Theatre on Granville Street closed. It had opened in 1891 as the Opera House; reopened on March 17, 1913, as the Orpheum (not the present theatre), with vaudeville acts; and opened a third time, on July 26, 1935, as the Lyric with talking pictures.

Also in 1960

During construction of the Trans-Canada Highway through the Fraser Valley, a man named Charlie Perkins stood guard over his ivy-covered fir tree, directly in the path of the new road. He had dedicated the tree to fallen comrades in World War I, and the public outcry resulted in the engineers curving the road around it. That may be a unique circumstance in the construction of a national highway. You can see the curve on the Trans-Canada to this day.

New Westminster built the Queensborough highway bridge over the North Arm of the Fraser, giving the city access to the suburb of Queensborough and the Annacis Industrial Estate. Previously, highway traffic used the BC Electric Railway bridge, built in 1913, which is still used for rail freight service to Annacis Island.

A Lulu Island–Sea Island bridge was demolished this year. This bridge, the first over the Middle Arm of the Fraser, was built at the north end of No. 3 Road, joining Sea Island to the Bridgeport area of Lulu Island, as an extension of the first Marpole Bridge (for road traffic).

Highway 17 to the Tsawwassen ferries opened.

Great Northern Way was named in honour of the railway company that donated much of the land the street is on.

Vancouver police reported that 84 bootleggers were in operation in Vancouver.

The Garibaldi Lift Company was formed to develop Whistler as a ski mountain. There was no road, no hydro, no water supply and no money at the time.

MacLean Park, a block-square park at Union and Jackson, was relocated to the block bounded by Heatley and Hawks Avenues and East Georgia and Keefer Streets. The original had been taken over for Vancouver's first urban renewal housing. Today seniors use the "new" park—where houses, apartments and a bakery once stood—for daily tai chi.

Maple Grove Park (on Yew between West 51st Avenue and Marine Drive) became the site of Vancouver's first recreation program for blind children.

Left: Arch competitor. At the same time that malls were racing to expand, competition for the best lowly grocery store was fierce too. This detached building on Victoria Drive, formerly a Super-Valu store, now a Value Village, was innovative in its use of arches, which allowed for a significantly more open floor plan.
Cristopher Wright

St. Paul's Hospital performed its first open-heart surgery. The hospital also opened BC's first biomedical engineering department.

Grace Hospital, under the direction of the Salvation Army at the time, celebrated its 50,000th birth. (Its 100,000th birth came in 1977 and its 200,000th in 1993, by which time it was the BC Women's Hospital and Health Care Centre.)

The farms at Essondale in Coquitlam were transferred to the control of the BC agriculture ministry.

CKWX started the open-line radio show format so popular in metropolitan Vancouver today. Barrie Clark was an early star.

The United Players were born as the St. James Drama Group, created by the St. James United Church Women. They still perform at the Jericho Arts Centre.

Hy Aisenstat, restaurateur, moved to Vancouver from Calgary and opened Hy's at the Sands. The son of a Russian émigré wholesale grocer in Calgary, Aisenstat and his wife, Barbara, had opened Hy's Steak House in Calgary in 1955 with a $3,000 loan. After his arrival in Vancouver he vastly expanded his restaurant empire.

The average person in the Vancouver area was eating 23 dozen eggs (276) a year in 1960. By 1997 that had dropped to 15 dozen (180).

Blanche Macdonald (née Brillon), entrepreneur and Native rights activist from Alberta, opened a modelling agency and self-improvement school in Vancouver. She later expanded into fashion, esthetics and makeup artistry training, but all this was almost a sideline. Proud of her French Canadian and First Nations heritage, she became CEO of the Native Communications Society of BC, was a founding member of Vancouver's First Woman's Network, and was a board member of the Professional Native Woman's Association and Vancouver Indian Centre as well as the Better Business Bureau and the Modeling Association of America.

Pearl Steen, who had had a distinguished career of public service, was the sole Canadian woman delegate to the UN General Assembly in 1960. She also became the only woman director of the PNE this same year, remaining on the board until 1968.

Comings and Goings

Roy Kenzie Kiyooka arrived in Vancouver to teach painting at the Vancouver School of Art. In the late 1960s he began working in poetry, photography, video, film and music, and by the mid-1970s he was involved in the Japanese Redress movement, which called for recognition of the injustice done to Japanese Canadians during World War II. During this period he was exploring issues of Asian Canadian identity in his art. He taught in the fine arts department at UBC from 1973 to 1991.

Notable deaths: Hockey's Patrick brothers died this year, **Lester Patrick** on June 1, aged 76, and **Frank Patrick** on June 29, aged 74. Both brothers were top defencemen, coaches, administrators and builders, literally and figuratively. They built the first two artificial ice rinks in Canada and also formed the Pacific Coast Hockey Association. They contributed several rules still in use and supported women's hockey. Other deaths: **Eric Hamber**, businessman, philanthropist, Lieutenant-Governor (1936–41) and UBC chancellor (1944–51), died in Vancouver on January 10, aged 79; **James Lyle Telford**, CCF MLA for Vancouver East (1937–39) and former mayor (1939–40), on September 27, aged 71; **J.W.G "Jock" Macdonald**, one of Canada's finest abstract painters, head of design at the Vancouver School of Decorative and Applied Arts (1927–33) and co-founder of the BC College of Arts (1933–35), died in Toronto on December 3, aged 63.

August 23 *Empress of Japan II* was the largest liner ever to dock in Vancouver.

1961

Right: Fast mover. Jim Pattison poses at the GM dealership that launched his career. From there he went on to become one of the wealthiest people in Canada, with his Jim Pattison Group holding such diverse companies as Save-On-Foods, the Ripley's Believe It or Not franchise, and multiple radio and TV stations. Vancouver Sun

Vancouver's 75th birthday was a milestone for two men who would do much to shape the city: business mogul Jimmy Pattison mortgaged his house to buy a car dealership, and Arthur Erickson earned a reputation as a distinctive architect. The station that became BCTV moved to its signature channel 8. And you could now phone long distance without talking to an operator.

January 1 Norm Grohmann got into radio at CHWK in Chilliwack in the 1950s and joined CKNW today.

For four decades he cut a goofy swath through local radio with a range of voices, culminating in a daily bit with NW's morning man, Brian "Frosty" Forst, where he played a vast variety of people—none of them normal, all of them loud and funny—discussing the weather. BCTV asked him to do the same, and viewers loved him. He stayed 25 years. Then switched to stage acting.

January 14 Gertrude Guerin was elected chief of the Musqueam Indian band, the first woman to hold that position.

January 15 The Coquitlam River flooded, prompting an extensive program of diking and drainage.

March 1 Ian Dobbin became manager of the Queen Elizabeth Theatre. He was there until 1982.

April 22 North Vancouver's Lions Gate Hospital, the fifth largest in the Greater Vancouver Regional Hospital District, opened at its current site with 285 beds.

Elsewhere in BC

August 1 The BC government bought BC Electric, which had been a private company, and merged it with the BC Power Commission to form a new provincial Crown corporation, the BC Hydro and Power Authority. The 21-storey BC Electric Building at 970 Burrard, at the time the tallest building in Vancouver, was renamed the BC Hydro Building. (*Province* columnist Eric Nicol, noting the monumental St. Andrew's-Wesley United Church across the street, called the intersection "The Power and the Glory.")

Elsewhere in Canada

June 8 Tommy Douglas and the Co-operative Commonwealth Federation (CCF) won a fifth consecutive majority in the Saskatchewan election.

A Montreal judge ruled that *Lady Chatterley's Lover* by D.H. Lawrence was obscene.

Elsewhere in the World

April 13 The Soviet Union's Yuri Gagarin orbited Earth, the first human into space.

May 8 Jimmy Pattison began his business empire by purchasing a GM dealership with a $40,000 bank loan from the Royal Bank, using his home and life insurance policy as collateral. Today Pattison runs BC's largest privately owned company, the Jim Pattison Group.

June 1 In the *Province*: "A permanent sales force has been set up by the Greater Vancouver Tourist Association to sell Vancouver as a convention centre...staffed by a man and 2 women, financed by district hotels and motels."

June 5 It was now possible to direct-dial long-distance calls from Vancouver.

July 28 Albert Edward "Dal" Grauer, former president of the BC Electric Railway, died in Vancouver, aged 55. He was born on Sea Island in 1906, the sixth son of a Lower Mainland pioneer, Jacob "John" Grauer (1861–1936). After earning a BA in economics at UBC and a PhD at Berkeley, he won a Rhodes scholarship in 1927 and went to Oxford for a second BA. He taught at the University of Toronto, then was appointed secretary of the BCER in 1939 and rose to become president in 1946. The company expanded tremendously under his leadership until his retirement in 1960. Grauer was also active in the community, particularly with the Vancouver General Hospital, Vancouver Symphony and UBC.

September 18 Alexander Russell Lord died in Vancouver, aged 76. Lord's career in education began as principal of Kelowna Elementary, then school inspector for the Prince Rupert/Peace River districts, Okanagan and Vancouver. He joined Vancouver Normal School in 1924 and remained until 1950, retiring as principal. Then he was a special lecturer for the College of Education (1950–58). He was a member of the UBC senate (1936–50), president of the Canadian Educational Association and the Children's Aid Society, and an educational adviser to the UN. He was awarded the Fergusson Memorial Award in 1950 for "outstanding contribution to education in BC" and received honorary doctorates from UBC and Queen's. An elementary school in Vancouver is named for him.

October 9 Anna Ethel Sprott died in Vancouver, aged about 82. After the death of her husband, R.J. Sprott, in 1943, she became the president of the Sprott-Shaw Schools of Commerce, Radio and Telegraphy. Sprott was elected a Vancouver city councillor in December 1949 and served on council to 1959, the first female alderman elected to three terms. On her retirement, she admitted to writing secret letters on council's behalf to those celebrating their 50th and 60th anniversaries and 90th or 100th birthdays.

Also October 9 Alice Frances Crakanthorp (née Patterson) died in Haney, aged 97. She was a student in the first class at Hastings Mill School, Vancouver's oldest school, which was built to educate the children of the workers at Hasting Mill.

October 13 The RCMP raided Vancouver bookstores and the main library to seize copies of Henry Miller's novel *Tropic of Cancer*.

October 31 Vancouver's first private television station, CHAN-TV, began broadcasting on channel 8. In May it had moved from its original home at the corner of Richards and Davie to a sprawling complex in Burnaby's Lake City.

Prohibited prose. Originally banned in Canada in 1958, the Henry Miller novel *Tropic of Cancer* came under police scrutiny only after a library employee phoned in to ask about its status. Now alerted, the police raided the library and a couple of bookstores on October 13, searching for the novel and its sequel, *Tropic of Capricorn*. *Vancouver Sun*

November 2 S.W. "Sam" Randall, thoroughbred racing promoter, died in Vancouver, aged 79. Sometime after he arrived in Vancouver from Toronto in 1908, two friends got him involved in racing. He took over Exhibition Park in 1920, operated Lansdowne Park on Lulu Island from 1924 to 1945, then managed Victoria's Willows Track until 1947. Randall was the first Canadian track owner to adopt the photo finish and the first western manager to install an electric starting gate (1939). He was inducted into the BC and Canadian Sports Halls of Fame and was known as "Mr. Racing" in BC.

December The Carol Ships began their Christmas Parade of Lights tradition.

House of memories. The University of British Columbia Graduate Student Centre, also known as the Thea Koerner House, was built by long-time patron Leon Koerner in memory of his wife. Featuring Koerner's Pub, a popular watering hole, the centre also has several function rooms available for rent. *University of British Columbia Archives [UBC 1.1/1461]*

Also in 1961

By 1961 the metropolitan Vancouver population had climbed to more than 800,000, double the figure of 20 years earlier, and pushing Vancouver's share of the population down to 46 percent. For the first time there were more people outside the city proper than in. Meanwhile, 60 percent of Richmond's population was of British descent this year, but that now began to change.

Transcendence, a Bronze sculpture by Jack Harman, was placed at the Thea Koerner Graduate Student Centre at UBC. Cast at his North Vancouver foundry, this piece was the sculptor's first commission. "When he suggested the design should be larger to balance the bulk of the building behind it," journalist Elizabeth Godley wrote, "the Koerner family doubled his budget."

There were 15,223 Chinese in Vancouver (298 of them in Richmond), double the number of a decade earlier. The number doubled again by the next census in 1971.

One branch of the Taylor family of Delta ended a 56-year tradition of running the post office in Ladner. They began in 1905, passing control from father to son to daughter-in-law.

The Crescent Apartments were West Vancouver's first high-rise condominium.

Vancouver: From Milltown to Metropolis, a history of Vancouver by *Sun* journalist Alan Morley, was published to commemorate the city's 75th birthday.

Surrey's Senator Reid Elementary School opened. It was named for a Surrey pioneer, Senator Tom Reid, originally from Scotland. Reid gave the municipality land that is now Bear Creek Park.

The BC government approved a plan to establish the province's first technical training institute. However, the British Columbia Institute of Technology did not open its doors in Burnaby until the spring of 1964.

The last lobotomy was performed at Essondale in Coquitlam.

Trans-Canada Airlines and Canadian Pacific Airlines bought pure-jet DC-8s this year. The switch to jets meant a major overhaul of Vancouver International Airport. A figure of $100 million was cited. The city voted to sell the city's share of the airport to the federal government for $2.5 million.

Brentwood Mall opened in Burnaby.

At 12 hectares (30 acres) it was the largest of its kind in BC at the time. In contrast was the supermarket built this year at 6415 Victoria Dr. Architectural historian Harold Kalman noted that, "in this day of sprawling mega-stores, we sometimes forget that the post-war common supermarket represented an ambitious architectural program. The Super-Valu chain, which originally erected and operated [the Victoria Drive] building, developed the best local solution. Large glued-laminated timber arches provide a broad expanse

Mega-mall. Its parking lots full on opening day, Brentwood Mall in Burnaby gets an auspicious start as the largest mall of its time in British Columbia. It has since been outstripped by several more recent developments. *Vancouver Public Library, Special Collections, VPL 49522. George Allen photo*

Arthur Erickson and Vancouver Architecture

This year was an architectural turning point for Vancouver according to historian Sean Rossiter in *The Greater Vancouver Book* (1998): "The history of Vancouver architecture consists of everything before Arthur Erickson, and everything since. In 1961 Erickson and Woodruff Wilson 'Bud' Wood were teaching a more design-oriented architectural approach at the University of Oregon. Erickson was already designing houses in Vancouver that he regarded as experiments; one, for example, entirely out of concrete blocks.

"Ron Thom, the outstanding designer in Vancouver before Erickson, was off to Toronto that year to build Massey College and thus become the first local architect with a national practice. Thom was a protege of the most influential architect ever to work in Vancouver, C.E. 'Ned' Pratt, whose firm, Thompson Berwick Pratt & Partners, had by then become the dominant office in the city.

"The founders of many of today's important firms were either working for Pratt or about to work for Erickson in 1961."

Vancouver-born Erickson began practising architecture in 1953. He had pursued fine arts in his youth—Lawren Harris was a friend and mentor—and considered a diplomatic career before studying architecture at UBC and McGill. Erickson and his work gained international renown in the mid-1960s, first with the publication of some of his house designs and then with his design for the new Simon Fraser University on Burnaby Mountain. Not only was the SFU design visually striking within its setting, it redirected thinking about university structures by placing all departments in joined rather than separate buildings.

Major building projects followed through the 1960s and 1970s: the keynote pavilion at Expo 67 in Montreal, the University of Lethbridge, the MacMillan Bloedel office building in Vancouver, UBC's Museum of Anthropology, and Robson Square and the Law Courts.

Erickson's best-known buildings, including SFU, typically combine openness, light and balance with his rhythmic repeating shapes in concrete, steel and glass. In his Robson Square and Law Courts, instead of a forbidding tower, he created low, linked structures that spanned three blocks and formed an urban refuge of water and greenery that encouraged passersby to pause amid the city rush. Zen Buddhism informed much of his design with a grace and fluidity that defied the limits of the massive concrete that formed it.

Despite his many national and international honours—including the Order of Canada as well as honours from France and the United States—and his ease at mixing with the international elites, Erickson was equally at home taking them to task for developments with a negative impact on Third World cultures. And in his 70s he agreed to design the Portland Hotel, a housing complex in Vancouver's Downtown Eastside for homeless people struggling with mental illness and drug abuse.

Having re-created the city he loved in a finer form, Arthur Erickson died in Vancouver in 2009, age 84.

"I am a Canadian, open to the broad world, and my work draws on universal sources to make a cultural mesh," Erickson told Nicholas Olsberg a few years before his death. "But cultures must find their contexts, and those contexts must be recognized in the elusive as well as the apparent."

---

of unobstructed, column-free space. Note the remarkably small metal connectors, which bear the full weight of the structure where the arches meet the ground."

Entrepreneur Hugh B. Sutherland established Mohawk Oil. By the time Mohawk was acquired by Husky Oil in 1998, it was the largest retailer of alternative fuels in western Canada.

Lansdowne Park was sold for real estate development, and all Lower Mainland racing was concentrated at Hastings Park.

Landscaping in the second quarry at Queen Elizabeth Park was finished.

Gordon Hilker was appointed artistic director of the Vancouver Festival. He held that post until 1967.

Calgary-born (1914) Marianne Linnell won her first civic election, running as a councillor for the Non-Partisan Association (NPA). She served five terms to 1974.

UBC opened the School of Rehabilitation Medicine to help relieve a shortage of therapists. The university also founded its Department of Asian Studies. The department's library is the largest of its kind in Canada, with more than 300,000 volumes in Chinese, Japanese, Urdu, Sanskrit and other Asian languages. It has an important collection of Chinese rare books and manuscripts dating as far back as AD 986.

Comings and Goings

Mountaineer Elfrida Pigou, most well known of local female climbers of the 1950s, was killed in an avalanche on Mount Waddington.

With choirmaster Charles Findlater, Vancouver's Elgar Choir (established in 1934) was the first Canadian cultural group to visit the USSR. The choir had previously travelled to Europe in 1957.

1962

The storm known as Hurricane Frieda was the talk of the town for decades: windows were smashed, trees uprooted and power knocked out. Comedian Lenny Bruce also caused a stir when he appeared at Isy's Supper Club; the Vancouver police morality squad ran him out of town. Meanwhile the PNE drew more than a million visitors for the first time, and many city residents attended the world's fair in Seattle.

February 26 The Queen Elizabeth Playhouse (now the Vancouver Playhouse) opened right next door to the Queen Elizabeth Theatre. Artist Toni Onley installed a mural in the form of a canvas collage in the brand-new building. This big work sparked controversy, with one outraged citizen claiming, in a letter to the *Province*, that it was "a Communist plot."

March 1 The first Vancouver International Amateur Film Festival began.

June 18 Native people in Greater Vancouver voted in their first federal election after Parliament extended the franchise to them in 1960. Some local election results: Arthur Laing, 57, former MLA and BC Liberal Party leader, who had left politics in 1959, emerged from retirement to run federally. Laing was one of only two BC members in Lester Pearson's cabinet after the 1963 election. Bob Prittie of the NDP was elected MP for Burnaby–Richmond. He served for six years and then became Burnaby's mayor in 1969.

Also June 18 The original Grouse Mountain Chalet, opened in November 1926, burned down.

Vancouver's Mr. Baseball

June 17 Robert Paul "Bob" Brown, "Mr. Baseball," died in Vancouver, aged 85. Born in Scranton, PA, Brown excelled on the diamond and the gridiron during his teen years, even playing college football for the fabled Notre Dame Fighting Irish in the 1890s. From 1900 to 1909 he played professional baseball in Montana, Oregon and Washington state, leading the Spokane Indians to a Pacific Coast League pennant in 1908.

In 1910, Brown moved to Vancouver to become the owner/playing manager of the PCL's Vancouver Beavers. Under his reign, the club captured three pennants (1911, 1914 and, in the new Western International League, 1922, the club's final season). He built Athletic Park (opened April 18, 1913) on land leased from the CPR and organized the first night games played under lights in Canada.

Brown served as president of the Western International League from 1938 to 1953. In 1939, with the help of Capilano Brewery, he purchased the Vancouver Capilanos from Con Jones. He sold the ball club six years later but stayed on as vice-president and general manager, and initiated the building of Capilano Stadium (1951). The Capilanos' last season was 1954. When a new franchise, the Vancouver Mounties, joined the reborn Pacific Coast League in 1956, playing out of Capilano Stadium, Brown was named honorary president.

In all, the adopted Canadian was involved in baseball for more than 60 years and was rewarded by being named the first member of BC's Baseball Hall of Fame in 1966.

June 25

The Haida section of Totem Park opened at UBC. It included a 19th-century large family dwelling, a smaller mortuary house, and works by many contemporary First Nations artists of the Northwest Coast, including Bill Reid, Douglas Cranmer, Norman Tait and Mungo Martin.

June 29 Kosaburo Shimizu, United Church minister, died in Winnipeg, aged 68. Born September 13, 1893, in Tsuchida, Shiga-ken, Japan, he came to BC in about 1906. At Royal City High School in New Westminster (1910–11), Shimizu won a gold medal for attaining the highest average of a first-year student. He attended UBC (1915–19) and in 1924 earned an MA at Harvard. Shimizu was ordained by the United Church in 1927 and served in Vancouver. He was committed to bringing first- and second-generation

Elsewhere in BC

June 18 The federal election left John Diefenbaker's Tories in power but with a minority government—only 116 seats, down from the record majority of 208 they had elected in 1958. The Liberals, under Lester B. Pearson, more than doubled their presence, from 48 to 99 MPs.

July 30 The 7,821-kilometre (4,860-mile) Trans-Canada Highway, the longest national highway in the world, was opened to traffic at Rogers Pass in the Rockies. It had taken 12 years to build, and more than 3,000 kilometres (1,860 miles) were still to be paved, but it was now possible to drive right across the country on one highway. The official opening was September 3.

Elsewhere in the World

August 5 Actress Marilyn Monroe was found dead of an overdose of sleeping pills.

Vancouver's G.P.V. Akrigg saw his *Jacobean Pageant: The Court of King James I* named one of the 10 best books of 1962 by the *New York Times*.

Seattle held a world's fair. Many Lower Mainland residents attended.

Japanese Canadians and Anglo-Saxons together. During World War II he was relocated to an internment camp at Kaslo, BC. In 1945 he was transferred to Toronto and organized Japanese United Church work there. He received an honorary Doctor of Divinity degree from Union College (now the Vancouver School of Theology). Shimizu died while chairing a conference of Japanese ministers.

July 21 A photo caption in the *Sun* described Mountain Institution, which opened this month: "On a lonely hillside seven miles north of Agassiz stands the new federal maximum security jail that will house convicted Sons of Freedom Doukhobor terrorists. 49 inmates will be transferred to the $300,000 prison next month from New Westminster penitentiary." As the *Sun* noted, many of the Doukhobors convicted of arson and terrorism in the 1960s were interned at this prison. Designed to house special inmates, the institution now serves as an incarceration centre for a high percentage of sex offenders.

August 12 Buda Hosmer Brown (née Jenkins), MLA, died in Vancouver, aged 68. She was born June 10, 1894, in Bellingham, WA. In 1958 she was elected Social Credit MLA for Vancouver–Point Grey. In 1960 she entered Premier W.A.C. Bennett's cabinet as minister at large, the first woman in a Bennett cabinet since Tilly Rolston. Her interests included traffic safety and youth. Formerly a Vancouver parks commissioner, Buda Brown was the first woman president of the International Northwest Parks Association.

October 4 UBC had taken over responsibility for training BC's teachers in 1956, but there was no central facility for instruction until the education building opened today. Additions and renovations occurred in 1965, 1972 and 1996, and in 1973 the building was renamed to honour Neville V. Scarfe, the first dean of the faculty (1956–73).

October 19 UBC students protested closure of the Hotel Georgia pub, a favoured hangout.

October 22
Scuba divers found the drive shaft of the SS *Beaver*, which sank off Stanley Park more than 70 years earlier.

November 17 A new Surrey municipal hall was opened on Highway 10.

November 23 Ira Dilworth, scholar and broadcast executive, died in Vancouver, aged 68. Born in High Bluff, MB, on March 25, 1894, Dilworth came to the Okanagan as a boy. He taught English at Victoria High School from 1915 to 1934 and then moved to UBC, where he was a popular associate professor of English from 1934 to 1938. He directed the Bach Choir (1938–40), was first president of the Vancouver Community Arts Council (the first organization of its kind in North

Hurricane Frieda Comes to Town

October 12 (and continuing into the early hours of October 13) Hurricane Frieda wreaked enormous damage in Greater Vancouver. Gusts reached 125 kilometres per hour (78 mph) at the Sea Island Weather Station. Windows of downtown department stores were shattered, and 3,000 trees blew down in Stanley Park. One person was killed when a falling tree crushed her car. There were five other deaths in BC. More than 1,500 trees were lost at the Vancouver Golf Club in Coquitlam, making VGC the hardest hit by far of all local courses. The storm lasted about four hours. The Lower Mainland was dark from Horseshoe Bay to Hope. Thanks to CKNW's Jack Gordon, an engineer with more than the usual helping of smarts, who had created an emergency broadcast system long before the storm hit, that station was the only one on the coast north of California to stay on the air during the crisis. CKNW became a coordination and information centre.

Was Frieda a hurricane, or was it a typhoon? We put that question to Sylvain Boutot of the Meteorological Service of Canada, who sent this response: "There was indeed a hurricane called Frieda that hit Vancouver on October 12, 1962. You'll hear some folks refer to Frieda as a typhoon and others as a hurricane and both terms are a little right and a little wrong. As storm aficionados are aware, the term 'hurricane' refers to severe Atlantic weather systems and those in the eastern Pacific. The term 'typhoon' is the designation for Pacific storms west of the International Date Line. Frieda had the distinction of starting as a typhoon and then moving east (instead of west, which is the usual pattern for typhoons) and becoming a hurricane while merging with another tropical storm. Weather professionals like to call it an extra-tropical storm and it proved its strength when it slammed into the coastal cities of Portland, Seattle and Vancouver."

Aftermath. Over the course of four hours in October 1962, Hurricane Frieda caused one death and tremendous damage all over Vancouver. Frieda was one of the worst storms to ever hit the city. *PNG*

1962

Hot spot. The Union Steamship resort on Bowen Island, its main building seen in this 1920s photo, was a popular destination from the 1920s to the 1940s. Tourism dropped off after World War II, however, in part due to the rise of the automobile age, and the hotel was demolished in 1962.
City of Vancouver Archives, CVA 99-3059. Stuart Thompson photo

America) and joined the CBC in 1938, rising through the ranks to become director of all CBC English networks in 1956. Dilworth was also a friend of Emily Carr, encouraging and editing her writing and ultimately becoming her literary executor.

November 29 The Vancouver Mounties PCL baseball club folded, though the team returned for the 1965 season.

December 9 Bill Rathie was elected mayor, the first born in Vancouver.

December 10 The old Union Steamship hotel on Bowen Island was demolished, and the resort was closed.

Also in 1962

The Metropolitan Theatre Co-operative, an organization of local community theatre companies, opened its first theatre on 4th Avenue in Kitsilano. It moved to a new home at 1370 SW Marine Dr. in 1963, and in 1966 began producing its own shows. Now known as Metro Theatre, it's one of Vancouver's most prominent community theatre companies, producing an average of 10 shows per season.

Highway 99 was completed, providing a continuous link between the US border and Vancouver through Richmond.

Attendance at the PNE passed the 1 million mark. It has rarely dropped below this level since.

The Japanese Friendship Garden was created in New Westminster as a tribute to its sister city, Mariguchi, Japan. A hundred ornamental flowering cherry trees were planted in this informal Japanese-style garden. Waterfalls, ponds and streams added to its charm.

CP Hotels, unwilling to spend more money on a hotel it didn't own, decided not to renew its Hotel Vancouver management contract with CN, which delegated the hotel's management to Hilton. CN resumed sole management in 1983. And in 1988 the hotel's ownership came full circle as Canadian Pacific Hotels once again acquired the Hotel Vancouver.

Edward Cecil "Cece" Roper became the first principal of the British Columbia Institute of Technology, which opened in the spring of 1964. Roper came to BCIT from teaching in the commerce department at UBC. He served until June 1967.

UBC's new president, John B. MacDonald, proposed building a system of community colleges across the province. BC had a poor record in providing post-secondary training and educational opportunities for residents, so the government began to act on MacDonald's recommendations.

The University Women's Club purchased Hycroft (built 1909), one of Shaughnessy's premier homes. Inside and out, it is one of the most beautiful buildings in the city, and they keep it that way.

The Evangelical Free Church of America opened Trinity Junior College in Langley with 17 students. The college dorms were portable housing units moved from a BC Hydro construction project in BC's interior. The dining hall was an old farmhouse; the barn was converted into a gymnasium called the "barnasium."

North Shore residents began clamouring for a second crossing over the First Narrows, claiming that, without one, "the Lions Gate Bridge will become the world's largest parking lot." It hasn't happened yet.

Mrs. Flora Bingham won the Order of Merit for Scouting in Canada after 20 consecutive years as Lady Cubmaster of the Cloverdale Wolf Cub Pack.

Willy Schaeffler, an Austrian ski resort consultant, reported favourably on

Whistler's potential as a world-class ski area.

Former mayor Fred Hume bought the Vancouver Canucks, then in the WHL. He owned the team until his death in 1967.

Katherine M. Freer compiled her thesis, *Vancouver, a Bibliography*, from material in the Vancouver Public Library and the Special Collections of the UBC Library.

The Vancouver Stock Exchange traded more than 100 million shares this year, the first time it had reached that level since 1937. A mining assay scandal and World War II had combined to keep the exchange quiet for many years.

Hugh Keenleyside, co-chair of BC Hydro, received the first Vanier Medal from the Institute of Public Administration of Canada. The medal is presented annually to a person who has shown leadership in or made a significant contribution to public administration in Canada.

The Abbotsford International Air Show was born. Forty enthusiastic members of the Abbotsford Flying Club passed the hat and came up with $700 to put on the first one, which attracted 15,000 spectators. Since then the show has become one of the world's premier flying and aviation-technology extravaganzas, attracting more participants and bigger audiences each year.

Frank Panvini, who had opened the Commodore Lanes on September 7, 1930, and who owned several other bowling alleys, died. In the 1920s, bowling was almost exclusively a male sport. Panvini changed that by running a promotion that allowed women to bowl free in the mornings. He was also the first to rent out shoes.

Mitz Nozaki, who had been with Panvini since the 1920s, became the owner of Commodore Lanes when his boss died. Nozaki's career in five-pin bowling began in 1927 at the Abbott Bowling Lanes when he was 13 years old. When Panvini opened Commodore Lanes, Nozaki became the cashier and learned as much as possible from his boss. When Japanese Canadians were removed from the coast during World War II, Nozaki was sent to Blind Bay on Shuswap Lake, but he returned to Vancouver and Commodore Lanes after restrictions were lifted in 1949. He became "Mr. Bowling," one of the biggest promoters of the sport in Vancouver. Nozaki rented shoes to such celebrities as Roy Rogers, Clark Gable, Jack Benny and Buster Crabb. He retired in 1990 at age 77.

Comings and Goings

May 30 There was a near riot at the Forum as Prime Minister John Diefenbaker addressed a rowdy crowd at an election rally.

July 30 Comic Lenny Bruce (author of *How to Talk Dirty and Influence People*) opened to a packed house at Isy's Supper Club. In the next day's *Vancouver Sun*, Jack Wasserman attacked Bruce's caustic performance. That evening the VPD Morality Squad showed up at Isy's and, after the performance, informed Bruce and club owner Isy Walters no further shows would be permitted, citing a bylaw that prohibited or prevented "any lewd or immoral performance or exhibition." Walters was told his operating licence would be suspended unless Bruce was cancelled, so he killed the balance of the engagement. The operator of the Inquisition Coffee House stepped forward with an offer to present the remainder of the performances. Bruce agreed, but the city's licensing boss announced the Inquisition's licence would be lifted if he performed. Bruce, who is now viewed as a hugely influential, ground-breaking comic, finally threw up his hands and vowed never again to perform in Vancouver. He died August 3, 1966.

November 1 Bob Smith, host of CBC's *Hot Air* jazz program, interviewed Duke Ellington at the Georgian Towers Hotel.

Notable deaths: **Francis James "Frank" Burd**, newspaperman (*Winnipeg Free Press, Whitehorse Tribune, Vancouver News-Advertiser, Province*), on January 6 in Vancouver, one day short of his 92nd birthday; **Mungo Martin**, Kwakiutl master carver, aged about 83.

Left: Air show takes off. Proving that big birds attract big crowds, the Abbotsford International Air Show drew 15,000 spectators in its first year in 1962. The show, held annually on the second weekend in August, has since gone on to become the largest in Canada. *Harbour Publishing Archives*

1963

It was a busy year in local media. Pat Burns shook up the talk radio world with his *Hot Line* show on CJOR. Jack Webster was still a popular radio host: rioting prisoners used a hostage to get on his open-line show. The *Ubyssey* was named the best college newspaper in Canada, the *Vancouver Sun* was sold to out-of-town owners and a local adman vowed to start a new paper to replace that local voice.

January 2 The *Ubyssey*, the student newspaper at the University of British Columbia, was named the best college newspaper in Canada by Canadian University Press. Editor Keith Bradbury accepted the award, and as if to justify the choice, later in the year he published an exposé on undercover RCMP agents spying on student political groups.

April 2 Tolls came off the Lions Gate Bridge

under its new owner, the provincial government, which had bought the bridge for $6 million. A new wrinkle was added: overhead lane-control signals allowed managers to reverse the direction of traffic in the centre lane of the three-lane bridge according to traffic flow.

April 18 The Iona Island Sewage Treatment Plant opened in Richmond. At the time residents of Richmond were really unhappy with the decision to put it there: they wanted Vancouver to keep its own sewage. But according to the GVRD's 1992 annual report, "the tides were against [them]—Iona was the best location to get a good tidal flushing action." The plant provides primary treatment to wastewater from approximately 600,000 people (in Vancouver, the University Endowment Lands and parts of Burnaby and Richmond) before discharging it through a 7.5-kilometre (4.5-mile), deep-sea outfall into the Strait of Georgia. One of the major connectors to the plant, the Highbury Tunnel, is named for the westside street that runs above it.

After the riot. Prisoners at the BC Penitentiary in New Westminster rioted in 1963 after three inmates were detected trying to escape. The three took a guard hostage, and insisted on negotiating with popular radio host Jack Webster. Among their grievances was a demand not to be placed in "the hole," the solitary confinement space that terrorized the prison population for decades. Vancouver Sun

Elsewhere in BC

July 1 Victoria College, which had been affiliated with McGill University (1903–15) and then UBC (1920–63), became the University of Victoria and moved to the Gordon Head campus in Saanich on Vancouver Island.

September 30 W.A.C. Bennett and the Social Credit Party won their fifth election, with 33 seats to the NDP's 14 and the Liberals' 5. During this term, Bennett passed Richard McBride's 12 years, 197 days in office to become the longest-serving BC premier.

Elsewhere in Canada

April 8 Lester Pearson and his Liberals won 129 seats in a federal election to form a minority government. The election was called after the Diefenbaker government collapsed on February 5, a day after the Conservative defence minister resigned as a result of a cabinet split over accepting nuclear weapons from the United States.

April 20 The Front de libération du Québec set off its first bombs in Quebec.

Canada's first national modern dance festival was held in Toronto. The lone BC participant was Vancouver's Norbert Vesak, born in Port Moody in 1936 and called by Max Wyman "Vancouver's first modern dance professional."

Elsewhere in the World

November 22 US president John F. Kennedy was shot dead in Dallas by Lee Harvey Oswald.

November 24 Nightclub owner Jack Ruby shot Lee Harvey Oswald dead in Dallas.

In some places the pipes are 90 metres (300 feet) beneath the surface.

April 19 There was real drama at the BC Penitentiary when rioting inmates, holding a hostage (prison guard Patrick Dennis), insisted on speaking in person to CKNW open-liner Jack Webster. The gutsy Webster met with them under extremely tense conditions and aired their grievances.

June 8 The Agrodome exhibition hall opened at the PNE. The fair's original proposal was for an 8,000-seat combined facility: a livestock arena that could be converted to an ice rink for a hockey team. Vancouver city council balked and what was built was a 3,500-seat arena with a 70-by-30-metre (230-by-100-foot) ring, covered by a domed roof.

July Donald Cromie, son of Robert Cromie, the founder of the *Vancouver Sun*, sold the paper to FP Publications, leaving Vancouver with no locally owned newspaper. In 1964, Stuart Keate returned to his hometown to become publisher of the *Sun*. He remained in that post until his retirement in 1978.

Summer The first Vancouver Sea Festival was held.

It was the brainchild of Harold Merilees, head of the Greater Vancouver Tourist Association.

Summer In response to the sale of the *Vancouver Sun* to out-of-town owners, local adman Val Warren decided to start up a new locally owned paper, the *Vancouver Times*, and began looking for investors. He named Victor Odlum, former owner and publisher of the *Vancouver Star* (1924–32), chairman of the board.

September 3 Maureen Chant began working for Jimmy Pattison at 18th and Cambie as the night switchboard operator of his Pontiac/Buick dealership. "Jimmy was doing a fair bit of public speaking then," she said in a 2002 interview, "and because of my proximity to his office I would listen to and critique his talks. The chemistry between us worked. I took courses and became his secretary—and then he got on the acquisition trail." Over the years she has handled Pattison's personal finances; overseen operation of the company airplane, the yacht *Nova Spirit* and "Frank's Place" in Rancho Mirage; arranged schedules for 100-plus meetings a year, etc., etc. and etc. In 2011 her title was Administrative Assistant to the Managing Director and CEO.

September 19 The newly built Frederic Wood Theatre opened its doors with the English musical comedy *Salad Days*. Up to that point, the theatre's home had been an old army hut on West Mall. The new theatre, built at a cost of $600,000 (half of which was paid by the Canada Council), contained three 50-seat classrooms and a 400-seat theatre complete with revolving stage, the first at a university theatre in Canada. UBC theatre grads have played a major role in the Canadian theatre scene, especially in Vancouver. They include Bruce Greenwood, Richard Ouzounian, Eric Peterson, Goldie Semple, Dennis Foon and Jeremy Long.

October 2 The curtain went up on Brendan Behan's *The Hostage*, the first production by the newly formed Vancouver Playhouse Theatre Company. Michael Johnston was managing producer during the 1963–64 season, acting as producer, manager and designer. *The Hostage* was directed by Malcolm Black, who served as artistic director of the Playhouse from 1964 to 1967. Built by the City of Vancouver to provide a facility for local arts groups, the Playhouse also became home to the Friends of Chamber Music, the Festival Concert Society and the Vancouver Recital Society.

The popular Vancouver Sea Festival was launched in 1963, celebrating all things maritime. Getting into the spirit, these canoes race off Kits Beach on June 25, 1966. *Vancouver Public Library, Special Collections, VPL 43195. The Province newspaper photo*

October 26 Donald Cameron Brown died in Vancouver, aged 71. He was born February 22, 1892, in Winchester, ON, and came to Vancouver in 1910. Brown served as a pilot with the Royal Flying Corps in World War I. He was elected twice as a Coalition MLA in Vancouver–Burrard (1945 and 1949), but was defeated in 1952. He and his wife joined the Social Credit Party in 1954. He was prominent in local organizations such as the Vancouver Board of Trade and Kiwanis, and was a director of Theatre Under the Stars.

October 30 William Moore died in Burnaby, aged 75. Born December 11, 1887, in Bryson, QC, he came to Vancouver in 1912 from Banff, and set up a photographic studio in his home on East 21st Avenue. He later moved to Sophia Street. He was one of two panoramic photographers in the city, specializing in photos 20 centimetres (8 inches) high and up to 250 centimetres (eight feet) wide. He took hundreds of views from 1913 to 1953, including English Bay, sporting events and cityscapes. From 1920 to 1946 he photographed the annual New Westminster May Day celebrations. His camera was a Kodak No. 8 Cirkut, and he donated 370 Cirkut images to the Vancouver City Archives.

November 21 Marathon Realty was incorporated to manage the Canadian Pacific Railway's vast real estate holdings. Pacific Logging Company Limited was formed to develop tree farms on CPR's timberlands.

November 26 A memorial service for assassinated US president John F. Kennedy was held at UBC.

November 30 Alexander Campbell DesBrisay, chief justice of BC, died in Vancouver, aged about 75. Born in 1888 in Winnipeg, DesBrisay was elected president of the Vancouver Bar Association in 1941, was treasurer of the BC Law Society from 1953 to 1955 and became chief justice of the BC Court of Appeal in 1958. In 1962 he was appointed to head a one-man royal commission on workers' compensation. When he died he had produced 6,000 pages of transcripts for the as-yet-unfinished inquiry. His wife, Ella Helen, died the following morning of a heart attack.

November The Greater Vancouver Tourist Association (formerly the Vancouver Information and Tourist Association, Greater Vancouver Publicity Association and Vancouver Tourist Association) moved to new premises at 650 Burrard and got a new name: the Greater Vancouver Visitors and Convention Bureau.

A young man walks across Simon Fraser University's distinctive quad in 1995. Construction of the university, designed by Arthur Erickson and Geoffrey Massey, began in 1963 in response to baby boomers reaching college age.
Ian Lindsay / Vancouver Sun

Also in 1963

The phone-in radio talk show as a local ratings phenomenon had its beginning this year on CJOR with the sudden and volcanic appearance of a man named Pat Burns. Burns wasn't new to radio: he'd been a news broadcaster for years. But when CJOR's Peter Kosick put Burns on air with his *Hot Line* program, the change in local radio was convulsive. Within weeks, seemingly everyone was listening to, as Jack Webster described him, this "gruff-voiced, well-informed, first-class demagogue." In fact, it was Burns' success on OR that sparked CKNW's counterattack with Webster, and talk radio has been a local staple ever since. Astonishingly, the Burns phenomenon was over in less than two years. By the end of 1965 CJOR's owners, fearing loss of the station's licence, had released him. Burns later returned to the talk-show format, but his ratings never matched the earlier numbers. Webster, on the other hand, went on to garner excellent ratings and later repeated his success on television.

Construction began on Simon Fraser University, one of the new universities popping up across Canada in the 1960s as the baby boomers reached college age. Architects Arthur Erickson and Geoffrey Massey won the competition to design the university, with Erickson as principal designer. They conceived the university stretched out along the ridge of Burnaby Mountain, organized by use rather than faculty, with a huge central mall that served as a meeting place and campus buildings branching off from it.

Sherwood Lett, chief justice of BC, ruled that the expropriation of a private company (BC Electric) by the provincial government's BC Hydro and Power Authority was illegal. The province was forced to pay far more to acquire BC Electric.

Bruce Hutchison became editor of the *Vancouver Sun*. He had started his lifelong career in journalism as a sports reporter for the *Victoria Times* in 1918.

David Suzuki became a professor of zoology at the University of British Columbia, specializing in genetics. Suzuki was born in Vancouver in March 1936, but he and his family had been interned in the Slocan area during World War II and had moved to Ontario after the war. He attained his PhD at the University of Chicago in 1961.

New Westminster–born radiologist Ethlyn Trapp was recognized by the Canadian Medical Association for her cancer research. In 1937, using her own money, she had set up a centre in Vancouver to prove the benefits of radiation therapy. She was also director of the BC Cancer Institute from 1939 to 1944 and actively involved in provincial and national medical associations.

UBC Press began publishing the *Canadian Yearbook of International Law/Annuaire Canadien de droit international*, which contained articles on international law and Canadian practice in international law, as well as a digest of Canadian cases in public international law.

Earle Birney, 54, who had been teaching literature at at UBC since 1946, started Canada's first creative writing department.

Theatre Under the Stars, which had been presenting musical productions at Malkin Bowl since the 1940s, closed—to be revived by enthusiasts in 1969.

Hugh Forrester, who in 1925 bought Purdy's Chocolates from founder Richard Purdy (who started the firm in 1907), sold it in turn to Charles Flavelle. Under Flavelle's stewardship and that of his daughter Karen, Purdy's grew from 4 stores to a chain of 59 locations in BC, Alberta and Ontario. It is now the largest manufacturing retailer of chocolate in BC, and the second largest in Canada.

The BC Lions got into the Grey Cup, but lost to Hamilton Tiger-Cats 21–10.

The backup electrical source for Metro Vancouver during peak hours or when the reservoirs for hydroelectricity are running low, the gas-powered Burrard Thermal generating plant was completed in 1963 near Port Moody. It has served faithfully ever since, but with concerns over having clean sources of power, its fate may be in question. *PNG*

The Chessmen, featuring singer Terry Jacks, made their first recordings.

The movie *The Bitter Ash*, directed by Lawrence Kent, was made with a UBC student cast and crew. Movie reviewer Michael Walsh wrote that Larry Kent's directorial debut drama "upset censors across Canada with its despairing portrait of a would-be playwright (Alan Scarfe) lost in a world of sex and drugs."

Lawyer Angelo Branca, who had been practising in Vancouver since 1926, became a judge on the BC Supreme Court.

Two Stó:lō women, Mary Peters and Adeline Lorenzetto, revived the ancient art of Salish weaving. Their work received international recognition.

Pollution coming down the Nicomekl and Serpentine rivers put an end to oyster farming, which had flourished for decades at Crescent Beach.

BC Hydro's Burrard Thermal generating plant at Port Moody was completed. Some years much of Greater Vancouver's electricity (and about 12 percent of total provincial supply) comes from Burrard Thermal. You can see its six tall stacks emitting steam just west of the Ioco refinery on the north shore of Burrard Inlet. Construction cost $150 million.

Comings and Goings

October It was all-star time at the opera as Vancouver Opera's production of Bellini's *Norma* had a young Joan Sutherland and Marilyn Horne singing together, with Sutherland's husband, conductor Richard Bonynge, in the pit.

Australian-born author James Clavell, whose novel *King Rat* was a 1962 success, moved to West Vancouver.

Author Eileen Kernaghan, who was born in Grindrod, BC, in 1939 and grew up on a farm, moved to Burnaby. She was coordinator of the Burnaby Arts Council (1974–84) and then ran a used bookstore, but she is best known for her young adult fantasy novels, including *The Alchemist's Daughter*, short-listed for the 2005 Sheila Egoff Prize in Children's Literature.

1964

Right: The Port Mann Bridge is seen under construction. It opened in 1964 with the distinction of being the longest arch bridge in Canada, and the most expensive to build. *Vancouver Public Library, Special Collections, VPL 41338. Province newspaper photo*

The BC Lions won their first Grey Cup, the Beatles came to town, and the Vancouver Aquarium captured and displayed a killer whale, beginning a long and controversial tradition. In the eastern suburbs, construction of Simon Fraser University was being fast-tracked, the BC Institute of Technology welcomed its first students and the Port Mann Bridge opened.

February The new Grandview Community Centre was opened by Aldyen Hamber, widow of Eric Hamber.

Elsewhere in Canada

The Lyall Dagg rink of Vancouver won the World Curling Championship in Calgary. Dagg's teammates, also from Greater Vancouver, were Loe Hebert, Fred Britton and Barry Naimark.

Elsewhere in the World

May 2 Northern Dancer became the first Canadian-bred winner of the Kentucky Derby, and set a record of two minutes flat while doing it. That record held for nine years, until Secretariat won the race in 1973 with a time of 1:59 2/5, three-fifths of a second faster.

Fall CBS-TV's Thursday evening schedule started with two series with locally born actors. Vancouver-born Yvonne De Carlo starred as Lily Munster in *The Munsters* at 7:30, followed by New Westminster–born Raymond Burr as *Perry Mason* at 8:00 p.m. These programs were available to us on KIRO-TV, channel 7, Seattle.

October George Hungerford, of Vancouver, and Roger Jackson teamed to win double sculls gold at the Tokyo Olympic Games. Harry Jerome won bronze in the 100 metres at the Games, despite a severe hamstring injury.

April The Association for Social Knowledge (ASK), the oldest homophile organization in Canada, first published the *ASK Newsletter*. A group of academics and feminists had established ASK a few months earlier to, as its newsletter explained, "help society understand and accept variations from the sexual norm." ASK has been described as the first gay and lesbian discussion group in the country. The newsletter ceased publication in February 1968.

May Construction was under way on Simon Fraser University. "The whole mountain is swarming with men and equipment," a reporter wrote. "At 9 a.m. officials signed a contract to build the $1 million gym; at 10 a.m. the government granted approval to build the gym and a $3 million library; and an hour later they were pouring concrete for the footings." Patrick McTaggart-Cowan was named the first president of SFU this year. He shared responsibility for building and opening the university on schedule in 1965, and he chaired and endured "long, arduous and torn" meetings until he resigned the post in 1968.

Spring The British Columbia Institute of Technology welcomed its first class: 37 medical laboratory technology students. By September, with the institute's first 17 two-year technology programs in place, about 645 more students were enrolled, less than half the number who had applied. BCIT's original three-storey building was designed to accommodate 1,200 students, but first-year capacity was set at 750. First-year fees were between $150 and $190, and second-year fees were $60.

June 12 The Port Mann Bridge opened. It is the longest arch bridge in the country and at the time was the most expensive piece of highway in Canada. The first "civilian" to drive across the bridge was CKNW reporter Marke Raines—he wasn't authorized, so he put the pedal to the metal and drove across at teeth-clenching speed.

June 30 BCIT announced that "Deeley Harley-Davidson Canada has donated three Harley-Davidson motorcycles: a 2002 Fat Boy, 2003 VROD, and a 2004 Sportster, valued at about $60,000 retail, to BCIT Polytechnic." Malcolm Hunter, president of Deeley Harley-Davidson Canada, said, "It's our pleasure to contribute to such a worthwhile program, and institution, as BCIT. We want our donation to encourage further knowledge and safety for all students in all power motive programs."

July 24 Sherwood Lett, judge, died in Vancouver, aged 68. Born August 1, 1895, in Iroquois, ON, Lett was the goaltender for UBC's 1914–15 hockey team and was with the Vancouver law firm Davis and Co. from 1922 to 1955. After distinguished service in both World Wars (he reached the rank of brigadier), Lett was named the first Canadian representative (1954–55) on the International Control Commission to oversee the ceasefire and disengagement of French forces in North Vietnam and the country's political stabilization. Lett was UBC chancellor (1951–57) and chief justice of BC (1955–64).

September 5 The *Vancouver Times* launched a bid to become Vancouver's third daily newspaper. The paper hired radio talk-show host Jack Webster and sportswriter Jim Taylor, installed the latest offset printing presses in its plant at 3350 East Broadway, ran colour photos every day and spoke proudly of being locally owned and operated.

September 14 From the *Province*: "Highways Minister (Phil) Gaglardi says his department is buying land along portions of the Upper Levels Highway to make room for a four-lane freeway from Horseshoe Bay to Taylor Way. He said expansion of the highway—to cost at least $5 million—will begin within two or three years. 'A lot of people try to hold me up (on land prices) but we're very fair," Gaglardi said. 'It would have been cheaper to build a four-lane highway ten years ago when it was first built. I fought night and day with the so-called experts. I said let's at least build four-lane bridges, if not highways. They said no, this will do for 20 years.'"

September 28 The Burrard Bridge Civic Marina officially opened. Half of its 628 boat spaces were already taken. Of those, 450 were on the water, 178 in dry storage. There were 350 boats at the marina on opening day.

Up and running. Live in the studio at the British Columbia Institute of Technology in 1969, these students were among the first to benefit from the opening of the new trade school in 1964. *Courtesy* Vancouver Sun

October 6 Premier W.A.C. Bennett formally opened the British Columbia Institute of Technology.

He promised to double the institute's size, a promise that was fulfilled when a new laboratory and classroom building opened in September 1967. Today the main campus of BCIT at 3700 Willingdon Ave. in Burnaby includes 55 permanent buildings and a few portable structures. BCIT also has campuses downtown, on Sea Island and in North Vancouver.

November 12 The Woodward Biomedical Library at UBC was officially opened. Its Charles Woodward Memorial Room contains a large collection of rare and aged medical texts, some of them hundreds of years old.

November 28 The BC Lions defeated the Hamilton Tiger-Cats 34–24 to win their first Grey Cup.

Six players of that 1964 Lions team are members of the Canadian Football Hall of Fame: Norm Fieldgate, Tom Brown, By Bailey, Willie Fleming, Joe Kapp and Tom Hinton.

November 29 Thousands welcomed the BC Lions home from their Grey Cup win over Hamilton.

December 7 The William Tell Restaurant opened on Richards Street under the expert control of Swiss-born Erwin Doebeli. In 1983 the restaurant moved to the Georgian Court Hotel, and in 2005 Erwin's son Philippe took control. The William Tell remained in the top tier of Vancouver restaurants until it closed on December 31, 2010.

December 27 Regina-born (December 12, 1927) Chris Gage, a Canadian jazz pianist whose technique was considered second only to Oscar Peterson, committed suicide in North Vancouver. At age four, Gage had stood on tiptoes to play the family pump organ; at six, he performed on Regina radio; at 11 he performed all-nighters with an adult band; at 14 he had his own six-piece band; and when he was 17, he came to Vancouver, appearing in clubs and on radio and TV. He declined many offers to tour with such stars as Louis Armstrong, Peggy Lee and Gerry Mulligan, and remained in the Vancouver area until his death. According to jazz musician Don Thompson, Gage's death destroyed the local jazz scene: "Everybody was so sad and depressed and everybody just stopped doing anything. Everything stopped being fun because Chris Gage was just such a fantastic person and such a fantastic musician...Well, it just messed up a lot of cats...and the scene really collapsed."

Also in 1964

Tolls were removed from the Deas Island Tunnel, which was renamed George Massey Tunnel this year in honour of the MLA for Delta (1956–60), who had long advocated for a tunnel to replace the ferry that crossed the Fraser here.

The Vancouver Public Aquarium captured the first killer whale ever to be studied alive in captivity. He (yes, he) became known as Moby Doll. They originally thought he was a female.

Open wide... Perhaps unsure if this is the correct way to feed a killer whale, Vancouver Aquarium founding director Murray Newman holds out a fish for Moby Doll, the first orca to be captured and studied in captivity. *Brian Kent photo. Courtesy Vancouver Aquarium*

Vancouver's mayor, Bill Rathie, and park board chairman, George Wainborn, drove the last spike in the Stanley Park miniature railway.

Carrie Cates was elected mayor of North Vancouver City. She was re-elected in 1965 and 1967.

The Islamic Centre was established at 655 West 8th Ave.

The first colour feature movie made in BC was filmed on the North Shore.

The Trap starred Oliver Reed and Rita Tushingham as a burly trapper and a mute orphan, respectively.

The new Steveston Buddhist Temple was built at 4360 Garry St. in Richmond. The first temple, built in 1928 on Second Avenue, had been dissolved in 1942 when Japanese Canadians were forced to leave the West Coast. After families started to return, the temple was re-formed in March 1952.

Whistler got its first paved road. Closer to Vancouver, Grouse Mountain Resorts Ltd. was formed, and in 1965 the directors decided to build Canada's largest aerial tramway and a new chalet (the original one burned down in 1962). Grouse Mountain Ski School later became Canada's biggest.

Leonard Marsh became a professor of educational sociology at UBC. Marsh had joined UBC's School of Social Work in 1947, becoming director of research in 1959. He was hugely influential in the formation of Canada's social security system.

A $2-million addition to the building finally made it possible for all Vancouver Vocational Institute classes to return to the downtown campus. Student enrolment had rapidly increased, and some of VVI's programs, like plastering, bricklaying, drywalling and aircraft repair, had been forced to relocate to such places as the poultry and livestock buildings at the PNE.

The New Westminster Museum opened. One of its most interesting holdings is the material on New Westminster's annual May Day celebrations, a tradition since 1870.

Thanks to the efforts of Yvonne Firkins, "BC's first lady of the theatre," the Arts Club Theatre opened on Seymour Street in a converted gospel hall and became an instant theatrical institution. The first production, Moss Hart's *Light Up the Sky*, won high praise. Now the largest regional theatre in western Canada, the Arts Club added a stage on Granville Island in 1979. The Seymour Street theatre was demolished in the 1990s.

Ethel Wilson, Vancouver novelist and short story writer, was awarded the Lorne Pierce Medal from the Royal Society of Canada.

Margaret Atwood started as a UBC English department lecturer and began to write the first draft of her novel *The Edible Woman*.

Helen Goodwin founded an experimental dance company, TheCo, at UBC. It took part in many of UBC's contemporary arts festivals.

Entrepreneur Jim Howe set up a west Burnaby club called The Lamplighter. Local country music fans went there to hear performers like Waylon Jennings and Bobby Bare and the Canadian Sweethearts. And in an era when nightlifers were still brown-bagging it, the club featured BC's first liquor licence.

Kapoor Sawmill in Barnet ended operations. It had started around 1900 as the North Pacific Lumber mill. When that plant was destroyed by fire in 1909, a modern mill was constructed in its place to handle 150,000 board feet a day. The mill was closed during the Depression, then reopened as Kapoor Sawmill.

The Canadian Progress Club established a Greater Vancouver chapter on the North Shore. The aim of this service club is to advance the community in which individual chapters are located, so the three branches that now exist in Greater Vancouver each conduct their own affairs and run their own projects. The Greater Vancouver Club provided the first $40,000 to help launch the BC Special Olympics.

Grandview, Forum, Empress and Hastings taxi services amalgamated to form Forum Empress Taxi. Yellow Taxi took over the company on August 17, 1977.

Dynamic Engineering Inc. began servicing turbocharged diesel engines on vessels in the Port of Vancouver. In the late 60s and 70s it started working on turbochargers in cars, trucks and motorcycles as well. Today the company's engineers travel anywhere in the world to troubleshoot and repair everything from 10-ton marine engines to 5-pound motorcycle engines.

Comings and Goings

September 16 US president Lyndon B. Johnson and Prime Minister Lester B. Pearson met at Peace Arch Park to sign the Columbia River Treaty. The treaty dealt with hydroelectric developments and flood control on the Columbia River, which flows through BC and the states of Washington and Oregon.

Toronto's George Knudson drew 5,000 fans to Capilano Golf Course for a filming of *Shell's Wonderful World of Golf*.

Notable deaths: **Angus MacInnis**, original CCFer, city alderman (1926–30) and MP for Vancouver East (1930–56), in Vancouver on March 2, aged 79; **Laura Emma Jamieson** (née Marshall), juvenile court judge (first BC woman in that position), CCF MLA for Vancouver Centre (1939–45), alderman, peace activist and suffragette, in Vancouver on June 29, aged 80; **William George Murrin**, president of the BC Electric Railway (1929–46) and governor of UBC, who was actively involved with community arts groups, in Vancouver on July 25, aged 88; **Elmore Philpott**, *Vancouver Sun* columnist (1943–61) and Liberal MP for Vancouver South (1953–57), in Penticton on December 9, aged 68; **Charles H. Scott**, artist, teacher and administrator at the Vancouver School of Art, aged about 78.

I Want to Hold Your Hand

August 22 The Beatles hit Vancouver. They were in Seattle the night before, in Los Angeles the next night. Allan Fotheringham described the pre-concert ritual in *Maclean's*: "The Beatles press conference has become as memorable an institution as President Roosevelt's fireside chats; and at the Vancouver session, Paul, John, George and Ringo were at their flippant best. Eighty-nine newsmen crowded into a room designed for forty, including the travelling Beatle experts from the Liverpool *Echo* and London *Daily Mirror*, the CBC's royal tour expert, several writers from the U.S. and Eastern Canada, a score or so of electronic journalists and disk-jockeys, five reporters from Victoria—the Empire's last anti-Beatle outpost—and a thirteen-year-old Beatlemaniac named Susan Lomax whom the *Sun* sent along to get the Youthful Viewpoint. All of them were...charmed by their now-familiar Liverpudlian cockiness...Asked about the customs delay, John Lennon replied: 'We had to be deloused.'"

As when Elvis performed at the same venue seven years earlier, Red Robinson emceed the show at Empire Stadium. Opening acts, including Jackie DeShannon and the Righteous Brothers, began singing at 8:14, and the Beatles came on at 9:23. They played seven minutes longer than Elvis had done, but neither audience was able to hear much over the screams of the fans. Both Red Robinson and Beatles' manager Brian Epstein interrupted the performance to appeal for calm, but it was no use. Thousands of teenagers rushed the stage and hundreds were crushed against the restraining fence. After 29 minutes the Beatles bolted from the stage and were whisked away in limousines with a police motorcycle escort.

The classical music critics sent by the newspapers to review the show griped, "Seldom in Vancouver's entertainment history have so many (20,261) paid so much ($5.25 top price) for so little." Jack Wasserman, who with Jack Webster was on the field, covering the show for Jack Cullen's *Owl Prowl* on CKNW, said it was "a damned disgrace" and "the most poorly organized advance gouge in the history of Vancouver." The commentary of the three Jacks, who were astounded by the number of "casualties" being carried away from the stage, seemed more appropriate for a battlefield or the apocalypse.

A day in the life. Seen taking questions at the airport, the Fab Four—(from left) Paul McCartney, George Harrison, John Lennon and Ringo Starr—later caused a near riot as fans went wild at their concert.
Top: Deni Eagland / Vancouver Sun; bottom: George Diack / Vancouver Sun

Right: A polar bear lunges for the water in the Stanley Park Zoo in 1965 while another looks on. The zoo was started in the 1890s out of the animal collection of the first park superintendent, Henry Avison, but Vancouverites voted to phase it out in a 1994 referendum and it closed for good when the last animal, an elderly polar bear named Tuk, died in December 1997 at age 36. Now the only local zoo is the Greater Vancouver Zoo in Aldergrove.
Province newspaper photo, Vancouver Public Library VPL 42902

1965

Vancouver installed its first curb ramps for wheelchairs, an innovation that became standard procedure. Simon Fraser University opened in Burnaby with a new approach to academics and athletics. And Whistler ski resort opened.

February 15 The new Canadian flag was hoisted at 6 a.m. at Vancouver City Hall. Because of the time differential, this was the first appearance of the flag in Canada after its official proclamation.

February 17 A testimonial dinner was held at the Hotel Vancouver for Premier W.A.C. Bennett on the occasion of his becoming the longest-serving premier in BC history: 13 years.

March 19 Violet Pooley Sweeny died in West Vancouver, aged 78. Known as "the Queen of Northwest Golf," in 1905 Sweeny won the first of seven Pacific Northwest and nine BC championships. She married Sedley Campbell "Bimbo" Sweeny, a famous rugby player and rower, in 1915 and sold cars for Consolidated Motors on West Georgia before becoming a golf demonstrator for McLennan, McFeeley and Prior sports and hardware. She was inducted posthumously into the BC Sports Hall of Fame in 1974.

May 10 Work commenced on clearing a portion of a 23.5-hectare (58-acre) site for the Gardens of Gethsemani in South Surrey. Financed by the Archdiocese of Vancouver, it was the first regional cemetery and mausoleum to serve the needs of Catholics and their families in the Lower Mainland.

August 6 Eleven months after its first edition appeared, the *Vancouver Times* ended publication. By early 1965, with just 50,000 subscribers, the newspaper was in financial trouble. It signed *Hot Line* host Pat Burns as a columnist after he left CJOR, but it wasn't enough. In May 1965 the paper slashed staff, asked shareholders to purchase more stock and offered an annual subscription rate of $15—down from $18—"to furnish needed working capital." On June 23 the single-issue price dropped from ten cents to five. Nothing worked.

August 16 The largest crowd in BC racing history turned out to

Elsewhere in BC

July 8 The crash of a Canadian Pacific Airlines flight near 100 Mile House killed all 52 passengers on board. The cause of the crash was determined to be "an explosive substance foreign to the normal contents of the aircraft," but the source of the explosion remains unknown and charges were never laid.

July 9 The Hope slide, the largest landslide ever recorded in Canada, killed four.

The provincial government established the regional district concept. The Greater Vancouver Regional District was created in 1967.

Elsewhere in Canada

March 11 The National Hockey League admitted six new teams and doubled in size.

November 9 A failure at an Ontario power station caused a blackout stretching from Florida to Chicago and all of southern Ontario.

Elsewhere in the World

January 24 Sir Winston Churchill died, aged 90.

watch as Johnny Longden rode his 6,000th winner at Exhibition Park. The *Province*'s Alf Cottrell reported: "Longden reached the historic milestone on local industrialist Art Fouks' steady veteran Prince Scorpion, after a masterful ride climaxed by a stern stretch drive. The little Englishman was the first jockey in history to ride 4,871 winners, for that was the point at which he passed England's Gordon Richards... in 1956... Now word of his latest feat will flash all over the world, including Taber, Alberta, the little town where he was raised." Longden, originally from England, had started his racing career in Canada and wanted to record this historic riding achievement before the "home folks."

September 9
Simon Fraser University enrolled its first students (2,500 in number) on Burnaby Mountain.
The university, designed by Arthur Erickson and Geoffrey Massey, had been built in less than two years thanks to the hard-driving Dr. Gordon Shrum, who was appointed the first chancellor in 1962. The official opening was presided over by Lord Lovat, whose name was Simon Fraser and who was the 24th head of the Fraser clan. He told an audience of 5,000 about the Fraser family crest, which had been adapted and adopted by the university: "There are strawberries all over our crest because the name Fraser came originally from 'la fraise,' French for strawberry. Our ancestors came to Scotland by way of Normandy and England." Simon's second great-grandson, Donald Fraser of Fargo, ND, beamed proudly from the audience.

SFU pioneered the year-round trimester system—self-contained 16-week semesters—a radical departure from the traditional academic year, with new possibilities for work and study. It developed the "Oxbridge" system of tutorials, in which students, guided by tutors, were left to their own resources. Large lectures were supplemented with small discussion groups. Admission requirements were relaxed for bright high schoolers and mature students. Whiz kids and grandparents have always shared classes. And in 1965 SFU was the only university in Canada to offer athletic scholarships for academically qualified students.

September Vancouver City College (VCC) opened at the King Edward Centre at Oak Street and West 12th Avenue, in a 1905 building that had housed King Edward High School. VCC was the first two-year community college in Canada. It was formed by bringing together the Vancouver School of Art, established in 1925, the Vancouver Vocational Institute, established in 1949, and the King Edward Senior Matriculation

SFU opens. The construction wasn't quite finished when Simon Fraser University—designed by a then-young professor of architecture, Arthur Erickson, and colleague Geoffrey Massey—opened its doors to fresh minds on Burnaby Mountain.
The Province

and Continuing Education Centre, established in 1962. In 1974 it became Vancouver Community College.

October 22 "Alvo" von Alvensleben, one of BC's first millionaires and an important Vancouver realtor, died in Seattle, aged 86. It is estimated he pumped $7 million into the provincial economy in the years before World War I. He was also one of our most colourful characters. One of my favourites of many, many stories about Alvo: He arrived in Vancouver with about $3 in his pocket and made a living partly by selling game birds he had shot in the Fraser Valley, which he sold to a haughty head waiter at the back door of the Vancouver Club. A few years later, now a millionaire through his real estate dealings, he proudly entered the front door of the club as a member...and snubbed the waiter. One of Alvo's homes is now Crofton House School for Girls.

October 30 Actor John Drainie died, aged 49. He was born in Vancouver on April 1, 1916. Many called him the greatest radio actor in the world. Not just in Canada—the world. "He mastered nearly every accent and dialect in the English world," said a cohort. "Not only could Drainie imitate the voices of six different people in one program, he was able to simulate the sound of a telephone ringing, telephone dialling, a busy signal and even the sound of a bell over a grocery store door." He was Jake on CBC Radio's *Jake and the Kid*, he played Stephen Leacock to perfection and there were hundreds of other roles.

November 22 Edith McConnell Stewart-Murray died in Victoria, aged about 65. She was born in Montreal in 1900, lived in Vancouver from 1904 to 1958, then moved to Victoria. Her father, John P. "Black Jack" McConnell, with brother-in-law T.S. Ford, founded the *Morning Sun*, the forerunner of the *Vancouver Sun* (1912). She was a columnist and women's page editor for the *Sun* and *Vancouver News-Herald* for 40 years. Her best-known column was *Let's Go Shopping*. She was a life member of the Canadian Women's Press Club.

November 26 BC-bred George Royal was named Canada's Racehorse of the Year. Among the dumber questions ever asked (I know, because I asked it) was this one of Jim Coleman, doyen of Canadian sportswriters and *the* writer on thoroughbred racing in this country: "Remember when George Royal was named Canada's Racehorse of the Year?" Jim remembered because he was on the committee that selected him. Writing earlier in 1965 about a journey George Royal took to Woodbine track in Toronto, Jim said: "He accepted his first-class flight accommodations with the lordly boredom of an Oriental potentate. He's a cool one...he even tipped the stewardess a bale of hay."

December 27 The *Vancouver Sun* and the *Province* began publication in new, shared Pacific Press premises at 2250 Granville St.

They stayed there for a little more than 30 years. Curiously, although that building is now gone—replaced by upscale condos—the earlier homes of both papers are still around: the *Province*'s old home was the Carter-Cotton building at the southeast corner of Cambie and Hastings, and the old Sun Tower is just a couple of blocks away at 100 West Pender. The two papers had been virtually next-door neighbours for more than 50 years already. When the *Sun* started in 1912 it was at 125 West Pender, just around the corner from the *Province*. In March 1937, when a fire destroyed the *Sun*'s business and editorial offices, the owners simply bought the World Building across the street at 100 West Pender, a funky green-topped skyscraper that had once been home to the now-vanished *Vancouver World*. The *Sun* staff walked across the street, set up shop and stayed until the 1965 move.

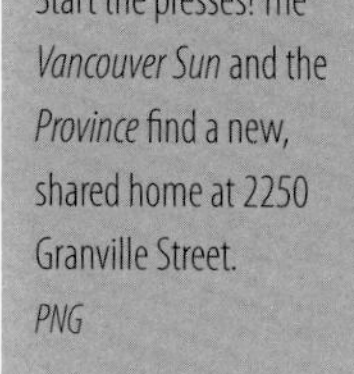

Start the presses! The *Vancouver Sun* and the *Province* find a new, shared home at 2250 Granville Street. *PNG*

Also in 1965

Grace McInnis became the first woman from BC elected to the House of Commons. She sat as the NDP member for Vancouver–Kingsway until her retirement in 1974. Politics was a family tradition: her father, J.S. Woodsworth, was the founder of the Co-operative Commonwealth Federation (CCF), forerunner of the NDP.

The Variety Club started a Vancouver chapter, thanks to the efforts of businessman Harry Howard. Hearing of the efforts of Howard and others, Jockey Club president and philanthropist Jack Diamond invited the group to the Clubhouse at the Track. He sponsored the dinner meeting and became a charter member of Tent 47, one of the most productive tents in Variety's world. Today, with the word "Club" dropped to indicate the openness of the group, Variety—the Children's Charity of British Columbia, continues to raise money for BC's children with special needs. Its major fundraising endeavour is the Show of Hearts telethon. The 2010 event raised over $7 million.

Al Reusch of Aragon Recording built what became Mushroom Studios at 1234 West 6th Ave. as an orchestral recording room for special sessions by the CBC. The state-of-the-art facility quickly became a favourite recording location for pop performers. Among the earliest clients were Motown artists Diana Ross and the Supremes. Legend has it that they cut their tracks here in the dead of winter, even before heating had been installed in the building.

Back in 1915 a musical comedy, *50 Years Forward*, premiered at the Imperial Theatre in Vancouver. Among its predictions for Vancouver in 1965: a woman mayor. We checked: it didn't happen.

The Vancouver Playhouse, presented its first original Canadian play, Eric Nicol's *Like Father, Like Fun*. It told of a crass lumber baron's attempt to contrive his son's initiation to sex. It was a success here and was taken to Broadway in 1967 with a new title: *A Minor Adjustment*. It was not successful there, but Nicol, unbowed, even had fun with that misfortune.

The Dorothy Somerset Scholarship Fund was established. Dorothy Somerset, born in Perth, Australia, in 1900, was an actor/director and teacher celebrated for her encouragement of young talent in the theatre. In 1958 she helped found UBC's drama department.

Playboard began life as a program guide for the Vancouver Little Theatre, published by Vienna-born theatre enthusiast Harold Schiel and his wife Irene. Over the years *Playboard* became part of the theatre- and opera-going experience for Vancouverites, with a mix of movie industry news, theatrical trivia and guides to current productions. It is now published by Archway Publications in Surrey.

The Fraser River Harbour Commission replaced the New Westminster Harbour Board. All municipalities adjoining the river sent representatives to the new commission, which dealt with issues like water pollution and industrial growth.

Surrey adopted the concept of "five towns" within the municipality—Guildford, Whalley, Cloverdale, Newton and Sunnyside—with sub-units designed as villages and "green bands" around each area.

Erickson/Massey Architects designed the Smith House, at 5030 The Byway in West Vancouver. It won the 1967 Massey Medal for Architecture.

The tunnel at the main Vancouver post office, built to carry mail to the CPR station, was closed permanently for that purpose, having proved impractical. It is now used for storage and creepy movie scenes.

H.Y. Louie Co. acquired the IGA chain of stores. The company, founded by Hok Yat Louie in 1903 and now under the stewardship of Hok Yat's son, Tong Louie, also bought the nine-store Dominion supermarket chain in 1968.

The Lions Bay development went into receivership. It had been battered by Hurricane Frieda in October 1962 and suffered slowing lot sales.

Charlie Crane, one of the most interesting people in Vancouver's history, died. He lost his sight and hearing as a result of spinal meningitis when he was nine months old, but he accomplished much. Charlie was a bright student at the Halifax and Jericho Hill schools for the deaf, and a special student at UBC from 1934 to 1937—the first deaf-blind person to attend university in Canadian history. He was also outstanding in athletics, particularly in wrestling. Later in life, due to lack of public awareness and support, Charlie settled into a life of manual work and personal study. He read voraciously, became an avid collector of Braille books and with help from others created his own Braille books. He bequeathed his personal collection of several thousand books to UBC on his death.

Early Whistler. Named for the vocal marmots that make their home on the mountain, Whistler Mountain Resort is now home to all kinds of wildlife, including ski bunnies and powder hounds. It is considered by many to be one of the Top 10 ski resorts in the world. *Whistler Museum and Archives Society*

That collection formed the basis of the Crane Resource Centre and Library.

Vancouver built its first curb ramps for wheelchair users. (Today virtually all the sidewalks in the downtown core have sloping ramps, called curb cuts, for easy access.)

The Great Northern Railway station, next door to the CN terminal and unused since 1962, was demolished. Using the CN station, the American railway continued to operate a Vancouver–Seattle train service for 15 years.

The Vancouver Mounties baseball team, which had disbanded in November 1962, returned for the Pacific Coast League's 1965 season. The club would, alas, fold for good at the end of the 1969 season.

Vancouver's Joan (Rocco) Haines was chosen the world's best female bowler.

Whistler Resort was born. It was originally called London Mountain, but the name was changed, apparently inspired by the alarm call of the whistling marmots that reside in the area. The first paved road had gone in just a year earlier, and the inaugural ski runs at Whistler Creek opened this year. They were built by the Garibaldi Lift Company, later renamed the Whistler Mountain Ski Corporation, which was bought out by Intrawest (also the owner of Blackcomb Mountain) in 1997. Franz's Run, named after founder and first president Franz Wilhelmsen, still exists.

Closer to home, skiers bemoaned the fate of Hollyburn, a skiing favourite since the 1920s: the chairlift shut down and the lodge was destroyed by fire.

Comings and Goings

March Famed opera singer Marilyn Horne appeared in the Vancouver Opera production of Rossini's *The Italian Girl in Algiers (L'Italiana in Algeri).*

October 29 Christy Clark was born in Burnaby. She grew up in a political home—her father Jim was a three-time candidate for the Liberals in Burnaby—and in 2011 she became BC premier.

Notable deaths: Drugstore pioneer **George Cunningham** in Palm Springs, CA, on March 7, aged about 76; **Duncan Bell-Irving**, Canada's first World War I flying ace, in Vancouver on April 24, aged 70; **Elizabeth "Betsy" Flaherty**, pilot (when she got her licence in 1931 she was the oldest female pilot in Canada) and co-founder of the Flying Seven Canadian Women Pilots, in Vancouver in June, aged about 87; **Austin Cottrell Taylor**, owner of the Bralorne gold mine and one of the city's wealthiest men, in Vancouver on November 1, aged 76; **Mary Isabella Rogers**, widow of Benjamin Tingley Rogers, founder of the BC Sugar Refinery, aged about 96.

1966

Various sports-related stories were front and centre this year as the city cheered the swimming exploits of a 15-year-old "Mighty Mouse" from West Vancouver, who became the country's youngest-ever Athlete of the Year. The first ski lifts opened on Whistler, and the BC Sports Hall of Fame opened at the PNE. Football fans, meanwhile, rioted in the street, and baseball players brawled on the field.

January 6 Yvonne Millicent Firkins, BC's "first lady of the theatre," died in Vancouver in her 70s. She was born in Worcester, England, and came to Vancouver in 1920. She was a founding member of Vancouver Little Theatre, Vancouver Ballet School and the Vancouver Dance Festival; president of the BC Drama Association; and founder of the BC Dance Festival. She also directed shows at Theatre Under the Stars. During World War II she was production manager of service shows for Pacific Command, and in 1964 she opened the Arts Club Theatre. What a lot of activity she crammed into her years!

January 7 The Right Reverend James Francis Carney became the first Vancouver-born Catholic to be named a bishop. He was appointed auxiliary bishop today and archbishop on January 8, 1969 (installed February 11.)

February 15 The first ski lifts opened to the public on Whistler Mountain, and mass-marketing of the resort began.

February 26 Health Minister Eric Martin opened the 132-bed Richmond General Hospital, situated next to a cow pasture. The first patient was admitted March 17 and the hospital's first baby was born later that day.

April 6 On Vancouver's 80th birthday a "Paint-in" began in front of the Vancouver Courthouse. Hoardings were built around the space on which a fountain was being installed, and, encouraged by Mayor Bill Rathie, amateur and professional artists began to paint on them in a wide and wild variety of styles.

May 11 A dark day for baseball's Vancouver Mounties, who had re-entered the Pacific Coast League in

Elsewhere in BC

December 14 The second Bank of British Columbia, the 1960s version, received its federal charter, exactly one year after the Senate banking committee rejected Premier W.A.C. Bennett's proposal to create a BC-based bank, with the provincial government as a major shareholder. Bennett felt financial institutions headquartered in Toronto and Montreal could not understand the pressing need to finance private development in BC. "Vancouver is farther away from the head office of a chartered bank than any other city of comparable size in the whole free world," Bennett told the banking committee in July 1964. But the committee turned Bennett down, concerned about the influence the BC government could have on a new bank if it were the major shareholder. In March 1966 the committee approved a different, totally private, proposal. The new Bank of British Columbia began full operations in 1968.

The Confederation of Native Indians of BC was established.

Elsewhere in Canada

July to December Canada's Parliament passed the Medical Care Act establishing universal health care programs.

Elsewhere in the World

August 29 The Beatles played their last live concert in San Francisco's Candlestick Park and started work on *Sgt. Pepper's Lonely Hearts Club Band.*

Mao Zedong launched the Cultural Revolution in China.

The United States more than doubled the number of troops it had in Vietnam, from 180,000 to 385,000.

Both the Soviet Union and the United States soft-landed lunar probes on the Moon. The probes sent back the first photographs from the lunar surface.

Yet to be surpassed in achievement, 5 ft. 3 in. swimmer Elaine "Mighty Mouse" Tanner was dynamite in the 1960s. Among her accomplishments, she set five world records, and was the first Canadian to win three medals in a single Olympic Games, as well as the first Canadian female swimmer to win a medal. Yet expectations were so high for a gold that when Tanner had to settle for a silver due to poor coaching, her achievements were ignored and Tanner was left traumatized. She retired the following year from swimming at the age of 18, and suffered two decades of depression, divorce, anorexia and eventual homelessness in Vancouver, before finding her way back to healing and life.
Bill Cunningham / The Province

1965. The Mounties' Santiago Rosario hit catcher Merritt Ranew of the Seattle Rainiers in the head with a baseball bat during an on-field brawl.

May Abbotsford's Matsqui Institution opened for the custody and treatment of drug addicts. This medium-security facility was built to hold 312 inmates.

May Allard de Ridder, first conductor of the Vancouver Symphony Orchestra, died in Vancouver, aged about 79. He was born in 1887 in Dordrecht, Holland, and received his musical education in Holland and Germany. Before being named the Vancouver Symphony's first conductor in 1930 he had conducted orchestras in Europe and the United States. In 1941, he moved to Toronto, where he joined the Hart House String Quartet and taught at the Royal Conservatory of Music, before founding the Ottawa Philharmonic Orchestra in 1944. He retired to Vancouver in 1951.

June 17 BCIT's first 400 graduates received the two-year National Diploma of Technology.

June 23 The *St. Roch* historic site opened adjacent to the Maritime Museum. The tough RCMP schooner, which had gone through Arctic waters twice (the first ship to traverse the Arctic in both directions), and which had gone through the Panama Canal (the first ship to circumnavigate North America), was put on display and made available to tours.

July 16 West Vancouver's Elaine Tanner, 15, was named Amateur Swimmer of the Year by the Canadian Amateur Swimming Association.

This was one in a string of honours for "Mighty Mouse." She won four golds and three silvers at the 1966 British Empire and Commonwealth Games, an individual Games record for women to that time. She was the youngest person ever named as Canada's Athlete of the Year. Later, at the Pan-American Games, she won two golds and three silvers, then went on to the 1968 Olympics and won two silvers. Tanner retired from competitive swimming at age 18, the best woman swimmer in Canadian history.

September 12 Some merchants in Block 42 (around Georgia and Howe in downtown Vancouver) launched a court case against the city's expropriation of their properties for the Pacific Centre development.

October 17 Frederick Laughton Townley, architect and designer, died in Vancouver, aged about 79. The son of Thomas O. Townley (Vancouver's mayor in 1901), Frederick was one of only five architects in Vancouver when he set up practice in 1911. He designed Vancouver City Hall ("a proud, modern, 1936 streamlined building") and more than 1,000 other buildings including the Great Northern Railway station, Capitol Theatre, Vancouver General Hospital, Vancouver Stock Exchange Building and the CNIB Building.

October 29 First annual Christopher Columbus banquet was sponsored by the Sons of Italy.

The BC Sports Hall of Fame

August The BC Sports Hall of Fame and Museum opened its doors, just two months after it was founded. Originally located on the PNE grounds, it relocated in 1992 to BC Place Stadium, the home field of the BC Lions CFL team, one of the many franchises and teams whose history is carefully archived within the museum's walls.

Founded by Eric Whitehead and run as a non-profit organization, the hall memorializes BC's rich sports history, from ancient First Nations games to modern athletic events. Among the first inductees were sprinters Harry Jerome and Percy Williams, boxer Jimmy McLarnin, rowers George Hungerford and Robert "Bob" Johnston, hockey players Frank and Lester Patrick and Fred "Cyclone" Taylor, swimmer Mary Stewart McIlwaine, cyclist William John "Torchy" Peden, weightlifter Doug Hepburn and golfer David Lambie "Davey" Black.

Here the stopwatch used to time the Miracle Mile rests alongside a torch from the 2010 Olympic Winter Games, and the struggles of resilient small-town teams like the 1908 New Westminster Salmonbellies—the first western lacrosse champions—share attention with the travails of multi-million-dollar professional sports franchises such as the Vancouver Canucks. The story of the amateur Trail Smoke Eaters, who in 1961 advanced on a technicality to the ice hockey world championship and won the tournament without a single loss, is recounted in vivid detail, as are the feats of individual Olympic and Paralympic medallists.

Stars of canoeing, rodeo, ice dance, hockey, judo and golf rub shoulders on the hall's list of 319 inductees. Displays feature local heroes including Cyclone Taylor, rover for the Stanley Cup–winning Vancouver Millionaires, and Grey Cup–winning Lions centre and guard Al Wilson.

Hall of Famer. Looking every inch his nickname of Mr. Baseball, Bob Brown, seen here in his Vancouver Beavers uniform, was a key organizer of Vancouver baseball from 1910 to 1962, when he died. In 1966 he became the first inductee to BC's Baseball Hall of Fame. *Harbour Publishing Archives*

November 25 A riot followed the Grey Cup game in Vancouver (Saskatchewan Roughriders beat the Ottawa Rough Riders 29–14).

November The provincial government bought the Queensborough Bridge and removed the tolls drivers had paid to use the bridge since it opened in 1960.

November Vancouver city council established the Department of Social Planning "to plan, develop, coordinate and integrate health, education, welfare, recreational, and community renewal programs and to foster self-help and community-betterment programs." A personal note: I have a special spot in my heart for the Social Planning Department. Away back in 1974 its staff arranged a grant from the city that allowed me to compile *The Vancouver Book*, which I described as an urban almanac. My thanks to Maurice Egan, who led the department back then, and to Ernie Fladell, who actually got the ball rolling on the book, which appeared in 1976.

December 12 Mathias Joe Capilano, Squamish chief and carver, died in Vancouver, aged about 81. He was born ca. 1885 on the north shore of Burrard Inlet, the son of Chief Joe and Mary Capilano. A prominent leader and internationally famed carver, he attended the coronations of both George VI (1937) and Elizabeth II (1953), wearing full tribal regalia. A lifelong campaigner for the rights of First Nations people, in 1949 he and his wife Ellen cast the first Native ballots in BC.

December 14 Tom Campbell was elected mayor of Vancouver, served a couple of turbulent terms and came to be known as "Tom Terrific."

Grey Cup follow-up. Rioting and sports seem to go together more often than preferred, as proved by a riot following the Grey Cup game in Vancouver on November 25, 1966. *Province newspaper photo, Vancouver Public Library VPL 42731C*

Also December 14 William George "Uncle Billy" Hassell, broadcaster and collie breeder, died in Vancouver, aged about 73. He came to Vancouver in 1919 after serving as a wireless operator in the Royal Navy. Hassell was the first Canadian radio newscaster to sign off with his own name, and possibly the first to make a singing radio commercial. He was known as Uncle Billy on his kids' program, *Squareshooters*. In 1946 he retired to breed collies in Langley.

December 15 Premier W.A.C. Bennett opened the first Grouse Mountain skyride. It carried 50 passengers. Ten years to the day later, Bennett's son, Premier Bill Bennett, opened Grouse's Superskyride, which more than doubled the uphill capacity. (Earlier this year, the Grouse Mountain Restaurant opened.)

On the same day, the busy premier opened Centennial Fountain, built on the Georgia Street side of the Vancouver Art Gallery, to commemorate the 1866 union of the crown colonies of British Columbia and Vancouver Island. The installation of this and several other fountains in Vancouver this year prompted an outburst by alderman Aeneas Bell-Irving. "There is one thing we don't need," he said, "and that is more fountains, because God has given us a perfectly wonderful supply of rain." Bell-Irving suggested bonfires would be more appropriate.

Also in 1966

The Amalgamated Construction Association (ACA) was founded. The organization's roots actually extended back to 1929, with the formation of the Building and Construction Industries Exchange of BC. The exchange's members helped build some of Vancouver's greatest landmarks, including the Lions Gate Bridge and the Hotel Vancouver. The ACA brought together the Victoria Building Industries Exchange, the Vancouver General Contractors Association, the Heavy Construction Association of BC and the Vancouver Construction Association, encompassing more than 650 companies. (It's now known as Vancouver Regional Construction Association.)

Construction began on the mammoth, fully automated, $20.4-million Saskatchewan Wheat Pool elevator in North Vancouver. The five-million-bushel terminal in North Vancouver, which opened in 1968, was the most expensive single capital project handled by the Wheat Pool up to that time.

The Marpole rail bridge was heavily damaged by a barge. Built in 1902 for the CPR, the bridge was now leased by the Southern Railway of BC. It was rebuilt with full main-line capacity and a longer, hydraulically operated swing span and went back into operation in 1967.

Angelo Branca, who had been a judge on the BC Supreme Court since 1963, was appointed to the province's highest court, the BC Court of Appeal.

St Paul's Hospital opened its intensive-care unit.

Phil Nuytten (pronounced "newton") founded Can-Dive to supply divers to oil companies and to develop deep-diving techniques and underwater technology. Nuytten started diving when he was only 12, designing his own scuba equipment. At 15 he opened a scuba diving store on 4th Avenue in Vancouver—the first in western Canada—and made good money as a freelance diver even before he finished high school. His best-known product, the Newtsuit, allows divers to work at 300-metre (1,000-foot) depths without having to undergo decompression after resurfacing.

In book news: *Bennett*, Paddy Sherman's biography of Premier W.A.C. Bennett, was published. James Clavell, who had moved to West Vancouver in 1963, had an international bestseller in *Tai-Pan*. Another hugely popular title

Right: Undersea entrepreneur. Phil Nuytten, already diving at the age of 12, put his aspirations to the test and opened his own scuba store at the tender age of 15.
Courtesy Phil Nuytten

was Christie Harris' *Raven's Cry*, which related the history, some of it mythological, of the Haida.

Elie Savoie of the CBC began producing *The Bill Kenny Show*. Kenny was an early member of the Inkspots, a popular singing group of the 1940s and '50s. Regulars on this light entertainment/music series, headlined by Kenny, were the Accents, Fraser MacPherson, Marty Gillan, Judy Ginn and Fran Gregory.

Director/producer John Juliani, who, according to the *Province*, "pioneered experimental theatre in Vancouver during his days as theatre head at Simon Fraser University," established Savage God, an experimental theatre company. The productions were so notorious one local critic accused Juliani of corrupting innocent youth.

The 718-seat Centennial Theatre Centre opened at 2300 Lonsdale Ave. in North Vancouver. One of many theatres built across Canada as part of the country's centennial celebrations, the Centennial is home to the North Shore Light Opera, the North Shore Chorus and the Greater Vancouver Operatic Society. Another North Shore centennial project, jointly funded by the City and District, was the North Vancouver Recreation Centre, which opened this year.

Gerhard Class created a granite monument to the Old Hastings Mill at the north foot of Dunlevy Street, site of the original mill. The Vancouver Historical Society commissioned the monument for $1,500 as a centennial project.

Carver Tony Hunt created the Kwakiutl Bear Pole at Horseshoe Bay.

The "Playground of the Gods" was installed at Burnaby Mountain Park, on an open slope looking west over Coal Harbour. The spectacular setting inspired Nuburi Toko and his son, Shusei, to carve 50 totem poles to represent the story of the gods who descended to Earth to give birth to the Ainu, Japan's first inhabitants. The poles honour the ties between Burnaby and its Japanese sister city, Kushiro.

The City of Vancouver bought Roedde House and made it the centrepiece in what came to be called Barclay Heritage Square, bounded by Barclay, Nicola, Haro and Broughton Streets in the West End. The square features nine historic houses built between 1890 and 1908. Roedde House, at 1415 Barclay, was built in 1893 for Vancouver's first bookbinder, Gustav Roedde. It's operated by the Roedde House Preservation Society, a non-profit volunteer group, and has been handsomely restored.

Stan McDonald, a Canadian-born Seattle businessman, developed a taste for cruising when he ran a charter ship during the Seattle World's Fair in 1962. This year he chartered two larger Italian ships and set about building his company, Princess Cruises—visiting Alaska in the summer, Mexico in the winter.

Department store founder Charles A. Woodward (1852–1937) was named to the Canadian Business Hall of Fame.

Residents of Lions Bay created the Lions Bay Water Improvement District, an umbrella agency that not only collected and distributed the water from the mountainside but also dealt with garbage, recreational facilities and fire protection.

Roedde House, built for bookbinder Gustav Roedde in 1893, was bought by the City of Vancouver and restored for use as a museum. *Roedde House Museum*

Comings and Goings

March 26 Bob Dylan performed at Vancouver's Agrodome. This was his last North American concert for eight years. He started a world tour on April 13 but on July 29 was badly injured in a motorcycle accident and spent a long time convalescing. It's a tribute to Dylan's staying power as a superstar that he attracted full houses in a string of Vancouver appearances in July 2005—39 years after his first show here!

Marilyn Horne returned to Vancouver to star in the VOA's production of *Il Trovatore*.

Notable deaths: **Sedley Campbell Sweeny**, nicknamed "Bimbo," a celebrated rugby player and rower, in West Vancouver on February 12, aged 77; **Charles Edwin Thompson**, teacher, rancher, car dealer and mayor of Vancouver (1949–50), on April 19, aged 75; **Samuel Joseph Cohen**, the founder of Army & Navy stores, in Vancouver on December 21, aged 69.

1967

Canada's Centennial was a year for protest and generational politics in Vancouver. The *Georgia Straight* newspaper was established. There were anti-Vietnam War marches and a "Human Be-In" in Stanley Park. When city hall proposed a waterfront freeway, it sparked an outcry that eventually scuttled the plan. There was also controversy over the statue of a naked boy.

March 26 A big anti–Vietnam War protest was held in Vancouver. On the same day there was a "Super Human Be-In" in Stanley Park. And on April 15, there was a peace march.

Be-In. To underscore and support a large anti-Vietnam protest happening on the same day, over 1,000 "hippies" took a page from San Francisco and converged on Stanley Park for the first Human Be-In in Vancouver. *Ken Oakes* / Vancouver Sun

May 17 The Canadian Lacrosse Hall of Fame opened in the Centennial Community Centre at 6th Avenue and McBride Boulevard in New Westminster.

June 1 The first McDonald's restaurant in Canada opened in Richmond at 7120 No. 3 Rd. It was take-out only, and hamburgers cost 18 cents.

Also June 1 VanCity Credit Union introduced North America's first daily interest savings account, known as Plan 24.

June 14 Squamish chief August Jack Khahtsahlano died. His grandfather was the man for whom Kitsilano was named, but August Jack

Elsewhere in BC

July 1 Not local, but must be reported: Pamela Anderson was born today in Ladysmith, on Vancouver Island.

In partial fulfillment of the Columbia River Treaty, the Duncan Dam was built on the Duncan River to control the flow of water into the Kootenay River.

Frank Calder and the Nisga'a of northwestern BC took the BC government to court, arguing that aboriginal title to ancestral lands in the province had not been lawfully extinguished. BC courts ruled that title had indeed been extinguished, but the Nisga'a appealed to the Supreme Court of Canada.

Elsewhere in Canada

April 28 Expo 67 began in Montreal.

July 1 Canada celebrated its 100th birthday.

Sprinter Harry Jerome won gold in the 100-metre race at the Pan-American Games in Winnipeg. He was also inducted into the Canadian Amateur Athletic Hall of Fame this year.

Canadian immigration laws were changed to evaluate potential immigrants using a points system, and all restrictions specifically directed against Asian immigration were lifted. The universal points system was created to encourage professionals and skilled workers from all over the world to immigrate to Canada, resulting in an increasingly diverse immigrant population.

Elsewhere in the World

March 26 Skier Nancy Greene won the first Women's World Cup title.

New Westminster–born actor Raymond Burr, already famous as TV's Perry Mason, began a new series, *Ironside*, as a wheelchair-bound investigator. It was a hit and lasted to 1975.

Victoria-born Lynn Patrick became general manager of the St. Louis Blues hockey team.

The first man to undergo a heart transplant (Louis Washkansky, age 55) died in Cape Town, South Africa, after living for 18 days.

The prices may have changed from 18 cents for a burger, but McDonald's has remained as a bastion of fast food since it opened its first Canadian restaurant in Richmond, BC. *City of Richmond Archives Photograph 1987 61 3*

The *Georgia Straight*

May 5 The first issue of the *Georgia Straight* appeared with stories about art censorship, Haight-Ashbury and the youth movement in Amsterdam. The first issue was produced in publisher Dan McLeod's apartment. Then the paper moved into an office at 432 Homer...and McLeod was jailed for vagrancy. College Printers refused to publish the second issue.

This radical newspaper (published every two weeks at first) stirred up a great deal of attention in the following months, before the city settled down and accepted it.

It's wonderfully ironic that McLeod—who in the paper's earliest days fought Mayor Tom Campbell and the right wing and the police and the prudes and was occasionally jailed for his pains—would in 1998 win the Bruce Hutchison Lifetime Achievement Award for his "contribution to journalism in BC." He deserved to win, but it's astonishing that he did. Circulation of the free, ad-fat *Straight* is way up (110,000-plus claimed), but the paper's calmer. It still does investigative stories, wins awards, has good writers and gets scoops. McLeod leaves editing chores to others. But he started it all, and local news was forever altered because of it.

Left: Ski sensation. Nancy Greene, for whom several ski runs, roads and hot-chocolate recipes are named, won top honours in the first Women's World Cup ski event. *Harbour Publishing Archives*

made a name for himself as one of the most fruitful and dignified sources of information on early Native life here, thanks to his long conversations with archivist J.S. Matthews, transcribed and accessible at the archives. (They are occasionally a source of unintended humour: sometimes Matthews has him speaking in the measured tones of an English professor, elsewhere he makes him sound like Tonto.) August Jack was born July 16, 1867, at Snauq (also spelled Sun'ahk), about where the H.R. MacMillan Space Centre is today.

June 19 The first four notes of "O Canada" played from four huge cast-aluminum airhorns atop the BC Hydro Building at Nelson and Burrard. Robert Swanson designed them. Unsuspecting pedestrians could be visibly alarmed when the horns blared out. Today they are atop Canada Place and aimed out over the water. They signal the noon hour.

June Vancouver businessman Harry Con published the first history of Canada written in Chinese.

July 4 Chief Dan George of North Vancouver's Burrard band moved a crowd of more than 30,000 people to silence with his eloquent "Lament for Confederation" at Empire Stadium.

It began: "How long have I known you, Oh Canada? A hundred years? Yes, a hundred years. And many many seelanum [lunar months] more. And today, when you celebrate your hundred years, Oh Canada, I am sad for all the Indian people throughout the land.

"For I have known you when your forests were mine; when they gave me my meat and my clothing. I have known you in your streams and rivers where your fish flashed and danced in the sun, where the waters said, 'come, come and eat of my abundance.' I have known you in the freedom of your winds. And my spirit, like the winds, once roamed your good lands.

"But in the long hundred years since the white man came, I have seen my freedom disappear like the salmon going mysteriously out to sea. The white man's strange customs which I could not understand pressed down upon me until I could no longer breathe."

July 6 Jack Harman's statuary group *The Family* was installed outside the Pacific Press Building at 2250 Granville. The figures were elongated, Harman explained, to lend them a spiritual quality. Controversy arose over the boy in the group: he was naked. That "spiritual quality" didn't deter the vandal who attempted one night to hacksaw away the boy's penis. The next day an embarrassed welder insisted on being screened from public view while he repaired the damage. "The work is intended," Harman said, "to depict the role of a newspaper in the family and the importance of the family in the community."

July 12 The board of the Greater Vancouver Regional District (GVRD) met for the first time. The GVRD is a voluntary federation of 20 municipalities and two electoral areas that make up the metropolitan area of Greater Vancouver. These communities, branded in 2007 as "Metro Vancouver," work together through the GVRD to deliver essential services more economically, efficiently and equitably at a regional level. It is one of 27 regional districts in British Columbia and with more than 2 million residents—a little more than half the population of the province—is easily the largest. The creation of the GVRD meant the Lower Mainland Regional Planning Board was disbanded, as the regional districts served a coordination and planning function for groups of municipalities. And the Greater Vancouver Regional Hospital District was incorporated, becoming responsible for hospital planning and construction in the region.

July 30 The first Nanaimo-to-Vancouver bathtub race was held today, with 212 powered bathtubs entered. The race was the wacky inspiration of Nanaimo mayor Frank Ney. It continued until the 1990s as part of Vancouver's Sea Festival.

July Vancouver writer Chuck Davis wrote, on a scrap of paper, a sudden idea: "should do urban almanac on Vancouver." That notion would—albeit many years later—lead to the 500-page *The Vancouver Book*, published in 1976 by J.J. Douglas Ltd., and, in 1997, to the 912-page *The Greater Vancouver Book*, published by Linkman Press.

September 27 Jack Harman's Bannister–Landy statue was unveiled, commemorating the famous "Miracle Mile" of the 1954 British Empire

Bathtubs are usually thought of with water on the inside, but not according to the inspiration of Nanaimo mayor Frank Ney, who instituted the first bathtub races. Hopefuls traversed the course between Nanaimo and Vancouver in all manner of clever, cobbled-together vessels, with this winner, Richard Mellis, roaring in in 1997 with a time of 1:17:17. Now, with the end of Vancouver's Sea Fest, the race is held entirely within the Nanaimo harbour. *Peter Battistoni* / Vancouver Sun

Stopping the Freeway

October 16 A headline in the *Vancouver Sun* read: "Chinese seethe over Freeway." This was a reference to the anger in the city's Strathcona neighbourhood over plans to run a freeway through an area where many of the residents, who had lived there for decades, were Chinese.

Urban renewal had already hit Vancouver's Chinatown/Strathcona district, which planners saw as a slum neighbourhood and a blight. Beginning in the late 1950s, the city started acquiring blocks of the neighbourhood and levelling houses, with the idea of replacing them with blocks of identical high-rises to be used as social housing. A citizen group, the Strathcona Property Owners and Tenants Association (SPOTA), formed to fight the demolition of their neighbourhood, the dispersing of residents and the disappearance of Chinatown. SPOTA spokespeople Mary and Shirley Chan, Bessie Lee and Harry Con negotiated with the three levels of government to persuade them that rehabilitation was possible. Their movement resulted in a community rich with heritage homes and pride that "you can fight city hall."

When the city announced it would place a 10-metre-high (30-foot) overpass over Carrall Street (right through the centre of Chinatown) and use the blocks between Union and Prior for the freeway, connecting them to a new Georgia Viaduct and a network of roads carving up the downtown, cries of protest rose from SPOTA but also from every other part of the city. A crowd of 800 people gathered in city hall to shout down the consultants' proposals. The chairman of the city's planning commission resigned on the spot, and a year later the plan was scrapped as Vancouver residents denounced the lack of consultation and the intended destruction. The Georgia and Dunsmuir viaducts were eventually built, the only pieces of the plan that came to fruition.

Games. Both Roger Bannister and John Landy attended the sculpture's unveiling. Today the statue is at the main entrance of the Pacific National Exhibition.

November 14 An anonymous donation of $100,000 allowed the installation of a pipe organ in the recital hall of UBC's Music Building, part of the new Norman MacKenzie Centre for Fine Arts, which opened January 12, 1968.

November 22
We got a new arterial route when Canada Way was named in tribute to Canada's centennial. Parts of the new route had been Douglas Road.

December 1 The Powell Street Dugout opened as a day centre for homeless men in the area.

Also in 1967

Vancouver businessman George Patey bought the wall from the Valentine's Day Massacre. Back on February 14, 1929, in Chicago seven members of "Bugs" Moran's criminal bootlegging gang were lined up against a wall in a North Side garage and shot down by members of rival Al Capone's gang, some of whom were dressed in phony cop uniforms. The wall, with its bullet-scarred bricks, was preserved and, in 1967, auctioned off. Patey, who heard about the auction while listening to his car radio, was the high bidder. He had the wall, 2 metres (6.5 feet) high by 3 metres (10 feet) wide, taken apart and shipped to Canada, where he reconstructed it and displayed it in shopping malls, museums and galleries. In 1971 he opened a bar in Vancouver in the style of the Roaring Twenties and installed the bricks (behind plexiglass) inside the men's washroom. After the bar closed in 1976, Patey eventually sold the bricks one at a time, keeping one for a keepsake.

The Vancouver Museum moved from its musty crowded home at the former Carnegie Library at Main and Hastings to brand-new quarters in Vanier Park. Museum officials took the opportunity to create four curatorial departments: archeology, ethnology, history and natural history.

Grandview United Church, at the northwest corner of Victoria and Venables, closed. It had opened in 1909 as a Methodist Church. In 1968 it became home to the Vancouver Free University and storefront law offices for such tenants as future premier Mike Harcourt. In 1973 it reopened as the Vancouver East Cultural Centre (the "Cultch"), a venue for music and live stage performances.

The Vancouver Aquarium expanded to three times its original size, becoming the largest public aquarium in Canada and one of the five largest in North America. Two killer whales, Skana and Hyak, began performing for visitors under chief trainer Klaus Michaelis.

Fairacres, the Ceperley mansion at Deer Lake, became home to the Burnaby Art Gallery. And the formal Century Gardens were installed at the park.

Vancouver received a gift of Yoshino cherry trees from the Japanese city of Yokohama. They beautify Cambie Street between West 41st and 49th Avenues.

Park and Tilford Distillers commissioned the Park and Tilford Gardens, at 333 Brooksbank Ave. in North Vancouver, as a centennial year beautification project. The small space contains eight separate theme gardens, including a native woodland garden, a rose garden, a herb collection, an Asian garden and a greenhouse with tropical plants.

The North Vancouver Youth Band, founded in 1939, won five first-place trophies at the National Band Competition, an unprecedented achievement.

W.P. Weston, an important figure in the Vancouver art scene, died, aged about 88. In addition to teaching art, he joined the BC Society of Fine Arts and exhibited regularly. He was the first artist in western Canada to be made an associate of the Royal Canadian Academy of Art.

The *George Cunningham Memorial Sun Dial* was created by sculptor Gerhard Class. The bronze and granite memorial, near the foot of Denman Street at English Bay, was commissioned by Cunningham Drug Stores. It commemorates the three greenhorns, who settled in the West End around 1867, as well as the first drugstore built in the area in 1911.

George Ryga's powerful play about the abuse of Native women, *The Ecstasy of Rita Joe*, electrified Vancouver Playhouse audiences with its strong message. Chief Dan George and Ann Mortifee were the stars.

The Surrey Arts Centre, a very much more modest structure than it is today, was built at 13750 88th Ave. as a centennial project at a cost of $225,000. In 1981 it was rebuilt by the municipality and the province at a cost of $2.1 million.

The "Barn" at UBC became a faculty, staff and student cafeteria after a long battle to save the heritage building. Built in 1917, it was originally used as a classroom for returning World War I soldiers and later became the horticulture facility for generations of undergraduate students in agriculture. While the building's original cost was just $5,250, the 1967 renovations cost more than $62,000. Forestry and agriculture students at UBC got a new home this year as well, when the H.R. MacMillan Building was completed and dedicated to the forest company executive who had contributed more than $12 million to the university.

Vancouver's Talonbooks published its first book. Publisher Karl Siegler says that in the early days of the company, staff members met once or twice a month in each other's homes to read and vote on what work to accept for publication.

Five teaching assistants were fired by Simon Fraser University's board of governors for supporting a student who had criticized a teacher at Templeton High School. The BoG recanted when a howl for academic freedom erupted.

An 8-hectare (20-acre) site in the northeast corner of Langara Golf Course was purchased to provide space for a new campus to replace the crowded King Edward Centre of Vancouver Community (City) College, established just two years earlier.

The first of what are now five Bentall Buildings went up in downtown Vancouver. Architects for the 22-storey One Bentall Centre were Frank Musson and his partner Terry Cattell. The first four towers of Bentall Centre, completed in 1982, formed the biggest superblock development in western Canada. A fifth building was added in 2007.

Comings and Goings

May 23 Queen Juliana of the Netherlands visited Vancouver.

Joan Sutherland appeared in the Vancouver Opera Association's production of *Lucia Di Lammermoor*.

Among the acts that played Vancouver in 1967: Marilyn Horne, Don Ho, Petula Clark, Danny Kaye, Maureen Forrester, Wayne Newton, Victor Borge, the National Ballet of Canada, the American Ballet Theatre, the Royal Winnipeg Ballet, the New York Ballet and the New York Philharmonic under Leonard Bernstein.

Two people who would have a great influence on the local dance scene arrived from England. Dancer and choreographer Anna Wyman established a dance company. Max Wyman, an expert on dance who was married to Anna at the time, became an arts critic for the *Vancouver Sun* and the *Province*, and wrote books on dance. (He is also the fastest two-finger typist I have ever seen. It's an awesome sight!)

Notable deaths: **Frederick J. Hume**, former mayor of Vancouver and New Westminster and owner of the WHL Vancouver Canucks, on February 17, aged 74; **Wanda Biana Selma Ziegler (née Muller)**, president of the 11-store chain of Ziegler Chocolate Shops, at Fort Langley on March 3, aged about 93; **Ellen Harris**, broadcaster and educator, in Vancouver on June 15, aged about 63; **Mildred Valley Thornton**, artist and writer, in Vancouver on July 27, aged about 77.

1968

It was a year of parties and protest as the Pacific Coliseum opened (paving the way for an NHL team) and the city held a big parade for Olympic gold medal skier Nancy Greene. In other parts of town, student protestors occupied the administration building at SFU and the faculty club at UBC. And Vancouver got an official, federally funded Town Fool.

January 8 Pacific Coliseum opened. Federal, provincial and municipal governments had joined forces to fund the building. At the opening, Vancouver civic chaplain George Turpin offered the prayer: "Please God, bring us the NHL." And lo, He did! The $6-million, 15,600-seat, state-of-the-art arena became best known as the home of the Vancouver Canucks. (Their first game was on October 9, 1970.)

March 7 Nancy Greene, who had just won gold and silver at the Winter Olympics, returned home to a victory parade.

Elsewhere in BC

January 18 CP Air took delivery of its first Douglas DC8-60, to be used on the Vancouver–Tokyo–Hong Kong run.

July 2 John Robert Nicholson, lawyer, businessman and Liberal MP for Vancouver Centre, was sworn in as BC's Lieutenant-Governor.

December 14 Premier W.A.C. Bennett made the front pages today with a proposal that Canada be reshaped to consist of five provinces: British Columbia, Prairies, Ontario, Quebec and Atlantic. The 60th parallel would disappear as a boundary too, with both BC and Prairies extending right up to the Arctic Ocean. Bennett claimed this would result in an immediate 300 percent increase in living standards for residents of the Yukon and the Northwest Territories. The plan, which involved extending the Pacific Great Eastern railway (now BC Rail) from Fort Nelson to Whitehorse, was hooted down in Ottawa and in the media, but Bennett said public reaction to the notion was decidedly favourable.

The first phase of the Peace River hydroelectric development was completed with the construction of the 183-metre (600-foot) W.A.C. Bennett Dam, initially bringing 681,000 kilowatts of power on line. Williston Lake Reservoir, created by the dam, displaced the Tsay Keh Dene people.

The Keenleyside Dam on the Columbia River became operational, creating the Arrow Lake Reservoir.

BC's population topped 2 million this year. It had reached 1 million in 1951.

Elsewhere in Canada

April 20 Pierre Elliot Trudeau was elected prime minister. One of his BC MPs, Len Marchand, was the first Status Indian to serve as MP. In 1984, Marchand was appointed to the Senate.

Provincial and territorial First Nations groups, representing Treaty and Status Indians, came together to form the National Indian Brotherhood, which advocated for Native rights. In 1982 it changed its name to the Assembly of First Nations. Groups representing Métis and non-Status Indians formed the Native Council of Canada (now the Congress of Aboriginal Peoples) in 1968.

Elsewhere in the World

February 15 BC skier Nancy Greene won gold in the giant slalom and silver in the slalom at the Winter Olympics. She also successfully defended her World Cup title, racing to 10 titles on the tour.

October Swimmer Elaine Tanner went to the 1968 Summer Olympics in search of two golds but had to settle for two silvers. Harry Jerome, world-class sprinter, also competed in the Mexico City Olympics, his final attempt for a medal. He raced home in the 100-metre final just two-tenths of a second slower than the winner, who set a new world record time of 9.9 seconds. Jerome finished seventh.

Dr. Har Gobind Khorana won the Nobel Prize for Medicine for his work in DNA research that opened up several new areas of research. In interviews he acknowledged the important influence of his work in 1952 at BC Research on the UBC campus.

Pacific Coliseum, located on the PNE fairgrounds at Hastings, was the previous home to the Vancouver Canucks. Now it hosts everything from rock concerts to Superdogs at the PNE, and is home to the Giants, Vancouver's Western Hockey League team.
Vancouver Sun

Also March 7 Voters in the school districts of North and West Vancouver, and Howe Sound, overwhelmingly supported a community college, the fourth two-year college approved in the province. At the first meeting of the college council, members voted on a name for the new institution. From among 40 ideas suggested by North Shore residents—including Evergreen, Alpine, Sunset, Muskrat and Seagull—the clear winner was Capilano.

March 12 The Electors' Action Movement (TEAM) held its inaugural meeting at Grandview Community Centre; it went on to become a real force in Vancouver's civic politics. Among the prominent people involved at the time were Arthur Phillips, Walter Hardwick, May Brown and Marguerite Ford. Walter Hardwick, whose influence was immense—urbanologist Gordon Price calls him "arguably the most influential alderman in Vancouver's history"—was the first TEAM member to be elected, later this year. When TEAM finally gained a majority on council in 1972, Art Phillips became mayor. Hardwick topped the polls.

April 1 Joachim Foikis, armed with a grant from the Canada Council, became Vancouver's Town Fool. He sported a jester's cap and bells and strolled around warning of impending nuclear destruction. In April 1969 he spent the last of his grant money on a party in Gastown for Skid Road residents.

April 26 Premier W.A.C. Bennett and Vancouver City Archivist Major J.S. Matthews dedicated New Brighton Park. One eyewitness reported that Major Matthews, who was a very forceful fellow with a stentorian voice, frightened some of the smaller children in the audience to tears.

May 20 West Vancouver was "twinned" with the Montreal suburb of Verdun. Six delegates from Verdun, including Mayor J. Albert Gariépy, participated in the twinning ceremony, during which a Verdun Park was inaugurated by West Vancouver officials. On June 24, a West Vancouver Park was established on Nun's Island in Verdun in a similar ceremony.

May Simon Fraser University was censured by the Canadian Association of University Teachers (CAUT). The charge: interference by the board of governors in academic affairs regarding promotion, tenure and renewal of academic contracts. The controversy centred on events in the political science, sociology and anthropology department, described by one observer as "a madcap collection of brilliant New Left academics." The censure was lifted in November, but the unrest in the PSA department continued.

July 18 Opening day for the Bank of British Columbia.

A mob of customers descended on the brand-new bank at the corner of Pender and Burrard. Opening capital of the bank: $12.8 million in shareholders' equity. In a big newspaper advertisement the new bank let everyone know that all its female employees wore "smartly tailored sea-blue uniforms" featuring mini-skirts. "But don't let them fool you into thinking they're without brains," the ad continued. "They've all been hand-picked for their secretarial, executive, teller or other banking duties. They're smart in the head, too."

September 10 On the first day of classes at Capilano College, some 750 students had enrolled—twice the anticipated number. Classes were held in temporary quarters at West Vancouver Senior Secondary School, and later in several church basements, a warehouse and even a bowling alley. The college operated on an after-hours basis, from 4:00 p.m. to 10:30 p.m., and initially offered 23 courses in four different career and vocational programs. Fees were $100 per semester.

Left: Heavy style. A local brutalist landmark, the MacMillan Bloedel, or MacBlo, building at Thurlow and Georgia was designed by Arthur Erickson. It opened in 1968, during the period when the brutalist style of architecture—which the *Canadian Oxford Dictionary* calls a "heavy plain style"—was flourishing. *Esto Photographics. No. 85EE-1*

September 22 Evelyn MacKechnie of Vancouver's Community Arts Council led a group of about 200 people on a walking tour—in the rain—of Vancouver's derelict Gastown area. Gastown had been in decline for years, and the CAC thought public awareness of the historical importance of the area could arrest that decline. They were right. Media coverage was good, and the walk, the first of many, caught the attention of retailers and developers. The CAC organized more tours, and the prospect of Gastown's demolition began to fade. The area got a big boost in 1970 when the Old Spaghetti Factory opened on Water Street. Its funky ambience drew crowds.

There's a funny story about one development firm, Town Group Ltd., which had been involved in negotiations to purchase the old Alhambra Hotel on Maple Tree Square long before the CAC tour. Apparently Town Group had just about closed the deal for $80,000. The day after the Arts Council walk, the price jumped to $89,500.

September Stanley E. Higgs, Anglican minister, was named the executive head of Vancouver's Central City Mission. From 1960 to 1968 he had been chaplain of Haney Correctional Institute. Higgs retired from the Mission in April 1974 after 47 years of service to the church and the community.

October 14 George Norris's famous Crab fountain sculpture was installed in front of the Planetarium and Centennial Museum in Vanier Park. The striking stainless-steel sculpture recalls a Native legend that says a crab guards the entrance to the harbour.

October 24

American Yippee Jerry Rubin and a number of UBC students invaded the Faculty Club and took it over for 22 hours, after which they left voluntarily.

Also October 24 The first kidney transplant in BC was performed at Vancouver General Hospital.

October 26 The Centennial Museum and H.R. MacMillan Planetarium were officially opened. Mayor Tom Campbell was there; so was H.R. MacMillan himself. The planetarium, which cost $1.5 million,

Home to Harold the Star Projector and the Vancouver Museum, the H.R. MacMillan Planetarium and Centennial Museum buildings are an architectural treat at Vanier Park in Kitsilano. *Vancouver Public Library, Special Collections, VPL 54588*

was his gift to the city. Today the complex is known as the Vancouver Museum and the H.R. MacMillan Space Centre. And, yes, that famous roof really was inspired by the shape of the traditional woven basket hats worn by First Nations people on the coast.

October 29 HRH Prince Philip was on hand to open the east wing of city hall, a four-storey annex constructed to make room for the growing civic bureaucracy. It was raining heavily, and legend has it that Philip said something like "I'm very pleased to officially open this building, whatever it is, on behalf of Her Majesty—now let's get the hell inside out of the rain!" Townley and Matheson designed the original city hall. Townley, Matheson, and Partners designed the annex.

November 1 Central Heat Distribution was founded. Chances are good that if you work in downtown Vancouver, or attend a performance at the Queen Elizabeth Theatre, or take in a Lions game at BC Place, or settle down to read at the Vancouver Public Library, you're being warmed by the folks at CHD. They heat more than 180 buildings in the downtown through a network, many kilometres long, of subterranean pipes, bringing steam (converted from natural gas) from their cavernous building on Beatty Street at the west end of the Dunsmuir Viaduct (formerly home to the Pacific Press printing plant) to big clients like the Shaw Tower all the way down to the tiny bursts of steam that sound the pipes on the Gastown Steam Clock. Customers include hotels, office buildings, small manufacturers, condominiums, shopping centres and civic buildings.

November 25 Students protesting admissions policy ended a three-day occupation of the administration building at Simon Fraser University after a squad of 100 unarmed RCMP officers arrested 114 people. SFU's brand-new president, Dr. Kenneth Strand, had called the RCMP in and used a bullhorn to warn the students to vacate the premises. The *Province* printed the protesters' names, ages (most were from 18 to 22) and addresses and noted that Strand said the university had adopted a "get tough" policy in the wake of the occupation.

Also in 1968

A referendum in the two North Vancouvers on the question of amalgamation was overwhelmingly approved by voters in the district (90 percent), but given just a razor-thin Yes vote in the city (50.5 percent), which had split away in 1907. The rules said there had to be 60 percent approval in both places, so they remained separate. Heavily influencing the city's vote was Mayor Carrie Cates, who was against amalgamation.

Adman Jimmy Lovick, described as "the true giant" of Vancouver ad men,

Sit-in. After a rather hasty debut in 1965, Simon Fraser University's admissions practices with respect to transfer credits came under fire when students erupted in protest and occupied the administration building in 1968. "Remember the 114" became a rallying chant for future protests in response to the students arrested that day. *Dan Scott / Vancouver Sun*

died. The agency he had started in 1948, which by 1958 was the biggest in the country, did not long survive its founder's death, becoming Baker Lovick, then McKim Baker Lovick and finally being gobbled up by New York–based BBDO. "Lovick seemed to live on airplanes," wrote business writer Michael McCullough, "becoming the first customer of Trans-Canada Airways to log a million air miles... [He] once flew to Toronto to pitch the Toronto-Dominion Bank account. In the middle of an Ontario snowstorm, he drove down Bay Street in his pinstripe suit, in a rented convertible with the top down. Launching into his presentation to the bank's brass, he took off his trousers, opened a window and threw the pants out, trying to impress upon the bankers the need to change their pinstriped image. It worked."

Nat Bailey and wife Eva sold 13 White Spot Restaurants and other related interests to General Foods for $6.5 million.

UBC's Ladner Clock Tower was built near the university's main library. Named after Dr. Leon J. Ladner, QC (who donated $150,000 of its $160,000 construction cost), it was "built in honor and memory of the pioneers of B.C. and in particular Thomas Ellis and William Henry Ladner." The tower, which houses a 330-bell carillon, has been the butt of several engineering week pranks. One year a Volkswagen Beetle was put on top of the clock tower. No one knows how they got it up there, but we do know how it was brought down: the university rented a crane large enough to lift it off and sent the bill for the crane to the Engineering Undergraduate Society!

The federal and provincial governments agreed to begin a $40-million program for bank and dike protection on the Lower Fraser and other Lower Mainland rivers subject to flooding. The City of Richmond reached an agreement with the provincial government to share the cost of building and maintaining the dikes, taking the care of the dikes away from individual landowners.

The *Silver Ann* was the last vessel built at Britannia Shipyard.

Richmond Minoru Chapel was rededicated and reconsecrated this year for the use of all denominations. It began its life in 1891 as a Methodist chapel at the corner of Cambie and River Roads. When the Methodists and Presbyterians united in 1925, the chapel became known as Richmond United Church. In 1961 the Municipality of Richmond purchased the property on which the church stood in order to relocate the railway through Brighouse Industrial Estates. The church stood boarded up, its fate unsettled. Finally, with strong support from the former Reeve Henry Anderson, the church was moved to its present location in Pierrefonds Gardens.

Vancouver magazine and *Pacific Yachting* began publishing. They're still going!

Author Ernest Perrault produced a thinly disguised biographical novel about the early days of rogue BC timber baron Gordon Gibson Sr., *The Kingdom Carver*.

Comings and Goings

August About 1,200 professionals, students, writers, artists and service industry workers, among others, arrived in British Columbia from what was then Czechoslovakia after the Soviet army invaded and put an end to what has become known as the Prague Spring.

September 7
Jimi Hendrix and the Jimi Hendrix Experience played at the Pacific Coliseum. He acknowledged his grandmother, who lived in Vancouver and was in the audience.

October 27 Bandleader Guy Lombardo, 66, with "the sweetest music this side of heaven," appeared in Vancouver to a capacity audience at the Queen Elizabeth Theatre. Lombardo's Royal Canadians was the most popular orchestra in North America: over 50 years they sold 300 million records.

Marilyn Horne, who liked Vancouver, returned to star in the Vancouver Opera Association staging of Rossini's *Barber of Seville*.

Notable deaths: **John Emerson**, actor and pianist, in Vancouver on May 2, aged 57; **George Clark Miller**, mayor of Vancouver (1937–38), on May 17, aged 86; **Thomas Reid**, Surrey reeve (1924–34) and Liberal MP for New Westminster (1930–49), who was devoted to rehabilitation of the Fraser salmon run, in Surrey on October 11, aged 82; **Kew Ghim Yip**, Chinatown physician (1927–68) and philanthropist, in Vancouver on December 13, aged 66; **Gordon Wismer**, lawyer and BC attorney general (1937–52), in Victoria, aged 80; **John Henderson**, a long-time Vancouver school trustee (1943–64) and Vancouver's Good Citizen in 1961, aged about 88.

1969

Vancouver gave the world "The Peter Principle," Swangard Stadium opened for soccer, and the city was awarded an NHL franchise. An overflow crowd turned out to open the Bloedel Conservatory, but a rock musical about hippies had patrons walking out of the Playhouse.

January 26 Fifteen days after her 100th birthday, Charlise Naud had her gallbladder removed, making her the oldest person in BC to undergo such a serious procedure. Charlise had lived in Vancouver since 1900.

January 31 Kenneth Hare stepped down after seven months as president of UBC, and Walter Gage, who had been interim president from 1967 to 1968, took on the position officially. Gage began his career at the university as a student, graduating with a BA in 1925 and an MA in mathematics (with physics minor) in 1926 before going on to graduate studies in math at the University of Chicago and the California Institute of Technology. He taught mathematics at Victoria College (1927–33), a UBC affiliate, and also served as registrar for the institution (1929–33). In 1933 he returned to UBC's mathematics department, becoming a professor in 1943. Gage served as Dean of Administrative and Inter-Faculty Affairs in 1948 and later as Dean of Inter-Faculty and Student Affairs.

February 1 The Nine O'Clock Gun in Stanley Park was "kidnapped" by UBC engineering students, who returned the 680-kilogram (1,500-pound) cannon for a "ransom," which was given to the Children's Hospital.

March 8 Voters in the school districts of New Westminster, Burnaby, Langley, Coquitlam, Delta, Richmond and Surrey decided in favour of establishing a regional college, the seventh in the province, to be named Douglas College after BC's first governor.

March 29 A nine-year-old boy, Larry Richard Ehrenholz, survived a 365-metre (1,200-foot) fall down the icy slope of Grouse Mountain. A friend with him was killed.

March 31 Vancouver was granted its first legal coat of arms. Through

Elsewhere in BC

The Union of BC Indian Chiefs (UBCIC) was created as 144 chiefs and delegates from all over BC met to discuss the federal government's White Paper and its effects on Native people in BC. The group was incorporated under the *BC Societies Act* in 1971.

Elsewhere in Canada

Significant changes to the Criminal Code of Canada meant that the federal and provincial governments could now use lotteries to fund beneficial activities (for example, the 1976 Montreal Olympic Games). Parimutuel wagering on horse races, small lottery schemes for charitable purposes and limited gaming at agricultural fairs continued to be allowed as well. Other Criminal Code changes legalized contraception and abortion (in some circumstances), and decriminalized homosexuality.

Prime Minister Pierre Trudeau and his Minister of Indian Affairs, Jean Chrétien, introduced a white paper on Indian policy. It proposed that the Indian Act be abolished, land claims be rejected and Native people be aggressively assimilated into the general population. Indigenous leaders quickly dubbed it "The White Paper."

Elsewhere in the World

July 20 US astronaut Neil Armstrong walked on the Moon.

September 2 The phenomenon that ultimately became the internet was activated when UCLA professor Leonard Kleinrock and his team succeeded in sending a message from one computer to another via a refrigerator-sized switch, or router, known as an Interphase Message Processor. The message was "login."

Dorothy Lidstone of North Vancouver won the world archery championship at Valley Forge, PA, beating a field of 40 women from 27 countries with a record 2,361 points—110 points more than the previous world record.

Judith Forst, born in Fraser Mills, Coquitlam, was awarded a five-year contract with the Metropolitan Opera Association of New York. She became a world-renowned mezzo-soprano.

the 1950s and '60s, long-time city clerk Ronald Thompson had quietly and persistently pushed council to petition the Crown to have its emblem approved by the College of Heraldry. The city had had an unofficial coat of arms since it was founded, although the original design was supplanted in 1903 by a more attractive and appropriate version by James Blomfield. The official arms were based on the Blomfield design. Changes included making the central "V" green, instead of red. The caduceus of Mercury was replaced by a Kwakiutl totem pole, one of the most familiar and dramatic of the art forms of the West Coast First Nations. The upper part of the shield was coloured gold and set with two dogwood flowers. Finally, the word "air" was added to the motto—"By sea, land and air we prosper"—acknowledging the increasing role of air transport in the city's history.

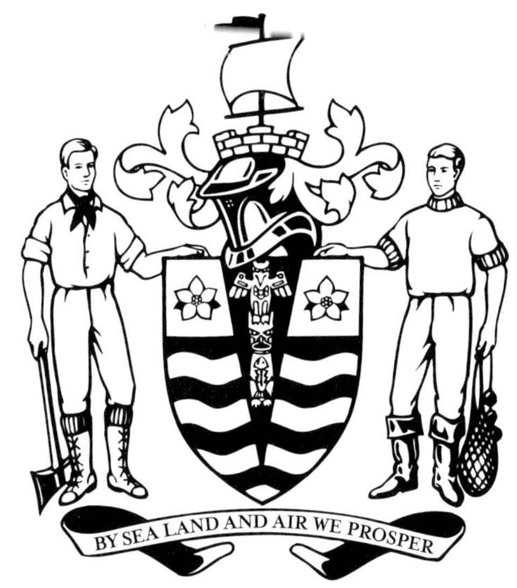

City crest. Vancouver's long-awaited coat of arms was officially granted in 1969. The logger and fisherman stand for Vancouver's traditional industries, the Kwakwaka'wakw totem pole for the city's aboriginal heritage, and the wavy blue and white for the ocean. The crown on top of the helmet is the traditional heraldic emblem for a city, and is topped by a ship to show Vancouver's importance as a seaport.
Courtesy of the City of Vancouver

March A new YWCA building opened on Burrard.

April 16 Albert O. Koch, the "father" of Congregation Beth Israel, died aboard a ship crossing the Mediterranean, aged 74. He came to Vancouver in 1925 and launched the National Dress Company, Vancouver's first garment manufacturing plant. In 1940 he began Lauries, a chain of dress stores. He was a founder of Beth Israel Synagogue at 4350 Oak and of Beth Israel Cemetery, and he served two terms as president of the synagogue. Koch sold Lauries on January 31,

Brief hover. On a cushion of air, Pacific Hovercraft began its service between Vancouver and Nanaimo on February 23, 1969. However, it lasted only three months. As future entrepreneurs will likely also find, this is a tough route to make a profit on.
The Province

1969, and on his retirement trip to Israel with his wife, Henrietta, suffered a stroke and died aboard ship.

April Champion skier Nancy Greene married Al Raine. Their twin sons, Charley and Willy, were born in January 1970.

April A 4.8-kilometre (3-mile) causeway to the artificial island of Roberts Bank, in Delta, opened to provide access to a deep-sea port being developed to ship Alberta and BC coal to Japan.

July 21 The *Vancouver Sun* and the *Province* both issued special supplements commemorating the first Moon walk the previous day.

July 29 Arthur Clarke became the first black man to become a Vancouver police officer.

August 31 The Vancouver Mounties came to an end. Only 1,101 fans saw their last game. After 11 seasons and two second-place finishes, the Mounties found a new home in 1970 in Salt Lake City.

August Early stirrings of what would become Greenpeace International began in Vancouver.

The US announced this month that it planned to test a one-megaton nuclear bomb in October on Amchitka Island, in Alaska's Aleutian Islands. Anti-nuclear and peace activists feared that such a test might trigger an earthquake and tsunami, or that radiation might leak to the surface or into the sea. A protest against the test, organized by Gwen and Derrick Mallard (who had formed SPEC, the Scientific Pollution and Environmental Control Society, in 1968), was held at the US consulate in Vancouver. According to Greenpeace historian Rex Weyler, among the people attending this protest "were Bob and Zoe Hunter, Irving Stowe, Bob Cummings, Lille d'Easum, Paul Watson, Ben Metcalfe, Rod Marining, Paul and Linda Spong, and others who

The sweetest-smelling place in Vancouver, the Bloedel Floral Conservatory opened in 1969 as a domed indoor garden decorating Queen Elizabeth Park.
Les Bazso / The Province

A Jungle on West 33rd

December 6 The Bloedel Floral Conservatory opened at Queen Elizabeth Park. Organizers expected about 3,500 people to visit on opening day, but more than 11,000 showed up.

The conservatory was built thanks largely to a $1.25-million donation through the Bloedel Foundation from lumber magnate Prentice Bloedel and his wife Virginia. The city and provincial governments kicked in smaller amounts. This is Canada's largest single-structure conservatory. Its domed design is based on the geodesic principle, which allows a large interior volume to be enclosed without the need for internal supporting columns. The conservatory dome consists of 2,324 pieces of aluminum tubing and 1,490 triodetic plexiglass "bubbles" (the bubbles were designed by Thorson and Thorson, structural engineers).

It's a great place to visit, especially on a wet, chilly winter day. Some 500 species of jungle and desert plants bloom year-round in the moist heat, a fine home for dozens of species of colourful tropical birds, from tiny, flitting button quail and gold-breasted waxbills to the big Moluccan cockatoo and the blue and gold macaw. The birds fly freely through the foliage.

In December 2009 the Park Board and the City of Vancouver cut funding to the conservatory. The Friends of Bloedel, an ad hoc lobbying and fundraising group, was quickly formed to fight the cuts, and the conservatory found new life as part of the VanDusen Botanical Gardens.

would eventually form the core of Greenpeace."

October 29 Lester Pearson, prime minister of Canada from 1963 to 1968, was named an honorary member of the Vancouver Club.

December 1

Vancouver was awarded an NHL franchise and history began for the Vancouver Canucks. Their first game was October 9, 1970.

December 2 Lily Laverock died in Duncan, aged about 89. Laverock came to Vancouver as a child with her parents. She was the first woman to graduate in moral philosophy from McGill University and in 1908 was the first woman employed as a general reporter by a Vancouver newspaper (the *World*). She moved to the *News-Advertiser* in 1910 and became editor of the women's page. Quiet, shy, ethereally attractive, she made her greatest local contribution when she became an impresario. An avid arts supporter, she promoted her first Celebrity Concert in 1921. The world-famous performers she brought to the city in the 1920s and 1930s make for an eye-popping list: Kreisler, Heifetz, Melba, Gigli, Casals, Chaliapin, Maurice Ravel at the piano...and on and on. She packed the Denman Arena with acts like the Ballet Russe de Monte Carlo and Belgian Royal Symphonic Band. World War II ended her efforts as a promoter. Today, despite her immense contribution to the city's cultural life, she's almost totally forgotten.

Also in 1969

George Ryga's *Grass and Wild Strawberries*, a "pop culture phenomenon," appeared at the Vancouver Playhouse. This musical about the hippie culture featured live music by the Collectors (who later became nationally famous as Chilliwack). Apparently when many unsatisfied Playhouse subscribers left the theatre at intermission, their places were taken by local hippies flocking to the empty seats to watch the second act.

Malkin Bowl in Stanley Park, which had been closed since Theatre Under the Stars folded in 1963, reopened when a semi-professional company, Theatre in the Park, began producing two musicals each summer. The company assumed the TUTS name in 1980.

G.P.V. (Philip) and Helen B. Akrigg, British Columbia historians, produced a marvellously useful book, *1001 British Columbia Place Names*, a fascinating trove of information about how our cities, lakes, mountains and more got their names. It was published by Discovery Press, owned and operated by the Akriggs. They published a second, expanded version in 1997.

Vancouver Cablevision (later Rogers Cable) initiated the Lower Mainland's first community cable channel. Radio man Vic Waters, along with partners Dave Liddell and Gerry Rose, operated the service on a shoestring budget—and the attitude was rather casual. Martin Truax, who joined in 1970, recalled that when Waters received calls from viewers who had missed a show, "Vic would say, 'No problem. I'll just run it again for you right now!'"

Construction began on Pacific Centre, the most ambitious construction project undertaken in Vancouver up to that time.

W.J. VanDusen, forestry industry executive, retired from the board of MacMillan Bloedel, aged about 80. He had been with the firm and its predecessors for 50 years.

The value of annual trading on the Vancouver Stock Exchange exceeded $1 billion for the first time.

Bob Prittie was elected mayor of Burnaby and served until 1973. The city's very attractive main public library was named for him.

Jimmy Christmas, mayor of Coquitlam, who was first elected in 1945, died in office after almost 25 years as mayor.

A garden shop owner named Bill Vander Zalm became mayor of Surrey.

Delta got a new coat of arms. According to Rob Watt, Canada's chief herald, "The green field represents Delta's rich farmlands... The silver disc represents the sun, enclosed by the silver triangle, referring to the Greek letter...The two silver horses represent Delta's foundation industry, agriculture, and its ongoing importance to the community as well as the corporation's strength. Each horse is distinguished by collars and medallions referring to two industries, grain growing and fishing." When the new municipal hall was built in 1994, designers used computers to create a sculpture of the coat of arms in concrete that is seen by motorists on their way to the Tsawwassen ferry terminal.

Swangard Stadium opened in Central Park in Burnaby. It was named for journalist Erwin Swangard, who had raised nearly $1 million for its construction. The stadium is the centre for professional soccer in BC.

Work on the Stanley Park seawall was financed with an annual $70,000 allotment. In 1968, that had added 365 metres (1,200 lineal feet). This year it paid for just 106 metres (350 feet).

The Sapperton Fish and Game Club began, with great success, to restore salmon stock in the Brunette River, flowing out of Burnaby Lake. The river had been badly polluted.

The Sisters of Providence, who had been administering St. Paul's Hospital, appointed a lay administrator and medical staff to run the hospital.

The Ross Street Gurdwara (Sikh temple) was built. This architectural gem originally stood unpainted and in isolation, but by 1995 it was brightly painted and surrounded by look-alike additions to the east.

The Peter Principle: Why Things Always Go Wrong rocketed to the top of the bestseller list. Dr. Laurence Johnston Peter might have toiled forever in obscurity as a teacher at UBC if he hadn't bumped into Vancouver writer Raymond Hull in the Metro Theatre. They were standing in the lobby during the intermission of an amateur production, and Hull—who didn't know Peter—casually commented that the production was a failure. Peter responded with an observation that people in any hierarchy invariably rise to their level of incompetence. As a result of that conversation, Hull and Peter collaborated on a book, a satire on corporate structure, that went on to sell more than 8 million copies.

Terry Jacks and the Poppy Family had a smash hit (it reached No. 2 in the US) with "Which Way You Goin' Billy?"

Jon Washburn, Ray Nurse, David Skulsky, Hans-Karl Piltz and Cuyler Page formed the Vancouver Early Music Society with the aim of fostering interest in medieval, renaissance and baroque music.

Empires and Nations was published, a book of essays in honour of retired University of British Columbia history professor Frederic Soward. He taught there from 1922 to 1966 and was head of the history department from 1953 to 1963. Fourteen Canadian historians contributed and there was a preface by Lester Pearson, a lifelong friend of Soward's.

The Great Northern Cannery, which had been active since 1891 near Sandy Cove in West Vancouver, closed. The site was purchased by the federal government for the Pacific Coast fisheries research station. Also this year, the Anglo-British Columbia Packing Company, a major player in the coastal canning industry since 1891, sold its assets.

The Charles Crane Memorial Library, now a unit of the Disability Resource Centre, was established at UBC as a reading room with the donation of a personal collection of about 6,000 Braille books belonging to the late Charles Allen Crane. Starting in 1970 the library's dedicated volunteers have recorded talking textbooks and background materials. A special disbursement was established in 1974 as a continuous funding base for the library, and by 1981 the centre had expanded to house nine soundproof studios with state-of-the-art professional recording equipment and high-speed duplicating and editing equipment. Hundreds of cassettes can be copied per hour, serving 35 to 50 blind, visually impaired or print-handicapped UBC students per year. Talking books produced at the Crane Library are sold on a non-profit basis to libraries and schools in such places as New Zealand, Australia, Japan, Hong Kong, Papua New Guinea, Ghana, South Africa, the US and Sweden.

Comings and Goings

A future opera star, Spanish tenor Placido Domingo, sang in *Manon*, a Vancouver Opera production. He had appeared here in 1968 in *Tosca*.

Golf Hall of Famer Carol Mann won her fourth straight tour title when she captured the Canadian Open title at the new Shaughnessy, the LPGA's first official event in western Canada.

Notable deaths: Haberdasher and impresario **Harry Mackenzie Hilker**, who formed Vancouver's first concert agency, Hilker Attractions (1936–50), with his son Gordon, on March 26, aged about 89; **Dr. Leonard Klinck**, UBC's first faculty member (dean of agriculture) and the second president (1919–44), in West Vancouver on March 27, aged 82; **James M. McGavin**, baker and founder of McGavin Bakeries, in Vancouver on April 17, aged 86; **Violet Alice Dryvynsyde**, founder of Athlone School for Boys, in Vancouver on October 29, aged 69.

1970-1979

1970

The sixties continued in Vancouver: there were street protests, student unrest and environmental action by a group that became known as Greenpeace. The Canucks began playing in the NHL, and architects came up with the economical house design known as the Vancouver Special. Major J.S. Matthews died; without the city's long-time archivist, this book would not exist.

January 30 Trans Canada Glass was incorporated under the name TCG International. The company, which had its beginnings in New Westminster in 1946 with one automotive glass store, now owns Apple Auto Glass, Speedy Auto Glass and hundreds of NOVUS windshield repair and replacement franchises and is heavily into satellite and cellular phones and paging systems.

February 10 John Davidson, botanist and conservationist, died in Vancouver, aged 91. He was born August 6, 1878, in Aberdeen, Scotland, and as a boy was hired by the University of Aberdeen's botany department. By 29 he was in charge of its botanical museum. However, his class (he was the son of a cabinet maker) and lack of formal education blocked his advancement to an assistant professorship. After a near-fatal flu/pneumonia attack in 1909, he was advised to move to a "more merciful" climate. He chose Vancouver, leaving Scotland in April 1911. Hired by Henry Esson Young, he was soon named provincial botanist. Davidson started the gardens at Essondale mental hospital in Coquitlam and at UBC. He was a botany instructor and professor at UBC (1916–48) and founded the Vancouver Natural History Society in 1918.

Renewable resource? *Vancouver Province* reporter Maurice Chenier explores the marijuana situation on the University of British Columbia Endowment Lands.
Ken Allen / The Province

February 16 David Y.H. Lui staged his first event as an impresario: the Phakavali Dancers of Thailand. For an all-too-brief and luminescent period, Lui imported many distinguished and exciting dance companies.

February A strike began at the two major Vancouver dailies, the *Vancouver Sun* and the *Province*.

Province staffer Mike Tytherleigh, who had newspaper production experience, suggested to the striking workers that they start their own newspaper and publish it three times a week until the strike ended. The first issue of the *Vancouver Express* appeared on February 21.

April 1 At the first annual conference of the Canadian Information Processing Society and the Canadian Operational Research Society, held at the Hotel Vancouver, Justice Minister John Turner warned of the threats to citizens' privacy posed by the new "computronic age."

April 7 Jana Jorgenson, an 18-year old Centennial High School student from Coquitlam, won the Miss Teen Canada contest.

April 30 CP Rail's first computer-commanded coal train from Alberta reached the new Roberts Bank superport in Delta.

Prime Minister Pierre Trudeau and Premier W.A.C. Bennett officially opened Westshore Terminals on June 15.

August 14 "Marijuana," wrote *Province* reporter Maurice Chenier on page 1, "is alive and well and growing in the Vancouver area, thank you." The *Province* had checked out a tip from a young person who claimed that there was a bumper crop of the illegal plant in the Vancouver area. "You'll find a lot of pot—potted or otherwise—growing in the University of B.C. area, in Stanley Park, and up on Burnaby Mountain at the back of Simon Fraser University," said the unidentified tipster. Chenier and photographer Ken Allen went out looking and found marijuana in a dozen spots. (As far as we know, the first reference to "marihuana" in a Vancouver newspaper was a March 5, 1937, *Province* item about a dead man with the stuff in his stomach.)

September 24 George Wootton, principal of still very young Douglas College, spoke to the college's

1,600 charter students from the ice rink of Queen's Park arena. The students attended classes at high schools in the evenings until late October and early November, when the three campus sites—a remodelled warehouse on Minoru Boulevard near Westminster Highway in Richmond, a 6.4-hectare (16-acre) campus with 10 portable buildings at 92nd Avenue and 140th Street in Surrey, and a 3.2-hectare (8-acre) campus with 13 portable units at McBride and 8th Avenue in New Westminster—were ready to receive them. Douglas College's first 175 graduates received their two-year diplomas in a ceremony at New Westminster's Royal City Curling Club in 1972.

October 1 Vancouver city archivist James Skitt Matthews died in Vancouver, aged 91. The city of Vancouver owes a huge debt to the Major: he and his wife Emily started the city's archives in 1933. For more than three decades he relentlessly and tirelessly amassed photographs, artifacts, books, newspapers, magazines, civic records, diaries and more. You can see it all at the City Archives. This book, not to mention all the post-1933 books on local history, rely heavily on the work Matthews did. Donna Jean MacKinnon, who once worked at the archives, described him as "a natural archivist, keeping meticulous track of his activities and of those around him who he thought were making an impact on society. It was a short step for him to start collecting general historical material from others in Vancouver. As the collection grew, he developed his own cataloguing systems, in the end amassing more than 500,000 photographs and hundreds of civic records and personal papers."

October 9 **The brand-new Vancouver Canucks played their first regular-season NHL game,**

Elsewhere in BC

At its second General Assembly, the Union of BC Indian Chiefs issued *A Declaration of Indian Rights: the BC Position Paper.*

BC's attorney general began licensing gaming conducted by charitable and religious groups and at fairs and exhibitions.

Elsewhere in Canada

October 5 Front de libération du Québec (FLQ) terrorists in Montreal kidnapped British trade commissioner James Cross, and the October Crisis began. On October 16 the federal government imposed the War Measures Act, and on October 17 the FLQ murdered Pierre Laporte, Quebec's vice premier and minister of labour. UBC's student newspaper printed statements and commentary suppressed by other papers fearful of reprisals under the War Measures Act.

Canada adopted the metric system of land measurement.

Elsewhere in the World

January 10 *Sun* business writer Phil Hanson travelled to Seattle to report on a new phenomenon in passenger aviation: Boeing's 747 jumbo jets. Pan American Airways, the first airline to use the 747, introduced them on January 22 on its New York–to–London service. Air Canada had them by spring 1971; CP Air by 1973. The 747 changed air travel forever by making it affordable to millions of people who'd never flown before. Phil Hanson was one of the first Canadians to fly in a 747 when Boeing flew him and a few other reporters down to Seattle in one.

September 18 Guitarist Jimi Hendrix died in London, England, at age 27. Hendrix had a direct, if brief, connection to Vancouver. One of the city's more prominent black citizens in the 1940s was Tennessee-born Zenora "Nora" Hendrix, Jimi's grandmother. Her son Al, Jimi's father, was born in Vancouver in 1919. Nora Hendrix—who was of Cherokee Indian descent and died in 1985 at age 100—lived from 1942 to 1952 in a small house at 827 East Georgia. In 1949, aged about seven, Jimi Hendrix lived very briefly with his grandmother at that East Georgia home.

December 29 North Vancouver's Chief Dan George was named best supporting actor by New York film critics for his role as Old Lodge Skins in *Little Big Man*. That terrific performance, funny and warm and dignified, also earned him an Oscar nomination.

Debbie Brill, 17, of Maple Ridge won gold in the high jump at the 1970 Commonwealth Games in Edinburgh. She was the first woman in North America to clear 6 feet in that event (she was 16 at the time).

Canuck moment. Driving the puck home, Barry Wilkins (number 4) scores for the Canucks in the third period during their inaugural NHL game against the Los Angeles Kings. Sadly, though historic, it was not enough, as the Kings won 3–1. The Canucks would finish their first season second to last of the East Division, only one point ahead of the Detroit Red Wings. *BC Sports Hall of Fame and Museum*

against the Los Angeles Kings, in the Pacific Coliseum and came out at the wrong end of a 3–1 score. General manager Bud Poile blamed it on the players' nervousness. The team's first captain, their second pick in the expansion draft, was Orland Kurtenbach (who later coached the Canucks). Their fourth pick was defenceman Pat Quinn (who took over coaching duties in 1987). The first coach was Hal Laycoe. Tickets ran from $3.50 to $6.40. (Incidentally, the Canucks were admitted to the league along with the Buffalo Sabres at an expansion fee of $6 million, three times what the cost had been when six teams joined in 1967.)

October 13 The Langara campus of Vancouver Community College, consisting of a five-storey library block and a three-storey instructional block, was completed in September, and the move to the new campus was marked by a "great trek" today. About 3,000 students, teachers and administrators walked or drove from the old King Edward Centre at Oak Street and 12th Avenue to the new campus at 100 West 49th Ave. (Langara became an independent college on April 1, 1994.)

October 23 Hungarian organizations in British Columbia persuaded Vancouver, North Vancouver and West Vancouver to declare this date, the anniversary of the 1956 Revolution, Hungarian Day. Thousands of Hungarians who died in the revolution are acknowledged on plaques in Vancouver's Queen Elizabeth Park and Burnaby's Forest Lawn Memorial Park.

October Vancouver City Police and hostel dwellers from Jericho clashed on West 4th Avenue.

Also in October Unrest continued at Simon Fraser University as the Canadian Association of University Teachers (CAUT) reinstated its 1968 censure of the university's board of governors for "interference in academic affairs." The beef this time: eight faculty members were dismissed from the political science, sociology and anthropology department after they went on strike, refusing to teach classes. This censure was not lifted until 1977.

November 3 Vancouver City Council approved the sale of land for multi-purpose development in Champlain Heights, the last large undeveloped tract in Vancouver.

Also in 1970

The Abbotsford Air Show, a success from its beginning in 1962, officially became Canada's national air show. That first event attracted 15,000 spectators; in recent years on average 250,000 to 300,000 have turned out during the show's three-day run at Abbotsford International Airport.

The first part of BC Ferries' "stretch and lift" program began. Four of its major vessels were cut down the middle so that 25-metre (84-foot) midsections could be "spliced" in. Similar

Left: Air attraction. Heads are officially in the clouds as the Abbotsford Air Show becomes Canada's national air show.
The Province

operations had been performed on smaller boats, but this was the first time BC Ferries' larger ships were subject to such extensive alterations. The fleet was now at 24 ships.

Graybeard, an ocean racer/cruiser designed by Vancouver marine architect Peter Hatfield and owner Lol Killam, began its racing career under the flag of the Royal Vancouver Yacht Club. The boat won the Swiftsure Lightship and Victoria–Maui races this year. "Graybeard" is the name given to huge waves that circle Antarctica, occasionally capsizing freighters.

Two ballet companies were established this year. Norbert Vesak launched his Western Dance Theatre, though it closed midway through the second season. Vesak went on to choreograph *The Ecstasy of Rita Joe* for the Royal Winnipeg Ballet and had an international career as choreographer and director. Morley Wiseman founded Ballet Horizons, which survived until 1974. Wiseman's group sowed the seeds for today's Ballet BC.

The decades-long tenure of many industries on False Creek's south shore ended as their leases expired, and the debate over the future of the area began.

Eaton's built a new store in Pacific Centre at the southwest corner of Georgia and Granville, having moved up from its previous location on West Hastings (the building now known as Harbour Centre). The new store's stark white and mostly windowless facade garnered much criticism. A year later, Pacific Centre connected Eaton's to the Bay, kitty-corner across Granville, with an underground shopping network.

In 1970 the entire book publishing industry in British Columbia earned $350,000 in sales.

Greenpeace emerged from the Don't Make A Wave Committee, which was founded to protest US nuclear tests in the Aleutian Islands. According to Rex Weyler, an early Greenpeace director, the participants were people "who thought such weapons should not be allowed to make waves through the oceans or atmospheres of the world ever again." Committee members had debated whether they should continue protesting nuclear tests or expand their efforts to fight against all threats to the environment. As Quaker Irving Stowe left one meeting, he said "Peace," the traditional salutation of anyone involved in the peace movement. "Make it a green peace," said Bill Darnell, a field worker for the federal government's Company of Young Canadians. That was the inspiration for the group's new name.

Thomas Davis Coldicutt died at about age 91. Born in England, he came to Canada from Birmingham in 1900 to take part in the Klondike gold rush but ended up staying in Victoria, where he was a ship's navigator, before moving to New Westminster and then to east Burnaby, where he was a city councillor. He donated 90 hectares (222 acres) for Central Park and secured the money to build Kingsway. In 1912 he bought a home in Crescent Beach; 20 years later he bought an additional 200 hectares (500 acres) and built homes, a villa with lodges, a stable and tennis courts—today's Ocean Ridge townhouses. Coldicutt Street was named for him.

Badminton champion Eileen Underhill (née George) and her husband Jack, another champion in the sport, were inducted into the BC Sports Hall of Fame, the first husband-and-wife team to be so honoured.

A plebiscite on incorporation in Lions Bay drew more than the requisite

All sails taut in the wind, the ocean racer/cruiser *Graybeard* slices through the water in this March 1, 1971, picture. Launched in 1970 from the Royal Vancouver Yacht Club, this was the largest fibreglass boat in the world.
Bill Cunningham / The Province

Synonymous with the words "mass market," "cheap" and "lots of floor space," the Vancouver Special architectural style hit the streets in the early 1970s. These examples are from either Ross or Elgin Streets in East Vancouver. *Cristopher Wright*

60 percent majority vote from the 250 residents. The community officially became a village municipality in the spring of 1971. Also this year, the Lions Bay Property Owners' Association acquired a fire truck, staffed by the village's newly created volunteer fire department, after fire destroyed a Lions Bay home.

This may have been the year the Vancouver Special originated. According to architectural historian Dr. Harold Kalman, "this new model for mass-market housing...maximized floor area and site coverage at an attractive price," putting living space on the second floor and utility rooms, garages and often in-law suites on the ground floor. They popped up everywhere on the Lower Mainland, to the dismay of architects and aesthetes. Kalman says the 6100 and 6200 blocks of Elgin and Ross Streets in Vancouver are good places to see them.

The Old Spaghetti Factory opened on Water Street, and its funky ambience drew big crowds to Gastown. After a spaghetti dinner, people could visit the new Gastown boutique Fox and Fluevog Shoes, opened by partners Peter Fox and John Fluevog.

A count of seagulls taken by the Vancouver Natural History Society recorded more than 20,000 birds of seven species. In his book *The Birds of Vancouver*, John Rodgers wrote that four other species can be seen from time to time. The most common, and the only resident, is the glaucous-winged gull, identifiable by its white head, pale grey mantle, yellowish bill with a red spot, and strident voice.

Comings and Goings

Meteorological writer Timothy Oke, born in Devon, England, began teaching at UBC in 1970 and was head of the geography department until 1996. Oke, a Fellow of the Royal Society of Canada and the Royal Canadian Geographic Society, wrote *The Climate of Vancouver* and co-edited (with Graeme Wynn) *Vancouver and Its Region*, an overview by 19 UBC geographers.

Notable deaths: **Lawren Harris**, Canadian artist and a member of the Group of Seven, in Vancouver on January 29, aged 84—he dominated the local art scene in the 1940s and '50s; **John Wallace deBeque Farris**, Vancouver's first Crown prosecutor (1903), attorney general (1917–22) and senator, on February 25, aged 91—he took more appeals to the British Privy Council than any other Canadian; **Fred Deeley Sr.**, motorcycle dealer, on May 9, aged about 89; **Paul Rand**, landscape painter and commercial artist for most of his working life, aged about 74; **Alexander Saba**, owner of Saba Brothers, silk merchants, in Vancouver, aged about 89.

The Old Spaghetti Factory opened on Water Street in Gastown in 1970, featuring a decommissioned trolley car that is seen here being moved in. According to the Ghosts of Old Vancouver website, the trolley came with a ghost, sometimes seen after hours by staff. *Courtesy The Old Spaghetti Factory*

1971

Pro-marijuana demonstrators and police on horseback fought in Gastown in what was later officially labelled a "police riot." Two Greenpeace boats sailed out of Vancouver to protest nuclear tests in Alaska: they missed the explosions but created enough waves that future tests on Amchitka Island were cancelled. And Prime Minister Trudeau married Margaret Sinclair in a secret North Vancouver ceremony.

January 8 Seaspan International was chosen as the name for the company formed by the merger of Vancouver Tugboats and Island Tug and Barge. The North Vancouver company operates tugs and specialty barges from Alaska to Mexico.

January 15 Vancouver purchased the old Shaughnessy Heights Golf Course lands, which were later developed as VanDusen Botanical Garden.

February The provincial government designated Gastown and Chinatown as historic sites, protecting historically significant buildings and streetscapes. But this silver lining had a cloud. While the designation protected neighbourhoods from demolition, it also hindered less-destructive growth.

March 4
Prime Minister Pierre Trudeau, 52, married Margaret Sinclair, 22, at St. Stephen's Catholic Church in Lynn Valley, North Vancouver.

April 4 Victor Wentworth Odlum died in Vancouver, aged 90. He arrived in Vancouver in 1889 with his scientist/writer father, Edward Faraday Odlum. Victor served in the Boer War and World War I. Between the wars he worked as a journalist with several newspapers, including a stint as editor-in-chief of the *Vancouver Daily Star*. He was the *Star*'s publisher from 1924 to 1932 and was publisher of the short-lived *Vancouver Times* (1963–65). Odlum was Liberal MLA for Vancouver City from 1924 to 1928. A brigadier, he commanded the 2nd Canadian Division in 1940–41. He served as high commissioner to Australia, Canada's first ambassador to China (1943–46) and ambassador to Turkey (1947–52).

Below left: Private affair. Heads bowed in prayer, local lass Margaret Sinclair and sitting Prime Minister Pierre Trudeau marry in a secret ceremony at St. Stephen's Catholic Church in North Vancouver. *Fred Schiffer / Vancouver Sun*

Elsewhere in BC

May 4 BC's first 29 ecological reserves received protected status, a conservation landmark for the province.

Canada Post issued a stamp celebrating the BC centennial, designed by E.R.C. Berthune of Kamloops.

Elsewhere in Canada

August 28 Canada's first gay rights demonstration, organized by George Hislop, took place on Parliament Hill.

Canada became the first country in the world to adopt multiculturalism as an official policy, recognizing the diversity of the Canadian population and preserving and promoting cultural pluralism. The policy also confirmed the rights of the country's aboriginal people and the status of Canada's two official languages.

The federal government formally withdrew its white paper on Indian policy.

Elsewhere in the World

Starbucks opened at its first location, in Seattle at Pike Place Market.

The Four Seasons' All Seasons Park

June 23 Vancouver mayor Tom Campbell visited "All Seasons Park" to, in his words, "poke the hornet's nest" and vocally spar with the young people squatting there.

In late May a few dozen hippies and Yippies had occupied the site at the entrance to Stanley Park where the Four Seasons hotel chain planned to build three 33-storey apartment buildings, three 8-storey buildings and a 14-storey hotel. Vancouver voters were split on the project, with half wanting to turn the land into a public park. The Yippies acted on this, planting trees and creating a children's playground. When a city vote to buy the land fell short of the 60 percent majority needed, Mayor Campbell visited to gloat.

However, the mayor was reluctant to use force to remove the squatters, saying it was a problem for the Four Seasons hotel and the federal government to deal with (the hotel site was on federally owned land), so the hippies remained until spring 1972. Public opinion turned strongly against the Four Seasons development during that time. Independent alderman Harry Rankin described the plebiscite as "a vote of nonconfidence in council," commenting that the mayor and his supporters on council had been "remarkably irresponsible and unresponsive to the wishes of the people."

In August 1972 Four Seasons announced it would not proceed with the project. Later in the year, Tom Campbell, who was criticized for being too easy on the squatters and too hard on young people during the Gastown Riot, announced he would retire from civic politics. And in 1977 the land that had been All Seasons Park was officially annexed to Stanley Park.

Above right: Various people stroll through All Seasons Park in 1971, a squatters' campground on a lot near the entrance of Stanley Park, erected in protest of plans to turn the site into a Four Seasons Hotel development. Mayor Tom Campbell was furious at the squatters but largely did nothing, and the development was cancelled in 1972 as public opinion turned against it. The land is now part of Stanley Park. *Gordon Sedawie / The Province*

April The railway through White Rock (now called the Burlington Northern) ended its passenger service. A few years later a BC Hydro "fastbus" commuter service linked White Rock with Vancouver.

May 4 Peter Basil Pantages died in Hawaii. Pantages ran the Peter Pan Cafe on Granville Street with his three brothers from the early 1920s. He was the founder (1920) and director (for 51 years) of the Polar Bear Club, which promoted outdoor swimming on New Year's Day. He swam every day, no matter where he travelled.

June 21 George Tidball opened his first Keg Restaurant in North Vancouver. In 1987 he sold his Kegs and other restaurants (76 in all) to Whitbread PLC of London, England.

June 28 The Georgia Viaduct opened in a ceremony presided over by Mayor Tom Campbell. Its Dunsmuir twin, to the north, opened in November. Cost for the two was $11 million. The old Georgia Viaduct, which had been

Right: Joint effort. A riot over marijuana seems counter-intuitive, but more than 1,000 people showed up at the "Battle of Maple Tree Square" in Gastown to protest the recent crackdowns by Mayor Tom Campbell. *Glenn Baglo / Vancouver Sun*

dropping chunks of concrete onto the roadway below for much of its 56 years, was finally demolished.

July 31 Foon Sien Wong, a well-known spokesperson for Chinese Canadian rights, died in Vancouver. Born in Canton, Wong immigrated to Vancouver Island with his family around the turn of the century. After graduating from the University of British Columbia, Wong worked as an interpreter and translator. As member and later president of the Chinese Benevolent Association, Wong advocated for Chinese Canadian immigration and rights, lobbying politicians in Ottawa and elsewhere. He was instrumental in winning the vote for Chinese Canadians in 1947. Wong was known as "the unofficial mayor of Chinatown."

August 7 The "Grasstown Smoke-In" turned into the Gastown Riot, also known as the Battle of Maple Tree Square. More than 1,000 people gathered in Maple Tree Square at the centre of Gastown to smoke pot and call for the legalization of marijuana. The riot squad and a mounted patrol charged the crowd, 79 people were arrested, 38 were charged and at least 12 were hospitalized. A later judicial inquiry headed by Justice Thomas Dohm criticized the action, characterizing it as a "police riot." (In 1996, proponents of legalized marijuana marked the 25th anniversary of the riot with a memorial smoke-in at Maple Tree Square. Police redirected traffic and observed the festivities.)

August 14 A "Gastown Festival," held exactly one week after the riot and meant to repair the area's image, drew 15,000 peaceful participants.

August 24 Yasutaro Yamaga died in Beamsville, ON. Born in 1886 in Japan, Yamaga came to BC from Seattle in 1907. After working as a CPR labourer, in 1908 he bought 4 hectares (10 acres) near Haney. There he organized Japanese social clubs and imported Japanese schoolbooks from the US to replace Japanese government textbooks. He led the Japanese Farmers' Union in the Fraser Valley. After being released from World War II internment, he ran a sawmill at 70 Mile House, then moved to Beamsville, where he established Nipponia Home, the first Japanese Canadian senior citizen's home in Canada.

September 7 City School opened, "providing an education alternative to Vancouver students."

September 15 The *Greenpeace* sailed from Vancouver to the island of Amchitka to protest a nuclear test on the remote Aleutian island by the US Atomic Energy Commission. On October 6 more than 10,000 secondary school students from all over the Lower Mainland massed in the 1000-block of Alberni—near the US consulate—to protest the test. The students sang, chanted and listened to speeches, ...and when the demonstration was over, some of them stayed behind to sweep up and collect litter. On October 29, while the *Greenpeace* was still en route to Amchitka, the atomic blast went ahead. Activists organized a second ship, the converted Canadian minesweeper *Edgewater Fortune*, which was rechristened *Greenpeace Too*. It set off for Alaska as well, passing the *Greenpeace* near Campbell River and continuing north. The US Atomic Energy Commission detonated a second five-megaton explosion under Amchitka Island when the *Greenpeace Too* was still a few hundred kilometres away, but it was the last nuclear test at Amchitka. The attention the Greenpeace voyages focused on the tests led the AEC to cancel further tests.

September 26 The Stanley Park seawall was officially opened, and the ashes of Jimmy Cunningham, the brawny little man who supervised the wall's construction between 1917 and his retirement in 1955, were buried in

Setting out to prove that peace-lovers can change the world, the *Greenpeace* sets off on its maiden voyage to protest nuclear testing near Amchitka Island, Alaska.
Courtesy Greenpeace / PNG

Jimmy Cunningham was the person most closely associated with the building of the Stanley Park Seawall. A Scottish stonemason, Cunningham cemented stones together and supervised hundreds of workers over 38 years. When the seawall was officially opened in 1971, Cunningham's ashes were also enclosed in an unmarked location in the wall, a tribute to the man who had given so much. *City of Vancouver Archives, CVA 392-1044, Gordon Sedawie, via* Vancouver Sun

an unmarked location within the wall. Cunningham had hefted thousands of its 45-kilogram (99-pound) blocks into place over 38 years, as did unemployed workers during the Great Depression, prisoners in work gangs and sailors from HMCS *Discovery* on "punishment detail." The wall was originally built to protect the foreshore from erosion, but it has become a popular roadway for walkers, cyclists, and rollerbladers. A portion of the wall remained uncompleted until 1980, when there was a second official opening.

October 21 The British Columbia Sports Hall of Fame opened in the BC Pavilion at the PNE. Newspapers paid tribute to sportswriter Eric Whitehead as the man most responsible "for the splendid collection of memorabilia, not to mention various splendid collections of money which made the Hall possible and will ensure its future." The hall is now in bigger quarters at BC Place—and well worth a visit.

November 5 Evlyn Fenwick Keirstead Farris, teacher and women's education activist, died in Vancouver, aged 93. She was a founder of UBC's University Women's Club, which was formed to stimulate intellectual activity, and served as the club's president in 1907–9 and again in 1925–26. She was also the first woman elected to the UBC board of governors, in 1917.

November 19 Heritage Village (now Burnaby Village Museum) was opened by Governor General Roland Michener. With costumed townsfolk, historic buildings, self-guided tours and a beautiful old carousel, the museum provided entertainment as well as education.

December 15 Bernice R. Brown, activist, died in West Vancouver, aged 66. Brown worked at the *San Francisco News*, then married and settled in Vancouver in 1930. She was an early editor of the *Jewish Western Bulletin*. In 1939 she organized a Red Cross unit to enable Jewish women to do war work. She received a Canadian Red Cross Distinguished Service Award in 1946. Through the media she urged Parliament to change immigration policy and accept orphans of the Holocaust. She was later an active member of the Canadian Institute of International Affairs.

December 23 Sister Charles Spinola died in Montreal, aged 86. She came to St. Paul's Hospital in Vancouver in 1906, graduated from the hospital's School of Nursing in 1912 and became supervisor of surgery. In 1918 she invented the "St. Charles Ether Machine," a device described by the hospital's archives as "a vaporizing machine designed to reduce the dangerous aftereffects of anaesthesia." Following the advice of many doctors, she applied for a patent that was granted February 12, 1924. The machine was eventually widely used throughout the country. Sister Charles retired in 1963, after spending 57 years at St. Paul's.

December 31 *Province* publisher Fred Auger buried a time capsule near the reception desk in the editorial department. It was to be opened on BC's 200th birthday. This was when the newspaper was at 2250 Granville St., before its move to Granville Square in 1997. Wonder what happened to that time capsule?

Also in 1971

The 1971 census showed the metropolitan population had topped the 1 million mark. One remarkable finding of that census was that Delta's population had tripled in 10 years.

The Capilano Fish Hatchery opened. The Department of Fisheries and Oceans built the hatchery after construction of the Cleveland Dam blocked access to the spawning channel of the Capilano River for coho, chinook and steelhead. The hatchery produces 3 million salmon a year for release below the dam.

Vancouver's first fireboat, *J.H. Carlisle*, built in 1928 at Burrard Dry Dock, was taken out of service by the Vancouver Fire Department. It was replaced by four "Super Pumps" that could provide 6,800 litres (1,500 gallons) of water per minute. They were stationed in the firehalls around False Creek, which by then was more easily accessible to land-based fire companies. The *Carlisle* was converted to a workboat and moved to Port Edward on the Skeena River.

The University of British Columbia began offering the first credit courses in women's studies in Canada.

Students at the Langara campus of Vancouver Community College, who had been pushing unsuccessfully for a crosswalk at 49th Avenue and Ontario Street, stopped traffic to paint their own crosswalk on the street. The city eventually gave in to the students' demands and installed two crosswalks.

The 41-kilometre (25-mile) Baden-Powell Trail was built on the North Shore by various Boy Scout and Girl Guide troops.

The trail was named in honour of the scouting movement's founder.

Prime Minister Pierre Trudeau and wife Margaret opened the whale pool at the Vancouver Public Aquarium.

The Jericho Youth Hostel was created in what had been a barracks for the old Jericho air station.

The Hyack Festival Association of New Westminster began its activities, which include the annual FraserFest, the Christmas Parade of Lights and the Miss New Westminster Ambassador Program.

The Port of Vancouver processed 22,800 cruise passengers this year. Total numbers passed 170,000 in 1981, 423,000 in 1991 and 600,000 in 1995. Since then they have fluctuated, from over 900,000 in 2004 to about 580,000 in 2010.

Among the locally shot films released this year were Mike Nichols' *Carnal Knowledge* and *McCabe and Mrs. Miller*, directed by Robert Altman.

Western Living magazine first appeared, founded by Liz Bryan and her husband, photographer Jack Bryan. With a circulation of 165,000, it is Canada's largest regional magazine.

Several cultural institutions started up this year. Some lasted; others didn't. The Vancouver Chamber Choir, led by its founder/conductor/music director Jon Washburn, is still making great music (in 1973 it was the first Canadian choir to win a first-place award in the prestigious BBC competition Let the Peoples Sing), and Pulp Press (which became Arsenal Pulp in 1982) still publishes gender-bending and provocative books. Tamahnous Theatre, founded by John Gray, the late Larry Lillo and others, presented new and challenging work for more than 20 years, then folded. And five former Royal Winnipeg Ballet dancers launched Ballet Horizons, which lasted a year.

J.J. Douglas Ltd. published two books this year: *British Columbia Coast Names*, by John T. Walbran (which first appeared in 1909), and *Cooking for One*, by Norah Mannion Wilmot. Walbran's book is still in print under the D&M imprint, and *Cooking for One* went on to sell some 50,000 copies. The company was off to a great start! In 1978 it became Douglas & McIntyre, the largest English-language Canadian-owned publisher outside Toronto.

The 35-member CBC Vancouver Chamber Orchestra, conducted by John Avison, became the first Canadian orchestra to perform in the Arctic.

Gertrude Weinrobe, the first Jewish child born in Vancouver (on May 12, 1893) received the 1971 BC Pioneer Centennial Medal.

Salmon aid. The Capilano Fish Hatchery opened in 1971, after it was found that the Cleveland Dam was blocking salmon from their spawning grounds. The site is now also a family-friendly interpretative centre where visitors can learn about and observe the life cycles of the fish.
Gord Croucher / The Province

Comings and Goings

July 2 Writer Evelyn Lau was born. By age 12 her fiction and poetry were being published. Now her books (*Runaway*, *Fresh Girls*, *Other Women*, *Choose Me*) are bestsellers.

July Roy Forbes, an 18-year-old lad from Dawson Creek, came to Vancouver and began to sing professionally. He called himself Bim. He was sensational. More than 40 years later Roy is still entertaining (and still sensational).

October 24 Soviet premier Alexei Kosygin made a state visit to Vancouver.

1972

At city hall, three decades of NPA rule ended with the election of a TEAM council while, provincially, 20 years of Social Credit ended with the election of the NDP. This was also the year Howard Hughes holed up in the Bayshore Hotel. At the Pacific Coliseum, Muhammad Ali fought George Chuvalo and Rolling Stones fans fought police.

March 18 The first purpose-built martial arts centre, or dojo, outside Japan opened in Steveston. The Martial Arts Centre was built as a centennial project and offered training in both kendo and judo.

June 18 Western Canada's first multilingual radio station, CJVB, started by Jan van Bruchem, signed on at AM 1470.

Most of its programming is now in Cantonese and Mandarin, but an early star was Sushma Sardana, the first Hindi and Punjabi announcer.

July 31 Ethlyn Trapp, radiologist, died in West Vancouver, aged 81. She was born July 18, 1891, in New Westminster, studied at McGill and in Europe, worked in military hospitals during World War I and then came to Vancouver to practise, where she used her own money to set up a centre to prove the benefits of radiotherapy. Trapp was also an art collector and a friend of Emily Carr. In her will, she bequeathed her home, Klee Wyck, to West Vancouver for use as an arts centre.

Elsewhere in BC

April 1 The Pacific Great Eastern Railway, which ran from North Vancouver to Fort Nelson, was renamed the British Columbia Railway. In 1984 it became BC Rail. (The line from Prince George north was later abandoned.)

August 30 Dave Barrett and the NDP won the provincial election. Barrett, a 43-year-old social worker from Coquitlam, became the province's 26th premier and served until December 21, 1975, when Bill Bennett, son of the man Barrett defeated, defeated him in turn. Barrett was leader of the opposition from 1976 until his retirement from politics in 1983.

November 10 Permanent licence plates began appearing on cars in BC, with stick-on tabs to indicate the renewal date.

December 4 A new minimum wage of $2 an hour went into effect in BC. Labour minister Bill King announced that further increases to $2.25 and $2.50 would take place in two stages over the following 18 months.

The Union of BC Indian Chiefs submitted its report *Claim Based on Native Title to the Lands Now Forming British Columbia* to Prime Minister Trudeau, proposing that Canada establish a claims commission to adjust reserve size and determine the amount of compensation to be paid to indigenous peoples for the loss of their territories. Trudeau ignored the proposal.

Elsewhere in Canada

November 10 Telesat Canada launched the world's first commercial domestic communications satellite, Anik 1, into geostationary orbit from Cape Canaveral in Florida. (*Anik* means "little brother" in Inuktitut.)

Elsewhere in the World

Karen Magnussen won a silver medal in figure skating at the Winter Olympics in Japan, while Vancouver's Bruce Robertson was outstanding at the Summer Olympics in Munich, swimming the second-fastest time ever. He won a silver medal in the 100-metre butterfly, second only to Mark Spitz. Combined with his bronze medal in the 4x100-metre medley relay, Bruce brought home two of the five medals Canada won at the games. David Miller of Vancouver won Olympic gold in yachting.

The Summer Olympics were overshadowed by tragedy when 11 Israeli athletes were taken hostage and then killed by Palestinian gunmen.

Greenpeace III (originally the *Vega*) sailed to French Polynesia to protest against French atmospheric nuclear tests. The boat, a 12.5-metre hand-built ketch, belonged to David McTaggart, chairman of Greenpeace International from 1969 to 1973. When McTaggart retired after being severely beaten, with others of his crew, during the 1972 protest, he retired the *Greenpeace III* as well. McTaggart died in a car accident on March 23, 2001, near his home in Italy.

Girl in a Wetsuit

June 9 Elek Imredy's *Girl in a Wetsuit* sculpture was unveiled on a rock off Stanley Park. (She's often misidentified as a mermaid, but if you look, you'll see the *Girl* has feet rather than a fishtail.)

Tom Butler, a former public relations professional, tells us that "the project was conceived by the late Vancouver lawyer Doug McK. Brown, who hired me to stick-handle the [unveiling]. After the obligatory speeches, when the denouement arrived, Brown announced that, since the *Girl* belonged henceforth to everyone who used the park, it would be inappropriate for himself or any of the politicians present to do the unveiling. Rather, the honour should go to the first citizen who strolled into view along the seawall. The assemblage waited for 10 minutes in the rain, while the Sea Cadet Band from HMCS *Discovery* tootled its entire repertoire. Finally, two girls came along arm-in-arm and were startled when Brown told them the honour was to be theirs. The girls together pulled a string on shore that reached out to the canvas covering the *Girl*—and the historic unveiling was accomplished."

Those girls, who "quite accidentally strolled into Vancouver history," were Sharon Lockhart and Mary McGowan, both 15 and both Navy League Wrenettes. According to Peggy Imredy, the artist's widow, the *Girl* "represents Vancouver's dependence on the sea and the necessity to use the sea for the benefit of all."

September 9 Dominic Charlie, Squamish leader and weather forecaster, died, aged about 87. He was born or baptized on Christmas Day in 1885 near Jericho Beach. Old-timers remembered Dominic Charlie (or, to give him his Salish name, Tsee-Qawl-Tuhn) for his frequent appearances in local newspapers predicting, with impressive accuracy, the long-range weather. More importantly, he and his half-brother August Jack Khahtsahlano collected stories and saw them published as *Squamish Legends: The First People.* He decided late in life to learn to read and write English and sat in with the kids in a Grade 1 class. He was 85 at the time.

September 30 John "Gassy Jack" Deighton's body, which had lain in an unmarked grave in New Westminster's Fraserview Cemetery for 97 years (he died in 1875), was finally located. A headstone was erected today, thanks to the Gassy Jack Memorial Fund.

September Harold Merilees, "Vancouver's first great ad man," died. He got his start in 1925 at Spencer's Department Store, then moved in 1931 to the BC Electric Railway Company. During World War II he promoted the sale of Victory Bonds. After the war he focussed his talents on public projects, including Vancouver's Diamond Jubilee celebrations (1946), the British Empire and Commonwealth Games (1954) and the BC Centennial (1958). He worked for the Greater Vancouver Tourist Association, where he came up with the idea for the Vancouver Sea Festival. And in 1969 he was elected Social Credit MLA for Vancouver–Burrard. He died in office.

Still a gas. Gastown visitors enjoy the sun and atmosphere in Maple Tree Square on June 22, 1978. It has proved to be a series of good decisions that three levels of government made in 1972 to give money for Gastown to be remodelled after its old self.
George Diack / Vancouver Sun

December 13
Art Phillips led his TEAM players to a big win on city council: Phillips won the mayor's chair in a landslide and was joined by eight aldermen (out of 10 on council) from The Electors, Action Movement (TEAM), ending 32 years of Non-Partisan Association domination.

December 29 Outgoing mayor Tom Campbell officially opened the Vancouver City Archives, housed in a building at Vanier Park that was named for the late archivist Major J.S. Matthews. (Also this year, the Public Archives of Canada published *The Great Vancouver Fire of 1886* by J.S. Matthews.)

Also in 1972

Three levels of government granted money for the beautification of Gastown. Utility wires were buried, trees were planted and old-fashioned street lights—modelled somewhat after the originals—were installed. Subtle, unobtrusive touches were added: the chain-linked bollards between the sidewalks and the roadways, for example, are there to discourage jaywalking. That they happen to look good is a bonus. The streets were paved with brick. The city's planner for Gastown, Jon Ellis, said it was the first time a North American city had torn up good streets to rebuild them in the old style.

Gary Bannerman, a *Province* columnist, was lured away by CKNW to become one of "The Investigators." He and Shirley Stocker and a large cast of others conducted hundreds of ratings-boosting investigations over the next 16 years.

The Canadian Wildlife Service bought much of Reifel Island, and George Henry Reifel donated the rest of the island to the Crown to maintain the George C. Reifel Migratory Bird Sanctuary, named for his father. The sanctuary is one of Canada's premier birdwatching sites and is a winter home of the lesser snow goose. More than 60,000 people visit annually.

The musical *Jacques Brel Is Alive and Well and Living in Paris* opened at the Arts Club Theatre in a co-production with David Y.H. Lui that changed the face of entertainment in Vancouver. Over its initial run it drew 40,000 people to the Art's Club Seymour Street theatre—even selling out Sunday matinees at 11 a.m. The show starred Leon Bibb, Ruth Nichol, Anne Mortifee, Pat Rose and Brent Carver.

This was also the year Bill Millerd became the Arts Club Theatre's artistic and managing director. As of 2011, he still is!

Neighbourhood pubs were approved by the provincial government, breaking the hotel industry's monopoly on the sale of draft beer.

The Vancouver Opera Guild began its Opera in the Schools program, designed as an introduction to opera for children in Grades 1 to 7. Each year more than 50,000 schoolchildren see a performance by the ensemble.

Kazuyoshi Akiyama was appointed music director of the Vancouver Symphony Orchestra.

The insanely surreal *Dr. Bundolo's Pandemonium Medicine Show* debuted on CBC Radio. Taped before university students, who revelled in its irreverent and raunchy humour, it ran until 1980, then moved to CBC-TV for two seasons. The show was produced by Don Kowalchuk and written by Jeffrey Groberman and Dan Thatchuk (the

Herring bounty. The captain of the *Royal Bounty* instructs crew members as they prepare to pump herring from their net during a herring roe opening in Baynes Sound near Union Bay on Vancouver Island. After herring stock rebounded in the early 1970s, fishing for the Japanese market was quite lucrative at $3,500 a tonne. *Nick Didlick* / Vancouver Sun

latter now known as Colin Yardley). Stars included Steve Woodman, Bill Reiter, Norm Grohmann, Marla Gropper and Bill Buck.

Impresario Sam Feldman launched S.L. Feldman & Associates. Before long the one-time doorman commanded the majority of club and concert business west of the Manitoba/Ontario border.

Simon Fraser University provided a futuristic background for *The Groundstar Conspiracy*, a science fiction thriller directed by Lamont Johnson.

The literary landscape of the province was mightily enhanced this year when Howard White began publishing the periodical Raincoast Chronicles, which told the stories of the pioneers of the BC coast. The Chronicles became a successful series of books, and by 1974 White's company, Harbour Publishing, was up and selling. White's crowning achievement was *The Encyclopedia of British Columbia*, and his impeccable taste is illustrated by the fact that he will be the publisher of *The Chuck Davis History of Metropolitan Vancouver*.

Lars Hansen, a 6-foot-10 centre from Coquitlam's Centennial Secondary, led his high school's basketball team to the BC title.

He went on to play four seasons at the University of Washington in Seattle and also became the only BC-born and -schooled player to end up in the NBA. He played 15 games for the Seattle SuperSonics during the 1978–79 season, averaging just over five points per contest. Seattle went on to win the NBA title that season, but Hansen did not play in any of the playoff games. Meanwhile, the UBC men's basketball team won its fourth national championship.

Bronze trio. Vancouver-based David Miller and crew celebrate after taking bronze, Canada's first "legitimate" Olympic sailing medal, in the Soling class at the 1972 Munich Olympics. Previously, in 1932, Canada had taken silver and bronze in sailing, but one race had only three competitors, and the other only two, making medals inevitable. From left: John Ekels, David Miller (skipper) and Paul Cote.
Courtesy Dave Miller

The North Vancouver Museum and Archives collected the holdings of the Lower Mainland's first museum, which had been at the Moodyville mill. NVMA features outstanding early photos and changing exhibits about the North Shore's lively social and industrial life, including the shipyards that fitted out 70 percent of the Victory ships for World War II.

Tonari Gumi, the Japanese Community Volunteer Association, was founded. With the support of the local Japanese Canadian community and a grant from the federal Local Initiative Program, the association developed basic services for seniors.

Harold Steves, a great-grandson of Richmond pioneer Manoah Steves (after whom Steveston is named), was elected the NDP MLA for Richmond. He was a member of Richmond council from 1968 to 1972 and then again from 1975 to the present, and was actively involved in preserving Steveston's heritage.

DeCosmos Village, the city's first co-op housing development (named for an early BC premier), opened at East 49th Avenue and Boundary Road in the Champlain Heights neighbourhood. The designer was architect Francis Donaldson. Champlain Heights was the last undeveloped acreage within city limits to be built up.

Kiichi Kumagai was elected to Richmond City Council, the first Japanese Canadian on board. He served until 2005.

There was a huge fuss when the "Black Tower" went up. The TD Bank Tower at 700 West Georgia was not an instant hit with the public. Its glossy black facade, 30 storeys and 127-metre (over 400-foot) height were greeted with cries of derision and dismay. Then there are those who say it's quite elegant.

The provincial government delegated responsibility for air-quality management to the Greater Vancouver Regional District, creating a regional focus for clean-air initiatives. Since then the GVRD has been responsible

The Sun

VANCOUVER, BRITISH COLUMBIA, WEDNESDAY, MARCH 15, 1972 — PRICE 15 CENTS

ALIVE AND WELL AT BAYSHORE

Howard Hughes arrives here

The Hughes Story, Pages 14, 15

'Came by private plane'

'Paying full rate'

Turbo-jet landed

MYSTERY MAGNATE Howard Hughes has checked into top floors of Bayshore Inn's tower block.

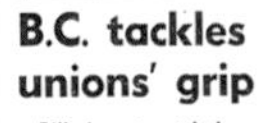

B.C. tackles unions' grip

Bill aims at restrictions in building trades pacts

ALIMONY CHEQUE GIVES EX-WIFE THE NEEDLE

HUSSEIN PLAN Linked Jordan proposed

112 missing in crash of Danish airliner

Lost freighter aground on reef

Navigational aids out but 38 seamen rescued

Famous billionaire and recluse Howard Hughes arrived in Vancouver in 1972 for a six-month stay, but this sketch in the *Vancouver Sun*, drawn with much speculation, was the most that anyone ever saw. He arrived at the Bayshore Hotel early in the morning, and never left his room.

Top left: Vancouver Sun; *top right:* The Province

for air-quality monitoring and the regulation of pollution sources.

UBC won a North American competition with an electrically powered car, the "Wally Wagon," named for university president Walter Gage (who was a favourite among engineering students).

A 13.7-hectare (34-acre) site in the Lynnmour area of North Vancouver between Lynn Creek and the Seymour River was chosen as the site for Capilano College. When workers began clearing the site for the college's first permanent facility, they found a hibernating bear.

Joe Martin of Agency Press launched *BC Business*, a monthly business magazine. It passed through the hands of several owners until it was taken over in 1990 by Canada Wide Magazines. The magazine's writers, staff and freelance, have won many awards. The editor from 1985 to 2004 was Bonnie Irving; her 19 years at the helm is possibly the longest tenure of any general-interest editor in the lower mainland. She once said that when she took over, the magazine was "remarkably dull and boring, with an emphasis on guys in suits standing next to their big corporate widgets."

Comings and Goings

March 14 From an article by Aaron Chapman, published in the *Courier* on December 16, 2004: "On an early and rainy Tuesday morning, March 14, 1972, an older man in an old bathrobe, pajama bottoms and sandals walked into the side lobby of the Bayshore Inn in Vancouver. Surrounded by a half-dozen bodyguards and staff, the tall, oddly dressed gent casually strolled around the nearly unoccupied lobby, commenting, 'This is pretty nice.' He moved into the elevator with the men and up to the penthouse suite where he would remain unseen, never leaving his single room for the duration of his six-month stay. Howard Hughes had arrived in Vancouver." Hughes remained ensconced in a blacked-out bedroom until September.

May 1 Muhammad Ali defended his North American Boxing Federation heavyweight championship at the Pacific Coliseum, winning a 12-round decision over George Chuvalo. Vancouver stock market player Murray Pezim arranged the match.

June 3 The Rolling Stones held a concert at the Pacific Coliseum. A riot broke out and 21 police officers were injured.

September 6 Website designer Stephanie Davis was born in Vancouver.

Joan Sutherland performed in the title role of *Lucrezia Borgia* for Vancouver Opera. It was her debut performance in this role.

Notable deaths: **Shin Shimotakahara**, community leader, who with her husband, Dr. Kozo Shimotakahara, ran a TB hospital and clinic for Japanese immigrants, died in Toronto on September 12, aged about 81; **Leon Joseph Koerner**, forestry industry innovator and executive, and philanthropist, in Vancouver on September 26, aged 80; **Wallis Walter Lefeaux**, fur trader, grocer, realtor, barrister, and CCF president and MLA, in West Vancouver on November 24, aged 91; **Dorwin Baird**, radio announcer and commentator for CJOR and CKWX, died in North Vancouver on December 8, aged just 56.

1973

The city underwent a lasting physical transformation as industrial False Creek began to be redeveloped as housing, and Granville Island was reborn as a tourist mecca. A spike in fire deaths lead to new sprinkler-system bylaws. And the new mayor hired an assistant named Gordon Campbell.

January 12 Ron Basford, federal minister of urban affairs and Liberal MP for Vancouver Centre, announced that Central Mortgage and Housing Corporation, a federal body, would acquire Granville Island and develop it as an urban park, with a seawall, trees...and the old industrial buildings spruced up and repurposed. By 1970 CMHC had bought out the leases of all the businesses on the island and owned the land and everything on it. Then it started looking for new tenants—shops, artist studios, restaurants—to fill the funky old buildings. In 1979 the Public Market opened as well as the Arts Club Theatre and Arts Umbrella. The next year Emily Carr College of Art arrived. In 1992, Performance Works. The island is a huge attraction today, second only to Stanley Park for both visitors and locals. Ron Basford Park on the island was named for the man who pushed hard for the concept.

January 18
The Creekhouse opened on Granville Island, the first building on the island to be converted from industrial use.
Bill Harvey and Mitch Taylor had bought a complex of former chemical plants and a distillery on Granville Island, renovated them and now offered space in the buildings to retailers and artists for rents as low as $1.50 per square foot.

January Sedgewick Undergraduate Library opened its doors at UBC. It was one of the largest branches in the UBC Library system, and one of the most innovative in design. When the student population increased rapidly in the 1960s, UBC decided to construct a new library building devoted entirely to undergraduate

Elsewhere in BC

March 29 The Mica Dam on the Columbia River became operational, creating Kinbasket Lake.

April 18 The Insurance Corporation of British Columbia (ICBC) was created. On March 1, 1974, all motor vehicles in BC would be required to have ICBC insurance.

Walter Owen, lawyer and co-founder (with Frank Griffiths) of Western International Communications, was appointed Lieutenant-Governor.

Elsewhere in Canada

November 13 A jury refused to convict Dr. Henry Morgentaler for performing abortions.

The Royal Canadian Air Farce was formed.

The Supreme Court of Canada ruled in *Calder v. British Columbia (Attorney General)*, the Nisga'a land claim case. It found that there was an aboriginal right to land, though the judges were evenly split on whether that claim had been extinguished or not. As a result of the case, aboriginal rights were discussed for the first time in the House of Commons, and the Liberal government changed federal policy to allow negotiation of aboriginal land claims.

Elsewhere in the World

March 3 Karen Magnussen, who trained first at Kerrisdale Arena, then at the North Shore Winter Club, won the World Women's Figure Skating Championship, held in Bratislava in what was then Czechoslovakia.

Vancouver's George Athans Jr. won the world crown for water-skiing at Bogota, Colombia.

Drought hit Point Roberts, the small chunk of land south of the 49th parallel and accessible by land only through BC. The 850 Canadian residents were in danger of having their water cut off in favour of American residents. Signs appeared, reading "Canadians Go Home." Water was trucked in from Blaine until the problem eased. A permanent water supply (from Canada) became available by 1986.

Augusto Pinochet led a military coup in Chile, overthrowing the government of Salvador Allende. Many Chilean refugees came to Vancouver.

needs. Students' traffic surveys indicated the best location would be the Main Mall, close to the main library. To preserve the area's open space, architects Rhone and Iredale decided to build the new library partially underground. The eight magnificent oaks that had lined the Mall for decades were incorporated into the design.

March 9 George Conrad Reifel, brewmaster, died in Vancouver, aged 79. He was born in Vancouver on May 15, 1893, the eldest son of brewer Henry Reifel. During Prohibition, George sailed his liquor down the coast. His brother Henry (known as Harry) raised purebred Jerseys in Milner, BC. The brothers built and owned the Commodore Block on Granville (1929) and the Vogue and Studio Theatres in the 1940s.

April 1 The federal government gave title to the Jericho Defence Lands to the City of Vancouver. The city created 29-hectare (72-acre) Jericho Beach Park.

April 18 The BC Land Commission Act, which established the Agricultural Land Reserve (ALR), was introduced. Richmond MLA Harold Steves was instrumental in developing the concept of an agricultural "land bank" to protect BC's dwindling supply of farmland, drafting the initial resolutions for NDP policy conventions in the mid-1960s. As an MLA he was active in getting the legislation passed by Dave Barrett's government, and over the following decades he was one of its strongest defenders. Initially the ALR comprised 4.7 million hectares (11.6 million acres), about 5 percent of the province. Despite boundary changes over the decades, its area remains approximately the same.

June 14 Henry Herbert "Harry" Stevens died in Vancouver, aged 94. Born in Bristol, England, Stevens and his family emigrated to Peterborough, ON, and in 1894 moved to Vancouver. Stevens clerked for $12 a week at City Grocery at Main and Pender. He was an alderman for Ward 5 in 1910, and in 1911 was elected MP for Vancouver, an office he retained until 1930. (He went on to represent East Kootenay from 1930 to 1940.) Stevens was president of the Vancouver Board of Trade from 1952 to 1953. He was effective in getting improvements to Vancouver Harbour, the Stanley Park seawall, False Creek and Granville Island.

Reflecting the desperation to inject some life into the franchise, Vancouver Blazers centre Claude St. Sauveur scores a first-period breakaway goal against Cleveland Crusaders goalie Bob Whidden on January 24, 1974. It wasn't enough, however, and after twice failing to make the playoffs, the World Hockey Association team was moved to Calgary in 1975. Vancouver Sun

June 23 The opening of False Creek Park marked the official start to redeveloping the False Creek area.

Like Granville Island, the rest of the creek had long been an industrial area—the site of sawmills, rail yards, shipyards and factories. By the 1960s, however, what had been the city's engine was becoming a polluted eyesore. The development of the Roberts Bank superport meant the creek was no longer needed as a working harbour, and an agreement between the province and the city gave city officials free rein to start developing South False Creek (including Burrard and Fairview Slopes) as a residential/commercial neighbourhood.

June West Vancouver, which had held May Day celebrations since 1931, discontinued them under that name. The new title was Community Days, and there were no more May Queens... because the celebrations were now held in June.

August Burnaby and New Westminster co-hosted the Canada Summer Games. Preparations included the creation of a 2,200-metre rowing course on Burnaby Lake, then one of only three such competitive courses in North America. The New Westminster venue was Queen's Park.

Summer Businessman Jimmy Pattison bought Philadelphia's World Hockey Association franchise and moved it to the city. The Vancouver Blazers played two seasons, losing games and fans, before moving to Calgary and becoming the Cowboys. Some Blazers trivia: the first professional goaltender to use a curved stick in a hockey game was the Blazers' Don Mcleod.

September 3 The last movie played at the Strand Theatre.

October 15 The Vancouver East Cultural Centre opened at 1895 Venables, on the city's east side, in what had been a church. It was transformed into a theatre, recital hall and community facility. The "Cultch" is now a popular performing-arts venue that attracts people from far beyond East Vancouver. Besides founding director Christopher Wootten, who was at the time an arts project officer for the federal program Opportunities for Youth, others involved in the creation of the Cultch were politicos Darlene Marzari, Jonathan Baker and Gary Lauk.

October 20 The *Province*'s Chuck Poulsen wrote that Jim Pattison wanted to buy a second sports team. "The multimillionaire Vancouver businessman and owner of the World Hockey Association Blazers launched a bid to buy the BC Lions—which is nothing new—and some of the Canadian Football League club executives say they're more than willing to listen." The sale never did go through, but Pattison had said he was prepared to renovate Empire Stadium, "increasing the capacity to 52,000 with two tiers on both sides of the field and covered end zone seats."

November 24 "I want everyone in BC to know I am my own man," Bill Bennett, the brand-new leader of the provincial Social Credit party, told delegates at the Socred leadership convention in the Hotel Vancouver. The line was a reference to Bennett's father, W.A.C., ensconced in a 14th-floor suite of the hotel, deliberately keeping away from his son's moment of triumph. The elder Bennett had been defeated in 1972 by the NDP's Dave Barrett after 20 years as premier. His son, in turn, defeated Barrett in the 1975 election.

Also in 1973

Some other community groups and activity centres that started up this year: Raminder Dosanjh, a prominent human rights and women's rights activist, co-founded the India Mahila (Women's) Association for women of South Asian origin; the United Chinese Community Enrichment Services Society (SUCCESS) is now one of the largest immigration and social service agencies in British Columbia, providing social, educational and health services, business and community development, and advocacy; and the Edmonds Community Centre for Older Adults (7282 Kingsway) and the Senior Citizen's Activity Centre (1475 Kent St.) opened in Vancouver and White Rock, respectively.

McDowell's Drug Store, which had opened in 1905 at 1st Street and Lonsdale in North Vancouver, was no more. It had been run by the same family for 68 years.

From Skid Row to Downtown Eastside

The Downtown Eastside Residents' Association (DERA) was born. Historically, decisions in the Downtown Eastside were made by city council or the province, church groups or planners—people who did not live in the area. In 1973 the situation changed. The city's Social Planning Department sent Peter Davies to deal with some of the problems in the area, including health and safety concerns. Davies decided that the neighbourhood needed a democratic community organization to permanently alter the situation.

Many residents were single, older men, which was seen as a drawback, but Davies realized those who had lived through the Dirty Thirties had been involved in unemployment or anti-poverty organizations at that time. One of these men, Bruce Eriksen, was a retired member of the Canadian Seaman's Union. He had no formal education, but he knew the people in the neighbourhood, and he knew the conditions there. Eriksen began to organize community meetings to identify the problems of the community. One early initiative was lighting laneways to prevent robberies, an accomplishment that convinced residents of the value of a community association and collective action. Another was the fight for fire-sprinkler bylaws (see below).

Eriksen and others set up a formal association to give residents a voice and self-esteem. They also decided to give the neighbourhood, which had always been known as Skid Road, a name that recognized it was a community. They chose the Downtown Eastside, and the organization became the Downtown Eastside Residents Association, or DERA.

When 40 people died in house fires this year, the worst toll in the city's history, DERA acted, as described by Jim Green, DERA director in the 1980s: "Neither the province nor the city made it mandatory for SRO [single room occupancy] hotels to have sprinkler systems. Approximately 25 people died every year, 40 in 1973. DERA worked hard to have the bylaw changed. The struggle was ignored by the city and fought against by the landlords who threatened to close permanently if they were required to put sprinkler systems in. The fire deaths of five people in the Commercial Hotel on Cambie Street allowed Bruce Eriksen to corner the mayor at the site of the burning building in front of the media and demand he bring in sprinkler laws to stop the unnecessary deaths. This incident led to the passing of the Fire Sprinkler Bylaw, responsible for the saving of many lives." (By 1982, deaths by fire were down to eight.)

Much different from today, this is an aerial view of the Vancouver skyline as seen from the Westcoast Transmission building in 1973, looking toward the Bayshore Hotel and Stanley Park.
City of Vancouver Archives, CVA 1435-160

Wakayama, Japan, became the sister city of Richmond. Mio-mura, a village in the same prefecture, was the native home of many of Steveston's earliest Japanese immigrants.

Granville Square was built at 200 Granville to house the headquarters of Canadian Pacific. Now the *Vancouver Sun* and the *Province* are there. At a height of 123 metres (400 feet), with 30 storeys, it is still one of the city's tallest buildings.

The Vancouver Whitecaps were formed in 1973 and joined the North American Soccer League in time for the 1974 season.

The John Davis family began to restore 166 West 10th Ave., the oldest (1891) woodframe house in Mount Pleasant. Then they began to restore other houses in the block. The result is one of the finest, most attractive streetscapes in the city.

The last class of psychiatric nurses graduated from Riverview (formerly Essondale), the mental hospital in Coquitlam.

In a report on commercial crime on the West Coast, the RCMP said: "Law enforcement agencies have estimated that approximately 20 to 30 percent of the mines and local, junior industrial stocks listed on the Vancouver Stock Exchange are manipulated." That report, the NDP governments' mining royalties and other factors led to a sag in VSE trading. The exchange lost money this year, for the first time in almost 40 years.

The Western Front, one of the first artist-run centres in Canada, was founded by a multi-disciplinary group of artists and became the centre of experimental and performance art practice in the city.

So far as we know, Chuck Davis' *Guide to Vancouver*, published this year by J.J. Douglas, was the first general guidebook to the city.

Fred Rogers' book *Shipwrecks of British Columbia* became a BC bestseller. Rogers had done 20 years of research into the subject, and he chronicled more than 100 shipwrecks and their discoveries. Rogers' *More Shipwrecks of British Columbia* appeared in 1992.

Comings and Goings

Gordon Campbell, born in Vancouver on January 12, 1948, returned from working for CUSO as a secondary school teacher, and basketball and track coach in Yola, Nigeria, and became an aide to new Vancouver mayor Art Phillips.

Notable deaths: **Dick Diespecker**, journalist, poet and novelist, who wrote more than 400 radio plays for CJOR, CBC, BBC and the South African Broadcasting Corporation, died in San Francisco on February 11, aged 65; **Anne Sugarman (née Wodlinger)**, Jewish organizer and activist, died in Toronto in May, aged about 78; **Jonathan Webster "Jack" Cornett**, shoe merchant, last reeve of the municipality of South Vancouver, and mayor of Vancouver (1941–46), died August 19, aged 90.

1974

The city began its first attempt to convert portions of Granville Street into a pedestrian mall. The year was also marked by the opening of the Aquatic Centre, the Knight Street Bridge and the fist neighbourhood pub. Vancouver scientist and environmentalist David Suzuki, meanwhile, began his television career with *The Nature of Things*.

January 8 Construction began on the Asian Centre at UBC, though it was not officially opened until June 5, 1981. The centre has an unusual history: Shotaro Iida, a professor of religious studies at UBC, went to Expo 70 in Osaka, Japan, and thought the Sanyo Electric Company's pavilion would make a great Asian Centre for UBC once the fair was over. He asked Sanyo for the building, and the company donated it to the people of the province of British Columbia in honour of BC's centennial. Since the cost of shipping the entire dismantled building would have been astronomical, only the supporting beams and girders were sent. UBC, however, did not know about the shipment and only learned of it when Canada Customs called saying they had some "white pipes" waiting to be picked up. The dismantled pieces were numbered to make reconstruction easy and efficient. Unfortunately, the beams were left on the site for a few years while UBC recruited sponsors for the construction, and rain washed the numbers off. Putting the beams together was rather like trying to solve a 172-ton jigsaw puzzle.

January 15 The Knight Street Bridge opened, replacing the Fraser Street Bridge, 1.6 kilometres (1 mile) to the west, which closed February 10. This is now one of the busiest

Serene centre. A place of Asian elegance, the Asian Studies Centre at the University of British Columbia began to take shape in 1974 and was finally completed in 1981. Also housing the Asian Studies Library, the centre—originally the Sanyo pavilion at Expo 70 in Osaka, Japan—has proved to be a popular hub for research, learning and serenity.
Deni Eagland / Vancouver Sun

Elsewhere in BC

March 1 From this date, all motor vehicles in BC were required to have coverage from the Insurance Corporation of British Columbia. ICBC got off to a robust start with 1 million policies. Today this Crown corporation collects vehicle and driver premiums from more than 2 million motorists and invests the money to provide insurance benefits for its customers and for victims of crashes. Also effective this date, all BC drivers were required to keep their licence plates when they bought, sold or traded their vehicle. Previously, motorists had retained their plates only as long as they owned a particular vehicle—when a vehicle was sold, the plates remained with it.

Elsewhere in Canada

July 2 Ralph Steinhauer was appointed Lieutenant-Governor of Alberta, the first aboriginal person to hold that position in a Canadian province.

The federal government commissioned Justice Thomas Berger to head the Mackenzie Valley Pipeline Inquiry, which was to investigate the social, environmental and economic impact of a gas pipeline that was to run through the Yukon and Northwest Territories. Berger travelled extensively in the north and released his report in 1977, recommending a 10-year moratorium to deal with the environmental and social effects such a pipeline would have.

Vicki Gabereau, latterly a Vancouver talk-show personality, ran in the Toronto mayoralty race as Rosie the Clown.

Elsewhere in the World

August 9 Richard Nixon resigns as US president to avoid impeachment as a result of the Watergate break-in. On September 8 his successor, Gerald Ford, grants him a full pardon.

Bottoms up! The Dover Arms opened in 1974 in the West End, the first neighbourhood pub following legislation in 1972 that ended the hotel industry monopoly over the sale of draft beer. Thankfully, it wasn't the last, and independent pubs can now be enjoyed all throughout Vancouver. *Stuart Davis / Vancouver Sun*

stretches of road in the city, with hundreds of trucks using it daily. The four-lane concrete bridge provides access to Lulu and Mitchell Islands and serves Routes 91 and 99 to the south. Innovations included the use of electric heating cables in the deck to minimize the need for de-icing salt in the winter. Construction took five years, and the cost, including approaches, was about $15 million. With the bridge opening, Knight Street became a more distinct dividing point between the western Sunset and eastern Victoria/Fraserview districts.

January 22 Granville Street north of Nelson closed to automobile traffic while it was converted to a pedestrian mall that opened August 22.

March 8
The Dover Arms, Vancouver's first neighbourhood pub, opened in the West End.

Legislation had been passed in 1972 allowing the establishment of pubs, an astonishing example of common sense.

March 19 Vancouver City Council voted to buy the Orpheum Theatre, at 884 Granville St., for use as a new concert hall after Famous Players revealed plans to transform the heritage building into a multiplex cinema. The Orpheum cost the city $3.9 million and was then renovated for an additional $3.2 million. It now hosts various touring shows and is home to the Vancouver Symphony Society, the Bach Choir, the Vancouver Chamber Choir and the BC Entertainment Hall of Fame.

March 26 David Lambie "Davey" Black, "the Wee Scot," died in Vancouver, aged about 90. Born in 1884 in Troon, Ayrshire, Scotland, Black came to Canada in the early 1900s and worked at Outremont and Rivermeade golf clubs (1905–20) before moving west to become the golf pro at Shaughnessy Heights Golf Course, a post he held for 25 years (1920–45). He won four national titles, the first in 1913; won the first BC Open in 1928; and in 1929, with Duncan Sutherland, beat Walter Hagen and Horton Smith at the Point Grey Golf Club. In 1935, Black and Sutherland bested the great Bobbie Jones, partnered with Davey's son Kenny, the BC amateur champion. Davey Black was inducted into the BC Sports Hall of Fame in 1966 and the Canadian Golf Hall of Fame in 1972.

May 3 Vancouver's Aquatic Centre, built to replace Crystal Pool, was officially opened. Swimmers started using it May 6, and the first paying swimmer to use the pool was 18-year-old Jeff Veniot.

May 5
The Vancouver Whitecaps played their first game,

debuting for a crowd of 18,000 at Empire Stadium against the San José Earthquakes. They lost 2–1 in a shootout. One of the players was

Right: The long, twisty road of the Vancouver Whitecaps began here, with this original squad, in 1974. With much of his own career tied to the Whitecaps, current president Bob Lenarduzzi is pictured here as player no. 5, in the back row, second from the left. *Vancouver Whitecaps FC*

Bobby Lenarduzzi, who had turned 19 four days earlier and who became one of the best soccer players Canada has ever produced. Born in Vancouver on May 1, 1955, Lenarduzzi started playing for Reading Football Club in England at age 16, eventually appearing in 67 Football League games and scoring two goals. He made his international debut for Canada against Poland in Toronto in 1973.

June 20 BC Rail's *Royal Hudson* steam train made its inaugural run from North Vancouver to Squamish, pulling 1940s-style passenger coaches, baggage cars and a dining car through some of the most picturesque mountain and ocean scenery in Canada. The big, beautiful locomotive was an instant hit with locals and tourists alike. It ran till mid-September each year, carrying as many as 70,000 passengers a season.

July 8 Simma Holt, a well-known *Vancouver Sun* reporter and author, was elected MP for Vancouver–Kingsway, becoming the first Jewish woman to serve in the Canadian Parliament. Art Lee was elected to represent Vancouver East, the second Chinese Canadian MP to serve in the House of Commons, after Douglas Jung. (Lee had been the leader of the BC Liberal Party from 1984 to 1987, the first Chinese Canadian leader of a party in Canada.)

August 24 The Grand Lodge of British Columbia (Freemasons), established in 1871, officially opened at its present location, 1495 West 8th Ave. The Grand Lodge serves as a kind of administrative body for the other lodges in BC and rents meeting space to about 25 of them.

September 1 Pauline Jewett, 51, became president of Simon Fraser University, the first female president of a major Canadian university. During her tenure, which ran until October 9, 1978, women's studies, a seniors program, distance education into BC's Interior and an innovative child-care centre were established.

September 30 Canadian Pacific ended its ferry service to Seattle.

October 16 Official opening of the St. Roch National Historic Site beside Vancouver's Maritime Museum. It was 30 years to the day since the *St. Roch* had returned from its historic voyage through the Northwest Passage, and some of the former crew were on hand for the ceremonies. An RCMP vessel, the *St. Roch* is unique because it was the first ship to traverse the Northwest Passage in both directions, and the first ship to circumnavigate North America.

October 29 The *Seaspan Commodore* was registered, becoming the flagship of the Seaspan International fleet based in North

Sea trip. Heading for the ocean, the *Seaspan Commodore*, registered in 1974 and Seaspan International's flagship tug, pulls the *Seaspan Forester*, the world's largest self-loading barge, down the Fraser River under the Port Mann Bridge. *Ian Smith / Vancouver Sun*

Vancouver. The 142-foot, deep-sea tug, with a speed of 14.5 knots, was built at Vancouver Shipyards. The *Commodore* towed the *Seaspan Forester* (the world's largest log barge) and barges of lumber, salt, gravel and clinker between Vancouver and Californian, Mexican and Alaskan ports.

November 12 Arbutus Village Square opened in Vancouver. The 12-hectare (30-acre), $20 million complex at 4255 Arbutus, built by Marathon Realty, included 450 housing units, a park and a 30-store shopping centre. The project had a rocky beginning, with its neighbours evenly divided over whether they wanted it or not.

November 30 The last movie played at the Capitol Theatre before its renovation as a multiplex.

November With the slogan "Elect a nut," Mr. Peanut ran for mayor on the art platform: "P for Performance, E for Elegance, A for Art, N for Nonsense, U for Uniqueness and T for Talent." William S. Burroughs, who was visiting Vancouver at the time, endorsed his candidacy. The *Vancouver Sun* reported: "Mr. Peanut managed to make his statement at the [candidates'] meeting by posing a 'visual question' to the other candidates during the question period. A retinue of his followers, including pretty girls in leotards [the Peanettes] and a band with kazoos disguised as leopard-skin covered saxophones, marched down the aisle of the auditorium...The girls flashed glittering letters spelling out Mr. Peanut's name while singing 'Peanuts from Heaven' along with the band. Mr. Peanut did a little tap-dance at the end, but did not explain what his 'visual question' meant." Art Phillips easily won re-election, but Mr. Peanut (aka Vincent Trasov, a performance artist and co-founder of the Western Front Society) received 2,685 ballots, or 3.4 percent of the vote.

December Vancouver began a program of designating "heritage buildings"—structures that, for various reasons (historical, architectural, aesthetic), were protected from demolition or exterior change. Among the first 20 buildings so designated were the mansions Gabriola, Shannon, Hycroft, Glen Brae and Aberthau; the churches St. James' Anglican, Christ Church Cathedral, St. Andrew's-Wesley United, and Holy Rosary Cathedral; and such historic sites as the old post office and the Hastings Mill Store.

Also in 1974

Jack Blaney came to Simon Fraser University as dean of education. In 1997 he was named president, and later he helped establish both the downtown Harbour Centre campus and the Morris J. Wosk Centre for Dialogue.

The Native Indian Teacher Education Program (NITEP) began at UBC. This program prepares and challenges people of aboriginal ancestry to be educators in public, band and independent schools. Seven students graduated with their bachelor of education degrees in 1985, and the program admitted its first master's students in 1986.

Vancouver City College became Vancouver Community College when it separated from the Vancouver School Board.

Popular Steve Woodman, "the man of 1,000 voices," was badly injured when, driving home after appearing on a telethon, his car hit black ice, went over an embankment and rolled out of control. He sustained severe head injuries and was in a coma for a long time. He did emerge from the coma but did not regain his voice, which ended an outstanding career in which his voice skills had been called on often. He died in his sleep on March 13, 1990.

Perry Goldsmith began Contemporary Communications Ltd. One subsidiary is a personal management division; another is the National Speakers Bureau, which offers celebrated Canadians who will speak to groups of all kinds. Goldsmith—born September 22, 1947, in Vancouver—has a lot of high-profile people in his stable, like Olympic gold medallists Alexandre Bilodeau and Mark Tewksbury, soldier and human rights activist Lt. Gen. Romeo Dallaire, newsman Don Newman and more than 100 others. "When I started in this business," Goldsmith says, "the demand for Canadian speakers was limited, now our clients have a strong interest in hearing Canadian perspectives."

Richard Bonynge (pronounced *bawn-ing*) took over from Irving Guttman as artistic director of Vancouver Opera. A bonus of his tenure was the appearance in many operas of his wife, the great soprano Joan Sutherland, "La Stupenda." Bonynge established the company's own orchestra and a resident training program, but his tenure ended in 1978 with the last half of the season cancelled because of growing debt. He was succeeded by Hamilton McClymont, who brought financial stability back to the opera company.

Advertising agency Griffiths Gibson Ramsay Productions and Western International Broadcasting invested $500,000 to open Little Mountain Studio. Among the celebrated groups that recorded there before the studio's demise in 1994 were Aerosmith, Bon Jovi and AC/DC.

A huge rock attraction was born when Bachman–Turner Overdrive, managed by Bruce Allen, exploded out of Vancouver.

The group's first LP came out May 17, 1973, but it was the 1974 release of *Not Fragile* that made BTO internationally known. Their biggest hit single, "Takin' Care of Business," is still played nearly 40 years later.

Mushroom Records was founded by brothers Wink and Dick Vogel. An early Mushroom LP, Heart's *Dreamboat Annie*, sold 4 million copies. The label declared bankruptcy in 1980, a year after the death of its vice-president and creative sparkplug, Shelly Siegel.

Five book publishers came together to found the Association of Book Publishers of BC. Today the ABPBC has over 30 members, many based in the Greater Vancouver area, who engage in every type of book publishing, including literary, poetry, educational, scholarly and a full range of trade books.

Well-known garden expert David Tarrant became education coordinator at UBC's Botanical Garden.

Dr. David Suzuki began as host of CBC-TV's *The Nature of Things*. He's still hosting it!

Michael Harcourt, a young Vancouver lawyer and alderman, criticized city police for their "Eliot Ness–style raids" on gay bars and bathhouses.

James McFarlane founded McIlhenny Offshore Surveying and Engineering in Port Moody. McFarlane spent 18 years in the Canadian Navy building manned submersibles. After leaving the navy he had a notion to build a "revolutionary" tethered vehicle but discovered that eight or nine companies were already working on that. So he began to concentrate on remotely operated vehicles. McFarlane started with two people. He employs over 100 today at International Submarine Engineering (ISE) of Port Coquitlam.

Left and above: Underwater Hunter. Seen here being transferred, the Dorado Semi-Submersible Minehunting Vehicle is designed to autonomously travel under water with only its mast above the surface. It is one of many vehicles and robotic systems developed by International Submarine Engineering Ltd., founded in Port Moody in 1974, and now based in Port Coquitlam.

Courtesy of ISE

The Red Book first appeared. This was an initiative of the Community Information Service (known today as BC211) that actually began back in 1957 when CIS realized its comprehensive card catalogue of community services in the Lower Mainland would be useful to many other agencies and began publishing it as a directory every two years. In 1974 the directory was published in a red, three-ring binder, and thus was born *The Red Book.* Three years later the organization began publishing annually because of rapid changes in the information, and it now has an online version and a 24/7 phone help line (just dial 211). *The Red Book* contains listings for more than 5,000 social, community and government agencies and services and is used by doctors, lawyers, educators, clergy, human resources staff, emergency services workers and others.

The BC Cancer Institute changed its name to the Cancer Control Agency of BC, and the Workmen's Compensation Board became the Workers Compensation Board (it's known today as WorkSafe BC).

Harold Scanlon Foley, forestry executive, died in Vancouver, aged about 74. He was the head of his family's Powell River Company (est. 1905) and oversaw its merger with MacMillan Bloedel in 1959. The pulp mill PRC established at Powell River was, for a time, the largest in the world. Among other firsts, the company created BC's first medical plan. Foley was respected both by executives and by workers and their unions. He was a significant (and often anonymous) philanthropist.

Minneapolis entrepreneur Tom Scallen, owner of the Vancouver Canucks since 1970, found himself in financial and legal trouble and sold the team for $9 million to Frank Griffiths' Vancouver-based telecommunications company, Western Broadcasting.

The Jericho Sailing Centre began operating at Jericho Beach as a non-profit, self-supporting association, under the aegis of the city's park board. It bills itself as "Vancouver's Ocean Access Community Centre." Completely land based, the centre has 3,000 members, 13 affiliated clubs and four schools and is a site for launching kayaks, canoes, sailboards and sailboats. A unique affiliate is the Disabled Sailing Association, whose members take to the water in specially modified boats.

Will Senger took over as chairman of the Cloverdale Rodeo and helped orchestrate a 10-year turnaround.

In 1983 the Cloverdale Rodeo attracted more contestants than the Calgary Stampede and packed 20,000 spectators into the arena, and in 1984 it was voted the Number One Performance Rodeo in North America by the Professional Rodeo Cowboy's Association.

The original, bellows-operated diaphone foghorn at the Point Atkinson Lighthouse was replaced by diesel-powered airchimes, the sound of which carried 8 to 16 kilometres (5 to 10 miles). There was unhappiness in 1996 when these were replaced by a solar-powered electronic signal rated for 3 kilometres (2 miles)—it was "like replacing an oboe with a penny whistle," said one old salt.

Island Princess and *Pacific Princess*, which became famous as TV's "Love Boat," began sailing out of Vancouver's harbour for the Alaska cruise trade. The 20,000-ton vessels, owned by P&O's Princess Cruises, continued in that trade until 1991.

The handsome terracotta Birks Building, at the southeast corner of Granville and Georgia since 1912, was demolished to make way for the Vancouver Centre development. This generated the most anger and sadness for a lost building since the 1967 demolition of the Pantages Theatre at 20 West Hastings.

The Greater Vancouver Housing Corporation was incorporated as a wholly owned subsidiary of the GVRD. The GVHC is a non-profit organization that manages more than 3,600 rental units around the Lower Mainland and provides affordable housing for more than 10,000 people at a mix of income levels.

Comings and Goings

Johnny Carson came to Vancouver to plug his new restaurant chain, Here's Johnny! He had a long lunch with Red Robinson.

Notable deaths: **M.Y. Williams**, professor of geology and one of UBC's original faculty members, on February 3, aged 90; **John Edward "Jack" Underhill**, badminton champion, on July 14, aged 71.

1975

A hostage-taking at the BC Penitentiary turned deadly and the murder of a distinguished poet by her husband made headlines. The Arthur Laing Bridge to the airport and the VanDusen Botanical Garden were both opened, while the Penthouse Cabaret was closed down in a police raid. A second-generation premier, Bill Bennett, meanwhile, began a decade in power.

January 22 The Granville Street Mall was closed to all but transit, emergency and taxi traffic.

April 14 Vancouver Co-operative Radio CFRO-FM 102.7 signed on at 3 p.m. with community-based programming. The station was and is non-profit, community based and run by its members.

Left: The Granville Street Mall opened in 1975, closing off the section between Hastings and Nelson to most traffic except for buses, taxis and emergency vehicles. With scores of new trees planted along the meandering road, the move proved popular with pedestrians who were out for a show at one of the many theatres.
Rob Straight / PNG

June 9 Three prisoners at the BC Penitentiary took 15 hostages.

The prisoners were about to be returned to solitary confinement and, as one of them said, "Going back to solitary confinement was a 100 percent chance of ending up dead...taking hostages was a 95 percent chance of dying and a 5 percent chance of getting out." The standoff with prison officials lasted 41 hours and ended June 11 when an emergency response team stormed the hostage-takers. During the raid, one of the guards accidentally shot and killed one of the hostages, classification officer Mary Steinhauser, 32. Ironically, she had been working at implementing courses for prisoners to make solitary confinement more bearable. Christian Bruyère wrote a play, *Walls* (1978), based on the incident. It was made into a movie in 1984.

Elsewhere in BC

September 6 The provincial legislature established the Resort Municipality of Whistler. This unique designation took account of the special problems faced by the developing resort.

December 23 Bill Bennett, who had defeated Dave Barrett in a general election on December 11, took office as BC's 27th premier. He was the son of the 25th premier, W.A.C. Bennett. Bill Bennett was born in Kelowna on April 14, 1932. He served to August 6, 1986.

Elsewhere in Canada

January 1 Product labelling using the metric system was introduced.

April 1 Environment Canada began giving temperatures in degrees Celsius rather than Fahrenheit.

April 2 The CN Tower was completed in Toronto. It opened to the public on June 26, 1976.

Elsewhere in the World

February 11 Margaret Thatcher became leader of the Conservative party in England.

April 4 Bill Gates founded Microsoft Corporation.

April 30 The last helicopter left the US embassy grounds in Vietnam; Saigon surrendered. The first Vietnamese refugees began arriving in Vancouver.

November 10 The *Edmund Fitzgerald* sank during a storm on Lake Superior, taking all 29 crew on board to the bottom. Gordon Lightfoot immortalized the event in "The Wreck of the Edmund Fitzgerald."

Pleasing puzzle. The VanDusan Botanical Garden opened in 1975, on what used to be, in 1910, "an isolated acreage of stumps and bush." Thankfully, it is no longer that. Pictured here is the maze, modelled after those created in Renaissance England. It was planted in 1981. *Courtesy PNG*

August 27
The Arthur Laing Bridge opened and immediately improved traffic flow to and from the airport

(it was officially opened on May 15, 1976). The crossing was originally to be called the Hudson Street Bridge, but Prime Minister Trudeau had announced in September 1974 that it would be named for Laing, a senator and former Liberal MP for the area. The south end of the bridge is near Eburne, in Richmond, where Laing was born on September 9, 1904. Sadly, Laing died in February 1975, just seven months before the bridge was finished.

August 30 VanDusen Botanical Garden opened on the old Shaughnessy Heights Golf Course lands. Eleven pieces of stone sculpture were created over the summer during the International Stone Sculpture Symposium at the garden.

September 13 Architect C.B.K. Van Norman died in Vancouver, aged 68. Van Norman graduated in architecture from the University of Manitoba in 1927 and came to Vancouver in 1928. He designed the Burrard Building, the Vancouver Maritime Museum and mansions for General A.D. McRae, H.R. MacMillan and F. Ronald Graham. He was also a design consultant for Royal Centre and many Park Royal stores. Van Norman specialized in post–World War II schools and pre-fab homes and won the Canadian Housing Design Council's Centennial Award for Beach Towers (1600 Beach).

September 24 Poet Pat Lowther was murdered by her husband. Her body was discovered in Furry Creek, near Squamish, three weeks later. (Her husband was convicted of the murder in June 1977 and died in prison in 1985.) Born Patricia Louise Tinmuth in Vancouver on July 29, 1935, Lowther had her first poem published in the *Vancouver Sun* when she was 10. She was becoming known as a poet, having published three books, and was also active as a teacher at UBC and in literary organizations. Her best-known work, *A Stone Diary*, was published posthumously in 1977 by Oxford University Press. In 1980, the League of Canadian Poets established the Pat Lowther Award, an annual prize to honour a new book by a Canadian woman poet.

September 25 The *Ubyssey*, the three-times-a-week paper for students at UBC, published a sort of interview with "Ace" Aasen, well known locally as the "Mayor" of Gastown. Ace, who was quite pleased to accept a drink from you at any time, strolled around the Gastown streets in a somewhat tattered top hat, sporting a cane and passing along his thoughts on life. In this *Ubyssey* interview, which at times approached coherence, he gave us his thoughts on pollution: "It will disappear."

November 23 The last movie was shown at the Orpheum Theatre. Ivan Ackery, longtime manager of the theatre, tells the story in his autobiography *Fifty Years on Theatre Row*: "Projectionist Bill Field pressed the button that drew the final curtain on the Orpheum Theatre's last picture show. Orpheum manager Ted Bielby wanted to show the Oscar-winning nostalgia film *The Last Picture Show*, but he had to run *Return to Macon County* instead. Impresario Hugh Pickett attended that last movie and held a closing party for Ted and his staff." What makes that item doubly interesting is that Hugh Pickett had been in the audience for the first movie at the Orpheum on November 7, 1927, when he was 14.

December 26 A runaway logging barge, driven by a westerly gale, carried away a 116-metre (380-foot) span of the Fraser River Swing Bridge at New Westminster. Fortunately Burlington Northern had drawings for a modern 114-metre (374-foot) span recently built at Spokane. This speeded the repair and reopening of this busy but obscure railway bridge.

December 31 Police raided the Penthouse Cabaret on Seymour and charged the Filippone brothers with living off the avails of prostitution (they allegedly received kickbacks in the form of cover charges and tips paid by the 80 to 100 prostitutes who were entering and re-entering the club to pick up customers). Joe Philliponi, the oldest brother (his name was misspelled by an immigration officer), who had opened the Penthouse as a dinner club in 1945, pleaded for leniency, claiming "it would kill my mother" if he were sentenced to a jail term. "The trial was a sensation," according to Greg Middleton of the *Province*. "There were undercover tapes, liquor inspectors on the take." Philliponi and his brothers were convicted and then won the case on appeal, but the Penthouse was closed for three years during the investigation and trial. Vancouver City Council reinstated the brothers' licence to run the Penthouse in 1979.

Also in 1975

BC Heritage Day celebrations included the third annual grand prix bike races in Gastown and the 1875 Burrard Inlet Dominion Day Festival at the Centennial Museum.

Cypress Provincial Park was created in West Vancouver.

At its creation, the park covered just over 2,100 hectares (5,190 acres). Today it's 3,012 hectares (7,440 acres).

Dr. Louis Miranda, a former Squamish chief, began working with Dutch ethnographer Aert Kuipers to create a written language for the Squamish Nation. Miranda, who was born in 1892 and was one of the foremost experts on Squamish culture and language, received an honorary doctorate from Simon Fraser University for that initiative.

Alvin Balkind, who had been curator of UBC's Gallery of Fine Arts (1962–73), became the chief curator at the Vancouver Art Gallery. He held the post to 1978.

In 1969 Maria Lewis formed an eponymous ballet ensemble in Vancouver. This year the former board of directors of the defunct Ballet Horizons approached her and asked her to organize a new company, to be called the Pacific Ballet Theatre. She directed it until 1980, when she was succeeded by Renald Rabu. Today the company is called Ballet BC.

The Strand Theatre on the south side of Georgia Street just east of Granville came down to make way for Vancouver Centre.

A woman named Charlie Galbraith had the idea to hold an awards show for local country music. That idea turned into the non-profit BC Country Music Association, which presented its first awards in 1977. The BCCMA held its 35th awards show in 2010.

Vancouver's second firehall (at 280 East Cordova) began answering alarms in 1906. This year the hall closed, the last fire truck drove away and a group called Actor's Workshop attempted to turn it into a theatre. Actor's Workshop folded, but the Firehall Theatre Society was formed in 1982 to try again, and it now operates the old firehall as one of the busiest venues in Vancouver.

Impresario David Y.H. Lui opened his own venue, the David Y.H. Lui Theatre. It closed in 1979, but during its brief existence, theatregoers enjoyed appearances by Dame Joan Sutherland, the National Ballet of Canada, the Royal Winnipeg Ballet and others. The building was reincarnated as a punk club, the Laundromat, for a year (1981), hosting legendary bands like Black Flag, Subhumans and DOA, and then became Richard's on Richards, first a glossy disco nightclub and in the 1990s a venue for live music. The building was demolished in 2009, to be replaced by condos.

Press Gang, an all-woman printing collective, published its first book, *Women Look at Psychiatry*. Press Gang began as a left-wing printing cooperative in 1970. In 1974 it became an all-women collective, offering printing services to local community and women's groups. The printing business was discontinued in 1993. The publishing collective published more than 50 books before it declared bankruptcy in 2002.

Vancouver's Robert Bringhurst received the Macmillan Prize for Poetry from the University of BC.

A view from Cypress Provincial Park overlooking Howe Sound. The park was created above West Vancouver in 1975 and is bordered on the north and east by Mount Strachan and Hollyburn Mountain. *Ministry of Environment*

1975

Right: Location: Vancouver. George Segal, playing RCMP Cpl. Timothy Shave in the 1975 film *Russian Roulette*, takes aim from the roof of the Hotel Vancouver. The film, about a Mountie engulfed in a KGB conspiracy to kill renegade Russian premier Alexei Kosygin, received middling reviews but for Vancouverites does have the bonus of showing Vancouver playing itself in a dramatic thriller.

Courtesy PNG

Helen Potrebenko fictionalized a female cabbie's struggle to earn a living in Vancouver in her novel *Taxi*.

The movie *Russian Roulette* was released, based on a 1974 novel, *Kosygin Is Coming*, by *Vancouver Sun* journalist Tom Ardies, who also wrote the screenplay. The movie's climax took place atop the Hotel Vancouver's steep green copper roof. One visitor to the online review site IMDB commented: "George Segal is well-cast and looks genuinely scared in the vertiginous rooftop shootout." He was genuinely scared, as anyone would be clambering around the roof of the Hotel Vancouver! No special effects.

Donald Gutstein's book *Vancouver Ltd.* was published. It was an economic study of Vancouver, with special reference to the CPR's influence on the city and its development.

Businessman Winston Malt imported a steel-and-plastic shield, strong enough to stop a bullet from a .38-calibre revolver, from New York. It was installed in a Yellow cab driven by John Adam.

The Vancouver Canucks won their first division title.

Much credit goes to goalie Gary "Suitcase" Smith, who had six shutouts and led the team to a 38-32-10 record.

The Native Sons of BC named Ben Wosk Good Citizen of the Year.

Doreen Braverman opened the first Flag Shop, believed to be the first specialty flag retailer in the world. There are 13 Flag Shops today, all the way across to Dartmouth, NS. Their product line has broadened over the years to include custom banners, a full line of flag hardware, pins, crests, decals—anything flag related.

The Great Northern Railway—now the Burlington Northern—withdrew passenger service from White Rock.

A major sewage plant was built on Annacis Island, handling waste from Burnaby, Surrey, Coquitlam, Port Moody, Delta and parts of Richmond. At first it offered only primary treatment. It was upgraded in 1999 to provide secondary treatment. The treated effluent is discharged into the Fraser River.

At the behest of Attorney General Alex Macdonald, Hugh Keenleyside undertook a study and published *The Fire Fighting Services in British Columbia*. He came down hard on the province's record in the report that was tabled in the provincial legislature in June 1975. We found a passage from *Hansard* for May 4, 1976, in which NDP MLA Bob Skelly quoted statistics from the report: "In the 10 years from 1963 to 1972, we lost 94.8 lives, on the average, to fire, which is 75 per cent above the national rate. The per capita financial loss to fire in B.C. was $12.33, some 751 per cent above the national rate for Canada. Residential fires were 88 per cent above the average rate for all the other provinces. Per capita losses through manufacturing plants were 50 per cent above the rate for the rest of Canada. For institutions and buildings of public assembly, again British Columbia's loss was $1.03 per capita. The average for Canada was 55 cents. So our record, as far as fire protection in this province, has been the worst in Canada—worse than any other province, worse than the United States which has the worst record in the industrialized world, and it's been deteriorating, according to Mr. Keenleyside's statistics, over the year since the fire marshal's office was established."

Comings and Goings

April 8 Pink Floyd appeared at the PNE in Vancouver.

May 21 The Australian cricket team, at the time probably the best in the world, stopped on its way to England for the World Cup and played a BC team at Brockton Point.

October 7 Moshe Dayan, Israel's former defence minister, spoke to an audience at UBC. "The Middle East is still the powder-keg of the world," he said. A chair-throwing battle broke out between political factions in the audience, while anti-Zionist demonstrators stomped and chanted outside. Dayan, whose dramatic black eye-patch and gleaming baldness made him one of the most familiar faces of the tension-filled 1970s, dealt with the disruption "in the manner," one reporter wrote, "that helped make him a general." "SIT DOWN AND BE QUIET," he roared. And everyone did.

1976

Housing took centre stage this year as delegates from around the world gathered in Vancouver for the UN Habitat conference and its free-wheeling spinoff, Habitat Forum. The Museum of Anthropology at UBC got a spectacular new home. And Chuck Davis published a book on Vancouver!

January 1 Cloverdale Raceway opened and quickly became one of the premier harness-racing centres in North America under the management of James Keeling Sr., proprietor of Orangeville Raceway in Ontario. In 1996 it underwent a $3-million renovation and was renamed Fraser Downs.

January 2 The Social Credit government ordered that auto insurance rates in BC be increased by as much as three times the current rates, starting March 1. ICBC chief Pat McGeer told motorists that if they couldn't afford the new rates, they should sell their cars. That sympathetic advice prompted the overnight appearance of bumper stickers reading *Stick it in Your Ear, McGeer*.

February 9 Prime Minister Trudeau officially commissioned the TRIUMF (Tri-University Meson Facility) nuclear accelerator at UBC. *Ubyssey* reporter Chris Gainor, covering the event, wrote that Trudeau's speech "included several pauses while he appeared to be at a loss about what to say next. 'I'm excited that Canada, has one of...uh... these things,' he told a crowd of 700 at the opening ceremonies. 'I'm not sure if I could understand this even if we spent some time inspecting it.'" After the ceremony, Trudeau went on an hour-long tour of the facility. When Gainor asked if he now understood how TRIUMF worked, Trudeau replied, "Perfectly. I'm going to work here after I'm no longer prime minister."

The TRIUMF cyclotron was built by UBC and the Universities of Victoria and Alberta (hence the Tri-University in its name), although six universities are now involved and another seven are listed as associates. The facility holds the world's biggest cyclotron, which is used to accelerate 1,000 trillion particles each second. TRIUMF is also a centre for the practical application of this basic research to treat eye cancers and brain cancers, provide brain scans, and

Below left: TRIUMF, "one of the world's leading subatomic physics laboratories," is opened by Prime Minister Pierre Trudeau in 1976. The facility contains the world's largest cyclotron, part of which is seen here while under construction; it accelerates 1,000 trillion particles each second.
The Province

Elsewhere in BC

May 16 An earthquake measuring 5.3 on the Richter scale jolted southwestern BC and adjacent Washington state.

Mica Dam on the Columbia River added 870,000 kilowatts to the BC Hydro power system.

Elsewhere in Canada

July 17 The Summer Olympic Games began in Montreal. During the games, Romanian gymnast Nadia Comaneci earned seven perfect scores of 10—the first time any gymnast scored 10 in Olympic competition. Canadians won five silver and six bronze medals.

August Vancouver's Greg Joy won the silver medal in the high jump at the Montreal Olympic Games.

Elsewhere in the World

January 21 The *Concorde* took off on its first commercial flight.

April 1 Steve Jobs and Steve Wozniak established Apple Computer Company.

April Pol Pot became prime minister of Cambodia (Democratic Kampuchea).

July 4 The United States celebrated the 200th anniversary of the Declaration of Independence.

develop new radio-pharmaceuticals, microchips and computer software, among other innovations.

Also February 9 H.R. MacMillan, lumber magnate, died in Vancouver, aged 90. Harvey Reginald MacMillan was born September 9, 1885, in Newmarket, ON. He attended the Ontario Agricultural College and Yale Forestry School. In 1908 he was hired as assistant inspector of the western Canada forest reserves but had to spend two years in a TB sanatorium. In 1912 he was named chief BC forester, and during World War I he worked for the federal timber-trade commissioner and the Imperial Munitions Board. In 1919, backed by British timber merchant Montague Meyer, he launched H.R. MacMillan Export. His manager (and later partner) was W.J. VanDusen. In 1951 MacMillan merged his company with Bloedel, Stewart and Welch to form MacMillan Bloedel Ltd. He resigned as chair in 1956 and as a director in 1970.

March 10 Twelve-year-old Abby Drover was abducted while on her way to school from her Port Moody home.

She was finally found in September 1976. Abby had been confined for six months in a bunker underneath the garage of Donald Hay's home, less than a kilometre from her own home, and tortured and repeatedly raped. Hay was given a life sentence for the abduction. In 2001 Abby Drover consented to having her name published. She said she was moved to go public by a recent spate of attempted abductions of children in the Vancouver area. She said she wanted to make sure that those hurt by crime, especially children, knew they could get help through victim services. "They certainly have made a difference in my life," she said. "If we're all honest with ourselves, we can all remember the victim's name second, and I want to change that."

March 16 Artist B.C. Binning died in Vancouver, aged 67. Bertram Charles Binning was born in 1909 in Medicine Hat, AB, and moved to Vancouver with his family in 1913. He attended the Vancouver School of Art and art schools in Oregon, Greenwich Village and England. Binning joined UBC's school of architecture in 1949, was a founder and head of the UBC fine arts department (1955–68) and an instructor there (1968–73). He developed UBC's Fine Arts Gallery, launched the Brock Hall Canadian art collection and was involved in planning the Nitobe Memorial Garden at UBC. Thousands of locals see his work daily in the intricate pattern of tiles on Electra (formerly the BC Hydro Building) at Burrard and Nelson Streets.

April 7 Rebecca Belle Watson, community activist, died in Vancouver, aged about 65. She was born about 1911 in Kitsilano, taught in the Cariboo, then trained as a nurse at Vancouver General Hospital. In 1958, as spokesperson for Save Our Parklands Association, she rescued the Shaughnessy Heights Golf Course from development. She was elected to the Vancouver Park Board in 1968, was an executive member of TEAM (The Electors' Action Movement) and in 1971 became president of the BC Progressive Conservative Party. She was named to the City of Vancouver's Civic Merit Board of Honour, the 22nd inductee in its 34-year history.

April 23 The Four Seasons Hotel at 791 West Georgia opened with a benefit to raise funds for the Vancouver Symphony Orchestra.

May 18 *The Komagata Maru Incident* opened at the Playhouse Theatre. This play by Sharon Pollock explored the 1914 standoff in which Sikh immigrants were forbidden to land in Vancouver.

May 20 The Joe Fortes Branch of the Vancouver Public Library—named for the beloved English Bay lifeguard—opened at 870 Denman St. in the West End.

Above and right: Habitat happening. Vancouver hosted the United Nations Habitat conference in 1976, drawing crowds that included Margaret Trudeau, Paul Manning, Ron Basford and Barney Danson.
Vancouver Sun

May 27 Habitat, a United Nations Conference on Human Settlements, convened in Vancouver. Hundreds of delegates attended from all over the world. The event ran to June 11. An alternative conference, the hugely popular Habitat Forum, run by Alan Clapp, was held at Jericho Beach Park. There was music, entertainment, talk and the world's longest bar.

May 31
UBC's Museum of Anthropology moved into a stunning new building designed by Arthur Erickson.

The MOA was founded to preserve and display existing material, while continuing to collect archeological and ethnographical artifacts from British Columbia and the rest of the world. For almost 50 years the collection remained in the basement of UBC's main library, tended by a devoted Dr. Harry Hawthorn and Audrey Hawthorn. Now the collection came out of the basement and moved into its 6,500-square-metre (70,000-square-foot) home on the bluffs of Point Grey overlooking the Strait of Georgia. The museum was a gift from the federal government to the people of BC, to celebrate the 100th anniversary of BC entering Confederation in 1871. The entrance area features a dramatic sculpture, *Raven and the First Men*, by Haida artist Bill Reid (commissioned by the museum in 1980). In 1975, Walter and Marianne Koerner had made a gift of their extensive Northwest Coast art collection to the MOA, which substantially helped the museum in its efforts to acquire financial commitments from the federal government and UBC itself.

May The eight-year-old Community Music School (which became the Vancouver Academy of Music in 1979) moved from West 12th Ave. to the Music Centre in Vanier Park, a former RCAF warehouse that had been reconstructed at a cost of $1.8 million. The centre contains classrooms, practice studios and rehearsal rooms, a library and the 284-seat Koerner Recital Hall.

June 10 The Musqueam Indian Band, whose traditional territory once occupied much of what is now Vancouver, wrote and released the Musqueam Declaration, which set out the band's intention to seek compensation for lost resources and to establish control of their communities and remaining resources. The declaration began: "We, the Musqueam people openly and publicly declare and affirm that we hold aboriginal title to our land, and aboriginal rights to exercise use of our land, the sea and fresh waters, and all their resources within that territory occupied and used by our ancestors."

June 27 The first Greek Days Festival was held on West Broadway, sponsored by the Hellenic Community Association.

The Museum of Anthropology gets its new digs, designed by Arthur Erickson.
Ricardo L. Castro, 2005, from Arthur Erickson: Critical Works at the Vancouver Art Gallery

July 21 Black Top Taxi bowed to the BC Human Rights Branch and lifted a 9 p.m. ban on woman drivers that had been contested by owner-operator Terry Bellamy, a mother of three who needed to work nights.

August 8 Wilson Duff, anthropologist, died by suicide in Vancouver, aged 51. Born March 23, 1925, in Vancouver, Duff was the curator of anthropology at the provincial museum from 1950 to 1965 and a founding member of the BC Museums Association in 1957. He helped preserve the last remaining totem poles at Kitwancool and villages on the Queen Charlotte Islands in the 1950s. He had moved to Vancouver to teach and do research at UBC's department of anthropology and sociology, and had appeared in court as an expert witness for Nisga'a land claims cases. Duff's entire career centred on the study of Northwest Coast Indians.

September 5 CKVU-TV went on the air with its flagship program: a five-day-a-week, live talk and entertainment magazine called *The*

The Skyride carts mountain lovers up and down Grouse Mountain in Vancouver.
Jon Murray / The Province

Vancouver Show. CKVU, Vancouver's second privately owned television station, was the brainchild of former CBC producer/director Daryl Duke and writer/producer Norman Klenman. Duke served as president, CEO and chairman of the board until 1988, when he sold the station in order to devote full time to his film and television career.

September 7 BC Tel began direct-distance-dialling overseas. To mark the occasion Vancouver mayor Art Phillips called the mayor of King's Lynn in England, the birthplace of Capt. George Vancouver.

September 12 The old Central School/City Hall building in North Vancouver opened as Presentation House, housing the North Shore Museum and Archives, a small theatre and a photographic gallery.

Fall Douglas College opened a Richmond campus in a converted warehouse at 5840 Cedarbridge Way.

November 30 Nearly 1,000 people jammed into Vancouver's 800-seat Christ Church Cathedral to witness the ordination of the Rev. Virginia Briant and the Rev. Elspeth Alley. They were among the first six women ordained as Anglican priests in Canada today. Anglican Archbishop David Somerville officiated at the ceremony, which also saw the Rev. Michael Deck become a priest. During the ceremony the rector of St. David's parish read a protest against the ordination of the two women, saying it was a "sponge [sic] to women's lib."

December 15
Grouse Mountain Resorts' "Super-skyride" was opened by Premier Bill Bennett, more than doubling the uphill capacity. It was 10 years to the day since his father, Premier W.A.C. Bennett, opened the first Grouse Mountain Skyride.

Also in 1976

Tong Louie, head of H.Y. Louie and Company, bought London Drugs— which was, at the time, owned by an American company, the Daylin Corporation. His competition for the purchase was the American firm Payless. Payless held the option to buy the chain but was being thwarted by federal regulations forbidding foreign companies from taking over Canadian companies without a Canadian partner. In 1976, Payless came to Vancouver looking for just such a partner. The search came down to two contenders: H.Y. Louie and Shoppers Drug Mart, based in eastern Canada. Louie met with the Payless representatives, but, the story goes, because he was not accustomed to working with partners, he decided instead to buy the option—for $500,000. Louie's son Brandt was there and remembers: "His accountant and his lawyer warned him in no uncertain terms that there had been no due diligence. My father puffed on his pipe and thought about it for 30 seconds, and extended his hand. 'Okay,' he said, 'it's a deal.' From the moment they all sat down until they shook hands, the meeting took 20 minutes." Tong Louie bought the chain for $9 million. The privately held company now has stores in more than 35 major markets throughout BC, Alberta, Saskatchewan and Manitoba, and its annual sales are estimated to exceed $1 billion.

London Drugs, from cough syrup to curling irons, was bought from an American company by H.Y. Louie and Company, which brought it back to the country of its birth and made it a Canadian institution. *City of Vancouver Archives, CVA 447-86. Walter Edwin Frost photo*

The Terminal City Dance company was launched. Initially a collaboration between Karen Rimmer and Savannah Walling, both students of American modernist Iris Garland, its focus was experiment and exploration. The ensemble broke up in 1983.

BC Ferries launched three double-ended "jumbo ferries."

The Vancouver Book appeared. This "urban almanac," conceived and edited by Chuck Davis, was just under 500 pages long and had dozens of articles on the city's history, neighbourhoods, environment, architecture, government, ethnic groups, media, transportation and more.

The local book-publishing trade was beginning to make an impression. *The Vancouver Book* listed more than 35 local book publishers with an annual total of 100 new titles.

After the Vancouver Stock Exchange's worst year in more than a decade (1975, with just 190 million shares traded), the exchange got a new president, tough-minded securities lawyer Robert Scott. According to David Cruise and Alison Griffiths, who wrote the book on the VSE (*Fleecing the Lamb*), Scott "created new regulations and saw to it that the old ones were enforced."

The Richmond Nature Park opened to preserve the last remaining section of Burns Bog—81 hectares (200 acres) of raised peat bog habitat that once covered large portions of Lulu Island. Walking trails give visitors the chance to get up close and personal with plants and animals of the bog.

Vancouver designated the Marine Building a heritage property, citing it as "one of the most accomplished and complete examples of Art Deco style in the world. In addition, the literal interpretation of the Vancouver environment in its form and details gives it a special architectural significance."

The landfill in Langley City was closed. It was full.

Whistler opened a new school named for pioneer Myrtle Philip. She and her husband Alex had opened Rainbow Lodge on Alta Lake in 1914, and Myrtle had been instrumental in establishing the area's first school in 1920. When the government turned down her request for a school she arranged to lease land from the railway and built her own.

Jack Short, about 68, wrapped up his race-calling career nicely: he was named BC's Broadcast Performer of the Year. In 1980 he was named to the BC Horse Racing Hall of Fame.

Two major local firms, Benndorf Office Equipment and Verster Business Machines, merged to become Benndorf Verster. Today the company is known as Ikon Office Solutions.

Comings and Goings

Notable deaths: **John Arthur Clark**, lawyer, soldier, and Progressive Conservative MP for Vancouver-Burrard (1921–26), died on January 18, aged 89; **Frederic Gordon Campbell "Freddie" Wood**, teacher, theatre director, founder of University Players' Club, co-founder of Vancouver Little Theatre, died on June 3, aged 89 (Wood was the first BC-born educator at UBC when it opened in 1915 and was there until he retired in 1950).

1977

This was the year a young Terry Fox lost a leg to cancer and formed the plan that would make him a national hero. The Orpheum Theatre reopened as a concert hall, and ferry service to the North Shore returned with the launching of the SeaBus. The Wreck Beach Preservation Society, meanwhile, began its work to keep part of the waterfront safe for naked people.

Right: The forerunner of the Wreck Beach Preservation Society was created in 1977 to protect Vancouver's only clothing-optional beach from development and other such interference. *George Diack* / Vancouver Sun

January 1 The British Columbia Ferry Corporation (BC Ferries) was established as a provincial Crown corporation, successor to the British Columbia Ferry Authority.

January 25 Judy Williams and other activists formed the Citizens Concerned for Wreck to protect clothing-optional Wreck Beach from efforts to control erosion of the cliffs above it. In 1983 that committee became the Wreck Beach Preservation Society, which continued the fight to preserve the beach from development.

January Newspaper executive Erwin Swangard, 69, was appointed president of the Pacific National Exhibition, a post he held for 13 consecutive annual terms. He came to be known as "Mr. PNE."

February 16
Marjorie Cantryn was the first Native woman to become a judge in BC.

Elsewhere in BC

August 23 The British Columbia Resources Investment Corporation (BCRIC, pronounced "brick") was created by the Social Credit government and promoted as an experiment in peoples' capitalism. BCRIC took over ownership of various sawmills and mines that had been bought and bailed out by the NDP government. Every British Columbian was offered five free shares in the company (which Premier Bill Bennett said were probably worth about $50 in total) and was encouraged to buy more. The idea was that they would earn a healthy return, and this would promote investment in the province. Nearly 90 percent of BC residents took up the offer of free shares. Unfortunately, BCRIC started making risky investments in resource industries rather than remaining a more conservative but safer holding company. Share prices plummeted, ending up at pennies rather than dollars. Eventually the company was bought by Jimmy Pattison.

Elsewhere in Canada

January 26 Katimavik was founded as a volunteer service organization for Canadian young people.

February 28 Canadian passenger rail services were amalgamated into VIA Rail.

April 7 The Toronto Blue Jays played their first game. The Jays beat the Chicago White Sox 9–5.

Elsewhere in the World

May 25 The movie *Star Wars* premiered in the US. *TIME* listed this as one of 80 days since the magazine was established in 1923 that changed the world.

August 16 Elvis Presley died.

September 6 Stephen Biko, anti-apartheid activist and founder of the Black Consciousness Movement, died in police custody in South Africa.

Orpheum Rising

April 2 The restored Orpheum Theatre opened with a special concert by its new tenant, the Vancouver Symphony Orchestra. Reaction to the refurbished theatre was wonderfully positive.

Design architect Paul Merrick tells a nice story about Tony Heinsbergen, the man who gave the theatre its exotic and colourful look back in 1927. Merrick had gone to Seattle to talk to architects at the firm founded by the theatre's original architect, Marcus Priteca. These architects told Merrick that the man who had embellished Priteca's architecture in 1927 was still, 50 years later, professionally active and living in Los Angeles. Merrick went down to California to see Tony Heinsbergen in his LA studio, which "was the size of a three-car garage and twice as high." Heinsbergen agreed to create a large mural, oval in shape, that would surround the massive chandelier in the centre of the auditorium ceiling.

The mural was painted during the winter of 1975–76 on 24 large canvas panels that were shipped to Vancouver and glued to the dome.

Orpheus was associated with music, so Heinsbergen conceived of a mural that would celebrate music, and although the work is peopled with mythical and fanciful figures, many of the figures are based on real people. The bearded man serenading the muse is Paul Merrick (who is beardless today), and the Merrick kids—Natasha, Nika, Maya and Kim—are up there too. Maya is the angel. The man conducting the orchestra is project architect Ron Nelson, not, as is sometimes suggested, former conductor Kaziyoshi Akiyama. The music he's conducting is Brahms' "Lullaby." The tiger in the mural represents Heinsbergen's Nova Scotian wife, Nedith, whom he called his "little tiger."

The new home of the Vancouver Symphony Orchestra, the lovingly renovated and absolutely gorgeous Orpheum Theatre graces the corner of Granville and Seymour Streets. *Courtesy Vancouver Symphony Orchestra*

February 21 North Vancouver's Carrie Cates died. Married to John Henry Cates of the famed tugboat firm, she was elected mayor of North Vancouver three times (1964, 1965 and 1967).

March 9 An 18-year-old Port Coquitlam student and star basketball player, Terry Fox, lost his right leg to osteogenic sarcoma. While Terry was in hospital waiting for the operation to remove his cancerous leg, his basketball coach Terri Fleming gave him a sports magazine that included a profile of one-legged runner Dick Traum, who had competed in the New York Marathon. The Traum story inspired Terry to take on a challenge that would eventually raise tens of millions of dollars for cancer research. He planned to run across the country, asking every Canadian for a one-dollar donation.

April 6 Jack Wasserman died of a heart attack while speaking at the Hotel Vancouver during a roast for Gordon Gibson, Sr. He was 50 years old. Born February 17, 1927, in Winnipeg, Wasserman came to Vancouver with his family in 1935, aged 8. He dropped out of law school to take a reporter's job with the *Ubyssey*. After graduating from UBC in 1949, he joined the *Vancouver Sun*, becoming a police reporter. Starting May 12, 1954, the *Sun* gave him a man-about-town column, and he hit his stride. His column on "the second front page" of the afternoon paper, often detailing the city's underbelly, became a hugely popular feature. His biggest scoop was the 1959 death of Errol Flynn in a West End apartment. Four months after Wasserman's death, on August 12, a plaque by artist Stjepan Pticek was installed at the northwest corner of Georgia and Hornby Streets, dedicating a section of Hornby Street (between Georgia and Dunsmuir) as "Wasserman's Beat." The Cave, a now-vanished nightspot, and a favourite haunt of Wasserman's, was down the block on the east side of Hornby.

May One of the largest state-of-the-art, electronic, automatic telephone exchanges ever put into operation by BC Tel began service in Whalley.

June 8 Vancouver Harbour Centre was officially opened. At 146.6 metres (481 feet) it was the tallest building in Vancouver. (Today the tallest is the Shangri-La Hotel, at 197 metres/646.5 feet, although loftier buildings are coming.) There's a funny story related to its construction. Jeff Veniot, a young tour guide, happened to be going by the construction site one day and saw the building's lofty mast lying on the ground, waiting to be lifted into place. Jeff whipped out an indelible pen and wrote his name and the date on the top of the mast. Later he watched in pleasure as the mast was lifted atop the building. For a time, his name was the highest in the city.

June 17 The first SeaBus went into service.

As the population of the North Shore grew, so did the demand for a "third crossing" of Burrard Inlet to ease the pressure of traffic on the two bridges. Instead of a third bridge or a tunnel, a high-speed marine passenger service appeared. Built completely in BC, SeaBus was the first marine transit service of its kind in the world. Each of the catamaran-style SeaBus ferries is 34 metres long, with a capacity of 400 passengers. Constructed of lightweight aluminum, the vessels are powered by four diesel engines with a cruising speed of 11.5 knots. Travel time from terminal to terminal: 12 minutes. Highly manoeuverable, the double-ended ferries can move in any direction and turn in their own length.

Lofty landmark. In the spirit of one-upmanship, the Vancouver Harbour Centre at its opening was the tallest building in Vancouver. *Glenn Baglo* / Vancouver Sun

August 13 Margaret Elinor Rushton died in White Rock, aged 69. She was born September 28, 1907, in Wigan, England, and came to Canada in 1930, the same year she married author and historian Gerald Rushton (1898–1993). She joined Vancouver Little Theatre, serving as its president from 1949 to 1954. Her interest in children's theatre led her to Holiday Theatre, where she was tour coordinator. A member of the Dominion Drama Festival national executive, she was also a president of the BC Drama Association. She retired in 1971.

Also August 13 The Vancouver Lookout opened high atop the Harbour Centre.

Neil Armstrong, first man on the Moon, ascended to the top in one of the building's famed outdoor glassed-in elevators and left his footprint as an official memento of the opening. It's still on display there.

Summer The Italian Cultural Centre opened in East Vancouver on Slocan at the Grandview Highway (the official opening was September 25). The centre, built mostly by volunteers, included a restaurant, banquet hall, art gallery, daycare centre, television production centre and even an indoor bocce court. Every summer the centre hosts a weeklong Italian festival. Italian-born Anna Terrana of Burnaby, later the MP for Vancouver East, was a strong force behind the construction.

September 18 Michael Leo Sweeney died in Vancouver, aged 91. As an infant in 1888 he came to Victoria, where his father founded Sweeney Cooperage, a barrel-making firm. Leo was named managing director in 1912. Two years after buying Canadian Western Cooperage in 1921 he moved to Vancouver.

Talk Minus Action Equals Zero

July The short-lived Furies and Victoria's all-female Dee Dee and the Dishrags headlined Vancouver's first punk concert at the Japanese Hall on Alexander Street.

Punk music had exploded on the musical landscape in 1976 in reaction to a popular music scene that had become increasingly commercialized and pretentious. Starting with bands like the Sex Pistols and the Clash in Britain, and the Ramones in the United States, punk quickly inspired young rockers in and around Vancouver.

The July 30 show encouraged a group of suburban youths headed by Joey "Shithead" Keithley to form the Skulls, which became Vancouver's most prominent punk band for a few months. In 1978 Keithley formed DOA. Despite numerous lineup changes and breakups, DOA anchored Vancouver's punk scene with its anarcho-political stance and still plays today. Others might be credited with bringing punk to Vancouver, but DOA brought Vancouver punk to the world, playing shows across North America and the UK. Their album *Hardcore '81* is widely believed to be the first use of the term "hardcore" in relation to the punk genre. Their relentlessly political message and their dynamic motto and slogan, "Talk Minus Action Equals Zero," cemented them as heroes of the Vancouver scene long after they'd graduated to a bigger stage

Another prominent Vancouver punk band in the early years was the Subhumans, whose bassist Gerry "Useless" Hannah wrote two Vancouver punk anthems, "Fuck You" and "Slave to My Dick." He later joined a group of political activists who carried out bombings and other actions that led to his being jailed for five years.

Punk helped spawn a lively alternative music scene in Vancouver that included bands such as the Pointed Sticks, the Modernettes U-J3RK5, 54-40, No Fun and many others. A fanzine, *Snot Rag*, was launched November 4, 1977, to cover the evolving culture and released issues until 1979. At Expo 86, officials shut down a concert by the Vancouver punk band Slow, causing fans to riot. Although punk was already in decline by then, it is periodically revived, helped by newer bands and reunions of bands from the late 1970s. Its spirit lives on in current local punk bands like Japandroids and in the work of documentary filmmakers like Melissa James (No Fun City) and Susanne Tabata (Bloodied But Unbowed).

Sweeney served on many civic boards and committees. As president of the Vancouver Tourist Association he wore a straw boater when it rained "to prove it was liquid sunshine." The company operated at the east foot of Smithe Street until 1981, when the land was expropriated for BC Place and the cooperage, one of the oldest industries in False Creek, was torn down.

September 24 The Gastown Steam Clock was dedicated. It was conceived as a solution for the problem of steam venting into the Gastown air from the Central Heat Distribution Plant, which supplies steam to hundreds of downtown buildings...and which vents excess steam through manholes here and there throughout the downtown. Jon Ellis, the city planner for the Gastown area, had the notion to have clockmaker Ray Saunders devise a steam-powered clock. It's easily the most-photographed object in Vancouver even if (*pssst!*) it isn't really steam-powered and, we learned within the last few years, never was.

September L'Ecole Bilingue Elementary school was born when Cecil Rhodes School was renamed. This was one of the first bilingual French/English schools in the province, created because many Vancouver parents wanted a French-immersion program for their kids.

October The White Rock Hotel, a 50-room, four-storey hotel that had opened on July 1, 1912, with a luncheon for 300 guests, was torn down for development.

November 25 The first World's Worst Art auction was held. This became a strange and funny annual event. It's nicely described by Elizabeth Macleod (in a witty article about one of her own paintings) in the Winter 2001 edition of *Life Writing from Brock House*. "Dr. Norman Watt, a UBC professor... while visiting an antique store in New York City in 1969 came upon an oil painting which he immediately labelled 'The World's Worst Oil Painting.' The owner sold it to him for $5.00. When Dr. Watt returned to Vancouver he showed it to his

Marine commute. The SeaBus goes into business, adding a little seafaring to the morning commute.
Dan Scott / Vancouver Sun

friend William Goodacre. Together they decided to visit flea markets, garage sales and second-hand stores and build up a collection, agreeing that they would pay no more than $5.00 for any one purchase. In time they persuaded Doug Mowat, then the Executive Director of the British Columbia Paraplegic Foundation, to sponsor an exhibition. The 24th Annual Exhibition and Auction of the World's Worst Oil Paintings was held in November 2000 at the Vancouver Convention and Exhibition Centre. To date this project has raised $600,000 for the Paraplegic Foundation."

December 6 Josephine A. Dauphinee, special education pioneer and women's activist, died in Vancouver, aged 102. She helped found the Vancouver Business and Professional Women's Club (1922) and was its president (1928–29) and also helped establish the Canadian Federation of Business and Professional Women's Clubs (1930) and was its president (1932–35).

Also in 1977

Jack Volrich became mayor, succeeding Art Phillips. Vorich, originally from Anyox, BC, had been a founding member of TEAM, but his outlook often seemed closer to that of the free-enterprise mayors of the Non-Partisan Association of earlier years. He was later a member of both the Progressive Conservative and Social Credit Parties. As mayor he proposed a rapid transit system for the city, as well as the trade and convention centre and BC Place Stadium.

The British Columbia Women's Hospital and Health Centre celebrated its 100,000th birth.

The City of Vancouver established its Equal Employment Opportunity (EEO) program, which helped city departments recruit and retain a workforce that reflected the city's diversity. Since 1989 the program has been administered by the city-owned Hastings Institute.

The city also established BC's first Advisory Committee on Disability Issues. In addition to seeing that past access problems were corrected, the committee closely monitored new development projects.

Japanese Canadians commemorated the centennial of Manzo Nagano's arrival in Canada. Nagano, who worked as a cabin boy on a British ship travelling from Nagasaki to New Westminster, was the first Japanese person to immigrate to this country. A mountain in the Rivers Inlet area was named for him, and the first Powell Street Festival took place to celebrate the centennial. The festival took place at Oppenheimer Park in Vancouver's Downtown Eastside, which was, before World War II, the largest Japanese Canadian community. Today, the festival is the longest ongoing community event in Vancouver, and Canada's largest celebration of Japanese Canadian culture, featuring martial arts, folk and modern dancing, traditional and contemporary music, literary events, food and much more. Centennial celebrations were soon followed by the organization of informal groups to discuss the idea of seeking redress for World War II internment.

White Rock bought its famous pier from the federal government for one dollar and put in new pilings to strengthen the pier. The feds still own the end of the wharf and are responsible for maintenance of the breakwater installed in 1953.

The Vancouver Pound sold a record number of dog-licence tags: almost 25,000.

Burnaby's Christmas junior hockey tournament featured 98 teams and 1,600 players. It had become the largest event of its kind in the world and was listed in the *Guinness Book of World Records*. Many talented players were produced by Burnaby's hockey program.

The main Rainbow Lodge building at Whistler burned down after 63 years of operation.

Samuel McCleery's 1891 farmhouse at 2510 Southwest Marine was demolished.

A vice-president of the Vancouver Stock Exchange fled to Britain to evade an RCMP investigation. He had been charged with 94 counts of conspiracy and taking bribes.

Comings and Goings

Fall Harry Ornest won a Pacific Coast League minor baseball franchise. He put the Triple-A Vancouver Canadians on the field in 1978.

October 18 Willy de Roos arrived off Point Grey in his 13-metre steel ketch *Williwaw*. He had come through the Northwest Passage (east to west) in the smallest boat to make the journey. It was also the first time a sailing vessel had made that voyage since Amundsen in 1906.

Cartoonist David Boswell, born in London, ON, in 1953, came to Vancouver to contribute cartoons to the *Georgia Straight*. His best-known work was *Reid Fleming, World's Toughest Milkman*.

1978

The first folk festival and the first children's festival were held, and the first of the Vietnamese "boat people" arrived in the city. Capilano Stadium and the Vancouver School of Art got new names. This was also the year the Canucks introduced their new and controversial yellow, orange and black uniforms.

January 1 The 58th annual Polar Bear Swim was the biggest to date, with 1,000 participants and 20,000 spectators.

Cold record. People have been throwing themselves into icy seas since 1920, and this year marked the largest throng of gluttons for punishment ever to participate in the annual Polar Bear Swim, following the lead of the Pantages family and friends.
Bill Keay / Vancouver Sun

Also January 1 Marjorie Cantryn, Canada's first aboriginal citizenship judge, swore in 30 new Canadians in Whalley in Surrey.

February 12 The Hellenic Cultural Community Centre opened today next door to St. George's Greek Orthodox Church on Arbutus Street. The number of Greek immigrants to Vancouver had doubled through the 1960s, which led to construction of the centre and to the establishment of the Burnaby chapter of the Anglo-Hellenic Educational Progressive Association, the largest Greek heritage organization in the world.

Also February 12 Vancouver's Variety Club Telethon raised $1,152,000, a world record to that time for any telethon sponsored by Variety.

March 27 Nathaniel Ryal "Nat" Bailey, restaurateur and White Spot founder, died in Vancouver, aged 76. Bailey was born January 31, 1902, in Saint Paul, MN. His itinerant family arrived here from Seattle in 1911. Nat sold peanuts at baseball games, then served snack food from the back of his truck at Lookout Point on Southwest Marine Drive. In June 1928 he opened his first drive-in at Granville and West 67th Avenue. From 1930 into the 1960s, his second wife, Eva (née Ouelette) co-managed his restaurants. The Baileys sold 13 White Spots and other business interests to General Foods in 1968 for $6.5 million.

April 2 The Vancouver Park Board voted to rename Capilano Stadium after Nat Bailey, a lifelong promoter of local baseball.

April 12 Leon Ladner, lawyer and MP, died in Vancouver, aged 93. He was born November 29, 1884, in Ladner, a settlement founded by his father and uncle. He was admitted to the bar in 1910 and began his Vancouver law practice in 1912. Ladner was a founder in 1912 of UBC's convocation, a founder of the law firm Ladner, Carmichael and Downs (later Ladner Downs) and a Liberal-Conservative MP for Vancouver South from 1921 to 1930. (The Liberal-Conservative Party was later renamed simply the Conservative Party, and in 1942 it became the Progressive Conservative Party.) He donated the Ladner Carillon and Clock Tower to UBC in 1969 in honour of BC pioneers.

April 26 The Triple-A Vancouver Canadians baseball club made its home debut, beating the San José Missions 9–4 before a crowd of 7,128 in newly named Nat Bailey Stadium.

May 14 Geordie Tocher, friend Richard Tomkies and navigator Gerhart Kiesel set out for Hawaii from West Vancouver in a native-style log canoe. Tocher had carved the canoe himself, to prove Hawaiians could have originated in BC. *Maclean's* magazine of March 5, 1979, reported that the travellers faced 10.5-metre (35-foot) waves. Tomkies described it as "sheer terror interspersed with moments of boredom."

Elsewhere in BC

May 18 Henry Bell-Irving, soldier and executive, was sworn in as BC's Lieutenant-Governor.

Vancouver's Triple-A baseball club, the Canadians, won their debut game against San José at Nat Bailey Stadium. Good baseball, good hotdogs, great afternoon.
Ross Kenward / The Province

May 29 The first Vancouver International Children's Festival began in big, colourful tents at Vanier Park. Since the festival began, more than 1.5 million children have attended.

July Brock House, a big handsome mansion built at 3875 Point Grey Rd. in 1911, was declared a heritage building by the City of Vancouver. In 1952 the owners had sold the house to the federal government, and it served as the RCMP's Vancouver subdivision headquarters until 1971. On May 1, 1975, the federal government turned the property over to the City of Vancouver as part of the transfer of the Jericho Waterfront Lands, and since 1977 the Vancouver Park Board has leased the house and grounds to Brock House Society, which operates a seniors' activity centre.

August 11 to 13 The first Vancouver Folk Music Festival opened in Stanley Park with Stan Rogers, Leon Redbone, Odetta, Leon Bibb, Pied Pear, John Hammond and Roosevelt Sykes among the performers. About 10,000 people came to hear them. Organizers of that first event were Mitch Podolak and Colin Gorrie of the Winnipeg Folk Festival; Ernie Fladell, Frances Fitzgibbon and Lorenz von Fersen of Vancouver's Social Planning Department; and Gary Cristall, who continued as artistic director and festival coordinator until 1993. The next year, and every year since, the festival has been held at Jericho Beach Park.

September 3 An Air West Airlines Twin Otter crashed in Coal Harbour, killing 9 of the 11 passengers and both crew members.

September 8 Dave Brock died in West Vancouver, aged about 68. This gentle, delightfully funny, mutton-chopped writer and CBC broadcaster was a true original. David Hamilton Brock was born in Ottawa in 1910 and came to Vancouver with his parents when he was four. (They lived in Brock House, mentioned above, from 1922 until 1938.) Dave attended UBC and Harvard and was called to the BC bar but never practised law. He was best known for CBC radio and TV shows, talks and documentaries, notably CBC-TV's *Seven O'Clock Show*. He wrote a column for the *Victoria Times* in the 1960s and was regularly published in *Punch*, *Saturday Night* and *Atlantic Monthly* in the late

Right: Musical milestone. Vancouver's first annual Folk Fest begins lulling listeners at Brockton Point, Stanley Park.
Glenn Baglo / Vancouver Sun

1930s and 1940s. I interviewed Dave on my CBC radio show sometime back in the 1970s, and he told me a story that I have treasured ever since. He'd been visiting a friend, a woman who worked in a meat-packing plant making sausages. They were sitting outside on the factory's lawn during her lunch break, and she said to Dave, "Oh, Dave, I'm so hungry I could eat a sausage."

October 2 Jack Webster, whose open-line radio show (CKNW) was a ratings force for years, moved to television (BCTV) and repeated his success.

October 3 Walter Gage, mathematics professor and president of UBC, died in Vancouver, aged 73. A scholar and revered instructor, he was associated with UBC for more than 50 years. They called him the Dean of Everything. Students liked him, and he liked them. He was a superior teacher, remembered their names throughout the years and was famous for helping students in crisis. Engineering students paid tribute to him by dubbing their fuel-efficiency vehicle the "Wally Wagon." Gage was the sixth president of UBC, serving from 1969 to 1975 (he had been interim president from 1967 to 1968). He was awarded the Order of Canada in 1971.

October 24 The Stormont Connector was officially opened. It pushed McBride Boulevard (which links to the Pattullo Bridge) through Burnaby to hook up with Highway 1 at Gaglardi Way. Highways Minister Alex Fraser cut the ribbon.

October Taylor's shoe store in Ladner closed after 66 years. Begun as a harness repair shop, the business switched to shoes when automobiles begin to replace horses.

Hearing about their dire situation, Canadian Forces assisted in the rescue of Vietnamese refugees from the *Hai Hong*, a rusty bucket denied landing and stranded off the coast of Malaysia.
Vancouver Sun

Fall Three British Columbians were sipping coffee in the anteroom of the Cavalry Club in London, England. Social Credit cabinet minster Grace McCarthy wanted "something dramatic" for Vancouver's centennial in 1986, eight years in the future. ("Could we borrow the Mona Lisa?" was one of her first ideas.) Lawrie Wallace, agent general for British Columbia at the time, knew that the third person in the group—Patrick Reid, then running Canada House—was also president of the Paris-based International Bureau of Expositions. The BIE, to give it its French initials, had awarded the hugely successful Expo 67 to Montreal. "Why couldn't Vancouver have one?" In November 1980 the bureau approved the idea, and six years and $1.5 billion later—despite some loud nay-sayings, and labour unrest during construction in 1984 that nearly cancelled the whole event—what began as Transpo 86, a modest transportation fair to celebrate the city's centennial, went on to huge success as Expo 86, a special exposition with a theme of transportation and communications, reflected in its motto (World in Motion—World in Touch) and its logo (three concentric circles symbolizing transportation by land, sea and air). Some 22 million tickets were sold.

November 1 The *Province* and the *Vancouver Sun* were closed by a labour dispute that lasted until June 26, 1979, just under eight months. The *Province* lost 16 members of its editorial department as a result of the strike; the *Sun* lost eight, including columnist Doug Collins, who joined the *Daily Courier*, and sportswriter Jim Taylor, who later joined the *Province*. The union launched the *Vancouver Express* to fill the gap, just as it had done during an earlier strike in 1970.

November 11 *Billy Bishop Goes to War*, playwright-composer John Gray's two-man musical about Canada's World War I flying legend, opened at the Vancouver East Cultural Centre. It starred Gray and Eric Peterson (who played 21 different parts) and became a huge hit, earning Gray the 1981 Los Angeles Drama Critics' Award, the 1982 Chalmers Canadian Play Award and the 1983 Governor General's Award for English Drama.

November The first 15 Vietnamese "boat people" arrived in Vancouver. The refugees were fleeing the aftermath of the Vietnam War, and 2,500 had crammed aboard the dilapidated freighter *Hai Hong*. They got as far as Malaysia, but the government there was already overwhelmed with refugees so did not allow them to disembark. When TV news shows broadcast images of the boat and its human cargo, there was an immediate response from the Canadian and other governments. Canada agreed to welcome 600 of the refugees, and 150 ultimately came to Vancouver. In August 1980 the city opened a special refugee coordinating centre at 16th and Cambie, where local residents could donate furniture and clothing or get information on sponsoring a Vietnamese refugee. The City of North Vancouver declared September 1980 Boat People Rescue Fund Month, and the Greater Vancouver Regional District asked member municipalities to contribute funds and other support for the boat people.

Also in 1978

Dr. Patricia Baird became head of the department of medical genetics at the University of British Columbia. Under her leadership the department grew from a small group of pioneer scientists and clinicians to an internationally known resource. Baird was the first woman to chair a clinical medical school department at UBC, and the first woman to be elected to the board of governors. Her medical genetics course, regularly voted the best course by UBC medical students, has been used as a model for teaching genetics to physicians of the future by the American Society of Human Genetics.

The Ocean Engineering Centre opened at BC Research on the UBC campus. Naval architects and ship builders frequently consult the centre and use its 67-metre (220-foot) towing tank as an interactive design tool to optimize hull lines. Researchers have tested the performance of tugs, barges, planing hulls, sailboats, offshore supply boats, hydrofoils, ferries, catamarans and even submarines. The centre also gets into the movies: its large wave basin (30.5 metres/100 feet long) with a 29-tonne (32-ton) wave maker has proven ideal as an aquatic sound stage. Features filmed on location at OEC include *The First Season*, *Jason Takes Manhattan* and *The Sea Wolf*.

Greenpeace bought a converted North Sea trawler, *Sir Williams Hardy*, renamed it the *Rainbow Warrior* and began to campaign against whaling in Iceland and Spain.

Jim Kinnaird, who was assistant deputy minister of labour in the NDP government, was elected president of the BC Federation of Labour. He was credited with uniting the divided body and served three terms as leader of 250,000 unionized workers.

The BC Film Commission was formed to promote and market BC to the world as a location for moviemaking and as a source of skilled professionals who could work in front of or behind the cameras.

After being hounded by a young North Vancouver singer, Bruce Allen agreed to become his manager. Good move. The young man was Bryan Adams.

Quintessence Records—an outgrowth of Ted Thomas' Kitsilano record store of the same name—became a focal point for the emerging punk and new wave scene, introducing such bands as the Pointed Sticks and Young Canadians. Quintessence closed in 1981, but staffer Grant McDonagh opened Zulu Records at the same location and also created the Zulu record label.

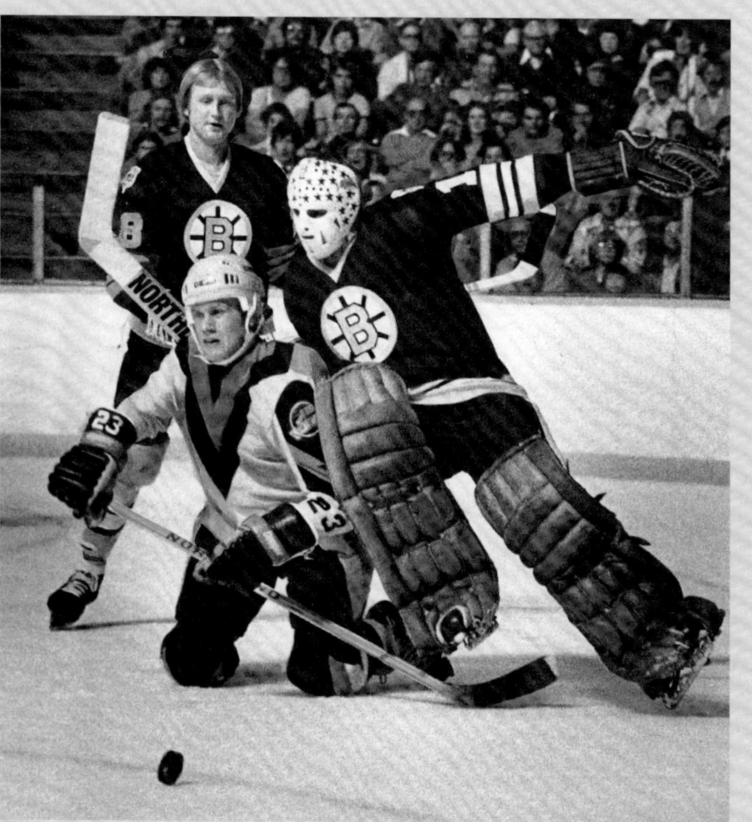

Right: Disputed duds. The Canucks have undergone a few uniform changes, but one of the most notable was the switch from the attractive blue, green and white to a controversial combination of yellow, orange and black. Is Bruins goalie Gilles Gilbert falling over with laughter? *Deni Eagland* / Vancouver Sun

Two new Indo-Canadian newspapers appeared this year: *Indo-Canadian Times*, a weekly with text in Punjabi, and *The Link*, a biweekly, the first Indo-Canadian English paper to be published in Vancouver. Another new publication was *Online/Onward*, an irregular publication of the Vancouver Online Users Group that covered events and information of interest to local librarians and others who worked with computerized information retrieval and database management systems.

Andrea Eng of Vancouver, the first Chinese Canadian Miss Canada, represented Canada at the Miss Universe competition.

Punchlines, western Canada's first comedy club, opened in the basement of the Queen Elizabeth Theatre. Founder Rich Elwood later moved the club to Gastown, where it lasted until 1995.

The Vancouver Whitecaps finished the NASL season in first place in the National Conference, Western Division, with a 24–6 record, which included winning the season's last 13 games in a row. The Whitecaps were drawing crowds of close to 30,000 at Empire Stadium.

The Canucks revamped their uniforms, changing the team colours from the original blue, green and white (with hockey stick logo) to a yellow, orange and black outfit that some people thought looked like loud pyjamas. A San Francisco marketing firm claimed it would strike fear into the hearts of opponents, but sports reporters thought they looked like clowns.

After a quarter century in the forest industry, Irving K. "Ike" Barber formed his own company, Slocan Forest Products. Slocan employed more than 4,000 people, including contractors, won awards for its sustainable forestry practices and achieved sales of nearly $1 billion. Barber became a prominent philanthropist and in 2002 made a $20-million donation to UBC to help establish the Irving K. Barber Learning Centre in the university's old main library.

Financial consultants Brown Farris and Jefferson prepared a report on the Vancouver Stock Exchange for the provincial government. "The odds of losing, overall, are 84%—about five times out of six," they concluded. "The chances of investors doubling their money each year for more than four years by buying and holding an issue appear to be nil."

Passenger service ended at the CPR's Port Moody station at 2734 Murray St. The Port Moody Heritage Society restored the building, which is now the Port Moody Station Museum.

Robin Mayor was appointed principal of the Vancouver School of Art in 1972. In 1978, thanks largely to Mayor's efforts, the school gained its independence from Vancouver Community College and became the Emily Carr College of Art (later the Emily Carr College of Art + Design). The new name was not a unanimous choice. Painter Gordon Smith, a former student and teacher at the school, was among those who opposed naming it after Carr. Smith was on the school's board at the time and says there had been fear that no one would know who she was. "In retrospect, I think it was a good idea," says Smith. "Emily Carr was one of the greatest artists in Canada. Her name has become synonymous with the school."

Vancouver's Planning Department took a series of panoramic views of the city intended for a special study. Some 25 years later, matching photographs were taken. The result is a fascinating illustration of how the city has changed. The camera seems to "pan" along the various skylines shown, and you see forests of new buildings rising.

Comings and Goings

October 19

***National Geographic* did a cover story on Vancouver** and sent one of its photographers, Charles O'Rear, to take some photos. An indication of the magazine's scale of preparation: O'Rear took more than 10,000 pictures, yet a mere 21 got into the magazine. For a shot of the magnificent interior of the Orpheum, O'Rear had special lights brought in by chartered plane from Washington, DC, but his Orpheum pictures were among the 9,979 that didn't get in.

Notable deaths: **Dorothy Gretchen Steeves**, a founder in 1932 of the Co-operative Commonwealth Federation (CCF) and CCF MLA for North Vancouver (1934–45), one of seven original CCF members in BC, died on May 9, aged 82; **Claud Detloff**, *Province* photographer, who took the famous Second World War photo *Wait for Me, Daddy*, died on July 18, aged about 79; **W.J. VanDusen**, forest industry executive who worked with H.R. MacMillan, died on December 15, aged 89; **Charles Edward Borden**, "Grandfather of BC archeology," died on December 25, aged 73; **H.D. Stafford**, educator, who served the Langley area as district superintendent of schools for 19 years and the education system for 30 years.

1979

The city got a Sunday newspaper, but the year's most sought-after information was never published: a prostitute's list of hundreds of high-society customers that was sealed by the court. A huge crowd met the Vancouver Whitecaps when they brought back the North American soccer championship, and the street photographer who had worked Granville forever retired after 45 years.

May 22 Svend Robinson was elected MP for Burnaby–Douglas, the youngest member of the NDP caucus (born March 4, 1952). He continued to represent Burnaby until 2004 and retired as one of the longest-serving members.

Also May 22 The *Vancouver Sun* won a long-running case against GATE, publishers of *Gay Tide* newspaper. It began in the mid-1970s when the *Sun* refused to run a two-line classified ad promoting *Gay Tide*. GATE had won a BC Human Rights Commission complaint and a subsequent challenge by the *Sun* in BC Supreme Court, but that decision was reversed in the BC Court of Appeal. Finally the Supreme Court of Canada ruled in the *Sun*'s favour.

June 9 Frederick Wellington "Cyclone" Taylor died in Vancouver, aged 95. Taylor was born June 24, 1883 (or was it 1884? or 1885?), in Tara, ON. He played with the Ottawa Senators in 1909 when they won the Stanley Cup and was the key player with the Vancouver Millionaires when they won the cup in 1915, beating Ottawa in three straight games, with Cyclone scoring seven goals. Taylor gave the Pacific Coast Hockey Association the credibility it needed. He played for Vancouver from 1913 to 1921, then retired. One of the great hockey players, he scored 194 goals—or was it 205?—in 186 games. His speed on the ice earned him his nickname.

During his professional hockey career Taylor was also employed by the Immigration Department. On his retirement he was Commissioner of Immigration for British Columbia and the Yukon Territory. Taylor was

Elsewhere in BC

May 10 The Social Credit party was re-elected under Premier Bill Bennett.

The Union of BC Indian Chiefs drafted the *Aboriginal Rights Position Paper*, outlining a basis for all discussions relating to land claims and Native rights. The paper advocated First Nations gaining exclusive control over larger reserves and included an "Indian Government Manifesto" that set out the principles of nationhood, self-determination and equality of peoples. The UBCIC also created and adopted a flag that symbolized First Nations' determination and power to safeguard their territories.

The provincial government, in part prompted by the dire situation refugees from Southeast Asia faced, passed a special act to help refugees resettle in BC.

Elsewhere in Canada

May 22 At only 39 years of age, Progressive Conservative Joe Clark won a minority government in the federal election and became Canada's youngest prime minister.

July 2–6 Native chiefs and elders from across Canada travelled to England and met with politicians, the Archbishop of Canterbury, staff at foreign embassies and media. They were making the case that the British Parliament still had final say over the Canadian constitution and should pressure the Canadian government to involve Native people in constitutional discussions. The Native delegation also presented petitions to the Queen and the British prime minister.

August 16 Former prime minister John Diefenbaker died in Ottawa. A special funeral train carried Diefenbaker back to Saskatoon, where he was buried.

Elsewhere in the World

March 28 The Three Mile Island nuclear plant in Pennsylvania overheated and suffered a core meltdown, releasing contaminated water and gases into the buildings and atmosphere.

July 1 Sony introduced the Walkman portable cassette player.

Greenpeace began to go international, with organizations forming in Australia, France, Holland, New Zealand, the United Kingdom and the United States. Today, Greenpeace International is headquartered in Amsterdam.

president of the Pacific Coast Hockey League from 1936 to 1940 and helped form the British Columbia Hockey Benevolent Society, which he served as director from 1954 until his death. He is, of course, in Canada's Hockey Hall of Fame. His oldest son, Fred, started Cyclone Taylor Sports in Vancouver, a retail outlet for sports equipment, in 1957.

June 16 Richmond celebrated 100 years since incorporation as a municipality and honoured pioneers who had lived in the community for more than 60 years.

July 12 Granville Island Public Market opened and became an immediate hit, one of the great Vancouver experiences. Some 10.5 million people visit Granville Island every year now, and a big chunk of them go to the market. Denny Boyd raved about it in his *Vancouver Sun* column the day after the opening. "I want to be able to poke a red snapper in the gills. I want to hear a good trumpet player blow a couple of choruses of Yellow Dog Blues while I'm looking at the scallions. Dammit, I want to buy a warm cookie." The market is in a building erected by BC Equipment Ltd., the island's very first tenant (1916). Part of the offbeat charm of that building is the travelling cranes that hang from the rafters, which were retained by the architects, Hotson Bakker.

August 6 Surrey Council invited "one and all" to the city's 100th Birthday Party Centennial Week at Bear Creek Park.

Granville treat. The place to be for buskers, baguettes and bass, Granville Island Public Market opens to the delight of locals and tourists alike. *Ian Lindsay* / Vancouver Sun

August 12 The *Province* first appeared on a Sunday.

August 16 Coquitlam Centre, a shopping mall, opened at 2929 Barnet Highway, bordered by bush, a trailer park and houses scattered amid trees. Population growth in Coquitlam had been shifting north in the late 1970s, and the mall was a response to that. The centre won the Governor General's Award for Excellence in Architecture for Edmonton architect B. James Wensley. The centre's collection of 27 sculptures and other work by BC artists also garnered praise.

August 22 The Village of Belcarra was incorporated, covering just over 5.5 square kilometres (2 square miles), with an estimated population of 2,000. It's under the watchful eyes of the Coquitlam RCMP detachment and the Sasamat Volunteer Fire Department.

August Richmond hosted the BC Summer Games, the first to include disabled athletes.

September 8 The Vancouver Whitecaps pounded out a dramatic win over the Tampa Bay Rowdies in New York to win the North American Soccer League Championship. Trevor Whymark scored both goals (one off each foot) in Vancouver's 2–1 victory. *Province* sports columnist Jim Taylor wrote, "Whymark has been the catalyst, the trigger, the missing piece in the marvellously improbable soccer story that has taken Vancouver by the heart and squeezed it as no other

Winners! The Vancouver Whitecaps bend it hard to win the North American Soccer League Championship against the Tampa Bay Rowdies.
Ken Oakes / Vancouver Sun

sports event has before." One hundred thousand fans greeted the team on its return.

October 28 Chuck Davis' columns on local history began to appear in the *Province* Sunday editions. In all, there were 194 of them. Then the paper went tabloid.

December 16 The Steveston Museum opened in a 1905 building that had been a bank, then a doctor's office. The Steveston Historical Society also operates a post office there.

December 21 *Province* "Consumer Alert" columnist Chuck Poulsen wrote, "In a month or so, supermarkets should be serving up a large batch of rabbits for sale. Chinese rabbits. For Canada Packers, it will be the first test run of the low-cost, imported rabbits

Foncie's Last Foto

September 27 Vancouver street photographer Foncie Pulice took his last picture. Foncie and his Electric-Photo camera had been a familiar sight on city streets for an astounding 45 years. He'd begun as a 20-year-old way back in 1934 as an assistant to street photographer Joe Iaci and had taken millions of photographs since. (It is quite possible Foncie Pulice photographed more people than anyone who ever lived.) "I said I'd retire at 65, and I kept my word," he said in a November 21, 1979, interview in the *Province*.

Did he save all those millions of negatives? They'd likely be worth a small fortune now. "I never did," he said. "I didn't really think about it at the time. I'd keep 'em for a year, then throw 'em out. I realize now I should have saved them, but it's too late."

All across Canada and in other countries there are thousands and thousands of Foncie's Fotos, showing thousands and thousands of people striding along the street, captured in motion in unposed moments that may be closer to the spirit of the people shown than any carefully composed studio portrait.

People even made appointments for street pictures! "Oh, yes. They'd phone ahead and tell us what time they'd be walking down Granville. Dr. Peter Bell-Irving had members of his family photographed every year. I have shots showing one little tyke in that family growing all the way up to six-foot-five."

Foncie's camera, made of war surplus materials, was preserved at the Vancouver Museum, accompanied by a slew of Foncie's Fotos, as part of the 1950s gallery.

Foncie Pulice was the last of the street photographers. He died January 20, 2003, at age 88, but his work lives on...everywhere.

Last Stop on the Line

October 27 The last scheduled passenger train departed from the CPR station at the foot of Granville Street. Trains had been arriving and leaving here since 1914, and for 65 years the handsome building had been the site of reunions and farewells. I first saw Vancouver from this building, having just arrived from Winnipeg with my father in December 1944. My first visual memory of the city was of the World War I statue in front of the station, which depicts an angel lifting a fallen soldier into heaven. That statue is still there, with later wars added to its words of dedication.

Station baggage master Doug Taylor had worked there for 39 years. When he started in 1940, Taylor said, the baggage department had a hundred employees. On this last day it had six.

There was disappointment that VIA Rail passenger service would operate from the CN station on Main Street. "The CN is just a barn," train patron George Copeland told the *Province*. "This place has got character."

The building still has character. It's been beautifully restored, as thousands of SkyTrain, West Coast Express and SeaBus patrons well know.

which are expected to sell for about half the price of the B.C. bunnies. The Chinese rabbits will be coming at a time when a government survey predicts that we'd eat rabbits faster than they multiply if there was a reasonable supply and the price wasn't too much higher than chicken."

Also in 1979

Art Cameron, resident manager at the Hotel Vancouver for decades, retired. What made Art—born in January 1910 in New Westminster—distinctive was his style: he was a naturally funny guy, a never-exhausted font of sly humour and wicked ripostes. How many hotel managers are also gag writers? Art wrote gags for Bob Hope (a lifelong friend), Jack Benny, Edgar Bergen, Phil Harris, Ed Gardner, Alan Young and others. Among the more notable events of his long career: he was manager of the Sylvia Hotel in 1959 and was one of the guests at a West End apartment when screen star Errol Flynn died there on October 14 that year.

The Office of the Ombudsman was established by provincial legislation. The Ombudsman receives inquiries and complaints about the practices of and the services provided by public bodies. He or she can investigate to determine if the public body is being fair to the people it serves.

Ballard Power Systems was created. Dr. Geoffrey Ballard developed the fuel cell technology that led to its creation, but he left the company in 1997. In 1999, with Paul Howard, he formed a new company, General Hydrogen. *TIME* magazine named him a Hero of the Planet that year.

Power business. Developers of the portable 1kW power unit, Ballard Power Systems charges up for business in Vancouver. *Courtesy Ballard Power Systems (www.ballard.com)*

The wooden auxiliary schooner *Maple Leaf* began to provide educational/environmental cruises between the Strait of Georgia and Alaska. The *Maple Leaf* was the oldest BC vessel in the Canada Registry of Ships, built at Vancouver Shipyard in Coal Harbour in 1904 for lumber baron Alexander McLaren. It was also the first vessel to fly the colours of the Royal Vancouver Yacht Club in an open race. (From 1916 to 1979 the schooner was used in the halibut fishery under the names *Constance B* and *Parma*.)

The provincial government sold the buses it had inherited from the BC Electric Company to Pacific Coach Lines.

Harold Lenett, a Vancouver businessman, approached Levi Strauss with an offer to make leather jackets but was asked to make denim instead. He borrowed $5,000, bought some used Levi's equipment and launched Pimlico Apparel. The company grew to become North America's leading denim jacket producer, supplying Levi Strauss and the Gap from a 6,970-square-metre (75,000-square-foot) factory. In 2001 Lenett's son Gary bought a local clothing company called Dish and began producing Dish jeans, now an international hit.

The 460-seat Arts Club Theatre: Mainstage opened at 1585 Johnston Street on Granville Island and became one of the earliest landmarks on the island, as well as a personal triumph for managing director Bill Millerd, who had always dreamed of having a theatre on the

Function meets form. Vancouver's new court-house designed by Arthur Erickson presides over Robson Square.
John Denniston / The Province

waterfront. Now the island is home base for the company, which regularly tours its shows throughout the province.

The 240-seat Waterfront Theatre opened at 1410 Cartwright on Granville Island. Originally the home of Carousel Theatre, the New Play Centre (now Playwrights Theatre) and the defunct Westcoast Actors, the Waterfront is now primarily a rental venue and home to Carousel, which produces three shows for family audiences each year.

Arts Umbrella was also established on Granville Island, offering visual and performing arts education for children. It now reaches more than 30,000 young people annually and offers classes in theatre, dance, painting, sculpture, architecture, film, new media, photography and more.

A study showed that Surrey had become "Vancouver's bedroom," as more than 50 percent of its residents worked elsewhere. A hundred years earlier, almost everyone who lived in Surrey worked there.

Vancouver's new provincial courthouse and Robson Square complex were completed, changing the face of downtown. The site was originally supposed to hold a 55-storey office tower for provincial government offices (a tower that, 30 years later, would still have been the tallest building in the city). When the New Democratic Party came to power in the 1972 provincial election, they changed course and changed architects, bringing in Arthur Erickson. The result, according to historian Harold Kalman, was "a low, multi-block courthouse that is symbolically and physically more accessible—so accessible that we can walk on it! All this shows how architecture can provide a powerful political symbol."

White Rock's first Great Canadian Open Sandcastle Competition took place, the idea of Tom Kirstein, a chartered accountant, and his friend Chip Barrett. With prizes amounting to $10,000 and scores of teams competing, the annual event drew international attention, attracting crowds estimated at 150,000 to the waterfront. Unfortunately, by 1987 community dismay at the crush of people, unruly elements and rising police costs forced the cancellation of the competition.

Elisabeth Hawley and her three grandchildren willed Haney House to Maple Ridge. Elisabeth was the daughter of Thomas and Annie Haney, area pioneers, after whom Haney—now a part of Maple Ridge—was named. The house, at 11612 224th St. in Maple Ridge, was built in 1878. It was restored as a museum and displays many furnishings and artifacts used by three generations of the Haney family.

Police seized a little brown book at the apartment of a well-known Vancouver prostitute. In it were 800 names of men, a who's who of high society, including a high-ranking member of the BC judiciary. Wendy King pleaded guilty to keeping a bawdy house and was fined $1,500. The notebook was sealed by a BC Supreme Court judge and the names were never revealed.

Pender Guy, Vancouver's only English-language radio program focusing on Chinese Canadian issues, went on the air at Vancouver Co-operative Radio. Conceived at the "Between us Chinese" conference at UBC, the program ran weekly for five years, airing skits, oral histories and documentaries and providing creative space for a number of activists including writer Paul Yee, poet Jim Wong Chu and future politician Tung Chan.

Comings and Goings

February 23

Former premier W.A.C. Bennett died in Kelowna, aged 78.

1980-1989

1980

Vancouver cheered, and then cried, when Terry Fox set out to cross the country on his prosthetic leg but had to stop after 143 days when his cancer returned. There was a summer beer strike and the city was chosen to host a world's fair in 1986. It was also the year a young singer named Bryan Adams recorded his first album.

Frustrated by how little money was dedicated to cancer research, Terry Fox—who had lost his own leg to cancer—embarked on his Marathon of Hope, taking him across Canada to raise funds.
Ed Linkewich / The Terry Fox Foundation

January Premier Bill Bennett announced that a new domed stadium would be built on the north shore of False Creek, continuing the redevelopment that began on the south shore with Granville Island. It would house the city's football and soccer teams and, proponents hoped, a major-league baseball team. Teams including the Toronto Blue Jays and Seattle Mariners have played exhibition games there, but no permanent resident has appeared.

January 20 The Carnegie Building at Main and Hastings reopened as the Carnegie Reading Room, open 7 days a week, 12 hours a day, 365 days a year.

February 18 Patricia Carney was elected Conservative MP for Vancouver Centre. In her 2000 memoir *Trade Secrets*, she wrote, "Like Alice in *Through the Looking Glass*, I walked through the mirror and found my political passion, politics, and the rest of my life." Carney, born with twin Jim in Shanghai on May 26, 1935, earned national attention in the 1960s, writing from Vancouver on business issues. Years as a business consultant in the Northwest Territories were followed by her election. She was appointed to the Senate in 1990, the first Conservative senator from BC in 59 years.

February Architects McCarter and Nairne moved to a new location, having been Marine Building tenants for just under 50 years. They designed the building.

Also in February Bryan Adams released his first album, called simply *Bryan Adams*.

April 12 One-legged runner Terry Fox of Port Coquitlam began his cross-country Marathon of Hope to raise money for cancer research. Fox had lost his right leg to osteogenic sarcoma in 1977. While waiting for the operation to remove his leg, Fox read a magazine profile of Dick Traum, a one-legged runner who had

Elsewhere in BC

Power from the Peace Canyon project came on line, and BC Hydro's province-wide capacity increased to 7,948,000 kilowatts (83 percent of it hydroelectric), more than five times its capacity two decades earlier.

Elsewhere in Canada

June 27 "O Canada" became the country's official national anthem.

August 16 Vancouver's Lois Wilson was the first woman to be named moderator of the United Church of Canada.

Elsewhere in the World

May 18 The eruption of Mount St. Helens in Washington state rattled windows in Greater Vancouver. The eruption, at 8:32 a.m. PDT, was triggered by a 5.1 earthquake centred beneath the mountain. Mount St. Helens was 2,950 metres (9,677 feet) high before the eruption, 2,550 (8,363 feet) after. The eruption caused the largest landslide in recorded history. The massive ash cloud grew to 18 kilometres (60,000 feet) in 15 minutes and reached the east coast in three days. Although most of the ash fell within 500 kilometres (300 miles) of the mountain, finer ash had circled the earth within 15 days and continued to stay in the atmosphere for many years. Fifty-seven people were killed as a result of the eruption. Twenty-one bodies were never recovered.

competed in the New York Marathon. Inspired by the story, Terry began to run daily after his operation, painfully short distances at first, but increasing steadily as he developed strength and technique. His running style was his own: two hops on his remaining leg, then a long stride on his artificial leg while lifting his torso and shoulders for leverage. "It takes more courage to fight cancer than it does for me to run," said a determined Fox. In 1979 he joined a wheelchair-basketball team, after being recruited by Rick Hansen. Part of his self-designed exercise routine was pushing his chair up Gaglardi Way, a long, steep climb up Burnaby Mountain toward Simon Fraser University at the top. Now, after planning his route and gaining support from the Canadian Cancer Society, Ford Motor Company (which donated a camper van), Imperial Oil (fuel) and Adidas (running shoes), he was in St. John's, NL. As he dipped his artificial leg in the Atlantic, then turned his face to the west to run across the nation, Terry's dream, the "Marathon of Hope," began.

April 18 Actress Dorothy Stratten (born Dorothy Ruth Hoogstraten on February 28, 1960, in Vancouver) appeared on the *Tonight Show* with Johnny Carson. Four months later, on August 14, she was shot to death by her husband, Paul Snider, in a West Los Angeles apartment. Snider then shot himself. The *Province* ran a feature November 30 that told how young and pretty Dorothy Hoogstraten, who had been working at a Dairy Queen on East Hastings, was "discovered" by Snider, a promoter. He arranged to have her participate in Playboy's Great Playmate Hunt in 1978. She was named *Playboy* playmate for August 1979, which led to a promising movie career. As she rose, Snider apparently became a handicap...and his anger and frustration ended in murder. A movie about the tragedy, *Star 80*, starring Mariel Hemingway, was made in 1983.

Summer Greater Vancouver brewery workers went on strike. It happened to coincide with an unseasonably hot summer. Groan.

August 27 Southam acquired ownership of the *Vancouver Sun* and now owned both dailies in the city, the *Sun* and the *Province*.

August The Transpo 86 Corporation Act was given royal assent in the BC Legislature, paving the way for Expo 86.

September 2 Terry Fox had to stop near Thunder Bay, ON, 143 days after he began his Marathon of Hope. His cancer had returned and spread to his lungs. Terry was flown home and taken to Royal Columbian Hospital in New Westminster. On September 18, at age 22, Terry Fox became the youngest companion of the Order of Canada (the highest of three levels of the order). In a special ceremony, Governor General Ed Schreyer flew to BC to invest Terry with the honour in the municipal council chamber of his home town, Port Coquitlam. "The Order of Canada awards," the *Province* reported, "normally are presented twice a year. But Schreyer and the council which advises him on selections decided that, because of his illness and because of his contribution to the country, a special award should be made to Fox." This marked the first and only time a Governor General travelled to the recipient of the award. On December 3, Fox was made a freeman of the City of Port Coquitlam. He was also admitted to the Order of the Dogwood.

September 21 A plaque on the Stanley Park seawall gives this as the official opening date for the 9-kilometre (5.5-mile) wall. It marked completion of the final portion of the wall between Third Beach and Second Beach.

October The Emily Carr College of Art and Design officially opened in its new home: three abandoned industrial buildings on Granville Island that

New home. The Emily Carr College of Art and Design takes up its permanent residence in three old, abandoned industrial warehouses on Granville Island.
Emily Carr University of Art and Design Library and Archives

were transformed as part of the federal government's urban renewal project on the island. The words "and Design" were added to the college's name.

November *The Look of Music* opened at the Vancouver Museum and proved a hugely popular show, featuring old, rare and beautifully made musical instruments and illustrating the evolution of Western musical instruments from 1500 to 1900. The guiding force behind the show was Dr. Phillip T. Young of the School of Music, University of Victoria.

Also November The Canadian Fire Underwriters Survey declared the Vancouver Fire Department had achieved Canada's first-ever and only Class I rating.

December Blackcomb opened with a capacity of 4,000 skiers per day, on four triple chairs and a beginner double chair, serving 1,240 metres (4,068 vertical feet). It grew slowly at first, as it was still much smaller than its largest competitor and neighbour across the valley, Whistler Mountain.

Not to be outdone by its bigger counterpart—Whistler Mountain—Blackcomb Mountain opened in 1980 to welcome up to 4,000 skiers a day. The two ski resorts would later join together into one mega-resort, but until that time it was like the Capulets vs. the Montagues. *Courtesy PNG*

December 31

Thanks largely to an earlier CTV telethon honouring Terry Fox, more than $24 million had been raised for his cause by year's end. Terry's goal of raising one dollar for every Canadian had been surpassed, and he had more than doubled the Canadian Cancer Society's 1980 research allowance. The Port Coquitlam post office reported that Terry received more mail this month than everyone else in town—residential and business—combined.

Also in 1980

Leila Getz founded the Vancouver Recital Society. Her aim was to feature outstanding local and international musicians in Vancouver performances, and she launched and supported the careers of many artists from BC, Canada and abroad.

Citing health concerns, John Avison resigned as music director of the CBC Vancouver Chamber Orchestra (which was renamed CBC Vancouver Orchestra this year). Succeeding him as principal conductor was the renowned English conductor John Eliot Gardiner.

Vancouver entertainer Barney Potts, 70, released an album titled *Barney Potts, Live—Just Barely*. Potts had led bands in the 1930s in such Vancouver nightspots as Happyland, Cinderella Ballroom, Mandarin Gardens and The Narrows. He performed in musicals in the 1940s and spent 12 years with Theatre Under the Stars. He was also a CBC-TV star for many years. Ten years later he was inducted into the BC Entertainment Hall of Fame for his decades of performing.

Debra McPherson, a nurse at University Hospital, looked at her first 1980 paycheque from the hospital and wondered out loud why it didn't reflect what she had earned for three years of identical experience in Edmonton. Manitoba-born McPherson became an activist at that point and has been involved with the BC Nurses' Union (president from 1990 to 1994 and again from 2000 to now) and the Canadian Federation of Nurses Unions. "Sure we can settle for less," she said, "but why should we? Why should I be paid less than a freaking plumber?"

The Cascades Drive-In Theatre, a Burnaby landmark since August 30, 1946, closed. The site is now occupied by the Cascade Village condominium development.

The 13-minute NFB film *Nails*, made by Vancouver film director Philip Borsos, was nominated for an Oscar. It won the 1980 Canadian Film Award for Best Short. "Who'd have thought the subject could be so interesting, or so exciting photographically?" asked the reviewer from the *LA Times*.

The TheatreSports League, an improvisational group, began performing late-night shows on weekends at City Stage. In 1986 the group took over the space, renaming the venue Back Alley Theatre. Some members of the ever-evolving cast: Jay Brazeau, Garry Chalk, Roger Fredericks, Dean Haglund, Christine Lippa, Colin Mocherie, Louise Moon, Morris Panych and Veena Sood. The troupe evolved into the acclaimed Vancouver TheatreSports League.

Ramona Mar became Vancouver's first full-time Chinese Canadian female newscaster.

She joined the CKNW/CFMI news department and later moved to CBC-TV to co-host a series on Expo 86. In 1996 she co-hosted and created *Spilled Milk*, a parenting program that ran nationally on CBC-TV for five seasons.

Two great books of Vancouver history came out this year. One of them, *Vancouver: An Illustrated History*, by Patricia E. Roy, is a solid piece of work, part of the History of Canadian Cities series co-published by James Lorimer and the National Museum of Man. The other, Rolf Knight's *Along the No. 20 Line: Reminiscences of the Vancouver Waterfront*, published by New Star Books, is a lively, exceedingly readable chronicle of life in the areas of Vancouver where loggers tended to hang out in the 1930s and '40s.

The BC Penitentiary, a federal maximum-security facility and the largest prison in the province, was phased out.

It was replaced by Kent Prison in Matsqui and other institutions as part of a decentralization plan.

The Downtown Eastside Residents Association (DERA) hired organizer Jim Green. DERA had been having financial problems, exacerbated by non-supportive provincial and civic governments. But then both Bruce Eriksen and Libby Davies, DERA founders and activists, were elected to city council, and with other supporters, such as Harry Rankin and Mike Harcourt, the association was able to obtain the funding to hire the organizer it needed. Green went on to help DERA establish non-profit housing projects and has become a prominent consultant and activist.

The north side of Whistler Mountain opened. So did the first phase of Whistler Village, with hotels, restaurants, pubs, shops, the Whistler Conference Centre, banks and tour companies.

Mohawk Lubricants began operating a used-oil re-refining plant in North Vancouver. Mohawk's used oil division collected over 33 million litres (7 million gallons) of used lubricating oil a year, which removed 30,000 tonnes of potentially hazardous waste material from the western Canadian environment every year.

The indoor pool at UBC's Aquatic Centre opened at a cost of $5.4 million, largely paid by students, alumni and the community. The Olympic-sized pool holds up to 738 swimmers and allows several different activities to take place at one time. The centre also houses a well-equipped exercise room, physical fitness testing centre, two saunas and a whirlpool.

Langara College began a co-operative education program that combined academic studies with practical work experience.

The Greater Vancouver Information Referral Service (formerly the Community Information Service) purchased its first computer, thanks to grants from BC Lotteries and the Vancouver Foundation, and began to digitize its famous *Red Book* database of social and other helping agencies in the region.

The Knowledge Network was created.

This BC government–funded educational channel made its on-air debut in January 1981. During that year the Knowledge Network staff increased from one to 30.

Award-winner. The address may be as lucky as it sounds: the architectural firm Musson Cattell Mackey won the Governor General's Award in architecture for designing this building, which stands at 888 West Hastings. *Courtesy Musson Cattell Mackey Partnership*

Ennui, a bimonthly art magazine produced by Ennui Publications of Vancouver, debuted this year. We could check to see if it's still around, but we're just too tired.

The BC ferry *Queen of Surrey* (bought in 1974 for $13.8 million and retired after two years) was refurbished at

Bill Reid's *Raven and the First Men*, depicting the Haida myth of human creation, took two years to complete. It was dedicated in 1980 and can be seen in the UBC Museum of Anthropology.
Jason Payne / The Province

a cost of more than $10 million, renamed *Queen of the North* and put into service on the Queen Charlotte run. The ship—with 99 passengers and crew aboard—sank on March 22, 2006, after hitting a rock about 135 kilometres (85 miles) south of Prince Rupert. Two passengers died.

AirBC was formed when the Jim Pattison Group purchased six small commuter airlines and amalgamated them into a larger, more efficient operation to serve destinations across western Canada (connecting BC, Alberta, Saskatchewan and Manitoba) and the northwestern US.

The CN Station (1917–19) and its rooftop neon sign were designated Schedule A Heritage Structures by Vancouver city council. Today that handsome building is Pacific Central Station, the terminal for Greyhound Lines, Pacific Coach Lines and two passenger railways: VIA Rail and Amtrak. The 1932 Coroner's Court at 238–240 East Cordova and Firehall No. 2 (1907) at 280 East Cordova were also designated heritage buildings this year. They now house the Vancouver Police Centennial Museum and the Firehall Arts Centre, respectively.

The Boeing plant on Sea Island was demolished. Built in 1939 to produce Canso and Catalina and later B-29 superfortress aircraft, the plant employed 6,000 people at the peak of production.

HRH Prince Charles unveiled the striking Bill Reid sculpture *Raven and the First Men* at the Museum of Anthropology.

The work, commissioned by Walter and Marianne Koerner, was carved by Reid from a 4-tonne block of yellow cedar. Haida people brought the sand at the base of the sculpture from the beach where the trickster Raven is said to have discovered the first humans in a clam shell. The beautiful boxwood prototype, small enough to fit snugly into a person's hand, is now in a permanent display of Reid's smaller work in gold, silver, argillite and wood at the museum.

Comings and Goings

Notable deaths: **William John "Torchy" Peden**, racing cyclist, on January 26 in Northbrook, IL, aged 73 (in 1929, Peden set a cycling world speed record of 81 mph [130.3 km/h] that stood for 12 years); **Lynn Patrick**, hockey player and executive, on January 26 in St. Louis, MO, aged 67 (he played championship basketball and CFL football, and won a Stanley Cup with the New York Rangers in 1940); **Ethel Wilson**, writer, in Vancouver on December 22, aged 92 (BC's top fiction prize is named for her).

1981

Real estate prices tumbled as the economy slid into recession. The city reflected on the best of humanity when Terry Fox died and was repulsed by the worst when the arrest of Clifford Olson revealed him to be a serial killer who had been murdering children in the Fraser Valley. The Cave nightclub, meanwhile, closed after decades of entertaining Vancouver.

April 1 The Fraser Valley college district served by Douglas College was divided into two smaller regions: one on the north shore of the Fraser River; the other on the south shore. Douglas College retained its campuses in New Westminster, Coquitlam and Maple Ridge. The new college took charge of the campuses in Langley, Surrey and Richmond. A contest was held to find a name for the new South Fraser regional college. Over 200 names were suggested, including Tillicum, Dogwood, Surdel–Langrich and Salish. The clear winner was Kwantlen, which means "tireless runners" and refers to the Native people who lived in the South Fraser region. The winning entry was submitted by Stan McKinnon, news editor of the *Surrey Leader*. Today Kwantlen Polytechnic University is a degree-granting institution with four campuses.

May 2 The diving charter vessel *Huntress* exploded in Coal Harbour while refuelling, killing two and injuring eight. Fuel had leaked through substandard PVC piping, causing the explosion and subsequent fire.

Elsewhere in BC

July 17 The BC government named a 2,639-metre (8,660-foot) peak in the Rockies after Terry Fox.

The Union of BC Indian Chiefs organized the Constitution Express, which sent trainloads of First Nations people from BC to Ottawa to lobby Prime Minister Trudeau and the premiers to guarantee Native peoples' right to self-determination in the Canadian constitution. When Canada passed the Constitution Act, 1982, it did recognize "existing aboriginal and treaty rights" in Section 35. Three years later, after a series of unsuccessful first ministers' conferences, the task of defining aboriginal rights was left to the Canadian courts.

Elsewhere in Canada

January 1 Gas stations began selling gas and diesel by the litre rather than the gallon.

July 30 The section of the Trans-Canada Highway near Thunder Bay where Terry Fox was forced to end his run was renamed the Terry Fox Courage Highway.

September 13 The first Terry Fox Run, named for the late cancer fighter, was held in more than 880 Canadian communities with more than 300,000 participants. They ran, walked, cycled, rollerbladed, swam and wheeled—and raised $3.5 million. Still an annual event, the run is now held in many countries and has raised millions of dollars for cancer research.

November 5 The federal government and all provinces except Quebec reached an agreement on patriating the constitution from Great Britain.

Joy Kogawa's novel *Obasan* was published in Toronto. It was the first novel to deal with Canada's internment of its Japanese citizens during and after World War II.

Elsewhere in the World

January 20 Within minutes of Ronald Reagan being sworn in as president of the United States, Iran released the 52 Americans who had been held for 444 days, since November 4, 1979, ending the Iran hostage crisis.

March 30 John Hinckley Jr. shot President Ronald Reagan in an attempted assassination outside a Washington, DC, hotel.

May 13 Pope John Paul II was shot by Mehmet Ali Agca.

June 5 What were later recognized as the first cases of AIDS were reported in Los Angeles.

July 29 Lady Diana Spencer married Prince Charles.

October 6 Egyptian president Anwar Sadat was assassinated by army members belonging to the Egyptian Islamic Jihad organization.

November 13 The Canadarm, a remote-controlled mechanical arm developed by Canada's SPAR Aerospace, was first deployed aboard the space shuttle *Columbia*.

The Devonshire Hotel, in business since 1925, is demolished in one final blast of glory. It took 6.5 seconds to fall. *Deborah Cameron* / Vancouver Sun

May 29 The Vancouver Indian Centre Society opened its new facility, with Chief Simon Baker officiating. The centre provided programs in health and welfare, social services, human rights, culture, education, recreation and equality for aboriginal people of all age groups and genders. Today it's known as the Vancouver Aboriginal Friendship Centre.

Spring Vancouver members of the Canadian Union of Public Employees (CUPE) went on strike, and garbage piled up at tennis courts and other makeshift collection sites throughout Greater Vancouver. The strike lasted 90 days. A strike by Richmond civic employees this year also lasted three months.

June 2 During a riot at Abbotsford's Matsqui Institution, 300 inmates seized control of the prison and set fire to seven buildings, causing millions of dollars in damages. During the riot, Corporal Patrick Aloysius Kevin McBride rescued eight staff members from a burning roof. As a result of his actions McBride received a second Governor General's Medal of Bravery.

June 28 Terry Fox died at dawn in Royal Columbian Hospital in New Westminster, one month before his 23rd birthday. His family was at his side. Canada mourned a genuine and beloved hero. Flags on all federal buildings across Canada were flown at half-staff. Terry's campaign had raised over $24 million for the fight against cancer. His dedication, courage and selflessness were perpetuated through the annual Terry Fox Run and the Terry Fox Foundation, which keep the Marathon of Hope alive.

June A new floating dry dock arrived at Burrard Dry Dock. It had been designed by Swan Wooster Engineering of Vancouver but built by Mitsubishi Heavy Industries of Hiroshima, Japan.

July 5 The Devonshire Hotel was demolished. The hotel opened at the northeast corner of Georgia and Hornby Streets in 1925. It took two years to put the building up. It took 6.5 seconds to bring it down. On this Sunday morning in July 1981, hundreds of people crowded (at a prudent distance) onto adjacent streets and waited for Arrow Demolition's big bang. The windows of nearby buildings, including the Vancouver and Georgia hotels, were jammed with onlookers. At 7:05 a.m. Chris Charles, the wife of Arrow's Brian Charles, pushed the button and, with a muffled crack from a hundred kilos of dynamite, the hotel's central elevator shaft began to collapse. The rest of the seven-storey building fell inward, and a vast cloud of white dust rose up as the crowd cheered. Not long after the dust settled, work began on the HSBC Bank Canada building.

July 20 The Cave closed its doors with a farewell performance by the Bobby Hales Orchestra.

With its dark interior and famous papier-mâché stalactites, the Cave had been a fixture on the Vancouver club scene for decades, run in its heyday by the towering Ken Stauffer. It had hosted acts ranging from Mitzi Gaynor, Milton Berle, Mel Torme, Lena Horne, Jack Carter, Henny Youngman and Louis Armstrong to Eric Burdon and the Animals and the Doors. The club was demolished the next day.

August 21 Clifford Olson, 41, a self-employed contractor from Coquitlam, appeared in Chilliwack court, charged with the murder of 14-year-old Judy Kozma. On August 31 he was charged with eight more counts of murder. These charges involved the killings of eight other young people, aged 9 to 18. He eventually stood trial on 10 counts of first degree murder in January 1982. He pleaded not guilty, but two days later he changed his plea to guilty and admitted he was responsible for yet another murder. On January 14, 1982, Olson was sentenced to 11 life terms. The judge hearing the case noted,

"My considered opinion is that you should never be granted parole for the remainder of your days. It would be foolhardy to let you at large."

September 23 Chief Dan George died in Vancouver, aged 82. He was born July 24, 1899, in North Vancouver. His birth name was Tes-wah-no, but he was known in English as Dan Slaholt. At age five he entered a mission boarding school, where his surname was changed to George. In 1959 he began his acting career. He appeared to great acclaim in the first production of *The Ecstasy of Rita Joe* by George Ryga (1967). His films included *Little Big Man* (1970), for which he received an Oscar nomination, and *The Outlaw Josey Wales* (1975). He was the chief of the Squamish band from 1951 to 1963 and honorary chief of the Squamish Nation. He wrote *My Heart Soars* (1974) and *My Spirit Soars* (1982).

October 17 Vancouver police broke up a Ku Klux Klan rally celebrating the assassination of Egyptian leader Anwar Sadat. It was the first Klan activity in the city for nearly 50 years.

November 17 Mike Harcourt was elected mayor of Vancouver, defeating Jack Volrich by 3,000 votes. "Vancouver," wrote the *Province*'s Jan O'Brien, "will never be the same after the weekend's upset civic election. A ward system in 1982, more housing and an immediate push for light-rail transit are on the agenda of the new city council." Topping the aldermanic vote with the largest number of votes ever cast for a Vancouver civic politician was lawyer Harry Rankin. Well down the list of aldermanic hopefuls who didn't make it was a fellow named Philip Owen. His turn would come. (The ward system's wouldn't.) Harcourt later became the leader of the New Democratic Party in BC and then premier in a landslide victory over Social Credit in 1991.

December 8 Premier Bill Bennett announced that construction of the downtown convention centre, planned for Pier B-C, on the city's central waterfront, had been postponed indefinitely. The facility, to be funded by the three levels of government, was initially projected to cost $25 million when it was first announced in May 1978. By 1980, with construction not yet begun, the price had soared to $52 million, then, within months, to $80 million. By November 1981, it was $135 million and politicians were panicking. On April 1, 1982, the federal government announced that it would build the Canadian Pavilion for Expo 86 on the pier—and when the fair was over, it would turn the pavilion over to the city and province to be used as a trade and convention centre.

December Poland's Communist government began its crackdown on the Solidarity trade union, and Polish seamen jumped ship in Vancouver. About 1,000 demonstrators, chanting "Solidarity Forever," marched from Robson Square to Pier B-C.

Also in 1981

The 1981 census was sobering for Vancouver: it showed a drop in absolute numbers, with 12,000 fewer people in the city since the 1971 census. That was only a 3 percent difference, but it was a decline. In contrast, most of the suburbs were leaping ahead: Langley Township had more than doubled in population in a decade, Surrey had grown by more than 50 percent, Richmond by more than 55. Delta was now five times bigger than it had been 20 years earlier. Two-thirds of Greater Vancouver's population now lived outside the central city. Only New Westminster joined Vancouver in bucking the trend: its population had dropped 10 percent during the 1970s.

A deep and protracted recession began in BC. Economist Michael Goldberg noted that the recession made it clear British Columbia "had to diversify its resource-based economy."

A decline in house values began and continued into 1982. Chartered accountant Don Young commented: "House values in Vancouver declined by 30 percent or more and many people were hurt, some bankrupted, because they were caught with two homes (bought one and couldn't sell the one they owned) when interest rates were at an all-time high—first mortgages at 20 percent and more—and the demand for new and used homes plunged from the unrealistically high levels achieved by the end of 1980. Other people had mortgage renewals come due and

The beautiful Burvilla, a Queen Anne–style home built for the Burr family in 1905–6, is relocated from the south side of River Road to the Deas Island Regional Park in Delta. *Colin Price / The Province*

Peace not war! Beginning with 10,000 in 1981 and growing exponentially each year—until the event became the largest event of its kind—marchers mobilize in a massive peace march in Vancouver to protest against nuclear weapons and other causes of conflict. By 1983 there were 100,000 participants. *David Clark / The Province*

found it difficult, sometimes very difficult, to keep up the new higher monthly mortgage payments with current interest rates."

Vancouver's St. Paul's Hospital introduced a computerized medication service that became a model for other acute care hospitals.

Julia Levy formed Quadra Logic Technologies, now QLT Inc., a biotechnology company. It was while teaching microbiology at UBC that Dr. Levy first became interested in the idea of using photosensitive drugs to treat diseases. The photodynamic therapy she developed involves a drug that is activated using light from a laser. Dr. Levy served as the company's president and CEO from 1995 to 2002.

MacMillan Bloedel began producing Parallam at a pilot plant on Annacis Island. MacBlo had spent $45 million over 20 years on research and development of this parallel strand lumber product, which created large beams out of small trees. Parallam was manufactured by bonding long strands of wood, under pressure, into uniform structural beams, using a waterproof adhesive. The bonding resin was cured with microwave energy—somewhat like cooking in a kitchen microwave. In 1987 MacBlo spent $100 million to bring the Annacis Island plant into full commercial production and to build a similar plant in Georgia.

George Wainborn, former Vancouver Park Board commissioner, started the Stanley Park Christmas Train, with strong support from the Mount Pleasant Legion.

The hedges that make up the walls of the Elizabethan maze at VanDusen Botanical Garden were planted.

Zool Suleman, a Richmond High School student, won the Canadian debating championship. He was the first BC high school student to win that championship, held in Montreal.

Richmond received 188 days of rain in 1981, the highest annual level since 1939. Farms produced only 56 percent of normal yield.

A 1981 peace march, protesting nuclear proliferation, was a success, drawing nearly 10,000 participants. The march attracted 35,000 the next year and more than 100,000 in 1983. The annual event grew to become the largest of its kind in North America.

In 1792 Lieutenant Peter Puget, one of Captain Vancouver's crew, named a small point near the tip of Point Grey "Noon Breakfast Point." The name was finally officially adopted this year.

Minnekhada Farms in northeastern Coquitlam, once the homesteaded property of Obe and Bertha Pollard, was made a regional park. Covering more than 200 hectares (nearly 500 acres), the park is home to the Minnekhada Lodge, one of the Greater Vancouver Regional District's premier heritage buildings and the site of many weddings and other functions. Tours of the park are welcomed—but be aware that there are bears there.

The Burlington Northern Railway (originally the Great Northern Railway, now the Burlington Northern and Santa Fe) discontinued passenger service. The line went through White Rock, although passenger service to and from that point had ended in 1975, and the railway gave its station to the City of White Rock that year. Passenger service between Vancouver and Seattle was restored by Amtrak in 1995. Amtrak's trains passed by the old station's door, but they didn't stop because in 1991 the station became the White Rock Museum and Archives.

Comings and Goings

April 19 Hayden Christensen, who played Anakin Skywalker (the future Darth Vader) in the *Star Wars* movies, was born in Vancouver.

August 21 Nanaimo-born bandleader Charlie Pawlett died, aged about 79.

1982

There was controversy when the RCMP admitted they had paid $100,000 to the family of Clifford Olson so he would lead police to his victim's bodies. The roof of BC Place Stadium was inflated for the first time, and the Vancouver Food Bank was founded. The Canucks made it to the Stanley Cup final for the first time, but lost.

January 14 A front-page headline in the *Sun* announced "Olson was paid to locate bodies." This was in reference to the RCMP's agreement to pay Olson's family $100,000 so that Olson would reveal where his victims' bodies were buried. The next day's *Sun* headline reported "Olson deal greeted with disgust." However, lawyers from all points of the political spectrum supported the payment, and in 1984 a *Sun* headline read "Families [of the victims] not critical of deal with Olson, lawyer says."

January 15 The Arts, Sciences and Technology Centre opened in temporary quarters at Granville and Dunsmuir streets. In 1977 the Junior League of Greater Vancouver and the City of Vancouver Social Planning Department had joined forces to establish a science centre for the city. Barbara Brink, community leader and fundraiser extraordinaire, worked tirelessly to make that dream a reality. Within six years the Arts, Sciences and Technology Centre had attracted more than 600,000 visitors. Another 400,000 benefited from the centre's outreach programs, which travelled around the province. In 1987 the centre moved into the big silver sphere at 1455 Quebec St. and was renamed Science World.

January 16 An arsonist's fire heavily damaged Malkin Bowl in Stanley Park, destroying, among other things, the signatures of hundreds of performers and the names and dates of shows that had been pencilled on the old wooden walls. The arsonist was never found, but the Bowl was rebuilt and shows are still presented there.

March 1 Ground was broken for the original SkyTrain line (now the Expo Line). The city had long needed a rapid transit system, and this system, developed by an Ontario Crown corporation, was seen as a perfect addition for Expo 86, with its focus on transportation.

March 8 Students, teachers and administrators, accompanied by a marching band, walked or drove from the Queen's Park campus of Douglas College at McBride and 8th Avenue to the new downtown site at Royal Avenue and 8th Street. Leading the trek on his black motorcycle was the college's second president, William L. Day. A pine tree uprooted from the old campus and transported by wheelbarrow was replanted on the new campus. Also transported during the trek was the wooden college entrance sign. A few years later that sign was given legs and turned into a bench.

April 2 Health Minister James Nielsen opened the 120-bed New Grace Hospital at 4490 Oak St. It's now known as the BC Women's Hospital and Health Centre.

September 11 Arthur Delamont, bandleader, died in Vancouver, aged 90. He was born in Hereford, England, on January 23, 1892, but came to Vancouver in 1922, where he led the West Vancouver Boys Band and the Kitsilano Boys Band. According to one of the Kitsilano alumni, Norman D. Mullins, QC, "Mr. D., as we called him, and his family were raised in the beliefs and traditions of the Salvation Army and it was with one of its bands that he learned to play the cornet. His irrepressible zest for motorcycle racing and dance hall music brought him to his first crucial decision: fun or faith. He left the band and committed himself to a career in music—with the occasional bike ride on the side...Mr. D. settled in Vancouver and in 1928, on the eve of the Great Depression, it occurred to him he might make a living and a contribution to his newfound community by organizing footloose boys into a band." The long list of awards won by the band under Delamont's direction is astonishing.

October 6 Alan Morley, journalist, died in North Vancouver, aged 77. He was born August 15, 1905, in Vancouver but grew up in Armstrong and Penticton. He first worked with his father, manager of the Sally Dam in the Kettle Valley, as a mucker and miner. He attended UBC in the early 1930s, supporting himself by writing

Elsewhere in Canada

April 17 Queen Elizabeth II signed a proclamation in Ottawa to bring the Constitution Act, 1982, into effect, patriating Canada's constitution.

Elsewhere in the World

Maple Ridge athlete Debbie Brill won gold in the high jump at the Commonwealth Games in Brisbane. She'd done it before, in 1970, at the Commonwealth Games in Edinburgh.

No surrender. Unhappy with the officiating during a Vancouver Canucks–Chicago Blackhawks game in 1982, Vancouver coach Roger Neilson waved a white towel tied to a hockey stick in frustrated protest. He was kicked out of the game, the Canucks lost 4–1, and thus was born an enduring tradition of waving white towels in support of Vancouver's beloved hockey team. *PNG*

Towel Power

May 16 There was no joy in Vancouver (nor the rest of Canada) on May 16, 1982, when the Vancouver Canucks were defeated by the New York Islanders in four straight games in their quest for the Stanley Cup. Not even "towel power" had helped.

For hockey fans, 1982 was "the miracle on Renfrew Street." Under interim coach Roger Neilson (filling in for Harry Neale who had been suspended after getting into a fight in the stands in Quebec), and with the heroic goaltending of "King" Richard Brodeur, the Vancouver Canucks beat Calgary in three straight games in the first round of the Stanley Cup playoffs, then took out Los Angeles four games to one but ran into trouble in game two of the Campbell conference final against the Chicago Blackhawks. The Canucks were losing 3–1 in the third period and were frustrated by a series of calls by referee Bob Myers, including a disallowed goal. Neilson showed his dismay by hoisting a white towel atop a hockey stick in a sign of surrender. Players Gerry Minor and Tiger Williams joined in and "towel power" was born. Neilson was ejected from the game and the Canucks received a bench penalty. They went on to lose the game 4–1, but the sarcastic gesture galvanized the team, and when they returned to Vancouver the fans were *all* waving white towels.

Vancouver T-shirt entrepreneur Butts Giraud is credited with realizing immediately the significance of what Neilson had done. Within 36 hours he had silk-screened and handed out 5,000 white towels with sponsors' names. A few days later Giraud was able to sell 15,000 towels at a Canucks–Blackhawks game. "Towel power" had begun.

The Canucks won the next three games and the series, which brought them to the Stanley Cup final against the Islanders, the closest the Canucks had ever come to hockey's top prize.

When they lost, the team was inconsolable. The fans were not. A piece by the *Vancouver Sun*'s Ian Haysom, headlined "Cinderella Heroes Lost Stanley Cup But Won Our Hearts," gave a sense of the atmosphere. "Stan Smyl," Haysom wrote, "eyes red, choking back the tears, said: 'Yes, it hurts. I guess it hurts a lot.' Outside the Canucks' dressing room, a crowd of almost 200 diehard fans chanted 'Next year! Next year!' and 'Stan-ley, Stan-ley!' That wasn't for the Cup, but for team captain Stan Smyl. The Canucks' captain, after regaining his composure, was persuaded to go out and meet them. They mobbed him, told him he was the greatest, they held aloft a foil-wrapped Stanley Cup, shook both his hands and cheered themselves hoarse. Smyl managed a smile and said, simply: 'Thanks, guys. You're the greatest. You've all been incredible.'"

for the *Vancouver Sun*, then wrote for 21 other newspapers before returning to the *Sun* in 1957 and working there until his retirement in 1970. He wrote *Vancouver: From Milltown to Metropolis* (1961), which is still our favourite book-length history of Vancouver because of his storytelling ability and his affection for the city.

October 7
Construction began on the Expo 86 site.

October 24 William Arthur "Bill" Pritchard, labour activist, died in Los Angeles, aged about 93. Pritchard was born in 1889 in Salford, England, and came to Vancouver in 1911. He was head of the Vancouver Longshoremen's Union and involved in the Vancouver Trades and Labour Council, the Socialist Party of Canada and the One Big Union. Convicted of sedition for his speech during the Winnipeg General Strike (June 12, 1919), Pritchard spent a year in jail. He was reeve of Burnaby during the Depression, from 1930 to 1932, and ended up in court again after using municipal funds to help the jobless. A judge agreed that Pritchard's action was illegal but argued it was necessary "to avert the possibility of revolution." Pritchard ran for election provincially for the Co-operative Commonwealth Federation (predecessor to the NDP) in 1933 and 1937 but lost both times, at which point he began working as a baker. A musician, he organized youth orchestras, choirs and operatic productions.

November 6 The BC Lions played their last game at Empire Stadium (and defeated the Montreal Alouettes). Coming up for the team: a new home at BC Place Stadium.

November 14
The roof of BC Place Stadium, the largest air-supported dome in the world, was inflated. It took less than an hour. The dome was made up of two layers of fabric with a 1-metre (3-foot) space between them. When it snowed, hot air was pumped between these layers to melt snow at a rate of 15 centimetres (6 inches) per hour. Each layer of fabric was only 8 millimetres (1/30th of an inch) thick, so the roof let in 20 percent natural light. The fabric weighed 255 tonnes, covered 4 hectares (10 acres) and had a circumference of 760 metres (2,490 feet). The stadium opened seven months later, on June 19, 1983.

False Creek to world fair. Construction begins for Expo 86 at the site on False Creek. *The Province*

November 20 Vancouver was declared a "nuclear free zone" in a plebiscite. Voters also okayed Sunday shopping.

Also November 20

The UBC Thunderbirds, coached by Frank Smith, won the CIAU (Canadian Interuniversity Athletic Union) football championship, the Vanier Cup. According to the UBC Sports Hall of Fame, TSN football analysts called this team "the greatest in CIAU history. It went undefeated in Canadian competition (12–0), often dominating by more than 40 points, winning the Canadian championship with a 39–14 victory over Western Ontario. This team had five first rounders selected in the CFL draft, 14 players placed on the league All-Star team," and 12 of its players played professionally in the CFL.

November 22 Firebombs went off at three Red Hot Video outlets. A group calling itself the Wimmin's Fire Brigade claimed responsibility. Five people (who became known as the Squamish Five) were arrested January 20, 1983, and, for this and other acts (including bombing a Litton Industries plant in Toronto), were jailed for terms ranging from six years to life.

Airy dome. The world's largest air-pressure-supported dome is proudly inflated at BC Place, Vancouver's 60,000-seat stadium. *PNG*

November 29 Percy Williams, a double gold medallist at the 1928 Amsterdam Olympics, died by suicide in Vancouver, aged 74. He came out of nowhere at the 1928 Amsterdam Olympics to win both the 100-metre and the 200-metre races. This wasn't a fluke. He set a world record for the 100-metre dash in 1930, and held it for 10 years. Only an injury kept him from succeeding at the 1932 Olympics. But he was shy and reclusive. "I didn't like running," he told a reporter once. "Oh, I was so glad to get out of it all." He never married and his later years were marked by constant pain from arthritis.

Harry Jerome, sprinter, was the second athletic legend to pass away this year. He died by seizure, aged 42, while a passenger driving northbound over the Lions Gate Bridge. Seen in 2010 with a sculpture of her brother is Valerie Jerome.
Mark van Manen / PNG

December 7 The sports fraternity in BC was shocked by the sudden death of sprinter Harry Jerome, 42.

He was riding as a passenger in a car northbound over the Lions Gate Bridge when he suffered a seizure and was dead when brought minutes later to Lions Gate Hospital. Jerome had been at Vancouver General Hospital just four days earlier after experiencing several seizures. He was the first runner to simultaneously hold world records for the 100-metre and 100-yard events and was co-holder of the 100-metre world record for eight years after setting a mark of 10 seconds flat in Saskatoon in 1960. He received the Order of Canada in 1970.

December A group called Canadian Ecumenical Action, meeting in the basement of Chalmers United Church on Hemlock at West 12th Avenue, established the Greater Vancouver Food Bank Society in response to the needs of workers hit hard by a continent-wide recession that began in the late 1970s and continued into the early 1980s. The group included Reverend Val Anderson, later a member of the BC Legislature, and Sylvia Russell, first executive director of the Food Bank. Within a few months the Food Bank moved into its own warehouse and began distributing food each week through five depots, most in churches. Elsewhere in the Lower Mainland this year, the White Rock–South Surrey Food Bank began in a small room in a church basement, and the New Westminster and District Labour Council founded the Unemployment Action Centre to help unemployed people. Seeing that claimants often needed food, the Action Centre, with the help of local labour unions, established the New Westminster Food Bank.

December Peter Toigo's company Shato Holdings, which had run through a rough patch in the mid-1970s, had recovered enough to buy the White Spot restaurant chain.

Also in 1982

The Renfrew Trojans won the Canadian Junior Football League title...the first local junior team to win the championship since the Vancouver Blue Bombers took it in 1947. (The team has been the Vancouver Trojans since 1994, even though their home field today is the Burnaby Lake West Sports Complex.)

Hassan Khosrowshahi founded Future Shop in Vancouver, building it into Canada's biggest consumer electronics retailer before selling to Best Buy in November 2001. Khosrowshahi had fled to Canada with his family from his native Iran in 1979, when it was evident Ayatollah Khomeini would be taking over. Khosrowshahi stays out of the limelight, but his wife Nezhat is a major financial backer of the Vancouver Symphony Orchestra.

Vince Ready switched careers and began to work in private mediation and arbitration. The consensus from management and labour nearly 30 years later: he's the best, a man whose skill at arbitration has made him famous. Ready, born June 25, 1943, in Pembroke, ON, fibbed about his age to get a job in an Ontario mine at 15. He was a union organizer (Steelworkers) and troubleshooter for more than a decade. He does his present work calmly and thoughtfully, appealing to the best in people through hundreds of collective agreements and labour disputes.

Muni Evers' 13-year career as mayor of New Westminster ended after seven terms. Evers, a pharmacist, was first elected in 1969. When he announced his retirement, Evers told the *Royal City Record*: "I'm very satisfied with my term. I'm not saying I'm perfect, but I'm close to it." He was grinning when he said it, but the consensus was that he had been a very good mayor. Evers died in 2004.

The young Salish artist Susan Sparrow (now Susan Point) was guest of honour when the City of North Vancouver received its new coat of arms. Sparrow's representation of a salmon and a bear were embedded in the arms, and copies of her print featuring the two representations were presented to Lieutenant-Governor Henry Bell-Irving and to Conrad Swan, York Herald.

BC Children's Hospital was completed at West 28th Avenue and Oak Street at a cost of $60 million. It had 29,730 square metres (320,000 square feet) of space and 250 acute care beds, an adolescent unit, a modern isolation facility, a rehabilitation unit, a 10-bed psychiatric unit and a 60-bed special care nursery.

Hamilton McClymont stepped down as general manager of the Vancouver Opera Association to work on Expo 86. The VOA was $725,000 in debt when McClymont took over; he cut that debt in half during his term. In 1978 he convinced the VOA board not to sell the company's rehearsal/office building—and in 1982 BC Transit expropriated the building, which resulted in a capital fund of nearly $2 million.

EDAM (Experimental Dance and Music) was founded by seven young independent dancers who wanted to explore improvisation. By 1989, Peter Bingham, a pioneer of Contact Improvisation, remained as EDAM director. Other members had broken away on their own. Jay Hirabayashi and Barbara Bourget created Kokoro Dance, and Jennifer Mascall and Lola MacLaughlin set up eponymous companies. (MacLaughlin died in March 2009.)

Dal Richards, musically active since the 1930s, went into hotel management in the late 1960s. He recorded a pair of swing revival albums in 1982 and 1983...and they brought him back into the music biz with a bang. In 2011, at 93, Dal is *still* active.

Leonard Schein initiated the Vancouver International Film Festival.

Philip Borsos released his first feature film, *The Grey Fox*, about legendary train robber Bill Miner. It was a huge success, commercially and critically, and won seven Genies, including best picture and best director. It was also nominated for Best Foreign Film at the Golden Globes, and Richard Farnsworth, who played Miner, was nominated for a Golden Globes acting award.

Ron Stern and his partners sold *Vancouver Magazine* to Comac Communications. This publication had changed the face of magazine publishing in the city. It began in 1967 as Dick MacLean's *Greater Vancouver Greeter Guide*. In April 1974 MacLean was fired by owner Agency Press, and new editor Malcolm (Mac) Parry was hired. The first issue under his guidance featured five bylines—all of them Parry, in various disguises. Journalist Sean Rossiter joined Parry for the second issue, and for the next two years they produced most of the magazine's articles. When Agency Press pulled the plug on the magazine, Parry and Rossiter brought a group together to buy it. With Paul Grescoe as editorial director, Ron Stern as publisher and a strong lineup of writers (including Susan Musgrave, William Gibson and Jack Hodgins), the magazine gained a new lease on life.

Comings and Goings

Notable deaths: **Leonard Charles Marsh**, social scientist and UN welfare adviser, died in Vancouver on May 10, aged 75; **Tsutae Sato**, educator who ran the Japanese Language School from 1917 to 1942, died in Vancouver on May 23, aged about 91; **Harold H. "Torchy" Anderson**, *Province* reporter and editor, died on June 28 (his bright red hair earned him his nickname); **Margaret Grant Andrew**, arts activist and school trustee, in Vancouver on July 30, aged 70; **Clarence Wallace**, shipbuilder and former Lieutenant-Governor (1950–55), in Palm Desert, CA, on November 12, aged 89; **Allan McGavin**, UBC chancellor (1969–72), president of McGavin Toastmaster and active community volunteer, died December 8, aged 71.

Saskatchewan-born (1908) Sinclair Ross, best known for his 1941 novel *As For Me and My House*, moved to Vancouver. He mostly lived at the Brock Fahrni Pavilion, a new veterans' wing of the former Shaughnessy Hospital, and died in 1996, aged 88.

Writer Russell Kelly, born in Toronto in 1949, came to Vancouver. In 1986 he wrote *Pattison: Portrait of a Capitalist Superstar*, which sold more than 20,000 copies, and in 1991 he became editor of *BC BookWorld*. Kelly died of cancer in 1997.

1983

Much of the year was marked with labour strife as protests against provincial government actions built toward—and then stopped short of—a general strike. BC Place Stadium was opened and hosted its first Grey Cup, with the Lions losing. And the Vancouver Art Gallery moved to a new home in the old courthouse.

February 3
The first Earls restaurant opened in Vancouver.

It was named for Leroy Earl Fuller, who in 1954 opened his first restaurant in Sunburst, MT. The first Earls with that name opened in 1982 in Edmonton. There are now more than 60 restaurants in the chain throughout western Canada, southern Ontario, Arizona, Colorado and Washington state. And Earl is still with us as chairman of Earls Restaurants Ltd.

April 20 There was a large demonstration at city hall organized by ASP, the Alliance for the Safety of Prostitutes.

June 19 Premier Bill Bennett opened Canada's first domed stadium, the 60,000-seat BC Place. On June 20 the Vancouver Whitecaps soccer team defeated the Seattle Sounders in the inaugural event at the stadium. After BC Place opened, Empire Stadium fell into disuse and was demolished in 1993.

BC Place is open for business as home to the BC Lions, the Whitecaps and countless rock concerts, boat shows and other large events.
Peter Hulbert / The Province

June The Surrey Self-Help Society for the Under-Employed was formed after the Surrey Co-ordinating Centre, the United Way and other groups joined to address the growing problem of hunger in Surrey. Today the Surrey Food Bank Society helps about 13,000 residents of Surrey and North Delta monthly.

August 2 The *Province* newspaper came out for the first time in a tabloid format. Prior to this time it had been what in newspaper circles is called a broadsheet. The *Vancouver Sun* still is.

September 18 Joe Philliponi (born Filippone) was shot to death, aged 70. He was born January 1, 1913, in southern Italy and came to Vancouver in the early 1930s, where he started Eagle-Time Delivery Systems (1934), later acquiring taxicabs. In 1945 he opened the Penthouse dinner club at 1019 Seymour, presenting big names like Sammy Davis Jr. and George Burns. On December 31, 1975, the club was closed by the vice squad, and in 1977 Philliponi was convicted of living off the avails of prostitution, although the conviction was overturned later that year, and the club was licensed and operating again by 1979. Philliponi's murder was linked to a robbery attempt. Some 800 people attended his funeral, a crowd described as including "Supreme Court justices,

Elsewhere in BC

The Sechelt Festival of the Written Arts was established. Vancouver-born writer Betty Keller was the prime motivator of the first major annual literary festival in BC.

Robert Rogers, formerly chairman and CEO of the forest company Crown Zellerbach Canada (1975–82), was appointed Lieutenant-Governor.

Elsewhere in Canada

July 23 The Gimli Glider: Air Canada Flight 143 made an emergency landing in Gimli, MB.

December 23 Jeanne Sauvé was appointed Canada's first female Governor General.

The Canadian Radio-Television and Telecommunication Commission licensed pay television. The first licences went to a pair of movie networks—Superchannel and First Choice.

Elsewhere in the World

Military forces in El Salvador were brutally cracking down on citizens and many people fled. Nearly 3,000 came to Canada this year, thanks to a special refugee program for Salvadorans instituted by the federal government. Some settled in Vancouver.

Solidarity For a While

August 10 A Solidarity rally at Empire Stadium was attended by more than 40,000 public and private sector workers, who took the day off work to protest the government's restraint policy. Some background: in July, responding to the lingering recession, Bill Bennett's Social Credit government introduced 26 bills that did away with the provincial Human Rights Commission and Rentalsman, increased the government's control of school boards and colleges, cut back health services and enforcement of employment standards, extended wage controls indefinitely and gutted public sector collective agreements, eliminating workers' job security.

Public and private sector unions came together with social justice advocates and community activists to protest the legislation and fight for long-established rights that suddenly appeared tenuous. Led by Art Kube of the BC Federation of Labour; Renate Shearer, a human rights worker; and Father Jim Roberts, a Catholic priest, the Solidarity Coalition organized rallies and other events, including a "Stone Soup Luncheon" outside the home of Grace McCarthy, minister of human resources. In the legislature, MLAs endured all-night sittings as the government tried to force the legislation through, and NDP leader Dave Barrett was ejected for challenging the speaker.

On October 15, 60,000 protesters marched through the streets around the Hotel Vancouver, where the Social Credit Party was holding its convention. People began calling for a general strike, and by early November 35,000 government workers (members of the BC Government Employees Union) and most of BC's teachers were on strike. Employees at Crown corporations, ICBC and BC Ferries were to walk out next, then municipal workers and bus drivers, and finally health care workers.

But on November 13 the showdown between organized labour and the provincial government was averted by Jack Munro, head of the province's largest private sector union, the 40,000-member International Woodworkers of America. The BC Federation of Labour had planned to order the IWA out on strike, but Munro felt his membership alone was responsible for when it would choose to strike. (He later said that he "would be damned if he'd let community groups, feminists and church leaders make decisions about his members going on strike and losing wages.") Munro also felt that "if you call a general strike, you'd better be in good enough shape to win it—which means, basically overthrowing the government." In his view, the long, bitter confrontation ahead would result in economic losses harmful to both sides. The IWA leader headed a labour delegation that met with Premier Bennett in the premier's home in Kelowna and agreed to a package that included no reprisals against those who went on strike and vague promises of consultation. There would be no general strike.

businessmen and dancers." Two men were convicted of the murder, Scott Ogilvie Forsyth and Sydney Vincent Morrisroe. Both were jailed. Morrisroe was released from prison in 2003 after 19 years. Forsyth was granted full parole in April 2004.

October 15
The Vancouver Art Gallery moved into the old courthouse.

After a hugely successful fundraising campaign to "take the art gallery to court"—$8 million was raised, twice the intended target and more than any other arts organization had ever raised in the city—the new gallery now found itself in immensely larger and more attractive surroundings. The 1906 provincial courthouse, originally designed by Francis Rattenbury, was redesigned by Arthur Erickson's architectural firm, with Eva Matsuzaki the associate-in-charge. One excellent innovation: escalators. The gallery is the largest in western Canada, with nearly 8,000 works in its collection, valued at more than $100 million. This was also the year the gallery finally bought an Emily Carr painting. It had declined to earlier because, according to arts reviewer Tony Robertson,

Ronald McDonald House Opens

October 4 Ronald McDonald House opened in Vancouver at 4116 Angus Dr. in Shaughnessy. The three-storey renovated house had 13 bedrooms, a playroom, a fully stocked kitchen and more and was on a beautiful piece of land about 15 minutes from the Children's Hospital. Ron Marcoux, head of McDonald's in western Canada, officiated and helped Canadian prima ballerina Karen Kain cut the ribbon. (Ms. Kain happened to be in town with the National Ballet and quickly agreed to make an appearance.)

How it began: In 1973 Fred Hill, a linebacker with the Philadelphia Eagles, and his wife Fran were told their three-year-old daughter, Kimberly, had leukemia. The Hills took Kim to St. Christopher's Hospital for Children in Philadelphia. For the next few months they slept in chairs in Kim's room, ate out of vending machines and tried not to show sadness in front of her. Hill talked to his teammates and asked for help in raising funds, not just for Kim but for all kids whose parents needed help.

Out of that painful experience came the idea for Ronald McDonald House. (The McDonald's franchise owners in Philadelphia got behind the idea in a big way.) There are now more than 300 of these houses, described as homes-away-from-home for families with children undergoing life-saving treatments at nearby hospitals. Locally owned and controlled, and supported by donations from the community, they offer the children and their families a place to stay for a nominal overnight fee.

Ronald McDonald House BC continues to expand its services for families in need with plans to build a new house on the grounds of BC Children's Hospital that will serve 60 families.

Home-away-from-home. Ronald McDonald House, provided by a charity organization for families with seriously ill children undergoing medical treatment, opened in Vancouver in 1983. *Courtesy Ronald McDonald House*

The Ten-Thousand-Hand-Ten-Thousand-Eye Avalokitesvara Bodhisattva statue inspires awe at the Kuan Yin Buddhist Temple in Richmond, the first in North America built in the authentic Buddhist tradition. Avalokitesvara is the bodhisattva of infinite compassion (a bodhisatva being one who delays nirvana to seek enlightenment for others). *Sam Leung / The Province*

"It wasn't art as they understood art." Today the gallery boasts, proudly, that it holds the world's largest collection of paintings by Carr.

October 23 The Kuan Yin Buddhist Temple at 9160 Steveston Hwy. in Richmond was dedicated. It was the first architecturally authentic Buddhist temple in North America. The architect, Vincent Kwan, produced a building that has been called "the most exquisite example of Chinese palatial architecture in North America." Operated by the International Buddhist Society, the temple served regular attendees as well as being open to the general public for lectures, meditation classes and tea ceremonies.

October 29 The Terry Fox Library in Port Coquitlam was officially opened by Terry's parents, Betty and Rolly Fox. A commemorative plaque was unveiled, and a statue of Terry—created by George Pratt from Nelson Island granite—was unveiled.

November 13 It was announced that the old 1910 post office building and adjacent buildings at Hastings and Granville were to get a $40-million facelift. Effective November 14, they also got a new name, Sinclair Centre, chosen to honour prominent businessman James Sinclair of West Vancouver, a former Liberal MP and federal fisheries minister (and father of Margaret Trudeau).

November 15 In New Westminster the *Columbian*, BC's oldest newspaper (established in 1861), published its last edition. Growing costs and non-growing revenues forced it into bankruptcy after 122 years. One of its writers, Douglas Todd, moved to the *Vancouver Sun*, where he became an award-winning writer on religion and ethics.

November 22 A violent and costly riot erupted at the Lower Mainland Regional Correctional Centre (formerly Oakalla). Rioters caused over $150,000 damage in a two-day spree.

November 25 World light-heavyweight champ Michael Spinks, 27, kayoed Peru's Oscar Rivadeneyra in the Pacific Coliseum. This was a title fight for both the WBC and the WBA crowns.

November 27 In the first Grey Cup game played at BC Place Stadium, close to 60,000 fans watched the Lions lose a squeaker, 18–17, to the Toronto Argonauts. Coverage of the game by both CBC and CTV television, CBC Radio and French-language CBC attracted 8.1 million people, the largest audience in Canadian broadcast history for a Canadian sports program to that time.

Also in 1983

St. Paul's Hospital admitted its first AIDS patient, and AIDS Vancouver was founded. The latter was one of the first AIDS service organizations in Canada. Although the disease wasn't confined to gay men, news items and articles on AIDS had appeared in *The Body Politic*, Canada's leading gay news magazine, in September 1981.

Canada's first cochlear implant was performed at St. Paul's.

Construction was under way on Canada Place, which was to be the Canadian Pavilion at Expo 86. However, enthusiasm for the world's fair was tempered by nagging unemployment. Among other gloomy news came word that none of the five shipyards on the North Shore (Burrard Yarrows, Vancouver Shipyards, BelAire, Allied or Matsumoto) had any new shipbuilding contracts pending. Burrard Yarrows had just completed work on an icebreaker, the MV *Terry Fox*, but it was expected that

2,500 workers would be unemployed by July.

Ballantyne Pier, a cargo terminal on Vancouver's east side, was temporarily put into service for cruise passengers while Canada Place was under construction.

Dr. K. George Pedersen, who had been president of Simon Fraser University since 1979, became president of the University of British Columbia, succeeding Douglas Kenny, president since 1975. Pedersen served until 1985.

William Saywell took over from Pedersen at SFU. He was immediately faced with financial cutbacks—the "worst financial crisis for universities since the depression"—and responded with painful, painstaking tuition increases, program and staff cuts, salary rollbacks and hiring freezes.

Paul George and Adriane Carr founded the Green Party of British Columbia. George had founded the Western Canada Wilderness Committee in 1980.

The Pacific Bell, a gift to the University of British Columbia by the Japanese government, was made and presented to UBC by Masahiko Katori, a master craftsman who has constructed 105 bells, two of which are in North America. (The other, the Friendship Bell, is in San Diego.) The tower housing the bell is built of BC western yellow cedar—very similar to hiba, or Japanese yellow cedar. Its design dates back more than 800 years to the Kamakura period. Prefabricated in Japan and assembled here, the structure—built at an estimated cost of $80,000—is held together without a single nail, with the exception of the eaves and the roof. Its location was chosen by Mr. Katori while on a visit to UBC, with special attention to the acoustics of the site. Construction costs were high because UBC imported skilled tradesmen from Japan to assemble the structure. The three characters on the bell mean "Clear thoughts lead to a tranquil mind."

Mario Bernardi succeeded John Eliot Gardiner as principal conductor of the CBC Vancouver Orchestra. Bernardi, born in Kirkland Lake, ON, was best known for establishing and shaping the National Arts Centre Orchestra in Ottawa. He was at the helm of the orchestra until 2006.

Bryan Adams began his ascent to superstardom with the album *Cuts Like a Knife*.

The Phoenix Chamber Choir was formed by conductor Cortland Hultberg. It immediately established itself as one of the finest of Canada's choirs, winning first place in the Contemporary and Chamber Choir categories of the CBC choral competitions. In 1995 Hultberg was succeeded as artistic director by Ramona Luengen.

Simon Fraser University alumna Terri Nash won the Oscar for Best Documentary Short for *If You Love This Planet.* The 26-minute film presented a lecture Dr. Helen Caldicott, founding president of Physicians for Social Responsibility, had given to American students in 1981. In the film, Dr. Caldicott outlined the effects of detonating a single 20-megaton bomb.

The 225-seat Arts Club Revue Theatre opened with the show *An Evening with Ruth and Leon*, a concert of songs performed by local stars Leon Bibb and Ruth Nichol.

Salim Jiwa joined the *Province* as a reporter. He became known for his crime stories and for his coverage of the bombing of Air India Flight 182. He was also the inspiration for his colleague Don Hauka's two murder mysteries featuring Indo-Canadian detective Hakim Jinnah.

In Lions Bay two teenage boys died and five homes were destroyed or damaged when a debris torrent poured tons of mud and logs down Alberta Creek. The creek was later channelized with a concrete lining.

Comings and Goings

March 9 The Royal Yacht *Britannia* sailed into Vancouver with Queen Elizabeth and Prince Philip aboard. At BC Place the Queen, in an international hookup, invited the world to Expo 86. On this same voyage she initiated the first pour of concrete in the construction of Canada Place.

Notable deaths: **Jim Kinnaird**, president of the BC Federation of Labour, died in office in Vancouver on February 17, aged 50; **Bill Rea**, who had started CKNW Radio in 1944, died in Santa Barbara, CA, on April 4, aged 74; **Stanley E. Higgs**, Anglican minister who served overseas with the Royal Canadian Corps of Chaplains (1941–46) and as chaplain of Haney Correctional Institute (1960–68), died in Vancouver on April 16, aged about 79; **John Avison**, conductor of the CBC Vancouver Chamber Orchestra from its inception in 1938 to 1980, died in Vancouver on November 30, aged 69.

1984

Vancouver wrestled with the impact of the world's oldest profession as protests and bylaws moved prostitutes around the city. While another one-legged runner began a cross-country journey, a Terry Fox memorial at BC Place was widely panned. The stadium itself, meanwhile, showcased Billy Graham, Michael Jackson and his brothers, and the Pope.

February 3 Dal Richards Day.

Mayor Mike Harcourt proclaimed this day in tribute to the man who's been a Vancouver musical fixture since the 1930s.

March 28 A seven-week strike began at the *Vancouver Sun* and *Province* newspapers.

May 25 West End residents organized a "Shame the Johns" operation in an attempt to drive prostitutes' clients from the West End. However, most of their anger and attention was directed against the prostitutes themselves. The women did leave, but simply moved to other neighbourhoods: Mount Pleasant, Strathcona, Kensington–Cedar Cottage and Grandview–Woodlands. Concerned Residents of the West End (CROWE) was formed in the early 1980s to oust the streetwalkers. City council, led by Mayor Mike Harcourt, passed a street-activity bylaw, imposing fines up to $2,000. But like so many attempts to legally control prostitution, it failed to stick in the courts.

The journey continues. Steve Fonyo, inspired by Terry Fox, began his cross-Canada "Journey for Lives" in 1984 to raise funds and awareness for cancer, to which he'd lost his leg at the age of 12. *Gerry Kahrmann / The Province*

Elsewhere in Canada

March 31 Steve Fonyo, inspired by Terry Fox, began to run across Canada. Fonyo, a 19-year-old from Vernon who'd lost his leg to cancer at age 12, dipped his artificial leg into the Atlantic Ocean at St. John's, NL, then faced west. The journey took him 14 months, and it ended May 31, 1985, at the Pacific Ocean in Victoria. By then Fonyo had travelled 7,924 kilometres (4,925 miles), crossed 10 provinces and raised almost $9 million for cancer research, education and patient services, including $1 million pledged by the federal government. (More millions were to follow.) On the way he wore out six artificial legs and 17 pairs of running shoes. Fonyo wasn't as photogenic as Terry Fox, his personality wasn't as attractive, his run wasn't as well organized and his post-run life was marked with trouble with the law. But he did two extraordinary things: with only one leg he ran across the entire country, and he raised those pledges in the fight against cancer to more than $13 million.

June 16 John Turner succeeded Pierre Trudeau as leader of the Liberal Party and prime minister, beating Jean Chrétien on the second ballot at the Liberal leadership convention by about 500 votes. He lost the federal election to Brian Mulroney and the Progressive Conservatives on September 4 after less than three months in office.

November 1 The Supreme Court of Canada rendered a historically significant decision in the case of *Guerin v. the Queen*, in which Chief Guerin and other members of the Musqueam band successfully sued the federal government for $10 million in damages for the surrender and improper lease of 162 hectares (400 acres) of reserve land to the Shaughnessy Heights Golf Club. The court ruled that the federal government, namely the Department of Indian Affairs and its agents, could be held legally responsible for improprieties in their dealings with surrendered Indian lands when they clearly failed to act in the best interest of the Indian band.

In the House of Commons, Vancouver Member of Parliament Margaret Mitchell raised the issue of repaying the racist Chinese Head Tax for two of her constituents. The modern era Head Tax redress movement began. Many Chinese and groups lobbied for a refund of the head tax, and an apology, or formal acknowledgment, from the Government of Canada.

Elsewhere in the World

December 19 The signing of the Sino-British Joint Declaration mandating the return of Hong Kong to China in 1997 caused Hong Kong capital to start flowing into Vancouver.

The Olympic Games held in Sarajevo were the first in which athletes based in Vancouver won gold in totally separate sports. Lori Fung, Vancouver's first-ever gold medallist, was the winner in rhythmic gymnastics (this was the first time that sport was an Olympic event), and UBC medical student Hugh Pisher teamed with Quebecker Alwyn Morris to win the two-man, 1,000-metre kayak final.

Granville Island Brewery opens, catering to Vancouver's love of beer. The brewery boasts beer brewed locally and with a love for the craft, and it produces such delights as Island Lager, Winter Ale and Honey Lager. *Courtesy Granville Island Brewing*

May 26 Mae Garnett, senior court reporter, died in West Vancouver, aged about 109. Born in London, ON, about 1875, Garnett was a PR officer for CPR and then the Calgary Exhibition and Stampede before becoming a newspaper reporter for the *Albertan*, *Edmonton Bulletin*, *Vancouver News-Herald* and, finally, the *Vancouver Sun* in 1930. She retired in 1962 as the *Sun*'s senior court reporter. Garnett was one of the first female news reporters in western Canada and was also one of the first women to get a mortgage from Central Mortgage and Housing.

June 28 Official opening of the Granville Island Brewery, Canada's first microbrewery.

Granville Island's first beer, Island Lager, was brewed in traditional Pilsner style, "according to the Bavarian Purity Law of 1516."

June Former BC premier Dave Barrett started a talk-show stint on CJOR. He left in January 1987.

June 20 Christ Church Cathedral was occupied by 12 members of the Alliance for the Safety of Prostitutes who were protesting the Supreme Court injunction prohibiting soliciting west of Granville Street. Cathedral staff had been warned about the occupation a couple of days earlier, so they were ready for the protest and the resulting media attention. After the women held a press conference, the church was locked, with the women inside and their supporters and the media outside. Several parishioners stayed with the protesters in the church. Sunday services took place as usual, with the protestors attending the morning Eucharist. They gave a presentation to about 70 members of the congregation that afternoon, and the sit-in continued until noon on Monday. Neale Adams, Christ Church historian, wrote, "After a Eucharist and another press conference, the protesters left peacefully, holding balloons...[They] had made their points (to little avail, it turned out—the injunction was later upheld). The Cathedral, while not condoning prostitution, presented itself as a place of refuge and concern."

June 24 Masajiro Miyazaki, doctor and community activist, died in Kamloops, aged 84. He was born November 24, 1899, in Japan, and arrived in Vancouver in 1913. He took part in UBC's Great Trek and graduated from the university in 1925 but had to go to the US to study medicine because of Canadian laws restricting Japanese Canadians' entry into professions. Miyazaki practised osteopathic medicine in Vancouver until his 1942 internment in the Bridge River–Lillooet area, where he served as doctor for 1,000 internees. In 1945 the town of Lillooet petitioned for his release to replace the town's doctor, who had died. The Miyazakis rented the main floor of the Casper Phair home for use as a clinic, but he also made house calls, travelling through the area on horseback, by railway speeder or rowboat and on foot. After Japanese residents were legally able to buy property, Miyazaki bought the Phair house, donating it to the town as a heritage site in 1983. He was awarded Scouting's Medal of Merit in 1970, published his autobiography, *My Sixty Years in Canada*, in 1973, and became a member of the Order of Canada on April 20, 1977. His citation reads: "Retired osteopath who, over a period of 35 years, has given unselfish service to the residents of Lillooet, British Columbia, particularly those of Japanese and Indian backgrounds and who continues to serve his community in spite of ill health."

Vancouver musician Bryan Adams, winner of four Juno awards, solidifies his international popularity at a concert in Moscow. *PNG*

September 29 Richmond's Gateway Theatre opened at 6500 Gilbert Rd. It houses two theatres, an art gallery and a photo gallery. Each year the Gateway Theatre Society produces a season of professional productions and presents material geared toward a multicultural audience.

October 3 Angelo Branca, judge, died in Vancouver, aged 81. Angelo Ernest Branco was born March 21, 1903, in Mount Sicker, near Chemainus on Vancouver Island. He began practising law in Vancouver in 1926 and became a leading defence attorney, defending high-profile cases, including more than 60 murderers. "I lost only two," he said, "...to the hangman." In 1932 he became Canadian amateur middleweight boxing champion. Seven years later he was BC's youngest-ever Crown prosecutor. He was a BC Supreme Court judge from 1963 to 1966 and BC Court of Appeal judge from 1966 to 1978. Vancouver's Italian community erected a statue of Christopher Columbus on Clark Drive in his honour.

October 14 The new Danish Evangelical Lutheran Church (the "Evangelical" was later dropped) opened on Kincaid Avenue in Burnaby. A model ship was suspended from the ceiling in this replica of an 800-year-old Danish church, and the church bell was donated by the church of Skovshoved, north of Copenhagen in Denmark.

October Vancouver entrepreneur Edgar Kaiser Jr. became president and CEO of the Bank of British Columbia, and the bank raised $153 million through a private sale of shares and then a public offering. Also this year, bank chairman Trevor Pilley announced the bank would build a new head office at the northeast corner of Georgia and Hornby. It transformed the downtown. In 1985 the bank bought the assets of collapsed Pioneer Trust, and opened nine new branches in Alberta, Saskatchewan and Manitoba. In spite of the rosy outlook, however, the bank failed two years later and was taken over by the Hongkong Bank of Canada (HSBC).

November 12 Red Robinson's last day at CKWX after 27 years spinning rock 'n' roll records.

November The Cambie Street Bridge was closed to traffic so its new $50-million, six-lane replacement—the third in that location—could be built. It opened December 9, 1985.

December 5 Bryan Adams won four Juno Awards for his 1983 album *Cuts Like a Knife*, which made him an international star. His 1984 album, *Reckless*, was his best seller in the United States. That album also made Adams the first Canadian recording artist to sell 1 million albums within Canada.

Also in 1984

This was a worrisome year for Expo 86 officials as strikes delayed the pace of construction.

Meanwhile, landscape architect Don Vaughan brought together a large team made up of past associates and partners, among others, to tackle the largest landscape project in Vancouver's brief history: the site of the 1986 fair.

Diane Farris opened her first art gallery in Gastown. With an alert and discerning eye, she launched the careers of many West Coast artists, including Attila Richard Lukacs, Chris Woods, Angela Grossmann and Graham Gillmore, and represented such luminaries as Dale Chihuly, Phil Borges, Judith Currelly and Gu Xiong. She moved to a 604-square-metre (6,500-square-foot) location on West 7th in 1987, but closed that gallery and went online in 2011. In the here-today-gone-tomorrow world of the private art gallery, Diane Farris' longevity was astonishing.

Bill Reid's magnificent bronze killer whale was unveiled in the presence of Lt.-Gov. Robert Rogers at the entrance to the Vancouver Aquarium.

The Terry Fox Memorial, created by Franklin Allen, was unveiled at the east end of Robson Street, at BC Place Stadium. Public reaction was mostly negative. For one thing, there was no representation of Fox. The memorial was demolished in 2010 during the BC Place revitalization, and a new one, designed by Douglas Coupland, was completed in 2011.

The UBC bookstore opened its doors this year, replacing a much smaller shop. It covered 3,250 square metres (35,000 square feet) of selling space, and sold about 225 tonnes of books each year, or 4.5 million volumes. Course books made up about half that number.

The Douglas Kenny Building (named after the university's seventh president [1975–83]) opened on the UBC campus to house the psychology department. The Whaler's Pole outside the front entrance was designed and carved by the Nuu-chah-nulth people and depicts a harpooner, assistant whaler, shaman, Puk-Up and Grey Whale.

The Downtown Eastside Residents Association (DERA) established the DERA Co-Op at 638 Alexander St. Jim Green, DERA organizer, described it as "an outstanding example of community development. This co-op, in which 50 percent of members do not speak English and 50 percent are over 65, has never had staff. It is run entirely by its members, a powerful example of the abilities of low-income peoples." The co-op provided 56 completely wheelchair-accessible units.

Karim Rai, a student at McNair High School in Richmond, became the Canadian national debating champion.

Woodward's became the first major Vancouver department store to open on Sundays.

There was a recession under way in western Canada. One of the results: the largest Surrey tax sale list on

Killer sculpture. *Chief of the Undersea World* is one of Bill Reid's larger creations. It depicts an orca whale and was unveiled in 1984 at the entrance to the Vancouver Aquarium.
PNG

Pope John Paul II was the first pope to visit Vancouver. Judging by the crowds who came to see him, it was well worth the trip. Years later, in recognition of his historic visit and his beatification by the Catholic Church, Mayor Gregor Robertson declared May 1, 2011, to be "Blessed John Paul II Day in Vancouver." *Gerry Kahrmann / The Province*

record. A total of 633 properties went up for sale for delinquent taxes.

Park Place, one of the city's more attractive office buildings, opened for business at 666 Burrard, next to Christ Church Cathedral. Some years earlier the Anglican diocese had decided it could no longer afford to maintain the cathedral, the oldest surviving church in Vancouver, and planned to demolish it. A better solution was found in the transfer of unused density rights to the adjacent property to the north, where Park Place was built, which provided the diocese with cash for its social programs and maintenance of the building.

Sts. Nicholas and Dimitrios Church was built on Boundary Road to serve the growing Greek community in East Vancouver and Burnaby.

This was the last season for a while for soccer's Vancouver Whitecaps, and for its parent organization, the North American Soccer League. When the NASL folded, the Whitecaps—and other teams—also died. They were revived in 1986 as the 86ers...and become the Whitecaps again in 2001.

The *Tymac No. 2*, a water taxi built in 1938, which in the 1940s and '50s ran passengers from the foot of Columbia Street to Britannia Mines and to church camps and summer resorts around Howe Sound, became a False Creek ferry. It had a capacity of 24 passengers.

The Loewen Group of Burnaby acquired 14-hectare (34-acre) Victory Memorial Park cemetery. Its big white cross had been a landmark in the South Surrey–White Rock area since the late 1950s. By the mid-1990s Loewen Group was the second-largest publicly owned funeral corporation in North America, but in 1999 it filed for bankruptcy.

The Asia Pacific Foundation of Canada, an independent, non-profit organization headquartered in Vancouver, was established to enhance awareness and understanding among the peoples of Canada and the Asia Pacific region.

Comings and Goings

September 18–19

Pope John Paul II came to British Columbia as part of the first papal visit to Canada. Some 200,000 people came to see and hear the Pope speak at Abbotsford, and there was a capacity crowd of 65,000 at an evening event in BC Place.

October Evangelist Bill Graham spoke to 46,000 people at BC Place Stadium.

November 16

The Jackson Five—Michael Jackson and his brothers—performed the first of three shows at BC Place. It was the most successful entertainment event in Vancouver's history to that point, attracting more than 100,000 fans to BC Place and grossing nearly $5 million, a new Vancouver entertainment record for a three-night stand.

Notable deaths: **James Sinclair**, federal cabinet minister and Pierre Trudeau's father-in-law, died in West Vancouver on February 7, aged 75; **Bill Duthie**, book sales rep and bookseller, died on April 6, two days before his 64th birthday (the Bill Duthie Booksellers' Choice Award, awarded each year at the BC Book Prizes for the best book in terms of public appeal, initiative, design, production and content, was named for him, and the Bill Duthie Memorial Lecture is delivered annually at the Vancouver International Writers Festival); **Lorraine McAllister**, singer, actress and wife of bandleader Dal Richards, died on April 27, aged 62; **Everett Crowley**, Avalon Dairy founder and Collingwood neighbourhood activist, died on November 25, aged 75 (Ev Crowley Park on Southeast Marine Drive is named for him).

1985

Crowds cheered the success of Steve Fonyo's one-legged trek across the country, while Rick Hansen left in a wheelchair to circle the globe. And the Lions won the Grey Cup. But amid the celebrations, a bomb placed on an Air India flight leaving Vancouver resulted in the country's worst mass murder, a case that would haunt the justice system for decades.

January Hall's Prairie School in South Surrey celebrated its 100th anniversary.

Man in Motion

March 21 Rick Hansen began his Man in Motion tour to the cheers of a crowd at Oakridge Mall in Vancouver. Rick's target: to travel around the world by wheelchair, covering 40,075.16 kilometres (24,902.7 miles), equal to the circumference of the earth.

Rick had been grievously injured in June 1973 when a truck he'd hitched a ride on overturned. He was a paraplegic at 15, a kid with, in his own words, "three obsessions: fishing, hunting—and sports. Always sports. If you could throw it, hit it, bounce it, chase it or run with it, I wanted to play it. And usually I could do it pretty well." He had just been named his school's athlete of the year, so the long, painful stretch of rehab that followed his accident was also sometimes angry and self-pitying. Then Rick got into wheelchair sports. And then he met Terry Fox, whose heroic Marathon of Hope—and the millions it raised for cancer research—inspired Rick. He became an activist and conceived of the Man in Motion Tour as a means to raise funds for research into spinal cord injury but also to raise public awareness about people with disabilities.

Rick's journey ended successfully on May 22, 1987, to the cheers of thousands at Oakridge, where it had started 26 months earlier. Today the Rick Hansen Foundation continues to raise money for research: over $200 million to date.

Rick Hansen kicked off his Man in Motion world tour in 1985 to raise funds and awareness for spinal cord injuries, showing that his accidental paralysis was no handicap.
PNG

Elsewhere in BC

Whistler, with a 1985 population of 6,000 people, got a cemetery.

Elsewhere in Canada

February 10 Bryan Adams, his song-writing partner Jim Vallance and producer David Foster co-wrote "Tears Are Not Enough," which was recorded today at an all-star session to raise funds for Canada's aid-to-Ethiopia campaign.

September 25 The Royal Tyrrell Museum of Palaeontology opened in Drumheller, AB.

November 27 In a terrific sports year marked by many national titles (see right) won by local athletes, the biggest prize of all was gained when the BC Lions won the 1985 Grey Cup, defeating Hamilton Ti-Cats 37–24 at Olympic Stadium in Montreal. The street in front of the football club's Whalley headquarters was renamed Lions Way.

The federal government passed Bill C-31, which eliminated discriminatory provisions of the Indian Act. In particular, it ended the practice of removing Indian status from Native women who married non-Native men, or automatically transferring Native women who married a member of another band to the husband's band. It also gave Native bands the right to set their own membership rules.

Elsewhere in the World

Some of the other metro Vancouver sports achievements this year: North Vancouver's **Linda Moore** skipped her team to the world women's curling championship in Jonkoping, Sweden, becoming the first BC women's rink to accomplish that feat (March 22); **Michael Olajide Jr.** won the Canadian middleweight boxing title over Winnipeg's Wayne Caplette (April 10); **Jennifer Wyatt** of Richmond, **Patty Grant** of Mission and Beach Grove's **Joli Pereszlenyi** defeated a team from Ontario to take the Canadian amateur women's golf championship (August 21); the Vancouver Canadians won baseball's Pacific Coast League title, the first for the city after 20 years of trying (September 10); Burnaby runner **Lynn Williams** won the Fifth Avenue Mile in New York City (September 28); **Vancouver Croatia** won the six-team Canadian senior soccer championship over Montreal (October 14); the **BC rugby team** defeated Ontario 31–11 to take the national crown for the third year in a row (October 20); Richmond's **Dave Barr** and Dan Halldorson of Brandon, MB, teamed up to win the World Cup team golf tournament in La Quinta, CA (November 24).

May 27–29
More than 20,000 people greeted Steve Fonyo for a nationally televised event at BC Place Stadium.

Fonyo was very near the end of his cross-Canada run, a trek inspired by Terry Fox. He paused at Terry Fox Plaza to place a single white rose beside the memorial arch before walking into the stadium and crossing a giant map of Canada. Just after midnight he was on a Canadian navy ship bound for Victoria and the May 29 finish at newly named Fonyo Beach. At 4:15, in a pelting rain, he poured into the Pacific Ocean the water he had collected from the Atlantic 14 months earlier.

Air India Flight 182

June 23 Canada's worst case of mass murder occurred when a bomb hidden in a suitcase aboard Air India Flight 182 exploded in the plane's forward cargo hold as it approached the coast of Ireland. Everyone on board—329 people, including 82 children—was killed. Most of them (280) were Canadian citizens of East Indian descent. The suitcase had been transferred to the flight from an airplane that had left Vancouver International Airport a few hours earlier.

Less than an hour later, a second suitcase exploded. This one was at Narita Airport in Japan and killed two baggage handlers. It had been put on an airplane in Vancouver and was about to be transferred to an Air India plane leaving Tokyo for Bangkok. In 1991 Inderjit Singh Reyat was convicted of two counts of manslaughter as well as explosives charges for the Narita Airport bombing. He was sentenced to 10 years in jail.

Members of a militant Sikh group were suspected of the bombings, but it was 18 years before Inderjit Singh Reyat pleaded guilty to one count of manslaughter and was sentenced to five years for manufacturing the bomb on Air India Flight 182. Two other men accused of that bombing were tried in 2003–4 but acquitted for lack of evidence. In January 2011 Inderjit Singh Reyat was found guilty of perjury at their trial and sentenced to another nine years. The Canadian government finally apologized to the families of the victims in 2010 after an official inquiry found a "cascading series of errors" had led to the bombing and subsequent fruitless efforts to catch the perpetrators.

June 8 Blanche Macdonald (née Brillon) died in Vancouver, aged 54. A housewife and mother of two, she opened a modelling agency and self-improvement school in 1960, later expanding into fashion, esthetics and makeup artistry training. Macdonald launched a journalism program for Native students and was a founding member of Vancouver's First Woman's Network and a board member of the Better Business Bureau, Modeling Association of America, Professional Native Woman's Association and Vancouver Indian Centre. In 1985 she received the YWCA Woman of Distinction Award for Business and the Professions.

June 17 The Mess Hall of the World War II military base at Point Atkinson in West Vancouver reopened as Phyllis Munday House, a Nature House for use by the West Vancouver Girl Guides. Phyllis Munday, a well-known mountaineer, had had a lifelong association with the Guide movement.

June 20 One of the most remarkable men in our local history, Dr. Gordon Shrum, died in Vancouver, aged 89. A graduate of the University of Toronto, Shrum was the head of the UBC physics department from 1938 to 1961 and dean of graduate studies from 1956 to 1961. Forced to retire at age 65, Shrum instead took on projects for the provincial government, co-chairing the BC Power and Hydro Authority (1961–72), serving as the first chancellor of Simon Fraser University (1962–68) and pushing through construction of its campus in 18 months, overseeing construction or redevelopment of the Vancouver Museum/Planetarium complex, the courthouse and the waterfront convention centre. He was awarded the OBE in 1946 and was inducted into the Order of Canada in 1967.

August 2
The flame at the Stanley Park war memorial commemorating the Japanese Canadian contribution during World War I was relit.

It had been extinguished since December 8, 1941. Masumi Mitsui, now 98, one of two surviving Japanese Canadian soldiers who had served Canada so bravely during the Great War and then been forced from his home and interned during World War II, was brought in to turn the light on again. Mr. Mitsui died in 1987, five months short of his 100th birthday, and one year before Ottawa issued an official apology to Japanese Canadians for the injustices done them during World War II.

October 30 To mark Orpheum Theatre manager Ivan Ackery's 86th birthday, the lane behind the theatre was titled Ackery Alley as a tribute to the master showman.

November 3 Nan Cheney, portrait painter and UBC's first medical artist, died at 88. Anna Gertrude Lawson Cheney was born June 22, 1897, in

Windsor, NS. She enjoyed a close relationship with Emily Carr in the period before Carr's work gained fame. The letters the two women exchanged have been collected in *Dear Nan: Letters of Emily Carr, Nan Cheney and Humphrey Toms*, edited by Doreen Walker.

December 9 The third, and present, Cambie Street Bridge opened today. The first bridge at this location, a two-laner built in 1891, cost $12,000. The second (actually the Connaught Bridge, named for the Governor General at the time), with four lanes, opened in 1912 and cost $740,000. The third cost $50 million—some 4,167 times the cost of the first. Mayor Mike Harcourt officiated at this opening with a very special guest of honour. Isabelle Duff-Stuart had been the child who presented flowers to the Duchess of Connaught at the opening of the preceding bridge 73 years earlier.

December 11 SkyTrain began running from Vancouver to New Westminster. During December it ran only on weekends, offering free rides. The *Province*'s Don Hauka spoke to Kyla Daman-Willems, one of the line's 81 attendants. "It's very exciting to be involved in something from the time it was on paper to when it goes into operation," she told him. "I just can't wait to see what happens. Everyone's dying to see it carry passengers and do what it was designed to do."

December 31 The runaway winner of the award for Canadian Newsmaker of the Year? Steve Fonyo. According to the newspapers, the amputee runner from Vernon "easily out-distanced Prime Minister Brian Mulroney in the balloting for top Canadian newsmaker by the country's newspaper, radio and television editors." Fonyo, 20, said he was "shocked" by the news. He didn't realize he'd made so many headlines during his Journey for Lives.

It's a go! The SkyTrain, light rapid transit with a sonically unique three-toned startup rev, began regular service between Vancouver and New Westminster in 1986. Vancouver Sun

Also in 1985

L.R. "Bunny" Wright published her first mystery novel, *The Suspect*, set on the Sunshine Coast and featuring RCMP officer Karl Alberg. It won the 1986 Edgar Award for best novel. She went on to publish eight more books featuring Alberg and became Canada's leading female author of mysteries. Born in Saskatoon in 1939 and raised in Abbotsford, she left a newspaper job in Mission to work for major newspapers in the prairies. In 1979 she received the Alberta First Novel Award for *Neighbours*, and she published three more literary novels, but her greatest success came with mysteries. Wright, who lived in Vancouver, died in 2001.

John Bishop started his now-famous restaurant at 2183 West 4th. He opened it in the middle of a recession but it didn't seem to matter: people came anyway. "We let the ingredients tell us what to cook," Bishop said. "A supplier brings in a load of razor clams, and they become our evening special. Someone picks a bunch of elderberry blossoms from a tree growing wild, and their distinctive fragrance inspires a sauce. Blackberries come into season, and we consider the possibilities of using them different ways, perhaps in a meat dish. That's the fun of running a small restaurant."

George Pedersen, president of UBC, resigned to protest cuts in government funding. He was succeeded by Robert H.T. Smith, who served very briefly before David Strangway took over. He would remain in the position until 1997. Strangway's tenure at UBC was marked by success in fundraising, which sparked a leap forward in the university's research. Dr. Strangway was born June 7, 1934, in Simcoe, ON, and spent his childhood in Angola. He received a PhD in physics from the University of Toronto in 1960 and 10 years later joined NASA as chief of the Geophysics Branch, responsible for the geophysical aspects of the Apollo missions. In 1972 he was awarded NASA's Exceptional Scientific Achievement Medal, "given for an exceptional scientific contribution toward achieving the NASA mission." He worked for the University of Toronto before coming to UBC.

A study of pollution in the Fraser River estuary resulted in the Fraser River Estuary Management Program (FREMP), which brought together federal, provincial and regional

Fantasy world. Before becoming premier of British Columbia, Bill Vander Zalm opened Fantasy Gardens, designed like a medieval village around extensive and well-kept gardens. *Rick Loughran / The Province*

agencies that set environmental policy, enforced regulations and managed the the land and water around the river. The aim was to to protect and improve environmental quality, provide economic development opportunities and sustain the quality of life in and around the Fraser River estuary. Another benefit: the public now had access to kilometres of walking trails along the river's channels, islands and rich tidal backwaters.

Lynn Headwaters Regional Park was created, making 4,685 hectares (11,580 acres) of watershed suddenly accessible to hikers. The rugged wilderness park offered 40 kilometres (25 miles) of marked and backcountry trails in North Vancouver's backyard.

The 23-kilometre-long (14-mile) BC Parkway began linking about 30 parks, paralleling the SkyTrain route between downtown Vancouver and New Westminster.

The Strathcona Community Garden was established at Campbell Avenue and Prior Street, one of many vibrant community gardens in the city.

Wallace "Wally" Oppal, an Indo-Canadian, was appointed to the BC Supreme Court.

The BC Packers cannery at Steveston canned more salmon this year—11 million kilograms (24 million pounds), with a further 5.5 million kilos (12 million pounds) frozen—than all the Steveston canneries together in the boom year of 1901 (7.25 million kilos/16 million pounds).

The last mill on Granville Island, a vestige of the island's industrial past, shut down.

A dwarf-tossing contest at the Flamingo Hotel in the Whalley neighbourhood of Surrey led to newspaper stories and comment all over North America.

Former Surrey mayor and MLA Bill Vander Zalm and his wife, Lillian, began transforming Bota Gardens, which they had bought in 1984, into Fantasy Gardens, complete with biblical theme park and miniature railway. In 1987 they added a castle, which became their home. The castle, a replica of one in the Netherlands near the ancestral home of Captain George Vancouver, was donated to the people of Vancouver by the city of Coevorden for Expo 86. The Vander Zalms bought it for an undisclosed amount after the fair was over.

The Royal Vancouver Yacht Club acquired colourful Wigwam Inn at the north end of Indian Arm. It was built in 1906 by Vancouver realtor Gustav Constantin "Alvo" von Alvensleben as a resort for his moneyed friends. He opened it with a lavish party for 600. It changed hands several times and was once raided by the RCMP as a gambling casino. Among its many guests were John D. Rockefeller and John Jacob Astor.

A small company called TheatreSpace, led by artistic director Joanna Maratta, produced the first annual Vancouver Fringe Festival, described as "a non-juried performing arts smorgasbord." The festival provided venues, technical support and publicity, and anyone who wanted to put on a show could do so. It has become an annual event and a September ritual.

Comings and Goings

Hugh Pickett, the grand old man of entertainment in Vancouver, officially retired at age 72 from Famous Artists, the firm he began in 1947. (Pickett died February 13, 2006, aged 92.)

Notable deaths: **Frederick Soward**, "boy wonder" of UBC's history department, who taught there from 1922 to 1966, headed the department (1953–63) and served as dean of graduate studies (1961–65), died on January 1, age 86; **Thomas Moore Whaun**, ad man for two of Vancouver's Chinese newspapers and Chinese activist, died March 5, aged 91; **Sydney John Risk**, actor, teacher and founder of Everyman Theatre, the first professional company in western Canada, died in Vancouver on September 5, aged 77; **Neville Scarfe**, the founding dean of the Faculty of Education at UBC, died October 8, aged about 78.

1986

Vancouver celebrated its centennial at the Expo 86 world's fair, a six-month party that had a lasting impact on the city's development and self-confidence. Controversy over displacing the poor provided a lesson that eventually helped the city host the Winter Olympics. Bill Vander Zalm became premier and Gordon Campbell became mayor. And SkyTrain started carrying commuters.

January 3 SkyTrain commenced regular operation between Vancouver and New Westminster, following the same route through Burnaby as the old interurban tramline. The inauguration of rapid transit sparked an influx of residents and businesses in South Vancouver and Burnaby, echoing the original settlement of the area. Along the line just east of Central Park, newly opened Metrotown Centre mushroomed to include high-rise apartments, multiple-dwelling complexes, office towers and a huge shoppers' destination. In 1989 the line was extended to Surrey, and in 2002 to East Vancouver and North Burnaby. The Canada Line, which runs through South Vancouver to the airport, opened in time for the 2010 Winter Olympics.

February 19 The Lions Gate Bridge was illuminated, a gift from the Guinness family, who built the bridge.

February VanCity Savings Credit Union launched the country's first socially responsible mutual fund—the Ethical Growth Fund (now known as Ethical Funds Inc., a nationally based entity). The fund has investment guidelines based on ethical principles—it cannot, for example, invest in companies that manufacture weapons or tobacco products, and all companies with which it invests must maintain good labour relations and high environmental standards.

April 6 The City of Vancouver celebrated its 100th birthday.

Elsewhere in BC

May 22 BC Premier Bill Bennett announced his retirement after 10 years as premier of BC. He was succeeded August 6 by Bill Vander Zalm, who won a provincial election on October 22, nine days after Expo 86 ended, winning 47 seats over the 22 held by Bob Skelly's NDP.

Adnan Khashoggi, then known as the world's richest man, popped up this year as a director of a VSE-listed company, Skyhigh Resources Ltd. Its shares went from 60 cents to $72 before evaporating. This was one of the events that caused Vancouver's stock market to be viewed with derision and suspicion elsewhere.

BC's population topped 3 million this year. It had reached 1 million in 1951, 2 million in 1968.

Victoria beat Vancouver's record of 28 straight days of rain this year with 33 days straight!

Elsewhere in Canada

The United Church of Canada was the first institution to apologize for the treatment of Native children at residential schools.

Elsewhere in the World

January 28 The space shuttle *Challenger* broke apart 73 seconds after launch. All seven crew members were killed.

September 25 Activist Darshan A. Sangha, also known as Darshan Singh Canadian, was murdered in Punjab, India, aged about 69. He was born in 1917 in Langeri in the Punjab and came to Canada as a young man. In 1942 he was the first person in the Sikh community to be drafted. As an organizer for the International Woodworkers of America, he fought for the rights of BC's East Indian woodworkers. After 11 years in Canada, he returned to India in 1948. He represented the Communist party for three terms in the Punjabi state legislature. After speaking out against Sikh extremism, he was murdered by unknown attackers.

Debbie Brill won gold in the high jump at the 1986 Commonwealth Games in Edinburgh. She had won gold as a 17-year-old at the same games in Edinburgh in 1970, and again in Brisbane, Australia, in 1982. To win gold in three attempts over 16 years was an astonishing achievement.

It marked the special year by hosting Expo 86, which opened May 2. Under the direction of Vancouver businessman Jimmy Pattison, construction finished one month before opening day and was $8 million under budget.

May 7 West Fraser Timber was incorporated. The company started in 1955 when three brothers—Henry, William and Samuel Ketcham—purchased a small planer mill in Quesnel. In 2006 it became the second-largest lumber producer in North America.

May 28 Members of the Vancouver Fire Department celebrated a "Century of Service" to the citizens of the City of Vancouver.

July 18 Gordon Gibson Sr., lumberman and politician, died in West Vancouver, aged 81. Born November 28, 1904, at Goldbottom Creek, YT, Gibson left school at 12 to work in fishing and logging and was nicknamed "The Bull" as a young man. In 1939 he and his father and three brothers started three logging companies. He was elected Liberal MLA for Lillooet in 1952 and was later elected in North Vancouver. He had a stormy political career, once accusing Premier W.A.C. Bennett of thinking he was God, and he was almost single-handedly responsible for exposing scandal in 1955, accusing Robert Sommers, the forests minister, of accepting "considerations" from large forest companies in return for granting cutting rights. In the end, Sommers was sent to jail—the first time a cabinet minister in the British Commonwealth was jailed for misconduct in office—and reforms were instituted.

July 19 Westminster Quay Public Market opened. Historic boats and buildings reminded shoppers of the area's century and a half of maritime history. On the North Shore, Lonsdale Quay opened this year as well to help revitalize the Lower Lonsdale area of North Vancouver.

September 22 The Alex Fraser Bridge opened, crossing the main channel of the Fraser River to link Delta with Lulu Island. When it opened, the 930-metre (3,050-foot)

The Province
YOUR EXPO PAPER
Vancouver, B.C.
Friday, May 2, 1986
35 cents
60 cents minimum outside Lower Mainland

IT'S ALL YOURS!

Gates open today at the world's fair
Page 3

EXPO RAVES
Page 31
Quebec pop star Veronique Beliveau sings for the royal couple tomorrow.
Page 51
Sunday and Monday evenings opera diva Kiri Te Kanawa performs with VSO.
Page 55
VERONIQUE
All the events
Pages 63-70

CROWDS SWOON
Pages 4, 5
Where to see royals
Pages 26-28
Prince Charles and Princess Diana flank Premier Bill Bennett as their ferry approaches Canada Place in Vancouver harbor yesterday.
Staff photo by Gerry Kahrmann

Royal touch. The Prince and Princess of Wales, Charles and Diana, grace the opening of Expo 86 in Vancouver, kicking off the fair and placing Vancouver on the world stage.
The Province

Expo 86: The World Comes to Vancouver

May 2 Expo 86 began, officially opened by Prince Charles and Princess Diana and by Michael Conway Baker's "Expo Fanfare." A retired couple who had driven their trailer from Newfoundland clicked through the turnstile to become Expo's first visitors. Over the next six months, 22,111,600 more people came through the gate, a huge success.

Some 54 countries participated, along with 10,000 journalists from 60 countries. Americans raved. Royalty and heads of state appeared regularly. Innovative provincial and international pavilions drew steady crowds, and for the first time China, the Soviet Union and the United States exhibited together at a North American fair. Audiences grew hushed during performances of "Spirit Lodge" and sang along with international stars of opera, rock, jazz and country music. Visitors travelled around the extensive Burrard Inlet site by boat and the brand-new SkyTrain, and sampled world cuisines at the many restaurants.

Ironically, the only consistently sour notes came from eastern Canada. Robert Fulford, writing for *Saturday Night*, found Expo 86 a dream that never came true. And as Jim Green of the Downtown Eastside Residents Association made clear, Expo was destructive for Vancouver's poorest citizens: "One thousand people were evicted from their homes. Eleven people died in the first month of the evictions including Olaf Soldheim who, according to the city's Medical Health Officer, died as a direct result of being evicted from his residence of 62 years...Networks and social relations were destroyed that to this date have never been rebuilt. Expo could have been a great opportunity for the community if it had offered opportunities to leverage people from welfare into working on the Expo site. There was no attempt to do this."

For many the event that captured the heart and soul of Expo 86 was the July 27 final performance of the World Drum Festival, when 140 percussionists from 17 nations—from Inuit with caribou drums to Indonesian gamelan orchestra and American drumset player Steve Gadd—played to standing ovations.

Expo 86's legacy is still visible in Greater Vancouver and farther afield, primarily in Science World (housed in what was the Expo Centre), Canada Place (formerly the Canada Pavilion), BC Place Stadium, SkyTrain's Expo line and annual dragon boat races in False Creek.

bridge with a total span of 465 metres (1,525 feet) was the longest cable-stayed bridge in the world. Originally the six-lane deck was restricted to four lanes, the outer lanes being reserved for cyclists and pedestrians. In about a year the bridge had generated sufficient traffic to justify opening all six lanes to vehicles. Pedestrians and cyclists were moved outside the cables.

September City council adopted the Vancouver Heritage Register (formerly the Vancouver Heritage Inventory), a listing of buildings, streetscapes, landscape resources (parks and landscapes, trees, monuments, public works) and archeological sites that have architectural or historical heritage value. The city's Heritage Management Plan was established as the blueprint for identifying, conserving and raising awareness of Vancouver's heritage.

October 12

A record 341,806 visitors showed up for one last visit on Expo's second-last day (120,000 was a daily average).

October 13 Expo 86 closed. Attendance at the exposition, originally projected to reach 14 million, topped 22 million.

November 27 The Hongkong Bank of Canada—a wholly owned subsidiary of HSBC Holdings (based in London, England)—announced it had bought the assets and liabilities of the Bank of BC, which was failing. The transaction was aided by a $200-million cash injection from the Canada Deposit Insurance Corp., to protect the Hongkong Bank from future losses resulting from acquiring the Bank of BC's assets. The purchase gave the small Vancouver-based Hongkong Bank, which had received its federal charter on July 1, 1981, an additional $2.6 billion in assets and 41 branches in BC and Alberta, making it the ninth largest bank in Canada. The Hongkong Bank of Canada is known today as HSBC Bank Canada.

December 8 Chung Chuck, potato farmer, died in Ladner, aged about 88. He was born ca. 1898 in China, came to Vancouver at age 13 and farmed with his father. He worked as a CPR labourer, then farmed near Ladner's Delta Dike. In the 1930s, when the BC Coast Vegetable Marketing Board instituted measures to squelch Chinese farmers, Chung and another Ladner farmer, Mah Lai, appealed to the Supreme Court. In January 1937 the Judicial Committee of the Privy Council in England, at the time the highest court of appeal for Canada, ruled the laws invalid. White farmers protested "unfair Chinese competition" and blocked Vancouver bridges. Chung attempted to cross, was attacked and later charged seven men with assault. He knew his legal rights, and he fought for them.

Left: The Alex Fraser Bridge spans the Fraser River at 465 metres (1,525 feet) in length, which at the time was the longest cable-stayed bridge in the world. Vancouver Sun

Also in 1986

Former realtor and businessman Gordon Campbell became mayor of Vancouver, succeeding Mike Harcourt, who left to become the leader of the provincial NDP. Campbell served two terms, during which "civic government worked more closely with development than community interests," according to historian Donna Jean MacKinnon. At the end of his second term in 1993, Campbell became leader of the provincial Liberal party and was premier from 2001 to 2011.

Richmond's population was 96,154, up from 26,000 in 1956. At that time, 60 percent of the city's residents were of British descent. Now the number of people claiming British heritage had fallen to 27 percent, while those of Chinese descent made up 8 percent of the population, and 5.6 percent had an Indo-Pakistani heritage.

A study showed that Vancouver's Kerrisdale neighbourhood was one of the most affluent in North America. Average household income in Kerrisdale was $59,474, nearly twice the $32,403 average for Vancouver city.

The Vancouver Canucks incorporated the Canuck Foundation, their community fundraising organization. Renamed Canucks for Kids Fund in 2002, it has raised more than $18 million and since 1995 has administered Canuck Place, the children's hospice.

Vancouver feature-film pioneer Larry Kent cast local broadcasting legend Jack Webster as a television anchorman in *High Stakes*, an action-comedy about newsgathering and a lost Nazi treasure.

Impresario Hugh Pickett received the Order of Canada. Recipients are commonly nominated by their friends, co-workers and so on. The committee in charge of selecting the honourees was startled, in Pickett's case, to receive recommendations from close friends such as Marlene Dietrich, Lillian Gish, Mitzi Gaynor, Katharine Hepburn, Ginger Rogers, Leontyne Price, Carlos Montoya, Sir Laurence Olivier, Vincent Price, Phyllis Diller and others.

The exquisite Dr. Sun Yat-sen Classical Chinese Garden opened in Vancouver's Chinatown. The architect was Joe Wai, and the garden was designed by specialists brought from China. It re-created the retreat of a scholar of the Ming Dynasty and was based on a prototype in Suzhou, China's City of Gardens.

The Dr. Sun Yat-Sen Classical Chinese Garden is an oasis for quiet contemplation in the midst of busy downtown Vancouver. Vancouver Sun

City Shapes: Vancouver Centennial Sculpture Symposium 86 took place during the summer in Vanier Park, organized by the Sculptors' Society of British Columbia, endorsed by the Vancouver Centennial Commission and funded by the federal Department of Culture and Communications. The legacy: 10 sculptures were created and dispersed throughout Vancouver. One of them, *Anchor* by Christel Fuoss-Moore, is near the west end of the pedestrian path along Spanish Banks. It metaphorically marks the spot where Spanish explorer Don José Maria Narváez dropped anchor in 1791. He was the first European to see the future site of the city of Vancouver.

Kevin Head, a student at Emily Carr College of Art and Design, was commissioned to create a life-sized bronze statue of Walter Draycott, the "father of Lynn Valley" and author of *Early Days in Lynn Valley*, who had died in 1985 at age 102. Draycott called himself "Your Ancient Scribe," which is also the name of the statue, located in Pioneer Park, at Lynn Valley Road and Mountain Highway.

Summerland-born Alan Storey created what is easily the most well-known kinetic sculpture in Vancouver: *Pendulum* is a big and hypnotic feature of the 995 West Georgia HSBC Building atrium. Oddly, when he conceived the piece the artist wasn't thinking of a pendulum but of "a column that could break free of its base."

The *Centennial Rocket* sculpture was installed in a plaza at the southwest end of the Cambie Street Bridge, a gift of the Vancouver Transportation Club and the Sheet Metal Workers Union 280. It was a replica of an earlier sculpture that graced Local 280's float in the PNE Jubilee Parade for Vancouver's 50th birthday in 1936 and then was installed at the Vancouver airport from 1939 to 1972, when it was scrapped. The Vancouver

Transportation Club decided to build a replica for the city's 100th birthday. It located Lew Parry, who'd designed the original rocket and still had the plans. Terminal Sheet Metal and Local 280 members used more durable materials to build the new ship, and it was exhibited at Expo 86, then donated to the city. A centennial time capsule in the base of the rocket will be opened in 2036.

The 1888 CPR Roundhouse in Yaletown was restored, another Vancouver Centennial project. Engine 374, which pulled the first CPR passenger train into Vancouver in May 1887, was also restored and sits proudly within a portion of the roundhouse.

Yet another centennial project was the creation of 100 oval plaques that described historic events, concentrated in Chinatown, Gastown and downtown areas. Many plaques have been placed well up the sides of buildings to prevent theft.

A few of the centennial books that appeared include *Vancouver: An Illustrated Chronology*, by Chuck Davis and Shirley Mooney (sponsored by the Vancouver Board of Trade, this book looked at the city's events in chronological order from its earliest days to 1986); *A Century of Service: Vancouver Police 1886–1986*, by retired Vancouver Police staff sergeant Joe Swan; *Centennial of Vancouver Jewish Life: 1886-1986*, by Cyril Leonoff and published by the Jewish Historical Society of British Columbia.

The Saltwater City exhibition opened at Vancouver's Chinese Cultural Centre. Curated by Paul Yee, the exhibit celebrated 100 years of Chinese Canadian history in Vancouver and inspired Yee's book *Saltwater City: The Chinese in Vancouver*, which won the inaugural Vancouver Book Award in 1989.

The Vancouver Police Centennial Museum was opened—its appropriate location the old Coroner's Court Building at 240 East Cordova. The museum, created to commemorate the centennial of the city's police force, has many grimly fascinating exhibits, from wanted posters to a forensic pathology exhibit of a preserved larynx fractured by a fatal karate chop. Errol Flynn's body was once stretched out here, and there was a crime scene re-creation of the still-unsolved 1953 Babes in the Woods murder.

The original White Spot restaurant on Granville Street, opened in June 1928, was destroyed by fire.

The city stopped selling plots at Mountain View Cemetery. There are 90,000 graves there, many at double depth to hold two deceased, and the cemetery is spread over 42.5 hectares (105 acres) west of Fraser between 31st and 41st Avenues. In Burnaby, Ocean View Cemetery's mausoleum underwent a $1.2 million addition. There are more than 4,500 entombments in the mausoleum, one of Canada's largest, and 86,000 buried on the 36 hectares (90 acres) of the cemetery, at 4000 Imperial St. Incidentally, among the people buried here are former world heavyweight boxing champion Tommy Burns (1881–1955), actor Miles Mander (1888–1946) and Victoria Cross recipient Cecil Merritt (1908–2000).

The *Georgia Straight*, which had started in 1967 as a weekly newspaper, became a magazine that looked like a newspaper. Charles Campbell was hired as managing editor, and the *Straight* began to expand its coverage of the arts and cultural scene.

UBC Thunderbirds, coached by Frank Smith, beat the University of Western Ontario Mustangs to win their second national championship. They had beaten the same team, to win the same title, in 1982.

Police memorabilia. Strange homemade street weapons, old uniforms, amazing photos and a very informative walking tour are just of a few of the amazing things you'll find at the Vancouver Police Centennial Museum. *Jason Payne* / Vancouver Sun

The Vancouver Park Board instituted a program of commemorative benches. Hundreds of benches have now been financed by members of the local public, in memory of loved ones, friends, colleagues, etc.

Comings and Goings

Legend has it that the title of rock group Bon Jovi's best-selling 1986 album *Slippery When Wet* was inspired by the band's numerous visits to a Vancouver strip bar where on-stage showers were a popular part of the routine.

Notable deaths: **Norman "Larry" MacKenzie**, international adviser and UBC president (1944–62), died January 26, aged 92; **Ron Thom**, one of the most highly regarded architects ever to work in Vancouver and a pioneer in the "West Coast" style, with its lavish use of wood and glass and informal integration into the distinctive coastal landscape, died in Toronto on October 29, aged 63; **John Henry Cates**, boat builder and Liberal MLA (1945–53), died in North Vancouver, aged 90.

1987

What had been the Canada Pavilion at Expo 86 began its life as the city's convention centre, while the Expo "golf ball" at the head of False Creek became Science World. Crowds cheered Rick Hansen's return from a 26-month wheelchair journey around the world. And Vancouver officially celebrated the longevity of the *Georgia Straight*, a newspaper it had tried to kill at birth.

February 7 Ida Halpern died in Vancouver, aged 76. Through the 1960s, '70s and '80s she studied and recorded the songs of BC's coastal Native people, publishing between 1967 and 1987 eight volumes of their songs. Without her work they might have been lost. She was also the founding president of the Friends of Chamber Music in Vancouver, sat on the boards of several key musical organizations and wrote music criticism for the *Province*.

March 15 West Vancouver received its new coat of arms from Dr. Conrad Swan, York Herald, in a ceremony at West Vancouver High School attended by Lieutenant-Governor Robert G. Rogers. The date was chosen to celebrate the anniversary of the city's incorporation on March 15, 1912. A special highlight of the ceremony was the unveiling of a magnificent armorial sculpture by local artist Dennis Sedlacek, which is on permanent display in council chambers. Surrey's new coat of arms was also introduced this year. Among the elements it contains are a beaver, a Salish canoe, a Thoroughbred horse, a farm horse, a communications tower and a variety of local plants.

May 5 Vancouver Mayor Gordon Campbell declared May 5, 1987, to be *Georgia Straight* Day, as the paper

Elsewhere in BC

July BC Premier Bill Vander Zalm's Social Credit government brought in the Industrial Relations Act (Bill 19). The BC Federation of Labour instituted a province-wide boycott of the act, describing it as "viciously anti-union." The Fed refused to appoint any of its members to the Industrial Relations Council, the tribunal appointed to administer the act, and refused to attend the council's hearings. Among the IRC's powers: it could declare workers essential and thus limit the right to strike and set up secondary picketing. The act was repealed December 15, 1992, when the NDP took office, ending a period of bitter labour relations in the province.

In 1985 control of public gaming, with the exception of parimutuel wagering, had been ceded to the provinces. This year the BC Gaming Commission was established to carry out licensing and policy-making functions.

Elsewhere in Canada

June 30 The Royal Canadian Mint released the new one-dollar "Loonie" coin for circulation.

December The federal government amended the Canadian Income Tax Act to designate Vancouver and Montreal as international banking centres. This legislation permitted financial institutions operating in these IBCs to be exempt from federal income tax on the profits earned from lending non-resident deposits to non-resident borrowers.

Elsewhere in the World

June 11 Margaret Thatcher won the UK election, the first British prime minister in 160 years to win a third consecutive term.

August 30 Canadian sprinter Ben Johnson set a new world record in the 100-metre dash...then tested positive for steroids and was stripped of the record and his gold medal.

September 17 The US House of Representatives passed the Civil Liberties Act of 1987, offering an acknowledgement and $1.37 billion in redress to Japanese Americans interned during World War II—$20,000 to each of the estimated 66,000 survivors and a $50-million fund to educate the American public about the uprooting. This spurred the Canadian government to offer a similar agreement.

Movie actor John Ireland (*A Walk in the Sun, All the King's Men, Spartacus, Red River,* dozens of others), born in Vancouver on January 30, 1914 or 1915, placed a famous ad in *Variety*, the showbiz weekly. "I'm an actor," the ad read. "Please let me work." The ad snagged him the role of Captain Aaron Cartwright, the younger brother of Ben Cartwright in the TV movie *Bonanza: The Next Generation*.

Left: Triumphant Hansen. Rick Hansen raised awareness for spinal cord injuries and inspired millions, crossing the finish line of his two-year, 34-country Man in Motion tour that covered over 40,000 kilometres. *Jeff Vinnick / PNG*

celebrated the release of its 1,000th issue. When the *Straight* hit the streets in 1967, Mayor Tom Campbell (no relation) was determined to shut it down.

May 22 Rick Hansen completed his 26-month 40,000-kilometre (24,800-mile) around-the-world Man in Motion tour, when he wheeled his chair into the Oakridge Shopping Centre, from which he had started March 21, 1985. He was met by a huge, cheering crowd, and the next day 50,000 people turned out at BC Place to welcome him back. His tour had raised $24 million for the Man in Motion Legacy Fund, but as the banner at the welcoming ceremonies said, "The End is Just the Beginning." For Rick, life since the tour has been equally rewarding. He established the Rick Hansen Foundation to continue the quest for an accessible and inclusive society and a cure for spinal cord injury. The foundation is recognized as an innovator, collaborating with researchers and funders internationally to pursue its goals.

May Roberts Bank set a world record when 239,084 tonnes of coal was loaded on the *Hyundai Giant*. The facility is able to handle dry bulk vessels of 260,000 DWT.

July 4 What had been the Canada Pavilion at Expo 86 became Canada Place, the city's convention centre. The first event in the $144.8 million structure was the International Culinary Olympics. They crammed a lot in here: the Vancouver Convention Centre East, the Pan Pacific Hotel, the Vancouver Port Authority corporate offices, Cruise Ship Terminal (operated by the Vancouver Port Authority), the CN IMAX Theatre (since closed), World Trade Centre Office Complex and Citipark parking facility.

July 26 The Federation Cup, the women's world team tennis championship, was held at Hollyburn Country Club in West Vancouver. It was the first time in the cup's 25-year history that it was played in Canada.

Summer Construction began on the SkyBridge, which extended SkyTrain across the Fraser River into Surrey. On October 28 a 100-tonne bridge deck section was lifted to deck level. The

Sails up. During Expo 86, it was the Canada Pavilion. The year following, it became the city's convention centre, Canada Place. Its signature five sails have defined the Vancouver harbourfront view ever since. *Deni Eagland / Vancouver Sun*

The beloved "golf ball," originally the Expo Centre, was secured as a home for Science World after much lobbying, persuasion and government support. *Les Bazso / The Province*

first day of operation for this transit-only bridge was March 19, 1990.

September

Following Expo 86, an intensive lobbying campaign was launched to secure the Expo Centre for Science World. With three levels of government backing its proposal, the Arts, Sciences and Technology Centre succeeded in persuading the provincial government to designate the exposition's famous "golf ball" as the new facility. The announcement was made this month. A massive fundraising campaign ensued, with donations from the federal, provincial and municipal governments, the GVRD, the private sector, foundations and individuals contributing $19.1 million to build an addition to the Expo Centre, redesign the interior and construct exhibits. Queen Elizabeth II dedicated the Expo Centre as "Science World, a science centre for the people of British Columbia" in October. It's known today as Science World at Telus World of Science.

October 15 Queen Elizabeth II opened the Commonwealth Heads of Government Meeting in Vancouver. One of the outcomes was the establishment in 1989 of the Commonwealth of Learning, an organization based in Vancouver that encourages the development and sharing of open learning/distance education resources and technologies to help developing nations improve access to quality education and training.

December 7 The Village of Anmore held its first council meeting today. The village occupied what had once been unincorporated territory on the northeast bank of Indian Arm, and the 800 people living there decided they would rather be on their own than absorbed by Port Moody. (That city had been casting covetous eyes at the area for some time.) Mayor Hal Weinberg described the residents of the "idyllic" community as "a core of highly individual, self-supporting people." Anmore at creation was 798 hectares (nearly 2,000 acres). Today it's 2,873 hectares (over 7,000 acres). Population is about 1,800.

December 27 There was a riot at the Lower Mainland Regional Correctional Centre (once known as Oakalla).

Also in 1987

The Vancouver Public Library celebrated its 100th year.

The Seymour Demonstration Forest (now Lower Seymour Conservation Reserve) was created in the District of North Vancouver, opening the lower Seymour Valley to recreationalists for the first time in 59 years. Most of the Capilano, Seymour and Coquitlam watersheds remained off limits in order to protect Greater Vancouver's drinking water, but miles of trails were available to hikers, cyclists, rollerbladers, picnickers, canoeists and fishermen. Visitors saw examples of integrated resource management such as timber harvesting, fish and wildlife management, and reforestation (much of the forest here was harvested more than 60 years ago, so the present forest is a prime example of second growth). More than 100 species of animals and birds live within the valley, and salmon and trout use the Seymour River to spawn. More than a quarter of a million people visit annually.

Forest gem. In keeping with its reputation for some of the most beautiful natural terrain in BC, North Vancouver is home to the 5,600-hectare (almost 13,850 acres) Seymour Demonstration Forest.
Stuart Davis / Vancouver Sun

Portside Park, by the Main Street Overpass, was opened. Eastside residents had squatted here for three months, fighting for a waterfront park between Second Narrows and Stanley Park on land belonging to the National Harbours Board. Two Chinese lion statues guard the entrance. Locals continued to call this spot CRAB Park (Create a Real Available Beach), and in 2004 the name was changed to CRAB Park at Portside.

Students and faculty in education and landscape architecture at UBC created the Neville Scarfe Children's Garden, designed to be a model learning environment for children, as well as a beautiful retreat for faculty, staff and students. The West Coast forest grotto, clover meadow, stream, pond, vegetable and flower gardens appeal to daycare, preschool and school groups of children, while the cedar carving of *Raven Bringing the Light* symbolizes the Native Indian Teacher Education Program, the department that donated this carving to the garden.

The University of British Columbia established a chair of Sikh and Punjabi Studies. Dr. Harjot Oberoi was the first incumbent.

The Vancouver Canucks hired Pat Quinn away from the LA Kings to become the team's president, general manager and occasional coach. Quinn, born in Hamilton in 1943, had been the Canucks' fourth pick in the 1970 draft, a defenceman. He was with them for two years. As president and GM he inherited 11 consecutive losing seasons. He took over coaching duties in 1991 and by the following year had led the Canucks to records for wins and points in a season.

The Vancouver 86ers soccer club rose from the ashes of the Whitecaps and under the coaching of Bob Lenarduzzi soon became the most successful soccer team in Canada. The 86ers won four consecutive Canadian Soccer League championships (1988–91) and set a string of records.

The provincial government launched a Liquor Policy Review this year. Expo 86 had opened the door to a new level of liquor service in BC, and the government began to change the archaic and paternalistic laws of the past, adopting a more liberal attitude. Among the recommendations in the review: expand the present system, which was working well; finance alcohol-abuse programs; improve the staff's knowledge of the product; and allow no beer or wine sales in supermarkets and corner stores.

Two university students, Paul Beaton and Timothy Wittig, who had been working as waiters, went into the specialty brewing business, producing British-style draft ales. When the first keg of Shaftebury was tapped, Beaton was 22 and Wittig was 26.

The Vancouver Board of Trade established its Business Hall of Fame, recognizing the important contributions made to Greater Vancouver by organizations active in BC for more than 100 years. Inaugural winners included Hudson's Bay Company, Vancouver Public Library and Oppenheimer Brothers.

The Easthope Brothers Steveston shop closed. For decades the company had built marine engines used by BC's fishing fleet. Brothers Ernest and Percy built their first marine engine, for a canoe, in 1900. They set up a factory in Vancouver and from 1913 to 1961 built 6,000 two- and four-cycle marine engines, valued for simple design, long life and reliability. In 1930 they opened an assembly and repair shop on No. 1 Road in Steveston, where much of the fishing fleet moored.

Vancouver doctor Jean Carruthers had been treating a patient for a spasm condition when one day the

À la Sylvia. As an accessory to the Sylvia Hotel, the adjacent apartment building was designed by architect Richard Henriquez to complement the 75-year-old landmark. *Stuart Davis / Vancouver Sun*

patient told her, "Every time you treat me I get this beautiful, untroubled expression." Dr. Carruthers was using a medication called Botox, used to treat facial spasms, headaches and other neurological conditions. She told her husband, Alastair Carruthers, also a doctor, about Botox's surprising side effect and mused about whether it might be good to treat wrinkles. "You only need to try it on one person to know that it works," her husband told *Vancouver Magazine*. "I was completely converted...I'm not sure if she blows her own horn enough. She was the one that brought Botox into Canada."

Architect Richard Henriquez designed a residential tower adjacent to the Sylvia Hotel. It opened for use this year, 75 years after the hotel itself opened, and was described as "accomplished and witty," looking as if it might have been built at the same time as the hotel.

Expo's flagpole, at the time the world's tallest at 85 metres (280 feet), was purchased by Guildford Town Centre's Chev-Olds dealership, which was renamed Flag Chev-Olds. Measuring 40 by 80 feet, the flag can be seen from 16 kilometres (10 miles) away.

Surrey bought the Kodak Bowl from Expo 86, moved it to the Surrey Fair Grounds and renamed it the Stetson Bowl. There is seating for 4,200 with room for an equal number of portable seats.

Sushma Datt established Rim Jhim, Canada's first Indo-Canadian radio station, which broadcast in Hindi and Punjabi.

Alan Twigg founded *BC BookWorld*, a free quarterly that has become Canada's largest-circulation, independent publication about books. *BC BookWorld* maintains the ABC BookWorld website, an invaluable directory of BC's books and writers, with reviews and biographies. Twigg has also published 15 books between 1981 and 2009, including *Strong Voices: Conversations with 50 Canadian Writers* (Harbour, 1988), *Intensive Care: A Memoir* (Anvil Press, 2002) and *Tibetans in Exile: The Dalai Lama and the Woodcocks* (Ronsdale, 2009).

Chris Wootten and Jane Howard Baker started the Vancouver International Comedy Festival, inspired by the success of the street performers at Expo 86.

The Vogue Theatre, a 1,200-seat art deco theatre at 918 Granville St., was sold to a development company. It remained closed until 1992, when it reopened as a live performance venue.

The Vancouver Symphony Orchestra began a collapse into bankruptcy, cancelling half its 1987–88 season. In 1989, city council approved a "rescue package" that, in part, allowed the symphony to lease the basement of the Orpheum Theatre at an annual rent of $100,000, to be offset by a grant of $100,000 from the city. The symphony used the city's contribution as leverage in its fundraising efforts and survived. In 1991 the orchestra hired a new music director, Sergiu Comissiona, whose arrival was described as a "musical rebirth" at the VSO. Popular, charming and dynamic, Comissiona pushed the musicians to new heights.

Comings and Goings

New York–born science fiction writer Spider Robinson and his wife (and occasional collaborator) Jeanne arrived in Vancouver from Halifax.

Notable deaths: **John Prentice**, co-founder and president of Canfor, chairman of the Canada Council for five years, president of the Chess Federation of Canada (1955–71) and Canada's representative at the World Chess Federation (1957–87), died on February 19 in Vancouver, aged 79; **Geoffrey Andrew**, professor of English, dean and assistant to the president of UBC (1947–62), died in Vancouver in February; **Stu Keate**, journalist and publisher of the *Vancouver Sun* (1964–78), died March 1 in Vancouver, aged 73; **Walter Mulligan**, Vancouver police chief (1947–55) who fled the country in the midst of a corruption scandal, died in Oak Bay in May, aged about 82; **John Qualen** (born Johan Mandt Kvalen in Vancouver), film actor, died September 12 in Los Angeles, aged 87; **Masumi Mitsui**, World War I hero, died in Vancouver, age 99.

1988

A new chapter in the city's development began when Hong Kong billionaire Li Ka-shing purchased the 80-hectare (200-acre) Expo site. The year was marked by a historic hotel fire, the opening-day collapse of a supermarket and a broken-pipe flood at Vancouver's central library. The Canucks, meanwhile, drafted Trevor Linden.

January 1 The year began with unrest in local prisons. On January 1, 13 maximum-security prisoners escaped from Oakalla four days after a riot at the prison. And on January 24, 80 inmates were involved in a riot at Kent Prison in Agassiz. Three were injured.

April 23 The roof of the new Save-On-Foods store at Metrotown collapsed during opening ceremonies, only minutes after Burnaby mayor Bill Copeland, who was presiding over the grand opening, had directed the evacuation. There were no fatalities. Copeland had become alarmed by cracks in the ceiling and personally escorted dozens of customers outside just before the roof caved in, bringing several automobiles down with it into the store. There were about 1,000 people in the store, and it was believed that Copeland, a former firefighter, had saved many lives.

April 24 The Vancouver Fire Department's first six-alarm fire occurred at the Fraser Arms Hotel. According to VFD historian Alex Matches, the first alarm came in at 9:41 p.m., and the fire had been upgraded to six-alarm within an hour (by 10:37). Off-duty firemen were called in to fight it. They had it under control by 11:45 and it was "struck out" by 12:11. The department stayed on the scene for several hours to extinguish smaller fires. They believed the fire started in a garbage container under a wooden stairway behind the building. Damage was estimated at $1 million.

May 5 The Biomedical Research Centre opened at UBC, a joint project of the Terry Fox Medical Research Foundation and the Wellcome Foundation (funded by Burroughs-Wellcome, a pharmaceutical company). Supporting organizations included the University Hospital, the TRIUMF research laboratory and the Imaging Research Centre, all on campus. The $23-million facility focuses on treatment for cancer and other disorders such as arthritis, allergies and asthma.

June 8 The Vancouver 86ers (formerly the Whitecaps) began an astonishing 46-game (37–0–9) streak without a defeat. It lasted until August 8, 1989. The 86ers won the 1988 Canadian Soccer League championship and went on to win it for three more consecutive seasons.

June
While the Prairies suffered from drought, there was a record rainfall in the Fraser Valley this month: 144 millimetres (5.7 inches).

Elsewhere in BC

September 9 Philanthropist David See-Chai Lam was sworn in as BC's Lieutenant-Governor, the first Chinese Canadian to be appointed to that position in any Canadian province.

Elsewhere in Canada

February The 1988 Winter Olympics were held in Calgary.

September 22 Prime Minister Brian Mulroney formally apologized to Japanese Canadian survivors and their families for the wrongful incarceration, seizure of property and the disenfranchisement of thousands of Japanese Canadians during World War II and after. Art Miki, of the National Association of Japanese Canadians, called the apology and $300-million compensation package "a settlement that heals."

Elsewhere in the World

Celine Dion won the Eurovision Song Contest representing Switzerland. Switzerland??

The Soviet Union began its program of *perestroika* (economic restructuring). It also began withdrawing its army from Afghanistan, where it had been fighting since 1979.

Science! Commune with dinosaurs, dip a balloon in liquid nitrogen and learn about "Grossology" at Science World, originally built as the Expo Preview Centre.
The Province

Summer Science World opened in the former Expo Centre, the "golf ball," at 1455 Quebec St. The first show, a four-month smash titled *Dinosaurs! A Journey through Time with White Spot*, brought in more than 350,000 visitors. The centre closed for refurbishing after its run and then opened for good on May 6, 1989.

August 19 A high-pressure water main feeding the new sprinkler system in the main branch of the Vancouver Public Library burst, soaking hundreds of rare books and bound periodicals.

According to a newspaper report, "more than 200,000 books and newspapers in the basement of the Robson and Burrard Building were doused in the 10-minute shower... Workers mopped up much of the mess, using 2,000 kg of newsprint to blot the moisture out of the less severely damaged items. Chief librarian Barbara Bell said staff stacked the most badly soaked items into 236 milk crates and sent them off to be freeze-dried, which stops water damage and mold growth." BC Ice and Cold Storage froze the books to prevent mildew until they could be shipped to BMS Catastrophe Ltd., in Fort Worth, TX. There, the books were freeze-dried, and the resultant ice crystals removed, preserving fragile paper and bindings. Though quick action preserved much of the collection, losses included 400 books, as well as several art periodicals printed on clay-coated paper stock that turned to muck in the flood. Totally lost was a 23-year bound collection (1939 to 1961) of the *Province* and *Vancouver Sun* newspapers. By January 11, 1989, the freeze-dried books were back on the shelves. Three months later, on November 10, Mayor Gordon Campbell promised the city a new main library.

Right: What's worse than dropping a library book in the bathtub? A tragic story at the Vancouver Public Library at Robson and Burrard when the new sprinkler system malfunctioned and soaked over 200,000 books and newspapers.
The Province

August 26 Tara Singh Hayer, editor of the *Indo-Canadian Times*, was shot by 17-year-old Harkirat Bagga. The shooting left Hayer partially paralyzed and confined to a wheelchair. Bagga was sentenced to 14 years in jail for the shooting and was eventually deported. Hayer continued writing hard-hitting columns in his paper, supporting moderate Sikhism and condemning militants, such as those behind the 1985 bombing of Air India Flight 182. He was fatally shot by an unknown assailant on November 18, 1998.

September 27

A plaque commemorating the opening of Stanley Park a century earlier was unveiled on the right side of the park drive at the north foot of Pipeline Road. That's where Mayor David Oppenheimer declared the park open on September 27, 1888.

September IFC Vancouver opened its offices with Michael Goldberg, from the commerce faculty at UBC, as executive director. Its aim was to establish Vancouver as an international financial centre (IFC), a location for international investment, in order to diversify the economy and broaden trading patterns and products. IFC BC (as it's been known since 2004) promotes international investment in BC and lobbies government for favourable tax treatment for these investors.

November 1 A county court judge dismissed a prostitute's earlier conviction of communication for the purpose of prostitution when she argued she had simply been asking an undercover policeman for a ride to work.

November 22 Workers on a False Creek construction site at the foot of Hornby Street were stranded on pilings when an unexpectedly high tide flooded the site with 1.5 metres (5 feet) of water. They had to be rescued by boat.

Also in 1988

The vacant Expo site was sold in one of the largest real estate deals in Canadian history. Li Ka-shing, a Hong Kong billionaire whose assets in 1988 made up one-tenth of the stock exchange in Hong Kong, purchased the site for CDN$320 million, to be paid over 15 years. The *New York Times* commented that this was evidence "of the Hong Kong capital now pouring into Vancouver in anticipation of the 1997 deadline for turning over control of the British Colony to China." The *Times* added that "some critics say... developers other than Mr. Li were not given an opportunity to bid on the property...The Government [headed by Premier Bill Vander Zalm] says it wanted to complete the sale with a minimum of delay, to a developer with enough capital to complete a project large enough to cover the old Expo site." Li's $3-billion Concord Pacific development transformed the site into a 67-hectare (165-acre) community of offices, townhouses and parks.

A study showed that between 1980 and 1988, people from Hong Kong, Taiwan and China accounted for 23 percent of all foreign immigrants coming to Richmond.

Amid considerable controversy, approximately 500 Kerrisdale residents were dispersed when a number of low-rise rental apartments were demolished to make way for condominium developments. Some of the sites were still vacant 10 years later.

BC Tel reported that 40 percent of all new homes built in BC this year were located in Surrey. The phone company also began constructing its portion of the cross-Canada lightguide transmission system—3 million metres (1,864 miles) of fibre

Too much land to stay vacant for long, the old Expo 86 grounds now contain high-rise condos, a beautiful seawall and a venue for Cirque du Soleil when it comes to town. *PNG*

The Burnaby Incinerator burns garbage generating 15 megawatts of power. *Gerry Kahrmann / The Province*

optic cable that provided British Columbians with rapid interactive voice, data, image and video transmission on one circuit. The system was completed in March 1990.

Point Roberts, the little tip of Washington state that's accessible by land only through BC, finally got its own US-based telephone service. BC Tel had been serving the area up until this year.

BC Gas was formed when Inland Natural Gas (incorporated in 1952) acquired the mainland natural gas division of BC Hydro. By far the largest natural gas utility in the province, it distributed its product through 30,000 kilometres (18,640 miles) of pipeline running from the Peace River Block through the centre of the province to about 700,000 residential and corporate customers in more than 100 communities throughout mainland British Columbia. BC Gas is now called FortisBC, a subsidiary of Fortis Inc.

Whonnock Industries Ltd.—which had started in the 1930s with a sawmill in Whonnock, east of Haney—changed its name to International Forest Products Limited (Interfor). Today it's one of the biggest forest companies in Canada.

The GVRD opened the Burnaby Incinerator. Costing just over $63 million, this was one of the most advanced municipal waste incinerators in North America. It now handles about 20 percent of all the solid waste disposed in the Lower Mainland, 280,000 tonnes of it every year, and generates 900,000 tonnes of steam, a portion of which is sold to the nearby Norampac paper recycling mill to reduce the mill's use of fossil fuels. The plant operators and GVRD engineers saw the excess steam as an opportunity to make the plant more sustainable, so they generate electricity from the steam and sell the power—enough to heat 15,000 homes—to BC Hydro.

A $40-million wastewater treatment plant and deep-sea outfall was built on Iona Island near Sturgeon Bank. It improved the quality of water at nearby Sturgeon Bank and served as the foundation for a popular public promenade and cycle path extending 4 kilometres (2.5 miles) into Georgia Strait...on top of the outfall pipes!

Pacific Regeneration Technologies Inc., now Canada's largest forest nursery company, was established. It consists today of a network of nurseries in Canada and the US. Collectively, these nurseries produce more than 220 million forest seedlings per year.

CCI Learning Solutions Inc. was incorporated to produce "courseware for instructor led classes, e-learning courses, blended training solutions and official certification exams."

In 1949 the Matsumoto family purchased a small shipyard on Dollarton Highway in North Vancouver, building fish boats and firefighting boats for Mexico. They sold the company this year to Pacific Western Shipbuilders.

Surrey's Farm Fair celebrated its 100th birthday this year and changed its name to the Cloverdale Exhibition.

The former Ferry Building at 101 14th St. in West Vancouver, built in 1913, was rehabilitated by Howard/Yano Architects to become an art gallery.

Right: Still a beauty. The beautifully restored Port Coquitlam City Hall, built originally in 1913. *The Province*

The clapboard structure had served as the West Vancouver ferry terminal until the service was discontinued in 1947.

Another 1913 building very attractively reshaped for 1988 was the Port Coquitlam City Hall at 2580 Shaughnessy St. The project was part of PoCo's Diamond Jubilee (75 years). Architects Toby Russell Buckwell and Partners integrated the old municipal hall with a very fine new addition.

W.T. Whiteway, from Newfoundland, was an important early-century architect in Vancouver. Among his works was the Kelly Building, begun in 1905 in what is now Gastown. This year, rehabilitated by Soren Rasmussen, it became The Landing.

An envelope with a "28" postmark was sold at auction this year for more than $3,000. Postmaster Maximilian Michaud, who bought the Brighton Hotel on Burrard Inlet early in 1869 and changed its name to the Hastings, used a grid-lined hammer enclosing the number "28" to cancel the mail. His was the only postal outlet in colonial times within Vancouver's current boundaries.

Pearl Steen, women's activist, died in Vancouver, aged about 95. Born Pearl Soper in Victoria in 1893, she was educated in Vancouver and had a distinguished career of community service. She was president of the National Council of Women, the Vancouver Council of Women and the Vancouver Women's Canadian Club, president of the Canadian Federation of Professional and Business Women's Clubs in 1935, president of the Point Grey Conservative Association (1936–37). She spent six years on the Vancouver School Board (1947–52) and was elected chair in 1950. She was a member of the BC Centennial Committee (1958), a member of the BC Human Rights Council, the sole Canadian woman delegate to the UN General Assembly in 1960 and the only woman director of the PNE (1960–68). Ms. Steen received Vancouver's Good Citizen Award in 1967. No kidding!

BC Research, since 1944 a non-profit government-subsidized research facility at UBC, incorporated as a private company. Revenues soon reached more than $10 million annually, but by 1992 the company reported a loss of $700,000 on revenues of $11 million. In 2007 the facility closed.

An SFU team synthesized a queen bee pheromone (message-carrying chemical) that others had been trying to replicate for 25 years. It was used to boost production in North America's $20-billion fruit and vegetable industries.

University Hospital came into existence when Shaughnessy Hospital merged with the UBC Health Sciences Centre and George Derby Centre. This partnership dissolved in 1993 when the Shaughnessy site closed and the UBC site merged with Vancouver General.

Meanwhile, in keeping with a 40-year trend in Western countries away from institutional care and toward community care, Riverview Hospital began reducing its in-patient numbers. People with serious, long-term mental illnesses were moved from Riverview to care in or through psychiatric departments in acute-care hospital, care homes or outreach services in the patients' own communities. A historical review of Riverview noted that the benefit the seriously mentally ill would receive from these changes would "largely depend upon the degree of integration of the various components of this community model and the adequacy of their funding."

Trevor Linden was Pat Quinn's first draft pick as president and general manager of the Vancouver Canucks. He was a good choice. Voted *Hockey News* Rookie of the Year that season, Linden became team captain in 1991 and team ironman in 1996. His 482 consecutive games surpassed Don Lever's streak of 437.

Ray Murao of the Steveston Kendo Club won the Best Fighting Spirit Award at the world kendo tournament.

Larry Lillo, 41, became the artistic director of the Vancouver Playhouse. "Audiences should be challenged as well as entertained," he said. "Some theatre-goers want to see plays with meat on their bones." Under his direction, Playhouse subscriptions rose from 5,800 in 1988 to nearly 12,000 by the 1992–93 season.

The Vancouver Out On Screen Film Society organized the first of what became known as the Vancouver Queer Film Festival.

Douglas Coupland wrote an article for *Vancouver Magazine* in which he referred to people born between 1961 and 1981 as "Generation X." He moved to Palm Springs shortly after and wrote the best-selling book of the same title.

Comings and Goings

Notable deaths: **Eileen Underhill**, badminton champion, on July 31, aged 99; **Hy Aisenstat**, restaurateur and founder of Hy's Steak House, on August 11, aged 62.

1989

Simon Fraser University opened a downtown campus, and a huge swath of the former University of British Columbia endowment lands was turned into the world's largest urban park. The 86ers capped an incredible winning streak by taking the professional soccer league championship, and the tradition of dragon boat racing in False Creek began.

Right: Distinctive medal. The Order of British Columbia is bestowed upon high-achieving British Columbians in the name of the Crown, and was introduced by Lieutenant-Governor David Lam. *Province of British Columbia*

March 23 Ranjit Mattu, star athlete and coach, the "Gretsky of his time," died in Malibu, CA, aged 72. He was born July 17, 1916, in Jullunder, Punjab, India, and came to Vancouver in 1924. He coached Canadian high school and junior football until 1949 (one of his teams, the Vancouver Blue Bombers, were the Dominion Champions of 1947). He joined his father's firm, Best Fuels, and later established various business interests including Ocean City Sawmills (renamed Hem-fir Lumber) on Mitchell Island. A community leader, Mattu was the organizer and host of Indian prime minister Jawaharlal Nehru's visit to BC in 1949.

April 3 Edward Gilbert Nahanee died in North Vancouver, six days before his 92nd birthday. He was born in North Vancouver of Kanaka (Hawaiian) and Squamish ancestry. Famed as a pitcher for the North Shore Indians baseball team, Ed worked on the docks from age 14. He was active in the longshoreman's union after World War I until clashes with RCMP and company police in 1923 broke the union. From 1946 he served as business agent for the Native Brotherhood of BC. He was awarded the Canada Confederation Medal in 1967 for his work with Native people.

April 21 The Order of British Columbia was established to recognize people who had served with the

Elsewhere in BC

BC Hydro launched its highly successful Power Smart conservation program. In five years Power Smart and the associated Resource Smart program (which enhanced existing production facilities) saved enough electricity to supply 233,200 homes.

The Cache Creek landfill opened. This 48-hectare (120-acre) site in an industrial area south of the village of Cache Creek, was the first landfill in western Canada to be designed and operated as a state-of-the-art, environmentally secure landfill facility. About 16 percent of the Lower Mainland's solid waste is taken there.

Elsewhere in Canada

June 3 The SkyDome (now Rogers Centre) opened in Toronto.

December 6 A gunman shouting that he hated "feminists" roamed the corridors of Montreal's École Polytechnique and shot 14 female engineering students to death. The Montreal Massacre became a galvanizing moment all across Canada as mourning turned to outrage at all violence against women. In 1997 a monument to the murdered women was unveiled in Vancouver's Thornton Park, at Main Street and Terminal Avenue.

Elsewhere in the World

February 14 Ayatollah Khomeini imposed a fatwa on Salman Rushdie for his book *The Satanic Verses*.

March 24 The *Exxon Valdez* ran aground in Alaska's Prince William Sound, spilling 240,000 barrels (11 million gallons) of oil.

June 4 Chinese troops massacred protesters in Beijing's Tiananmen Square.

October 17 A major earthquake struck central California. More than 60 people were killed, and damage was estimated at almost $3 billion in San Francisco alone. The effect in Vancouver: a lot of engineering work began to upgrade local bridges and dams with an eye to seismic hazards.

Communist governments in Romania, Czechoslovakia and East Germany resigned or were overthrown, and Hungary and East Germany opened their borders to travel to the West.

Pacific Spirit Park

April 23 Pacific Spirit Park was named. Richmond resident Sherry Sakamoto was at the ceremony because she had won the province-wide competition to name the park, made up of 763 hectares (1,885 acres) that had previously been part of the University Endowment Lands. She explained that the name "was inspired by the First Nations belief in the Great Creator and their connection to Mother Earth...It is the gateway to the Pacific and a spiritual ground to becoming one with nature." Sakamoto won a Helijet ride over the park and North Shore mountains, attended a reception to meet Premier Bill Vander Zalm and his wife, Lillian, and had one of the park's trails named for her.

Pacific Spirit, the largest urban park in the world, has 34 multiple-use trails that traverse coniferous and deciduous forests, ancient bogland, ravines and the Point Grey foreshore. Walking trails through this second-growth forest are shared by strollers, cyclists, dogs and horses.

During the 1960s there had been plans to build large housing developments in the Point Grey forest surrounding the UBC campus, but the locals protested. One resident, Iva Mann, had been fighting to keep the area forested since 1951, when a tree behind her property was cut down during an attempt to subdivide the area. By 1970 she was working with the Regional Park Committee and BC Outdoor Recreation, volunteer groups that were converting old logging skid roads into hiking trails to bring hikers to the forest. It took many more years, but the provincial government finally transferred title in the land to the Greater Vancouver Regional District in December 1988.

Joggers' haven. Considered one of the best places for a daytime jog with friends, the Pacific Spirit Park covers a huge portion of the University Endowment Lands at UBC—not to mention its proximity to Wreck Beach for an after-hike dip in the sea. *Abdallah*

greatest distinction and excelled in any field of endeavour benefiting the people of BC or elsewhere. The order, which is awarded annually, represents "the highest form of recognition the province can extend to its citizens."

May 5 Simon Fraser University opened a downtown Vancouver campus

in the Spencer Building on West Hastings Street. This unique campus, now known as Harbour Centre, was originally financed by the private sector and designed to meet the challenge of mid-career education in the emerging global, knowledge-based economy. Within its first five years of operation the busy "intellectual heart of the city" was serving more than 50,000 people annually, who were taking advantage of new opportunities in lifelong learning.

May 28 The handsome old Georgia Medical-Dental building, which went up on the northwest corner of Georgia and Hornby Streets in 1929, was demolished by a controlled explosion viewed by a huge throng in the surrounding streets. The demolition followed an intense but unsuccessful public campaign to save the building.

June 3 Garry Point Park in Steveston opened. The park, at the southwest corner of Richmond, is a popular spot for strolling, watching ships go by, kite flying and more.

July 12 The NAMES Project AIDS Memorial Quilt went on display at

Final stand. The Georgia Medical-Dental building, built in 1929, takes its last stand before being demolished.
Vancouver Sun

the Vancouver Art Gallery, Robson Square and Pacific Centre Atrium. The quilt contained 2,000 Canadian and US panels, including more than 24 from BC.

August 28 Delta council vetoed an application by Tsawwassen Developments to establish a big housing development along the shores of Boundary Bay. The proposal—hotly opposed by many residents—had been debated at a 25-session public hearing that lasted from May 1 to July 17, the longest public hearing in Canadian history. More than 400 speakers were heard and 3,700 written submissions received. The battle divided the community, pitting newcomers against old-timers.

September 7 A Russian drug gang was rounded up in Vancouver on charges of conspiring to sell cocaine. More than 25 pounds of coke valued at $9 million was seized along with machine-guns and luxury cars. Two weeks later, Premier Bill Vander Zalm vowed to step up the attack on the illicit drug trade. He told more than 1,400 mayors and aldermen attending the annual meeting of the Union of BC Municipalities that he was setting up and chairing a cabinet committee on drug abuse. "It's our intention," Vander Zalm said, "to develop a drug-attack program that will be the envy of Canada." We wonder how that worked out.

October 29 An era in Vancouver entertainment ended with the death of Ivan Ackery, one day before his 90th birthday. He was born Ivor Frederick Wilson Ackery in Bristol, England, on October 30, 1899. (In later years he changed the Ivor to Ivan because that's what everybody in Vancouver called him anyway.) He moved to Vancouver in 1914. As manager of the Orpheum Theatre from 1935 to 1969, he was known as Mr. Orpheum, Atomic Ack and Little Orpheum Ackery. Promotional stunts earned him two Motion Picture Quigley Awards, the theatre promoters' equivalent of an Oscar. To plug one of his under-performing movies, he once paraded a cow down Granville with a sign: "There's a great show at the Orpheum and that's no bull." Theatre managers in the 1930s were more than just administrators. They frequently chose the films they showed, they were expected to promote them—and, boy, did Ackery promote them—and they devised special attractions to make their theatres stand out and bring customers in. Ackery was so good at all of this, and he was good for so long (35 years), that it's fair to say he was the single most influential person in the Orpheum's history.

November 21 Frank Baker died in Vancouver, aged 67. Frank Madill Baker was born June 24, 1922, in Vancouver. He opened Baker's

Frank Baker, owner of the Attic restaurant in West Vancouver, poses with Kenneth Luscombe-White in front of his beautiful Aston Martin, the car driven in the James Bond film *Goldfinger*. Baker—a showman—showcased the car outside his restaurant.
George Diack / Vancouver Sun

Catering (at 25th and Kingsway) and Spring Gardens (at 41st and Boulevard) in 1946. With partner Frank Bernard he opened two restaurants in the Georgian Towers and bought the Park Royal Hotel. After the partnership ended he opened the 1,200-seat Attic in West Vancouver. Guests were entertained by Lance Harrison and His Dixieland Band. A showman, Baker played the trumpet (learned at the Four Square Gospel Church) and always wore a trademark white suit. Outside the Attic he showcased the Aston Martin driven in the James Bond movie *Goldfinger*. He was briefly a Vancouver alderman.

Also in 1989

The Vancouver Food Bank had started in 1982 as a temporary facility for needy people. By 1989 there were six depots distributing to 15,000 people every month. Also this year, the Langley District Help Network began to operate the Langley Food Bank, helping hundreds every week with their food needs. The Help Network also operated a furniture bank, a laundromat and a free store.

Harold and Barbara Morgan opened the Exotic World Museum (and paint business) on Main Street after 45 winters of travelling and collecting curios. When Harold died, the collection was purchased by antiques dealer Alexander Lamb, and at Barbara's request it remained at the back of the store for viewing. There are now two more boxes on display, containing the ashes of Harold and Barbara.

The Vancouver Canucks took the Calgary Flames to the seventh game of the first playoff round in NHL action before losing on a disputed overtime goal by Joel Otto (assisted by Jim Peplinski) that sent the Flames on to their first-ever Stanley Cup. Canucks fans believed Otto had kicked the puck in. That it still rankled long after was obvious when Canucks GM Brian Burke spotted Otto and Peplinski in Calgary in February 2002. "That puck was kicked in!" Burke yelled, and the room exploded in laughter. It had happened *13 years* earlier.

In professional soccer the 86ers' incredible 46-game winning streak (37-0-9) that had started June 8, 1988, finally ended with a loss in Edmonton. Vancouver stormed into the playoffs, winning the western division championship. In the title game at Swangard Stadium before a record crowd of almost 8,000 fans, the 86ers won the league championship with a 3–2 victory over the Hamilton Steelers.

The University of British Columbia soccer Thunderbirds began a terrific stretch of victories in Canadian Interuniversity Sport Championships. They won again in 1990, 1991, 1992 and 1994.

The Whalley All Stars competed in the final baseball game of the Senior Little League World Series. They lost to the defending champions from Taiwan.

Dragon boat races were held for the first time in False Creek. The Canadian International Dragon Boat Festival is now a three-day event held every June.

The federal fisheries department, in co-operation with the Musqueam band and Vancouver Park Board, began to stock Tin Can Creek (or Musqueam Creek) with chum salmon fingerlings raised by children in their classrooms. The creek, which rises in Pacific Spirit Regional Park and enters the Fraser River from Musqueam reserve land, needs constant protection from urban abuse such as effluent from storm drains.

Emily Carr College of Art and Design began offering bachelor's degrees in fine arts and design through the British Columbia Open University.

The Adbusters Media Foundation began publishing *Adbusters Quarterly* with the mission of raising consumer alarms about the advertising industry. Another magazine that began this year was the weekly *Business in Vancouver*, published by Peter Ladner and George Mleczko.

North Shore Studios was built in North Vancouver City by Hollywood writer/producer Stephen J. Cannell (*The Rockford Files* was one of his creations). It contained seven sound stages, production offices, on-site shooting facades and technical production services. The studio was later home of the TV series *The X-Files*, *The Commish* and *21 Jump Street* and the feature movies *Little Women* and *Intersection*.

In spite of the title, much of *Friday The 13th Part VIII: Jason Takes Manhattan* was filmed in Vancouver and Britannia Beach. The hockey-masked slasher added 19 notches to his machete, dispatching victims on locations that included a SkyTrain dressed to look like the New York subway.

The Classical Joint, Vancouver's oldest jazz club, closed. It had started at 231 Carrall Street in Gastown in 1970 with the arrival of Swiss-born Andreas Nothiger, who ran it for 18 years.

Comings and Goings

July 19 Major leager Sammy Sosa arrived to play for the Vancouver Canadians of the Triple-A Pacific Coast League.

Sosa had started with the Chicago White Sox at a red-hot pace, then went into a colossal slump. With his average hovering at the "Mendoza line" (.200), Sosa was sent down to Vancouver. He wasn't here long. He was recalled August 27 (after playing 13 games) and finished the season with a .203 average, 10 homers and 33 RBI—along with 98 strikeouts in 116 games. Then things started picking up. In 1998, Sosa and Mark McGwire battled to surpass Roger Maris' home-run record.

Planes from the Soviet Union (remember them?) appeared for the first time at the Abbotsford Air Show. The *Province*'s Don Hunter wrote: "They showed off their sleek MiG 29s, an IL-76, and the enormous AN-225, the world's biggest aircraft. Canadian Armed Forces Major Bob Wade became the first western pilot to fly the MiG 29. The Soviets attracted so much interest that 60,000 would-be spectators were turned away."

Heavyweight boxing champion Mike Tyson came to Vancouver to see his ex-wife, Robin Givens, who was shooting a TV movie called *The Penthouse*. According to film reviewer and historian David Spaner, Givens was stayed at the Hotel Vancouver, and there was a crowd of media to greet Tyson when he arrived. He grabbed a *Vancouver Sun* photographer's camera, threw it against the wall, then ripped the viewfinder from a BCTV camera and smashed it on the floor.

Christopher Erienbeck, BC's three-millionth citizen, was born at Burnaby Hospital.

Notable deaths: **J.V. Clyne**, lawyer, Supreme Court judge, and CEO of MacMillan Bloedel, died in Vancouver August 22, aged 87; **Agnes Watts**, known as the Telethon angel for her generous gifts to children's projects through the Variety Club of BC, died October 30 in Vancouver, aged about 90 (Watts was the first female employee when Scott Paper opened a mill in New Westminster and stayed with them for 22 years, "rolling toilet paper" and saving every penny; her wealth came from her own frugality and smart investments in the stock market and real estate); **John Napier Burnett**, teacher, administrator and inspector of schools in the Interior, and district superintendent for the Richmond School District, died, aged 89; **Gertrude Lawson**, teacher, artist and daughter of West Vancouver pioneers John and Christina Lawson, died. It's in her handsome stone-fronted home at 680 17th St. that the West Vancouver Museum and Archives has made its home since 1994.

Life's rough at the Chateau. Built in the French manor-house tradition started in the 1880s by CP Railway, the Chateau Whistler Resort remains a haven for skiers and non-skiers alike. *Mark van Manen* / Vancouver Sun

1990-1999

1990

The transit system made two important advances: the completion of a special bridge extended SkyTrain service into Surrey, and regular buses became the first in Canada to carry wheelchairs. Vancouver hosted an international "gay games," and this year was also the first Indy race on city streets and the first Bard on the Beach presenting Shakespeare in a tent.

February 8 Richard Loney (famous for singing "O Canada" at Canucks games) sang *two* versions of the national anthem at a meeting of the Canadian Club in Vancouver. The first had words written in 1909 by Ewing Buchan, a Vancouver banker. His version was popular a century ago but was eventually beaten out by the R.S. Weir version we know today. Loney sang the Weir version to close the meeting. The first public singing of the Buchan version of "O Canada" took place at a Canadian Club luncheon meeting in Vancouver on February 9, 1910.

March 19 The first full day of operation of the SkyBridge, built to carry the SkyTrain across the Fraser to Surrey. The 616-metre (2,020-foot) structure was part of a $179-million, 3.1-kilometre (2-mile) SkyTrain extension into Surrey that opened in 1994. The bridge, set aslant the Fraser River to ease the curve coming from New Westminster, was the world's longest cable-stayed bridge designed solely for rapid transit. The 104 deck sections were built in Richmond, barged up the Fraser and then lifted into place by heavy equipment.

April 27 Charles Nanby Wynn "Chunky" Woodward, retailer, died in Vancouver, aged 66. Grandson of Charles A. Woodward, who founded the Woodward's department store chain in 1892, Chunky fought in World War II, joined the family company in 1946 and in 1956 was named president of Woodward's BC and Alberta chain, a position he held until 1988. Woodward was involved in the development of BC Place Stadium and Whistler Mountain. He worked with horses at his 220,000-hectare (543,600-acre) Douglas Lake ranch and established rodeo circuits across western Canada. He received the W.A.C. Bennett Award for sports contributions from the BC Sports Hall of Fame in 1986.

June 6 Marianne Linnell, civic leader, died in Vancouver, aged about 76. She was an NPA alderman from 1961 to 1974, the only woman on Canada's Centennial Commission and a spokesperson for small business, municipal affairs and "that forgotten individual, the housewife." She also chaired the BC Aviation Council in the 1960s.

August 4 20,000 people marched into BC Place Stadium for the opening ceremonies of Celebration '90: Gay Games III and Cultural Festival. This "tourist bonanza" for the local economy (bringing in $15 million

Speed with a view. The SkyTrain, opened in 1986 and extended to Surrey in 1990, is still the fastest inter-borough transportation in the city, making its way across the Fraser River on the stunningly engineered SkyBridge. *Mark van Manen / Vancouver Sun*

for local business, according to some estimates) was also the world's largest sporting and cultural event in 1990, with 8,500 participants in 29 sports and 14 cultural events. The games made "queer culture" more visible in politics, media, entertainment and advertising than ever before.

August 23 The Surrey campus of Kwantlen College officially opened. Several divisions of Kwantlen's Newton campus moved to the new site.

September 2 The first Vancouver Indy car race took place on a 2.65-kilometre (1.6-mile) track in the shadow of BC Place Stadium and Science World. More than 25,000 visitors came to Vancouver and spent

The fast track. Al Unser's car is one of the many bees that buzzed their way around downtown streets during the Molson Indy Vancouver. To this day, it's a little hard not to accelerate one's own car along Expo Boulevard, used as an S curve in the race. *Denise Howard / PNG*

Elsewhere in BC

The federal and provincial governments abandoned a 119-year-old policy of refusing to acknowledge aboriginal title and created the BC Claims Task Force with First Nations. The province of BC also joined the Nisga'a and the federal government in the negotiation of the Nisga'a land claim.

By 1990 BC Rail's total length of track was 2,232 kilometres (1,387 miles), making it the third-largest railway in Canada.

Elsewhere in Canada

January 15 VIA Rail cut half of its passenger network. Included in these cuts was a decision to run just one transcontinental train between Toronto and Vancouver via CN's route through Winnipeg, Saskatoon, Edmonton and Jasper.

March 6 The National Gallery of Canada purchased *Voice of Fire*, by US abstract expressionist Barnett Newman, for $1.8 million, causing an uproar.

July Mohawk warriors barricaded a road to "The Pines" near Oka, QC, to stop a golf course expanding into their traditional burial ground. When police attempted to take down the barricade, one officer was killed and the Mohawks blockaded all roads and bridges leading into their territory. Local non-Native residents rioted at the barricades, and the Canadian Army was called in. In September the barricades were dismantled and 150 Mohawk people were arrested, but the golf course proposal was abandoned. Indigenous communities across BC erected blockades in support of the Mohawks.

December 17 Brian Mulroney's Conservative government imposed the Goods and Services Tax.

Canada banned the use of leaded gasoline—except in cars used for drag and stock-car racing.

Elsewhere in the World

February 11 Nelson Mandela was released from prison in South Africa after 27 years.

March 22 Canadian arms designer Gerald Bull was assassinated in Brussels.

August 2 Iraq invaded Kuwait, an action that eventually led to the Gulf War.

October 3 East Germany and West Germany reunited in a single Germany.

December 25 Tim Berners-Lee created the first webpage on the first web server.

as much as $25 million in the city; millions more watched the race live around the world. By 1996 the event drew more than 170,000 people over three days. The Vancouver course became notorious among drivers. It was short, narrow and had tight turns, making it extremely hard to pass. The 1990 event got off to a tragic start when volunteer worker Jean Patrick Hein was killed after he was struck by the car driven by Willy T. Ribbs. Hein had jumped on the track to push the stalled car of Vancouver driver Ross Bentley in a tight corner known as a chicane.

September "Dr. Peter" (Dr. Peter William Jepson-Young) began a weekly diary of his life with AIDS on the CBC evening news. A documentary of his TV diaries, *The Broadcast Tapes of Dr. Peter*, won many awards and gained an Academy Award nomination.

October 16 The District of North Vancouver was granted its coat of arms, designed by Robert Watt, the chief herald of Canada. The stylized shield includes references to snow-capped forested mountains and the curving lines of the mountain streams and rivers flowing down to meet the waters of the harbour. The crest is a 19th-century sailing ship. A silver bear and deer represent the riches of the natural environment, and a golden Salish salmon salutes the First Nations. The motto *Montes Rivique Nobis Inspirant* means "The Mountains and Their Streams Are Our Inspiration."

November 7 The British Columbia Entertainment Hall of Fame was established—63 years to the day after the Orpheum Theatre opened.
The founding ceremony paid special tribute to the late Ivan Ackery, who was manager of the Orpheum from 1935 to 1969. In 1994 the hall created Starwalk on the Granville Street sidewalk, and in 1996 added Starwall inside the Orpheum.

November 19 On the occasion of Douglas College's 20th anniversary, all 18 babies born at Maple Ridge, Burnaby and Royal Columbian Hospitals today received Douglas College entrance scholarships.

Also in 1990

Bard on the Beach was established to provide Vancouver residents and tourists with affordable, accessible Shakespearean productions of the finest quality. The first year's production was *A Midsummer Night's Dream*. Artistic director and founder Christopher Gaze said he got financing from "my dentist, my insurance man, anyone. We raised $36,000 and cleared $1,300 at the end of the season." Bard on the Beach is now a fully professional theatre company, and the productions, staged

When the Bard on the Beach tents appear in Vanier Park, it's officially summer. The seasonal theatre stronghold keeps Shakespeare alive, affordable and best of all, comprehensible.
PNG

in open-ended tents at Vanier Park, with a view of mountains, sea and sky, consistently receive both critical and audience acclaim. From a first-season attendance of 6,000 patrons, the festival has grown to more than 90,000 in 2009.

We have a hunch that Jack Bell will not be best remembered for the business ventures (including peat-harvesting technology) that made him a millionaire many times over, but for his imaginative philanthropy. UBC gave him an honorary degree this year, describing him as "a man whose heart is in the right place." The Jack Bell Foundation started the Vanpool/Carpool Program to reduce pollution and traffic congestion. He donated $1 million to the construction of the First Nations Longhouse at UBC, gave $4 million for a research centre and gerontology unit at VGH, gave money to the Downtown Eastside Women's Centre, etc., etc. He was made a Freeman of the City of Vancouver, and awarded the Order of British Columbia in 1991.

The Mary Pack Arthritis Society Chair in Rheumatology was established at UBC, named in honour of teacher and arthritis campaigner Mary Pack, who devoted her life to arthritis and rheumatism care and research. In 1945 she had established the organization that became the BC Division of the Canadian Arthritis and Rheumatism Society.

Vancouver became the first city in Canada to provide scheduled bus service to people with disabilities. BC Transit (now TransLink) began to install wheelchair lifts on buses on scheduled runs throughout the system. This was the first time wheelchair users could be accommodated on regular buses. (Trolley buses never had them.) Today, the newest trolley buses ordered by TransLink are all low-floor with ramps, and the system is fully accessible.

Roberta "Bobbie" Steen, a tireless promoter of BC and national sporting opportunities for women, became founding chair and executive director of Promotion Plus, the BC organization for girls and women in sport and physical activity.

Geist: the Canadian Magazine of Ideas and Culture began publishing.

Evelyn Lau, 21, was the youngest Canadian to be nominated for a Governor General's Award for Poetry.

Jon Steeves, a Vancouver computer consultant, began marketing and selling MooT (as in "a moot question," because the answers can often be debated), a word game he devised back in 1987. It's still selling more than 20 years later. A sample MooT question: According to the *Concise Oxford Dictionary*, its name probably derives from the Sanskrit word for the number five. What type of drink is it? Comment: The word "punch" probably derives from the Sanskrit *panca*, "five," as the drink properly had five ingredients—similarly, the Punjab is the land of the five rivers.

The Pacific Baroque Orchestra was founded this year by a group of West Coast musicians experienced in the performance of classical and baroque music on instruments of the period. Led by violinist Marc Destrubé, the ensemble played instrumental concerts and also collaborated with choirs.

The Vancouver Board of Trade launched the federal debt clock, which made news right across the country—especially after it travelled the nation and visited Ottawa. The clock, designed by the Vancouver architectural firm Matsuzaki

Future shock. The BC Provincial Debt Clock is not a doomsday device, but it certainly displays a daunting dollar amount, as the expression on the face of this young future taxpayer seems to reflect. *PNG*

Wright, was a massive 360-kilogram (795-pound), 4.5-by-3-metre (15-by-10-foot) computerized calculator that tracked the rise in federal debt. It inspired the Canadian Taxpayers Association to create similar clocks for the provinces of BC, Alberta, Saskatchewan and Ontario.

The Vancouver Board of Trade launched another initiative this year: its Business and the Arts Awards, which encouraged corporate involvement with the arts. The awards continued the successful work initiated by the Vancouver Society for Business and the Arts.

In a sign of the decline of the fishing industry the Campbell Avenue fisherman's wharf, east of the BC Sugar Refinery, closed down.

An anonymous donation of $10 million was made to UBC this year, but someone tattled and it was learned the donation came from the Chan brothers, Tom and Caleb. The Chans arrived in Vancouver in 1987. Tom had visited the city in the 1960s and 1970s when he was at Berkeley, and he returned for Expo 86, a trip that inspired him and his wife to move to the city. The brothers started Burrard International Holdings, a company that developed golf courses and properties. Caleb, the president, handled the business side and Tom looked after the charitable foundation. In 1997 they financed the building of the Chan Centre for the Performing Arts at UBC.

The sale of houses in Vancouver dropped an astonishing 40 percent from the previous year. Sales rebounded sharply in 1991. On the other hand, 1990 marked the beginning of a surge in downtown construction. On average, in the first three years of the 1990s, a major new office building went up in downtown Vancouver every 84 days.

Larco Investments purchased Park Royal shopping centre and gave it a $20-million facelift, including new shops, fashion galleria and marketplace.

Ruling on a case brought by Musqueam litigant Ron Sparrow, the Supreme Court of Canada determined that the aboriginal right to fish was constitutionally protected and overrode all other interests except conservation. Further, the court decided that section 35 of the Constitution Act, 1982, provided a "strong measure of protection" for aboriginal rights. It also ruled that aboriginal and treaty rights were capable of evolving over time and must be interpreted in a generous and liberal manner.

The Arctic Canada Pavilion was opened at the Vancouver Aquarium. It included a two-million-litre (439,900-gallon) beluga whale pool and the Jean MacMillan Southam Arctic Gallery. The gallery featured sounds of Arctic marine mammals.

The City of Vancouver began a composting program. Residents received subsidized compost bins so organic waste (otherwise destined for landfills) could be recycled into a usable soil conditioner. Within five years the city had distributed more than 15,000 compost bins (at $25 each), diverting about 3,800 tonnes of organic material annually. This was also the year Surrey adopted the Blue Box recycling system for metal, glass and plastic, and the GVRD and its member municipalities switched to a policy of buying only recycled motor oil (a study showed that an estimated 5-million litres/1-million gallons of waste oil was disposed of annually by "do-it-yourselfers" in Greater Vancouver).

The city purchased the old Children's Hospital in Marpole and began its restoration as a residence for seniors.

Coquitlam's Westwood Motorsport Park, which was the only European-style racetrack in Canada when it opened in July 1959, closed down.

Comings and Goings

Notable deaths: **Laurence J. Peter**, co-author of *The Peter Principle*, died in Palos Verdes, CA, on January 10, aged 70; **Elod Macskasy**, UBC mathematics professor and champion chess player, died on January 21 (thanks to the generous support of the UBC Department of Mathematics, the inaugural Macskasy Memorial chess tournament was held in 2005); **Steve Woodman**, TV and radio broadcaster, entertainer and the first Ronald McDonald in Los Angeles—"the man of 1,000 voices"—died on March 13, aged 62; **Phyllis Munday**, mountaineer, died on April 11 in Nanaimo, aged about 95; **Tom Alsbury**, former Vancouver mayor (1959–62), died July 21, aged about 86.

Chanel opened a Vancouver location. Normand Pitre, president of Chanel Canada, called Vancouver "the Canadian city of the future."

1991

Canuck Pavel Bure skated his way into Vancouver hearts as "the Russian Rocket" while another city favourite, place-kicker Lui Passaglia, became the longest-playing Lion. Rita Johnston became the first female premier after being elected by the Social Credit caucus and then was defeated by the voters when former Vancouver mayor Mike Harcourt and the NDP won.

April 2 Rita Johnston, Social Credit MLA for Surrey, became premier of BC, succeeding Bill Vander Zalm, who had resigned. She served until November 5, 1991. She had been an MLA since 1983. During that time she was minister of municipal affairs (1986–89), highways minister (1989–91) and deputy premier (1990–91). Before that she had served on Surrey council for eight years (only the second woman to be elected to council), including a period when Vander Zalm was the mayor. As MLA for the area, Johnston was instrumental in bringing SkyTrain to Surrey—a move that heralded the municipality's arrival as the Greater Vancouver Regional District's second city centre.

June 30 The Lower Mainland Regional Correctional Centre (which until 1970 had been called Oakalla Prison Farm) closed. Originally designed to house a maximum of 484 prisoners, the prison population had peaked in 1962–63 at 1,269 inmates.

July 10 Grace MacInnis died in Vancouver, aged 85. Winona Grace Woodsworth was born July 25, 1905, in Winnipeg, the daughter of J.S. Woodsworth, one of the organizers of the Co-operative Commonwealth Federation (CCF). Grace was a delegate to the party's founding convention in Regina in 1933. A lifelong socialist, she was active in the CCF and its successor, the NDP. MacInnis was elected a BC MLA (Vancouver–Burrard) and served

Elsewhere in BC

The Union of BC Indian Chiefs established the Institute of Indigenous Government, which became a degree-granting institution in 1995. In 2007 the Nicola Valley Institute of Technology took over the IIG.

The Hatzic Rock archeological site was discovered near Mission. It is one of the oldest intact Native villages in North America, dating back to 7,000 BC. A museum has been established there.

Scotland-born ultra-marathoner Al Howie of Victoria ran the 7,295.5 kilometres (4,533.5 miles) from St. John's, NL, to Victoria in 72 days, 10 hours and 23 minutes, a world record. That's about 101 kilometres (63 miles) a day...every day...for 10 weeks. Not bad for a 45-year-old diabetic. He raised $750,000 for children with special needs.

Elsewhere in Canada

Federal legislation called for the total elimination of ozone-depleting chlorofluorocarbons (CFCs), found in many appliances and some hospital equipment, by 1996. Hospitals and the Greater Vancouver Regional Hospital District put out tenders for new CFC-free equipment. Savings in the first year: $3 million. Annual savings since: $1 million.

Ukrainian Canadians across the country celebrated the centennial of Ukrainian immigration this year.

The Royal Canadian Mounted Police introduced new regulations that allowed Sikh constables to wear elements of their religious attire as part of their official uniform. Constable Baltej Singh Bhillon was the first RCMP officer to wear a turban and other Sikh symbols.

Canada established a Royal Commission on Aboriginal Peoples to examine the relationship between Canada and indigenous peoples. The commission visited 96 communities, held 178 days of hearings and completed more than 350 research projects over four years.

Elsewhere in the World

January 16 Operation Desert Storm, the military action to liberate Kuwait, began with US air strikes against Iraq. On February 26 Saddam Hussein announced Iraq's withdrawal from Kuwait.

June 25 Croatia and Slovenia declared their independence from Yugoslavia.

December 26 The Supreme Soviet met in Moscow to formally dissolve the Soviet Union. Most republics had already seceded from the 73-year-old union, and Mikhail Gorbachev had resigned the previous day. The new country was renamed the Russian Federation.

from 1941 to 1945. She "emerged from the backrooms" in 1965 to win the Vancouver–Kingsway seat for the federal NDP, becoming BC's first woman MP. She retired in 1974 and was appointed an Officer of the Order of Canada the same year in recognition of her service to others. She was named to the Order of British Columbia in 1990.

Right: Soccer heavy-weight. Hockey isn't the only game in town. The 86ers, with scoring led by Domenic Mobilio, dominated national soccer as they won four Canadian Soccer League Championships in a row. Who needs a Stanley Cup? *Ralph Bower / Vancouver Sun*

September 16
The *Vancouver Sun* became a morning daily.

September 17 Henry Angus died in Vancouver, aged 100. Henry Forbes Angus was born April 19, 1891, in Victoria. He joined the University of British Columbia in 1919 as an assistant professor of economics. He was head of economics, political science and sociology from 1930 to 1956, the first dean of graduate studies (1949 to 1956) and dean emeritus from 1956 to his death. Angus was one of the few public figures in BC to oppose internment of Japanese Canadians during World War II.

September 25 The Stanley Theatre, built in 1931, ran its last movie, *Fantasia*, and then shut its doors. It reopened in October 1998 under the auspices of the Arts Club Theatre with Dean Regan's hit production of *Swing*. Beginning with the 2000–2001 season the Industrial Alliance Pacific Life Insurance Company became a sponsor of the theatre, which on April 5, 2005, became the Stanley Industrial Alliance Stage. The restoration of the art deco venue received a 1999 City of Vancouver Heritage Award.

September Rick Watson, an activist for the rights of people with disabilities, began a column for the *Province*. Disabled by cerebral palsy, he pecked out one letter at a time with a wand attached to a headband.

He won a Canada 125 medal for his activism, and a BC Newspaper Award for a column critical of telethons, one of which he'd appeared on as a child. He died in 1994, aged 41.

October 6 "Canadian soccer," wrote the *Province*'s Jack Keating, "has never seen the like of the Vancouver 86ers. Dominating Canadian soccer like no other franchise, the 86ers added to their prestigious record Sunday, October 6, winning a fourth consecutive Canadian Soccer League Championship with a resounding 5–3 victory over the Toronto Blizzard."

November 5
Michael Harcourt, NDP MLA for Vancouver Centre, became premier.

He had been mayor of the city from 1980 to 1986 and then ran provincially, becoming leader of the NDP and leader of the official opposition in 1987. He led the NDP to their first election win since 1972 but was forced to step down in 1996 in the midst of the "Bingogate" scandal involving inappropriate use of charitable donations. While Harcourt was not personally involved in the scandal, he took political responsibility for it.

Also November 5
Pavel Bure jumped on the ice for his first NHL game against the Winnipeg Jets

and stunned fans and players alike with his dazzling speed, prompting

Sun reporter Iain McIntyre to label him "the Russian Rocket." Bure had been the Vancouver Canucks' sixth-round draft pick in 1989, perhaps the best sixth-round pick in NHL history. There was a bit of a dust-up at the beginning because it appeared Bure had not played the requisite 11 games at the elite level to be eligible for the draft. Canucks scouts claimed he had, and an investigation by the NHL proved they were right. Bure was named the league's best rookie at the end of his first season, and he helped the Canucks to the 1994 Stanley Cup finals. He was also the league's leading scorer in the 1993–94 season. After seven seasons in Vancouver, Bure was traded to the Florida Panthers, where he continued to lead the league in scoring. He struggled with knee injuries throughout his career and finally retired in 2005, although he had not played since 2003. He averaged better than a point a game in his NHL career (779 points with 437 goals in 702 NHL games).

November Mi-Jung Lee, the first Korean Canadian media personality, joined BCTV, where she produced and anchored the *Weekend News Hour*. She had launched her TV journalism career in 1990 as a reporter and part-time anchor at CHEK-TV in Victoria. From 1998 to 2001 she was with Vancouver Television and then moved to CTV, where she was anchor and producer of *CTV News at 11:30* (2001–10).

December
South Surrey's new ice arena opened. It was the only Olympic-sized arena in BC.

The Warehouse Studio, a recording facility established by hometown musician Bryan Adams, inhabits the Oppenheimer Bros. grocery warehouse. For restoring the warehouse, which is the oldest brick building in the city, Adams received the City of Vancouver Heritage Award in 1998. *PNG*

Also in 1991

The District of North Vancouver marked its 100th birthday.

Rock superstar Bryan Adams bought the old Oppenheimer Brothers grocery warehouse at Columbia and Powell in Gastown and turned it into a recording studio. It's the oldest brick building in Vancouver.

One of the pioneer automobile retailers in the city, Plimley's—active for 98 years—closed. Thomas Plimley had started a bicycle business in Victoria in 1893, the year he arrived from England. He sold the first car in Victoria, an Oldsmobile, in 1901. His son Horace started Plimley Motors on Howe Street in 1936; it became one of BC's largest dealerships. Horace's son Basil, who ran the company from 1957 to 1986, was one of the few

Longest-playing Lion. Lui Passaglia is hoisted to glory after kicking the field goal that won BC's team the 1994 Grey Cup. *Gerry Kahrmann / The Province*

third-generation executives of a BC business.

Frank Iacobucci, born in Vancouver on June 29, 1937, was appointed to the Supreme Court of Canada. He served to June 30, 2004. Justice Iacobucci gave an interesting interview to Fiona Story of *Il Postino* in 2001, while he was still on the court, in which he admits: "I would have liked to have been the manager of a major league baseball team."

Microsoft bought Vancouver-based electronic mail specialist Consumer Software, a Vancouver software development laboratory, and in 1994 transferred its operation to Redmond, WA.

Dean and Sherri Duperron took over Sprott-Shaw College, which had been around since 1903. Under their leadership the college expanded rapidly. The Duperrons sold the college in 2007, and the new owners continued to expand throughout BC as well as internationally.

Leadership Vancouver, established this year, was a program to develop, promote and encourage effective community leadership. It sprang from a US concept that was, in turn, sparked by a horrific 1962 plane crash that wiped out nearly every major cultural leader in the city of Atlanta, GA. The grieving city established a leadership program in a volunteer community effort "to foster successive generations of community leaders." The idea caught on in other American cities and came this year to Vancouver, the first Canadian city to pick it up. Leadership Vancouver was a joint effort by Volunteer Vancouver and the Vancouver Board of Trade.

Stan Smyl, at the time the Vancouver Canucks' all-time leading scorer (262 goals and 411 assists in a team-leading 896 games), retired. His number 12 was retired too, making him the first Canuck so honoured. Smyl later joined the team as an assistant coach. (Trevor Linden and Markus Näslund have since passed his goals, assists and games-played records.)

James Delgado became the executive director of the Vancouver Maritime Museum. Delgado, born January 11, 1958, in San Jose, CA, and the author of many books, was the first underwater archeologist to visit the *Titanic*. In 2006 he dismayed the locals when he left to become executive director of the Institute of Nautical Archaeology.

Lui Passaglia of the BC Lions set a new professional football scoring record, finishing the year with a lifetime 2,312 points. Passaglia also became the longest-playing Lion in history (1976–2000), appearing in a total of 236 games, overtaking Al Wilson's previous mark of 233 games. Passaglia retired in 2000 and spent seven years as the Lions' director of community relations before resigning to work in his family's property development company.

Cornelia Oberlander, landscape architect, was named a Companion of the Order of Canada. Her work on the Robson Square/provincial courthouse, Vancouver Public Library's central branch and UBC's Museum of Anthropology have made Vancouver a greener and lovelier city. Born June 20, 1924, in Muhlheim, Germany Oberlander escaped with her family from Nazi Germany in 1939. Years later she returned to Germany to design the gardens for the Canadian embassy in Berlin.

The *Globe and Mail*'s urbane glossy magazine *West*, inaugurated in 1990, was named Western Magazine of the Year. It died in 1992. A similar fate awaited *Step*, an independent arts magazine launched this year by neophyte publishers Ray Dearborn and Philip Aw. It won the Western Magazine of the Year title in 1992 and folded the following year. It's a tough town for magazines.

A two-storey, $6.9-million facility housing the Networks of Centres of Excellence opened at the University of British Columbia. Designed by architect Zoltan Kiss, it sat atop the university bookstore and was designed to accommodate laboratories and offices. This was the building that housed Michael Smith's laboratory, and where he shared a champagne toast with colleagues the day it was announced he had won the 1993 Nobel Prize for Chemistry.

Coquitlam's Town Centre Stadium opened in time for the district's 100th anniversary and its metamorphosis into a city.

Dr. Jean Barman and Linda Hale of UBC co-produced a bibliography of local history books from BC, under the auspices of the BC Library Association, for BC Heritage Trust. Some 800 communities were included, and 1,044 local history titles cited, in *British Columbia Local Histories: A Bibliography*.

Bowen Islanders voted no to municipal status in a referendum. The island remained unincorporated and under the jurisdiction of the Greater Vancouver Regional District (GVRD).

In 1991 about 23 percent of municipal solid waste generated within the GVRD was recovered for recycling. Based on a population of 1.7 million residents at that time, the per capita waste generation rate for all GVRD residents was about 860 kilograms (1,900 pounds) per year and the recycling rate was about 200 kilograms (440 pounds) per year. Between 1988 and 1991 the municipal solid waste recycling rate had increased significantly: during that time the quantity of waste generated increased by more than 22 percent, but the amount recovered for recycling increased by almost 300 percent.

Glen Brae was bequeathed to the City of Vancouver. The stately Shaughnessy mansion at 1690 Matthews Ave. had spent the last few years as a seniors' long-term care facility. The house was given to the city by its owner, Elisabeth Wlosinski. It reopened in 1995 as Canuck Place, a hospice for children with life-threatening illnesses, sponsored by hockey's Canuck Foundation.

The BC Rail car shop in Squamish, built in 1914 when the line was called the Pacific Great Eastern, was hauled the short distance from the BCR yards to the new West Coast Railway Heritage Park. It was the largest building—24 by 46 metres (80 by 151 feet)—ever to be moved in the province and it formed the centrepiece of the 5-hectare (12-acre) railway museum, which features a fine collection of locomotives and rolling stock representing the railways that have operated in British Columbia.

There was trouble in Mount Pleasant when local residents took to the streets to try to remove hookers from their neighbourhoods. Vancouver Police released the names of johns nabbed in the area, but the city newspapers refused to publish the names.

Richmond's population was growing at a tremendous pace. In 1956 the population was just 26,000. That increased to 43,323 in 1961 and hit 62,120 in 1971. Then the boom began, as Richmond grew to 96,154 people in 1986 and jumped to 126,624 in 1991. In 1971 some 83 percent of the city's population had listed English as their first language; by 1991 that had fallen to 69 percent. Richmond declared itself Canada's first multicultural city and began offering city services in a wide variety of languages.

Book worthy. The Newton Library, an internationally renowned architectural undertaking, beautifies Surrey.
Colleen Kidd / Sterling News Service courtesy of PNG

Between 1981 and 1991 some 18 percent (28,585 people) of immigrants to the Lower Mainland were from Hong Kong, 14.1 percent (22,405) from China, 9.3 (14,845) from India and 6.9 percent (10,910) from the Philippines. Immigrants from Great Britain dropped to fifth place at 5.8 percent (9,295).

The 1991 census also reported that of a total Vancouver population of 465,300, those with aboriginal origins or First Nations registration numbered 13,360.

The first anthology of contemporary writing by Chinese Canadians, *Many-Mouthed Birds*, was published, edited by Bennett Lee and Jim Wong-Chu.

Comings and Goings

Notable deaths: **Gordon Hilker**, concert promoter, artistic director of the Vancouver Festival and director of the Expo 67 World Festival of Entertainment, died in North Vancouver on April 28, aged 77; **Dorothy Somerset**, actor/director, who helped found UBC's drama department, died in Vancouver on August 11, aged 91.

1992

Right: Built to last. At 100 years old the Britannia Heritage Shipyard received the National Historic Site distinction. *PNG*

The city chose a Roman Colosseum design for its new central library. Hundreds attended the funeral of Dr. Peter Jepson-Young, whose TV diary on the CBC evening news had done much to educate people about AIDS. This was also the year Vancouver introduced sprinkler regulations and began aerial spraying for the gypsy moth.

January Britannia Heritage Shipyard in Steveston was declared a National Historic Site. Built in 1889–90 as a cannery and converted into a shipyard in 1918, it was the oldest surviving collection of cannery/shipyard buildings on the Fraser.

February 16 White Rock city council commemorated the 35th anniversary of the city's incorporation (April 15, 1957) by becoming the first municipality in Canada to request a grant of arms from the newly established Canadian Heraldic Authority. The milestone anniversary was marked April 10, 1992, by the visit of Governor General Ramon Hnatyshyn.

February The three finalists in the competition to design Vancouver's new main library submitted their visions to public scrutiny, and Moshe Safdie's great ellipse, reminiscent of the Roman Colosseum, was the favourite with approximately 70 percent of the 7,000 Vancouverites who commented. Critics were less enthusiastic (Adele Freedman described it as "falling somewhere between a joke and a folly, both monumental") and the city's quantity surveyor estimated the building would run more than $25 million over budget. The judges awarded the commission to Safdie with the proviso that the architect resolve the structural and financial shortcoming, which he was able to do.

April 11 Harry Farnham Germaine Letson, soldier, died in Ottawa, aged 95. Born September 26, 1896, in Vancouver, he was the first graduate in mechanical engineering at UBC. In 1917, during World War I, he won the Military Cross "for conspicuous gallantry and devotion to duty." King George V presented the medal to him at Buckingham Palace. From 1923 to 1936 Letson was a member of UBC's mechanical and electrical engineering department, then left to run Letson and Burpee, a machinery manufacturing company co-founded by his father. In 1939 he was put in charge of defences for the Vancouver and Fraser Valley areas, but by August 1940 had been appointed military attaché to the Canadian legation in Washington, DC, and in February 1942 was called to Ottawa to take over the duties of Adjutant-General, responsible for recruiting and training the Canadian armed forces. He was ultimately appointed chairman of the Canadian Joint Staff in Washington. After the war, when Viscount Alexander became Governor General of Canada, Major-General Letson was his secretary. An outstanding career, an outstanding man.

May 23 Burnaby celebrated its 100th birthday with a Centennial

September 21 Federal and provincial governments and BC's First Nations established the BC Treaty Commission and a process to negotiate modern-day treaties. Chief Joe Mathias of the Squamish Nation signed the agreement on behalf of the province's First Nations, along with Chief Edward John, Sophie Pierre, Miles G. Richardson and Tom Sampson. Prime Minister Brian Mulroney and Tom Siddons, minister of Indian Affairs and Northern Development, signed for the federal government, while Premier Michael Harcourt and Andrew Petter, minister of Aboriginal Affairs, signed for the province.

Elsewhere in Canada

The CRTC, the governing body of the communications industry, opened the long distance market to full competition.

New regulations decreed that it was no longer necessary for beer to be brewed in the province where it was sold.

Left: Model libraries. When the library at 750 Burrard became unable to support the volume of users, the call went out for a new, bigger library. These are two rejected proposals for the design of the library, ultimately won by Moshe Safdie, Richard Archambault and Barry Downs, resulting in the unique Colosseum-inspired building at 350 West Georgia.
David Clark / The Province

Parade to Swangard Stadium as fireworks blazed from atop the BC Tel building at Kingsway and Boundary Road.

May The Canadian Craft Museum opened. This small architectural gem, designed by Paul Merrick, was part of the Cathedral Place complex, with its own tiny green courtyard. The museum closed in 2003.

June 20 The Burnaby Centennial Quilt was unveiled at the Bob Prittie Library in Metrotown. Celebrating Burnaby's history, it had taken 18 seniors one year to create.

July 1 The Vancouver International Airport Authority took over control of YVR from Transport Canada. David Emerson, former president of the BC Trade Development Corporation, was appointed president and chief executive officer. The VIAA described itself as a community-based, not-for-profit corporation whose primary objective was to "expand the contribution which Vancouver International Airport makes to local economic development, and to improve the cost-effectiveness and commercial orientation of the airport." To achieve this, the authority instituted "airport improvement fees" on May 1, 1993. All travellers departing from the airport paid a $5 to $15 fee depending on where they were going. In a 1996 interview with *Equity* magazine, Emerson explained that someone had to pay the $500 million for the airport's expansion, and the VIAA decided to make the fee visible so the public associated the money with the project. He promised that once the additions were completed, the fee would disappear and further expansion would be funded by 20-year bonds. (By June 1, 1996, when the new international terminal opened for business, the AIF program had raised approximately $100 million toward the cost of the building.)

August The Richmond campus of Kwantlen College opened just over a year after construction began in March 1991. The $37-million campus was built on the 4-hectare (10-acre) site of the former Lansdowne racetrack at the corner of Garden City and Lansdowne Roads. (Kwantlen is known today as Kwantlen Polytechnic University.)

Summer Vancouver experienced water shortages and regulations were put in place to limit lawn sprinkling.

September 22 The District of Burnaby turned 100 and became the City of Burnaby. (It had been a municipality to this time.)

September 23 This was not a good year for the BC Lions. They lost eight straight games before finally vanquishing Ottawa 33–27 on September 3 under quarterback Danny Barrett. Team owner Murray Pezim declared bankruptcy, and the CFL took over the team. On September 23 Bill Comrie became the new owner, but the team's losing ways continued. They finished the season with a dreadful 3–15 record and an average attendance of 14,000. Head Coach Bob O'Billovich was fired.

September 27 Hugh Llewellyn Keenleyside, diplomat and executive, died in Saanich, aged 94. Born July 7, 1898, in Toronto, he moved to BC with his family as a child. After high school he served with the 2nd Canadian Tank Battalion in World War I, then went to university, earned his PhD, taught history at UBC from 1925 (the first year the university was on the Point Grey campus) and joined the Department of External Affairs in 1928. He served in Tokyo from 1929 to 1936 and was the Canadian secretary of the Permanent Joint Board of Defence from 1940 to 1944. (Keenleyside opposed the forced internment of Japanese Canadians during the war.) The next two decades were varied: he was, consecutively, Canada's ambassador to Mexico, federal deputy minister of mines and resources, federal commissioner for the Northwest Territories and director general of the United Nations' Technical Assistance Administration. In 1959 he returned to BC and served as chair or co-chair of the provincial hydro utility until 1969, playing an important role in BC's development of hydroelectric power. He was on the UBC senate from 1963 to 1969 and was chancellor of Notre Dame University in Nelson from 1969 to 1977.

September The Japanese Canadian Cultural Centre opened in Steveston alongside the existing Martial Arts Centre and the Steveston Community Centre. It was one of the first buildings to be funded from the Japanese Canadian Redress Foundation, negotiated in 1988 to revitalize Japanese Canadian communities across Canada.

October 5 Surrey Metro Credit Union angered some traditionalists when it introduced a new share structure, and non-voting ownership shares began trading on the Toronto Stock Exchange. The traditionalists feared this could shift control of the credit union to out-of-province interests. Surrey Metro had gained a reputation in the field as BC's maverick credit union.

October 26 In New Westminster two patents, one for the city's coat of arms and flag, the other for the badge of the city's police department, were presented by Governor General Ramon Hnatyshyn at a special ceremony at city hall during a visit celebrating the 125th anniversary of Confederation and the Silver Jubilee of the Canadian honours system. "Thus," wrote Canada's chief herald, Robert Watt, "122 years after incorporation, BC's first capital was granted a coat of arms which enshrined a good part of its symbolic heritage."

October Home-Coming '92 commemorated the 50th anniversary of the wartime expulsion of Japanese from the West Coast in 1942. More than 700 delegates from across Canada, the United States and other countries, including Japan, attended. Robert Ito was on one of the buses touring the sites of BC's detention camps. Ito was born July 2, 1931, in Vancouver and was sent to Tashme internment camp. In 1944 his family moved to Raymond, AB, and later to Montreal where he began his dancing career with the National Ballet of Canada. In the mid-1960s he turned to acting and was probably best known for his seven-year stint as "Sam Fujiyama" on the popular TV series *Quincy, M.E.* opposite Jack Klugman.

November Vancouver initiated its CityPlan process, with city council inviting a broad range of people—including members of clubs, business associations and resident groups as well as interested individuals—to meet in small groups called City Circles. Their task was to propose ideas for Vancouver and suggest how to make them happen. More than 450 City Circles, involving over 5,000 people, were formed, including 150 youth circles and more than 70 multicultural circles, with people participating in languages other than English. This fulfilled city council's wish that the process involve people who did not normally participate in city planning. The city won national and international awards for the innovative public process.

November 15 "Dr. Peter" (Peter William Jepson-Young) died. A medical doctor, he had started a weekly diary of his life with AIDS on the CBC evening news in September 1990. It ran for 111 instalments, which were edited into an Oscar-nominated documentary. Until his death, he continued to educate viewers, becoming Canada's leading HIV/AIDS spokesperson. Born June 8, 1957, in New Westminster, he was 35 when he died. More than 900 people attended his funeral on November 24.

December 1 Coquitlam, incorporated July 25, 1891, became a city. Its coat of arms was affirmed for continued use. The predominant colours of blue and white were chosen for esthetic reasons, although the blue does refer to the rivers which define several of the municipal boundaries.

December 21 Alvin Balkind, curator, died in Vancouver, aged 71. Balkind was born March 28, 1921, in Baltimore, MD, and came to Vancouver in 1954. His New Design Gallery, founded in 1955, was a centre for the avant-garde. He was the curator of UBC's Fine Arts Gallery from 1962 to 1973 and chief curator at Vancouver Art Gallery from 1975 to 1978. Then he turned freelance. "I got sick to death," he said, "of being in an institution. As Dennis Wheeler once said, 'They can't exist without your energy, but they use it up and they know it before you do.' A gallery's programming is so intense, the exhibitions are so many and complex, and then there's the internal politics to deal with. After a while it's exhausting." Balkind won the first $50,000 VIVA award from the Vancouver Institute for Visual Arts, presented to an artist or art worker who has made a lasting contribution to the art scene in British Columbia.

December The North Vancouver Division of Versatile Pacific Shipyards laid off its last employees. The company would have celebrated its 100th anniversary in 1994. (The Victoria division closed in 1994.

Also in 1992

Vancouver-born Tim Stevenson became the first openly gay person to seek—and achieve—ordination in a mainline church denomination in Canada. He was ordained by the British Columbia conference of the United Church of Canada.

First Nations House of Learning opened at UBC. Architectural historian Harold Kalman wrote that the building, designed by Larry McFarland Architects, was "inspired in its shape and structure by the longhouses of the Coast Salish, while the gabled roof, supported by massive cedar logs, recalls the traditional cedar housing of all coastal native groups."

Cates Tugs, a fixture in this area since 1913, was sold to US entrepreneur Dennis Washington, owner of Montana-based Washington Corporation. Washington left day-to-day operations in the hands of local management.

Jessie Wowk Elementary School in Richmond was named to honour the area's Ukrainian pioneers.

Vancouver residents were sprayed with a deluge of newspaper, radio and television stories about gypsy moths. Mark L. Winston, a biologist at SFU, described the pest as "Vancouver's most publicized insects. These forest-eating moths originated in Europe and Asia, and regularly arrive today from two directions, eastern North America and Siberia. They may do minor damage to our forests if they become established, but present a major threat to our lumber export industry: importing countries would require fumigation of all BC wood products if gypsy moths were declared resident." The city instituted an aerial spray program, releasing moth-killing bacteria over much of the city, which was greeted by vociferous protests.

Cates Tugs, a visual staple of the North Vancouver shoreline, is owned by Dennis Washington, who is also the owner of Southern Railway of BC, Montana Rail Link and Seaspan.
Top: David Clark / The Province Left: Bill Keay Photo / Vancouver Sun

A study showed that the average annual household income in Vancouver was $49,938. The same study showed that the average household spent $196 per year on cable TV, $77 on live sports, $60 on live performances and $54 on movies.

The provincial ministry of agriculture, fisheries and food did a study, too. It announced that the average Vancouver family of four spent close to $10,000 on meals per year.

Cleaner cars. AirCare, BC's plan to reduce harmful car emissions by testing cars yearly as a requirement for insurance, wasn't everyone's favourite way to spend a morning. AirCare has since modified the rules based on the age of the car and remains as a way to weed out the heaviest-polluting offenders. *Gerry Kahrmann / The Province*

The *Vancouver Sun* reported there were 1,500 prostitutes working in the city and estimated they generated $63 million in revenues to the local economy.

AirCare started. All vehicles in the Lower Mainland had to pass emissions testing before they could be insured.

The Jantzen swimwear company began an annual cleanup day campaign at Sunset Beach with volunteer staff.

The Sunny Trails Club for nudists, which had been in Surrey since 1952, moved to Lake Errock.

John Alleyne, Barbados-born National Ballet School alumnus with extensive performing experience in Germany, became artistic director of Ballet British Columbia following the death of Barry Ingham. He raised the company's profile with his innovative choreography.

In the movie *K2: Journey to the Top of the World*, directed by Franc Roddam and released this year, Vancouver played Seattle, and Blackcomb stood in for the "Savage Mountain" of the Himalayas that challenged the endurance of rival climbers.

This was a good year for the BC book publishing industry. In 1970 the entire industry earned $350,000 in sales. By 1992, total provincial book revenue climbed to $25 million, more than 70 times the 1970 figure.

One of the great Vancouver books appeared this year. Bruce Macdonald, born in Vancouver in 1948, got the idea for *Vancouver: A Visual History* in the summer of 1984. The 1992 book (10,000 hours of work, partially subsidized by the Vancouver Historical Society) comprised a series of maps showing the development in 10-year increments of Vancouver from the 1850s to the 1980s, with accompanying text. Other maps show ethnic heritage, religious affiliation, etc. It's terrifically interesting and sometimes surprising, and the introduction is very funny.

Rolf Knight published *Homer Stevens: A Life in Fishing*, the autobiography of Homer Stevens, former president of the United Fishermen and Allied Workers' Union, which is a history of the BC coast and the portrait of a complex man. Knight interviewed Stevens and ended up with 90 hours of tapes to transcribe and then compile. According to the author, "Here is an account of a person who represents an amalgam of different peoples: his ancestors were Croatian, Finnish, Greek, Native—but Homer's radicalism was very much indigenous to British Columbia."

Comings and Goings

March 1 The CBC Vancouver Orchestra and the Vancouver Recital Society joined to present Italian diva Cecilia Bartoli in the Orpheum—the first of what would be three appearances together. Bartoli is now one of the world's most popular and successful opera singers.

Notable deaths: **George H. Reifel**, farmer and distiller, died in Palm Desert, CA, on March 7, aged 69; **John Ireland**, movie actor, died in Santa Barbara, CA, on March 21, aged 78; **Mary Pack**, "angel of mobility," who devoted her life to arthritis and rheumatism care and research, died in Vancouver on May 11, aged 87; **Pauline Jewett**, political scientist, president of SFU from 1974 to 1978, MP for New Westminster–Coquitlam from 1979 to 1988, died in Ottawa on July 5, aged 69; **Beatrice Wood**, daughter of Lieutenant-Governor John William Fordham-Johnson and wife of UBC drama teacher Freddie Wood, died in Vancouver on July 18, aged 92; **John Richard Collister "Jack" Short**, racing broadcaster, died August 4, aged 83; **William Bruce Hutchison**, journalist, *Vancouver Sun* editor (1963–79), and three-time Governor General's Award winner, died on September 14, aged 91 (Hutchison coined the phrase "Lotusland" to describe BC); **Earl Marriott**, educator and Surrey School District superintendent, died November 16, aged 86.

1993

A Vancouver institution was lost as the Woodward's chain declared bankruptcy. A UBC professor won a Nobel prize, and the city hosted a summit meeting between Bill Clinton and Boris Yeltsin. Vancouver electors, meanwhile, elected the country's first Indo-Canadian to Parliament and defeated the first female prime minister when Kim Campbell lost her own seat.

January 15 Woodward's, a retail institution in Greater Vancouver for more than 90 years, closed its original downtown store at Hastings and Abbott. The Woodward's chain had filed for court protection from creditors on December 11, 1992, but there was no escape. The company owed more than $65 million and declared bankruptcy in June, the victim of a fast-paced retail market. It collapsed with 26 department stores, 33 Woodwyn discount outlets, 20 travel agencies, 4 Abercrombie & Fitch specialty stores and 3 Commercial Interiors divisions in BC and Alberta. In 1993 another Canadian retail institution, the Hudson's Bay Company, purchased the Woodward's assets and quickly converted the old stores into new Bay or Zellers outlets.

The famous big "W" sign atop the store was a landmark which the people of Vancouver refused to lose. Charles Woodward put a lofty tower atop his store in 1923. It was 23 metres (75 feet) high, patterned after the Eiffel Tower and topped with a revolving

The iconic "W" sign marked the original downtown location of Woodward's for over 90 years. *PNG*

Elsewhere in BC

Sue Rodriguez, who was diagnosed with amyotrophic lateral sclerosis (ALS or Lou Gehrig's disease) in 1992, applied to the Supreme Court of BC to strike down the section of the Criminal Code that made assisted suicide illegal. The Supreme Court of Canada ultimately ruled against Rodriguez, but her struggle galvanized the public. Rodriguez committed suicide in 1994 with the help of an anonymous doctor.

The BC government and the Union of BC Indian Chiefs signed a Memorandum of Understanding that established a government-to-government relationship between the province and BC's First Nations. The MOU ensured that discussions with the province would not interfere with First Nations' negotiations and relationship with the federal government.

Elsewhere in Canada

June 25 Kim Campbell, MP for Vancouver Centre, took office as the first female prime minister in Canadian history. She didn't last long: the Conservatives were soundly defeated in the October 1993 election and Jean Chrétien took over as prime minister.

Changes were made to the electoral act this year that allowed all Canadians living overseas, including those who had returned to Hong Kong and Taiwan for fewer than five consecutive years, to vote in Canadian federal elections.

Elsewhere in the World

January 1 Czechoslovakia peacefully spilt into two countries, the Czech Republic and the Slovak Republic.

After playing college hockey at the University of Maine, Paul Kariya was drafted fourth overall in the first round of the National Hockey League draft by the Anaheim Mighty Ducks. Kariya was born in Vancouver on October 16, 1974, to a Japanese Canadian father and a Caucasian mother. He firmly established himself as one of the most skilful athletes of the NHL, winning Hockey East Player of the Year (1993), Hockey East Rookie of the Year (1993), Hobey Baker Memorial Award (1993), a silver medal with the Canadian Olympic team (1994) and the Lady Byng Memorial Trophy (1997). He led the NHL with 429 shots during the 2000 season, shooting 86 more times than anybody else in the league.

Cranbrook-born Brent Carver (November 17, 1951) won a 1993 Tony Award (Best Actor in a Musical) for his starring role in Broadway's *Kiss of the Spiderwoman.*

searchlight that could be seen as far away as Vancouver Island. At the base of the tower sat a huge letter W, a red neon sign that featured 660 flashing bulbs. When World War II began, the federal government ordered the light removed, so William Woodward put the W—5 metres (16 feet) high and weighing 2.7 tonnes—on top of the tower, 91 metres (300 feet) above the street. It had been up there ever since. The building was demolished in 2006, but the W was reinstalled on the new Woodward's Building.

January 28 Mandrake the Magician (Leon Mandrake) died in Surrey, aged 81. He was born April 11, 1911, in New Westminster. At age eight he performed at the Edison Vaudeville Theatre and the New Westminster Civic National Exhibition. From 1927 he toured North America with his magic show, and by the 1940s he was a top box-office draw. He married his partner/assistant, Velvet, in Chicago in 1947. They toured worldwide, setting the trend for large, elaborate illusion shows; he was the first magician to play nightclubs. In the 1950s he had two TV series and performed on the CBC. Mandrake lectured at Canadian universities in the 1970s. Whether he inspired the popular comic strip *Mandrake the Magician* (which premiered in 1934) or it inspired him is a subject of interest to entertainment buffs to this day.

January The *Spirit of British Columbia,* an S-class superferry, was launched this year for the BC Ferry Corporation.

It measured 167.5 metres (550 feet) long and could carry 2,052 passengers (and 48 crew) and 470 vehicles. Service speed was 19.5 knots, and the ship still travels regularly on the Tsawwassen–Swartz Bay route. It was built in five modules by three shipyards—Allied Shipbuilders and Pacific Rim Shipyards of Vancouver and Integrated Module Fabricators/Yarrows in Victoria—then joined together.

June 2 Larry Lillo died in Vancouver, aged 46. He was born September 20, 1946, in Kinuso, a tiny village in Alberta northwest of Edmonton. Lillo was the co-founder of Tamahnous Theatre and a director and actor with the company from 1971 to 1981. After several years as a freelance theatre director and the artistic director of the Grand Theatre in London, ON, he became artistic director of the Vancouver Playhouse in 1988. Within four years he had doubled the number of subscriptions sold. He won a Jessie and a Dora award for his 1988 direction of Sam Shepard's *A Lie of the Mind*, and he directed and developed many new Canadian plays.

July 10 Anne MacDonald died in North Vancouver, aged 63. Anne Elizabeth MacDonald was born March 18, 1930, in Vancouver. She established North Vancouver's Presentation House Arts Centre and saved the historic Church of St. John the Evangelist as a recital hall (named Anne MacDonald Hall in 1977). She founded the North Vancouver Community Arts Council and the BC Arts and Crafts Fair. As the first executive director of the Vancouver Community Arts Council, she set up the Assembly of BC Arts Councils. Ms. MacDonald sat on many boards and commissions including the UBC

The *Spirit of British Columbia*, the first of two "Spirit Class" superferries and the largest ship in the BC Ferry Corporation's fleet (along with its sister ship, the *Spirit of Vancouver*) graces the Tsawwassen to Swartz Bay run, and boasts one of the best buffets in BC. *Debra Brash* / Victoria Times Colonist. *Courtesy PNG*

senate, North Vancouver School District and Canadian Conference of the Arts. She was a member of the Order of BC and in 1990 received the YWCA Woman of Distinction Award for Community Service.

August 12 Momiji Garden was built in Hastings Park to commemorate the Japanese Canadian internment during World War II. Japanese Canadians were processed at the PNE site before being moved away from the coast. The Vancouver Japanese Gardeners Association designed and created the garden with upper and lower sections divided by a stone wall reminiscent of ancient castles in Japan. The use of azaleas, irises, hydrangeas, day lilies and Japanese maples provides year-round colour.

Beautiful reminder. The stunning Momiji Garden, a little piece of heaven nestled in Hastings Park, was designed by the Vancouver Japanese Gardeners Association and built to commemorate the internment of Japanese Canadians.
Colin Price / The Province

August 27 The 200,000th baby was born at New Grace Hospital (now the BC Women's Hospital and Health Centre).

September 11
The Municipality of Surrey officially became a city.

Surrey's population is expected to eclipse that of Vancouver as it moves toward becoming the urban giant of the South Fraser area.

October 6 Peter Toigo died in Los Angeles, aged 61. Peter Claude Toigo was born September 9, 1932, in Powell River, BC. At age seven he sold eggs door-to-door in Powell River. Ten years later he bought the Wildwood Grocery and worked there as a butcher. He married his childhood sweetheart, Elizabeth Rowher, in 1950 and completed his first major land transaction. In 1960 he bought downtown Powell River from MacMillan Bloedel and built its first shopping centre. In the mid-1970s his company, Shato Holdings, almost went bankrupt but survived and expanded, buying the White Spot restaurant chain in December 1982. An intensely private man, he was dogged by controversy around labour issues and Social Credit Party connections.

October 13
UBC professor Michael Smith (born in Blackpool, England, in 1932) won the Nobel Prize in Chemistry.

The prize was $500,000 but Smith didn't keep it. He gave away half to the Schizophrenia Society of Canada and the Canadian Alliance for Research in Schizophrenia, then gave away the other half to establish an endowment fund whose income, among other things, helped support the Society for Canadian Women in Science. Dr. Smith died of leukemia at age 68 on October 4, 2000.

October 25 Dr. Hedy Fry, born August 6, 1941, in San Fernando, Trinidad, was elected as Liberal MP for Vancouver Centre, defeating Prime Minister Kim Campbell. "I ran against a white, blonde, blue-eyed fifth-generation Canadian prime minister and I beat her," Fry stated after the election. "I beat her because whites, Chinese, Asians, everybody voted for me." Dr. Fry was a past president of the Vancouver Medical Association and president of the BC Medical Association. She was re-elected in the 2011 federal election, marking 19 years in office. The first Indo-Canadians were also elected to the federal Parliament this year, and one of them was from BC. Harbance "Herb" Dhaliwal won the Vancouver South riding. He became the first Indo-Canadian to assume a cabinet post when he was appointed minister of national revenue in 1997. Gurbax Singh Malhi, from Malton, ON, was the first turbaned Sikh in Parliament. Raymond Chan, who was elected in Richmond, became the first Chinese Canadian cabinet minister when he was appointed minister of state for multiculturalism in 2004.

November 12 Gerald Rushton died in Tsawwassen, aged 95. Gerald Arnold Rushton was born July 20, 1898, in Liverpool, England. After winning a scholarship to Liverpool Collegiate School, he took officer training (1915–19), learning world trade shipping. He came to BC in 1920 and joined the Union Steamship Company, where he worked for 38 years. His knack for research made him a sought-after expert on the maritime heritage of the West Coast. Rushton wrote *Whistle up the Inlet: A History of the Union Steamship Company* (1974) and *Echoes of the Whistle* (1980), an illustrated history of the company.

November Philip Owen became Vancouver's 42nd mayor. He got into politics in 1978 as a Park Board commissioner and was on council by 1986. He was the first mayor of Vancouver elected to a three-year term of office, a cost-saving measure approved at the previous election. He was elected twice more and ultimately served nine years, the longest uninterrupted mayoral term in office since the city began.

Old thriller. Built in 1912, the Parker carousel thrilled riders at the PNE for over 50 years before its restoration and relocation to the Burnaby Village Museum, where it resides still in full working order.
Top: The Province; below: Ric Ernst / The Province

Also in 1993

The Musqueam filed a statement of intent to negotiate a treaty with the BC Treaty Commission. It was one of the first bands to enter the new process established in 1992. Negotiations began in 1994. The Musqueam negotiated and initialled a framework agreement in 1997, but it was rejected by band members in 1998 after BC and Canada indicated that compensation was not open to negotiation. No agreement was reached on a framework for negotiation, the third of six steps in the treaty process.

The Squamish Nation also entered the BC treaty process this year, proceeding slowly to the third stage.

This year's Fraser River sockeye salmon run was the largest since 1913: 24,195,000 fish counted (compared to 6,493,000 the year before and 17,241,000 the year after.)

A big, aging barn, last remnant of the Frasea Dairy Farm on Sea Island, once Richmond's largest dairy farm, was torn down when Vancouver International Airport began building its third runway. The farm had been established in 1922 by Jake Grauer and at one time was home to 500 cows.

The City of Vancouver began installing distinctive plaques on its heritage buildings. The bronze markers incorporated the city crest with text briefly outlining the building's history and architecture. Today there are more than 100 plaques (with more being added); the Heritage Department at Vancouver City Hall will provide you with a locations list.

Dr. Murray Newman, director of the Vancouver Public Aquarium, retired and was succeeded by Dr. John Nightingale, former deputy director of the New York Aquarium. The aquarium is now the largest in Canada, and one of the five largest (of about 50) in North America, with an annual budget of about $13 million.

Capilano College marked its 25th anniversary by opening a new $10.9-million library. The three-storey building had a shelving capacity of 200,000 books and included an audio-visual centre, a media production lab and an Achievement Resource Center (ARC) that provided services and courses for students wishing to develop their learning and study skills.

St. Paul's Hospital established North America's first Chair for AIDS research with funding from the St. Paul's Hospital Foundation and the University of British Columbia.

Research started this year by Burnaby Hospital senior nurse Peg McIsaac led to insights into the standard hospital policy of waking all long-term patients three times during the night. Instead, nurses quietly checked all patients every half hour, giving assistance only to those who were awake and in need. Patients who enjoyed uninterrupted sleep showed improved appetite and less agitation, belligerence and confusion during the day. Other hospitals that adopted the system have praised it, and the provincial health ministry urged widespread adoption of the changes.

The provincial government launched the first public inquiry into the BC Securities market. In spite of more aggressive policing by the Securities Commission and the Vancouver Stock Exchange itself, stock market abuses were continuing, and James Matkin, who headed the inquiry, recommended substantial reforms that held brokerage firms much more responsible for weeding out poor-quality listings and market manipulations.

A study showed that even though farms within the Greater Vancouver Regional District (GVRD) occupied just 2 percent of BC's farmland, they generated 23 percent of total farm income. GVRD farms produced half the province's greenhouse vegetables most farm-grown vegetables, and most of our cranberries, mushrooms and greenhouse flowers. With food processing and distribution, the study continued, the region's agricultural industry added about $3 billion to the economy. Half the 2,647 farms in the region were in Langley, the rest in Surrey, Richmond, Delta and Burnaby.

Former NHL star Tiger Williams introduced professional roller hockey to BC as co-owner and coach of the Roller Hockey International League (RHI) franchise Vancouver VooDoo. The VooDoo were RHI division champions in 1993 and 1994, but the team folded in 1996 and the league itself ended in 1999.

The Canadian Soccer League folded and the Vancouver 86ers moved to the American Professional Soccer league.

Carol Montgomery—hospitalized in 1988 after being hit by a truck while cycling—was named world women's duathlon champion and Canada's triathlete and duathlete of the year.

Comings and Goings

March Mikhail Gorbachev, former president of the Soviet Union, participated in a student forum at Vancouver's Expo Centre prior to speaking at a fundraising dinner for Science World.

April 3 Vancouver hosted a two-day summit meeting between US president Bill Clinton and Russian president Boris Yeltsin, the first of several summits attended by both men. A marker in front of Seasons in the Park restaurant in Queen Elizabeth Park notes that Yeltsin and Clinton dined there. A funny note: Wreck Beach was briefly in the news during the summit. President Clinton's advance team discovered, to its horror, that directly below a spot where the two presidents would be strolling were signs showing the way to the nude beach. The signs were immediately covered over.

June Dr. Stephen Hawking, the famous physicist, spoke to some 150 disabled students about how he manages his disability, amyotrophic lateral sclerosis (ALS).

Notable deaths: **Harold Winch**, CCF MLA for Vancouver East (1933–53), leader of the provincial CCF (1938–53) and CCF/NDP MP for Vancouver East (1953–72), died February 1 in Vancouver, aged 85; **Barney Potts**, musician, died in Vancouver February 6, aged 82; **Erwin Swangard**, journalist, *Vancouver Sun* editor, sports promoter, PNE president for 13 years, died in Vancouver May 5, aged 84; **Raymond Burr**, born in New Westminster in 1917, actor and star of *Perry Mason* and *Ironside*, died at Dry Creek, CA, on September 12, aged 76.

1994

Sports gave Vancouver a reason to cheer in 1994. The Canucks had a memorable run to the Stanley Cup final, coming up only one goal short in game seven, and the Lions won the Grey Cup. Civic pride was marred by one night of shame when a downtown riot after the Stanley Cup series left injuries and property damage in its wake.

January 21 The movie *Intersection* premiered, starring Richard Gere and Sharon Stone, but to locals the star was the city of Vancouver. Gastown, Deep Cove, West Vancouver and UBC provided the visuals for this US film with no claims to being set anywhere but Vancouver. Upping the Vancouver credibility was the film's use of Arthur Erickson's architecture (Museum of Anthropology) and persona—Erickson's old pal Richard Gere called on him to provide some character advice for the film's architect hero, Vincent Eastman.

January 27 Dock workers at the Port of Vancouver walked out in the first widespread labour disruption on the coast since 1986. Outbound consignments of grain, potash, sulphur and minerals clogged storage facilities while ships sat waiting. Rival ports in Washington enjoyed extra business as Canada's railways diverted container shipments south. Vancouver port officials estimated the daily loss to the national economy at more than $1 million. On February 9 the federal government passed legislation to send 3,500 members of the International Longshoremen's and Warehousemen's Union back to work. Vancouver Port Corporation chair Ron Longstaffe called on Ottawa to appoint an

Elsewhere in BC

September Hikers on Mount Cheam near Chilliwack discovered the wreckage of a Trans-Canada Airlines plane that had disappeared on April 28, 1947, with 15 people on board.

Emery Barnes, former defensive tackle for the BC Lions, vigorous anti-poverty crusader and MLA for Vancouver–Burrard (1972–96), became the first black speaker of the BC Legislature.

Sue Rodriguez, a Victoria right-to-die advocate suffering from Lou Gehrig's disease, died February 12 in an assisted suicide. Present at her death was Svend Robinson, MP for Burnaby–Kingsway.

Over 300 Kanaka descendants gathered on Saltspring Island for a modern-day luau. During the celebration they dedicated a bronze plaque, since installed at St. Paul's Roman Catholic Church, which gives a brief history of the Kanakas on Saltspring and the Gulf Islands.

Elsewhere in Canada

American retailing giant Wal-Mart opened its first Canadian stores in March.

In September, Quebec elected the separatist Parti Quebecois, led by Jacques Parizeau, who pledged to move the province toward sovereignty with a referendum in 1995.

At year's end the American dollar was worth $1.41 Canadian.

Vancouver-based Chan Hon Goh became the first Chinese Canadian principal dancer of the National Ballet of Canada. She joined the company in 1988, and in 2009, after a 20-year career, she made her final appearance as the lead in the classical masterpiece *Giselle*. Her autobiography *Beyond the Dance: A Ballerina's Life* was a finalist for the Norma Fleck Award for Canadian Children's Non-Fiction in 2002.

Elsewhere in the World

Apartheid officially ended in South Africa in April as 23 million voters participated in the country's first multi-racial elections.

In Rwanda, the death of President Juvenal Habyarimana in a plane crash on April 6 precipitated a massacre of Tutsi tribespeople and months of bloodshed between Hutu and Tutsi fighters. The death toll in the civil war was estimated at more than 1 million.

The breakaway Russian province of Chechnya challenged the authority of the Kremlin, but by year's end the Russian army had closed in on the rebel stronghold of Grozny.

industrial inquiry commissioner to examine the bargaining process.

February 9 On Chinese New Year's Eve at 9 p.m., "Memory Music" CHQM AM 1320 ended more than 34 years of playing nostalgic and easy-listening music with Bob Hope's "Thanks for the Memories." Moments later the station became CHMB, with an all-night Chinese-language program and a new multilingual format. After experimenting for seven months, it moved to all-Chinese programming.

The Garage. General Motors Place, later renamed Rogers Arena, became home ice to the Vancouver Canucks in 1995. Nicknamed "The Garage," it hosts big-ticket shows ranging from professional wrestling to Cirque du Soleil during non-hockey season.
Jason Payne / The Province

February 17 **Two key by-elections involving Vancouver politicians changed the face of provincial politics.**

When Gordon Campbell, mayor of Vancouver from 1986 until 1993, became leader of the Liberal Party in 1993 he was without a seat in the legislature. On by-election night he won the riding of Vancouver Quilchena and soon took his place in the house as opposition leader across the floor from Premier Mike Harcourt (also a former mayor of Vancouver). Campbell became premier in 2001 and served until 2011. On the same night the leader of the Social Credit Party, Grace McCarthy—a resident of Campbell's Quilchena riding—ran in the Fraser Valley riding of Matsqui but was defeated in what had been a safe Socred seat. She tried to lead the party from outside the legislature, but her electoral defeat triggered defections by three of the six sitting Socreds in the assembly. She resigned on May 3. By October the party was down to one sitting member in the legislature, and the once-mighty Socreds lost status as an official party.

February 29 The Salvation Army, founder and operator of Grace Hospital since 1928, turned control of the facility over to the province. The hospital, Canada's busiest maternity centre, was merged with the Women's Health Centre and became BC Women's Hospital and Health Centre, with a mandate to deliver specialist services to patients from all parts of the province.

March 29 Arthur Griffiths, president of Northwest Sports (the Canucks owners group), announced

The 1990s

With its 125th anniversary imminent in 2012, the Vancouver Board of Trade has much to celebrate as one of the city's leading civic and business organizations. From its beginnings in 1887 as a group of concerned businessmen helping to rebuilt Vancouver after its devastating 1886 fire, the Board has continued to shape local business and social life, and to promote Vancouver internationally.

Among its early contributions to Vancouver were the lobbying for a regular steamboat route to all points north to open up business opportunities, and a telegraph cable connecting Vancouver to Australia, which would open communication with the rest of the world. Both were achieved in 1901 and 1902 respectively. The Board also first suggested daylight savings in 1913, donated land for Capilano Park in 1924 and provided funds to establish the Faculty of Commerce at UBC in 1926. In 1983 the Board joined the World Trade Centers Association, creating stronger business links worldwide. These exemplify the long-standing mandate of the Board, which past chair for 2009-10, Sue Paish, defined as "to promote individual, business and community well-being as a vehicle for building a strong province and country."

The 1990s is perhaps best known for the Debt Clock, which was a graphic reminder of the ever-increasing federal debt. Worried about rising business taxes as a result, and needing a way to raise public awareness in order to spur change, the clock did the trick as it was paraded around the country making government officials very uncomfortable. In 1998, after presenting a balanced budget, Finance Minister Paul Martin finally got to hit a gong and stop "that damned clock." Unfortunately, since stimulus spending began in 2009, the clock has been resurrected, and is still waiting the next gong.

The 1990s were also a decade for leadership programs launched by the Vancouver Board of Trade, aiming for a strong foundation for Vancouver to build upon. 1991 saw the Leadership Vancouver program begin, the first of its kind in Canada, co-founded with Volunteer Vancouver. This program brought together emerging professionals from business, government, labour and non-profits into a six- or nine-month experiential program, focussed on community leadership. The end of the decade then saw the Leaders of Tomorrow Mentorship Program begin in 1999, which has brought soon-to-graduate post-secondary students into contact with senior business leaders.

Dragon boats. Over 100,000 spectators turn out yearly to get a tan and watch the dragon boat races in False Creek. The tradition began in 1989. *Les Bazso / The Province*

that Vancouver's new hockey arena, then under construction on the north shore of False Creek between the Georgia and Dunsmuir Viaducts, would be called GM Place. The Canucks moved from their former home, the Pacific Coliseum on the PNE site at Hastings Park, and played their first game in the new arena on September 23, 1995. Their new downtown venue, designed to seat 18,860 hockey spectators, also accommodated 19,700 fans of Griffiths' second major sports franchise: the National Basketball Association's Vancouver Grizzlies. General Motors Canada maintained its sponsorship until 2010, a relationship that inspired fans to refer to the arena as "The Garage."

April 1 Langara College became an independent public college. Originally part of Vancouver City College, in 1994 it provided academic courses for 5,000 students, career training for 1,500 and continuing education for 8,400.

April 17 The Vancouver Museum turned 100.

A birthday party at the museum's site in Vanier Park was followed by a three-month exhibition of *The Jade Canoe*, a monumental work by Haida sculptor Bill Reid, commissioned by Vancouver International Airport for the new terminal under construction at Sea Island. The museum's celebratory mood evaporated later in April when trustees outlined plans to cut staff and programs. A strike began June 28 that shut down the museum until December 15, when it reopened with staff reduced from 36 to 16.

April 25 By a vote of 4–2, Port Coquitlam municipal council approved a controversial proposal to build a nine-storey, 40-unit complex. Residents in an adjacent four-storey apartment, until then the highest structure in the area, objected that the new building would block views. Councillor Ron Talbot, a supporter of the new development, remarked, "Ten years ago you couldn't have bought an apartment in downtown Port Coquitlam to save your soul. People used to say, what's wrong with Port Coquitlam? Nothing ever happens here."

May 4 Birks announced plans to vacate its 87-year-old premises at Granville and Georgia and relocate to an even more historic site three blocks north at Granville and Hastings. By renovating the Canadian Imperial Bank of Commerce building, constructed in 1908, Birks preserved part of the city's architectural heritage and renewed its connection to the Hastings corner where it had started business in 1907.

May 22 Randy Stoltmann, environmentalist, was killed in an avalanche while skiing through remote ranges west of the Kitlope River. Born September 28, 1962, in Vancouver, Stoltmann became an active environmentalist while still in his teens, conducting an exhaustive exploration of mountain country within 200 kilometres (125 miles) of Vancouver and searching for record-sized trees. In April 1994 he drew up a formal proposal to preserve the Elaho–Upper Lillooet wilderness under the BC government's protected area strategy. The 260,000-hectare (642,500-acre) roadless area is now known as the Randy Stoltmann Wilderness.

May Ninety local teams competed with many other Canadian and international teams in the Canadian International Dragon Boat Festival.

June 16 The Canucks lost the seventh game of the Stanley Cup finals 3–2 to New York.

When television coverage finished, more than 60,000 people headed into the downtown, a few of them angry, inebriated and looking for trouble. The centre of the crowd coalesced on Robson Street between Thurlow and Burrard and the after-game party turned ugly. Some participants rolled parked vehicles, broke store windows and began looting. By 10:30 the riot squad moved in, firing tear gas and plastic bullets. Despite the arrival of more police from Burnaby, Surrey and Richmond RCMP detachments, a crowd estimated at 3,000 continued to

Night of shame. After the Vancouver Canucks' upsetting loss to the New York Rangers in the 1994 Stanley Cup finals, "fans" took to the streets to express their disappointment in a riot resulting in smashed windows, brazen looting and broken hearts.
Steve Bosch / Vancouver Sun

roam the city centre after midnight, leaving damage and debris behind. From there, the year went downhill for hockey in Vancouver. A league-wide contract dispute resulted in a player lockout that began in September and delayed the season start until early 1995. The Canucks didn't skate for home fans again until January 19, and significantly higher ticket prices depressed attendance.

June 25 The Gulf of Georgia Cannery in Steveston celebrated its centenary by reopening as a National Historic Site with exhibits commemorating the West Coast fishing industry. The cannery had been the major source of canned BC salmon for most of the early 20th century. Production ended in 1979, but volunteers preserved the building and nearby homes of cannery workers.

June 29 Premier Harcourt was cheered by 200 workers at Vancouver Shipyards in North Vancouver as he announced construction of five new ships for the BC Ferries fleet, including three fast ferries to reduce travel time between Vancouver Island and the Lower Mainland. The shipyards of Greater Vancouver were struggling to survive against competition from shipbuilders in Asia, and the premier predicted that the $800-million overhaul of the BC ferry fleet and terminals would create 3,400 new jobs, 1,000 of them in the shipyards. The project was ill-fated. The fast ferries came in three years late and extravagantly over budget, and they were underpowered, uncomfortable and prone to breakdowns. After less than five years they were removed from service and were sold in 2003 for about 13 percent of their development cost. Their failure contributed to the fall of the NDP government in 2001.

Active afterlife. The over 100-year-old Gulf of Georgia Cannery in Steveston, once a major hub for Canada's West Coast fishing industry, is now home to an extensive and thoughtful museum. Also, at Halloween, it hosts one of the best haunted tours in the city.
Photo from The Gulf of Georgia Cannery Society / PNG

June 30 Writing Thru Race, a four-day conference of Canadian writers, generated controversy by restricting workshop admission to writers of colour and First Nations. Conference coordinator Roy Miki praised the city and provincial governments for maintaining their financial support after the minister of Canadian Heritage cut off federal funding. Miki defended the conference as a space where writers with experience of racism could meet and share their stories.

July 1 West Vancouver's Museum and Archives opened in Gertrude Lawson House. Later in the year, West Vancouver's library was named the most popular in Canada with an annual circulation of 23.5 books per citizen.

July 24 The BC Entertainment Hall of Fame inaugurated Starwalk outside the Orpheum Theatre on Granville Street. Memorial plaques set into the sidewalk honoured pioneers of music, dance, theatre and radio who had brightened the lives of Vancouver's early citizens.

August 24 A fire at the Alberta Wheat Pool dock forced closure of the Ironworkers Memorial Bridge for six hours. The threat of a grain dust explosion led to the evacuation of 25,000 fairgoers from the Pacific National Exhibition at nearby Hastings Park.

September 9 A gala fundraiser at the Orpheum marked the 100th birthday of the Association of Neighbourhood Houses of Greater Vancouver. From its beginning as the Alexandra Orphanage in Kitsilano, the ANH evolved into a network of volunteer-based community centres. In 1994, neighbourhood house programs included summer camps for inner-city children, after-school day care, assistance for new immigrants and leadership in community development projects such as children's recreation facilities and low-cost housing. A milestone during the year was a new neighbourhood house planned in Mount Pleasant, part of a community revitalization that included the region's first neighbourhood crime prevention office and a Mount Pleasant area network of social services.

October 4 Robert Swanson died, aged 88. What a great deal of noise he made. In the 1940s Swanson invented the Nathan-AirChime horn, which mimicked the sound of a steam train's whistle. When diesel trains began running on BC railways, motorists didn't always associate the single note of their airhorns with the potential danger of an approaching train. Swanson used the US Navy Band at Annapolis to identify frequencies

The main man. BC Lions place-kicker Lui Passaglia leads his teammates in celebration after his game-winning field goal defeating Baltimore for the Grey Cup, thus ending a nine-year dry spell. *Mark van Manen* / Vancouver Sun

that would make the train horn distinguishable from truck horns but still audible inside an automobile. The horn he developed sounded a five-note chord. Swanson also designed the horns that blare the first four notes of "O Canada" over Vancouver at noon. These horns, a daily tradition since 1967, were moved from the old BC Hydro Building to Canada Place and first tested there on October 13, 1994. The test was timed to coincide with a memorial service for Swanson. Another of his talents was poetry; two collections inspired by his days as a BC logger, *Rhymes of a Western Logger* and *Whistle Punks and Widow-Makers*, were bestsellers.

November 8

A sniper lurking outside the home of physician Gary Romalis shot and seriously wounded the well-known gynecologist.

Dr. Romalis, an abortion provider, had previously been a target of protests by anti-abortion activists. Police never found his assailant.

November 13 Thousands of onlookers watched the dawn demolition of the 23-storey Pacific Palisades Building in the West End. The 20-year-old apartment complex went down in 10 seconds after coordinated blasts collapsed the floors. Work began immediately on two new residential towers.

November 27 Football gave Vancouver another chance to cheer. The 82nd Grey Cup was played in the city, and the hometown BC Lions won it, beating the Baltimore Stallions 26–23 in the first Canadian Football League final to feature one of the short-lived American franchises. For the Lions, it was the first Grey Cup victory in nine years, and the third in the team's 40-year history.

December 20 Arguments ended in a 42-day legal battle between Canada Customs and Little Sister's Book and Art Emporium, a West End gay and lesbian bookstore. The store used the Charter of Rights and Freedoms to challenge the government's seizure of imported books suspected of obscenity. Notable writers, including Pierre Berton, Jane Rule and Nino Ricci, defended the store's right to free speech. In 2000 the case went to the Supreme Court, where the justices affirmed customs legislation but criticized Canada Customs for improper procedures. They found Little Sister's Bookstore had suffered "excessive and unnecessary prejudice" and awarded court costs to the shop.

Also in 1994

The first Slam City Jam brought skateboard enthusiasts to the Plaza of Nations for skating competitions and music from 17 bands in May. There were ups and downs for skateboarders in Greater Vancouver this year. South Surrey planned a $30,000 street park to augment the recently opened skateboard bowl at 20th Avenue and 148th Street, and North Vancouver city council budgeted $20,000 toward a skateboard park near Parkgate Mall. However, the City of Vancouver continued to enforce a bylaw against skateboarding and rollerblading on any sidewalk or roadway in the city and drafted a tough amendment allowing police to seize the board of any skater caught using city pavement.

Greater Vancouver community health nurses went on strike for seven weeks. They had been without a contract since the end of 1991.

A labour dispute at Pacific Press curtailed production of the *Sun* and *Province* newspapers, depriving the city of its daily papers for the first two weeks of November.

The Royal Bank reported that Vancouver had the least-affordable housing in the country, with an average detached bungalow costing $279,600. The same house in Toronto, the next most expensive market, cost $201,200; in Montreal, it was $116,700.

Comings and Goings

Notable deaths: **Roy Kiyooka**, poet and artist, died January 4, age 67; **J.J. Johannesen**, music entrepreneur and founder of the Festival Concert Society, died in Victoria on March 14, age 65; **Harry Adaskin**, violinist, author, teacher and broadcaster, died on April 7, age 92; **Frank Griffiths**, pioneering entrepreneur of Vancouver television and radio, who had owned the Canucks since 1974, died April 7, age 78; **Rick Watson**, columnist in the *Province* and long-time cerebral palsy sufferer, died April 30, age 41; **Elek Imredy**, sculptor of *Girl in a Wetsuit*, the statue off Ferguson Point in Stanley Park, died on October 12, age 82; **Rory Ralston**, arts administrator and AIDS activist, died on October 23, age 43; **Bill Rathie**, first Vancouver-born mayor, who held office 1963–66, died on November 26, age 80; **Tony Pantages**, lawyer and advocate of stricter gun control, age 59; **Alan Chung Hung**, sculptor of *Clouds* at 983 Howe St. and *Goddess of Democracy* at UBC, died on July 21, age 48.

1995

Three impressive new buildings transformed the face of east downtown in 1995. The Colosseum-like central library, the Ford Theatre and the multi-purpose GM Place arena, located within a few blocks of each other, revitalized the surrounding area and created an attractive central hub of arts and culture.

January 19 The YWCA opened its new Program Centre at 535 Hornby. Faced in the early 1990s with a need for expensive renovations at their aging building at Burrard and Dunsmuir, YWCA directors opted instead for a land swap involving the City of Vancouver, the Downtown Parking Association and the Bentall Corporation. The Y emerged from the deal with the new site on Hornby and $12-million cash to invest in an elegant new health and fitness

Elsewhere in BC

March 31 Vancouver businessman and philanthropist David Lam ended his term as a popular Lieutenant-Governor of BC, the first Canadian of Chinese ancestry to hold a viceregal post. He had worked enthusiastically to link the office to all citizens of the province, making 808 trips to communities far from Victoria and entertaining 79,000 visitors to Government House. A keen gardener, he invested his $250,000 salary in the resurrection of the gardens of Government House and rescued its deteriorating groves of ancient Garry oaks. On April 21, his successor, Garde Basil Gardom, was sworn in. Gardom had been MLA for Vancouver–Point Grey from 1966 to 1987 and Agent-General for BC in the United Kingdom and Europe from 1987 to 1992.

An investigation into alleged wrongdoing at Nanaimo bingo halls brought into the open a long history of misappropriation of charity funds by Nanaimo NDP power broker Dave Stupich and a party-linked organization, the Nanaimo Commonwealth Holding Society. By November the ensuing scandal, which became known as "Bingogate," had tarnished the government. Premier Mike Harcourt, who was not personally implicated, announced his resignation. Stupich, a former MLA and cabinet minister, pled guilty to fraud and breach of trust in 1999 and served two years of at-home electronic monitoring in Nanaimo. He died in 2006, aged 84.

Elsewhere in Canada

October 30 Voters in Quebec narrowly defeated a proposal for separation from Canada. The sovereignty referendum failed with 50.56 percent of the voters saying "no" and 49.44 percent saying "yes." A disappointed Premier Jacques Parizeau bitterly blamed "money and the ethnic vote" for the defeat of his sovereignty campaign.

Paul Bernardo was sentenced to life in prison with no chance of parole for 25 years after he was convicted of the sex-slaying of schoolgirls Leslie Mahaffy and Kristen French. Bernardo's wife and accomplice, Karla Homolka, made a deal with prosecutors and went to jail for 12 years on a manslaughter charge. Her testimony helped convict Bernardo.

Wayson Choy's first novel, *Jade Peony*, set in Vancouver's Chinatown during the 1930s and 1940s, spent 26 weeks on the *Globe and Mail* bestseller list, won the City of Vancouver Book Award and was co-winner of the 1995 Trillium Award in Ontario. It was released in the United States in 1997 and was one of 11 books chosen by the American Library Association as Notable Books for 1998.

Elsewhere in the World

February Vancouver filmmaker Mina Shum's *Double Happiness* won the award for Best First Film at the Berlin International Film Festival. The movie's star, Sandra Oh, won a Genie for Best Actress.

April 19 Timothy McVeigh and Terry Nichols used a truck loaded with explosives to destroy the federal building in Oklahoma City. Their act of antigovernment terrorism killed 168 people, including 19 children under the age of six, and injured more than 680.

October 3 After a controversial trial that generated widespread racial tension, American football hero O.J. Simpson was acquitted of the murder of his ex-wife Nicole Brown and her friend Ronald Goldman.

Vancouver DJ Red Robinson was inducted into the Rock and Roll Hall of Fame. His career stretched over 47 years, from 1953 to his retirement from CISL with his last broadcast on November 8, 2000.

Moshe Safdie's ambitious design for the Vancouver Public Library main branch, modelled on the Roman Colosseum, was finally realized after two years of construction. The library also has a private rooftop garden designed by landscape architect Cornelia Oberlander. *Jon Murray / The Province*

facility as well as other service centres, including Munroe House for battered women, a new 155-room hotel residence at 733 Beatty St., the Crabtree Corner emergency family service centre in the Downtown Eastside and the Semlin Gardens affordable housing project for single mothers.

January 25 About 4,000 post-secondary students and their supporters rallied at rush hour outside the Vancouver Art Gallery and marched through downtown in protest against the federal government's proposed funding cut to universities and colleges. Students said they feared a dramatic rise in tuition fees and student debt burdens. Fear became reality in October when UBC president David Strangway said a 50 percent tuition hike would be necessary once federal cuts began. The leaders of Simon Fraser University, the University of Victoria and the colleges of Greater Vancouver issued similar warnings.

March 20 The Gathering Place opened at 609 Helmcken St. and began providing food and health care, along with social, recreational and educational opportunities, to residents of nearby hostels and hotels and people living on the street in the Downtown South area. Soon 1,000 people a day were using it.

April 9 A human salmon run slithered from the Vancouver Art Gallery over False Creek to Vanier Park as the first Wild Life Youth Conference weekend finished.

More than 500 secondary school students from across the province showed their commitment to environmental causes by creating a street-theatre enactment of salmon trying to get up coastal streams to spawn. Some students pretended to be fish. Others were costumed as parts of a log jam, and one dressed as toxic waste. The parade reflected growing public concern about precipitous declines of BC salmon stocks. The Fraser River, Greater Vancouver's lifeline into the Interior, usually produced more than half of the commercial fish caught in the province, but on August 11 federal fisheries minister Brian Tobin shut down all sport and commercial salmon fishing in the Fraser and the Straits of Georgia and Juan de Fuca in an effort to conserve unexpectedly low numbers of breeding fish. Fishermen objected to the ban, saying there were more fish in the river than federal officials indicated, and painting a False Creek boat with the slogan "Save a salmon. Can a Tobin."

May 26 The new main branch of the Vancouver Public Library opened on a square block bordered by West Georgia, Robson, Homer and Hamilton Streets. Its radical design by architect Moshe Safdie featured curved exterior walls resembling the colonnades of the Flavian Amphitheatre in Rome, and the interior welcomed patrons to a glass-roofed concourse filled with light even on rainy days. There were 1,400 comfortable new chairs for readers

Addressing the Past

This was a year of tension and struggle for First Nations groups in BC. An ongoing RCMP investigation into child abuse at Indian residential schools in BC identified more than 90 former or current clergy and teachers suspected of committing crimes, including murder and physical and sexual assault. The investigators outlined their progress at a special meeting of BC band chiefs at the end of June. During the summer, Native protesters set up road blockades at several sites in the province to draw attention to land claims and other grievances. At Gustafsen Lake in the Chilcotin, a Native occupation of sacred lands escalated into a standoff between protesters and police. (In 1997, 13 of the Native participants were convicted and sentenced in BC Supreme Court to terms ranging from six months in the community for spiritual leaders Percy Rosette and Mary Jane Pena to 4.5 years in jail for Jones Ignace, known as "Wolverine.")

and 2.25 million books and other items for them to peruse. The library square development, the largest capital project ever undertaken by the City of Vancouver, had been built by PCL Construction between 1993 and 1995 at a cost of $106.8 million.

June 5
In an interview in *Maclean's* magazine, Vancouver writer William Gibson told journalist Brian D. Johnson how he conceived the idea of "cyberspace." Gibson said that while walking down Granville Street one day he looked into one of the video arcades there and realized from the physical posture of those playing the games that they really believed in the space the games projected. They seemed to sense "some kind of actual space behind the screen, some place you can't see but you know is there." Said Gibson, "I took that home and tried to come up with a name for it. I literally did sit down at a typewriter one night and go, 'Dataspace? Noooo. Infospace? Boring. Cyberspace? Hmmmm. It's got sibilance. It sounds interesting.' What did it mean? I had no clue. It was like an empty chocolate cup awaiting the whipped cream."

June 6 Vancouver city council approved CityPlan, the first comprehensive long-range development vision drafted by the city since 1928. After consulting citizens in a three-year public process, city planners recommended guidelines for "a city of neighbourhoods" where population increase would occur not as urban sprawl but as increased density around pedestrian-friendly village centres. CityPlan's 30-year timeline projected Vancouver would grow from a city of 500,000 in 1995 to 660,000 in 2021. The 1994 Greater Vancouver regional plan, which included the city as well as 27 suburbs and other municipalities in the Fraser Valley, had predicted the region would grow from the 1994 level of 1.7-million inhabitants to more than 3 million by 2021.

June 30 Lorne Davies, founding director of the Simon Fraser University athletic department and the first coach of its football team, the Clansmen, retired after 30 years at the helm of SFU's sports programs. By implementing Canada's first university athletic awards program, he showed how athletic scholarships could encourage top Canadian athletes to study at home rather than in America. He had coached a young Terry Fox, counselled him during his cancer treatments and helped him launch his subsequent Marathon of Hope. In 2006, SFU honoured Davies by naming its new sports facility the Lorne Davies Complex.

July 23 At the Vancouver Aquarium, a female beluga, Aurora, delivered a female calf weighing 70 kilograms (154 pounds). The baby cavorted with its mother within four hours of birth. It was later named Qila—and in 2008 gave birth to its own baby, Tiqa.

July 27 Vancouver-based Hollinger Inc., controlled by media baron Conrad Black, bought 19 Canadian newspapers from the Thomson Newspapers group and began rolling toward ultimate dominance of the Canadian publishing world. By January 1999, Hollinger had gained control of 33 papers in the Southam chain, which included Vancouver's two dailies, the *Vancouver Sun* and *Province*. Black sold Hollinger's holdings to CanWest Global in 2000 and renounced his Canadian citizenship in 2001 in order to take a seat in the British House of Lords. In 2007 he was tried in Chicago on charges of fraud and obstruction of justice. Black was ultimately convicted and sentenced to six years in a Florida penitentiary where he deployed his well-known erudition in jailhouse tutoring. In 2010 he was granted bail pending appeal, and two of his four convictions were overturned, but in 2011 he was resentenced to a reduced term of 42 months and a fine, which meant he had another 13 months to serve in prison.

August 12 BC's fraternity of horse owners and breeders celebrated the inaugural BC Cup Day at Hastings Park. The day's six feature races were restricted to horses bred in BC or Canadian-breds sold in BC. "Any time you have a restricted race, you leave yourself open to the charge that you're rewarding something other than the very best," said Pacific Racing Association chairman Mohan Jawl. "But I look at it as an incentive to our breeding industry." BC Cup Day subsequently became a popular annual fixture.

Left: Hoop dreams. The short-lived Vancouver Grizzlies basketball team was the third Canadian NBA team ever. In their inaugural season, the Grizzlies set the league record for most games lost in a row: 23. After six seasons at GM Place, the team moved to Memphis. *Colin Price / The Province*

September 17 General Motors Place, Canada's first privately funded arena since Maple Leaf Gardens opened in Toronto in 1931, had a gala launch party, with 75,000 visitors touring the new home of the Vancouver Canucks hockey team and the Vancouver Grizzlies NBA basketball team. They got a glimpse of the 88 luxury suites, 12 hospitality suites and 2,195 club seats that supplemented regular seating of 19,700 for basketball and 18,860 for hockey. Two days later, pop superstar Bryan Adams headlined the arena's opening concert. The Canucks took to the ice for the first time on September 23, beating the Anaheim Mighty Ducks 4–3. The Grizzlies played their first home game on November 5, beating the Minnesota Timberwolves 100–98 in overtime before a sold-out crowd, but they ran into ticket trouble soon after. They had a dismal five and a half years in Vancouver, played their last game on April 18, 2001, and moved to Memphis.

November 1
The West Coast Express train made its first run,

offering commuting workers a welcome alternative to car travel on clogged roads. The rail service took 77 minutes from its Mission terminal to Waterfront Station in downtown Vancouver, with five trains running to the coast in the morning and five back in the evening. Almost 7,000 riders tried it on the first day, and some on the middle train on the morning run had the bad luck to be delayed by the system's first engine breakdown. Transport minister Glen Clark enthused, "The train runs spectacularly, notwithstanding this small problem we've had today." Pressure for more public transit was growing throughout the Fraser Valley. The suburban cities of the Greater Vancouver Regional District had growth rates from 6 to 25 percent between 1990 and 1995, and the GVRD was expecting to absorb 1.2 million more people by 2020.

November 2 The first event at the Ford Centre for the Performing Arts was a concert featuring BC

Convenient commute. The West Coast Express made its inaugural run in 1995 and has since provided residents of the Greater Vancouver corridor a welcome alternative to car travel. From its Mission terminal to downtown Vancouver, the trip is just 77 minutes—enough time to offer commuting workers a fighting chance at solving the day's crossword puzzle. *Charlie Hayes / PNG*

vocalist Brent Carver. Moshe Safdie, the project architect, commented, "The auditorium is more intimate and warm than even I expected." Vancouverites had a chance to tour the Homer Street showpiece for free the following weekend, and the theatre's first major Broadway-style production, *Showboat*, opened on December 3 with a $2-million sound system in operation. Subsequent shows included *Sunset Boulevard*, *Phantom of the Opera*, *Joseph and the Amazing Technicolour Dreamcoat*, *Riverdance* and *Ragtime*. The centre closed in November 1998 after Garth Drabinsky's Livent Entertainment, which owned the facility, went bankrupt, and it sat dark until it was sold in late 2001 to Four Brothers Entertainment, a company owned by the Law family of Denver. They reopened the theatre with a production of *Of Heaven and Earth* in August 2002.

November 30 Canuck Place children's hospice welcomed its first families to the renovated Glen Brae mansion in Shaughnessy. The house was a warm, comforting place where children with terminal illnesses could stay together with family members during their last days. Brenda Eng, a Vancouver registered nurse, began campaigning for a children's hospice in 1988. She won the support of George Jarvis, a local advertising and marketing executive, and together the two enlisted the Vancouver Canucks in their cause. The City of Vancouver arranged a one-dollar lease on Glen Brae, volunteers spent three years renovating it, and with a lot of community support the dream became a reality. Canuck Place has nine beds and four family suites, and it operates at full capacity. In 2011 construction began on a second hospice facility at Abbotsford, Dave Lede House (named for a major corporate donor), to address the regional need for pediatric palliative care.

December 6 Every seat in GM Place was filled for a performance by legendary Italian tenor Luciano Pavarotti. The 60-year-old opera superstar thrilled his audience with arias from *Turandot*, *La Boheme* and *Madama Butterfly*. A gala after-show fundraising dinner at the Wall Centre was marred by Pavarotti's distress at the toothache suffered by his female travelling companion, but Vancouver endodontist John Diggens stepped forward to offer immediate assistance in his downtown surgery.

Also in 1995

Photographers at the *Province* and the *Vancouver Sun* started showing up for assignments with no film in their cameras. It wasn't a matter of lapsed human memory, but rather improved computer memory. The Pacific Press newspapers became the first in Canada to convert to digital photography. Hard drives in the new cameras held up to 76 images, and pictures could be sent by phone line direct from a news scene within

Respite. Children with life-threatening illness and their families are welcomed at Canuck Place, a renovated Shaughnessy mansion. The children's hospice is regularly visited by Canucks players and other professional athletes. *Courtesy Vancouver Canucks*

Learning About Discrimination

Internal dissension at the University of British Columbia erupted into national controversy with the release of an investigative report by Vancouver lawyer Joan McEwen, who looked into some graduate students' allegations of racist and sexist behaviour in the political science department. The 177-page report, for which McEwen billed $246,364.24, recommended that the university shut down new admissions to the political science graduate studies program until the department purged itself of alleged discrimination against women and racial minorities. When UBC president David Strangway and dean of graduate studies John Grace immediately shut down graduate admissions to political science, department head Don Blake took leave of absence. A fierce debate about feminist scholarship, academic freedom and due process began inside the university and on editorial pages across Canada. On July 13 the student newspaper, the *Ubyssey*, returned to publication after a 15-month political hiatus with a strong editorial comment: "No matter your stand on political correctness, academic freedom or sexual harassment, UBC's image has been badly tarnished by this debacle." The allegations remained unproved when admissions were reopened in October. Tom Berger, a former justice of the BC Supreme Court and a member of UBC's board of governors, resigned in protest at the handling of the matter, saying the university had acted "hastily and unwisely" on the basis of a "flawed" report and had neglected due process in treating unsubstantiated allegations. Fallout from the issue continued for years. In November 1998 the BC Human Rights Commission dismissed student complaints of racism and sexism as unfounded, and Strangway's successor as president, Martha Piper, apologized to the political science professors for the university's inappropriate response to the 1995 charges.

minutes of deadline. Previously, photographers had to take their film to the office darkroom to develop and print it before a picture could be considered for publication. Noting the potential to use the new technology to alter images, *Province* editor-in-chief Michael Cooke said, "We will never manipulate a news photograph, and that's a promise."

***Andy Warhol: Images* drew almost 100,000 visitors in its three-month run at the Vancouver Art Gallery** and ended up being the most popular exhibition in the gallery's history. A centrepiece of the show was a famous set of 10 pictures of Marilyn Monroe created by Warhol in 1968.

Vancouver city council demanded that the University of British Columbia include significant community amenities, such as park and school space, in its plans to develop 10,000 new housing units on its endowment lands. Councillor Jennifer Clark suggested the Greater Vancouver Regional District could act as a watchdog to ensure the university respected concerns of residents in nearby communities, but GVRD chairman Greg Halsey-Brandt predicted the lack of a local government structure for UBC residents would create problems unless an amalgamation with Vancouver occurred. "It is about time that they take some responsibility for themselves," he told the *Vancouver Sun*, pointing out the university did not have to deal with the impact of its development on city infrastructure such as transit, sewer and road systems.

Comings and Goings

October 24 The American aircraft carrier USS *Constellation* sailed under Lions Gate Bridge into Burrard Inlet carrying a ship's complement of 2,000 sailors and 40 planes. The crew members enjoyed shore leave until the weekend, and Vancouverites were invited to tour the gigantic vessel.

Notable deaths: **Julius Balshine**, 84, New Westminster hotelier and philanthropist; **John Conway**, 79, scholar, awarded the Military Cross for valour while serving with the Seaforth Highlanders in Italy during World War II; **Bev Fyfe**, chorus director at Vancouver Opera for 32 seasons; **Don Garcia**, 58, former leader of the International Longshoremen's and Warehousemen's Union; **Bob Hallbauer**, 64, former president of Cominco; **John Kirkwood**, 62, *Vancouver Courier* columnist; **Walter Koerner**, 97, industrialist and patron of the arts; **Bill Lewame**, 68, mayor of Burnaby (1981–87); **Assa Manhas**, 44, Howe Street stock promoter; **Bob Nicholson**, 86, long-time *Vancouver Sun* gardening columnist; **Karl Norman**, 79, former manager of the Vancouver Opera Association and a gifted tenor whose voice and comic flair captivated Malkin Bowl audiences from 1947 to 1969; **Lorne Parton**, 63, reporter, editor and about-town columnist at the *Province* for 38 years; **Allan Sawyer**, 70, local soccer great; **Robert Wenman**, 54, independent-minded former MLA from the Fraser Valley; **George Woodcock**, 82, celebrated author and anarchist; **Ben Wosk**, 81, philanthropist and furniture business entrepreneur.

1996

Vancouver had many reminders this year of how far it was from Ottawa. Although overlapping land claims by local First Nations bands covered the entire metropolitan area, municipal authorities in Greater Vancouver had little or no voice in treaty negotiations under way between the bands and the federal government. Local anger grew when federal fisheries minister Fred Mifflin forced many BC fishermen to abandon their salmon licences. Ottawa churned the waters again with an unpopular plan to phase out lighthouse keepers in the Strait of Georgia.

January 26 The Greater Vancouver Regional District, the union of 21 municipalities and one electoral area in the lower Fraser Valley, adopted the Livable Region Strategic Plan to manage land use and transportation through 2021 for the nearly 2 million people living in the lower Fraser Valley between Squamish and the American border. All local governments agreed to four core strategies: protect the green zones, build a network of regional town centres, achieve a compact metropolitan centre in the Vancouver core and create alternatives to car travel in the region. The initial consensus lasted only until April, when city councillors in Richmond and Surrey balked at changing their development zoning to conform with the plan.

February 18 Glen Clark, MLA for Vancouver–Kingsway, won the support of 70 percent of delegates at an NDP leadership convention, succeeding Mike Harcourt as party leader and premier.

BC fishermen burn applications for area licences in protest against federal fisheries minister Fred Mifflin's plan to retire more than 2,000 boats. *Ian Smith* / Vancouver Sun

Elsewhere in BC

March 15 In New Aiyansh, BC, chiefs of the Nisga'a First Nation joined federal minister of Indian Affairs Ron Irwin and BC minister of Aboriginal Affairs John Cashore in signing an agreement-in-principle for the Nisga'a land claim settlement, the first modern-day agreement on lands, resources and Native self-government. The ceremony brought hundreds of the Nisga'a people together in the school gym for an emotional morning of songs, dances, speeches and gift-giving.

March 29 Federal fisheries minister Fred Mifflin, a Newfoundlander, responded to persistent declines in West Coast salmon stocks by announcing a draconian plan to retire half the BC fishing fleet of 4,400 boats. He offered a carrot (fishermen were asked to sell their licences back to the government in an $80-million voluntary scheme) and a stick (fishermen, formerly free to range along the coast, would have to buy separate licences for designated areas). With each licence costing upward of $70,000, many independent fishermen would be priced out of the fishery. Mike Emes, a fourth-generation Vancouver fisherman, angrily told the minister, "I might just as well put a match to my boat." The fleet reduction was in addition to a complete closure of the Fraser River sockeye fishery and earlier shutdowns of BC fish hatcheries during a federal cost-cutting drive.

September 12 Rocky Mountain Railtours ran the longest passenger train in Canadian history. Three GP40 locomotives hauled 34 cars from Vancouver to Kamloops.

Elsewhere in Canada

February 19 Canada adopted a new coin worth two dollars. Since the dollar coin with a loon on its face was known as a "loonie," the new coin immediately became known as the "toonie."

Elsewhere in the World

March 13 Former Scout leader Thomas Hamilton opened fire in the gym of the primary school in Dunblane, Scotland, killing 11 girls and 5 boys before shooting himself.

July 19–August 4 Athletes from Greater Vancouver won glory at the 26th Olympiad in Atlanta, undeterred by a terrorist bombing on July 27. Medal winners from Greater Vancouver were Vancouver's Janice Bremner and Coquitlam's Christine Larsen, silver in synchronized swimming; North Vancouver's Jessica Monroe, silver in the rowing eights; Delta's Brian Walton, silver in the cycling points race; Vancouver's Kathleen Heddle, gold in double sculls and bronze in quadruple sculls; North Vancouver's Alison Sydor, silver in cross-country cycling.

August 28 Prince Charles and Diana, Princess of Wales, completed divorce proceedings.

Left: Resolute rowers. Not to be deterred by a terrorist bombing that took place earlier during the Olympic Games, gold-medal rowers Marnie McBean and Kathleen Heddle hoist the Canadian flag at the closing ceremonies of the Games in Atlanta, Georgia. *Nick Didlick* / Vancouver Sun

in 1998, Simon Fraser University gave Davis its Chancellor's Award for distinguished service to BC.

May 27 Federal work crews moved into the Point Atkinson Lighthouse in West Vancouver to begin installing automated equipment, part of a cost-cutting move to eliminate human lighthouse keepers along the BC coast. In spite of protests from boat operators and persistent objections from the provincial government, coast guard authorities proceeded with their plan. Later in the year, four of the recently automated weather stations in Georgia Strait failed at the onset of a violent storm. If not for the efforts of a remaining lighthouse keeper at Entrance Island off Departure Bay, boaters on the water on October 18 would have been without essential weather data.

In a move to reduce overhead, Point Atkinson Lighthouse in West Vancouver is refitted for automation, along with all the other lighthouses on the BC coast. Visiting MP Brian Tobin (second from left) tours the facility with the primary and assistant keepers, Gerry Watson (left) and Don Graham (fourth from left). *Glen Baglo* / Vancouver Sun

February 22–25 Vancouver and North Vancouver hosted the 18th annual BC Winter Games, and 2,700 amateur athletes aged 13 to 70 came from all corners of the province to compete in 29 events. At some venues, warm temperatures depleted the snow pack, but organizers managed to complete most competitions.

March Eddie the Engine and his companion Chough, a tiny steam locomotive, travelled by sea from England to Surrey. After a brief tune-up, they began delighting children at Surrey's Bear Creek Park, where they have been pulling the miniature trains ever since.

April 1 About 500 volunteers turned out for the first Keep Greater Vancouver Spectacular cleanup campaign. The grassroots effort saw workers of all ages fanning out through the region to pick up garbage in public areas, clean graffiti and remove old posters. It became a popular annual event, involving more than 26,000 citizens by 2010.

April 30 *The Greater Vancouver Book*, edited by Chuck Davis, was launched at a gala evening at the Orpheum Theatre. The CBC Vancouver Orchestra, conducted by Bruce Rodney Dunn with soloist Roger Cole, performed *Vancouver Variations*, a specially commissioned concerto for oboe and orchestra by Michael Conway Baker. The original plan was to introduce the book during the concert, but the 904-page tome didn't actually appear until June 11, 1997. It included articles from 237 contributors on subjects from the Abbotsford Air Show to zoning and Zoroastrians, and it won the 1998 City of Vancouver Book Award. Also

May 28 **A provincial election confirmed Glen Clark as premier and gave the NDP a majority with victory in 39 seats,**

renewing the party's mandate to govern (although the Liberals won a slightly larger share of the popular vote—41.82 percent against the NDP's 39.45 percent). The fledgling Green Party fielded 71 candidates and garnered 30,000 votes. Greater Vancouver elected the first woman of Chinese descent to sit in the legislature (Jenny Wai Chin Kwan of the NDP in Vancouver–Mount Pleasant, who, before she was elected to provincial office, was the youngest person elected to Vancouver city council) and the first two openly gay members (United Church minister Tim Stevenson of the NDP in Vancouver–Burrard, and Whistler mayor Ted Nebbeling of the Liberals in West Vancouver–Garibaldi). Stevenson replaced veteran MLA Emery Barnes, who retired after holding the riding for the NDP for 24 years.

June 1 **The new international terminal at Vancouver Airport opened on time and on budget**

with a spectacular display of West Coast aboriginal art enhancing the greatly expanded facilities for travellers. The centrepiece of the terminal was the sculpture *The Spirit of Haida Gwaii*, popularly known as "*The Jade Canoe*," by Haida artist Bill Reid. The airport inaugurated more components of its expansion later in the year. On November 2 about 10,000 people, led by sprinter Donovan Bailey and wheelchair athlete Rick Hansen, imitated planes and rumbled down the new 3-kilometre (2-mile) runway. By year's end, the airport was able to accommodate up to 7 million additional passengers and 125,000 additional takeoffs and landings annually.

Rick Hansen and Donovan Bailey break in the runway at the new international terminal at YVR. The terminal boasts increased comfort and capacity, and an impressive display of aboriginal art, including *The Spirit of Haida Gwaii*, by Bill Reid. *Colleen Kidd / The Province*

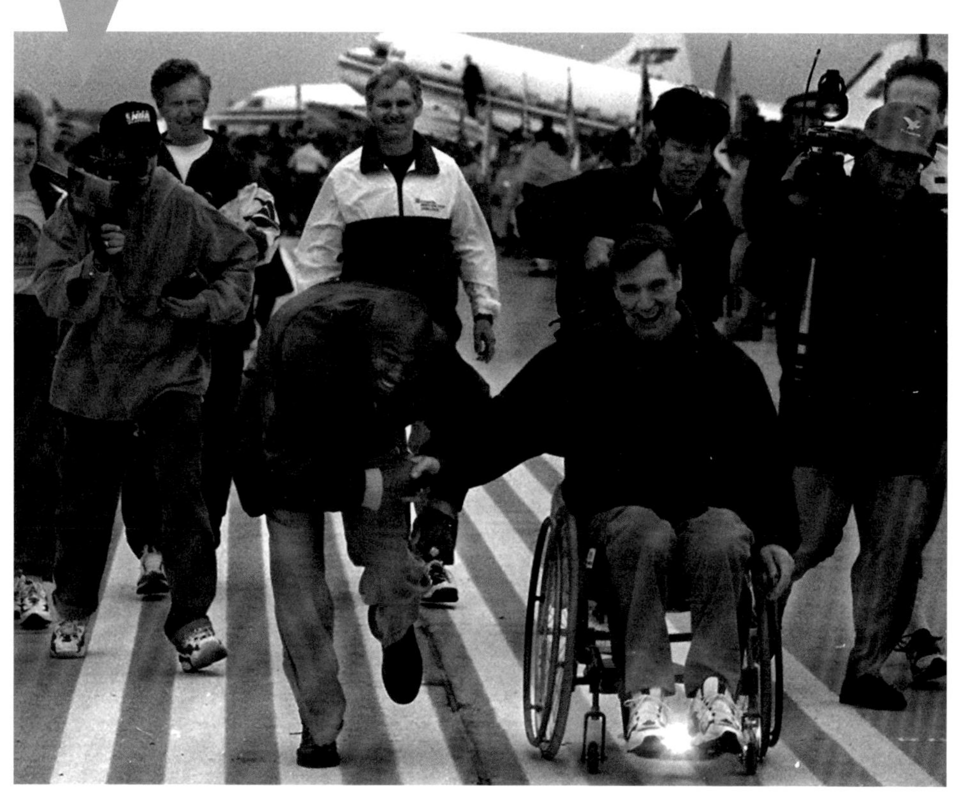

June 28 McCleery Golf Course reopened after a redesign. Challenged by its location on the Fraser River flood plain, it had suffered since its opening in 1959 from occasionally waterlogged fairways. The new McCleery featured a system of 15 ponds developed by course architect Ted Baker to improve course drainage and, coincidentally, swallow golf balls. The renovation was part of an ongoing effort by the Vancouver Park Board to upgrade the three municipal courses—McCleery, Fraserview and Langara—and provide the general public with access to top-quality golf facilities. Across Burrard Inlet, the District of North Vancouver opened Northlands Golf and Country Club for public play in 1997, winning accolades for its Les Furber design.

June 29 The Commodore Ballroom on Granville Street, the hub of Vancouver's music and dance scene since 1929, closed its doors because of a legal battle between operator Drew Burns and leaseholder Morguard. The historic nightclub, famous for its dance floor padded with horsehair, remained dark for two years.

July 7–12 Vancouver hosted the 11th International Conference on AIDS. More than 15,000 delegates from around the world listened to 4,800 presentations from medical researchers and frontline caregivers describing the latest advances in the battle against the spread of HIV and AIDS. Prime Minister Jean Chrétien refused to attend to open the conference, and Premier Glen Clark told a first-day audience, "There needs to be a national AIDS strategy. Having the conference here serves to highlight that there isn't the kind of initiative and support we should be seeing from the federal government." A keynote address by federal health minister David Dingwall was drowned out at times by heckling from activists angry at a looming withdrawal of federal research money.

June 8 An experimental bike lane on the Burrard Bridge shut down early after the first week of trials showed 870 more people than usual cycled over the bridge each day but 8,840 vehicles were being displaced to other routes into downtown. The Bicycle People, a bikers' activist group that had lobbied for the bike lane, threatened to stage a mass ride-in on the bridge after city council suspended the experiment. "You can expect to have big traffic delays," biking spokesman Guy Wera warned. "They are doing nothing for cyclists. If they want people not to pollute, they have to give us ways to do that."

Peaceful party. Twenty-five years after the Maple Tree Square riots in Gastown, hundreds of people gather under the Gassy Jack statue to commemorate the 1971 protesters and to continue to advocate for the legalization of marijuana.
Arlen Redekop / The Province

July 16
Fire started in Delta's Burns Bog and spread quickly in high wind, casting a pall of smoke over the metropolitan area. Firefighters and water bombers struggled to contain the blaze and called in forestry service crews for help. Flames scorched more than 150 hectares (370 acres) of the environmentally sensitive area, a 4,000-hectare (9,900-acre) domed peat bog of compressed sphagnum moss that is home to several species of indigenous plants and wildlife.

August 26 For the first time in 30 years Vancouver hosted an event on the Professional Golf Association tour, the inaugural Greater Vancouver Open at the Northview Golf and Country Club. More than 1,500 volunteers joined Canucks staff to run the competition and support Canuck Place children's hospice.

September 2 This was the last day of a Group of Seven exhibition, *Art for a Nation*, at the Vancouver Art Gallery, and 3,500 viewers passed the turnstiles to set a one-day attendance record. The VAG followed that hit with another. *Topographies: Aspects of Recent BC Art* opened on September 29 and showcased work by leading BC artists.

September 30 The Vancouver Park Board let the Vancouver Aquarium keep its whale exhibit despite pressure from the No Whales in Captivity coalition. The aquarium could no longer acquire healthy new whales from the wild but could still take in those that were sick, stranded or endangered.

October 28 The provincial government announced 24 new parks for the Lower Mainland and new wildlife-management areas at the Squamish estuary, Roberts Bank, Sturgeon Bank in Delta, Steveston Island and McDonald and Swishwash sloughs in Richmond. The additional parks meant 14 percent of the land in BC's most heavily populated area was reserved for environmental conservation and recreation, more than in any other region of the province.

November 14 Vancouver's penguins flew. The Stanley Park Zoo, preparing for closure, sent its 22 Humboldt penguins to a new home in Chicago's Brookfield Zoo, keeping only its geriatric polar bear, Tuk, as the last animal resident. Tuk lived until December 10, 1997.

November 16 The civic election drew low turnouts of about 30 percent in almost all the municipalities of Greater Vancouver.
Voters dismissed the left-leaning Coalition of Progressive Electors in Vancouver and gave centre-right candidates from the Non-Partisan Association all 27 seats on council, school board and park board.
In Surrey, one-term councillor Doug McCallum defeated veteran incumbent mayor Bob Bose.

November 27 Vancouver novelist and songwriter Michael Turner won a Genie award for best song, "Who the Hell Do You Think You Are?" from the movie *Hard Core Logo*. The film, shot in Vancouver and released in October, was an adaptation by Bruce McDonald of Turner's novel of that name.

Gaining Some Freedom

The year began auspiciously for First Nations in the northern areas of Greater Vancouver. On February 12, Chief Joseph Becker of the Musqueam band and Chief Joe Mathias of the Squamish band joined 11 other chiefs from across Canada and representatives of the federal government at a ceremony to sign an agreement that affirmed the right of the First Nations signatories to manage, lease and develop their lands and resources without prior approval from the minister of Indian Affairs. On March 6, the 335-member Burrard band of North Vancouver became the first group in the Lower Mainland to achieve a treaty framework agreement with the governments of BC and Canada. Robin Dodson, the chief federal negotiator, commented, "This is the first framework agreement that we've signed in an urban area, and I think that's certainly significant because the ingredients of a treaty in an urban area are not clear-cut to any of us." No such progress was evident south of the Fraser River, where the Tsawwassen band was in ongoing conflict with Delta council over construction of an 83-unit condominium on band land adjacent to the Tsawwassen ferry causeway. When the band refused to allow the municipality a say in the development, Delta retaliated and refused to provide a sewer connection. During the summer, the band built its own sewage treatment plant and discharged waste into a nearby salt marsh. In November, Chief Sharon Bowcott and the band's Tsatsu Shores development company were charged under the federal Fisheries Act for destroying fish habitat.

December 29 The last weekend of the year brought a record snowstorm, dumping 34 centimetres (13.5 inches) in 24 hours at Vancouver Airport and stranding 250 people on the Trans-Canada Highway between Abbotsford and Chilliwack. Avalanches in the Fraser Canyon cut off the communities of Lytton, Yale, Spuzzum and Boston Bar. Ferries stayed in their berths because crews could not get aboard, and planes were stranded at the airport when de-icing crews could not keep up with the snow. Bus service throughout Greater Vancouver became sporadic or stopped altogether as snow clogged many thoroughfares, and there were skiers on Robson Street. Large roofs collapsed, most greenhouses suffered damage, and the Fraser Valley was on flood alert because of the volume of snow about to melt into the river. When the river stayed within its banks, it brought some New Year relief to the area.

Also in 1996

Volunteers in Mission founded the Mission City Farmers' Market. They opened the first stalls for business in June at the West Coast Express parking lot. Now operating on a park-like site near Lane Creek from late spring to early autumn each year, the market has become a Fraser Valley institution offering locally grown produce, crafts, artwork and entertainment to urbanites in search of farm-fresh food and rural peace.

The dismissal of Vancouver Canucks coach Rick Ley on June 4 signalled ongoing major changes at the hockey team. Ley was replaced by former Olympic coach Tom Renney. Throughout June and early July, principal shareholder John McCaw of Seattle took over negotiations to sign Wayne Gretzky but couldn't reach a deal. In November the Griffiths family, long-time owners of the team, relinquished ownership and control to McCaw and his Orca Bay organization. On the ice, the Canucks had a disappointing year, making the playoffs but losing to Colorado in the first round.

The Pacific National Exhibition did away with the PNE parade. After 60 years of marching bands and floats winding through downtown Vancouver and along East Hastings Street, the parade disappeared when general manager Shirley Nutbrown deemed the event "tired and tacky" and saved $150,000 by cancelling it. She invited bands to participate in a marching competition at the PNE grounds instead. The PNE also said it planned to leave its traditional site at Hastings Park after 1997, a move that never occurred.

Canada's Competition Tribunal blocked a move by Montana billionaire Dennis Washington to dominate the Canadian West Coast tugboat and barge market through his purchase and merger of three long-established operators: Seaspan International and C.H. Cates and Son of North Vancouver, and Bahamas-based Norsk Pacific Steamship Co. The tribunal imposed an interim order preventing the Seaspan sale from going through. After a 10-month standoff, Washington agreed to sell a group of ship-berthing assets in the Port of Vancouver and Roberts Bank as well as a dozen Seaspan barges serving the forestry industry in exchange for clearance on his $100-million Seaspan takeover.

Comings and Goings

Notable deaths: **Pat Burns**, 75, the veteran voice of talk radio; **Prentice Bloedel**, 95, co-founder of forestry giant MacMillan Bloedel; **Don Lanskail**, 79, former West Vancouver mayor and developer of the West Vancouver Centennial Seawalk; **Nancy Malloy**, 51, Red Cross nurse from Vancouver who was shot to death while on a mercy mission in Chechnya.

1997

There was a lot of fire but less smoke when municipalities in Greater Vancouver compelled smokers to butt out in public places during 1997. On the water, the Great Salmon War escalated when Premier Glen Clark raised his dukes against the US military, and Canadian fishermen threw a blockade around an Alaskan ferry. On the home front, there were fierce engagements between municipal governments resisting big casinos and provincial politicians eyeing easy revenue from gambling.

January 1
At one minute after midnight in Pitt Meadows, it became illegal to smoke indoors in any licensed restaurant or pub.

In Vancouver, a municipal ban on smoking in restaurants was enforced in spite of a legal challenge from restaurant owners. The ban caused embarrassment at the gala opening of the Planet Hollywood restaurant on March 16 when visiting co-owner (later governor of California) Arnold Schwarzenegger nonchalantly lit up a giant stogie inside the restaurant and sparked complaints from anti-smoking activists. In Burnaby, city council banned smoking in restaurants as of March 1, but elsewhere in Greater Vancouver chaos reigned as municipalities introduced a patchwork of bylaws and some reconsidered smoking bans under pressure from business owners. What did have an impact were Workers' Compensation Board regulations which ordered that workers be protected from second-hand smoke by April 15, 1998. All workplaces in BC had to be smoke-free by New Year's Day 2000.

January 11 A theological dispute within the Sikh congregation of the Guru Nanak Temple in Surrey escalated into a bloody melee involving members wielding ceremonial swords and daggers. Four people were injured, and two days later police charged three participants with offences including attempted murder. The problem started when attendees at a post-worship meal could not agree on whether all should sit on floor mats or some should be free to sit on chairs.

January 22 Premier Glen Clark, who had promised during the 1996 election to leave gambling regulations alone, signalled a change of plan when he told a Vancouver radio talk-show audience he wanted to expand the gambling industry. "If we had the same gambling policy as Alberta, we'd have $750 million a year more in revenues," he said. Within one day, anti-gambling campaigners organized a rally in Vancouver that drew city politicians, church leaders and Liberal Party leader Gordon Campbell together to oppose casino expansion in the Lower Mainland. After the province approved resort-style casinos with slot machines and video-lottery terminals, the City of Vancouver used new zoning restrictions to block development of large for-profit casinos. The province went to court to overrule municipal authorities, and casino battles continued for years.

January 28 The Arthur Erickson House and Garden Foundation paid off the first mortgage on the home of the famous but bankrupt architect at 4195 West 14th in Point Grey. Erickson lived and worked in the cottage studio on the property until his death in 2009 at the age of 84. The foundation continues to offer summer tours of the site.

February 20 The musicians of the Vancouver Opera orchestra heaved sighs of relief as the Vancouver Symphony and Vancouver Opera called off their plans to merge. The idea had elicited a public outcry from patrons and performers wanting to keep the opera productions independent. Merging would have killed the jobs of 50 to 80 freelance musicians in the opera orchestra.

Erickson enclave. The president of the Arthur Erickson Home and Garden Foundation, Michael Jeffery, takes in Erickson's home and garden, purchased from the bankrupt architect by the foundation to be preserved as a heritage site. *Bill Keay* / Vancouver Sun

May 5 The *Georgia Straight* newspaper celebrated its 30th birthday, having evolved from a 10-cent radical rag famous for libel suits to an influential weekly featuring award-winning investigative journalism and authoritative coverage of Vancouver's arts and entertainment scene. Dan McLeod, still owner and publisher after 30 years, reminisced about his days as a hippie firebrand

Elsewhere in BC

January 29 The Botanical Garden at UBC offered help to the people of Haida Gwaii after transient protester Thomas Hadwin chainsawed through their beloved Golden Spruce, a unique 300-year-old tree whose needles turned bright gold in sunshine and symbolized a myth of endurance for the Haida First Nation. UBC admitted that 30 years earlier its biologists had secretly taken cuttings from the sacred tree and generated two seedlings that were now two metres (6.5 feet) tall. It offered the trees to the Haida. Said Haida spokesman Guujaww, "It all seems kind of sneaky. But we'll probably take their tree and put it in the old site if it is from the original tree. That would keep the Golden Spruce alive." Meanwhile, Hadwin said he would paddle from Prince Rupert to Haida Gwaii for a court appearance on April 22. He failed to appear, and his kayak was later discovered wrecked on a Hecate Strait beach.

After a misguided individual unceremoniously sawed down the sacred, 300-year-old Golden Spruce that was the symbol of endurance for the Haida First Nation, Bruce Macdonald of the UBC Botanical Garden admitted that cuttings had been taken secretly 30 years ago. The resulting saplings (partly visible here) may now be the only two of these beautiful trees left in the world. *Peter Battistoni / Vancouver Sun*

November 14 Despite Premier Glen Clark's 1995 promise to hold ferry fare increases to 2 percent above inflation, the government announced ticket price hikes of between 30 and 40 percent on most routes. Angry island dwellers and commuters reliant on the ferries pointed out the government subsidy of the West Coast Express commuter train in the Lower Mainland amounted to $15 per rider while the per-rider ferry subsidy was 21 cents. Vociferous protests caused the government to back down, and on December 22 it reduced tariffs for frequent users of local routes—though large increases remained for occasional travellers and those on the long-distance routes between the Lower Mainland and Victoria or Nanaimo on Vancouver Island.

Elsewhere in Canada

June 2 It was a rare thing—a federal election in which the country waited for BC to decide the outcome. After the Liberals took five seats in Greater Vancouver (Richmond, Vancouver Centre, Kingsway, Quadra and South Burnaby), Jean Chrétien formed a majority government. Outside Vancouver, most BC ridings went to the Reform Party.

The Supreme Court of Canada ruled in *Delgamuukw* that aboriginal title to the land of BC had not been extinguished. The court clarified that federal and provincial governments could infringe upon aboriginal title for such reasons as resource extraction, economic and infrastructure development or environmental protection, but governments must consult with aboriginal people and compensate them for any infringement.

Elsewhere in the World

February British researchers introduced the world to Dolly the sheep, the world's first higher mammal cloned from the cells of an adult.

June 2 Greg Moore, 22, of Maple Ridge became the youngest driver to win an Indycar race when he led the field at the Champ Car (CART) Milwaukee 200. One week later he won the Detroit Grand Prix. Moore's career ended on October 31, 1999, on lap 9 of the Southern California Marlboro 500 when he suffered fatal injuries after his Player's Forsythe car spun off the track into an infield wall. Moore was remembered by his hometown fans for his good humour, courage and passionate commitment to racing. Maple Ridge opened the Greg Moore Youth Centre in 2003, and the Greg Moore Foundation, established by his parents, Ric and Donna Moore, continues to support the Youth Centre and other community projects.

July 1 Hong Kong ended 150 years as a British crown colony and returned peacefully to Chinese rule. Many wealthy Asian immigrants to Vancouver decided to return home, and the upscale properties they had bought in the years before the handover flooded the city's real estate market. By early August, the average house price had dropped by 27 percent from the previous year's price on Vancouver's west side and by about 14 percent in West Vancouver.

August 31 Diana, Princess of Wales, died in a car crash in Paris while being pursued by paparazzi.

Rockin' and Rollin'

June 24 Two earthquakes shook the Lower Mainland. The first, a magnitude 4.5 tremor under the Strait of Georgia between Vancouver and Nanaimo, occurred at 7:40 a.m. and rattled dishes and windows around Vancouver. So many people called 911 to report it that they briefly disabled the emergency response system. That afternoon another quake near Bremerton in Washington state shook homes in southern parts of Greater Vancouver. Three days later the provincial government gave the go-ahead to a long-needed regional emergency centre in Vancouver. The specially reinforced building at 3301 East Pender opened on November 4, 1998. Meanwhile the BC auditor general's office investigated earthquake preparedness in BC and reported in December 1997 that the Greater Vancouver area was ill-prepared to respond to a large earthquake.

Triumph and tragedy. Talented and competitive, Maple Ridge's Greg Moore became the youngest driver to win an Indy car race when he was just 22 years old. The year 1997 was a banner one for Moore, who also drove at Vancouver's Molson Indy car race that summer. Only two years later, the racing star lost his life when he lost control of his car at California Speedway and hit a wall. *John Denniston / The Province*

putting out the paper from his apartment: "I would often go out and sell papers if someone couldn't do a route or if we were banned in a certain area. It was the only way of doing it. You had to go out there and be a victim."

May 6 Vancouver city councillors voted 9–2 to increase the height limit for buildings downtown from 135 metres to 187 metres (from 440 feet to 610 feet, about 60 storeys), but they preserved view corridors between buildings to ensure people in the core had views of the North Shore mountains.

May 23 Simon Fraser University president John Stubbs fired head swim coach Liam Donnelly after an internal tribunal accepted the claim of student Rachel Marsden that the coach had sexually harassed her. Donnelly responded with a wrongful-dismissal suit and publication of proof that Marsden had stalked him, harassed him with sexually explicit emails and delivered provocative photographs to his office. As Marsden's credibility crumbled, the university re-evaluated its handling of the case and changed its harassment policies. Donnelly was reinstated on July 25. Patricia O'Hagan, the harassment policy coordinator who had handled the Marsden case, left the university. President Stubbs took stress leave and resigned in October. Marsden later became a conservative political commentator for Fox News, CNN and the *Daily Telegraph*.

June 22 About 60 decorated backsides flashed down Wreck Beach in the first annual Bare Buns Run.

Clothing was optional and not much in evidence at the event sponsored jointly by the Wreck Beach Preservation Society and

The first annual Bare Buns Run at Wreck Beach took place on June 22. About 60 runners participated on the famous clothing-optional beach, and Richmond runner Mark Chesser took first prize. *Ian Smith / Vancouver Sun*

Right: Clash on campus. The Asia-Pacific Economic Co-operation summit took place in Vancouver in the fall of 1997. The progress achieved over a week of talks between 10,000 delegates and official visitors was overshadowed by the run-in between the RCMP and 1,000 human rights protesters at UBC. The clash climaxed when officers blasted students with pepper spray. *Stuart Davis / The Province*

the Greater Vancouver Regional District. Richmond runner Mark Chesser finished first in 27 minutes and explained, "The guys in the pub challenged me to do it."

June 25 The Port of Vancouver doubled its container-handling capacity as it opened Deltaport, a 40-hectare (100-acre) container terminal at Roberts Bank. The expansion offered shippers excellent connections to the national railway systems and an alternative to US ports for container traffic to and from Asia.

July 18 Newsroom staffers at Pacific Press, publisher of the *Province* and the *Vancouver Sun*, moved north from their old haunt at 2250 Granville St. to Granville Square at the north foot of Granville Street, an office tower with water views of Burrard Inlet. The old presses downtown were phased out and new presses at Kennedy Heights in Surrey took over paper production on October 23.

July 29 Marathon Realty opened bids on the Coal Harbour lands, a 33-hectare (80-acre) parcel of undeveloped downtown waterfront. Originally part of the Canadian Pacific Railway land grant, Coal Harbour offered stunning views of Stanley Park and the North Shore mountains. Marathon expected to make more than $300 million on the sale.

August 6 It got stinking hot in Vancouver when the city's outside workers began a strike that left garbage piling up in alleyways until September 17. Other city employees, including cemetery workers and city hall staff, walked off, slowed down or were shut out of jobs for varying periods. In the last week of August a wildcat strike by bus drivers stranded commuters, and readers found the libraries shut as the city saved money by suspending all library operations until September 2.

August 21 A Vancouver jury took only 15 minutes to deliberate and deny serial killer Clifford Olson early parole. Olson, the unrepentant murderer of 11 BC children, had served 15 years of his 25-year sentence.

October 15 David Duchovny, star of the TV science-fiction serial

The X-Files, generated hundreds of letters to the editors of Vancouver's papers when he slagged the city on a US talk show. Duchovny, who lived in Kitsilano for five years during filming, complained on *Late Night with Conan O'Brien* that "Vancouver is a very nice place if you like 400 inches of rainfall a day. It is kind of like a tropical rain forest without the tropics. More like an Ice Age rain forest." The show moved to Los Angeles in 1998.

November 4 Even with newly recruited star Mark Messier, the Canucks were on a 10-game losing streak, and the first man on the firing line at GM Place was general manager Pat Quinn. Next was vice-chairman and former owner Arthur Griffiths, who criticized the Quinn firing and was told to clear his office and sever ties with the team. On November 14, coach Tom Renney got the boot, to be replaced by Mike Keenan. The firings marked the end of the Griffiths family's long association with Vancouver's hockey team. Family patriarch Frank Griffiths had owned and supported the team from 1974 until his death in 1994, and his sons had tried to continue the association, finally selling out to John McCaw's Seattle-based Orca Bay Sports and Entertainment in 1996 when their debt load, acquired from building GM Place and expanding into basketball

A hot mess. At the end of the summer of 1997, the City of Vancouver CUPE outside workers went on strike, suspending garbage pickup for more than a month. The city's alleyways became trash-strewn—and pungent. *Les Bazso / The Province*

with the NBA Grizzlies, became too much for the family.

November 19 The Asia-Pacific Economic Co-operation (APEC) summit drew leaders from Pacific Rim countries to Vancouver for a week of talks that cost the city, the province and the federal government almost $60 million. The event drew 10,000 delegates and other official visitors and ended in a notorious cloud of pepper spray when the RCMP subdued 1,000 human rights protesters during a November 25 meeting of heads of state on the UBC campus. Dismissing criticism of summit security, Prime Minister Jean Chrétien said, "For me, pepper, I put it on my plate."

December 29 Since January 1, Vancouver airport had measured 1,500.8 millimetres of rain, making 1997 the wettest year on record and beating the old record of 1,490.5 millimetres set in 1983.

Also in 1997

It was the little engine that could. Great Canadian Railtour, operator of the successful Rocky Mountaineer tour train between Vancouver and Jasper, fought a bid by Crown-owned VIA Rail to retake the business VIA had deemed a failure and sold to Great Canadian in 1990. Great Canadian had spent seven years building up the route with international marketing and investment in Kamloops and Jasper. Now VIA applied to run three competing trains a week in the summer season. Transportation minister David Anderson listened to objections from the premiers of BC and Alberta and shot down VIA's proposal.

The provincial government received a confidential engineering report warning the Lions Gate Bridge needed to be repaired or replaced within 16 months. The 59-year-old structure had significant deterioration in the beams running under the deck. Transportation Minister Lois Boone proposed a new four-lane bridge built by a public-private partnership and paid for by tolls, but the City of Vancouver objected to the increase in traffic pressure a four-lane flow could create. After debate, a renovation in 2000–2001 replaced the bridge deck, preserving the original superstructure and creating three widened traffic lanes and better pathways for pedestrians and cyclists.

Environmentalists applauded when German automaker Daimler-Benz AG invested $198 million to buy 25 percent of Ballard Power Systems, a Burnaby-based pioneer of hydrogen fuel cells. Later in the year, Ford Motor Company injected $650 million into the company's technology. In spite of this early optimism, Ballard acknowledged by 2007 that the fuel cell could not compete against the global fossil fuel infrastructure, and the company shifted its focus to fuel cells for forklifts and stationary generators.

The Vancouver/Richmond Health Board declared a public health emergency among intravenous drug users in Vancouver's Downtown Eastside. The number of people with the AIDS virus was increasing faster in Vancouver than anywhere else in the developed world. Among the estimated 5,000 drug addicts living in downtown lodgings, the HIV infection rate was approaching 50 percent, up from about 2 percent in 1990. Within a month, Mayor Philip Owen announced plans for a drug treatment centre in the Downtown Eastside, a new residence for the homeless and stepped-up police efforts to combat a wave of drug-related thefts and home invasions.

Fishy Business

July 6 Hundreds of thousands of Fraser River sockeye salmon migrating through the North Pacific died in the nets of Alaskan fishermen who claimed to be harvesting low-priced pinks while taking the high-value sockeye as "accidental" bycatch. The Pacific Salmon Treaty signed by Canada and the US in 1985 entitled the Alaskans to 120,000 fish, but after renegotiation talks collapsed in 1992, they had escalated their catch of Canadian-spawned species, taking an estimated 400,000 in early July 1997 while some Canadian fishermen, abiding by conservation measures, took none. On July 19 nearly 200 Canadian fish boats formed a blockade around the Alaskan ferry *Malaspina* and kept it penned into Prince Rupert harbour for three days. Retiring UBC president David Strangway was asked to resolve the dispute, but acrimony continued and the treaty was not amended until 1999.

Comings and Goings

April 15 Statistics Canada released census figures for 1990–96 which showed that 442,439 newcomers had arrived in BC, about 80 percent of them settling in the Greater Vancouver area. Of immigrants from outside Canada, most came from Pacific Rim countries. In Vancouver, almost one in three residents had declared Asian descent.

Martha Piper became president of UBC when David Strangway retired on June 30. Jack Blaney became president *pro tem* of Simon Fraser University on September 15.

Notable deaths: **Nathan Nemetz**, former chief justice of BC and past chancellor of UBC; **Len Norris**, virtuoso cartoonist; **Bob Tharalson**, veteran staff member of the Vancouver Public Library.

1998

Vancouver's environmental health was improving: compared to 1988, the city's air was cleaner, the water quality in False Creek and English Bay was better, and there were nearly 35,000 more trees and 65 more kilometres of bike routes (40 more miles).

February 18 A casualty of redevelopment at the Pacific National Exhibition in Hastings Park was the great topographic relief map of BC that had fascinated viewers since its 1954 installation in the BC Pavilion. A crew dismantled 564 square metres (6,000 square feet) of plywood mountains and river valleys that woodworker George Challenger had cut painstakingly in his basement over seven years, and Challenger's ashes were removed from a niche under the map where they had been placed after his death in 1964. The map went into

Right: Pot brouhaha. North Vancouver's Ross Rebagliati won the world's first Olympic gold medal in slalom snowboarding, then nearly lost it when a drug test found THC in his circulatory system. The decision was eventually overturned and Rebagliati returned to Whistler a winner.
Mark van Manen / Vancouver Sun

Elsewhere in BC

Summer In the BC Interior, forest fires compelled thousands to flee their homes in the Okanagan and Shuswap regions.

November 13 An avalanche swept Michel Trudeau, 23, off a cross-country ski trail and into Gibsons Lake in Kokanee Glacier Park, where he drowned. The experienced outdoorsman was the youngest son of former prime minister Pierre Trudeau.

Elsewhere in Canada

October 27 The *National Post*, Conrad Black's new national daily newspaper, hit the streets with the aim of giving voice to Canadians of a conservative bent. Its publisher was Don Babick, formerly of Vancouver's Pacific Press, and its motive force was Black of Vancouver-based Hollinger Inc. (later Lord Black and later still a convicted felon serving time in the US). The *Post* challenged the established print news hegemony of the *Globe and Mail* and *Toronto Star*.

Jane Stewart, the federal minister of Indian Affairs, acknowledged the damage done to Canadian Native people by residential schools and made a statement of reconciliation. A $250-million Healing Fund was established to address the legacy of residential schools. Also this year, the United Church of Canada apologized for its involvement with residential schools.

Canada Post honoured Phyllis Munday, a Vancouver mountaineer and nature photographer who died in 1990, in a stamp series on legendary Canadians.

Elsewhere in the World

February 8 Whistler's Ross Rebagliati won the world's first Olympic slalom snowboarding competition at Nagano, then nearly lost his gold medal when a post-race drug test revealed traces of marijuana in his urine. The 26-year-old racer maintained that he must have inhaled second-hand smoke. He was allowed to keep the medal because pot was not on the Olympics list of performance-enhancing drugs.

Allan MacDougall, head of Vancouver's Raincoast Publishing, was at the 1998 Frankfurt Book Fair when he learned Canadian rights were available for a fantasy novel featuring a then-unknown hero called Harry Potter. MacDougall negotiated the rights, and Raincoast later made millions on the phenomenally successful series.

storage, and in spite of lobbying efforts by three former premiers and other backers trying to find it a new home in Greater Vancouver, the huge image has remained in darkness. During the 2010 Olympics, the Sea-to-Sky segment saw daylight briefly when it was used by security staff and viewed by visiting dignitaries.

March 13 It was a fateful Friday for the Griffiths family of Vancouver, inheritors of a broadcasting and sports empire built up over 42 years by patriarch Frank Griffiths. News broke that his widow Emily had sold her shares in Western International Communications to Shaw Cable and the Allard family of Alberta. Frank's death in 1994 had sparked a struggle between rival corporate giants Shaw Cable of Calgary and CanWest Global of Winnipeg for control of the BC television and radio stations owned by the Griffiths family. CanWest got the television assets in 2000 but ultimately sold them back to Shaw a decade later.

March 20 Municipal leaders of the Fraser Valley temporarily forgot their squabbles and united against Fish Protection Act changes requiring expensive environmental protection for even the smallest watercourses running toward the river. Chilliwack mayor John Les said he would go to jail before complying with the legislation, and Langley engineering services manager Mick Gottardi warned the new provisions would apply to "virtually every drainage ditch in the township" accessible to fish.

March 22
GM Place rocked as the stars of Canada's music industry gathered for the Juno Awards. Vancouver's Sarah McLachlan took home the statuettes for best album (*Surfacing*), best female vocalist, best songwriter and best single ("Building a Mystery").

March 26 Canadian Forest Products (Canfor) closed the Eburne Sawmill on the Fraser River by the Arthur Laing Bridge, but 200 angry workers took over the plant, demanding that it stay open until the company guaranteed their jobs. They pointed to Canfor's employment obligations under its 1960 timber licence, but resistance proved futile. By October 1, three other major mills along the lower Fraser had shut as the province-wide lumber price collapse hit home in Greater Vancouver. One in six jobs in the region had been tied to the forest industry.

April 16
Celebrated Native carver Robert Davidson began shaping two totem poles to commemorate the 125th birthday of the RCMP. Conceived by White Rock RCMP constable Mike Lane and funded by the White Rock and Surrey RCMP detachments, the poles were erected on East Beach in White Rock in 1999 as a cultural link between First Nations and the RCMP.

June 18 The Barrett Commission investigating BC's leaky condominiums recommended financial aid from federal, provincial and municipal governments for homeowners facing extensive repair costs due to hidden defects in buildings erected in the 1980s and 1990s. Chairman (and former provincial premier) Dave Barrett chastised developers for causing building envelope failures and criticized all levels of government for lax building codes and poor

Leaky condo crisis. The Barrett Commission recommended financial aid for the owners of condominiums like this one on West 6th Avenue in Vancouver. Constructed in the 1980s and '90s, the buildings let water in, triggering decay, rust and rot. The sellers were not upfront about the hidden defects, strapping the buyers with debilitating repair bills.
Wayne Leidenfrost / The Province

Bill Millerd and the Arts Club Theatre Company spread their wings as the refurbished Stanley Theatre reopens with its inaugural production of *Swing*.
Bill Keay / Vancouver Sun

enforcement of building standards. In response to his recommendations the province passed the Homeowner Protection Act, which created a mandatory new home warranty program, a dispute resolution process for owners of defective homes and new licensing requirements for builders and contractors.

June 22 After rancorous public meetings and protests from anti-gay objectors, the Vancouver Park Board approved installation of a steel memorial at Sunset Beach to bear the names of British Columbians killed by AIDS. Commissioner David Chesman remarked, "Tonight we said no to bigotry and in that regard we made the right decision."

July 4 The New Sakura-so seniors housing complex for Japanese Canadians opened. It was the first component of Nikkei Place at Kingsway and Sperling in Burnaby.

July 27 Alumni of the renowned Kitsilano Boys Band gathered for a reunion concert at the Kitsilano Showboat, exactly 70 years after the band was founded by the beloved and famously tyrannical Arthur Delamont, who directed the band until its last season in 1974. While leading them to many Canadian championships and memorable gigs in England, Europe, Russia and the United States, Delamont introduced several generations of Vancouver youngsters to the pursuit of excellence. Delamont died in 1981, aged 90. Though the band had not played in 23 years, 83 former members took to the stage on reunion night under the batons of Dal Richards and Ken Sotvedt. Soloists were Arnie Chycoski, Jimmy Pattison, Brian Todd, Roy Johnson, Donnie Clark and Wayne Petty on trumpet; Chris Startup and Jack Bensted on clarinet; Brian Bolam on post horn, Bill Trussell on trombone and Dale Peterson on alto saxophone. Architect Bing Thom (clarinet) and retired MacMillan Bloedel chairman Raymond Smith (trumpet) attended but didn't play, claiming to be out of practice.

August 24 Gillian Guess, a jury member in the 1995 trial of accused murderer Peter Gill, was convicted of obstruction of justice for beginning an affair with Gill during the seven-month court case, then convincing fellow jurors to acquit her lover. Sentenced to 18 months' incarceration, Guess spent four days in jail before being released pending her appeal. "I have been convicted for falling in love and nothing more," Guess said. Her appeal was dismissed in November 2000.

October 1 Barb Fellnermayr, manager of the Vancouver City Pound, introduced a no-kill approach that guaranteed stray dogs would not be euthanised if they were adoptable. The pound partnered with a West Vancouver volunteer group, Animal Advocates, to find temporary homes for the furry homeless and welcomed an army of volunteer walkers who ensured animals got daily exercise outside their kennels.

October 28 After being dark for seven years, the Stanley Theatre on Granville Street at 12th returned to life with a sparkling production of *Swing!* by the Arts Club Theatre Company. The art deco entertainment palace had been Vancouver's oldest operating movie theatre when it closed in 1991 after 61 years of screening films. Heritage-conscious citizens formed the Stanley Theatre Society and began a "Save Our Stanley" campaign to preserve the historic building. With support from the province, the federal government, the city, the Arts Club, Vancouver TheatreSports and major donors Peter Wall and duMaurier, the Stanley was renovated to become a home for live theatre. In 2005, ongoing sponsorship from the Industrial Alliance Pacific Life Insurance Company provided long-term security, and it was renamed the Stanley Industrial Alliance Stage.

November 18 Tara Singh Hayer, publisher of the *Indo-Canadian*

Times and a well-known voice of Sikh moderation, was shot dead as he struggled out of his car and into his wheelchair at his home in Surrey. He had survived an assassination attempt in 1988 that was apparently linked to his editorials condemning violence in the Sikh community and its role in the 1985 Air India bombing. Although that shooting left him partly paralyzed, Hayer continued to speak out against terrorism and religious extremism. He won awards for his journalism and was named to the Order of British Columbia in 1995. At his funeral, 45 police officers in bulletproof vests patrolled for bombs with sniffer dogs. His murder, like the Air India case, remains unsolved.

December 1 Cheering filled the Robson Square Conference Centre as hundreds of volunteers heard the Canadian Olympic Association choose Vancouver/Whistler as the Canadian bid city for the 2010 Winter Olympics. Bid society chairman Arthur Griffiths warned, "This is a bit like scaling a mountain. We've made it up the first leg." In 2001, after Toronto lost its bid for the 2008 summer games, Vancouver launched its own ultimately successful campaign for international votes.

December 5 At 8:18 p.m. Vancouver police arrested Frank Paul, a Mi'kmaq man, for being intoxicated in public, held him briefly at the Main Street jail, then deposited the barely conscious man in an alleyway in East Vancouver where he was found a few hours later, dead of hypothermia. In 2000 an internal police disciplinary proceeding gave one officer involved a suspension of two days for discreditable conduct and another a suspension of one day for neglect of duty, but no charges were laid in the death despite investigations by the Police Complaints Commission and the provincial justice department. In 2007 a new public inquiry began. Closing submissions were heard in December 2010, and a report was expected in 2011, more than 12 years after Frank Paul's death.

A legacy begins. On December 1, the Canadian Olympic Association chose Vancouver/Whistler as the bid city for the 2010 Winter Olympics. Bid society chairman Arthur Griffiths and Premier Glen Clark show the jubilation of the crowd of hundreds at Robson Square Conference Centre.
David Clark / The Province

December 31 Ernie Campbell, incoming Musqueam chief, vowed immediate enforcement of a court decision that tenants on band lands along the Fraser River should pay the band's new annual lease charges of $28,000. Tenants had built their homes on Musqueam land after the federal government set an annual lease charge of $375 on behalf of the band about 10 years earlier, and they claimed the 7,000 percent increase in lease charges made their homes almost unaffordable and unsaleable.

Also in 1998

In January the Fraser Valley prepared for a possible eruption of Mount Baker, which had begun one of its periodic steam-venting events. Emergency response teams set up field centres in Langley and Abbotsford and coordinated efforts by riverside communities practising for the earth tremors, mud slides, ash falls and flash floods that could accompany an eruption of the mountain. Mount Baker's last major eruption was in 1843.

Vancouver's immigrant organizations came together in February to denounce proposed revisions to the Canada Immigration Act that would restrict in-migration by people not fluent in French or English. Vancouver architect Bing Thom, Hong Kong–born designer of the Canadian pavilion at the 1992 world's fair in Spain, said at a news conference the new proposals would have kept him and half of his staff out of the country at the time of their families' arrivals. "It is a complete reneging on what Canada is all about," he said. "Canada was built by immigrants who did not speak English or French."

MacDonald Dettwiler and Associates of Richmond won a federal contract to build and operate the $305-million

Radarsat II earth observation satellite. The Canadian Space Agency said the project would launch in 2001 and create about 150 high-technology jobs in BC during construction.

There was unrest in Vancouver hospitals as first doctors and later nurses withdrew services. On March 6, doctors refused to perform surgery, except for emergency operations, and closed their offices as part of a province-wide protest to back a demand for $180 million more in fees from the government. Doctors withdrew services again on March 18 and March 31, and most practitioners offered reduced service periodically for the rest of the year. In November, nurses began targeted, rotating strikes to win a new collective agreement. In January 1999, nurses accepted a provincial contract offer that partly addressed their complaints of overwhelming workloads and understaffing.

Gentrification in formerly rundown neighbourhoods meant the supply of low-cost rooming houses and hotel rooms for Vancouver's least wealthy residents was shrinking. In March the Downtown Eastside Residents Association showed off a model living space that was 19 metres square (204.5 square feet) with a rudimentary bathroom and kitchen. DERA asked for support from Vancouver's civic and provincial politicians to convert a heritage building into 291 similar suites that would be rented to locals struggling with poverty, mental disabilities and addictions. Elsewhere in the troubled neighbourhood, the provincial ministries of housing and health bought Downtown Eastside hotels, cleaned them up and protected current occupants from eviction. First to be renovated were the 55-room Sunrise Hotel and the 89-room Washington Hotel at Hastings and Columbia Streets.

The Greater Vancouver Transportation Authority (later renamed TransLink) was born amid grumblings from municipal councillors in Surrey, Richmond, Coquitlam and Langley Township. The new regional authority accepted responsibility for major roads in Vancouver and much of the Fraser Valley and took control of all transit services, including municipal bus companies, SkyTrain, SeaBus and the West Coast Express. In 2007, provincial legislation extended TransLink's operations to include transit in the Whistler corridor and the entire Fraser Valley east to Hope.

Jacqui Cohen, whose grandfather founded the Army and Navy Department Stores, became president and chief operating officer of the family business. In May she opened a new store in Langley, the chain's first in 22 years, and gave the venerable company a fresh image with cheeky advertising (a headline for a sale of canned beans read "Cheap Gas").

Bankers and economists in Vancouver pointed to a dramatic rise in mortgage foreclosures in the Greater Vancouver region as a sign of general economic difficulties throughout BC. Home values, particularly condo prices, were dropping as unemployment rose. The province's August jobless rate of 8.3 percent was the highest in Canada west of Quebec and well above Alberta's rate of 5.5 percent.

Comings and Goings

March 23 Charles, Prince of Wales, and his teenaged sons, Prince William and Prince Harry, arrived in Vancouver to begin a six-day official visit and private ski holiday. Thousands of teen girls from throughout the Lower Mainland flocked to venues where the handsome young princes were scheduled to appear. Corie Hausner, 14, asked her parents for a lift to the Pacific Space Centre where she stood outside, hoping, she said "to just breathe the same air" as Prince William.

August 15 Lions owner David Braley brought NFL football to Vancouver for a one-night stand in the hope of increasing enthusiasm for Lions ticket sales. An exhibition game between the Seattle Seahawks and the San Francisco 49ers drew more than 45,000 fans to BC Place for a hard-hitting game the 49ers won 24–21.

Notable deaths: **Kathleen Shannon**, 62, founder of Vancouver's Studio D, the women's studio of the National Film Board; sculptor and carver **Bill Reid**, 78, whose work graces the Vancouver airport, the UBC Museum of Anthropology and the Canadian embassy in Washington, died March 13; **Tong Louie**, 84, son of one of the city's pioneer grocers and chairman of both the province's giant food distributor, H.Y. Louie Co. and London Drugs, died April 28 (an energetic philanthropist, Louie once remarked, "Money does not go to heaven, but, I'll tell ya, it certainly performs a lot of heavenly miracles on earth"); flamboyant Howe Street stock promoter **Murray Pezim**, 77, died of a heart attack on November 11; **Donalda Smith**, 92, whose work set the standard for synchronized swimming internationally, died November 13; artist **Jack Shadbolt**, 89, died November 22.

1999

In early 1999, police began investigating an apparent exchange of favours between Vancouver MLA and premier Glen Clark and Dimitrios Pilarinos, a Burnaby hotel associate who was applying for a provincial casino licence. By the end of the year Clark had resigned and the governing NDP had a caretaker premier, Dan Miller, at the helm as a hard-fought leadership contest got under way.

February 1 BC Tel and Alberta's provincial phone company, Telus, merged to form a new company

with a head office in Vancouver and control of 22 percent of national telecom business. Second in size to Bell Canada, Telus began challenging eastern-based companies for a larger share of the rapidly expanding communications market. It has grown

Elsewhere in BC

February 24 Independent auditor Hugh Gordon reported to Gordon Wilson, the minister responsible for BC Ferries, that the "fast ferries" project was going to cost $445 million, more than double the government's previously announced budget. Gordon's 70-page study detailed persistent government and corporate mismanagement since the project's inception in 1996. Two of the fast ferries made their maiden runs this year, and a third had a sea trial in 2000, but all had problems, and the new Liberal government was reluctant to invest more money in their development. By the end of 2000, all three were docked permanently, awaiting sale.

April 22 The BC Legislature ratified the Nisga'a Treaty, which was also debated in the federal Parliament, becoming law in early 2000. It was the first modern-day land claims agreement. The Nisga'a surrendered 92 percent of their territory in exchange for expanded reserve lands and $190 million. The Nisga'a Lisims government was subject to provincial and federal laws, and Nisga'a people living in the settlement lands were subject to BC, Canadian and Lisims taxation. Also this year, the Sechelt Indian Band signed an agreement in principle that formed the basis for a treaty with BC and Canada. In 1986, the Sechelt had become the first Indian band in Canada to attain self-government.

November 1 American forest industry giant Weyerhauser bought Vancouver-based MacMillan Bloedel, known familiarly as "MacBlo" in towns and timberblocks throughout BC. From 1908, when its corporate ancestor opened the world's largest pulp and paper mill in Powell River, the company grew through a series of mergers to become one of the largest employers in the province, holding $4 billion in assets at its peak. In the 1980s and 1990s MacBlo struggled to cope with changing world markets, environmentalism, a demanding government regulatory environment and declining profitability. As a result, most company shareholders supported the Weyerhauser takeover offer.

Elsewhere in Canada

April 1 The Territory of Nunavut was created on April 1, and Inuit leader Paul Okalik became its first premier.

October 20 One of Canada's pioneer retail businesses, Eaton's, went out of business after declaring bankruptcy.

November 4 A group of BC fishermen appeared before the House of Commons fisheries committee and said that the 1999 collapse of the Fraser River sockeye run should be declared a natural disaster. The delegation, which included provincial fisheries minister Dennis Streifel as well as Native and non-Native fishermen, reported that although federal officials had estimated at the beginning of the summer that 8.25-million sockeye would return to the river, only 3.6 million showed up, the smallest run in 110 years. The group pleaded without success for federal income support for fishing families whose livelihoods had been devastated.

Journalist and broadcaster Adrienne Clarkson became the first Chinese Canadian Governor General.

Elsewhere in the World

April 18 Wayne Gretzky retired the famous number 99 after 20 years as a professional hockey player.

July 16 John F. Kennedy Jr. died with his wife and her sister when a small plane he was piloting crashed into the sea near Martha's Vineyard, Massachusetts.

Difficult cats. Three so-called fast ferries—sleek, over-budget catamarans—unfortunately caused trouble for the BC government and contractors alike. Two went to sea in 1999, including *PacifiCat*, shown here, but all three would be awaiting sale by the end of 2000.
Tanya Vaughan / The Province

into a major provider of national telephone, wireless, internet and television services.

March 2 A BCTV camera crew, acting on an anonymous tip, appeared in front of Premier Glen Clark's home in Burnaby and provided live coverage as three commercial crime squad officers arrived with a search warrant and were admitted by the premier's wife. The police were already going through drawers and cupboards when Clark himself arrived home. It was the start of a scandal that became known as "Casinogate." In August, Attorney-General Ujjal Dosanjh revealed that the premier was the subject of a criminal investigation into the casino-licensing process for a hotel in Burnaby. A co-applicant, Dimitrios Pilarinos, had renovated an outdoor deck on the premier's home around the time his casino application was approved by cabinet over the objections of Burnaby municipal council. Clark resigned Saturday, August 21, and was later charged with criminal breach of trust. A government commission ruled in 2001 that he had violated conflict of interest guidelines, but he was acquitted of the criminal charge in 2002. Clark's legal bill of nearly $1.3 million was paid by the government.

Also March 2
Legendary reporter, radio hot-line host and television personality Jack Webster died

at 80 of congestive heart failure and Alzheimer's disease. After beginning his journalism career in 1932 as a 14-year-old copy boy at the *Glasgow Evening Times*, Webster served with the British army in the Middle East during the war before immigrating to Vancouver in 1947. He covered the labour beat for the *Vancouver Sun*, then moved into radio in 1953, pioneering hot-line talk radio in the city at CJOR. For 25 years his acerbic wit and inquisitorial fearlessness made him an audience favourite and the scourge of politicians and leading citizens of Vancouver who agreed, perhaps unwisely, to be interviewed. Former prime minister Pierre Trudeau inquired plaintively after his session with Webster, "Why does that man hate me?" In 1978, Webster switched to television with an hour-long

Some days following a televised search of his home by members of the RCMP, Premier Glen Clark read a brief statement to the media. The search was the start of the scandal, "Casinogate," which would lead to Clark's eventual resignation and permanently tarnished his premiership.
Ian Lindsay / Vancouver Sun

interview program preceding the nightly news on BCTV. He retired in 1986 and became a panellist on CBC TV's national *Front Page Challenge* from 1990 until the show's demise in 1995. The Jack Webster Foundation, which presents the annual Jack Webster Awards, was established in his honour in 1986 to support journalistic excellence in BC.

May 30–June 5 Efforts by politicians, concerned citizens and city planners to make Greater Vancouver more bike-friendly coalesced during Bike Week. Events in the Greater Vancouver area included the opening of the Sunrise Bikeway in East Vancouver that brought the total distance of city bike paths to 104.2 kilometres (65 miles); the extension of Burnaby's Urban Trail to the Fraser Foreshore Park; Pitt Meadows Day volunteers providing free bicycle valet parking at Harris Road and Lougheed Highway; and Port Coquitlam announcing upgrades to the downtown stretch of the PoCo Trail to make it bike-friendly. Responding to public pressure for safer cycling routes in the downtown core, Vancouver city council started planning for dedicated bike lanes, with Pender Street between Hamilton and Carroll a likely first route. Unlike most North American cities, Vancouver entirely lacked downtown bike lanes and lagged behind most, including Toronto, in the proportion of commuters using pedal power.

June 5 At the end of a week in which she closed all but one of her bookstores and filed for protection from creditors, Celia Duthie blamed the decline of her family's 42-year-old bibliophilic empire on the rise of big-box chain stores she bitterly called "outlets for American trash." At its peak, the well-known Vancouver company had 10 stores and the contract to supply BC Ferries shops. Duthie's was noted for its focus on Canadian books and its support of BC publishers. The last Duthie's store, in Kitsilano, closed in 2010.

Juan Montoya eats spray on the wet pavement of Vancouver's new Indy track through False Creek. Celebrating its 10th anniversary, the Vancouver Indy Championship Auto Racing Teams race welcomed almost 200,000 spectators with a need for speed.
Chris Relke / The Province

June Bill C-49 became federal law, giving the Squamish Nation the opportunity to control and manage its reserve lands and resources and make its own laws regarding resources.

September 2–6 The Vancouver Indy Championship Auto Racing Teams race celebrated its 10th anniversary on a new track looping around the east end of False Creek from BC Place Stadium to Science World and Manitoba Street. Road closures accommodated 170,000 fans who turned out to watch North America's top drivers peel rubber legally.

September 17 In a bittersweet game, the Vancouver Canadians Triple-A baseball team won the Pacific Coast League title as they played at Nat Bailey Stadium for the last time in their 22-year run as Vancouver's

In their last game as a Triple-A baseball team, the Vancouver Canadians defeated the Oklahoma Redhawks to win the Pacific Coast League title before moving to Sacramento. The Vancouver Canadians would be reincarnated, and in 2011 became a Northwest League affiliate of the Toronto Blue Jays.
Steve Bosch / Vancouver Sun

boys of summer. They went on to win the World Triple-A Championship on the way to their new home in Sacramento for the 2000 season. In 2004 the Park Board threatened to demolish the empty stadium, named for the baseball-loving founder of the White Spot restaurant chain, but it was saved after a lobbying campaign led by the city's premier baseball fan, Bud Kerr. Local investors Jeff Mooney and Jake Kerr brought a Single-A team to the city in 2007 to make Nat Bailey a home field again and revive the name of the Vancouver Canadians.

October 20 Bud Osborn, a volunteer and former addict in the Downtown Eastside community, won the City of Vancouver Book Award for his volume of poetry about life in his neighbourhood, *Keys to Kingdoms.* Mayor Philip Owen presented the $2,000 prize at the opening gala of the Vancouver International Writers Festival.

November 12 The Commodore Ballroom on Granville Street, which originally opened in December 1929 and had languished empty since 1996, was reborn as a dance and concert venue with Blue Rodeo headlining the evening. It marked the triumphant culmination of a $3.5-million revival project by partners Roger Gibson, Bruce Allen and Don Simpson. They said they hoped their renovation of the Commodore, one of Vancouver's best examples of art deco style, would initiate a revitalization of the whole Granville Street entertainment district.

November 20
Civic elections drew only 36.7 percent of eligible voters to the polls in Greater Vancouver.

Re-elected Vancouver mayor Philip Owen, disgusted by the low turnout, called for a system of compulsory voting. "One-third or slightly more is really not good enough," he said. "It's annoying when you think about the great system we have." Mayoral victors in other municipalities were Clint Hames in Chilliwack, Marlene Grinnell in Langley City, Kurt Alberts in Langley Township, George Ferguson in Abbotsford, Doug McCallum in Surrey, Doug Drummond in Burnaby, Greg Halsey-Brandt in Richmond, Lois Jackson in Delta, Joe Trasolini in Port Moody, Helen Sparkes in New Westminster, Don MacLean in Pitt Meadows, Jon Kingsbury in Coquitlam, Len Traboulay in Port Coquitlam, Al Hogarth in Maple Ridge, Barbara Sharp in North Vancouver City, Don Bell in North Vancouver District, Ron Wood in West Vancouver and Lisa Barrett on Bowen Island.

December 26 About 4:30 a.m., an intruder ignited a Molotov cocktail in the southeast Vancouver constituency office of Attorney-General Ujjal Dosanjh, but damage to the office and a nearby vegetable market was minimal. Dosanjh, a leading candidate in the provincial NDP leadership contest, was no stranger to political violence. He had suffered a vicious assault in 1985 after he spoke out against the extremism of advocates for Sikh independence from India. Dosanjh won the party leadership in February and served as premier from 2000 to 2001, when he was defeated in the Liberal electoral sweep. Later entering federal politics, he served as a Liberal MP from 2004 until 2011.

Also in 1999

Jamie Lee Hamilton, spokesperson for a group of sex workers from the Downtown Eastside, appealed for a police investigation into the mysterious disappearance since 1995 of 21 women from the East Hastings Street prostitutes' stroll. "There appears to be a particular block where almost all of them worked before they disappeared," she said. She suggested a serial killer could be at work, but police said there was no evidence to support her claim. Women continued to disappear, and Vancouver police and the RCMP eventually collaborated on an investigation after resolving jurisdictional disputes. In 2002, Port Coquitlam pig farmer Robert Pickton was charged with the murders of 26 women, most of them prostitutes from the area identified earlier by Ms. Hamilton. Pickton was convicted on six counts in 2007, with charges being stayed on 20 remaining documented deaths. Pickton had murdered his first victim in 1983, and evidence indicated he processed bodies at his farm abattoir for nearly 19 years afterward, despite being arrested for attempted murder of a sex worker in 1997. Prosecutors said they had not proceeded with that charge because they judged the victimized woman to be unstable.

The Hastings Park Sanctuary opened as a nature reserve on the site of recently demolished PNE exhibition halls in East Vancouver. The sanctuary incorporated walkways, marshes and a large pond in a 4-hectare (10-acre) refuge for birds and aquatic life. As the park matured, it attracted an expanding population of animals. By 2007 the Hastings Park Conservancy had documented 100 different bird species in the former industrial area.

CP Rail announced plans to build townhomes, stores and green spaces along 10 kilometres (6 miles) of disused rail line between False Creek and Steveston. Known as the Arbutus Corridor, this narrow strip of land, originally granted to the railway in 1886, was much used by hikers and bikers in spite of its weeds, potholes and old railway ties. CP's announcement was a counterblast to a recent declaration by city planners that the old rail corridor would be restricted to rail, transit and park uses. CP challenged the city's right to determine use of the strip and fought the case up to the Supreme Court, where it was dismissed in 2006. With the railway and the city administration locked in a stalemate over land value and appropriate use—a situation not without precedent in Vancouver's history—the Arbutus Corridor remained undeveloped.

In December, Vancouver police constable Mel Millas learned he would get to keep $1 million he had found in April while walking his dog in Clinton Park. When the dog showed insistent interest in a garbage can, the off-duty officer investigated and discovered a backpack stuffed with cash. He turned it in to his employer, but after no claimants could prove ownership, Officer Millas became a millionaire.

Comings and Goings

August 9 Jimmy Pattison's gleaming new 150-foot yacht *Nova Spirit* left New Orleans for her maiden voyage through the Panama Canal to Vancouver. Built at a cost of about $30 million, the yacht was the largest registered in Canada and featured gold and platinum trim in some of the 15 bathrooms, Italian marble floors and countertops, a grand piano and a white carpet in the lounge.

The *Nova Spirit* is Jim Pattison's 150-foot yacht, quite possibly one of the most expensive on the Pacific West Coast. It is rumoured that celebrities, dignitaries and prime ministers alike have been asked to remove their shoes to spare the white carpeting.
The Province

December 14 Ahmed Ressam, a 32-year-old illegal immigrant from Algeria, loaded his car trunk with explosives and checked out of the 2400 Motel on Kingsway, where he had been staying for four weeks. He took one ferry to Victoria and another to Port Angeles in Washington state, where an alert US Customs officer investigated the vehicle. Ressam tried to flee but was apprehended, and his arrest led to discovery of a terrorist plot, organized in Montreal and Vancouver, to bomb Los Angeles International Airport on New Year's Eve of the new millennium.

December 31 Victoria Anne Taggart was born at 11:53 p.m. in Abbotsford, the last baby of the 20th century born in BC. Her parents, Christie and Collin Taggart of Mission, were delighted but surprised—Victoria was seven weeks early.

Notable deaths: **Clark Bentall**, whose Dominion Construction Company had erected many Vancouver landmarks including the MacMillan Bloedel Research Centre, the BC Pavilion at Expo, the Rogers Sugar Refinery building, the old Vancouver courthouse and the four Bentall towers; **Dr. Peter Hochachka**, an eminent research scientist at UBC in the fields of zoology and biochemistry; **Major-General Bert Hoffmeister**, who commanded the Seaforth Highlanders in the World War II campaign through Italy and later became chairman of MacMillan Bloedel; **Hide Hyodo**, a schoolteacher who had been director of schools in the Japanese internment camps during the war and a passionate voice for redress of the wrongs done by the province and Canada to citizens of Japanese ancestry.

2000-2011

2000

The end of the millennium came more peacefully to Vancouver than city administrators had predicted, and the feared Y2K computer bug failed to affect local systems because most were well shielded. The year's major troubles came in later months when strikes by public service workers closed the region's schools, prevented garbage collection and shut down the public transit system.

January 1 On the millennium night, police anticipated trouble on the streets. The number of officers on patrol was five times normal and the new emergency dispatch centre (known as E-Comm) was double-staffed in readiness. However, while the rest of the world partied hearty, Vancouver had an unusually quiet Friday night and Saturday morning. Earlier the city had dampened enthusiasm by refusing to stage a fireworks display, and police spokesperson Constable Anne Drennan had issued a stern warning on December 28: "Don't think you're going to come down and party on the street. If people come downtown on New Year's Eve, they better have a place to go."

February 20 The NDP leadership convention drew more than a thousand delegates to Vancouver's Pacific Coliseum to elect a replacement for Glen Clark and his interim successor, Dan Miller. Attorney General Ujjal Dosanjh, MLA for Vancouver–Kensington, defeated his principal challengers Gordon Wilson, Corky Evans and Joy MacPhail. On February 24 Dosanjh took the premier's oath of office and became Canada's first Indo-Canadian provincial leader, serving until his defeat in the Liberal election sweep of May 16, 2001.

February 21 Fans at GM Place witnessed one of professional hockey's most infamous incidents of violence.

With only three seconds remaining in a game marked by fighting and taunts, defenceman Marty McSorley of the Boston Bruins slashed Canucks left-winger Donald Brashear, knocking off Brashear's helmet. Brashear fell, his head hit the ice and he suffered a serious concussion and seizure. The NHL gave McSorley an indefinite suspension and the RCMP charged him with assault with a weapon.

IT apocalypse? The technological practice of using two digits to represent the year caused everything from end-of-days predictions to nerd rage when it was discovered that rolling over from 99 to 00, known as the millennium bug or Y2K, could cause major glitches in computer systems worldwide. The midnight countdown had new meaning for many, but 12:01 came and went without issue.
Diana Nethercott / PNG

Elsewhere in BC

March Students got an extra week of spring holidays when a strike by school support workers, including administrative employees, janitors and special-needs service providers, shut down most public schools in Greater Vancouver. Teachers showed solidarity with the strikers by refusing to cross picket lines. Under pressure from angry parents, the NDP government called an emergency session of the legislature on April 2 to pass back-to-work legislation.

Elsewhere in Canada

May Bacterial contamination of the water supply in Walkerton, ON, left seven residents of the town dead and more than 2,000 seriously ill.

September 28 Former Canadian Prime Minister Pierre Trudeau died of prostate cancer. At his state funeral in Montreal, honorary pall bearers included Cuban Premier Fidel Castro and former US President Jimmy Carter.

In company with other former tech darlings on the stock market, Canadian industry leader Nortel Networks began a January slide in value that was accelerating by year-end.

Elsewhere in the World

March Vladimir Putin was elected president of the Soviet Union.

November George W. Bush won a cliff-hanger of an election to become president of the United States, although the result was not official until December.

On October 4, a Vancouver jury found McSorley guilty and he was sentenced to 18 months' probation. He never played in the NHL again. Brashear returned later in the year to play for the Canucks but was traded to Philadelphia during the 2001–2 season.

February 21 Vancouver Mayor Philip Owen presented a City Heritage Award to the Vancouver Heritage Foundation for its "True Colours" Program. In partnership with paint company Benjamin Moore, the Foundation offered incentives to property owners in older neighbourhoods to paint their homes in historically accurate colours.

Art Turmoil

April 10 The resignation of Vancouver Art Gallery director Alf Bogusky triggered a revolt in the ranks of the arts community. Bogusky officially left for health reasons, but many observers sensed he was forced out after a series of disagreements with the VAG board, which then named Joe McHugh interim director. McHugh was a former board member and art collector, and some saw the board's appointment of a former colleague as unprofessional. Marie Lopes, curator of education at the Burnaby Art Gallery, told *CBC News*, "I'm very bothered by the conflict of interest of having a board member take over as director of the gallery. I feel strongly that a board's role in a public institution should be much more removed. You need to hire the staff you're confident can do those jobs, and then let them do them." After more than 100 prominent artists, writers and curators signed a petition asking for McHugh's immediate resignation, the board agreed to form a search committee for a new director with consultation from the arts community, but the dispute had a dire impact on the gallery's community support and fundraising throughout 2000. In March 2001, Kathleen Bartels became director of the VAG and undertook a long-term restoration of its financial and aesthetic health.

March 4 Vancouver Opera celebrated its 40th birthday with a gala night of vocal music at the Orpheum. Among the soloists were BC's Kathleen Brett, soprano, and Judith Forst, mezzo-soprano. Forst, a Port Moody resident, first sang with the Vancouver Opera chorus in 1967 before becoming an internationally famous diva.

April 11 It was the beginning of the end for the Grizzlies, Vancouver's six-year-old National Basketball Association franchise, as owner John McCaw announced the team's sale to Chicago businessman Michael Heisley for US$160 million. Although Heisley initially said the team would stay in Vancouver, on July 4, 2001, he won NBA approval to move the perennially bottom-ranked team to Memphis.

April 15 Among young singers from across North America participating in the Canada Sings! festival at the Plaza of Nations, none were prouder than the children of the Kids Sing Chorus from Vancouver's east side. Founded in 1998 by Elva Fitzpatrick-Walters, a retired music teacher who wanted to give youngsters from the city's less wealthy neighbourhoods a free music education, the choir was a flourishing group of 30 elementary-school-age singers by mid-2000. Elva supported the group until her death in 2005 at the age of 93, and her son, Dr. Don Fitzpatrick, has worked with other dedicated volunteers to maintain the choir in the years since.

April 14–16 Members of the Cheam band of the Stó:lō First Nation blockaded a road in the Fraser Valley between Agassiz and Rosedale and talked of charging motorists a $10 toll to cross a bridge on Highway 9 in an effort to win provincial recognition of Native fishing rights in Ferry Island Provincial Park. More than a dozen protesters in army camouflage and face masks guarded barricades throughout the weekend, disregarding Aboriginal Affairs minister Dale Lovick's threat to take the band to court. Nervous residents of Fraser Valley communities along Highway 9 expressed concern about access to emergency health services in Chilliwack. Chief June Quipp said the Cheam band's claim to ownership of the parkland was being ignored.

In a dispute with the provincial government over First Nations fishing rights, the Cheam Band of the Stó:lō Nation blockade a residential access bridge. By imposing a toll on the bridge, impeding access to residents, protesters hoped to gain recognition, despite threats of legal action. *PNG*

April 20 Satnam Kaur Reyat, wife of Air India bombing suspect and convicted terrorist Inderjit Singh Reyat, was fined $10,000 and sentenced to one year of house arrest for defrauding the BC government of more than $100,000 in welfare payments. She had collected welfare since 1991 when her husband was incarcerated for the killing of two baggage handlers in the 1985 bombing at Japan's Narita airport. Mrs. Reyat claimed to be destitute while concealing regular payments totalling more than $109,000 from a wealthy associate of her husband, Ripudaman Singh Malik. On October 27, Malik and Kamloops priest Ajaib Singh Bagri were charged with multiple counts of murder and conspiracy in connection with the 1985 bombing of an Air India aircraft over the Atlantic.

June 3 Attired in a gold lace gown that complemented the $2.6-million diamond pendant gracing her neck, Jacqui Cohen welcomed guests to the 10th edition of the city's glitziest private charity gala at her mansion in Point Grey. Cohen, president of Army and Navy Department Stores and one of Vancouver's best-known socialites, expected her "Face the World" dinner and auction would raise about $400,000 for several local causes, including a YWCA shelter for battered women and children and a Downtown Eastside daycare. Cohen was in the news again July 11, when Robert Harrison pleaded guilty in provincial court to cutting down trees in Pacific Spirit Park. He said he had been hired to improve the view for a Cohen family mansion on Marine Drive. Cohen said she was unaware of the cutting but paid the GVRD $50,000 to settle.

June 25 The Vancouver Japanese Language School and Japanese Hall at 475 Alexander St. was designated a historic site by the city of Vancouver.

August David Stadnyk bought the Vancouver 86ers soccer club. During his tenure as owner the team became the Whitecaps again. Stadnyk also launched the Vancouver Breakers women's soccer team and was an early investor in the Ravens, a lacrosse team. However, Stadnyk dropped out before they began to play, and in 2003 he relinquished ownership of the soccer teams, citing severe financial losses.

September 20 The once-derelict Toronto Dominion Bank building at the corner of Hastings and Seymour shone like a downtown jewel once more when Simon Fraser University opened the Morris J. Wosk Centre for Dialogue in the restored edifice. Retiring SFU president Jack Blaney, whose vision had inspired construction of the centre, said the high-tech convention centre was designed to encourage public policy discussions in a non-confrontational setting. Key supporters were Morris Wosk, who donated $3 million for interior renovation, and Peter Eng of Allied Holdings Group, who donated the building and land. SFU's downtown campus grew again in 2002 with philanthropist Joseph Segal's gift of the abandoned Bank of Montreal building at Granville and Pender for conversion into the SFU Centre for Graduate Management Studies.

September 22 The National Nikkei Heritage Centre officially opened at Nikkei Place in Burnaby. The Centre houses the National Nikkei Heritage Centre Society, the Japanese Canadian National Museum, the Japanese Canadian Citizens' Association, the Nikkei Seniors Health Care and Housing Society, ICAS Nikkei TV, the Gladstone Japanese Language School, and the Japanese Immigrants Association. In 2002 Nikkei Home also opened at Nikkei Place, offering assisted living based on the principles of independence, dignity, individuality and choice.

September 27
CUPE Local 15, representing 2,500 parks and city inside workers, went on strike

over management control of work scheduling. Until November 15, when CUPE members voted to return to work, Vancouverites lacked access to city ice rinks, swimming pools, cemeteries, garbage pickup and water connection services. Children were

CUPE Local 15 workers walked off the job at 8 a.m. on September 27. Mayor Sam Sullivan helped the city reach an agreement with the workers on November 15, restoring garbage pickup, water connection services and access to municipal pools and ice rinks. *Ward Perrin* / Vancouver Sun

The Lions Gate Bridge, a major headache for many North Shore commuters, underwent a major overhaul to widen the deck and make the three narrow lanes into three less narrow lanes. The bottleneck remains, but the trip is safer with more room for transit.
Craig Hodge / Vancouver Sun

disappointed by cancellation of the Hallowe'en Ghost Train through Stanley Park. The City announced residents still had to pay their taxes, but they couldn't do it at city hall.

November 26

Placekicker Lui Passaglia finished a quarter century of professional football with a 29-yard field goal that clinched Grey Cup victory for the BC Lions over the Montreal Alouettes. Retiring after the game, the 46-year-old Passaglia said, "I'm excited. I'm sad. I don't want to take this uniform off."

November 27 In the federal election Greater Vancouver sent four Liberals to the government benches and two NDP candidates to the opposition. All other ridings in the region went to candidates of the recently formed Canadian Alliance, which became the Official Opposition.

Also in 2000

Maureen Whyte, vice-president of clinical services at Vancouver General Hospital, declared in January that emergency room wait times at the province's biggest hospital were at crisis point. While patients with life-threatening conditions were being treated immediately, many others with acute illness experienced hour-long waits, and sometimes ambulances delivering patients were lined up in the parking lot. She attributed the space crunch to a shortage of nurses and a high number of patients waiting in hospital beds for long-term care openings in the Lower Mainland. St. Paul's Hospital said it also was experiencing extreme space pressure in its emergency department.

A survey of 218 cities suggested that Vancouver had the highest quality of living in the world. International consulting firm William M. Mercer measured 39 factors such as environment, personal safety, education and economic health and ranked the city at the top ahead of Zurich, Vienna and Bern. Toronto and Montreal tied at 15th.

Bad downtown traffic became awful on January 15 after a crane being barged under the Knight Street Bridge clipped the bridge deck, rupturing a water conduit and a natural gas pipeline. Closing this major cross-Fraser link to Richmond, Surrey and Delta created headaches for thousands of commuters on Monday morning. Richmond mayor Greg Halsey-Brandt said that the communities south of the Fraser had been frustrated for decades by an inadequate vehicle transportation network and a lack of rapid transit alternatives.

Traffic woes made news again on January 31 when Vancouver's struggle to reconcile cars and trees became the focus of a raucous Vancouver Park Board meeting lasting five hours. Angry citizens excoriated park commissioners for agreeing to cut down trees in Stanley Park to widen the vehicle causeway between Georgia Street and the Lions Gate Bridge. Tree-lovers outnumbered car-lovers in the packed meeting room as 64 speakers lined up for the microphone, including one dressed in a red dinosaur suit. The board agreed to reconsider its tree-killing decision.

Drivers' frustrations increased in May when work started on the Lions Gate Bridge deck-replacement project.

Although traffic continued to flow across the bridge each day, temporary closures and lane reductions occurred until the project's completion at the end of 2001.

Vancouver stood first in Canada for film production activity and third on the continent,

behind Los Angeles and New York. About 35 production crews were working regularly in the city. The province's film and television industry reported that 1999 had been its best year ever, with revenue in excess of $1 billion. Much of the money stayed in Vancouver, where local service providers did well supporting the film crews.

For $25 and an hour of their time, Vancouver apartment dwellers received a 50-litre (11-gallon) plastic tub containing 500 red wiggler worms and an instructional session in how to use the creepy crawlies to convert their organic garbage into compost on their apartment balconies. The worm adoption program run by the City of Vancouver aimed to reduce pressure on local landfills. It was estimated that, given an opportunity, enthusiastic worms could recycle about 30 percent of the city's household waste.

Burnaby-born actor Michael J. Fox announced he was ending his film career because he had been diagnosed with Parkinson's disease. He became a courageous public advocate for research into the progressive and debilitating condition.

Comings and Goings

January 1 BC's millennium baby was born in Royal Columbian Hospital in New Westminster at one minute past midnight. Bradley Phillip Parks, son of Brenda and Glenn Parks of Port Coquitlam, came three days later than expected but right on time to make history.

April 27 The Vancouver Aquarium's board decided its last killer whale, 23-year-old Bjossa, would be moved to a new home at Sea World in San Diego. Bjossa had been alone and in ill health since her companion, Finna, died three years earlier, and aquarium staff said the move would give her a chance to live with members of her own species. David Mate of Whale Friends, who had locked himself in a steel cage outside the aquarium for six days in 1999 to protest Bjossa's ongoing captivity, said animal rights activists would continue criticizing the aquarium for keeping captive dolphins and belugas.

October 3 Daniel Igali of Surrey received a hero's welcome from more than 1,500 cheering supporters when he returned home from the Summer Olympics in Sydney. He had won Canada's first Olympic gold medal in freestyle wrestling. Born in Nigeria, Igali immigrated to Canada in 1994 and attended Simon Fraser University where he held a 116–0 competition record.

November 8 Pioneer broadcaster Red Robinson retired from daily radio after a career of 46 years on air. As a teenaged DJ in the 1950s at CJOR, he introduced rock and roll to Vancouver and interviewed rock stars Buddy Holly and Elvis Presley. In 1964 he was MC for the Beatles at their memorable concert in Vancouver. Robinson's fans held a gala celebration for him at the historic Commodore Ballroom following his sign-off.

December 14 After leaving Vancouver 169 days earlier, the RCMP patrol boat *St. Roch II* completed its circumnavigation of North America, a journey that honoured the historic 1954 voyage of the original *St. Roch.*

Hollywood North. The local film industry skyrocketed, making Vancouver the third busiest city for film production in North America, just behind Los Angeles and New York. *Peter Blashill / The Province*

Carrying the old *St. Roch* flag, the *St. Roch II* dodged ice as it crossed the Arctic Ocean, then travelled down the east coast, through the Panama Canal and back along the Pacific coast to get home for Christmas. Vancouver Maritime Museum director James Delgado praised the four-person RCMP crew for their courage and resourcefulness but noted their voyage of rediscovery had failed in its attempt to raise money to preserve the old *St. Roch*, which was suffering from dry rot in her berth at the museum. The federal government had cut off the vessel's maintenance funding to save money, and major Canadian corporations had refused the museum's appeal for donations.

Notable deaths: **Himie Koshevoy**, a veteran Canadian journalist who began his career in his native city; **Joe Mathias**, hereditary chief of the Squamish Indian band and a leader of the historic land claims negotiation process; **Barbara Pentland**, composer and key figure of the post-war musical avant-garde in Canada; **Al Purdy**, the BC-raised poet of Canada's unsettled edges; **Dr. Michael Smith**, UBC cancer researcher and winner of the Nobel Prize in biochemistry for his contributions to the study of genomes.

2001

The terrorist bombing of New York's World Trade Center in September overshadowed all other events in 2001, but Vancouver had been having a bad year even before September 11. From April to August the city functioned without a bus system while the region's recently formed central transit authority, TransLink, struggled to resolve a strike by transit workers and a funding dispute with the provincial government. Provincial politics were also in turmoil: voters turfed the NDP government and replaced one Vancouverite, Ujjal Dosanjh, with another, Gordon Campbell, in the office of the premier.

Right: The family that built Vancouver. Seen in this 1965 photograph are Charles Bentall (far right) and his sons (from left) Howard, Clark and Robert (Bob). Clark and Bob continued the family construction empire started by their father, remaining until 2001. The only one of the men still alive, Bob, now focuses on philanthropy with his wife. Howard became a Baptist minister. *PNG*

January 1

The death from meningitis of a 23-year-old Abbotsford nursing student was the harbinger of an outbreak of the serious infectious disease in the central Fraser Valley. By late July there were nine reported cases among young adults in Abbotsford and Mission, and one additional death. A mass vaccination campaign of residents between the ages of 18 and 29 halted the disease spread until late October. Four new cases in Abbotsford before year's end led to the deaths of two more victims, both of them older than the vaccination campaign's target population.

January 15 After nearly a century of shaping the downtown skyline, the Bentall family announced the sale of its remaining stake in Bentall Corporation to a Quebec pension fund. The company had been founded three generations earlier by Charles Bentall, a structural engineer who arrived in Vancouver in 1908 and became the head of

Elsewhere in BC

October 29 The ship was named HMCS *Vancouver*, but it sailed from Victoria, carrying 235 Canadian service men and women to a six-month deployment in the Arabian Gulf, part of Canada's response to the terrorist action in New York on September 11. Vancouver mayor Philip Owen, Defence Minister Art Eggleton and Deputy Premier Christy Clark joined Lieutenant-Governor Iona Campagnolo in a farewell to the troops as they headed to California to join an American aircraft carrier battle group going to the Middle East.

Iona Campagnolo was appointed BC's first female Lieutenant-Governor. She was the Liberal MP for Skeena riding in northern BC during the 1970s, serving as federal minister of sport. She had also been involved in a number of non-governmental agencies and was the first chancellor of the University of Northern BC in Prince George.

Elsewhere in the World

On the morning of September 11, terrorists highjacked four commercial flights in the eastern United States and flew them at targets in Washington and New York. One hit the Pentagon and two hit the twin towers of the World Trade Center. The towers caught fire and collapsed, killing about 2,750 occupants and emergency service personnel. Air traffic across North America was disrupted and many American planes landed in Canada, where passengers were sheltered and fed by concerned citizens. Osama bin Laden, a Saudi Islamist extremist, was identified as the architect of the attacks, and America began a pursuit that led to the invasion of Afghanistan by NATO and other allies of America. The search for Bin Laden finally ended in 2011 when he was killed by American special forces in Pakistan.

Out with the old, in with the new. SkyTrain cars for the new Millennium Line were unveiled by Premier Ujjal Dosanjh and cabinet minister Mike Farnworth in a public ceremony at the Burnaby Works Yard. *Colin Price / The Province*

Dominion Construction. He and his descendants helped build the Stanley Park causeway, the old Vancouver courthouse, the BC Sugar refinery, the four Bentall towers, the BC Pavilion at Expo 86, the MacMillan Bloedel Research Centre and the Telus building in Burnaby, among other city landmarks.

January 30 Premier Ujjal Dosanjh and transit minister Mike Farnworth hosted a jolly public unveiling of new SkyTrain cars for the nearly completed Millennium Line,

but key TransLink officials were conspicuous by their absence from the platform party. One week earlier, the province had refused to implement TransLink's unpopular levy on Greater Vancouver vehicles while also denying the road and transit authority a bigger share of regional gasoline taxes. Now TransLink faced an operating budget shortfall of $30 million, the loss of $95 million from the levy and the pain of service cuts, just as it was expanding bus and rail transit routes and initiating major road upgrades. TransLink chairman George Puil and many other municipal politicians didn't feel like celebrating with the premier, whom they accused of reneging on a promise made in 1998 to implement a vehicle tax if necessary. The failure of the vehicle levy coincided with the resignation of TransLink chief executive Ken Dobell, an architect of the TransLink system and a long-time public transit advocate. A few months later he became the premier's deputy in a new Liberal government.

February 17 Residents of Chinatown joined officials from three levels of government in the Dr. Sun Yat-sen Chinese Garden to celebrate plans for revitalization of the neighbourhood and construction of a traditional gate at its entrance. The promise of $750,000 in funding for the project helped ease some pre-existing tensions between government and the community that had been aroused months earlier by the announcement of a controversial addictions treatment facility for Hastings Street. "We need some good news in this area because we've been inundated with bad news for a while," commented Kelly Ip, vice-president of the Millennium Gate Society. As part of the revitalization project, in April the city opened "The Silk Road," a walking route linking Library Square and Robson Street to Chinatown through the new Millennium Gate.

March 1 Cypress Bowl ski resort on the North Shore got a new owner, Boyne Resorts of Michigan. The company said it would upgrade the resort's facilities with a new gondola, alpine and nordic base area and 100-seat restaurant.

April 1 More than 675,000 bus riders in Greater Vancouver had to find alternative transport when all the buses stopped.

Drivers for Coast Mountain, TransLink's main bus-operating system, went on strike to support a demand for an 18 percent wage hike over three years. The company's office workers soon joined drivers on the picket lines. It had been 17 years since Vancouver's last bus strike. SkyTrain and the West Coast Express continued to operate, but heavy traffic snarled the roadways and frayed tempers throughout the metropolitan region. By June, when negotiations were still stalled, placard-waving protesters took over the TransLink board meeting, and other angry citizens set up a tent camp at

Not in service. Protesters called for the firing of TransLink chair George Puil when the exec failed to settle the three-month bus strike that left 675,000 bus commuters stranded. *Bill Keay / Vancouver Sun*

Vancouver city hall. Labour mediator Vince Ready submitted a compromise recommendation on June 14 for an 8.5 percent hike, which the drivers accepted, but Coast Mountain held out until the recently elected Liberal government legislated both unions back to work on August 1. The 123-day transit strike, the second-longest in Canadian history, hurt transit users but created a budget windfall for TransLink, which saved about $5 million a week during the strike in unexpended operating costs.

April 14

The Vancouver Grizzlies NBA basketball team played their last home game, losing 100–85 to the Houston Rockets at GM Place (later renamed Rogers Arena). Since arriving in the city in 1995, the team had seen three owners (Arthur Griffiths, John McCaw, Michael Heisley) and five head coaches (Brian Winters, Stu Jackson, Brian Hill, Lionel Hollins, Sidney Lowe). After finishing last in its division in 2000–2001 with 23 wins and 59 losses, the team moved to Memphis on July 4, and Vancouver basketball fans left the arena to return to their television sets.

May 16 It was an electoral tsunami. In BC's 37th provincial election, the Liberal Party under leader Gordon Campbell won 77 of 79 seats in the legislature, ending more than nine years of rule by the NDP. Premier Ujjal Dosanjh lost his seat in Vancouver–Kensington, although the city re-elected two of his cabinet members, Joy MacPhail (Vancouver–Hastings) and Jenny Kwan (Vancouver–Mount Pleasant), as the only two NDP representatives. Acknowledging impending defeat, Dosanjh had resigned as party leader one week before the election. When the house reconvened, Premier Campbell refused to recognize the two NDP members as an official opposition party. MacPhail served as the NDP's appointed interim leader until 2003, when she stepped down and the party elected Carole James.

June 13 Vancouver civil rights lawyer and federal Liberal activist Mobina Jaffer, 51, became the first Muslim named to the Senate of Canada. She was also the first senator born in Africa, and the first of South Asian descent.

July 10 Ken Lyotier, entrepreneurial leader of the United We Can recycling operation for "binners" in the Downtown Eastside, saw another of his bright ideas succeed when the federal government gave $120,000 to the non-profit Save Our Living Environment society, an organization of street-level recyclers founded by Lyotier in 1990. SOLE proposed to pay about 120 Downtown Eastside residents between $100 and $200 a month to clean graffitti off walls of boarded-up buildings in the city's poorest neighbourhood. "If you don't have a nickel, you are willing to do what it takes to get that nickel," said Lyotier, a former street dweller.

Dead end. Struggling to remain positive despite defeat, the Vancouver Grizzlies meet their end. Typically one of the worst teams in the NBA over their six seasons in Vancouver, and with plummeting attendance, the basketball team moved to Memphis in 2001. Diehard fans continue to agitate for a Vancouver team, but that seems unlikely. *Arlen Redekop / The Province*

July 28 to August 8

Fireworks lit up the night sky over English Bay, but it had been tough finding the matches.

When Benson & Hedges, the former main sponsor of Vancouver's annual Symphony of Fire, withdrew funding for the $1.5-million event at the end of 2000 because of new federal rules against tobacco advertising, the city said it would support the festival only if private sponsors could be found. A new organization called the Vancouver Fireworks Festival Society coalesced in the nick of time to save the popular summer show. The resurrected "Celebration of Light" attracted participating pyrotechnic teams from Asia, Africa and Europe and provided a spectacular free show for thousands of viewers perched on the beaches and bridges downtown.

In 2000, Benson & Hedges withdrew funding for the Symphony of Fire annual fireworks and music competition, which it had sponsored for a decade. New advertising regulations had forced the tobacco company out. In 2001, new sponsors stepped in and the summer light show over English Bay became the Celebration of Light. *Craig Hodge* / Vancouver Sun

August 1 to 14 Within a two-week period, the Liberal government passed three pieces of legislation that had a heavy impact on public-sector labour unions in the Lower Mainland. On August 1, striking transit workers in the Greater Vancouver area were ordered back to work. On August 9 the government imposed a contract on recalcitrant members of the BC Nurses Union and the Health Sciences Association (the union of 11,000 X-ray technicians, pysiotherapists, pharmacists and other health professionals). On August 14 it was the turn of militant teachers to feel pressure when the legislature passed a law confirming the right of teachers and school support workers to strike, but also enshrining the right of students to receive classroom instruction during a strike.

August 25 Port Moody MLA Christy Clark, minister of education and deputy premier, became the first BC cabinet minister to give birth while in office. Clark's son, Hamish Marissen-Clark, accompanied his 35-year-old mother when she returned to work in early autumn and slept in a temporary nursery adjacent to her office so she could breastfeed him.

September 10 Mayor Philip Owen and members of city council led an enthusiastic party of walkers on a new waterfront path along Southeast False Creek to mark the completion of a 28-kilometre (17-mile) walkway linking Kitsilano Point to Coal Harbour. With the opening of the False Creek section, Vancouver became the only city in North America with a waterfront walkway system of such magnitude. Vancouver Molson Indy race organizers were main sponsors of the False Creek section.

September 17 At noon, a squad of rappelling dancers used the walls of the new Scotiabank Dance Centre as performance surfaces in an aerial dance event choreographed to celebrate the public opening of the seven-storey rehearsal and administrative building at the corner of Davie and Granville. In the weeks following the opening, the centre's 150-seat production and performance studio showcased new works commissioned from six Vancouver choreographers: Cori Caulfield, Jai Govinda, Katherine Labelle, Naomi Lefebvre, Jennifer Mascall and Wen Wei Wang. The city's arts community welcomed the centre, designed by Arthur Erickson, as a much-needed downtown venue for independent, innovative dance making.

November 3 The Nikkei Fishermen's Reunion dinner brought together 300 retired Japanese Canadian fishermen and their spouses for a banquet at the Steveston Buddhist Temple to commemorate over 100 years of Japanese Canadians in the fishing industry.

December 19 At the end of a bitterly disappointing year, George Puil said he would not stand for re-election as chair of TransLink. The

71-year-old chairman of the Greater Vancouver Regional District had led the transit authority through a difficult bus strike and corporate reorganization, enduring physical threats. Protesters had even dumped a pile of manure on the lawn of his Kitsilano home, but he said the last straw for him was having to fund regional transportation initiatives from an increase in property taxes after the provincial government refused to implement a vehicle levy. Puil had promised to avoid hiking property taxes. He said, "I had to break my promise, something that does not come easily. I could have stepped down and avoided it. But that would have meant quitting when the going was roughest. And whatever else I may be, I am not a quitter." The veteran of 32 years of politics with Vancouver Park Board, Vancouver City Council and the GVRD stayed on as GVRD chair.

December 26 Dariusz Blachnio, a construction worker from Surrey, was one of five winners nationwide of a $5-million Lotto 6/49 jackpot. Blachnio played six special numbers—3, 6, 9, 10, 13 and 20—that he said had come to him in a dream three years earlier. He had been buying lottery tickets with them ever since. The father of nine-year-old twin daughters, who had immigrated with his wife from Poland 11 years earlier, said, "I had the dream, so I must win." Odds of his numbers coming up were about one in 14 million.

Also in 2001

Gordon Houston (pronounced *hoost'n*) was appointed president and CEO of the Vancouver Port Authority in March. Under his leadership, the Vancouver, Fraser and North Fraser ports amalgamated in January 2008 to form Port Metro Vancouver, Canada's largest port. The port trades more than $75 billion in goods annually with more than 160 nations, generates more than 45,000 local jobs and 132,700 port-related jobs across Canada, and contributes $970 million in taxes annually (2008 statistics). Houston retired in February 2009, ending a 44-year career in marine transportation.

Jack Diamond, called the father of modern-day horse racing in BC, died at age 91. Diamond was a poorly educated farm boy from Poland who became a self-made millionaire and philanthropist in Vancouver. A Jewish community leader and prodigious fundraiser, he was co-owner of Hastings Park race track, a meat-company owner and former chancellor of Simon Fraser University.

Dr. Wah Jun Tze, founder of Canada's first alternative medicine clinic connected to a hospital, died at age 65, in Beijing, after a heart attack. Tze was an internationally recognized pediatric endocrinologist and founder of the Tzu Chi Centre for Complementary and Alternative Medicine at Vancouver General Hospital. Earlier in 2011, Tze had published *HQ* (for "Health Quotient"), which examined how the latest high-tech advances of mainstream western medicine could be integrated with mind/body medicine, spirituality and ancient remedies.

The Fraser Valley Buddhist Temple in Aldergrove was partly destroyed in August by a fire set by an arsonist. The shrine survived the fire and was taken to the Buddhist Temples of Canada headquarters at the Steveston Buddhist Temple for safekeeping. On June 6, 2003, it was returned to the Fraser Valley in time for the celebration of the Buddhist festival, Obon.

Passenger traffic through YVR plunged 250,000 in September after the World Trade Center attacks.

David Masuhara, a Vancouver *sansei* (third-generation Japanese person), became the first Japanese Canadian to be appointed to the British Columbia Supreme Court.

Comings and Goings

Notable deaths: former Squamish Nation chief **Simon Baker**, age 90; environmentalist **David McTaggart**, 68; radio disc jockey **Rick Honey**, 53; mystery novelist **L.R. Wright**, 61; sportswriter **Jim Coleman**, 89; **Norma Macmillan**, who got her start on the stage in Vancouver in the 1950s and was best known as the voice of Casper the Friendly Ghost, at age 79 in Vancouver; **Bob "Hopper" Scarr**, who played on the UBC basketball team that represented Canada at the 1948 Summer Olympics, 74; **Ruth Wilson**, athlete (she excelled at tennis, golf, basketball and softball), coach, administrator, writer, teacher, mentor and the first woman to referee basketball in the province, 82.

Bjossa, for many years the star attraction at the Vancouver Aquarium, died in San Diego at about age 24. The glistening black-and-white giant killer whale entertained by floating sideways, propelling herself forward with hefty flaps of her tail, soaring into the sky, then soaking people on the sidelines as she settled back into the pool. A necropsy report issued by SeaWorld in San Diego, where she had been moved to be in the company of other killer whales, confirmed she died of broncopneumonia, an inflammation of the lungs.

2002

In early February, residents of Greater Vancouver were shocked by pictures of hundreds of police and forensic anthropologists, supported by teams of volunteer university students, digging through the dirt of a Coquitlam-area pig farm in search of the remains of women missing from the city's Downtown Eastside. Later in the year, Lions Gate Bridge closures ended and the Millennium SkyTrain line opened.

February 3 Dozens of city dog owners competed in the third annual "Dress Your Dog in Style" fashion show at the Playhouse Theatre. A packed house of dog owners and furry friends in frou-frous turned out to hear Mayor Philip Owen open the show with praise for the Vancouver pound's no-kill policy, the first in Canada. Fashionista and actor Veena Sood introduced each dog parading down the runway, only one christened the red carpet, and the 12 dogs with the best togs went on to a photo shoot for the 2003 dog calendar produced by City Animal Control. Proceeds supported the city's rescue program for abandoned animals.

February 5 Police used a firearms warrant to enter the Port Coquitlam pig farm of Robert "Willy" Picton and began searching for evidence in the BC Missing Women investigation. Picton was charged February 22 with two counts of first-degree murder, and an archeological dig conducted at the farm throughout 2002 and 2003 unearthed gruesome evidence of more slayings. Ultimately charged with the murders of 26 women, Picton went to trial in 2007 on six charges and was convicted of second-degree murder in December 2007, receiving a sentence of 25 years with no parole. When a publication ban on evidence was lifted in 2010, it was revealed he had admitted killing 49 women. The police investigation cost nearly $70 million. Picton unsuccessfully appealed his conviction to the Supreme Court of Canada.

February 6 Students at UBC marched from the Students' Union Building to the home of university president Martha Piper to protest an announced rise in tuition fees of 25 percent starting in fall 2002. It was the beginning of a trend

The RCMP and the Missing Women Task Force began the search for evidence on Robert Picton's pig farm. The search was a major breakthrough in the investigation of the 50 women missing from the Downtown Eastside. *Les Bazso / The Province*

Elsewhere in Canada

The provincial government held a referendum on the principles to guide BC treaty negotiations with First Nations, but the referendum questions were widely denounced as biased, divisive and unjust. Angus Reid, co-founder of the polling company Ipsos-Reid, told a CBC interviewer that it was "one of the most amateurish, one-sided attempts to gauge the public will that I have seen in my professional career." Indigenous leaders across the province organized a boycott of the referendum, and only about 33 percent of the mail-in ballots were returned. Of those, over 80 percent indicated the respondents supported the government's position.

Elsewhere in Canada

Peter Gzowski, journalist, genius radio interviewer and Canadian patriot, died of emphysema in January at the age of 67.

Elsewhere in the World

In February, both the women's and men's hockey teams won Olympic gold for Canada in Provo, Utah, with ice legend Wayne Gretzky managing the men's effort. It was the first Olympic gold medal for the men in 50 years. After the competition, it emerged that Canadian ice-maker Trent Evans had buried a lucky loonie at centre ice.

Scandal rocked financial markets and boardrooms throughout 2002 as pervasive executive fraud was uncovered at corporate giants Enron and WorldCom, accounting firm Arthur Andersen was prosecuted for obstructing justice, and home design doyenne Martha Stewart was charged with insider trading.

Fight over fees. When the province's six-year tuition freeze was lifted by the newly elected BC Liberal government, post-secondary students spoke out.
Nick Procaylo / The Province

across the country to escalate most postsecondary fees.

February 20 Mayor Philip Owen cut the ribbon on a new walk-in freezer at the Vancouver Archives, where thousands of the city's historic photographs would be preserved at minus 18 degrees Celsius. The 45-cubic-metre (1,600-cubic-foot) freezer was one of only three in Canada built to keep historic images from fading and wrinkling.

May 29 An act of the provincial legislature made possible a new liberal arts and sciences university in Squamish. Sea to Sky University, rechristened Quest University Canada in 2005, was the brainchild of former UBC president David Strangway, whose vision of a private residential university with students drawn from around the world became reality when 74 students arrived for classes in 2007. The first bachelor degrees in arts and sciences were bestowed in 2011.

August 15 Drivers and cyclists sighed with relief as the Lions Gate Bridge closures ended after two years,

during which the vehicle deck underwent a gargantuan rebuilding and extension. The project cost $125 million ($47 million over budget) and took twice as long as planned, but the result was improved carrying capacity and a handsomely refurbished city icon. The bridge, which had first opened to traffic in November 1939, was designated a National Historic Site in 2005.

August 31 Passengers rode SkyTrain's new Millennium Line for its entire length for the first time, travelling a loop from Waterfront Station south through Burnaby and New Westminster to Lougheed Town Centre and back to Commercial Drive by way of north Burnaby and the Simon Fraser University area. The new line's Bombardier cars could carry 119 passengers, 44 more than cars on the older line, and the design of the new stations improved safety for visually impaired riders. The line's planned extension to Coquitlam, later known as the Evergreen Line, was postponed due to a lack of funding and was later delayed again when the Canada Line to the airport and Richmond took precedence for the 2010 Olympics.

October 6 Queen Elizabeth II, attired in an elegant burgundy suit complemented by strands of pearls, dropped the puck at an exhibition game at GM Place between the Canucks and the San Jose Sharks. She got to keep the puck.

Queen Elizabeth II drops her first NHL puck at a San Jose Sharks/Vancouver Canucks game while the team captains and The Great One (a.k.a. Wayne Gretzky) cheer her on.
Ian Smith / Vancouver Sun

September 26 When the City of Vancouver and the Corporation of Delta won the 2002 Energy Aware Award at the Union of BC Municipalities convention, it was a real gas. The two governments got the prize for partnering with Maxim Power and CanAgro Produce to harvest methane and carbon dioxide produced by the Vancouver landfill's decaying garbage and convert the gases to heat and electricity for use in CanAgro's greenhouse operations.

October 22 Vancouver honoured its First Nations roots when *A Stó:lõ-Coast Salish Historical Atlas* won the City of Vancouver Book Award. The book's team of six editors, led by Keith Carlson, used maps, archival photographs and traditional narratives to trace the history of the Stó:lõ people from its beginnings in their origin myths. The book described how the nation's culture changed as its home territory was transformed into the urbanized environment known as Greater Vancouver.

October 23 More than 40 men and women lined up early Saturday morning on Robson Street, ready to get naked for at least 30 seconds in winter temperatures to win a free yoga top and bottom at the opening of Vancouver marketing phenomenon Lululemon's first downtown store. Since opening his original outlet in 1999 in Kitsilano, owner Chip Wilson had watched his line of comfortable exercise wear become a global sensation after television star Oprah called her Lululemon outfit one of her "favourite things." By 2010 Vancouver-based Lululemon Athletica was one of the top performers on the Toronto Stock Exchange.

November 9

Vancouver photographer Jeff Wall, famous for images combining his city's natural beauty with revelations of urban blight, received the world's most prestigious photographic prize, the Hasselblad Award, from Princess Lilian of Sweden at a ceremony in the Gothenborg Museum of Art.

November 11 Ottawa named the country's first poet laureate: Vancouver resident George Bowering, 67, twice a winner of the Governor General's Award (for poetry and for fiction), once a vice-president of the Canadian Nihilist Party, until recently a professor at Simon Fraser University and still an ardent baseball player. Asked to define a poet, Bowering said the poet was "the person waiting under the tree, waiting for lightning to strike. Waiting with pen in hand."

November 16 The municipal elections brought a landslide victory for the left-leaning Coalition of Progressive Electors when its candidates in the City of Vancouver ousted the administration of the Non-Partisan Association, and COPE candidate Larry Campbell won the mayor's chair. Campbell, a former Mountie, was also the former chief coroner of BC and the reputed model for the crusading coroner on the popular television drama *Da Vinci's Inquest*. Mayor Philip Owen had resigned after a rift with his own NPA party over his championing of a safe injection site for the Downtown Eastside. Campbell carried Owen's drug strategy forward.

Also in 2002

Homeless people and community activists occupied the historic but empty Woodward's building between Cordova and Hastings Streets in Vancouver's east end on September 13, demanding it be dedicated to social housing for the area's poor. Evicted after one week, the squatters erected a tent city on the sidewalks around the building for three months, setting up a communal kitchen at the corner of Hastings and Abbott. The protest came to be known as "Woodsquat" and drew 280 homeless persons and supporters to the street until the city offered a deal to those wanting shelter. On December 14, 53 homeless squatters moved into the nearby Dominion Hotel after the city agreed to pay their rent for up to four months through the Portland Hotel Society. Squat participants led a clean-up of the sidewalks, and leader Jim Leyden commented, "I have a lot of hope for this. This is something new, something that hasn't been tried before, but it is the way getting people off the

Thousands of squatters made the abandoned Woodward's store their home for three months as the fate of the Hastings Street building remained undecided. The occupation of the building and the surrounding sidewalk led the way for social housing at the site. *Ian Smith / Vancouver Sun*

streets should be done." By 2010 the Woodward's site had been redeveloped with a combination of market housing units, subsidized social housing, retail shops, civic offices and Simon Fraser University's new School for Contemporary Arts.

New Westminster city council let light into a dark place in the history of Greater Vancouver when it approved a new housing development and park for the site of the old Woodlands Institute, BC's largest institution housing the mentally disabled from its founding in 1878 to closure in 1996. Where once the Woodlands patients lived in grim wards, cut off from the growing city outside, there were plans for housing for between 2,000 and 3,000 residents, built around 5 hectares (about 12 acres) of open spaces and parkland. The cemetery, where more than 3,000 former patients were interred in mostly unmarked graves, became a memorial garden with a central sculpture titled "Window Too High," a reference to the barred windows placed high in the old walls to prevent patients seeing out or being seen. Richard McDonald was a resident of Woodlands from age 9 to 19 (1952 to 1962). As president of the Self Advocacy Foundation and a leading proponent of the memorial garden project, he commented, "It was not so pleasant to live at Woodlands. It was quite scary most of the time. We need to tell these stories. We need to be in history."

The year ended with the city's housing picture reflecting the tension between old and new, preservation and renovation. In Fairview, the neighbourhood's oldest Queen Anne-style heritage home was saved from destruction. The dilapidated James Shaw house at 550 West 7th Ave., built in 1895, had to make way for a $20-million biotech office tower to be built on the site, but Cressey Developments lifted the house and trucked it around the corner to Ash Street, where it was restored and incorporated into the new development. Meanwhile, downtown in Coal Harbour, there was a surge in construction of condominium towers, and Concord Pacific continued development of the former Expo lands along False Creek.

A Turbid Discharge

Vancouverites watched their tap water turn yellow as silt and organic material washed into the Seymour reservoir after heavy winter rain. Turbidity at the North Shore lake, one of Greater Vancouver's main water supplies, rose to nearly 10 nephelometric turbidity units (NTUs), well above the maximum acceptable level of 1 NTU posted in national water guidelines. Regional medical health officer Dr. John Blatherwick warned HIV sufferers, cancer patients and other Vancouver residents with weakened immune systems to boil their drinking water. Squamish also posted a boil-water advisory when district officials noted turbidity levels approaching 10 NTUs. The safety of the region's water supply became an issue again in February when the province released an independent panel's review of the new Drinking Water Protection Act. Chaired by David Marshall, executive director of the Fraser Basin Council, the panel warned a Walkerton-style public health disaster could hit BC unless threats to community water supplies from intensive farming, logging and septic system concentrations were addressed by more comprehensive legislation than the new act provided. The report noted BC had the highest rate of waterborne disease outbreaks in Canada, and 240 community water supply systems were on permanent boil-water advisories because of persistent contamination hazards.

Room of One's Own celebrated 25 years of publication. Founded in the early days of Vancouver feminism by a group of women interested in reading and recognizing female writers, the literary journal's team of volunteers looked back on nearly 100 issues featuring influential women writers like Carol Shields, Dorothy Livesay and Nicole Brossard as well as emerging younger talents.

Vancouver geneticist Marco Marra, working with a team at the Genome Sciences Research Centre of the BC Cancer Centre, succeeded in mapping the mouse genome, a crucial step toward understanding how human genes interact with disease triggers. The city team received international recognition when the journal *Nature* outlined progress of the global mouse genome project.

Comings and Goings

Notable deaths: **Kat Craig**, 54, pioneering video artist; **Jack Cullen**, 80, disc jockey of late-night radio for five decades; **Christie Harris**, 94, author of *Raven's Cry* and other books retelling Haida legends for children; **Douglas Jung**, 77, the first Canadian of Chinese heritage elected to Parliament; **Homer Stevens**, 79, legendary president of the United Fishermen and Allied Workers, nationalist and environmentalist.

Howe Street learned of the death of its princess, Tammy Patrick. The flamboyant former broker cut a swath through the financial district in the 1980s and for eight years was the love interest of the late, legendary Murray Pezim. Patrick passed away suddenly in the home of a Kelowna friend after years of fighting drug addiction. She was 40.

2003

Vancouver won its bid for the 2010 Winter Olympics. TransLink got the green light for a rapid transit line to Richmond and Vancouver Airport. And Canada's first safe injection site for drug users opened in September on East Hastings Street.

January 1 Nearly 100 racers left Brockton Oval in Stanley Park at 8:45 a.m. in the 10th annual Fat Ass Run—a misnomer, because participants covered 50 kilometres (31 miles) and tended to be serious athletes. Participants ran along the shoreline from the park to Spanish Banks, followed muddy trails through Pacific Spirit Park, then retraced their path to finish with a plunge into Burrard Inlet.

January 10 Premier Gordon Campbell, MLA for Point Grey, took a holiday in Maui and came home with some undesired travel pictures—his police mug shots.

After leaving a dinner with friends, he was stopped for speeding and arrested for drunk driving. Campbell was fined and ordered to take part in a substance abuse program. The police photos adorned Vancouver's coffee mugs for years afterward.

January 23 The city and private developers Amacon and Onni Group shared the honours at a groundbreaking ceremony for the Vancouver International Film Centre, under construction between two residential towers at Davie and Seymour. In exchange for a density bonus granted by Vancouver, the developers built a 1,300-square-metre (14,000-square-foot) facility with a 170-seat theatre for the Vancouver International Film Festival. The centre was one more element, with the Scotiabank Dance Centre and Granville's theatre row, in an emerging cultural hub in the downtown.

February 25 The Squamish First Nation signed a deal with Eaton Power of North Vancouver to develop a run-of-river hydroelectric project on Furry Creek in Squamish traditional territory on Howe Sound. The

Elsewhere in BC

In BC's longest province-wide state of emergency, three pilots lost their lives fighting forest fires, and 334 homes burned, most of them in the Okanagan region.

The province sold BC Rail to CN Rail for $1 billion in November, but scandal plagued the sale when police raided the offices of ministerial aides Dave Basi and Bobby Virk looking for evidence they had conveyed secret details about the sale to other potential purchasers. After a protracted judicial process, Basi and Virk pleaded guilty to corruption charges in 2010.

In November, the provincial NDP elected Carole James as its new leader.

Elsewhere in Canada

Prime Minister Jean Chrétien signed the Kyoto agreement on climate change and endorsed same-sex marriage and the decriminalization of marijuana, then retired, to be succeeded as Liberal leader and prime minister by Paul Martin in November. Meanwhile, the Progressive Conservative Party merged with the Canadian Alliance to unite the right on the federal political spectrum.

Elsewhere in the World

February 1 Space shuttle *Columbia* disintegrated as it re-entered Earth's atmosphere, the result of damage to the protective heat shield covering its wing during launch. All seven crew members died in the disaster.

April 13 Left-handed golfer Mike Weir of Ontario became the first Canadian to win the Masters golf tournament.

David Radler, right-hand man of Conrad Black, resigned as deputy chair, president and chief operating officer of Chicago-based Hollinger International in the midst of a scandal over misappropriation of funds. Radler later pled guilty to a lesser charge in a plea bargain that saw him testify against his former boss, former owner of the *Vancouver Sun*, who went to jail in the United States.

The much-maligned PacifiCat fast ferries were auctioned off by the Ritchie Brothers Auctioneers. Washington Marine Group bought the Fast Cats for just $19.4 million; the boats cost almost $460 million to build. *Peter Battistoni / Vancouver Sun*

agreement gave the Squamish Nation equity ownership, a share in revenues and a training program for workers in the nation's construction company. The 10-megawatt plant was expected to generate enough power to light 5,000 area homes.

March 1 Gasoline taxes rose 3.5 cents a litre across the province, and drivers in the Lower Mainland, already paying the highest fuel taxes in the province, were now paying a total per-litre provincial tax of 20.5 cents. Drivers in Victoria paid 17 cents; those in the rest of the province, 11 cents. The premier said new tax revenue of about $175 million would help pay for improvements on the Sea to Sky Highway to Whistler, a key element in Vancouver's Olympic bid.

March 11 The United Nations awarded the City of Vancouver an Innovation in Public Service Award for its Neighbourhood Integrated Service Teams, which help residents work together with the city to solve local problems.

March 24 The story turned out to be "buy high, sell low" when the PacifiCat fast ferries, mothballed for months, sold at auction to the Washington Marine Group of the United States for $19.4 million. The provincial government had built them at a cost of nearly $460 million between 1998 and 2000, but they were plagued by budget overruns, engine problems and high fuel consumption. In 2009 the vessels were sold to a company based in the United Arab Emirates.

April 24 Vancouver Public Library named author Timothy Taylor's book *Stanley Park* its must-read book of the year and organized a lecture series, book club meetings and a dinner gala to celebrate it.

May 22 In a sign of hope for an old building at the heart of Vancouver life for generations, Mayor Larry Campbell relit the big "W" atop the old downtown Woodward's store.

Yes! Though there were mixed reactions, the general feeling was positive when Vancouver received the news that the city had been chosen to host the 2010 Winter Olympics. Vancouver Sun

The Downtown Eastside's Insite is Vancouver's first supervised injection site. Since opening its doors in 2003, Insite has served 12,236 and reduced overdose mortality within 500 metres of the facility by 35 percent. *Peter Battistoni* / Vancouver Sun

At its installation in 1958 the "W" dominated the city's night sky, but it went dark in 1993 when Woodward's went bankrupt. A coalition of private interests, community groups and the city were working to revitalize the building and its neighbourhood.

May 29 The controversial Richmond/Airport/Vancouver (RAV) rapid transit line narrowly won approval from directors of the Greater Vancouver Regional District. They concurrently, but ineffectively, passed a motion asking TransLink to build the Millennium Line extension to Coquitlam in conjunction with RAV. The matter was not settled, however, as the RAV line underwent a few near-death experiences in 2004.

July 2

The International Olympic Committee met in Prague and selected Vancouver as the host city for the 2010 winter games. Bid team chairman Jack Poole and president John Furlong, supported by Mayor Larry Campbell, Premier Gordon Campbell and Prime Minister Jean Chrétien, celerated with their volunteers when the IOC gave Vancouver three votes more than the rival bidder, Pyeongchang in South Korea. The games took place in Vancouver and Whistler from February 12 to 28, 2010, and the Paralympic Winter Games followed on March 12 to 21.

July 29 As sockeye salmon started their annual run, the Department of Fisheries and Oceans closed the Native-only commercial fishery on the Fraser River after a ruling by Vancouver provincial court judge William Kitchen that the race-based fishery was "racial discrimination" and violated Canada's Charter of Rights. Defiant members of the Stó:lō First Nation set their nets the following weekend between the Port Mann Bridge and Sawmill Creek above Yale. Said Stó:lō spokesman Bob Hall, "We're going to continue, we're going to exercise our fishing rights, continue to barter and sell and trade our salmon; it's a way of life for us." Musqueam First Nations councillor Wayne Sparrow called on Ottawa to appeal the ruling and said the Musqueam were consulting with their own lawyers.

September 1 TransLink, with sponsorship from VanCity, implemented the U-Pass program, which gave students at Simon Fraser University and the University of BC unlimited use of the Lower Mainland transit system in exchange for a charge embedded in their total student fees at the start of each term. The U-Pass became a great success, cutting down vehicle traffic near the universities and increasing transit ridership. Langara College and Capilano University adopted the program in 2009, and U-Pass became a province-wide initiative in June 2010, with a provincial student transit rate of $30 per month.

September 20

An open house on Burnaby Mountain introduced prospective purchasers to UniverCity, Simon Fraser University's planned community for about 10,000 residents, which was under construction within a ring of 305 hectares (753 acres) of parkland. With guidelines for energy conservation, water conservation and protection, and environmentally friendly landscaping, UniverCity became a leader in green neighbourhood growth, but it drew the ire of Arthur Erickson, the original architect of SFU, because it failed to preserve his brutalism principles of bare concrete, flat roofs and monumental horizontal planes. The first settlers took up residence in 2004 and enjoyed access

The price of protection. After years of negotiations the Greater Vancouver Regional District, the Corporation of Delta, and the provincial and federal governments pitched in nearly $78 million to purchase Burns Bog and establish the 2,042 hectares as an ecological conservancy area. *PNG*

to the university's sports and library facilities as a feature of purchase.

September 21 North America's first government-run supervised injection site for drug users opened at 139 East Hastings Street

in Vancouver's addiction-afflicted Downtown Eastside. (In 2000, the DTES had 4,700 chronic drug users.) Called Insite, the injection site operated from 10 a.m. to 4 a.m., seven days a week, under a special exemption to the Controlled Drugs and Substances Act, offering clients a clean, anonymous place where they could inject the cocaine, heroin, morphine or prescription drugs they brought to the site without fear of prosecution. Medical assistance was available as well as drug and alcohol addiction counselling. Proponents pointed to the reduced harm to addicts and society in general that would come from a decline in infections from dirty needles and an increase in the use of detoxification services and addiction treatment. Initially funded by Health Canada and the Vancouver Coastal Health Authority, Insite continued operating past the end of its three-year pilot project term, drawing ongoing opposition from critics who saw it as an encouragement of the city's drug culture. In 2010, the site recorded 312,214 visits (an average of 855 visits per day) by 12,236 unique users; an average of 587 injections a day; and 221 overdoses with no fatalities, due to intervention by medical staff.

December 11 Delta's Burns Bog, a peat bog with a unique ecosystem more typical of subarctic zones than a temperate climate like the Lower Mainland, was protected and preserved when four levels of government united in a purchase offer of $77.8 million for 2,042 hectares (about 5,050 acres) held privately by Western Delta Lands. The deal was finalized in March 2004.

Also in 2003

Fresh off a flight from Hong Kong, BC's first victim of Severe Acute Respiratory Syndrome (SARS) checked in to Vancouver General Hospital on March 7. Though there was no outbreak in the general population, local tourism declined 13 percent from March to July and cruise-ship bookings fell for the first time in 20 years. Americans especially seemed to think Vancouver was a suburb of Toronto, where the SARS outbreak was much more severe. Dr. Lyne Filiatrault at Vancouver General Hospital was credited with preventing a SARS catastrophe. On April 12 at 4 a.m., a team of 30 scientists at the BC Cancer Agency cracked the genetic code of the virus causing SARS. A spokesman for the World Health Organization in Geneva hailed their discovery as "an extraordinary step" in the global fight to stop the plague-like new illness that had killed 13 and sickened 274 in Canada since emerging in China earlier in the year.

A public outcry over the division of Vancouver's telephone directory into five separate books signalled the start of a long, hot summer and fall for Telus Corp. Trying to bounce back from a dismal 2002, in which stock plunged and bond-rating agencies downgraded its $4.3 billion in debt to junk status, the company announced a plan to cut its workforce by 40 percent (11,000 positions) through early retirement and voluntary buyout packages. Customers widely viewed the move as a cash grab by the company, which charged 95 cents for every directory-assistance call. But there was worse to come as Telus grappled with service disruptions attributed to staff cuts and Interior fires, generating a public relations debacle. CEO Darren Entwhistle belatedly apologized to British Columbians as the furore peaked in October.

A coalition of environmental groups, including the Sierra Club, the David Suzuki Foundation, Greenpeace and West Coast Environmental Law, issued a report accusing the provincial Liberal government of bad environmental stewardship in its first two years in office. Their report pointed to weak drinking-water regulations, cuts to parks and conservation enforcement staff, and a rollback of environmental protections in the Forest Practices Code.

Bishop Michael Ingham of the Anglican Diocese of New Westminster announced that he had issued a rite of blessing of people in committed same-sex unions and had given some priests permission to bless gay and lesbian unions, even though the Anglican Church of Canada had not agreed to allow such blessings.

Aboriginal bands who supported Vancouver's successful bid for the 2010 Olympics named Squamish First Nation hereditary chief Gibby Jacob as their representative director on the 19-member board of the Vancouver Olympic Organizing Committee. In return for aboriginal permission to let Olympic events occur in traditional First Nations territories, an agreement in November 2002 committed Olympic organizers and the government to a transfer of 120 hectares (about 300 acres) of land in the Callaghan Valley to the Lil'wat Nation and funding for a First Nations cultural centre in Whistler. The Squamish and Lil'wat bands received ownership in several legacy sports facilities, contracting opportunities at event sites and, eventually, 50 houses from the Whistler athletes' village.

The world went into panic at the outbreak of SARS. At YVR, passengers arrived from Hong Kong wearing the medical masks so closely associated with the virus. A Vancouver research team finally cracked the genetic code in April; by that time, tourism to Vancouver and Toronto had been dramatically curbed. *Les Bazso / The* Province

The Vancouver Asahi Baseball team (1914–41) was inducted into the Canadian Baseball Hall of Fame. A film by Canadian filmmaker Jari Osborne, *Sleeping Tigers: The Asahi Baseball Story*, was released by the National Film Board of Canada and premiered at the National Nikkei Museum and Heritage Centre in Burnaby.

Comings and Goings

November 26 Delegates from First Nations involved in treaty negotiations arrived in North Vancouver for a three-day summit in the recreation centre of the Squamish Nation on Capilano Road. National Assembly of First Nations chief Phil Fontaine was a featured speaker.

Notable deaths: **Rosemary Brown**, 72, the first black woman elected to a Canadian provincial legislature; **Paul Gallagher**, 73, former head of Capilano College and Vancouver Community College; **George Wainborn**, 91, Vancouver's longest-serving park board member, who sat from 1956 to 1990; **Leon Kahn**, 78, Holocaust survivor, Vancouver developer and philanthropist; **Ron Longstaffe**, 69, a former Canfor executive and donor of 800 artworks to the Vancouver Art Gallery over a 20-year period.

2004

Right: Despite protests and bids from local shipbuilders, the provincial government opted to give the contract for three Super C-class ferries to German company Flensburger Schiffbau-Gesellschaft.
Wayne Leidenfrost / The Province

The Winter Olympics were still six years away, but two major infrastructure projects—a rapid transit line from Vancouver to Richmond and the international airport, and the upgrade to the Sea to Sky Highway from Horseshoe Bay to the Olympic venue at Whistler Village—were already making news and causing controversy in the Lower Mainland. Both were expected to have a significant impact on the region, and while both were the darlings of the provincial government, some locals dug in their heels to resist them, while others dropped their pants. This was also a hot year for the local economy: housing starts hit a record high in Vancouver, the Canadian loonie reached new heights (80 cents) in relationship to the US dollar and the price of a barrel of oil was on the rise. This was the year slot machines were approved in Vancouver. And it was the year yet another referendum was held on the ward system of municipal government—the sixth in the city's history.

Elsewhere in BC

September 13 The BC Ferries board announced that the German company Flensburger Schiffbau-Gesellschaft had won a $325-million contract to build three Super C-class vessels. Several hundred of the province's shipbuilders, including those working in North Vancouver, travelled to Victoria to protest the deal in front of BC Ferries' offices, to no avail.

Meanwhile, down on the farm: the US *Journal of Science* warned that farmed salmon contained much higher concentrations of toxins than wild salmon, possibly elevating health risks. And avian flu struck the Lower Mainland in March. Its rapid spread meant the eventual destruction of virtually every bird in the Lower Mainland's poultry industry.

Elsewhere in Canada

January The Canadian cattle industry was dealt a huge blow after DNA tests positively linked a mad cow in Washington state to Alberta.

February 10 Auditor General Sheila Fraser released a report that launched the sponsorship scandal and led to the demise of the federal Liberal party. Fraser's report showed that up to $100 million of the Liberals' $250-million sponsorship program was awarded to Liberal supporters at advertising firms and Crown corporations who hired Liberal fundraisers or donated to the party but did little or no work for the money. In response to the report, Prime Minister Paul Martin appointed Justice John H. Gomery to head an inquiry into the allegations.

March 20 Stephen Harper became leader of the Conservative Party of Canada.

Elsewhere in the World

February 4 Facebook was founded in Cambridge, MA.

December 26 An earthquake in the Indian Ocean generated a tsunami that inundated coastal communities (and beach resorts) of Thailand, Indonesia, India, Sri Lanka and other southeast Asian countries. At least 186,000 people died—some estimates put the number of casualties as high as 227,000.

Elsewhere in the universe

NASA's rover *Opportunity* landed on Mars and discovered indications there was once water on the red planet. And the *Cassini-Huygens* spacecraft arrived at Saturn.

Left: Yaletown boom. Vancouverites are known for their love of athletics, nature—and real estate. Hundreds of prospective homebuyers lined up to buy condos in Yaletown Park, one of two new residential towers in the tony neighbourhood. *Jon Murray / The Province*

April 15 Burnaby NDP MP Svend Robinson confessed to stealing a ring from an auction firm. He took immediate medical leave, and in August pleaded guilty to theft over $5,000. He received a conditional discharge, avoiding jail time and a criminal record, but was required to perform 100 hours of community service.

January The year started with city council ending a prohibition on slot machines that it had created in 1997, the year Victoria first allowed slots into the province. The first site to get the one-armed bandits was the Edgewater Casino at the Plaza of Nations, owned by the Great Canadian Gaming Corporation. In July, Great Canadian celebrated city council's approval, in a 6–5 vote, of slot machines at Hastings racetrack.

February Condo-mania returned to Vancouver. In a scene resembling a Boxing Day Sale, people lined up early to get a chance to buy a condo in the Yaletown Park project.

March 8 Vancouver Canucks' Todd Bertuzzi sucker-punched Steve Moore of the Colorado Avalanche from the rear, driving him headfirst into the ice. Bertuzzi then piled onto Moore, followed by other players, leaving Moore unconscious on the ice for 10 minutes. The assault was in retaliation for Moore's hit on Canuck team captain Markus Näslund on February 16. In that game, Moore ran his shoulder into Näslund's head, leaving the captain with a concussion and a bone chip in his elbow that caused him to sit out three games. There was no penalty. Officials declared the hit by Moore was legal, but the Canucks were livid and swore revenge. One team member offered a reward to anyone who took out Moore. As a result of Bertuzzi's hit, Moore suffered a concussion and three broken vertebrae in his neck. He wore a neck brace for the next year and never played professional hockey again. Bertuzzi was suspended for 20 games, pled guilty to assault causing bodily harm in a BC court (he received a conditional discharge and was required to do community service) and was eventually traded in a deal that brought goalie Roberto Luongo to Vancouver.

April Doman Industries Ltd., once one of BC's largest lumber companies, declared bankruptcy, the victim of crippling debt (as much as $1 billion), insider trading allegations, the collapse of the Asian economy in the 1990s and increased competition from Europe and South America. In June the company emerged from bankruptcy as Western Forest Products, under the control of bondholders who had agreed to a debt-for-equity swap with the Doman family.

June Great Canadian Gaming opened the glitzy River Rock Casino in Richmond.

The River Rock Casino drew crowds to its grand opening. The glitzy resort lent gaming and glamour to Richmond. *Ian Lindsay / Vancouver Sun*

August 13 Nancy Trang Nguyen was jailed for nine months after pleading guilty to defrauding her North Vancouver employer, the travel insurance company TIC Agencies, of $53,500. Three months earlier the 35-year-old Surrey mom had been voted employee of the year by her co-workers.

October North Vancouver RCMP tracked down "bargains" at a garage sale where they seized 100 allegedly stolen home computers worth thousands of dollars. Police reported that a sign inside the home where the sale took place read: "If an item cannot be found, it will be arriving soon."

October 16 For the sixth time in Vancouver's history, voters were asked if they wanted to elect their councillors by neighbourhood wards instead of at-large. The ward system of government was brought in shortly after the city's incorporation in 1886 and, except for a three-year hiccup in the 1920s when there was a system of proportional representation, wards remained in place until 1935. That's when Mayor Gerry McGeer promoted and won a referendum to return to the at-large system. The Non-Partisan Association, which governed the city for much of the next 70 years, and a sympathetic provincial government managed to thwart subsequent attempts to bring in the ward system, making Vancouver the odd one out when it came to major cities in North America. This year, though, with the centre-left COPE party in the majority at city hall, the issue went to referendum again. COPE had campaigned in favour of wards since its founding in the late 1960s. But when it was finally in power and able to act on the matter, it found itself in serious disarray, deeply divided on a number of issues. NPA councillor Sam Sullivan, long the poster boy for the at-large system, amassed a coalition behind the "No Wards" banner and prevailed with 54 percent.

November In the fight to stop the Sea to Sky Highway from ploughing a path through the Eagle Ridge Bluff, a group described as West Vancouver moms and two men stripped naked to pose for a fundraising Back the Bluffs calendar. They wanted a tunnel instead. But BC's transportation minister, Kevin Falcon, was unmoved by the fleshy objections and said the overland route would be cheaper and safer and would last longer. His view prevailed.

November 6 Long-time West Vancouver resident and arts philanthropist Kay Meek died, age 98, the day of the first public performance at the Kay Meek Centre for the Performing Arts, to which she had contributed $2.5 million. Born Kay Menelaws in England on August 6, 1906, she was a social studies teacher in Vancouver until she married George Norgan in the early 1940s. Norgan was an executive with Lucky Lager and had an ownership interest in Harrison Hotsprings Hotel and Lansdowne racetrack. They moved to Kew House in West Vancouver in 1953. After George died, Kay married Reginald Meek and they worked together on many philanthropic projects, including the Academy of Music, the Vancouver Symphony, the Vancouver Art Gallery, the Lions Gate Hospital, the Vancouver Foundation and the West Vancouver Foundation. She was awarded the Queen's Golden Jubilee Medal in recognition of her community spirit.

The community of Horseshoe Bay came together to protest the development of the Sea to Sky Highway, which would disturb the residents—human and animal—on the route from Vancouver to Whistler.
Wayne Leidenfrost / The Province

Also in 2004

Secondary suites were legalized in Vancouver, ending a long-standing controversy over this housing option with a whimper rather than a roar. Secondary suites were encouraged immediately after World War II to deal with the city's housing shortage, but for the next 30 years folks in single-family neighbourhoods considered them a nuisance as they sucked up resources from parking space to garbage collection. In the 1980s the

To Hell and Back with the RAV Line

Among the most expensive public infrastructure projects built in BC, the Canada Line was conceived in controversy, rejected at birth, went through several near-death experiences at the hands of municipal politicians and regional transit authorities, was resurrected, reviled, went half a billion over budget, was sued by disgruntled business owners and yet survived to become an indispensible component in Vancouver's transit system, moving more than 100,000 people a day within two years of completion.

The RAV line, as it was initially named (for Richmond/Airport/Vancouver), was conceptualized in the 1990s as a logical expansion to Metro Vancouver's rapid transit inventory, but it languished on the agenda of TransLink (the regional transit authority that had succeeded BC Transit) behind a proposed Evergreen Line that would link Coquitlam, Port Moody and Burnaby.

By 2004, spurred by the people-moving demands of the coming Winter Olympics, provincial and federal governments joined Vancouver's airport authority to push for a $1.35-billion rapid transit line linking the international airport in Richmond with Vancouver's downtown. They sweetened the proposal with promised infusions of cash. Ottawa would put up $450 million, the province $300 million, Vancouver airport $300 million and TransLink $300 million. Two consortiums, Bombardier Inc., builder of SkyTrain, and SNC-Lavalin Inc., were shortlisted and asked to submit their bids. The winner would build, operate and maintain the line for 35 years. SNC-Lavalin won.

Municipal councils were divided from the outset. When hearings opened in 2004 it quickly became clear that almost no one was on the same page. Some wanted the Evergeen Line built first; some wanted an elevated line like SkyTrain; some wanted a surface line; others wanted to take the line underground. In the end, the Canada Line included elements of all three. Nine of its stations in Vancouver were underground, seven stations in Richmond and at the airport were above ground, and at various places the trains ran below, at or above grade.

In-fighting between and within councils and TransLink was fierce. Vancouver mayor Larry Campbell, who wanted the line, called TransLink director and fellow COPE politician Fred Bass, who favoured expanding bus service, a "backstabbing son of a bitch." After TransLink's second attempt to approve the project failed on a tied vote, Richmond East MLA Linda Reid lamented, "I have never seen such a public display of stupidity in my life." Burnaby mayor Derek Corrigan worried the new line was too expensive, that taxpayers would be left holding the bag and that it would pre-empt the Evergreen Line.

The RAV proposal survived a Greater Vancouver Regional District vote in February 2004 when TransLink's $4-billion, 10-year capital plan, which included the line, was passed by a narrow margin after nine hours of wrangling. But in May, facing opposition from mayors of North Vancouver, Burnaby, Coquitlam and Pitt Meadows who wanted the Evergreen Line, TransLink voted it down by a margin of seven to five. "I hope it's not dead. I don't think it's dead," said Richmond mayor Malcolm Brodie. He was right. In June, Premier Gordon Campbell breathed life back into the near corpse with a promise that the province would assume all financial risk for the line—whose cost had increased to $1.7 billion—and offered $170 million for the Evergreen Line. TransLink voted again. The project failed again on a 6–6 tie vote.

Finally, a report from Vancouver city council concluded that a surface rapid transit line could not work in downtown Vancouver. On December 1 the weary, battle-scarred directors of TransLink met again and, after several hours' debate, voted to approve the Canada Line project by a margin of eight to four.

"Let's look at the reality of the facts. The reason the Canada Line was built was because of federal money, airport money and provincial money," the *Vancouver Sun* quoted Port Moody mayor Joe Trasolini as saying. "The Canada Line was the No. 2 priority. But we were told if we didn't build [the Canada Line] the money [for the Evergreen Line] would not be there."

On August 17, 2009, at a final cost of $2 billion, the Canada Line opened three and a half months ahead of schedule and six months before the Winter Olympics it was built to serve. Taxi companies complained that it was hurting their business by capturing travellers to and from the airport. But by 2011, sharp increases in values were reported for properties around Canada Line stations, a signal of its popularity with the public.

Above left: Green light. The Greater Vancouver RAV line was finally approved at TransLink. The project would exhaust the available funding, test the patience of commuters and business owners, and ultimately change the way Vancouverites move. *PNG*

city had legalized just under half the existing suites and attempted to clamp down on illegal ones, but their numbers continued to grow. The new law was a bow to the inevitable.

Comings and Goings

April The Dalai Lama visited Vancouver for three days. He attended an academic conference on Tibet and gave the keynote address, gave a spiritual teaching at the Pacific Coliseum, enjoyed a musical tribute at the Orpheum Theatre and took part in public talks. With Professor Shirin Ebadi, an Iranian judge and human rights activist, and Archbishop Desmond Tutu of South Africa, he took part in the convocation ceremonies of Simon Fraser University and the University of BC. The three Nobel laureates each received honorary degrees from both institutions.

Notable deaths: **Toni Onley**, artist and arts activist, February 29; **Doug Bennett**, singer (Doug and the Slugs) and musician, October 16.

2005

There were dramatic changes in the political leadership of BC's two largest cities, Vancouver and Surrey, and provincially the Liberal party, while holding on to power, dropped from its stunning 77–2 majority of 2001 to 46 seats, with the NDP moving up to 33. And the saga of the Canada Line continued as Cambie Street merchants realized construction was going to block access to their stores.

Right: Rapid transit to Richmond. Construction to build the RAV Canada Line restricted access to the commercial strip of Cambie Street. The project's cost to the city was almost $2 billion; for some local business owners, the cost was their livelihoods.
Ian Smith / Vancouver Sun

January 26 Merchants and residents along Cambie Street got an unpleasant surprise when they learned that the rapid transit line from Vancouver's waterfront to Richmond and the airport would not be built in a bored tunnel along that busy commercial stretch of the city. Instead, the most expensive infrastructure project in the city's history (at almost $2 billion) would be built using a much more disruptive "cut and cover" process that would eliminate or reduce access to dozens of businesses for three to six months. In reality, construction dragged on for years. Shops moved or went out of business, and their owners launched both private and class-action lawsuits seeking compensation that continued to make their way through the courts after construction was completed in 2009.

January Provincial Education Minister Tom Christensen visited New Westminster to tour the site of

Elsewhere in BC

January The December 26, 2004, earthquake and tsunami that devastated southeast Asia touched the lives of people in Richmond when the body of former Richmond resident Rubina Wong was finally positively identified. The 25-year-old teacher had been vacationing on an island in Thailand with her boyfriend, Michael Lang, when the tsunami struck.

May 17 The citizens of BC were asked to vote in a referendum on an alternative way of selecting representatives in provincial elections. A provincially financed Citizen's Assembly had examined voting methods from around the world and decided that the "single transferable vote" system (STV) was the best choice to replace the "first past the post" system used throughout the country. STV was used in only a few countries, but proponents argued it would better reflect the choices of the electorate. Following an intense campaign by both sides, the referendum passed by 57.7 percent but fell just short of the 60 percent threshold set by Gordon Campbell's Liberal government. There was a second referendum on STV in 2009, but the option failed to achieve a majority of support.

Also on May 17 Gordon Campbell and the Liberal Party held on to power in the provincial election, but their majority was cut severely, from 75 seats to 13.

Although BC billionaire businessman Jimmy Pattison came in a poor 107th on Forbes' list of the World's Richest People this year, he still had $4.8 billion tucked under his mattress. Pattison trailed Toronto businessman, art collector and *Globe and Mail* owner Kenneth Thomson, who was ranked 15th, worth $17.9 billion. Other Canadians on the list were Paul Desmarais, worth $3.3 billion (164th place) and Charles Bronfman, a distant 235 out of 691, with $2.8 billion.

Elsewhere in Canada

March 3 Four members of the RCMP—Peter Schiemann, Lionide Johnston, Anthony Gordon and Brock Myrol—were killed by James Roszko during a drug raid on his farm near Mayerthorpe, AB.

Elsewhere in the World

August Hurricane Katrina hit the US Gulf Coast, causing severe damage. The storm surge breached the levees protecting the city of New Orleans, and 80 percent of the city flooded. At least 1,836 people died.

a proposed $50-million high school. Christensen wouldn't say exactly what the province would contribute to the project, but he assured school officials the government would do everything it could to ensure the school was among the best in the province. "I'm pretty confident this is going to be a pretty impressive school in two-and-a-half years," Christensen said. He was optimistic. The project has been chronically stalled by the fact that the school shares a site with a historic graveyard.

February Tsering Luding, a 39-year-old carpet cleaner from Richmond, became the biggest lottery winner in BC history when he hit the $26.6-million jackpot from Lotto Super 7.

March 8 Grant DePatie, a gas station worker in Maple Ridge, was killed when he tried to stop a teenager who drove away without paying for $12 worth of gas. DePatie, the lone attendant on the night shift, fell under the stolen van the teen was driving and was dragged 7 kilometres (4.5 miles). In 2007 the provincial government passed a law requiring BC drivers to pay before they pump 24 hours a day, becoming the first province in Canada to enforce this law.

March 17 Justice Ian Bruce Josephson of BC Supreme Court delivered a not-guilty verdict in the cases against Ripudaman Singh Malik and Ajaib Singh Bagri for the bombing of Air India Flight 182. That event, which took place 20 years earlier, was the biggest terrorist attack in Canadian history and killed 329 people, 278 of them Canadian. Dissatisfied relatives of those who lost their lives repeated demands for a public inquiry into the federal police agencies' bungled investigation, which cost $130 million and caused the judge to conclude that the "evidence has fallen markedly short of the standard."

May 2 Bob Hunter, a founder of Greenpeace and the organization's first president, died of prostate cancer at age 63. He was best remembered for his work with the environmental group that started out in Vancouver in 1971 to protest underground nuclear testing in Alaska and grew to become a global movement that changed the way we think of our place on the planet. In the mid-1970s Hunter was involved in protests against Soviet whaling and the seal hunt on the east coast of Canada. Former comrade-in-arms Paul Watson recalled one incident from that time: "In March of 1976, he and I stood on the heaving ice floes off the coast of Labrador as a large sealing ship bore down on us. The ice cracked and split beneath our feet as I said to Bob, 'When it splits, I'll jump to the left and you to the right.' Bob looked straight ahead and calmly said, 'I'm not going anywhere.' And he meant it, and because he stayed, I stayed and we brought that seal-killing ship to a dead stop."

May 14 Tracy Hinder, a 13-year-old West Vancouver student, won the provincial CanWest CanSpell spelling bee with the word "apotheosis," which means "to elevate to transcendental position." She went on to the national spelling bee in Ottawa, where she came fifth after stumbling on the Jewish word "daven," which refers to the act of praying.

Greenpeace founder. Wearing sunglasses, Bob Hunter is pictured here at the waterfront in Vancouver in September 1976, while president of Greenpeace. He died three decades later, in 2005, of prostate cancer. *Rob Straight / Vancouver Sun*

May The Lower Mainland got its first taste of a batch of new and free daily newspapers, including *24 Hours*, *Metro* and *Dose*, all designed primarily to capture a growing market among public transit commuters. Many local city councils were not impressed with the proliferation of newspaper distribution boxes and the resulting litter that accompanied these new publications, and Port Coquitlam put forward a bylaw to limit the number and placement of the boxes.

July For as little as $10, people could own a piece of the historic lacrosse floor at Queen's Park Arena, which bore the battle scars of more than 72 years of box lacrosse. The New Westminster Minor Lacrosse Association was selling pieces of the floor as a fundraiser to finance a new wooden floor that it hoped to have in place for the 2006 season.

Missing sockeye. The expected bumper catch of sockeye salmon never arrived this summer, leaving market vendors with nothing to put on the scale. Only a small number of fish made it to the Fraser River and in the interest of saving the stocks, the Department of Fisheries and Oceans closed the season for commercial fishing. *Sam Leung / Vancouver Sun*

August Fishermen eagerly waited for what was to be a bumper catch of 11 million Fraser River sockeye salmon. The run was expected to peak August 8, but by the third week of August the fish still hadn't arrived. The Department of Fisheries and Oceans eventually closed the commercial fishery because by the time the fish did arrive, their numbers were depleted and they were mixed in with the Cultus Lake salmon, which is an endangered species. Some angry fishermen organized an illegal fishery.

August 3 Ernest "Smokey" Smith, New Westminster's greatest war hero and Canada's last surviving recipient of the Victoria Cross, died at the age of 91. Smith's remains were flown to Ottawa to lie in state in the House of Commons foyer for a day, and Canadian flags were lowered to half-staff. His body then lay in repose in Vancouver's Seaforth Armoury on August 12, and a full military funeral was held on August 13.

October 10 Over 42,000 teachers defied back-to-work legislation and went on strike, closing down 40,000 schools and giving 600,000 students an extra holiday. Other workers participated in rotating "regional days of action" in support of the teachers. While most of these supporters were members of public sector unions and striking Telus workers, other private sector workers also joined the walkouts, and a general strike in Victoria on October 17 brought 35,000 public and private sector workers to a rally at the Legislature, closing down public transit, post offices and construction sites. The militancy brought the government back to the bargaining table, and on October 24 the teachers returned to work. They later voted to accept the new contract offer by 77 percent.

November 19 The Vancouver election produced a dramatic shift in power as the Non-Partisan Association regained control with a majority on council, school board and park board. Sam Sullivan, the only NPA member on council for the previous three years, was now mayor with the slimmest of majorities. On his way to that win he had beaten former BC cabinet minister and future BC premier Christy Clark for the NPA nomination. The previous COPE administration under Mayor Larry Campbell had literally torn itself in two through internal wars over members' differences concerning transit, gambling and other issues. Campbell and his allies formed a new party called Vision Vancouver, but Campbell bailed out of municipal politics before the election when he was offered a Senate seat by Prime Minister Paul Martin. Of that appointment, the popular mayor, who was the model for the titular character in the TV series *Da Vinci's Inquest*, observed: "I'm looking forward to not being recognized on the street in Ottawa." The ex-Mountie and former provincial coroner left behind his lieutenant, Councillor Jim Green, to suffer the humiliation of defeat.

November 19 Meanwhile, south of the Fraser in Surrey, another dramatic power shift was taking place. Nine-year councillor Dianne Watts busted free from the establishment coalition controlling council to win the mayor's seat in BC's fastest-growing community. Three years later she won again, bringing her six-member Surrey First slate with her. She inspired her community with her vision of a new downtown core and a new city hall to go along with it. When Gordon Campbell stepped down as premier in 2010, Watts was touted as a replacement, but she remained in Surrey.

Also in 2005

St. John of Shanghai Orthodox Church became Vancouver's first English-speaking Orthodox Christian parish. In 2006 a second all-English Orthodox church was established, named after St. Nina of Georgia. Alas, Vancouver proved too expensive for twin efforts, and the two congregations merged in 2008 as St. John's, located in a former Franciscan convent near Commercial Drive.

When the latest homeless count numbers were released in April, the news was not good. While the number of shelter beds provided in the region had gone up in the three years since the previous count, the number of people sleeping in doorways, behind dumpsters or under trees, bridges or cardboard boxes was soaring. In Burnaby it was up 300 percent, in Langley 600 percent, and in Vancouver 500 percent. In 2002 there were 93 people in this city who slept outside. That number was now officially up to 591, and the people doing the counting admitted their figures were low. Clearly, as Michael Goldberg of the Social Planning and Research Council of BC (SPARC) said, there was something "terribly wrong" with our social safety net to cause such dramatic increases, and homelessness became a growing concern for municipal councils, particularly Vancouver's, for the rest of the decade and beyond.

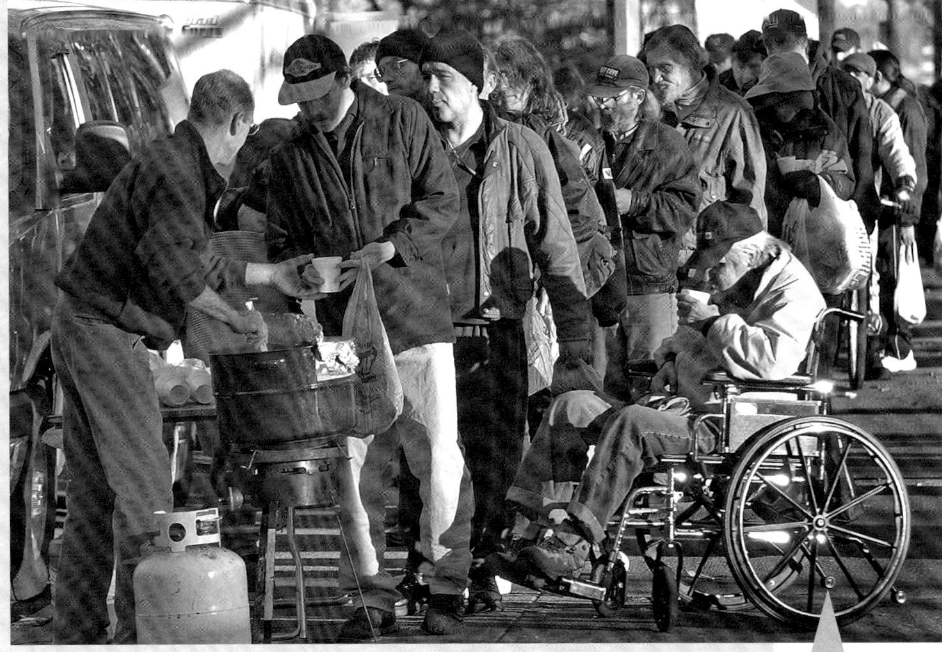

Vancouver's Homeless. The region's latest survey found that homelessness had soared since the last count. The shelter beds and services like these at Oppenheimer Park were much in demand. *Ian Smith* / Vancouver Sun

Gladys Radek, a 48-year-old Aboriginal woman living in Native housing in downtown Vancouver, successfully brought suit against the Tinseltown shopping mall and Securiguard (the security agency patrolling the mall) for violating her rights to public space and for systemic discrimination against aboriginal people. In 2001, Radek had been harassed by security personnel, a practice she had often observed at the mall, and called police, who failed to act. The BC Human Rights Tribunal heard that guards sometimes required Aboriginal people to show that they had money to enter the mall. Guards would also follow Aboriginal people through the mall or force them off the sidewalk in front of the mall. The tribunal awarded Radek damages of $15,000, the largest in tribunal history, and required the retraining of security personnel. The decision was later cited in federal court cases regarding racial profiling. Radek went on to become a major Aboriginal leader and one of the driving forces behind the Highway of Tears inquiry into missing women. She co-founded Vancouver-based Walk4Justice in 2008, and was honoured by CBC in its Champions of Change initiative in 2011.

Vancouver was seriously bitten by the sustainability bug as city council declared all future municipal buildings would meet LEED (Leadership in Energy and Environmental Design) gold standards, which also figured prominently in the design of the 2010 Olympics' Athletes Village. LEED was developed in 1968 by the US Green Building Council, and the LEED Green Building Rating System™ has become the accepted benchmark for the design, construction and operation of high-performance green buildings. It is a point-based rating system to assess new and existing commercial buildings for a variety of Earth-friendly features. Kierstin De West, CEO and founder of Conscientious Innovation (CI), a Vancouver-based marketing and branding firm, noted that "sustainability is to the 21st century what the tech boom was to the 90s. Businesses that don't get it will be at a disadvantage."

Comings and Goings

Notable deaths: **Chuck Cadman**, politician, activist against youth violence and victims' rights advocate, July 9; **James Doohan**, actor (Scotty on *Star Trek*), July 20; **Long John Baldry**, blues singer, July 21.

2006

It was a year of storms, both political and natural. Stephen Harper's federal Conservatives ended 12 years of Liberal rule, and Vancouver Kingsway Liberal MP David Emerson caused a scandal of sorts when he crossed the floor to join Harper's government. Then weeks before Christmas, in a year that had already had some of the

Right: Ferry disaster. At approximately 12:25 am on Wednesday, March 22, 2006, the *Queen of the North* hit Gill Island on its journey from Prince Rupert to Port Hardy. The ship sank, and while most passengers were able to evacuate, two were presumed drowned. *Courtesy BC Ferries*

Elsewhere in BC

March 22 BC Ferries' *Queen of the North* sank in choppy seas after ramming into Gill Island, 135 kilometres (84 miles) south of Prince Rupert. It was the first ferry in the fleet's history to sink. Residents of the nearby First Nations village of Hartley Bay were the first to respond in their trawlers before search-and-rescue crews got to the scene. Initially BC Ferries reported that all on board had been rescued, but it later determined that two passengers, Shirley Rosette and Gerald Foisy, were missing and presumed drowned. In the court actions that followed, BC Ferries was ordered to pay $200,000 to each of the victims' families. Three crew members were fired following the incident, and in 2010 Karl Lilgert, the navigating officer responsible for steering the vessel at the time, was charged with criminal negligence causing death.

Elsewhere in Canada

June 26 Prime Minister Stephen Harper offered an apology and compensation to Chinese immigrants who had to pay a head tax to enter Canada between 1885 and 1923. Survivors or their spouses would receive $20,000, although only 20 Chinese Canadians who paid the tax were believed to be alive in 2006.

June The Union of BC Indian Chiefs sent an open letter to the prime minister urging the federal government to "actively encourage the adoption without amendment or qualification of the Chair's proposed text of the UN Declaration on the Rights of Indigenous Peoples." That declaration was adopted on September 13, 2007, with the support of 143 countries, but Canada was one of four nations (the others were Australia, New Zealand and the United States) to vote against it. In November 2010 Canada said it would endorse the declaration, and by the end of 2010, the other three countries had also accepted it.

Elsewhere in the World

March The work of a North Shore resident was honoured onstage at the 78th annual Academy Awards. Bill Vince, a resident of West Vancouver, was one of the producers for the film *Capote*, which was nominated for five Academy Awards, including best picture. The film portrayed US writer Truman Capote's efforts to write about a set of murders that rocked a Kansas town in the mid-20th century. Philip Seymour Hoffman, who played the role of Capote and received an Oscar for his performance, acknowledged Vince in his acceptance speech.

August 10 Airport security in Vancouver and across the country was cranked up several notches after British police announced they had foiled a terrorist plot to bomb commercial aircraft using liquid explosives. Passengers on all flights, including domestic ones, were now prohibited from having beverages, shampoo, suntan lotion, creams, toothpaste and hair gel in their carry-on luggage.

November 5 Saddam Hussein was convicted of "crimes against humanity" for his role in killing 148 Shiite Muslims after a failed assassination attempt in 1982. He was sentenced to hang. The sentence was carried out December 30, 2006.

most extreme weather in recent memory, the Lower Mainland was devastated by hurricane-force winds that slammed the coast and uprooted or snapped thousands of trees in Stanley Park and across the region, causing millions of dollars in damage and leaving thousands of regional residents without power.

January The Wet Coast earned its name this year. January was the soggiest month on the Lower Mainland since Environment Canada began keeping records, with 283.6 millimetres of rain. That's almost a foot of water and enough to give any kid a soaker. The previous record of 281.8 millimetres (11 inches) was set back in 1982.

January 5 There was no rain on the parade of the folks in the Fraser Valley opposed to the Sumas 2 Energy plant. They celebrated when they got the news that the Supreme Court of Canada would not allow the Washington state company building the plant to construct a needed power line to Abbotsford. Fraser Valley residents were against the power plant because pollutants from it would have drifted up the valley to Canada.

January Downtown Port Coquitlam lost one of its favourite shops. After 75 years as a local landmark the Batty Shoe Clinic closed when John Sousa and his wife Maria decided to call it quits. The shop had been a fixture since 1929, when a cousin of Augusto Battistoni started a shoe repair business in a Port Coquitlam woodshed. In 1939, Battistoni opened the company's first store on a lot next to the Masonic Hall on Shaughnessy Street at Elgin Avenue. John Sousa was in his 20s when he immigrated to Canada in 1957 after learning to make orthopedic shoes in his native Portugal. Within months of his arrival he found work at Batty's. In 1971 he and a partner bought the company. When his partner died two years later, Sousa and his wife took over. Sousa said the store drew faithful customers from Prince George, Toronto and even China—grateful for the comfort his orthopedic shoes provided.

January 31 Premier Gordon Campbell unveiled an ambitious $3-billion transportation plan, dubbed the Gateway program, that included twinning the Port Mann Bridge and widening Highway No. 1. The proposal was well received south of the Fraser River, but opponents claimed that some Coquitlam neighbourhoods, such as Maillardville, would bear the brunt of increased traffic. Other municipalities, including Vancouver, objected to the twinning of the bridge and widening of the highway; they argued that more asphalt would bring more traffic that would inevitably flow into the city and choke its streets, a complaint that failed to convince the province. Other criticisms were that more roads would only increase urban sprawl, pollution and greenhouse gas emissions.

February 3 Federal inmates in Fraser Valley prisons found themselves on the outside, after the Correctional Service of Canada decided it was time for incarcerated smokers to butt out or get out. Inmates weren't impressed. "It's bull—," said Lucky Belliveau. "This is our residence, but I guess we have to follow the rules in prison."

February 6 Two weeks after Stephen Harper and his Conservatives won the federal election with enough seats to form a minority government, sending former prime minister Paul Martin to the opposition benches, Martin's former Industry minister and Liberal MP for Vancouver Kingsway David Emerson crossed the floor to join Harper. Observers at Rideau Hall were surprised to see Emerson turn up for the swearing-in ceremony for Harper's first cabinet. The former head of the giant forestry company Canfor picked up the portfolio of Minister of International Trade with responsibility for the 2010 Winter Olympics in Vancouver. Emerson said he would not be paying back the money that was spent so he could win a second term as a Liberal, adding, "I fundamentally went through the thought processes many times over and came to the conclusion I can be more helpful to the people of my riding, the people of my city, the people of my province and the people of my country doing this, as opposed to being in opposition and trying to become a powerful political partisan which I have never been." This was a change from the view he held on election night, when he told reporters: "I would like to be Stephen Harper's worst nightmare." Emerson did not stick around to fight for a second term as a Tory in the 2008 election.

April 30 Trombonist and conductor Alain Trudel was named musical director of the CBC Radio Orchestra (formerly the CBC Vancouver Orchestra), replacing Mario Bernardi. He was the fourth conductor of the orchestra, which was now the only remaning CBC orchestra in Canada and the last radio orchestra in North America.

April Members of the Coalition to Save Eagleridge Bluffs at Horseshoe

Highway protest. In their efforts to save Eagleridge Bluffs, environmental activists erected a tent city above West Vancouver. Despite the 70 squatters' protests, the four-lane route through the ecologically fragile area—and the Olympics—would come to fruition. *Mark van Manen / Vancouver Sun*

Bay set up an urban tent city above West Vancouver. The permanent camp, which had about three dozen tents and about 70 campers, was intended to let the province know its plans for the Sea to Sky Highway were unacceptable. A four-lane overland route was set to run adjacent to Eagleridge Bluffs and the Larsen Creek wetlands, and the coalition asked for the road to be replaced with a tunnel. A month later police arrested two dozen protesters who refused to leave the site, including veteran environmental protester Betty Krawczyk, 78. Krawczyk was ultimately arrested three times and spent three weeks in jail over the summer for violating a court injunction banning her from the site. Krawczyk and one other Eagleridge protester, Andrew Teasdale, faced charges of criminal contempt of court when they disobeyed a May injunction ordering protesters to stay away from the construction site. The road went through.

April 18 A fraction of a gram of old feed that might have contained some animal by-products may have been enough to infect a six-year-old dairy cow in the Sumas Prairie with mad cow disease, the first reported case in the Lower Mainland.

May The Land Conservancy of BC (TLC) purchased Joy Kogawa House with the intention of restoring the property to its appearance between 1938 and 1942, when author Joy Kogawa lived there as a child. Kogawa and her parents were removed from Vancouver and interned with other Japanese Canadians during World War II. TLC hoped the house would serve as a reminder of this incident and as a historic literary landmark. The organization runs an annual writers-in-residence program from the house.

June Blame the rising price of commodities: metal thieves broke into West Vancouver's Capilano View cemetery sometime between the evening of June 3 and the morning of June 5, prying 17 bronze plaques from graves. The plaques were valued at about $250 each. Copper, the main component of bronze, had jumped in price over the previous year, suggesting the likely motivation for the thefts from Capilano View.

September 7 John "Jack" Edwin Loucks, former mayor of the City of North Vancouver and one of the longest-serving and most-respected mayors in the province, died at his home in North Vancouver at the age of 88. Loucks served as mayor from 1977 until his retirement in 1999 and was widely respected for his ability to gain consensus. Loucks also had a long career in education.

October The Evergreen Line appeared to be going off the rails. TransLink threatened to shelve the long-promised project to provide rapid transit to the northeast sector of the region if senior levels of government didn't plug a funding gap of $400 million. TransLink chose April 2007 as its deadline to receive the funds, but the appeal was met with silence from both the provincial and federal governments.

October 11 John Turvey, whose activities as an outspoken and energetic street worker in Vancouver's Downtown Eastside earned him the Order of Canada and the Order of BC, died at age 61. Turvey, the adopted son of fundamentalist Baptist parents, grew up in Alberta and the Fraser Valley. He ran away from home at 13 and became a heroin addict but turned his life around by his early 20s. As a social worker in the 1970s, he began working with street kids who saw in him a kindred spirit, someone they could trust. He founded the first needle exchange in Canada, providing free needles to Vancouver drug addicts to reduce the spread of disease, and in 1988 was recognized for his groundbreaking work by the US Centers for Disease Control. He was the founder and executive director of the Downtown Eastside Youth Activities Society but was forced to resign in the early 2000s when he was diagnosed with mitochondrial myopathy, a degenerative disease that interferes with nerve and muscle function. That disease ultimately took Turvey's life.

November 16 Water, water everywhere but not much to drink, at least safely. The GVRD issued a boil-water advisory for the entire Greater Vancouver area after torrential rains washed huge quantities of mud into the region's reservoirs. Residents and businesses were told to boil tap water for at least a minute or buy it in bottles, as filtering would not be enough. This meant that many restaurants, which don't tend to boil water for drinks, couldn't serve their usual fare. The advisory was lifted for much of the Lower Mainland a couple of days later but remained in place for Vancouver, Burnaby and the North Shore until November 27. As if that wasn't enough, snow wreaked havoc on the North Shore as 30 centimetres (12 inches) fell near Burrard Inlet and as much as 65 centimetres (25 inches) at higher elevations. The results were power outages, school closures, delayed transit and chaotic traffic.

December 15

Barges broke free from their anchors in Burrard Inlet and smashed into docks on the North Vancouver waterfront, huge trees crashed down on the Stanley Park causeway and 31,000 homes were left without power in the wake of a dramatic windstorm that slammed the North Shore with gusts of more than 94 kilometres per hour (58 mph). Much of North Vancouver remained in the dark all day, with 22,700 homes without power in the District of North Vancouver alone. (250,000 homes lost power across the province.) The storm, which peaked about 3 a.m. Friday morning, sent trees and power lines down all over the North Shore and caused traffic havoc after both the Lions Gate Bridge and Dollarton Highway were closed because of fallen trees. Cates Park, Lynn Canyon Park and all the parks in West Vancouver were closed because of danger from falling trees. The West Vancouver Seawalk and Ambleside Pier were heavily damaged and were also closed due to danger from crashing surf. Hardest hit was Stanley Park, where an estimated 3,000 trees were destroyed and the seawall destabilized. Governments and individuals responded almost immediately to fundraising drives to support the park's restoration, which raised millions of dollars.

Also in 2006

one cool word hit the streets, published by 20-year-old Tracy Stefanucci and co-founder Ken Yong. The magazine focused on Vancouver content, ranging from art to literature, and included a full-length compilation CD. It was relaunched in 2011 as *OCW Magazine*, a self-described "biannual

Storm damage. Parks crews got to work removing fallen trees from wind-battered Stanley Park. Winds swept through the city like a hurricane, taking down an estimated 3,000 trees in the Vancouver landmark. The cleanup took several months. *Peter Battistoni* / Vancouver Sun

interdisciplinary art project dedicated to the cultivation of new ideas, new voices, and new ways of experiencing art."

Graham McMynn, a student at the University of BC, was abducted at gunpoint and held captive for eight days in Vancouver and Surrey before being rescued as more than 100 police officers carried out 14 raids on homes in Nanaimo, Surrey and Vancouver. Police suspected the kidnappers had planned to ask for a ransom from McMynn's father, a wealthy Vancouver businessman, but when they carried out the abduction on a Vancouver street in broad daylight, there were too many witnesses, making it impossible for the kidnappers to negotiate in secret. They never made contact with the parents to ask for payment, but the police were able to capitalize on witness statements and some lucky breaks. Five adults and one juvenile were ultimately charged. Three adults were convicted and the juvenile pled guilty to unlawful confinement.

Right: Paperclip trader. Proving that bartering still works, Belcarra native Kyle MacDonald leaps in celebration in front of his new house in Kipling, SK. MacDonald started with a red paperclip, and quickly became an internet sensation.
Courtesy Kyle MacDonald

Richmond city council took steps to legalize secondary suites while cracking down on unauthorized multiple suites. The Richmond Poverty Response Committee was thrilled to see the issue addressed, as it had made affordable housing a major political issue. Prior to the approval of the new policy it was estimated there were between 2,700 and 5,000 non-approved suites in the city.

A year after 50 butchered eagle carcasses were discovered dumped on Tsleil-Waututh land in North Vancouver, the BC Conservation Officer Service charged 11 men under the provincial Wildlife Act with trafficking in eagle parts. The men were from several communities in the Lower Mainland and Vancouver Island and were thought to be part of a larger poaching and smuggling ring. Investigators alleged they shot the eagles to obtain feathers and talons to sell for ceremonial use by First Nations in Canada and the United States. Two men pled guilty and were fined and sent to jail.

West Vancouver police officer Const. Lisa Alford was promised a promotion just months after crashing into another vehicle with her car while driving with a blood alcohol level nearly three times the legal limit. Alford later pleaded guilty to impaired driving and was given a $600 fine and a licence suspension. She subsequently beat out 13 other officers to win the number 2 spot on the department's promotion list. BC's police complaints commissioner called in a Vancouver police officer to investigate the West Vancouver police department's response to Alford's drunk driving conviction after it was revealed that Alford's drinking took place at the West Vancouver police station.

Comings and Goings

July Kyle MacDonald, who grew up on the North Shore in Belcarra, achieved his goal of turning one red paperclip into a house. The 26-year-old blogger received the keys to a home in Kipling, SK, in exchange for a role in the movie *Donna on Demand*, ending a year of trading up random items that began when he swapped a single red paperclip for a fish-shaped pen. The pen yielded a sculpted doorknob, which led to a Coleman stove, then a red generator, then an instant party (including a keg of beer and a neon Budweiser sign). After that, MacDonald traded up for a snowmobile, then an all-expense-paid trip to the town of Yahk, BC, a cube van, a recording contract, a year-long contract to live in Phoenix, AZ, an afternoon with rocker Alice Cooper, a KISS snow globe and finally the movie role. Book and movie deals eventually followed.

October 25 Krista and Tatiana Hogan, conjoined twins, were born in Vancouver.

November 4 Frank Calder, the first Native person elected to the BC Legislature, died.

2007

Serious rehabilitation of Stanley Park began following the severe windstorm in December 2006. Another storm in January deflated the roof of BC Place Stadium. More turbulence followed as municipal workers walked off the job, and then the RCMP, already facing criticism for their lack of accountability, tasered a Polish immigrant at the Vancouver airport, claiming he had been violent—their statements were contradicted by a video of the event taken by a young man passing through the airport at the time.

January 5 When two workers separately noticed that the roof of BC Place Stadium was sagging, they turned on some of the buildings fans to reinflate it. However, the rapid inflation combined with a flaw in one of the roof's fabric panels and the gusting winds of yet another winter storm to cause a tear in the roof, which grew quickly as air gushed out of the building. Maintenance staff deflated the entire roof to prevent further damage. Rain and melted snow flooded the stadium. A temporary panel was installed two weeks later, and a permanent one later in the year, and the stadium continued to be used for trade shows, BC Lions games and the 2010 Winter Olympics, but after the games the roof was removed and replaced with a retractable one for $365 million...then $458 million...then $563 million.

June 21 Jim Chu was named Vancouver's chief of police, Vancouver's first non-white chief constable and the first Chinese Canadian to head a major city police force in Canada.

July 20 Just over 1,800 Vancouver outside workers walked off the job in what ended up being the most wide-spread strike in the city's history and, at 12 weeks, its second longest. For the first time, the city's library workers hit the bricks. The strike was provoked in part by a rarely used "final offer vote," in which the employer has the right to present its offer to

Elsewhere in BC

October 1 Steven Point was sworn in as BC's 28th Lieutenant-Governor. His Honour is a member of the Stó:lō Nation. He served as an elected chief of the Skowkale First Nation for 15 years and also served as the tribal chair of the Stó:lō Nation Government. He was honoured as Grand Chief by the Chiefs of the Stó:lō Tribal Council. Steven Point was appointed a provincial court judge in February 1999 and was Chief Commissioner of the British Columbia Treaty Commission from 2005 to 2007.

Elsewhere in Canada

June Prince Harry, third in line to the Canadian throne, spent time in Alberta, training alongside soldiers of the Canadian and British armies at Canadian Forces Base Suffield, near Medicine Hat. In February 2008 the British Ministry of Defence confirmed that Harry had served a tour of duty in Afghanistan as part of the NATO-led forces fighting the Afghan War. Other Royals visited Canada this year: Prince Andrew visited Nova Scotia and Ontario in April, and Princess Anne was in Saskatchewan in June.

Elsewhere in the World

July 21 *Harry Potter and the Deathly Hallows*, the last book in the Harry Potter series of novels, is released and becomes the fastest-selling book in history, with more than 11 million copies sold on the first day.

November 5 Members of the Writers Guild of America, who write for film, TV and radio in the United States, went on strike. Issues involved payment for material used on DVDs and in new media. The result of the strike, which lasted until February 2008, was that no scripted television shows or movies were produced for 14 weeks, costing the entertainment industry an estimated $500 million. The cost to the economy of Los Angeles was said to be somewhere between $380 million and $2 billion.

December 27 Benazir Bhutto, the former prime minister of Pakistan, was assassinated at an election rally. At least 20 others were killed in the bomb blast. In November the prime minister of Pakistan had declared a state of emergency, and Bhutto's assassination led to postponement of the election scheduled for January 8, 2008. When the elections were held February 18, Bhutto's Pakistan Peoples Party won a majority of seats.

Photographer Fred Herzog gets his own picture taken during a retrospective of his work at the Vancouver Art Gallery. *Glenn Baglo / Vancouver Sun*

Photographic Witness

January 25 The Vancouver Art Gallery launched a spectacular three-month exhibit of the photographic works of Fred Herzog, a man who brought the everyday scenes on the city's streets to life.

Perhaps it was the viewpoint of an outsider, an immigrant. Perhaps the technical skill of a trained biomedical photographer. Or maybe it was the combination of Kodachrome slide film and some particular Vancouver light. Whatever the reason, the work of street photographer Fred Herzog, born in Stuttgart in 1930, seemed to capture a Vancouver not often seen on film.

Herzog immigrated to Canada in 1952 and soon afterward began shooting what he saw, though his serious documentation of Vancouver's streets did not begin until 1957. Shooting in colour was, at the time, unthinkable for art photography, so Herzog was something of an outsider in artistic circles, though he showed in some Canadian galleries with other photographers.

For decades Herzog captured the resonances of life in Vancouver and abroad with an eye somewhere between documentary and cinematic, and his photos often contain a sort of spontaneous truth, much like those of another street photographer, Foncie Pulice of the sidewalk portrait-studio.

Some see the Vancouver of Herzog's images as "lost," a historical fact, but his photographs also serve to remind us of what lies immediately under the surface of the Vancouver we know: a rougher, poorer, less-polished town, and for all these things, still beautiful.

the employees without approval from the union bargaining committee. Employees rejected the offer, and the ensuing job action by a number of CUPE locals was quickly referred to as "Sam's Strike," as unions blamed Mayor Sam Sullivan for intransigence. Sullivan lashed back, saying the strike was all about trying to force his Non-Partisan Association out of office in the upcoming municipal election, which was still a year away. He said the union just wanted a "CUPE mayor." Strong pressure to settle the strike came from the fact that the 2010 Winter Olympics were less than three years away. The municipality of Richmond, which was also the site of Olympic venues under construction, but which was not part of the regional bargaining strategy, offered its workers a five-year deal with a rich 17.5 percent increase—an arrangement that would keep the region strike-free well beyond the Olympics. While the regional government bargaining committee resisted, the Richmond agreement ultimately set the pattern for settlements. Vancouver workers finally agreed to a similar offer.

August West Vancouver police busted a 35-year-old Sunshine Coast resident after they discovered what appeared to be a functioning grow-op in the rear of the man's Toyota RAV 4—the first of its kind,

Grow-op on wheels. West Vancouver police discovered a unique grow-op when they flagged a Toyota RAV 4 lined up for the ferry at Horseshoe Bay. The back of the vehicle had about 140 marijuana plants, electrical wiring for lighting and a watering canister, apparently assembled by the 35-year-old Sunshine Coast driver. *PNG*

Robert Dziekanski

On October 13, Polish citizen Robert Dziekanski arrived at Vancouver International Airport at 3:12 p.m. for an extended visit with his mother, Kamloops resident Zofia Cisowski. Within 12 hours he was dead.

His mother was at the airport to meet him but could not enter the international arrivals area and, hampered by the fact that she did not have her son's flight information, was unable to discover if he had actually arrived. She convinced a customer service agent to page her son twice, but the announcements could not be heard in the secure customs hall. Cisowski's husband used a wall phone to contact Canadian Border Services in the secure zone, but Dziekanski was nowhere to be found. Finally Cisowski returned to her home in Kamloops, believing her son had not arrived.

In fact, Dziekanski was wandering around the secure zone, increasingly distraught. He spoke only Polish, and except for an agent who pointed him to some written instructions in Polish for filling out forms, he appeared to receive little help to navigate the customs and immigration maze. Between 11 p.m. and midnight, Dziekanski had a couple of encounters with immigrations officials, who processed his documents and allowed him to exit to the area where his mother had been waiting. When he didn't find her there, he returned to the international lounge, appearing more upset and frustrated all the while.

It was now past one in the morning and people were cautioning Dziekanski to calm down. Instead he threw a computer on the floor and overturned a small table. The RCMP were called and told about someone who was "drunk" and throwing suitcases around.

Four RCMP officers arrived. Observers say they told Dziekanski, who was pacing, to stand near a counter and place his hands on top of it. He complied but then picked up a stapler. About 25 seconds after the police arrived, one constable tasered Dziekanski, who writhed in pain. He was tasered several more times, including at least one time when an observer believed two charges were applied simultaneously, and fell to the ground, where the police handcuffed him and continued to use their tasers. Within minutes, Dziekanski stopped moving. Paramedics arrived about 15 minutes later and declared Dziekanski dead at the scene at 2:20 a.m.

In the wake of his death, the RCMP claimed that Dziekanski had threatened the officers and that the use of tasers was necessary. These claims were contradicted by a video of the event that had been filmed by another traveller, Paul Pritchard, who was passing through the airport at the time. Pritchard voluntarily handed his camera to the police, but when the RCMP did not return the film as promised, he went to court to regain possession of it. After the government of BC ordered a full public inquiry into Dziekanski's death, the actions of the RCMP, and police use of tasers in BC, this film became a crucial piece of evidence.

On November 19, at the same time he announced the public inquiry, Premier Gordon Campbell offered an apology to Dziekanski's mother, Zofia Cisowski, on behalf of the people of British Columbia, saying: "That was something that was devastating to her in more ways than I can even begin to imagine."

Justice Thomas R. Braidwood headed the inquiry. When he reported back on Dziekanski's death in 2010, he concluded that the four RCMP constables were not justified in using their tasers on the man and that they deliberately misrepresented their actions on the night of October 13, 2007. The four have since been charged with perjury related to their testimony during the inquiry.

In an earlier report, Braidwood stated that the provincial government should establish province-wide standards for taser use and that the threshold for use should be "significantly revised from 'active resistance' to the much higher standard of 'causing bodily harm.'"

according to the police. They discovered the vehicle during an impaired-driving investigation at the Horseshoe Bay ferry terminal. The two officers who made the arrest estimated there were about 140 plants in various stages of growth in the rear of the car, with a street value of $62,000 at maturity. The police also found the back of the vehicle contained light fixtures set up with electric wiring, a watering canister, fertilizer and a transformer to boost the electrical input.

September 8 Elanor Yearwood made it to the altar to marry Aaron Franks on time, thanks to the North Vancouver Fire Department. The firefighters rescued her and one of her bridesmaids from a three-car collision and, after checking with their supervisor, allowed the two of them to hitch a ride on the pumper truck while the rest of the wedding party climbed into the department's SUVs.

October 19 Six people were murdered in a highrise apartment in Surrey. Four were drug dealers while two were innocent bystanders—a resident of a neighbouring apartment and a gasfitter who had been cleaning fireplaces in the building. In 2009, Dennis Karbovanec, a member of a local gang, pleaded guilty to three of the murders and was sentenced to life in prison. Three other gang members have been charged.

December 5 Arthur Erickson's Graham house in West Vancouver was bulldozed in spite of a months' long protest from both residents and heritage groups. The homeowner, Shiraz Lalji, had applied for a demolition permit a month earlier following a debate among architects, Lalji, the city's mayor and heritage groups about the possibility of restoring the structure.

Gridlock. A report released by the province suggests rush-hour traffic jams in Greater Vancouver will quadruple by 2021.
Ric Ernst / The Province

Also in 2007

The city of Vancouver decided to accept the province's offer to build new supportive housing to reduce the city's chronic homeless problem and provided 12 plots of city land. As well as paying for the cost of construction and the cost to have non-profit societies operate the buildings, the province also committed to paying for pre-development costs related to municipal approval.

Thanks to a generous donation from Dr. Yosef Wosk, George McWhirter, professor emeritus at UBC, was installed as Vancouver's first Poet Laureate.

Automobile traffic congestion continued to plague the region, and a provincial report predicted that it would only get worse. By 2021, the report forecast, the amount of traffic on the Lions Gate Bridge would have quadrupled, and traffic jams during rush hour would also quadruple.

2008

Vancouver experienced two startling art thefts, involving part of a public installation in Queen Elizabeth Park and several Bill Reid creations from the Museum of Anthropology. And in preparation for the Olympics, the beautiful and environmentally friendly Richmond speed-skating oval, showcasing BC wood killed by pine beetles, had its grand opening.

February 13 Taking into consideration various differences of doctrinal and biblical interpretation, members of the congregation at Canada's largest Anglican church, St. John's Shaughnessy, voted to separate from the Diocese of New Westminster and align with the Anglican Network in Canada. Two other congregations, at the Church of the Good Shepherd (Vancouver's largest Chinese Anglican church) and St. Matthias and St. Luke's, followed about two weeks later.

May 14 Police conducting a drug raid in the West End were surprised to find a hoard of medals from the World Wars. They were stolen from Lt.-Col. Aeneas Bell-Irving in 1962, from a house on Point Grey Road. Bell-Irving had served in both wars, and as he had died in 1966, the medals were returned to his 78-year-old son.

June 11 After 19 seasons in the National Hockey League, 1,140 games of which were spent with the Vancouver Canucks, well-loved professional hockey player Trevor "Captain Canuck" Linden announced

The Great Museum Robbery

May 23 Thieves broke into the Museum of Anthropology (MOA) and stole 12 priceless pieces by BC artist Bill Reid.

The theft itself showed ingenuity and a dash of Hollywood style. During the day, MOA security staff received a call from someone purporting to be from the museum's security firm. The caller claimed there was a problem with the alarm system and told the MOA not to be concerned by false alarms. Then, knowing that an alarm would not produce an instant response, the thieves disabled the security cameras and burst into the museum late at night while the guard was on a cigarette break, sprayed the entranceway with pepper spray, and made off with the loot, apparently knowing where to go, what to get and how to get it. All told, the haul was worth $2 million.

Most upsetting was the loss of the works by Bill Reid, which consisted of two sets of cufflinks, three brooches, five bracelets and a small box, all worked in gold, along with a pipe carved from argillite, a type of stone frequently used by Haida artists. The initial fear was that the gold would be melted down and sold (its value was estimated at $15,000). This prompted the museum and UBC to offer a reward of $50,000 for the artworks' return, though they acknowledged that the real value was cultural and artistic.

Bill Reid was, of course, a central artist for the MOA. He was born in Vancouver in 1920 to an ethnically Scottish-German father and a Haida mother. After becoming acquainted with his maternal heritage as a young man, he set out to almost single-handedly resurrect Haida art. The MOA has over 200 pieces of his art and jewellery in its possession, including the large cedar carving *Raven and the First Men*, which is in a place of honour in the museum's rotunda.

Thankfully, all the pieces were later recovered. Police were reluctant to release details, and charges have yet to be laid, but with international help and more than 50 officers on the case, most of the items were found within a couple of weeks after houses in Burnaby and New Westminster were searched. The final two items were found in August. All pieces were in good repair except for the argillite pipe, which was missing a couple of inches, and three Mexican gold necklaces that were also taken.

Elsewhere in BC

BC Games extinguished its natural gas–fed torch, which had been lit in host communities since 1981. In 2009 a "green" replacement was unveiled. Devised by a team at Camosun Collage, the new torch was lit by over 300 LED lights.

Elsewhere in Canada

June 6 CBC announced that it would not renew its licence to use Dolores Claman's much-loved "The Hockey Theme," also known as "Canada's second national anthem," for the opening of *Hockey Night in Canada*. Outrage and shock rippled across the country. CTV quickly picked up the rights to the song, which it broadcasts on its TSN and RDS sports channels.

June 11 Prime Minister Stephen Harper formally apologized to Canadian First Nations for the residential school system that operated from the 1840s to 1980 and forcibly separated children from their families with the intention of assimilating the Aboriginal peoples into European-Canadian society. In many instances, children were physically and sexually abused by the system as well.

October 14 Stephen Harper won his second federal election, beating Liberal leader Stéphane Dion, and increasing his minority hold on Parliament. Just over a month later, he almost triggered another election when he tried to eliminate the per-vote subsidy (which gave each political party a $2 allowance for each vote it received in the previous election) as part of a financial bill that would cause the government to fall if it were voted down. The opposition responded to this blatantly partisan move by offering to form a coalition that the Governor General could call on to form government if Harper's Conservatives were voted out. Facing the threat of losing power, Harper asked the Governor General to prorogue Parliament, which she did. Parliament was shut down from December 4 to January 26, 2009; Harper avoided the confidence vote; and he dropped his plans to eliminate the subsidy, for the moment.

Elsewhere in the World

January 21 In response to the subprime mortgage crisis and fears of a US recession, stock markets around the world began a roller-coaster ride that continues today and ultimately resulted in a number of bailouts of banks and countries around the world.

February 24 Fidel Castro resigned as president of Cuba, to be succeeded by his brother Raúl.

May 12 Sichuan province in China was hit by a devastating earthquake that killed an estimated 70,000 people.

November 26 Mumbai, India, endured four days of terror as Pakistani militants carried out 10 shooting and bombing attacks throughout the city, targeting hotels, a train station and a Jewish centre, among others, and killing 164 people.

his retirement. Linden ended his career with the most assists in franchise history; he was also the team's second-highest points-scorer and the leader in games played with the Canucks. On December 17, Linden was honoured by having his number, 16, retired. Vancouver city council declared the day Trevor Linden Day.

June 16 A sneaker-clad foot was discovered near Westham Island, Delta. It was the fifth found along the BC coast since August 2007 and sparked a media storm around the world. Five more feet have since been found in BC and Washington waters, though only a few have been identified.

July 1 In response to a distraught woman who was threatening to jump, Vancouver police closed the Ironworkers Memorial Second Narrows Bridge for six hours on Canada Day. Although a partial closure was considered, they decided that a full closure was the best option given the circumstances. Traffic chaos and frustration followed as drivers were rerouted to the narrower Lions Gate Bridge. In response to harsh criticism, Vancouver police constable Tim Fanning stated: "People were inconvenienced. We are very sorry for that but a life was in the balance and that's why we did what we did yesterday...And we were able to get her to safety and get her some help."

July 14 Downtown Vancouver went dark, with traffic lights, office towers and even the internet, in some places, losing power. Some BC Hydro customers were without power for up to three days. The cause turned out to be an underground fire affecting a connector and power cables.

August 20 Vancouver Monopoly diehards let out a collective groan as Montreal scored the most expensive property in Hasbro's new Monopoly Here and Now: The World Edition. Based on voting by over 5 million Monopoly fans, Vancouver was relegated to a middling position (though beating out Toronto) to be in the orange set where New York Avenue usually features.

September 1 Five BC post-secondary institutions, including four in the Lower Mainland, started the school year as brand-new universities, thanks to the BC government amending the University Act in April. The new universities were Emily Carr University of Art and Design, Capilano University, Kwantlan Polytechnic University, University of the Fraser Valley and Vancouver Island University.

November 15 Incumbent mayor Derek Corrigan surprised even himself, and made Burnaby history, when he led his party, the Burnaby Citizens Association, to a clean sweep of all council and school board seats over their rivals, Team Burnaby.

November 25 Catching Vancouver's arts community off guard, Ballet BC laid off all 38 of its dancers and staff today, citing debts and low ticket sales. The next week the company formally began the process of declaring bankruptcy. All was not quite lost, however. The company pinned its hopes of a revival on a crowd-pleaser, *The Nutcracker*, produced by Ballet BC but performed by the Moscow Classical Ballet. Thankfully, the show, and the public, delivered.

December 8 Gregor Robertson—former MLA for Vancouver–Fairview and co-founder of organic fruit beverage company Happy Planet—took office as the 39th mayor of Vancouver. Robertson and his Vision Vancouver colleagues just about wiped out their NPA rivals. His predecessor, Sam Sullivan, later edged past Premier Gordon Campbell and took first place in the "Vancouverite closest to hell" category in the *Georgia Straight*'s annual Best Of Vancouver 2008 edition.

Gang violence. After a rash of shootings opened citizens' eyes to the Lower Mainland's gang problem, the Vancouver police as well as the RCMP and the province vowed to tackle the issue and get tough on gangs.
Ian Lindsay / Vancouver Sun

Also in 2008

Every few days in the first four months of 2008 there seemed to be another story in the newspapers about a gangland hit. Cars were sprayed with bullets at busy intersections, daylight attacks occurred in restaurants and parking lots, and gang bosses were gunned down in front of their homes. Statistics back this disturbing trend, showing 13 gang-related homicides in BC in 2006, 24 in 2007, and 34 in 2008. Several gangs were involved, including the Red Scorpions, the United Nations Gang, the Hells Angels, the Independent Soldiers and the Bacon Brothers.

Citing the rise in the Canadian dollar, Raincoast Books, Canadian publisher of Harry Potter, announced that it would cease its publishing program in favour of its more profitable distribution business.

The Richmond Olympic Oval opened in December. It featured a unique "wood wave" roof, built out of BC pine beetle-killed wood. In July, the Doug Mitchell Thunderbird Sports Centre at UBC, site of the Olympic and Paralympic hockey games, opened. Both facilities were awarded the LEED silver certification for their green designs.

The Peak 2 Peak Gondola in Whistler opened for business in December to the delight of tourists. The lift links Whistler and Blackcomb Mountains and holds the record—3.03 kilometres (nearly 2 miles)—for the longest free span between ropeway towers.

Mayor Sam Sullivan and Park Board chair Korina Houghton were among those present to officially open the newly constructed Southeast False Creek seawall. This was the final piece of a continuous 22-kilometre (13.5-mile) public shoreline stretching from Coal Harbour (Burrard Inlet) around Stanley Park and False Creek to Kitsilano Beach.

The first annual Car-Free Vancouver Day was held, continuing a bold grassroots experiment that began with the inception of the Commercial Drive Festival in 2005. The initiative has grown to become a popular annual event in a number of neighbourhoods across the city, drawing thousands of visitors.

A gondola linking the Whistler and Blackcomb Mountains made tourists marvel at its views and record-breaking engineering. *Ric Ernst / The Province*

While playing in the semi-finals of St. Cristina Bocce tournament at Grand Boulevard Park, North Vancouver mayor Darrell Mussatto and his sporting partner, firefighter Jim Barbieri, resuscitated a 92-year-old spectator who had collapsed during the event. After the spectator was safely taken to the hospital, they returned to their bocce match and won the game.

Police announced in August that they had recovered a life-sized bronze statue stolen from Queen Elizabeth Park in June. The statue was part of a set called *Photo Session*, which depicts three people posing for a cameraman and is one of the most photographed pieces of public art in the city.

Comer William "Bill" Parnell died September 6, age 80. The North Vancouver native stunned the track-and-field world and became a local celebrity when he ran the mile in 4 minutes, 11 seconds, at the 1950 British Empire Games in New Zealand. He went on to carry the flag for Canada at the 1952 Summer Olympics and opened the 1954 Empire Games, held in Vancouver. However, it was at those 1954 games that the "Miracle Mile" was run,

Left: Legacy building. The Richmond Olympic Oval would serve as a multi-purpose civic centre after the Olympics. The roof makes use of wood salvaged from the pine beetle epidemic. *PNG*

Jumbo ferry. Decked in Olympic imagery, the MV *Coastal Renaissance* sails into Vancouver Harbour. The ship is one of a trio of German-built Coastal-class ferries that are currently the largest double-ended ferries in the world.
Jason Payne / The Province

shattering Parnell's record. He retired and became a teacher.

In the midst of a cold spell, and as part of their attempt to reduce homelessness before the Olympic Games, Vancouver mayor Gregor Robertson and Premier Gordon Campbell announced an agreement in mid-December to immediately open up 200 new shelter beds for the homeless. The new shelters were to be as rules-free as possible to attract those people who would otherwise not use them.

Heavy snowfall followed by rain paralyzed Vancouver the last two weeks of December,

causing great disruption for locals and holiday travellers, but also raising questions about how Vancouver would cope if the same thing happened during the Olympics. Officials assured the public that they were using this as a learning experience, and hoped that this was a 1-in-10-years experience.

Comings and Goings

March 8 MV *Coastal Renaissance* began its service for BC Ferries. The vessel, the largest double-ended ferry in the world, had arrived from Germany, where it was built, in late 2007. Its sister ships, MV *Coastal Inspiration* and MV *Coastal Celebration*, went into service on June 16 and November 21, respectively.

March The CBC announced that the CBC Radio Orchestra would be permanently disbanded after performing its final concert on November 16, 2008, at Vancouver's Chan Centre. The orchestra had been founded in 1932 by John Avison, and over the intervening 76 years had been conducted by Avison (until 1980), John Eliot Gardner, Mario Bernardi and, since 2006, Alain Trudel. It was the only remaning CBC orchestra in Canada and the last radio orchestra in North America, and news of its demise brought protests from the classical music community, politicians from all parties and thousands of music lovers, who gathered outside CBC locations across Canada. On November 1, 2008, CBCRO musical director Alain Trudel announced that the orchestra would attempt to continue independently of the CBC, as the National Broadcast Orchestra of Canada with plans to perform 6 to 10 concerts a year with a contingent of between 35 to 50 players.

Notable deaths: **Allan McEachern**, chief justice of BC and UBC chancellor (2002–8), on January 10, age 81; **Lenny Gibson**, Canada's first internationally known black dancer, and renowned teacher, choreographer, director, and producer, on February 11, age 81; **Jim Skelton**, Vancouver tennis champion in the 1940s who went on to twice captain the national Davis Cup team and become president of Tennis Canada, on March 5, age 87; **Lyle Thurston**, Vancouver-based medical doctor and early environmental activist, who went on the first Greenpeace voyage, on March 25, age 70; **Ian Berry**, a fixture of the Vancouver club scene since the 1960s, playing in such bands as Sweet Beaver (later The New Breed), Cement City Cowboys, 6 Cylinder and Wildroot Orchestra, on May 2, age 65; **William "Bill" Vince**, Vancouver film producer of such films as *Air Bud*, *Capote* and *The Imaginarium of Dr. Parnassus*, on June 21, age 44; **Bob Ackles**, lifelong BC Lions fan, who rose through the ranks from water boy in the inaugural season to GM for their 1985 Grey Cup win to president and CEO, on July 6, age 69; **N. Robin Crossby**, creator of the Hârn fantasy world and role-playing games, on July 23, age 54; **Geoffrey Ballard**, hailed as the father of the fuel cell industry and *Time*'s 1999 Hero for the Planet, on August 2, age 75; **Ray Perrault**, longtime embattled BC Liberal MLA, MP and senator, on November 24, age 82; **Hubert Jacques "Pit" Martin**, Chicago Black Hawks captain who ended his NHL career with the Canucks, on November 30, age 64.

2009

The chickens came home to roost as Vancouver city council passed a bylaw allowing people to keep hens in their backyards. Council also opened the first bike lane on Burrard Street Bridge. Meanwhile, 9 million sockeye salmon did not return to the Fraser River as expected. And the Woodward's Building reopened with a mix of housing and commercial spaces.

January 2 J. Michael Miller became the new Catholic archbishop of Vancouver after Raymond Roussin resigned, citing an ongoing battle with depression.

February 5 West Vancouver's Rockridge Secondary School grabbed national attention when it was placed

Elsewhere in BC

May 12 Gordon Campbell led the Liberal Party to a third provincial election victory in an election that saw the lowest voter turnout in BC history—only 50 percent of eligible voters cast a ballot.

July 23 Premier Gordon Campbell announced that British Columbia would implement a Harmonized Sales Tax (HST) on July 1, 2010. The new 12 percent sales tax would combine and replace the previous 5 percent federal goods and services tax and the 7 percent provincial sales tax. The announcement was met with strong opposition from all facets of BC society and ultimately led to Campbell's resignation in November 2010.

Elsewhere in Canada

October 20 Super-centenarian Margaret Fitzgerald, the oldest person in Canada, died at the age of 110.

Elsewhere in the World

January 7 Three Canadians, Ray Zahab, Richard Weber and Kevin Vallely of Vancouver, broke the world record for an unsupported trek from Hercules Inlet on the Ronne Ice Shelf to the geographic South Pole. Covering a distance of over 1,100 kilometres (683.5 miles) and powered by a 7,000-calorie-per-day diet that included a lot of Gatorade, the trio arrived in 34 days—five days quicker than the previous record holders.

June 11 The outbreak of the H1N1 influenza strain, also known as "swine flu," was deemed a global pandemic. Not since the Hong Kong flu of 1967–68 had such a condition been given this designation.

June 25 Legendary pop icon Michael Jackson died at his rented mansion in Los Angeles, causing several outages on major websites due to historic levels of internet traffic. America Online Instant Messenger collapsed for approximately 40 minutes and called it a "seminal moment in Internet history...We've never seen anything like it in terms of scope or depth." On February 8, 2010, Jackson's personal physician, Conrad Murray, was charged with involuntary manslaughter by prosecutors in Los Angeles.

June 29 Bernard Lawrence "Bernie" Madoff, chairman and founder of the Wall Street firm Bernard L. Madoff Investment Securities LLC, was sentenced to 150 years in prison as a result of a massive securities fraud scheme that stole billions of dollars from thousands of investors.

October 9 The Norwegian Nobel Committee named US president Barack Obama the 2009 Nobel Peace Prize winner "for his extraordinary efforts to strengthen international diplomacy and cooperation between peoples."

October 22 The Vancouver 2010 Olympic Winter Games flame was lit in Olympia, Greece.

December 22 Brandon Yip, son of Gail and Wayne Yip of Maple Ridge, scored the first goal by a Chinese Canadian NHL hockey player. Yip was playing for the Colorado Avalanche against the Anaheim Ducks. He finished the 2009–10 season with 11 goals and 8 assists for 19 points in 32 games played. He scored his first playoff goal and added an assist for a total of 3 points on April 16, 2010, in the second game of the playoff series against the San Jose Sharks. He also had his second playoff goal during the sixth and final game of the Avalanche season.

December 30 Vancouver-born journalist Michelle Justine Lang died in a roadside explosion along with four Canadian soldiers. Lang was on a six-week assignment covering the Afghanistan war. She was the first Canadian journalist to die in the war.

Polar record-breakers. Canadian adventurers Kevin Vallely, Richard Weber and Ray Zahab shattered the world record for an unsupported journey to the South Pole, arriving five days quicker than the previous record holders. Their diet included a healthy portion of deep-fried bacon. *Courtesy the trekkers*

HST rage. After denying plans for a new Harmonized Sales Tax in the 2009 election, the Liberal government flip-flopped and brought in the HST. Protests led to Premier Gordon Campbell's resignation in November 2010.
Ian Smith / PNG

under lockdown after two people were seen walking toward the school with a rifle. Three tense hours later, students were released from the sealed classrooms in which they had sought refuge. Police later determined that the two people in question were carrying a tripod, not a firearm. In response, some students planned a "Bring A Tripod To School Day" event.

March 5 Vancouver city council unanimously approved a controversial proposal that allowed people to legally keep urban chickens in order to have fresh eggs. The city joined the likes of New York City, Seattle, Portland, Victoria, Burnaby and Richmond, among others, that allow backyard hens.

March 12 Richmond hosted the World Single Distance Speed-Skating Championships in the run-up to the Olympics.

April 3 Wendy Ladner-Beaudry, sister of Vancouver city councillor Peter Ladner, was found dead on a trail in Pacific Spirit Park, where she had been jogging a few blocks from her West Side home. The murder was deemed to be a "random attack." The unprovoked crime has yet to be solved.

May 12 **Exactly 60 years after Japanese Canadians won the right to vote in BC elections in 1949, Naomi Yamamoto became the province's first Japanese Canadian MLA.** Yamamoto, president and owner of Tora Design Group for over 20 years, represented North Vancouver–Lonsdale. New Democrat Mable Elmore was the first Filipino ever elected to the BC legislature, representing Vancouver–Kensington.

The 2009 provincial election saw numerous South Asians victorious, including Raj Chouhan (Burnaby–Edmonds), Jagrup Brar (Surrey–Fleetwood), Harry Bains (Surrey–Newton), Dave Hayer (Surrey–Tynehead), Kash Heed (Vancouver–Fraserview) and Harry Lali (Fraser–Nicola). There were also three Chinese MLAS: Richard Lee (Burnaby North), John Yap (Richmond–Steveston) and Jenny Kwan (Vancouver–Mount Pleasant).

May 30 Ebisu Park opened at 72nd Avenue and Osler Street in Marpole. Ebisu is the Japanese god of fishermen, luck and the working man, the protector of young children. The name acknowledges the history of this area of Marpole, which was home to a thriving Japanese fishing community until 1942. David Suzuki's parents had a dry-cleaning business in the neighbourhood until they were relocated to Bay Farm in the Slocan area.

July 12 **Bike lanes opened on the Burrard Bridge for a summer trial period.** The west curb lane and the east sidewalk on the bridge became dedicated bike lanes, while the west sidewalk was reserved for pedestrians only. The lanes caused no traffic disruptions, dispelling months of complaints and predicted failure, which caused cyclist and former city councillor Fred Bass to declare: "If sex was like the Burrard Bridge, there would be no population in the world, because it would be all foreplay and nothing much later." In November, the city announced the lanes would remain in place until after the Olympic Games, and as of summer 2011 they are still there.

August The Department of Fisheries and Oceans and other environmental specialists were baffled

Urban chickens. Vancouver joined the likes of New York City, Portland and Victoria when city council approved the keeping of chickens for fresh eggs.
Ward Perrin / PNG

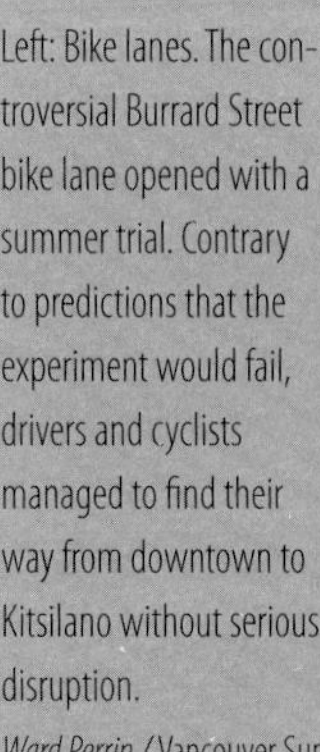

Left: Bike lanes. The controversial Burrard Street bike lane opened with a summer trial. Contrary to predictions that the experiment would fail, drivers and cyclists managed to find their way from downtown to Kitsilano without serious disruption.
Ward Perrin / Vancouver Sun

by the disappearance of approximately 9 million sockeye salmon that were expected to travel up the Fraser River. The mysterious collapse hit local fisheries hard. In November the federal government appointed Justice Bruce Cohen to head an inquiry into the declining salmon stocks, which had necessitated closing the salmon fishery for three consecutive years.

August 13 Jim Parsons was struck by lightning outside his house in North Vancouver as he was covering his work tools. The strike sent him flying 3 metres (about 10 feet), but aside from an earache, a headache and some dizziness, Parsons was fine. He admitted he would be more cautious the next time, stating: "I'll be running for cover."

August 17 TransLink's SkyTrain network expanded with the opening of the 19.2-kilometre (12-mile) Canada Line connecting downtown Vancouver to Richmond's No. 3 Road and Vancouver International Airport. Exceeding all projected ridership targets, 30,000 passengers took the train in the three hours of operation on opening day.

August 20 After decades of heated debate and years of construction and renovation, the Downtown Eastside's renowned and historically significant Woodward's Building opened its doors to tenants. With a unique mix of market and non-market housing as well as institutional and commercial functions, the opening was met with conflicting emotions. There was concern about how the area's impoverished residents would deal with an influx of newcomers (and vice versa), and fear that they would be pushed out of their home neighbourhood, but also optimism that the development would revitalize the Downtown Eastside and support existing residents.

September 1

A harbour seal acrobatically jumped 1.2 metres (4 feet) out of the water and grabbed five-year-old Caleigh Cunning from the Thunderbird Marina dock in West Vancouver

as her father cleaned fish a few feet away. Fortunately, Caleigh was wearing a lifejacket at the time and suffered only minor injuries, but after she was rescued, she reportedly told her father that she thought it was very rude of the seal not to ask if she wanted to go for a swim. Caleigh and her father had been feeding the seals fish earlier, and the rare attack may have been caused by pieces of fish remaining on her clothes. Caleigh no longer wants to feed the seal or be its friend.

December 2 Amidst much controversy and protests from neighbouring residents, the Squamish

Left: Canada Line. Trains made their way between Richmond's No. 3 Road, YVR and downtown Vancouver on opening day of the Canada Line. In just three hours of operation, 30,000 passengers got on board, shattering projected ridership targets.
Ian Lindsay / Vancouver Sun

A landmark returns to the Vancouver skyline. Workers prepare a new red "W" before it is hoisted onto the redeveloped Woodward's building. *Arlen Redekop / PNG*

First Nation erected the first of six electronic billboards on reserve land adjacent to the Burrard Street Bridge. Measuring 9 metres wide by 3 metres tall (29.5 by 9.8 feet) and created to generate revenue for the Squamish Nation, the billboards were approved at the federal level since local and regional governments have no control over reserve lands.

Also in 2009

David Suzuki received the Right Livelihood Award for outstanding vision and work on behalf of the planet and its people. He was honoured "for his lifetime advocacy of the socially responsible use of science, and for his massive contribution to raising awareness about the perils of climate change and building public support for policies to address it."

Pivot Legal Society filed a human rights complaint against the Downtown Vancouver Business Improvement Association on behalf of street people, including Natives, who, they claimed, were harassed by the "Ambassadors" hired by the DVBIA and denied their rights to public space on the basis of race, colour, ancestry, and physical and mental disability. The ambassadors were said to prod street people out of commercial areas frequented by tourists.

The heritage Pennsylvania Hotel, complete with its signature turret, reopened in the Downtown Eastside. The renovations were guided by the non-profit Portland Hotel Society, and the Pennsylvania—formerly known as the Rainbow Hotel and then the Portland Hotel—was set to provide apartments and on-site support for low-income residents.

Vancouver's tallest building and latest luxury hotel opened at the corner of West Georgia and Thurlow. At 201 metres (660 feet) and 62 floors, the Living Shangri-La edged out One Wall Centre by 51 metres (167 feet) to redefine the city's skyline.

Brad Cran was named Vancouver's second Poet Laureate, taking over from George McWhirter.

The Vancouver East Cultural Centre re-opened in East Vancouver after renovations and quickly found its place again as a quirky theatre and concert hotspot.

Comings and Goings

May 20 Renowned Vancouver-based architect Arthur Erickson died at age 84. His well-known works include Roy Thompson Hall in Toronto, Simon Fraser University in Burnaby, Vancouver Law Courts/ Robson Square in Vancouver and countless international commissions.

July 1 North Vancouverite Breanna Watkins, 21, left town to officially start her Australian adventure as girlfriend to British man Ben Southall, winner of the Best Job in the World competition. The six-month, US$100,000 position organized by Tourism Queensland required that Southall "explore the islands of the Great Barrier Reef, swim, snorkel, make friends with the locals and generally enjoy the tropical Queensland climate and lifestyle." About Watkins, Southall commented, "She's a lucky girl. I think she's got the best job in the world because she doesn't have to do any work."

July Emperor Akihito and Empress Michiko of Japan visited Vancouver. The first visit by then-Crown Prince Akihito was in 1953.

September 27–29 The Vancouver Peace Summit was sponsored by the Dalai Lama Centre for Peace and Education, an international charitable organization. Held at UBC's Chan Centre for the Performing Arts and the Orpheum Theatre, the event was attended by 5,000 people, including Nobel Laureates Jody Williams, Mairead Maguire, Betty Williams and Murray Gell-Mann, and the Dalai Lama; spiritual writer and teacher Eckhart Tolle; and Mary Robinson, former president of Ireland and UN High Commissioner of Human Rights.

2010

After years of planning and counting down the days, Vancouver finally played host to the 2010 Winter Olympics and Paralympics. Canada won its first gold medal on home soil, and the nation rocked as the home team won the men's hockey gold medal over Team USA. The post-game hangover wasn't so fun, however. Vancouver city council had to step in and take control of the Olympic Village in an effort to recoup its investment.

January 1 **A North Vancouver sporting goods store lost $2,600 in hockey jerseys to crafty burglars who slid a 3.5-metre (11-foot) hook through the mail slot to snag the merchandise.**

January 27 Police arrested two North Vancouver men in connection with a 60-kilogram (130-pound) shipment of opium smuggled across the border in a tombstone. It was the largest opium bust in BC's history.

February 11 Rush hour was knocked off-kilter the day before the Olympics opened when police brought in a bomb-disposal robot to destroy a suspicious package at North Vancouver's SeaBus terminal. The package was later revealed to contain a fishing rod.

February 15 Reflecting some of the discontent with the games, and protesting the ongoing problem of homelessness, the Olympic Tent city was established in an empty lot in the Downtown Eastside. It remained for a month and was deemed a success after dozens of residents found permanent housing.

February 24 Vancouver composer John Oliver debuted his *Chamber Concerto* at the Vancouver Playhouse. Commissioned by the Cultural Olympiad, Oliver sought to capture the essence of curling, speed skating, skeleton, freestyle skiing and hockey in five movements.

Elsewhere in BC

November 3 In the face of plunging popularity and constant attacks over his introduction of the HST, Premier Gordon Campbell announced that he would step down as leader of the BC Liberal Party. Campbell became leader in 1993 and premier in 2001. A month later, a revolt in the caucus of the NDP opposition forced its leader, Carole James, to step down as well.

Puget Sound, the Strait of Georgia and the Strait of Juan de Fuca area were collectively named the Salish Sea by the Washington State Board of Geographic Names and the BC Geographical Names Office in recognition of the long-time presence of aboriginal peoples.

Elsewhere in Canada

July The federal government provoked controversy when it decided to scrap the mandatory long-form census in favour of a shorter, voluntary census. Critics claimed that indispensible data would be lost and StatsCan's international reputation would be ruined, but the government pressed ahead, arguing that Canadians deserved privacy and the right to withhold personal information.

Elsewhere in the World

January 12 A catastrophic 7.0 magnitude earthquake struck Haiti, pushing the Caribbean nation to the brink of collapse amidst its ongoing issues of political corruption and poverty.

April 15 Volcanic ash from the eruption at Iceland's Eyjafjallajökull glacier reached northern Europe, closing European air space for five days and stranding millions of passengers.

April 20 An explosion at the Deepwater Horizon—a BP-leased oil rig in the Gulf of Mexico—killed 11 workers and triggered the fifth-largest oil spill in history. With an estimated 4.9-million barrels of crude oil leaked over three months, the spill caused extensive damage to the ecology and to the fishing and tourism industries in the area.

April 3 Apple released the first iPad tablet computer and sold 3 million devices in 80 days.

October 13 Thirty-three miners near Copiapó, Chile, were trapped 700 metres (2,297.5 feet) below ground by a cave-in at the San José Mine. They were brought back to the surface after surviving for a record 69 days.

Gold at Home

February 12 to 28 More than 2,500 athletes from 82 countries competed at the 21st Olympic Winter Games in Vancouver and Whistler. As 1.8 billion people watched on TV, holders of 1.49 million tickets costing as much as $1,100 took in the 15 sports in person. Vancouver streets were jammed with tens of thousands of celebrants, many wearing souvenir red mittens and waving Canadian flags. That it cost Canadians an estimated $6 billion to build and operate the venues for the games was temporarily forgotten.

The idea to bring the "Games of Ice and Snow" to Lotusland was hatched in 1960 by a group of Vancouverites, dazzled by the Squaw Valley Olympics in northern California, who put together an unsuccessful bid for Whistler to host the 1968 games. In 1972 the BC government turned down the International Olympic Committee's offer to host the 1976 games after Denver, CO, citizens balked at the rising costs.

It was more than two decades later, in 1996, that Tourism Vancouver and Sport BC decided to attempt another bid. The groups figured Vancouver could hold either a summer or winter games but chose winter because Toronto was bidding for the 2008 Summer Olympics (which eventually went to Beijing). In December 1998, Vancouver received the Canadian Olympic Committee's endorsement for its bid over proposals from Calgary and Quebec City. Then, in response to residents who did not support spending billions on the games when the province was cutting social spending (some vocal opponents believed the money would have been better spent on housing the Downtown Eastside homeless; others were angry that the games were being held on "stolen Native land"), the city held a plebiscite in February 2003 on Vancouver's bid: 64 percent of the voters supported holding the games on the coast.

Finally, on July 2, 2003, Vancouver's bid was chosen by the IOC at a convention in Prague, beating Pyeongchang, South Korea, and Salzburg, Austria. The Vancouver 2010 Bid Corporation became the Vancouver Organizing Committee for the 2010 Olympic and Paralympic Winter Games (VANOC). Sadly, VANOC chairman Jack Poole, a veteran real estate developer, died of pancreatic cancer in Vancouver on October 22, 2009, the day after the Olympic torch was lit at a ceremony in Greece. By then the committee's day-to-day affairs were already in the hands of John Furlong, an Irish immigrant who had managed the exclusive Arbutus Club before the bid.

Venues for sliding and Nordic sports were built in Whistler. UBC got a new hockey arena. A curling rink at Hillcrest Park and the marquee Richmond speed-skating oval were created with the aim of turning them into community centres after the Olympics. VANOC incorporated energy-saving measures in the new venues and promoted the use of existing rinks. The Pacific Coliseum was renovated for figure skating and short-track speed skating, and Rogers Arena (formerly GM Place) avoided a major overhaul because Olympic hockey was played on the smaller NHL ice surface for the first time.

The Sea to Sky Highway was widened and SkyTrain's Canada Line linked downtown with Vancouver International Airport. The Vancouver Convention Centre also expanded for the games amid an economic boom. However, in the wake of the 2008 global economic crisis, the City of Vancouver took over the $1.1-billion Olympic Village on False Creek to insure it was completed in time for the games.

First Nations were a major focus of the games. Chiefs of the Squamish, Tsleil-Waututh, Musqueam and Lil'wat tribes received the same privileges as heads of state, and the tribes received money and land for cultural centres, museums and other uses as

Bottom left: Olympic flame. Wayne Gretzky lights the Olympic outdoor cauldron after riding through Vancouver in the back of a pickup truck. *Jason Payne / Canwest News Service*

Bottom right: First gold. Alexandre Bilodeau's victory in men's mogul freestyle skiing made him the first Canadian to win an Olympic gold medal on home soil. Bilodeau's win led the way for an impressive showing by Canadian athletes at the 2010 Games. *Gerry Kahrmann / Canwest News Service*

part of the Olympic legacy. However, Quebec snowboarder Caroline Calve, whose great-grandmother was Algonquin, was Team Canada's only aboriginal link. The games were also without ski-jumping women, who couldn't convince the Supreme Court of Canada to force the IOC to allow their event.

The federal government budgeted $900 million for security as 16,000 police, military personnel and security guards from across Canada and the United States converged on the region. Riot cops quashed a violent downtown protest by anarchists the morning after the opening ceremony. The biggest incidents, however, were a $2-million ticket fraud and the collapse of a barrier at an outdoor concert.

Tragedy marred the start of the games on February 12 when Georgian luger Nodar Kumaritashvili flew off his sled and died after striking a pole while training at the Whistler Sliding Centre. The opening ceremony went on later that day at BC Place Stadium, but flags flew at half-staff and the crowd gave the grief-stricken Georgian athletes a standing ovation. Hockey legend Wayne Gretzky, basketball's Steve Nash, gold-medal skier Nancy Greene Raine and speed skater Catriona Le May Doan lit the ceremonial indoor cauldron, but Gretzky alone lit the permanent outdoor cauldron, ending the 106-day, 45,000-kilometre (28,000-mile) cross-Canada torch relay.

Freestyle skier Alexandre Bilodeau, of Quebec, made history on February 14, 2010, when he became the first Canadian to win Olympic gold at home. It was the first of 14 trips to the top of the podium for Canada, a record for a Winter Games host. Bilodeau's gold came on Cypress Mountain, where mild El Niño rainstorms had washed snow off the slopes. Replacement snow was trucked 160 kilometres (100 miles) from Manning Provincial Park.

North Shore snowboarder Maelle Ricker became the first Canadian woman to win gold on home soil. Skeleton's Jon Montgomery marched through Whistler with a pitcher of beer after his surprise gold, and perhaps figure skater Joannie Rochette's bronze felt like gold. Rochette was mourning her mother, who had died of a heart attack after arriving in Vancouver.

The Canadian women's hockey gold medal was expected. Overtime in the men's gold-medal hockey game on February 28

The golden goal. The gold medal men's hockey game between Canada and the US was dramatic and emotional. Sidney Crosby is seen raising his arms after clinching Canada's victory by scoring at 7:40 in overtime. Canada won 3–2, and the cheers could be heard across the country.
Arlen Redekop / PNG

was not. An estimated 26.5-million Canadians viewed the most-watched hockey game in history, which ended when Nova Scotia's Sidney Crosby scored the golden goal 7 minutes and 40 seconds into overtime for a dramatic 3–2 victory over Team USA. Vancouver and Canada celebrated through the night.

Mayor Gregor Robertson and Premier Gordon Campbell both got their 15 seconds of fame on February 28: Robertson when he passed the Olympic flag to the mayor of Sochi, Russia, host of the 2014 Olympics; Campbell as he waved the Canadian flag from the VIP box during the CTV and NBC telecast.

Olympians departed, but winter returned and a new batch of athletes arrived March 12 for the 10-day Paralympics. North Vancouver's Lauren Woolstencroft became Vancouver 2010's queen of the hill with five gold medals in para-alpine skiing.

VANOC eventually claimed it balanced a $1.884-billion operating budget, but it needed additional taxpayer subsidies to accomplish that feat. Vancouver was left with fond memories, better transportation and sports facilities, but questions remain about the legacy and cost of the games.

April 28 Deep Cove's Markus Pukonen made a remarkable 10-hour paddleboard trip from West Vancouver to Nanaimo.

May 17 The Squamish Nation and Vancouver governments formally agreed to co-operate on a variety of issues, such as economic development, tourism, environmental protection, and cultural and heritage protection. Mayor Gregor Robertson and Chief Gibby Jacob signed a historic memorandum of understanding and protocol agreement that called for the two councils to meet together at least once a year.

June 28 Vancouver realtor Sebastian Albrecht set a record by hiking the Grouse Grind 14 times in one day to raise money for the Royal LePage Shelter Foundation.

Summer Bike lovers celebrated the joys of cycling during Vancouver's first Velopalooza, featuring themed bike rides over 10 days.

July 8 A microphone mix-up caught Mayor Gregor Robertson swearing after a contentious committee meeting in council chambers. He quickly issued an apology, but not before the video went viral on YouTube.

August 20 Fraser Health officials issued a boil-water advisory for White Rock that lasted 12 days after low-level *E. coli* contamination was discovered during routine testing. Unlike the rest of Metro Vancouver, which gets its water from North Shore reservoirs, White Rock is supplied by a groundwater source. The contamination, attributed to bird droppings, ultimately led to the controversial decision to chlorinate the water in early 2011.

September 8 Police recovered an ATM from the bottom of the ocean near the Langdale ferry dock after thieves accidentally dropped it while attempting to lower the machine from the ferry into a waiting Zodiac.

September 22 Grouse Mountain's massive "Eye of the Wind" wind turbine was hooked up to the province's electrical grid.

November 17 The City of Vancouver placed Millennium Development Group, owner of the troubled Olympic Village project, into receivership in an effort to recoup $740 million in taxpayer funds.

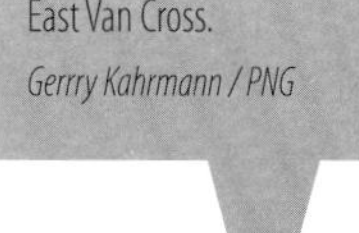

East Van Cross.
Gerry Kahrmann / PNG

Also in 2010

Phase one of Vancouver's food scraps collection program was launched on Earth Day. The resulting compost was sold to local nurseries and the public. The program was an element of Vancouver's Zero Waste Challenge, which aimed to divert 70 percent of solid wastes from landfills by 2015. Compostable food scraps make up an estimated 35 percent of the city's garbage.

The renamed Museum of Vancouver, employing a newly created repatriation policy, returned what the museum called the "Sechelt Image," a stone sculpture 51 centimetres (20 inches) high, 32 centimetres (12.6 inches) wide and 32 kilograms (70.5 pounds), to the Sechelt Indian

The East Van Cross

Art is not wallpaper. It's not uplifting propaganda. Art emerges from the cultural wallpaper, from the background murmur of elevator music and the visual white noise of the commonplace, to make a statement that cannot be ignored, like it or not.

An example is homeboy artist Ken Lum's 20-metre-high (65-foot-high), white-LED-lit East Van cross, which was installed on a rise at the corner of Clark and East Sixth Avenue in early 2010. Almost two years later the stylized icon was still triggering arguments about what it represents, its symbolic origins, who owns it and whether it's a triumph or an eyesore.

"It's bad. It's rad. It's a bit mad," wrote award-winning *Sun* columnist Douglas Todd shortly after the cross, which emerged from the tags of street graffiti artists, was unveiled. "The striking quasi-religious Monument for East Vancouver has the best qualities of effective outdoor sculptures: It's simple but complex, historic but contemporary, irreverent but meaningful." A year later, East Vancouver resident Karen Litzcke was complaining on the newspaper's op-ed page that the illuminated cross served as a tribute to vandals and was an offensive monstrosity.

In 2011, controversy erupted when an art gallery selling photographs of the cross was confronted with a claim that the symbol belonged to the East Enders, a bike gang associated with the Hell's Angels, and that it had been copyrighted as such in 2010, after the installation went up but before the city registered it as a trademark.

Not so, countered Lum: "The East Van cross dates back to at least the late '40s (as there are no formal records of this, I glean this from speaking to old-timers). I recall kids scrawling the East Van cross when I was a student in the 1960s. The symbol well precedes its adoption by any East End gang. I altered it from its traditional form, softened the corners, rounding them, widening the perimeter outline around the words and adopting a very neutral font (often the font was gothic). This is the version the city copyrighted. Others can do as they wish with other variations, but not this particular design."

Commissioned on a budget of just over $200,000 by the city as part of its Olympic and Paralympic Public Art Program in conjunction with the 2010 Winter Olympics, the illuminated neon cross is a clever visual and textual pun in which a crossword spells out East Van. It was part of an $800,000 section of the program named Mapping and Marking, which differed from other public art programs in that the ideas came from artists not bureaucrats.

Lum, one of Canada's leading international artists, works in a variety of media. He is acclaimed for innovative and provocative installations, including sculptures made from rented furniture, photographs that combine portraits with faux corporate logos, mirrors inscribed with text, and images that mimic and evoke the signage of working-class mini-malls. Lum's work has been widely exhibited since 1978, with shows at the Vancouver Art Gallery, the National Gallery of Canada and in Germany, Japan, Switzerland, the Netherlands, Italy, Cuba, China, Turkey and the United Kingdom.

Born in Vancouver in 1956, Lum earned his undergraduate degree in science at Simon Fraser University before completing a Master of Fine Arts degree at the University of British Columbia in 1985. He taught in the department of art history, visual art and theory at UBC between 1990 and 2006. Other teaching posts include École Nationale Superieure des Beaux-Arts in Paris, the Akademie der Bildende Kunst in Munich, the China Academy of Art in Hangzhou and the School of the Arts at Bard College in New York State.

Vancouver Sun critic Kevin Griffin described a 2011 exhibit of Lum's *Mirror Maze with 12 Signs of Depression* at the Vancouver Art Gallery as "a fantastic work of art worth the price of admission all on its own."

"I don't want my art to be confused with non-art," Lum once told a critic. No fear of any such confusion with his thought-provoking East Van cross.

Band. Wilson Duff, a former UBC anthropologist, regarded the prehistoric sculpture as preeminently important. The Sechelt Band, which had long sought the return of the piece, which was purchased by the museum in the 1920s, greeted what they call "Our Grieving Mother" with several days of celebration. The museum also repatriated a cloak to the Maori of New Zealand in 2010, and a large boulder with many petroglyphs to the Canoe Creek First Nation in 2011.

Vancouver became the first large city in Canada to be designated a Fair Trade Town by Fairtrade Canada. The designation recognized the city's use and support of fair trade products and principles. A year later, UBC became Canada's first Fair Trade Campus.

Nat Bailey Stadium got a name change after the city signed a naming rights agreement with a major sponsor. The new mouthful is Scotiabank Field at Nat Bailey Stadium, which most fans will probably ignore. And "GM Place" disappeared as General Motors gave up naming rights and Rogers Communications signed a 10-year sponsorship deal. The stadium was rebranded as Rogers Arena.

Just a year after one of the smallest runs on record, an estimated 30 million Fraser River sockeye returned to BC waters in August, the largest salmon run in nearly a century. Prices dropped and BC's fish-processing infrastructure was overwhelmed by the bonanza. As excitement mounted, journalist Stephen Hume called for "humility rather than hubris," describing the runs as "a reminder that we still don't understand the dynamics of salmon ecosystems."

Hornby bike lane. Downtown got even more cycle-friendly with the completion of the Hornby Street bike lane.
Ian Smith / PNG

The Dunsmuir Street bike lane—the second separated bike lane into the downtown core, running across the Dunsmuir Viaduct to Hornby Street—began its trial period on June 16. On October 5, Vancouver city councillors voted unanimously to build the Hornby Street separated bike lane to link the Burrard and Dunsmuir bike lanes, despite strong opposition from the Downtown Vancouver Business Improvement Association and the Canadian Federation of Independent Business, who claimed that removing 150 metered parking spots along the street would cost businesses from 5 to 25 percent in sales. The bike lane was officially completed on December 6 and fully operational the following day.

The Vancouver International Children's Festival moved to Granville Island after 33 years at Vanier Park. Beloved but financially troubled, the festival moved in order to save about 40 percent on production costs and to have access to venues capable of hosting more technically challenging performances.

Two giant sinkholes disrupted traffic. The first, 4 metres (13 feet) wide, appeared in North Vancouver on July 5, blocking the intersection of Lynn Valley and Hoskins Roads for more than 12 hours. The second, 9 metres (30 feet) long by 4.5 metres (15 feet) wide and 6 metres (20 feet) deep, showed up in Vancouver on December 12 and closed Southeast Marine Drive between St. George and Fraser Streets until Christmas.

As part of the Canucks' 40th-season celebrations, Markus Näslund, former captain and franchise leader in goals and points, was honoured by having his number, 19, retired, joining other greats Stan Smyl and Trevor Linden.

Rare whale sighting. Vancouverites were wowed by a gray whale that hung around English Bay for a few days and even entered False Creek. Experts speculated the massive mammal was drawn by a school of herring near Olympic Village.
Glenn Baglo / PNG

Comings and Goings

May 5 Hundreds of people gathered along False Creek to catch a glimpse of a gray whale that entered the busy urban waterway.
Many suggested that this event was directly related to the recent completion of Habitat Island, constructed as part of the Olympic Village development and designed to foster the growth of herring.

June 12 Vancouver enthusiastically welcomed Ultimate Fighting Championship 115, after a reluctant city council approved a two-year trial period on December 17, 2009. UFC returned to Vancouver a year later for UFC 131.

Three independent bookstores closed in quick succession, raising questions about the viability of booksellers in Vancouver. Duthie Books closed after 52 years, the children's store Once Upon a Huckleberry Bush after two, and multilingual Sophia Books after 35. Biz Books also decided to close its Gastown presence in order to focus on online sales. Ardea Books and Art was hailed as a successor to Duthie's when it opened in the spring, but it too closed in May 2011.

"Prince of Pot" Marc Emery was extradited to the United States to face charges of selling marijuana seeds to American residents. Under a plea bargain, Emery was jailed until July 2014.

Notable deaths: **Joe Rimmer**, graphic designer, typographer and proprietor of New Westminster's Pie Tree Press, on January 8, age 75; **Eva Markvoort**, New Westminster cystic fibrosis activist, March 27, age 25; **Devon Clifford**, drummer for the Abbotsford dance-punk band You Say Party, after collapsing from a brain hemorrhage during a concert at Vancouver's Rickshaw Theatre, on April 18, age 30; **Jack Volrich**, mayor of Vancouver between 1976 and 1980, on May 31, age 82; **Charles Thomas Beer**, organic chemist who helped to discover anti-cancer drug vinblastine in 1958, and then moved to the UBC Cancer Research Centre in 1960, on June 15, age 94; **Jim Bohlen**, on July 5 at age 84, and **Dorothy Stowe**, on July 23 at age 89, co-founders of Greenpeace; **David Lam**, 25th and first Chinese-Canadian Lieutenant-Governor of British Columbia, November 22 in Vancouver, age 87.

2011

By the time this book went to press, 2011 was shaping up to be a year of public celebrations. Vancouver turned 125 in style with a plethora of city-sponsored events, exhibitions, festivals and artistic projects. The one-year anniversary of the Olympics was also marked, and the public clean-up after yet another Stanley Cup riot highlighted Vancouver's true spirit in an otherwise dark moment.

February 12 Seeking to re-create the Olympic high, Vancouver threw a one-year anniversary party to relive the glory. Former VANOC CEO John Furlong kicked things off with a breakfast where he launched his memoirs. The lighting of the Olympic torch was a highlight, as was the Lunar Fest Parade down Granville.

Elsewhere in BC

All of BC's major parties got new leaders. Four months after Gordon Campbell resigned, Christy Clark was elected premier and leader of the Liberal Party. Adrian Dix took the helm of the provincial NDP in April, and, not to be left out, the BC Conservatives chose former MP John Cummins as leader in May.

Elsewhere in Canada

May 2 Prime Minister Stephen Harper finally got his Conservative majority. The other parties were also shaken up in the federal election, with the NDP gaining official opposition status after a surprise sweep of Quebec, and the Liberals and the Bloc Quebecois posting their worst showings ever. Green leader Elizabeth May won her party's first elected seat.

June 3 Canada Post workers began rotating strikes, starting in Winnipeg, over wages, benefits and safety concerns. Canada Post insisted that it could not meet union demands due to lost revenue and locked the workers out on June 14. Parliament passed back-to-work legislation on June 27. Most pundits were more interested in debating the relevance of the postal system in our internet age.

June 25 Vancouver native Zachary Yuen became the first Chinese Canadian defenceman drafted into the NHL, joining the newly reconstituted Winnipeg Jets. The only other Chinese Canadian NHLer was fellow Vancouverite Brandon Yip, a forward for the Colorado Avalanche.

June 30 Newlyweds Prince William and Katherine Middleton, now the Duke and Duchess of Cambridge, were warmly received in Ottawa at the start of their first official overseas trip. Between June 30 and July 8 they visited eight Canadian cities, starting in Ottawa for Canada Day celebrations and ending in Calgary, AB, where they kicked off the Calgary Stampede.

Elsewhere in the World

Spring Sparked by the success of a Tunisian revolution, uprisings in Egypt, Yemen, Bahrain, Libya and Syria rocked the Middle East.

March 11 The fifth-most-powerful earthquake ever recorded—9.1 in magnitude—and subsequent tsunamis hit the east coast of Japan, killing over 15,000 and leaving another 8,000 missing. Emergencies were declared at four nuclear power plants, and thousands of residents had to be evacuated.

May 1 US president Barack Obama announced that Osama bin Laden had been killed during an American military operation in Pakistan.

July 20 The UN declared famine in southern Somalia, estimating that 10 million people were affected. The UN also passed a non-binding resolution calling for happiness to be a "development indicator." Initiated by Bhutan, which is known for its Gross National Happiness index that takes a holisitc approach to measuring quality of life, the resolution aimed to encourage member states to look beyond mere economics in development goals.

July 22 Norway was stunned by a car bombing in downtown Oslo and a shooting at a youth camp, the worst attack in the country since World War II.

August 5 Credit rating agency Standard and Poor's downgraded the credit rating of the US federal government from AAA to AA+, the first time the US credit rating had been downgraded since it was given a triple-A rating by Moody's in 1917. The downgrade followed a month of wrangling in Congress over a proposal to raise the federal government's debt ceiling.

White Is the Colour, Soccer Is the Game

March 19 The new Vancouver Whitecaps FC played their first game in Major League Soccer (MLS), North America's professional soccer league. They beat Canadian rivals Toronto FC...then failed to win in their next 11 games, losing 5 and playing to a draw in 6.

It was the third incarnation of the Whitecaps. In 1979 the Vancouver Whitecaps drew an estimated 100,000 fans onto the streets of Vancouver as they paraded in open cars, triumphantly waving the Soccer Bowl as champions of the North American Soccer League. "White is the Colour, Soccer is the Game," featuring the somewhat inebriated voices of some of the players, rocketed near the top of the local radio hit parade and it seemed the love affair would last forever.

Five years later, they and the NASL were history. Other Vancouver teams played in other leagues over the next 25 years—the 86ers played in the Canadian Soccer League, winning four straight championships (1988–91) and setting a North American professional sports record by playing 46 consecutive games without a loss. When the CSL folded in 1992 the 86ers bounced around various North American professional soccer leagues and in 2001 became the Whitecaps again. In 2006 and 2008 they won the United Soccer Leagues First Division championship, but when the MLS announced plans to add two expansion franchises in 2011, team owners and management put together a winning bid.

The new league is at a much higher financial altitude, which must make Herb Capozzi smile ruefully. In 1974 he purchased the original NASL franchise for $25,000. Exact price for the new MLS franchise was never disclosed, but given that Toronto FC paid $10 million in 2005 and Montreal will reportedly pay $40 million in 2012, a mid-$20-million tab guesstimate for Vancouver would not be out of line. Plus, of course, the cost of building the team itself.

Which raised the question: in an NHL-mad city, could the old love affair be rekindled? On early evidence, yes. Fans packed the temporary Empire Field facility, some 17,000 of them as season ticket holders. The team was slated to move downtown in late 2011, under cover in the refurbished BC Place Stadium, which will provide easier access and walk-by customers.

The new 'Caps knew going in that they'd have a difficult time matching rosters with the players who captured the city in the Soccer Bowl year. They would have to find their own Willie Johnston, their own King Kevin Hector, their own John Craven, the no-quarter defender known as the Elegant Thug. In the minds of soccer fans, no one ever plays as well as the legends of memory.

But they were well-financed by a triumvirate whose net worth featured a lot of zeroes before the decimal point: West Vancouver's retired software designer Greg Kerfoot; Victoria's Jeff Mallett, first CEO of the Yahoo internet empire; and Steve Luczo, part owner of the NBA's Boston Celtics. And for a face younger fans would happily identify with, Victoria's Steve Nash, two-time NBA most-valuable player and current star with the Phoenix Suns.

Given the enormous dollars involved, it was clear the owners weren't in the game to make money. "They love the game," said club president Bob Lenarduzzi (speaking of Canadian soccer legends), "and they're in it for the long term."

All together now:

White is the colour, soccer is the game;
We're all together, and winning is our aim...

Given the classic impatience of Vancouver sports fans, they'd best aim true.

April 6 Vancouver let loose and celebrated 125 years to the day after incorporation. The city hosted a party for thousands downtown at the Jack Poole Plaza. Billed as Birthday Live, it kicked off at 2 p.m. with a street hockey tournament, and festivities continued on into the night with a giant birthday cake, video and light installations, the lighting of the Olympic torch, and live music from such bands as 54-40, Bend Sinister and Leela Gilday. The celebrations continued in Stanley Park during Summer Live from July 8 to 10.

April 19 Taking their cue from the Vancouver Not Vegas! coalition, city council unanimously voted to deny the Edgewater Casino the right to expand, stating that Vancouver as a gambling destination was incompatible with Vancouver's "global brand" as the most liveable city in the world.

Also April 19 After heated debate between the municipality and neighbourhood community members, Vancouver city council approved tall towers in Chinatown—12-storey buildings in Chinatown South and up to 15-storey buildings in select locations on Main Street south of East Pender. Heights throughout the area were previously limited to 7 to 9 storeys (21 to 27.5 metres/70 to 90 feet).

May 20 Al-Jazeera journalist Dorothy Parvaz returned home to her family in North Vancouver after being detained in Syria and Iran. First taken into custody on April 29 for attempting to report on the unrest in Syria, Parvaz was then deported to Iran, where she was eventually released.

June 8 A new 15-bed hospice was finally approved by the UBC board of governors after an additional review in response to complaints by primarily Asian-Canadian neighbours. The issue of declining property values was raised, and resident Janet Fan explained that, "In Chinese culture, we are against having dying people in your backyard. We cannot accept this. It's against our belief, against our

Home-Ice Disappointment

In the late spring of 2011, as the Vancouver Canucks completed the best season in their 40-year history in the National Hockey League, fans began savouring the possibility of the city's first Stanley Cup championship since the Vancouver Millionaires swept the Ottawa Senators in 1915.

The Canucks had finished first overall in the league standings, had won the scoring title for the second year in a row and had earned home-ice advantage throughout the playoffs. They dispatched the Chicago Black Hawks in a nail-biter, then the Nashville Predators and the San Jose Sharks before reaching the final series against the Boston Bruins.

During the series, CBC set up big screens outside its studio and headquarters a few blocks from GM Place, and fans gathered in a genial party atmosphere to watch the games. Bars and restaurants did a rip-roaring business.

On June 15, the Canucks were soundly defeated 4–0 by the Bruins in the seventh game. Although stunned fans were quiet when the game ended, some of the crowd—estimated by media observers to be as large as 150,000—erupted into violence. Police responded with tear gas, pepper spray and flash bombs. In less than an hour, youths had damaged at least 15 vehicles, including two police cars set afire in a Cambie Street parking lot, overturning some and burning others. Then the mob began smashing windows and looting stores, all while curiosity seekers watched and took countless photos with their digital cameras and phones, making it the best-recorded riot in city history. Among the most seriously damaged premises were the Hudson's Bay, London Drugs, the Bank of Montreal, Sears, Future Shop and Chapters on Robson Street. Police, using dogs and batons, gradually pushed the mob along Georgia Street from Hamilton to Cambie, and the rioting finally subsided.

Vancouver police chief Jim Chu reported that the crowd had been three times the size of the one that rioted after the Stanley Cup loss in 1994. More than 100 people were arrested; 85 were charged with breach of the peace, 8 with public intoxication, and 8 with Criminal Code offences ranging from theft and mischief to break and enter or assault with a weapon. City officials reported 29 businesses damaged, and damage estimates ranged as high as $5 million.

The aftershocks of the riot continued for days. The next morning hundreds of volunteers turned out to clean up broken glass and write their remorse and condolences on boarded-up windows. Others vented outrage online and posted photos of rioters and looters. Participants overcome with shame and remorse turned themselves in to authorities and returned their loot. Some businesses dismissed employees who had been identified as rioters or looters. Controversy arose when the Insurance Corporation of British Columbia volunteered the face-recognition technology it used in licensing to help police identify rioters and looters from photos submitted by the public or posted to the web. Critics suggested it was a breach of civil liberties that broke new ground.

Eventually, as was the case following the 1994 hockey riot, an independent inquiry was struck to investigate the causes.

Hockey high. The Canucks finish the 2011 season as the top team in the NHL then score playoff wins over the Chicago Blackhawks, Nashville Predators and San Jose Sharks to win the Western Conference.
Ric Ernst / PNG

culture. It's not culturally sensitive." After considering various options, the BoG decided to press ahead anyway, noting the urgent need for palliative care in Vancouver, and offering to screen the hospice from view and to help residents relocate if they so wish.

June Showing its true colours, Boston Bar, a small town in the Fraser Canyon, changed its name to Vancouver Bar for the duration of the Stanley Cup finals.

June 15 After a controversial, roller-coaster ride of a series, and with tens of thousands of fans waiting to celebrate in the streets of downtown Vancouver, the Vancouver Canucks were shut out 4–0 by the Boston Bruins in the seventh and final game of the 2011 Stanley Cup finals. In a replay of events after a similar disappointment in the Stanley Cup run of 1994, riots, fires, looting and violence broke out along the streets of downtown Vancouver after the game. Stunned, Vancouverites rallied the next morning to clean up the downtown and turn the boarded-up windows of the Hudson's Bay Company store into a wall of remorse and hope.

Left: Hockey low. After the Canucks lose to the Boston Bruins in game seven of the Stanley Cup final, violence and looting erupt among a crowd of 150,000 swarming the downtown core, casting a pall over the city.
Ric Ernst / PNG

Riot City

Maybe it's something in the water, maybe it's in the air, maybe it's in the social conditions or maybe it's just programmed into the anti-authoritarian DNA of some of those bold spirits who uproot and trek to the end of the line that British Columbia represents in Canadian migration patterns. Moral decay, race prejudice, booze, low-lifes, politicians, the ruling class, anarchists, louts, teenagers, media hype, rock-and-roll music, professional sports and the police have all been blamed for riots. Whatever the source, Vancouver has a tradition of public mayhem that dates from its founding as a city.

1887—A mob of 300 (the city's population is about 5,000) marches from City Hall to Coal Harbour; shelters and possessions of Chinese workers are burned and 25 are beaten before the mob moves to Carrall Street, where it burns the homes of 90 more. Three people are arrested; all are released for lack of evidence.

1907—Members of the Asiatic Exclusion League invade Chinatown and smash every window. The mob continues up Powell Street, overwhelming a small contingent of 25 policemen reinforced by firefighters, until the Japanese fight back. With many casualties, the mob retreats. Thirty-seven shops, nine hotels, a bank and a newspaper office are damaged.

1912—A city bylaw bans all outdoor meetings. Members of the Industrial Workers of the World and the Socialist Party of Canada are told to stop giving speeches on Carrall Street. They refuse to comply. Mounted police charge into the crowd, swinging clubs, and 30 are arrested in the Free Speech Riot.

1918—Labour organizes a general strike, the first in Canada, to protest the police shooting of labour leader Albert "Ginger" Goodwin, pursued as a draft evader despite a national amnesty. Returning soldiers sack the Vancouver Trades and Labour Council building. Several people are beaten, others are threatened.

1935—Unemployed men from relief camps—where they are paid 20 cents a day—march through department stores, including the Hudson's Bay Company. In a melee with police, display cases are smashed and six officers injured. Windows on Hastings are also smashed. Later, police battle longshoremen in the Riot of Ballantyne Pier and fire tear gas into a nursing station set up by women to assist the injured.

1938—Homeless and unemployed men occupy the post office for six weeks. Police fire tear gas. Squatters smash plate-glass windows to disperse the gas. RCMP assault the building and are met with a hail of bricks. A mob marches down Hastings, smashing store windows.

1942—Canadian citizens of Japanese descent surrender for relocation from the West Coast and are jailed in unacceptable conditions. After three weeks, inmates turn fire hoses on the guards and smash windows. Soldiers respond with tear gas and live ammunition to quell the Jap Riot.

1963—A woman is struck by a bottle after the Grey Cup game. Police attempting to nab the bottle thrower are the targets of a barrage of bottles and rocks. Dogs are set on rioters. Fighting rages into the wee hours. Police arrest 300 and charge 249, mostly aged 18 to 24. Police promise to be better prepared next time.

1966—An hour after Friday's Grey Cup Parade, pitched battles erupt on Georgia Street between Hornby and Seymour, where a mob faces off against 150 city police, reinforced by RCMP, who march shoulder-to-shoulder banging truncheons on shields. They are showered with bottles hurled from hotel rooms above. Windows are smashed, streets left ankle deep in broken glass and 37 go to hospital.

1971—"Hippies" gather for a smoke-in to the music of psychedelic bands. City police are sent to disperse them. Firemen are asked to turn their hoses on the demonstrators but refuse. Mounted police charge the crowd; 12 demonstrators are hospitalized, 79 arrested and 38 charged in the Gastown Riot.

1972—At the first concert of the Rolling Stones' North American tour, those without tickets storm the gates and force their way inside. Plate-glass windows and doors are smashed. Police are attacked with rocks, bottles, Molotov cocktails and homemade guns; 20 officers are injured, some seriously. A formal review is ordered to answer the question, "How can we prevent it from happening again?"

1994—After a Stanley Cup loss, 70,000 people are on Robson Street when rocks are thrown at police, windows smashed, cars overturned and shops looted. Police respond with dogs, tear gas and rubber bullets. Afterward, arrests are made using videotape. Most rioters are young, single males; half are jobless; three-quarters are not from Vancouver. The riot is blamed on troublemakers who are said to have ruined Vancouver's world-class reputation. A study is ordered.

1997—A human rights protest against Asian dictators at the APEC summit goes sour when students are too slow to clear a road and RCMP resort to pepper spray. There are 40 arrests. There's an inquiry.

1998—When protestors gather outside a Liberal Party fundraiser with Prime Minister Jean Chrétien, police deploy 175 officers. Twenty demonstrators break through security lines, and police wade into the protest; 11 civilians and eight police are injured in the Riot at the Hyatt.

2002—Ten minutes after a Guns N' Roses concert is supposed to start, the doors remain locked. Speakers aren't working. Staff must yell to let the restive crowd know that the show has been cancelled. Concertgoers then smash $350,000 worth of glass at GM Place. Two people are seriously injured.

2011—After the Vancouver Canucks lose a Stanley Cup final series they were expected to win, a disappointed mob erupts into a ferocious binge of car burning, window smashing, looting and violence. Yet another review to determine causes of the upheaval is ordered, although one thing is different about this riot: social media and cell phone cameras make it easier to identify the participants.

June 25 Forty-eight new Canadians were sworn in at the Musqueam Cultural Educational Resource Centre during the first citizenship ceremony in BC to be held on First Nations reserve land.

June 28 At approximately 4:30 a.m., a tugboat hauling a load of gravel along the Fraser River struck the railway bridge between New Westminster and Queensborough, disabling the rail link for a month.

July 14 Endorsing Vancouver's goal of being the greenest city in the world by 2020, Vancouver city council voted nearly unanimously to accept the Green City Action Plan. Mayor Gregor Robertson first announced this goal

A World-Class Board

June Wendy Lisogar-Cocchia, chair of the Vancouver Board of Trade, visited New York and was surprised to find that instead of learning from the various chambers of commerce there, she was answering questions about how the Vancouver board had been so successful in recruiting and retaining members. Proportionally speaking, having over 5,500 members is "absolutely phenomenal."

The answer, it seems, is to be socially engaged, beyond the regular business concerns. As outgoing chair Jason McLean put it, "We have realized that we can bring more value to our members by making the connection for them of a healthy community and their success." And from its beginnings in 1887 as a group of concerned businessmen helping to rebuild Vancouver after the devastating fire of 1886, the board has been doing its best to shape local business and social life, and to promote Vancouver internationally.

Among its early contributions, the board lobbied for a regular northern steamboat service to open up business opportunities and for a telegraph cable connecting Vancouver to Australia, which would open communication with the rest of the world. Both were achieved, in 1901 and 1902 respectively. The board also first suggested implementing daylight saving time in 1913, donated land for Capilano Park in 1924 and provided funds to establish the faculty of commerce at UBC in 1926.

In 1983 it joined the World Trade Centers Association, creating stronger business links worldwide. This exemplifies the long-standing mandate of the board, which past chair Sue Paish (2009–10) defined as "promot[ing] individual, business and community well-being as a vehicle for building a strong province and country."

During the 1990s, the Vancouver Board of Trade was perhaps best known for its debt clock, a graphic reminder of the ever-increasing federal debt. Board members were worried that business taxes would rise as a result of the debt and devised the clock to raise public awareness and spur change. In 1998, after presenting a balanced budget, Finance Minister Paul Martin finally got to hit a gong and stop "that damned clock." When stimulus spending began in 2009, the clock was resurrected and is still awaiting the next gong.

The 1990s were also a decade for leadership programs launched by the board, which aimed to create a strong foundation for Vancouver to build upon. In 1991 it co-founded Leadership Vancouver with Volunteer Vancouver, the first program of its kind in Canada. Leadership Vancouver offered emerging professionals from business, government, labour and non-profits a six- or nine-month experiential program focused on community leadership. The Leaders of Tomorrow Mentorship Program, which begin in 1999, brought soon-to-graduate post-secondary students into contact with senior business leaders.

A flurry of socially aware initiatives marked the first decade of the 21st century. In 2000 the Vancouver Board of Trade Foundation was established as its own charity, and the Spirit of Vancouver initiative was launched in 2001, with the aim of revitalizing civic spirit and public celebrations through increasing business involvement. In its first year, Spirit of Vancouver saved the Celebration of Light fireworks display from closure and initiated the Stanley Park Symphony in the Park event. The Spirit of Vancouver 2010 campaign was launched in 2004. It encouraged community involvement in the Olympics to make them a success.

The board commissioned and issued several reports on a variety of issues including crime, airport governance, the convention centre expansion, arts and entertainment, health care (offering suggestions to government on how to reduce the rise in expenditures) and early childhood development, making the argument that investing in children will cost the government less in later years.

In addition to these social activities, and staying true to its business roots, the Board of Trade continued to expand its offering of mentorship and learning opportunities. Foremost among these was the Company of Young Professionals, a leadership development program for professionals under the age of 32, which was launched in 2006 to foster volunteerism and networking. The Women's Leadership Circle, inaugurated in 2007, gave female leaders a place to connect and grow. Throughout, the board continued hosting speakers and workshops, such as its Managers' Toolbox series.

Moving on to a new decade will bring challenges. For one, long-time managing director Darcy Rezac retired in April 2011 after serving for 24 years. However, as the Vancouver Board of Trade celebrates its 125th anniversary in 2012, it is sure to find its way.

in 2009, the same day chickens were allowed in the city and a section of the city hall grounds was converted into a garden. Since then a committee had been working on pinpointing goals and recommendations, and the city implemented further green initiatives, such as bike lines to the downtown core and encouraging the use of tap water over bottled water. With the new action plan, Vancouver hoped to double the number of green jobs between 2010 and 2020, work toward carbon neutrality in new buildings, and promote a zero-waste culture, among other initiatives.

July The Rosewood Hotel Georgia, first opened in 1927 as Hotel Georgia, one of Vancouver's swankiest hotspots, reopened after four years and $120 million in renovations. The current owners hoped the makeover would restore the Georgia's former glory.

Also in 2011

In conjuction with Vancouver's 125th anniversary celebrations, the Department of Canadian Heritage designated the city one of three Cultural Capitals of Canada for 2011. The other two cities were Charlottetown, PEI, and Lévis, QC.

Local architect Scott Kemp raised the bar for sustainable living when his new house received LEED platinum certification, the highest level possible for sustainable building. Located in

Mayor Gregor Robertson and a unanimous city council turn down the Edgewater Casino expansion, April 19, 2011. *Les Bazso / PNG*

the small riverside community of Port Guichon, near Ladner, Kemp's 204-square-metre (2,2000-square-foot) home was built for $650,000, entirely out of scrap wood. It is rare for a house to receive LEED certification, but Kemp hoped that his efforts proved that it was possible to incorporate sustainable features even within a budget.

UBC geneticist and physician Michael Hayden won the 2011 Canada Gairdner Wightman Award for his groundbreaking research into Huntington's disease, a neurodegenerative disorder that affects muscle co-ordination and leads to dementia.

George Bowering, the "utility infielder of the Canadian literary world," former parliamentary Poet Laureate and prolific author with 80 books and counting, hit another home run as he recieved the Lieutenant-Governor's Award for Literary Excellence.

David Boswell, cartoonist of the iconic underground strip *Reid Fleming: World's Toughest Milkman*, was inducted into the Canadian cartooning hall of fame. The strip debuted in the *Georgia Straight* in 1978, and the complete adventures were published in two collections in 2010 and 2011.

The for-profit Vancouver Harbour Flight Centre, located at the Vancouver Convention Centre, opened amidst a storm of controversy as the province's biggest floatplane operators complained about the centre's high fees, which would force them to raise their ticket prices. Harbour Air and West Coast Air, who fly 85 percent of floatplane passengers, led the opposition, but with the temporary terminal set to close and no other options, they were forced to sign up with VHFC.

A team of four Surrey high school students were among 12 finalist teams from around the world to go to NASA's Lyndon B. Johnson Space Center in Houston in July to take part in the prestigious International Space Settlement Design Competition. It was the first Canadian team to make the finals in the competition's 18-year history.

St. Mary's Kerrisdale, on the corner of Larch and West 37th, celebrated "one hundred years of grace."

Shift Delivery Co-op launched a downtown delivery service, using pink trikes capable of hauling up to 272 kilograms (600 pounds). The five post-secondary entreprenuers who started Shift aimed to bypass traffic and provide emissions-free courier service for this green-conscious city.

Chuck Davis' final book went to press!

Comings and Goings

West Broadway's high-end restaurants Lumière and db Bistro Moderne closed. The pair was originally opened by local celebrity chef Rob Feenie (db Bistro Moderne was then called Feenie's), but New York super-chef Daniel Boulud was brought in as co-owner in 2007 after Feenie fell out with majority owners David and Manjy Sidoo. The owners attributed their decision to a market more interested in casual dining. Confirming this, Nicli Antica Pizzeria opened in Gastown and became the new hotspot, with eager customers lining up for hours for a table and authentic Neapolitan pizzas (baked for 90 seconds in a birch-burning brick oven imported from Naples).

Disney-owned Propaganda Games closed in January, shortly after releasing the game *Tron: Evolution*. This was another blow for a city and industry hoping for a comeback after the recent economic downturn.

Buschlen Mowatt Galleries closed after 30 years as a leader of the local contemporary arts scene. Owner Barrie Mowatt said he wasn't retiring exactly, but at age 65 he wanted more time for himself and his partner, and time to devote to his other major contribution to Vancouver public art, the Vancouver Biennale.

Hampered by an aging membership, the Franciscan Sisters of the Atonement left Vancouver after 85 years of service. A fixture in the Downtown Eastside on Cordova Street, the Sisters had most recently been serving daily lunch to 500 people and providing men with clothes, toiletries and workboots. The work continued, however, as the building was sold to the Catholic Archdiocese of Vancouver, and the Missionaries of Charity, the order founded by Mother Teresa, was slated to move in.

Notable deaths. **Eileen Dailly**, provincial NDP education minister in the 1970s, who courted controversy with initiatives such as banning corporal punishment, introducing sex education, and establishing the first Aboriginal school district, on January 17 on Saltspring Island, age 84; **Lois Smith**, Vancouver native, who in 1951 became the first prima ballerina at the National Ballet of Canada and later became a famed dance teacher, on January 22 in Sechelt, BC, age 81; North Delta childhood cancer advocate **Megan McNeil** died at age 20 from the rare adrenalcortical carcinoma, January 28; following through on his saying "Writers never retire, they just die," Canada lost one of its great humourists when **Eric Nicol** died February 2 at age 91; Bowen Island's unofficial mayor, **Mallory "Mal" Smith**, former CEO of forestry-products firm Koppers International Canada, died February 24 of multiple myeloma at age 80; **Allan Williams**, BC attorney-general from 1979 to 1983 and West Vancouver politician, on February 28, age 88; **Donald Brenner**, chief justice and reformer of the Supreme Court of BC from 2000 to 2009, on March 12, age 64; **Nancy Hall**, provincial mental health advocate from 1998 to 2001, and tireless activist and researcher, from cancer on March 24 in Vancouver, age 60; **Wayne Robson**, Vancouver-raised actor best known for playing Mike Hamar in the Canadian sitcom *The Red Green Show*, on April 4 in Toronto, age 64; **John Bottomly**, Canadian singer-songwriter, best known for his 1995 album *Blackberry*, of suicide on April 6, aged 50, near his Brackendale home after dealing with depression; **Betty Fox**, mother of Terry Fox and founder of the Terry Fox Foundation, died June 17 from complications of diabetes and arthritis at the age of 71; **Gaye Delorme**, Canadian songwriter, composer and virtuoso guitarist, known for the Cheech and Chong anthem *Earache My Eye*, on June 23 of a heart attack shortly before performing at the Calgary Bluesfest Warmup with his Vancouver band; **Barry Wilkins**, an original Canuck (1970–74), who scored the team's first goal, on June 26 in Arizona, aged 64.

Downtown Vancouver today. In 2011 the city celebrates 125 years of incorporation.
Arianna McGregor

Davis honoured. Vancouver broadcaster, author and history maven Chuck Davis was the recipient of the George Woodcock Lifetime Achievement Award for his many contributions to BC culture. *Les Bazso / PNG*

Chuck Davis, 1935–2010

Chuck Davis loved facts. An amateur historian, he frequented archives and libraries, where he mined documents and yellowed newspaper clippings for nuggets of information.

He had an anecdote for every occasion. In the fall of 2010, shortly after he received a diagnosis of untreatable lung cancer, he made a public announcement about his illness, asking for help to complete this book. Afterward, he told reporters about one of his recent finds: A century earlier the city acquired the first mechanized ambulance in the Dominion. The crew proudly took it on a tour of the downtown, during which it struck and killed a pedestrian. The absurdity of that tragedy struck him as humorous, and one could not help but admire a man whose appreciation of the macabre was undiminished in the face of his own death sentence.

Davis was one of Vancouver's most familiar figures, an avuncular presence for nearly half a century as author, lecturer, quizmaster, cruciverbalist, television host and radio announcer. No person knew more about the city and its past, earning him the nickname Mr. Vancouver, which he hated. He could name a half-dozen others from the city's past more worthy to carry the name.

An amiable man with a hearty laugh and a magnificent, stentorian voice, Davis was, in the words of one of his many friends, a "delightful shambles." His many passions did not extend to his wardrobe, which often consisted of rumpled shirts and formless sweaters of unappealing pattern. He worked from a home office through which passage was made treacherous by paper stalagmites of uncertain stability.

Though such an appearance could hint at carelessness, Davis was devoted to facts, wasting no effort to track down details. Such painstaking research caused some of his projects to stretch beyond deadline, testing the patience of publishers.

He was a natural storyteller who possessed little ego and was so self-deprecating he eagerly retold tales in which he was the butt. Some years ago, he informed a colleague about his ambition to write an omnibus history of the Lower Mainland, promising the book would be "fun, fat and filled with facts." "Just like you," the co-worker replied. No matter how many times he repeated the exchange over the years, Davis would end the anecdote with a hearty guffaw.

Charles Hector Davis was born in Winnipeg on November 17, 1935. His parents' marriage soon collapsed, and he saw his mother only once after that. In December 1944 his father moved with the boy to the West Coast. They lived in a former squatter's shack built over the Burrard Inlet shoreline. It lacked electricity and shook ominously when freight trains rumbled past. Two years later, fire destroyed the shack and the homeless boy appeared in a photograph on the front page of a local daily.

A teacher's etymological examination of the origins of "breakfast"—the act of breaking, or interrupting, a fast—sparked in the schoolboy a lifelong fascination with words. (Davis was a demon at Scrabble.) He also began compiling lists of such facts as the rivers of Australia and the prime ministers of Hungary. Lists brought order to an untidy life. His father jokingly suggested he compile a list of his lists, which became much of his working life.

Davis' formal education ended at age 13, midway through Grade 8. At 17, by which time he had held 23 different jobs, he decided he wanted to fight in Korea. He enlisted with the Princess Patricia's Canadian Light Infantry in June 1953. "That war ended in July," he wrote, "so I guess someone notified the North Koreans. They didn't tell me when I joined that you had to be 19 to go over anyway." He found his calling while stationed overseas in West Germany. At 5 p.m. on March 21, 1956, Private Davis had the honour of making the inaugural broadcast on CAE, a 250-watt Canadian Forces radio station.

On discharge later that year, he returned to Canada to launch a radio career in Ontario, working for stations in Kingston, Kitchener and Kirkland Lake before accepting a job at CJVI in Victoria. He worked for the CBC in Prince Rupert before being transferred to Vancouver.

Over the years he produced 17 books, including an unreleased history of the Orpheum Theatre. His most financially successful book was *Turn On to Canada*, a Grade 3 textbook. His great brainstorm was to prepare an "urban almanac" on the occasion of Vancouver's debut on the word stage as host of the United Nations' Habitat conference in 1976. He recruited dozens of top writers for a compendium of history and information. Printed on cheap newspaper stock, which gave it the semblance of a telephone directory, *The Vancouver Book* proved enormously popular. (The library staff told Davis that it was the second-most-purloined title in the collection after Hitler's *Mein Kampf*.) Twenty-one years later, Davis revived the model for an even more all-encompassing look at the city and its thriving suburbs. The *Greater Vancouver Book* proved a critical success, winning two major literary prizes, but a financial disaster—the only black ink in the enterprise was on the book's 904 pages.

The announcement of his ill health sparked tributes, many of which were overdue. The city declared a Chuck Davis Day, and he was awarded the George Woodcock Lifetime Achievement Award for his literary work. A plaque in his honour was placed on the Writers' Walk at the main branch of the Vancouver Public Library.

The writer Daniel Wood recounts Davis being surprised and overcome by the tributes that came his way in his final days. Touched by the honours he was afforded, he said to his wife, Edna, of his impending death, "I should have done this sooner!" Typical Chuck.

—Tom Hawthorn

Index

Illustrations are **bold**

Published by the Vancouver World Printing and Publishing Company, Limited.
PANORAMIC VIEW OF THE
CITY OF VANCOUVER
BRITISH COLUMBIA
1898.
UPPER FALSE CREEK FLATS
BURRARD